THE WELL OF ETERNITY

Richard Gotshalk

University Press of America,® Inc.
Lanham · Boulder · New York · Toronto · Oxford

Contents

PREFACE

As an undergraduate senior at Harvard University (1951-1952), I spent some time in the Eliot House library reading through an eighteen-volume translation of Friedrich Nietzsche's complete writings, curious about what I would find. It was not my first encounter with Nietzsche, nor was it needed for the undergraduate honors thesis on a theme in *Beyond Good and Evil* which I was then writing under the direction of Henry Bugbee. But a responsive chord had been struck, an affinity sensed, and a curiosity aroused. In the fifty-odd years since my first reading of Nietzsche's complete writings, I have periodically returned to that body of work with anticipation and in the hope not simply of better understanding his thinking but of learning under the stimulus and challenge to my own that he presented. During my twenty years teaching at Pennsylvania State University (1957-1977), I used works of Nietzsche's fairly often in my classes; and as my own reflection evolved, the opportunity to reconsider his thought enabled my perception of it to expand and grow more penetrating. In the first years after retiring from teaching there, I brought to completion (in 1979) the first form of this current study. Since then it has passed through a number of metamorphoses, and finally has reached its present form.

My concern with Nietzsche over the years has been part of a philosophic concern with the problematic of existence and meaning that is endemic to the human condition. Because philosophical inquiry seeking understanding of this problematic is both personal and concrete, the thoughts which a philosopher-- any philosopher-- develops reflect much that is particular to his/her own times and to his/her own person; this is so because inquiry, while it aims at gaining an understanding of the human condition which is universal and not relevant only to one's own time and person, must seek its goal within a milieu that is indelibly marked by particularity. Nietzsche's was a times separated from my own by over a century, to say nothing of a continent and a different family and social setting. His was also an individual being quite different from my own. And yet, as my thinking evolved in my own times, I began to feel a significant kinship, both in our sense of the times in which we found ourselves and in our sense of how we needed to proceed reflectively in them. We both felt ourselves to be living in the midst of what seemed a turning point in the history of human existence on earth, and as philosophers we were concerned to understand the nature and import of that embracing happening. Moreover, we shared the sense that, however different the conditions of their lives, human beings all know life as an affair of growth and maturation, and that philosophical reflection must expressly situate itself in this changing matrix as we know it in our own person and seek to comprehend human being and life from out of it. Finally, what emerged eventually in both of us, sharing those two things, was a recognition that, if we would understand what we sought to understand, we must reach back in reflection to the temporal ground of human being and life, and understand the time and temporality enabling and conditioning it.

The following study is issue of an extended dialogue with Nietzsche that has been marked by the above-described shared perspective. It attempts one thing above all, namely, to set forth his thinking and thoughts on time and temporality as he communicated them in his published writings. The presentation however, has certain unusual features. To orient a reader to what is to come in the main body of this work, and what is not, let me indicate several of them here.

To elicit Nietzsche's thinking and thoughts on time and temporality is not as simple a task as it sounds. The difficulty of his published writings is well recognized, and attested in the variousness of the interpretations they have received in the mass of scholarly material that has accumulated in the intervening years since their publication. Indeed, Nietzsche himself was already taking note in his own day of the variety of readings to which his works were being subjected, and in response to his sense of being continually and fundamentally misunderstood, he eventually composed a work, entitled *Ecce Homo*, in which he directed his readers to his writings in a way that was intended to clear up misunderstanding, supposing that those readers were of good will and were willing to follow out his delineation of what is required for a reading that would properly grasp his meaning. For whatever reason(s), that work has been almost universally ignored or dismissed; the present study, however, is fruit of an effort that over the years has approached his writing in keeping with his counsel in *Ecce Homo*, and that has eventually found his pointing there quite helpful.

As a result, this study begins with two Chapters on *Ecce Homo* and on Nietzsche's directive to us there concerning his writings, namely, that we are to take up with them as communicating his thought as an evolving affair. What does that mean? Nietzsche thinks of his own reflection as more than an intellectual affair whose evolution might simply be a matter of accumulation of evidence and refinement of themes and ideas over time from the unchanging standpoint of reason. It is rather a reflective venture whose developing issue in ideas and written works expresses-- and is enabled by-- an evolution and changes in his own being and experiencing. In particular, his thinking has concerned itself with a problematic that is being disclosed in his life-experience; in consequence, that inward evolution and those inner changes have made for an altering and (so he claims) expanding and deepening standpoint at which his reflection has gained freer and more apt access to its continuing problematic and to evidence for understanding what needs to be understood. His writings are communicating, at different stages along the way, the changing fruit of such a venture in living and in thinking upon life. Thus when he wanted to clear up misunderstandings of them, he composed the autobiographical work *Ecce Homo* and sought to show that-- and how-- his changing life-experience, as visible to him retrospectively, was the enabling basis for the thinking and thoughts conveyed in his writings and the key to their understanding.

If we seek to honor Nietzsche's attempt to help us and, heeding this pointing, seek to test his claim about the way to address his writings and to understand the thought being conveyed in them, then we find ourselves entered into an attending to the written word which makes certain demands on us. As we seek to meet those demands and undertake the complex reflection called for, we also find ourselves in a quandary not unlike that which Nietzsche himself must have known. For we are being asked by him to acknowledge the personal character of philosophizing, and to recognize our own philosophic concern (including our concern with his writings) as depending for its success above all on our own participation in-- and recollective drawing upon-- the maturational evolution of ourselves as human beings. That our effort to understand him must necessarily be personal in this maturational vein may not be something we readily acquiesce in. But supposing we have accepted and followed his directive, at the very least as an experiment, what does that mean when it comes time for us to communicate to others what we are finding? Is he asking not only that we read him in personal vein but also that we write in that same vein about his thinking and thoughts? If so, what would that mean? Must we write something like *Thus Spoke Zarathustra*, or even *Ecce Homo*?

In the case at hand, I have settled on a form of writing which in order to accomplish its central purpose sacrifices several important things. The chosen form is dominantly expositional, and its overriding aim is to focus the reader on Nietzsche's thoughts. True, there is Chapter 3, in which I offer one fruit of my own experience and thought, namely, some ideas on time and life and on a re-flective understanding of these, and use it as a preparatory framework for the discussion to come. And critical or questioning passages appear here and there amidst the exposition, before a concluding chapter (14) provides some assessment of the thinking we have encountered. These elements all remind not simply of my side of the dialogue that has been involved in my reading Nietzsche as he requests but also of the reflective nature of the efforts of the original writer (Nietzsche) and of the au-thor of this study (myself) both, that they address a shared problematic and that all the writings in question are ultimately meant to foster a reflective understanding of that problematic. Nowhere, how-ever, is this dual reminder filled out: the problematic itself remains incompletely addressed in what is written here, and no indication is given (say) of the life-experience which has given me my access to Nietzsche's thought and which, as developed reflectively, has led me to make the reading and the expositional presentation that I do. But then, in regard to this-- the first of the sacrifices I alluded to earlier-- and to all that is missing as a result, that absence could become a blessing if, as part of read-ing the present book, you were experimentally to test what is being said in it by yourself going back to Nietzsche's writings and reading them in accordance with his wishes. For in that way you would recall first-hand the things in your own life that are cognate to those to which I have had recourse in forming my understanding of Nietzsche, and would be in the best position you could place yourself in not only to assess what is offered in the present work but also (and more importantly) to understand and critique Nietzsche as he would have you do.

As readers of Nietzsche who wish to follow his directive in *Ecce Homo*, we are summoned not simply to a personal reading of his other works but to a consideration of them in series, so that what is presented in a particular work such as *Thus Spoke Zarathustra* is seen and understood by us in the appropriate developmental and published-work context. Thus after the initial focus on *Ecce Homo*, this study considers eight further writings of Nietzsche's, beginning with his first published work and proceeding with the others in the order of their publication. The treatment of time and temporality in them undergoes a complex and uneven development but eventually comes to what seems at first like a sudden eureka-like culmination in the eighth work, namely, *Thus Spoke Zarathustra*. To main-tain focus in a treatment of so many different writings, the exposition made in this study presents only those themes and thoughts in these works which need attention if one is fully to make evident Nie-tzsche's developing thinking on the basic theme that concerns us. Because Nietzsche's reflection in each work has its own internal coherence and in no case is devoted simply to the theme that concerns us, we must be selective while at the same time being fair. That is not easy, and it has led to a selec-tion of thematic material that, if it has erred, has done so on the side of inclusiveness.

The expositional address to Nietzsche's thought sketched out above has made for a rather lengthy work, all the more so because of its abundance of paraphrased and cited passages, included in the belief that the tone and style of Nietzsche's words are important in carrying his thought and that hearing first-hand earlier ways of speaking and thinking giving way to later ones gives a reader an irreplaceable access to the character of the development of that thought. To prevent the length being intolerable, two further sacrifices have been made. For one, this study has minimized (indeed, almost wholly eschewed) the introduction into the text of materials from Nietzsche's lectures, his unpub-lished youthful writings, and his later published works, to say nothing of his preserved notes and his letters. It has sought to keep the focus on the various published writings being considered, and when such further material appears, it is usually in the Notes. For a second thing, this study has left out of express account the extensive and growing body of scholarly material treating Nietzsche's thought. The intent has been to convey the issue of such a direct engagement with Nietzsche himself as he would have us undertake, and given the time and space needed for that, the attempt to connect the approach, ideas, and criticisms, being undertaken here with the body of such scholarship would have made this work unacceptably long. As a result no attempt of that sort has been made.

PRELUDE

RETROSPECT AND REFLECTIONS

CHAPTER 1
Ecce Homo

Late in 1888, at the peak of his creativity and just before the madness struck which prematurely ended the productive phase of his life, Friedrich Nietzsche took a bold, even desperate, step to deal with what seemed to him widespread misunderstandings of his earlier writings. He composed a work (*Ecce Homo*) that was meant not only to counter such misunderstanding, but to do so in a way that would also avert misreading of writings he was to be publishing in the near future.[1] In the preface to that work, he explains why it is important not simply to himself but to others for him to do this. He sees himself at present as entered upon a mission in which he is about to confront his fellow human beings with a weighty demand, indeed the weightiest ever placed upon them. It concerns the unprecedented future humanity is entering upon at present. For as he sees it we have reached a critical turning-point in human history when human beings need for the first time to assume full responsibility for human existence on earth, and he is the first to have become aware of this in its basic nature and truth. In his previous works, he has been speaking forth his thoughts and disclosing himself and his evolving vision with sufficient clarity and fulness that others ought by now to know who he is and to understand what he has been saying and thinking. Yet he has persistently been misunderstood. Because of the importance of what he has to say, he is feeling pressed to do something radical so as to counter the prevailing misunderstandings and to improve the possibility that others will hear and understand appropriately the demands he will be making. Thus despite the fact that declaring openly who he really is runs against his grain, he now feels it as his duty to write and call out: "Hear me! for I am such-and-such-a-one. Above all, do not mistake me for someone else!"

It is not immediately clear how the work so prefaced, an autobiography of a peculiar sort, could be expected to clear up confusion about his earlier works and prepare the way for a better understanding of his coming works. Presumably knowing the author better would enable us to interpret his writings as coming from *him* rather than someone else, and thus as meaning 'this' rather than 'that'. Then too, knowing the experience and capacities out of which he speaks, we would presumably be better able to judge how, and how seriously, we should take him. In any case, you and I are about to embark on a study of Nietzsche's writings; they are not easy to understand, and since their author has offered us a guide, let us prepare for our consideration of his thoughts on time and temporality by noting how he would himself retrospectively point us into the writings which convey his ideas. In this chapter, we will concentrate on who Nietzsche is revealing himself to be, and how he conveys this who-he-is to us in this autobiographical work; in Chapter 2, we will expand this account of the who-he-is, supplementing the sketch in *Ecce Homo* with material from prefatory writings which he added when earlier writings were being republished, and we will also observe how he characterizes the various writings we will be taking up with as he relates them to his own evolving being.

Given the gulf of misunderstanding which Nietzsche saw between his readers and himself, his writings, and the thinking which he was trying to convey in the latter, we might expect that this clarificatory work would be simple and straightforward, introducing us to him in a way that would make it relatively easy for any reader to understand him and thus his writings. This is not what we find. Instead we have a rather complicated autobiographical presentation of himself, even more demanding than many of his previous works. As autobiography it is unusual in structure and form, different from most works of that genre. And in its style it is marked by an extremism that seems almost bound to obscure rather than to facilitate understanding. Let us begin our consideration with some obvious features which indicate how we are to take up with the work.

A. Title, subtitle, preface, and note

The title reads: "Behold, the man!"[2] It is a striking pointer to a singular human being as the subject of the work. The subtitle reads: "How one becomes what one is". It extends the pointing of the title in two main directions.

First, the "I am such-and-such-a-one" [*ich bin der-und-der*] which Nietzsche would have others understand him as being is a temporal being who not only is not static throughout the time of his being but *is* in an *essential becoming*. That means: Of the essence in the currently ongoing and singular being of himself as a temporal being is a character and constitution fitted to realize his being in-- and as-- a *coming* to *be* himself *out of himself* over time. Having his being in a gradual appropriating of it in actuality over time, he is eventually to have it as a full actuality whose potential and meaning have been his from the start. Being himself in this 'ongoing and unfolding-from-a-starting-point' fashion also means that the being he actually is at any time along the way inherently integrates two things: one, a have-become-actual-so-far, and the other, an able-yet-to-be that is marked by a destined-to-be. In virtue of the temporality of his being, then, he *is* only ongoingly and unfoldingly, in the course of (and as continuing and evolving issue in) a living that takes time. In presenting his being, then, he would have to recount its essential becoming, and include what is essential both in his having-become-actual-so-far and in the destined-to-be immanent in his able-yet-to-be.

Second, the singular becoming-being whose story is to be told is one unique realization of a becoming which every human being is involved in as human. The impersonal "one" in the subtitle is an indication that the story will hold a level of meaning that is to concern us all as ourselves caught up in an essential becoming. This means that the story of Nietzsche's singular life is not told, nor to be taken, in a merely personal reference to his singularity. In what way or ways universality is involved, and what elements have such universality, are open questions at the moment. But we can say at least that the individual man (Friedrich Nietzsche) is presenting himself as, in his becoming (that is, in his coming to be the individual philosopher he currently is with the distinctive task and mission he has), attesting something universal in the becoming essential to any human being as human.

The preface extends in a further direction the pointing of the subtitle into something more than the singularity signified in the title. Our first-personal being as human beings is plural as well as singular, with a plurality that is not exhausted by the fact that *all* human beings (past, present, and future) share a common nature and condition as human. It involves as well a being-together which, concretely, is historical in character. As being with a limited selection of particular other human beings, we are implicated in, and our present having-to-do-with each other is the medium for, the happening of a particular 'time' or 'age' that inflects the 'with' of our being-with; that being so, the actualization of our individual being, and in particular, of such relation to others as is implicated in that being, is conditioned by elements and factors of the embracing historical happening in which we are involved in our particular historical age. Now a 'time' is not something going on simply 'out there' apart from our own individual becoming, to which we are perhaps helplessly subject and are merely passive parties, or which we might remain unaffected by through ignorance and/or choice. Rather, it exists as entering into ourselves in the inwardness of our becoming and as inflecting our very own personal being. Yet how we are complicit parties in the existence of our 'time' is *not* a function simply of what is given in this entry and inflecting. Rather, precisely because a 'time' exists as entering into and conditioning our very being as we *in some way* assume, bear, and respond to it *out of ourselves* in our becoming, *how* we come to be in the actualization of ourselves in our own becoming (including our relations to others) and *how accordingly* we are participants in the being of such a 'time' depend as well on our nature and the becoming of ourselves rooted in this; and these make it possible for us to be merely 'timely' in our being-with and our involvement in affairs, but also to be more or less 'untimely'.

Now the singular human being who is telling us the who-I-am of himself did not simply live in a time, and in relation to us who live a century or so later, in a time which in basic ways is still our time. But he lived there in a becoming of himself that meant his eventual entry into inquiry as a philosopher. As he became a philosopher, he sought insight into the truth of the human situation, of the reality of life and existence, and his seeking operated in and probed the present situation and condition of humanity on earth while striving to reach beyond what is merely timely in the immediate matrix of his life and inquiry and to gain 'untimely' insight into what is universally human. Now as Nietzsche came to see it, that time in which he and his contemporaries were caught up was at bottom precarious and unsettled in a way that no one else had yet discerned; for in it a critical change was underway that concerned the collective human future and the meaning of human existence on earth. As his philosophic inquiring took him into the heights and depths of experience and reality and as he thereby became 'untimely' in his being and discerned things in 'untimely' fashion, he came to see through the ideals which governed human life in the present, to see them as not simply false but as mendacious inventions. An important part of his work as philosopher was to challenge and overthrow such ideals, to bring them to light as the lies they are, to uncover the hidden side both to them and to those who proposed and those who cleave to them. But the work of a philosopher is ultimately constructive, realized initially in insight into the truth of life and life's meaning; and because the present was at bottom such as it was, his inquiry issued in such insight into the present and the future implied in it as disclosed it to be unique in what was at bottom taking place in it and to be decisive for the future character of all human life on earth. Out of his insight, Nietzsche would communicate to his contemporary audience (and we are an indirect part of that audience), and would communicate to them/us as participants-- even if unknowingly-- in that crisis. In this communication, he would bring the crisis to our attention in its nature, meaning, and future, so that we might participate *wittingly* in the historical process in which the crisis reached some-- and hopefully, a constructive-- resolution. It is this herald of a crisis that is being presented to us in this autobiography; or more fully, the latter presents us with a singular human being who, involved in a becoming in his being, has become a philosopher whose insight has come to implicate him in being such a herald.

Finally, the note places the pointing of the title, subtitle, and preface, into a reflexive perspective. It reads as follows.

On this perfect day, when everything is ripening and not only the grape is turning brown, the glance of the sun just fell upon my life. I looked back, I looked forward, and never saw so many and such good things at once. It was not for nothing that I buried my forty-fourth year today; I had the *right* to bury it; whatever was life in it has been saved, is immortal. The first book of the *Revaluation of All Values*, the *Songs of Zarathustra*, the *Twilight of the Idols*, my attempt to philosophize with a hammer-- all presents of this year, indeed of its last quarter! *How could I fail to be grateful to my whole life*?-- and so I tell my life to myself.[3]

Two points emerge in this note that are important for us to mark here.

The first point: When the author of this autobiography writes about himself and his becoming and points to a universality implicit in that becoming, he writes from a definite mid-life standpoint, that of a condition of being which has been achieved through the movement of his life up to the present time and from out of which, given the capacities he has developed, he can see and bring to speech the whole becoming in question. According to this note, from that standpoint he is cognizant of his life in both retrospective and prospective veins: it is his life in its wholeness-- a temporally expansive wholeness-- that comes into view from this particular middle on "this perfect day". From that middle he can not only see it as bounded by beginning and end, but can see in it manifold good things that belong to it, in particular, certain recent achievements in virtue of which he can not but feel grateful to his whole life-- to a life currently harboring a special destined future for him as well as his past realization of destiny. Now the standpoint for seeing life whole which he has reached on his forty-fourth birthday is defined by an achieved peak in his fruitfulness; he knows his present being as that to which belongs a cumulatively formed mature capacity and which from the start has held a destined future that is now clearly discernible from the present but that began its drawing closer forty-four years ago as his life began its concrete unfolding. Only in and by the particular ingatheredness which harbors capacities that have become formed in him over those years and which holds his cognizance of certain recent manifestations of his creative power, does he find his life disclosed as it is, in retrospect and in prospect, and can he speak of himself as presently being such-and-such in issue of his essential becoming.

The second point: The telling of his own life that occurs out of that condition and expresses a sense of gratitude toward that life as a whole, is a telling first and foremost *to himself*. Yet as a tale told out loud (in print), it is one *meant for* the hearing of others, even if it is *not* told directly *to* them. What meaning does that have for the telling and for the listening of the hearer-reader? Life is always lived in a peculiar first-hand fashion such that each of us alone has direct access to the living of our own life. To overhear someone speaking to himself of his own life, addressing himself to what he alone is privy first-hand, is to find a kind of voicing of life in its inwardness which, when overheard, appeals to be listened to in kindred inward fashion.

What do all these pointers mean for us as readers of this autobiographical work? What are we being invited to do, what is our task, as readers? If, in response to the appeal of the 'telling to himself' remark which ends the note, we attend to Nietzsche's immediately ensuing telling of his life-story out loud, and if we do this on the strength and background of our own being recollected into our own life and becoming, we would find ourselves being directed and drawn into a complex (at least four-sided) act of reading by the various pointers we have enumerated.

To begin with, following the title, we would be directed and drawn to take the story of this singular human being to ourselves in our own singularity, and to register and grasp that being and life in its contrasting singularity over against our own. Here our task is simply that of accurately registering and discerning the singularity being communicated.

Secondly, as we note such singularity, we could not help but at the same time discern various differences in factuality between ourselves and the person we are being introduced to. Factuality here includes circumstance, deeds and sufferings, course of life, and overall, determinate singularity and particularity. But following the subtitle, we would not leave the matter simply in this state of recognizing a factual contrast in singularity; we would be drawn to attend to his life as factually realizing (in one way) a becoming which is being claimed as obtaining also in our own lives. Any such commonality of ourselves as human beings, involving as it would meanings which are universal but whose concrete actualization would be different in the lives of different persons, would presumably be accessible to us in and through our own lives; since the invitation recalls us to those lives and we are privy to them in their inwardness, we could expect ourselves thereby to be in a position to discern any such meanings as something immanent in our own life and being realized as we live it. Heeding the subtitle, then, we would be drawn to attend to-- and to test by way of what is directly accessible to us-- whatever of commonality in meanings, thence in actualization of these, is being implied or expressly claimed in the speaker's account of his life as an affair of becoming as a human being. Here our task as readers is not simply that of registering and noting something (a claim) but that of reflecting on this matter of our commonality as human beings and of testing a claim being made about that.

Thirdly, as we proceed in this reflective way we would find ourselves being summoned to expand our reflective response, this time in connection with the crisis which in the preface Nietzsche is claiming embraces his contemporary world and which concerns us as sharers in a common 'times'. Presented with an 'untimely' thinker, we are called to such careful reading of this present self-disclosure as would make of us fellow-philosophers and that means: we are called ourselves to engage in our own careful and thoughtful probing of our times, searching it out with his claim to prophetic insight and his claims concerning its nature and meaning in mind, and seeking to see how and why he claims our times to be critical for all humankind and its future on earth and attempting to confirm or disconfirm his various claims. If there is this common involvement in a historical crisis and both how we are involved and how it may be resolved depend on us in some measure, then for the sake both of our own individual becoming and of the human future on earth, we need to know the man making such claims and to join him in the seriousness of a reflective dialogue, an 'untimely' thinking with and against him, that will involve our confirming or contesting those claims.

Finally, as we are being drawn to register and note, to test and to reflect, in these ways, our response to the 'telling to himself out loud' of the note would not only bring us to read and respond on the background of a recollection to our own life. But in that being recollected, we would be made aware (and forcefully so, if we have grown much with time) of this, that since it is the powers and capacities formed in our own first-hand and first-personal participation in life that always mediate our receptivity to and understanding of another human being and since the registering-and-testing-and-reflecting resources that they provide themselves change, accumulate, and (hopefully) amplify, with time and with our own growth and becoming, in our effort we are unavoidably placed into the question of whether we are, at the time of our responding to this work of Nietzsche's, yet sufficiently experienced and endowed with resources to be able (first of all) to hear what he is saying as something registering and resonating in ourselves and (secondly) to recognize and understand it with any assurance and effectiveness. Do we as yet have the 'ear' to "*hear* aright the tone that comes from this mouth"[4], or instead, do we need more time-- and more than time, of course-- to be ready and able in this fashion? Here our task as readers is that of being self-aware to how, and how well, our own being is functioning to enable us to do the reflecting and testing which form our second and third tasks. We are being asked not simply to reflect on the matters being presented in this work but also on our own preparedness to discern and understand the thought being conveyed to us.

B. The four parts, and the title again

The main body of *Ecce Homo* consists of a story-telling which is to disclose to us who this Friedrich Nietzsche is. For a reader who responds in the inward fashion and takes seriously the four-sided task just sketched out, its revelation is effected in complex fashion. To grasp it, we need to consider the work in three aspects: its embracing structure, its determinate content, and its mode of presentation.

1. The embracing structure of the work

Seen in structural terms, the story has four titled parts. The first two concern Nietzsche's personal development in certain regards up to the present, and the third speaks of the published books composition of which has had a place in that development so far. The fourth part concerns the future that is being anticipated to emerge out of (because it is currently destined within) the present, thus the sense of himself as a fatality for humankind and human history. In this overall structure, the account is in important respects unlike what one would find in an autobiography in other cases. Three such differences are significant clues for us. First, one of the four major parts addresses a future which has not yet come to be. Thus it is life in some sense not reducible to past life which is the subject of his story. Second, the exposition of his past life does not follow through the unfolding of that life as it happened (chronologically), nor in fact does it concern itself with many of the events and happenings that a chronological account would normally include. Thirdly, the separating out of his books from his life, yet the inclusion and treatment of those books in a separate part, underlines that they have a character, standing, and destiny of their own, not to be identified with that of their mortal author, at the same time as they, in their production and character, belong to the story of his life.[5]

Together these structural features point us into this life-story as one recounted selectively, with attention focused in a definite direction and under a definite sense of relevance and importance. According to the larger or overall perspective pointed to in the embracing structure, the story-teller is telling us of that being out of which he is composing this work, and is saying: it is a being which is defined by a cumulatively-formed potency and centered in a task of discovery and creation whose decisive issue (both personal and in regard to human affairs at large) is as yet futural. If this in-the-midst-of-his-work character of his present being, with its presentiment of his own and humanity's future inherent in it, makes intelligible the inclusion of his future in the fourth part of an autobiographical self-presentation, it also points us to the reason for the kind of selectivity in the first two parts. Nietzsche knows the life of the human being as a mortal whole which is centered in the temporal realization of a creative self which forms the nucleus of that whole being. Since in his case that self is the philosopher in the midst of a profound task, his recounting of his past is focused on the past becoming-himself of this self, that is: of this soul and spirit, and of these capacities drawn together and harnessed into this task. The first two parts thus treat only of those past aspects of the story of the becoming of the whole individual which concern and make intelligible the capacities involved in that creative self, their fitting him for a certain task, his development of those capacities and his eventual discovery of that task. If this focus and sense of importance make intelligible the selectivity in the first two parts, they also help us understand the separating out of his writings, and the kind of separation effected in the third part. For while these are not his self nor his task, their composition and publication are important in his achievement of his task, or more precisely, are expressive elements in the rehearsal of his task which he has been undertaking as he has been becoming himself. Since that 'himself' is an ongoing issue taking shape in that becoming, they are valuable in helping us to understand where he has been philosophically and where he is at the time of the composition of *Ecce Homo*. Unfortunately they have been subject to varied but persistent misunderstanding. Thus the third part begins with a preliminary word on the understanding or lack of understanding with which his books have been received, and then turns to a recall of those writings, one aimed mainly at making them intelligible by placing them in the context of the development of his creative self, his own spiritual evolution, and by focusing on what seems important now from his later standpoint. Presumably, if one takes up with them assisted by such retrospective envisaging, one will be better able to understand them, and with the context of misunderstanding which threatens communication being thereby dissipated, the works which he presently envisages as immediately to come and as culminating his calling as prophet and herald will be capable of better understanding from the start.

2. The determinate content of the work

Let us expand our grasp of Nietzsche's self-presentation within the sense of it pointed to in the work's structure by briefly noting the major determinate features of the who-he-is that is being conveyed in his presentation of the becoming (past and futural) of his individual creative self.

a. The first two parts

As their titles suggest, these parts ("Why I am so wise", "Why I am so clever") are complementary voicings of the working of a certain "wisdom" and "prudential cleverness" in Nietzsche's life up to the time of his writing *Ecce Homo*. Seen in retrospect, his life has harbored a becoming of himself, in issue of which he now finds himself centered in a task-- that of his maturity, one for which he was fitted by nature and for which (although unknown to himself at the time) his nature was cunningly (that is, 'wisely' and 'cleverly') preparing him in the course of his youth.

The first part focuses mainly on two things, both treated as matters of inheritance from his father. One is a capacity to find himself, quite without his having consciously willed this, entered into "a world of lofty and delicate things", and to find himself "at home there", his "inmost passion" becoming free only there.[6] This is that sensibility and sensitivity within which his reflection could move and develop; yet it was also something to which he gained fuller access by the second of the two things. That was a condition of ill-health, and more precisely, the decline to a low point in his over-all vitality at the age of thirty-six (the age at which his father died). Because that decline took place in a fundamentally healthy human being, he was able to draw on remedial resources in such way as not simply to survive (unlike his father) but (in the perspective of later life) to find his ill-health "an energetic *stimulus* for life, for living *more*"[7].

Several things took place as he responded to his ill-health. One was that "everything in me became subtler [*sich ... verfeinerte*]-- observation itself as well as all organs of observation."[8] This gradually opened up more richly than ever that 'world of lofty and delicate things' mentioned above. A second was that he found in himself "an absolute instinctive certainty about *what* was needed above all at that time". Thus he found, for one thing, "the energy [*Energie*] for absolute solitude and detachment from situations to which I had become accustomed", and taking himself in hand, he was able to make himself healthy again.[9] For another thing, he ceased to be a pessimist, his instinct for self-restoration forbidding him a philosophy of poverty and discouragement. Finally, he knew not to let himself be drawn in his sickness and weakness into *ressentiment* and to burn up his energy-- and wear out his authentic remedial instinct (his fighting instinct)-- in acting on the affects of *ressentiment* (anger, lust for revenge, etc.). Rather he was able to cease reacting to the hurt, and to respond with "Russian fatalism" to various "all but intolerable situations, places, apartments, society".[10] Thus he was able to avoid the rapid consumption of nervous energy, and the pathological increase of harmful excretions, that come from such reaction and any attempt to rebel against the barely tolerable. Put more broadly, he learned to live under various prudential imperatives. One was "not to see many things, not to hear many things, not to let many things come close"[11]; a companion one was to separate himself from anything that necessitated defensive expenditures of energy; and third was to react (negatively or positively) as little as possible, "to avoid situations and relationships that would condemn one to suspend (as it were) one's 'freedom' and initiative and to become a mere reagent"[12]. Together such prudential imperatives were effective self-defense mechanisms operative while his recuperative powers slowly enabled a sufficient recovery from the low-point he had reached that he came back to life again, this time equipped with the more subtle capacity for registering things which he sees as having arisen out of his sickness.

Something more particular of what was involved in this response to ill-health comes out in the early sections of the second part. As he became more subtle in his observations and powers of observation, he also became attentive to, and developed the needed knowledge of, matters of nutrition, of climate and place, and of rhythms in life's processes, as these related to his own unique being, capacities, and development. For such matters, while often thought of as not worthy of much attention (and so he himself had learned to think, until his illness forced him to change), have a great bearing on our vital-energy, and in particular, on the metabolic functioning which makes it possible to draw again and again on great quantities of energy. Thus he was able to eat better, and to live in places and climates more conducive to his nature, and to change the ways he used his days to better accord with the needs of his nature. As a result, he "discovered life anew, including myself" and, living life now at previously unattained heights and with 'one foot beyond life', he made his philosophy out of his "will to health, to *life*".[13]

If Nietzsche stresses the positive role of his sickness in his life-- and in particular, its giving him access to questions and perspectives of health and illness, of ascending and declining life and vitality, and its awakening him to his previous obliviousness and inattentiveness to many things important for life and for health--, it is as contributing to something else that he sees all this as important. That 'something else' is his growth and maturation humanly, his 'becoming himself'. That in turn means: the way his functioning amidst circumstance was developing him and bringing him, quite unawares, toward a place and a time when he would awake to himself ready and prepared for the self-aware pursuit of that unique task which he, by nature and circumstance, was suited to carry out. Put in the metabolic-terms just used above, it means his functioning and development was enabling his animal vigor to become great enough to bring the freedom which, overflowing into the most spiritual regions, allowed him to recognize '*this*, I alone am capable of'.[14]

In the second part, he speaks of this growth process (this 'becoming what one is') as taking place in someone meant to be oblivious for a long while in the conscious side of his being to what is going on. At the same time as "the whole surface of consciousness-- consciousness *is* a surface"-- is "kept clear of all great imperatives", the organizing "'*Idea*'" destined for dominance [*Herrschaft*] is continually growing in the depths.[15] It is part of the 'prudence' and 'reason' of his nature that initially the un-conscious development of this 'idea' was accompanied in consciousness by a misunderstanding of himself that subserved the development of himself in a smaller, narrower, being than the one actually belonging to him by nature. Thus he blundered along, taking side roads and wrong roads, wasting seriousness on tasks that were removed from *the* task. Such is the understanding Nietzsche has in retrospect (1888) of his having become a philologist (1867) and then a professor (1869).

On the un-conscious side of this blundering he was developing skills and aptitudes that would (although he did not recognize this at the time) one day prove to be indispensable as subservient capacities he could employ in his engaging in the eventual dominant task which, during all this while, was still invisible to him.[15] Then too, in fortuitous fashion he happened on what proved to be important stepping-stones to self-discovery. These were his initial encounter with Schopenhauer's works (1865) and his meeting with Wagner in person (1868). At the time, these seemed more; to him who "at an absurdly early age, at seven" "already knew that no human word would ever reach"[16] him, these seemed encounters with other individuals kindred to himself and with whom sharing in regard to the most important human matters was possible. In particular, he speaks of his first contact in person with Wagner as "also the first deep breath of my life: I experienced, I revered him as a *foreign* land"[17], as a sharp contrast to and protest against the 'German' as it surrounded him and seemed suffocating to him. In both cases, however, while excited and enlivened by something that touched him in those men, he made something of these encounters which could not stand up long, and disillusion eventually followed. Important as they were for a while, he needed to grow beyond what he was able to be in connection with them.[18]

In this unwitting way-- misled into 'idealism' by his education and continually inattentive to physiological matters at least partly because of that, mistaking the sense of his task and becoming a philologist as if that was his future, growing closer to what he was with the help of Schopenhauer and Wagner but misinterpreting their meaning and aid in both cases-- Nietzsche finally came to himself under the pressure of his sickness and the change of his mode and place of life that it required. For then what had been forming in himself unknowingly was able and ready finally to surface and to disclose itself to a 'him' who could now recognize 'this was his task, something he alone could do'.

b. The fourth part

The dual retrospective account of the first two parts has sketched out the past becoming which has engendered him in his current being; that becoming has brought his mid-life entry into an Athena-like birth of himself and his matured capacities in the midst of his life-task, much of which lies ahead of him.[19] The counterpart to the account of that phase of his life up to the present, is his prospective account of his future in the fourth part, "Why I am a destiny [*Schicksal*]". In it Nietzsche speaks of himself and his future in connection with that happening in which he and his contemporaries are caught up and which it is his life-task to address. Thus speaking out of a knowledge both of what he has come to see in the world around him and of what he is himself attempting, Nietzsche anticipates that something tremendous will some day be recalled and be joined together with his name-- "a crisis such as has never existed on earth, the most profound collision of conscience, a decision that was conjured up *against* everything that had been believed, demanded, hallowed so far. I am no man, I am dynamite."[20] For

> what defines me, what sets me apart from the whole rest of humanity, is that I *uncovered* Christian morality. ... The *uncovering* of Christian morality is an event unlike any other, a real catastrophe. He who sheds light on that [morality] is a *force majeure*, a destiny-- he breaks the history of humankind in two. One lives *before* him, or one lives *after* him. The lightning bolt of truth struck precisely what was up to now highest: let whoever comprehends *what* has here been destroyed see whether anything is left in his hands. Everything that has hitherto been called 'truth' has been recognized as the most harmful, insidious, and subterranean form of lie; the holy pretext of 'improving' humankind, as the ruse for *sucking the blood from* life, for making it blood-poor. Morality as *vampirism.*[21]

More broadly:

> The truth speaks out of me.-- But my truth is *fearful*; for so far one has called *lies* truth. *Revaluation of all values:* that is my formula for an act of supreme self-examination by humanity, become flesh and genius in me. It is my lot that I have to be the first *decent* human being: that I know myself to stand in opposition to the mendaciousness of millennia.-- I was the first to *uncover* the truth by being the first to feel-- to smell-- lies as lies. ... Only starting with me are there hopes again. For all that, I am necessarily also a calamitous human being. For when truth enters into a fight with the lies of millennia, we shall have upheavals, a convulsion of earthquakes, a moving of mountains and valleys, the like of which has never been dreamed of. The concept of politics will have merged entirely with a war of spirits; all power structures of the old society will have been blown up-- all of them rest on lies: there will be wars the like of which have never yet existed on earth. Only starting with me does the earth know *great politics.*[22]

In looking to his future, then, Nietzsche sees his as a destined being, not simply in the sense of the becoming we have seen him setting forth in the first two parts (the realization of what he was destined to be out of his own being), but more profoundly in the sense that his life-task, and the commitment to carry it forward concretely in works of the immediate future (recall the preface and his reason for writing his book), implicate him in furthering a happening which concerns the destiny of the human race in its existence on earth. In that furthering, his will be a crucial role: so he anticipates. It is this-- his priority in the intellectually conscientious discovery and promoting of truth, his leadership in the war against mendaciousness-- that he anticipates being remembered and honored for.

Given such a sense of the collective future and of his role in what is to come, Nietzsche's urgent desire to be heard and understood becomes discernible in its rationale. At the same time, the place and function of the third part in this story of his life and becoming also become intelligible.

c. The third part

In this part ("Why I write such good books"), Nietzsche prefaces the one-by-one recall of his writings by a brief consideration of their being understood or not understood.[23] Writing is a matter of communicating; a style of writing is a use of signs ("including the tempo of these signs") to communicate "a state, an inward tension of pathos". A style is good which "really communicates an inward state, that makes no mistake about the signs, the tempo of the signs, the *gestures*"[24]. To understand writing, then, is more than to find some meaning in the words which can be grasped intellectually; it is to come to have "really experienced [*erlebt*]"[25] the writing, that is, to have found it articulating one's experience. But for that, experience is required. Writing can communicate only if "there are ears", if "there are those capable and worthy of the same pathos", if "there is no lack of those to whom one *may* communicate oneself".[26]

Ultimately, nobody can hear more in things, including books, than he already knows. One has no ear for what one lacks access to from experience. Now let us think of an extreme case: that a book speaks of nothing but experiences that lie altogether beyond the possibility of any frequent or even rare experience, that it is the *first* language for a new series of experiences. In that case, simply nothing will be heard, but there will be the acoustic illusion that where nothing is heard, *nothing is there*. This is, in the end, my typical experience and, if you will, the *originality* of my experience. Whoever believed he had understood something of me, had made up something out of me after his own image-- not uncommonly an antithesis to me; for example, an 'idealist'-- and whoever had understood nothing of me, denied that I need be considered at all.[27]

In the third part, Nietzsche claims that it is intelligible and right that there are no "ears *and hands* for *my* truths today"[28]. This claim does more than recognize the fundamental basis for his 'thoughtful' words having been thoughtlessly taken and mis-taken in the past. It raises a question for us, about whom it is that he is seeking to communicate with and be understood by in this present work. If the basis upon which his contemporaries misunderstand him is, basically, a lack of certain experience on their part and, secondarily, the lack of skill in reading, how could an author clear up such misunderstanding by anything he could write? Would not anything he wrote inevitably be misunderstood for the same reasons as before, supposing that a written work could not itself change the basis Nietzsche is pointing to for the misunderstandings? In particular, would he not have to await the entry by others into the needed experience, through maturation in themselves and/or further development of the crisis, before he could expect to have understanding readers, or to bring clarity of understanding to replace misunderstanding in the minds of his readers?

If in fact Nietzsche does think that his being misunderstood has these roots and that his writing can not by itself change that, then he is not writing for anyone and everyone in the sense that he wants to be understood, and thinks he could be understood, by any reader whatever. He is instead placing in the public domain a work expected by him to be intelligible (at best) only to a few but shaped so as to be apt for eventual understanding by them when they encounter it and take up with it aptly. Yet because the public domain through which alone he could reach such a few is open in principle to any and all, because any work is subject to interpretation by anyone and to being claimed to be understood by that person, and because his previous works have suffered manifold misinterpretation, this work has an element addressed to all in this respect, that it utters to readers (both good and bad) an emphatic disclaimer, a rejection of the way he has been understood, mistakenly classed together with others, and dismissed before even being heard. As addressed to most readers, this rejection of misconceptions is a bit of malice; but it has a different meaning for the few who have the resources to be able to understand him and the skill to read well.[29] For the misunderstandings of Nietzsche's writings that pervaded the intellectual world of his time could turn those few to and for whom he is writing away from him before they have ever really given him their ear-- at least, if those misconceptions are not contested.[30] Thus this work, and its rejection of how he has been understood so far: and more, its autobiographical form. For even as addressed to good readers, no work can achieve communication by itself alone; readers must not only have the skill and experience but also apply these. In this regard, an author can be helpful by virtue of the form he uses, as well as by more direct urging. Nietzsche's recourse to the autobiographical form and his inclusion of the third part within that, is an experiment, a final attempt, bold and risky, to discover and help good readers (even among his contemporaries) before his culminating works are produced and put forth. It does this by writing in a way fitted directly to encourage readers to draw upon their own evolving experience in their reading, to read with their own 'blood' what is written with Nietzsche's own 'blood'-- a necessary effort if reading is to issue in understanding. And within the work so composed, it extends this attempt to communicate his being by bringing his other works, none of them composed in this autobiographical form, into that same light, that shed by the evolution of his own life; for those works too were written with his blood, and need for their understanding a reading with the reader's blood. His retrospects on them are to help the reader to see them in this light.

3. The mode of presentation

Such thoughts bring us to the place where the third sort of consideration of the body of the work, that relating to its mode of presentation, can profitably be entered upon. By this I mean, whether the account presents the individual directly and straightforwardly, or involves the use of guises and masks which complicate and symbolically enrich the disclosure of the individual. In this work, the elements of direct and straightforward presentation are as if framed by those which present him in a guise, a mask. For the title, and the concluding line of the fourth part, and recurrent places in between (including the beginning of the fourth part), present this atheist in a religious reference and under a religious guise. More specifically, they do so in a religious contrast: both in recognition of the kinship in claim to decisive position in reference to human history, and in reference to the historical character of his present position, Nietzsche takes Jesus as that religious figure polar opposition to which is to dominate his presentation of himself in this work.

That he should present himself in religious guise and reference is in keeping with the sense that the matter at issue is, broadly speaking, religious in import, as concerning the founding of human life and the centering of human concern in accord with a tie back to ultimate reality. Such a guise is also not without precedent in Nietzsche's work. For the Yes-saying book in which his mission first found its own words to express itself has a religious figure as its main character: Zarathustra, the Iranian transformed by Nietzsche into a follower of Dionysus so that his drive to truth may reach deeper and be brought through self-transformation into an 'immoralism' that undoes his initial 'moralism'. It is, nonetheless, somewhat peculiar for this vocal atheist to present himself in a religious guise. Let us note how it happens in this work and what its meaning might be.

We have noted already the bold claim which Nietzsche makes for himself in the preface, to a priority as witness of a world-historical happening and to the centrality of being a prophet and herald who, in seeing before others what is happening, warns human beings and summons them toward an undertaking of their life on earth that differs radically in nature and style from that involved and implied in the currents of 'modernity' that dominated human life at his time. This claim of Nietzsche's to a world-historical task and thus to a larger-than-individual meaning to his being has often been taken, merely because of the extreme nature of the claim it makes on his own behalf, to be expressive of insanity. Yet in making such a daring claim Nietzsche has notable company among the great: there is Gautama, there is Socrates, there is Jesus, all are his kin in basic respects, although in different contexts of course and witnessing the divine in different forms. The making of such a claim as Nietzsche makes is not itself a sign of madness unless we are to consider all these men to have likewise been madmen. What we seem to have in all these cases is, at a minimum, human beings with an unusual subtlety and depth to their awareness of reality, with a sharp sense of truth, and with a strong love of human beings which draws them to seek to help others to find such truth and to re-orient life in accordance with such discovery on their own part.

The difference in divine powers involved is crucial. Nietzsche claims to be "a disciple of the philosopher Dionysus"[31], and to live amidst and himself to share in a reality which is Dionysian in character. What would that mean for the way he would present himself in a work intended to reject the previous misunderstandings of himself and to reveal himself truly and clearly to those whom he was addressing in this work? How, consonantly with his own sense of truth and reality and his sense of teaching as such a disciple, could he best disclose himself, and if that involved an autobiographical mode, how could he best recall his very self and his life-story and make his true being manifest in its individual character and in its larger human meaning?

Consider the following four things.

Consider, to begin with: The religious contrast Nietzsche makes emphatic in this work is not with Socrates or Gautama, but with Jesus. The import of the use is put succinctly in the one-line section that ends the whole book: "Have I been understood?-- *Dionysus versus the Crucified*."[32] But it is apparent as well in the title. For *ecce homo* is the Latin for the words of Pilate in reference to Jesus, as recorded by John (Chapter 19, Verse 5). The context of those words is this: Jesus is being brought before Pilate by the Jews, and in the course of Pilate's examination, Jesus acknowledges: "I was born for this, I came into the world for this: to bear witness to the truth." Pilate responds, "Truth? What is that?" When read in the light of this context, the title of this work suggests (and the body of the work confirms) that throughout a contrast is being drawn between two human beings with a sense of *mission*, each with a sense of *bearing witness* to *truth*. What is different, most fundamentally, is the god which each follows, and with this, also the reality and the truth envisaged, the way a human being needs to live in the light of that truth, the way this all must be witnessed for other human beings, and the way human beings are called to respond to this witnessing and revealing of truth.

Consider, secondly: When Nietzsche uses "the Crucified" as his contrast-symbol at the end, he means this Jesus, of course, in particular regard to his suffering for truth. But what is symbolized by "the Crucified" is something broader, namely, humanity as perfectly obedient to the will of its divine creator, receiving grace and revelation of truth from beyond itself, and living according to that truth and in conformity to that will, in faith and in trust in that divine power: in short, the saint. Who is the opponent to the Crucified, who is this anti-Christ? Nietzsche presents himself as a disciple of Dionysus, thus as a satyr, not a saint. What does that mean? Among the Greeks Dionysus was known as a god who drew up his followers beyond the ego in their ordinary selves (effecting an *ekstasis*) and who possessed them by indwelling within them (engendering an *enthusiasmos*). In his entering into, possessing, and elevating human beings beyond themselves, Dionysus opened up for his followers, in visions, what would otherwise remain hidden, what is terrible as well as what is joyful at the very heart of reality itself. But there is more than immediate awareness involved, at least as Nietzsche means that god when he characterizes him in a distinctive way, as a philosopher. This divine power as Nietzsche knows and means him does not simply elevate his followers beyond conventional limits in the realms of passion and of awareness, but also enters them into the search which is philosophical, into thoughtful exploration of what was opened up in such awareness and immediacy. Speaking of philosophy, Nietzsche says: "Philosophy as I have hitherto understood and lived it, is living voluntarily among ice and high mountains-- seeking out everything strange and questionable in existence, everything hitherto placed under a ban by morality."[33] The philosophical satyr-follower of Dionysus is the polar opposite to the saintly Jesus in most ways, but particularly in this matter of philosophical questioning. Dionysus does not demand faith and proscribe inquiry, but quite the reverse, elevates the human capacity for immediate awareness of reality and fosters the human love of truth, the dedication of human effort to an unrestricted seeking out of truth wherever it may be found.

The satyr-image of himself as engaged in philosophy amidst (and as part of) a Dionysian reality, is central to *Ecce Homo*. In the preface he hints: "I should prefer to be even a satyr to being a saint. But one should merely read this essay. Perhaps I have succeeded: perhaps this essay has no other meaning than to express this contrast in a cheerful and philanthropic manner."[34] In his presenting himself through that contrast, there is good-humor, and a love of humanity.[35] Yet it is a love that would affirm a quite different sense of human being than that affirmed by the saint, and a cheerfulness that is sometimes expressed in malice, in polemic, as necessary elements in that love and as supportive of that rejoicing in life and its possibilities which is the primary expression of his good-humor. Why polemic and malice? Nietzsche has come to feel that the 'truths' of the past are-- all of them, in one fashion or another-- lies: not just falsehoods, fictions, but visions and conceptions that were, and are still being, offered *mendaciously* as truth. This vision of life as normally dominated by illusory 'truths' and 'ideals' has been reached as he himself attained to certain heights in his own truth-seeking. These heights have been reached, following Dionysus into the deeper and broader awareness of reality, not by intellectual cleverness but first and foremost by the courage, self-discipline, honesty, and purity that informed his living his life and his use of mind in that search. The truth in these matters is not something far away and distant from human beings, it is nearby; but it takes courage to find it, courage to acknowledge it as truth, and courage to bring it to utterance. Thus Nietzsche claims: "How much truth does a spirit *endure*, how much truth does it *dare*? More and more that became for me the authentic measure of worth. Error (belief in the ideal) is not blindness, error is *cowardice*. Every attainment, every step forward in knowledge, *follows* from courage, from hardness against oneself, from cleanliness in relation to oneself."[36]

If the discovery of truth requires a courage that can sustain one in the movement beyond the ordinary, the conventional, and into the presence of elements of profound negativity, what of listening to the truth-speaker and following out his pointing oneself? How much truth can a listener endure? To Nietzsche's mind human beings have been-- and still are-- afraid of truth, and with good reason. For there is much that is terrible and terrifying in truth. But if that fear dominates in a listener, if the pointing touches too closely upon what one does *not want* to see, does not feel *strong* enough to look at and acknowledge and live with, what then? What can an author do to encourage in his readers the desire for truth and to foster in them the courage to pursue and look at it? and if not in all (and Nietzsche disclaims writing for the masses[37]), then at least in those few who have the potentiality for reaching to the place of insight and decision but who need encouraging? Yet these, of course, are not the only persons who will read the book. What of those others, the many who perhaps should not be encouraged, indeed should even be discouraged, because they lack the capacity, the courage and the strength, the desire and love of truth, needed for genuine insight into truth in these matters?

Consider, thirdly: In entering into his followers, possessing and drawing them beyond themselves, Dionysus not only entered them into visions and philosophical inquiry, but sponsored a release from conventions which brought not simply freedom from the constraints and inhibitions associated with convention but a kind of extremism in action. It was such action that was in keeping with the reality disclosed through him. Is not the religious guise of being a follower of this divine power aptly developed in the several forms of extremism found in Nietzsche's account of himself, his development and his future? Simply to read the titles of the four parts is to be faced with one expression of such extremism: "Why I am so wise", "Why I am so clever", "Why I write such good books", and "Why I am a destiny". That, however, is only the beginning: the work is filled with apparently extravagant if not arrogant claims, and with a vehemence in opposition to many things which seems excessive. How are we to take these features of his autobiography? There is a temptation, seemingly authorized by Nietzsche's own procedure in this work, to read these in a merely reductive vein, and take the unrestraint expressed in them as a sign of oncoming madness. But that is to ignore the *artistic* character and function of those elements in the work, to fail to see their meaning *in* the work itself. Equally, it is to betray one's inability to allow the human being disclosing himself in the *work as a whole* to come home in his complexity, and to connect (for one thing) this masking feature of his self-presentation with that strong resistance which in the preface he says his habits and the pride of his instincts offer to what he is doing in this work.

Consider finally: At the start of the fourth part ("Why I am a destiny"), Nietzsche expresses the premonition of his future we noted earlier, that he will eventually be recalled in connection with a tremendous crisis in human existence, and he continues: "Yet for all that, there is nothing in me of a founder of a religion. ... I *want* no 'believers'... . I have a terrible fear that one day I will be pronounced *holy*... ." Finally he says: "You will guess why I publish this book *beforehand*; it shall prevent people from doing mischief with me."[38] There are a number of things which this last phrase might mean, and probably does mean. But that he follows immediately with "I do not want to be a holy man; sooner even a buffoon.-- Perhaps I am a buffoon", suggests that Nietzsche is presenting himself as satyr in part precisely because of the jester or buffoon side to the satyr character. Under the guise of a buffoon, with all that this conventionally involves in the way of acceptable license of speech, he can say something of himself which is true but he can say it in a way that would ward off in advance any sanctification of himself. A man who writes a work with part-titles like "Why I am so wise" and "Why I am so clever" and who makes outrageous claims for himself: surely no one could treat such a man as a holy man! No one could take him seriously in that vein! Besides, his own sense of himself, and in particular of his previous self-deceptions, made it possible for him to feel that in reality he might be a buffoon; he might be quite mistaken now, just as (so he now felt) he had been before. The satyr-guise was apt for conveying this possibility as well, together with the sense of assurance which he had that nonetheless he was at the heart of things, that something of critical importance was voicing itself in him.

In the light of the preceding four considerations and this reading of the religious guise in which Nietzsche presents himself in *Ecce Homo*, an intimate complementary relationship emerges into view between *Thus Spoke Zarathustra* and *Ecce Homo*. Both present Nietzsche in forceful Dionysian guise. The more indirect presentation is in the figure of Zarathustra, the transformed Iranian religious prophet. First introduced in *Gay Science* in an aphorism that later becomes the initial portion of the Prologue in *Thus Spoke Zarathustra*, Zarathustra (in Nietzsche's portrayal) is a follower of Dionysus and a tragic figure, as the title to the aphorism in question hints ("*Incipit tragoedia*" [in English, "the tragedy begins"]). He shares much with the satyr-figure in *Ecce Homo*. Both are truth-sayers who are saying terrible truths. Both claim to be aware of being misunderstood. Both disavow the implications of being a prophet in the traditional sense; that is, neither is a fanatic who preaches and demands belief, and perhaps ends up founding a religion. Both want companions and fellow-thinkers, not believers. Both see that a pervasive mendaciousness holds human existence in its grip and that language itself has become corrupted as a result. Thus both put their terrible truths in language that is polemical and provocative, in terms that cannot readily be taken back into the perspective of morality and twisted so as to protect the complacency of the mendacious. Now if Zarathustra is a tragic hero, and *Thus Spoke Zarathustra* is a tragedy of sorts, would not the satyr in *Ecce Homo* be the main figure of the satyr play that follows the performance of tragedy and presents a comic, or at least contrasting and lighter (a "cheerful"), exhibition of the theme of the tragedy? Since the satyr is the more obviously exaggerated figure, assumption of such a 'cheerful' guise would fit nicely with the more personal, the more intensely polemical, the more open and direct, manner which Nietzsche seemed to feel was needed in order to make clear who he really was and what he really was about.

In sum, what is the import of the mode of presentation of himself Nietzsche adopts in *Ecce Homo*, namely, the placing of all that is straightforward and direct concerning his individual being within the frame of a self-presentation in the guise of a satyr, and in particular, of the satyr in contrast with the saint? By presenting himself in this way, two things may be conveyed at once.

First, he may place his sense of himself as a philosopher out of whom the truth speaks within a figuring forth of his being which can make emphatic, by its elements of extremism and buffoonery, the ambivalence involved in his bold claims. On the one hand, the claims are ventured as an issue of his life and life's-work so far, and are issue in an effort of deeply skeptical and self-critical reflection which he would encourage in others who have the courage and capacity for it. So far, he would be taken with utmost seriousness, for his is a work grounded closely in matters of experience, the outworking of a complex sensibility and a determined effort to seek truth, and the fruit of wide-ranging and persistently self-critical efforts whose advances have a moral as well as a reflective basis. On the other hand, he knows that the main way of encouraging others in the needed reflection and its animating love is through the force of one's own being and example.[39] He knows from his own early experience with Schopenhauer and Wagner the dangers in this, that those who can respond to the vitality, the energy and life, the intensity, the love of truth, of the philosophical man may respond in such way as to venerate and follow him in the wrong sense. Then would emerge a disciple who has lost his or her own selfhood and become a bad imitation of someone else, rather than having become strengthened in his or her own being, to become a companion and fellow-thinker. Zarathustra might constitute a presentation of himself that would lend itself to such mistaken following, even despite the fact that internally to *Thus Spoke Zarathustra* (at the end of Part I) such following as a believer was expressly rejected as unwanted. Where the force of personality is strong, however, the danger remains. In addition, he knows his own efforts, as ventures, to be tentative: however assured he has been at any time, he has outgrown much that he was once sure of, and he has become convinced that his truths reflect his weaknesses as well as his strengths, his limitations as well as his capacity. Thus the sense of authenticity, of truthfulness, of earnestness, and the present credibility of his truths to himself, can not be translated into the achievement of some absolute truth valid for himself even, let alone for others, to say nothing of for all. Thus inward to the seriousness with which he would be taken is need for something to counteract possible veneration and the temptation to mis-take his truths for absolutes. The elements of extremism and the buffoonery would surely work in this counteractive vein, to help any potential 'disciple' to become companion instead.

Second, he may make apparent in religious terms that the truth which he would voice is fundamental and far-reaching enough to call into question the foundations of Western life (Christianity) and, given that such life represents human life in its highest form so far, of human life on earth up to the present. What is at stake is the future of human life on earth, and one in which the best up to now must be transcended in fundamental ways. If that transcending future is hinted in what the Greeks achieved, it is not a return to the Greeks that is called for but a transfiguration of the Greek whereby its vanquisher (Christ, the Crucified) is in turn vanquished and the best of both is retained in sublimated form. It is this which Dionysus stands for in *Ecce Homo*, and this future which his satyr-follower, the philosopher Nietzsche, would proclaim as his good tidings.

C. Concluding thoughts

What has this initial consideration of *Ecce Homo* revealed to us that is relevant to our study? Two main things.

The first: When the author of the works we will be studying attempts to clear up misunderstandings of his previous writings and to prepare us to understand writings of his to come, he seeks to make us acquainted with the who-he-is whose thoughts are embodied in the works, as if our knowing him would be the best way in which to help us understand those writings. But what does it mean to 'know him'? As he presents himself, that who-he-is is a person who *is* in a *becoming* of himself, and in that becoming up to the time of his composition of *Ecce Homo*, he has been an evolving philosophical inquirer who, on the strength of the resources he is acquiring and the experience he is undergoing in the course of his development as a human being and as a reflective agent, has been gaining increasing insight into the present as a time of fundamental crisis for human life on earth, with radical implications for the future of humankind. To know him means we must understand the evolution he was undergoing, the resources he was developing, and the experience enabling him to gain his insights.

The second: This philosopher, become author, would communicate the insight that has eventually emerged, but he has found himself in a situation fraught with difficulty in that regard, given the conditions under which that insight could be truly shared and given the history of unsuccessful communication in regard to his previous writings. He has composed this self-disclosure in an effort to surmount the difficulty, and his understanding of the problem has dictated an autobiographical communication of himself, using a form and providing a content that are suited to enable a good reader to know him well and appropriately enough that the good reader could read his writings, past and to come, understandingly. His thinking, and in particular the insight he has gained in the course of his inquiring, has not been a function simply of an intellectual capacity and a reference to evidence which can be apprehended regardless of the first-hand experience and the moral strength of the person in question. It has been something gained in dependence on a skillful functioning of such capacity amid evidence access and address to which requires development over time of various resources and capacities for taking part (first and foremost) in life and (secondly) in reflective inquiry. Specifically, the resource needed has been a cumulatively-formed moral strength, and the capacity required has been a skill in exploring life's self-disclosure to an inquirer whose living of life and conduct of inquiry are centered in such moral strength. Without a cognate first-hand access to evidence and skillful address to the matters at issue which depend on the maturation of ourselves as human beings, readers will not be in a position appropriately to understand and assess the author's ideas.

If Nietzsche is to be our guide, then what is called for on our part is a thoughtful attempt to make our own the meaning of his writings by centering ourselves back in such access and address to evidence as we know in our own being and lives. To us who are about to venture on a study of certain basic facets of his thought, *Ecce Homo* says: 'behold the author of this and other works; if you would understand his works, see them as having come from the author's evolving being, conveyed in all its essentials to you in this work. Here is how, in retrospect, he sees that being and connects his works with it. Take it into account, and as you read the writings yourselves keep the connection he points out in mind. But above all, drawing on what your own lives, experience, and reflection, have opened you to in the way of evidence, think along with-- and against-- him from out of where you are in life and out of life's self-disclosure to you there'.

Before we plunge into our own work-by-work study of Nietzsche's thoughts on time and temporality in the writings up to and including *Thus Spoke Zarathustra*, let us look at how, in his retrospects upon them, he makes his own life an illuminating background for them and presents them in their character and claim to truth as these have become visible to him from his later (mid-life) perspective.

CHAPTER 2
Nietzsche's Expanded Retrospect on his Life and his Writings

In *Ecce Homo*, Nietzsche briefly characterizes the movement and the dynamic of the development of his life, and thus of the growth (with its elements and circumstances) that formed the generative matrix for his writings. In the third part, he concentrates attention on those writings, and his recall there suggests that because of the way they are rooted in his life they are grouped in a certain way. For the writings manifest phases in the development of a thinking whose standpoint changed several times as he maintained his effort of reflection in and through a radical transformation in his being and experience. Seen in this perspective, the published works fall into four sets, each representing a phase in his thought and the first three phases preparing the ground for a fourth which, at the time of *Ecce Homo*, is only beginning to take shape. The first phase is embodied in *The Birth of Tragedy*, and four *Untimely Meditations* (*David Strauss, the Confessor and the Writer*; *The Utility and Harmfulness of History for Life*; *Schopenhauer as Educator*; *Richard Wagner in Bayreuth*). These are the works of his youth. The second phase is embodied in *Human All-too-human* (Volumes I and II, the latter originally being two appendices to the original *Human All-too-human*, entitled *Mixed Maxims and Opinions* and *The Wanderer and his Shadow*); *Dawn*; and *Gay Science*. These are works carrying out his youthful rebellion against his youth, or at least, against fundamental elements in it. The third phase is initiated by *Thus Spoke Zarathustra*, and includes all but two of the remaining works completed by the time of the composition of *Ecce Homo*, some of which had already been published, and one of which was ready for publication but not yet published. These works are *Beyond Good and Evil*, *Toward a Genealogy of Morals*, *Twilight of the Idols*, and *The Case of Wagner*.[1] This phase was to be followed by a fourth and culminating phase, one being prepared for by *Ecce Homo* but to be achieved (at least in its start) in a work which was never completed but whose first part was finished by the time of *Ecce Homo* and was entitled *The Antichrist*.[2]

Now at the peak of his productive years Nietzsche not only composed EH (1888) but, two years before that, he composed and affixed prefaces to some of his earlier works, a number of which were being reprinted. Thus in the spring of 1886, he composed a Preface to HAH-I; in August of that year, he completed a new Preface to BT and added it to the previous editions of the work; then by September, he had composed a Preface to HAH-II (the two aphorism-collections that were originally appendices to HAH but are now being put together and made into Volume II of the work). Finally, in October, he composed a Preface for D, which was now being published in a second edition, and another one for GS, which was likewise being published in a second edition.[3] The thrust of four of these five prefaces (all but that to D) was not simply to introduce the writings as they now seemed to him but also to convey that earlier state of his being out of which he composed them and which they manifest and express. In fact, the prefaces form first steps toward the sort of retrospective account of his life and works which we see in EH.[4] They give us a fuller sense of the life-matrix for his works than does EH, and they expressly consider the works in that matrix. That same sense is embodied in them as in EH: that of an author who has grown beyond what he had been when he wrote his earlier works, and who is looking back on them and calling them back to mind as expressions of earlier conditions of his being. Because that 'beyond' means 'more deeply and fully into himself', the earlier works are visible to him now as distinctive landmarks on the path toward himself-as-he-now-is, and the prefaces are to help the reader to understand those works better by understanding them as such.

In this chapter, we will take up with the pointers into his works offered us in EH, but in such way as also draws heavily on these prefaces. Thus first, we will sketch out the fuller account of the who-he-is which emerges when we integrate what these prefaces say with what is said in EH. Second, we will take note of what Nietzsche says in all these places about his various writings as they appear to him in mid-life retrospect and when seen as works of different times of his becoming. Finally, we will conclude with a closer consideration of the sort of connection Nietzsche is asserting to hold between his becoming and his writings, and of the bearing of that connection on the truth-claim of the thinking conveyed in the writings.

A. Nietzsche's account of the intelligible dynamic of his own life[5]

As Nietzsche calls back to mind his life both in its wholeness and in its reflective side, his presentation in EH and in the prefaces emphasizes the crucial role in his becoming of two factors. One is his health, and the other is his work, his task.

To throw light on the most important feature of his health, he has recourse to his parentage: thus we have seen him[6] tracing his healthy basic constitution and instincts back to his mother, whereas the severe decline in vitality which he experienced at thirty-six (the age at which his father died) is rooted in his inheritance from his father. That decline, and his eventual recovery with the help of healthy recuperative instincts after a lengthy period of illness, enter with far-reaching impact into the way he can and does live his life and pursue reflection.

That life itself, however, was taking shape like any human life, in an out-of-itself unfolding whose concrete movement and course were being accomplished in the interplay with circumstance The becoming of himself, effected in the encounter with an environment that included much that was not favorable to him but also certain significant favorable chance encounters, was inherently meant to eventuate in his entry into a task or work, that is: a creative endeavor, passionate devotion to which would draw upon and concentrate his native and acquired strengths and enable their discharge in a disciplined and productive vein. Such a task or work, whatever its determinateness, was to be an affair of adult life, and thus was something the capacities for which need to have been developed and trained in earlier life in order for him to be prepared and ready for carrying out the endeavor he was fitted by nature to carry out. Life's movement thus ultimately had its course and meaning made intelligible by reference to this task or work that was meant to be his: beginning with the preparation for such a work, it culminated with the discovery and carrying of it out.

1. Pre-youth

In his recollection of early moments and features of that preparation in his life up to and into his youth, the most important thing which Nietzsche recalls is his immersion in an education-- a system at school (at Pforta, then at university), but confirmed in important respects at home-- that taught him to "ignore realities" and to focus instead on "idealities". As we saw in Chapter 1, the realities he means are what he calls physiological matters: questions of nutrition, place and climate, recreation, as these bear on us in our unique being, in our individual animal-and-psychic vigor.[7] It is this vigor, when great enough, that enables the growing human being eventually to attain the spiritual freedom which makes it possible for such a being to recognize the creativity of which he/she is uniquely capable.[8] Learning about and paying attention to such 'realities' could foster such increasing vigor and facilitate the achievement of such freedom and its discovery of a work, a task, unique to his nature; but ignorance and inattention, while they would not preclude such growth altogether, would mean leaving it wholly to chance, and in his case-- since education was leading him in an opposed direction that lessened the likelihood of success, and particularly since he seemed also to lack a commanding instinct and appropriate self-concern strong enough to counter the lead he was incorporating into himself via his education-- such ignorance and neglect in fact led to a misuse of his extraordinary energies and strengths. Indeed, he locates the calamity of his life in this idealistic ignorance, for the latter led to all the blunders, the instinctual aberrations, and the 'modest' selling himself short, which for a good while led him away from his life-task: led him to become a philologist, for example.[9]

2. Early youth

As Nietzsche recalls his youth[10] and particularly the time when, entering upon university education, he finally focused on philology and the Greeks, his musical aptitude and sensitivity played a particularly important role in his life. Especially was this so due to his becoming drawn to the music of Wagner. "All things considered, I could not have endured my youth without Wagner's music."[11] But it was not the music alone which counted; as he came to know the man, a certain affinity with him became important, so that Nietzsche can speak of "the most profound and cordial" relaxation-and-recreation of his life[12] and say: "Beyond a doubt, that was my intimate association with Richard Wagner. I'd let go cheap the whole rest of my human relationships; I should not want to give away out of my life at any price the days of Tribschen-- days of trust, of cheerfulness, of sublime accidents, of *profound* moments."[13] The heart of their affinity, he judges to have been "that we have suffered more profoundly, also from each other, than human beings of this century are capable of suffering"[14].

His long-standing sensitivity to and aptitude for music, including composing and improvising on the piano, and what this brought eventually in the way of association with Wagner, the man and artist behind the music which by his mid-twenties was strongly touching him: this musical thread became interwoven with that of his growing concern for the Greeks and for philosophical matters. Both were significant parts of a larger two-sided happening which dominates his sense of his evolution in youth.

The one side: Reflective questioning, often carrying with it suspicion and doubt of some strength, seems to have been his naturally from early youth on, and was an early part of his gradual taking responsibility for himself and his life. With it went the courage needed, even the audacity, to bring into question the Christianity, and in general the Germanic ways, in which he had been brought up and educated and amidst which he was living in an alienation he was feeling with increasing force. Courage summoned forth by a love of truth, a kind of drive toward purity, a strengthening emphasis on intellectual conscience and moral rectitude leading to contempt for what did not seem to measure up: these mark the youthful Nietzsche, and form the initial manifestation of what lies behind his claim: "In fact, I do not believe anyone has ever before looked into the world with an equally profound suspiciousness."[15]

The other side: Love of music, then the love of the man who came across with exceeding force when Nietzsche first read the major work of Schopenhauer, and then the love evoked when he met and associated with Wagner the man and creative artist-- these three loves joined with his love of truth to provide a positive and animating force complementary to (but also at some odds with) his reflective suspicion and questioning, his doubts and increasing awareness of pain and suffering both in the world and inside himself. In virtue of this love-side of his being, youth was a time in which (characterized from the perspective of what happened to him later) his probing and suspicioning spirit became fettered. Speaking of himself and other persons "of a high and select kind", he comments on the "duties" which early on fetter spirits who eventually become "free": "that reverence proper to youth, that reserve and delicacy before all that is honored and revered from of old, that gratitude for the soil out of which they have grown, for the hand which led them, for the holy place where they learned to worship-- their highest moments themselves will fetter them fastest, lay upon them the most enduring obligation."[16]

The profound suspicion he knew developing in himself was isolating in its effect. And the linking of the two sides of himself which dominate his youth-- this suspicioning, and those loves-- had a particular outworking, reflected in the following passage.

> Anyone who could divine something of the consequences that lie in every profound suspiciousness, something of the anxieties and frosts of the isolation to which every unconditional *disparity of view* condemns him who is marked by it, will also understand how often, in order to recover from myself, as it were to temporarily forget myself, I sought shelter in this or that-- in some piece of veneration or enmity or scientificality or frivolity or stupidity; and why, where I could not find what I *needed*, I had artfully to force, falsify, invent, it for myself ... . What I again and again needed most for my cure and self-restoration, however, was the belief that I was *not* thus isolated, not alone in *seeing* as I did-- a bewitching suspicion of relatedness and identity in eye and desire, a reposing in the trust of friendship, a blindness to a second person without suspicion and question-marks, a pleasure in foregrounds, surfaces, things close and closest, in everything possessing color, skin and apparentness [*Scheinbarkeit*]. Perhaps in this regard I might be reproached for many sorts of 'art', many sorts of refined false-coinage: for example, that I knowingly-willingly closed my eyes to Schopenhauer's blind will to morality at a time when I was already sufficiently clear-sighted about morality; likewise that I deceived myself over Wagner's incurable romanticism, as though it were a beginning and not an end; likewise over the Greeks, likewise over the Germans and their future-- and perhaps a whole long list could be made of such likewises?[17]

We will consider more precisely later, in connection with specific writings, this matter of Nietzsche's 'self-deception' and his 'inventing and falsifying'. For the moment, we need simply note that there was something in the way of a genuine and reinforcing connection being formed between the youthful Nietzsche and Schopenhauer, but even more, between him and Wagner. Yet Nietzsche's own need to see something more as being there seems to have dominated what was strengthening in the connection and also (so Nietzsche sees in retrospect) to have drawn him astray, away from the path toward his own task, his own work. Thus he can speak of the time spent with Wagner at Tribschen and characterize it as "the fairest, but also the most perilous period of dead calm [*Meeresstille*] of my voyage"[18]. His movement-forward toward his own work was brought to a stop. Yet

> supposing ... that all this were true and that I was reproached for it with good reason, what do *you* know, what *could* you know, of how much cunning in self-preservation, how much reason and higher protection, is contained in such self-deception-- or of how much falsity I shall *require* in order that I may continue to permit myself the luxury of *my* truthfulness? ... Enough, I am still living; and life is, after all, not devised by morality: it *wants* deception, it *lives* by deception.[19]

In retrospect, then, Nietzsche recalls these early love-affairs with Schopenhauer and Wagner as having been ambivalent: finding in the two great men a sufficient kinship to himself in his youth that he was strongly moved by them and their work and was excited by the apparent kinship, he nonetheless initially subordinated himself to them and their language, thought, and projects, and did this in such way that (seen in retrospect at least) he lost himself for a while.

3. Mid-youth: the crisis

In the light of what happens subsequently, Nietzsche speaks of the whole period of early youth as one in which, having been exposed to a contagious disease (romanticism), he had become sick and suffered a temporary attack of the most dangerous form of romantics.[20] The outward event that opened the way for him to regain his health-- or to change the expression, for him to be liberated from the fetters on himself and his thought which his youthful love (including his youthful love of truth) had formed-- was his experience at the first festival which Wagner put on at Bayreuth, in May of 1876. In the several years leading up to that time, he had been distancing himself privately in this or that regard, first from Schopenhauer's thought, then from Wagner, even as in his recently published writings he had been presenting the two in an idealistic and uncritical vein. But at this festival, he was overcome by a feeling of "profound alienation from everything that surrounded me there".

> Whoever has any idea of the kind of visions that had come across my path by then may guess how I felt when one day I woke up in Bayreuth. Altogether s if I were dreaming! Wherever was I? There was nothing I recognized; I scarcely recognized Wagner. In vain did I leaf through my memories. Tribschen-- a distant isle of the blessed: not a shadow of any similarity. The incomparable days when the foundation stone was laid, the small group of people that *had belonged*, had celebrated, and of which one did not have to wish 'if only they had fingers for delicate matters'-- not a shadow of any similarity. *What had happened?*[21]

Whatever had happened to Wagner (he had changed, the Wagnerian had come to dominate over him), the feeling of alienation forced Nietzsche to raise questions about himself-- himself now, but also himself as he had been over these previous years. It seemed to him now that for years he had been wandering out of touch with what was genuinely himself, the genuine in himself; in his 'professorship at Basel' as well as in 'Wagner', he had been venturing on paths distant from what was central to his genuine self, and what was worse, in the course of that "total-aberration" of his instincts, he had been wasting time [*Zeit ... verschwendet sei*], not developing as he should have been as regards what was truly his own.[22] Forgetting his essential being, not attending to and nourishing it over these years as a philologist, he was now saddened and revulsed at himself and the state he was in.[23]

> It was then that my instinct, without any pity, decided against any longer yielding, going along, and confounding myself. Any kind of life, the most unfavorable conditions, sickness, poverty-- anything seemed preferable to that unseemly 'selflessness' which I had originally got myself into from ignorance, from *youth,* but in which later on I had remained fastened from inertia, from the so-called 'feeling of duty'.[24]

The experience of that day and the days to follow had come suddenly and like the shock of an earthquake. How was this to be understood? In retrospect, Nietzsche frames it in large perspective.

As part of life as an affair of growth, youth is the time when we are to assume our own life upon ourselves as our responsibility. For this, we need to be able to think for ourselves, and Nietzsche's recollection indicates that this part of the maturational work came to him early. But such assumption is not merely a matter of thinking for oneself, let alone doing this only in certain regards; it is a matter that involves standing on one's own feet in the undertaking of one's life, and for that one needs a strength that is not given simply with the capacity and strength generally to think for oneself. Moreover, the thinking that is called for is one concerned and commensurate with this assumption of responsibility for ourselves. Apparently the strength for this life-assumption had been growing unawares in the youthful Nietzsche, and its surfacing (given the fettering hold that Wagner had had over him and to which he himself had willingly contributed) was initially traumatic. Nonetheless, Nietzsche can speak of the decisive moment at Bayreuth as "this first outbreak of power [*Kraft*] and will to self-determination [*Selbstbestimmung*], to one's very own valuations [*Selbst-Wertsetzung*], this will to *free*-will"[25]. It had a decisive maturational meaning, signifying a crucial step in his coming into his genuine selfhood.

Nietzsche expands upon and deepens this point by placing this turn of youth in the movement of life as a whole. To his mind, the life in us is an affair of growth which is oriented beyond the initial aim at independence, at assuming our own lives as our own and living them as such; it is oriented ultimately to a goal that presupposes the achievement of independence, but is a task, a work, a passionate involvement in some endeavor on the part of the independent human being. Grasped in this longer perspective, Nietzsche speaks of what "must happen to everyone in whom a *task* wants to become incarnate and 'come into the world'" and claims:

> The secret force [*Gewalt*] and necessity of this task will hold sway among and in his particular destined-turns like an unconscious pregnancy-- long before he has caught sight of the task itself and knows its name. Our calling [*Bestimmung*] governs-and-disposes-of us [*verfügt über uns*] even when we still do not know [*kennen*] it; it is the future which gives the rule to our today.[26]

Now (as he puts it in 1888) assuming that "the task, the destiny, the *fate* of the task, transcends the average very significantly",

> in that case, nothing could be more dangerous than catching sight of oneself *with* this task. That one becomes what one is, presupposes that one has not the remotest suspicion *what* one is. From this point of view, even the *blunders* of life have their own meaning and value-- the occasional side roads and wrong roads, the delays, 'modesties', seriousness wasted on tasks that lie beyond *the* task. All this can express a great prudence, even the supreme prudence: where *nosce te ipsum* would be the recipe for ruin, forgetting oneself, *misunderstanding* oneself, making oneself smaller, narrower, mediocre, becomes reason itself. ... So many dangers that the instinct comes too soon to 'understand itself'--. Meanwhile the organizing 'idea' that is destined to rule keeps growing in the depths-- it begins to command; slowly it leads us *back* from side roads and wrong roads; it prepares *singular* qualities and fitnesses that will one day prove to be indispensable as means toward a whole-- one by one, it trains all *subservient* capacities before allowing any hint of the dominant task, of 'goal', 'aim', 'meaning'.[27]

Or putting it in the earlier (1886) language in which the task or work in his own case is eventually centered on the problem of order of rank:

> it is only now, at the midday of our life, that we understand what preparations, bypaths, tests, temptations, disguises the problem had need of before it was *allowed* to rise up before us, and how we first had to experience the most manifold and contradictory states of joy and distress in soul and body, as adventurers and circumnavigators of that inner world called 'man', as survey-ors-and-measurers of that 'higher' and 'one above the other' that is likewise called 'man'-- pene-trating everywhere, almost without fear, disdaining nothing, losing nothing, tasting everything, purifying everything of what is chance-and-accident in it and as it were thoroughly sifting it-- until at last we had the right to say, we free spirits: 'Here-- a *new* problem! Here a long ladder upon whose rungs we ourselves have climbed and sat-- which we ourselves have at some time *been*! Here a higher, a deeper, a beneath-us, a tremendous long ordering, an order of rank, which we *see*: here-- *our* problem!'--[28]

Returning to the 1888-language and speaking now of the task as that of the revaluation of all values:

> Considered in this way, my life is simply wonderful. For the task of a *revaluation of values*, more capacities may have been needed than have ever dwelt together in a single individual-- above all, even contrary capacities that could not be permitted to disturb and destroy one anoth-er. An order of rank among these capacities; distance; the art of separating without introducing hostility; to mix nothing, to 'reconcile' nothing; a tremendous variety that is nevertheless the opposite of chaos-- this was the precondition, the long, secret work and artistry of my instinct. Its *higher protection* showed itself so strong that in no case did I even suspect what was growing in me-- that suddenly one day all my capacities, ripened, *leaped forth* in their ultimate perfec-tion. I cannot remember that I ever tried hard-- no trace of *struggle* can be demonstrated in my life; I am the opposite of a heroic nature. 'Willing' something, 'striving' for something, en-visaging a 'purpose', a 'wish'-- I know none of this from experience. At this very moment I still look upon my future-- an *expansive* future!-- as upon calm seas: there is no ripple of longing. I do not want in the least that anything should become different than it is; I myself do not want

to become different.[29]

The language used in these passages varies slightly, but the thought coheres. The burden of the delineations in each case is to call to mind the evolution of an agent whose life is eventually to center in a major task or work; along the way to the discovery of this task, much is hidden to the agent, the preparation for what is to be his taking place mostly in an ignorance, an obliviousness, a mis-taking. In every case, the venturing of oneself-as-agent and oneself-as-(say)-philosopher is at once conscious and unconscious (with multiple meanings to these terms, and different emphases to the different matters severally intended under each). In his own case, venturing as agent was a matter of becoming responsible in a personal fashion for a destiny and future-- basically, a task or work-- which is at first unclear and is initially misunderstood in its character and what it calls for; thus he felt himself tasked (concerning German culture and the reform of the German educational system) even before he became involved with Wagner, and then under Wagner's influence the task became reconstrued, its goal becoming an overall cultural revolution among the Germans. In both cases, he was misreading something more fundamental, reading it prematurely and with foreshortened focus. Similarly, venturing as philosopher involved a guiding problematic (that of existence and meaning) which was likewise unclear and misunderstood in its initial apprehension (understood as a metaphysical problem). From his later place of retrospect, the 'earthquake' at Bayreuth is the second beginning that calls into question his initial (early youthful) interpretation and venturing in both regards and initiates that recall to himself which eventuates in a clearer discovery of direction in both cases.[30]

All this concerns the event as seen retrospectively and in a larger significance that was invisible at the time. In the event itself, the experience was one of confusion, disorientation. "The young soul all at once becomes convulsed, torn loose, torn away-- it does not know what is happening."[31] The immediate path ahead was complex. For inward to this condition of being at sea were two different but connected drives which would carry onward and expand the dynamic of the movement being initiated; at the same time, the conditions under which the young Nietzsche could move ahead soon included an worsening health which required, but also made graceful, his withdrawal from the professional side of life and a fairly radical change of life-style. Above all, however, the time of confusion and disorientation was marked by a sense of loss. For in it his early sense of having a task, linked closely with certain limited and limiting interpretations of what that task was that were made under the impact of Schopenhauer and Wagner, disappeared, leaving him feeling at sea. Later, he can say:

> That concealed and imperious something for which we for long have no name until it finally proves to be our *task*-- this tyrant in us takes a terrible retribution for every attempt we make to avoid or elude it, for every premature decision, for every 'identification' of ourselves with those with whom we do not belong, for every activity, however respectable, if it distracts us from our chief undertaking, even for every virtue that would like to shield us from the severity of our ownmost [*eigensten*] responsibility.[32]

But what in retrospect seems only the undermining of something "premature", at the time involved dissolution of all sense of a task, so closely identified had that sense been with what he had been making of it before. Thus he can say: "My *task*-- where had it gone? What? did it not now seem as if my task had withdrawn from me, as though I would for a long time to come no longer have any right to it? How was I going to be able to endure *this* greatest of privations?"[33] As it turns out, of course, the sense of loss and of being undermined, however painful, had been necessary if he was ever to return to himself out of the 'identification' (i.e. mis-identification) of himself with certain figures and events beyond himself and to regain his task in some form genuinely his own.

4. Mid-youth: the way forward

Speaking in generalization from his own case about the moving-forward in the midst of this confusion and disorientation, Nietzsche points to the complementary forward-impelling drives and their interweaving as he then experienced these. The young soul found in itself a

> sudden terror and suspicion of what it loved, a lightning-bolt of contempt for what it called 'duty', a tumultuous arbitrary volcanically-erupting longing for travel, strange places, estrangements, coldness, soberness, frost, a hatred of love, perhaps a desecrating blow and glance *backwards* to where it formerly loved and worshiped, perhaps a glow of shame at what it is doing, yet a rejoicing *that* it is doing it-- and a drunken inwardly-exultant shudder which betrays a triumph: a triumph? Over what? Over whom? An enigmatic, question-packed, questionable triumph, but the *first* triumph all the same:-- bad and painful things like these are part of the history of its great liberation.[34]

Accompanying the reaction-against was a longing-for which defined itself on two paths. On the one hand, his longing-for (the strange) was part of a desire to get away from the world as it had become familiar to him.

> A drive and impulse rules and becomes master over (the young soul) like a command; a will and desire awakens to go off, anywhere, at any cost; a vehement dangerous curiosity for an undiscovered world flames and flickers in all its senses. 'Better to die than to go on living *here*'-- thus sounds the imperious voice and temptation: and this 'here', this 'at home', is everything it had hitherto loved![35]

The 'away' here was not altogether indeterminate; for "a truly burning thirst took hold of me: henceforth in fact I pursued nothing more than physiology, medicine, and natural sciences-- and I did not return even to properly historical studies until my *task* compelled me to, imperiously."[36] On the other hand, taking this path forward on unfamiliar routes through the sciences was made part of an exploration of matters that had belonged to the world he was rejecting, but an exploration with new eyes, an exploration of strange and fantastic other sides, an exploration animated by his deepening suspicion and skepticism turned back more searchingly now on himself as well as on what he had been involved in. Perhaps "exploration" is not quite the word for what took place, i.e. for the turning over and looking differently at what had been 'near and dear' before and the probing of what had been overlooked about it previously. For "alone now and miserably self-distrustful",

> weary of the unending disappointment with everything we modern men have left to inspire us, with energy, labor, hope, youth, love everywhere *dissipated*; weary from disgust at the femininity and wild-and-fantastic lack of discipline of this romanticism, weary in face of the whole idealist pack of lies and softening of conscience that had once again carried off the victory over one of the bravest; weary, last but not least, from the bitterness of an inexorable suspicion-- that, after this disappointment, I was condemned to mistrust more profoundly, despise more profoundly, to be more profoundly alone than ever before; ... I thus-- and not without a sullen wrathfulness-- took sides *against* myself and *for* everything that hurt *me* and was hard to *me*, and in this way I again found my way to that courageous pessimism that is the antithesis of all romantic mendacity, and also, as it seems to me today, the way to 'myself', to *my* task.[37]

Nietzsche was not simply exploring, then, but he was working with an animus in virtue of which he was not altogether free to allow his insights to transform themselves and to evolve in unconstrained fashion beyond their initial forms.

In his determined seeking to prove himself no longer dominated by others and to be master in his own life and thought, he concedes in retrospect having gone to extremes, and becoming sick in another way that was potentially debilitating psychologically. This time, it was an excessively rationalistic thrust, counter to the romanticism he would dissociate himself from. His reflective bent being marked by deepening suspicion, he sought to overturn all that he found veiled or guarded by a sense of shame, and sought to see what it looked like when reversed. For such a young soul in this condition, "it is an act of willfulness, and pleasure in willfulness, if now he perhaps bestows his favor on what had hitherto had a bad reputation-- if, curious and the tempted to experiment, he creeps around the things most forbidden." In this way, proceeding restlessly and aimlessly as if wandering in a desert, there developed in him an "increasingly dangerous curiosity: 'Cannot *all* valuations be reversed? ... In the final analysis is everything perhaps false? And if we are deceived, are we not precisely thereby also deceivers, *must* we not also be deceivers?'"[38]

In this desert of experiment and testing to unmask anything and everything, his solitude deepened into a morbid isolation, and to keep himself alive spiritually, he had recourse-- and this time, apparently, more knowingly and transparently than before-- to the same fictionalization that he had earlier engaged in with Schopenhauer and Wagner. Thus

> when I needed to, I once also *invented* for myself the 'free spirits' to whom this melancholy-valiant book with the title *Human all-too-human* is dedicated: 'free spirits' of this kind do not exist, did not exist-- but, as I have said, I had need of them at that time for company, so that good things remain amidst the ills (sickness, solitude, unfamiliar places, *acedia* [Greek for "indifference"], inactivity): ... as compensation for the friends I lacked. That free spirits of this kind *could* one day exist, that our Europe *will* have such vigorously-active and audacious fellows among its sons of tomorrow and the next day, physically present and palpable and not (as in my case) merely phantoms and hermit's phantasmagoria: *I* should wish to be the last to doubt it.[39]

While this was taking place spiritually, his physical illness worsened.

> Here, in a manner that I cannot admire sufficiently and precisely at the right time, my father's *wicked* heritage came to my aid-- at bottom, predestination to an early death. Sickness *detached me slowly*: it spared me any break, any violent and offensive step. Thus I did not lose any good will and even gained a good bit. My sickness also gave me the right to change all my habits completely; it permitted, it *commanded* me to forget; it bestowed on me the *necessity* of lying still, of leisure, of waiting and being patient.-- But that means, of thinking.-- My eyes alone put an end to all bookwormishness-- in brief, philology: I was delivered from the 'book'; for years I did not read a thing-- the *greatest* benefit I ever conferred on myself.-- That nethermost self which had, as it were, been buried and grown silent under the continual *having-to-listen* to other selves (and that is after all what reading means) awakened slowly, shyly, dubiously-- but eventually, it *spoke again*. Never have I felt happier with myself than in the sickest and most painful times of my life: one only need look at *Dawn* or perhaps *The Wanderer and His Shadow* to comprehend what this 'return to *myself*' was-- a supreme kind of *recovery*.-- The other kind merely followed from this.[40]

Nietzsche's physical illness not only induced or invited such changes in the way he spent his days, but that illness and in particular the pain he suffered in its course had a major role in how his thought developed, for the changes it entered into the responsive matrix of his reflections.

On the level of life itself, in face of the pain he responded with the determination to retain his composure, to maintain his equilibrium and even a gratitude toward life. And against the conclusions which are wont to grow like poisonous fungi from pain and disappointment, isolation, and the like, he was determined to defend life and strike down such conclusions.[41] On the level of reflection, his response was just as courageous and determined, and was able to turn the occasion to good use.

> Only great pain is the ultimate liberator of the spirit, being the teacher of *the great suspicion* that turns every *U* into an *X*, a genuine *X*, the letter before the penultimate one. Only great pain, the long, slow pain that takes its time-- one in which we are burned, as it were, with green wood-- compels us philosophers to descend into our ultimate depths and to put aside all trust, everything good-natured, everything that veils, that is mild, that is medium-- things in which formerly we may have found our humanity. I doubt that such pain makes us 'better'; but I know that it makes us *more profound*. Whether we learn to pit our pride, our scorn, our will-power against it, equaling the American Indian ..., or whether we withdraw from pain into that Oriental Nothing--

called Nirvana-- into mute, rigid, deaf resignation, self-forgetting, self-extinction: out of such long and dangerous exercises of self-mastery one emerges as a different human being, with a few more question marks-- above all with *the will* henceforth to question further, more deeply, severely, harshly, evilly, and quietly, than one had questioned heretofore. The trust in life is gone: life itself has become a *problem*. Yet one should not believe that this necessarily makes one gloomy. Even love of life is still possible, only one loves differently. It is the love for a woman that causes doubts in us. The attraction of everything problematic, the joy in an *X*, however, is so great in such more spiritual, more spiritualized human beings, that like a bright blaze this delight ever again enfolds all the distress of what is problematic, all the danger of uncertainty, and even the jealousy of the lover. We know a new happiness.[42]

In this time of 'sickness'-- the spiritual sickness of extreme response to internal upheaval, the physical sickness of deteriorating bodily condition--, Nietzsche became physician and patient in one, and in retrospect prides himself on his fundamental health and his healthy decisions.

I have always instinctively chosen the *right* means against bad [*schlimmen*] states ... . The energy for absolute solitude and detachment from situations to which I had become accustomed; the insistence on not allowing myself any longer to be cared for, waited on, and *doctored*-- that betrayed an absolute instinctive certainty about *what* was needed above all at that time. I took myself in hand, I made myself healthy again: the condition for this-- as every physiologist would admit-- is *that one be healthy at bottom*. A typically morbid being cannot become healthy, much less make itself healthy. For a typically healthy person, conversely, being sick can even become an energetic *stimulus* for life, for living more [*Mehrleben*]. This, in fact, is how that long period of sickness appears to me *now*: as it were, I discovered life anew, including myself; I tasted all good and even little things as others cannot easily taste them-- I made my philosophy out of my will to health, to *life*.[43]

If, then, the 'earthquake' initiated-- and made clear the need for-- a fundamental reassessment and shift, and if his increasing illness forced upon him numerous changes in life, Nietzsche's physician-like response to these pressures amounted to transferring himself-as-patient into totally strange surroundings "in order that he be removed from his entire 'hitherto', from his cares, friends, letters, duties, stupidities and painful memories, and learn to stretch out his hands and senses after new nourishment, a new sun, a new future"[44]. This self-removal from the old and reaching for the new marked not simply his way of life, but also what was central to that, his reflection. It is not so much his immersion in the sciences, and in things that were new for him and distant from the old in that vein, that is involved here. It is, even more, his exploration of the phenomena behind (and explanatory of) the 'world' he had inhabited before. He entered himself upon "a wandering on by-ways amidst strange things, in *strangeness* itself, upon a curiosity for every kind of strange thing"[45]-- in the world beyond the accepted and conventional. In the course of this wandering, he also discovered and prescribed (in virtue of his still-healthy instinct) an anti-romantic self-treatment that would bring a spiritual cure,[46] and sought not simply to undermine the romanticism that seems to him now a disease that had infected him, but also to conduct "with myself a patient and tedious campaign against the unscientific basic-tendency of every romantic pessimism to interpret and inflate individual personal experiences into universal judgments and, indeed, into condemnations of the world"[47]. In this, he enlisted his expanding studies of the sciences, and "turned my perspective around. Optimism, for the purpose of restoration, so that at some future time I could again *have the right* to be a pessimist... ."[48]

Once he began to define and enact his self-prescription for his 'disease', the path of convalescence and recovery took "a long, all too long, series of years", and involved "relapse, decay, the periodicity of a kind of decadence".[49] In the first of those years, his path took him through

this stretch of desert, exhaustion, disbelief, icing up in the midst of youth, this old age inserted at the wrong place; this tyranny of pain even excelled by the tyranny of pride that refused the *conclusions* of pain-- and conclusions are consolations--; this radical recourse to solitude as a self-defense against a contempt for men that had become pathologically clear-sighted [*hell-seherisch*]--; this principled self-limitation to what was bitter, harsh, and hurtful to know, prescribed by the *nausea* that had gradually developed out of an incautious and pampering spiritual diet, called romanticism ... .[50]

But after a long process of roaming, seeking, changing, with a dietary and discipline that supported the high-flying of the soul, there came in time a great spiritual strengthening, a growing joy and fulness of health; and finally recovery:

> Life itself *rewards* us for our tenacious will to life, for such a long war as I then waged with myself against the pessimistic weariness of life, even for every attentive glance of our gratitude that does not let escape even the smallest, tenderest, most fleeting of life's gifts. In the end we receive for that life's *great* gift, perhaps the greatest it can bestow-- we receive back *our task*.[51]

Along the way of this uneven path of convalescence and gradual recovery, there are certain landmarks which Nietzsche recalls. The first is a mid-way condition of delicate light and sunshine happiness, unfettered from love and hate.[52] A step further and life has drawn nearer, and it has grown warmer around the recovering spirit; feeling has gained depth, and thawing winds pass lightly over such a one. The near and nearest things have changed, acquired bloom and magic, and what surprises he experiences as he sees himself, finds himself having slowly become healthier, and feels his will to health venturing to clothe and disguise itself as health already achieved although in fact his was only a condition health*ier* than it had been.[53] But eventually, the return to health occurs, this time in the form of a "tremendous overflowing assurance [*Sicherheit*] and health": a "*mature* freedom of spirit which is just as much self-mastery and discipline of the heart and which permits access to many and contradictory modes of thought", an "inner encompassingness and indulgence which belong to superabundance and which exclude the danger that the spirit may even on its own road perhaps lose itself and become infatuated and remain seated intoxicated in some corner or other", a "surplus of formative, curative, molding and restorative forces which is precisely the sign of *great* health, that surplus which grants to the free spirit the dangerous privilege of living *experimentally* and of being allowed to offer itself to adventure: the privilege of mastery [*Meisterschafts-Vorrecht*] that belongs to the free spirit!"[54] Health here is that fulness of life's vitality when this involves an extraordinary native endowment brought to actual creative functioning in its fullest realization.

5. Mid-life elicitation of meant-to-be's

The beginning of the path which eventually reached this point was in a confusion and disorientation, and a not knowing what was happening. Harbored there at the time, and reflecting the character of what was taking place, were certain questions: "Why so apart? so alone? denying everything that I revered? denying reverence itself? Why this hatred, this suspicion, this harshness toward my own virtues?" For long the enigma of that 'earthquake' had "waited dark, questionable, almost untouchable in his memory"; he did not dare to pose the questions to himself expressly. But finally, "under the sudden illumination of a still stressful, still changeable health", the spirit which was growing ever freer asked them aloud, and as he heard in reply something like an answer, the enigma of what had been happening to him-- of "this great liberation" that was now nearing its consummation-- began to reveal itself to him. The answering voice pointed now to what had been the meaning, the rationale, implicit in the transformation that began back then, what had been *meant to come of* the start that was being made in the confusion and disorientation he experienced.

> 'You were supposed to [*solltest*] become master over yourself, also over your virtues. Before, *they* were your masters; but they are permitted [*dürfen*] only to be your instruments along side other instruments.
> 'You were supposed [*solltest*] to get control over your For and Against and to learn to know

how, each time in accordance with your higher purpose [*Zwecke*], to display and hide them.

'You were supposed [*solltest*] to learn to grasp the what-is-perspectival in every value judg-ment (the displacement, distortion, and seeming teleology of horizons and whatever else pertains to the perspectival)-- also the portion of stupidity that marks opposed values, and the whole intellectual loss which every For, every Against, costs us.

'You were supposed [*solltest*] to learn to grasp the *necessary* injustice in every For and Against, injustice as inseparable from life, life itself as *conditioned* by the perspectival and its injustice.

'You were supposed [*solltest*] above all to see with your own eyes where injustice is always greatest, namely, there where life has developed in the least, narrowest, neediest [*dürftigsten*], most initial [*anfänglichsten*], fashion, and yet cannot avoid taking *itself* as the purpose and mea-sure of things and for the sake of its own preservation secretly and pettily and ceaselessly crumbles away and calls into question the higher, greater, richer.

'You were supposed [*solltest*] to see with your own eyes the problem of the *order of rank*, and how power [*Macht*] and right and encompassingness of perspective grow into the heights together.

'You were supposed [*solltest*] ... ': enough, from now on the free spirit *knows* what 'you shall' [*du sollst*] he has obeyed [*gehorcht hat*], and he also knows what he now *can* do, what only now he *is permitted to* do ... .[55]

For all the focus on change, the becoming which Nietzsche has been recalling, being a 'become what you are', has its peculiar sameness-in-and-amidst-difference, both as regards life itself and as regards the reflective development of Nietzsche as a philosopher. In regards the latter, his return to himself is a return to what he had begun being in youth, the 'tragic philosopher'. For

there is a will to the tragic and to pessimism that is as much a sign of severity as of strength [*Stärke*] of intellect (taste, feeling, conscience). With this will in one's breast one has no fear of the fearful and questionable that belongs to all existence; one even seeks it out. Behind such a will there stands courage, pride, the longing for a *great* enemy. This has been *my* pessimistic perspective from the beginning-- a novel perspective, is it not? A perspective that even today is still novel and strange? To this very moment I continue to adhere to it and, if you will believe me, just as much *for* myself as, occasionally at least, *against* myself.[56]

But the 'himself' to which he returns is not identical with the earlier form of himself, for

from such abysses, from such severe sickness, also from the sickness of severe suspicion, one returns *newborn*, having shed one's skin, more ticklish and malicious, with a more delicate taste for joy, with a more sensitive tongue for all good things, with merrier [*lustigeren*] senses, with a second dangerous innocence in joy, more child-like and yet a hundred times subtler [*raf-finierter*] than one has ever been before.[57]

In particular,

there are a few things we now know too well, we knowing ones: oh, how we now learn to forget well, and to be good at *not* knowing, as artists! And as for our future [as inquirers], one will hardly find us again on the paths of those Egyptian youths who endanger temples by night, em-brace statues, and want by all means to unveil, uncover, and put into a bright light, whatever is kept concealed for good reasons. No, this bad taste, this will to truth, to 'truth at any price', this youthful madness in the love of truth, is spoiled for us; for that we are too experienced, too seri-ous, too merry, too burned, too profound. We no longer believe that truth remains truth when the veils are withdrawn; we have lived too much to believe this. Today we consider it a matter of decency not to wish to see everything naked, or to be present at everything, or to understand and 'know' everything. 'Is it true that God is present everywhere?' a little girl asked her mother; 'I think that's indecent'-- a hint for philosophers! One should have more respect for the *bash-fulness* with which nature has hidden behind riddles and brightly-colored uncertainties. Perhaps truth is a woman who has reasons for not letting us see her reasons? Perhaps her name is (to speak Greek) Baubo? Oh, those Greeks! They knew how to *live*. What is required for that is to stop courageously at the surface, the fold, the skin, to adore appearance, to believe in forms, tones, words, in the whole Olympus of appearance. Those Greeks were superficial-- out of profundity. And is this not precisely what we are again coming back to, we daredevils of the spirit who have scaled the highest and most dangerous peak of present thought and looked around from up there-- we who have *looked down* from there? Are we not, precisely in this respect, Greeks? Adorers of forms, of tones, of words? and therefore-- artists?[58]

Such is Nietzsche's account of his life up to the time of his recounting, put to a great extent in his own words and thus framed for the most part in the terms which he thinks are relevant at the mid-life perspective from which he is recalling things. Or more precisely: framed in the terms needed for presenting himself publicly to his readers in the way he wanted to. It is in the light of this sense of his being as the growing and changing one just sketched out that we are to understand his writings. Let us see how this is so.

B. Writings as expressing his life

In the retrospect of the prime of both his life and his reflective life, Nietzsche sees the writings from earlier times in his life as the work of reflection *as he was capable* of pursuing it *in those times*. Thus since philosophy is a transformation of one's being into 'light and flame',[59] the earlier writings expressed and reflected his being *as it was then*, or in his retrospect, *as it appears to him now to have been then*. Because of the 'becoming'-character of that being-- and that means, of his capacity for living and for engaging in the work his life ordains for him--, the *fuller* being of himself at the time of his mid-life retrospect enables his past works to appear to him at that place as having characteristics which were not-- and could not have been-- visible to him at the time of their composition and publication. Since our concern in the main body of this study will be with the works of the first two phases of his thought and the beginning of the third, let us note how he represents those works *as seeming to him now* in retrospect. In particular let us note how, having grown through those times and grown beyond the capacity he had then, and being ready for and on the verge now of a culminating venture, he would bring them and what they attempted to our attention and would connect this with his evolving being and the movement of his life as he could see these now.

1. First phase

Philosophical writings arise out of philosophical reflection. Now the reflective mode of thought emerges at the earliest in youth, when we are entered by ongoing life into the need to take responsibility for our lives and to reflect on life's meaning in connection with that responsibility. When that reflection broadens to become philosophical, and when it becomes animated by the need to talk with others about the matters in question, to challenge the ideas of others and to submit one's own ideas to challenge, then writing can gain a role in the ensuing dialogue. In this first phase Nietzsche's thinking and writing do not simply express certain things which belong inherently to youth and which we all might find in youth; but they are also marked by various things which are particular to himself and his circumstance and which became important occasions and foci for his reflection at the time: his experience of the German educational system, for one, and the claims of Christianity which his deepening suspicion was bringing into altered light for him; likewise his particular sensitivity to music, and his discovery of the Dionysian phenomenon among the Greeks, his happening on the writings of Schopenhauer, and his intense and promising involvement with Wagner. From early on, his reflection was also intimately tied up with the sense of needing to act on what insight was disclosing and thereby to *live* the philosophy that was emerging in his thought; with his own educational experience and then his experience of teaching, this meant initially the need to achieve educational reform. Then with the increasing dominance of Wagner in his life and thought, the activist outworking of his reflection became broadened into practical concern with a basic cultural revolution, so that writing's function as sharing and as fostering discussion and practical action became developed to serve the furthering of such revolutionary change.

In his retrospect on the writings of this phase, Nietzsche sees himself having composed works most of which were deeply ambivalent. In most cases his retrospects on them seek to sort out the aspects and reasons of that ambivalence, and to acknowledge the limitations he sees now as well as to affirm the strengths, and to note the type of continuity which he sees and which leads him to claim that from the start and up to where he is at the time of his retrospect he has been and is the 'tragic philosopher', the follower of the philosopher Dionysus. This continuity is not one of sameness: he is Dionysian at the end only under a transformation of his initial Dionysian being and only as issue of a re-forming of his thought and a re-interpreting of evidence which have amplified and purified that beginning. His books up to the time of his retrospects bear witness to such a process, and with it, to eventual insight and claims to truth the character of which amounts to the fuller and more apt appropriation of matters he was dealing with at the start but doing so in a way flawed by (among other things) certain defects of youth.

a. *The Birth of Tragedy*

Of his first published work, *The Birth of Tragedy out of the Spirit of Music*, Nietzsche later says:

> What I then got hold of, something frightful and dangerous, ... today I should say that it was *the problem of science itself*, science considered for the first time as problematic, as questionable. But the book in which my youthful courage and suspicion then found an outlet-- what an *impossible* book had to arise from a task so uncongenial to youth! Constructed from a lot of premature, overgreen personal experiences, all of them hard on the threshold of what can be communicated, presented in the context of *art*-- for the problem of science cannot be recognized in the context of science-- a book perhaps for artists who have the added-penchant and capacity for analysis and retrospection ... ; a youthful work full of the courage and moody melancholy of youth [*Jugendmut, Jugend-Schwermut*], independent, defiantly self-reliant even where it seems to bow before an authority and personal reverence; in sum, a first book, also in every bad sense of that label. In spite of the problem which seems congenial to old age, the book is marked by every defect of youth, above all by its 'much-too-long' and its 'storm and stress'.[60]

Being the time of life when maturationally we are initially to assume our lives upon ourselves and take responsibility for them, youth is also the time when by nature our capacity for such assumption is meant to be amplified by the discovery of the pointer into the future which is aspiration. In Nietzsche's case, in virtue of the particularity of his nature a musical sensitivity was drawn into play during this time, so that his encounter with Schopenhauer's writings, which spoke of music as uniquely voicing the very heart of reality and in particular voicing the suffering present there, could appeal strongly on that basis. But what appealed most about Schopenhauer was the candor and honesty Nietzsche seemed to see in him; and reinforced by this, his own youthful response to the call to reflection initially being felt at this time of life under the pull of aspiration was deepened in the suspiciousness ingredient in it and was strengthened in the courage inward to it as a venturing. Knowing in this way an ardent and idealistic love of truth, he knows also a moody-melancholy that is characteristic of youth, that is, the youthful mood arising when the apparently inherent and unremediable suffering at the heart of reality comes to be registered against what aspiration is summoning one to reach for and seems to promise is possible here at the start of life.

How Nietzsche experienced and understood youth when he was himself young comes out especially in UHH and SE. When composing his retrospect, however, he finds himself at some distance from youth, and sees it somewhat differently than he did at the time. At this mid-life distance he says of the work which was the first work of his youth:

I do not want to suppress entirely how disagreeable it now seems to me, how strange it stands before me after sixteen years-- before a much older, a hundred times more demanding, but by no means colder eye which has not become a stranger to the task which this audacious book dared to take on for the first time: *to look at science in the perspective of the artist, but at art in that of life.*[61]

Much has changed in him since then; his maturation in the intervening time has made him differently capable and differently constituted, so that what he is now is a considerably fuller realization of himself when compared with what he was then. The "fuller" realization retains in modified form the ardor and earnestness of the lesser, and also maintains touch with the task which earlier effort found itself facing and undertook; but it involves (among other things) a more patient and demanding address to the matters at issue, one less ready to take the disclosure of the time as ultimate and as needing little in the way of close attention and scrutiny for its meaning to be grasped.[62]

In virtue of the difference between himself-now and himself-then, this first book of his seems to him now "exceedingly strange". Its original core was his thoughts about the Greeks, and its basic new insights concerned the Dionysian phenomenon and Socrates. He emphasizes the former: why did the Greeks need tragedy, and more broadly, art? What need called these forth and made them so important? This was "a fascinating question of the first rank, and in addition to that, deeply personal"[63]. "I had *discovered* the only counterpart and likeness in history to my inmost experience--- and thus became the first to comprehend the wonderful phenomenon of the Dionysian."[64] In this work, he sees himself as having spoken with the voice of an initiate, for he knew first-hand through his experience something which gave him illuminating entry into Greek life[65]; but the disclosive experience was a youthful one, as was his capacity to deal with it at the time.

> Today I find it an impossible book: I consider it badly written, ponderous, painful, image-mad and image-confused, sentimental, in places saccharine to the point of effeminacy, uneven in tempo, without the will to logical cleanliness, very convinced and therefore disdainful of proof, mistrustful even of the *propriety* of proof, a book for initiates, 'music' for those dedicated to music, those who are closely related to begin with on the basis of common and rare aesthetic experiences, 'music' meant as a sign of recognition for blood-relatives in the arts-- an arrogant and rhapsodic book that sought to exclude right from the start the *profanum vulgus* of 'the cultured-and-educated' even more than the 'people' ... .[66]

But there was a second part to the work, and above all, in that part (but in some measure, throughout) he seems to "bow before an authority and personal reverence"[67]. Yet whether the authority-figure is Schopenhauer (in places) or Wagner (throughout), he knows-- as still being privy to his own condition at the time-- the independence and defiant self-reliance that were at work in him even if the written discussion masks this and betrays nothing of it on its surface. Thus: "How I regret now that at the time I still lacked the courage (or immodesty?) to permit myself in every way *my own individual language* for such individual views and hazards, and that I tried laboriously to express by means of Schopenhauerian and Kantian formulae strange and new valuations which were basically at odds with the spirit and taste of Kant and Schopenhauer!"[68] And yet,

> there is something much worse in this book, something I now regret still more than that I obscured and spoiled Dionysian premonitions with Schopenhauerian formulations: namely, that I *spoiled* the grandiose *Greek problem*, as it had arisen before my eyes, by intermixing the most modern things! That I appended hopes where there was no ground for hope, where everything pointed all too plainly to an end! That on the basis of the latest German music I began to tell tales about 'the German essence' as if it were just on the point of discovering and finding itself again-- at a time when the German spirit, which not long before had still had the will to dominate Europe and the strength to lead Europe, was just making its last will and testament and *abdicating* forever, making its transition, under the pompous pretense of founding a *Reich*, to a leveling mediocrity, democracy, and 'modern ideas'![69]

It is this sense of having allowed Wagner to have too great and inappropriate a role in steering the expression of his thought in the work that most reflects the distance between the author of this retrospect and the author of the original work.

In short: looking back on his first published work, Nietzsche recalls it as the work of a time in his life at which his capacity for reflection and his experience of life were youthful, meaning: not simply were they limited and relatively undeveloped, but they were infused with a spirit characteristic of the immaturity of the time of life he was in. There was potency there, indeed, but impotence as well. Judged from his later standpoint, the book does not express well even the thoughts he was developing at the time; but more deeply, those thoughts were still not getting adequately to the heart of the matter which, nonetheless, had registered in him in youthful fashion and which he was attempting to address. However much, then, he was able in his youth to find himself at the heart of things and to address matters of central philosophical importance, his was a youthful being-there and one whose immaturity not only limited his achievement but, given the insufficiency of his youthful courage to enable him to establish himself there simply as himself, implicated him in a yielding to others of a role which, however supportive it also was, distorted that achievement.

b. The *Untimely Meditations*

Untimely Meditations is the name for a series which Nietzsche projected and of which he completed four works. About these four, he recalls that "they are thoroughly warlike"[70]; and that is in keeping with the sense he had (from beginning to end) of the natural relation of the philosopher to his times, namely, that of a critic and bad conscience. In particular, it squares with his sense of himself at the time as participating in the cultural revolution in which Wagner was the major figure and as composing works that would further that revolution.

Of the three essays our study will concern itself with, the earliest-- *The Utility and Harmfulness of History for Life*-- carries through his attack in the primary spheres that were of interest to him long before he met Wagner, namely, culture and education. Its point is to bring to vocal consciousness the resistance, the protest, of youth against the current educational system in which it finds itself enmeshed. That system is marked by two presumptions which run counter to youth's needs: that culture is an addition to oneself, an adornment acquired by incorporation from without, rather than a transformation of the life evolving within oneself; and that this incorporation was mainly of knowledge, so that the cultured human being was the learned scholar and the transformation of historical study by its development as science was unconditionally a positive affair. In this work Nietzsche expressly situates himself in youthful experience, but in a somewhat different side of it than that which gave him access to what was central to BT. It is the side of youth's hopefulness, of its reaching for fuller life in future and for that self-transformation of life which issues in culture; it was this side that the educational system was failing to serve. Not only does this work show little trace of Schopenhauer and Wagner-- here Nietzsche comes as close as he ever did in the published works of early youth to speaking his own voice directly--, but he has nothing to say self-critically about it in his retrospect and little to say overall.[71]

In contrast with UHH, SE and WB are not only closely linked expressly with their ostensible subject-figures (Schopenhauer, Wagner), but are also linked with them in a way not acknowledged in the works and of which Nietzsche seems to have been only half-aware at the time.

> In the *third* and *fourth* Untimely Ones, two images of the hardest self-love, self-discipline, are put up ... as pointers to a *higher* concept of culture, to the restoration of the concept of culture-- untimely types *par excellence*, full of sovereign contempt for everything around them that was called 'Empire', 'culture', 'Christianity', 'Bismarck', 'success'-- Schopenhauer and Wagner *or*, in *one* word, Nietzsche.[72]

Put more fully, in the two essays

an unequaled problem of education, a new concept of *self-discipline, self-defense* to the point of hardness, a way to greatness and world-historical tasks, longed for its first expression. Broadly speaking, I caught hold of two famous and as yet altogether undiagnosed types, as one catches hold of an opportunity, in order to say something, to have at hand a few more formulae, signs, means of language. This is really suggested with a perfectly uncanny sagacity [near the end of section 7] in the third Untimely Meditation. Plato employed Socrates in this fashion ... . Now that I am looking back from a certain distance upon the conditions of which these essays bear witness, I do not wish to deny that at bottom they speak only of me. The essay *Wagner in Bayreuth* is a vision of my future, while in *Schopenhauer as Educator* my innermost history, my *becoming*, is inscribed. Above all, my *promise!*[73]

What does it mean that "at bottom" the two works speak only of Nietzsche himself? We noted above, in considering Nietzsche's life-movement and the dynamic and decisive turns in it, that in retrospect Nietzsche felt that in his early years he had allowed the Schopenhauer and Wagner who had resonated in him and his youthful aspiration to gain a hold over him and to draw him astray, away from the path to his own task and work. In these two meditations as illuminated by his retrospect upon them, we see more fully how he understands that this was so. On their face the two essays are focused on two individuals other than Nietzsche, and accordingly attend to particularities of *their* natures, *their* actions and thoughts, *their* circumstances. Even if that treatment sets forth the thoughts and being of the two persons in such way as to make of them types and not simply individuals, even these types are presented as expressly involving Nietzsche only as someone inspired by them, not as himself *being* either or both of them. But in retrospect he acknowledges: the two figures came across to him in his youth as bodying forth in their way of being and thinking a way of engaging with things which evoked a resonance in him at the time because they seemed to express on a grander scale and higher plane something kindred to, and reinforcing for, the aspiration which he felt to be central to himself then. Or more fully and precisely, they expressed something kindred to, and reinforcing for, a complex sensibility in himself, focused perhaps in the reaching of aspiration but harboring sensitivities to various facets of the world. These sensitivities were a sounding-board sufficiently set in vibration by them that in Wagner and Schopenhauer he seemed to find spirits kindred to his own in ways important to him at the time, and what is more, spirits attesting settled lives that had sustained the way of being and thinking in question quite beyond the youthful time he knew in himself-- indeed in Schopenhauer's case, throughout a life lived to the end in that spirit. Reinforced in his own reaching by the felt kinship in spirit, Nietzsche could also find that ideas which these revered figures advanced, as he understood these at the time, were helpful in interpreting the matters that were at issue in his youthful reflection. In retrospect however, it seems to him that he did not so much draw on his own experience to understand *them* as 'project' himself[74] into them-- or perhaps better, implicitly transform them into (alien) versions of himself. Thus in speaking later of WB and the tragic attitude adumbrated in it, he says: "This is the strangest 'objectivity' possible: the absolute certainty about what I *am* was projected on some accidental reality-- the truth about me spoke from some gruesome depth."[75] And again:

A psychologist might still add that what I in my youth had heard in Wagner's music had nothing at all to do with Wagner; that when I described Dionysian music I described what *I* had heard-- that instinctively I had to transpose and transfigure everything into the new spirit that I carried in me. The proof of that, *as strong as any proof can be*, is my essay on *Wagner in Bayreuth*: in all psychologically decisive places I alone am discussed; and one may ruthlessly put down my name or the word 'Zarathustra' where the text has the word 'Wagner'. The entire picture of the *dithyrambic* artist is one of the *pre-existent* poet of *Zarathustra*, sketched with abysmal profundity and without touching even for a moment the Wagnerian reality.[76]

Or finally:

What I am today, *where* I am today-- at a height where I speak no longer with words but with lightning bolts-- ah, how remote from this I still was at that time!-- But I *beheld* the land-- I did not deceive myself for a moment about the way, the sea, the danger-- *and* success. ... How I understand the philosopher-- as a terrible explosive, endangering everything-- how my concept of the philosopher is miles apart from any concept that would include even a Kant, not to speak of academic 'ruminants' and other professors of philosophy-- this essay (SE) gives inestimable information about that, although at bottom it is admittedly not 'Schopenhauer as Educator' that speaks here, but his *opposite*, 'Nietzsche as Educator'.[77]

Thus works which, on their face, delineated others and (in the case of SE) also Nietzsche's response to someone other to himself, were in actuality media in which, in the mis-taking and mis-representing presentation of those others, he was indirectly and in disguised fashion expressing and working through matters he was involved in in his own becoming, matters of his own nature and promise and future. Just as in responding to Wagner's music, he was transposing it into his own spirit and making 'Dionysian music' out of it, so in his treatment of Schopenhauer and Wagner in these two work, he was transmuting them into his own spirit while nonetheless presenting them as themselves, without hint of the transmutation that was going on. How much he was self-conscious to this *at the time*, how (and how far) he understood *then* what was taking place, Nietzsche indicates only to the extent revealed in the quotation of the first HAH Preface which we cited above[78]: apparently, he was half-aware at the time that his need for company and connection was overmastering the complex awareness that he had, and when it came to writing, this need was leading to his dismissing differences as unimportant and to stretching likenesses into identities. Thus he was agent half-wittingly drawn to "force, falsify, invent" the Schopenhauer and Wagner of these two essays, and to offer a rendering of them which was made possible by the entry into them that his own nature at the time permitted but which was given its ultimate shape by an uneasy but necessitated stretching and dismissing which amounted to pretense. Put differently: at the time he lacked the courage to make the difference apparent, and thereby to do something which violated the reverence which he felt for those figures.

The matter here is complex: if (as we saw earlier[79]) Nietzsche makes courage central to philosophy and its seeking for the truth of the meaning of human life, and claims that every step forward in knowledge follows from courage, this 'following from' only means that courage is a necessary condition, not that it is a sufficient one. SE and WB may express his own youthful cowardice in the face of truth, and not simply the truth of Schopenhauer and Wagner but the truth which the philosopher seeks, the truth of the meaning of human life. But even if he had been wholly courageous at the time (supposing that that is possible for youth), he would not have been *able* both to see and to understand the truth of that matter. For as he has pointed out in recalling BT, youth involves other insufficiencies which mean that youthful seeing is unavoidably slanted and incomplete, and youthful understanding unavoidably premature and limited. Whatever measure of moral and reflective insufficiency are expressed in SE and WB, however, in his retrospective eye there was at work in himself (along with all that was merely youthful) a power, a destining power, which, functioning in the unconscious side of his decision-making and -executing at the time, was effectively leading him, even as he was going astray. And that power's presence and working is attested in the kinship he felt with Schopenhauer and Wagner, in the inspiration stemming from them, in the reinforcement by them of his 'seeing'-- a genuine 'seeing' despite his having been disposed toward a mis-taking of the disclosure taking place in it by his incapacity to stand his ground effectively against the two powerful presences and to develop his very own understanding and find the proper words for its expression.

2. Second phase

According to Nietzsche's retrospective view, the second phase of his thinking and writing takes its start from the crucial experience of disillusionment at Bayreuth which we have noticed in our recall of his life course. In that earlier discussion, we noted that the shock of this experience was two-sided: one, it was a challenge to him in his personal becoming, a challenge to complete the act of assuming personal responsibility by entering upon the path that would regain his 'work' as 'his own';

and two, it was a challenge to him in his reflection, not simply to modify ideas he had developed but more deeply to alter the very way in which he had been involved in reflection. On the personal side, the shock was the beginning of a gathering of himself back out of what he had become involved in doing with his life (being a philologist, a teacher) and back to what was needed for him to evolve out of himself in his own way as the budding philosopher he was. The completion of his assumption of his own life on himself demanded an effective re-commitment of himself to his own philosophical work. This in turn demanded both a change in life-style to one that would support this and a venturing in reflection to hold fast more effectively to his own immediate sense of reality and life and to ground his interpretative thought better in this sense. On the side of reflection, the shock was the impetus to his thinking's breaking free from what his various loves and his reverence for certain men had done to generate a horizon and framework which, while it had seemed to aid his thinking, was imprisoning it and limiting the way he had been able to address the matters he needed to address-- the way he had been able to carry out the reflection that was his life-commitment.[80]

In short: the disillusionment disclosed that a transformation was underway in his reflection-centered being and needed to be completed in an effective way, bringing with it an altered way of life; and inward to this, in the reflection that was to be central still in that changed way of life, it disclosed the need for an altered way of addressing matters in that thinking, and that means: in the responsive taking up into reflection of what he was opened and opening to in the altering disclosive matrix for that reflection which the underway-transformation of his being was providing. In their overall character, the works of this phase are the fruit of the concerted self-criticism and self-purification which ensued. But as the restoration of himself to himself succeeded, and within this, as the disclosive matrix of his reflection altered and as his developing thought-capacity gained strength and confidence in the attempt to go at things reflectively in this significantly different fashion, the changes eventually entered him upon another (third) phase of his thought, and with it, need for a further alteration in his mode of writing.

a. *Human all-too-human*

The initial writing to express the re-focusing of attention and energy after the disillusionment at Bayreuth was HAH. The work published in 1878 under that title was the "monument of a crisis"; in it "I liberated myself from *what* in my nature *did not belong to me.*"[81] If it was in a youthful involvement that Nietzsche had acquired what he felt the need now to free himself from, the effort that gradually achieved this liberation was youthful as well. Thus in an aphorism in BGE, Nietzsche observes:

> In one's youthful years one venerates and despises without that art of nuances which constitutes the best gain of life, and it is only fair that one has to pay dearly for having assaulted men and things in this manner with Yes and No. All is arranged so that the worst of all tastes, the taste for the unconditional, is cruelly fooled and abused before a human being learns to place a bit of art into his feelings and preferably still to risk trying the artificial: as the rightful artists of life do. The wrathful and reverent attitudes which belong to youth do not seem to give themselves any rest until they have falsified men and things in such a way that these attitudes may be vented on them. Youth in itself is an affair of falsification and deception to some extent. Later, when the young soul, tortured by nothing but disappointments, finally turns suspiciously against itself, ever still hot and wild even in its suspicion and pangs of conscience-- how angry it is with itself now! how impatiently it tears itself to pieces! how it takes revenge for its long self-delusion, just as if it had been a deliberate blindness! In this transition one punishes oneself with mistrust against one's own feelings; one tortures one's own enthusiasm with doubts; indeed, one feels even a good conscience as a danger, as if it were a way of veiling one's eyes and of exhausting one's subtler honesty; and above all one takes sides, takes sides on principle, *against* 'youth'.-- Ten years later and one comprehends that all this, too, was still youth.[82]

In the effort to free himself from what no longer bore even the appearance of belonging to and expressing himself, Nietzsche recalls his reflection's having moved within an altered experiencing;

for under the combined force of physical illness and mental weariness, the life-alluring haze over things had disappeared from the disclosive matrix. Within that matrix 'cold reason' pursued a reflective attention to what was given, but animated by self-mistrust, nausea, and bitterness, 'reason' was determined upon undermining, negating and rejecting. While the role of feeling in many emotional inflections was mistrusted, there was in fact a strong and emotional animus animating such 'reason', and in particular, an extreme of suspicion which was bent on finding acceptable only such insights as undermined his previous 'idealism' in a plausible 'rational' fashion. Enlisting his developing interest in the sciences in service of this animus, and along with that interest enlisting a renewed intellectual conscience and an intense determination not to be fooled by anything or to deceive himself again, Nietzsche seemed to himself at the time to have strengthened in himself the spirit of enlightenment. Thus in the book itself,

> the tone, the voice, has completely changed: you will find the book clever, cool, occasionally hard and mocking. A certain spirituality of *noble* taste seems to be continually holding itself on high ground against a more passionate current. ... On closer inspection you will discover a merciless spirit that knows all the hideouts where the ideal is at home-- where it has its secret dungeons and, as it were, its ultimate safety. A torch whose light never wavers is beamed with incisive brilliance into this *underworld* of the ideal. This is war, but without powder and smoke, without warlike poses, without pathos and strained limbs: all that would still be 'idealism'. One error after another is placed on the ice; the ideal is not refuted-- it *freezes* to death.-- Here, for example, 'the genius' freezes to death; at the next corner, 'the saint'; under a thick icicle, 'the hero'; in the end, 'faith', so-called 'conviction', freezes to death; 'pity' also significantly cools down-- and almost everywhere 'the thing in itself' freezes to death.[83]

Nonetheless, the effort which appealed to 'reason' manifested an extremism, a sickness, which if left unchecked would destroy the inquirer.[84] Even so, the inquiry which marks this "monument of rigorous self-discipline with which I put a sudden end to my being infected with 'higher swindle', 'idealism', 'beautiful feelings', and other effeminacies"[85] is continued unabated in the two original appendices which later form Part II of the republished work. Throughout all these works, the ultimate horizon of inquiry that is acceptable is time and the temporal; life and experience no longer are allowed to lead back to the timeless, or to be seen against the background of the timeless. Not only is the metaphysical rejected, so that the physical (including the psychological, even making it central) is now the exhaustive field for inquiry; but the 'romantic' reading of experience which sees in certain 'mystical' encounters an opening into the heart of true being and an immediate grasp of the latter's nature is rejected as hasty and unfounded. As alternative to that 'romantic' tendency to interpret in inflated fashion the disclosive force of certain individual personal experiences, Nietzsche turned to something which he saw in the sciences, a methodical procedure in which small but well-established empirical truths were key and formed the basis for building a solid structure by the patient accumulation and putting together of such truths.[86] And yet the 'scientific', however important now for its content as well as method, is filtered for a mainly critical use, as vehicle for rejecting what seemed to him now grandiose and pretentious.

In short: Nietzsche recalls HAH as representing a shift which is of such character that "to no psychologist or reader of signs will it remain hidden for a moment what state in the evolution [of the 'free spirit'] the ... book belongs to ... ."[87] While the disclosive matrix for the insights presented is colored now by disillusion, disgust, self-mistrust, and the like, the thinking is released to develop itself in new fields and within an altered horizon, and to understand itself differently. In Nietzsche's own retrospect, HAH is the work of a 'sick' man determined to free himself from an earlier 'illness' that has infected him, even if it means introducing as inoculant a power (reason, science) which carries disease of another sort. There emerges, indeed, a fictional companion to this courageous but illness-beset man, namely, the 'free spirit'; and in the image of such a spirit, a future health is anticipated in the way a sick man might anticipate it-- in an anticipation which projects only a pale version of what health eventually turns out to be like. The book then embodies insights such as a person of this sort (youthful, sick, courageous) could achieve under such conditions-- those of a morbidly-solitary wanderer[88] making his way in the desert, looking for companions but finding only 'science' and a fictive 'free spirit'. Those insights will receive further transformation and refinement as convalescence and recovery of health proceed; but it is only with D (or perhaps a bit with WS, the second original appendix to HAH[89]) that the wanderer begins to return to himself and to feel the flush of reviving life registering in and modifying the disclosive matrix for his thought. By then certain patterns of interpretation have become established in this re-formed address to reflective matters, and further exploration of the expanding disclosure-matrix carries them forward.

b. *Dawn*

Nietzsche says little in EH or in the later added Prefaces about the condition out of which he thought and composed this work. Both the recall in EH and in the Preface added to the work itself point primarily to its thematic focus and achievement, not to the experiencing which enables its insights.[90] Of the latter, however, he does speak in two ways.

First way: The turn taken and manifest in HAH is continued in D, but there is a considerable concentration on one matter central in the thought of his first-phase works (especially UHH and SE), namely, morality. Thus he points out that within the disclosive matrix that was now his[91], his was the inquiring of a "solitary mole" who, "going forward slowly, cautiously, with gentle inexorableness" on his own individual path, found himself commencing the investigating, the digging out, the undermining of "our *confident trust in morality* [*Vertrauen zur Moral*]".[92] Put more pointedly, his was the concerted effort, in the presence of morality, not to simply entrust himself to it and to obey its commands but rather to regard morality as a problem and to address it critically-- and thus to act immorally (for in its presence, morality does not allow of any moral response but that of obedience to its commands). Yet what animated this effort was in fact a 'thou shalt', a "stern law over us", "the last moral (law) which makes itself audible even to us, which even we still know how to *live*"--

> in this if in anything, we too are still *men of conscience*: namely, in that we do not want to return to that which we consider outlived and decayed, to anything 'unworthy of belief', be it called God, virtue, truth, justice, neighbor-love; that we do not permit ourselves any bridges-of-lies to old ideals; that we are hostile from the ground up to everything in us that wants to mediate and mix; hostile to every kind of faith and Christianness existing today; hostile to the half-and-halfness of all romanticism and fatherland-worship; hostile, too, towards the artists'-pleasure-seeking and artists'-lack-of-conscience which would like to persuade us to worship where we no longer believe-- for we are artists; hostile, in short, to the whole of European *feminism* (or idealism, if you prefer that word), which is forever 'drawing us upward' and precisely thereby forever 'bringing us down':-- it is only as men of *this* conscience that we still feel ourselves related to the German integrity and piety of millennia, even if as its most questionable and final descendants, we immoralists, we godless men of today, indeed in a certain sense as its heirs, as the executors of its innermost will-- a pessimistic will, as aforesaid, which is not afraid to deny itself, because it denies with *joy*! In us there is accomplished-- supposing you want a formula-- the *self-sublimation of morality*.[93]

Such a conscience-- a trust in reason[94] and our intellectual conscience, which is internal to a trust which cleaves to life's pointer into fuller life and into the out-lived character of the past-- forms the moral core of the effort to undermine morality and lies at the heart of the reflective effort which generated the thoughts of this book.

Second way: In the course of explaining that his campaign against morality[95] begins with this book, Nietzsche characterizes both the dominant mood that is bodied forth in the work and the way in which its insights serve to express and reinforce that mood. Despite the fact that the effect of the book is negative, in that one is meant to take leave of it "with a cautious reserve about everything that has so far attained honor and even worship under the name of morality", its way of achieving this is not that of a frontal attack: "the whole book contains no negative word, no attack, no malice", but rather "lies in the sun, round, happy, like some sea animal basking among rocks".[96] Appealing to the Vedic inscription which prefaced the whole work ("There are so many dawns that have not yet glowed") and claiming that the author was pointing to a new day that would dawn with the liberation from moral values, he characterizes the liberating act as involving a "saying Yes to and having confidence in all that has hitherto been forbidden, despised, and damned" and says of this book itself: "This Yes-saying book pours out its light, its love, its tenderness, upon ever so many wicked things; it gives them back their 'soul', a good conscience, the lofty right and *privilege* of existence. Morality is not attacked, it merely comes no longer into view."[97] The ideas which carry this illuminating light were the issue of an art which is no small art, namely, that of "making fast in some measure things which flit by lightly and noiselessly, moments which I call divine lizards"[98]. This capacity to register and attend to nuances in experience and to catch their nature and meaning to some extent in words is a skill of maturing reflection, and of a reflection which (in the case of this book: so Nietzsche emphasizes retrospectively) was a concerted moral effort honestly to bring to light and think through on behalf of life the otherwise neglected, denied and suppressed, sides of the phenomenon of morality. If this work is still youthful (with the 'youth' which rejects 'youth'), it is also marked by a quieter, more assured and self-confident, more patient and alert, and more demanding, application of mind, which is wiser and more capable in this matter of reflecting and reflective inquiry than what was at work and is apparent even in HAH, to say nothing of his first-phase works.

c. *Gay Science*

Recalling in his EH-retrospect the verse inscription to Book IV of the original work[99], Nietzsche speaks of GS as emerging out of a health sufficiently restored that the life in him has begun to over-flow once again from inward depths and the 'knowledge' which is being carried from those depths to others on the outflow of life's creative love has become "gay": it is "gay science". That is, it is knowledge developed within and with the disclosures of the disclosive matrix of life-revived. Again, at the opening of his later-added Preface to the original work, he speaks of the language in which the work is written as that of "the thawing wind: high spirits, unrest, contradiction, and April weather are present in it, so that one is constantly reminded of the nearness of winter no less than of the *victory* over winter that is coming, must come, perhaps has already come".[100]

> Gratitude pours forth continually, as if the unexpected had just happened, the gratitude of a convalescent-- for *convalescence* was unexpected. 'Gay Science': that signifies the saturnalia of a spirit who has patiently resisted a terrible, long pressure-- patiently, severely, coldly, without submitting, but also without hope-- and who is now all at once attacked by hope, the hope for health, and the *intoxication* of convalescence. Is it any wonder that in the process much that is unreasonable and foolish comes to light, much playful tenderness that is lavished even on problems that have a prickly hide and are not made to be caressed and enticed? This whole book is nothing but a bit of merry-making after long privation and powerlessness, the rejoicing of energy-and-strength [*Kraft*] that is returning, of a reawakened faith in a tomorrow and the day after tomorrow, of a sudden feeling and anticipation of a future, of impending adventures, of seas that are open again, of goals that are permitted again, believed again. And what did not lie behind me then![101]

The condition which Nietzsche points to as the matrix of this work is complex, not simply as many-sided but as encompassing in itself a past over against which the present is registering and a future which is being opened out into with anticipation and reawakened hope. The strengths which mark this present have been developed in the course of "long and dangerous exercises of self-mastery". In virtue of such development, he has emerged "as a different person, with a few more question marks-- above all with the *will* henceforth to question further, more deeply, severely, harshly, evilly and quietly" than he had questioned up to then. Not only that: on the side of the responsive-matrix for reflective effort, the person who has emerged "from such abysses, from such severe sickness, also from the sickness of severe suspicion", has returned a hundred times more subtle than before.[102] Thus as Nietzsche recalls it, the generative matrix for this work was both a more sensitive and delicate responsiveness and a more determined, more demanding, and more capable, effort of reflection and reflective inquiry; the insights set forth in the work-- the 'gay science' intended in the title-- reflect his more subtle probing of experience, and his greater capacity to attend to nuances and to frame new and fruitful questions. Animating both the sensitive and the reflective powers available to him now was a resurrected life, meaning in particular: the vitality of someone who feels himself able again to take part in things joyfully, playfully, and skillfully, more so than ever before, and to find that taking part invested once again with a 'future' as well as strengthened in virtue of its difficult past.

Due to this complex matrix and his ability to work within it, the insights and glimpses of truth in GS, and the increasingly coherent and connected exposition of these by means of apparently merely separate and serially presented aphoristic units, represent not simply further developments on the path set by HAH and D; they represent the initial fruit of another transformation of reflection that is beginning to take shape but that has not advanced far enough to require a different written form for its apt expression. That transformation is rooted in a deepening in the being of the man who is forming the thoughts. In virtue of that deepening, he is leaving behind the condition (in particular, the responsive matrix) out of which HAH took shape. But unlike in the case of the traumatic transition between the first and second phases of his thought, the transition that is beginning to appear in GS does not involve bringing into question of the terms of the second phase. The advance being achieved involves, instead, a movement ahead which is accompanied by the revival in himself of much of the self of his early youth, that behind the first phase of his thought; but even though the expanded and revivified capacity for participation in reality brings an altered sense of truth, thus of reflective inquiry, of its animating love of truth, and of the relation of inquiry to truth, neither the advance nor this accompanying revival generates a questioning relating back to the horizon of the second phase. It is rather full speed ahead on a path beginning to become clearer and exciting as he makes his way on it.

In short: As Nietzsche recalls GS, it continues the course set in HAH but reflects a deepening and amplifying of his being and capacity, and effects-- if in a gradual way-- a transition into another phase of his thought and writing. The 'nethermost self' which is beginning to speak here not only maintains the time-bounded horizon of the second phase and accommodates in the conceptual framework that was formed at the start of that phase the revival of the self speaking in the first phase; it is also already beginning to form and utter ideas which will be central to the re-formulation and re-expression of the early tragic vision that was embodied in BT.[103] In the retrospect of his later-added Preface to BT, Nietzsche spoke of his regret that in that work he had not "sung": "What I had to say then-- too bad that I did not dare say it as a poet: perhaps I would have been capable of it."[104] The deepening of his capacities and revivification of his experiencing has brought him to the place of a cognizance of reality and truth within which he is being summoned to penetrate them more profoundly and re-form his understanding of them and consequently to transform once again his style of writing. GS expresses that point in the transformation of Nietzsche's being and thinking at which he is on the verge of bursting into song and poetry and of singing the tragic song which he regretted not having attempted in BT. That song, that poetic creation, in which he makes fully his own his youthful tragic vision, is TSZ.

3. Beginning of the third phase

The work which forms the first expression of the third phase of Nietzsche's thought, TSZ, is a poetic drama whose central figure is named Zarathustra. The Zarathustra of TSZ is an actual historical figure (in this case an ancient Iranian religious reformer) who has been transmuted into a fictional idealization of Nietzsche himself. The poet-author of TSZ composed this work out of his own recovering health, which had advanced to such a point that the persistence of elements of physical ill-health was simply a condition-- and often a fruitful one-- for his expenditure of an overflowing spiritual power and fullness. Projecting himself and elements of his own being into the figure of Zarathustra, Nietzsche sees the latter as bodying forth the ideal of a type of spirit who knows a "great health", a health that a person never acquires as a possession but must ever continue acquiring because one is-- and must be-- continually giving it up again and again in creative effort. To explain this concept-- and "I don't know how I could explain this concept better, more *personally*, than I have done it in one of the last sections of the fifth book of my *gaya scienza*"-- he quotes aphorism 382 of GS (the next to last aphorism of the Book V which was added in 1887 to the original four-Book work).

> Being new, nameless, hard to understand, we premature births of an as yet unproven future need for a new goal also a new means-- namely, a new health, stronger, more seasoned, tougher, more audacious, and more joyful than any previous health. Whoever has a soul that craves to have experienced [*erlebt*] the whole range of values and desirabilities to date, and to have sailed around all the coasts of this ideal 'mediterranean'; whoever wants to know from the adventures of his own most authentic [*eigensten*] experience how a discoverer and conqueror of the ideal feels, and also an artist, a saint, a legislator, a sage, a scholar, a pious man, and one who stands divinely apart in the old style-- needs one thing above all else: the *great health* ... . And now, after we have long been on our way in this manner, we argonauts of the ideal, with more daring perhaps than is prudent, and have suffered shipwreck and damage often enough, but are, to repeat it, healthier than one would like to concede, dangerously healthy, ever again healthy-- it will seem to us as if, as a reward, we now have in front of us an as yet undiscovered country whose boundaries nobody has surveyed yet, a 'beyond' in relation to all the lands and nooks of the ideal so far, a world so overrich in what is beautiful, strange, questionable, fearful, and divine, that our curiosity as well as our craving to possess it have got beside themselves--- alas, now nothing less will sate us! After such vistas and with such a burning hunger in our conscience [*Gewissen*] and science [*Wissen*], how could we still be satisfied with *present-day humanity*? It may be too bad but it is inevitable that it is only with an ill-maintained seriousness that we look at its worthiest goals and hopes, and perhaps we do not even bother to look any more. Another ideal runs ahead of us, a wondrous, tempting, dangerous ideal, to which we would not want to persuade anybody because we do not readily concede *the right to it* to anyone: the ideal of a spirit who plays naïvely-- that is, not deliberately [*ungewollt*] but from overflowing power [*Mächtigkeit*] and fulness-- with all that has hitherto been called holy, good, untouchable, divine; for whom those supreme things that the people have (and fairly so) in their value standards, signify nothing more than danger, decay, debasement, or at least recreation, blindness, and temporary self-oblivion; the ideal of a human-superhuman well-being [*Wohlseins*] and benevolence [*Wohlwollens*] that will often appear *inhuman*-- for example, when it places itself side-by-side with all earthly seriousness so far, all solemnity in gesture, word, tone, eye, morality, and task so far, as their most incarnate and involuntary parody-- and in spite of all this, it is perhaps only with him that *great seriousness* first begins, that the real question mark is posed for the first time, that the destiny of the soul takes a turn, the clock-hand moves onward, the tragedy *begins*.[105]

TSZ is a work centered in the idea of eternal recurrence, which he recalls having occurred to him in August 1881, eighteen months before the first burst of inspired creativity (in February, 1883) that resulted in the Prologue and Part I of the work. Later ten-day bursts of kindred inspiration gave rise to Parts II and III, so that within roughly a year the three Part version came into being. The inspiration involved--- the Dionysian overflow enacted in deed-- was the concentrated expression of the spiritual health he had achieved by then. He spends some time in EH characterizing that inspiration, stressing the involuntary character of what happens in its rapture, and that the dominant sense is of one's being beside oneself and of oneself receiving and being given, not seeking and acquiring: "Everything happens involuntarily in the highest degree, and yet as in a furious rush [*Sturme*] of the feeling of freedom, of being-unconditioned, of power, of divinity."[106] But there was more than inspiration involved in finding the images and metaphors and words that went into the creating of TSZ; the surplus of strength [*Kraft*] involved, the "tremendous passion and height", were those of someone who has seen further, willed further, been *capable* further, than any other human being. In every word he contradicts, this most Yes-saying of all spirits; in him all opposites are blended into a new unity. The highest and the lowest energies of human nature, what is sweetest, most frivolous, and most terrible, streams forth from *one* fount [*Born*] with immortal assurance. Till then one does not know what is height, what depth; one knows even less what truth is. There is no moment in this revelation of truth that has been anticipated or guessed by even *one* of the greatest.[107]

This sense of achieved heights is essential to the condition of health that Nietzsche was speaking out of and projecting into Zarathustra, as is the integration of the "highest and lowest energies of human nature"[108]. Further, Nietzsche characterizes the soul of Zarathustra as one

> that has the longest ladder and reaches down deepest-- the most comprehensive soul, which can run and stray and roam farthest within itself; the most necessary soul that plunges joyously into chance; the soul that, having being, dives into becoming; the soul that *has*, but *wants* to long for and will; the soul that flees itself and catches up with itself in the widest circles; the wisest soul that folly exhorts most sweetly; the soul that loves itself most, in which all things have their sweep and countersweep and ebb and flood.[109]

Inspiration did not engender any of this-- the heights, the internal diversity and tension, the complexity, the venturesomeness-- but infused a person who had reached into such an elevated place and had come to be able to draw on such capacity.

We have been speaking of a condition of recovered health, but these periods-- times of 'great health'-- were only one element in it; as discharges of overflowing energy they were preceded and succeeded by long periods marked by unequalled distress. When the functioning which attests 'great health' is exhausted and the overflowing energy is discharged, one is weak again for a while, and in Nietzsche's case, subject to suffering and distress. Health persists, but now in the form of a capacity to endure: the capacity to cope with the negative responses of others to the work, say, or with the small stings to which one is now extremely sensitive. Such sensitivity is unavoidable, because in virtue of "the tremendous squandering of all defensive energies which is a presupposition of every *creative* deed, of every deed that issues from one's most authentic, inmost, nethermost regions", "our *small* defensive capacities are ... as it were, suspended; energy no longer flows to them."[110] The aftermath of times of creativity, when "something one was never permitted to will lies *behind* one, something in which the knot in the destiny of humanity is tied"[111], mean also having to labor under the burden of the deed and its achievement: it almost crushes one, especially in one's weakened condition.

Regardless of how we understand and assess Nietzsche's claim that TSZ is a work which "stands altogether apart"[112]-- indeed, above all other works of any previous human being--, our point here is simply to note how Nietzsche focuses his recall of it upon the responsive matrix within which it took shape, the concentration and integration of capacities whose nature and refinement are such as to establish a standpoint, a place on inward spiritual heights high above correlative depths, from which a 'world' is visible, an ideal of the human, and a task.

C. Life, being, and truth-claims

In these retrospects upon his life and his writings, Nietzsche points to a connection of his writings with his life and being, and gives particular body to a general claim concerning philosophical reflection and its discernment of truth.

Put in simplest form, that claim is as follows. There is a necessary condition for our thinking's arrival at truth, namely, that we have both adequate access to the evidence that is needed for determining truth in the case in question and sufficient skill in interpreting and concluding from the evidence that we can determine truth aptly. In regard to the truth a philosopher seeks to understand (that of the problematic of existence), access is provided by the responsive capacities with which the life

on which that problematic bears-- the inquirer's life-- is being lived. But the functioning of these capacities provides the form of access needed for reflective understanding only when the dynamic of
our life's movement has brought life to unfold far enough and has brought the responsive capacities
through which we act and live to evolve sufficiently that two things hold: first, life in its *temporal
wholeness* can disclose itself *expressly* in and to ourselves, and second, the disclosure of this wholeness is to a *mature and spiritually healthy* human being. Access, however, is only one element in the
necessary condition for arriving at truth. We also must avail ourselves of this access with the reflective skill needed to discern truth. Thought's arrival at truth depends on the moral and disciplined use
of reflective capacities by the mature human being who knows such express self-disclosure and who
in inquiry can well and skillfully gather in and interpret the needed and accessible evidence and make
apt conceptual discernment on that basis.

Put more at length: Nietzsche conceives the endeavor of philosophy to be a human activity which,
as in all such activity, is undertaken in response to the at-stake which makes existence a problematic
affair. But in the reflective inquiry in question, this problematic is *also* something to which the inquiry is responsively attuned so that in it we are reaching for an understanding of its truth, the truth of
reality, life, meaning. While being engaged in, then, our reflective activity is the central ingredient
in our own current overall engagement as human beings with circumstance, and is at once three
things: an effort appropriately to be answering (in and with our own person, by way of activity) to
the problematic as it presently concerns us as human beings; the current medium (for the while of our
actual pursuit of inquiry) for the living of our life; and a particular outworking in activity of our creative energies. As such a several-sided ingredient in our overall engagement, reflection has an embracing disclosive matrix provided for it by the vital responsive powers (sense and feeling, for example)
at work in that overall engagement itself; that is, this agential matrix itself gives us our openness to
the interacting we are entered into and to the various factors at work in it, including the problematic
of there being something at stake in existence. What is involved in reflection is that we have express
recourse to this access, and make our reflective activity address, as a matter of concern for its effort
to understand, the very problematic to which our venturing to reflect is our own current answering.
As in our reflective activity we register and attend expressly to what is being disclosed within this
openness, our thought searches out what is being received, and interprets and brings to concept the
facets of it that seem relevant for true understanding of the problematic in question. This means that
it is due to our active engagement with circumstance and its enacting of life that we inquirers have
not only the immediate access to the problematic to which our thinking is responsive but also direct
access to evidence bearing on the matters at issue. According as our vital energies, disclosive powers,
and decision-making capacities, are functioning in the enacting of our life in that engagement, then,
the matters at issue are enabled to come out into the open for-- and to be registered and responded to
in-- thought.

Now such an endeavor of reflection was a natural and important activity for Nietzsche from early
youth on, and from the time he retired from teaching to the end of his productive life such effort was
the dominant channel for the outworking of his creative energies and the living of his life. In his
retrospects, he presents the dynamic of his life-course from youth up to mid-life as having involved
an augmenting and developing of what functioned as the responsive matrix for his reflection: not
simply an increasing (an adding on to and enriching quantitatively) of his capacity to receive and register, to interpret and understand, and to enact life's unfolding in his active engagement with circumstance, but a deepening and broadening (a qualitative transforming) of this capacity, an amplifying
that complexified, intensified, subtilized, and the like, and over time made reality in its various aspects differently-- and in particular, more fully and more clearly-- available for thought. The reflection which first became possible in the transition time of his youth took its rise in the early phase of
such a developing and augmenting responsiveness, and as he sees it in later retrospect, because of the
determinate nature of that responsiveness at the time, his reflection had a direct access whose initial
quality was imperfect so far as the matter of its allowing truth to emerge clearly and purely. Not only
that, but in this time of his novitiate as a thinker, the capacity for reflection which was being sum-

moned into action also still needed training, disciplining-- needed exercise in which it could learn, and learn well, how to operate so that truth might be discerned and be the issue of the effort made. Because of a certain lack of confidence and courage in his thinking on what was being disclosed, the venturing, trying-out, experimenting, which took shape in his initial reflective efforts (the first phase of his thought) was ambivalent in its character and in its issue. As the disclosive matrix in himself amplified during that time and this initial ambivalence became eventually discovered with sufficient clarity and force that he was impelled to react against fundamental facets of what he had been doing and how, there was (in the second phase of his thinking) an animus that emerged initially with great force and for a while strongly affected his openness to what was being disclosed in that matrix; and there was a companion constraint upon his self-critical effort and its results which affected the way he addressed and interpreted disclosure and which made 'science' an important vehicle that he would integrate into his thinking throughout this phase. It is when the self which had been realized in constrained fashion in the first phase and was seeking to free itself in the second began to revive in strength and to disclose itself with pressing openness to him, that in retrospect he sees himself having moved beyond the second phase and having entered in intense and striking fashion into a realization of mature reflection.

Looked at from a place reached even later in his evolution-- one involving thus his more fully developed responsiveness, and his more skillful and capable address in reflection--, the writings which he had composed along the way of this reflective effort appear as the manifestation and embodiment of this evolving effort of thought and this uneven realization of his self. In each case, the writing had been shaped in such way as best to convey to others truth so far as he could see it at the time and could determine an appropriate way of communicating it. If a reader would understand these writings, then his/her response to them needs to recognize two things at once. One is the constancy that lies at the defining center of the reflective effort in question, that of a continually experiential thrust to his pursuit of the truth of the problematic of existence. The other is the adaptability of his reflection as ongoing life, and the experiential disclosive matrix for his reflection, brought transformations of capacity and presence and made the problematic he was concerned with accessible differently over time. Because of the change of presence and changing access which such transformations brought, a reflection constantly concerned with a matter of experience was required to proceed in altered ways if it was to make best use of current presence and access. The method of such evolving reflective effort, its 'way-after' the to-be-thought so as effectively to bring thinking into the relation to it which would allow truth to emerge and insight into it to be gained, could not be a settled pattern or set of procedures for thinking as an isolated or self-contained act, as if we were mere thinking beings intrinsically complete in our power of thought and antecedently secure in our knowledge how to apply it to any subject-matter. It must be a developing approach in which reflection is ready and able to be equal to the challenge of an expanded range of evidence and a different appearance and meaning to all the evidence that is available at the current place of reflection. The retrospects and the writings themselves both attest that Nietzsche sought to carry out this constant experiential orientation in a love of truth and in an openness and disciplined attention to the immediacy of life's concrete disclosure, but also in a readiness to proceed in adaptation to the matter to be thought and to the way it comes to disclosure. He is continually seeking to appropriate the current evidence interpretatively in such way as best enables for the time being the true nature of the problematic to manifest itself, and to test thought's claim to insight into truth in the immediacy of ongoing life-experience.

Let us leave to one side for the present what he himself acknowledges in his retrospects, that he did not always carry out reflection well and in effective keeping with its own nature-- witness the way Schopenhauer and Wagner functioned in his first phase, and science in his second, so that the experiential thrust of his thinking was constrained and filtered. Instead, let us ask about the evolution of capacity and amplification of presence which was taking place. Given the changes he has been through, given his sense that life is an affair of growth and maturation and thus involves essentially a changing standpoint upon itself as well as upon all else, what basis does he believe he has for thinking that when composing EH he was operating from the standpoint at which life had come *fully* to itself in truthful self-*awareness* in his person and was gaining truthful self-*understanding* in him?

The question can be reframed by reference to one matter which is strongly stressed in his retrospects and which in virtue of his own experience he sees as impacting in general the connection of life-matrix, reflective address, and truth-claims. As reflective effort takes shape along the way, this maturing capacity for engaging with things is not unconditioned as it is at work amplifying and refining its enabling disclosive matrix and giving changing shape to the standpoint for reflection. In turn, in the effort of reflection itself, how this capacity-for-engaging is constituted and conditioned, both in its own decision-making and in regard to the particular capacities that are being drawn into play in its functioning, gives to the reflective effort in question an animating and dispositioning power of one sort rather than another. Thus "in some, it is their defects and deficiencies [*Mängel*] that philosophize, but in others, it is their riches and strengths [*Kräfte*]."[113] Or more encompassingly: it is health or sickness that philosophizes. When Nietzsche affirms this, he has in mind a rather complex idea of "health" and "sickness". For there is the health of the whole being, in contrast with the health of a part (an organ, a capacity, or whatever). And within the whole being, there is both physical and psychic health, different yet not unconnected. But there is also the difference between the fundamental health of the whole being and various kinds of unhealthy (or healthy) states in that person; for someone with a fundamentally sound constitution may still become sick and thus be at the same time (but in different references) healthy and sick. Finally, since the living being is involved in growth and maturation, and since such development involves a natural augmentation of its original vigor, there is the health of the mature being, with its overflowing vigor, energy, strength, in contrast with the health of earlier times of development and the measure of augmentation achieved in them.

Now in addition to affecting the disclosive matrix for reflection, different conditions of health and sickness influence the way we dispose ourselves in our reflection. For example, sickness pressures thought-- unconsciously, perhaps, but in fact-- toward an interpreting which sees reality and meaning in this-light rather than in that-light, especially if there is pain involved in the distress of sickness. In such interpreting and rendering, a reason so moved is not fully free to move toward truth but, invited and even compelled to see things with the eyes of sickness, it is pushed toward rationalization instead.[114] Only if there is a certain measure of health (of courage and strength, say, as well as of inherent vitality) can such pressure be resisted and thinking free itself sufficiently to place what is visible under that pressure into a sounder perspective. Ultimately, the sufficient freedom for seeing the truth that a philosopher seeks is granted only out of the healthy strength and overflowing vigor of full maturity, and the philosophizing in which such strength and vigor "inscribe (themselves) in cosmic capital-letters on the heaven of concepts" is one which can avail itself of such freedom.[115] But of course freedom to see is not the same thing as skill to apprehend or as skillful apprehension of what is visible. Skill of that sort, and skillful apprehension, need good judgment as well, judgment adept at guiding itself according to the lead provided by truthful presence. We may rephrase our question then: on what basis does Nietzsche think that when composing EH he was operating out of a fulness of health sufficient that life could come to itself in truthful self-awareness in his person and that it could gain truthful self-understanding in him?

However he might answer either form of the question, what *Ecce Homo*, in its form and its content, suggests, and what the later-added Prefaces confirm, is at least this: that Nietzsche would have us understand his thinking by seeing it as issuing out of a living, a way of taking one's stand reflectively in the midst of such living, and a way of skillfully addressing what is accessible there in the form of disclosure. He would claim for the living, and for the stand eventually taken in reflection, an adequacy for disclosing the problematic of existence that reflection is to bring to understanding, and would claim for the address to the matters to be grasped an aptness and eventually an achieved thought-issue which is sufficient as an apprehension of truth. Finally, he would have us approach his writings and assess the claims of his thought embodied in them out of a thinking by us which situates itself in kindred fashion in our own lives and which, as we are doing our best to test his claims, is at the same time entering us into a testing of ourselves in who-we-are and in whether we are as yet capable enough to test those claims aptly and justly. Let us proceed to put ourselves to the test.

CHAPTER 3
Life, Time, and Reflection:
Initial Thoughts

In *Ecce Homo* Nietzsche invites us to allow his account of his own life to sound against the life in ourselves, against the sense of life's movement and meaning as this has taken shape in our own participation in human life. To accept this invitation is to find ourselves recalled to (among other things) our own involvement in the problematic of existence and to attend to what has taken-- and is taking-- place in our lives in that reference. The recalled immediacy of the problematic nature of our existence in turn places us under the summons to become philosophical ourselves and to reflect on this matter of meaning as a human affair. At the heart of our puzzling out that matter would be thought on the temporality of our own lives, and on time as an enabling condition for our existence, our life and activity. Before we turn to Nietzsche's own thoughts on these matters as they took shape in his writings up to and including TSZ, let us bring forward what we are drawn to think when, accepting the invitation of EH and letting what we find in the recall to our own lives orient us, we think on life as a human affair and on temporality and time as we know these first-hand in our living. Such a preliminary reflective rehearsal of the matters we will see Nietzsche considering will best prepare us for our study of his thoughts if we can not simply bring to mind the most fundamental facets of the phenomena themselves but can also explore this matter of our understanding itself, of the conditions under which an understanding of life and time is possible to us as temporal living beings.

A. 'My' life

When we think of our own lives, we tend to think first of all of the things we have done and the things which have happened to us in life's course. For life is something we live in our interaction with what belongs to our circumstance. In that interacting, we are active, but we also suffer; and both the doing and the suffering-- and through them, elements of circumstance-- enter into our living and contribute their own character to our life in its concrete reality. Even so, life is not for us simply the series of our particular doings and sufferings. For while our lives do exhibit something like such a series in their concrete course, that course is importantly shaped by an inherent dynamic and directionality belonging by nature to us humans. For example, we all were once children and have since grown up into our adulthood; that is, we know our lives as affairs of growth and maturation as human beings. The determining ground for this is the inherent nature of human life, not circumstance nor particular deeds and/or sufferings. So however differently our lives may take shape concretely in view of circumstance and the particularities of our doings and sufferings, they have a kinship based in an inherent maturational inflection which enters naturally into the shaping of their course and which works together with circumstance and our doings and sufferings to bring those lives to unfold as they do and be what they are.

The activity which is central to the ongoing actualization of life is a dramatic affair-- thinking "drama" here in reflection of its derivation from the Greek *drama*, meaning "deed" (from *dran*, to do, to act). In its connotation the English word "drama" conveys two essential features of our activity. The first is that in it there is something at stake, something that concerns us and that depends for its securing (at least in some measure) on our activity. The second is that, invested with concern to see to such securing, our activity is a venturing amidst circumstance beyond and independent of ourselves, an essaying which in particular fashion seeks-- but may fail-- to help secure what is at stake. For us, then, to act is to make an attempt at helping secure something at stake, a try which runs the risk of failing in this regard. Because it matters to us how things turn out, and because the outcome may not represent success, all of our activity exhibits something which we may call a dramatic tension, sometimes to a greater degree, sometimes to a lesser, depending on the importance of what is to be secured, on the risk the doer runs, on the difficulty introduced by circumstance, and so on.

When we consider more closely this matter of what is at stake in our action, we find the need to make a distinction. For activity is a straining and striving, a venturing, whose reference to the at-stake is at least two-sided. In activity we find ourselves attempting to secure various particularities (desirable ends, say) as something at stake in our effort. Here we know activity as an attempt at achievement, as bringing our powers and skills into play in focus on results/outcomes which we join in producing. The tension and drama of activity in this reference concerns the success or failure of effort as so directed. Yet at the same time, activity has another and concomitant meaning and function, in which something rather different is at stake from produced results. For as it is seeking results, activity is also the medium for the actualization of our lives and of the vital-energy native to those lives. Crucial to how this dual actualization is accomplished is both the capacity with which we accomplish the decision-making and -executing whereby we engage in activity and the way in which that capacity is exercised. Because this capacity and our way of exercising it are meant to evolve, the lives we lead are affairs of growth and maturation in which what is at stake in this reference is a mature and perfected form and functioning of such capacity. Because such form and functioning are eventualities which arises by exercise and by learning in and from that exercise, the forming and carrying out of that result-seeking active involvement is also the medium of such growth and maturation. In its actualization of life, then, activity not only gives shape and character to the life being lived by the particular result-seeking activities undertaken but enters into that life a maturational quality reflecting the decision-making and -executing capacity in its current form and manner of functioning.

If we consider this matter still more closely, we find need for an even finer discrimination. For entry into our grown-up humanity, involving as it does assuming our own lives upon ourselves as our responsibility, unavoidably involves us in such a question as 'What are you going to do with your life?' It is as if the development of our decision-making and -executing capacity up to and within this time of transition has a preparatory meaning, being a readying of ourselves to enter upon and to live an adult life in which a commitment of ourselves to ... , a giving ourselves over to ... , a dedicating or devoting of our lives to ... , is central; and concomitantly, it is as if underlying this "to" is some recognition and acknowledgement that what is at stake in life is more-- is deeper and more inclusive-- than our own growth and achievements. At the same time, that adult life for which we have been being prepared involves our taking part in extended undertakings and courses of action, careers trades and professions, causes and movements, as forms of activity and institutional channels which ask of us-- or at least, provide the opportunity for-- sustained commitment and concerted effort. In living our adult life and availing ourselves of opportunities of this and other sorts for disciplined and lasting adult engagement in activity, we are venturing to participate in the securing of that deeper and more inclusive something which we now recognize as at stake in our activity. Yet if such a focus on discipline and long-term commitments and such a participation in the securing of what is most basically at-stake in life is what is meant to emerge in us in time, how this happens and how successfully we enact the life of mature responsibility depends on the contingent conjunction of circumstance and the continued evolution of our capacity for engagement. To the end life's venturing knows an at-stake which still involves us in circumstance, active achieving, and continued actualization of our maturity.

If we think of our lives in this way, then three factors seem most important in defining a life. First, is the activity of the person, as this enacts his/her life in an engagement with circumstance. Second, is the person's growth and maturation humanly, as it introduces into his/her activity and life at their decision-making and -executing heart its own dynamic and directionality. Third, is what is at stake in existence and is of concern to us human beings, both as this is interpreted by the person and as it is truly the case. In virtue of what is involved in these three references, life as we live it is a dramatic affair whose drama involves this, that as active beings we know our activity from the start as referred to something at stake, and thus as an affair of care and concern, but that at the start and for a long while as we grow, we do not know *what* is at stake nor *how* it can be secured. Seen in this perspective, life is a venturing and risking which is lived eventually by an adult under some sense and interpretation of what is at stake, and lived in a more or less self-aware and self-directed effort to take part concretely in the securing of this.

To be most helpful for the study which follows, we need to expand this sketch of life's nature by attending more closely to life's temporality, and with that, to time and space as conditions which enable-- but also bound and limit-- life's distinctive temporality. This will require us to attend to matters we readily ignore and/or mistake in our ordinary thought, but a few words about them are needed before we consider the understanding which life enables us to have of itself.

1. The present as enabling active existence

The living and acting in which something is at stake is a complex temporal affair. More precisely, it is an affair conditioned by space and time so as to take place with all its tensions and drama centered in a bounded and ongoing present. Let us then focus first on expanding our understanding of the present.

As locus of our active engaging with things the present is two-sided. For each of us, it is ever the same, the same as it has been from the beginning of our living and acting and presumably also the same as it will be to the last, the steady present of our ongoing involvement in affairs. It is always in the present in this stationary side of itself that we find ourselves alive and active. Yet this side of the present of our engaging is ever matched by the flow and fluctuation, the newness and difference, of an ongoing side of that present. Now what passes in this sense does so *only in tension and contrast with* the stationary, and is what it is -- namely, passing-- *only in* that tension and contrast.

Correlative to such tension and contrast and enabling to the ongoing in its movement are bounds internal to the present: an end introducing the future and the futural as the direction of time's movement, and a beginning introducing the past. Time is actual as an ongoing-now which has ever already left behind the one bound of its present and has ever not yet reached the other bound, and which is continually transforming into itself the not-yet of its end-bounded future and continually being transformed into the no-longer-current-now that is augmenting the actuality of its beginning-bounded past. In this actualizing of itself as bounded, the present is continually making itself last, and this, by diminishing and increasing (respectively) the future and past harbored in its bounds. In the form of such an internally complex present, time functions (co-ordinately with space) as an enabling condition for agency and activity, and for an agent's continual initiative or initiating its own activity out of itself. We *are* such active beings, agents in whom activity is continually taking shape in the ongoing of our present. But for the most part, we are oblivious or inattentive to the futural and past bounds which belong to the present of our living and acting. Yet as our life lasts and we grow more capable in our living, there can come to be more or less extended stretches of time when, whatever be the occasioning and enabling reasons, we can know the intense self-aware register in which the beginning and end expressly haunt the ongoing as its own enabling limits. Then we see the actuality of time (of the present of existence, activity, life) as involving its ever and continually being concentrated into this ongoing-and-lasting that is going on somewhere between its own beginning and its own end.

Because the actualization of life takes place by way of activity which is part of an interacting, there is a third bound which enters into the constitution of the present.[1] I mean here, the bound of concurrency or contemporaneity. For life, while being realized under the conditioning concentration of temporal beginning and end, future and past, is lived in activity which is an engaging with what is other than ourselves, what exists, lives, and acts, *out of itself* in *its own* enabling present. Because what is other is 'there' spatially to ourselves 'here', such interacting is enabled by space in conjunction with time. Now not all that ever so exists, lives, and acts, enters concretely into the present of our life-time, let alone into any particular ongoing moment of that present. Concurrency is the interactively-concrete connecting of the presents of different active beings, a joining via their current moments which is limited in its reach. We *are*, then, as situated beings, placed amidst others and interacting with some of these, and our interacting brings the participants, each active out of its own present, together and into a sharing of our being and time which includes some beings (but not all) as situationally compresent participants. The song sparrow whose song, long ago in my youth, evoked a return call on my part and with whom I 'sang' back and forth over several summers, is not a concurrent part of life in Ruby valley in my old age; and many are the things which were before I came to be and have no element of concurrency with my being, though of some of them I know something historically. The concurrent forms the limited and limiting circumstantial field within the totality of existence which is the primordial matrix of my engaging, so that this life, extending itself in the 'between' of futural and past bounds, knows its unfolding in the continual engagement with the concurrent circumstance that bounds my present being.

As the discussion of concurrency indicates, the temporal structure of the present gains a complex inflection due to the spatiality of beings and of the interacting they are involved in. For the latter involves each of us participants, living and acting out of ourselves and our own present, interacting with the others who are living and acting out of their own presents. Now in regard to ourselves, we are directly cognizant of inward and private aspects of ourselves and our activity, as well as directly cognizant of outward and public aspects of these; but in regard to those others who confront us as factors in our circumstance, we are open directly only to their presence as effective in the interacting, and concomitantly with this, to outward aspects of their face. By conditioning our being and our living and acting so as to introduce (among other things) contrasting public and private sides into these, space enables us to interact as each acting out of ourselves with inwardly-formed initiative, as encountering each other in an interactive way made possible by the outer and public sides of our being, and as connecting in that interacting without dissolving our own different being and initiating.

Now due to the way that this spatial differentiation structures the participants and the interacting, we are cognizant of time in two different but connected ways.

One way is in refraction of the public face of things. For example, as I move amidst the landscape in this part of the western United States, I see not only the things which confront me but also the visible marks of the seasonal rhythm on their face. At the moment, vegetation wears the changing colors of autumn. The immediate basis for this rhythm-- the sun-- is at present hidden behind the grey clouds of an overcast day, which in turn reminds that the passage of the seasons is something experienced in a life which is lived day by day. Because our lives are outwardly oriented in our interacting with others, and because that interacting is a temporal affair as connecting ongoing beings enacting their own presents, we have developed measures of the passage of time in each of us by reference to standard units accessible in the commonly discernible public aspect of our interacting, namely, those relating to the movement of the sun: days, seasons, and years. But measures of time's passage are one thing, time itself is quite another. In the case of sun-time-- or more precisely, the sun-based measures of time's passage--, little of time's nature and character is made manifest in the formulating and using of those measures.

There is another medium refractively disclosive of time, one more intimate to ourselves even than what is immediately present outwardly, and one making manifest time's own nature and character more fully in the measures harbored in it. That medium is the inwardness of that active participation of ours in whose ongoing present the outward face of our interactive partners and of ourselves is directly disclosed, its presence and features noted, and (for one thing) the movement of time measured in sun-referent terms. In its own nature and function, time is a condition of existence for beings active out of themselves, and such an enabling condition as (together with space) determines for each of us that-- and how-- our existence is an active involvement with others. Because for us earthlings the sun's rhythmic presence and functioning in that involvement provides a reference point for measuring time's passage that is public and accessible to us all, our living of our lives as a daily affair leads to our measuring that living indirectly, by years, say. But that living nonetheless has its own intrinsic measures and they are not sun-based. I mean this.

It is in activity as immediately and in first-hand fashion conditioned and enabled by time that we live our lives, extend them into the future, make them endure and last for a while. While that extending and making-last are continual so far as activity continuously accompanies the ongoing of time in the present of our existence, in virtue of the initiative-nature of the activity in which our lives are realized those lives are actually lived in stretches of time which are given distinctness and shape by the activities that are being initiated and are going on in them and are the current but shifting medium of our life's actualization. Because the conditioning of activity by time and space makes activity first-personal in its character, taking place in an out-of-oneself fashion that means (because of the privacy and inwardness that are involved) its initiating and essential aspects of its carrying-through are not directly public and visible in their own nature and being, such measures of time are not themselves public and directly visible either. This is so even though, given the interactive character of activity, we may time-and-date our activity in an external reference and relate it via its public facets to such outward measures-- so long, that is, as we can connect its inward beginning and end with things manifest in the public side of the activity and the situation in which it is undertaken. In this time-refractive medium to which each of us alone in our privacy is privy with immediacy, then, the measures of time's ongoing are activity-referent stretches. There are stretches of time (of the ongoing that realizes in its movement the stable-but-bounded present of my life and life-time) when I am fishing, and others when I am walking and observing; and the extending of time (the time of my present) that enables such initiative as makes of my activity now fishing and later walking and observing makes actual the continual ongoing of the present in diverse stretches of time and does so in activity that is not (in its own terms) simply continuing and continually the same but is taking shape and gaining articulation according to a shifting initiative at work in the present.

2. The present and human life

Enabled by the 'between' of the ongoing present bounded in future and past directions, and by the 'amidst' of that ongoing bounded in the presence of what is concurrent, the life we live and enact as our own is individual, unique, and this is so for each of us, universally so. It is also realized in a way that enters all manner of particularity into it via the interacting, so that one person's life is indelibly distinguished from another's due to the personal particularity with which-- and the concrete circumstantial matrix in which-- it is taking (and has taken) shape. Yet when we are considering ourselves and our own lives, it is in every case a *human* life which is being realized in this medium of particularity. Working within the first expansion of our understanding of the present, let us here make a second expansion, this time focusing on the growth and maturation which, taking place under the three-sided present of our ongoing activity, introduce further temporal aspects to the human life which in the coursing of time is being actualized by way of our active initiative.

To begin with, that life is human as being realized through a distinctive decision-making center of ourselves. At that center, in that deciding, factors from out of all three dimensions of the present are selectively integrated into the shaping of effort and made somehow ingredient in the activity that issues from and en-acts that forming. Within the bounds of our futural end, our present harbors possibility and potentiality, as the 'not yet actualized but (under appropriate conditions) able to be' which inherently belongs to our life; and in the forming of our activity, that reservoir becomes drawn upon in some fashion as our own and bounded by our end. Likewise within the bounds of our past begin-ning, our present harbors both developed capacity and accumulated resources, the 'already actualized and (under appropriate conditions) able to be drawn upon' which also inherently belongs to our life; and in the forming of our activity, that reservoir becomes drawn into play in some fashion. Finally, within the bounds of the concurrent, our present harbors our current actual being and an immediate context-and-matrix which, however favorable, opportune, and congenial, or unfavorable, misfortu-nate, and difficult, for us in its mixture of actual and potential, constitutes the concrete medium and context-and-matrix for enacting what is meant to be our responsible participation in the securing of what is at stake.

What is decisive for the distinctively human, however, is not the fact of the integrating of possibil-ity from one's future, resources from one's past, and the concurrent-matrix, taking place in the form-ing of activity, but something further, relating to the manner of such integrating. That 'something' is threefold.

First: Our diverse capacities as active beings all inherently harbor common meanings as meant-to-be's that intend from the start a development over time of those capacities, and in particular, a devel-opment that is integral to the distinctive centered agency that is ours.

Second: The powers which function from the start at the center of that distinctive agency, as the decision-making and -executing essence of our being as active beings, are responsive in nature. And they are powers whose responsiveness is meant to develop in virtue of their exercise in the forming of our initiative and of a learning in and from such exercise. Thus we know a kind of 'on the job' training in this matter of engaging in activity as a human being.

Third: The responsive powers operating at our decision-making center are inherently referred in their practical functioning here to an at-stake, and register it in the imperative mode. Our acting out of ourselves, then, is a responding to this claiming force of the at-stake, this obligating presence.

In sum: The initiative which takes shape in us through the functioning of our evolving responsive capacity brings factors from our own past, present, and future, into play as it responsively takes in and appropriates the at-stake as claiming, and thereby our engagement with things is a responding and answering which seeks to contribute to what ought to-- needs to-- be coming to pass concretely, al-though it may not actually happen to come to pass. We ourselves are evolving centers of such claim-responsive activity, ordained to the eventual fulfillment of our initiating-power in a capacity for re-sponsibility commensurate with the at-stake. It is this responsive and responsibility-consummated manner of our decision-making and -executing that makes us human, and it is in relation to the evo-lution of ourselves as centers of activity so initiating that our lives are affairs of growth and matura-tion as human beings. Such growth and maturation are not automatic, nor is success in them inevita-ble. Yet because growth and maturation depend most fundamentally on the way in which (out of our-selves, in our decision-making) we make something of the at-stake, determine ourselves to activity, and are able gradually to learn the 'how' of responsible decision-making and -executing, we have some effective share in the more-or-less-successful evolution in ourselves of our capacity for respon-sible participation in the affairs of life.

If life harbors meanings which intend that the essential capacities by which the living human be-ing decides and initiates activity and realizes its life are themselves meant to evolve, so that decision-making and -executing are meant to become rather different affairs as life goes on, then life is not realized simply as a continuous affair continually taking shape in the ongoing of the present, nor even simply as an articulated affair shifting and changing in close connection with the variable initiative and the different stretches of time integral to the activity in which it is being realized. Life is realized in present activity as an affair that also unfolds, doing so as a phased affair. The phases in question here are those relating to the evolution and development, the growth and maturation, of the human being as a distinctive center of initiative and life; in particular, they are phases together ordained to the enabling of a certain eventual and overall *telos* or completion of and fulfillment to such evolution and maturation. Phases are times-- expanses of time, of our life's time-- meant from the first for the realization of various facets of such growth and maturation. Thus the development in question (that of the essential and of its functioning components, and of ourselves as centers of initiative of the sort in question) is meant to (and does) take time, its own time. Since the development is mediated by activity and primordially concerns the capacity for decision-making in the interacting with circumstance, that time-- that natively intended expanse of time-- is ordained initially to a development that involves variable complicity with concurrent circumstance over that time, but one sufficiently favorable that the development called for can actually occur with the help of circumstance and on the strength of the acting as an interacting. If in fact circumstance is not favorable and an adequate or even a constructive development is not possible, the capacity to learn, unlearn, relearn, can perhaps subsequently retrieve the potentiality from this initial failure and enable the development to take place later in some form. But later realization is never the same as timely realization to begin with. And in any case, the disharmony may not provide opportunity for the needed unlearning and relearning.

Development/maturation-phases and the expanses of time allotted to them impart to the ongoing actualization of life in the present a distinctive character, one intrinsic to the nature of human life and central to the directionality that belongs to the realization of that nature over time. As with stretches and activities, so with the expanses and the development-phases of growth and maturation: however much the times in question relate to the development of an agent interacting with circumstance and of his/her capacities for initiative, they are not intrinsically measured by sun-time measures-- the phase of adolescence, say, by an age-period set off in months and years. Rather they are defined in an inward reference, above all in relation to meanings which apportion and allot the developmental work meant to take place over time; that apportioning and allotting concerns the work as meant to contribute to an intended eventual issue (a *telos*) and as belonging to the orderly development and integrating of the functional components and the forming of the enduring center of initiative that make a living being a living *human* being: that is, a being who is living and acting in a distinctively *human* fashion in the course of his/her life-time. In the expanse of time initially meant for any phase of growth and for development of the capacities and functioning involved in such growth, no matter what the measure and manner of actualization taking place the life being lived and the activities being undertaken are inflected by (and somehow responsively taking shape within and sensitively to) the dynamic of the phase and its intended transformation of the decision-making and -executing capacity of the person toward maturity and perfection. Thus it would be important for an understanding of the movement of our lives to gain insight not simply into the actual activities involved but into the meanings that make human life be an affair of growth and maturation and into how such growth is (or is not) taking place and how well-or-ill the living being is evolving toward being the center of mature capacity for responsible engagement which is the *telos* of growth implicit in human nature.

B. Understanding 'my' life

In our response so far to the invitation extended in and by *Ecce Homo* to reflect on life and its meaning, we have begun a provisional sketch of the nature and temporality of human life, one that has been issue of our own reflection; that sketch is still incomplete, since it scarcely touches on some of the most important elements: for example, what is at stake most fundamentally in human life? But for our present purposes the sketch will suffice as a preparatory step for our main undertaking. Yet what we have done has a peculiarity needing notice and some attention in its own right.

In our effort to understand life (his life, our life, human life) by utilizing our only direct access to the matter to be understood (our only access to the life in others is indirect, by way of our own life), we find ourselves concerned with understanding something which is still going on in ourselves. That seems promising in many respects: for example, what we are trying to understand is ever present to us. And yet, the phenomenon in question is unfinished, incomplete; and moreover, its going on is at times by way of our very effort at understanding, so that we have no distance, no separation, of ourselves-as-inquiring from the matter we are inquiring into. These aspects of the situation provoke questions. For example: What sort of understanding could be possible under such conditions? How would it be possible to understand 'human life' by way of a life that has not been lived out to its end?

EH suggests that if we need to be alive to understand life ('dead men tell no tales'), the tale we could tell (certainly about our own life, and surely also about human life generally) would depend on where in our own life we are, what resources we have there for insight, and so on. Could life, then, make possible a full and universal understanding of itself? How?

Let us look in a provisional and preparatory way into this matter of our understanding our own life, bearing in mind both what we have seen Nietzsche saying and claiming and the sense of life and its temporality which we have just developed. What would be the nature of such understanding, and how would it be possible to us who are still living?

1. Capacity for understanding

Reflectively understanding our own life is, in the following respect, like understanding anything else of which we have some direct awareness. On the one hand, it is a matter of applying our mind to the matter (here, reflecting on it) and of forming ideas which seem to give insight into it. On the other hand, it is a matter of testing and confirming the claim of those ideas, doing so ultimately in immediate experience and here, in the reflecting person's experience of his/her own life. Thus our capacity for understanding this matter is two-sided.

As regards the side of immediate experience, we all have direct access to the matter to be understood in our own case, since we are still living the life to be understood and have experienced it all along the way as we were living it. Relevant evidence thus is open to each of us, and indeed, the most essential and decisive evidence regarding our own lives is directly open only to each of us alone, being so disclosed only to ourselves in our own inwardness.

As regards the side of reflection, we have a capacity for a reflective use of our minds but only as something which we enter upon and make our own in the course of our lives and first do so well after the beginning. Moreover, this capacity is one which itself develops with use and practice, so that as we make it our own by repeatedly making the effort to reflect, we develop this capacity in certain ways and hopefully learn better how to reflect and how to gain understanding. In virtue of the development and learning involved in such repeated effort, our actual reflection alters in character over time; and our exercise of it at any time often carries the sense of as yet unrealized potential: we can still develop our capacity further and learn better how to reflect.

The emergence of our native capacity for reflection into availability for use is part of our development as human agents, and the development of that now-available capacity in actual use depends on an employment of it entered upon in the exercise of our decision-making and -executing capacity, such as this latter capacity is in its own development at the time when we enter upon this activity. Since it is with this development of our essential capacity that we grow and mature as human beings, our maturing is the matrix for our exercise and development of the particular capacities involved in our activity, including our reflective capacity. This means that the development of our capacity for reflection is intimately related back to and qualified by the maturing of ourselves as human agents. Three different connections of these two developmental processes call for attention here.

The first connection: In reflecting rather than (say) playing basketball, we have entered upon that activity of reflection and maintain ourselves in it on the strength of a decision-making capacity which in its operation has availed itself of a determinate horizon of interpretation-and-understanding which is already our own, current to our active being at the time. If we are to reflect on and gain truthful understanding of anything at all (including our own lives), we need to elicit and bring into reflective question the character of this guiding horizon. For even though this horizon is an actual and functional element in our current practice and life-perspective, what so operates is not necessarily true because it enables us to live on. Fictions of all sorts enable us successfully to live. Reflection that would gain understanding of anything needs to be self-critical; for simply carrying over that horizon of our own practical life and assuming it as the horizon for our reflection on anything without making clear to ourselves its mixture of the truthful and fictional leaves our reflective effort captive to unreflective presumptions which may well not be true. More specifically, in our reflecting upon and understanding our own life, we need to understand this guiding horizon not only because it is itself part of our lives and thus part of what we are seeking to understand; but more importantly even, we need to bring that horizon forward in self-critical fashion in our address to the life we are reflecting upon, in order to enable our very effort of reflection to free itself (where these are present) from pre-conceptions and prejudices carried in our own engaging in activity (here, in reflection), and to address our own lives with the confidence of a self-aware openness. Otherwise our 'understanding' of our own lives would simply be an inadequately reflective apprehension which is being steered by our un-examined or unexplored preconceptions.

The second connection: The development of our capacity for reflection toward a self-critical ad-dress to what we are reflecting upon takes place in activity which is realizing the maturation process in our own persons. Now that process, itself a developmental affair relating to the decision-making and -executing capacity in ourselves, may be inadequate in its realization of the meanings defining it. For the meanings involved (the meant-to-be's defining the development and its phases) are mean-ings whose realization may occur in many ways and modes, almost none of which are fully adequate to the meanings even if they achieve their realization in some form. So far as such more-or-less in-adequate realization marks our growth and so far as our decision-making and -executing capacity becomes developed in such manner as is not fully or sufficiently functional for adequate maturation, not only does maturation become flawed and distorted but the particular capacities we are drawing into play, exercising, and developing, through it in our engagement with things become inflected and disposed toward future use in a fashion that reflects such flawed and distorted maturation. For exam-ple, our engagement in reflective thought may become marked by a fear and animosity that have come to mar our maturation; and these may not simply color the thinking but affect the openness to evidence and the entertaining of possible ways of interpreting and understanding the evidence, to say nothing of limit the degree to which our reflection is able to become self-critical. In the measure in which distorting factors reflecting inadequate maturation bias and prejudice our reflective efforts, and color our openness to what evidence is available to us in the immediacy of our own lives, the demand for honesty and dispassionate weighing of the evidence becomes compromised, and reflection serves not so much as a means for understanding as (say) a vehicle for a protective rationalizing, one that (say) secures our safety and peace of mind rather than serves the truth.

The third and final connection: If our reflection upon our own lives is to issue in truthful insight, it must not only be aptly self-critical and be able to be conducted in freedom from the biasing factors which inadequate maturation introduces; it must also be able to address, as something accessible first-hand in our own person, our own lives as realizing life as an affair of growth and maturation. As we continue to live life and do it as an affair of growth, it is directly accessible to us in this regard all along the way; but since that access is provided by our own maturing capacity-- that whose develop-ment means our growth and maturation--, life as an affair of growth is not only itself different in char-acter over time but is also accessible to us differently at different places along the way, and not simply differently, but also both in different fashions and more or less fully. For as we grow and know a growing capacity for taking part in the affairs of life, our augmenting capacity gives us expanded access to life as such a phenomenon, providing both a fuller manifestness of it and also a fuller capac-ity for seeing and understanding it. "Augmenting" and "expanded" and "fuller" have a specific mean-ing here, given that the maturation we are speaking of is a transformational process. That means it is not a process defined by quantitative increase in units of uniform character, but one defined by a change that is at once qualitative and quantitative. In virtue of the character and meaning of trans-formation here, the whole process can not become fully visible (let alone understood) in its true char-acter and meaning, except to one who has realized the *telos* in capacity for taking part in life in which such transformations become completed. Short of that completion and what it brings-- first-hand access to the full character of life as a maturational affair and to the capacity to register it in its full maturational character--, we have not lived long enough to have available to us in immediate evidence the full reach of life as an affair of growth. For that reason, we do not have sufficient basis in evi-dence for understanding our own lives, let alone the needed capacity for seeing the evidence in its proper revealing force-- leaving aside the additional matter of whether we also have the self-critically developed reflective power needed for such understanding. For what is available to us first-hand is two things. First is a reflection which, given the transformational character of the matter to be understood, can not accurately and aptly apprehend the matter on the basis of the incomplete evidence that one alone has; for while reflection may anticipate and generalize, its anticipations and generalizations may not transcend the experiencing of life we know first-hand except in conjecture. Second, the evidence as we have it in our experiencing of life so far is not simply incomplete but may in reality not be evidence in the way it currently seems to us to be for life as we have already lived it, let alone for what belongs to life in the way of future transformation. For further transformation of ourselves may well bring presently available evidence into altered light and disclose what now seems evidential in one way to be in reality evidential rather in another way. Think back on our youth, say, and on how life seemed to us then-- not simply life as we had experienced it up to then and were experiencing it at the time but also life as it stretched out ahead of us. The idealistic register of life at that time may have been appropriate enough for that time of beginning and appropriately disclosive of life itself to youth for life's purposes at that time-- for inviting us into an active adult participation in things in which we might perfect our capacity for mature participation in life. But that disclosure offered no clue-- and discloses itself now in retrospect as having indeed provided none, despite what we thought at the time-- with regard to the transformations which belong by nature to the adulthood and old age of life. Youth's anticipations of adulthood and old age can not truly transcend the experiencing of life in the youthful person. But in the person in whom those later times of life have become matters of experience, not only do youth's anticipations of being old seem oddly mistaken (being old is nothing like it seemed it would be to us in youth), but youth itself, recalled in the immediacy of its own experience of life and its anticipations, seems rather different to ourselves now than it seemed to us when young. For we can now see (say) the energy and idealism of youth as part of a phase of life other phases of which are now known by us as having been lived through, so that that energy and idealism are no longer apparently at one with life itself as at that time they seemed to be. The traditional sense of wisdom as the fruit of age and experience has its relevance here in this sense, that short of having lived into the time of completion when we know at least the meanings which define the *telos*, if not also know their adequate realization in ourselves, reflection on our own life can only attain insight which brings life-not-yet-fully-realized-in-its-developmental-movement to light for an incompletely-grown human being. Such a being is unable to take what has come to light and to place it in the fuller life-context in which it belongs and find it appearing there (and to see it fully) in its truth as what it is and not as (say) what it seemed to us to be when we were younger.

To sum up: a two-sided capacity for understanding is native to us, but as something needing development; and if that capacity is to become equal to the task of understanding our own lives, its development would seem to require a number of things at the very least. We have to learn to exercise it in self-critical fashion; and eventually we have to complete our maturation as human beings and to learn to reflect both as freed from the distorting factors that inadequate maturation introduces and as open from the place of maturity to the full phenomenon of life as an affair of growth. Without apt maturation and the self-critical development of our capacity for reflection in that matrix, we find our efforts to understand our own lives hindered and obstructed by the absence or concealment of relevant accessible evidence, by the distorting and coloring of the available relevant evidence by extraneous emotional and other factors, by the development in ourselves of ways of proceeding in thought which are prejudiced and inapt to the matter to be understood, and by the deflection of our application of our mind in its intent for truth so that our thinking belies its claim to be serving truth.

2. Standpoint for apt reflection

In speaking of the nature and development of our capacity for reflective understanding, we have noted how the character of reflection changes with exercise, and have pointed toward a mature and self-critical reflective understanding of our lives as eventually open to us by our nature. Because our effort at understanding is an activity of a being who is continually on the move temporally, ourselves changing and our lives evolving amidst changing things, it would seem that achievement of such understanding would depend on there being a stable enabling foundation on which, as reflective agents who are still moving and changing, we may steadily move to gather in relevant evidence, apply ourselves in thought, and gain (in principle, at least) an adequate understanding of our own lives. What would be the nature of that foundation?

a. A temporal foundation for reflection

In our opening sketch of life, we spoke of the present as enabling active existence. The present's stationary side, together with its constant temporal bounds (its beginning and end), make time's actuality into an ongoing-that-extends; and under this actualization of time, active beings are continually forming and initiating activity out of themselves as agents whose temporal bounds-- whose impending end and receding beginning and circumscribing circumstance of determinate active beings-- are enabling them to be. In ourselves (the human type of active being), that forming and carrying out involve a responsive integration of these bounds themselves; this occurs as what is given within them is being selectively integrated into our decision-making and -executing. By maintaining our activity (as it is taking shape and being carried out) in such responsive touch with the three-fold limit as limit, that integrating anchors it in the structure of time itself. While such responsive anchoring may be characteristic of human activity, it is not itself definitive of any particular activity in its particular character, nor is it normally recognized and acknowledged expressly as part of the distinctive activity it is anchoring. It is possible, however, for the responsive integrating in which our activity takes particular shape to involve bringing such anchoring to an express recognition and acknowledgement and for the resulting express cognizance of the three-fold limit to be integral to a determinate form of activity.

This happens naturally, for example, when reflection on our own lives becomes integral to our maturing as human beings. Thus in that transition-time of our maturational development when we are initially assuming our own lives upon ourselves and are faced with the question of what to do with them, we find ourselves entered upon thought as having become aware for the first time of our *lives* as *our own* and as something the responsibility for which is *ours* from now on. In the express receptivity which ushers in such reflection, our lives are brought to our attention as temporally-bounded wholes. In such receptivity, we characteristically discover death, say, as ours now in a register and feel that is new: it strikes home now as *indeed our* end, we *feel* its impending as directed precisely at us and as to be *owned up to* as such. As well, we characteristically discover *our own* childhood as something gone by now, *ours* indeed in this beginning-again-of-life which is the beginning of adult life, yet ours as no-longer and not something we are living now, rather something we are assuming in the assuming of our lives upon ourselves. And with this, we find as well the past limit to our being and recall, our own having begun, that increasingly distant starting-point beyond which the 'our own' of our childhood does not reach. In the discovery of our own lives as our own in which our own future and past bounds register expressly, we find ourselves emerging for ourselves in *this mid-point* between beginning and end as *on our own* now, *here amidst these things* as the given immediate matrix in which, assuming the burden of this life of ours in such aloneness, we are beginning *our own life as our own responsibility.* This is the beginning-in-the-middle which forms the opening of adult life, within which beginning we are emerging-- and are discovering ourselves as so emerging-- as no longer ourselves as we were (yet 'our' childhood is being assumed), and as not yet ourselves as we are yet to become and be. To ourselves as such beginners, this yet-to-become-and-be is disclosed at best in aspiration, thus in a meant-to-be which we are assuming in a want-to-be and are to work out concretely (as actuality) in our exercise of our responsibility. In complicity with circumstance, the meant-to-be is to be realized in some fashion, and this, in a 'to-be-(realized)' which we are accepting as part of our responsibility in the course of life to come.

In the reflective thought evoked within the transformation in cognizance being considered, we can do more than simply put our attention to-- and our minds on-- our own lives as manifest in this initial way in the here and now of the present of this transitional time of life; we can do so within an express accepting-into-ourselves and acknowledging of the bounds inherent to our life and making it a finite affair. That means, more fundamentally, within an express accepting-into-ourselves and acknowledging of the three-sided temporal limits to the present which constantly ground life as a finite affair and which we are already responsively integrating as such in the forming of our effort to reflect. So attending to our lives within such awareness and acceptance of bounds, we are able to explore and think on them as something which we are in the midst of realizing and whose realizing we are now to take part in as responsible party. As far as we are able in our reflection to establish and maintain such accepting-and-acknowledging touch with our enabling temporal limits and to attend thoughtfully on that basis to our lives as finite affairs being lived and unfolding within those bounds, so far we are able to make our reflection proceed on a stable foundation, one on which we are firmly supported as we move in the activity in question. For time as the present is *ever* enabling us to be and to act so long as we are and are active, and in the measure in which we can recognize and acknowledge this constant enabling condition in *sustained* fashion as we reflect we are *steadily* establishing ourselves in and on that stable foundation. In so proceeding, we are firmly aligning our reflection with its own enabling condition, doing so from out of its very forming and undertaking and doing so self-aware. Such aligning, however, even when it is effective and successful, does not guarantee that whatever insight arises in such thinking is truth itself. At best it assures that such reflection, addressing life with poise from that standpoint, is able to be apt in its address.

b. An agential foundation for reflection

In speaking of our capacity for understanding our own lives, we have noted how the reflective side of this capacity is one calling by nature for development, and how such development is interwoven with the development of our capacity for decision-making and -executing, that is, with the medium of our growth and maturation as human beings. Then in considering the standpoint for reflection, we have focused on reflection as something which emerges naturally in the transition-time integral to our maturation. If the reflection which emerges then is to develop in apt fashion, it needs to find a stable basis on which to conduct its exploration of life. One element in such a basis is to be found in time itself, as the constant enabling condition for our active existence and activity. A further element is found in the constants which determine the active existence and activity of the human being to be human. I mean the following.

As conditioned by space and time, we find ourselves active beings, agents involved interactively with each other out of our own presents. What defines us as human agents involves two constants: one is the responsive character of our initiative, and the other is something at stake in existence and concerning us as beings whose initiative is responsive in its nature. Now the capacity for such initiative is one that is meant to evolve and to do so in and through its own functioning. In virtue of such evolution we know transformations of our capacity to initiate and of the way our responsive initiative relates us to the at-stake. The reflection which, as we have seen above, is called forth first in the time when we first take life upon ourselves as our own is thought that has been evoked to serve the practical function there of aiding in this initial assumption of responsibility for ourselves. As such, it is thought which inherently involves the express self-aware apprehension of ourselves as agents whose power of initiative is responsive to the at-stake, since it is thought clarifying matters within that condition. As with time, so with the two constants here: the reflective thought called forth can find a stable and facilitating foundation in these constants for its pursuit of understanding by its accepting and holding fast to them. But the reflection which does this not only itself develops by use over time; it also finds those constants in a changing fashion in virtue of its own larger matrix, namely, that evolution and those transformations of our essential capacity as a whole which constitute our growth and maturation as human agents. Thus for example, reflection initially can establish itself on this constant foundation by holding to the at-stake and the responsive-initiative of ourselves in a matrix marked by aspiration and its animating force; such aspiration colors not only youth's receptivity to the at-stake but the youthful undertaking of reflection and the character of the holding to the constants (the at-stake and our responsive initiative) whereby reflection at that time maintains a foundation for its pursuit of what needs understanding. This latter is, overall, our own lives as what we are assuming on ourselves and taking responsibility for, and more narrowly, what is of practical concern here and now in those lives, including this matter of taking responsibility. Now the centrality of aspiration in the matrix for youthful reflection does not obtain throughout life; and since reflection has a continuing role in our agency as a functional element in our power of initiative, as we grow and undergo further transformation in our agency the immediate matrix for reflection becomes colored differently. The reflection of later times, then, must maintain its touch with the constants in question in a way colored by whatever dominates in those later times-- the impending of death, say.

The reflection which arises in youth as part of the completion of capacity-formation being effected in the first transformation of our power of initiative, needs development as a practical element in that power; and it can gain its apt development by founding itself in its practice in the two constants, keeping them in mind in its address to whatever needs thinking on. But in that development, it needs not only to learn how to maintain that touch in the changing matrix which our maturation involves, but also to learn what to make of the changes in the matrix, how to understand the transformational nature of maturation, and how to understand life's nature and movement as an affair of growth. Now while the reflection in which such learning is to be effected is to achieve this in and for a practical address to life, to what is at stake in it, and to the matters in need of practical clarity in the time of life in question, it is possible for such reflection to develop quite beyond this practical function and become itself the central element in a particular form of activity undertaken by ourselves as agents.

For example, philosophy seems a development of such reflection, one in which the address to the problematic of existence becomes realized in a seeking for universal understanding-- what it means to be (say) a human being, and not simply to be myself or be ourselves in some particular historical grouping and reference. Practicality remains, but only in an indirect and distant fashion, to the extent that the attainment of clarity in such a universal reference can make a difference in the reflection operating in the immediate practical context and thereby also-- to the extent that reflective ideas have an effective role in our decision-making and -executing-- in the way we take part in life in determinate practice. If such reflective inquiry as philosophy is would remain faithful to the two constancies the holding to which enables the apt development of practical reflection, it would be also not simply the reflection *of* an agent-- whatever shape it takes, it is that-- but something being expressly undertaken from the standpoint of an agent, in self-awareness to its own aim at understanding as being an agent's effort, on a universal plane, at the self-clarification and self-illumination of active existence. Of course, philosophic reflection may be pursued in ways that do not involve or allow its remaining effectively so faithful, even though it remains the reflection of an agent and is responsive somehow to the problematic of existence.

Another example of a development of such reflection would be found in the pursuit of that understanding of our lives which telling the story of those lives would require.

c. A maturational foundation for reflection

The reflection which arises in youth and has a continuing role in human initiative can develop aptly in its exercise by holding fast to the ever-present bounds of time as the enabling condition of active human existence and thus of itself as an activity, and by holding fast to the constant conditions which define active existence as human, the at-stake in existence as concerning and claiming us, and the responsive initiative which is ours as human beings. But as we have just seen, reflection can reach the constancies of the second foundation (and likewise with regard to the first) only in its own maturational matrix and amidst the responsive register of the factors (such as aspiration, in youth) that are part of that matrix at the time. Is it possible that the structure of the maturational process is such as to enable, as an eventuality in maturation, a matrix in which there is a third foundation upon which reflection may establish itself, one stable perhaps in a different way from the first two since it would not itself be constant (as they are) but stable as enduring even if having only emerged in the course of time? Is this foundation needed to provide the final element of stability that enables reflection to be fully apt?

Maturation is a transformational process which we have so far spoken of in a vein that emphasizes life's forward movement and that sees growth as an augmentation, an increase in capacity. If we have recognized in the movement of life a direction which is not simply the more-and-more adding up in the course of the onward-and-onward and constituting the increase, it is in pointing to a *telos*, as if our maturation involved a culmination of the augmentation in capacity at a place of completion, of a completeness which is not simply the sum of the more-and-more. In so pointing, we enter into a way of speaking of this matter which, while giving a place to the onward-and-onward and more-and-more, develops the notion of completion and completeness in a qualitative and transformational context, which includes bounds and phases innate to human life and complicit with its being a finite affair bounded ultimately by beginning and end. Let us draw out this way of speaking a bit farther.

The crux of the matter here is an enabling structure of meant-to-be's which, implicit in the life we live as human beings, make of life a qualitatively self-transforming affair at its heart. Such meanings do this as harbored in our decision-making and -executing capacity, and as intending its development as (in large) a transformational affair. Such meanings thus apportion times and intend both phases in development and transitions that differentiate and connect those phases.

To speak only in terms of the largest and crudest expanses and only sufficiently for the point in question here: there is the initial time of infancy and childhood in which our original capacity takes shape by developing various elements in it in the interacting with circumstance. Development in this time is preparatory and meant to culminate-- its work is meant to be brought to completion-- during a transition period in which the developing decision-making and -executing capacity undergoes its initial fundamental transformation. The transformational work of that period is meant to yield a complex capacity for initiative in our active engagement in things, one which has come to completion in its elements and their integration to function in a different sort of decision-making and -executing from before, and one which has gained in aspiration an animating directional factor for its operation. The sort of decision-making and -executing emerging now is one in which, in forming our initiative, we are not simply shaping action but are expressly taking our lives upon ourselves, assuming responsibility for them, in that acting.

In our entering into such expanded and transformed capacity, we have completed an initial growing up and are entered upon life ahead as that of an adult or grown-up human being. But by itself alone the transformation leaves us simply as beginners in this affair of living life as adults with adult responsibility. In the movement that continues the adult living we have begun here, we need to complete our growing as a growing up, and to do this under aspiration's animation of us to reach upward and toward a different sort of completion, another completeness, this time not of integrated elements in a complex capacity, but a completeness or perfection in that functioning with this capacity wherein we take on our lives as a responsibility in our action and engage responsibly with things. In assuming responsibility for our lives and responding to aspiration's urging, we find that the at-stake that we have known from the start as concerning our activity now appears to concern it not simply in its reference to particular achievements but also in regard to what is at stake in life as a whole; thus it seems to concern activity now as the medium in which we do something with our lives over time and find meaning in living in this way rather than in that. As beginners who now have a life-time (our own life-time) as expansive horizon within which to look at our current and future efforts, and who now recognize the at-stake in its commensurateness with our living (and not simply with this or that activity) as a reference for our sense of 'what really matters and why' and for our doing-this rather than doing-that, we need to find concretely the best way for us to take part in the securing of the at-stake in its now recognized form. Let us speak of this, in shorthand, as our life's work, task, vocation, to allude in a brief phrase to the matter of our doing something with our lives in a concerted effort that answers to the at-stake visible now in the horizon of life.[2] In this second time of development (that as adults now, instead of as children), we are meant to be perfecting our capacity for engaging in activity in such way as to discover and begin to live life as a vocational affair. Such perfecting in our essential capacity and discovery of an involvement that is vocational in nature is meant to eventuate in a second transformation, in virtue of which we are meant to have come into that perfection of our capacity for active participation in affairs in which we are not simply grown up and adult, but fully grown up and mature as human beings, so far as concerns our capacity to take part in affairs and bear our lives as human agents. And as so capable, we are to find ourselves already venturing in concrete fashion on activity vocational in its meaning.

It is this perfected capacity and initial involvement in our life's 'work' that form maturation's intended *telos*, that consummation in the development and transformation of our capacity for responsive initiative in virtue of which we have finally grown up fully and are able finally to engage in activity as fully mature human beings entered upon the calling and into the responsibility that belong to being human. Carrying with it now a vocational sense, our engaging is concerned with the human contribution to the securing of what is at stake as this may be effected concretely by way of our own particular activities. If the perfecting of this first adult phase of our lives means the filling out and sensitizing-to-reality of the moral seeds implanted first in the aspiration of youth, the development of our capacity to engage in particular activity in the adult world, and the provisional discovery of this vocational meaning to such engagement, in virtue of this perfection we find ourselves beginners again (for a third time); and as beginners in vocational effort by a fully mature human being, we know a capacity still needing the further development in exercise which the idea of a 'beginner' imports. Even so, we have reached a certain end (that of growth as 'up'); we have become one part of what aspiration pointed us into becoming. To that extent, from now on we know a stable element in our being and activity, that of a poised and perfected maturity. At this end aspiration transmutes into anticipation of involvement at the 'heights' which youthful aspiration pointed to as to be made our own, and of a strengthening sense of the vocational meaning of our effort. Ourselves settled in our inward self-becoming, we now can settle into our 'work'.

Now from the time when reflection first emerged as element in this maturational process, it has been situated in the developmental matrix of its own time and developmental-phase. In bringing us into the culmination and end of growth "up", the maturation process has engendered another matrix for reflection, and not simply 'one more'. For if indeed this culmination is fuller than before, it is also at once an end to our growth up and a beginning of full maturity; and if in this (in that sense, enduring) matrix our cognizance and self-awareness can also reach more deeply and widely into life and its movement and into reality itself, the process has provided reflection with a fuller (but this time also, enduring and settled) purchase and foundation for pursuing the activity of reflection, one at a 'height' which enables a far-ranging vision of life and reality and which is to be ours for the rest of our lives.[3] If accepted and acknowledged in such pursuing, that condition could provide a steady basis which, in virtue of its character and its function as completing and disclosive matrix for reflection, could also mean the bringing of the other two foundations into their fullest presence and the facilitation of our holding fast to them as well as to this maturational basis itself as an enduring and stable one. It is such a three-fold basis that would seem to provide the best foundation for the apt pursuit of reflection and achievement of reflective understanding.

3. Apt reflection at this standpoint

Even if as reflective agents we could keep the discursive movement of our reflection grounded in the three-sided foundation just sketched, we would not automatically be effective in our reflection and able eventually to discern the truth. Effective discernment of truth would depend, partly, on how fully and well the matter to be understood is disclosed to us there, and in part, on what resources we can actually bring to bear in our attending to things there and how well we can employ them.

We have already sketched out our sense of the phenomenon and its structure, and in particular, that aspect of its structure due to which the phenomenon of life enables (in principle) its own self-disclosure in and to ourselves as living human beings whose being is so structured. From what we have seen, that structure centers our being in activity, in the present ongoing of which our life is actual as going on and extending itself in the present over time. Our reflecting, as a form of such active engaging, takes place somewhere along the way in the middle of this ongoing-and-extending of life, at a place where, because of the way life is being temporally concentrated whole there, life is immediately accessible indeed, but in its temporal being: ongoingly, in its continuing present actualization; futurally, as mortal and in some measure still only potential and with a potential that is being entered as such into the present ongoing actualization; and past-wise, as in some measure already actual in its course, as having been actualized in some measure in its resources and energies, and as being inflected in its present actualization by such developed resources and energies. Thus at that mid-life place where we have available the three-fold stable foundation for reflection and seem to know as mature human beings the fullest in-the-midst-of-ongoing-life reach of life's temporal self-disclosure, reflection that would aptly address matters would seem to have the needed disclosure of our life-whole, but would face three questions (among others).

For one, has life actually become open in its fullest differentiation for us, or will the close of this phase of life disclose (at least, potentially) further differentiation to life's developmental character than we now see first-hand? We have grown up, indeed, but life is not over; there is old age, and (at least potential) deterioration and disintegration (inward and outward) ahead: will life show itself more fully then? It would seem that we cannot know yet whether the phenomenon is fully disclosed to us in mid-life-- not simply disclosed as a whole, but in all its facets. If so, how would reflection that would be apt to the phenomenon proceed in the light of such an acknowledgement? How would it see its insights (such as they turn out to be) in relation to its aspiration to understand the phenomenon well (including "fully")?

For a second, since the phenomenon is complex, itself structured in its own nature, is there a better or more fruitful point of focus for our inquiry, if we would appropriate this matter of our own life-- in its particularity, but even more importantly if we are philosophers, in its disclosure of human life universally-- and gain such reflective understanding of it as would reveal it in its truth? Is the phenomenon itself natured and structured in such way that attention to certain facets would better advance our inquiry toward the understanding we seek? If so, if an apt address to the phenomenon would be most effective by concentrating on a particular point of focus, what would that focus be, and do we have the resources for turning what in this sense is potentially most disclosive of life in its nature as a dramatic affair into the understanding we seek?

For a third, while the resources available to different persons will differ and that will make a difference in inquiry, there is in every case still the question of how we would employ our given resources if we would employ them well. Our earlier discussion suggests that the 'well' would in every case involve certain variables as relevant. Among the relevant would be the following commonalities: the degree to which our manner of searching out presence, assessing its disclosive force, and in general, of employing such (native and developed) resources and capacities for thought and understanding as we have in the various component activities of reflective inquiry is self-critical; the measure in which we can avail ourselves of the moral elements needed to gain insight in the face of various difficulties: elements such as courage, honesty, strength, freedom from self-deception, self-discipline, required to enable us to face and gain insight into truth despite (say) whatever in the way of fear, anxiety, resistance, and the like, assail us at this place of thought; the degree to which we can maintain our effort in a way that keeps it fully faithful to our human condition, to our being agents responsive to the at-stake as obligating and responsively involved thereby in the drama of existence.

Let us conclude our discussion of this matter of understanding our life by a brief consideration of the second question, taking up with the three potential points of focus which have emerged in previous discussion.

a. The series of activities: the best focus?

According to our initial sketch, our life is an ongoing affair which is realized in various activities that take place along the way. That suggests that we might best understand life by focusing on activity. Now taking our reflective stand somewhere in the middle of a life that is still going on, we are aware of it as going on now as we are thinking but at the same time as still futural (unfinished, with things still to do) and as having already become actualized in some measure in activity from our beginning up until this time of our reflection. Because that past course is now gone, if we focus on activity in our effort to understand life our approach will unavoidably be predominantly (but not wholly) recollective in nature, and will depend heavily on memory and memory-aids for recalling the activity of earlier life. What we will be attending to in this way is a roughly serial set of dramas, for each activity is as something more-or-less dramatic. [I say "roughly serial" because we are usually, perhaps always, doing several things at once, so that activities overlap in their temporal realization: the ongoing of time may be continuous, but in the course of that ongoing activity actualizes life in a temporally complex fashion.] Without essential modification in its focus, our recollective attention might expand to note threads and connections relating different activities earlier and later in the ongoing of time. Indeed, it might even regard the development of particular capacities in the course of the series, such that later activities become visible as made possible by earlier development of capacity, not simply by earlier achievements in their own character.

Let us note three things about the understanding of our lives that might arise given such a focus.

First: There are a range of ways in which memory brings back the past to us in the present. At one end are those times when earlier incidents come back in such way and with such force that we find ourselves as if caught up in them again, reliving them, called back into them and their feel so that we live them through again. At the other end from such vivid return of the past are those times when we look back on past incidents clearly at some distance from them, and often enough with such attention to what we are recalling that we note it only partially, for some aspect of it only-- its result, say, so that we attend to the recalled activity simply as it was the means for bringing about that result. It is the fuller and more vivid form of recall that we need if we are to know and understand our past activity and the actualization of our life being accomplished in our taking part in activity. For that form brings home activity as it was, as it took shape in its own ongoing present and at the (then) forward edge of time; such activity has a futural reference: for instance, it involves an at-stake that is futural to the undertaking of activity; it involves the agent's ignorance (at the time of the undertaking) of what will actually come to pass; and it harbors anticipations and expectations which, whatever their accuracy turns out later to have been, enter into the forming of our activity and help make it what it is as we are undertaking it. It is only in activity as so entered upon and carried through that we live life and give determinate shape to life's actualization. But if so, then in recalling past activity and life in such fashion, our reflection would proceed aptly by endeavoring to make self-conscious a journeying-in-the-dark of ours, a journeying which is now being recalled from a later perspective that includes much knowledge that was not part of the acting at the time, but which is being brought forward now for an understanding that would grasp how *in the activity as it took place* life was being actualized and our life-path being defined.

Second: In the activities in which life is being realized, life's actualization is continuous, but the activities are many and diverse, each with its beginning and ending, often overlapping but roughly serial, and without later focal activity necessarily having any particular ground in immediately preceding focal activity. To the extent that we are dependent on memory for reflective access to what we seek to understand, we find ourselves hindered to this extent: even if we are recalling as openly and honestly as we can, we are not capable of recalling *all* our activities, let alone *all* that was taking place within their forming and executing at the time. Our power of recall, even of the vivid sort just spoken of, is fragmentary in both regards. But that means, our access to the continuous actualization of life in the variety of our activities up to the time of our reflection is fragmentary, with gaps and omissions. If the sought-for understanding of our life involves grasp of the concrete actualizing of life in us, then such fragmentary recollective register makes impossible a thoroughgoing understanding of life in its actuality and actual course.

Third: In the rough series of activities being recalled as it was even if only in disconnected fragments, each activity involves something at stake in it, but the series is not itself an activity and so far has nothing at-stake activity-wise in it as series. Insight into the one-after-another then would presumably discern the different matters at stake in the different activities, and judge the measure of activity's securing of this in each case. It might also note how earlier and later activities relate to each other, and perhaps even build on each other such that what is at stake in later activity can be so because of the achievements of earlier activity. And finally, if there were a standard by reference to which one might form one's judgment, one might be able to say 'this-achievement was more important than that-one in this-regard'. But unless life harbored in itself a standard of importance relating to its own actualization in activity, no activity would be more important than another *in and for our lives* simply because it was more important in this-regard or that-regard, that is, as regards the particularities of achievement. Looking only to the different activities themselves, we would instead be drawn to conclude that life is being lived equally throughout the series of little dramas, even as we acknowledge that the dramas themselves differ in regard to achievement-matters and in that way differ in the character they give to the ongoing life in ourselves.

In sum: Although activity is an integral part of life and a medium through which the living of life gains character, taking activity as our focus for understanding our lives has certain limitations. Activity and life are not identical; activity is only the complex shifting medium for the continuous actualizing of life, and what is important in achievement-terms for activity is not necessarily important for life. There is this one significant connection, that in maintaining itself and doing this in conjunction with supportive circumstance, activity continually enables life's ongoing and contributes to its character. But to understand fully how this medium (this rough series of activities) enters into the living of life so as to contribute to life's character and to the shape of life's concrete course, we need to focus our attention beyond activity itself, at least in its achievement-side, and to attend to life itself as being continuously realized in and through activity, but even then, not necessarily realized equally and in simple function of the fact or the achievement-character of activity itself.

b. Our maturing: a better focus?

Our initial sketch of the life that is realized in and through activity delineated it as-- in its own nature in our (the human) case-- an affair of growth and maturation. For as it becomes actual via activity, life has a dynamic and directionality native to itself, a vital energy that ebbs and flows and animates ourselves as active beings, and a meant-to-be that bears on activity as a to-be-realized by way of active effort and that intends-and-means the maturational evolution of the agent. Central in and for such evolution is the very decision-making and -executing capacity with which we engage in activity as something initiated from out of ourselves. Its development, and its transformation as such development advances, not only impact the employment of capacities and the particular activities entered upon through it but concretely inflect life as a lived affair. As regards the life we are to realize in this developmental vein, we know (as at-stake for our activity) a complete and perfected capacity for the responsible engaging in activity and actualization of life, and the integration of our functioning through this capacity back into the living so as to give character to it as an affair of growth and maturation.

Given such a relation of these three (our decision-making and -executing capacity, life's meant-to-be for this power by which its own actualization is to be accomplished concretely, and activity itself), we can see how life itself offers at least an initial pointer into how one little-drama of activity might be more important in and for life than another little-drama. The reason would lie in the relation of the activity involved to the maturation of the agent being effectuated in the decision-making and -executing that bring the activity into being. It is in this reference to what is happening to our decision-making and -executing capacity in them that such activities bear immediately on our growth and maturation, and relate more or less importantly to what is at-stake in life in this regard.

If we would focus attention, then, on the embracing drama of maturation that gives to the series of little-activity-dramas a larger and more inclusive context and a role in a more inclusive affair, to what would we attend if we would understand life as such an affair? There are two things in particular. One relates to this evolution itself, namely, the meanings which define it, and with them, the tension of meanings and actuality. The other concerns activity as, in its being the vehicle for achievement and the medium for such evolution in our capacity as agents, involving more than both achievement and maturation as what is at stake for itself, and eventually, as maturation is reaching its culmination, involving our entry self-aware into participation in the securing of something even more inclusive, more profound and far-reaching, something that is at stake in existence at large and that concerns us as active participants in existence. Of this latter-- the largest of dramas, that of existence itself--, we will speak in the next sub-section; here, let us concern ourselves with the meanings determinative of growth and maturation.

There are, for example, the meanings that determine a phase of human life such as adolescence. Implicit in life and intending what they do from the start, they become registered in the immediacy of the responsiveness at work in the forming of activity and the making actual of ongoing life at the intended time of life; being at work there in that responsiveness as we live the time in question, such meanings can also be discerned later in retrospect as having been immanent in the happening of that time of life. But such later express discernment of the common meanings immanent in human life is in reality rather difficult. Among the reasons for this, three are important to point to here.

A first difficulty: The discerning of such meanings is not a matter of ascertaining a fact-- a pattern, say, visible in actual life and perhaps discoverable in the lives of other human beings, indeed of all if the meaning is indeed human and thus common to all of us. It is rather a matter of fathoming something whose realization in actual life can take quite different shape in different lives. For the meanings that are bodied forth concretely for integration into the forming of activity are determinative for a time of life only as *meant to be* realized in the enacting of that time; as responsively registered and being realized somehow, however, they are *able to be realized* there in a variety of ways: in the manner of neglect and resistance and dismissal as well as of receptiveness, for example, and also in ways whereby that realization is inadequate or incomplete, partial in one respect or another. Not only that, but their realization, in whatever mode or way, is for each of us ever in a diverse matrix and medium of particularity, and thus has a different character to it in each case as well as being (say) more or less adequate or as reflecting (say) greater or lesser receptivity and perceptiveness in the responsiveness involved in the realization. Now in actual human life, it is meanings that are common, not the form their realizations take; since adolescence, say, is realized in different persons quite differently, someone looking for 'empirical fact' (in the form, say, of instances of common features) instead of looking for diverse realizations of meanings would misconstrue actuality. It is sifting through experience, sorting out the immanent meanings harbored in actuality, and seeing actuality as realizing such meanings somehow, that is the task of reflection and understanding here.

A second difficulty: The meanings to be discerned are immediate ingredients in a first-personal living and acting out of ourselves as centers of initiative engaged actively with what belongs to our circumstance. In virtue of the complex spatio-temporal structure of our being, and the peculiar interweaving of the hidden and the open, the private and the public, which we have noted earlier as marking our interacting and the participants in it, such meanings are harbored and discoverable as such and directly in each case only in the immediacy of the inwardness and privacy of each of us. Living and acting out of ourselves, we encounter each other likewise so living and acting, but in virtue of what this means, we can never be privy in immediacy to meanings as they are operative ingredients in the living and acting of others. For while we encounter others and register them in their effective presence, such register takes place in a direct awareness which is otherwise limited to certain outward aspects to the bodily being, the activity and the life, of those others with whom we are concretely engaging. So far as the immediacy of our cognizance is concerned, we are forever closed off from the being of others *as they are*-- which means, as being *out of themselves*-- and with that, from the inwardness and privacy and all that belongs to the first-personal character of their being, of their living and acting out of themselves. But such meanings are common as belonging to our being as human; can we not help each other in their discernment? Indeed we can, but it remains that each of us would still have immediate and direct access to them only in our own persons. We can reach such factors in the being of others only indirectly, in inferences that are not (and can never be) based on, or confirmed to ourselves by, *our own* first-hand participation in that inward first-personal immediacy *of theirs* which is both integral to the actuality in question (their living and acting out of themselves) and alone *directly* disclosive of the most relevant evidence for any understanding of that actuality *as it is*. At best we can seek confirmation of our inferences from the others in question; but what we receive in response from them is also unconfirmable by us in its immediacy as evidence. And more than that: none of us, communicating with others likewise cognizant of life in their own persons, is able to confirm *first-hand* even that what we are seeking to understand is in fact the same thing others are addressing. We can be helped by others to understand such common meanings in our own lives, then, but only under conditions of considerable indirection and uncertainty.

A third difficulty: If we would ourselves apprehend directly the meanings that belong to human life and that come into play in the forming of life's actual ongoing, we must avail ourselves in first-personal vein of our own ongoing as that alone in which such meanings are (or in retrospect, were and remain) immediately accessible to us in their presence and working. If it is a recollective vein in which we are operating, then recalling the past in such way as enables discernment of meanings as they were at work in its forming means living through it again and in some measure rediscovering the forming of the actuality in question, but now as that same person who has lived beyond that time and is able to recall that earlier living from this 'beyond'. 'Beyond' may, of course, signify only a later time in life. But for humans, the 'beyond' is not simply the 'later' but carries with it further meaning. We who, in this later time, are still living that same life and can recall that earlier time in it from this later vantage point, may of course find ourselves in that 'beyond' as having expanded the capacities (the sensitivity, the know-how, the awareness of possibility and distinction, say) and outgrown the limits (the ignorance and restricted acquaintance, the obliviousness and inattentiveness, the elements of illusion and self-deception, say) that marked our developing selves in our living-through the earlier phase. But we may not; indeed, we may have become so entrenched in the distortions that have arisen in the past as to be unable (even from the vantage point of some later time) to free ourselves and our attempts at discernment from them. For the basis on which we have developed our capacity to discern (the process of growth and maturation) may at the same time have failed to generate-- or may have cut us off from-- what would enable us retrospectively to discern the truth undistorted or even at all. It may, for one thing, have developed our capacities in such way as has given fear an inappropriate strength in ourselves. While fear discloses aspects of things, it also closes off other aspects and distorts still others. If our capacity to discern is distorted by fears in ourselves, that may well mean we are unable to discern such meanings truthfully in our own person, let alone to infer truthfully to their presence in others.

If such difficulties are able to be surmounted, and we are able to maintain the grounding of our reflection on that three-sided foundation we spoke of earlier and to think there out of a matured capacity for taking part in affairs as human beings, our reflective address to our own life, operating within our recall of earlier life, could attend to the series of activities there as also involving an embracing drama, that of our own growth. Unlike in the little-dramas of activity as achievement-oriented, the evolution meant to take place here is only rarely and eventually brought to self-consciousness and made theme of awareness and reflection. But in retrospect, recollective attention could lead to discernment of what has happened in this regard in its overall character and, by reference to various growth-meanings, in the turning points and phases of our growth as human beings. And to the extent that we are able to trace out the ongoing resolution in the series of our activities of the tension of actuality with the meant-to-be's under which life takes the shape it does, we are in a position to notice certain activities and times as more important, even as decisive, and others as less important or indecisive, for life in this reference-- as a drama of growth and maturation. Such notice would not only follow life's own pointers into the more and less important, but provide an organizing basis for an autobiographical recounting of life. Even so, there is the limitation upon any effort to do this which we have noted in the preceding section: our inability to recall all of our activities means our inability also to trace out with assurance the thread of maturation in the concrete.

There is, however, a more fundamental limitation to our effort to understand our lives by this retrospective address to the actuality of those lives in the past. At the three-sided-foundation place that is reflection's potentially secure basis, we find ourselves in the middle of a life that is still unfinished. That means, for one thing: however fulfilled we are in respect to maturation as a matter of growing "up", the life we are living now is still pregnant with further meant-to-be's relating to our decision-making and -executing capacity. For while there is no further 'upward' evolution to be realized, there is an 'onward' marked by anticipation and the resolve to remain at the heights and to work out concretely something which we have become entered into in this *telos* we have reached. Thus the present is charged in its futural reference not simply with death but with a future of such working-out as well as with any as-yet-unrealized phases and turning points that life holds already as still meant-to-be. How is it possible to understand our lives, then, if here, in the middle of them, we only recollect the past and its actualization of life so far, and do not connect that with what we find when the current ongoing of our present becomes transparent, including not simply the living which is currently going on in the effort of recollecting and seeking understanding, but also that future which is already immanent in our ongoing life: a future whose defining meanings are harbored already in life, a future whose potential is already part of our being now, and a future the more or less self-aware anticipations of whose reality we already have and are acting on? Both the currently ongoing and the future that is aborning in it are integral to the life of the living being, and belong thus to the phenomenon to be reflectively understood. Must not our understanding of life be of life-whole, not just of the actually completed part of life but of life in that wholeness which is ever our own in the middle of time's bounds?

In sum, then: When we reflect upon life as an affair of growth and maturation and attend to the defining meanings for this as these are accessible to us there at that mid-life best place for reflection, we can understand ourselves to be involved in a life-long drama as regards our own growth and to have reached into the high-point of that drama. But there we find ourselves having entered self-aware into an even more inclusive drama. For the odyssey of our maturation up to this point has brought us to a mid-life 'home' at which we find ourselves, in the fulness of our being as responsible human agents, entered into a work (a 'task' and 'work to be done'); in that work, we have the larger responsibility that belongs to self-aware participants in the largest drama of all, that of the universe itself, that of existence at large as involving an at-stake for the securing of which the active venturing of all existents (including ourselves as human beings) is implicated as needed. If we would understand our lives, then-- indeed, even if we would only understand them in regard to this growth-drama--, we need ultimately to understand this matter.

c. Our life-'work': the decisive focus?

According to our initial sketch, human life in the first transition time of our maturational development enters us into the question of what we are going to do with the life which we are assuming on ourselves, and invests this time of question with a pointer into an answer, namely, aspiration. As our capacity for responsible initiative becomes responsively harnessed to aspiration and what it points us to in disclosive fashion, we are initially unaware of this power and disclosure in their full complexity and differentiation. Instead we initially discover aspiration in only a two-sided pointing: into a higher-and-better being of ourselves as moral beings, and in some contrast but connection with that, into activities-- thence professions, careers, trades, and more broadly, roles-- which potentially give us-with-our-particular-capacities a place in a concrete community of human beings and which facilitate our connecting with others in the medium of particularity out of this higher-and-better being of ourselves. But as aspiration becomes acted upon and we advance in our learning how to discharge our responsibility for our own lives in an adult setting, this pointing becomes more visible in its complexity and its meaning; thus we discover a third side to it, one previously undiscerned as a distinct side but now emerging as distinct from the other two in the awareness belonging to our evolving capacity of initiative. That pointing refers us in our higher selfhood to a participation in existence at large which is 'beyond', and is to condition, any fit and fitness of ourselves as functional members of the human community. As individual existent beings, we take active part in existence at large but in this as situationally determinate for us in the concrete confluence of ourselves and circumstance; in that interacting we are beings who connect concretely with others who are likewise active out of themselves and are connecting concretely with what is circumstantial to them. While there is a social element necessarily mediating any connecting between human beings, there is also in aspiration a summons which, becoming distinct in this developing and trying-out time, is a summons to take part in the connecting as beings whose very human being is more than social. At bottom, that connecting is dramatic because in existence at large there is something at stake and to be secured in this inter-acting, and such interacting is an experiment in connecting whose issue depends on the venturing of each party amidst what is independent of it and is not inherently constituted so as to guarantee success. Thus according to the growth-meanings determinative for human life, as we move toward becoming fully ourselves we are expressly to find such fulness under the guidance of aspiration's pointing us to a part in a larger drama, a part to be assumed by us as ours. The drama of our matur-ation is thus, in its earlier phases, a prelude and preparation of ourselves for this final assumption of responsibility, this time for an assumption not of our own lives as ours but of our part in a joint 'work' in which what is ultimately at stake in existence is to be secured. That part, in which we enter ourselves and 'our own' lives into the effort toward a realization that is more encompassing than our own, is the 'work' of our lives.

In the retrospect and prospect of this mid-life time, then, it seems that the meanings whereby life has intended our growth and the *telos* of that growth have intended our eventual discovery of a meant-to-be which is not that of our growth itself but of active existence itself-- and not simply of our own individual existence, but of that existence at large which includes us. According to the nature of ac-tive existence as an *interactive* affair, *all* beings are meant to be participants in the securing of some-thing at stake in existence at large; our existence is to be a participating in the securing of this at-stake, and ultimately, in virtue of our meant-to-be growth as human beings, a participating self-aware out of mature capacity for bearing our own lives. At this *telos* of our capacity, then, the at-stake which has concerned us and been registered by us from the start but which, at the start and for long after, we could discover and interpret only in limited fashion, has become disclosed more fully, and disclosed as part of a structure of existence in virtue of which (whatever our natures and whatever in the way of growth is meant internal to such natures) our active-functioning is meant to be a venturing in which we are contributing-- out of ourselves, and as we can-- to the securing of what is so at stake. In our case as human beings, we are meant eventually to discover (in virtue of our own maturation) this at-stake as concerning us simply as active human beings who, regardless of society, are related to existence at large in such way that in our having to do with anything and everything, a vital con-nection is to be secured and our own activity is to contribute to the securing of that connection.

But what is the nature of that inclusive existence and its larger drama? What is truly at stake in interactive existence at large? Indeed, how can existence be constituted so that there is something at stake in this way, in such way as implicates us as agents concerned by-- and with concern for-- what is so at stake? Our immediate cognizance of aspiration in this more differentiated disclosive pointing, and our responsive integration of presence as holding such difference, does not mean our under-standing, let alone our self-conscious understanding, of what is involved-- for instance, of the answer to these questions, or to the further question, What is this venture which with mature resolve and settled purpose we are committing ourselves upon? It rather means our finding ourselves beginners again, able now to *differentiate in immediacy* a 'work' to be accomplished in our interacting from the various activity-vehicles in and through which we can take part in the accomplishing of that work, and to glimpse how we may carry out that work by way of such vehicles-- if, indeed, we can utilize them. But the 'work' itself is still basically futural to us, our capacity for taking part in it is for the most part still untested, and we are by this time in our lives experienced enough in life's trans-formations and shifts in perspective to acknowledge that how it seems now may not last. Yet this seems so, that regardless of how in fact either of these matters turns out in future-- matters of our functional fit, and of the viability of various activity-vehicles for our taking part in a work deeper than that accomplished in reflex of such a fit--, we have discovered this further differentiation, and our aspiration now has become an anticipation which quickens the responsive commitment of ourselves (our energies and resources, our capacities, and the living of our lives) to the accomplishing of some 'work' that pertains to us simply as human participants in existence at large. In that commitment, we assume with mature capacity the larger responsibility which is ours as human, and discharging our responsibility for our own lives in this fashion, we participate in life now as a 'vocational' affair, as a 'calling' in which we are devoting our lives to ... something beyond just ourselves.

Although we are able to respond in this way to the urging force immanent in such immediacy, the questions which it raises for us and the need for some clarity to accompany commitment make some understanding of the answer to them be sought in reflection and ventured. Thus at this crucial mid-life turn and entry into our perfected capacity for bearing our own lives, reflection which would understand our own lives would be required indeed to look to what light active achievement up to that time might throw on them, and more importantly, to the light able to be shed by growth and maturation up to this time. But in our reflection we must also look futurally, and most importantly of all, because our maturation has issued in the kind of committing of ourselves it has, we must look beyond the human itself. For here in the fulness of our own being as human we are finding our own humanity inherently being referred to an at-stake which includes-- but is more than-- ourselves. In virtue of that, we are fully human only when taking an effective and responsible part in some inclusive 'work' in which we connect with all beings as jointly at work in the securing of something at stake in existence. That 'work' of ours is to be worked out in our being here and now, together, and being engaged in an interacting with these others. If understanding of our lives depends on reflectively fathoming that 'work' into which we are pointed and grasping its basis in reality and its nature and meaning as so based, then the dominantly recollective address to our life, appropriate when we seek understanding by focusing on activity and on growth, must be complemented by a different address apt to the mainly potential status (at the time of reflection) of this 'work' that we have been taking as our reference point. As our actual participation in that 'work' increases, the basis in evidence for understanding it and understanding life as meaning our involvement in it expands and an increasingly recollective address will emerge in this regard as well. But apart from some understanding of our lives in reference to what we are to devote our lives to, and why, our understanding of those lives remains basically at sea, and the apt advance we can make in it in other regards remains impaired.

And yet, what we are to understand in order fully to understand our own lives is something which, if not itself futural, implicates us in a work that is for the most part futural; as such, it is also not able to be understood in the way what is past and present may be, or at least, what is factual in these. If working on that futural task belongs inherently to our lives, and so to work is part of the meant-to-be for us as active human beings, then fully understanding our own lives depends on understanding this future and this meant-to-be. But what sort of understanding of these is possible-- keeping in mind that neither is fact? And on what basis is it possible? Can any understanding, as interpretative and related to a meaning that is as having futural bearing and implicating us in its own realization under some interpretation or other, be other than a pre-judgment, not a discernment of truth proven out by what actually ensues but an arbitrary pre-conception which we make to be, so that it is according to our whim that 'reality' and 'truth' are as they come to be?

More broadly: If we have been concerned here in our most recent discussion with the question of how reflection, when stably and steadily grounded in certain constant or stable facets of reality, might become apt in its address to life so that we might actually come to understand our own lives, it remains worth underlining: we may never be able actually to understand our lives fully, and this, for a number of different reasons. We have already noted some of these; here, at the conclusion of these reflections, we note the most fundamental one. Even if the at-stake in our active existence could come fully into disclosure in immediacy from the mature standpoint we have been considering, and life thereby come into immediate disclosure and visibility in this largest of references, the at-stake would not be disclosed as a fact but as meant-to-be belonging to reality as in-the-making. The meanings that determine not simply that reality holds an at-stake at its heart but what it is that is at-stake become available for reflective address only as in process of being realized concretely, and that means: only as being responsively integrated into our activity with the help of pre-reflective interpretation. Since they can become taken up into understanding only under a further and reflective interpretation which intends gathering them up in their truth, questions always remain about how adequately this complex act has been carried through and how well and substantiatedly truth itself has been claimed in any purported understanding. As regards this determining 'structure' of reality, the understanding of which is crucial for our fully understanding our own lives, not only do questions remain as regards the sort of understanding possible, but also as regards the living of life in the activity of reflection, along with all the other activities involved concretely. In particular, is it possible for reflection-- even out of a current condition of fullest maturity and capacity-- to bring fully into question and to diverge from the pre-reflective interpretation of the at-stake that guides our own living of life even in the very act of reflecting? Can it do this without substituting an alternative interpretation to rest on, but rather in such way as leaves the phenomenon reflectively in suspense as one ventures practically in an altered vein, trying out living life in somewhat different terms but without claiming (absolute) truth for those terms? Can one live (and think) experimentally in this way, without a premature settling for an 'understanding' which then militates against further experiment and possible changing insight? If one could, what would such tentativeness in our understanding of reality mean for understanding our own lives? What would it mean for telling the story of our own lives in a truth-revealing way? If the latter is not possible-- since we do not *have* the truth, but at best an attempt at understanding which is self-aware to its own status as an attempt--, then can we say nothing? Is that the same as remaining silent?

With such questions, it is time to close this preparatory chapter and, turning back to Nietzsche's writings, to set forth what emerges into view when we read them as we saw him calling us to in EH. How do we find him thinking the theme of time and temporality?

PART I

YOUTH'S STATEMENT

CHAPTER 4
The Birth of Tragedy

Our Prelude is completed, and keeping in mind Nietzsche's guidance and our own thoughts on life, time, and temporality, we turn now to carrying through our study of his writings according to their order of publication. In his very first work, whose original title is *The Birth of Tragedy out of the Spirit of Music,* Nietzsche points us to two things that are of primary importance for our understanding of the notions of time and temporality with which he works initially. The first thing is the nature of reality: Nietzsche's initial claim is that it is creational in its nature and that time is a conditioning factor entered into created reality. The second thing is a pattern in human history: Nietzsche's initial claim is that the most humanly meaningful collective realizations of existence in the creational whole are to be found (actually) in the Greeks of ancient times and (in process of coming to pass) in the Germans of modern times.

A. A creational reality

In his retrospect on this work, Nietzsche alludes to an "artist's metaphysics"[1] as the framework for the development of its claims about tragedy. For the sense of reality which he was setting forth was developed in connection with art, and with art grasped as an affair with metaphysical roots and a metaphysical significance. Present in the realm of art are two basically different art impulses, tendencies, forces, each with its own distinctive nature and function in the situation of its manifestation. Among the Greeks these two forces are represented by their two art gods, Apollo and Dionysus. As this representation by divine powers suggests, these art-forces have a relation to the ultimate ground in the nature of things and have a function to be understood in that reference.

In the vision being sketched out in this work, reality is a whole whose internal constitution harbors a differentiation and a dynamic that is purposive in structure and nature. The differentiation in question is that of a basic side from a derivative side. The basic side is a "truly existent primal unity" that is eternal, and the derivative side is the phenomena or appearances which are manifold manifestations of this unitary eternal ground and which constitute empirical reality: the world of our experience, a world of perpetual becoming which is subject to time and space and which is interactive in the manner of causality. Now the unity of the primal unity is such as harbors inward tension, conflict; and not only is it inwardly at odds with itself, contradictory, but this conflicted being of itself makes suffering be an eternal element in its being. Thus this "eternally suffering and contradictory" being knows inherently the need for redemption from that suffering, and its way of finding that redemption is the creative act. Thus phenomenal reality has been (more precisely, is continuously being) called forth into being as "the rapturous vision, the pleasurable illusion" which the source can contemplate and in contemplating find its continuous redemption from its suffering. More precisely, the source finds its redemption in its cognizance of the joy which attends its creating and which is reflexive element in its contemplation of the derivative reality which it is creating.[2]

Now this derivative and manifest many has its own kind of unity, that of a differentiated and individuated multiplicity interacting to form one order of empirically real beings. Like the source with its own eternal internal contradiction, it has as well its own inherent internal conflict, both within each of the various individual phenomenal beings and in their interaction with each other. Thus in our participation in existence, we know pleasure at times, but know pain and suffering as well and know them as inherent features of our existence. For there is death, inherently at odds with the life in ourselves and inescapably introducing loss and suffering into it; there are conflict, frustration of desire, pain and injury, all inevitable ingredients in our interacting with other beings. These are all marks of finitude, of individuation, of the deficiency in being which belongs to individual finite existence. Because in our participation in such existence we ordinarily are not aware of the "mysterious ground of our being"[3] and thus are *not* cognizant of this created reality *as created*, this horizon of space, time, and suffering seems to us ultimate, and that seeming, although it involves a mis-taking on our part of empirical reality for the whole of reality, intensifies the need in ourselves which suffering introduces, for redemption.[4] In keeping with the purposive structure of the act of creation, however, that act introduces into creation the powers which enable this need of ours to be met. For harbored within creation at large, and at work within human being as well as beyond it, are the two art impulses, the Apollonian and the Dionysian. Through them art is created, and by participation in the act of artistic creation and in contemplation of its work, creatures may attain a redemption of their own complementary to the self-redemption of the unitary ground.

In their most basic form and working, the two art-creating powers manifest themselves without the mediation of human artists, in physiological phenomena which are analogous to the artistic phenomena of sculpture and music, respectively. These are dreams and intoxication.[5]

In dreams, what is phenomenal reality projects an appearance of itself-as-appearance, an illusion within itself-as-illusion, into which the phenomenal can in turn become immersed *as illusion*. Dream reality is intense, intelligible in its immediacy, capturing and holding attention so that the onlooker lives and suffers with the dream-figures and dream-event, yet remains separate and other than them.[6] As we become immersed in dreams and lose sight of waking reality, we experience those dreams with profound delight. To these dream states belongs a higher truth or perfection in contrast with "the incompletely intelligible everyday reality"[7]. At the same time, such intense dream-reality glimmers with the suggestion of its being mere appearance, illusory; it is felt as image, as illusion, and because of that, one does not take it for reality itself and lose oneself in it as such. Rather, one remains oneself and distinct from it-- or better, one is a self like Apollo, individual and reposing calmly in oneself in contemplation of such individuated dream-reality and its beauty.[8]

In intoxication, there is a contrasting energy, impulse, drive, tendency, a release from restrictions and an overflow of feelings in which everything subjective vanishes into complete self-forgetfulness. Under the workings of this impulse the intoxicated human being reaffirms the union of him-/herself not simply with other human beings but with nature, and finds nature responding: "with the gospel of universal harmony, each one feels himself not only united, reconciled, and fused with his neighbor, but one with him, as if the veil of *māyā* had been torn away and were now merely fluttering in tatters before the mysterious primordial unity."[9] This ecstatic condition of waking existence, when it is expressed in song and dance, is one in which the human being functions as a "member of a higher community" (indeed, feels him-/herself to be a god); as such, the human being's being is transformed into a living work of art.[10]

In both of these cases, the Apollonian and Dionysian artistic energies have burst forth from nature itself, without the mediation of the human artist. Here nature's art impulses are satisfied in the most immediate and direct way, first in the image world of dreams, and second as intoxicated reality and its mystic feeling of oneness. But these contrasting energies find further outworking in art as the creation of individuals, in art-forms such as sculpture and music. Apollo works to inspire an art-creation (sculpture, or epic poetry such as in Homer) in which he "overcomes the suffering of the individual by the radiant glorification of the eternity of the phenomenon: here beauty triumphs over the suffering inherent in life; pain is in a certain sense obliterated by lies from the features of nature."[11] Dionysus, in contrast, works to inspire an art-creation (music) which of itself is the immediate phenomenal copy of ultimate reality, ultimate reality made manifest directly. Dionysian art seeks also to convince us of the eternal joy of existence, but of a joy which is to be sought not in phenomena, but behind them. In the working of both gods, as the artists participate as artists in the creation of works of art they are grasped by artistic energies that come from beyond themselves as individual human subjects in empirical reality, and are taken by those energies beyond themselves as such subjects (as conscious centers of willing and knowing). Indeed, in the working of those energies through the individual artists the latter become (as it were) media

> through which the one truly existent subject celebrates his redemption in appearance. For to our abasement *and* exaltation, one thing above all must be clear to us. The entire comedy of art is neither performed for us (our betterment or education, say) nor are we the authentic authors of this art world. On the contrary, we may assume that we are only images and artistic projections for the true author, and that we have our highest dignity in our significance as works of art-- for it is only as an *aesthetic phenomenon* that existence and the world are eternally *justified* ... .[12]

In this interpretation of art, and in particular, of the experience of art and art-works both from the creating side and from the enjoying-and-appreciating side, Nietzsche is attempting the clarification (among other things) of the sort of experiencing he knew as a youth that seemed to him to give him meaningful access to the phenomenon of Dionysus. His interpretation draws on Schopenhauer and Kant for some of its language and thought, and however it may have seemed to him at the time, this feature of his endeavor is seen in retrospect as contributing to the defects which he notes in his later-added Preface (see the discussion in Chapter 2 above). The language and thought are particularly confusing when it comes to the notion of time, which is crucial to the idea of creation that he uses to interpret the disclosure of reality achieved in art.

Within the Kantian framework, the objective world of experience is an issue of two things, namely, what we introduce in our apprehension of reality-beyond-us and what that reality contributes as we apprehend it. Included in the former are the forms of our sensible intuition, namely, space and time; these are ways in which reality-beyond, when it modifies our sensibility, is immediately apprehended by us: it is spatial and temporal in its appearance to us. As in our spontaneity we take up the given manifold and order it conceptually, we organize the contribution of reality-beyond in such way as to establish the objective world of a unified space-time of interacting substances over against ourselves as cognitive subjects. Now this world, while it is for human beings formally one and the same and in that sense there for all of us, is something which actually exists only in the intermediate realm 'between' (so to speak) reality-beyond and ourselves; that is, it exists in dependence on our human powers of apprehension (sensibility and spontaneous conceptuality), and has standing only in the relation between reality-beyond and ourselves, in our interacting. As for reality-beyond in its own being (as contrasted to it in its relation to us), we can never know it, for knowing is a relational affair. At best, in virtue of the moral law and its binding character on us, we may think (but not know) this much of reality beyond appearance, that it is constituted in ourselves by a rational will.

There is, however, according to Schopenhauer's modification of Kant, a way in which we 'know' reality in its ultimate side, beginning with a direct inward apprehension under the immediacy of time as contrasted with the outward apprehension achieved under the immediacy of space *and* time. Such knowing is *of* our bodily being-- not of that being as it is an object of outward perception, for in that way it is simply one object among others out there, filling space and located in various spatial relations to other things. Rather, in an immediate inward apprehension we know our body in its being uniquely 'mine' (indeed, it constitutes my individuality as I 'identify' with it), and more profoundly even, we know will and willing as constituting ourselves as such bodily beings, and know will and willing (in some meaning of those terms) as the 'in itself' of ourselves and (by inference) of all things. This 'in itself' is thus 'energetic' and (so it would seem) 'interactive' in virtue of its own character.

Leaving aside the question of how Nietzsche understood the Kant and Schopenhauer whose language and thought he drew upon, and attending simply to the (in part borrowed) language that he uses to articulate the nature and meaning of the disclosive experience that concerns him, we see him making use of a temporal language in his account both of true reality and of the unfolding of such experience as brings an "identification" of ourselves with that reality. Thus in interpreting true reality as a "primordial one"[13] and accepting that this "one" involves an inherent internal contradiction or conflict, Nietzsche attributes to it primordial suffering, pain, and joy.[14] But if that self-conflicted one is "eternal"[15] in the sense of "timeless", how is such an attribution meaningful, since joy, suffering, and pain, all seem to involve time? If such talk is meaningful as metaphorical only, and the dynamic which such attributions carry is not truly temporal but (say) structural and dialectical, is that likewise the case when he speaks of the primordial one's life, its abiding indestructibly through the change and destruction of things, and its raging desire for existence and joy in existence and its eternally being creative and eternally finding satisfaction in the change of phenomena?[16] For in all these cases, the attributions are intended to capture facets of the source revealed to a (human) manifestation's immediate experience of it, such as in the experience of Dionysian art when "we actually [*wirklich*] are, for a brief moment, the primordial being [*Urwesen*] itself and feel its unrestrained desire for existence and joy in existence."[17] Is this the temporal experiencing of a non-temporal reality? Or ... ?

From the language he uses, it is clear that creation as Nietzsche means it is not some long-ago event, but is something going on all the time, that is, wherever there is time and (with time) the phenomenal reality he calls appearance. Here another difficulty arises. Creation is not itself a temporal act, something occurring *in* time; and the source is not phenomenal, something coming and going *in* time. For there to be time in the Kantian sense, there must *be* ourselves and other things and *interaction* (of some sort) between us. For time is no more than a condition of our 'experience', and that 'experience' is engendered in the interaction of 'already existing' human beings with other beings, being issue of the latter's giving themselves to our intuition and ourselves apprehending them in virtue of the forms (intuitive and conceptual) under which we can do this. If nothing is 'given', if we 'receive' nothing from beyond ourselves so that there is no empirical content entered into our power of receptivity under its spatial-and-temporal forms, there would be no such world. Not only, then, do the creational act and the created world 'precede' time, but time's being actual depends upon that 'antecedent' *being* of creatures-deriving-from-their-creator and upon an 'antecedent' *interacting* (of some sort). To speak of *experiencing* our source and our own creatureliness, then, is not only to speak of experience in a non-Kantian sense, but it is also to invoke a meaning of "time" as a condition of our activity (at the very least, of the receiving and conceiving that make for 'experience' in the Kantian sense), and not simply as a subjective condition of objective knowledge (including the subject's knowledge of its own subjectivity in the Schopenhauerian sense). But as to that creaturely activity (or more precisely, interacting) in which 'experience' is constituted: what are the time and temporality which mark it, if they are other than the time and temporality which belong to the intuition which forms a constitutive element in experience and objective knowledge? There is confusion here and need for greater clarity, as Nietzsche will eventually recognize.

Leaving that for future consideration, but tracing out further here the conception seemingly involved in the creational account Nietzsche is offering: According to its rationale, the creation of creatures which goes on 'all the time' does not reach its end and satisfy the creative urge simply with the emergence of the things which compose creation. There is, indeed, redemption of the creator in the joy of creating, a joy deeper than its suffering; but the initial issue of creation is finite creatures individuated and existing under conditions which make suffering an unavoidable element in that existing. The redemptive meaning of the act of creation is not complete except as creatures know redemption, and as it turns out, except as creatures can be creative in the likeness of their creator and indeed, be creative in a creating in which they become 'one' with that creator in the joy of its creating. In order to secure what is at stake in the original act of creation, then, art is needed as the medium of the creaturely creating, and in particular, tragic art, as the vehicle for a disclosure of truth which can accept the negativities of creaturely life while facilitating a self-aware participation in life and life's inherent creativity. Only in this does the creature know redemption. But if this is so, if it is only through time (and space) that the atemporal source and its atemporal act of creation can issue in its actual and full culmination, that would seem to make time essential in a further sense to the religious meaning of existence. For not only is time entered into creation in the act of creation so that the joy of the source in creating is an affair that involves the temporal (even if it is not itself temporal), but both tragic drama and creative life, if they are integral to the culmination of creation, take time, involving as they do temporal human agents and an affair and a drama that unfold in time. Whatever else may be said of such a culmination, it means a peculiar connection of the temporal and the timeless. What sort of domain could constitute the locus of any such culmination?

The questions raised by such an account of reality as Nietzsche gives in this work, and especially by the nature and role of time in that account, are things which Nietzsche himself will in some measure deal with in the course of the development of his thought. For the moment, his initial account is one which he developed out of his own youthful experiencing, and in particular, in an interpretation which sought to make sense of "a lot of premature, overgreen personal experiences, all of them hard on the threshold of what can be communicated"[18]. Within the complex and rather overpowering matrix of experience, he brought to speech as best he could what was visible, and he sought an intelligibility sufficient at the time and seemed to himself to have found it in an interpretation of its disclosure as evidencing a creational act whose telic structure gives to existence an aesthetic and metaphysical meaning. According to the understanding thus developed, human life gains insight into reality and a meaningfulness to itself in the living being's self-aware participation in the artistically-and-aesthetically achieved consummation of the act of creation, in the immediacy of its art-shaped experiencing. The rendering which he achieves of the disclosure of such experience, however, utilizes ways of speaking that do not readily cohere with each other, though each separately may seem to catch something important, even essential, in experience and therefore to need to be present. At the very least, there is lacking the precision which the more mature reflective person demands-- one that would establish consistency as well-- but which in this beginning has not yet been attained. This seems in part to be what Nietzsche has in mind when, in the later-added Preface, he speaks of the work as "image-mad and image-confused" and lacking the "will to logical cleanliness".

B. Tragic ages in human history

We human beings are participants in the temporal order which is existence, and because the enabling conditions of space and time make that participation finite, ours is a mortal and passing existence. But in virtue of our human nature we are involved also in reproduction, so that while we as individuals come and go, we leave progeny behind and make it possible for generations of human beings to succeed one another. During our individual existence, we find ourselves associating with others, and as involved in various associative groupings, we find ourselves being raised and operating within social traditions which have been formed by predecessors and inherited by us and the members of our groups, and which we can ourselves perhaps add to or modify during our lifetime. Thereby we know our existence as temporal not simply because we are mortal but also because our mortal existence gains some of its character from the traditions we inherit and the way we enact them and engage with others who likewise are enacting a tradition-- perhaps our shared tradition, but perhaps a different one. We *are*, then, temporal in traditional and historical as well as mortal fashion.

For Nietzsche in BT, we also know a trans-historical power, namely, art, which has metaphysical roots and a capacity to invest the temporal with eternal meaning. Not only does it open the artist in his/her present ongoing to time-less depths and to eternal meaning for mortal life; but art is a cultural force which operates in the tradition-marked associating of humans and in its fullest form-- that of religion and myth-- can gather up members of a community and help them participate together in the time-less depths, in the creaturely consummation of creation. In this regard, the Greeks of archaic and classical times have a fascination for him, for their accomplishment in art is (so he judges) superior to all others, although it is on the verge of being equalled by the Germans of his own times. That working of art among the Greeks which establishes the highest form of their human superiority is the participative disclosure of reality and life achieved in the tragic stage-drama that celebrates Dionysus.

1. The Greeks and the birth of tragedy

To explain his understanding of the Greeks, Nietzsche sketches out in quasi-Hegelian fashion[19] stages in the historical Greek involvement in art, and sees the dynamic that generates those stages as the strife, the mutual antagonism but also mutual incitement, of the two art-powers, the Apollonian and the Dionysian.

The first period is one dominated by Dionysus, or rather, one in which the knowledge declared by Silenus, the companion of Dionysus, prevails. What Silenus voices is knowledge of an order of terror in which Moira and the Titans hold sway. The second period emerged in response to the need that stemmed from this Silenic knowledge. Here the Apollonian art-impulse, particularly manifest in Homer, gave such shape to the world of the Olympian gods as effected a different emphasis within the mythical horizon of the Greeks. Within the "Olympian divine order of joy" being achieved thereby, the focus on beauty successfully veiled much of the negativity of existence. The power of this order to enable the Greeks to endure the terror of existence lasted until the onslaught of the Dionysian from outside the Greek world brought on the third period. The incursion of the barbarian form of the worship of Dionysus, with its extravagance, its cruelty, its savagery, resonated against the negativity still present in the Greeks but now hidden by the Olympian vision; thus even as the sane Greeks took up the barbarian Dionysian incursion and transformed it, the Apollonian Greek had to recognize his inner kinship with the Dionysian in this form. For despite all its beauty and moderation, his existence rested on a hidden substratum of suffering and of knowledge revealed to him by the Silenic side of the Dionysian. Where the Greeks were able to resist and surmount this invading barbarism and maintain the Apollonian as dominant, we find the fourth stage, that of the Doric city-state and Doric art, that of the dominance of the Delphic form of Apollo. In Athens, however, even this was eventually surmounted; for there, in a fifth stage, a resurgence of the Dionysian led to an integrating of Apollo and Dionysus in which neither power dominated to the exclusion of the other but the two together achieved a joint issue in which the force of each was sustained and heightened. The offspring in which this revivifying union of these two divine art-impulses was consummated, a child both Dionysian and Apollonian, was Attic tragedy.[20]

Tragedy developed in Athens as part of the worship of Dionysus. In that worship generally, the followers of Dionysus, seeking truth and nature in their most forceful form, find themselves changed; under the god's spell they are drawn beyond themselves and possessed by him. Transformed by the power [*Macht*] of such moods and insights as he engenders, they become aware of themselves differently-- here, as restored geniuses of nature, as satyrs; and they become entered into those visions which the god engenders in his followers. The first step in the Attic accomplishment was to turn the dancing satyrs, the possessed followers of Dionysus, into the chorus, which formed the original element of tragedy. In tragedy, this satyr-representing chorus functioned as mediator between the public, assembled in the theatre to worship Dionysus, and the rest of what was involved in this worship, namely, the god and the action. The second step was to transform the god present to the worshipper into a visible reality; this was achieved by making the world of the stage, the scene and the action, be the vision in which the satyr-chorus beholds its lord and master Dionysus. With this use of the

Apollonian impulse to present the god as something visible for every eye, we have drama, not merely chorus. But if this drama was an Apollonian element, it was one that served the Dionysian; for the enacted drama embodied and conveyed the Dionysian in its fullest truth. The Dionysian wisdom bodied forth in tragic drama was one which, looking clearly at the terrible destructiveness of existence (of world-history and nature both), pronounced nonetheless the comforting insight that "life is at the bottom of things (despite all the changes of appearances) indestructibly powerful and pleasurable."[21]

From its earliest form through to the form it took at the hands of Euripides, Greek tragedy had for its sole theme the sufferings of Dionysus. But over time, the tragic hero began to appear in a variety of forms, and in particular, the Greeks began to draw upon their myths-- the Homeric, the Apollonian, story-accounts-- and invest them with a new and profound significance by making them be the guises and disguises for the appearing of Dionysus on stage. For in those stories the suffering Dionysus of the Mysteries appeared as a fighting hero entangled in the net of the individual will, and with the destruction of the hero the stories symbolized the restoration of oneness, the hope for which casts a gleam of joy upon this world torn asunder and shattered into individuals.

What was tragedy, then, to the Greeks?

It was an element in the celebration and worship of the god Dionysus. That god induces in his worshipers an annihilation of the ordinary bounds and limits of existence and opens their vision into reality beyond that of ordinary personal existence. Initially the emerging insight reaches beyond the appearances of ordinary experience into the eternal nature of the world of appearances as horrible, fearful, terrifying. Such insight in turn calls forth a nausea at that world, and a weakening of the will to action in it, given that nothing can be changed at bottom, so that there is nothing that action can really accomplish with regard to 'reality'-- "to action belongs being veiled by illusion."[22] But the insight opened up by the god does not stop with this Silenic vision of existence in its horror and absurdity. It reaches beyond appearances to the eternal life of the source of appearances, to ultimate reality as a life which abides joyfully in and by the perpetual creation and destruction of appearances in the world of appearance. Now tragedy is the work of the art-impulse of Dionysus which, in an artistic enactment that is part of the ritual celebration of the god, bodies forth this deeper insight, this 'wisdom from the very heart of nature'. Its origin lies ultimately in the power of music, the Dionysian art-form which gives rise to song and dance and which moves the dancing satyr-worshippers of Dionysus who are figured forth in the chorus of tragic drama. Its full form is achieved when, engendering a form of worship of Dionysus which (with the help of the Apollonian art-impulse) is centered on the performance of a visible and audible drama before an audience of worshiper-spectators, it ends by transforming the mythical horizon of the Greeks at the time when it was otherwise dying and making it be the vehicle for the enactment of the Dionysian insight into the truth of reality and life. In virtue of this form of worship, the audience-member worshipers are enabled to enter into, to see and feel, that deeper truth. Thereby they share in a mystery teaching which, while regarding individuation as the primal cause of evil, sees deeper into the nature of things than individuation, seeing the oneness of all that exists. The drama, embodying that teaching in a symbolic vehicle, evokes the joyous hope that the spell of individuation may be broken. In this way, the participants know the redemptive power of art and realize its metaphysical meaning.

Such was the tragic art-form for the Greeks, as Nietzsche understands it here in his first book. In regard to "the profound Hellene, uniquely susceptible to the tenderest and deepest suffering", here "art saves him, and through art-- life."[23]

2. The death of tragedy among the Greeks

Tragedy arose and persisted among the ancient Greeks for a while, but eventually it was undermined by another force that had arisen among them. The poet at whose hands tragedy died was Euripides, but the figure who embodies and symbolizes the daimonic power which accounted for that death was Socrates.

Euripides was not poet alone, but thinker as well. Indeed, not only was his productive artistic impulse stimulated by his critical talent, but understanding was for him the real root of all enjoyment and creation. So he made himself-as-thinker, together with that man whom he regarded as his equal as thinker, namely, Socrates, the judges of works of art, his own included. Demanding clarity, he could see Aeschylus and Sophocles only as lacking this, in form and content both; and not understanding them, he initiated-- in alliance with Socrates, who likewise did not comprehend or esteem tragedy-- the tremendous struggle against the art of Aeschylus and Sophocles, and did this not with polemical essays but as a dramatic poet who opposed his conception of tragedy to the traditional one. His aim: to separate the primordial Dionysian element from tragedy and to reconstruct tragedy purely on the basis of an un-Dionysian art, morality, and world view. "The deity that spoke through Euripides was neither Dionysus nor Apollo, but an altogether newborn daimon, called Socrates."[24]

How did Euripides accomplish this aim of reconstituting tragedy? First, by making music, thus the chorus, secondary; thereby he divested tragedy of the Dionysian and was left with only dramatized epos. But in this Apollonian domain of art, the tragic effect is unattainable. So to attain a tragic effect he had to make use of stimulants outside both art-impulses, the Apollonian and the Dionysian: "these stimulants are cool, paradoxical thoughts (replacing Apollonian contemplation) and fiery affects (replacing Dionysian ecstasies)." But more: "thoughts and affects copied very realistically and in no way dipped into the ether of art"[25]. Thus in reforming tragedy Euripides became naturalistic, and inartistic. For this, his 'aesthetic Socratism' was responsible, since it led him (via the dictum 'to be beautiful everything must be intelligible', the counterpart to the Socratic dictum 'knowledge is virtue') to measure by the standard of clarity all the separate elements of the drama (language, characters, dramaturgic structure, and choric music) and to correct them accordingly. Thus as to form, he introduced the prologue; as to content, he reconceived the hero by bringing the everyday human being onto the stage and in image showing him to himself-as-spectator. In short: in Euripides, no longer was the spectator to be caught up in the transformation of Dionysus-worship, nor is the vision of the Dionysus-worshiping-chorus any longer Dionysus-in-disguise, thus grander than the everyday.

Through his 'audacious reasonableness' Euripides only succeeded in destroying tragedy. Yet if he represented an aesthetic Socratism-- if he as poet was essentially an echo of his own conscious knowledge-- what did Socrates himself stand for?

Socrates represents the emphasis on knowledge: not instinctual knowledge, but knowledge as self-conscious. So strong is the contrast here that "in this utterly abnormal nature, instinctive wisdom appears only in order to hinder conscious knowledge occasionally. While in all productive men it is instinct that is the creative-affirmative force, and consciousness acts critically and dissuasively, in Socrates it is instinct that becomes the critic, and consciousness that becomes the creator ... ."[26] Socrates was the typical non-mystic whose excessively developed logical nature is central: "wherever Socratism turned its searching eyes it saw lack of insight and the power of illusion; and from this lack it inferred the essential perversity and reprehensibility of what exists. Basing himself on this point, Socrates believed he had to correct existence."[27] But the logical urge that became manifest in Socrates was not turned against itself; it proclaimed the logical drive in un-self-critical fashion, making dialectic, argument and counter-argument, with their optimism prevail under the three optimistic maxims 'virtue is knowledge; human beings sin only from ignorance; he who is virtuous is happy'.

The eye of Socrates, in which "the fair frenzy of artistic enthusiasm had never glowed" and which had been denied "the pleasure of gazing into the Dionysian abysses", could (when turned on tragedy) see only "something rather unreasonable, containing causes apparently without effects and effects apparently without causes; the whole, moreover, so motley and manifold that it had to be repugnant to a sober mind, and a dangerous tinder for sensitive and susceptible souls".[28] To such an eye, too, the chorus-- and indeed, the whole musical-Dionysian substratum of tragedy-- appeared as accidental, a dispensable vestige of the origin of tragedy. True, it was not Socrates who was the first to turn such an eye on tragedy: an anti-Dionysian tendency was operating even prior to Socrates, and merely received in him an unprecedentedly magnificent expression. Still, in Socrates and Euripides the musical foundation-and-generating-force for tragedy became dismissed, in favor of a focus on verbal content and the like.

In short, Nietzsche sees in Socrates the embodiment of the rationalism which ended tragedy and more broadly the cultural life of the tragic-age Greeks. And yet, about this Socrates, there is a question which he also feels impelled to ask, "whether there is necessarily only an antipodal relation between Socratism and art, and whether the birth of an 'artistic Socrates' is altogether a contradiction in terms"[29]. The occasion for this question is a profound experience in Socrates' own life; Nietzsche is here referring to Plato's *Phaedo* and its portrayal of Socrates in prison. In the dialogue Socrates speaks of himself as having often experienced in dream a dream-figure urging him to "practice music", and says that he had previously interpreted that as urging him to be a philosopher (for philosophy is the highest music, that is, Muse-inspired activity). But now he has reinterpreted it so that he has become a musician-poet in prison, putting some fables of Aesop to music, and composing a hymn to Apollo. Nietzsche comments: "The voice of the Socratic dream-apparition is the only sign of any misgivings about the limits of logic: perhaps-- thus he must have asked himself-- what is not intelligible to me is not necessarily silly and stupid? Perhaps there is a realm of wisdom from which the logician is exiled? Perhaps art is even a necessary correlative of, and supplement for, science?"[30] Was Socrates perhaps more than the naive rationalist he seemed to be?[31]

However that may be, Socrates symbolizes the end of the ancient Greek cultural and artistic achievement, but also the beginning of a historical development which has extended up to Nietzsche's own day.

3. The Germans and the re-birth of tragedy

In the time since the Greeks, a modern European world has arisen which reflects two major and decisive events. To one of the two-- the rise of Christianity and its permeation of the Western world, in particular, the Christianization of the German people, and thus the dominance of an alien myth in German life--, Nietzsche makes only covert allusions.[32] It is on the other-- developments stemming from the ancient Greek world and decisive for the character of modernity-- that he concentrates his attention. For understanding this second matter, Socrates is once again crucial.

> He who once makes clear to himself how after Socrates, the mystagogue of science, one school of philosophy after another was loosed like wave after wave; how the desire to know, in a never-suspected universality, has reached into the widest realm of the cultured and educated world and has driven science (as the authentic task for every person of higher gifts) out onto the high seas from which it has never again been able to be driven altogether; how due to this universality, a common net of thought has become spread over the whole globe, indeed over the lawfulness of the whole solar system; he who makes all this present to himself, together with the astonishingly high pyramid of knowledge in our own time-- he cannot refrain from seeing in Socrates the one turning point and vortex of so-called world history.[33]

Seen from this perspective, we may say that modernity, and in particular, nineteenth century Germany, has taken on the character of the Socratic or Alexandrian culture which arose among the Greeks after the death of tragedy and from which this development stems. For in our world science-- that is, disciplined rational knowledge-- has been made master of the life of the peoples of modern Europe and an attempt thereby has been made to establish culture on a different basis from myth. The ideal of this culture is a human being-- theoretical man-- who

> combats Dionysian wisdom and art, [who] seeks to dissolve myth, [who] substitutes for a metaphysical comfort an earthly consonance, in fact, a *deus ex machina* of [his] own, the god of machines and crucibles, that is, the powers of the spirits of nature recognized and employed in the service of a higher egoism; [he] believes [he] can correct the world by knowledge, guide life by science, and actually confine the individual within a limited sphere of solvable problems, within which he can cheerfully say to life; 'I want you; you are worthy of being known'.[34]

Within a culture bent on such a dominance of reason, every other form of existence than that embodied in theoretical man can only struggle on laboriously, at best tolerated, at worst combated. The result is that, in modern culture since the Renaissance (fifteenth century) reawakening of Alexandrian-Roman antiquity, we have come to approximate our Greek forefathers of that ancient time. Thus

> on the heights we meet with the same overabundant lust for knowledge, the same unsatisfied delight in discovery, the same tremendous secularization, and beside it a homeless roving, a greedy crowding around foreign tables, a frivolous deification of the present, or a dully dazed retreat-- everything *sub specie saeculi*, of the 'present age'. These same symptoms allow us to infer the same lack at the heart of this culture, the destruction of myth.[35]

Or again, in drawing a contrast with a culture in which myth is alive and the healthy natural power of its creativity is preserved:

> By way of comparison let us now picture the abstract human being, guided without myth; abstract education; abstract morality; abstract law; the abstract state; let us imagine the lawless roving of the artistic imagination, unchecked by any native [*heimischen*] myth; let us think of a culture that has no fixed and sacred primordial-site but is doomed to exhaust all possibilities and to nourish itself miserably on all other cultures-- there we have the present age, the result of that Socratism which is bent on the destruction of myth. And now the mythless human being, eternally hungry, stands amid all past ages and digs and grubs for roots, even if he has to dig for them among the remotest antiquities. The tremendous historical need of our unsatisfied modern culture, the assembling around ourselves of countless other cultures, the consuming desire for knowledge-- what does all this point to, if not to the loss of myth, the loss of our mythical home, the mythical maternal womb? Let us ask ourselves whether the feverish and uncanny excitement of this culture is anything but the greedy seizing and snatching at food of a hungry person-- and who would care to contribute anything to a culture that cannot be satisfied no matter how much it devours, and at whose contact the most vigorous and wholesome nourishment is changed into 'history and criticism'?[36]

There is one anomalous element in this modern development. For some reason the German spirit has not been so wholly absorbed into this culture as to be inextricably entangled in it. Quite to the contrary, there is a noble core [*Kerne*] to the character [-*charakters*] of the German people, "a lordly [*herrliche*], intrinsically healthy, primeval power [*uralte Kraft*]", that lies concealed beneath this "restlessly palpitating cultural life [*Kulturleben*] and cultural convulsion [*Bildungskrampfe*]".[37] Thus the present (especially in the German part of it) is marked by a profound mixture and ambivalence.

On one side are the signs of an end to the vitality of the culture that has gained an "attenuated form of transfiguration" under the dominance of "the Socratism of science that impels toward life".[38] Thus if we look around sensitively, we see a contemporary culture that is desolate and exhausted, without a single vigorously developing root or even a spot of fertile and healthy soil: a desert, in which the critic has gotten the upper hand in the theater and concert hall, the journalist in the schools, the press in society, and art has become imitative of productive periods and natures and not productive itself. Moreover, ours is a culture of optimism, committed to the rational scientific guidance of life, to the solubility of any problems that face us, to the correction and improvement of the world by way of knowledge[39]; and yet, as this optimism has permeated through society from highest to lowest strata, we find the emphasis on earthly happiness and on this as attainable by all awakening 'wanton agitations and desires', unsettling demands that all become educated and cultured and share in such happiness. Finally, ours is also a culture which, despite our fine talk to the contrary, requires for its permanent existence a slave class; but with its optimistic view of life it denies the necessity of such a class. As the fine-sounding talk of the 'dignity of man' and the 'dignity of labor' become less and less effective in the face of the reality of modern life, we find ourselves drifting toward destruction at the hands of the 'class of barbaric slaves' who have come to regard their existence as unjust, and clamoring for 'justice', are prepared to avenge themselves and overthrow 'the system'. Thus despite its intentions, the optimism at the heart of this culture is ripening fruits that are threatening it, and the society is drifting toward a dreadful destruction. In the face of such threatening storms, as the logical consequences of our optimism become visible and the upheavals these threaten begin to frighten modern man, our search for ways of averting danger can have no confidence in any appeal for support and remedy to 'our pale and exhausted religions'. In their foundations, they have degenerated into scholarly and rationalized religions as myth has become mastered by the optimistic spirit and the feeling for myth has vanished; and in any case, the myth involved in them (the Christian myth) is an alien one without power to move the genuine spirit of the people (the German spirit, least of all).[40]

On the other side are the recent signs of this German spirit beginning to awaken and come to itself. There is German music, beginning with the chorales of Luther. "Out of the Dionysian root of the German spirit" has risen this power-- the only "genuine, pure, and purifying fire-spirit" present in all our culture, itself hostile to and inexplicable by Socratic culture. This is "German music as we must understand it, particularly in its vast solar orbit from Bach to Beethoven, from Beethoven to Wagner"[41]. Then there is German philosophy in the persons of Kant and Schopenhauer. They have used the paraphernalia of disciplined knowledge to point out the limits of science and the relativity of objective knowledge to appearance; thus they have undermined in principle the claim of science to universal validity and to universal aims. In so doing, they have undermined the optimism of modern culture and realized the deeper meaning of the illusion which guides theoretical man, namely: it is meant to drive him to the 'boundary points' of knowledge, and to open up, in the recognition of the limits of knowledge, a new form of insight, that which the Greeks attained, namely, tragic insight. With the insight into knowledge as limited to appearance and as unequal to fathoming ultimate reality,

> a culture is ushered in that I venture to designate a tragic culture. Its most important characteristic is that wisdom takes the place of science as the highest end-- wisdom that, uninfluenced by the seductive distractions of the sciences, turns with unmoved eyes to an all-embracing image [*Gesamtbilde*] of the world, and seeks to grasp, with sympathetic feelings of love, the eternal suffering as its own.[42]

This accomplishment of Kant and Schopenhauer in undermining the illusion at the basis of the complacent delight of scientific Socratism in existence has introduced an infinitely profounder and more serious view of ethical problems and of art, which Nietzsche designates "Dionysian wisdom grasped in concepts"[43]. But the question remains: Can this turning of optimism into tragic insight lead to something deeper than Silenic pessimism in the face of negativity, and lead instead (say) "to ever-new configurations of genius and especially of the Socrates who practises music"[44]? That is, can this modern realization of tragic insight be deep and strong enough not only to transcend Silenic negativity but also to *incorporate* the drive which Socrates epitomized and to maintain that otherwise-tragedy-killing drive *within*-- and in *subordination to*-- the deeper acknowledgement of Dionysian truth? Can it maintain that drive within a new culture of human beings who, possessed of such clear-sighted vision, are resolved (in view of their "self-education for seriousness and terror")"'to live resolutely' in wholeness and fulness"[45]?

For a tragic culture to arise, a modern version of that which the Greeks once achieved, another force, powerful and positive, would be needed. At present, most of what we see is modern Socratic culture-- shaken "from two directions, once by the fear of its own consequences which it at length begins to suspicion, and then because it is no longer convinced with its former naive confidence in the eternal validity of its foundation"-- rushing here and there, mistrustful and timid, seeking the new and the old without wanting "to have anything whole, with all of nature's cruelty attaching to it"[46]. In its midst, however, we do find something else, and indeed, precisely such a force as could bring tragic culture as its eventual issue. That is Wagner's music, taken not simply as music but as the medium of the revival of German myth. Recall the Greeks here: out of music was born the tragic drama which bodied forth Dionysian insight and revived Greek myth by making it a symbolic vehicle for conveying such insight. Is it possible then that Wagner's music could do likewise, in this case revive

Germanic myth, and thereby point the way to and assist in the realization of the return of the German spirit to itself and in the reinstatement of Germanic myth as the horizon for the healthy creativity of the German people? Can we see in Wagner's music, then, a restoration of music to its "Dionysian-cosmic mission"[47]? This is the hope whose expression Nietzsche so much regretted in his later retrospects upon BT. Let us see what it amounted to in its original assertion.

Speaking of this mysterious oneness of German music and philosophy, Nietzsche claims it points to a new form of existence, the character of which Hellenic analogies can help us see. In passing backward, so to speak, from the Alexandrian age to the period of tragedy, we have the feeling that

> the birth of a tragic age simply means a return to itself of the German spirit, a blessed self-rediscovery after tremendous powers intruding from the outside had for a long time compelled it, living as it did in a helpless barbarism of form, to servitude under their form. Now at last, upon returning to the primordial source of its being, it may venture to stride along boldly and freely before the eyes of all nations without being attached to the lead strings of a Romanic civilization; if only it can learn constantly from one people-- the Greeks, from whom to be able to learn at all is itself a high honor and a rare distinction. And when were we in greater need of these highest of all teachers than at present, when we are experiencing a *rebirth of tragedy* and are in danger alike of not knowing whence it comes and of being unable to interpret to ourselves whither it wants to go?[48]

If what we face now is an endeavor to attain to culture and to the Greeks on the same path, it remains that in the midst of the desolation and exhaustion of contemporary culture and with the cultural power of our higher educational institutions never feebler than at present, we will not find the Greeks on what would seem to be the most direct path, that of Hellenic scholarship. For even the best of our Hellenists in the present day are not able to penetrate into the core of the Hellenic nature. The renovation and purification of the German spirit must rather take place "through the fire magic of music" and in particular the "mystic tones of reawakened tragic music"[49]. Wagner's music, his grand opera, is to be understood in the likeness of Greek tragedy, as the music which transforms the stories of Germanic myth and, at the same time as it revitalizes myth in that sense, makes those stories symbolically embody Dionysian insight into reality and life. Grand opera then would be the modern version of the tragic art-form. But this is only a first step in the creation of a tragic culture. In his enthusiasm for this idea, Nietzsche pays little express attention to differences that are significant. For example, Greek tragedy emerged in an already extant religious matrix as part of a religious ritual, whereas Wagner's music and use of Germanic myth in his grand opera had no such setting, Germanic myth not being the religious center for the German polity of the time. Nonetheless, in BT Nietzsche points to the future as involving the revival, in the Germans, of this religious center to the life of the people.

If the analogy with the Greeks has a bearing here, that means the Germans of the immediate future will not only find their way back to their own myth as a living affair, but find in their own way that middle path between Rome and Indian Buddhism which the Greeks achieved. For the connections between art and the people, myth and custom, tragedy and the state, are close and fundamental. Through myth a people (and individuals) dip into the current of the timeless, to find rest in it from the burden and the greed of the moment.

> And any people-- just as, incidentally, also any individual-- is worth only as much as it is able to press upon its experiences the stamp of the eternal; for thus it is, as it were, desecularized and shows its unconscious inward conviction both of the relativity of time and of the true (that is, metaphysical) significance of life. The opposite of this happens when a people begins to comprehend itself historically and to smash the mythical bulwarks that surround it. Connected with this is usually a decisive secularization, a break with the unconscious metaphysics of its previous existence, together with all its ethical consequences.[50]

Now the Greeks knew myth as the foundation for a communal life that was realized in and through the city-state [*polis*] as its medium. This, like tragedy, involved an integration of Dionysian and

Apollonian. For a diminution of, indifference to, indeed hostility to, the political instincts is the up-shot of the Dionysian without the Apollonian (see Indian Buddhism, reflecting the excessive Diony-sian excitement of preceding times), just as where the political drives are taken to be absolutely valid, a people must take the path of the most extreme secularization (see the Roman empire as an ex-pression of this). Between the two, the Greeks invented a third form, uniting the extraordinary strength of their Dionysian and political instincts so as to be fiery and contemplative at the same time.[51] Thereby they formed at their height a living and creative people, organized politically and operating out of the homeland of its own native spirit, giving shape to itself and living life with eyes open to the Dionysian reality which is ours to live in.

If the revival of tragic music and tragedy in Wagnerian form is only a beginning point for the in-clusive revival of the German spirit and its expression in a tragic culture that permeates the life of a politically-organized German people, there is one important complication for any such revival. The Germans have become Christianized and lost their own myth as a guide to life; while Luther meant a rejection of one form of Christianity, he did not mean the revival of Germanic myth. In BT there is considerable hostility against Christianity as having mastered the Germans, although that hostility is relatively unobtrusive given its merely allusive expression. There is as well a strong sense of the need to throw off this alien myth-garb and to revive indigenous German myth. The rebirth of tragedy among the Germans would mean, then, that the German spirit, which during the time of the domi-nance of Christianity has been resting and dreaming still in some inaccessible abyss, would awake and manifest itself once again in its glorious health and Dionysian strength. Indeed, from the abyss where this profound spirit is now resting undestroyed, the Dionysian song is already rising to our ears

> to let us know that this German knight is still dreaming his primordial Dionysian myth in blissfully serious visions. Let no one believe that the German spirit has forever lost its mythical home when it can still understand so plainly the voices of the birds that tell of that home. Some day it will find itself awake in all the morning freshness following a tremendous sleep: then it will slay dragons, destroy vicious dwarfs, wake Brünnhilde-- and even Wotan's spear will not be able to stop its course! My friends, you who believe in Dionysian music, you also know what tragedy means to us. There we have tragic myth reborn from music-- and in this myth we can hope for everything and forget what is most painful. What is most painful for all of us, however, is-- the prolonged degradation in which the German genius has lived, estranged from house and home, in the service of vicious dwarfs.[52]

Because the revival of Germanic myth entails casting off Christianity and its myth as foreign to the German people and alien to the German spirit, Nietzsche claims:

> We think so highly of the pure and vigorous core of the German character [*Wesen*] that we dare to expect of it above all others this elimination of the forcibly implanted foreign elements, and consider it possible that the German spirit will be recalled to itself ... . This spirit must ... fight [to restore itself], but ... the inner necessity [that must animate such a fight is] the ambition to be always worthy of the sublime champions on this way, Luther and our great artists and poets. But let him never believe that he could fight similar fights without the gods of his house, or his mythical home, without 'bringing back' all German things! And if the German should hesitantly look around for a leader who might bring him back again into his long lost home whose ways and paths he scarcely knows anymore, let him merely listen to the ecstatically luring call of the Dionysian bird that hovers above him and wants to point the way for him.[53]

In sum: The present in modern Europe and in Germany in particular is an age in transition. Al-ready in principle the preceding (Socratic) culture has been undermined and a new age of tragic cul-ture is in process of dawning. For that dawning, it is the music of Wagner that is the critical happen-ing, leading toward a transformed culture of the German people which concretely embodies the Dio-nysian wisdom of the German spirit. In the parallel of Greek tragedy and Wagnerian music, of Greek culture and this aborning German culture, history exhibits not inevitable progress (Hegel) but comparable realizations of an eternal theme-- variant historical embodiments (in a temporality invested with eternity) of the meaning of human existence.

C. Enlarging our consideration

In the preceding discussion we have briefly set forth the larger development of ideas in BT-- those of reality and of the collective metaphysical meaning to human life-- within which Nietzsche has introduced ideas of time and temporality and employed them to help him make clear the nature of both matters. It is time now to look more closely and in detail at the experiential matrix within which Nietzsche is operating, so far as this becomes visible in and through the work, and to observe in particular how time and temporality come to light in it; it is also time to consider more fully the matter of the reflective inquiry which he is undertaking, and in particular, his own account of its standpoint and perspective on what becomes disclosed in immediacy in the experiential matrix, and his use in that account of notions of immediate and instinctive wisdom, reason, and illusion.

1. The dialectic and disclosure of
Dionysian experience

Nietzsche's engagement in philosophical reflection arose and gained its direction from his own life-experience, and it was to experience that he looked ultimately for confirmation of his thoughts. His reflection thus became disciplined to attend to immediate experiential disclosures both as revealing the problematic itself and as holding the direct evidence for such understanding as is possible of the matters at issue in that problematic. Thereby it had to attune itself to, and learn to sort out, an ongoing affair that was variable in character and whose variability had many dimensions and grounds. For experience takes shape in the interplay of ourselves with circumstance, and that interplay, while continual and ongoing, involves activities and encounters which range from the momentary to the life-long. There are rhythms and complexities within the ongoing interplay, and there is also development and evolution of ourselves, our capacities and our connections with things; and finally, the problematic itself involves in each case a variety of particular factors whose role in the problematic as something universal needs attentive exploration and discerning judgment so as to separate them out, identify and assess them, and interpret their importance and meaning in the problematic. Thus the present which is the persistent yet continually changing locus of the interplay and our experience of it forms a quite complex context for our reflection.

In Nietzsche's case, from an early time there was something characteristic in his interaction with the world which was not only central to the problematic and his reflection on it, but which also seemed to him to be sufficiently akin to the Dionysian phenomenon among the Greeks that it illuminated that affair for him in intimate and profound fashion. As we saw earlier (Chapter 2, page 31 above), Nietzsche speaks of the Dionysian as "the only counterpart and likeness in history to my inmost experience"[54]; and he calls the voice speaking in BT that of an "initiate" into the Dionysian mysteries. Let us then attempt to read back from that 'counterpart and likeness' as he sets it forth, and seek to divine the central ingredient in the experiential matrix which enabled him to characterize the Dionysian in that fashion and to think of himself as an initiate.

a. The dialectical dynamic of 'Dionysian' experience

The Dionysian as Nietzsche saw it represented an experiencing of the problematic of life's meaning which had a characteristic dynamic. That dynamic was constituted by an expansion and contraction of the disclosive register of things as they bear on life lived under the question of its meaning.

In an initial simplified way, we may formulate that dynamic as follows: Its beginning lies in an intensification of awareness and attentiveness, one which brings a veiling obscurity which marks our ordinary everyday involvement with things noticeably to dissolve. With this we find ourselves thrust into the middle of presences whose presencing registers in an altered way, namely, such that experience is pervaded by the insistent and fascinating impress of a negativity endemic to finitude-- of terror and threat, of anxiety and horror, of cruelty and destruction, of absurdity and pointlessness. If our experiencing develops beyond this immersion held captive to life-threatening and life-depressing factors, it does so with a deepening which is achieved in a welling up from greater depths within of a joy that seems instinct with the vital inwardness of natural things without. This development involves a dissolution of barriers, of separations, so that the culmination of the dynamic is a sense of unity and higher community in which all (self and world) seem a perfected manifestation of a single hidden source. In the achievement of such unity and community, life is being actualized in an amplified vitality that is not divisive but consonant and affirmative in its connecting with all else.

This initial adumbration can be elaborated so that a complex transcending and deepening or circling back is seen to mark the dynamic of such experiencing.

Thus in elaboration: There is, to begin with, our everyday waking experiencing of things. In our ordinary involvement with them, our sense of reality is formed through an attentiveness and awareness that are focused on sensible appearances with their evident and limited forms; and in that involvement, these appearances are something toward which we are oriented by our desires and under standards and norms (moral, social) which themselves determine patterns for our involvement. Such focusing defines a region of regard in contrast with one of dis-regard, so that an inescapable obliviousness is attendant upon the cognizance in virtue of whose mediation we develop our sense of reality. So far as this focusing enters into our activity, it is a delimiting and emphasizing whose instruments (whose interpretative ideas) must work to engage us in such way as enables us to live. It has this vital function. Yet the ideas developed, even if they succeed in supporting our vital existence, are not for that reason true. Indeed when we are able to give them careful scrutiny free from the need to believe them on practical grounds, they show themselves to be half-truths at best if not sheer falsehoods, illusions-- though we take them for true in our ordinary engagement with things and act upon them as such. But our involvement in falsehood and illusion is profounder than that. For this focusing is also determined by a self-deceiving whereby we not only pretend to the truth of what is (in all honesty, for any conscientious mind) false, but we also conceal and repress what we do not want to see or take as true. In this way our ordinary involvement in things, our everyday experiencing, is marked by a veiling, an obscuring, within which what becomes disclosed is being envisaged and mistaken in numbers of ways, including being mistaken for reality itself.

It is possible, in the development of our experiencing, to find occasions on which this veiling becomes dissolved, at least in some respects and in some measure. This first step in the transcending-and-deepening dynamic of experience is an amplified cognizance which discloses in particular a negativity in existence which we ordinarily would obscure to ourselves and which calls into question its possible meaningfulness: the negativity of the absurd, of the horrible and terrible, of the senselessness of mortal being and of existence at large. To the extent that we want to know truth and to live by it, to that extent we can become overwhelmed by the force of this negativity dis-covered in the immediacy of our experience, and find ourselves (at least for the moment) undermined in our involvement in things. If this movement of experience goes no deeper but rather circles back from this place to the engagement with things that belongs to our ordinary life, then we can find that undermining continued, providing that this circling-back does not amount to a retreat and success in losing ourselves once again in the obliviousness that ordinarily marks such engagement. For so long as we recall what we have experienced and maintain a will to truth, the recognition of the pervasiveness of falsity, of self-deception, in the determining of the ordinary back into the midst of which we are, e-vokes a nausea in us who have returned. To that extent, the desires which in everyday life move us to act and to maintain ourselves in existence become even more fully negated: the life, the will to life, becomes debilitated by the horror, the absurdity, the falsity and self-deception, intrinsic to finite existence. An ascetic mood then supervenes.

It is possible for the transcending-and-deepening dynamic of experience to move not only beyond the negativity but also beyond this retreat back to the ordinary, whether the latter issues in obliviousness again or rather has an ascetic issue in virtue of our inability or unwillingness to forget the horror and absurdity which we ordinarily screen out of our consciousness. In this further movement the will to life can reassert itself and resist even the ascetic conclusion. Here Nietzsche's own particular sensitivities and concerns discover to him powers which the will to life can draw upon to transcend the negativity but without deepening experience. For art can have a role, and (where it is present) science as well, in the measure in which one can be seduced and immersed, charmed and bewitched, by the appeal of either. Science can distract from the negativity by its focus of our attention on the surface as knowable, by the pleasure we take in the inquiry and the discovery of truths relating to that surface, and by its promise of the power eventually to correct various negative elements, to progressively remove negativity. Science is to that extent optimistic in its outlook and a force counter to the pessimism engendered by truthful recognition of negativity. Like science, art also can distract, and do this by its own type of focus on the surface, this time in glorification of it in its immediacy. Through the appeal of beauty, it has a life-enhancing function like that of science. But in contrast with science, this function is achieved by strengthening the hold of appearance, of illusion and delusion, of falsity, but of these as they excite, incite, activate and engage, and thus maintain and further the life of those responding to art's appeal.

The transcending-and-deepening dynamic of experience need not end with life being enhanced by these distracting powers. But at this point, two different directions of movement may take place. In the one case, we may push to the end the drive for truth which science embodies; but with this philosophical drive, there is the danger of undermining the optimism which science expresses, by bringing to light the limits of the power of knowing and thence of any progressive removal of negativity. This reintroduces the disclosure of the negativity from which science was to be a successful distraction, and enhances life only to the extent that the living being can take joy in the love of truth, can rejoice in the moral integrity and strength of such a lover. In the second case, we may find a way becoming opened beyond even this, if the well of creative joy hidden in the depths of the living becomes disclosed and released. With joy welling up from innermost sources comes a different movement beyond the negativity inherent in finitude and the separateness of individual existence, into a sense of the unity of all. With this, there is also possible another type of art which, rather than distracting from the negativity by beauty and illusion, would body forth and voice this joyful disclosure, this ultimate truth, and would thereby strengthen the ascending reaching of life in keeping with a clear-sightedness about life's inescapable involvement in negativity.

As Nietzsche himself grows and his experiencing evolves, and as his capacity for reflection develops and he becomes increasingly self-critical, two issues arise for him in connection with this experiencing which is central to his first book. One is: how adequate was his initial *interpretation* of this experiencing? The other: can any experiencing, however profound and illuminating, reach to the heart of being and be decisive, be *uniquely disclosive*, for the reflection that would understand life's meaning? Whatever questions may arise, however, this 'Dionysian' experiencing with its dialectical dynamic will endure as his inmost experiencing, and to the end will remain central for his reflection, even as it deepens and becomes clarified somewhat differently as time goes on.

b. The culminating disclosure of 'Dionysian' experience

As the above discussion of the dynamic of 'Dionysian' experiencing indicates, Nietzsche addresses our experiencing as a complicated affair harboring in its overall character a variety of different contributing factors and a complex and varying disclosiveness. As regards reality and with it time and temporality, the disclosiveness achieved in experience not only expands and contracts but its expansion can eventually arrive at a culmination. As part of his sorting out of this matter, Nietzsche avails himself of various ideas of "depth". Disclosiveness is not a matter of varying quantity and reach on the same level, but involves qualitative variables which he articulates with the help of the figure of "depth". There are at least three different things which he has in mind under that term.

There is, first of all, an inward sense of "depth", defined in reference to the attention and attentive awareness central to our engagement with things humanly. There is this, that our conscious regarding and register of disclosure, and the accompanying functioning of our attentive selves that is also conscious, represents only a part of us who are nonetheless active at the time *as wholes*, as *integrated* active centers. We are complex beings whose functioning as active centers always has *both* a conscious side *and* an un-conscious one. Because the latter does not register distinctly in the former and thus is not part of the conscious side, it is apt to be dismissed and ignored when we consciously think of ourselves; but it nonetheless holds much of that functioning of ourselves which enters into the forming and conducting of our activity at any time. In particular, it holds much of our receptivity to presence and registering of it, and this in such way that the conscious forms a foreground register whose character depends in important ways on (for one thing) the background dismissing and repressing taking place in accompaniment to-- but beyond-- the conscious regarding. Conscious and unconscious are not side-by-side and independent affairs, but compose a differentiated whole within which the conscious is continually being accompanied and conditioned by the unconscious. Nietzsche will speak of the conscious side as a surface, and speak of what else is involved in our functioning but is operating beyond and affecting this conscious side as taking place and lying in the unconscious depths. What is currently functioning unconsciously and is operative out of those depths in the forming of our activity (say) can of course enter consciousness at another time and function there, and the reverse. But it remains that as active beings we are marked in our functioning by the differentiation of conscious from unconscious and by the joint operation of factors in the conscious surface and in the unconscious depths in the determination of our engagement with things.

There is, secondly, a different inward sense and reference for the term "depth", relating this time to the character and reach of the conscious sphere. Our functioning as integrated wholes is such that most of the time we are operating in an everyday mode; in the imagery which Nietzsche is prone to use, this is a way of taking up with things and experiencing them and ourselves at the level of the flat land of the earth's surface. This way, involving a quick and simplified apprehending for practical purposes, is relatively crude and superficial, as well as relatively attenuated and subdued. In it, we know a kind of ordinary everyday intelligibility to what we encounter and to ourselves as selves involved with circumstance and encountering this-or-that; however otherwise it may seem to us when we are caught up in this everyday mode of operating, this intelligibility is incomplete. For not only is it perspectival and limited in reach to the surface, but more importantly it is only partial, involving as it does an ordinarily unconscious filtering and a disregarding (even repressing) which becomes disclosed to us expressly only occasionally when the obstruction or veil, the dampening down, that this introduces as an inherent (but normally unrecognized) feature of our ordinary consciousness dissolves in greater or lesser measure. Within this everyday mode of functioning, we seem to ourselves to be conscious egos with individual wills, subjects construing things and ourselves according to an intelligibility whose horizon is that of causes and grounds.

Now at times, we know a more intense and concentrated functioning of ourselves as wholes, and within this we know an encountering and conscious experiencing of things and ourselves which Nietzsche represents by images of height and depth. There are two different facets of this altered functioning as it is manifest in our conscious side: one is the expansion of the range of what enters into our conscious regarding, to reach beyond what we ordinarily register consciously and to include even things which in our everyday mode we are not consciously regarding but are nonetheless registering unconsciously while being consciously focused on whatever things are holding our attention. Conscious regarding is still a surface phenomenon (in the first sense), but its reach now includes things which were before never distinctly present to us or were present in the hidden depths (again in the first sense), factors of which we were previously unconscious. The other is a change in the quality of the regarding: we are more alert, more sensitive, sharper and more discerning, than ordinarily, so that even what we expressly regarded in our everyday awareness we now regard in qualitatively different fashion. The imagery of heights which Nietzsche uses to represent such heightened attentiveness with expanded reach intends it particularly in its operation within the sense of aspiration as a reaching upward, and as involving the spiritual as a higher side to ourselves. Thus this complex

extra-ordinary regarding, with its intensification and expansion, its attentiveness animated by aspiration, and its drawing spirit into more effective play, is spoken of as taking place on greater or lesser
heights (often those of the 'mountains') or at some elevation above the plains, and as open to things
in a perspective which allows other sides of things to come to our attention. This extra-ordinary and
deeper/more-elevated experiencing thus brings experienced appearance to be three-dimensional, so
to speak; it is no longer a set or series of apparent surfaces superficially apprehended. Here also imagery of flying is often introduced, and a sense of release from the burdens of gravity: the intensification and animation mean inwardly a functioning in which we are not weighed down by constraints
which otherwise and ordinarily limit our sight. What is intended in this second meaning of depth,
then, is both a more intense and wider-and-deeper attentiveness that reaches beyond (but also includes) the things encountered in ordinary conscious experiencing, and an altered presence in which
all things, even those met in ordinary experience, now appear extra-ordinary.

There is, thirdly and finally, an experiencing beyond this deeper and wider, this fuller, form, when
our functioning as wholes reaches an apex at which our inward vital energies are released into an
overflowing that animates us in that functioning. Such functioning discloses for our attentive regard
a reality that is fuller and deeper than appearance-- than what appears to us ordinarily as if it were
reality itself (things and ourselves in their/our surface appearance, the world of empirical reality), and
even than what appears to us in that heightened attentiveness which gives meaning to "depth" in the
second sense (things in 'three-dimensionality' that makes them more than surface, and ourselves rising to heights that enable us to see their 'dimensionality'). In this experiencing, we not only know
our own functioning as involving a flow from somewhere in the depths within ("depth" in the first
sense), from a depth unfathomed and even unsuspicioned in the conscious side of our ordinary experiencing; but as we experience *reality* in *its* depth, we know others and ourselves in a transformed and
fuller being, such that we are no longer able to localize ourselves in ourselves-as-'ego' nor localize
others in that being by which they are part of everyday existence for ourselves-as-'ego'.

'Dionysian' experiencing and its disclosure culminate in this fullest disclosiveness, this disclosure
of *reality* in *its* depth. To make his reading of its nature and meaning and to make intelligible the
'more' of ourselves and others that becomes disclosed in such experiencing, Nietzsche uses creational
terms. Under his interpretation, reality disclosed in its depth and fulness not only harbors a differentiation into a basic and timeless true-reality in contrast with what before had appeared to be reality
but which now seems mere appearance, only phenomenal-or-apparent reality; but as we noted in earlier discussion, this differentiation is of a creational nature: true reality is *source* of empirically real
beings, we are thus creatures existing here amidst creatures. Nietzsche has several ways of speaking
of true reality. In keeping with the sense that the discovery of it involves the transcending of what
we otherwise ordinarily take as reality itself, he speaks of it as being the "heart [*Herz*]" or "inner essence [*Wesen*]" of the world, the "innermost heart-and-marrow [*Kern*] of things", the "innermost
abyss [*Abgrund*] of things";[55] and if its nature is to be named, this heart is "will itself", which is alive
in an "eternal life" which "flows on indestructibly" "beneath the whirl of phenomena".[56] This life of
true reality is lived in an eternally bringing forth from out of itself all that is beyond itself (all creatures), so that Nietzsche may speak of "the eternal and original [*ursprüngliche*] art-power that calls
the whole world of phenomena into existence at all"[57]. Now we are, like our source but under conditions of finitude, living beings who live life in our activity of engendering (producing results, say),
and as living manifestations of this eternal power we harbor as immanent in ourselves this eternal life
which is not only engendering us (holding us into being) but is animating us and impelling us to continue in existence. If in ordinary experiencing we are oblivious of this immanent power and its crea-
tional-and-animating working, in Dionysian experiencing we (human creatures) not only find the
barriers separating us from each other as finite beings dissolving[58] but also become "as it were one
with"[59] this "indestructibly powerful [*mächtig*] and joyful"[60] creation-engendering life of our source.[61]
In this 'becoming one', we have a "direct [*unmittelbaren*] knowledge of the nature [*Wesen*] of the
world", a knowledge "unknown to" our "reason".[62] That is, we have an immediate noetic apprehension of ourselves as creatures and of that source in virtue of which this is so-- the source which is

"eternally" creating the phenomenal world, "eternally" impelling its beings to continued existence, and "eternally" knowing joy in this creation of the world of finite beings with its inherent and unavoidable elements of struggle, suffering, and the eventual destruction of each and every being.

In his subsequent thought, Nietzsche alters his interpretation of this experiencing and its disclosure, and in particular, rejects the metaphysical reading of reality in its depth being ventured in BT. But as we saw earlier, while Nietzsche seems intent on clarifying something fairly forceful and definite, the creational language he uses to interpret it, deriving from the Schopenhauerian reading of things, makes his reading waver, and does this precisely on the matter of time and (as correlative with it) of eternity. To expand on that point one step further than we did earlier: In Dionysian experiencing we are elevated "above space, time, and the individual"[63], and at the same time find ourselves-- in that selfhood of ours which is not 'ego' (or more precisely, which is deeper than 'ego')[64] one with a power that is eternal and is eternally creating things and eternally rejoicing in that creativity. Thus when we find ourselves no longer "individuals" but "happy living beings [*Glücklich-Lebendigen*]"[65] who are one with that creative joy, we find ourselves to be one with an eternal living power that is eternally dynamic. Now what could it mean to be elevated "above time", and to become one with a power which is eternally holding us into being-- we who *are* temporal and mortal in that being?

Let us look more closely at the difficulty Nietzsche has in expressing himself consistently here. There is (in Kantian-Schopenhauerian language) the "time" of the objective world and correlatively the "time" of our empirical experiencing of that world: it is this (objective/subjective) "time" above which we are elevated. That means, we are *beyond* the way of registering and making intelligible whose horizon is (in part) time as formal intuition; we are no longer 'knowing' objects and ourselves in our empirical interaction with things, but are finding ourselves and others given to ourselves in another vein. But we are elevated above time in that sense *for a while*, and for a 'while' *during which* we are *actively taking part in such rapture*; the 'while' in question is not a period of objective-and-subjective time, for we are 'beyond' 'experience' in that (Kantian) sense and are not simply cognizant of that but cognizant of *our own ongoing and enduring* in that state-- 'our own', however, not as 'ego' but as 'creaturely self'. At a later time we may seek to treat this experiencing as if it were 'experience' in the Kantian sense, and place it in a time-interval in the objective-and-subjective order of time; but that external approach, while possible to the extent that there are outward anchor-points for our determination of time, fails to catch the temporality of the experiencing itself in which we have been elevated 'above time'. However, it is not simply that in such experiencing we are 'above time': at that elevated height we find ourselves in the midst of *ongoing* creation. That is, creation or the holding forth of ourselves into actual being is taking place in-and-through the movement of time in some other sense (the 'ongoing' of it that pertains to creation); thus we find ourselves in our temporal being *continually emerging* as such a being in the *ongoing* of time in this other (non-objective, non-subjective) sense. Such continual emerging is *from the depths of being itself*; it is not our genesis from other and prior temporal beings that is being addressed in speaking of creation (that genesis is, in any case, one-time, not continual), but rather our *continual* coming-into-being as temporal beings.

Whatever this other sense of time is which Nietzsche is implicitly referring to, it is time as enabling condition of our being-and-being-active, not time as condition of our knowing ourselves and others in the objective order of phenomena. We who are so emerging are, as temporal, *continually actively involved* with each other in the course of the ongoing in which we are enjoying our being; and in that interacting, we may indeed be objectivizing and 'experiencing' in the Kantian sense, but we are unable as part of that to register, let alone to understand, the disclosure of the Dionysian, and in particular, its disclosure of the temporality of our own being and of time as enabling condition of that being. If the ongoing of time in this deeper sense is not the passage of (objective/subjective) time, then how is that ongoing to be understood, and how is that time constituted by which it is possible for us to be active beings involved 'for a while' in such ongoing? How can we *be* as active, that is, as *initiators* of activity, if we are not *at the start of* time in this sense? But what could that mean?

In short: Nietzsche is implicitly-- and apparently unknowingly-- availing himself of a different sense of time than the Kantian-Schopenhauerian, and indeed, than any sense which does not recognize how time functions in *creation* (as contrasted with in genesis, in the order of becoming as an objectively knowable affair). But what is there in the experiencing in question that might have lent initial plausibility to a *creational* interpretation? Is there something beyond the transformation in the self-hood and self-awareness of the participant? Or was Nietzsche simply forcing an interpretation, pursuing thought in this direction for other reasons than some confirmation present in his experience?

In BGE (aphorism 289), Nietzsche speaks of the writings of a hermit, and of a hermit's reading of the writings of other philosophers, and he claims:

> The hermit does not believe that any philosopher (assuming that every philosopher was first of all a hermit) ever expressed his authentic and final opinions in books: does one not write books precisely to conceal what one harbors in oneself? Indeed, he will doubt whether a philosopher *could possibly* have 'authentic and final' opinions, whether behind every one of his caves there is not, must not be, another deeper cave-- a more comprehensive, stranger, richer, world beyond the surface, an abyss [*Abgrund*] behind every ground [*Grunde*], under every attempt to furnish 'grounds' [*Begründung*]. Every philosophy is a foreground philosophy-- that is a hermit's judgment: 'There is something arbitrary in his stopping *here* to look back and look around, in his not digging deeper *here* but laying his spade aside; there is also something suspicious about it.' Every philosophy also *conceals* a philosophy, every opinion is also a hiding-place, every word also a mask.[66]

In this matter of the experiential disclosure of a creational meaning to reality in its depth, and in the matter of Nietzsche's later rejection of his initial metaphysical reading in favor of another and non-metaphysical one, we are at a place where this judgment the hermit makes needs to be addressed to Nietzsche himself. If, as he in retrospect contends, he had not been conscientious enough, subtle and courageous enough, in his initial reading and had failed to 'dig deeper *here*' and had arbitrarily 'stopped *here*', is that so in the way in which he claims it to be, so that the later-acknowledged absence of anything to substantiate the creational reading he had first offered meant the absence of *anything* to support *any* creational reading? Or is his later judgment also questionable, reflecting a second failure to have dug deep enough into the earlier disclosure and (in particular) to have found (for express understanding) time in its creational nature and structure?

There is at least this pointer to be followed out, that Nietzsche would make central to his account of the disclosure of experience the imagery of depth, and in particular would address the culminating form of disclosure by speaking of a "blissful ecstasy that rises up from the innermost ground-and-bottom [*Grunde*] of man, indeed of nature"[67]. The imagery, refined and amplified, will eventually bring us to the well of eternity, and to the mature Nietzschean vision of how a mature creativity, developed within the finite temporality which marks human life, can enable us to find life meaningful and to be equal to all the negativity which belongs to our temporality.

2. Reflection, reason and illusion

The disclosive matrix operative in the philosophical inquiry that generated the ideas in BT seems to have had as its decisive element the determinateness of such Dionysian experiencing as we have sketched out. Within the matrix that was opening him out in this fashion into the problematic of existence, Nietzsche's reflection gained its concrete direction from the disclosive facets registering with the negative and positive emphases we have seen, and it ventured to make sense of the complex disclosure taking place by responding directly and closely to the immediacy involved. That venture was (so he later admits) inexpert, but in this novitiate stage of his reflective effort, Nietzsche was not unaided; rather, he knew of Kantian and Schopenhauerian philosophical developments that seemed to him at the time attractive and sufficiently reliable that he could draw upon them in the interpreting by which he made sense of the disclosure of immediacy. As we saw earlier, he came to regret this, or at least, the way he did it: his inexpertness led to his using these helpers in a way that did not unqualifiedly help. Nonetheless, taking the work as we have it, how at that time did he pursue and concretely define reflection and reflective inquiry, and more pointedly, how well did he understand (and how much perhaps misunderstand) what he was doing at the time?

In BT Nietzsche does not do much directly to characterize for us the reflection he is engaging in, but instead as he carries it on he makes its character explicit mostly indirectly, by contrasting it with the mode of thinking which he speaks of under the name of reason. As first step toward a grasp of the nature of reflection as he was engaged in it, let us call back into mind the dual originating ground of reflection generally. That ground is, on the one hand, the problematic of the existence in which we ever find ourselves as living active beings, and on the other hand, the summons upon us in youth, given that we participate in existence with responsive decision-making capacities, to take thought as we accept and assume responsibility for our lives in this problematic affair. Reflective thought is then an activity of ourselves as ongoing living beings, a thinking begun in youth and undertaken *by* us *on behalf of* ourselves *as concerned by and concerned with* a problematic in all our activity and in the actualizing of our life which is being accomplished in that activity. That problematic not only bears continually on us as agents in whatever we are doing; but starting in youth it expressly presses upon us the question of what we are to do with our lives and how we are to find meaning in our doing and living in the future we are now responsible for. Such pressure provokes in us the effort to bring this problematic to mind in its intelligibility, to understand it, and thereby to make our way wittingly as we live out the lives we are taking responsibility for.

Now we have just been noticing the central disclosive force in the agential matrix that served Nietzsche's early reflection, namely, the dynamic of Dionysian experience. Our earlier discussion of it should have made clear that this disclosive matrix, being that of a complex and ongoing being, is always itself complex and to some extent changing, and such as includes at any time (and all the more, over time) elements that vary in their disclosive force. To speak of a "central" disclosive force, however, is not merely to reinforce that point but to suggest a further one. We human agents are always, as whole beings, involved actively in varying fashion with circumstance. Not only do we exercise there our capacity (both particular and decision-making) as individual agents, and enter into and carry on a responsive venturing with certain constituent capacities and factors to the fore at the time while others are then subordinate or accompanying; but we also carry into that current involvement with present circumstance our past experience as able to be drawn on expressly (but selectively) in such activity. Even when the activity is reflection that would center itself in ourselves whole and in what is human in the our being (not in our particularity, but in ourselves as sharing a human nature and the human condition), it is like every other activity in being a concrete affair involving an engaging as a whole being; but now the global disclosive matrix subtends the effort to think. Philosophical reflection thus takes place from a standpoint and within a concrete perspective whose current global experiential disclosure for registering and thinking through the problematic and its facets is *to* a particular human being *with this* present complex of (particular and decision-making) capacities and repository of experience, who is *entering into* present circumstances *engaging* with things in *this* particular way (as having entered into reflection, say) and in the exercise of *these* particular capacities (at present, of reflective thought). Whatever the character and components of the standpoint at which reflection is being undertaken at the time, the effort to think there brings into *further* play *some* of the disclosive factors that are already part of the global matrix, and that bringing into play involves a selecting out (within the global register of the diversity) of those whose disclosiveness seems relevant to the matter at issue, an assessing and interpreting of them which seeks to make clear how they are relevantly disclosive, and eventually a conceptual grasping of their significance as disclosive.

In virtue of this sorting out of presence and its register, the different factors are attended to in inquiry (or are dismissed) under an assessment of the bearing, the importance, the relevance, they are judged to have for understanding the matters to be understood. This means that in the taking up with matters of experience, interpreting them, forming the ideas which would clarify the matter at issue, testing the ideas, etc., what is at the time taken as important, as crucial, as decisive, in a disclosive reference thereby gains a role which other elements that are also present and are significant formative forces for the standpoint that could be drawn upon-- the ones judged unimportant, subsidiary or secondary, trivial disclosively-- do not. Given the judgment that effectuates this by making determinate in the situation the broad sense that disclosure does not take place to the same degree, fulness, clarity, strength, and the like, everywhere, the inquiring agent will thereby be disposed in his/her attention and awareness to take up with matters for thought-- to focus, emphasize, highlight, and draw upon in the forming of thought, but also to downplay, dismiss, disregard, and ignore in that forming-- accordingly. Depending on the strength and plausibility of that relevance-and-importance judgment at the time to the person reflecting, the inquirer is establishing inwardly a hierarchy of the reflectively relevant and important, a prioritized and weighted determination that may be merely temporary or may last for a while but that in some aspects may endure throughout the person's reflective life. Consider, for example, how his musical capacities and sensitivities, and his experience of music, seem to have functioned for the thinking we see Nietzsche engaged in in BT. These evidently came early to be not simply factors (one among many) giving determinateness to his being and in youth entering into the standpoint at which he was undertaking his reflection; but given that in his youthful judgment they seemed important for his understanding the problematic of meaning because (so it seemed) they opened the heart of reality itself to disclosure, it made sense to him to draw upon them in his thinking, to use what they seemed to disclose, and thus to think (say) of meaning as being secured by us in our participation in activity as an artistic-and-aesthetic affair.

The assessing, prioritizing, interpretative judging characteristically at work in the reflection conveyed in BT shows itself importantly in the way the work treats the matter of intelligibility. In it, intelligibility has two elements, one immediate in nature and one whose nature is that of conceptual apprehension.[68]

As regards immediacy, there are two different and variable dimensions involved. On the quantitative side, there is its range and the complexity included in its register; and on the qualitative side, there is its intensity and the concentratedness involved in the focusing whereby we receive and register presence in its immediacy. In the ordinary register of things, there is an incompleteness due not so much to a limited complexity but due basically to a filtering of presence combined with the lack of inward intensity and concentratedness in the receiving and registering. Thus what is present to us is deficient in the force of its presence, in the impressiveness of the impression it makes. There may indeed be considerable variability inwardly in the emotional factors involved, but there is no 'third-dimensionality' to the presence of things: they register as surfaces and the reach of attention and awareness into them is superficial. In some contrast there is the clarity and force of things in correlation with the contemplativeness which Nietzsche calls Apollonian. Here there is a forcefulness, a vivacity, a 'depth', that obtains in the connecting and interacting of ourselves with things, such that 'beauty' reveals itself *to* an individual who is, in the register of presence, both *moved* and touched and at the same time *removed* at some distance, distinct from what is registering. The distance is not that of presences present like mere shadows on a wall, which pass by without touching one and make no real impression on one. The incompleteness lies rather in a dis-connect which still obtains despite the inward intensity and concentratedness and the forcefulness of presence pregnant with typal meaning. The finality being achieved resonates then with the hint of mere seeming, semblance, of something more real than everyday presence (even if 'unreal' when taking everyday presence as standard), and yet not fully real either. Finally, there is that emergence of things and oneself into the closeness and connectedness which Nietzsche speaks of as holding in the culmination of the Dionysian: the bursting of the remaining dis-connect (the barriers and distance) that is inward to the emerging of the depths of being into conscious immediacy. Here intensity is at its greatest, disclosure at its fullest, and (so he claims) reality in its depth opens up for a participant whose own sharing in that reality is no longer that of an ego or of an individual but that of a creature.

All of these variations concern the disclosive quality of immediacy as we all may register it in our experience. But in his assessment of the variants, Nietzsche not only does as we might, namely, recognizes differences in that quality; he goes further and, like the Platonic Socrates, sees in them a kind of hierarchy of greater-and-fuller lesser-and-more-incomplete levels of disclosure. Above all, however, here at the start of his reflective life he interprets the immediacy of the Dionysian culmination not simply to be a disclosure of the heart of reality but more importantly to include a cognitively significant seeing-into which intuitively apprehends what is disclosing itself in that immediacy, directly apprehending it in its direct revealing of itself to and for that seeing. That is, in this fulness of immediate intelligibility we have Dionysian wisdom: the "instinctive unconscious Dionysian wisdom"[69] whose extreme is the mystic cognizance of unity. The intelligibility involved here is not that of conceptual apprehension, let alone of rational apprehension in terms of grounds, but that of a pre-conceptual intuitive seeing-into whose apprehending of what it apprehends gives one insight without bringing that insight to conscious sorting out, let alone itself being a result of such sorting out, a conclusion drawn from certain premises.[70]

Now if the standpoint of reflection is agential in the sense earlier described, and human agency has a developing character, gaining a characteristic and distinctive form in different phases of our maturation humanly, then the standpoint of reflection will undergo evolution beyond the agency of youth and what may be native to youth but not an enduring part of life. Thus in his retrospective perspective on this first work of his, Nietzsche can recall BT from a more mature perspective and can speak of it as "a book for initiates, 'music' for those dedicated to music, those who are closely related to begin with on the basis of common and rare aesthetic experiences", the speech of "something like a mystical, almost maenadic soul that stammered willfully, with difficulty, as in a strange tongue".[71] But he can also see, due to further experience and greater skill, that while the standpoint from which he was then operating in his reflection is something he still basically (if not in all regards) finds himself operating out of in later life, his initial reflective venturing there had been inexpert and lacking in the skill needed to operate well there. In particular, he sees himself having allowed himself in incautious youthful fashion not simply to judge certain elements of immediacy to be more fundamentally disclosive of reality but also to interpret the immediacy in question as a matter of immediate intuition of the heart of being (Dionysian wisdom) and to think of himself as in his reflection effecting (if with difficulty) a direct conceptualization of such wisdom. As a result, in BT he had spoken as someone "very convinced and therefore disdainful of proof, mistrustful even of the *propriety* of proof"[72].

In and for his reflection in BT, then, Nietzsche has not only entered into thinking from a certain standpoint and in his inquiry there given to experience with a certain disclosive dynamic a central place; but he has also regarded what seemed the deepest disclosive element in it as including a direct apprehension of ultimate reality and truth, in relation to which reflection is the effort of thinking to bring what has been apprehended into conceptual form. Within BT, Nietzsche sees only one alternative to philosophical reflection as such thinking grounded in such seeing; that is reason or the power of thought as a power of conscious reasoned apprehension. As he thinks it here, reason grounds itself in the disclosiveness of experience, indeed, but in its disclosure only of the apparent, not of ultimate reality. Reason also introduces a different sort of intelligibility, in function first of its interpretative conceptualizing but more definitively in function of its consequent recognizing of things in their intellectually apprehensible and comprehensible connection with each other. In this, he stood in a long line of thinkers, the most important early figure (for his discussion in this work) being Socrates, and the most recent figures being Kant and Schopenhauer.

From the same standpoint at which he speaks of the mystic Dionysian wisdom, Nietzsche speaks of Socrates as the paradigmatic figure for the love of knowledge, where knowledge is the conscious reasoned grasp of truth. As we saw earlier, Socrates seeks knowledge by utilizing the dialectical mode of inquiry and the apparatus of argument and counter-argument; and he seeks it fundamentally as a panacea.[73] The healing to be achieved thereby, both the outward correction and the inward, stems from reason become dominant as the guide to taking part in life; above all, reason can allay the fear of death, so that the dying Socrates (the human being whom conscious knowledge and reasons have liberated from that fear) epitomizes the rational human being possessed of the power of curing existence of its ills.[74] Nonetheless, it is a profound illusion that Socrates embodies in his person, the unshakable faith that thought, using the leading-string of causality, can penetrate the deepest abysses of being, and that thought is in a position not only to know being but even to correct it.[75] Socrates could maintain this illusion only because the logical urge that became manifest in him was prevented from turning against itself. In virtue of this, the ultimate meaning of reason and its drive was being frustrated in Socrates, for reason was meant eventually to turn back upon itself and bring a vision of its own limits. Within the unscrutinized blindness of his faith, however, Socrates developed a rationalist way of life, and this, not so much with the help of constructive knowledge of what-is but above all with the help of reason operating critically. For over and over again, wherever he looked closely, he found self-delusion and pretense to knowledge, and he conceived it to be his duty to expose this and to correct the existence corrupted by it.[76]

In his promotion of reason, Socrates may be an extreme: indeed, according to Nietzsche, the Platonic Socrates was the non-mystic *par excellence*, someone lacking any mystical disposition, someone in whom (due to a hypertrophy) the logical nature was developed to an extreme and as excessively as instinctive wisdom is developed in his polar opposite, the mystic.[77] Centering his life and being in his tremendous intellect, he could at best acknowledge instinctive wisdom only in the form of his *daimonion*, thus in a form which operated on occasion to *hinder* conscious knowledge. Yet while abnormal because of the extreme of his development of a component of the normal human being, there was this that still united him with the normal, that at the bottom of his engagement with things was illusion and self-deception. The most fundamental illusion he shared with his compatriots concerned reality: even the Socratic drive toward knowledge remained immersed in the apparent, oblivious to the creational meaning of things. That meant that it was self as ego and world as knowable appearance that constituted reality even for Socrates; and ego meant ourselves as wholly conscious centers, not as (for Nietzsche) centers whose functioning is always both conscious and unconscious and never simply conscious. Concomitant with this illusion concerning the real was a basic self-delusion concerning reason itself. In contrast with others, Socrates strongly developed and emphasized reason in contrast to the sensuous and emotional, the rational in contrast to the irrational, as the proper dominating and guiding factor within our conscious decision-making and -executing; and as part of this, he sought persistently to undermine a fundamental pretense which he saw lying at the heart of the way we ordinarily engage in life's affairs, a pretense to know what we do not in fact know. Yet while he was thus prone to bring into question the variety of illusions which we otherwise develop and function under in that engagement, he himself operated un-self-critically within the presumption that "reason" could know reality and serve as self-sufficient guide to life.

According to Nietzsche, it was not until Kant, and after him, Schopenhauer, that reason came to full self-consciousness and was able to discern its own limited character: that it was confined to appearance and could not attain the truth of true reality. This insight of reason in modern times opened the way to the (re-)discovery of Dionysian wisdom in its full reach, and thereby to the rebirth in modern form of the tragic age of the Greeks. In the culture of this new age, reason and science would be subordinate, no longer the highest end (as in Socratic culture), and wisdom and its vision would be primary.[78] In the 'resolute living' founding itself in such immediate intuition and its acknowledgement of reality in its fulness and wholeness, reason would not have the decisive place, nor be the guiding and decision-making power; yet such a living would not be mind-less, but rather (as the image of the artistic or musical Socrates conveys) would integrate 'reason' into a way of life shaped by such intuitive insight and its reinforcement in the reflective conceptualization of a Dionysian philosopher. The strength and courage that enabled such a person to see true reality in its depth would also enable an expansion of thought's critical functioning beyond that of Socrates, and even that of Kant. In both philosophers, reflection remained a work of reason, and while the 'reason' of Kant pointed beyond the 'reason' of Socrates, it was still only a naive conscious working of our power of thought which was oblivious to, and incommensurate with, reality and life in their truth.

At this point, certain questions emerge. Presuming a sufficing self-awareness of reality, Nietzsche undertook a reflection which presumed to transcend 'reason', and with it thus the illusion of reason's sufficiency for apprehending reality. But in his articulation of reflection as basically an affair of conceptualizing an instinctive wisdom which pre-reflectively apprehends in immediate fashion what it most fundamental in reality, he later sees, and acknowledges, an illusion on his own part, a mistakenness to his initial claim to such immediate insight. Now in our discussion of BT, we have seen that on the matter that most concerns us, namely, time, Nietzsche accords it an important role in enabling the finite created side of reality to be and be what it is; yet he speaks in a way that introduces a tension-- indeed, a conflict-- between his explicit account of the status and function of time in creation and a way of speaking of the experience that is disclosive in this regard which seems to imply a somewhat different account. Why this tension, this gap between what he expressly says and what is implied in his characterization of the disclosive experience? Does it have anything to do (directly or indirectly) with his way of carrying through and understanding reflection? Is the tension there because of (say) a youthful excitement and premature judging which can be outgrown in time but which, combined here at the start with a relatively undeveloped and as yet unskilled reflective capacity, initially led him not only to misread intelligibility and mistake what it is to have insight but also to speak prematurely and at cross purposes with himself on this matter of time? Or is there here some more enduring blind spot, some obliviousness or some proclivity or penchant, which for all his efforts to be self-critical as time goes on leaves him unable (not simply here at first, but even as youthful exuberance wears off and judgment and skill in reflection increase) to bring into apt conceptual rendering what is being disclosed in immediacy? These and other-- but connected-- questions will return as Nietzsche's thought evolves and he discovers out of that evolution the need to be more deeply self-critical. When we come to the works in which this takes place, we will come back to this matter.

CHAPTER 5
The Utility and Harmfulness of History for Life

In this meditation, Nietzsche's focus is on the temporality central to the human condition. In his discussion, he is silent about the creational structure of reality and the metaphysical meaning of life, and almost wholly disregards the Greeks and art; he also does not use the language of Schopenhauer and Wagner. Thematically, the only obvious connection with BT is that his discussion of temporality here centers on its enabling of history and tradition. Despite such obvious differences, his treatment of life, time, and temporality here coheres with that of his first work.[1]

Let us take up his thoughts on time and temporality in three stages.

A. Temporality and life

1. Historical, unhistorical, superhistorical

Like all living beings, we humans continually live and act in the present, but we know a distinctive temporality to our lives and active involvement with things. Memory contributes much to this distinctiveness. For example, animals live wholly absorbed in each transitory current moment as it comes along.[2] Without memory of the past, thus without sense of a 'today' in contrast with a 'yesterday', the animal knows a pleasure and displeasure connected with the current moment, but does not know such feelings as boredom and melancholy, which involve conscious register of an ampler present in which this contrast of 'yesterday' with 'today' is to be found. The animal, then, is continually involved with things in the present in a way that is "unhistorical".[3]

Even as children we human beings are unlike the animal. For while in this early part of our life we are oblivious to the historical past and future,[4] we are capable of more than an oblivious animal-like immersion in the current moment; we know also a recall of earlier childhood times. And as we grow up and enter youth and then adulthood, the differences between human and animal become greater and even more apparent. It is the case, indeed, that as adults we still know, in some form and at various moments, a child-like unhistorical immersion in the present. In fact, it is only because we retain the capacity for such immersion that we have "the foundation upon which alone anything right-and-just, healthy, and great, anything truly human, can grow. The unhistorical is like an enveloping atmosphere within which alone life engenders-and-produces itself [*sich erzeugt*], only to vanish again with the destruction of this atmosphere."[5] Nonetheless, only with the limiting of this unhistorical element by thinking, reflecting, comparing, distinguishing, drawing conclusions, only due to the arising within that encompassing cloud of a clear illuminating gleam of light-- thus only through the power of employing the past for life and making history [*Geschichte*] again out of that which has been done and is gone [*Geschehenen*]-- did the human being first become human. But with an excess of history the human being again ceases to exist, and without that envelope of the unhistorical he would never have begun or dare to begin.[5]

In contrast with the child, then, the adult human being has entered into a two-fold capacity. One is the capacity for recalling in the current moment a past moment of human history beyond its own personal experiencing, and for utilizing the capacity for reason which emerges as a possibility in youth to re-appropriate that past in a way that makes it serve life. The other is the capacity for a distinctive kind of unhistorical immersion in the moment. Let us briefly consider each of these.

As for the historical: Like the animal, our living and acting in the present means our involvement in a series of current moments which come and go, and an attending to current circumstance first and foremost. But unlike in the animal, in us when the current moment passes and no longer defines our present consciousness it does not become nothing to us, but is retained in mind. Yet from the start it is initially retained there outside current consciousness, forgetfully, as a 'nothing' for our conscious awareness but not an absolute nothing for us.[6] Thus our ongoing involvement with things ever bears with it *obliviously and latently* an accumulating past. Now the obliviousness in question can take two different forms. Initially it is simply the other side to an attentiveness and awareness that are concentrated on what is current or stretched out into the future; the past that is being retained is simply held unremembered, there in our unconscious depths. But there is an obliviousness which is different from this. We can also forget in an active and positive fashion, in a resisting any return of that forgotten past into the current present as something now being expressly recalled. We know a power of repression, as we would put it in more contemporary psychological language.[7]

Even in childhood, of course, we can find an element of the increasing "dark, invisible burden"[8] of the retained past of our own experiencing becoming consciously revived in us, entering again openly into the current moment like a ghost returned to life, and being acknowledged in an "I remember". When it is called (or allowed to come) back to mind and thus haunts the present and its current moment, it can function in many ways in that moment, but in all ways it introduces some sense of passage into the experience of the moment and it disturbs and complicates the conscious activity taking place there. For now the current moment is the locus not of our simple being but of our becoming, our passing. By the time of adulthood, however, we can also find ourselves recalling this-or-that part of the trans-personal past, and then we know a being of ourselves which is itself 'historical' in this sense, that in the current moment our conscious functioning connects and contrasts ourselves with a historical past whose recall now intensifies our sense of our own passing.[9]

Given the rise in adulthood of this possibility of dwelling historically in the moment, in self-consciousness to 'today' in contrast with 'yesterday', we can also connect this past with what is going on in our unhistorical immersion in the moment, and using the power of reason into which we come in youth and adulthood, we can appropriate the past conceptually and (guided by reason) bring it to bear on the current situation and the future implied in our current being and activity. With this introduction of the light of reason into the conscious side of our activity in the moment, we achieve one side of our adult humanity, that in which we live and act knowingly (and that means here, historically) and function quite differently as human beings from any animal or even from ourselves as children.

As for the distinctive kind of unhistorical immersion in the present: The cognizance of the 'it was' reviving in the 'now' of our ongoing involvement in things registers in our conscious cognizance the basic tension which ever marks human existence. Nietzsche speaks of such existence as "an uninterrupted has-been [*Gewesensein*], a thing that lives by negating and consuming itself, contradicting itself"[10]. When as adults we have advanced beyond personal memory and come to know the intensified sense of passage which the historical mode of being brings, we can also on occasion find a temporary resolution to this tension, one opened up for us by youth's aspiration and love and their pointer of us to an engagement with things which incarnates happiness. In the engagement that realizes aspiration and love, our resistance to remembering (the power of forgetting in the positive sense) has succeeded. By leaving ourselves behind as self-conscious beings aware of our passage and by becoming immersed in the ongoing moment forgetful of ourselves and of the past, we are able to feel *unhistorically* for a while in the manner of the *adult* human being. And with this type of unhistorical immersion, we achieve another (and the more basic) side of our adult humanity. This immersion is different from the unhistorical participation in things by animals, since it involves the positive exclusion of a retained past-- quite a different matter from the animal's having no power to recall its past. This is also not a return to childhood, to the time before we gained our sense of history and our reflective and rational capacity. Yet it involves a functioning whose encompassing character is that of a child-*like* immersion in the present. That immersion is only "like", however, since it presupposes a prior historical involvement which in the immersing is being subdued and since the capacities at play in it are ones amplified beyond the child's.

Because such happiness is only episodic in its achievement, the resolution to the tension of an existence inwardly at odds with itself is only temporary. Indeed, in some human beings, even this is not attained. For some find in themselves a difficulty in forgetting; their power of repression does not operate forcefully and well. Taken in the most extreme case, such a person would be continually recalling things, and be condemned to an involvement in the moment in which the person saw 'becoming' everywhere.[11] That is, such a person would not only be continually aware of passage inwardly (no moment is simply a current present to someone whose 'historical sense' is operating in it); but that person would also be aware of all things outwardly in like fashion. Thus such a person would be continually aware of the present as ever being shadowed in its current moments by a past which no longer is and thus would be aware of the moment as the place of passage alone, never of simple present being.

When Nietzsche speaks in this fashion of "being" and "becoming", one must be careful. For in these early meditations there are two rather different things involved in his use of the term "being" in a contrast with "becoming".

There is that being of each of us which includes a becoming *internal* to itself; the becoming of this being is simply the actualization of that being over time, and does not involve that we who have such being become something *different*, only that we come-to-be *more fully* the self we already are. Such becoming takes place in the moment when, in our involvement with whatever we are engaged with, we are wholly immersed in the present and the future it is pregnant with, and are acting unhistorically. In such actualization of our being, we are aware of ourselves as simply *being and being ourselves.*

In contrast with such being when actualizing our inmost being in its inherent self-becoming, we may (say) learn a (social) role and thereby take on a different character than before. By such learning we 'become' (and think of ourselves as 'being') president, say, of a company. In such role-playing as this implicates us in, however, not only are we *not being*-- or even any longer believing in-- our own *innermost self-or-being,* but we are also forced continually to remember the role we are playing, and thus to focus attention on the world that this role implicates us in, on others as playing complementary roles, and on how things are happening as regards such role-players-- all in such way that we can never simply *be* (that is, be ourselves) in the present moment but have *continually* to be *mindful* in this role-playing reference. That means: we are continually existing in the moment in historical fashion and continually aware of change and difference (of 'becoming' in that sense), both within and around ourselves.

Beyond the unhistorical and the historical modes of involvement in the present moment, there is a superhistorical mode open to adult human beings, and this, in two different forms.[12] If the unhistorical and historical concern our agency as doers, the superhistorical (in the form he initially treats) concerns our agency as thinkers and knowers whose only aim is truth (the scientist, say). This form itself has two sides.

One side pursues to its ultimate issue the knowing of the particularity of things, and here, of the historical. But any historical phenomenon, when not simply recalled but completely and purely known, is an affair which has become dead for the knower.[13] He has recognized the illusion, the injustice, and the blind passion which unavoidably belong to even the greatest of phenomena, despite the fact that the matrix generative for such phenomena includes not only a reaching for the true and pure and just but the belief in what is being undertaken as living up to such standards. As a result of this recognition of blindness and injustice as inherently marking all human undertakings, the life and vitality which give the phenomenon power to inspire others to action and to a furthering of life in their own turn can no longer do this effectively; it has been destroyed by the knowing. To make such historical study or education sovereign, then, would be an act antithetical to life.[14]

The other side is the knowing-grasp which focuses not on the particularity of things but upon the ever-presence of imperishable types exemplified in phenomena. For if the particular is always defective, the knower can ignore particularity and look instead to the past and present as one and the same because typically alike in their diversity. But since this leads to seeing the world as at every moment complete and attaining its end quite beyond and apart from the particularity of phenomena, such knowing divests the process of history once again of any power to engage one in further history-making effort. Since that process presents to such a knower a stable picture of unchanging values and an eternally identical significance, it offers no salvation in virtue of that process, as issue of it: it is going nowhere, only repeating patterns with insignificant variation. At best, the turn of the knower to a meditative apprehension of the imperishable types exemplified in the particulars brings an enjoyment to complement the unconcern or the satiety and nausea for the particularities of history. But as a sheer recognition of fact it gives no impulse to further life or work, and in particular none that answers to life's impulse toward higher and superior life.[15]

2. Time, temporality, and the moment

In our study of BT, we found Nietzsche treating time as a creational condition which makes the existence and being of creatures a temporal one. In that treatment he employs a Kantian/Schopenhauerian conception of time as a formal intuition which is constitutive for human experience and objective knowledge. The resultant tension between this idea and his exposition of the experiential disclosure of the creational pointed us to a cognizance in him of time and its nature which his explicit conceptualization was not succeeding in capturing. Something similar happens here in UHH, when apart from any express notion of creation Nietzsche is addressing the temporality of our active being and introduces his idea of the time which serves as enabling basis for our temporality's being what it is. Let us see how this is so.

Nietzsche's own exposition of the thought which we summarized in the preceding sub-section opens by employing the expositional device of first calling our attention to the activity of a herd of animals out there and to the presumed temporal consciousness the animal has, and then reverting to our own (human) activity and addressing its temporal consciousness as a more complex one in certain regards. Since he does not know the inwardness of the animal from within and directly, he accomplishes his initial step by empathetically projecting an inwardness into the other-being of the animal, using the only first-hand experience open to him (his own human experiencing) and projecting it under restrictions that seem appropriate in light of the animal's presumed less complex being. Specifically, he imagines it by taking as key a limited aspect of time as it conditions and enables human effort, namely, the moment.[16] As he renders it in this connection, the moment [*Augenblick, Moment*] is the current side of time taken as embodied primordially in a point-like stretch, one extremely brief in its duration, sudden in its coming and going, and wholly without past or future in its own character.[17] As he utilizes it with regard to the animal, he imagines not so much its being the locus of the animal's activity (although it is that) as its being the dominant temporal feature for understanding the awareness internal to its activity. Strictly speaking, it is the content of the current moment of its activity which is what the animal's awareness is ever immersed in and to which its register is limited-- so his portrayal claims.[18] Thus the feeling element central to its being (the displeasure and pleasure involved in its register of presence) is "bound on short tether to the tether-stake of the moment".[19]

When Nietzsche reverts to human experience from this phantasized starting-point in the world out there, he does not have recourse to that fulness of time and temporality which our experience can disclose and from which he abstracts when he projects the 'moment' as a feature of animal experience. Instead he maintains the initial interpretation in which he has selected and simplified our experience, and simply adds on further features to the initially abstracted feature. In particular, he adds three things. First, as moments pass and lose their currency, they nonetheless endure in us as a past which *somehow still is* and is a functioning part of our being. We human beings may forget and become oblivious to those past moments, but we nonetheless accumulate them as our past [*Vergangenen*], and that past (the moments and their content), weighing on us with increasing weight [*Last*], functions as an encumbering burden [*Bürde*] to our current moving ahead. Thus the accumulating past makes a difference, even if that difference-making is a hidden one; the difference it makes is in how the activity that is taking shape in the ongoing current moment does so and in how it carries us thereby into the future.[20] Second, we are able to discover certain moments from this hidden burden of 'it was' coming back into current consciousness as ghostly presences. This revival in current awareness of our personal past discloses to ourselves our 'are'-- our existence and our being-- as complex, in that it is being realized in the ongoing current present but realized there not simply in current (conscious) activity but in activity which has an increasing personal past hiddenly at work in it. In reality, our existence has never been a sheer being or mere 'is', but it has been from the beginning and will be to the end a being that retains its own (personal) past and harbors it as continuing to be operative in its current ongoing-- a *Gewesensein*, so we have seen Nietzsche calling it in a play on the German word that combines 'been' and 'being'.[21] Indeed, it is only because the past is still there, that we can at times expressly find it re-entering our current conscious awareness (entering now *as past*, as no longer the current present it once was in us) and can remember it. Third, in becoming adults, we can come to distinguish from our personal past a historical past going beyond our own person, and under such express recognition we can enter this more extensive past into our current conscious awareness. Indeed, by knowing this past with the help of our reason, we can even come to include it as a factor in the making of our future.

Accompanying the contrast which Nietzsche is drawing between the temporal character of experience in animals and in humans is a characterization of time in its fulness which he offers in this opening passage by way of an image. According to the image, time is a "scroll [*Rolle*] of leaves [*Blatt*]", whose leaves are unceasingly detaching themselves from it one after another and fluttering away.[22] That is, time itself is the present (= the scroll), which is being realized in a series of discrete moments (= the leaves) which come and go successively in that present. In virtue of this, the present is the only time of existence, but it is a different time according as the moments in which it is being realized are different. It is because time is such (so he claims), that the animal's experience can be as he proposes (in each passing leaf-moment absorbed wholly in what is current in that leaf-moment), and that human experience can involve memory in the way it does.[23]

Does the explicit account of time offered in this opening exposition succeed in doing justice to time as it is manifest in the temporal matters he is presenting? The answer to this is definitely 'No'. For if we take seriously the way Nietzsche describes the matter of our personal experience of time,[24] then the passing of any current moment in our experiencing of things transforms it into a *past* moment; such transforming gives to the no-longer-current moment a status which is *relative to* the *new current* moment in our ongoing experience and is relative *within* the *very same present* that is continuing to be realized there in further current moments. Having lost its previous standing as the current moment of our experiencing, this transformed-into-past moment not only *continues to be* within the present (now in the mode of 'was'), but in this new standing *as past* it is *latently operative in* the new moments which form the current ongoing actualization of the present in question. As implied in this way of speaking, time is thus a present (that of some being and its activity, say) which realizes itself primordially in a moving ahead (an onflowing current) and which in this moving is not only making new (previously future) moments current but is at the same time *transforming* the passing current moments into past moments *within* itself. Such transforming retains all such past moments as the increasing *actual past* that is harbored (as still-being) in that present and that continues to be at work in the current ongoing of the present. And this standing as still-being is maintained *so long as* the present in question continues being realized in further ongoing current moments. Past moments are not nothing, but neither are they the something they were when they were current. Theirs is a real-- but secondary and dependent-- being; in Nietzsche's imagery, theirs is the existence of ghosts which are continually entering hiddenly into and affecting current moments of effort and occasionally return openly to haunt them.

The idea of time implied in his exposition, then, is somewhat different from, and in conflict with, his explicit idea. For the former idea makes the present be realized not in the currency of the moment alone but in a complex way that involves (among other things) the still-being-and-functioning of previously-current-but-now-past moments that belong to this present. According to it, no moment is a simply current affair (a leaf-moment), for its currency latently harbors a past that is at work in it and that amplifies the current actualization of the present in this subordinate preterite direction.[25] Not only does this idea contrast significantly with the idea of time imaged in the scroll-image, namely, that of the present which is realized in successive completely discrete current moments; but it implies a different understanding of the phenomenon of memory than that conveyed by speaking of the fluttering back and landing in our lap of separate leaf-moments previously detached from the scroll-present.[26]

Nietzsche, however, seems oblivious of any disparity--- indeed, any tension at all-- between the matters as he is setting them forth and the idea of time he is presenting as if it sufficed to grasp time truly and to make those temporal matters intelligible in their true character. What is problematic in his account, however, goes deeper than this conflict between what is implied in his exposition and his explicit idea, and reaches to his interpretation of the ongoing side of time via his notion of "the moment". This interpretation (although in somewhat different forms) is a part both of his explicit idea of time and of the idea implied by his exposition of temporal matters. To critique the interpretation, we need to do two things: to distinguish the different emphases within what is presented by Nietzsche as if it were a single reading of the moment, and to recover the fuller sense of the ongoing of time from which he abstracted his notion of the moment. Let us attempt these two things together in the following fashion.

In our reflections in Chapter 3 we developed the beginnings of a conception of time as a two-sided affair: time as the present which is the enabling locus of our active engaging with things has both a stationary side which is ever the same as long as we are, and an ongoing or moving side which is ever different. Nietzsche's counterpart to this conception is his rendering of time through the image of a scroll (kindred to the stationary side) and its leaves (kindred to the ongoing side). If the ongoing side is not to be conceived as a succession of wholly current moments (as in his explicit image) nor as a succession of temporally-complex moments (as in his implied conception), how then is it to be conceived? To make that clear, we need to make visible more fully than before time's nature and complex structure as enabling condition for activity.

Let us approach this matter by calling to mind the experience of a mode of the unhistorical involvement in things which Nietzsche makes central to our being human and especially to our being creative. What is the character of those times when we are able to "dwell in the moment"? At such a time we find ourselves becoming immersed in and intensely registering presences in a striking and unusual immediate impress of them on and in us. In the contemplative ingatheredness and concentration of our attending at such times, we are not only attentively receiving, exploring, and noticing what is concurrent and present but are also cognizant of the going-onward or passing character of this encounter; more pointedly, we know ourselves and things being in the midst of something happening, of something going on in this ongoing coming-together here and now. Different facets of presence may dominate our register and feel of the time, but we are cognizant of what is happening then as not always marking our experience. If it is presence that comes to the fore in our attention, it contrasts with presence as we recognize it in the relatively inattentive receiving and acknowledging of our ordinary experiencing. If it is transiency that comes to the fore, reinforced by the rise to conscious notice of the bounds of our own temporality (with their implication of ourselves in impending death) and the wonder of finding ourselves here-and-now with these things and not (say) with others, this contrasts with the obscured bounds and bland obviousness of our ordinary experiencing, in which the givenness of things and presence of ourselves in their midst are both obtrusive surds, 'indeed so, but so what?' Whatever comes to the fore, to dwell in the moment means to be engaged with currently-present things aware intently of them and ourselves here and now, undistracted by anticipations and memories, immersed in what is going on in our encounter as going on in the ongoing now.

As we dwell in it in such fashion the moment may last for some time, or may not. Yet as it lasts, as it prolongs itself, it is not as if within that lasting we are finding other and later moments succeeding an initial moment. It is the moment itself which stretches out and lasts on and on for the while of our continuing immersion; and while much is happening during the time, some things before others, all this belongs to that moment. Eventually, indeed, the while of our dwelling in the moment ends, and our immersion lapsing, we find ourselves engaging differently with things. But in its enduring, it was one while-- a single while-- which our contemplating was taking shape within, and its end often brings the apparently self-contradictory sense that, with our shift to other ways of engaging with things in the continuing ongoing of time and with our recall of that dwelling as now part of our past, that time had lasted for an eternity and yet at the same time only for a moment. In both characterizations we are seeking faithfully (if only haltingly and elliptically) to mark something about the stretch side of time's actualization in that dwelling.

What are we to make of such times?

If we recognize them as peculiarly revealing and remain faithful to their disclosure of time in the experience in question, they seem times in which time's nature as enabling condition for activity is more fully uncovered than ordinarily. For it is not simply that in them time's continually-ongoing-now is disclosed as continuously integrating into its currency the beginning-and-end future-and-past and concurrent-presence with which the present that is being realized in that ongoing is currently marked. It is also that this temporally-concentrated ongoing is disclosed as moving forward in such way that for a while (for the while of our activity) time is also stretching out and thereby enabling activity to be as an affair which takes time. For there is no activity in an instant, not even in a series of instants; activity is an affair that *takes time to be* and that *occupies* time in *this* sense. Time can not be an enabling condition for activity if its nature includes only the integration of future-past-and-presence into the ongoing current in which the present is being realized; its nature must also include the institution of more or less lasting or enduring moments of itself, such that as time continuously goes onward during the stretch of any such moment that ongoing future-past-presence-integrating affair of activity takes shape and gains actuality and is thereby able to be the enduring-and-stretched-out-through-time affair which any activity is. In short, the complex temporality of activity involves a forming-and-executing by which activity can take shape as a time-taking affair; and such an affair is enabled (in certain respects) by an ongoing-now whose actualization of the present in the ongoing concentrates future, past, and presence, and is enabled (in other respects) by an ongoing-now whose actualization of the present is inflected by a moment that stretches out and lasts for a while. To 'dwell in the moment' is to engage with things in such way as both embodies and brings to disclosure in an enduring moment of (say) contemplation this complex ongoing-and-moment-nature of time; the lasting moment in which contemplation is taking the time it needs to be itself (to register presence in the way it does) enables not only the ongoing register of the temporal concentration of time's three-dimensionality in its ongoing but also that ongoing awareness of the lasting itself as a stretching of time which enables this time-occupying activity of contemplation to take shape and be its becoming-self in that while.

The moment in which we dwell when we 'dwell in the moment' is thus that side of time's ongoing in which it is being realized in a lasting stretch; like the stretch of any moment of activity, such lasting does not continue without limit but ends and (as we put it colloquially) 'life goes on'. Normally, we make of such times what we do, and read their disclosure as we do, in a functioning of ourselves in stretches of time which are outside-and-beyond the time of our contemplative 'dwelling in the moment'. This would be no problem if in our reflection then we fully recalled such an earlier time and stayed faithful to its immediacy and its disclosure. But with the immediacy of the earlier time now being part of our ongoing experience only as something being recalled in its transformed-into-a-past character, we are disposed to regard the recalled stretch of the past focused by what is continuing on in that outside-and-beyond stretch of time in which we now find ourselves in our recollecting and re-flecting. That means, usually, one of two things.

On the one hand, we focus on the ongoing that brought us through that stretch and is still taking us forward, and thence on the stretch as one stretch among others being actualized in the course of that ongoing; and as we note the time-taking activity which occupied our 'dwelling in the moment' and took the shape which it did during it, we above all have a regard for its lasting in a comparative vein. There are indirect measures to which we normally appeal here for comparing the greater or lesser lengths of moment-unified stretches of activity, and more about them in discussion below; but more importantly, there are direct measures as well. For in the initiative involved in our engaging with things, we are often active in a variety of ways *all at once*: for example, looking around me and taking in the stream, the trees, the rocks, the varied face of circumstance, I was also standing, then walking, and occasionally shifting my posture and position; and if one might say that all of this formed only different facets of the one activity of contemplation, that activity nonetheless was itself undertaken in a pause in my fishing, which quite different activity had begun earlier and would con-tinue later and was still going on now but as something held in suspense while I was contemplating. And then beyond the suspending of one activity while doing another which marked time's ongoing for me then, there were further activities I was engaged in during part of this same time, such as swatting a mosquito and scratching the itch of its bite, and altering my breathing first to slow and quiet it and then to deepen it. Enabling all of these in-the-middle-of-being-engaged-in activities which conjointly marked and complexified my ongoing initiative as an active being, the current of time in the course of which my initiative was being actualized was itself being inflected so as to stretch out as enabling condition for this complex functioning. In this context I can recall how the lasting of contemplative immersion endured, indeed, but as enfolded in a longer-lasting activity of fishing whose moment encompassed that of contemplation. In such a comparative vein, we can directly recognize moments which differ considerably in their enduring, and even reach a notion of a momentary moment which is quite kindred with one way in which Nietzsche speaks of the moment. For as we are considering the more or less extended moments of activity, we may find quite brief mo-ments; but like other moments of more lasting duration, they are continuing whiles of an ongoing which is temporally complex (continually integrating future-past-and-presence during the whole stretch). Thus such moments, brief though they are, could never be the merely-current moment of Nietzsche's explicit conception of time; but they would approximate to some of the brief moments to which Nietzsche alludes in his presentation of temporal affairs, namely, those which are living af-fairs fraught with future and past and of concern to Nietzsche precisely as such and due to the involvement in life (in becoming, in growth and maturation) which is taking place in them. Such lived moments form one implicit component of Nietzsche's notion of the moment.

On the other hand, in the course of sorting out the various stretches of life and activity, we regard them all as realizations in the course of the continuous ongoing of time and current existence-- an on-going which was going on and is still going on and which will continue to go on until the end of our time. This invites the effort to seek to correlate the ongoing with the various activities-and-stretches so as to see the latter as successively embodying the former. Given the particularization that is char-acteristic of our initiative, however, the idea of the ongoing of time as actualized in stretches of activ-ity that neatly follow on each other and occupy the whole of the continuous ongoing without gap is quite at odds (at least on the face of the matter) with the intricate temporal interrelation (of contem-poraneity, partial contemporaneity, preceding or succeeding) of the different initiative-elements involved in such particularization. And this divergence from reality is even more forcefully im-pressed on us when we recognize activity as something formed and carried out in a decision-making and -executing whose responsive beginnings (in good part, at least) may be unconscious to us at the time and may well involve matters that were initially part of life long ago but are making themselves felt in that forming and executing now. Nonetheless, we do seek to address this continuous ongoing which the various stretches of our activity inflect, but we do so indirectly, by focus this time on the outward and by the generation and use of other ideas, one of which is implicit in Nietzsche's notion of the moment and functions there in undifferentiation from the lived moment as we have just been discussing it. What I have in mind is this.

At the same time as our initiative is ever realizing our limited existence-time in an articulation of it into activity-formed stretches and is thereby providing activity-measures of the actualization of our time (of our life-time and existence-time), we are ever interactive with other beings and are attentive in some fashion to the present face of things as it is being continuously discovered to us in our inter-action. Given that something is at stake in our engagement, the temporal registering of others in their face is fraught not simply with our current interest, say, but also with anticipation and with recall, all reflecting ways in which we as active and concerned beings are realizing the futural and preterite sides of our own ongoing being in our attention to the face of things. Now if our activity is to be an interacting that links effectively with the activity of the beings that compose our circumstance, the focus for our register and notice needs to be one or another publicly-accessible feature of the chang-ing face of what we encounter. With its help we could determine an outward and public measure of time in contrast with the private and inward one provided by our own activity, and orient our activity accordingly. Since that face does not directly manifest time (time is not an evident feature of what we encounter, like color or shape or movement), we focus on phenomena whose regularity we can use to establish *indirect temporal* measures for the *time being actualized in our activity*: the phe-nomena of day and night, for example, which form an immediate basis for the sun-measures of time. In the notice which is definitive for the time-measuring that is taking place, we do not focus on these phenomena and their appearance in their own right, but connect the outward-and-changing (circum-stance as its face changes for our engaging) with the inward-and-ongoing (time as we are realizing it in the stretch of our engaging). We do this by marking certain concurrences: it-is-daylight-now in an earlier part of the stretch, it-is-night-now later in that stretch, say. In the register of concurrent inward (now) and outward (daylight), we reflexively apprehend the ongoing which is making possible our apprehending but do so *only in partial or abstract fashion*. For one thing, the full nature of the enabling ongoing (including, in particular, its futural and preterite dimensions, and its boundedness) is *disregarded*, and regard is given to *only one* dimension of time (concurrency) and (more narrowly) to the role of the inwardly current within concurrency as an inward reference point for a marking that starts from the outward phenomenon being noted and ends inwardly with ongoing time only with reference to the simple concurrency of that phenomenon with our noticing of it. In such abstraction as we are effecting, the 'current moment' as marking-ground is (properly speaking) represented as only a current point-instant-- the actual moment after it has been stripped of future and past, and in-deed of any stretch. And while the ongoing-into-the-future is reflected in time's directional move-ment being futural, the movement is now conceived as the successive displacement of such wholly current point-instants. Finally, given the beginning-and end-marks established in such marking, we can not only connect the stretch of the ongoing encounter between those marking-acts with the discrete outward markers (the beginning and end of daylight, say) and establish a *temporal period-be-tween* as holding between those markers; we may also proceed further under those abstractions and divide the resultant interval into lesser periods and grasp the period between the boundary-defining markers as holding a succession, an iteration, of lesser units, even ultimately of discrete point-instants, each instant being discontinuous with similar such preceding and succeeding instants but together occupying the interval between the period-markers.[27] That is, we can generate the abstract side which is contained in Nietzsche's explicit conception of time and the moment but is not differentiated by him from the lived side.

In this marking of points and establishing of periods, our measuring activity operates within a regarding *and* disregarding to establish public measures of time. The disregarding dismisses various facets of the concrete situation as irrelevant to its purpose, including enabling facets of time and space and components of our own measuring activity; and on that basis the regarding notices in only a very limited way (abs-tracts) various restricted features and connections of the actual ongoing of time, the noticing, and what is noticed. The establishing and use of the *indirect* and *outwardly-grounded mea-sures* does not require or involve an understanding of the *nature* and *full structure* of time, but stems from and depends upon a taking-into-account which is limited in the ways suggested in the previous discussion. Furthermore, those measures themselves do not provide us sufficient access to that nature and structure to be able to understand time by starting from them. Nonetheless, by establishing and using such measures publicly accessible to us in our interacting with things and each other, we can date and locate our activity temporally with respect to the public visibility of other things happening in our encountering of circumstance; and by refining those measures we can be enabled to proceed scientifically on the course of an enormous (even if still circumscribed) advance in our understanding of the phenomena we encounter.

To conclude this discussion of time, temporality, and the moment: The explicit idea of time Nie-tzsche offers in UHH represents the present as being realized in a succession of discrete current mo-ments. Not only does this representation stand at odds with the idea of time implicit in his character-ization of temporal matters, but the idea of the moment which he avails himself of in both cases-- an idea which holds in undifferentiated form two quite different conceptions, namely, the lived moment as a brief stretch of experienced time and the instant which abstractly represents a single facet of time useful in the public measurement of time-- does not allow even the fuller and more profound idea of time manifest in his exposition to do justice to time's nature in important regards. Nonetheless, it is with the help of such a representation, embodied in the image of the leaves of a scroll, that Nietzsche would grasp time's nature explicitly, while the phenomena to which he was attending and which he was making central for his analysis of the human condition were presented in a way that implied a somewhat different idea of time. It seems that as in BT, so here: as Nietzsche attends to certain phe-nomena and seeks faithfully to bring them to understanding, his characterization of them opens the way for a line of thought which implicitly (and seemingly unbeknownst to himself) points us to a different interpretation of time than he is at the same time expressly proposing and using to make sense of those phenomena. In considering BT, we could readily assent to Nietzsche's retrospective point concerning the untoward influence of Kant and Schopenhauer on his thought and language there. But in UHH, while the explicit idea offered in UHH fits (so far as it goes) with the perspective of the two, there is no sign here of the Kantian-Schopenhauerian language of BT, and no appeal to a creational, or a transcendental, status for time. Whatever of implicit influence there may have been, if any, at best seems to have served as reinforcement to what was (already here at the start of his re-flective life) distracting his thinking and making him oblivious to the more fundamental way in which time was coming to disclosure in his experience. As we shall see in considering subsequent works, his thinking continues to be centered in the matters central to UHH; as a result, there is opportunity for more self-aware and apt insight to emerge and bring an advance in his understanding beyond the explicit view of time offered here. What comes of that, we shall notice in succeeding chapters.

In the meantime, we need to ask again the hermit's question. Why was Nietzsche not able-- sup-posing that he felt the need (and if not, why not?)-- explicitly to explore time and temporality in an-other vein, within a different horizon? A more radical view of time, the basis and makings for which are present in UHH, continues to be present in his thought, and indeed, evolves as he sifts through the matters that concern him most (matters of values, of drives and ultimate ends, of reality and illusion); but that presence continues to be, as it was in BT, merely an implicit one. Even so, it re-mains strong enough that when in *Thus Spoke Zarathustra* he ventures a modification of the scroll-and-page view found in UHH and makes that modification the major idea of that (his major) work, he gives a form to that work and develops the various themes in it in a way that expresses his feeling for time in that fuller more radical nature which is being implicitly acknowledged here in UHH.

3. Life

At the same time as Nietzsche is setting forth his sense of ourselves as capable of participating in activity in both unhistorical and historical ways, he is also presenting the inclusive being of our-selves as that of living beings who, in the course of time, by nature evolve into adults capable of such varied participation in activity. As his presentation conveys it, life is (at its most inclusive) a temporal affair which each of us participates in and knows first-hand as a first-personal affair ('my own life').[28] The being of ourselves as capable of such participation is an internally ordered and structured one which makes the formation and execution of activity-- the exercise of initiative-- the medium of life's concrete realization in ourselves and thus of our participation in it. Now activity is a relational affair-- an interacting with others, with circumstance; and the enabling feature for this is that, under the con-ditions of space as well as time, we exist as bodily beings who, in our living and acting out of our-selves, are *situated* among other beings. Thus primordially we enact our own being and live our lives in an interacting with the concurrent beings and circumstance of our situation, those to which our bod-ily being directly opens us out and exposes us. In this interacting, the concrete context, the environs and environment, which our activity enters us into, become themselves integrated into our life and living. Thereby concurrent circumstance, including our 'times', has an integral (if happenstance) role in determining the concrete shape of the life we are living. But more basically and more essentially, the exercise of initiative that engages us actively with circumstance and that concretely realizes our life itself inflects the life we are living and the living of that life, so that in us life and living are hu-man affairs; and because our human power of initiative is by nature meant to evolve-- and with that evolution, we mature humanly--, life is for us not only an interactive and historical affair but above all one of maturation, of becoming as in the phrase "become what you are".

In the retrospect of EH, Nietzsche wishes he had paid more attention at the start of his reflective life to the aspect of life which is our being embodied and situated agents living our lives as such. For his purposes in UHH, what he does attend to about life in this regard are two things. One is some-thing which he calls life's "plastic power". The other is the evolving spontaneity which human life exhibits. Let us expand upon the account of life briefly sketched out in the preceding paragraph by noting what he says about these two matters.

a. Life's plastic power

In his account of our 'historical' mode of being as adult human beings, Nietzsche claims that life and action as adults demand a *measure* (but only a measure) of (historical[29]) remembering. If we are to live humanly, we *need* at *some times* to remember *some* things from the (trans-personal) past and to bring them via our rational consciousness to contribute to the character of our present and to the future we are reaching for in it. In keeping with the growth-character of human life, while as children we have no capacity for such remembering, as we grow and become adult we become capable of and need it. But if we need a measure of such remembering, we can not be healthy human beings, and ultimately can no longer retain our humanity, if there is *too much* memory of the historical past; beyond a certain threshold, the degree of remembering is harmful, and eventually fatal.[30]

Now "too much" is always a relative quantitative term; how much is too much *depends* ... . But relative to what? depends on what? The limits beyond which calling back the past in memory be-comes "too much" are set by the life in us. In particular, how much is too much depends upon, and is relative to, how great the "plastic power" [*plastische Kraft*] of the living being is at the time. Nie-tzsche explains this power in a complex phrase.[31]

It is, first of all, the power of growing [*wachsen*] in distinctive-and-characteristic fashion [*eigen-artig*] out of oneself [*aus sich heraus*]; thus it includes a power much like what Aristotle spoke of as the nature of a thing, its internal principle of motion. Our activity ever enacts our nature in its current state of development at the time of our engagement and is vehicle for its further development.

It is, secondly, the power of remolding [*umzubilden*] and incorporating the past and the alien; thus it includes the power of taking in what is around and subduing it to support this natural growth and development, and the power of subordinating the past to play a role in that growth and development as well. This includes that development of our nature which we have been noticing, from child to adult, with (for one thing) its evolution of the 'historical' as a mode of taking part in things.

It is, finally, the power of healing wounds, of replacing the lost, of repairing broken forms out of oneself; thus it includes the native power to restore and replace where there is injury and harm, so that life may continue to grow (within its natural limits) even in a relatively unsupportive environment or under harsh conditions.

The complex and internally ordered nature of this power is worth emphasizing. What is involved in the second and third aspects is subordinate in function to what is involved in the first. And if this in turn-- the power to grow and become ourselves in our own distinctive and characteristic way-- is centered in a growth in our initiative-capacity, and if such central growth should intend our becoming capable (say) of responsible and creative participation in affairs, then we could speak of life's plastic power as by its nature involving in us a drive to become capable as the individual and type of active being we are, and as involving a variety of powers through which, in interaction with our environment, we are to subdue all else to the whole and healthy development and exercise of that capability. Much later, under some refinement, this drive will be called by Nietzsche the will-to-power. In any case, there are several senses of power involved in this notion of a formative force or power, and they are ordered in their operation and functions.

When measured by this standard, the "too much" of the past will vary: it is relative to the current condition and power of the being in question. But the stronger the roots which a human being's innermost nature [*innerste Natur*] has, and the more that nature gives the living being capacity, power, strength, in its own innermost self, then the more from the past such a being can appropriate or subdue to itself [*sich aneignen oder anzwingen*]. As an extreme case, the most powerful [*mächtigste*] and tremendous [*ungeheurste*] nature would know no limit; it could draw to itself [*an sich heran-ziehen*] and draw into itself and assimilate or incorporate [*in sich hineinziehen*] and as it were trans-form into blood [*zu Blut umschaffen*] all the past, its own and what is most alien to it. In all cases less than such an extreme, a nature would show its power, strength, capacity also by being able to forget the past, to block out and repress it, in any and every case where it can not subdue it to such service. More broadly, it would show its power by being able to form a closed horizon around itself; this is a horizon which contains no sign of men, opinions, and the like, outside it: one has simply blocked these out, ignored and forgotten them, and shapes one's life and active involvement with things in reference to what lies within that horizon.[32]

Put generally: Life takes shape according to the following universal law, namely: a living thing can be healthy, strong and fruitful, only within a horizon, one either drawn around itself by itself, or one into which it is willing to fit itself and its own view [*Blick*].[33] In humans, cheerfulness, good con-science, joyful deeds, trust and confidence in the future, all depend not only on there being a horizon but on a suitable taking up with things within it. That is, they depend on there being a line which di-vides the surveyable and visible [*Übersehbar*] and the bright and clear [*Helle*] from the shadowy and dark [*Dunkeln*] and the vague [*Unaufhellbaren*]. But they also depend on the person's knowing equally well the right time to forget and the right time to remember, on the person's feeling [*heraus-fühlt*] with powerful instinct [*kraftigem Instinkte*] when it is needful [*nötig*] to feel [*empfinden*] his-torically, when unhistorically.[34]

b. Life's evolving spontaneity

From what we have just seen, the life which is structured to make activity the vehicle of its reali-zation introduces vital energies by which it pervades the whole living being and operates to condition the activity in question and to help sustain the living being in its interaction with circumstance. But it introduces as its central power the power to grow out of itself, and in the living being, the power of initiative by the exercise of which the living being acts and (among other things) realizes the life in itself is a power of this sort. In human beings this initiative-power (our decision-making and -executing capacity) is meant to evolve out of itself by its exercise over time; and as it evolves, it is to make the realization of our life different over time, especially by gradually actualizing what is initially only potential in our life and ourselves as living beings.

In earlier discussion, we considered from one perspective the initiative realized in the exercise of our decision-making and -executing capacity, and noted that in the forming and taking part in question, some of what is inwardly operative in us is functioning unconsciously, some consciously, some instinctively, some in a deliberate fashion. But as coming together within ourselves as agents ingathered into the forming and taking part, all that is operative functions in a structured *co-working* in virtue of which we engage concretely with circumstance and do so as singular and whole centers of initiative functioning *at once consciously and unconsciously*. There is another perspective from which Nietzsche addresses our initiative in UHH, and that is with a view to the powers that are operative in it and to the nature of the evolution of the capacity which is being actualized in their operation together. Let us take note of how this matter is being conceived here (Nietzsche will say more in SE), and then notice the distinctive temporality which the evolution in our capacity introduces into our being and life.

As to the powers involved and their operation together: The original and originative side in our human capacity for decision-making and -executing is a power of receptivity, that of feeling, sensation: the complex immediate responsiveness in virtue of which, within a sense of 'something matters', we not only receive and register (attend to and notice) but are initially moved, motivated, disposed, toward responsive action. Now feeling (using this term to stand for our overall responsiveness in its immediacy and immediate register) discloses in a first-personal way not only what is inward and enters in unique and private fashion into the initiation and carrying out of activity; it discloses as well circumstance, what is other than ourselves and out there, over there, public, and encountered as polar opposite in its standing to ourselves. Finally, it includes in its disclosure ourselves as part of the circumstance for others and not only as 'out there, over there, public' for them and encountered by them as polar opposite in our standing to themselves, but as in some measure present to ourselves in this aspect as well. Within its reach, then, this overall responsiveness discloses to us (inwardly) such things as the drives moving us, the capacities we are drawing upon, the vital energy which animates our activity and pervades the capacities of our active being, the life which is unfolding out of itself in us-- our own life-- as it currently is,[35] and in general, ourselves as engaging with others; it also discloses to us (outwardly) the things we are encountering and can register in our sense-openness as beings belonging to our situation and forming the evident element in the confronting conditions with which we have to do in our current acting and living.

Given this global and complex receptive sensitivity as (dynamically speaking) the starting-point in our spontaneity for the forming of activity, that forming advances beyond-- but back in reference to-- such a beginning by way of an interpreting and assessing which, giving a concrete determinateness to the 'something matters' and defining a horizon of sense-making within which (say) 'this' matters more than 'that', concern both the disclosive and the motivating sides of feeling and our register of the confronting conditions in our situation. In virtue of this, what bears on us within the global receptivity gains a determinate reading of its nature, importance, and relevance, for our initiative, which reading introduces its own emphasis and focus, acceptance dismissal and denial, beyond that marking the responsiveness of our immediate register. It is within this complex register and under this interpretative reading of relevance and importance, and as animated in our deciding by life's drive toward 'more life' (a drive which Nietzsche points to in his characterization of life as "that dark, driving power that insatiably thirsts for itself" [*jene dunkle, treibende, unersättlich sich selbst begehrende Macht*]), that decisions concerning our active response in a situation are made.

As to the evolution in our capacity for initiative: When the decision-making whose issue is ordered to arise through the dynamic in the working of these basic factors is seen in the perspective of the ongoing of time, we observe that at the start of life we are relatively impotent in our decision-making, because we are relatively primitive and crude, undifferentiated and undiscerning, in the reach and quality of our sensitivity, our noticing, and our interpreting, and because the initial decision-making reflects the unskilled working-together of such undeveloped powers. At best, our initial venturesome initiative is thus unavoidably limited in its grounding in the reality of existence. But aided by learning and further exploratory venturing, the exercise of our capacity can in time bring a more subtle, sensitive, and differentiated, receptivity, a more discerning noticing, and a more discriminating interpreting and assessing; and to the extent that we have learned how to bring such powers to work together skillfully in our decision-making, we can be entered with good judgment into a more complex and capable engagement with circumstance and with the inward facets of our own being.

Now this evolution into 'more capable' agents has a starting-point, namely, our nature or, more specifically, our 'inborn' 'first nature'.[36] In SE, Nietzsche will speak somewhat more precisely of this starting-point.[37] In UHH, he simply regards it as the complex of actuality and potentiality with which we are endowed at the beginning of life and which provides the matrix and constitutive powers for the initiative whereby the life in us gains its realization.[38] A moment ago we said "at the start of life we are relatively impotent"; this impotence is relative to the potency or power which is to be ours eventually in virtue of the development and evolution that it is in our nature to be involved in. Because we are natured beings, the initial activity for which the factors which compose our nature are the 'already given' basis takes us into the future by way of the relatively undeveloped capacity for initiative with which we begin. The exercise of that capacity for initiative is animated by life's drive toward 'more life' as what we by nature want; more specifically, given that at the start our being is not fully actual but is on balance dominantly merely potential, that exercise is animated by the drive toward 'more life' in the form of the desire to grow out of ourselves and, as the essential aspect of this, to mature in our capacity for engaging in activity. This "out of ourselves" [*aus sich heraus*] character of our growth means not simply that we seek more life on the strength of this *inherent-in-us* drive and seek it in ways that (if circumstance is favorably complicit) bring the actualization of our *natural inborn* potential; but more profoundly, it means that animated by that drive and operating in complicity with circumstance, our seeking for more life via the initiative of current activity brings ourselves forth *over time* as fully actual from what we *already were*-- but only *embryonically* were-- at the start. The potential in us is not potential for just anything, but involves a native stuff of our being and a natural direction for our growth, such that if and when that potential is eventually realized in effective fashion in and through our activity, we have become fully the potent (that is, morally and creatively powerful) human beings *we already were in embryo* at the start.

The maturational development at the heart of our growth not only has a starting-point and (within that) a prefigured end point which activity so animated is to eventually bring us to reach, but it takes place in a distinctive fashion.

To begin with, maturation is a form of our growth in which exercise and learning are the unique and irreplaceable vehicles whereby our capacity for initiative and activity is to amplify and transform itself in keeping with its native potential. In this particular sense, we are to bring ourselves to be more capable-- to be 'competent and capable' human agents-- by our own effort and first-hand learning, and to do so under the concrete conditions of our existence. Success in this does not, of course, depend simply on our wanting to grow and on just any exercise of initiative. Not only do circumstantial conditions necessarily enter into our striving and unavoidably affect our growth; but success depends also on our learning how to take part in our interacting with circumstance so that we are able to survive and grow within the concrete conditions of our existence. Because we begin with limited actual capacity and almost totally opaque to ourselves, we are not only a long time in building actual capacity out of what is originally given us mostly as potential but we are unable to succeed without much mis-learning and un-learning, and without learning to learn well.

By nature, however, the evolution of our decision-making and -executing capacity is not a matter of simple self-development in a cumulative exercise-and-learn way. That evolution is rather a phased transformational affair, whose phases relate to developments (qualitative as well as quantitative) in our capacity for effective participation in affairs so far as such participation embodies responsibility. The transformations which are decisive for the maturational phasing of life are those of a capacity for acting which is deepening, widening, integrating, and stabilizing, as we exercise it and learn how to take part in interaction with circumstance. But they concern this capacity in this particular respect, that by way of its exercise and its development we are becoming stronger in our humanity, and that means, in our capacity to assume responsibility in our participation in affairs, or more precisely, in our capability for participating as responsible beings in the securing of what is at stake in existence. So far as nature succeeds in its evolution here, the phases of our maturation are concluded and begun by developmental turns and transformations affecting this matter of responsibility in basic respects.

As to the distinctive temporality which the evolution in our capacity introduces into our being and life: In virtue of such developmental transformations, we know a temporality to life which implicates us in times of life which differ in important ways but first and foremost differ in the developmental phases meant for realization in such times; thereby the times differ in the ways in which we are able to take responsible part in affairs in them, given the form of the decision-making and -executing capacity we have developed by then. In UHH, Nietzsche's account of these differing times and phases is uneven, focusing mainly on youth.

First time and phase: The first time of human life, and phase of our becoming as human beings, is that of childhood. It is the time of a preliminary and preparatory phase marked throughout by a particular kind of unhistorical participation in affairs, and more deeply, by our potential for-- but as yet actual incapacity in regard to-- responsible participation in affairs. During this time, our initiative is an exploratory venturing which is founded in a global register of initially rudimentary feeling, relatively limited and crude in range and quality, and in an initially relatively naive and uninformed interpreting of the register of a feeling-complex which is for the most part undifferentiated and which for a while we are incapable of finding otherwise. At the same time as the receiving, registering, and interpreting at work in our forming of initiative and participating in activity are evolving and we are developing our inborn powers and capacity for relatively effective participation in affairs, we are incorporating into ourselves much that is initially merely circumstantial to us, other and alien. In particular, we are assimilating and incorporating the language and norms of our current society and associates. Now we do this from the start not only with incompletely developed capacities, but in ways that may not foster well the life within, even as what is incorporated is becoming a part of us and a continuing factor in our functioning. To the extent that we develop by an incorporating which does not succeed well in making what is being incorporated serve our own growth, we become simply 'a child of our times'. For a 'times' consists in a common framework of social meanings which is embodied and expressed in the current living and acting of our contemporaries. We become part of this in the measure in which our assimilation of that framework-- in terms of roles and role playing, language, conventional patterns of behavior, and the like-- leaves us a function of it, that is, leaves us functioning simply in reflex of such meanings. Finally, the time of childhood is one in which not only are we still relatively incapable human beings but we live in dependence basically on chance for the happenstance that what is given and there for our encounter (the people, the social circumstance, the life-conditions) is propitious for our growth and development. If we are fortunate, in our interacting with things we are able sufficiently to be equal to the impact of what happens to be our circumstance that we develop as nature would have us develop, as is outlined already in that nature. Whatever may be happening in fact, however, childhood is the extended time needed for the development work that brings us to the place of the first basic transformation in our capacity, in which we claim for ourselves an independence of sorts and enter upon responsibility in its first form, that of bearing and realizing our own lives in responsible fashion.

Transitional turn: The childhood-phase of our growth out of ourselves ends when we have grown to be sufficiently ourselves-- sufficiently capable of being what we 'already are' in potentiality-- that our wanting more life involves us in wanting to take our own lives upon ourselves and to live them on the strength of a decision-making and -executing which is 'our own'. To succeed in this venture in responsibility for ourselves, we need to know ourselves and to free ourselves from whatever of 'our times' has been incorporated into ourselves but *never effectively subordinated to* our growth out of ourselves. Youth then is a time of beginning-again in which we are (among other things) to dissociate ourselves from 'our times', to search within for what discloses to us further our own genuine being, and to establish our own way of living. This dissociating is directed toward what is outside us and marks circumstance, but even more importantly, toward what of this is by now within us but is yet untransformed, not effectively made 'our own'. Youth is inherently rebellious against its 'times'. But this rebelliousness-against is part of a fuller reality, of a rebelliousness-on-behalf-of, namely, of the life which is being taken now into youth's hands and which needs to evolve further under them.

In virtue of the growth native to our nature, we are naturally equipped in youth for the beginning-again and the liberation which nature is seeking in this time of life so that life may the better flourish. Nietzsche speaks of "the strongest instincts of youth, its fire, defiance, self-forgetting, and love"; he speaks as well of youth's "desire to mature slowly", and "its power to implant in itself in over-flowing confidence a great idea and to let it grow out of itself into a still greater idea". But above all, he speaks of youth in regard to a moral element. To youth belongs "a feeling for the right-and-just", an "honesty and boldness of feeling", and in particular, "courageous, uncalculating honesty" and the various moral qualities needed for this assumption of responsibility for ourselves-- needed, say, for the required reflective searching out of the genuine, and for the venturing that would help the life being assumed to evolve further.[39] That searching out and venturing require clear recognition of the difference noted earlier (see page 96 above), between the becoming-of-what-we-natively-are which is our growing as individual persons, and the 'becoming' involved in our assuming and learning to play roles. The latter is a matter of becoming something other than we were previously, becoming different; the former is just the unfolding of what we already are, the progressive development and eventual blossoming of one and the same being.

In youth as a transitional time, then, our evolving decision-making matrix of feeling and interpre-tation is meant to become altered by the emergence of two things that make possible an adult engage-ment in life's affairs. One is a power of reason by reason of which we can act with some apt under-standing of what we are doing. The other is a form of feeling (the passion of love) that opens the way to full maturity. With the former our unhistorical immersion in things as children knows a develop-ment which enables the self-conscious integration of the historical into that immersion; and with the latter, our originating power of feeling knows the directional force and the outflow which enables, as issue of the unhistorical immersion in which it is at work, the type of creative discharge of our capacity that marks maturity in ourselves.

Second time and phase: About the persons we are eventually to become in our adult life (ourselves when we have become fully what we are), Nietzsche speaks in UHH from the perspective of youth and selects out three main things. One concerns the capacities in us that need to be strengthened if the responsibility we initially venture upon in youth is to be carried through effectively. A second concerns the productive character of the life we are to lead, its productivity correlating with the uniqueness of each of us as persons. The third concerns our eventual being as a cultured one. In sum, we are responsible for becoming morally matured, cultivated, and productive, human beings.[40]

In our functioning as adults, the spontaneity in virtue of which we can participate in affairs is meant eventually to develop at its heart the kind of wisdom in virtue of which we live and act as ma-ture human beings. The capacity, the capability and skill, which constitutes the wisdom of maturity includes the power to feel what is happening within ourselves, in particular to feel and instinctively to respond to the growing life within ourselves, and guided by that feeling, to find that way of engag-ing with things (sometimes in one way, sometimes in another) which assists that life to grow further. It includes also the power to be selective and to focus, to exclude from attention and to concentrate on that range and variety accessible within our situation (things, people, teachings, opportunities) which can help us to grow from out of our own nature. It includes also the power to resist seductions and distractions, different passions and goals, and even other basic alternatives that other human beings have developed and that may be right for them but not for us. Even if there may be something attractive and tempting about them, still it is such as would undermine the pull of what is necessary for the development of our own distinctive life and might even induce a paralyzing relativism-- a sense that there are so many alternatives that there is nothing which we *have* to take seriously, and nothing which we can simply *take for granted* while attending to other things on that basis. Finally, it includes the power instinctively to know when we must plunge in and act and put an end for the moment to considering alternatives, puzzling out the meaning and character of things, and when we need to spend time assimilating from the past and from others and subduing what we are assimilating to serve the needs of the life growing in us.

What is conceived as eventual issue in our development as human beings, then, is a mature practical wisdom or capability whereby we are able to bear in responsible fashion our own individual life as a human affair. But not simply as a human affair. For youth's entry of ourselves into responsibility for ourselves is two-sided: we are human beings, and therefore becoming capable of a responsible participation in life means something the same for each and all of us; yet each of us is an individual human being, and if individual means unique, becoming capable of a responsible participation in life means becoming capable of a creativity that is open to us by our own distinctive individual nature. As individuals we are different, and for the achievement of such relevant creativity, we need different things both within and in regard to circumstance. But if adult life is in each of us to be a productive, creative, affair and, in virtue of our mature judgment, to be carried out responsibly in its creative work, it will involve for us all an integrating of the historical and unhistorical modes of taking part in adult life and activity which gives the dominant place to the unhistorical as it is centered in feeling in the form of passion. The life in us can be creative, can produce itself and be productive, only by such passionate involvement. Now the passion in question presupposes the development in us of the historical mode of functioning and what this involves of reason's working (its reflecting, comparing, distinguishing, drawing conclusions, and the like). Since these (reason, the historical) do not inherently, automatically, serve the life and creativity that is to be born, they can evolve and function in a way that undermines life. What is needed then is not just any development of the rational and self-conscious, but rather a becoming self-conscious and deliberate *within* the passionateness, one which refines and clarifies the passionateness from within rather than displacing or eliminating passion in favor of reason and the historical sense. What we are to find then is an unusual combination: we are to reach a responsibility for ourselves humanly which has a completion-condition which all could reach, but to assume responsibility for a creativity which in each case is unique and which might never reach a final point or end but might (at least in principle) involve continued increase and novelty so long as we live.

As we are assuming our individual lives in youth, then, we know a task (that of responsibility) and a path (that on which our becoming is to take place as issue of our responsible actualization of the life in ourselves). By the transformation of youth we are entered into the need for a further maturing as human beings toward a fully-grown-up being of ourselves, and for a carrying out of life in some unique creative endeavor. On this path and in accomplishing this task, we all (as beginners in adult life) need to learn how to live such a life, and that means: we must learn how, in our interaction with circumstance, to make all else (within and without) serve the whole and healthy development and exercise of our increasing capability as the unique human being we are. But if the path of further maturation takes us toward an achieved practical wisdom and an effective creative engagement of ourselves as individuals with circumstance, is our responsibility exhausted with such achievement? Or do we find opening up a further side to responsibility, not simply *for* our own lives but for those lives *in relation to* something more? That is, granting that youth involves only our initial capacity to be responsible for ourselves and that this capacity needs a perfecting that takes time, is responsibility for ourselves the limiting horizon for a life of responsibility? Or does the path that leads to the place of completed maturation involve our discovery both of the need to assume responsibility in some further sense and of the capacity in ourselves for this? If so, then the transformation in our capacity for responsibility that this would involve would mark a transition into a further phase of human life.

Nietzsche's youthful vision of the culminating form of the spontaneity of an active human being is of a kind of passionate vitality and intensity which is found especially in the human beings we think of as exceptionally productive. There are suggestions of what this would mean more concretely.[41] But because in this book he is a young man preoccupied with youth and its dynamic, he provides only minimal pointers into what later life is to bring. But we might ask here: according to UHH, responsibility points the individual toward creativity and culture, and culture is not simply a matter of individual perfection but of a community connectedness. Are we then to understand with BT: communal culture has a metaphysical meaning, and we human beings a responsibility for achieving a ('tragic') culture that culminates the act of creation?

B. Varying integration of the past into life's ongoing

1. Life-enhancing ways

When the actualization of life in us brings us into youth and its transition into adulthood, we find the aspiration which qualifies the spontaneity of that time of life forming the entryway into the adult phase of our lives. As we assume responsibility for our lives and venture upon activity under aspiration's directional appeal, we find ourselves reaching for and into the future in one way or another. In this meditation, Nietzsche distinguishes for attention three forms of reaching, different according as the current condition of the life in us differs. In connection with that understanding, he sees the integration of the transpersonal past and knowledge of that past-- the integration that would be life-enhancing-- as also taking three different forms, each one being suited to and supportive for one of the ways of reaching into the future.

Thus it may be that life in its unfolding is currently so constituted as to point us aspirationally into a higher and better that involves greatness realized in a new and different vein. Here the inmost drive of life-- to achieve more and fuller life-- would reach into the future by novel venturing. Or it may be that the life in us discovers itself to us at the time as under some constriction, in some oppression, by continuing tradition and heritage, and thus summons us into our future above all under the need for release from what constricts and oppresses. Here the inmost drive of life, finding itself inhibited, would cast off the burdensome obstruction so that the life in us could attain the more vital actualization it seeks. Or it may be that life's unfolding discovers to us our aspiration-intimated future as realizable through the instrumentality of an ongoing spiritually-alive way of life of which we already find ourselves a part, so that life summons us only to strengthening our touch with that way and continuing it into the future. Here life's drive would have us keep alive a past in our future and expand our receptivity to it.

Whatever the form of reaching the life in us knows in youth,[42] it knows a need for knowledge of the past (more precisely, of the transpersonal past) if it is to succeed in its aim at more and fuller life. But to answer to this need so that the knowledge can function in life-enhancing fashion, the historiographical recall of the past needs to be selective: different parts of it will be relevant, given the different needs and futures that are in question; and it needs to effect the recall in different ways of presenting the past selected, so that the relevance and meaning of the past for life at present is made apparent in effective fashion. The selectivity and the manner of presentation in each case will be suited to enable the past to bear supportively on the life in question, answering to its current neediness and assisting its reaching into the future and its achieving of fruitfulness there. To make clear what specifically he has in mind, Nietzsche spends some time delineating three modes of historiography, which he speaks of as monumental, critical, and antiquarian. Historiography is monumental as (say) recalling figures and events that would reassure and encourage by their own example and character the venturer who aspires to novel greatness; it is critical as (say) undermining an obstruction (an institution, perhaps) by recalling the injustice carried in it in virtue of its origin in the past; and it is antiquarian as (say) reinforcing the reverence and gratitude we feel toward our origins by recalling their original and/or earlier character and meaning.

What is involved in all three forms of reaching into the future is life seeking fuller life, and in youth that means: a fuller that includes some realization of the higher-and-better of aspiration. For that realization to take place, we must establish for ourselves, or must assimilate and accept from our environs, a limited horizon within which we operate, a horizon whose determinateness fits with, supports, and fosters, our own fruitful individual participation in life as adults. Such a horizon, opened out first in feeling but amplified and refined by attention and concern, interpretation and judgment, enables the concentration and commitment which are needed for such participation. Now given that we begin life with limited capacities and that in the course of our development into adulthood we form and accumulate numerous 'truths' which in reality are illusions believed in as true, whatever horizon we develop will unavoidably include various illusions belief in which is supportive to-- even crucial for-- our activity taking the shape it does.[43] Then in the crucial transitional time of early youth the life we are living opens out distinctively as aspiration and hope introduce into it an immediate directional intimation of a life-long future. Our horizon is thereby expanded and altered, first and foremost on the strength of the immediacy of feeling involved, then secondarily by such thoughtfulness as we are able to muster in this time of youthful questioning when our earlier beliefs are called into question and need to come under some scrutiny. In the measure in which this reaching-upward-toward persists and we form our activity responsively to it, our participation in life as adult human beings can unfold and be fruitful and productive within the amplified horizon in question in virtue of a love which the horizon supports and nurtures and out of which we are creative and productive in the way we are.

The need which we come to have in youth for knowledge of the past is for a knowledge which could enter into such a horizon and foster and support the life being born in us with that love. Depending on the condition of the life in question, the relevant and serviceable past will be made available historiographically in monumental, critical, and/or antiquarian vein. Now in the seeking out, sorting through, determining as the case, and capturing in writing, of the past with a view to serving current life's reaching for a future, we are entered upon a recall which is not at one with a recall that seeks truth simply, above all, at any cost. To make the past serve as we *need* it to serve, we will be disposed to tailor and shape it in our interpretive account-- to simplify and emphasize, to fill out and fill in, and thus, when judged by the standard of truth as an iconic representation of what is, to fictionalize the past to some extent. In this way, life-enhancing historiographical inquiry, the accounts of the past which issue from it, and our use of such accounts to enable life to achieve its fuller birth in ourselves, give a constructive life-enhancing standing to beliefs which often are in truth illusions.

This creates an inner conflict. For to the extent that youth is honest and genuine, to the extent that the reflection called forth in youth seeks truth as what it would found itself on in future, to that extent we are embarked by such seeking on an undertaking which runs counter to life's reaching for fuller life. For truth is not itself, as such, necessarily supportive of life-- Nietzsche's thought here joins with his discussion in BT of Dionysian experiencing, and in particular, of the life-depressing Silenic insight into finitude and the ills of finitude, including the inescapability of injustice and illusion in our lives. Instead, put in apparently paradoxical fashion: justly as we may condemn it, illusion has in truth an intrinsic and positive role in life, such that aspiration toward a life founded solely on truth is not only unrealistic but life-threatening.[44]

For one thing, the love which engages us with things in the unhistorical fashion needed for creativity and what it includes of a life-enhancing use of knowledge of the past involves (among other things) the unconditioned belief in the perfect and just. That is, in keeping with the aspirational element in it, such love has an unconditional affirmation at its heart, and it involves a commitment, a drawing into play of available resources, which depends upon the belief in the justness and perfection of what one is attempting to bring to pass and of the efforts one is making to achieve this. Yet such a belief, whatever it may be directed to in the way of determinate work or offspring, involves us in an illusion; nothing can be just and perfect with the unconditionalness which we hold to be true.[45] Moreover, because we are situated beings whose temporality involves us in the gradual development of what is only a finite capacity for understanding, we realize our lives only in an interacting which right from our earliest times enters numerous particular illusions into our being, to be functional there to the life we are realizing; and even as many such 'truths' reflect the incompleteness of ourselves as growing beings at the time we formed and made those beliefs our own, even the full maturity in which we have outgrown our earlier belief in many such 'truths' leaves us finite and limited in capacity and relying on other 'truths' for support even in our most fruitful participation in life's affairs.

Thus the fact that at times and in regard to certain 'truths' we can outgrow and see through them and reshape them does not mean we could eventually become free of illusion and injustice altogether. For life's finitude and the realization of its aspiration for fuller life by way of love means that any horizon that enables life's achieving this aspiration will involve not only the illusory belief in the just and perfect but various particular illusions, and will support our creativity only through its mixture of illusion and truth. From life's perspective what matters is not that we gain a horizon free of all illusion and injustice, but that the mixture of illusion and truth-- and any changes in the mixture-- works (and continues working) supportively to the unfolding life in the living being in question.[46]

Thus the conditions under which our inquiry into, understanding, and use of the knowledge of, the past can be life-enhancing include our involvement in illusion and dispose us to an integration of the past in which we engage in some measure of fictionalization. Now this actualizing of life under conditions which involve illusion does not mean that we should not be critical, and above all, self-critical. Indeed, life calls for this *at times*, and *at times* we can accomplish this-- even self-criticism-- in a life-supportive way. For example, as growing beings who are becoming more capable and alive in a life which is reaching for fuller life, we can grow to the place where we no longer need (say) some particular 'truth' or illusory belief; if and when we have gained the strength, we can then bring such a 'truth' into question, see through it, and, reshaping our belief, free ourselves from something which from that time on would not help but would hinder us, constrict the growing strength in ourselves, and in fact block us off from the fuller future we aspire to, despite having formed a needed and functional part of our life-enabling horizon up to the time.[47] But until we are alive and strong enough, and sufficiently well founded in the courage and honesty needed, exposure of such illusions by acting on our drive to truth no matter what the consequence is dangerous and can work counter to life's reaching. Thus self-criticism has a constructive meaning only so far as it opens the way to the actualization of fuller life which, in turn, depends on our being able to turn off such self-critical scrutiny for a while and, operating on the basis of a stable horizonal foundation that can be taken for granted (regardless of what illusions are part of it), engaging with things in an instinctive and unconscious (not deliberate and self-conscious) way. When self-criticism has any other meaning, it can well lead to an undermining of life and its reaching.

Self-criticism is particularly dangerous when it comes to the central illusion foundational for our creative love, the belief in the just and the perfect, in the justness and rightness of our creative doing in the particular forms it takes along the way. We need this belief *in* that doing, and as a result, we can never outgrow it and replace it with truth and *without further ado* still remain productive and flourishing. For whatever compels us no longer to love unconditionally cuts off the roots of our strength and energy [*Kraft*] and uproots the future of the creative or productive human being.[48] If seeing through this illusion does that, if it weakens the hold of that illusion upon us and threatens the creator's love and if such weakening and threatening persist uncountered, then it undermines life: we will inevitably wither and dry up inwardly, become dishonest and mendacious, and die humanly. Thus if at some time we grow to the place where we have the strength to see into the *illusory* character of this belief, then *if we are to remain vital* in our ongoing life-commitment, we can not simply condemn this illusion but instead must be able to avail ourselves of the "considerable strength" [*sehr viel Kraft*] that is required for us "to be able to live and to forget how far living and being unjust are one".[49] We must be able, that is, to live and act *beyond* our commitment to justice and in keeping with the truthful disclosure of justice's limited place in reality. This means being able to find the strength *at times* temporarily to suppress the condemnation with which the reaching for justice in us responds to such recognition, and to re-immerse ourselves *for a while* unhistorically, to love and create within that forgetfulness, and to bring a higher and better future into being, *even though at other times* we expressly recognize and condemn the illusion that is operative in us. It is only when this recognition and condemnation are made *unforgettable* to us, that we arrive at the unhealthy cynicism that undermines life's upward reaching, our own trust in the future, and our creative love.[50]

In short: the life in us needs some knowledge of the past, in order that its drive toward fuller life be facilitated. But the drive which calls forth inquiry into the past and use of accounts of the past so as to facilitate the realization of a "future which is already alive in the hope"[51] of the present provides a horizon for that inquiry and use which, by the direction and constraint it gives to them, invites fictionalization of the past. If we are to make constructive use of 'knowledge' of the past, we can not insist on truthful knowledge alone without risking the undermining of life.

2. A life-undermining way

The life in each human being, harboring a drive toward more and fuller life, contains also various vital energies, needs, drives, instincts, and powers, which are native to the living being. Each of us is moved by our own nature to develop out of ourselves and to develop our own distinctive nature. That means, more than anything else, acting on and developing and refining the genuine immediate feelings native to us, our own native responsiveness, and with the help of that responsiveness and of the working of spirit, seeking our own elevation and refinement and reaching for more and fuller life by that route. The path of development is not simply one of developing the multiplicity of factors separately but at the same time of organizing and integrating the multiplicity of developing inner factors so as to be building and eventually to achieve in ourselves a strong or powerful unified center of life and activity, a coherent and harmonious inwardness out of which we take part in things.

The development, elevation, and refinement, by which our nature is to become actual, and the integration of energies and directions of striving and achievement that are involved, are not simply internal matters. For not only does the inward development take place in our interacting with circumstance, and especially with other human beings, but the inward factors in question drive toward realization in our interaction with others, thus toward outer manifestation in acts, in appearances modified to reflect the inner, in patterns of intercourse, in expressive things created to function in the public world, and so on. More importantly, the integrating center drives toward realization and manifestation of itself as a whole, thus toward the visible expression of its integrated inwardness, of the wholeness of the person. The life in us thus drives toward culture, and that means: it drives toward that transformation of our nature whereby, in virtue of a process of cultivation, it has become realized in integrated and elevated form and expresses itself in public fashion.[52]

Because the life in individual human beings develops in the interaction of one human being with others, the process of cultivation of the individual has a complex communal dimension. Not only do individuals influence each other and contribute to the cultivation going on in each. But they share feelings, and the cultivation of such shared feelings in each reinforces that in others, especially when such feelings are expressed publicly and those public expressions (in deeds, works, etc.) are responded to by all. Seen in this perspective, culture is not simply the cultivated state of the individual, but the unity of artistic style (of style of creativity) in all the public expressions of the life of a people. The life in question here is a communal and shared life. What is included in culture is not simply the public aspect of such life; it also includes the inward shared spirit as it is expressing and manifesting itself in the outward. Thus in virtue of culture in this sense the members of the community are drawn together in a shared spiritual functioning out of their own being, and the community becomes self-conscious to itself as such with the help of the works of culture. Even though it is this connectedness of centers from out of the heart of themselves which is the embracing locus of the realization of culture, the prominent place of the public element in this realization, being the facet to which all participants in the realization have direct access, readily leads to taking the works, deeds, institutions and patterns, in question as of themselves constituting culture; but these are grasped in their cultural meaning only when they are seen as realizations and expressions of the life of a people, and in particular, of their higher or spiritual life (life beyond the matter simply of survival).

If the issue of culture in the individual reference is a transfigured fulness of the individual's nature, the issue of culture in a communal reference is the binding together of a whole community, effected on the strength of a differentiation of the few people creative on a grand scale and the many who are receptive and responsive to that creativity but not themselves creative except at best in a minor way. This binding together unites centers heart to heart; for it is rooted in the genuine feelings of the members, and it occurs by way of expressions of those kindred feelings which enable the life being realized in and through them to become shared. It is in the life of a people in this sense that its native spirit is made manifest-- that German spirit, say, of which Nietzsche made much in BT.

Now as Nietzsche sees it, in contemporary Germany something has happened which has changed in fundamental fashion the simple and natural relation of individuals to culture in both forms, that of their own cultivated being and that of the communally shared style of expressing their shared life. That is the presence and working of science, and in particular, the demand that the study of the past should be a science and that science should extend its historical range as far as possible.

In virtue of the response to this demand, several things have happened.

For one, when the need of the living for a knowledge of the past calls forth inquiry in natural fashion, such inquiry is guided and restrained by life's own aim in the present at more and fuller life. But as inquiry into the past becomes scientific and is undertaken as part of such disciplined effort to find truth, it is no longer regulated and confined by life itself. Inquiry seeks knowledge for its own sake, not for life. And the inquirers are no longer those who need such knowledge for the sake of the life in themselves or the shared life of the people to which they belong. Rather they are pure thinkers who only look on at life and who seek knowledge alone, regardless of its relevance to life in the present. In their case, the sheer accumulation of a knowledge of the past is itself the goal.

For another, the presence of human beings devoted to such a goal would have meant in any case the accumulation of more historical knowledge than would otherwise have been the case. But under a sense of reality as exhausted by the temporal and forming an arena of becoming, science has pushed to explore all things as 'historical': humanity and human values indeed, but also living nature, and even non-living nature. In virtue of this extension of the realm of the 'historical', the devotion of energies to gaining scientific knowledge has produced an enormous wealth of 'historical' knowledge. For example, in biology there has emerged the evolutionary vision of life on earth, so that the human past is only a late phase in the evolution of life on earth, humankind representing only an evolutionary continuation of plant and animal life on earth; and in geology and cosmology the discovery of 'history' has been extended to include the becoming of the earth, whose genesis is itself grasped as part of the genesis of the solar system, and so on backwards in time indefinitely. Because the scientific pursuit of knowledge has also brought a skeptical unlearning of much that had been essential in the horizons of human beings of the past, and furthermore, has involved a sense of "knowledge" which recognizes in it a tentativeness such that what claims to be knowledge at any time is always subject to future revision, the progressive work of science has not simply involved an altered vision of reality but has had the effect of a "madly thoughtless splintering and unravelling of all foundations" and of the introduction of a restless alteration of the lines of the horizon of a modern human being. What in the way of knowledge is to guide and support life now is only spider's webs which every new stroke of knowledge tears apart, so that it is difficult for us moderns to act creatively because the horizon we need lacks the required stability.[53]

For a third, the changed nature of knowledge, the immense detail and scope of knowledge produced as a result of such extensions of the range of the "historical", and the presence of learned humans whose lives are devoted to acquiring knowledge apart from the needs of life, together have constituted a force which has significantly altered the soul of modern man, including the modern German. This alteration has led to-- and has in turn been assisted by-- a reshaping of the educational system. The cultivated human being which that system is supposed to produce has been reconceived as the learned human; if education is not to make the student into a scholar-and-scientist, it is at least to prepare the student for a life which places the pursuit and employment of scientific knowledge at the heart of life generally and which perceives such pursuit and employment as the essence of the higher life. In virtue of the reshaping of educational institutions in their aim and in the means used to extend the practical relevance of scientific knowledge and to achieve that aim, the student being educated is inundated by a wealth of knowledge which far exceeds what could be taken in and remembered, and even more, which is not fully harmonious in its elements. For this reason the students of his day were forced to be selective and to organize what they took in, and even then they remained threatened by unresolved conflicts. Since knowledge was changing and new things were ever coming to light, this selecting and organizing was a never finished task.[54]

Nietzsche particularly stresses two aspects of the impact of such an educative process on a student.

One: Because the mass of knowledge far exceeds his hunger and because much of it runs counter to his need, he is overwhelmed and tends simply to 'turn off' rather than to select and organize. As a result, he does not really take anything in and take it seriously but only lets it register lightly and in passing.[55]

Two: In keeping with the modern emphasis on knowing, he has developed the penchant for immediately transforming all that is happening into knowledge ('instant analysis') rather than letting it sink in and feeling it for a while before analyzing it. As a result, what is happening to him becomes immediately related to knowledge which he already carries with him and becomes categorized without having ever registered deeply. As a result it never becomes met head-on in its own right, let alone becomes understood out of itself and the experience of it.[56]

In both of these forms of response, modern man does not let what he experiences or comes to know reach into the depths of his self, into his innermost feelings and instincts. Because he also does not develop the honesty and truthfulness that would make apparent this superficial character to his responses and would disclose his own feelings, needs, distress, and being, to himself,[57] he tends in effect to deny his own feelings and instincts and thus never to venture to develop under their impetus out of the deeper depths of his own being and to be a person, the unique person he is. By catering in this way to the inclination for comfort and ease, he develops that unsureness and lack of belief in himself due to which he eventually can not resist giving in to whatever comes along.[58] In these ways he forms a second nature which is weak, restless and somewhat unhealthy. It is a second nature of roles which he adopts and plays; he masks himself then as 'politician', 'poet' and the like, and learns to think and feel accordingly.[59]

This second nature, centered in various assumed roles, substitutes much knowledge-about and many learned-feelings for the personal power which is formed through belief in oneself, through self-development which draws into play one's own inner depths, and through one's native feelings trusted and developed so as to be strong and assured enough to be the measure for all that is taken in from the outside. Although the knowledge-about found in this second nature is often taken as itself an intrinsic mark of culture, so that modern man tends to equate the cultured person with the educated person (the learned person, the scholar), in fact it is not of itself intrinsic to genuine culture. Life harbors a drive to come to be out of itself so that the living being develops and manifests something of its very own, something coming to be from out of its own depths. In this development, knowledge has indeed a place and an important function: it is meant to help transform the vital elements within (including native feelings) as the life which is actualized through them expresses and manifests itself in the outward and in a transformation of the outward which makes it express the inward. This is genuine culture. But in modern man, the knowledge he acquires has no such function of transforming his own nature and its outward expression of itself. Instead it is carried around with him as "a huge quantity of indigestible stones of knowledge"[60]. For this reason there is no close connection of outer and inner in him. What is inner is the chaotic grab-bag of much knowledge together with a variety of different feelings, to varying degrees falsified (one feels what one is supposed to).[61] This feeble and disorganized inwardness, he may call "culture"[62], though it is not, and he may cultivate it in the sense that he seeks increased variety. But it is not only itself dysfunctional inwardly; it is also disconnected with what is outer.[63] For the latter, being a motley set of conventions adopted (with some modification) from elsewhere, is not expressive form but mere conventional pattern. Functioning as disguise, as garment to be put on or taken off, as covering, as adornment, the outer has no genuine cultural significance, no meaning as manifesting a transformed nature.[64]

In the modern educational system, then, we find the promotion of a way of integrating knowledge of the past into ongoing living beings which undermines rather than supports life and does not foster genuine culture. For amidst the excess of historical knowledge, as the latter relates to the student's need and capacity to take in, digest, and employ, it in life-enhancing fashion, the student is overwhelmed and unable to do this, and indeed, he is encouraged not to attempt this but rather to develop toward the ideal of the learned human being, and become someone fitted to play his role in a social order which stresses science and its application to the practical problems of life.

Now correlative with this, the very activity which has generated this knowledge (the disciplined inquiry of science) introduces into its practitioner a personal weakness of a connected kind. Science has succeeded in generating knowledge in virtue of its method and its objective approach to the matters to be known in its inquiry. This (historical) objectivity, modern man claims to be a strength, and more specifically, a proof of his capacity to sort things out and pass just judgment on them. He has learned to find and face the truth and to form just judgments better than man ever has up to now: so he claims. But does his objectivity really reflect his capacity to be just, does it originate in a heightened sense of the need for justice, does it show him to be just in a higher degree than humans of other ages? Or does that objectivity arise from sources quite other than his desire and capacity to be just?

We have already seen that, ultimately, in our striving to see truth, we must reach beyond even justice, for in this Dionysian world justice has a subordinate place to life itself. Nonetheless, in the hierarchy of strengths, justice holds a high place. It is the rarest of all virtues, indeed an impossible virtue. For while still a fallible human being, someone who would be just must have the will for truth as the truth of world-judgment, as ordering and punishing judge. The search for truth has something great in it only if, among other things, the seeker has the unconditioned will to be just; that is rare indeed, but rarer still is that the seeker also has the strength to be just, the self-conscious strength that gives him the right to judge. He must be able to hold the scales steadily, to place the weights in disregard of himself, to note the rising and falling of the scale with unclouded eye, and to pronounce a verdict with a voice neither harsh nor tearful.[65] Is this what lies behind modern man's objectivity?

Leaving aside the many who claim to seek and serve truth but who do not,[66] there are human beings who do in fact seek truth,[67] and achieve an objectivity in their search. But that objectivity is a condition of indifference in which (say) the historian envisions an event in all its motives and consequences so purely and with so little feeling that it has no effect at all on his subjectivity, on himself as subject.[68] Such truth-seeking as he might properly undertake in this condition is one requiring neither the will nor the power to be a judge in the most basic matters of existence. There are in fact many indifferent truths, there are problems about which judging correctly (giving an accurate iconic representation and a just assessment) requires no overcoming, let alone sacrifice. In this indifferent and safe realm a human being can succeed in becoming a cold demon of knowledge. Such persons seek 'pure inconsequential knowledge', and do so without any strict and great justice, without this noblest nucleus of the so-called drive to truth, being present.[69]

Now what sort of truth-seekers and judges are our historians today? Are they of this sort, or of another? At their best, they have a subtle and variegated passive receptivity, and they can achieve this objectivity of indifference-- a condition of personal weakness, of weakness as a creative human being, but one employable in this context as a virtue, a kind of strength. But they do not have the superior strength really to be judge, let alone to see beyond justice and into the deepest nature of things in its tragic meaning. The human weakness involved is reflected in the fact that their echoing of the past mutes it; while the original note sounded powerful, sounded of deeds, needs, terrors, its echo lacks this sound. Unlike the voice of even our best historians, the voice of justice is never pleasing and charming, but is hard and terrifying. Our historians not only lack the superior strength which alone could really judge; only a rare few can reach the much lower virtue of magnanimity or generosity. Many more attain only to tolerance, to allowing validity to what they cannot deny happened, to explaining away and extenuating in a moderate and benevolent fashion, etc. There is even greater weakness here, which must tolerate if it is not to be hypocritical and pretend to strength, and thus turn justice into a play-actress.[70]

At the heart, then, of the modern development of science and in particular of the modern effort to make the study of the past into a science, is the development and training of the practitioners of science for an objectivity of indifference. Such objectivity may be a strength in that under its aegis a many-sided knowledge of fact can be, and has been, developed. But such 'truths' do not disclose what lies at the heart of the actual, nor do they reach into the depths and heights of the past. Rather they are limited to the surface of things. This limitation is founded in, and counterpart to, the inquirer's weakness as a person, as a human being, and thus to his/her lack of the resources with which to fathom the depths of things.[71] The achievements of modern science, then, do not indicate that modern man is just in higher degree than human beings of other times. Quite to the contrary. They attest the absence of the personal strength and power required for justice. Their production has depended on the fostering of an enabling objectivity which reflects human weakness, indeed has depended on a preparation and training which does not allow the inquirer to mature humanly[72] but fits him for a pursuit which eventually disenchants, then saps the life from, the inquirer and finally destroys that person's humanity.[73] This is the human cost of the cultivation of objectivity as enabling factor in the unrestrained pursuit of scientific knowledge: the weakening and extirpation of the humanity in the individuals involved.

In sum: we modern human beings have placed science at the center of our life, and with it, the drive to truth-- but not that drive in its more noble forms.[74] Still, science has achieved a massive accumulation of knowledge about nature and human affairs (history). The impact of this endeavor, both from the side of those who assimilate such knowledge in their education and from that of anyone being trained to produce it by the objectivity of indifference, is the same in one regard: namely, the weakening of the humanity of the human being involved. Instead of developing ourselves as persons, instead of fostering mature and harmonized personalities in our educational system and in our search for truth, we modern human beings are venturing to refashion ourselves to play the roles whereby we can meet the needs of the times and can play a functional part in modern society. Even though we seem to ourselves to be advancing by this reshaping of ourselves and our society by science, we are unwittingly destroying our own humanity, all in the name of "progress" and the higher, indeed (so we claim) highest, actualization of the "human".

C. The 'times' and youth, morality and culture

The life in us is realized in our concrete interaction with other beings, and in such interacting we integrate our concrete context, our environs and environment, into ourselves and our lives. Thereby the particularity of the context becomes part of our life and helps determine the shape it takes as we live it. Now in virtue of the temporality of things, our immediate context and circumstance (so far as it is human) and the current state of our own being bear in themselves a latent past, and in particular, meanings which constitute a social tradition; thus in our ordinary everyday participation in the interacting we find ourselves bearers of a shared tradition as part of what enters into the interacting. In that everyday activity we carry this tradition as at work there unconsciously and sometimes consciously (in our 'historical' mode of participation), operative in providing direction and directives and in general disposing us to interact in certain ways. Thus we assimilate roles, for example, and develop so as to fit ourselves with others in a role-determined social context; such roles and such associating with each other enter more or less effectively and pervasively into the shaping of the second nature of the human beings involved. And at large, as the 'times', the 'age', this social power represents a disposing atmosphere within which and according to which we ordinarily encounter and take to ourselves what we meet.

The content of a 'times' is the tradition-relative facet of the present concrete interaction in which we are realizing our lives, and in that sense, is different for the Greeks of the 5th century BC and for the Germans of the 19th century AD. But however different the factors forming the 'times' in these cases (or any other), as part of a 'times' such factors in each case function in ordinary activity in the same way, as initially disposing their bearers to activity in keeping with themselves.

1. Nietzsche's characterization of his own 'times'

Nietzsche spends some time in UHH characterizing the 'times' in which he and his contemporaries find themselves, and offers a view which, while it complements what he set forth in BT, stresses what is relevant for this work with its focus on historical knowledge and education. To the fore therefore is modern science, its empirical method (its 'objectivity' in procedure), and its achievements. As this is operative in the everyday life and activity of himself and his contemporaries, its successful embodiment of 'reason' continues a tradition which goes back to the Greeks, among whom an element in the human decision-making and -executing capacity (the power of thought) received for the first time a particular rendering (*logos*, *nous*: 'reason') and under that rendering was claimed to be the humanity-defining power that should dominate our active participation in things.[75] In modern times this power has received widespread and effective development in the form of the disciplined inquiry of empirical science, and ongoing life is being increasingly adapted to the presence and centrality of this power in our affairs.

What marks the 'times' in which this is happening is a spirit whose contrasting two-sided character reflects (according to Nietzsche) a weakened and weakening humanity. One side-- its foreground side-- is a kind of pride and bravado. In the emerging 'historical' culture, 'timely' persons see a progress and the superiority of the present over what went before, indeed the arrival in principle at the culmination of humankind's reaching to elevate human existence on earth. The other side-- its background side-- is an undercurrent of a quite different sort. There is, paradoxically, a kind of hopelessness, pessimism, as regards the future. If there is not decline and increasing barbarism,[76] there is at least a sense that, mighty as the wingbeats of our knowing are, we have nonetheless not been able to soar aloft and descry a future fuller of life than the present is.[77] What the two share-- the sense of having arrived at an end (in the one case a culmination, in the other a termination)-- is expressed in an apparently conflicting fashion reflecting this dual meaning to "end"; but when the two are seen together, the excessiveness of the foreground side (the vaunting of achievement and progress) is visible as an exaggeration whose function is to distract from the background side (the hopelessness). Yet this is nothing that is acknowledged; indeed, intrinsic to this ambivalent sense of present achievement and of the future is an inability or unwillingness openly and honestly to acknowledge the full two-sided condition or the human weakness it attests. As a result 'modern man' is close to paralysis and drifting, and to allowing the future to become increasingly lifeless and empty within while presenting the outer appearance of energy and achievement.

If the basic meaning of the 'times' of Nietzsche and his contemporaries is that 'reason' has come into a predominant position in modern life and vitality is accordingly being sapped out of life, there are more visible elements of those times which Nietzsche would bring to attention. Four of these are of particular importance in his account and for our purposes.

First: The 'times' are such as have been formed in a reaction against the medieval accomplishment which had brought the Christian myth to a dominant place in life. Christianity still lingers on as the rationalizing of life has taken place, resisting it all the while as it is becoming itself undermined as myth and accepted in a 'rational' version of itself. In its persisting vision, Christianity sees no future for humankind in life on earth, but rather an eventual final judgment in which earthly life, lived at its best by looking backward to the decisive events as already having taken place, receives its otherworldly issue (its reward or punishment). So far as Christianity becomes integrated into ongoing life and forms part of the 'times', it offers no support to any love and hope, any venturing, that would involve new planting, bold experimentation, free longing; indeed it resists and opposes these.[78] To that extent, it reinforces the hopeless background-side of the modern spirit.

Second: In the philosophical strand of the complex modern development in which Christianity is losing its power, one particular philosopher has become recently influential, especially in the Germany of Nietzsche's times. That is Hegel. According to his sense history is the finite dialectically-formed process of god manifesting himself in human history, of self-aware spirit accomplishing its own progressive self-revelation in and through that history. According to this reading, "the race is now at its zenith, for only now does it possess knowledge of itself, only now has it become revealed to itself."[79] Thus the latecomer sees himself under this inspiration as raised to godhood and sees his more knowledgeable and more self-aware being "as the true meaning and goal of all previous events", as the "completion of world-history".[80] If the Christian vision reinforces a hopelessness concerning life on earth, the Hegelian vision invites a glorification of power and success. It has "accustomed the Germans to talk of a 'world-process' and to justify their own age as the necessary result of this world-process; such a point of view has set history, insofar as history is 'the concept that realizes itself', 'the dialectics of the spirit of the peoples' and the 'world-tribunal', in place of the other spiritual powers, art and religion, as the sole sovereign power."[81] Thereby Hegel's vision has

> implanted into the generation thoroughly leavened by him that admiration for the 'power of history' which in practice transforms every moment into a naked admiration for success and leads to an idolatry of the factual: which idolatry is now generally described by the very mythological yet quite idiomatic expression 'to accommodate oneself to the facts' [*den Tatsachen Rechnung tragen*]. But he who has once learned to bend his back and bow his head before the 'power of history' at last nods 'Yes' in mechanical Chinese fashion to every power, whether it be a government or public opinion or a numerical majority, and moves his limbs to the precise rhythm at which any 'power' whatever pulls the strings. If every success is a rational necessity, if every event is a victory of the logical or the 'idea'-- then down on your knees quickly and do reverence to the whole stepladder of 'success'![82]

Hegel's vision of history as an evolutionary movement or process in which spirit realizes itself in and through certain collectivities reinforces the foreground side of the modern spirit: we live in the 'times' in which this movement is achieving its end, that necessary culmination arrival at which gives purpose and meaning to all that went before. But if this is so, if 'whatever is rational, is real; and whatever is real, is rational'[83], then Hegel implicitly teaches a passivity in the face of powers-that-be. For not only had history to unfold precisely as it has and humankind to become so and not otherwise than it precisely is now, but in the movement into the future the 'rationality' of the present, being full and complete, will dominate. Over against the 'must' of such 'rational' movement, nothing (and certainly no human being) can stand. Thus a sense of powerlessness against the 'march of history' confirms the sense of hopelessness in regard to any future for humankind; there is nothing becoming in the present which would be in any basic sense different from simple continuation of the past; what a human being must do is simply surrender to the current of history and let himself be carried along.

Third: The historiography which, in modern times, has turned scientific not only manifests and promotes personal weakness in the way noted in earlier discussion; it has developed a way of looking at the historical process itself which is limited and is reflective of the weakness of the inquirer even though it offers itself as the objective and truthful rendering of the reality of human affairs.

One aspect of this way of looking at history is the reduction of all human motivation to egoistic motives.

> Men seem close to discovering that the egoism of individuals, of groups or of the masses, was at all times the lever of historical movements; but at the same time, one is in no way disturbed by this discovery but one decrees: egoism shall be our god. With this new faith one is now setting to work with the clearest intention of erecting coming history on egoism: only it should be a more prudent egoism, one which imposes certain restraints upon itself so as to ensure its enduring, one which studies history precisely to become acquainted with the imprudent egoism. In the course of this study one has learned that a quite special mission in the to-be-founded world-system of egoism falls to the state: it is supposed to be the patron of all prudent egoisms, so as to protect them with its military and police forces against the terrifying outbreaks to which imprudent egoism is liable. It is to the same end that history-- the history of animal and humankind-- is carefully inculcated into the dangerous, because imprudent, masses [*Volksmassen*] and working classes: one knows that a grain of historical culture is capable of breaking down dull and rude instincts and desires or of leading them into the path of a refined egoism.[84]

Not only does the past become represented as a field in which egoism has in fact dominated, but with the emerging dominance of rationality and the refinement of reason's practical relevance modern humanity is committing itself to egoism in what is claimed to be a more prudent form.

A second aspect of this way of looking at history, reflecting the Hegelian focus on peoples, considers the course of events from the standpoint of the masses and seeks to find those laws in it which derive from the needs of these masses. Now a people unites the few with the many, the creative and cultured with the uncultured (lacking in higher culture, at least). The masses are the many, and this, whether or not they form part of the community of a people. To Nietzsche's mind, the masses seem worthy of notice by the historiographer in three respects alone: "first, as vague copies of great men produced on bad paper and with worn-out plates; then, as resistance to the great; and finally, as instrument of the great; for the rest, let the devil and statistics take them!"[85] No doubt there are uniformities reflecting "how vulgar and nauseatingly uniform the masses are; but should the effects of inertia, stupidity, mimicry, love and hunger, be called laws?" Even if one should count them as such, such laws and such history are worthless; and yet the historiography which is currently prized takes "the great mass drives as the important and chief factors in history and regards great men as being no more than their clearest expression, as it were bubbles which become visible on the flood".[85]

In Nietzsche's view, the tendency of such historiography is mistaken in several respects. It purports to be concerned with the great but it misses greatness in its intrinsic character, in its character as the noble and elevated, and thus in its linkage with the heights and depths of being and time in priority to any linkage with the ongoing. It also mistakes the origin of greatness: as if it were the product of the masses, given birth to by them out of themselves. Finally in the absence of any idea of greatness in its own character, it confuses greatness with what has moved the masses for some length of time and has in this sense become what is called "a power in history"; that is simply to ignore quality and to reduce greatness to something quantitative, to what has enduring success in its impact on the masses. But apart from the fact that "the noblest and most exalted things make no effect whatever on the masses"[85], that would be to make greatness a retroactively attributed quality without attending to the intrinsic character of the creation itself.

In UHH, Nietzsche presents a view of the affairs which form history which is quite at odds with the view he claims historiography is offering, to say nothing of being at odds with the Hegelian and the Christian. Leaving unnoted any metaphysical meaning such as BT sees in human affairs,[86] and leaving aside also what we will find in SE of the evolutionary sense of the human, Nietzsche's presentation in UHH of the nature and meaning of history focuses on the achievement of greatness. More specifically: temporal existence is so ordered in the nature of things that the question of meaning receives its decisive resolution for the human being with the help of a linking together of human beings in center around the greatness of individuals creative in many different ways. That linking together is achieved in a people, which is not just a group, a collectivity, but a living community of suffering humanity which is brought together in virtue of a capacity to respond to higher aims, to sacrifice their ego (individual and collective) in service of higher things. The crucial linking factor is the high aims formed through the greatness of individuals who are thereby the spiritual leaders of the community that establishes itself. It is culture, then, in Nietzsche's distinctive sense of that word, that lies at the heart of community, and it is the creativity which functions in this hierarchical yet unifying way that is the significant content of history.

Contrary to Hegel, the achievement of such content does not take place in a dialectical or any other sort of progress from one 'times' to the next. Already in BT, we have seen Nietzsche summoning the Germans to return to and learn from the Greeks of the tragic age and to bring forth under their inspiration a new tragic age. Between such times of rising to comparable heights lies a long course of affairs, with the most significant connecting factor being the accomplishment of Socrates and the expansion of that example which he set in which knowledge is a lure toward continued existence and life.[87] But this interim time, starting with Socrates himself and his achievement, shows a decline spiritually from the heights of a healthy and vital creativity, and the revival of the tragic among the Germans would not represent progress but rediscovery of those heights at which humanity achieves its noblest realization. If anything from the interim made a difference to the character of the renewed greatness and the later achievement in the heights, it was not as producing the latter in virtue of a necessary process stemming from the earlier time. In the present meditation, Nietzsche's focus is on the threats in his own times to the new and renewed future of the Germans and the German spirit. His allusions to the "most living part of our culture"[88] as music, to the need of "every people ... that wants to become *mature*"[88] for a protective veil if it is to do so and become productive out of that maturity, and to art and religion as "true ancillaries" which could "combine to implant a culture which corresponds to true needs"[89], remind of his account in the earlier work. His allusion to the possibility that "no more than a hundred productive human beings educated and actively working in a new spirit"[90] could do away with present German 'culture' and raise a new culture points, however, in the direction of the notion of a people united in focus around the cultural creativity of a few which is developed in this meditation.

Under this notion, Nietzsche speaks of "all hope of a still coming national culture" as stemming from "belief in the genuineness and immediacy of German sensibility, from belief in a sound and whole interiority".[91] Within such a genuine and unified interiority dispersed among the Germans the "great productive spirit" could operate, secure in the unity of feeling among the cultivated who embody the art-spirit of a people and the uncultivated who can be responsive to the work of such a spirit and of the creators who embody it. In that context, with a "heart ... full of pity for all", creative spirits could reach out in longing and could work knowing their own necessary place in the body of the people and knowing the "instinct of the people" coming out to meet them.[92] Because the decisive initiative and achievement is that of the few individuals, and since that achievement is a realization of a greatness to the human, Nietzsche can also speak of great individual human beings as forming

> a sort of bridge over the desert [*wüsten*] stream of becoming. They may not perhaps continue a process, but living timelessly contemporaneous thanks to historiography [*Geschichte*] which allows such a working together, they live as that republic of genius of which Schopenhauer once spoke; one giant calls to the other through the waste [*öden*] intervals of time, and undisturbed by the noisy wanton dwarfs who creep along below them the high spiritual conversation proceeds. The task of historiography [*Geschichte*] is to be the mediator between these and so ever again to give impulse to the creation of the great and to lend strength to that creation.[93]

Keeping in mind that the historiographic mode which would be this mediator is monumental in nature, that it would recall the earlier under such falsification as would make of it a type and an exemplar for imitation, and that the new context for realization would make the latter not an instance but a novel variation of the theme adumbrated in the type, the point at issue is that history is no "process" which shows progress (in realization of the spirit, say). What is historically significant in the course of affairs is rather recurrent, and occurrent at various times along that course.[94] Thus Nietzsche can end the passage just quoted: "No, the *goal of humanity* can not lie in the end, but only in its *highest examples*."[95] The final point at which humanity arrives may in fact represent a decline from the achievement of earlier stages along the way.

Fourth: Emerging with the advance of science and important in the "universal history" that is becoming formulated in modern times is an evolutionary view of life on earth in general, such as that of Darwin. According to this general view, human beings belong in an evolutionary stream, and the life in us shares the nature of life generally, that it seeks adaptation and continued existence. This forms the ultimate limiting horizon of its striving. Within educational circles and (by the popularization of science) in the populace at large, the discovery and teaching of the notions of evolutionary becoming as ultimate and sovereign and of the lack of cardinal difference between man and animal have gained broad acceptance. To Nietzsche's mind, this has brought us to a dangerous place. Such teachings, "true but deadly"[96], are having a subversive impact on any sense of dedication, commitment, allegiance, which is other than egoistic, which expresses anything other than self-seeking. For in such teachings we are being taught that species-preservation is the limiting horizon of the reaching of the life in us; but if any other sense of that reaching is specious, then the evolutionary teaching in Darwinian form works counter to the notion of a people as well as to the individual creativity which embodies a sense of future. For in both cases, creativity is founded in aspiration toward the higher-

and-better, and the meaning to be found in a creative or productive life depends upon commitment to a "high and noble" purpose.[97] When our aspiration lapses from the higher-and-better and we collapse as individuals back upon ourselves, this brings dehumanization, and we then know only an ego-horizon to life. This holds not simply for us as individuals in our responsibility for our own life; it holds for us in the communal side to human existence, for us as individuals inherently involved in a collective reference in our actualization of our individual lives. Without shared aspiration, there is no people, only associations and groups, various forms of collectivity, whose bonds are ego-bonds. Thus Nietzsche anticipates: If such ideas as are offered in the evolutionary teaching in its Darwinian form are thrust upon the people for another generation with the current frenzy,

> no one should be surprised if the people perishes of egoistic pettiness and misery, ossification and selfishness, indeed above all falls apart and ceases to be a people; in its place then perhaps systems of individualistic egoism will step into the theatre of the future, brotherhoods for the purpose of rapacious exploitation of non-brothers and similar creations of utilitarian vulgarity.[98]

What can be done to counter this, at the same time acknowledging the element of truth in an evolutionary view? What counterweight to the force of the present educational system, including now as part of its force the teaching of such a view of life and the human, is available? How revive and keep open the sense of future which a vigorous people has and needs, and reshape the educational system to suit the way of life and youth of a vigorous people with a sense of a future for itself?

2. The counterforce to the 'times': youth

The life in us is temporal in its nature not simply as lived in the course defined by our active engagement with circumstance but also as unfolding in a developmental fashion, so that it is an affair of the growth and maturation of ourselves humanly. Because this development takes place in the actual interacting with circumstance and primordially in virtue of the exercise of our native and developed capacity such as it is at the time, and because it is in that exercise that the 'times' also enter into us and have their impact in that development, the forming and engaging in activity is the locus of the confluence of the disposing working of the 'times' and of the development of the native potential in ourselves. The latter not only has its own temporal meaning-- we know 'youth' not as a function of circumstance but in virtue of our nature's own unfolding; but it also has a specific meaning in regard to this matter of the incorporation of the 'times' into ourselves. For youth is the time of life in which our nature, having by its unfolding brought us to the place where certain native capacities (for reflection, for example) become available to us, brings us into the presence of life's summons to take responsibility. In life's call then, we are summoned (among other things) to our own way of engaging with things. That way, animated by aspiration as our native source of direction and directives-- one expressing life itself as a naturally unfolding affair--, is to take shape with the help of a sorting out and critiquing of what else offers itself as directional and directive beyond this immediacy. That sorting out is called to resist the disposing atmosphere of the 'times' and its pressure for acceptance: it is a new life and a new beginning, at the threshold for which what is to be accepted as directional and directive needs to enable and support the life to come. This is to be the natural standard for reflection's sorting out. In virtue of its maturational meaning, then, youth is a time of 'rebellion' whose issue is to be entry into and persistence in a way of engaging with things and bearing life which is responsive to-- and effectively answers to-- life's call to responsibility.

a. Youth's nature

It is youth-- the youth in himself, trusted by himself-- which Nietzsche claims has been the inspirational power which has guided him on this journey of reflective exploration of the condition of contemporary German culture.[99] It has urged him on to protest against the historical education of youth in present-day Germany and to demand that before anything else a person learn to live and to use history only in the service of that life the person is learning and has learned to live.[100] It is to youth as well-- the instinct of youth in others not yet fully moulded by German education-- that he would communicate these exploratory reflections. And finally, it is the condition and potentiality of youth that he would voice, the young speaking to the young about their common youthful condition.

As to that condition and potentiality, youth is a time and human condition that is naturally marked by certain things. As we noted earlier,[101] in this meditation he points to certain "instincts" as belonging to it: "fire, defiance, self-forgetting, and love ..., the ardor of its feeling for the right-and-just ..., the desire to mature slowly ..., the honesty and boldness [*Keckheit*] of feeling ..."[102]. And he adds, as the "fairest privilege" of youth, "its power [*Kraft*] to implant in itself with an overflowing confidence [*Glaubigkeit*] a great idea and to allow it to grow out of itself into an even greater idea"[103]. A human being in whom such instincts and such powers are intact and healthy would feel as he has expressed himself as feeling in the analysis set forth so far: the educational system in its present state is anti-natural in character. While it rightly treats culture as the aim of education, it takes culture as something added on like icing to a cake, and produces the scholar, the scientific person, who is socially useful as early as possible. Not only is that idea of culture false and unfruitful; the result of such an education is a cultural philistine, not a truly cultured human being. The instinct of youth urges instead toward a culture which arises and blossoms from life itself and toward an educational system which fosters this end, the free cultivated human being.[104]

Whoever would shatter the present educational system and foster such cultivated human beings must help youth to find the words which illuminate its unconscious counter-will and resistance to that system with the clearness of concepts and which thereby make the resistance into a conscious and articulate one.[105]

The first step in helping youth find those words is to destroy the superstition that the present educational system is the only one and thus is necessary. There *are* other possibilities than an education which insists that the youthful must begin not with living and experiencing themselves, not even with a knowing about life, but with a knowing about culture, and a knowing which is historical at that, not the direct knowing of culture in the present but an indirect knowledge of past ages and peoples. In reality the basic desire of the young is to experience something themselves, to feel a connected living system of their own experiences growing in themselves. Such a desire need not be drowned out, as it is in present education. Rather, education must begin with life, but also respect that life is a craft which must be learned continually and from the ground up and must be practised unsparingly if one is not to become a botcher and babbler. As it is, contemporary education wishes for the flower without the root and stalk, wishes for a culture without the first-hand-learning basis and the educational process that could form one.[106]

If there is to be change, the first generation educated differently must suffer because of the lack of an appropriate educational system already in place. It will have to educate itself, and do so even against itself, in order to attain a new nature and manner of life [*Gewohnheit*]. All members of this generation must overcome themselves, and in particular, must judge about themselves what they might more easily bear as a general judgment about a whole time:

> we are without culture; still more, we are corrupted for living, corrupted for correct and simple seeing and hearing, for happy grasping of the nearest and natural; and we still do not have even the foundation of a culture because we are not convinced of having in ourselves a truthful life. Fragmented and in pieces, half-mechanically fallen wholly asunder into inner and outer, sown with concepts as with dragon's teeth and bringing forth conceptual dragons, suffering from the malady of words and without trust in any feeling of our own which is not yet stamped with its word: as such an unliving and yet uncannily busy concept-and-word-factory, perhaps I still have the right to say 'I think therefore I am', but not 'I live therefore I think'.[107]

But "give me life, then I will create for you a culture out of it": so will every individual of this first generation call out, and all will recognize each other by this call. Who, however, will give them this life?[108] No god and no human being, only their own youth. Unchaining it, one liberates life-- the life merely hidden, in prison, not yet withered away and dead, but sick indeed and in need of being healed, sick with many illnesses but pre-eminently with the historical sickness (the excess of history). Although imprisoned and sick, it is life nonetheless, and thus harbors that plastic power which can and should make the past serve as a strengthening [*kräftigen*] nourishment but which no longer understands how to do this.[109] The beginning of education, then, is with an unchaining, a liberating, of the life already latent in one. But how?[110] As part of the life in itself youth has the clear-seeing gift of nature which can see this evil and see the paradise of health that is lost. It also has the healing instinct of this same nature through which it can divine how this paradise is to be won back. What can it see in the way of remedies? How can it utilize what it sees and restore the life in itself to health?

b. The remedies youth sees and their use

The historical sickness amounts to a disordering and unbalancing of life's essential factors. The basic antidotes which youth divines to that sickness are thus twofold: the 'unhistorical' and the 'superhistorical'. By 'unhistorical' Nietzsche means here, the art and power [*Kraft*] of being able to forget and of enclosing oneself in a limited horizon. By 'superhistorical' he means here, the powers which lead vision away from becoming to that which gives to existence the character of the eternal and identical-in-meaning, that is, the powers of art and religion.[111] It is by re-establishing the appropriate order, placing the unhistorical in its primacy, and by establishing the appropriate balance, making the historical subordinate and supportive, and reinforcing and consummating this order and balance with the help of the superhistorical,[112] that health could be regained and an elevated and cultured life become possible as a natural outgrowth.

Of course, science sees in these antidotes powers and forces hostile to it. For from its own perspective, the true and correct (hence scientific) view [*Betrachtung*]-- the only acceptable one-- is that view by which one sees everywhere something-become, something-historical, and never something-which-is, something eternal. Science lives in an inherent contradiction to the eternalizing powers of art and religion, just as it hates forgetting (the death of knowing) and as it seeks to cancel any limitation in horizon and to cast humanity into a boundless light-waved sea of becoming that is known-and-familiar [*erkannten*].[113] The unlimited drive of science is an absolutization of one element that is intrinsic to life itself. For life harbors the historical, but in inherent inner tension with the unhistorical and the superhistorical; and it gives its natural shape to itself through the ordered and balanced working of these three conflicting powers. What has taken place in modern times is a disordering and unbalancing wherein the historical, developed now as science, has sought to dominate rather than to be a subordinate but contributing factor to life itself. But human beings can not live at that place to which science pushes them. The avalanche of concepts which science starts takes from humans the foundation of all their certainty and rest, the belief in the enduring and eternal, and thus undermines life, making it weak and fearful. Yet no one doubts, life is the higher and decisive force, the mastering force. For a knowing which denied life would have denied itself, since knowing presupposes life and thus has an interest in its preservation so that it may itself exist.[114]

Science requires, then, a higher supervision and watching over. A hygiene of life belongs close by science, and one of its assertions would read: the unhistorical and the superhistorical are the natural antidotes against the overpowering of life by the historical, against the historical sickness.

c. History as itself helping to heal the sickness

Even if life harbors within itself, and more specifically, within the youth that belongs to it, the capacities for-- and the instinctive discernment of-- the remedies to the sickness it currently suffers, the application of those remedies and the recovery of health will still not be an easy matter. For the antidotes themselves will bring suffering. But such suffering is no proof against the correctness of the chosen means to health. For if properly applied recovery can eventually come.

What is involved in such application? What is the course of such recovery?

The first youthful generation of fighters have the mission of opening the way toward health and an elevated culture, but only that. That mission is accomplished mainly by negation: by shattering and creating scorn and hate for the concepts of 'health' and 'culture' of the present age. This mission will be animated by a presentiment and sense of promise, by a divinatory glimpse into the happiness and beauty which are to come eventually through its efforts-- into the "more beautiful and blessed humanity and culture" which constitute for it the promised land. But its own condition-- that of suffering from the sickness and from the antidotes both-- will be alleviated at best by the feeling of a fighting, excluding, and dividing power at work within itself, of occasional good hours of elevated life-feeling [*erhöhten Lebensgefühle*], and by that confirmation of its own sense of having a stronger health and more natural nature than that of its forefathers which is provided by its inability honestly to use any of the concepts and words of present existence to designate its essence. If such a youthful generation will have no culture yet and thus will be coarse and immoderate, it nonetheless will enjoy the privileges and consolations of youth, and "especially the privilege of brave uncalculating [*unbesonnenen*] honesty and the inspiring consolation of hope"[115].

For such a generation, beyond the superhistorical and unhistorical there is a dual way in which history and the historical may help them in their effort.

To begin with, we have already seen how the recall of the past can function in a life-supportive fashion. In a present in which an excess of historical knowledge is undermining any life which harbors a future, the first way in which such recall can help is to strengthen the moral resolve their youth harbors and thus the drive to oppose that cynicism and sense of powerlessness which acquiesce in the 'it was' and its apparently overwhelming momentum into the future. The invitation of the 'it was' which history teaches is to accept that as not simply fact but as justified fact; in the Hegelian phrase, the real is the rational and the rational is the real. However if history teaches 'it once was', morality teaches 'it should not have been'. There is much that is unacceptable, immoral, in all that is past. Nietzsche uses the early death of Raphael as an example: "morality is offended" here, "such a being should not die".[116] To an apologist of the factual who would say, for example, that Raphael had expressed everything in him, he had no new beauty to create, and so on, Nietzsche responds in scorn for the idolization of the factual and the insensitive ignorance of the creative nature of such a man as Raphael shown in such an apology. And he carries this over to a recent judgment that Goethe, at eighty-two years of age, had outlived himself.

> That the many live and those few no longer live, is nothing but a brutal truth, that is, an incorrigible stupidity, a sheer 'so it was once' over against morality's 'it should not have been so'. Yes, in opposition to morality! For whatever virtue one wants to speak of-- justice, magnanimity, bravery, the wisdom and the compassion of human beings-- in every case a person becomes virtuous by rising against that blind power of facts, against the tyranny of the actual, and subjecting himself to laws which are not the laws of the fluctuation of history. He always swims against the tide of history, whether by combating his passions as the most immediate stupid fact of his existence or by binding himself to honesty as the lie spins its glittering web around him. If history in general were nothing more than 'the world-system of passion and error', humans would have to read it as Goethe advised his readers to read *Werther*: as if it called to them 'be a man and do not follow after me!' Fortunately, however, it also preserves the memory of the great fighters *against history*, that is to say against the blind power of the actual, and puts itself in the pillory by exalting precisely these men as the real historical natures who bothered little with the 'thus it is' so as to follow a 'thus it should be' with a more cheerful pride. Not to bear their generation to the grave, but to found a new generation: that is what impels them ceaselessly forward; and even if they themselves are late-born, there is a way of living which will make this forgotten, coming generations will know them only as first-born.[117]

Historical recall may in a second way amplify its appeal to this moral nerve of human existence and reinforce the hope which life bears with it inherently concerning the future, by calling back to mind in monumental fashion a case of successful cultural achievement which can teach us that we can succeed and also how to begin. Contemporary historical culture makes the Germans of his time self-aware to themselves as coming late in a stream of tradition, and invites them to think of themselves as simply followers in the higher reaches of culture. Nietzsche has pointed to how this sense is given a particular twist: the decisive events have happened, we are latecomers, there is no future ... , but of course, we have arrived at the peak of existence, there is a future in the sense of improvement and progress understood in the terms achieved at that peak. Understood in the broader scope of history, Nietzsche sees this ambivalent attitude as one issue of the possibility which Socrates figured forth. But may not historical recall place this sense of heritage in an even more far-reaching context? Suppose that we contemporary Germans think of ourselves, indeed, as followers, yet not of late antiquity but of early antiquity? Let us congratulate ourselves with having brought the spirit of the Socratic and Alexandrian-Roman culture to a productive peak in our science, our universal history, and so far think of ourselves as successful followers. But then, let us not remain with that alone; let us set our aim higher and further, setting the more difficult task of striving back behind this Alexandrian world and above it, and seeking our prototypes by a courageous look into the original ancient Greek world [*Urwelt*] of the great, natural, and human. There we would find the reality of an essentially unhistorical culture that was unspeakably rich and full of life. In such a recall and in an effort to follow this people and their effort at that time of beginning, could we not find their success in creating a new and vital culture to be a reinforcement to the effort we need to make now and a support for our hope for a future of our own? In this way, could we not learn what it would be for us Germans to be and become ourselves? To be first-born in a new venture?

As Nietzsche grasps the situation of the Greeks, there were centuries when they were in a similar danger to that of contemporary Germans. Their 'culture' was a chaos of foreign forms and ideas (Semitic, Babylonian, Lydian, Egyptian), and their religion a battle of the gods of the whole (Middle) East, somewhat as 'German culture' and religion is in his age a struggling chaos of all the West and of all past ages. And yet, thanks to the Delphic Apollo and his saying ('know yourself'), the Hellenic culture that emerged was no mere aggregate. "The Greeks gradually learned *to organize the chaos* by (in accordance with the Delphic teaching) reflecting back on themselves (that is, on their genuine [*echten*] needs) and by letting what were merely seeming-[*Schein*-] needs die out." In this way they did not remain the overloaded inheritors and epigoni of the whole East, but regained possession of themselves. Indeed, after a difficult struggle with themselves in which they carried through a practical interpretation [*practische Auslegung*] of that saying, they became the most blessed enrichers and increasers of their inherited treasures and the first-born and model of all coming culture-peoples.[118]

This is a parable for each individual among us. We know a life in ourselves-- the life in the youth among us, a life not yet developed and expressed in a culture but only suppressed and weakened by the current 'culture' and educational system. Following the Delphic saying, each of us must reflect back upon our own genuine needs. Our honesty, our good [*tuchtiger*] and truthful character, must rebel against all that is being merely imitatively spoken, learned, done. Thus that honesty will open the way to the achievement of a culture which is something other than a decoration of life, that is, at bottom, a dissimulation and a disguise, for all adornment conceals what is adorned. It will make possible culture as a "new and improved nature", without inner and outer in dissociation from each other, without dissimulation and convention, culture as a unanimity [*Einhelligkeit*] between living, thinking, seeming and willing. In this way, we will learn out of our own experience that it was the higher strength [*Kraft*] of the *ethical* nature through which the Greeks gained victory over all other cultures, and that every increase in truthfulness must also be a preparatory furthering of *true* culture. And this is so, however much on occasion this truthfulness may damage the cultivatedness [*Gebildetheit*] currently respected, or even help in the downfall of a whole decorative culture.[119]

Nonetheless, for the first generation of fighters, Nietzsche anticipates only a preparing the way for such an achievement of culture, not the achieving itself. Thus until the cure is carried to this point of completion, such human beings will be more ignorant than the 'educated' human beings of the present. For they will have unlearned many things, and will have lost interest in much which the 'educated' human beings of today want to know-- even in good things. Eventually however, at the end-point of this healing process, they will have become "*human beings* again, and have ceased to be human-like aggregates"[120].

In short: it is the moral heart of youth-- of ourselves at the time of assuming responsibility for our own lives and for lives that are to be creative out of themselves--- which is crucial to the resolution of the crisis of the present and the coming of a new and vital future, and it is in reinforcing that heart by historical recall, particularly of the Greeks and their cultural achievement, that the history which otherwise is helping undermine contemporary life by its mass of knowledge can instead serve life well.

CHAPTER 6
Schopenhauer as Educator

This is one of a pair of meditations in which Nietzsche presents two figures important in his own life and thought. In the way he renders them he brings forward matters of consequence for understanding the becoming-- personal, historical, and evolutionary-- in which we each are involved. In the course of doing that, he adumbrates in further ways and in further contexts the initial ideas of time and temporality which we found being developed, explicitly but also implicitly, in UHH.

A. Youth and morality

As in UHH, so in SE: the youthful Nietzsche speaks about life from the perspective of youth, and concentrates attention on the maturational work of that time of life and on how we must conceive our nature to be if (as it seems) the becoming natural to us implicates us in morality.

1. Maturation, the call of conscience, and education

The onward movement of life realized in our active engagement with things brings us on a course of our own becoming in which we are meant eventually to come to be ourselves in the fulness of our selfhood. Central to that becoming is a maturation of ourselves as human beings that is focused in the evolution of the responsive powers that compose our decision-making and -executing capacity. That evolution involves transformations of this capacity, so that the course of the actualization of life in ourselves is not simply straightforward but involves metamorphic turns. Life takes its first crucial maturational turn in youth, and enters upon this in the voicing then of the call of conscience, that is, in the sounding of life's summons to take responsibility for ourselves as the unique individuals we at bottom know ourselves to be. The turn is continued in one way or another when upon hearing this call we make some type of response and move life onward accordingly.

The call of conscience is heard by us with an initial natural responsiveness which disposes us to heed it and to follow out its accompanying aspirational pointer, which intimates a higher-and-better selfhood as ours and a happiness which is open to us only by our coming to be ourselves in the intimated fulness. Despite the fact that our initial responsiveness disposes us to heed that call (we find it appealing, and want to secure what it intimates is meant for us), we ordinarily turn away from the assumption of responsibility called for and suppress the knowledge we have of our own uniqueness, in effect disavowing our individuality. We do this out of fear of the hardships which unconditional honesty would impose upon us. Responding to the call of conscience means, for example, liberating ourselves from what in ourselves is not really ourselves-- from the things which we have taken into ourselves from our environs as we have grown up and which we have allowed (and continue to allow) to function in such way that what we do, think, and desire, does not really come from ourselves, from our very own inmost selves, but rather from the ego which forms our everyday 'I' and whose determinateness reflects these inadequately-incorporated things. It means, as well, laboring at the tasks and duties which the uniqueness of our being implicates us in. Only profound honesty and commitment will enable us effectively to become the unique beings we are; but the difficulties such response would involve us in intimidate us. And so, instead of taking responsibility for ourselves in an honest and courageous way, we take an easy way out and allow ourselves to be ruled by convention and public opinion, in this way embodying an inertia in regard to our essential task as responsible beings. Thus we live as mass-men, timidly subject to our neighbors, imprisoned by public opinion without and by the components of convention that we have taken into ourselves and allow to dominate us.

This is not a comfortable condition for us, given the dishonesty, the cowardice, the self-deception, it involves us in. It is all the more uncomfortable because complicit with the call of conscience and the knowledge that we are unique is a recognition of our existence as a one-time affair. This-- and in particular, the wondrous and enigmatic fact that, with a brief today of our own, we exist now (and not at some other time) amidst the infinity of time-- means that our brief today is the only time we have in which to show why and to what end we came into existence now and at no other time. If our life is to mean anything-- and we stand under the pressure to live in a way that brings meaning--, it will be in terms of some larger purpose we serve and it is during this brief time of our present existence that we must find and serve that purpose. This recognition of the one-time character of our existence reinforces and adds urgency to the call of conscience to be answerable before ourselves for our existence and for some purpose which it serves, and thereby strengthens in us the will to take charge of our existence and not let it be like a thoughtless meaningless accident. Even so, we usually turn a deaf ear to this call of conscience and dismiss the ghostly reminders of it which the things of our present existence continually make.

If and when-- as happens on occasion-- we do find the courage attentively to listen to this call and to initiate a response to the desire arising in us to assume responsibility for ourselves despite the difficulties, we still need to interpret for ourselves the pointer of aspiration toward the higher-and-better, to find the standard and law under which our life is lived as our own, and to travel on the unique path for life's actualization which only we, as the unique individuals we are, can take. Nietzsche suggests that there are certain times which point us to our genuine selves in some emphatic and important way. Those are the times of love, times when we find some person, some activity, some place, that draws out our love and engages us actively on its strength. Thus

> let the young soul look back on life with the question, 'What have you truly loved up to now, what has drawn on your soul, what has dominated it and made it joyful at the same time?' Put up the series of these venerated objects before you, and perhaps they will show you, through their essential-being and their sequence, a law, the fundamental law of your authentic self. Compare these objects, see how one complements, broadens, surpasses and transforms the other. See how they form a stepladder on which you have climbed so far toward your self; for your true essential-being does not lie hidden deep inside you but immeasurably high above you, or at least above what you usually take to be your 'I'.[1]

In youth as the time when aspiration and the longing to be ourselves naturally emerge, our various loves (past and present) can be keys to our selfhood because our love is a responsive expression of something having touched that core in ourselves which is our very own essential-being, what we are given as being from the start. Thus in drawing us out and giving us some concrete shape, such loves are disclosing to us "the true original meaning [*Ursinn*] and the basic stuff [*Grundstoff*] of our own essential-being [*Wesens*]"[2]. That is, they are educating us, teaching us who we are, what we are made of, what we were meant to be. This is the beginning and basis of that further process of cultivating--

of shaping [*Bildung*]-- which eventually makes us cultured human beings. The secret of all such cultivating [*Bildung*] is that the educating whereby the cultural transformation to and of our being is brought about is not an adding on from the outside but a liberating of what is within, a releasing in the manner, on the one hand, of removing what would attack and threaten the budding growth, and on the other hand, in the manner of providing the supportive conditions-- the light and warmth and rain-- under which the bud may develop out of itself and eventually flower.

Ours, then, is a becoming which is meant to take place with the help of a learning on our part, and one to be achieved not simply within circumscribing circumstance but with the aid of circumstantial presences which support and foster that learning. Indeed, in recognition of this about ourselves as human beings, we create various educational systems by which we-- the grown-up-- give early assistance to our young. Thus other (the grown-up) human beings function as educators for us (the young) and thereby become important contributors to our becoming. Recalling his own initial youthful thinking on this matter of education as an affair by which we human beings are made to be human, each in our distinctive individuality, Nietzsche remembers in youth being already convinced that proper education for us in the time of youth and the crucial turn in our maturation which is taking place then is one that would help "transform the whole human being into a living, animated system of suns and planets" and would "discover the law of its higher mechanism".[3] Put less metaphorically, this means: in some cases, proper education at this time of life would develop the central force or strength in us, helping it to dominate and organize the others but not allowing it to disrupt them; but in most cases, it would develop and integrate the variety of forces involved in our being. In all cases, it would foster such development that the human being became in actuality an integrated active being who is centered in some particular productive activity (say, philosophy) but is marked by a variety of different and potentially conflicting particular capacities and drives; these latter have become so developed and integrated as to give each scope but to make of the whole being a harmonized, productive, and cultured, human being who is empowered as such a being to the extent of his/her own nature.

What is required of any apt educational effort by others is that it provide support for youth's following out the call of conscience, and thus for the moral effort required of the youthful if they are successfully to heed that call. As it turned out for the youthful Nietzsche thinking of education in this way, the main educative force which actually fostered this learning in himself was not the educational system current in Germany. It was rather individuals, and in particular, in his youth one individual, Schopenhauer. What was educative about him was not so much what he said (his book) as his own being as it was conveyed to Nietzsche. Speaking of "the first, as it were physiological impression, which Schopenhauer brought forth in me, that magical out-pouring of the innermost strength [*Kraft*] of one natural creature [*Naturgewächses*] upon another that ensues at the first and slightest touch"[4], he focuses on the moral character of the man as what impressed: his honesty, his steadfastness in being himself, and the cheering sense of him as a conqueror of the greatest difficulties. What was educative most fundamentally then was the moral character evident in him and his embodiment of that uniqueness which in meaning is what we are to learn in our own case. In contrast, in the educational system which was supposed to serve as supportive element in the learning needed, Nietzsche recalls finding nothing adequate to the task. What formed the central inadequacy as he sees it in SE (he emphasized another inadequacy in UHH) was the absence of thoughtful human beings who epitomized "creative morality" in the present and whose deep concern for moral problems ennobled them and made them moral exemplars-- precisely what he found in Schopenhauer.[5] This was an inadequacy especially significant for the educating of a human being whose dominant force is to find its outworking in philosophy. For the question at the heart of youth and of the responsibility for ourselves which it is the maturational task of youth to initiate-- the moral question, 'how ought I to live and act?'-- is the question central to philosophy as well.

2. Nature and morality

The morality which Nietzsche sees Schopenhauer attesting in his being and which he finds himself called to strengthen and perfect in himself in response to the call of conscience is a morality of responsibility. This is a morality which is meant naturally to take its first shape in youth. In its primordial reflexive side, it is one of a self-responsibility which is commensurate with the sense of our life and being as meant for an actualization to be achieved in and through our own activity and to be worked out by us concretely over our life-time. The beginnings of the moral life are in youth's response to the call of conscience, in its responsive wanting to bear responsibility for our own lives by taking them upon ourselves and seeing to their unfolding in accord with the primordial meaning meant to be realized in them. Our primordial obligation as moral beings, then, involves us in the self-aware acceptance of our lives upon ourselves and, with that, of the task of self-consciously guiding ourselves in the living of those lives in such way as to bring us to be in our fullest and deepest selfhood. Wanting to be responsible for our lives, accepting the claim of our own essential-being upon us as something meant to be realized in and through our activity, and resolving to carry out into the future this responsibility which none but ourselves can assume and carry out (for no one can live our lives for us or bring us to become ourselves apart from our own responsible participation): it is in the dynamic of this decision-making that we find ourselves in the midst of morality as something which emerges naturally from within ourselves. It is 'natural' in that it is called forth as ingredient in the dialectic of the unfolding of our human nature in the course of-- and in dependence upon-- our participation in activity, and therefore is nothing laid upon us from the outside, by other human beings, by our society, by a god, or whatever.

Because we awake to this responsibility only as already having lived for a while and having become readied (in our growing up) for such assumption, we find ourselves at the start under obligation to think on our natural becoming in both a future and a past reference. That is, even before we are capable of assuming responsibility for our lives we have already achieved a measure of our becoming, and in the course of that have also incorporated into ourselves much from the outside which we may or may not have made truly our own rather than simply submitted to and accepted into our development. Moreover, we are in the process of becoming-- needing to become-- something more than we currently are, of completing a becoming in directions which are at most intimated to us by our loves and now in our aspiration and longing for what is a higher self that is our own being as fulfilled, as fully ourselves. In this time of youth, we must sort out what is *genuinely* ourselves from what is not, and what are *genuinely* our own directions and what are not. Because this sorting out and the carrying through on our reaching toward our higher and fuller selves involves us in hardship and in a network of troubles and burdens, this effort requires of us certain virtues, certain strengths, a certain moral character: in short, a certain moral core to the way we live and act now that we are assuming responsibility for ourselves.

In this dynamic at the start of moral life, then, we find certain powers and strengths needed which every human being needs if the task of maturation is to be carried through to completion, and we find other powers and strengths which may be required or may not, depending on the singularity of the human beings involved. Thus the demands of the task which each of us faces as human beings are e.g. for honesty with ourselves, for attentiveness to the claims and nature of our own essential-being, for thoughtfulness and wisdom in the understanding of those claims and nature, for courage in the pursuit of such understanding and in the following out of our understanding in deeds. All of these represent universally-human moral values with roots in our nature as human beings, and the life in us summons us to develop and employ them in this reflexive reference. But this task is for each of us to assume our own life and essential-being, and when it comes to the components of the uniqueness in each case, then the virtues called for so that we may become that in particular, the strengths demanded for this, and the actions and directions of effort that must be pursued, will vary. Our own creativity and fruitfulness as distinctive human beings being what we must each realize, morality in this natural reflexive dimension must *also* in some measure be relative to our own distinctive natures and destinies, which call for different strengths in different human beings. What is a virtue in one of us may not be a virtue in someone else, for virtue here is a functional strength relative to our nature and what it demands for its actualization.

There is another element in our being-human which Nietzsche points to as coming to light as we discover ourselves in youth and find ourselves wanting to be responsible for our own lives. This element gives to the morality that is called for a communal side which complements the reflexive side and the meaning of responsibility as self-responsibility. We human beings are meant to interconnect and interlink with each other essentially, out of that very being-human which is our own. It is not simply that the powers which make up our distinctive natures are such as involve us with other human beings unavoidably, both for them to be developed and for them to be exercised (most involve us in joint undertakings with other human beings). It is also that the responsive power through which we share in action and life out of ourselves and through which we eventually find our own lives laying claim upon us also opens us to other human beings as claiming us as well. Wanting to be responsible for our own lives, we want also to reach out to and find others in their selfhood, in their being as developing centers of life and action existing in their own right, in their being as other and as (in that otherness) to be joined with as kin and companions. This is the moral element at the heart of what Nietzsche speaks of as a people, which is not simply a social group but an ongoing community of developing human beings connecting on this moral foundation.

Out of our own natures, then, we are meant to find ourselves wanting others to become and grow, and feeling their being as it registers in our feelings at this time in life calling forth in us (as responsive beings) a love toward them as companions in this venture of life, as themselves involved in the same coming-to-be under the demands of their own natures as we are. Morality in this natural communal reference has two aspects.

First: Assuming responsibility for one's own being and being responsible in one's recognition and acknowledgement of others are rather different things. We can not assume responsibility *for* others in regard to *their own* lives, for we all share this condition of having to become responsible for ourselves. Thus when others have the claim upon us which evokes our love as a natural response, a certain kind of respect is called for: the claim is e.g. upon us for our help, for our being responsibly concerned for a becoming which is not our own and yet which may well need us or be helped by us. But respect involves recognition of the limits of help, in the integrity of the person in question. Some sorts of 'help' are not help at all but attempts to impose things on others 'for their own good' but in violation of their integrity.

Second: We cannot assume responsibility for our own being, let alone be responsible in our acknowledgement of others, except in the concrete, in undertaking certain things. Most undertakings (indeed, all undertakings, in some degree) essentially involve us with other human beings as needing each other for the undertakings, the projects, to be pursued. Now whatever we do in such pursuit both affects others, makes demands on others, and at the same time draws ourselves forth into the concrete and helps us to become through our participation in them. Where our action involves us with others, then, it must not only come out of the reflexive dimension of morality, and not only express the moral qualities that are involved in respect for others, but it stands under the demand that it do justice to all concerned. Within the bounds of the individual destinies of each, then, we must join together in a just and vital ongoing community of ourselves as diverse.

3. The temporality of youth

In his discussion of the crucial maturational turn of youth with its focus on the emergence of the call of conscience and thence on the morality which our human nature enters us into at this time in our life, Nietzsche is developing in particular terms an account of one facet of the temporality of our being. To see more fully what he is doing and to elicit in greater detail the facet of temporality which is involved, let us consider more closely his interpretation of the maturational turn of youth and note how it is a kind of beginning-again of life.

As Nietzsche has been-- and continues, in SE-- accounting for it, ours is the temporal being of an active participant in existence whose activity is concerned by something at stake so that participation in activity is for us a venturing, a risking, a hazarding, in which something is to be secured. The initial side of our temporality is to be found in the continuous spontaneity or initiative whereby, as time actualizes itself in its own ongoing, we are accomplishing in and through our complex involvement in activity the concomitant forward moving of our own existence as active beings and thereby the continuing actualization of the life in ourselves. But that temporality has a second side, manifest in the fact that while our (human) capacity for initiative is ever being claimed by an at-stake and is ever responsive to such claiming in its forming and carrying out of activity, the powers that operate in such capacity, and such capacity itself, are not themselves constituted as identical from the beginning to the end of our lives. Rather with exercise they change, and do so as meant to develop from an initial form which represents a relative impotence in our capacity and to evolve toward and eventually into a fulness in capacity for our responsible participation in the affairs of existence. As the just-completed sketch shows, in SE Nietzsche's account of the phased development of this capacity and of the initial transformation taking place in youth expands on what was set forth in UHH, making it more determinate with such notions as the call of conscience and of the primordial meant-to-be and basic stuff of our being.

According to his account, such phased development is made possible by-- and intended in-- a temporal beginning of ourselves which harbors, as the core of our active being, what he calls our essential-being [*Wesen*]. This is the heart of the initial nature and constitution of ourselves as the determinate and individual active living beings that we are. That constitution is, overall, a complex unity of actuality and potentiality which is natured to be the enabling matrix for the temporally-ongoing spontaneity whereby we initiate and carry through activity. Included in this complex is not only the many-sided potential of our being which our initiative operates responsively amidst and whose actualization over time our initiative mediates, but also the primordial meant-to-be which relates to the development and integration of the varied stuff of that potential that is to occur over time in the course of and in dependence upon our activity. Finally, included in the initial actuality of our being is (among other things) the native impetus of the life in us toward 'more life' and its register in the responsiveness of our initiative.

Given our initial constitution and its core essential-being, we are fitted temporally for a 'becoming' in which, in virtue of our continuous active participation in existence and how that takes place and in complicity with what we are interacting with, we are meant gradually to come more fully to be ourselves and do so in such way that, supposing that circumstance allows and supports and our own participation enables this, we concretely actualize the potential in ourselves in keeping with the primordial meant-to-be. Central in this actualization and definitive for the maturation which pertains to our becoming is the gradual actualization of the decision-making and -executing capacity whereby we take part in activity; it is in virtue of the development of this capacity that we eventually come to be capable of hearing the call of conscience, of reflecting on the problematic of our existence, and of resolving one way or another to heed or evade the call to assume our lives upon ourselves and move ahead in them in this-way rather than in that-way.

As we have seen in discussing our spontaneity as it is set forth in UHH, the initially crucial factor for understanding the maturational development of our decision-making and -executing capacity, is the receptivity involved in that capacity. If we observe closely what constitutes this receptivity, it is first and foremost a three-sided power of feeling.

The first side is the immediate receptivity which is our openness to existence as involving an at-stake that concerns us in our active engagement, that is, that bears on us in the forming of our initiative and lays claim upon our efforts. In so bearing and claiming, the at-stake makes it such that in our engagement with things we are aware in our responsive initiative that something matters and that we are accordingly to take part in this-way rather than in that-way.

The second is the immediate receptivity with which we conjointly receive other active beings in their presence to us and receive ourselves as we are functioning in our interaction with others.

The third side is what makes our receptivity to beings be richer than mere sensation; for our register involves the immediate affective inflections whereby we are moved in initial inclination this-way or that-way toward this-or-that action (emotions, for example, or pleasure and pain). These moving-forces form our register of the apparent direct incitement toward activity internal to the confluence of circumstance and ourselves as active beings currently constituted and functioning as we are.

In virtue of the reach of this three-sided complex of feeling, we are continually receiving into ourselves and registering in the receptivity that is part of our initiative-capacity both the manifold of immediate presence (that of others and ourselves as active beings) and the at-stake in its immediate claiming force. In the decision-making and -executing which takes shape from this starting-point, we responsively admit this global register of immediately-felt claim and immediately-felt presence *in some fashion* and *under some interpretation* into the forming of a decision, and on the basis of that decision venture a response that reflects this admitting (somehow) of the force of such presence and such claim into the resolve with which we initiate activity.

Now our decision-making and -executing capacity has a developmental character, in virtue of which we begin in relative impotence. It takes time for exercise to build this capacity and develop the powers that operate in it, and by virtue of the nature of those incompletely developed powers we are unable (during the initial part of that time) to register in our conscious awareness the claiming of the at-stake *in differentiation from* the presence felt in sensation and affection, and then for a further while we are unable to relate any differentiated register of this to our own life as 'our own' so that the at-stake becomes apparent as bearing on our life, not simply on particular actions. During this time before youth, the development of our capacity for decision-making and -executing from its initial form involves, in the second and third sides of this three-sided receptive power, the amplifying of our register of others and ourselves to include more and more things and to involve qualitatively greater sensitivity to things, so that as we develop we become immediately responsive differently and in increasingly complex fashion to more and different things. But amidst all the change in what and how we are registering in this reference, there is the ever-presence of the drive of the life in ourselves toward 'more life', thus the register of our wanting to live and grow and gain fuller participation in life.[6]

Now the evolution of our receptivity is not restricted to the increasingly-different-and-complex register of things in the second and third sides of that receptivity, but involves also alteration over time in the character of the register on the first side, that of the claiming of the at-stake within our overall receptivity. There is indeed constancy here in this sense: the responsive receiving of the at-stake ever takes in the latter in the immediate mode of need (*Not,* in one of the many meanings of the term which Nietzsche's thought avails itself of). "Need" as meant here has the force of a *claiming*: the at-stake concerns us as claiming our energies and efforts. Now from the start of life on, we are ever venturing responsively to the at-stake as concerning us in this fashion, as registering in its claiming of us. But initially we are unable to register this imperative claim except in some *undifferentiated* fashion such that it is indistinguishable in our ears from the register of the sensual and emotional (for example, of the urgency of desire).[7] In youth, however, we have reached the developmental time when our overall receptivity is meant to have evolved in its elements to the place where our register of the at-stake in its imperative immediacy is for the first time able to appear within the global immediacy in clear differentiation from the impress of things in the (increasingly complex) sensual and emotional sides of our receptivity. This differentiated register takes place in conjunction with two other things which also belong to the time of youth, namely, the emerging aspirational inflection to life's drive toward 'more'-- its pointing to the higher-and-better which is to be realized as ours-- and the discovery of our own lives as 'our own'. In this conjoint manifestation with the emergence of our own life *as 'our own'* and a *distinctive affair* in its own right (not simply a matter of doing-this or doing-that) and of the aspirational inflection of life's drive toward 'more life', we find the distinctness of the register of the at-stake sounding in us as *obligating* us *expressly* to initiate activity in the attempt to realize the aspirationally-intimated higher-and-better selfhood in this life of '*our own*' and to make this selfhood the *to-be-secured-issue* of a responsibility we are taking on in assuming the life in us on ourselves as 'our own'.

According to Nietzsche's account, then, the initial maturational evolution of ourselves is by nature the evolution of ourselves in our practical capacity for feeling, thus of ourselves as sensitive human beings. And when this evolution has developed to the place where we enter upon the first basic transformation in our decision-making and -executing capacity, the leading edge for the transformation is one related to sensitivity.[8] Now in this account, the transformed register of the at-stake which initiates the maturational turn, while achieving in youth a differentiation from the sensual and the emotional registers, leaves its claiming still undifferentiated from the urgency of life's own drive toward 'more life' (and now, 'more' as 'higher-and-better'). This undifferentiation reflects that the receptive side of our responsive powers is still incompletely developed at this time in our growth. Because SE is a youthful work in which Nietzsche is seeking to speak in keeping with the experience of youth, we find him interpreting the imperative bearing of the at-stake and its register in youth as a matter of *life's summons* of ourselves toward an engagement with things which would not only involve our assuming our life upon ourselves but would also concretely begin the effort that brings us toward the fuller life which aspiration points us to. That is, in his idea of the call of conscience the imperative voice calling us to assume responsibility is *that of the life in ourselves*. In so reading the matter, his very faithfulness to the experience of youth perpetuates in his way of interpreting the matter the continuing undifferentiation of the urgent-toward-fuller-life and the imperative which is part of the experience of that time of life.

In virtue of this transformation in our receptivity in which life is found to summon us, the living, to assume responsibility, we are entered into a fairly radical development in the temporality of our lives. For in that summons as something first emerging for our hearing and heeding in youth, we are called to enter upon a peculiar sort of beginning-again of our life. For here, in the midst of a life we are already living and at some distance from its beginning, we have found ourselves for the *first* time awakened *distinctly* to the bounded life-whole in the middle of whose actualization we presently are; and in that awakening, we have found ourselves coming into immediate and distinct cognizance of the life in ourselves in its *temporal wholeness*: in its currently being lived, its having been lived from its beginning, and its yet to be lived before its end. But it is not simply that we find ourselves (at this in-the-middle place) aware of life in this temporal wholeness in that sense; because that wholeness includes the beginning and end that temporally enclose the living, we are aware of the impending of death and (implicitly to the meant-to-be that concerns our original basic stuff) of the givenness of our beginning. And in virtue of the character of that awakening to our over-arching temporality from this place in the middle of life's ongoing-- that in it we find ourselves as bounded beings *summoned* to *assume* our life on ourselves *as 'ours' and 'our responsibility'*--, we find ourselves venturing *now for the first time* on a self-aware *assumption of this whole* and committing ourselves, in the course of our concrete response in life ahead, to making life's actualization in keeping with its aspirational intimation be a *matter of our responsibility*.

This *beginning of life as our own* and *our responsibility* is at once a new beginning and a beginning again. It is new as a 'for the first time' self-aware relation to the life in us in its temporal wholeness. It is an 'again' as a recall back to the at-stake, the primordial meant-to-be and the basic stuff, that have been involved from the start in our living as the basis of our engaging with things: a recall whose register, in the responsiveness in our initiative, is accepting of this basis as one for 'our own' life ahead. In its newness, this beginning contrasts with the (original) beginning in virtue of its distinctive register of the at-stake and our primordial being: the distinct summoning or imperative presence of the at-stake and the bearing of our primordial being under that presence is significantly different from that in the undeveloped responsive capacities which were ours at that start. In its 'again', this beginning involves our commitment to carrying life forward in a re-affirmation of its original basis, but this time *with developed capacities and experience that were not ours at the start*; for we do not begin this new life in a personal void, but in an assumption of our past life as now 'our own', including thereby our experience of life so far and the dispositions and capacities that have been developed in our past. In our re-gaining the matrix of the original beginning and our acknowledging and re-affirming it now as ours into the future, we who are *now* an 'ourselves' defined by a summons, by an aspiration which points us into a future that is new and different from the past, and by such developed capacities as we actually have, find aspiration's pointer as a lure and standard which works in two-fold fashion on the past we are assuming. On the one hand, we find its pointer into the higher self implied in our original native stuff and its meant-to-be convoking various dispositions and capacities already built up in the past, and (perhaps also) confirming various extant loves which have an affinity to it and which are partially disclosive of the self in ourselves; in this way what in our past is genuinely our own already and most readily serviceable for the future becomes discernible. On the other hand, we find in its light much in ourselves that does not appear serviceable, and in its appeal for our commitment to its actualization we find the call to self-criticism, self-purification, and the dismissal of what is not alive with a life kindred to the higher life being intimated, that our future may be realized with as much of our energy and resources as possible, including those which we need to liberate from the forms that have captured them in the past.

Thus in our response to the call of conscience we find ourselves implicated in a task of self-development relating to our life-whole, and that means both to the futural side of our becoming and, for the sake of this, to the past that is being borne along with us and is bearing for better or worse on our venturing and on that realization of the higher-and-better which is our commitment now. Our task is to take charge of our own lives and to enter upon a responsible *way of life enduringly attentive to* the concrete securing of the at-stake in our *lives* and not simply to engage in a particular transient deed and do so aiming only at an achievement at-stake in that doing. This time, we begin with different actual capacity than we had at the start of life, and in particular, with an amplified capacity whose operation is conditioned by (and can draw upon) an experience of our own personal past and a development of our initial capacity which reflects and still carries that past-- none of which was available to us at the start. The precondition for the success of any such re-beginning is that this developed capacity, evolved in the course of that time of life that is now ending, be such as is empowered (in conjunction with current circumstance) to make an effective response to the summons in question.

To the challenge that confronts us now, we may or may not initially be equal. For there is no guarantee of our having developed to the place where the inward side of this empowerment-precondition is actually present in us.[9] But given this regaining of the original basis and the new actualization of life that is to be founded in this basis, and given the re-integration of the past into the ongoing of life under aspiration as well as the ongoing clarification of the basis itself and of what seems to point us concretely into the called-for future: given these things, then if we have strength enough to be equal to the summons, living 'our own' life will involve living in response to the at-stake in its immediacy as claiming and with ultimate regard (for a while, at least) to the aspirationally-disclosed potential in ourselves and the meant-to-be which has related to it from the start.

I say "for a while" with the thought in mind that for the moment and for a while into the future, what has opened up for us now, while it involves such capacity and such presence as make possible for the first time a basis for the unfolding of our life as 'our own' and with it the task of responsibility, may also intimate (but not disclose yet in fully differentiated fashion) a future transformation as radical or even more radical than that of youth. What we visualize in anticipation as the culmination of this venture toward the higher-and-better we are now undertaking has in fact unseen sides to it which, as they become visible in the course of time, portend the end of this (early adult) phase and the beginning of another. In SE, however, Nietzsche's attention is captured by the time of life in which he found himself in the reflection being shared in that work. Thus his account (so far as we have considered it) seems to intimate that in our re-beginning we have been opened up to a (potentially) boundless progress. At the very least, that is how in youth it does indeed seem.

B. Youth, the 'times', and the future

Nietzsche first encountered Schopenhauer when, in youth, discovering the call of conscience in himself and recognizing the need to learn how to live in keeping with this call, he was finding himself distressed by the lack in those around him of authentic reflection on questions of morality. The impact of this philosophic man on him was strong. Central to it was a sort of "magical outpouring" of "innermost strength [*Kraft*]" which inspired confidence. Here was a mature human being, a "whole harmonious unconstrained and uninhibited natural being that hangs and moves around his own pivot"[10], whose very being came across (even through a book) and touched Nietzsche in his own essential-being. He had by good fortune found an educator of the sort he was seeking-- so it seemed.

1. Schopenhauer and moral education

Important in the discovery was that it was a mature and thoughtful human being that he had encountered, someone who embodied in himself and in his life and actions a fulfillment of nature, of a moral and philosophical nature both. He *lived* the law of philosophy, as UHH claimed that a philosopher must do and as SE reiterates. But his educative force lay mostly in this manifestation and its attestation not simply of the positive elements of such fulfillment but of the moral strength to cope with the various dangers which a human being with such a nature and potential greatness must face. "To live at all means to be in danger."[11] And all the more is this so if the living being is a true and great philosopher.

Some of such dangers, Nietzsche speaks of as constitutional, and thus not peculiar to Schopenhauer but such as any other human being with a philosophic nature must face: dangers of isolation from other human beings, of despair of truth (especially in the face of the Kantian claims concerning the limits of knowledge), and of intellectual and moral hardening in the face of limitations (moral and talent-wise) in oneself and one's will. Indeed, at least two of these constitutional dangers (that of isolation, and that of intellectual and moral hardening) threaten each of us in some measure, even if our nature is not philosophic in its main bent. For isolation threatens each and all in the measure in which we are responsive to the productive uniqueness we each have; not only are we drawn by it on our own path apart from others, but we also find others-- the lazy ones among them-- responding in their feel for what is happening to us by feeling threatened and withdrawing, to make even more sharply apparent that solitude is now our lot. Likewise, the hardening which comes with losing touch with the aspiration and longing that alone enable the fruitful development of our productive capacity and uniqueness threatens because it is only by a venturing which is risky and liable to eventuate in our becoming lost that we can keep touch with our aspiration; and if we do become lost and are not able to regain touch and find our way again, our lot is that of the disenchanted, even cynical, the failed and the bitter, the non-productive. Having responsibility for ourselves means knowing ourselves to be endangered, threatened by things in our venturing and in danger of losing ourselves if we fail in that venturing. Thus despite the distance between ourselves and his being as genius, Schopenhauer can also support us by his attestation of moral character in facing such dangers and can help educate us to the possibility of surmounting them.

2. Education concerning the 'times'

Other dangers which Schopenhauer faced and surmounted were due to the times he lived in: for example, the valuelessness of the humanity around him, which valuelessness was liable to color his judgment and his assessment of the value of existence itself. Again, Schopenhauer can help educate those of us who can respond to him about our times, as well as about ourselves so far as we have incorporated the times into ourselves; for over against and in contrast to him, the times become all the more clearly apparent in their true character.

Nietzsche's sketch of the times in SE complements and echoes his accounts in BT and UHH, but as in those essays, so here: it has its own emphasis. While the focus is upon the complete uprooting and destruction of culture, he places that in the larger historical and social context.

> We live in the age of atoms, of atomistic chaos. In the Middle Ages the hostile forces were pretty much held together by the church and, through the strong pressure it exerted, were to some extent assimilated with one another. When the bond broke and the pressure relaxed, they rebelled against one another. The Reformation declared many things to be *adiaphora*, domains which were not to be determined by religious thoughts ... . From then on, the divide spread

wider and wider. Nowadays the crudest and most evil forces, the egoism of the money-makers and the military despots, determine almost everything on earth. In the hands of the despots, the state certainly makes an attempt (as does the egoism of the money-makers) to organize everything anew out of itself and to bind and constrain all those mutually hostile forces: that is, it wants human beings to render it the same idolatry they formerly rendered the church. With what success? We have still to learn; we are, in any case, even now still in the ice-filled stream of the Middle Ages; it has thawed and has fallen into violent destructive movement. Ice-floe piles on ice-floe, all the banks have been inundated and are threatened. The revolution is absolutely unavoidable, and it will be the atomistic revolution; but what are the smallest indivisible basic constituents of human society?[12]

And again, after painting a picture of modern life in its increasing worldliness and cultural barbarism he points to a darker side.

There are certainly forces there, tremendous forces, but savage, primal and wholly merciless. One gazes upon them with a fearful expectation, as though gazing into the cauldron of a witch's kitchen: at any moment it can spark and flash and herald dreadful apparitions. For a century we have been preparing for absolutely fundamental convulsions; and if there have recently been attempts to oppose this deepest of modern inclinations, to collapse or to explode, with the constitutive force of the so-called nation state, the latter too will for a long time serve only to augment the universal insecurity and sense of being threatened. That individuals behave as though they knew nothing of all these anxieties does not mislead us; their restlessness reveals how well they know of them; they think with a haste and with an exclusive preoccupation with themselves such as human beings have never before thought, they build and plant for their own day alone, and the pursuit of happiness is never greater than when it has to be caught today or tomorrow, because perhaps by the day after tomorrow there will be no more hunting at all.[13]

3. Education to culture

The dynamic in this movement that is engulfing modern man is an egoism that has been made the ultimate horizon of life. The issue of this movement in the times contemporary to Nietzsche is a widespread anxiety and insecurity which constitute a kind of emergency so far as concerns humanity and human greatness. For the human inherently involves-- as youth attests-- a reaching for the higher-and-better, for a nobility and greatness, which is quite contrary to any and all selfishness or egoism. In this regard, the Schopenhauer who inspired the young Nietzsche embodied one ideal type of humanity, although not the only one: there are types imaged by Goethe and Rousseau, for example, which have emerged in modern times and are also relevant to modern human beings. But for a philosophic nature, and indeed in some respects for modern man generally given the moral vacillation and vacuity at the heart of modern life, Schopenhauer's is the most compelling educative image. At the heart of Schopenhauerian man is the will to truth, the courage to assume the suffering that arises in virtue of the pursuit of truth, and the eventual transfiguration of his being in which, having heeded the admonition of conscience and realized the productive uniqueness at the core of his essential-being, he finally surrenders the will and ego involved and finds the authentic meaning of existence in resignation. This image, with its elements of belief in a true and pure existence reached by heroic endeavor and of courageous acceptance of the suffering which the striving for truthfulness brings on, envisions the eventual mortification of the ego by the suffering undergone and by a calm detachment at whose heart is a strong consuming flame which burns as it purifies.

The Schopenhauerian man takes upon himself the voluntary suffering involved in truthfulness, and this suffering serves to slay his own willfulness and to prepare that complete overturning and conversion of his being, to lead to which is the authentic meaning of life. This utterance of truth seems to other men a discharge of malice, for they regard the conservation of their inadequacies and humbug as a duty of humanity and think that anyone who disrupts their child's play in this way must be evil. ... But there is a kind of denying and destroying that is the discharge of that mighty longing for sanctification and salvation and as the first philosophical teacher of which Schopenhauer came among us desanctified and truly secularized men. All existence that can be denied deserves to be denied; and being truthful means: to believe in an existence that can in no way be denied and which is itself true and without lie. That is why the truthful man feels that the meaning of his activity is metaphysical, explicable by the laws of another and higher life, and in the profoundest sense affirmative: however much all that he does may appear to be a destroying and breaking of the laws of this life. Thereby must his doing become a lasting suffering ... . I would think that anyone who set such a life-direction before his soul must feel his heart open wide and an ardent longing arise in him to be such a Schopenhauerian man: that is, to be pure and wondrously composed about himself and his own welfare, in his knowledge full of strong consuming fire and far removed from the cold and contemptible neutrality of the so-called scientific human being, exalted high above all sullen and ill-humored reflection, always offering himself as the first sacrifice to perceived truth and permeated in profoundest fashion by the consciousness of what sufferings must spring from his truthfulness. He will, to be sure, destroy his earthly happiness by his bravery; he will have to be an enemy to those he loves and to the institutions which have produced him; he may not spare men or things, even though he suffers when they suffer; he will be misunderstood and for long thought an ally of powers he abhors; for all his striving after justice, he is bound (in virtue of the human measure of his insight) to be unjust: but he may console himself with the words once employed by his great teacher, Schopenhauer: 'A happy life is impossible: the highest that a human being can attain is a *heroic one*. That person leads it who, in whatever shape or form, struggles against great difficulties for a future that is somehow to the benefit of all and in the end is victorious, but who is ill-rewarded for it or not rewarded at all. ...'[14]

Now how can Schopenhauer-- or more precisely, the ideal type of humanity imaged by Schopenhauer-- educate us?

The beginning of his educating is with the kind of liberating impact which Nietzsche found Schopenhauer having on himself. Because everyone has a productive uniqueness of some sort at the core of his/her being, Schopenhauer can awaken each of us to that uniqueness. Or more precisely: he can awaken each of us to the inner admonition of conscience in ourselves, and exhibit for us in his own person the moral strength of the refusal to take the attitude toward himself and his fellow human beings that others ordinarily take. Knowing that the arrangements of common social life are so adapted that life, in a continual dispersion of thought, is not felt, he strongly wants the opposite, namely, precisely to feel [*spüren*] life, and that means, to suffer from life. For he notices the meaning of that adaptation of the social, that it is to deceive him about himself, to steal him away from his own cave; and he bestirs himself, and resolves: 'I will remain my own!'

It is a dreadful resolve; only gradually does he grasp that fact. For now he will have to descend into the depths of existence with a string of unaccustomed questions on his lips: Why do I live? What lesson am I supposed to learn from life? How have I become such as I am and why do I suffer from this being-such-and-such? He torments himself, and sees how no one else does as he does, but how the hands of his fellow human beings are, rather, passionately stretched out to the fantastic events which are visible in the theatre of politics, or how they strut about in a hundred masquerades, as youths, men, greybeards, fathers, citizens, priests, officials, merchants, mindful solely of their common comedy and not at all of themselves. To the question: 'To what end do you live?', they would all quickly reply with pride: 'To *become* a good citizen, or scholar, or statesman'-- and yet they *are* something that can never become something other-and-else, and why are they precisely this? and not, alas, something better? He who understands his life as no more than a point in the evolution of a race or of a state or of a science, and thus regards himself as belonging wholly to the history of becoming, has not understood the lesson which existence proposes to him, and will have to learn it at another time. This eternal becoming is a lying puppet-show in beholding which a human being becomes self-forgetful, the authentic distraction which disperses the individual to the four winds, the endless play of foolishness which the great child, time, plays before us and with us. That heroism of truthfulness consists in one day ceasing to be the toy it plays with. In becoming, everything is hollow, deceptive,

shallow and worthy of our contempt; the enigma which a human being is to resolve can be resolved only in being, in being thus-and-not-otherwise, in the imperishable. Now he starts to test
how deeply he has grown together with becoming, how deeply with being-- a tremendous task
rises before his soul: to destroy all that is becoming, to bring to light all that is false in things.[15]

But this first step expands when, awakening us to ourselves and to our need to search out the
genuine in us and to find the way to complete our authentic becoming in the future, Schopenhauer
also makes us cognizant, in virtue of his own embodiment of greatness, of the role of great men in
the scheme of things at large. According to the account in this essay,[16] nature at large is so constituted
as to aim at some end or goal, and more specifically, to be reaching beyond mere animal existence
toward a mode of existence which is self-conscious, one in which she would come to see herself in
all her joyous and suffering creativity. In particular, nature presses toward humanity as the medium
of her redemption, as that mirror in which life appears no longer senseless but in its metaphysical
significance, in its true meaningfulness. But humanity as that toward which we and the rest of nature
are impelled is humanity as something which stands high over-and-above us, humanity as more than
animal, more than a happiness-seeker.

> The tremendous coming and going of human beings on the great wilderness of the earth, their
> founding of cities and states, their waging of wars, their restless gathering and dispersing, their
> confused racing about, their learning from one another, their mutual outwitting and down-
> treading, their cry in need, their howl of joy in victory-- all this is a continuation of animality,
> as if man was being deliberately cultivated to retrogress and being cheated out of his meta-
> physical disposition, indeed as though nature, after having for so long longed and worked for
> man, now recoiled at his sight and would prefer to return to the unconsciousness of instinct.
> Alas, nature needs knowledge, and yet she has a horror in face of the knowledge she really
> needs; and so the flame flickers restlessly back and forth, as if it were afraid of itself, and seizes
> upon a thousand things before it seizes upon that on account of which nature needs knowledge
> at all. There are individual moments when we all know how the most extensive arrangements
> of our life are made only so as to escape our authentic task, how gladly we would like to bury
> our head somewhere as if our hundred-eyed conscience could not find us out there, how we
> hasten to give away our heart to the state, to money-making, to sociability or science-and-
> scholarship merely so as no longer to possess it ourselves, how we labor at our daily work more
> ardently and thoughtlessly than is necessary to sustain our life because it seems to us more
> necessary not to arrive at reflection. Haste is universal because everyone is in flight from him-
> self; universal too is the timid concealment of this haste, because one wants to seem content and
> would like to deceive the more sharp-eyed spectators about his wretchedness; universal is the
> need for new jingling word-bells bedecked with which life will be noisy and festive. We all
> know the peculiar state when unpleasant memories suddenly force themselves on us and we try,
> with vehement gestures and sounds, to drive them from our minds; but the sounds and gestures
> of life everywhere reveal that we are all in such a condition all the time, in fear of remembering
> and of turning inward. But what is it that assails us so often, what is the gnat that will not let us
> sleep? There are ghostly-spirits all around us, every moment of our life wants to say something
> to us, but we do not want to listen to these spirit-voices. We are afraid that when we are alone
> and quiet, something will be whispered into our ear, and so we hate the quiet and deafen our-
> selves with sociability.[17]

In those moments when we discover nature's aim at humanity, but at humanity as far above us, we
discover the 'above' as 'above even our higher self'. That is,

> we feel that we are too weak to bear those moments of deepest inward-turning for long and that
> we are not the human beings to whom the whole of nature is impelled for its redemption. It is
> already much for us, that we are at all able on occasion to stick out our heads a little and to take
> note of the river in which we are so deeply sunk. And even in this emerging and awakening for
> a vanishing moment, we are not successful in virtue of our own strength [*Kraft*]; we have to be
> lifted-- and who are they that lift us? They are those true *human beings, those no longer ani-*

mals, the philosophers, artists and saints.[18]

In such a man as Schopenhauer, nature has achieved one of those 'mirrors' of herself in which she is redeemed, in which she can see herself in the creativity which is her way of being. An artist is one type of such a mirror, whose mirroring takes place in images and brings to nature a self-enlightenment thereby; the philosopher is another, his mirroring involving thoughts and bringing to nature a self-knowledge thereby; the saint is the third such mirror, in which nature reaches such a transformation of herself as dissolves the ego, achieves a profound feeling of oneness with all that is alive, and knows "that final and supreme becoming-human after which all nature presses and drives for its redemption from itself"[19]. Now

> there is no doubt that we are all related and connected to this saint as we are related to the philo-
> sopher and the artist; there are moments and, as it were, sparks of the brightest love-filled fire,
> in the light of which we no longer understand the word 'I'; beyond our essential-being there lies
> something which in these moments becomes a here-and-now, and so we desire from the bottom
> of our hearts to bridge the distance between here and there.[20]

With this, with the discovery of the life in us straining toward the achievement of such human mirrors, we find the final component of the morality which our nature harbors and intends being realized in us, even if we are not ourselves capable out of our own being of such greatness and such mirroring. For implicit in the self-responsibility and the responsibility to others which our human nature calls us to is this, that whatever that nature of ours involves otherwise, it implicates us in duties and tasks which are set by Nature for ourselves and our productive capacities as individual members of a human community held together by the idea of culture. Such a community is nothing formed by social institutions, by external forms and regulations, but rather by an idea, the idea of culture as what is at stake in existence, as that fulfillment of Nature in the achievement of which nature within and without us gains meaning. It is by our participation in this community, which both includes and makes possible such great human beings, that the life in each and all of us-- whether our nature is made for greatness or not-- gains its fullest and deepest meaning and significance.

Not all of us can participate in such a community in the same way. Yet there is the same basic obligation devolving on us in this regard, the same basic responsibility we have, the same basic task set for each of us by the idea of culture, namely: to employ our own productive uniqueness in such way as to "further the production of the artist, the philosopher, and the saint, in us and outside us", and this, with the sense that in so working, we are working at "the consummation [*Vollendung*] of Nature". Whatever our individual nature and capacities, we can-- and are called to-- contribute by our activity to the production of human beings who do embody in themselves such greatness. Thus, reinforced in our reaching by such a great man as Schopenhauer, we can be led beyond ourselves in our ordinary ego-dominated self and drawn into taking part in this co-operative task that gives significance to our existence-- to the existence of the human race itself, and to our own individual existence, and indeed, to the striving of Nature at large.

In short: youth opens us by nature to a call to take responsibility for ourselves, for selves involved in an inward becoming which is to eventuate in a harmoniously integrated agency central to which is a productivity which realizes and manifests the uniqueness of our individual human being. That call summons us, in our execution of our responsibility, not simply to enact the aspiring and longing in ourselves toward our own true higher self, but to enact the recognition as well of our implication in a reaching of life toward a cultured existence as what is at stake in Nature itself and in human life both individually and as a communal affair. To respond well to this call we need to learn how to take part in life in keeping with it; and the educative powers most helpful in that regard are our own loves, and in particular, great human beings who evoke our love and whose inspirational power for us draws us out and enables us to pursue the understanding and living we need as ourselves being taught by someone who (among other things) embodies in him-/herself what we need to learn. Human greatness itself lies well beyond most of us but appeals to us because it expresses in grand form what we too are humanly in our own much lesser way-- or what we could be, if we could genuinely be ourselves. What we ultimately find as called for in face of individual great human beings-- whether or not by nature we ourselves belong among the potentially great-- is the entering of ourselves (as individual becoming-creative selves) into connection with others who likewise aspire both to enact their own individual being and to assist in this consummation of Nature, and that means: the joining of ourselves self-consciously with those others upon the task of realizing culture in the communal fashion Nature calls for. In such self-conscious alignment of ourselves with Nature's reaching for a community of human beings at work on the realization of culture, we carry out our responsibility for our own individual lives in such way as makes the most of them and gives them the most meaning. If the redemption of Nature at large, and the realization of the meaning of human life on earth, is to be found in a certain ongoing living interaction of diverse human beings, that community is only one element in the inclusive association of the human beings in question. Initially the participants in this creative community would work outside (and for the immediate future at least, work in conflict with) the current social system which otherwise connects them together, including in particular the established educational system which presumes (but fails) to promote genuine culture. If that working may indirectly call for and even promote a reform in the established educational system, it is because in its own being as an ongoing culturally-stimulating interaction of the creative members of a people, it is actually giving shape to what the current educational system only pretends to foster, the culture of a people which expresses the unity of its feeling and thus can resonate in all. For such a continuing creative community and such a people to exist, various institutions are required that would function as necessary but non-cultural support; but what Nietzsche would call attention to as decisive is the living culturally-productive heart of a whole people, which people in turn is responsive in some fashion to the works of its creative center.

4. The philosopher, an 'untimely' being

In his EH retrospect, Nietzsche points to his portrayal of the philosopher as central to SE, as might be expected since it treats of a philosopher (Schopenhauer) and of his functioning as educator for Nietzsche (himself a budding philosopher) and since the culture which it conceives as the proper issue of education is embodied in certain higher men including philosophers. As the previous discussion has made clear, however, the heart of this educating concerns morality and in particular the basic moral question the ventured answer to which is central to the maturational work of youth, the question concerning how one ought to live and act as one bears in responsible fashion 'one's own' life. Because philosophy is a kind of reflection which by nature takes its rise in that youthful moral question and which seeks to understand life's meaning and to grasp reality as the enabling matrix not only for life but therewith for life's question and the answer to that question, its reflection amounts to the effort to bring to self-conscious understanding in a living being matters the disclosure and understanding of whose nature depends first and foremost on the moral effort of the reflective person. If we can not, in our living, answer to the call of conscience and venture accordingly, if we can not be effectively responsible in our living, then our access to the matters to be understood and to the evidence relevant for their understanding and our very functioning in thought will all three be defective, and the greater this deficiency of access, evidence, and reflective functioning, the less we will be in a position to understand the matters philosophy is concerned to understand. A philosopher as Nietzsche is here conceiving him is "not simply a great thinker but also a real [*wirklicher*] human being", and can be the former only if he is the latter.[21]

The beginning of philosophy, then, lies in the youthful discovery, in the presence of the call of conscience, of a responsiveness to that call which involves a recognition of an inadequacy to ourselves in our current condition and a longing to be something higher-and-better than we are. Implied in that higher-and-better is a higher-and-better order of things: not simply our own higher-and-better self, but an interactive existence of ourselves with others that is in keeping with the higher-and-better that is involved. Thus implied is a 'metaphysical' meaning to life, a meaning found in participation in an order that is free of the inadequacy, of the limitations and deficiencies, of existence as we see it now. Such recognition of inadequacy and longing for the higher call into play the moral honesty which wants truth and truthfulness, and in particular, wants the fuller discernment of what within us is-- and what is not-- genuinely ourselves and what without us is unfavorable-- and what favorable-- to our becoming that higher-and-better self which is the evolved and consummatory form of the genuine in us. The drive for truth here, in service to the summons of life and our response to that summons, is so far directly serving the becoming-actual of our being. But if that being has as its greatest particular strength a philosophic capacity, a reflective capacity which would discern life's meaning not simply in our own life but universally, then the realization of this element in our individual meant-to-be amplifies the employment of this reflective capacity of ours beyond the practical discernment of the genuine-and-favorable in our own lives. That is, in the philosopher a capacity which is for all of us basically practical in an individual and decision-making reference for our own lives becomes extended in its functioning into *additional* employment in reflective fashion in a universal reference that includes but reaches beyond simply our own lives. In this extension, the drive for truth which in the personal-life reference is a commitment to honesty and truthfulness in the affairs of our own living and becoming-ourselves takes shape as a commitment to a truthful understanding of how life is in all of us, indeed how reality itself is which harbors life in many forms, including the human. Philosophy is the truthful bringing of life to self-awareness and self-understanding from within ongoing life and its active involvement with circumstance.

Nietzsche formulates the path of development he has in mind, and hence his vision of why the philosopher is not simply a great thinker but must be a real human being, in the course of distinguishing the philosopher from anyone (whether someone claiming to be a philosopher, or simply someone disciplined to inquiry in any field of science-and-scholarship) who "lets concepts, opinions, things-past and books come between himself and things, whoever is in the widest sense born to history"[22]. The stress on immediacy here is central: philosophical reflection gains its access to its problematic and to the evidence relevant for understanding it only in first-hand fashion, in the immersion of our aspiring selves in things themselves and in the attentive exploration and thoughtful discernment of what is disclosing itself in this way. Given his concern and his access to the matters at issue for his reflection, the philosopher "must take most learning from himself", not from others; in and for his reflection, "he himself serves as illustration [*Abbild*] and abbreviation of the whole world."[23] "Read only your own life and understand from it the hieroglyphs of all life."[24]

If our philosophical insight into life and existence as a whole takes its rise in connection with the youthful moral question and depends for its possibility on the way, in the living in which we are answering that question individually, we are able to avail ourselves of the moral strength and make our living answer effectively to the call of conscience, such insight is nonetheless not itself the ongoing living that is-- and is to continue-- taking place. It is rather a fruit in and of that living, the first issue of the productivity of the philosopher, in the form of a purported conceptual understanding which we have achieved as living beings in exploration of the complex circumstance in which we are involved in our living and acting, and of ourselves as so involved. What the philosopher strives for is an overall picture of life and existence as a whole, together with an interpretation of it as a whole which would enable us to see life's meaning and see it as it relates to all human beings. That picture, however, not only makes a claim to truth but is also meant to be entered into our ongoing living (and also into the living of others) as a help in guiding ourselves in our taking part in affairs.[25]

In UHH, Nietzsche claimed that there are many indifferent truths, and problems about which judging correctly requires no overcoming, let alone sacrifice. But the more basic truths, relating to life and its meaning, are not of that sort. Because philosophy deals with dangerous and difficult truths, it distinguishes itself in that way from other truth-seeking disciplines. Here in SE, Nietzsche suggests another basis for characterizing the difference of philosophy from other such disciplines. That is this, that philosophy is concerned with the whole, whereas other disciplines are focused on elements within the whole. To develop further this point, he speaks of the whole as caught by the philosopher in an image of itself, and likens the imaged whole itself to a painting. A painting consists of a canvas, colors, and an image formed by use of the colors on the canvas. Now it is one thing to isolate and understand the canvas and the colors: this, in effect, is the work of the various scientific-and-scholarly disciplines as they relate to the special subjects of their areas of study. There are those interpreters who think it is enough simply to bring together and organize the results of the various current sciences to have interpreted the picture. But to conclude that the whole is "a very intricately woven canvas with colors on it which are chemically unanalyzable" is not yet to have understood the painting. For that, one needs to attend to the image itself and to understand the painter, the organizing and creative power due to which the painting has the image which it does. What is it that gives to the whole its order and organization? What is the meaning of the latter, and thus of life lived in such a whole?[26]

We may understand better what Nietzsche is thinking philosophy is if we look at the philosophy we find him expounding in connection with Schopenhauer. What he offers in SE is a Schopenhauer-based account of the whole and an interpretation of the meaning of that whole. That account and interpretation may be briefly sketched out in two steps.

First: the extra-ordinary experiencing which transports us beyond our ordinary selves and provides the crucial openness for reflection[27] brings the disclosure in Nature at large of an ordering purposiveness whose culminating point lies in human beings. The pivotal feature of existence for interpreting such disclosure is the matter of suffering, and in particular, animal suffering, suffering which is senseless, meaningless. Need suffering be senseless? The sense of the disclosure is that Nature, seeking redemption from this curse of animal life, presses toward human life as that in which she can hold a mirror up to herself and see herself as released from that senselessness and as achieving a meaningful existence. And yet, while there are moments when we understand the necessity of the human for such redemption, those moments point us beyond ourselves in our ordinary mode of being, which is a merely animal mode oriented toward happiness and having no higher meaning. But those revealing moments do not merely point us back to ourselves in our own authentic being and its task, and into an authentic way of being which is genuinely human; they point us more profoundly into our own being as lesser than what Nature needs and is aiming at in needing and aiming at the human. For while we are, in our being, "evidence of the greatest and most wonderful intentions of this artist" (i.e. of Nature), we (almost all of us) reflect also her ineptness, her lack of skill. In us, she has made a "bad job" of it, made human beings inferior in their nature, whereas she had wanted and intended human beings superior in their nature.[28] Thus we (all but a few of us) are not the human beings to whom the whole of Nature is impelled for its redemption; those few-- the few "true *human beings*"-- are the "*philosophers, artists, and saints*".[29] As humans, we are indeed related and connected to these few, but we do not have in our own persons the stuff in virtue of which we *are ourselves* such beings. Thus if in our own realization of our own being we can come to feel this encompassing purposiveness of Nature, we find it pointing to a culmination formed directly by those few superior human beings who can, in their own living and acting, achieve the mirroring of nature that is the sign of and an element in meaningful existence.

Second: the human fulfillment of this purposiveness is not the same in the three types, and is also not equal in each case. The artist works in images, the philosopher in concepts; through the works of these two, Nature is made accessible for conscious appreciation in her intelligibility and meaning for human beings. Only in the saint and his manner of being-- holiness is his work-- does the element of purpose drop away and life become lived beyond purpose and thus in the fullest securing of meaning. Put differently: only in this "final and highest becoming-human" which is the saint does the "I" melt away and the saint live with the "deepest feeling of identity, sharing, and unity, with all that is living".[30] In this life of resignation and negated will,[31] the saint is the human being who "feels himself full and boundless in knowing and loving, in seeing and ability, and who with all his wholeness attaches to and belongs in Nature as judge and value-measurer of things"[32].

Given this account of the whole and our place in it, the Nietzschean-Schopenhauer claims to interpret for us the meaning of our lives. The consummating form of human life and existence is found in certain higher men, and more specifically, in the saint. Given the constitution of the whole which orients it toward such a human being, the saint is affirmed by such a philosopher to be the ultimate measure of value, "the judge of existence"[33]. In such an affirmation with such a rationale, we find the philosopher functioning in that ultimate directive fashion whereby he is the "legislator for the measure, stamp, and weight of things"[34], based on his insight into the nature of things and the place of the human in the order of things.

Now this view, including its interpretation of life's meaning, claims truth and thus relevance to us all. More specifically, it claims truth about what the call of conscience claims us to, namely, the at-stake as the intended issue in that effort we are obligated by the call of the life in us to make. Thus on encountering this philosophy we would most appropriately respond first of all by finding its relevance to ourselves, that is, by interpreting it

> individually, by the individual for himself alone, in order to gain insight into his own misery, needs, and limitations, and to know the antidotes and consolations; namely, sacrifice of the 'I', submission to the noblest intentions, and above all, to those of justice and mercy. He teaches us how to distinguish between real and apparent furthering of human happiness, how neither becoming rich, nor being respected, nor being learned, can raise the individual above his disgust at the valuelessness of his existence, and how the striving after all these goods is given meaning only by a high and transfiguring overall goal: to win power in order to lend nature a helping hand and to slightly correct her foolishness and clumsiness-- at first, admittedly, only for oneself, but through oneself eventually for everybody. It is true that this is a striving which when profound and heart-felt leads to resignation; for what, or how much, can it be improved at all, individually or generally?[35]

The basic test of a philosophy takes place when, having discerned its relevance to ourselves, we make the effort to live it, that is, to live guided by its interpretation of the meant-to-be of aspiration (what conscience calls one to assume and realize).[36] The touchstone for this test, the relevant standard that enables our assessment, is provided by life itself, in its own thriving (or not) under such a reaching for the higher-and-better. The judge who would be assessing life ventured under such an interpretation would be the whole human being, not the human being as simply a "clattering thinking-and-calculating machine [*Denk- und Rechenmaschine*]"[37]. In particular, the judge would be the human being whose vitality, in living, is being developed and strengthened in life lived under such guidance. But a question: if one is to measure the meaning of philosophy "by one's most holy innards"[38], is that a measure of its truth? Or because (as in UHH) both fiction and truth are needed for life to flourish, could the strengthening or weakening be only a reflection of the usefulness for life of the ideas in question, not of their truth? Is there a way of understanding the standard being appealed to, and the test under that standard, which makes the judgment formed on such a basis relevant to truth?

If the truth which the philosopher would understand is that of the meaning of life, its relevance is not restricted to the philosopher but relates to all human beings, both because each of us seeks a meaningful life and because that seeking involves thought and some guiding ideas that enter into the practical decision-making in which we live our lives and seek meaning. If the philosophic love of truth-- if the love of wisdom-- is indeed practical in import, then in keeping with its nature it wants to make a difference in human life generally. Indeed, in his EH retrospect, Nietzsche speaks of how SE gives "invaluable instruction" about "how I understand the philosopher (as a terrible explosive, endangering everything), how my concept of the philosopher is miles apart from any concept that would include even a Kant, not to speak of academic 'ruminants' and other professors of philosophy ... ."[39] In principle, the philosopher's love of truth is "something fearful and mighty"[40], for the insight he gains is into life as a phenomenon of development and creativity, and as he finds knowledge that clarifies this he acts upon it: his insight has consequences, not simply in his own life but (through his actions) in the lives of others. These consequences stem not simply from the critical side of his undertaking, that he is willing to operate on anything and everything with the scalpel of truth[41] and thus is dangerous to established ways of thinking and acting and established institutions; they stem also from the constructive side of his undertaking, that he is voice of a new life and a commensurately new future and, bearing an alternative vision of life and with it a new dominant value-center in life, is intent on reaching out to others and mobilizing them to live in keeping with that vision. This sense of the philosopher is epitomized by something which Nietzsche quotes from one of Emerson's essays:

> Beware when the great God lets loose a thinker on this planet. Then all things are in danger. It is as when a conflagration has broken out in a great city, and nobody knows what is really safe, or where it will end. There is nothing in science-and-scholarship which may not one morning have experience of a turn-around; there is likewise no literary reputation, not the so-called eternal famous names. All the things which are dear and of value to human beings at this hour are so on account of the ideas which have emerged on their mental-and-spiritual horizon, and which cause the present order of things as a tree bears its apples. *A new degree of culture would instantly subject the entire system of human pursuits to a revolution.*[42]

Indeed, these *Untimely Meditations* themselves are an embodiment of this sense of the philosopher and his task. In them Nietzsche is himself voicing a new sense of culture and, having discovered things which favor it and others which are hostile, is seeking to further life by offering support for that sense and being critical of what seems to hinder and oppose its realization. This view of the philosopher, then, makes him the 'untimely' human being *par excellence*, necessarily a critic of his times and an activist in achieving a change in those times. But it also makes him builder, constructer, and legislator, for that future which is to issue from such change.

5. The future

As law-giver concerning what things are important and what not, the philosopher-- the "great thinker"-- would speak to youth about the future by sorting through the tension, indeed the clash, between powers laying claim on youth's energies and efforts, and urging youth to an engagement in affairs that finds for itself, and accords itself with, one or another appropriate life-direction [*Lebensrichtung*].[43] In broadest terms, that tension is between two factors present in youth.

On the one hand, there is in each individual the future as locus for the outworking of life's native reaching in the individual and thus for the achieving, first, of the higher-and-better self of the individual person, but second, of a place in the higher-and-better community of individual persons which is the ring of culture within the complex set of rings which form a people. Nature intends and impels toward realization of a 'future' harbored in the present as a meant-to-be latent in the potentiality in itself, but that future achieves actual concrete realization in the future-as-locus only in the ongoing interaction of being(s) with circumstance. In this interacting the natural direction of the immanent 'future' is not simply registered, hearkened to, and interpreted, but is worked toward concrete reality or is ignored. It is in that interacting and working-toward that circumstance also makes its actual enabling/disabling contribution and what was 'future' finally becomes actual in the present.

On the other hand, there is the 'future' implicated in the 'times' which each individual assimilates from circumstance in growing up and whose meanings are maintained in the everyday social interconnecting of the human beings in whose interacting the native (individual and communal) 'future' relative to each is being brought toward reality in whatever measure it is. For the 'times', in including extant social (traditional) elements of the past being continued into the present, contains anticipations, plans, ideals and commitments, founded in and expressive of those elements. As operative in the assimilating individuals encountering each other, these futural factors dispose the ordinary involvement in activity of such persons to take shape in accord with themselves and thus point contemporaries into the future (individual and collective) in their terms.

Analyzed more closely, the tension between these two pointers into the future is more complex than the characterization so far indicates. We can make clear the relevant part of this 'more' here by differentiating two facets of the tension.

One facet is a moral one, centered in the response to the call of conscience and involving the summons of life to an authentic as contrasted with an inauthentic existence. The tension here, a being stretched in different directions, gains its resolution at any time from the character of the response to the call: it is one thing if we are willing to take responsibility and, seeking to sort out the genuine from the incorporated-but-not-made-our-own (within) and to diagnose the nature of the claiming pressure of circumstance and its components (without), resolve to align our effort with the genuine and what supports it; it is another if we are lacking in the courage to resolve in this way and instead turn away from the call, for whatever reason or mixture of purported and real reasons, and commit ourselves simply as mass-man. At least for a while after it emerges, this is clearly an ongoing tension, not resolved in the individual in any one decision and perhaps never resolved finally except so far as the individual gains an enduring strength to the resoluteness in question. But in any case, while the resolution of the tension seems clearcut-- we are authentic or inauthentic--, in fact it admits of a host of variations and compromises depending on the power of the call, the strength we have to respond, and how in our actual response we find ourselves able to give weight (say) to the fear which the prospective venture in one way seems to introduce and (say) to the urgency of the need to venture in that way on this occasion. In every case, both the future being anticipated and worked for in the resolve and the future that actually comes to be realized cooperatively with the actually-enacted resolve will differ in reflection of the authenticity, the inauthenticity, or the mixture, which is embodied in the decision-making in the how-of-its-response to the call of conscience.

The other facet is complex in principle, due to two different, but somewhat cognate, reasons. However determinate our nature may be, it is never such as achieves its realization except as integrating circumstantial conditions into itself through the activity in which that realization is occurring. Involved in such realization is, in internal reference, a meant-to-be and native meanings which are inherently somewhat indeterminate (in virtue of their character as meanings) and in need of a determining interpretation to gain realization in some form. Such meanings are realizable differently in the integration of different circumstances. Thus realization is not a matter of determinate instantiation of something determinate but of inherently variable actualization such that realization gives rise by its nature to what is somewhat different in actuality. Included in such meanings is that meant-to-be whereby our human nature intends the essential connection of one human being with others; integral to the concrete realization of such community of human beings-- and at its height, of the higher-and-better community of culture-- are particular meanings (particular historical specifications of this meaning) which facilitate in determinate ways our association with each other: social meanings, meanings which have entered into our being via socialization. The (historically) particular social meanings whose claim sounds in the everyday involvement of ours, in which they dispose us to act according to themselves, differ from social context to social context. But in each context they have this same standing and disposing-function. They are also themselves always interpretable in various ways and can be made effective in the concrete in variable ways. For example, we not only learn and play different roles in different situations, but we adapt our roles to our own particularities, and develop those particularities according to the interpretation we make of our role. At the level of our nature, then, and at that of our determinate social context, there is in each case the tension of alternative possibility and interpretation, and between the two sides, the tension of adaptability and suitability of particular social meanings as integrated elements in the concrete realization of the meanings of nature. Thus even if the moral tension were resolved purely on the side of authenticity, such resolution only enters us squarely into the tension of alternative interpretation of meanings (natural and social), and ultimately into the realm of finite judgment that, however well it would ground itself in the factors involved first-hand, maintains itself-- and the venturing which emerges with its help as answering to the at-stake-- amidst a measure of indeterminateness, alternatives, and continuing tension, concerning activity's answering to the claim of the at-stake.

Now in both UHH and SE, Nietzsche grasps youth (the initial transition-time and the early adult phase of life) as the time when the future-- at once the personal future of an individual and the collective future (in Nietzsche's case) of the German people as he has a part in making it what it will be-- first comes expressly into our decision-making and does so as to be worked for in one way or another amidst these tensions. The future that will actually emerge depends in significant measure on how such decision-making is constituted-- on its authenticity or inauthenticity, on its interpretative rendering-determinate of possibility and potential, on its integration of the actuality of circumstance into the resolve that makes our answering what it is concretely, and so on. Outlining for youth the collective future as he sees it in advance, Nietzsche sketches out contrasting futures, but in mainly contrasting ways: the one future-- implied in what is in process of happening, supposing that the momentum of the 'times' holds sway-- is sketched in some detail, while the other and different future that could arise if nature were heeded and the disposing force of the 'times' was opposed is given little determinateness.

If it is as 'timely' human being that a person gives form to him-/herself in the struggle and that he/she ventures upon this-future rather than that-future, the resolve to act has in that case been born out of turning a deaf ear to the call of conscience and a seeking refuge in meanings harbored in the 'times'; that turning and seeking refuge allows the impetus of the everyday to hold sway in that person's activity, and under that condition such a person anticipates and seeks to realize a future marked by some variant-enactment of the (social) meanings which form the horizon of the 'times'. The failure in courage that makes the carrying out of the roles involved be everyday in its spirit means that, regardless of the particular variant being enacted, activity is carried out as a role-playing which does not stem from and draw upon the person's very own selfhood. As such it exerts a re-inforcing pressure on others, to concede likewise to such role-playing: public opinion is an important facet of this. The future which is envisioned in this perspective, and is brought to actuality in activity of such sort, may involve change: as we saw above, Nietzsche sees revolution lying on the horizon in such a future, social and political upheaval, including the spread of democracy, and he sees (on the personal level) scholarly activity increasingly stunting the person in question even as more and more knowledge may be being acquired. But the limits of its variation lie in the horizon of the 'times'.[44] What is most problematic for Nietzsche in this case is something that would be present in all variations, that the same spirit of the conscience-less everyday, and the same weak and weakening vitality, would be constitutive in the future being realized. This degeneration-expressing-and-inducing vitality and spirit are not identical with (say) the institutional changes that might take place (in the educational system, for example), although they are at work in producing such changes. And not only "at work in": by the inauthentic decision-making involved, both are growing more powerful and are gaining a momentum in the persons in question and are impelling toward continuities and further changes which increasingly reinforce that spirit and vitality. To understand and anticipate the future that is in the making here, he would therefore point us not so much to the institutional changes themselves, but also not simply to the everyday spirit whose refuge-taking in roles is currently a key to the dynamic of such change in the persons in question; he would refer us to the conditioning matrix which the communication of this debilitating spirit is generating for the growth of human beings whose circumstance and whose involvement in circumstance hold such 'times'. Genuine maturity and creativity, genuine culture, are being smothered, and the future bodes the continuation and worsening of this, whatever the social surface may show in the way of change or stasis relative to the current horizon. We are on the verge of our own dehumanization-- all under the banner of 'progress'.

If, however, it is as a 'conscientious' and 'untimely' human being that the person gives form to him-/herself in such struggle and ventures upon a future, the resolve that takes shape reflects a successful struggle against the 'times' and a commitment to a novel future that is to emerge creatively.[45] In finding what genuinely belongs to him-/herself, such an 'untimely' person would not only have temporarily dissolved the everyday spirit within (the conventionalist and conformist spirit) which effectuated the soldering; but more importantly, he/she would have found the meant-to-be of his/her own nature and found it as needing a concrete realization in him-/herself amidst circumstance. Indeed, more broadly, he/she would have found the meant-to-be of Nature's own longing for true human beings and found it as entering him/her into the task of realizing culture. Given the creative nature of the resolve by which such realization-- individual, and communal-- would take place and with it the person's contribution to the forming of the collective future, what sort of determinate anticipation (if any) is possible of the future that would emerge given such enabling resolve? Its character as stemming from a responsible and creative appropriation of (natural) meanings would give some indication, relatively indeterminate as it may be, of what would arise, *supposing* that it did so on such a basis. But what (if anything) could then be said in advance of the concrete character of this future?[46]

In SE, Nietzsche speaks as participant in the decision-making that will make the collective future come to be and be what it is. As participant he is already connecting with his contemporaries in a way that involves social meanings, both as shaping what he encounters and as having been assimilated and integrated into his own being in the socialization by which he has become the member of German society which he is. But as participating in the way he is, he would warn his fellow Germans-- and in particular, the youth among them, for it is these he especially addresses as bearers of the future-- against allowing the urging of the 'times' to prevail in their decision-making. So far as concerns any particularity of that future he would advocate, however, he does not on the whole seek to project what he anticipates would come to be in that regard or even what he would urge. He speaks rather to reinforce the voice of nature's meant-to-be as what needs to be heeded, and thus to urge the responsible realization of natural meanings in the concrete.

What, however, of social meanings? Are new social meanings needed to enable the meant-to-be to become aptly realized? This matter is discussed in one place, in regard to the matter of education and the institutions formed to foster culture. Let us look a bit more closely at this matter.

We have seen above how nature, in its purposive reach, intends a humanity above-and-beyond ourselves, not only ourselves in our everyday 'I' but for most of us even in our higher-and-better self. It reaches for the creative figures who embody and give inward and outward shape to culture. And yet it seems clumsy, not adept in the achievement of its aim, and in need of human help, that is, of a purposive human effort self-consciously and knowledgeably aligned with the reaching of nature in ourselves and seeking nature's perfection, the realization of her intentions which nature only imperfectly achieves on her own.[47] The natural starting-point for what is called for is twofold: one is the chance arising of a great human being such as Schopenhauer, and the other is the reaching which is internal to the nature of every human being. The start is made when the encounter with the great human being evokes in others the love which is the crucial factor that opens up the higher-and-better future which is to be realized. In the measure in which such love is evoked, it is possible for those drawn out by such a person to have the fearless self-knowledge in which we see ourselves truly. Moreover, in such love (and only there)

> the soul gains not only a clear, analytical and contemptuous view of itself, but also gains that desire to look above-and-beyond itself and seek with all its might [*Kräften*] a higher self which is still hidden somewhere. Only he who has given his heart to some great human being receives thereby the *first consecration of culture*. The sign of this is shame without self-loathing, hatred of one's own narrowness and shriveled-up-ness, compassion with the genius who ever and again tears himself away from our dullness and dryness [*Dumpf- und Trockenheit*], presentiment [*Vorgefühl*] for all those who are in the process of becoming and for all fighters, and the most inward conviction that we meet nature almost everywhere in her need-and-distress [*Not*], as she presses [*sich ... hindrängt*] toward man, as she painfully feels her work failing again and again, as she nevertheless succeeds in the most wonderful beginnings [*Ansätze*], outlines [*Züge*], and forms, so that the people with whom we live resemble a field covered with fragments of the most precious sculptural projects [*Entwürfe*] which all call out to us: "Come, help, complete, bring together what belongs together! We long immeasurably ourselves to become whole!"[48]

That is, those caught up in love in response to the presence of a great human being find themselves involved in a task, that of fulfilling nature (in themselves and beyond) by purposive human effort. To work at that task-- that of culture-- means working in support of such true human beings as currently exist, but as well, seeking to produce those favorable conditions under which further such beings can arise and flourish in future; and correlatively, it means working against what is hostile to the existence and functioning of such human beings, both at present and in future.

Culture being something in which we are joined with other human beings in a concern for the becoming of each and all as whole human beings, the task in which we are involved demands of us all not only our own inner transformation (moral and cultural) but action in the form of a fighting for culture and being hostile to the influences, laws, and institutions, in which we do not recognize the goal [*Ziel*] of the production of higher culturally-productive human beings, true human beings. Now it is not that present society does not acknowledge something called "culture": indeed it does, and makes much of it. But it is not culture as Nietzsche understands it, nor is it fostered because it is what ultimately provides human life with meaning.[49] As Nietzsche understands it, culture (focused in the artist, philosopher, and saint) forms one of the set of interlocking rings which constitute a human community [*Gemeinwesen*].[50] Of the nature of the other rings, and of the relation and interplay of them all, Nietzsche says nothing directly in SE,[51] although his whole discussion of the 'times' in-cludes recognition of the social fabric as an interwoven affair and of (say) the pervasiveness of the everyday spirit in the operation of the various elements of the society. Within that fabric and struc-ture, however, there are institutions of higher education which are meant to foster culture. In the course of discussing these, Nietzsche contrasts the current form they have in Germany with those

> institutions [*Institutionen*] of a different and alien kind which the second and third generations will perhaps find necessary. Whereas through the efforts of current higher education, either the scientist-scholar, the civil servant, the money-maker, the cultural philistine, or, as is usually the case, a mixture of all these is produced, those institutions still to be invented would have a more difficult task-- not more difficult in itself, since it would in any event be a more natural and in that measure also easier task. And can anything be more difficult than the unnatural training [*abrichten*] of a youth for science-and-scholarship, as now happens? But the difficulty lies in re-learning and in setting oneself a new goal [*Ziel*]. It will take unspeakable toil to replace with a new basic idea the basic idea of our current educational system [*Erziehungswesens*] which has its roots in the Middle Ages and before which really hovers the medieval scholar as the goal of perfected cultural-education. It is time to put the contrast before our eyes, for some generation must begin the struggle in which a later generation will be victorious.[52]

Two things deserve notice here. One is the fact that, because we are concerned in culture about human being connecting with human being, social meanings are involved, and in this case, meanings tailored to assure the emergence (in virtue of the process of education) of this-or-that type of human being as issue of participation in the process in question. The other is the fact that the basic moving force that calls for meanings of that sort rather than of some other sort is nature's meant-to-be: this provides the 'end' and 'purpose' which the institution is to serve as means for.

Now in Nietzsche's eye, the present educational institutions in Germany, while nominally they have the right aim (culture), have taken on a form which is no longer suited to enable that issue as a function of participation in them. Thus while the 'timely' human being will find in present institu-tions a setting which is supportive of himself and those many others who, in virtue of their weakness and lack of courage, feel comfortable conforming to the aim, the person who has grasped the novel idea of culture which Nietzsche is presenting finds no support there and, refusing to go along, will rarely find companions there, and will be mocked by those who have taken that path and who would entice him over to themselves. To persons on the path being supported, the educational/cultural insti-tution will consist of rules and arrangements suited to accomplish the common end in orderly fashion; but to those who are looking for higher and more remote goals, the setting is antithetical. To them,

> an institution [*Institution*] would have a quite different purpose to fulfill. They themselves want, through the bulwark of a stable organization, to prevent themselves from being swept away and dispersed by the crowd and to prevent individual members being hurried into all-too-early creation or even from being alienated from their great task. These individuals must bring their work to completion [*vollenden*]-- that is the meaning of their cohesiveness [*Zusammenhaltens*]; and all who take part in the institution [*Institution*] shall be concerned, through a continual purification and mutual care [*Fürsorge*], to prepare in and around themselves for the birth of the genius and the maturation of his work. Not a few even of the ranks of the second and third rate talents [*Begabungen*] are destined for this co-operative task [*Mithelfen*], and it is only in submis-

sion to such a destiny [*Bestimmung*] that they feel they live a duty [*einer Pflicht zu leben*] and live with purpose and significance in their lives [*mit Ziel und Bedeutung zu leben*].[53]

In present circumstances, the few for whom this second path is suited-- especially those who are not themselves among the highest natures-- are seduced by appeal to their selfish impulses, to their weaknesses and vanities. What enables those who can resist this seduction is the influence of a certain heroic basic disposition-and-mood [*Grundstimmung*] and the degree of inner kinship [*Verwandschaft*] and cohesion [*Verwachsenheit*] with the great. "For there *are* human beings who feel it as *their* distress-and-need [*Not*] when they see the genius laboriously struggling and in danger of destroying himself, or when his works are indifferently put aside by the shortsighted selfishness of the state, the superficiality of the money-makers, and the dry self-satisfaction of scientist-scholars."[54]

Now in envisioning an institution of the sort he speaks of here, Nietzsche is entering into his idea of an institution not simply the sense of a concatenation of social meanings accepted by the parties involved as mediating framework for their intercourse; he is conceiving that set of meanings as they are being realized in creative persons whose moral bearing (whose responsible care and concern, for example) makes their association something which is founded in their higher-and-better self. Yet he is speaking as if those meanings, *in their own nature and functioning*, were creativity-supporting. But suppose that such an institution came into being; would it not, insofar as it was a set of accepted social meanings with a particular purpose to be achieved with their help, have the status of all such meanings, and becoming part of a tradition be liable to assimilation differently in various human beings, including in a realization by them in a functioning of the everyday spirit? No institution, not even one whose defining aim is cultural creativity-- indeed, no set of social meanings of any sort-- can by *their own* impetus *generate* creativity nor *assure* a participation on the part of the parties which is creativity-fostering. And none can, by their very nature, preclude an acceptance of themselves and their constitutive meanings which embodies the everyday spirit, which is not creativity-fostering.

What is at issue here is the status and function of social meanings (including institutions).[55] Thought generally, they are themselves specifications of the natural meant-to-be of human nature in virtue of which we are connected with each other as human beings; but they are such specifications as require further interpretation in their assimilation by the members of the society in question in order actually to function. Because this interpreting is part of a decision-making in each of us which may, or may not, involve opening up to and cleaving to our higher-and-better self, the interpreting may or may not involve making the meanings in question our own as we interpret them and thus enabling them to function as 'ours', in contrast with making ourselves a function of them and acting upon them in the everyday spirit of conformity. So far as the constitutive meanings of the sort of cultural institution Nietzsche speaks of are able to be (and are actually) brought to function in this 'our-own' way in a participant in the institution, then involvement in the institution could assist the person in a functioning that is creative and could enable the institution, to that extent, to function in a way that is in keeping with its defining end. But that is not simply because of the meaning itself; it is rather due to the moral power of the participant and the effectiveness of the person in question in making the meanings of the institution subservient to the realization of self in him-/herself-- the very self out of which creativity also stems. And in any case, the functioning of an institution is not localized in one individual, but in an interacting of individuals; and if, in that interacting, others are not operating effectively out of such self-realization, that impacts not only the functioning of the institution itself but even that functioning of the individual whose participation is self-realizing.

At best, Nietzsche is speaking elliptically and is not expressly laying out the distinctions needed properly to make the point he would make. Nonetheless, the path on which his thought seems to be venturing in conceiving of such a culture-fostering institution is still in the making and is being achieved in SE only in initial and provisional form. In WB, and in the idea of Bayreuth, we find another adumbration, another attempt at fathoming and formulating, the idea he has in mind, that of a community of the creative in virtue of whose working the future might take on a meaningful shape.

CHAPTER 7
Richard Wagner in Bayreuth

In the Schopenhauer meditation Nietzsche worked out matters of the becoming we are involved in-- the personal, the historical, and the evolutionary-- mainly by his account of the impact of Schopenhauer on his own becoming as a youth who was decisively being educated by Schopenhauer. In this present meditation, Nietzsche's focus is almost exclusively on Wagner and *his* becoming.[1] The sketch Nietzsche undertakes here has a structure which anticipates that of EH. For this work opens with a presentation of Wagner at the decisive moment in his life: at 60, laying the foundation stone at Bayreuth, his life up to then a preparation for this moment and the deed it initiates, and his gaze caught up inwardly in his life come together as a whole, making visible to him how he had become, who he presently is, and what he will be.[2] Since Nietzsche claims that it is only as we understand these matters of the temporal matrix in question that we can understand the great deed being undertaken here, the essay is structured accordingly: Sections 2-8 address how Wagner came to be, Section 9 what he presently is, and Sections 10-11 what he will be.

The organizing focus for this meditation's concern with Wagner and his becoming is an event to which Nietzsche refers under the shorthand term 'Bayreuth'. What is in the forefront of his mind here is the project which Wagner was undertaking at Bayreuth: to create the appropriate physical setting and establish the proper tradition of performance in virtue of which his work-- 'the total art-work' in its various forms-- could be appropriately presented and continued into the future in keeping with the composer's intent. About this event there is a certain greatness-- so Nietzsche claims. As he sees it, whenever someone does something, whether small or great, the doing aims at and depends for its success upon circumstance being constituted in such way as corresponds with the effort being made, its being natured adequately to support the deed and to enable it to achieve its aim. If an event such as 'Bayreuth' is to have greatness, this could be only if several things came together, and in particular, if there was a greatness of mind [*Sinn*] at work in Wagner, whose creating and art-works lay at the center of the happening, and there was a corresponding greatness of mind [*Sinn*] obtaining in those who participated in and experienced [*erleben*] those works and received the gift which he was giving in his creating. One pre-condition for this apt confluence would be Wagner's insight into circumstance, the correctness of his judgment that the time is right and the circumstances propitious for the undertaking he is venturing upon. Insight of this sort into circumstance, insight into the present ripeness and readiness of circumstance for this deed, is insight into the needful, the necessary, the 'must' whose holding sway in the confluence means the embodiment of greatness in the event. Nietzsche is confident that Wagner has the requisite vision [*Blick*] for necessity [*Notwendigkeit*]. But if he were perchance to be lacking in this regard and there were not such correspondence, then chance would master him, and his deed would be "brief, blunted [*stumpf*] and unfruitful". As it is, the correspondence is there (so Nietzsche believes), and a certain necessity is being realized, a certain needfulness successfully responded to.

But what necessity and what needfulness are in question? When this question is answered, it turns out that 'Bayreuth' has a meaning that goes quite beyond the present, beyond what is happening between Wagner and some of his contemporaries, beyond what has happened in the becoming of Wagner himself. For what the needful is which the project answers to in the present is itself, in significant measure, an issue of a history in which life-- and in particular, the life in human beings-- is visible as seeking something in the course of affairs. As affairs have taken shape in Europe since the ancient Greeks, a modernity has emerged and a humanity which has become needy due to the manner of its shaping of affairs. It is as addressing that neediness, and the life-based necessity which is its ground, that the event of 'Bayreuth' has its full meaning and its more-than-German significance.

To explain 'Bayreuth' according to this sense of it, Nietzsche does four things.

He delineates the historical matrix, and thus the double neediness of the present for a certain sort of transformation: a revolution in the theatre, and thus in all the spheres of life's expression of itself.

He sketches out the power which, in the person of Wagner, has responded (and is responding) to this dual neediness, and that means: the nature and power of Wagner as a dithyrambic dramatist, his capacity to communicate himself and move others in response. With the discharge by Wagner of a power that both overpowers and empowers others and makes for a mutual strengthening, the interplay involved forms a living community which is the initiating point of the revolution in question.

He sets forth the evolution of Wagner's being in virtue of which he has become such an artist and life-furthering force. In that evolution and its consummation, there is necessity at work, an inward necessity stemming from the life in him. Thus in the interplay of his evolving capacity with historically conditioned circumstance the necessity being worked out in Wagner's development becomes interwoven with the neediness of contemporary man in such way as leads to his achieving the power apt for the initiation of the cultural revolution needed in the present.

He points to the futural meaning of the event which is 'Bayreuth': the realizing in the present of a revolutionary impetus which needs to have-- and is being sought to be provided with-- a futural outworking, and which has thus a futural meaning, not simply a present one.

In short: there is at present need of ... ; there is the present capacity of Wagner for ... ; this capacity has come to arise in him in virtue of ... ; and the coming together in present day circumstance of this capacity with a correspondent receptivity is initiating a development which assures a future for ... . Let us consider each of these four points, and note how his development of them fits with and amplifies the ideas of time and temporality he is working with.

A. The historical matrix, past and present

In WB Nietzsche sees the present-day culture of modern man in the same historical context that he has pointed to in all his early writings, namely, one beginning with the Greeks and their cultural achievement. Following on the tragic age, then the Socrates-induced death of tragedy, is Alexander, the bearer of a twofold mission, to Hellenize the world and to orientalize the Hellenic. The history of culture which has followed shows the rhythmic interplay of these two factors. In particular, it exhibits the initial dominance of Christianity, a piece of oriental antiquity, and now, in modern times, the resurgence of the Hellenic cultural world. In this resurgence, it is the emergence of the rigorous sciences and their increasing dominance in modern life that most reflects the revival of the Greek, but in its Alexandrian-Hellenic form.

> The spirit of Hellenic culture lies endlessly dispersed over our present: while forces of all kinds crowd forward and the fruits of the modern sciences and skills are proffered in exchange, the image of the Hellenic dawns again in pale features, but still quite distant and ghostlike. The earth, which has been orientalized to the point of satiation, longs again for Hellenization; to be sure, he who wants to assist here has need of speed and a winged foot if he is to bring together

the most manifold and most distant points of knowing, the remotest continents of talent, in order to run through and command the whole tremendously-spread-out region. Thus it is that we now have need of a series of *counter-Alexanders* possessing the mightiest power to draw together and unite, to reach to the remotest threads and to preserve the web from being blown away. Not to cut the Gordian knot of Greek culture [*Kultur*], as Alexander did, so that its ends fluttered to all the corners of the earth, but *to tie it again after it has been loosed*-- that is now the task.[3]

Wagner is one of these counter-Alexanders, whose work it is to effect this creative integration which life needs now, to give form to and to animate the various threads of culture he brings together.

In his case, this general task of being a creative simplifier and refashioner is being accomplished by way of his accomplishing a narrower task, namely, the reform of the theatre. Today the arts are no longer vital affairs, a sign of the detachment of art from life in virtue of the degeneration of life in modern man; in particular, "our theatre is a disgrace to those who build and frequent it."

> Strange clouding of judgment, ill-dissembled thirst for amusement, for distraction at any cost, scholarly considerations, pomposity and affectation on the part of the performers, brutal greed for money on the part of the proprietors, vacuity and thoughtlessness on the part of a society which thinks of the people only insofar as it is employable or dangerous to it and attends concerts and the theatre without thereby any notion coming to mind of a duty-- all this together constitutes the musty corrupted air of the state of our art today. But if one is as accustomed to it as our cultivated persons are, one no doubt believes it necessary for one's health and feels ill if forced to be deprived of it for any length of time. There is really only *one* short way of convincing oneself of how vulgar, how peculiarly and oddly vulgar, our theatrical institutions are, and that is to compare them with the former reality of the Greek theatre. If we knew nothing of the Greeks, then the conditions that now obtain would perhaps not bother us ... . The way human beings are, it might perhaps be said, the kind of art we have is satisfactory and suited to them-- and they have never been any different!-- But they most certainly have been different, and even now there are human beings who are not satisfied with our present institutions-- as the fact of Bayreuth itself demonstrates. Here you will discover prepared and dedicated spectators, the emotional state [*Ergriffenheit*] of human beings who feel themselves at the summit of their happiness and feel precisely in it their whole essential-nature [*Wesen*] being pulled together to be strengthened for yet higher and wider willing; here you will discover the most devoted self-sacrifice on the part of the artists and, spectacle of all spectacles, the victorious creator of a work which is itself the encapsulation [*Inbegriff*] of an abundance of victorious artistic deeds.[4]

If Wagner could achieve the reform of the theatre, this would generate in others the strength for 'higher and wider willing' and begin to alter everything in our modern world; for things are so interdependent that removing a single nail would make the whole structure tremble and collapse.

> It is not possible to produce the highest and purest effect of the art of the theatre without innovating everywhere, in morality and politics, in education and social-intercourse. Love and justice, become mighty at one point, namely in the domain of art, must in accordance with the law of their inner need-and-necessity [*Not*] reach out around themselves more widely and cannot return to the inert condition of their former chrysalis stage.[5]

How could the spectator-participants in Bayreuth not be transformed and renewed, and thence in other realms of life, transform and renew those realms? How could they not seize every opportunity to bear witness to their transformation and renewal through their actions? And how could this not in turn rouse their natural allies, the many who suffer on account of the various institutions of the present (the educational institutions, for example)? Out of this current of transformation and renewal would arise then the broad revolutionary struggle against contemporary bogus culture and its representatives which is symbolized in the tragic art-work of Wagner: "the struggle of the individual against everything that opposes him as apparently invincible necessity-- his struggle with power, law, tradition, compact, and the whole established order of things"[6].

In the historical situation, then, the increasing resurgence of the Hellenic has this ambivalence: as BT and UHH have pointed out, Hellenization in the Alexandrian-Socratic form signified by the increasing scientization of modern life is sapping the vitality out of modern man. And yet at the same time, there is music and with it the manifestation of another side to the dynamic of life in modern times. In its more obvious features, modern life is "a mighty upward-striving existence fighting for *conscious freedom* and *independence of thought*"; what, then, is the meaning of the appearance of music-- of German music, as BT notes-- in this time which otherwise is so alien to music?

> Is it a chance event? Certainly a single great artist might be a chance event; but the appearance of a series of great artists such as the history of modern music discloses-- a series equalled only once before, in the age of the Greeks-- makes one think it is not chance but necessity [*Notwendigkeit*] that rules here. This necessity is precisely the problem to which Wagner furnishes an answer.[7]

In his analysis Nietzsche conveys Wagner's own diagnosis of the present as a time of *Not*-- here, distress-and-need, one affecting the health of current life. The distress of our unhealthy state is two-sided.

One side: Everywhere language is sick, and the oppression of this tremendous sickness weighs on the evolution of the whole human race. For language has this as its basic function (that for the sake of which alone it exists), that human beings (who are entered into an existence which inherently involves suffering) may make themselves understood to each other about the simplest life-needs/life-necessities/life-distresses [*Lebensnöte*]. But in modern times, the development and emphasis upon the sciences has meant a pressure that has forced language "to climb up to the highest rung of a-chievement possible to it", and there, "at the greatest possible distance from the excitation of strong feeling to which it is originally in all simplicity capable of corresponding, to encompass what is opposed to feeling, namely, the realm of thought".[8] Through the extreme effort in this direction made during modern times, the power of language has become exhausted, so that it is now no longer capable of carrying out its primordial function.

> The human being can no longer, on the strength of language, know himself in his need-and-distress [*Not*], and therefore can not truly communicate himself to others. In this obscurely felt condition, language has everywhere become a power in its own right [*für sich*], which now embraces humans with ghostly arms and impels them to where they do not really want to go. As soon as human beings seek to come to an understanding with one another, and to unite for a work, the madness of universal concepts-- indeed of the mere sounds of words-- seizes them, and as a consequence of their incapacity to communicate, the creations of their common mind bear again the signs of this not-understanding, inasmuch as those creations do not correspond to their real needs but only to the hollowness of those despotic words and concepts. Thus to all its other suffering, humanity adds suffering from *convention*, that is to say, from a mutual agreement as to words and actions without a mutual agreement as to feelings. Just as when every art goes into decline a point is reached at which its morbidly luxuriant forms and means gain a tyrannical domination over the souls of youthful artists and make them their slaves, so with the decline of language we are the slaves of words; under this constraint no one is any longer capable of show-ing himself, of speaking naively, and few are at all capable of preserving their individuality in struggle with a culture-forming [*Bildung*] which believes it proves its success not by the fact that it advances to meet in cultivating fashion [*bildend*] definite [*deutlichen*] feelings [*Empfindungen*] and needs [*Bedürfnissen*], but by the fact that it entangles the individual in the net of 'definite concepts' [*deutlichen Begriffe*] and teaches him to think correctly [*richtig*]: as if there were any value in making someone into a correctly thinking and reasoning being [*Wesen*], if one has not previously succeeded in making that person into a being that feels correctly.[9]

In the measure in which modern human beings have failed to mature in their capacity for feeling, and feeling in them has been corrupted, *incorrect feeling* rides and drills them unremittingly and does not allow them to confess to themselves their own wretchedness; when they want to put it into words, convention whispers something into their ear, at which they forget what they really wanted to say; when they want to make themselves understood with each other, their minds are paralyzed as by a magic spell so that they call happiness what is in fact their unhappiness and willfully unite with each other in their own adversity. They have become wholly transformed and reduced to will-less slaves of incorrect feeling.[10]

In this regard, the music of the German masters-- culminating in that of Wagner-- is the voice of a return to nature which is at the same time the purification and transformation of nature. That voice makes audible the *correct feeling* which is the enemy of all convention, of all artificial alienation and incomprehension between human being and human being. In the souls of these musical composers-- of these most-love-filled human beings-- the need for that return to nature has arisen, and in their art there sounds nature transformed in love.[11]

The second side: Feeling, and in particular, the transforming feeling which is love, wants expression, realization in deed and in the outward realm. As we have noted before, culture has meaning as the style of the outward expressions of life. Viewed in its appearance, modern cultural life seems a gaudy and motley spectacle, marked by the glitter and sparkle of countless little stones and fragments borrowed from earlier cultures; for it is a surface phenomenon only, and a borrowed surface which in fact conceals and dissembles, is wholly semblance. Rather than making the life in a person visible, and with it, his own genuine self, it conceals these and substitutes itself for them. It is not what genuine culture would be, namely, the form-and-configuration necessitated by the inward and manifesting and expressing it. In times dominated by such pseudo-culture the appearance of souls filled with music-- souls who in noble honesty and super-personal passion "move on the path to a grand free rhythm" and "glow with the mighty tranquil fire of the music that wells up into the light out of inexhaustible depths within them"-- has a purpose and meaning: it is a call for expression of genuine inward culture in appropriate cultural forms. In Wagner and his music, Nietzsche hears the cry "to all who can hear": "help me to discover that culture which my music, as the rediscovered language of correct feeling, prophesies; reflect that the soul of music now wants to form for itself a body, that it seeks its path through all of you to visibility in movement, deed, institution and custom".[12] The distress here-- of unfulfilled longing for the completion of what is begun in correct feeling-- demands action. When the person who can hear this call and feel this distress directs his gaze on modern life, his dissatisfied soul can only feel hatred and bitterness toward the 'culture' and 'cultured persons' he encounters. Even if he is capable of doing more by way of action than denying and mocking-- if he can himself love, and join in compassion in a building of a genuine culture--, "he *must* nonetheless at first deny, so as to create a pathway for his soul in its readiness to help."[13] If music is one day to move many human beings to devotion to that higher culture which it intends, much way-clearing work needs to be done.

According to the analysis so far, the twofold neediness and distress of the present has its roots in a historical development in which the Hellenic, in its revival in modern times, has worked out ambivalently so far; ironically, its strengths (including the development of modern science) have contributed to a weakening of the vitality of modern man, and that weakness, that neediness, has shown itself importantly in the two ways just noted. The rise of music in the midst of this modern development and stress represents life's attempted counteraction of this onesidedness and the sickness that has ensued; that counter-movement culminates in Wagner and his music, with the powerful light-bringing and love expressed in it operating with the urgency of a re-call of modern man to the distress-and-need of the life in himself, a life which otherwise is currently being weakened and dissipated. Liberated in his soul from the 'modern' soul and in his music liberating art to a realization of itself in its fundamental function, Wagner-- "compelled by the love out of which he was born"-- pursues and wants to compel modern man.

'You *shall* pass through my mysteries', he cries to them, 'you need their purifications and convulsions. Risk it for the sake of your salvation, and leave for once the dimly lit piece of nature and life which is all you seem to know; I lead you into a realm that is just as real, you yourselves shall say when you emerge out of my cave into your daylight which life is more real, which is really daylight, which cave. Nature inwardly [*nach innen*] is much richer, mightier [*gewaltiger*], more blessed, more fearful; in the way you usually live you do not know it: learn to become nature again yourselves and then with and in nature, let yourselves be transformed by the magic of my love and fire.' It is the voice *of Wagner's art* which speaks thus to humankind.[14]

But why now? Why this voice now? Why the presence of this saving figure and power in this time of need? Why is it that "we children of a wretched age are permitted to be the first to hear it"? "True music is a piece of fate and primordial-law; for it is impossible to derive its sounding at precisely this time from an empty, meaningless chance; a Wagner who appeared by chance would have been crushed by the superior-force [*Übergewalt*] of the other element into which he was thrown."[15]

There is, then, a confluence being exhibited here. On the one hand, we find a necessity and neediness which concern the history of human life on earth and which have necessarily brought to pass in modern man a condition of neediness which life must respond to; on the other hand, we find the development and evolution of a singular human being which exhibits a necessity and neediness of its own and which issues in a maturity of that human being and his creativity which not only make manifest and address the neediness of modern man but also open the way to a response on the part of the life in the human beings of the time which is apt to its own revival and to a flourishing in the future that would emerge on the strength of that response. As to why the latter-- the occurrence of Wagner and his maturation-- takes place in the present marked by the neediness in question, Nietzsche says enigmatically: as to the purpose for which this artist and art exist and exist now, we may have the presentiment and suspicion [*Ahnung*] that ... , and he expresses the direction of that suspicioning in the following two questions:

> should the greater really exist for the lesser, greatest giftedness for the good of the smallest, the highest virtue and holiness for the sake of the infirm-and-defective [*Gebrechlichen*]? Must true music resound because humankind *deserved it least but needed it most*? Let us immerse ourselves only once in the boundless miracle of this possibility: if one looks back on life from there, it lights up, however dark and misty it may have seemed before.[16]

If we recall the creational sense of reality in BT and the evolutionary-life sense in SE (something which Nietzsche does not himself do within WB), we may see implicit in what he is saying here: Wagner is the contemporary counterpart to Aeschylus,[17] and thus the initiating force for such communal self-aware participation in existence on the part of human beings now and into the future as redeems the creator and creatures both and as enables meaning-- a tragic meaning-- to be realized in the lives of human beings. Something like that same sense of the historical significance of Wagner as was expressed in BT is being reiterated here in WB.

B. Wagner, the dithyrambic dramatist

The initiating power which, in a creative rising above the 'times', responds to the neediness of contemporary humanity is Wagner the dithyrambic dramatist. Nietzsche's characterization of this power which has evolved in Wagner echoes passages in BT (Section 21, for example) and his characterization of the tragic as integrating the Apollonian and the Dionysian.

> In Wagner, the visible side of the world wants to deepen and inwardize itself into the audible and seeks its own lost soul; in Wagner likewise, the audible side of the world wants out-and-up into the light as appearance for the eye, wants (as it were) to attain bodilyness. His art always leads him on the double path, out of a world as play of sound into an enigmatically related world as play of appearance, and conversely; he is continually forced (and the observer with him) to translate visible movement back into soul and primordial-life and in turn to see the most hidden inter-

stices of the inward as appearance and to clothe it with a seeming-body. This all is the essence of the *dithyrambic dramatist*, taking this concept in its fulness such that he encompasses actor, poet, and musician, alike: a concept derived with necessity from the only perfect exemplar of the dithyrambic dramatist before Wagner, from Aeschylus and his fellow Greek artists.[18]

As dithyrambic dramatist, Wagner

stands in the midst of all the noisy summonses [*Anrufe*] and importunities of the day, of the necessities of life [*Lebensnot*], of society, of the state-- as what? Perhaps as though he were the only one awake, the only one aware [-*Gesinnte*] of the real and true, among confused and tormented sleepers, among the deluded, the suffering; sometimes no doubt he even feels as though a victim of a protracted sleeplessness, as though he had to spend his own life, so clear and conscious even through the night, together with sleepwalkers and creatures of a spectral earnestness: so that all that seems everyday to others to him appears uncanny and he feels tempted to meet the impression of this appearance with exuberant mockery. But this sensation [*Empfindung*] is crossed in characteristic fashion [*eigentümlich*] when, to the brightness of this shuddering exuberance, there is joined a quite different drive, the longing [*Sehnsucht*] out of the heights into the depths, the loving desire [*Verlangen*] for the earth, for the happiness of communion [*Gemeinsamkeit*]-- then, when he recalls all he is deprived of as a solitary creator, as if he should now immediately take all that is weak, human and lost and, like a god come to earth, 'raise it to Heaven in fiery arms', so as at last no longer to find worship but to find love, and in love to relinquish himself utterly! The crossing of sensations assumed here is, however, the actual miracle in the soul of the dithyrambic dramatist; and if his essential-being can be conceptually grasped anywhere, it must be here.[19]

If such is the inner condition of the dithyrambic dramatist, it is also that out of which he is creative. The creative moments in his art

are those when he is intensely-stretched-out [*gespannt*] in this crossing of sensations [*Empfindungen*], when the uncanny and exuberant alienation and amazement [*unheimlich-übermütige Befremdung und Verwunderung*] at the world is coupled with the longing pressure [*sehnsüchtigen Drange*] to approach this same world as a lover. Whatever glances he may then cast upon earth and life, they are always beams of sunlight which 'suck up moisture', gather mist, spread thunderclouds. His glance falls downward *at once clearsightedly-reflective and lovingly-selfless*: and everything that he now illuminates with the twofold light-force of this glance, nature drives with fearful rapidity to the discharge of all its forces [*Kräfte*], to the revelation of its most deeply hidden secrets: and to be sure, through shame. It is more than a figure of speech to say that with this glance he has surprised nature, that he has seen her naked: so that now she seeks in shame to flee into her antitheses. What has hitherto been invisible and inward escapes into the sphere of the visible and becomes appearance; what was hitherto only visible flees into the dark ocean of the audible: *thus, by seeking to hide herself, nature reveals the essential-being of her antitheses.* In an impetuously rhythmic yet hovering dance, in ecstatic gestures, the primordial dramatist speaks of what is now coming to pass within him and within nature: the dithyramb of his movements is as much shuddering understanding and exuberant penetrating-insight as it is a loving approach and joyful self-renunciation. Intoxicated, the word follows in the train of this rhythm; coupled with the word there sounds the melody; and melody in turn casts its sparks again into the realm of images and concepts. A dream apparition, like and unlike the image of nature and her wooer, floats by, it condenses into more human forms, it expands into the succession of a wholly heroic exuberant will, an ecstatic going-under, and no-more-willing:-- thus does tragedy come into being, thus there is bestowed upon life its most glorious wisdom, that of the tragic idea, thus finally there has grown [*erwächst*] the greatest sorcerer and happiness-maker of mortals, the dithyrambic dramatist.[20]

In those who receive and respond to the works whose formation gives such expression to such insight, a complex dynamic arises and is entered into play.

To begin with, a question is raised: involuntarily cast back upon our own pettiness and frailty by the greatness becoming manifest to us, we are entered into the question of the end for which we exist. So brought into question, we are alienated from our 'timely' being and all that seems essential to it. Thus Nietzsche can speak of the person who encounters a work of Wagner's as being "overpowered [*überwaltigen*] by it as by the uncanniest, most attractive magic", and as standing

> before a power which cancels [*aufhebt*] the resistance of reason, which indeed lets all else in which one has up to now lived appear irrational and incomprehensible: placed outside ourselves, we swim in an enigmatic, fiery element, we no longer understand ourselves, no longer recognize the most familiar things; we no longer possess any standard of measurement, everything regular and everything fixed begins to move itself, everything shines in novel colors, speaks to us in novel signs and symbols.[21]

Now secondly, this alienation of ourselves from our everyday 'I' and 'world' is achieved in a communicating of-- and a receptive participation in-- Wagner's own higher self and its greatness. In the working of this out- and over-flowing nature of his that is communicated in his works, we who are receiving this influx are taking part in an energy-and-force [*Kraft*] which is working to empower us to a feeling and perceiving that is our very own, a feeling and perceiving in which we are brought into touch with our own higher self and stand over against Wagner as called to-- and capable of-- a creative involvement of our very own, the accomplishing of a task which makes demands on our very own capacity. In this sense of ourselves as being tasked amidst the reality in which we find ourselves, there is a tension; and Wagner can redeem us from that tension, at least for the time of the performance of his work. For

> with him we ascend to the topmost rung of sensibility [*Empfindung*] and only there do we fancy ourselves again in free nature [*freien Natur*] and the realm of freedom; from this height we behold, as though in immense air-drawn reflections, ourselves and what is like ourselves in struggling, winning, and going under, as something sublime and meaningful; we have delight in the rhythm of passion and in its victim, with every mighty step the hero takes we hear the dull echo of death and in its proximity we know [*verstehen*] the highest stimulus [*Reiz*] to life:-- thus transformed into tragic men, we return to life in a strangely consoled mood, with a new feeling of security, as though out of the greatest dangers, excesses, ecstasies, we had found our way back to the limited and familiar [*Heimische*]: back to where we can take part in the traffic of life now in superior benevolence, or in any event more nobly than before; for everything that here appears as seriousness and need [*Not*], as progress towards a goal, is now, by comparison with the path we ourselves have traversed, even if only in a dream, more like strangely isolated fragments of that experience of the-all [*All-Erlebnisse*] of which we are conscious to ourselves with terror.[22]

As in Schopenhauer's communication of himself through his works, so with Wagner: the responsive animation of the receptive person by the power and energy of Wagner recalls the person to life's reaching for the higher-and-better and, in the presence of a greatness which is beyond the capacity even of that person's higher self, to its reaching for what the person is called to enlist his/her creativity in helping arise and sustain itself.

C. Wagner's becoming

Much of WB is devoted to tracing out the becoming of Wagner which eventuates in this culminating capacity and power. In brief compass, Nietzsche addresses that becoming as follows.

> There lies over the becoming of the real Wagner a transfiguring and justifying necessity. Beheld in its arising, his art is a most glorious spectacle, however full of suffering that becoming may have been, for reason, law, purpose, show themselves everywhere. In his joy at this spectacle, the beholder will laud this suffering-filled becoming and reflect with delight on how primordially-destined nature [*ur-bestimmten Natur*] and giftedness [*Begabung*] must [*mutz*] in every

case become prosperity and gain, no matter how hard the school it has to pass through; how every kind of peril makes it bolder [*beherzter*] and every victory more thoughtful [*besonnener*]; how it feeds on poison and misfortune and grows strong and healthy in the process. Mockery and contradiction by the world around it are a goad and stimulus; if it wanders into error [*ver-irrt*], it returns home out of error and lostness with the most marvelous booty; if it sleeps, 'its sleep only gives it new strength'. It even tempers and steels the body and makes it more robust; it does not consume life, however long it lives; it holds sway [*waltet*] over the person like a winged passion and at the moment when his foot has grown weary in the sand or is hurt against a stone it makes him fly into the air. It can do nothing other than communicate, everyone shall collaborate in its work, it is not niggardly with its gifts. If it is repulsed, it gives more abun-dantly; if the recipient misuses it, it adds to its gifts the most precious jewel it possesses-- and the oldest and most recent experience teaches that the recipients have never been altogether worthy of the gift. The primordially-destined nature [*die ur-bestimmte Natur*] through which music speaks to the world of appearance is thus the most enigmatic thing under the sun, an abyss in which force [*Kraft*] and goodness lie resting together, a bridge between self and non-self.[23]

In this brief description, Nietzsche's pointer into Wagner's becoming avails itself of certain ideas as the appropriate framework for making it intelligible. When the longer sketch which expands this pointer spells out the becoming and the dynamic obtaining in it, Nietzsche expands the framework of intelligibility as well, and employs in particular certain ideas of freedom, necessity, and chance. Let us first get before ourselves the longer sketch that Nietzsche presents, and then (in the next sec-tion) let us consider more closely the framework of ideas he is using here, and connect it with what we have seen in his other early works, particularly in SE.

1. Childhood and youth

As Nietzsche presents it, Wagner's life ran its course in the fashion of a drama, although the drama began unmistakably only in adulthood so that there was a pre-drama time in his life. In that early part of his life, before that 'self' which was genuinely his own announced itself, a variety of capacities and drives, tendencies and inclinations, showed themselves but did so simply side-by-side. He was highly gifted and talented, especially in the power of imitation. But he had a restless spirit and a nervous hastiness, leading him to seize hold of a hundred different things; and given that his sensibility was easily aroused and superficially satisfied, he seemed on his way to being a dilettante in many things, tasting this and that intellectually and developing the self-conceit which is bound up with much superficial knowledge. He also had a passionate delight in almost pathologically intense moods, and experienced abrupt turns from moments of the most soulful spiritual stillness into the most violent and noisy of moods. Because his family context lacked a traditional involvement in any single art, he did not know any restraint from that quarter when a diversity of arts-- painting, poetry, acting, music-- approached him and enticed him as holding a future for him. But the larger context of the world under whose spell he grew up was not a particularly favorable setting for an artist: it was filled with energetic busyness, indeed, but it was dull, with a dullness that contrasted sharply with the colorfulness of the theatre and the soul-compelling sound of music.

In all, the many-sidedness of modern life entered readily into Wagner the boy and Wagner the youth, and formed in him a serious childhood illness. Nothing of his authentic self showed itself in this developing 'little adult' who in erratic and superficial fashion was taking so much of the modern world into himself.

2. Adultood: the terms of the drama

When Nietzsche speaks of the dramatic character of a life's unfolding, he has in mind by "drama" a movement in which something is at stake but which by nature is a venturing in which the securing of what is at stake is not assured, in which there are turns and incidents which bear for better or worse on such securing (perhaps threatening it, perhaps supporting it), and which keep the venturer (and any onlookers) in suspense as to the final outcome of this effort to secure. As regards Wagner's life, what is at stake is basically an actualization of his native capacity for creativity, and along the way, in virtue of the major features of his nature, a maintaining of the wholeness of that nature and the development of his considerable talent for learning in such way as subordinated it to his creative powers.

According to Nietzsche's account, the drama began on his arrival at his spiritual and moral manhood, and began unmistakably when a dominating passion-- one that compassed his whole nature including his ownmost capacity for creativity and his intellect-- emerged in him and became conscious of itself. With this passion for what he was most capable of and most loved to do-- roughly speaking, for theatrical performance-- came a directionality, and a movement ahead which was dominated by a will and exhibited a unique inner lawfulness. This did not mean, however, that because the fumbling, straying, and the proliferation of secondary-shoots that had obtained before had given way to a sense of direction, the venturing was now simple and straightforward. Quite to the contrary: the concrete meaning of that directionality was not transparent, so that his venturing ahead was a trying out of what was meant, one whose 'ways and wanderings' were convoluted and often pursued in an adventurous sally under one or another plan that presumed to represent the direction.

By this time of early manhood, his nature had become simplified in this sense, that it was torn apart into two main drives and spheres.

Below everything else raged a vehement [*heftiger*] will in precipitous streaming [*jäher Strömung*], which (as it were) on all paths, ravines and crevices, wants to reach light and longs [*verlangt*] for power [*Macht*]. In order for this will to become pointed onto a path into the good and beneficial, a wholly pure and free force [*Kraft*] would be needed; bound up instead with a narrow [*engen*] spirit, such a will with its boundless tyrannical craving [*Begehren*] could have come to disaster. Whatever the case with the character of the force that would direct it, a way had [*mutzte*] soon to be found out for it into the open and arrival into pure air and sunshine. For if such a mighty [*mächtiges*] striving knew only repeated failure in this regard, it would become embittered, irritable and unjust, thus evil, and this, regardless of where the reason of the failure in any case lay: in circumstances, in the-unalterable of destiny, or simply in the lack of strength-and-energy [*Kraft*].

High above everything else, and as counterpart to this will, was a love-full spirit, abounding [*überschwenglich*] in goodness and sweetness and gentle in voice, to whom the act of violence and self-destruction is hateful and who wants to see no-one in chains.

Central to the drama of Wagner's life was the interplay of these two profoundest forces of his nature. More precisely, that drama involved this, that

> the two fundamental powers [*Kräfte*] of his essential-being drew ever closer together: their wariness of one another diminishes, and hereafter his higher self no longer condescends [*begnadet*] to serve its violent [*gewaltsamen*], more earthly brother, it *loves* it and cannot but [*mutz*] serve it. Finally, when the goal of this evolution has been reached, the most tender and pure elements are contained within the mightiest, the impetuous [*ungestüme*] drive goes its own way as before but along a different path, there to where the higher self is at home; and conversely, the latter descends to earth and in everything earthly recognizes its own likeness.[24]

In his growth as adult human being whose nature was evolving also in other respects, this interplay and development of a relationship between these two deepest powers in his nature meant the achieving and maintaining of a wholeness to that nature which was not in his control. The central feature of this interplay was rather "that marvelous experience and knowledge that one sphere of his essential-being [*Wesens*] remains loyal to the other, preserves loyalty out of free and most selfless love, the creative innocent more illuminated [*lichtere*] sphere to the dark, unconfined [*unbändigen*] and tyrannical"[25]. It was in this yielding of the higher to the lower that the "great necessity" lay "by which alone he could remain whole and himself"; he could only observe the interplay, feel the temptations to disloyalty that arose and the threats thereby to his wholeness, and submit to what was happening in this development of what was nonetheless *his own* nature.[26]

3. Adulthood: first phase

The course of Wagner's dramatic becoming exhibited three phases.

First phase: At first, it was the lower power's undirected and restless striving that drove him; in this "dark and restless" time, he stormily sought appeasement of this striving, and this, in such way that the "entire stream" of this power "plunged now into this valley, now into that, and bored its way into the darkest ravines". But in the course of this "night of his half-subterranean raging [*Wühlens*]"[27], he found the higher side overcoming its wariness and condescending to serve the lower.

This initial coming together of higher and lower, with its own uncertain issue, worked itself out amidst uncertainies and conflicts of various further sorts. On the one hand, he found (inwardly) each of his drives striving without limit, and each of his various talents whereby he could enjoy existence seeking to tear itself free from the others and to satisfy itself individually. So as his drives and talents multiplied and developed, inner tumult and conflict increased. On the other hand, this inward development was taking place as (outwardly) chance and circumstance were enticing him to acquire power and fame and to enjoy intense pleasure in the ways and forms which are open to a person in modern times. This seemed innocuous, in virtue of his having incorporated the 'times' into himself and his finding its voice within him. But in the measure in which those ways and forms ran counter to the honesty which the true artist in himself felt and to the seriousness which animated him as budding artist, giving in to the temptations which appealed to his lower will's circumstance-directed 'times'-supported striving and venturing on the path of those ways led over and over again to his eventual disgust with and thrusting aside of what before had seemed promising to him, now that its true character and its insufficiency in the face of his own seriousness had become apparent.

Nietzsche's characterization of the Wagner of this phase makes him a restless wanderer trying out this and that in a setting which never seemed to offer him the opportunity and support for any lasting achievement that matched his deepest desire and was deeply satisfying. Thus there developed in him a burdening weight, a half-hearted hope, an exasperation at continually disappointed hopes, and a penchant for letting hope intoxicate him without really believing in it.

During this time, as the drive which was moving him was taking him amidst and then beyond various traps and fetters and life was becoming ever more complicated, there was unfolding an extraordinary talent for learning which introduced "a new danger even greater than that attending a life apparently unstable and rootless and confusedly directed by restless illusion"[28]. His capacity for learning gradually led him from being an experimenting novice to being "an omni-sided master of music and of the stage and in all technical matters an innovator and increaser". Seen in the broadest perspective:

> The rejuvenator of the simple drama, the discoverer of the place of the arts in a true human society, the poetic elucidator of past views of life, the philosopher, the historian, the aesthetician and critic, the master of language, the mythologist and mytho-poet who for the first time enclosed the tremendous glorious and primeval structure within a ring and carved upon it the runes of his spirit-- what an abundance of knowing Wagner had to assemble and encompass to be able to become all that! And yet this extensive sum did not stifle his will to action, nor did particulars-- even the most attractive-- lead him aside.[29]

All this learning (even that in history and in philosophy) was made to serve his creative power [*bildende Kraft*] and not allowed to become an end in itself and threaten thereby his becoming as an artist. In this way he satisfied the demand of what had called for such learning (his higher self), its demand on him and his creative capacity for total-deeds which expressed his "many-voiced essential-being"[30].

In this first phase, the "ruling idea" of his life, the interpretative guide of the passion that gave him direction, took a form suited to the lower side of his nature: it was the idea of an incomparable influence that could be exercised through the theatre. Tempting and stirring this lower side, and galvanizing the dark personal will in himself which longed insatiably for power and fame, this idea nonetheless raised a question: incomparable influence over whom? and how? As he sought answers to this question, and began on the path of learning we have just noted, he sought to assess everything around him that enjoyed success and to understand even more those on whom influence was to be exerted. How could he best serve this will in himself "to conquer and rule as no artist had done before, and if possible to attain with a single blow that tyrannical omnipotence toward which his will so obscurely drove him"? A "glowing hope of supreme power and influence [*Wirkung*]" permeated him when his assessment led him to recognize, as counterpart and echo of his own experience, those "violent storms of the soul", that "sudden spreading intoxication of heart-and-soul, honest through and through and selfless", which are engendered in great crowds as they respond to certain rises in intensity of dramatic song.[31] Knowing such things in himself, he would be able to invent what would engender them in the crowd. Drawn to grand opera as the medium through which he could realize the ruling idea of influence, he sought and found the musical and theatrical means for achieving such a response and thus for mastering those spectators and listeners (the 'public') on whom he wanted to exert influence in this powerful way. In the intention which guided him here, and in its mobilizing of his capacity (creative, and learning) to an effort in keeping with his current sensitivity, Wagner was not yet "great and free" as he later became. But here at the start of his becoming, there was nonetheless enough conscience in him that eventually, when his eyes were opened to the kind of 'artifices' the artist was almost necessitated to employ if he was to wrest a success from the public, he grew ashamed and embittered.

> I doubt whether there has been another great artist in all history who started out so greatly in error and who engaged so unsuspectingly and naively in the most revolting form of his art: and yet the manner in which he did it had greatness in it and was therefore extraordinarily fruitful. For out of the despair he felt when he came to recognize his error he came to comprehend modern success, the modern public, and the nature of the whole of modern artistic falsity.[32]

This discovery and understanding, and his turning against what he had been doing and his becoming a critic of 'effect', meant a purification in himself, in virtue of which the spirit of music could speak to him now rather differently.

4. Adulthood: second phase

In the phase which took its rise out of such discovery and purification, the "ruling idea" which had governed in the first phase gained an altered form, one more powerful than before in the way it claimed him who had himself become altered by what had been happening. In this new form, the "over whom" gained a different answer, and the new direction was set for him when, having lost his naiveté about art and artists in modern society, he inquired more deeply into the nature of this 'public' he had been addressing. It was a society-- or the cultured element of one-- in which the 'people' had become deprived of its genuine nature and its members turned into serviceable functionaries ('workers') in a soulless or soul-hardened social order. The 'modern world', having lost its soul, had learned to turn its various constituent institutions-- Christianity, for one, and science-and-scholarship for another-- into vehicles for satisfying what it took as its needs but which were in reality only sham-needs [*Scheinbedürfnissen*]. In the course of this, the 'people' had been deprived of the greatest and purest things it produced out of its own profoundest urgent-need [*Nötigung*], things which communicated its soul: its mythology, its song, its dance, its linguistic inventiveness. In anger and disgust at what seemed to him the case, Wagner became a social revolutionary, out of compassion for the 'people'. And it was to the 'people' that he now turned in yearning, as the only spectator and listener who might be worthy of and a match for the power of his art-work as he dreamed of it.

Thus his reflections gathered around the questions of how a people comes into being, and how it might be resurrected. His answer: it is as suffering the same basic need-and-distress [*Not*] that a multiplicity is drawn together and forms a 'people'; where that need-and-distress is the same, the same impulse [*Drange*] and desire arise out of it, and the same kind of satisfaction of it is sought and the same happiness discovered in this satisfaction. Asking after what cheered and consoled him most profoundly in his own need-and-distress [*Not*], he recognized this in myth and music: myth, the product and language of a people's need-and-distress, and music, with a similar but even more enigmatic origin. In these two elements, he bathed and healed his own soul: they were what he needed [*bedarf*] most ardently. Inferring from this how closely related his need was to that experienced by a people when it came into being, he not only discerned the affinity but surmised that if there were to be many Wagners, a people would have to arise again.

Here Wagner heard clearly the command [*Befehl*] directed at him: restore to myth its manliness, and take the denaturing spell from music and bring it to speech. All at once, he felt his power [*Kraft*] for drama unfettered, and his lordship over a new realm-- that as yet undiscovered realm between myth and music-- grounded. What emerged in this phase in his creative efforts was a new form of art-work, into which he entered all that he knew of the powerful and effective and bliss-conferring [*Beseligende*], and which he offered with the question: 'Where are you who suffer and stand in need as I do? Where is the multiplicity which I long to see as a people?' Accompanying this compound question was an expectation: "I will recognize you by this, that you shall have the same happiness and the same comfort in common with me: your suffering shall be revealed to me through your joy!" But the works he offered were received in a way that made clear: no-one had understood the question. There was much talk about these new art-works, but nothing he could construe as an answer, as a response which had heard the question being asked. When he tried to help in the understanding of his question by a series of prose writings, there was again much talk, but nothing that really cor-responded to what he was saying. "His question had not been understood, his need-and-distress [*Not*] not felt, his art-works were like communications to the deaf and blind, his 'people' was like a phantom of his brain."[33]

With this turn [*Wendung*] in "his outward and inner destiny [*Schicksals*]", he contemplated the possibility of a total overturning of all things, with the hope that on the other side of revolution and destruction a new hope could be erected-- and if not, nothingness [*das Nichts*] would in any case be better than this repulsive order of things. Thus he became a penniless political refugee.

5. Adulthood: third phase

Again, despair and purification entered him into another phase, in which the dithyrambic dramatist that had been in the making over the first two phases finally appeared in his own form, without concealment. And once again, the "ruling idea" gained another form, this time a more deeply transformed form than previously. In the despair that forms the entryway into this phase, Wagner sees into the depths, to the very bottom of existence, and sees suffering in the very essence of things-- nothing that can finally be removed. Growing more impersonal and accepting his own share of suffering more calmly, he finds that longing for supreme power which marked his previous phases transmuted into artistic creativity. Thus in this phase he speaks no longer to a 'public' or a 'people', to exert influence over or to evoke an immediate response in; rather, he speaks now only to himself. Seeking to gain the greatest capacity on his part for such a colloquy and to bestow on his art the greatest clarity, he wants only to come to an understanding with himself, and to think the essential nature of the world in events, to philosophize in sound. His intentionality, then, is no longer bent on influence or immediate response, but upon ultimate insights. Thus *Tristan und Isolde* and *Meistersinger von Nürnberg*, and finally, his Bayreuth art-work, the *Ring des Nibelungen*.

While proceeding in this fashion, something happened which made him stop and listen: friends were reporting to him a movement of many hearts-and-souls.

> It was far from being the 'people' that was here in motion and announcing itself, but perhaps the germ [*Keim*] and first source of life of a truly human society to be perfected in the distant future; for the present no more than a guarantee that his great work could one day be placed in the hands and care of faithful men who would have guard over and be worthy of guarding this most

glorious of legacies in the years to come; in the love of friends, the colors in the days of his life became more radiant and warmer; his noblest care-and-concern, as it were to reach the goal of his work before evening and to find for it a shelter, was no longer his care-and-concern alone.[34]

Fortified by the exhibition of virtue by Germans in the war with France, he began to believe that one day there would be others beyond a few friends of his who would stand beside his work as a formidable power for its enduring (as the art-work of the future) into its pre-destined future-- a future which is possible but may in fact never happen and will not without such persons to bear it forward. He began to work all the harder to see that his work would be carried into that future as more than a mute score; he began pointedly to give instruction in the new style needed for its performance and to found a stylistic tradition of performance and to inscribe it upon the souls of human beings. As culmination of this effort we find the idea of 'Bayreuth' and the undertaking of the project involved.

D. Freedom and necessity

In the sketch just set forth, Nietzsche seeks to enter into and convey Wagner's becoming, at least up to the time of his venture at Bayreuth. His account sees that becoming as the purposive unfolding of a nature; activity-mediated and passion-motivated, and making the interacting with circumstance its medium, that unfolding is complicit with a purposiveness in the larger circumstance which is also grounded in life, but in the lives of contemporary human beings as well and not in Wagner's alone. In the complex temporal movement involved in all this, necessity reigns, or more precisely, necessity in conjunction with freedom. Let us consider more closely the terms of his account, with an eye both to their meaning and to the way they fit together.

1. Nature and internal destiny

The beginning is with our nature, or as Nietzsche characterizes it in Wagner's case, "primordially destined nature [*ur-bestimmten Nature*]". If in WB Nietzsche had simply used the language of UHH and SE, he would have spoken of this nature as that of a living being, and more specifically, of a singular living human being; and he would have grasped it as one which determines us to be active beings who take part in life by way of our activity and who form our activity in the exercise of a responsive decision-making and -executing capacity. Belonging to our nature would have been (as in SE) two things. One is an original endowment of powers or forces, including capacities and drives: the basic stuff of ourselves, much of which is only or mainly potential to begin with. The other is an original meant-to-be, complex in character and extensive in reach, an immanent direction-dispositioning power for the development of capacity, the operation of drives, and the integration of capacity and drive in the evolving human being as a whole. Belonging to our nature would also have been (as in UHH) the drive of life, life's seeking 'more life'. These three facets of our nature would have been treated as centering our being in a deciding-and-executing of activity which begins from a responsive (sensitive, interpretative, attentive) register, primordially, of an at-stake that concerns us in our being and activity (namely, 'more life'), and within that, of factors that bear on us with some kind of moving power: within, factors in the inclusive current actuality/potentiality of ourselves in our present state of becoming and, without, factors in the circumstance of our being. Animated by the drive to 'live life more fully', we would have been seen as active out of ourselves, and in that activity, what would have been decisive for it and thence for our development out of ourselves and the unfolding of our lives would have been how all this is interpreted, attended to, and brought to function in the forming of our initiative.

In WB, Nietzsche sees and affirms all these same things, but he speaks now with a distinctive new emphasis. Our initiative is, to begin with, now regarded as responsive to our being as a whole, and to itself in particular, as natively *destined* for development of various sorts, especially for development of a maturity in our capacity for taking part in affairs which is, in part, moral, and in part, a matter of creativity and creative working; it is, for a second thing, responsive outwardly to a determinate context as the *allotted* circumstance amidst which that native destiny is to be worked out. Finally, the parties which are entered into this resulting interplay marked by internal destiny and external lot are, for a third thing, at the same time working out a *larger and inclusive destiny* harbored in the nature of life itself. What is the meaning of such an emphasis? Let us look more closely at what these new terms add, and begin with the unfolding of our nature as taking place according to the distinctive necessity of destiny.

2. Concrete realization of internal destiny

By Nietzsche's account, the crucial players in the realization of the internal destiny of Wagner and Wagner's life emerge at-- even as-- the beginning of his adult life, and emerge as entering him into a drama. What came before, in childhood and youth, was basically preparatory stage-setting for this drama. But when the stage has been set, three players enter upon it to begin the drama. One is a 'self' to Wagner as an active being, where "self" means a determinate and identifiable center of will and decision-making out of which a person functions and moves into life ahead in some relatively focused and committed fashion. In SE, Nietzsche had stressed the moral element in our evolution as human beings, and the honesty and demand for understanding which obtain in a nature whose creative focus is philosophy. In the present meditation, he reaffirms the moral as important but pays extended attention to the creative capacity particular to Wagner (mainly musical and theatrical), and as a result dwells on those facets of his particular nature which are important conditions for the outworking of that creative capacity. Thus the early-adult announcement of a self passionate about theatrical performance-- the crucial player in the drama to come-- is delineated with reference to two further players that emerge at this time, namely, certain higher and lower sides of his self. These-- an elevated spirit of a certain sort, and a drive for power of a contrasting sort-- are naturally (but so far, only partially) evolved forms of forces in his original nature. Having developed out of their starting-points in his nature and gained significant realization and strength while he had been restlessly trying-this then trying-that during childhood and youth, they come on stage making competing claims on-- clamoring for incorporation as effective forces in-- the deciding-and-executing of that passionate self which is committing him to an exercise and development of his creativity in the arena of theatrical performance. These two players bear (as immanent in themselves) aspects of the true primordial-meaning of his nature as a whole, which intends for them a further development which includes their future transfiguration and integration. The natively-intended *telos* of that development is a trans-formed-higher-side submitting to a transformed-lower-side in such way as enables their harmonious working together and as makes Wagner's creativity that of the dithyrambic dramatist.

The drama of Wagner's adult responsibility for himself as individual creative being, beginning with these three players, with the clamoring of the two in the ears of the third, and with this natively intended *telos* of the development of the two players, is that of an unfolding taking place with the *necessity* ("great necessity") of a *destiny* that is being realized in ongoing activity. Let us consider in three steps what that means.

a. Destiny, not fate

The "must" involved here is not the "must" of an "inevitably will be" *despite* or *regardless of* effort. That is, it is not the "must" of fate, of something in and for whose coming to pass activity has no efficacy whatever and can make no difference, whether in fostering, prohibiting, altering, or evading, what is to come to pass. It is rather the "must" of destiny, and that means, a "must" that *depends on* a *concrete working out* in *activity that makes a difference in* the necessary realization taking place. But what sort of difference? And how does activity work out destiny and make that difference?

The "must" here is complex, with a structured dynamic that embraces and connects the three players. The first moment in it pertains to the meant-to and the stuff that are structurally 'already there' for activity and its working-out function. In virtue of the nature of our nature, the development toward the destined end is *natural* as an *unfolding* of the native basic stuff *out of itself* in *accord with* the primordial meaning; such development, so far as it takes place in keeping with that meaning, is a 'lawful' evolution, the embodiment of a 'natural tendency' and 'natural course' which, provided there is support and no obstruction or distortion, will arrive at its intended destination, its destined end. When I speak of this developing-out-of-itself as forming a moment in the "must" "prior to" activity, I do not mean temporally earlier, just structurally prior, expressing the nature of the nature for which activity is the realizing medium.

b. Activity as enabling vehicle for destiny

The "must" of destiny is realized only concretely, and that means: the destined natural evolution of the higher and lower sides of Wagner's nature-- the higher one, a capacity, the lower one, a drive-- actually takes place *only with the help of* activity as its *enabling* vehicle. More specifically, the final phases in the evolution of those sides come to pass only as the latter come to operate in the impassioned activity that is the adult employment of his capacity for creating some sort of theatrical performance. Since this operating depends on the way activity itself takes shape, the second moment in the structured dynamic of the "must" of destiny concerns this way. Three features of it are central to its expanding the dynamic of the "must" of destiny beyond the first moment just noted.

First feature: Our active engagement with circumstance is ever a responsive one which (as we saw above) is initiated in our decision-making amidst the global register (on the one hand) of an at-stake that concerns us and (on the other hand) of the factors in ourselves and in present circumstance that bear on our responsive capacity with a power to move us. Now this decision-making and -executing capacity of ours has a developmental nature and operates in a way inflected by the differentiation between conscious and unconscious. Due to our initial relative impotence in this capacity, a certain illusion arises early and becomes part of us, namely, that as active beings we *are exclusively* what shows itself of ourselves and our functioning in the conscious sphere. In the measure in which this illusion (of ourselves as 'ego') becomes an actual part of us and enters on the conscious side into the formation of our efforts, we form our initiatives and carry out our efforts thinking 'we' (meaning 'ourselves as ego') are able to steer (and are steering) them consciously: we are completely free and conscious agents in conscious control of what we do.[35] Nonetheless, our venturing, our functioning as initiating agents, is not what we are taking it to be; in reality, our initiating always involves us *as wholes*, and thus is formed and constituted by conscious *and* unconscious components *together*, and this, even though we are not conscious of that. Consciousness is a real factor, indeed, with a (more or less) efficacious part in the forming and carrying out of initiative; but our sense of ourselves as, in our agency, *wholly* conscious centers who are undetermined by anything that is not part of our consciousness, is an illusion. Nonetheless, this illusion not only arises in us but has a real place in our actions and conduct of life so long as we hold on to it and maintain it as truth in our functioning.

Nietzsche speaks of Wagner as having entered into adulthood able by then to form his initiative without confinement by the presumption that is central to the illusion of himself-as-ego, namely, that he could take conscious charge of his actions and what happens in himself, and, consciously aiming at this result, could bring about the evolution and integration of these sides of his nature *simply in function of effort guided by that intent*. Thus Nietzsche notes Wagner's acknowledgement that "he did not have it in his power" to command and control this evolution and continued wholeness of his nature. Yet such acknowledgement of the mistaken character of this ego-presumption was only the renunciatory side of a fuller recognition, whose other side was that we nonetheless *do have* (conscious-and-unconscious) *initiative,* and that the achievement of the 'natural' issue and the fulfillment of the dynamic-- the necessity-- of the evolving realization of our inward destiny *depends on* such initiative. Thus in Wagner's case the "must" of necessity involved activity entered upon in hopeful and trusting fashion, *risking* that his nature would develop further and hold together *of its own accord* as he ventured.

Second feature: In the risk-taking active engagement on whose enabling work the "must" of his internal destiny depended for its realization, Wagner responded to the clamor of the two competing sides of his self for incorporation as functioning forces in his effort by granting them both an effective place in it. But the formation of initiative did this only under an interpretation of them-- of their character, of their disparate and conflicting pressure, and of their appropriate relation to each other and their place in himself as a unitary being. Initially his interpretation gave priority as moving force to the one side, to the drive for power, and more fundamentally, grasped the reaching for power as the striving for influence upon and power over others. Governed by this ruling idea, he committed himself to mobilizing his creative capacities in the effort to achieve power over others in the medium he was by nature fitted best to be productive in. That was the medium of opera, with its unification of theatre and music and, in his case, also myth. In his initial interpretation the 'others' over which he initially sought power and influence were 'the public', that is, the cultured audience of the day.

While the operation of responsive initiative unavoidably involves interpretation, there is no assurance that such interpretation will be correct. In Wagner's case, his initial interpretation of what was involved-- both regarding the nature of the sides of himself and regarding the appropriate audience and connection with that audience-- was in significant respects a misinterpretation. But he learned of his mis-taking of matters only as he acted on his interpretation, and then learned what was mistaken only gradually. His initial efforts brought him success in creating what would capture audiences, but at the same time it brought disgust at what he saw himself doing and what was involved in succeeding as he did. The sense that for all his success he had guided himself awry in his initial effort reflected the centrality of a standard, a natural moral standard, in his judgment of that effort. Not only had there been something dishonest in what he was doing, but he had been addressing an audience whose concern with art (his included) was basically frivolous, lacking in moral seriousness. This was nothing he could accept.

Despite the guiding mis-reading of affairs, something had been happening to the two sides of his nature while he had been making his effort. Quite without any conscious willing of this on his part, they had not simply become dominating functional forces but had come to function together in his effort. In particular, he had found his higher self, out of itself, condescending to serve the drive for power he had interpreted as the drive for power-over and had made prior as moving force; and in virtue of this loyalty shown by the higher toward the lower, a beginning had been made on the integrated working of the two. But only a beginning, far short of the destined consummatory end.

Third feature: If the active engagement on which the "must" of destiny depends for its realization is something that can be formed and carried through under a mistaken interpretation, it is also something which harbors the possibility not simply of the agent's discerning the mistakes that are affecting his effort but also of his/her reforming that effort, having learned, unlearned, and relearned, so as better to grasp (say) the concrete meaning of the factors involved. When Wagner's disgust led him to look more deeply into the situation and to conclude that it was not 'the public' but 'a people' that was his proper audience, he was also able to learn what constituted the essence of a 'people', to form an idea of how a 'people' might be brought to life again out of the diminished form to which it had been reduced in modern society, and re-forming his creative venturing accordingly, to create works suited to exert influence and power-over by eliciting and uniting a people. During this second venturing, the two sides of his own nature evolved further and connected with each other, again without this happening as a result of his willing it. For in his higher side's reflective work of understanding the people, he had come to find a more elevated sense of the others he was to address in his art, their value and quality. Along with this elevated vision came greater refinement and transfiguration, if not of the lower side itself, at least of the effort that would express that lower side; for the longing for power-over was being directed now toward a higher entity (a 'people' and not simply the 'public'). Thereby the working together of the two sides of his nature in their more elevated and refined forms also became more intimate, and their destined integration was brought closer.

His learning, however, had not yet enabled him to see the full extent of the misinterpretation under which he had been acting. Thus further disappointment ensued, and yet because of the continuing strength of his initial passionate commitment and given the strength of his capacity to learn, he was able to respond to his failure by looking even more deeply into the nature of things, seeing the irremediable implication of beings in suffering, and in compassionate response to this implication, to re-form his creative efforts again. This time it was the previously unquestioned aspect of his interpretation of the drive for power that came into question; in the face of reality as he now saw it, he found himself called-- and able-- to abandon the ruling idea that heretofore had interpreted the meaning of the lower self. No longer was it credible that what was crucial in its reaching to rise upward and shine was the attainment of influence on and power over others. What seemed now its meaning was its reaching for the higher and, within that realm and in a disregard for the 'over others' of power, its striving toward the power which is realized in achieving the highest insight into life and its meaning. In the harnessing of his creative capacities to the striving for power so understood and to the task of embodying in his works the insights he came to, Wagner finally found himself creating from out of his whole nature in that meant-to-be integrated form in which both sides, fully evolved and transfigured, worked harmoniously. The result was the dithyrambic dramatist, creating out of a transcendent illuminated awareness of things and life in their strangeness and wondrousness (his higher self transformed) and out of a longing to draw close to this world and to those others as lover, and to give out of himself the gifts that are the outflow of his love-animated creativity (his lower self transformed). Creating out of his destiny-fulfilled self, Wagner participated in a power that overflows, at once realizing and discharging itself in its overflowing fulness, and knew as the issue of the necessity of destiny's realization a "doing with joyful freedom the necessary at every moment of creation"[36].

In sum: According to Nietzsche's account of Wagner's becoming-himself, the "must" whereby the internally destined end actually arrives is one whose natural directionality is able to be realized in virtue of the way the responsive medium of activity brings the three players in the drama into play in concrete effort. Activity's role in expanding the "must" is, first, as expressing a continuing commitment of the whole active being to creative effort; included in that commitment is a renunciation of the illusion of ego and thus of any pretense to take conscious charge of one's destiny and to bring the destined end about in function of the working of the conscious-ego. That role includes, second, the responsive entering of the two sides of his nature into the formation of such activity, doing this under an interpretation and, when reinterpretation is called for, continuing to give the sides a place for effective functioning under such reinterpretation as seems needed. Third and finally, that role includes a self-re-forming of activity that incorporates a learning, unlearning, and re-learning, ventured upon discovery of elements of mis-taking in the interpretations guiding ongoing effort. In activity which in this three-sided way enters a second moment into the realization of the "must" of destiny, the two sides of Wagner's nature were able to develop further out of themselves and eventually to reach their integrated fulfillment while the commitment, intention and attention, involved in the effort that entered them as functional elements in its forming were being directed toward the issue of that effort, namely, the theatrical performance being created.

c. Circumstance

While activity is crucial in these ways to the realization of the "must" of destiny, its own nature as a concrete and responsive affair means circumstance also is integral to that realization. For not only does circumstance constitute the context for an agent's activity and hold any other agents with whom the agent in question is interacting; but in the forming of activity by a being with responsive initiative, circumstance also becomes integrated into that forming, to make a difference there. There is, accordingly, a third moment in the structured dynamic of the "must" of destiny, one concerned with the way circumstance functions in the activity enabling the realization of the destined end. Nietzsche's account of Wagner's becoming brings out two sides to this moment.

First side: At least from the perspective of an agent, circumstance is basically happenstance, what he/she happens to have as the concrete context for living and acting and as circumstantial medium in which his/her active working out of the "must" of destiny must operate as its lot. Whatever particulars may compose circumstance for an agent, there are facets of it-- and of ourselves as agents-- which represent the "unalterable and unchangeable" in the determinate actuality-and-potentiality of the beings involved in this working out of our internal destiny. Suffering is something which Wagner eventually recognizes as of this sort in living beings: the nature of things is constituted in such way as makes it an inexpungible part of existence for any such being. Such a facet can not be eliminated from our lot as active beings, and represents necessity in the form of the unalterable power of fate within whose bounds destiny is to be realized.

Second side: When natured beings are part of the circumstance allotted to an agent, the out-of-itself character of the natural functioning of such beings, and their natural constitution, make for a context with an initial ongoing dynamic and determinateness rooted in other beings, not in the agent. For nature disposes them (as it does us) to certain forms of activity and development *from out of themselves*, while it also gives them a constitution with a determinate susceptibility to suffer a *limited range of changes* generated not by an impetus internal to their own nature but by the *working of others beyond* themselves. Thus depending on the chance of allotted circumstance and the way in which an agent ventures and gives character to his/her activity in the engagement with it, the efforts of that agent to effectively work out (internal) destiny in the given context can meet obstruction, constraint, channelling, distortion, and the like, in this engagement, due to the conflict and mismatch between the natural working and the constitutional susceptibility to change that mark both the natured beings that are part of the situation and the agent's own nature and susceptibility to change, together with his/her limited strength, skill, and capacity at the time. Inward to the concrete working out of internal destiny, then, is the character and impact of this dynamic, that of the circumstantial out of itself, both as it is and as it is responsively registered and taken into account and interpreted as being in the shape-taking and carrying-out of activity; whether the working out adapts to or modifies (so far as it can) the character of that dynamic medium, it defines itself in a context which of itself is more-or-less supportive of the working-out-of-internal-destiny effort taking place. In Wagner's case, it turned out that his allotted circumstance held such a sufficient support for his creative efforts that, in and by the (favorable and unfavorable) working of circumstance in relation to the character of his own commitment and engagement, it was possible for his destined self eventually to be realized and for him to establish an empowered-and-empowering creator-to-audience relation with others by way of his creations. Was this favorable conjunction mere co-incidence, chance? Did it just happen that what was allotted for his living and acting ultimately cor-responded to what was needed for him to work out his destiny successfully? Or was there further necessity at work here? And if so, of what sort?

3. Internal destiny and an inclusive destiny

In our consideration of the "must" of destiny so far, we have been focused on the individual agent Wagner, and have noticed in circumstance what initially seems simply a contingent conjunction of contemporaneous agents favorable to his working out his destiny in that context. Even when we note that the others in question, invigorated by the power instreaming from him and his works, are being fostered in their own capacity to function creatively and not simply as derivative followers, this still could appear as only another instance of the working out of internal destiny, in this case, that related to the natures of those others. But what seems chance when looked at simply in a contemporaneous reference appears to be more than that when looked at in historical perspective, and more broadly, in evolutionary perspective. Nietzsche claims that the life in us, being more than individual, is a destining power which holds a necessitating basis for an inclusive destiny, in which the *coming* of Wagner *at this time* and *into this present-day world* and the creativity sparked in the response of others to his works and presence has the significance of a conjunction that was itself meant to be, and more precisely, of a destined *telos* of life itself in its overall evolutionary development. In WB, Nietzsche gives only an occasional hint of what he has in mind.[37] But if we recall BT and SE, we can draw out the meaning of those hints and also more fully understand his idea of the "must" of destiny.

In SE, Nietzsche speaks of Nature, and the living beings composing her, as marked by a purposiveness. At bottom, this is an intent toward the realization of those true human beings (philosophers, artists, saints) in whose person she comes to self-awareness and thereby enables the life in them, a power that is unable to avoid suffering, to share in meaning. Yet while Nature is purposive in this regard in her action, she is clumsy and unskilled in the means she uses for achieving her purposes. Thus she can, on the strength of her blind but purposive reaching, eventually give rise to an artist here (a Wagner, say) and a philosopher there (a Schopenhauer, say). But because such blindly engendered beings are entered into circumstances in which they cannot have their full effect, "it often looks as though the artist, or especially, the philosopher, existed in his times *by chance*, as a recluse or wanderer who has become separated and been left behind".[38] Even if such blindness could be redressed by human beings with a knowledge of Nature's aim and of the means for its more skillful realization and with a commitment to its achieving guided by such knowledge, that would not suffice. For Nature's aim is not toward isolated figures that embody human greatness but toward a community which includes a multiplicity of true human beings whose cultural creativity reaches beyond the few to elevate the existence of the whole community. Culture has a meaning for all, even if all may not partake of it in the same fashion and degree; and if culture as nature transfigured and improved is the aim of life, and such greatness in any individual drives toward outward expression in a broader community, only the rise of such a community could suffice the reaching and intent that marks Nature.

Yet even this is not the full story. In BT Nietzsche focuses on the artist and sees the significance of the artist as a metaphysical one. Interpreting the metaphysical in a creational vein, he sees the tragic drama of the ancient Greeks as a vehicle for expressing and occasioning a coming to see the ultimate Dionysian truth of life, and in such seeing achieving for the tragic artist and the participants the redemption from the negativity and suffering which inherently threaten life and life's meaning. If in this celebration of Dionysus the god is also present and participant, then the significance of the celebratory event is more than human. In the second half of BT, Nietzsche understands modern times on the background of the Greeks, and sees the contemporary world as Socratic-Alexandrian and Wagner (in a reversal of the order of events in Greece) as reinstating tragedy, which among the Greeks came before the Socratic-Alexandrian. And in general, BT emphasizes affinities and approximations between (modern) Germans and (ancient) Greeks, and he even goes so far as to say "that one is reminded almost palpably of the very relative nature of all concepts of time: it almost seems as though many things belong together and time is only a cloud which makes it hard for our eyes to perceive their belonging-togetherness".[39] Now variations on an eternal theme are different, not identical, and only as such are they variations and not repetitions. But what is the meaning of the difference in the realization of the tragic drama and insight among the Greeks and its realization among the Germans? Is it only an indifferent difference? Or ... ?

In WB, there is something more about to emerge into view. WB implicitly carries the sense which has come forward markedly in SE, that life (inclusive of the life in each of us) has an evolutionary character, and that there is a movement in time beyond that taking place in each individual living being. The life in us, in the character it shares in its presence in all living beings, involves a drive toward 'more life' (UHH), and toward a 'more' that is ever on the way toward a culmination in the 'self-aware and joyfully creative life' (SE, BT) in which the nisus of creation and the dynamic of life's evolutionary nature achieve their destined *telos*. Because this drive animates a venturing, the achieving of this *telos* is not a matter of inevitability, but it is a matter of destiny, thus of a necessity of some sort. But of what sort? In WB Nietzsche is on the verge of voicing a view of the movement of collective human existence which advances beyond what we have seen in previous works. In particular, he is close to speaking of what is happening in the Germany of his day as embodying and manifesting a uniqueness that pertains to collective human venturing, a "for the first time" whereby modern man is not simply a variant-companion of ancient man but, in a destiny-embodying development which is building on the Socratic-Alexandrian drive to know and is reinstating something like the tragic insight known to the Greeks, is in truth entering into a time and condition that are fundamentally new and different. There is no name yet for this new time and condition, and no clear rendering of how (say) the artistic Socrates would significantly differ from the tragic poet and be something new and more profound, not simply something different. Nor is there yet any indication (except the hint contained in speaking of Wagner as dithyrambic dramatist) of whether the creator god under the figure of Dionysus would suffice as representation of the reality in which this novel self-awareness found itself and life's drive to 'more' gained its novel communal *telos*. Before greater clarity and definiteness on such matters gains public expression, a fairly radical break will have taken place, and the voice that eventually voices them will do so in a rather different key than it has sung in so far.

Overall, then, WB, with its stress on destiny (internal, and inclusive) and the differentiation of various facets of freedom and necessity, culminates Nietzsche's initial concerted attempt to be attentive to, and remain faithful to, the agential involvement of ourselves in affairs that began in BT. According to WB, our condition at its heart is marked by a complex necessity which conditions the free but responsive initiative which is ours as active beings. Through that initiative, we are to define the actual course of life in a concrete venturing in the dark amidst the "must" of internal destiny, the "must" of circumstance, and the "must" of an inclusive destiny that relates to humanity's life on earth. If WB voices Nietzsche's sense of something momentous happening in the present of his own day-- something communal that 'must' be, that was destined but not inevitable or predetermined actually to be--, his grasp of it in this work is still tied up intimately with Wagner, and still operates (except for brief hints of something else) within the horizon of intelligibility that has marked the three preceding works we have seen as part of this first phase of his thought. Nonetheless, WB is pregnant with thoughts which will be revived and reworked, some in the next phase of his thinking (as, for example, this matter of freedom and necessity), but others only in the third phase (for example, the matter of the full nature of his-- or here, Wagner's-- will-to-power).

E. The meaning of 'Bayreuth': the future

As we have seen, there came a time in Wagner's life when both his own becoming and his creativity came to fulness, and given the character of the man and his works and the at-odds-with relation of both to the times, if the work his works were to achieve was to be brought to fulfillment there was need for a place that could serve three connected but different purposes at once.

To begin with, as his own work and the idea governing his efforts had evolved, he had not only grown disenchanted with the contemporary world of art and 'success' with the public, but he had found his works being performed in theatres and for the public in ways that were so superficial and thoughtless that, while there was no malice or ill-will involved, the ineptitude and insensitivity repulsed him. All the more did he feel his lofty idea being denied and derided, even if innocently, when, under this repulsive form, his works began to 'succeed' at the theatre. Thus when the war between Germany and France revived hope in him that the genuine German spirit still survived deep down, and when friends conveyed to him the sense that there were a number of souls being reached and moved-- perhaps enough to form the "germ and first source of life of a truly human society to be perfected in the distant future"[40]--, he felt all the more strongly the need for a place in which, under his full control and guidance, his work could be performed in fully appropriate fashion. This was the first purpose that could be served by the construction and establishing of the place and institution he was attempting at Bayreuth.

In so establishing this place and performing his work there, Wagner was also accomplishing a second purpose: he was making possible "the morning consecration on the day of battle". The battle in question here was that involved in the overcoming and transforming of the 'times' of 'modern man'. What was at stake was a "better future" and "freer humanity" than anything which could come out of the triumph of the 'present age' and its 'unnatural humanity'. Now although the tragic artwork he was producing represented symbolically the struggle of the individual against the established order of things at present,[41] his art did not exist as a weapon useful directly in the broader struggle itself. It was rather to be useful for the intervals of quiet before and in the midst of battle, when the fighters on the broad front need symbolic reminders of what is involved and a quickening of the life and renewal of the energy in themselves.

> Everywhere else the individual finds his personal inadequacies, his half- and in-capacity: how should he have the courage to fight if he had not first been consecrated to something 'super-personal' [*überpersönlichen*]! The greatest suffering of the individual which exists-- that there is no community of knowing among human beings, that ultimate insight is uncertain, and that capacity is not equally distributed: this all makes him need art. One can not be happy so long as all that is around us suffers and brings suffering on itself; one can not be moral so long as the course of human affairs is determined by violence, deception and injustice; one can not even be wise so long as the whole of humanity has not struggled in competition over wisdom and led the individual into living and knowing in the wisest manner. In face of this feeling of three-fold dissatisfaction, how should one stand it if one could not recognize in one's struggling, striving and going-under, something sublime and meaningful and had not learned from tragedy to have pleasure in the rhythm of great passion and in the victim of the same?[42]

As symbolic, art does not educate directly: what the tragic hero strives for may well not be worth striving for in any absolute sense. And the struggles which art depicts are simplifications of the real struggles of life, its problems abbreviations of the infinitely complicated calculus of willing and acting. But by way of its simplified semblance of the world and solution of life's riddle, art can re-new us and strengthen our (re-)dedication to the super-personal. In particular,

> that is the meaning of tragedy; the individual shall unlearn the terrifying angst which death and time evoke in the individual: for already in the smallest moment, in the briefest atom of his life-course, the individual can encounter something holy which boundlessly outweighs all struggle and all need-fraught distress [*Not*]-- that is, he may become disposed tragically; and if the whole of humankind must one day die-- and who may doubt that?-- so the goal is set for it, as the high-est task for all coming times, to grow together into unity and community in such way that hu-mankind *as a whole* stands over against its impending going-under with a *tragic disposition*; in this highest task lies included all ennobling of human beings; the conclusive rejection of this task would yield the saddest picture a friend of humankind could put before his soul-- so I feel! There is only *one* hope and *one* guarantee for humanity's future: *that the tragic disposition not die out*! An unequalled cry of distress must resound over the earth if humanity should ever fully lose it; and in turn, there is no more blessed joy than to know what we know-- how the tragic idea has been born again in the world. For this joy is completely super-personal and universal, humanity's jubilation over the guaranteed connection and continuation of the human as such.[43]

While his dramas symbolized the struggle in its meaning, their revolution-supporting force did not reside simply in that. As we have noted earlier, modern cultural development and its institutions has stressed a development of language which has weakened its capacity to be commensurate with and to correspond to strongly aroused feeling and thus to carry out its most basic function, the expres-sion of strong feelings, of passion. Human beings no longer know how to communicate with each other and make themselves truly understood about their own life-needs, life-distresses, and that means in particular, the life-feelings and life-sufferings in which such need and distress register. But even more profoundly: we for the most part no longer know or let ourselves acknowledge feeling in that form, but rather feel as we are supposed to according to our roles-- such is incorrect feeling as Nie-tzsche understands it. But in German music generally, and in Wagner in particular, we find a restor-ation of touch with feeling and in particular a recovery of correct feeling, and thus a restoration of the basis for the natural power of language (musical and verbal) to achieve communication in regard to feeling. With the exercise of this natural power can come joint undertakings founded in shared and mutually-understood feeling. With works that unite music and word, and that embody and manifest nature's achievement (through love) of its own purification and transformation, there is also the sum-mons to the embodiment of nature so transformed in a culture which expresses itself visibly in deed and movement, in institution and custom.

This is the second meaning of Bayreuth, that as a place for the appropriate performance of the tragic art-work he was producing, it enabled those fighters engaged in the larger revolutionary struggle against the 'times' on behalf of genuine culture to know times of respite and reflection in which, as audience-participants in the performance of his art, they could find themselves brought back self-consciously into touch with the correct feeling in themselves, made self-aware through the symbolic meaning of the art of the character of the struggle they are engaged in, and instated with restored and renewed energy in the tragic disposition and mood needed for continuing the larger fight.

There is a third meaning as well, a third purpose to be served. Wagner's work spoke as a revolutionary voice in relation to present times and his contemporaries, and was meant to endure into the future as a continuing voice which would strengthen those fighters who could bring about that future in which many-- a people-- could eventually find his art to be their voice. His larger, culture-transforming task thus required of him the special task of founding for his art a stylistic tradition by means of which his work could live on, pure and unalloyed, into that future beyond his own lifetime, until it reached that future for which its creator has destined it. For that to occur, it would have to be others who would maintain his work. For unlike a philosopher, whose work can maintain itself in the form he gave it by being put into printed form, Wagner's musical work could not, but required for its endurance into the future those who could perform it and do so properly. The signs that some persons were responding to his latest music was an indication that it might be possible to place his work in the hands and care of faithful guardians, if he could but publicly demonstrate and give successful instruction in the new style needed for the proper performance of his work. But more: this present in which this work, addressed basically to men of the future, currently exists is one which, quite apart from Wagner's initiative and his power to effect, has about it an insecurity and instability which portends an apparently ineluctable revolution which may or may not lead to that freer humanity to whom his latest works could speak with the prospect of being heard and responded to. The problem arises, then, not simply how to preserve his art appropriately into the future, but just as importantly, how to dam the flood which is bringing the revolution and to do this in such way that this art, and what belongs to such a *better* future as his art promoted, are not also swept away by the revolution along with all that is worthy of destruction in our times. Wagner felt the need both for "human souls as mediators with the future" and for lasting "public institutions as guarantees of this future", that his works might be preserved through these coming times of earthquake and upheaval.[44]

In this situation, Wagner is confident in the capacity of the German people to provide the ongoing socio-political and institutional matrix within which his work could be maintained into the future for which it was meant. But as for carrying the music itself: his experience of its performance and reception had been anything but reassuring, so that if it was to be maintained *as he meant it to sound and to appear* he would have to awaken and train those to whom he would have to entrust his most precious possession. His answer was contained in the idea of Bayreuth as a place not simply for performance while he was alive but for continued performance into the distant future according to a tradition which he would establish there before his death.

'Bayreuth' then means an undertaking which, if successful, will carry onward into the future beyond Wagner's own lifetime a possibility, embodied in the properly performed music itself, that will speak to-- and help to give shape to-- a future of a rather different character than the present. That future is not characterized at any length in this meditation. But two pointers are interesting.

First: Wagner's art is different from all modern art because it does not speak the language of a caste (the cultivated) but speaks to all, cultivated and uncultivated alike.

> That it was in any way possible for an art to exist which was so bright and warm [*so sonnenhaft hell und warm*] that it would both enlighten [*mit ihrem Strahle zu erleuchten*] the poor-in-spirit and lowly and melt the arrogance of the learned [*Wissenden*]: this had to be experienced, and was nothing that could be guessed. But it must transform every notion of education and culture in the spirit of everyone who experiences it; it will seem to him that a curtain has been raised on a future in which there are no longer any highest goods and happiness-makers [*höchsten Güter und Beglückungen*] except those which all hearts share in common. The ill odor which has hitherto clung to the word 'common' will then have been removed from it.[45]

Second, but in a characterization of Wagner that departs from almost everything else said about him in the meditation, Nietzsche claims that, despite the Wagnerian emphasis on the German people and German spirit,

> the creative artist's urge [*Drang*] to help is too great, the horizon of his love of human beings too encompassing, for his vision [*Blick*] to remain attached to the confines of the national character. His thoughts are like those of every great and good German, *supra-German*, and the language of his art speaks, not to peoples, but to human beings. *But to human beings of the future.*[46]

These human beings will presumably be those he characterizes when speaking of Wagner's belief in the future; that belief

> means no more than that he perceives in present-day human beings qualities which do not belong to the unalterable character and bone-structure of the human being [*Wesen*] but are changeable, indeed transitory, and that it is precisely *on account of* [*wegen*] *these qualities* that art has to be homeless among them and he himself has to be advance messenger of another age. No golden age, no cloudless sky is allotted to this coming generation to which his instinct [*Instinkt*] directs him and whose vague features can, so far as it is possible to infer the nature [*Art*] of the need-and-distress [*Not*] from the nature [*Art*] of the gratification, be divined from the secret writing of his art. Neither will super-human goodness and justice span the fields of this future like an immovable rainbow. Perhaps this generation as a whole will even seem more evil than the present generation-- for, in wicked as in good things, it will be more open [*offener*]; it would be possible, indeed, that if its soul should speak out in free full tones it would shake and terrify our soul as if the voice of some hitherto concealed evil spirit of nature had spoken out loud. Or how do these propositions sound in our ear: that passion is better than stoicism and hypocrisy; that to be honest, even in evil, is better than to lose oneself in the morality of tradition; that the free human being can be good or evil but that the unfree human is a disgrace to nature and has no share in either heavenly or earthly consolation; finally, that he who wants to become free has to become so through himself, and that freedom falls into no one's lap like a miraculous gift. However shrill and uncanny all this may sound, these are sounds from that world of the future which has a *truthful need of art* and which can thus expect truthful satisfaction from it; it is the language of nature restored also in the world of human beings, it is precisely that which I earlier called correct feeling, in contrast to the incorrect feeling which predominates today.[47]

INTERLUDE

A PAUSE

CHAPTER 8
The Turn

The published writings which we have been attending to in Part I reflect a coherent initial phase of Nietzsche's thinking as he ventures upon the reflective task of a philosopher. Before considering in Part II the works which embody the second phase of his thought and noticing what happens there to his thinking on time and temporality, let us pause and take a brief look backward, then forward.

A. A look backward

In his retrospects, Nietzsche points us to one problematic feature of the writings and thought we have been considering, and makes it central to his own account of the turn his thought is about to take. But he seems oblivious of two others, which have a considerable bearing on the character of the ideas and the writings we will be considering next.

The feature he notes is this: in his early thought development Schopenhauer and Wagner were dominant figures whose lead he followed when he sought to clarify and understand the matters that concerned him; in retrospect, while valuing their inspiration he at the same time regretted the degree to which he had allowed his thought to take a shape determined by them so that it appeared in a somewhat alien guise and coloration. What Nietzsche acknowledges means that there is always a question of what in these early works represents his own thinking as it comes directly out of himself and his own experiencing, and what is his thinking as he was allowing it to be steered and colored by ideas assimilated from others and given some sort of meaning by him. But the ambiguity and uncertainty goes further: in retrospect Nietzsche also notes that, when he was treating expressly of Schopenhauer and Wagner in these early writings (especially in the meditations in which they were the central figures), he was not doing what he seemed to be doing, namely, attempting an accurate portrait of them, but to an important degree was projecting himself into them. Since the writings did not alert a reader to this fact (and perhaps he was not fully aware of it himself at the time), he charges himself in retrospect with a significant measure of falsification and forgery.

In our discussion, we have not attempted to sort out and disentangle these ambiguities and uncertainties in the presentation of his thought: our interest has not required this. Instead, while noting their existence, we have concentrated on eliciting the disclosive experience he operated within (so far as this is made accessible to us in the writings themselves) and on understanding the horizon of intelligibility, the nature and terms, of his account of time and temporality. There are, however, two further problematic features of his early writings of which he remains oblivious even in his retrospects. Let us consider each of these briefly.

1. Time and temporality

One of these features concerns the very subject of our study. In setting forth his thought, Nietzsche makes time and temporality central for his understanding of reality, life, and meaning. Recalling our accounts in Chapters 4-7, two things stand out about his treatment of this complex subject in the works considered.

First, each successive work expands his ideas of these matters. While characterizing time's creational function, BT starts his treatment off without speaking of time's own internal nature; rather, it focuses on a dual temporality stemming from it. One facet is passage: every temporal being knows an end to an existence which began for it, knows transience and (for the living) mortality. A second facet is tradition: a temporal being knows not only the passage between beginning and end but a continual interacting along the way which for humans includes, among other things, reproduction of the species, thus successive generations of human beings and the transmission of shared tradition through such generations.

In order to speak of the internal nature of time which BT ignored, UHH treats time as a condition of experience and addresses its nature by way of the current moment of the present of a being involved in the interacting of a transient existence. That nature is represented by a scroll-and-pages, with time's movement being imaged by the successive detachment of pages from the scroll. As for temporality, UHH expands and internalizes BT's concern for tradition, and makes central a certain mode of active engagement, namely, the historical. But this mode, in contrast with the unhistorical, is open to us only as we have grown into adulthood, and UHH addresses as crucial to the temporality of our humanity our growth and maturation. The connection of these two facets of our temporality is made evident in the two sorts of 'times' which enter into the forming of human initiative. On the one hand there is the 'times' which, as the contemporary social framework in which one is involved, is also internalized and influences the forming of our initiative; in addition, it harbors the traditions inherited from the past of the group we are being raised within. On the other hand, our power of initiative develops out of itself according to a native directionality which means that by our nature as individual human beings we evolve over time via phases-and-times of maturation; demarcated by transformative-transitions, these times are significantly different for us humanly, in a way defined by immanent meanings, not by the circumstantial-and-social. Youth is the time of life (in natural meaning) in which an altered relation to one's 'times' (in the social sense) is first possible and called for, and the way is opened (in principle) for the continuation of our maturational evolution-and-transformation toward the eventual full development and exercise of our capacity as human beings for responsible participation in the affairs of existence.

SE then expands this account of temporality by filling out in two ways the UHH-ideas concerning life as involving individual growth and maturation. Introducing the call of conscience, the morality of responsibility, and aspiration-and-love, as part of youth, and culture as their intended issue (individually and collectively), it speaks (first) of the toward-what of the movement of life in individuals (namely, culture) when this movement is seen in the larger temporal horizon of the evolutionary development of life on earth. So seen, we are not simply individuals but also represent and bear a line of life, life's development, and life's reaching; the life in each of us thus involves an at-stake and an evolutionary meant-to-be which is of more than individual-- indeed, more than human-- significance. For life reaches for those 'true human beings' in which Nature finds her redemption of herself. But SE speaks also (second) of the how of the moving-onward of life. The movement by which, in virtue of our decision-making and -executing, we realize the life in ourselves and its individual meant-to-be (maturity), is not automatic, inevitably bringing us to mature and our lives to unfold; it is the movement of a venturing, a risking, which is often enough unsuccessful, its non-inevitability being due both to circumstantial reasons and to various inward failures in the exercise of an evolving capacity. Now so far as it carries an evolutionary reaching and meant-to-be, the life in us makes us agents in and for its reaching; but in this role we living agents often show her as not adept but clumsy in her attempt to accomplish her own larger purpose, and as in need of ourselves, in the form of responsible, knowledgeable, and purposeful, human effort, if she is to reach her meant-to-be goal.

Then finally, in a gathering together but particularizing of the sense of temporal movement he has been gradually setting forth in these three works, in WB Nietzsche reformulates the character of the how of that movement, speaking now in terms of "necessity". Within us, the temporal becoming is one of a venturesome but natural 'become what one is'; and beyond us, the coming-to-be of evolutionary life eventually has brought a circumstance that cor-responds with the 'becoming' of a historically-decisive individual (Wagner). The outcome is a linking of within and beyond, one that embodies necessity throughout. Yet this necessity is that of destiny and lot, thus a necessity with several meanings, different but presumably consonant, all relating to a purposiveness as at work in life's temporal movement and in life's participation in meaning.

The second thing which stands out about this developing account of Nietzsche's is this: Although it has a certain coherence when understood from the agential and idealistic standpoint from which it is formulated, the exposition of it involves the introduction of an explicit idea of time which is at some odds with, and is unable to do justice to, time and temporality as he is making these visible to us in his presentation. The fact that what he was actually responsively aware of and working with (so far as his writing conveys this) and what he was seeking to make intelligible in certain explicit terms holds more than he was succeeding in eliciting conceptually, is nothing surprising. Rather, it is a normal part of the exploring and testing which belong to reflection as a venturing. Yet of this tension in his own thinking, between an explicitly formulated and utilized interpretation of time and the immediate sense of time and temporality being conveyed and developed in his exposition, Nietzsche seems oblivious even in retrospect. In our exposition, we have on occasion pointed out this tension and sought to suggest (at least in some measure) the idea of time and temporality which is only implicit in his presentation. We have done this not simply to make apparent the state of the matter, but because his exposition provides access to a profounder insight into time and temporality than what becomes expressed explicitly in his account. The immediate question raised by this tension is whether, in the turn of thought we are to be considering next, he becomes aware of this tension and succeeds in retrieving what was being missed. The fact that he does not, and the reason(s) for that, have profound consequences for the development of his thought in this second phase.

2. Space and spatiality

The second of the problematic features of his early writings which we wish to bring to attention here was not only unnoticed by Nietzsche himself in his retrospects but was not raised into view by us in our earlier discussion. Yet consideration of it becomes pressing due to the turn which Nietzsche's thinking takes in its second phase. In the case of time and temporality a tension arose within his thinking because Nietzsche presented and used an explicit concept of time inadequate to the matters of time and temporality as he was bringing these forward in his exposition; but in the companion case of space and spatiality Nietzsche does not even develop an explicit concept of these. Nonetheless, from the start (BT) space has belonged with time and individuality as distinguishing marks of the things of the (creaturely) world of appearance. Thus in his discussion of reality and life as matters to be understood, he presents these as involving space and spatiality and in that presentation leaves undifferentiated facets of space and spatiality which are in need of differentiation, especially in relation to the matter of the bodiliness of ourselves as agents. This absence of an explicit concept of space and spatiality and this undifferentiation marking his discussion of reality and life would not matter if they made no difference to the coherence and cogency of his thought. But they do. In the writings that express the first phase of his thought, the presence of what is problematic in this regard remained a dormant and peripheral one, in virtue of the way his thought followed out the disclosures of experience in a metaphysical direction. But in the second phase of his thought he rejects this type of understanding of the import of the immediate disclosures that lie at the heart of his thinking, and brings our bodily being as agents forward into a prominent place in his reflections. Since the expansion of attention to search out our being so as to make evident the bodily character of that being becomes accomplished without the rethinking of space and spatiality that are needed, the problematic nature of the failure to discern and make clear various differentiations when conceiving space and spatiality comes out into the open in this second phase, and an increasing tension emerges between the experience of our agency as he conveys it and the terms he would avail himself of to make it intelligible. It is important, thus, to enter upon some initial exploration of this matter of space and spatiality, and to note the main differentiations required for aptly treating the matters marked by them.

As he addresses life in the first phase of his thought, Nietzsche interprets it first and foremost as an affair which we live, and which each of us lives firsthand and first-personally. That living takes place in an interacting with circumstance, in a having-to-do with each other. And in this, space is inherently involved. If time directly enables and makes temporal the initiative and activity of ourselves as creaturely beings, setting the bounds of beginning and end and introducing the moment-forming stretching needed for the actuality of our continuing initiative and undertakings from out of ourselves, space directly enables and makes our activity spatial as an interacting of diverse agents who are situated in diverse heres over against the heres of others and who are constituted in their separateness for a contributing out of themselves to the connecting with each other which their interacting achieves. The finitizing work of space is apparent in the complex spatiality which makes our active being be bodily and our active engagement be an engagement out of our separate selves which links us with-- but maintains us as different from-- others likewise active out of themselves and bodily in their being.

In keeping with the dominant thrust of Nietzsche's reflection, that in it he is disclosing life *as we live it*, how do we discover our spatiality to be in this living, and more specifically, how do we discover our bodily being as it is involved in our living and acting? In the background of Nietzsche's thought lies a pointer of Schopenhauer's, made when he notes that we know our body in a dual way. There is that unique and intimate immediate awareness that each of us has, of our own body as our own, of our immediate openness to the world around us through our bodily being, and of our particularization as active beings in virtue of this bodiliness of our being; and there is that awareness of our body as it shows itself amidst other bodies, on the strength of which we can apprehend and know it in that appearance it has just as we do any other body, with no disclosure or even any hint of the unique relation we have to our own body. What are we to make of this duality? In his first-phase writings Nietzsche does not attempt to bring this matter into explicit conceptualization and make the differentiations called for, but in them he does take for granted and implicitly bring forward varied facets of our being as spatial. Let us seek to make explicit the basic structuring of this sort, and its condition, and bring the undifferentiation in what Nietzsche does say into that perspective. To think on this matter, let us take as point of focus any activity of ours, say, playing the piano, and begin sorting out the spatiality involved in this. In the following discussion, it is important that we maintain the perspective of ourselves clarifying *our own* activity from the standpoint of *our being the persons who are engaging in* it and who are therefore experiencing it in first-personal fashion.

Suppose we are playing a Chopin nocturne for some friends. Included in the situation along with ourselves are (among other things) the piano and piano-bench, the room, and the audience in the room, all entered into the situation so as to be connecting with each other from various distances and in various directions. Entering into our playing as obvious elements in it are our sitting on the bench, placing our feet at the pedals, reaching out our arms and moving our fingers: in short, a positioning and maintaining of ourselves posture-wise in a relation to the piano appropriate for our striking the keys and making the musical sound become audible. Entering more centrally into our playing are the attention and concentration under which we ingather ourselves and attend to the matter of producing the music; included here are (for example) a peripheral awareness of the surroundings, the piano, and our posture-relation to the piano, but inwardly also and more in the forefront so far as the actual playing is concerned, an awareness of our own readiness-condition as we compose ourselves, rehearse the beginning in anticipation, and then begin to play. At the same time as in that playing we are calling upon and releasing into actual functioning the skills of playing and the knowledge of the music developed in previous practice over time, we are receiving and registering the musical sound as it emerges and assessing it as more or less successfully making audible the music as we conceive it inwardly and are attempting to make it heard by all. None of this, the attention and concentration and the inward condition and functioning of ourselves as we play, is itself directly visible to others, yet it is central to the executing of an activity which is visible both as (overall) a performing and as (in its components) marked by various overt elements such as we mentioned above.

Let us take this as a sufficient initial reminder of important facets of the activity of playing the music we are performing for our friends, and let us now ask: what are the spatial elements involved here? How are we to understand the space which enables and conditions the activity, giving the beings and their activity the spatiality that marks the interaction and its various parties?

The initial and obvious spatial feature of the situation in question is that all the human parties enter into it as bodily beings situated for activity in relation to what is circumstantial to them and for interacting with each other in a playing and listening in the situation.

As regards the bodily aspect of the non-human focal point, the piano: it has an expansive bulk and in virtue of the area it occupies it is positioned in relation to all else within the room; and that bulk has a three-dimensionality and a delimiting surface, in virtue of which we speak of it in terms of its exterior (outside) and its interior (inside). More importantly, as a particular type of manufactured instrument the piano has a functional configuration to its bulk, whereby that bulk is articulated in such way as to be able to be struck on its keyboard and to be brought to operate so as to produce sounds which radiate out into the space beyond itself. As we encounter it, then, the spatiality of the piano, as a manufactured instrument, lies in its determinate three-dimensionality, in its location or occupation of an area and its positioning in relation to other area-occupying beings, and in the operational configuration of its bulk whereby it is arrayed for the approach to it and operation of it by others spatially beyond itself to produce sounds that carry spatially beyond it.

As for we ourselves who can approach it and strike those keys and hear those sounds: although we likewise have an expansive bulk, it is one articulated naturally in ourselves as active living beings, and articulated in such way that, under the condition of the outwardizing which orients us toward and exposes us to what is beyond ourselves, we are enabled to be active and initiate activity in which our own articulated bulk serves as enabling ingredient in and for that activity. We have hands and fingers, limbs, eyes and ears: all these functional instruments fit us for activity addressed to what we encounter beyond ourselves. And we know these *as enabling ingredients*-- that is, we know ourselves in this articulated-for-action outwardized bodiliness of ours-- first and foremost *in* our *acting*, in our employing of our articulated body in activity; and this self-knowledge consists above all in the immediate intimate self-awareness that is element in our being active and that discloses this bodily ingredient functioning in our activity as uniquely 'our own'. Now even though we know the bodily side of our being to be 'our own' in our cognizance (say) of our fingers and ears as we employ them in the playing and listening, still in virtue of the outwardizing or externalizing involved in making our bodily being be what it is, the exposure of our bodily side has a determinateness which is, like that of the piano, marked by the variables of interior-exterior (internal and external, inside and outside, and so on); and in this determinateness, there is no sign whatever of the 'our own', of 'our own' fingers playing or 'our own' ears hearing. For everybody else, and for myself when I consider these visible things as others do from the outside, there is at best 'his fingers' and 'his ears', or even 'its fingers' and 'its ears' (that body's). Even more importantly, when we look in this external way we do not find much of what belongs to our *activity* nor much of the enabling spatiality for it, *as enabling*. Even so, although the spatiality of our being makes us bodily in virtue of an outwardizing or externalizing which introduces an exterior-interior determinateness to our articulated-for-action bodiliness, our spatiality is not exhausted by this, and certainly not determined in primary reference to such determinateness. What is missing here? What is more fundamental?

Our activity is a complex and structured affair, and more central in it than the obvious facets (the striking of the keys with our fingers, say) are those facets of it which are decisive for its nature and occurrence as the activity which it is; we have recalled them in short-hand, so to speak, by referring to the concentration and attention, the awareness, and the other elements in the initiative in virtue of which we are (say) playing the piano rather than making supper, and are concentrating and attending in ways (say) that enable the key-striking by our fingers which is crucial to piano-playing taking place. We say of such elements that they are inward, and mean that they are inward to us *as those active beings* whose being involves an *outwardized bodiliness* that is likewise (but in a different way) enabling to our activity. It seems clear that we do *not* mean by characterizing those elements as inward that they are inside us, in our interior, in such way that (say) a surgeon could cut us open and expose what is inside us and find such factors and facets. Our attention and concentration, and the various facets of our initiative, are not discoverable like the bones, the joints, the muscles, which are (to an observer) hiddenly at work as instrumental factors in the striking of the keys and which, because they manifest themselves in the exterior-interior side of our bodiliness in general, can be discovered directly only by penetrating from the outside to the interior beyond the original surface. Rather they are like our cognizance of the bodily side of our activity as 'our own', inward in a sense which in principle makes any approach from the outside which seeks to find inwardness in the interior be futile and misguided. The inwardness in question is instead a spatiality *concomitant and polar to* the outwardly-orienting and the outward, and for that very reason the domain of the private. Inwardness is nothing public, or able to become public, and nothing discoverable to awareness and attention immersed in the outward alone.

The inwardness which is the place formed in the inwardizing which is the concomitant obverse to the externalizing or outwardizing which makes our bodily being complex as polar is indeed discoverable by us, and is discoverable directly, but only from within itself, in first-personal vein. And more, it is discoverable as the more fundamental pole of our spatiality in this sense, that it is not only that feature of our spatiality which harbors the capacity-- the potentiality as well as actuality and actual initiative-- that belongs to us as beings active with initiative out of ourselves, but that feature which has priority in the 'here' in which we operate as we shape the initiative by which we are active out of ourselves. If the inward were an interior, what takes place in it could be thought to be cut off from what is outward; but because the outwardizing thrust of our bodily being is enabling to activity whose formation takes place in the inwardness that is enabled by the inwardizing that is the polar obverse of that outwardizing, that forming involves inward receptivity to and register of the outward beyond the agent as well as to-and-of the agent in his/her own wholeness as agent. The prior inward side of the 'here' is the locus of all our discovering, above all of our discovering of the outward beyond ourselves and what it holds. For such discovering takes place in the inwardness of our being, in first-personal vein, in (say) the perceptual touch which registers in our striking the piano keys. As a result, there is privacy in the hearing of the music by each of us, privacy to the registering of the public (the sounding music) in our own listening; and this listening, in each of us our own and private, is an inward functioning made possible by the opening of ourselves-- 'our own' opening-- to what is spatially beyond ourselves, what is outward and public, achieved with the whole outward side of our bodily being but here, especially with our ears.

In spatiality as so far grasped, it is space as enabling to active-participating-in-an-interacting that is the conditioning and grounding factor for the spatial features in question. Space enables interacting as enabling diverse heres for the agents and their engaging, and enables those heres as distinct-yet-connected in virtue of a conjoint inwardizing-and-outwardizing whereby each here can be and maintain itself as the unique locus of an agent's initiative. The polarized spatiality obtaining in active beings in virtue of space's conditioning makes the bodily being of each be complexly structured, involving an outward side operating within-- and enabling-- the being's activity so as to connect the being (as distinct agent) with other beings who are able to be active out of their own 'here' in virtue of the bodily character of their own being. In that connecting, the outward is the public mediating component such as enables the inward and its privacy to be and be maintained in the connecting of center with center that is taking place. Now as regards this 'here' of ours, there is an ambiguity to saying that correlative with it is a 'there'. For if 'there' means the locus of space-conditioned agents other than ourselves, it must refer to the 'heres' which are those of other agents in their own participation in activity: 'there' signifies those other 'heres' from the perspective of another agent's own 'here'. But if 'there' means what manifests the *outward aspect* of our spatiality and what appears thus in the public realm, then *that* 'there' is not (properly speaking) correlative with the 'here' of inwardness, but refers rather to an aspect-- the outward-- which serves as orientation-field (and if the 'there' is specific, the orientation-point within that field) determined from out of some 'here' in and by an active being. The other beings who are participants out of themselves in the interacting which is existence are not found 'in' that 'there', as if that field *contained* them whole; for that field only harbors their face, while as agents whole, they have an inclusive (polar) spatiality one in virtue of which their own proper 'here' harbors-- and indeed, gives spatial priority to-- a center inward to (but not internal or interior to) that outward face. Only that 'here' of the *whole being as active* is the 'there' which is the proper correlative to some other agent's own proper 'here'.

Space, then, is the condition which determines, for diverse beings participating in interaction, a spatiality whose fundamental features are an inwardness and outwardness for each being; in virtue of the polarity of this differentiation, the activity of those beings involves an inwardly formed initiative which, gathering up the whole bodily being (including its outwardness) into activity, engages the agent with others in an interacting to which the whole bodily side of the being of each and all is integral. Making activity possible as an *inter*acting, the inward and the outward together make it a complex affair achieved in virtue of a dual polarity: that of outward and inward within each being, and that of agent-here interactively connecting out of its inwardness with agent-here in an interacting mediated by the outward. Spatially construed and collectively speaking, we are diverse agents able to interact with each other because, at the same time as we are outwardized in our being toward each other, we are inwardized so as to make our participation in the interacting be possible as-- and to maintain it as-- an acting initiated out of ourselves. If the spatial inwardness so characterized forms the most fundamental aspect of our structured spatiality, as being the abode harboring the deciding and determining powers and workings involved in the forming and carrying out of our activity and participation in the interacting of existence, these two-- that inwardness, and what it harbors-- are only (the fundamental) elements in an acting and interacting which require for their possibility the outwardness of our being, the other pole of our spatially shaped bodily being. Without this outwardness and its activity-articulation, we could not play the piano, we could not make the music audible and hear it: our activity could not be such as it is.

Now in virtue of the very nature of space and our spatial being as helping (along with time and temporality) to make possible an interacting in which something is at stake, we are primordially oriented in our activity toward what is beyond ourselves spatially and more specifically are initially directly exposed to the face of such beings which, together with that of ourselves, forms the outward and public side of what we must register and take into account in our activity. Building upon our attention to that face, we may abstract this outward side of things from the whole in which it is what it is, and may thereby gain purchase for a study of the character and operation of what we find: we can study "space" and "spatial relations", we can study "spatial things" in their various features, we can know "nature" as it manifests itself in this "spatial framework". But if in so proceeding we take up with *this one aspect* of "space" and "the spatial" and regard it as *exhausting* space and spatiality, we *mis-take* matters. What is so studied is neither itself what is fundamental and the basis of everything else, nor something which exists in that isolated fashion. What we are focused on exclusively in virtue of our abstraction exists in reality as one element in active beings and their interacting, and indeed, as only one aspect of a more inclusive space and spatial whole that holds such an element. For that whole of space and spatiality to be disclosed and discerned in its own nature as the activity-enabling whole it is, and for the fuller spatiality of such beings to be grasped, a broader and fuller attentiveness is needed.

Let that suffice as the beginning on a differentiating of the sides of the spatiality which belongs to us as human agents. Such a beginning is sufficient for the immediate purpose at hand, which is, in anticipation of the writings of the second phase of Nietzsche's thought, to note the absence of re-cognition by him of appropriate differentiations when space and spatiality enter into the discussions in the writings embodying the first phase of his thinking, and to ready ourselves for seeing how this absence affects the thought of the second phase in which space and spatiality become matters crucial to the focus of his concern. To carry this preparatory purpose further, let us consider Nietzsche's characterization (in UHH) of the plastic power that is harbored in life. Two sorts of non-differentia-tion mark his discussion, one concerning the structure our spatiality enters into our being, the other concerning the nature of the facets of this power and, given the different spatial status of such dif-ferent facets, the ways those come into play and operate in our activity.

To set the context for our notice of these non-differentiations, let us recall the place which this plastic power has in us. According to Nietzsche, we are active beings who realize the life in us in our activity; that activity carries us as whole beings into an interplay with circumstance, and its forming--our initiative, our decision-making and -executing-- takes place by way of responsive powers in such way as integrates not only circumstance but also our being and its inward complexity into the forming and carrying out of the activity in question. Now for Nietzsche the life in us introduces several fur-ther things into our being. First, it introduces a drive toward 'more life', which registers in the re-sponsiveness forming our active engagement and thereby animates the functioning of our capacities with a vital-energy so that they operate as 'vital powers' in and through which we are by nature reaching for fuller life. Second, it introduces into the spatially-outward and articulated-for-action side of our being we have just been thinking on that organ-ized constitution and physiological functioning whereby our outwardized vehicle for activity is an organic body. Finally, it introduces the plastic power we want now to consider again. In earlier discussion, we noted how it is a complex and struc-tured power: at its heart is the power to grow in characteristic fashion out of itself, and supportive of this are two further facets of the overall power, namely, the capacity to reshape and incorporate the alien and the past so as make these support our natural growth, and the capacity to restore and replace functional elements in ourselves as living growing beings when injury or harm is done to them. In his formulation of this power and these facets of it, Nietzsche makes no further determination of what he has in mind: apparently none seemed needed for his point in introducing reference to this power, namely, to provide the basis for a standard for understanding the use and misuse of history as regards life. But let us briefly consider them further, and look to them in the light particularly of our discus-sion of space and spatiality.

The crux of the matter of growing out of ourselves is the kind of complexity which belongs to our nature. At its heart are the decision-making and -executing powers in virtue of which our initiation of activity is a responsive affair. Operating in the inwardness of our being, they function in a respon-siveness which, in regard to the at-stake which they register, receives this in the mode of need and (eventually) obligation, and registers what else enters into the decision-making as exerting a claim to be heeded somehow in our response to the at-stake in the need in which it claims us. The growth out of ourselves in this regard (the maturation of ourselves humanly as we develop our decision-making and -executing capacity and the powers involved) has a distinctive character. The meant-to-be which destines the evolution of this capacity toward a moral issue and makes youth the crucial time for assuming life and life's unfolding on oneself as a moral affair is a meaning native to our na-ture. The realization of that meaning takes place by exercise and learning, and more precisely, by ex-ercise and learning accomplished by the very responsive powers that the meant-to-be means for an evolution. That is, its realizing medium is the responsive freedom by which, in our answering to the at-stake as needy, the meant-to-be in question gains such effective directive force as it does, and gains it in virtue of how we responsively register and respond to it. All of this-- the meant-to-be and the potential for which it is meaning, the actual responsive formation of initiative, the gradual realization of the meant-to-be over time, the emergence of the morality that is meant-to-be-issue in our matura-tion-- is harbored in the inward side of our being so that in the measure in which we mature we do so out of ourselves and on the strength of a responsive interplay that involves need and obligation.

However, maturation takes place only by way of the formation of activity in an interacting with outward circumstance; and it takes the shape it does within the matrix of our whole active being and in responsive activity which responds to other facets of the growth out of ourselves-- facets relating (say) to our bodily development, such as our growth in height. Now these facets and their meanings are latent in the outwardness of our physical being, and their actualization takes place differently from our maturation humanly. For the processes of actualization in question are not natured themselves to be an interplay of freedom and obligation and a decision-making amidst claims; nor is the interplay of outward conditions which directly affect such processes (both those conditions belonging to the outwardness of our body itself and those of circumstance) constituted in such way. And yet, at the same time, all such processes as belong to the outwardness of our bodily being are taking place *within* an encompassing whole-- ourselves as active beings--, and within a whole whose *operation as the whole it is* itself takes shape *on other grounds* and *in other ways* than those processes. As a result, according as the activity of ourselves as a whole takes shape in one way or another, these processes belonging to the bodily side of our being gain different circumstantial conditions for their functioning, and also become differently conditioned within our own body in virtue (ultimately) of differences in our inward functioning. Indeed, whether we grow or not in these physical regards, and how we do, depends indirectly and in part upon our inward initiative and the activity of ourselves whole that is initiated and carried through on inward bases: eating, eating what nourishes, exercising, are integral to the possibility of our physical existence and growth. Nonetheless, quite regardless of the degree to which our activity indirectly may impede or assist our physical growth, the evolution in question does not take place in the inwardness of our being (it concerns rather the outward side of our being), nor are the processes of growth in question themselves matters of responsive or moral activity.

The kind of interweaving of inward and outward factors which the spatial differentiation of inward and outward within the whole of ourselves makes possible is complex. Further facets of that complexity are evident in the other components of the plastic power. For example, in virtue of the organic constitution of our bodily being we are needy and dependent as regards circumstance for our continued existence and for what answers to our needs. Thus an important element of the plastic power is the capacity to re-shape and incorporate the alien-- say, food-- in order that, in virtue of the physiological processes of digestion, we may extract the nourishment we need for sustenance and for physical activity and growth. Yet while the re-shaping and incorporating (as ingesting) themselves are activities which issue from an inward initiative responsive to the claiming of the at-stake, and while the particular need which such activity responsively heeds is registered and thereby operates in our inwardness, the need itself and the processes of digestion which complete the 'incorporation' and eventually alleviate the physical need belong to our outwardness. In that status, they themselves have a character and a functioning which belong to the organic constitution of our outwardness and which operate in their own independent way *so long as* (external and inward) conditions are supportive or not disruptive.

The matter is equally-- but differently-- complex when it comes to the re-shaping and incorporating of the past. Nietzsche's main focus in UHH is on the trans-personal past. The starting-point for a recall of this is the initial (spatially-mediated) incorporation of factors from circumstance beyond ourselves in the present (the 'times' and, say, 'knowledge made accessible to the learner in the books and records accessible within the times'); in that incorporation, we make the knowledge of the past our own in some sense. But that appropriated knowledge, subsisting as retained in the unconscious side of the inwardness of our being where it has become part of that accumulating burden of the past we carry with us, can be recalled at some later time: we can 'recall' the past, and then scrutinize and reinterpret it, and in turn consciously enter it into our shaping of life's future. In all of this, it is our own inwardness as active beings that is involved, though the knowledge in question, in its content, reaches quite beyond us spatially and temporally. Now of the knowledge held unconsciously in this way, we have no distinct consciousness any more than of anything taking place in the unconscious side of our being as we are forming our initiative and carrying out our actions; yet as part of a burden, it exerts pressure and somehow functions in us unbeknownst in other regards. How are we to understand the impress of such knowledge on the forming of our initiatives when the impressing does not come to consciousness in us? Does the fact that our initiative is formed by a capacity responsive to the claiming of the at-stake mean that such functioning can not be of the form which belongs to the outwardness of our being, like the digestive processes or processes of physical growth? But if not like these, then like the functioning of powers in the conscious side of our being and of the formation of our initiative? But how do the powers that come into play there function? Or again: this time focusing on the personal past and the learning involved in the forming of dispositions-to-respond which we bear in the inwardness of our being and which can come into play later, how do such dispositions come to bear on the forming of our initiative?

Because in UHH Nietzsche does not need to raise and answer such questions for the purpose for which he introduced the notion of life's plastic power, the spatially-grounded differentiations we have been noticing never become part of his explicit thought. Indeed they might not have been so even if he had been confronted with the questions and had had to analyze more fully the matters he includes under the different facets of the plastic power and under the power as a whole. However that may be, Nietzsche does not expressly make the differentiation between inward and outward that we have been pointing to, and does not expressly distinguish within the components of the plastic power the very different things included in them and speak thus of an interweaving of factors very different in their spatial ground. In the second phase of his thought, a confrontation with some such questions will be part of what needs to take place, and what we have been discussing will help us to understand the meaning of what Nietzsche is urging at that time.

B. A look forward

As we have seen in Chapters 1 and 2, in the evolution of Nietzsche's personal and reflective life there came a time when the impetus which maintained him on the course of thought being developed in his earliest writings became undermined. Beginning in altered feelings, the transformation that took place in Nietzsche the human being and Nietzsche the thinker meant a significant alteration not only in his conduct of reflective inquiry and the terms he avails himself of explicitly in his pursuit of understanding but also in the manner of his presentation of his thought in writing. In his retrospects Nietzsche makes much of the change that takes place in him and that is carried into his works, and with good reason; for even beyond what he recognizes, how his thought now develops and the presence and absence of certain reflective themes in it (particularly in the implicit and explicit self-criticism in which he now engages) has its roots in the altered feelings involved and his response to and upon them.

In his later-added Prefaces, Nietzsche stresses the element of mistrust and suspicion which marks the works to which we are now turning. Whatever the elements of criticism that had been involved in the works of the first phase of his thought, those works embodied a thinking rooted in his own youthful experience and reinforced in important measure by a reverence for certain figures (Schopenhauer and Wagner, mainly) and by a faith-- a youthful faith-- which had brought commitment not only to reflection but more broadly, to duties and to a supportive engagement on his part toward Wagner. Despite the strength of the inspiration and the seeming support for his concerns and ideas coming from Wagner, Nietzsche had eventually become disenchanted with the latter and had been revealed to himself has having been involved in a significant measure of self-deception. Even though in retrospect he can speak of such self-deception as having been an element in his self-preservation and his movement ahead, the immediate disillusioning discovery led to a forceful, even extreme, turning against what he had been drawn into and, in response to an imperious voice from within, brought the awakening of a will and desire, a drive and impulse, to rebel and to liberate himself from what seemed to him now alien and polluting. According to his own account (see Chapter 2 above), in the flush of this "first outbreak of strength and will to self-determination" he sought to demonstrate his mastery over things by "wild experiments and singularities"; and in particular, wandering restlessly as if in a desert, he was tempted and moved by the thought that values needed to be reversed. He pursued that path with a vengeance.

The writings which emerge as this counter-current forms and, flowing initially in turbulent fashion, eventually grows calmer, manifest a mood noticeably different from that of the early writings. Gone is the innocent passion and sense of life-- especially youthful life-- reaching hopefully and confidently for the heights, whose companion critical address to what in the contemporary world lacks (or works against) the realization of the vibrancy, the love, the moral heart and task, of such life was infused with that same passion and an eagerness to assist in life's elevation. In their place, a more sober, cautious tone marks the speech, initially exhibiting at times a scornful and acerbic side that seems all the more harsh for the absence of the energy, the enthusiasm, and the confident passion, that marked the first phase and that imparted to the criticism and to the recognition of the negative sides of life found in that phase a constructive meaning. The sobriety infuses a determination which was born out of the shame and anger generated by disillusion and which now animates a persistent effort to unmask and expose. As deeper companion to the sobriety and determination, and giving these their intensity and guardedness, the embarrassment, shame, guilt, and anger, which emerged in reaction to the disillusion, turned the drive to truth in him into the drive to purify, unmask, and reject, using whatever seemed to be an effective weapon. These works convey above all diverse ventures on self-purification in which Nietzsche is trying out various things, pushing inquiry in certain directions and doing so to an extreme, not for the sake of truth alone but to find a truth which would perform this purifying function for himself-- or (as he puts it) which would hurt him. To the extent to which this is so, Nietzsche realizes in his own person a concern for truth which is of a piece with that of those who (as he puts it in *Dawn*) are seeking cures for themselves, not seeking truth.[1]

In the works themselves (as contrasted with in his later retrospects), he does nothing to make the reader aware of all this. Indeed, he remarks in a later-added Preface to HAH-II on how

> it was then that I learned the art of *presenting* myself as cheerful, objective, inquisitive, above all healthy and malicious ... . What perhaps constitutes the charm of this writing will nonetheless not escape a subtler eye and empathy-- that here a sufferer and renouncer speaks as though he were *not* a sufferer and renouncer. Here an equilibrium and composure in the face of life and even a sense of gratitude towards it *shall* be preserved, here there rules a rigorous, proud, constantly watchful and sensitive will that has set itself the task of defending life *against* pain and of striking down all those inferences that pain, disappointment, ill-humor, isolation and other swampgrounds usually cause to flourish like poisonous fungi.[2]

The writing itself does not expressly remark on this disparity of the presenting face of the written word and its actual root in the author. Yet even in the way Nietzsche presents the fruits of his current inquiries, as if we should regard them and their claims simply as truths, there is this almost defiant tone, conveying that the once-burned author feels himself to have secured himself finally (if belatedly) against the idealistic self-deception that had infected him before. He is telling us now how matters really are. At the same time, he alludes occasionally to the trying-out character of his effort and in general to the tentative, evidence-based and correctible, character of responsible thought; yet he scarcely attempts to indicate the reservations and tentativeness with which it would be appropriate for a reader to receive and think on thoughts that made a claim of such a nature. And the very form in which he presents his claims-- brief and compact, apparently disconnected and self-contained-- helps underline their nature as (in a double sense) pointed.

The first and unrestrained expression of his altered mood and frame of mind originally bore the name *Human all-too-human* (in the collection later reprinted under that name, it is Volume I); it was closely followed by two separately- and successively-published 'continuations and appendices' which later were gathered together as Volume II in the reprinted edition. There is irony in his stress at the beginning of the original HAH, on natural science as a paradigm of the spirit and method of an approach to truth, and as holding fruitful elements of content as well. For particularly when the sets of aphorims included in both volumes are read on the background of his retrospects concerning the work, they indicate that it was in a far from detached fashion that he was carrying through the effort to reject and break free from what he now finds embarrassing. It was more like he had suddenly found himself amidst great danger, and reacting quickly and forcefully and taking whatever seemed useful to extricate himself, he was trying to cope with the threat by attacking it-- or what he thought was it-- head-on. In virtue of this, while he is bringing into question fundamental elements in his prior sense of human agency and in his vision of the world-- elements which seem to him now linked to or expressive of what is alien--, the mood and attitude which animate the inquiry and determine its focus in these directions are not such as invite (or perhaps even permit) the scrutiny of much that needs reflection and subtle analysis.

An animus of considerable intensity marks his efforts for a while and, concentrating his attention, infects them with ambivalence. Life, by its very nature, involves something at stake, and with this, venturing and risking on the one hand and threat and danger on the other. There is no reflection that would address the problematic of existence which does not find, as part of the purchase which enables it, the responsive register of these matters in feelings of fear, anxiety, and the like. But if responsible reflection can not be well-founded without them, it remains that such feelings invite a consideration of things in thought which is unduly colored by their ambivalent concealing-and-unconcealing force if it is not countered by (say) courage and the immediacy of aspiration. Such misleading of reflection is all the more a potential in the case in point. Nietzsche's own retrospective account of what was happening and how he was initially responding indicate-- and convey his later recognition-- that his initial efforts were skewed by the animus which stemmed from the embarrassment, shame, guilt, and anger, which he was feeling. Dominated by this animus for an initial while, his reflection advances within a certain horizon whose plausibility is, to a significant extent, a function of the animus and of the power of thought, operating within the horizon, to effect the rejection and dissociation he was seeking. What Nietzsche does not recognize-- at the time, or even in retrospect-- is the full measure of the resulting ambivalence of his progress.

Three things are taking place at once in this second phase of his thought. One is the advance within a new horizon and an altered address to the problematic of existence, the advance being given direction and force by the animus in its initial strength; a second is the intensification of his health-problems, the reaching of a nadir in his health, and the beginning of recovery; the third is, as in time the initial strength and turbulence of the animus diminished, the beginnings of a return to himself and of a revival, in more refined and mature form, of that basic spirituality which had been his in the first phase of his reflection. By the time he was gaining-- in new form-- this sense of what was genuinely his own as the particular human being he was, the initial pursuit of inquiry and advance of thought, animated and hedged in by his animus, had developed a horizon whose initial plausibility had become reinforced and rationalized to the place where, even as the animus lost strength in its immediacy and as his evolving capacities and skill in inquiry became attended by an increasingly subtle sensitivity and discrimination, there was no apparent need for bringing the fundamental elements in that horizon into question. Thus the increasing strength of his resolve to question and not to be satisfied with the first seeming answer became channelled within it, and the new spirituality was explored without the needed critiquing of basic factors in the new horizon. The result was that he came to achieve a clearer, more subtle and broader, view of the problematic with which he had been dealing, and eventually admitted into it numbers of things that were important in the first phase of his thought. But the purification they undergo to gain admission makes them acceptable now only under an interpretation which would make them consistent with his newly-developed way of framing the problematic, and in particular, with the critical tools which he is focused on as the heart of the needed 'scientific' pursuit of inquiry into the problematic. If, then, in the course of his recovery of his health he was achieving a somewhat fuller, more complex, and more self-aware engagement with things and eventually discovering in himself with growing confidence a new form of his early sense of ourselves as active agents and of a crisis obtaining in contemporary life, the thought-terms in which he would now do justice to these make for an account which, while more refined and more complex and while drawing on somewhat deeper and more subtle experience in virtue of his maturer being, can even less do justice to their fundamental nature than before. For his initial animus has so skewed and slanted the framework, the horizon, in which he would make things intelligible now as to distort and belie (in ways he never sees) the fuller sense of things which is coming to be his. When at the end of this phase that fuller experiencing of things has begun itself to take the lead again and his concern for a positive vision on that basis has regained precedence, the reading of things-- of the nature and meaning of the disclosures accessible now-- by way of the 'purified' terms has become a melodic line which is being sounded in some contrast and dissonance against the ground bass of a countervailing 'fuller and more sensitive' feel for life.

The path through this second phase, begun in an extreme reactive turn, advances in the pursuit of insight over a variety of exploratory avenues, which are pursued more calmly in *Dawn* than in HAH until finally, in *Gay Science*, this period of 'winter' is passed through, and a spring thaw has arrived, bringing the breaking of the ice which allows the stream to flow once again.[3] GS leads directly into the major work of the third phase of his thought, *Thus Spoke Zarathustra*. Indeed, as Nietzsche notes in EH, GS "contains a hundred signs of the proximity of something incomparable; in the end, it even offers the beginning of *Zarathustra*, and in the penultimate section of the fourth book, the basic idea of *Zarathustra*".[4] In TSZ, the voice which we first heard in *The Birth of Tragedy* makes itself heard once more, now in mature form. But the overflow in which Nietzsche makes his first effective entry into the fulness of his maturity and reaches not only beyond youth *but also* beyond 'youth reacting against youth' transmutes once more the terms in which Nietzsche had been working in the preceding phase (this time, the second phase). But in this case, the transmutation involves not so much a rejection and replacement, as a sublimation and amplifying that enables the purified conceptual framework that has been being developed in the second phase basically to continue as horizon but to become much richer and more nearly apt to the immediacy of experience. In TSZ, we hear a Nietzsche who has matured considerably and who, having become master in his own house, is beginning the task of mastering the art of life and reflection lived and carried on in that house.

What are the thematic developments which take place in Nietzsche's thought in the works which emerge in the course of the spiritual dynamic we have just recalled? Let us consider those works and see.

PART II

YOUTHFUL REACTION
AGAINST 'YOUTH'

CHAPTER 9
Human all-too-human

As we have noted in Chapters 2 and 8, *Human all-too-human* is what Nietzsche himself calls the "monument of a crisis". The crisis is a personal one, calling into question what he is doing with his life (his profession, his involvement with Wagner, etc.) and in particular how he has been conceiving and pursuing philosophy. Let us consider how the ideas of time and temporality are being grasped and brought to function in the re-thinking Nietzsche is undertaking in this work, by focusing on its treatment of three things: the nature of philosophy, the nature of human agency, and the crisis-character of the present seen in relation to its past and its future.

A. Philosophy

What is philosophy? As we have been conceiving it, philosophy is reflective inquiry responsively attuned to the problematic of existence and seeking to understand the existence in which we find ourselves, the lives we are engaged in living, and what meaning is to be found in life and existence. This problematic comes forward concretely in different ways to claim thought, arising in experience differently not only for different persons but even for the same person at different times. If what one becomes entered upon in response-- namely, reflective inquiry-- is the 'same thing' amidst these differences, the 'sameness' is nonetheless not one of complete identity in character as it is found in all persons at all times but one of a determinate concrete realization of the same meaning. The response in each case takes shape as in some respects a necessarily different realization, but every realization is determined (say) to an aim at truth, and in particular, at the truth of these matters of the problematic of existence, life, and meaning.

In the early phase of his thinking that we have been considering in the preceding chapters, Nietzsche has been not only realizing philosophy in a certain fashion but (as part of this) developing and carrying with him a particular understanding of what he was doing. With the turn in his thinking which provides the impetus to the composing of HAH, Nietzsche not only alters the way in which he is realizing philosophy but also develops a rather different understanding of philosophy itself; as part of this alteration, he enters upon a self-criticism concerning the way he had previously been pursuing and understanding philosophy. The first chapter of HAH-I (entitled "Of first and last things") begins with a set of aphorisms which set forth the way he now understands philosophy and contrast his present approach with his previous one (as he now understands it). Thus he contrasts what he calls "historical philosophy" (philosophy as he is currently pursuing it) with "metaphysical philosophy" (traditional philosophy, including philosophy as he now sees himself to have been pursuing it in the first phase of his thought).

In his conception of them the two modes of philosophizing (of pursuing inquiry that seeks "the most general [*allgemeinste*] knowledge and the valuation [*Abschätzung*] of the totality of existence [*gesamten Daseins*]"[1]) are at one on this point, that philosophical reflection not only is attuned to a problematic that arises in and is integral to ongoing life and experience, but it also seeks a ground in experience for whatever insight into reality it purports to arrive at. The two differ, however, in the way they understand the possibilities of such grounding. Metaphysical philosophy seeks to found itself in experience as at times giving an immediate insight into the heart of reality and life, so that the reflective understanding claimed in it is said simply to be the conceptual rendering of the import of such immediate insight. In contrast, historical philosophy, while also proceeding by way of experience as a realm of immediacy, does not regard immediacy as itself a matter of cognitive intuition. Rather it takes any cognitive insight into reality to be a conclusion arrived at in conceptual reasoning which bases itself on an interpretation of the disclosive import of various experiences and which infers the insight as a properly drawn conclusion for which such experience provides sufficient evidence to warrant its acceptance as true. From the perspective of historical philosophy, the claim of metaphysical philosophy to found itself on direct and absolute insight is mistaken. The metaphysical philosopher lays claim to an intuitive cognition, that is, a sort of presentiment [*Ahnung*] which takes us beyond the field of 'appearance' and provides a miraculous eyeglass with which the philosopher sees directly into the essence of nature, or (phrased differently) "a direct view of the nature of the world, as it were through a hole in the cloak of appearance", a "miraculous seer's vision" which is achieving this glimpse through that hole and which can "communicate something conclusive and decisive about man and the world" on its strength "without the toil and rigorousness of science".[2] But in truth what he has is only the immediacy of passion and profound feeling-- moving indeed, elevated and significant indeed, but not cognitively disclosive in the way claimed, its profundity and strength only giving the deceptive semblance of enabling the 'seer' to penetrate into the interior of reality and arrive at the heart of nature. It is self-delusion to claim that such feeling reaches disclosively beyond the surface of things and brings the seer into cognitive touch with the world's heart.[3]

Founded in this different sense of the possibility of an immediate cognition of the heart of reality in experience is a second difference, in the account of reality itself. Metaphysical philosophy claims insight into a reality that is 'beyond' 'appearance', the latter being the reality delimited by space, time, and individuation, and manifesting itself directly to the (inward and outward) sensibility of ourselves who are part of that reality. The disclosure that is key to metaphysical philosophy not only opens us to a reality beyond appearance (a second and metaphysical world) but in particular discloses a creational nature to reality as a whole, so that the 'beyond' is source of (and explanatory ground for) 'appearance' or the world of the actual as we find it in the immediacy of our sensibility.[4] In contrast, historical philosophy addresses what we encounter in sense-immediacy (within and without) as exhausting reality. That means, the ultimate horizon of understanding is time (or more fully, time and space). Not only is there nothing eternal beyond the temporal (no source, no creator), but there are no 'eternal facts' within the temporal: reality is a continually changing affair, which makes the question of 'origins', 'beginnings', a primordial one for a philosopher, and a through-and-through temporal one. Therefore when the historical philosopher takes up with (say) those opposites in the world of appearance (good/bad, good/evil, right/wrong, just/unjust, rational/irrational, sentient/insentient, logical/illogical, disinterested-contemplation/covetous-desire, and the like) which the metaphysical philosopher sees as including a "higher" pole that derives from the "higher" metaphysical reality (from the very "kernel and essence of the 'thing in itself'"), he looks at them quite differently. For one thing, given that the horizon of his questioning now is time, he does not look for their intelligibility by reference to any trans-temporal (let alone also higher) origin. For a second thing, his inquiry has already discovered in some cases-- and believes it will probably find in every case-- that the idea of opposites, that of exclusive poles, is itself mistaken. What actually exists and is being mistaken by the metaphysician under the idea of opposites is rather a basic element and its various sublimations [*Sublimierungen*]-- refinements in which the lower becomes transformed into something higher. The historical philosopher, in his address to such matters, is thus free to follow out this sublimating and develop a "chemistry of the moral, religious, and aesthetic, representations and sensations, likewise of all those excitations we experience in ourselves in the large- and small-scale intercourse of culture and society, indeed in solitude"[5]. From this would arise a rather different sense of temporal things.

In HAH, then, Nietzsche is urging that while philosophy is an experiential inquiry it may be pursued in a way that mistakes reality and human capacity for understanding it, or in a way that is more apt in both respects. But his account of this more apt way of proceeding does not in fact faithfully reflect his actual procedure in this new phase of his thinking, for in truth his current approach, while he claims it is historical philosophizing, is not rooted simply in the disclosures of experience nor carried out in thoughtful reasoning that comes out of himself in simple and straightforward fashion. Rather something very kindred to what took place in his first phase is taking place again, although it is only in later retrospect that he recognizes-- or at least, acknowledges-- this. What is happening is this: in the thoughtful pursuit which is expressed in this work, his address to the disclosures of experience is unduly guided by an exemplar beyond himself. In his first phase, he had developed a reading of those disclosures-- in particular, those of Dionysian experiencing-- which was importantly inflected by the terms of Schopenhauer's philosophy, and given Schopenhauer's roots, by the terms of Kant's philosophy. As a result, the path of his reflection took shape in a way that did not simply follow out and guide itself by the disclosive emphasis of his own experience nor by the emerging clarity of a thinking which sought to define itself in the unassisted and direct interpretation of and reasoning with such disclosure. Instead, the path he made for himself reflected in important ways the character of-- the horizon in-- the borrowed framework of intelligibility which heavily influenced him at the time and which seemed to him then to aid him in making sense of what he was concerned to understand. Thus while the thinking involved was nominally his own, an originally alien framework and terms, reinforced by the persons of Schopenhauer (indirectly) and Wagner (directly), were accepted into his thought-appropriation of experience and gave it an important (but later regretted) coloration. Similarly, when the path of his life-experience brought the disillusion at Bayreuth and provoked in him the reaction in which, setting out on another path and (among other things) rethinking what he had been doing, he sought to free himself from the outside influence of the kindred figures (Schopenhauer and Wagner) he had before revered, he succeeded in that but only by giving undue weight to support from the alien-yet-kindred in another form. This time, he sought shelter in science and its rational spirit and methods, disguising himself as 'scientific'.[6]

1. Philosophy and science

In metaphysical philosophy, the basic disclosure goes beyond the temporal and the apparent, and in virtue of that, not only is such philosophizing different from science and scientific inquiry, which is seen as a disciplined objectivizing address to the things we encounter in the immediacy of experience (to 'appearance'), but because of its concern for a reality whose basis is time-less it finds art and religion of much greater significance than science. For art and religion thematize the reality 'beyond' 'appearance', although they do so only symbolically. In contrast, historical philosophy (at least as Nietzsche would now pursue it) operates within the horizon of time and is focused on appearance (the temporal); and for that reason, it is closely aligned with science. Indeed, Nietzsche speaks of historical philosophy as "the summit of the entire scientific pyramid"[7], as "philosophical science"[8] or "scientific philosophy"[9].

When Nietzsche speaks in this way, he has in mind what he takes to be central to science, its spirit and the embodiment of that spirit in the methods of inquiry whereby that spirit can lead confidently to reliable results. In HAH Nietzsche does not spell out in any detail what constitutes the "spirit" of science or the "rigorous methods" he has in mind, but his contrast of science with the spirit and methods of metaphysical philosophy points us indirectly to their nature. The heart of the matter is an intellectual conscience which, summoning into play doubt and suspicion and an unwillingness to accept anything without scrutiny, seeks such certainty as is possible (which means, as high a degree of probability as is possible, for certainty is unattainable).[10] Inquiry insists on taking up with nature in restrained fashion, as a book to be read for what it says straightforwardly, without presumption of second (allegorical or mystical, say) meanings.[11] Whatever the reading may seem to be at any time, inquiry insists on rigorous testing of any and all claims to truth, making appeal to evidence and to correct concluding from that evidence the key to accrediting them.[12] Such a laborious and cautious way of proceeding makes for a tentative holding-for-true of any 'truths' whose claims are substantiated by evidence, and for a continued scrutiny of those truths because absolute certainty is impossible.[13]

This sort of seriousness about truth, and the use of such methods of making claims be based on testable experience, did not belong to science from its start, with the Greeks of classical times. For there science began in metaphysical vein, indeed as (part of) philosophy. Among the ancient Greeks there were human beings who could not-- would not-- rest in myth but sought individual insight into the truth of the problematic of existence. The 'truths' gained, however, while they acquired the status of convictions in their authors, stood in conflict with each other. Because each individual was concerned with *his* 'truth' (i.e. his being in the right), the conflict of the claims of different individuals to unqualified truth led men to discover, step by step, incontestable [*unumstötzliche*] principles by which the justice of these claims could be tested and the contest decided. At first one decided according to authorities, then one criticized the ways and means by which the other's supposed truths had been discovered; in between, there was a period when one drew the consequences of an opponent's proposition and perhaps found it harmful and productive of unhappiness-- from which everyone was supposed to see that the opponent's conviction contained an error. It was this personal strife of thinkers that eventually sharpened the methods in such way that genuine truths could really be discovered and the aberrations of earlier methods could be exposed for all to see. The methods and spirit of contemporary science are the outcome and culmination of this war of convictions and this attention to procedure.[14] And in historical philosophy, this same seriousness about method and this same intellectual spirit reclaims philosophy itself from the metaphysical realization with which it began and which it maintained as inquiry in particular fields (the specialized sciences) detached itself from the enduring core of philosophy.

Although science, as spirit and method, appealed to Nietzsche for its pointer into the nature of responsible inquiry generally, when he comes to attend to and analyze science more closely, something else emerges as well. His further analysis takes up with science on two levels.

On the first level, he takes science as it seems to itself and gives itself out as being. Thus he notes that implicit in the methodical approach to truth adopted in the particular sciences is the conceptual delimitation of a field for exploration (some realm of nature, say) and the employment of the method on what appears within that field, with a concern simply for truth and in disregard of whether knowing such truth brings happiness or unhappiness in its train. Approaching its field in such fashion, scientific inquiry generates genuine truths which are solidly based in experience and the evidence it provides, and challenges pseudo-truths which are not so founded, however grand they are and happiness-producing when believed in. If the truths it generates are insignificant in appearance and do not seem to contribute much or anything to our happiness, they nonetheless are able to be built on as established facts and to contribute to an edifice of solid knowledge. To adhere to the small but solid objective truths which modern science is discovering in this way and to discard the grand metaphysical and other 'errors' that cannot be substantiated by such a methodical procedure is "manly" and manifests "courage, simplicity, and abstemiousness": in other words, a certain moral strength.[15] But to adhere to them is not to hold them as absolute truths: they are probabilities approximating more or less to certainties, reasoned opinions, and not convictions in which one believes oneself to be in possession of unconditioned truth on this or that point of knowledge.[16]

Like Kant, Nietzsche knows a second level, on which he looks at science rather differently. Reflecting back upon the enabling conditions for such truth-establishing inquiry-- the immediate or intuitional fields of space and time which enter into the experience of everything, the conceptualizations involved in the idea of the thinghood of any thing and the ideas of reason, logic, mathematics, and the like--, he finds that those enabling conditions have a surprising character and standing, given that on their basis inquiry seems able to establish factual truths. In his self-critical address to experience, Kant had developed a transcendental approach, and had sought to fix once and for all the conditions for the possibility of 'experience' or objective knowledge, treating them as *a priori* factors perpetually and necessarily involved in the constituting of experience. Nietzsche enters upon a cognate but somewhat different path. Attending to scientific inquiry as an activity of a living being who has emerged in the course of the evolution of life on earth and who is seeking to maintain and enhance the life in itself in its interaction with things, he develops what he calls "the physiology and history of the evolution of organisms and concepts"[17]. Thus he sketches out what seems to him a plausible account of the development of the cognitive faculty in human beings, and in particular, of the fundamental ideas which are foundational for the science of nature. According to him, nothing of what is essential for the establishing of scientific truths is itself truthfully disclosive of reality, even though, operating within such false or fiction-informed foundations, we are able in science to arrive at conclusions which have a perfect rigor and certainty in their connection with each other.

Nietzsche's account is two-sided.

On the side of nature:

1. In our (human) interaction with what is other than us, all things (including ourselves) appear to us within space and time, as spatio-temporal things. But "our sensations of space and time are false, for tested for their consequences they lead to logical contradictions."[18] In truth, space and time are qualities of human subjectivity, in virtue of which we can receive and register others and ourselves as presences to-and-for us. We find ourselves and the things of nature to be spatio-temporal entities not because we all *are* such *in reality* ('in ourselves'), but because we can not find (that is, register and apprehend) anything at all unless, in our receiving of it, our sensibility enables it to appear to us. Among the conditions which our own subjectivity introduces so as to enable things to appear to us are the intuitions of space and time; these, then, do not belong to things apart from our apprehension of those things, and are not thus disclosive of reality itself.

2. Within space-time as it holds us and what we interact with, things appear over against us, a multiplicity of different things. Now our concept of a thing-- any thing, as thing-- is a development of something discernible when we go back to the lower organisms. We must think that such an organism at first never registers any differentiation in what surrounds it, only (so to speak) a sameness to all; but when the various pleasurable and unpleasurable stimuli [*Erregungen*] become noticeable, it gradually distinguishes various different substances, each marked by one attribute (i.e. a single relation to the stimulated organism), and it forms the judgment and belief in different substances. Apart from the substance's relation to it in respect of pleasure and pain, the organic being has no interest in the substance, and no awareness of any alteration in it. It is from the period of the lower organisms that humanity has inherited the belief that there are *identical things*. But this belief is a false one: there is no 'same thing' which is identical with itself at different points of time, there are no such things as identical things. Rather, the organism, as part of its response to the stimulus, has fabricated an identity whereby the stimulus-source is apprehended as a distinct thing; but the identity attributed to it, while it may function as a reference point for use in the organism's response to the stimulus, has no genuine cognitive value as disclosing what is there, but at best has practical value in marking the relation of what is there to the organism, its way of appearing to that organism.[19]

3. Again, even at the level of primitive organisms, the formation of the concept of a thing involves a differentiating and distinguishing, and with this, the establishing of a multiplicity, a number of things different from each other. Sameness and difference go together. Now in our case, the estab-

lishing of the conclusions of science concerning spatio-temporal things involves a conceptualizing of the spatio-temporally present, and that conceptualizing utilizes (among other things) the concept of number.[20] But like the concept of a thing, that of number is founded on the error of unities which can occur more than once, the error of identity.[21]

> When Kant says 'the understanding does not draw its laws from nature, it prescribes them to nature', that is wholly true with regard to the *concept of nature* which we are obliged [*genötigt*] to attach to nature (nature = world as idea, that is as error), but which is the summation of a host of errors of the understanding. To a world which is *not* our idea, the laws of numbers are wholly inapplicable: these are valid only in the human world.[22]

On the side of reason:

1. As rational inquiry into the truth of nature, science makes use of concepts and words. In general, but in science as well, the 'things' which we conceptually fabricate as experienced unities are brought by us into language, so that we speak of such experienced 'things' as 'trees', 'animals', and the like. We are prone to treat the words whereby this happens not simply as designating them but as expressing a knowledge of reality: reality *is composed of such things*, and our way of speaking about it captures the truth of that reality. But this is mistaken.[23]

2. Moreover, as we have developed it, reason is a power which, because it operates with language, depends also on this belief-- that we can put the truth of things into language, indeed that such truth is reflected in the nature and structure of language. And logic too, the science of the laws of reason, depends both upon this false idea and upon the fiction that there are identical things, that identity is to be found in the real world.[24]

In sum: reflection upon the enabling conditions for scientific discovery of truth indicates that it is 'fabrications' which are false or fictional and do not genuinely disclose reality itself that make possible our establishing, within those conditions, of reliable 'truths' (of appearance). The idea of nature employed in the science of nature is in truth only a subjective organizing concept directive for our attention to what we are receiving-and-registering in immediacy, and not a concept which truthfully discloses either reality or the character of the presence being received-and-registered. In the ideas which unfold this concept (the idea of 'thing' or 'substance', for instance, and the idea of number) we are claiming a self-identity which has no counterpart in reality or immediate presence but which we are projecting in order that presence (which seems to us reality) have intelligibility to us. Not only does the concept of 'nature' have this character and standing, but the concept of our own nature as 'rational' beings ('subjects') likewise does not correspond with the reality of ourselves or our immediate presence to ourselves. In addition, the concepts of that thought-activity which is brought into play in our inquiring ('inference', 'logic', 'reason') involve fictions in essential ways. Yet, if our power of conceptualization does not render either reality or presence as they are in truth, it remains that the conceptual 'fabrications' which we project into the immediate content of sensibility do direct our attention along certain lines to the presence given in immediacy and lead us to connect our impressions of it in certain ways; and the result is that we are able to make presence *appear* to-and-for us in our experience as the approximate sensible realization of an ordered world of 'things' or 'substances' intelligible by way of the concepts in question. And so long as we are immersed in such 'things' brought to stand for us by way of these basic conceptual fabrications, we can explore such appearance ('apparent reality') and make our scientific determinations of 'truth'.

The second-level account which Nietzsche gives of science has an odd ring to it. For he would show that the determinate truths which we can establish by rigorous inquiry in the special sciences are established only on the strength of, and within, a framework of fictions and falsities which are being held as true but are not, even though they are effectively serving our practical involvement in affairs and enable the sciences to proceed. This would seem to mean that the determinate truths which the sciences establish are themselves *in reality* only 'truths' (that is, useful fictions relating to appearance), not truths (assertions validly claiming correspondence-with-what-is). Yet when, as historical philosopher in his pursuit of the truth of the problematic of existence, he would show how these framework-'truths' arose, he draws on truths being established by the special sciences (about life as an evolutionary phenomenon, in particular) and treats the latter as truths, not as 'truths'. This methodologically confused procedure is self-undermining. For how can the evolutionary account (a 'truth' of the useful-fiction sort[25]) function as a basis for a true (correspondent-with-what-is) philosophical explanation of how the fundamental conceptualizations in question came to be invented and, despite being falsities and fictions, came to be held as true (correspondent-with-what-is)?

Seen in its full reach, then, the account which Nietzsche is venturing of (historical) philosophy, science, and truth involves a three-level differentiation. On the highest or philosophical level, there are truth-claims substantiatable in the correspondence-with-what-is sense: for example, that reality does not exhibit the conception of identity. And on this level, the other two lower levels are truly (in a correspondence-with-what-is sense) discerned as constituted by falsities and fictions. On the most basic of these two, there are various conceptualizations which the philosopher recognizes as truly life-supporting and useful, but which he sees as in reality falsities and fictions, conceptualizations whose claims to truth are not substantiatable in a correspondence-with-what-is sense even if they enable scientific inquiry and work in a life-supporting sense. Finally, within the framework for more specific inquiry provided by these 'truths' when they are accepted as being true (in the correspondence-with-what-is sense), there is the development of the various scientific disciplines, and the establishment by methodical inquiry of more determinate 'truths' (useful fictions) as 'objectively' the case. And these are readily (if mistakenly) taken to be truths in the correspondence-with-what-is sense.

What seems taking place in HAH is the first step in an effort by Nietzsche to try out a skepticism which is one in spirit with what he sees embodied in scientific inquiry and to press it as far as he can, both to undermine matters that were important in his first-phase thought but also in order to explore carefully this matter of truth-seeking, both as regards philosophy and as regards this vehicle (science) which now seems promising to him in the pursuit of philosophy as he now needs to undertake it. But when, despite finding science attractive as regards its spirit and methods, he examines the concrete outworkings of the sciences, he pursues a dual path. On one path he takes the outworkings as experience-based truths, and enters them as such into his own reflective inquiry. On the other path, he carries his skepticism to the point of claiming that the truths involved in the framework of the various sciences and thus those achieved in the course the specific inquiries of those sciences are, like 'truth' in a practical vein, merely 'useful life-supporting fictions', in differentiation from truth as reflection might discern it in a correspondence-with-what-is sense. There is no problem with taking such a dual path except when, in bringing together the discoveries being made on them, one does not heed closely their differences. In fact, a certain incoherence or internal contradiction enters Nietzsche's discussion when, in claiming the inapplicability of "identity" to reality (in truth, there is nothing identical in reality), he does not seek to argue that point[26] but instead concentrates on explaining how the fundamental life-supporting (and science-founding) fictions arose in the context of life and living beings interacting with their environment. For in such explaining, he makes a 'truth' or *useful-fiction* of biological science (namely, life as an evolutionary affair) his basis for *truly* (in a correspondence-with-what-is sense) explaining the origin of the fictions fundamental for life and science. But such an explanation can not claim truth in any correspondence-with-what-is sense: at least, he has not yet found a way to make the case for that.

Even so, in maintaining a sense that philosophical reflection can discern truth in a correspondence-with-what-is sense, he keeps open the possibility that, provided this is consistent with its enabling conditions, such reflection could expand its range and gain truth in other areas (that of biological life, say). He also avoids the self-defeating step of seeking to expand the skepticism with respect to the scientific so as to include philosophy as well. Any case made for universally transforming truth-as-correspondence-with-what-is into truth-as-useful-fiction must include itself, meaning that its claim to truth would have to be only of that life-supporting sort. That could not be. For if we are to be able to judge according to this standard, this 'life-supporting' itself must be such as can both be understood and be applied as a standard, and such application is possible *only if* we can judge *truly* (in a correspondence sense) what *genuinely* measures up to the standard and what does not.

In all of this, the matter at issue is polar: at one pole, there is the question of the true nature of reality, and at the other, that of the true standard of truth which is at work in our apprehending and affirming reality such as it is. The matter itself, and Nietzsche's ventures which treat it, are both difficult, and somewhat more complex and not quite as straightforward as the preceding discussion suggests. Let us approach it from a somewhat different starting-point, that of reality itself.

2. Reality: an interactive affair?

Historical philosophy rejects any trans-temporal side to reality, and in particular, any "thing in itself". But what does reject mean here? Deny that we have any access to a "thing in itself", thus that we could have any knowledge of it? Or deny that there is a "thing in itself"? But if things do not exist "in themselves", and they are only "in relation", then is our knowledge addressed to things in their existence in relation only to us? What of them in their relation to other things, is that different from them in their relation to ourselves (human beings)? At this stage in his thought Nietzsche's discussion of these matters is emphatic in certain directions, but is marked by considerable unclarity.[27]

In HAH-I/16, Nietzsche takes up the matter of the contrast of "appearance" and "thing in itself" (the title of the aphorism).

> Philosophers are accustomed to station themselves before life and experience-- before what they call the world of appearance-- as before a painting which has been unrolled once for all and unalterably shows the same fixed event [*Vorgang*]: this event, they think, one must correctly interpret in order to make thereby a conclusion to the being [*Wesen*] which has produced the painting-- that is, to make a conclusion to the thing in itself, which is ever accustomed to be seen as the sufficient reason [*Grund*] for the world of appearance. Countering this, more rigorous logicians-- after they have established the concept of the metaphysical as that of the unconditioned (consequently also of what does not condition)-- have denied any connection between the unconditioned (the metaphysical world) and the world familiar to us: so that in appearance, the thing in itself does *not* in any way appear, and every conclusion from appearance to the thing in itself is refused. Both parties, however, overlook the possibility that that painting-- what we human beings at present call life and experience-- has gradually *become*, indeed is fully still in *the process of becoming* [*Werden*] and therefore should not be looked at as a fixed quantity from which one might make a conclusion concerning its author (the sufficient reason) or might also merely refuse to make any conclusion.[28]

Let us leave aside, for the moment, one misleading facet of the image, namely, that life and experience could be a painting out there in front of us, whether in a finished or a still-in-process state; for we are participants in the reality which is supposedly being imaged and can not see ourselves as out there as if we were not participants but simply members of the procession being observed.

The whole contrast of appearance (the thing in its appearance to us) and thing in itself (the thing in its being apart from everything else, including its relation to us) emerges in a reflective analysis of our experience as the disclosure to us of ourselves and the other things we live amidst and encounter in our surroundings. As initially undertaken by Kant, in whose thought the distinction that goes under these names was first formulated, that analysis recognizes that how reality appears to us in our encounter with other things is dependent in important regards upon our powers for receiving and registering it (our sensibility), and upon our power for conceiving it (our reason). According to Kant's account, "experience" is a disclosure to us of ourselves and other things in the fashion of a subjective knowing of an objective world. Kant's reflective concern is to elicit those immanent transcendental structures, activities, and powers, which give experience the formal constitution of such a subjective-apprehension-of-objects. His analysis in its most precise form suggests that in this eliciting we need to distinguish between three matters: (1) things as they are in themselves (as possessed of an independent and wholly self-contained being apart from anything else: this is ultimate reality in its own nature and character), (2) things as they act upon us and (in particular) affect our sensibility (this is such independent realities when they relate to each other in interactive fashion, and here, in the particular case that involves human beings), and (3) the things of experience that are manifest to us in virtue of the character of the experience-generating interacting of things with human beings and that constitute the objective world we are apprehending in our experience. Neither the first nor the second of these three matters appears in experience as a content and part of experience; they are only reflectively-required preconditions without which we would not have experience as the actually existent affair it is. Experience itself arises in an interplay between things-beyond-ourselves and ourselves which begins with things affecting our sensibility; in our register of this affecting, the sensible manifold which emerges as a result of the action of things on us becomes qualified by the formal spatial-and-temporal intuitions which belong to our own sensibility. What forms the given in our experience, then, will always be sensible and have spatial and temporal quality, because this is the way our receptivity to things works. We bring to completion this beginning of our experience and apprehend an objective reality-- the spatio-temporal things of our experience, such as trees, animals, houses, and in general, the world of appearance-- only as we take up the elements of the spatio-temporal sensible manifold and conceptually connect them in certain formal ways. The resultant things of experience are basically constructs of ours whose unity and coherence as distinct things have the formal features they do because those are the only ways our powers of conceptualization can grasp something over against ourselves (as an 'object' for knowing 'subjects').[29] Thus although it does not at first sight seem to us so, according to Kant's analysis our experience of the world is in reality an apprehension of constructs whose character is importantly a function of the way *our* sensibility and *our* reason operate in that interacting with reality beyond ourselves which generates the sensible starting-point of our reception-and-construction-process. Genuine knowledge on our part is limited to the things of our experience which we have so constructed, but that knowing presupposes a reality-beyond-ourselves, a reality-of-ourselves, and an interacting of such realities (in particular, one which affects our sensibility), none of which are known or knowable by us. What we know, then-- what we call the real world, the world of experience-- is circumscribed by what we can not know but which we must think to be if our knowing is to be what it is.

In short: according to Kant, the world of our experience is simply an appearance (to us, of reality-beyond and of the reality-which-is-ourselves) which does not itself belong to reality in its independent being apart from our receiving-and-judging and which does not either manifest directly or enable us to know indirectly that reality in itself or its action upon our sensibility; it is rather an intermediate realm which emerges between ourselves-and-other-realities when we interact and whose showing-and-shown are *simply relative* to us-who-are-perceiving-and-conceiving.

Nietzsche's pointing to an overlooked possibility-- that 'appearance' is an 'intermediary realm' taking shape in an ongoing and *changing* way in the interacting of certain beings-- reflects the movement of his thought beyond Kant. But the first steps he takes in HAH-- and they are only a beginning that will be continued and eventually reconceived in subsequent works-- are somewhat problematic. Nonetheless, let us note the character of these steps and the contrast with Kant being attempted.

If something called "experience" is what both Kant and Nietzsche would analyze, and if the analysis in both cases suggests that experience is issue of-- and in-- an interaction whose character depends on the nature and operation of the interacting parties, both the nature of the starting-point for analysis and the character of the address which pursues understanding of it are significantly different.

First step: Nietzsche treats experience as a much richer affair than the subjective apprehension of an objective world. As the phrasing quoted above suggests, it is life-experience that he has in mind, lived experience in all its variety and color. Experience in this sense is, indeed, an "intermediate world" (the apparent world) whose character is (as with Kant) an issue of the way the interacting parties function in the interacting itself. But Nietzsche rejects the idea of "thing in itself" as an idea useful for understanding experience and its status: nothing *is* as independent and wholly self-contained in its being, but all *is* only as *participant in an interacting with* other beings. But if being is interactive (interrelational) in its very nature, can such reality be known? For any being that attempted to know such reality would be a particular being who knew it as part of its participating in (that interactive) reality; but would not the particularity of its participant-status inevitably limit and bias its effort at knowing and render it unfit to know reality itself?

Despite the desire to move beyond Kant, here at the beginning of his effort to do so Nietzsche is still dominated by the Kantian distinction he is in process of rejecting, namely, that between the "in itself" and "in relation to".[30] In effect, he proceeds as if that disjunction exhausted the alternatives; that means that here at first he does not recognize the full meaning of "interactive reality" and of "participation" and does not carry forward their implications consistently and fully. Instead, he proceeds on a path analogous to Kant's path in this sense, that thinking in terms of the "in relation to" and stressing one party in the interaction (and in our case, that means the human), he ascribes a "relative to us" standing to the intermediate world of appearance, as if the most we could do as *participants* would be to discern the interactive from an "our side" or "human perspective" that is *encapsulated* by its own disclosive powers. We human beings can see other things and ourselves, indeed, but only from our own side of the interacting, only from our own perspective, and by the nature of the case that side and perspective are one-sided and partial, unable to be apt to any universal truth.[31] In the further development of his thought, Nietzsche will move beyond this sense of our own being as encapsulated by its disclosive powers and eventually recover more fully than here at the start the being of ourselves as that of *participants* who, *as participants*, are indeed determinate in many respects but not in a way that *encapsulates us and cuts us off from the uni-versal*. For the moment, however, he simply rejects the 'in itself' and tries to do his best with the 'in relation to'.

Second step: Because his "best" takes reality as through and through temporal, he eschews entering upon the sort of transcendental analysis which Kant undertook. Specifically, because he sees the 'intermediate world' of experience as a life-world and life-experience and sees our co-constituting work as that of living beings, not merely cognitive subjects, he is drawn to note the changing character of a living being's experience over time, and to recognize such change as a function mainly of the way the capacities in us as living beings-- capacities for engaging with things and for bringing into disclosure the interacting we are involved in-- themselves change over time. Now as we noted in discussing UHH, what Nietzsche meant in his first-phase thought under the term "life" was first and foremost something we lived: life as we live it in first-hand fashion and in a first-personal sense, thus life as marked in its fundamental nature by various immediately and inwardly disclosed features. Accordingly, the change over time which was of prime interest in the first phase of his thinking was that during one's personal lifetime, and in particular, that introduced by life's being centered in the growth and maturation of our individual selves humanly, and as part of this, that which reflects the incorporation of the historical into the development of capacities involved in growth. But as the notion of life's plastic power indicated, "life" meant something with a variety of sides to it. In our first Interlude, we pointed to how his rendering of this complex power which is life, while it saw an order to the complexity, failed expressly to differentiate the spatially quite different matters within that power that need differentiation and that have a different role according to their different spatial status. When Nietzsche looks to the change of our life-world in this second phase of his thinking, he makes as his main point of reference for interpretation of all else not the living being ordered to make the inward primary in its participation in interacting and in its living its life out of itself, but rather the living being in a secondary facet of itself. Treating life as *basically* a biological affair, he is drawn to look beyond the individual life-time as an affair primarily of an individual development which incorporates into the ongoing the past as it manifests the historical interconnecting of lives; he views the human primarily now as a continuing part of the evolution of life on earth. In doing this, he brings forward for emphasis what belongs to life in its subordinate and spatially outward side (the physiological and biological, and more temporally phrased, the evolutionary). Seeking to approach life in its more fundamental side (life as the living being lives it inwardly) via this, he does again as he did in UHH when time was the theme, namely: he projects into the life visible outwardly in its organic structure and processes an inwardness that he posits as harboring what lies at the heart of the living being's energy and vitality. Because in its temporal movement evolution seems visibly to build from simpler to more complex forms and to do this in a way that involves genetic inheritance and a maintaining of the simpler in some fashion within the more complex, the representation of the simplest inward life-activity (that of the simplest life-forms) projects only the lowest and most minimal elements of the inwardly experienced resources present in our own (complex human) psyche and experiencing; and where the life-forms are more complex, so the elements in ourselves abstracted and projected to represent the inwardness of other living beings are also more complex. Given the outward guide that now has priority in Nietzsche's reflection on life, this procedure eventually brings him back to us human beings as highly-evolved life-forms whose inwardness (in some form) we happen to know directly, as our own. But in recognition of the historical development of human inwardness from something primitive and simple to something sophisticated and complex, he would understand the human by supplementing such abstraction and projection with ideas such as sublimation (the transfiguration of something lower into something higher), and seek to understand historically-subsequent humanity as harboring various sublimations of the more primitive and simple historically-antecedent humanity.[32]

Thus Nietzsche's address to understanding experience contrasts with Kant's not simply because of its rejection of the "in itself" and its richer notion of what is meant by the term "experience" but because his is a genetic approach which would explain human experience today by making an extended detour through the evolution of life on earth. The initial significant issue of this procedure for our concerns is a conjecture as to the history of the creation of concepts as life evolves, which would understand the evolution of the higher and complex from the lower and simpler, and thus of the experience of today from the experience of life (including pre-human life) long ago. Thus he speaks of certain basic features of the way we receive, register, and respond to what we are encountering, as having been settled in us long before the four thousand years we more or less know about;[33] nonetheless, for the last two thousand years at least, in our operating we have made moral, aesthetic, and religious demands on the world, looked upon it with blind desire and passion and fear, and have abandoned ourselves to the bad habits of illogical thinking, to such an extent that this world has gradually become marvelously variegated and colorful.[34] Of late, we have developed a counter-force to all this, a truth-seeking in the form of science, whereby the objective face of this 'intermediate world' is looked to in order to determine its character; and one day, the steady and laborious process of science (this scientific participation in the interacting) will bring to light the history of the genesis of thought, and enable us to see that

what we now call the world is the result of a host of errors and fantasies which have gradually arisen in the total evolution of organic beings, grown intertwined with one another, and are now inherited by us as an accumulated treasure of the entire past-- a treasure, for the value of our humanity rests on it. From this world of representation, rigorous science is capable of releasing us only to a limited extent-- and it is not at all to be desired-- insofar as it is essentially incapable of breaking the force of primeval habits of sensibility-and-feeling; but it can, quite gradually and step by step, illuminate the history of the arising of that world as representation-- and at least for moments, raise us above the whole event [*Vorgang*].[35]

3. Philosophy as law-giving

The truth-seeking side of philosophy-- the search for an understanding of the problematic of existence-- seeks understanding of an interactive existence in which something is at stake, and seeks for an understanding of this that will enable life to be lived into the future under a self-guidance and in a self-understanding consonant with truth. As such it is inquiry which goes beyond the specialized sciences and their realms of fact, to concern itself with values and evaluation, purposes and goals, as important facets of life related to what is at stake. It asks after the truth relating to these matters.

By its very nature as the reality which it is, life is something to be lived in the living being's active participation in existence at large; and the living active being for whom there is an at-stake in its participation in things registers that initially in feeling.[36] At the same time as in his second phase of thought Nietzsche emphasizes reason and spirit as elements in our active being, he reiterates the focus of the first phase on feeling as the primordial side of that being and, given the new emphasis, addresses our being now as "irrational" and "illogical" at its very heart. Not only does our nature involve us in an "illogical basic stance [*Grundstellung*] toward all things"[37], but it also involves us in a continual evaluating of what we encounter, an assessing of its value for the life in us and for life's seeking (in and by our activity) to secure what is at stake.[38] But while our own being as living beings provides the standard for that assessment, not only is that being in actuality a changing and fluctuating one, but any evaluation of other beings and their bearing is based on incomplete knowledge: for example, no human being enters our experience so fully and openly and is accessible in sufficient fulness to our knowing that we would have thereby a logical right to any total evaluation of that person. All evaluations are-- and have to be-- premature and hasty, and thereby unjust.[39] But we cannot avoid evaluating: life involves us inescapably in inclination and aversion, in drives-toward and drives-away which involve not only the register in feeling [*Gefühl*] of the apparent bearing of things on the drive of life toward what furthers the life in us and away from the harmful but also some kind of cognitive [*erkennender*] evaluation concerning the value-for-life of various goals of any drive. "We are from the first [*von vornherein*] illogical, and therefore unjust, beings *and can know this*: this is one of the greatest and most unresolvable disharmonies of existence."[40]

At the same time as life ever (at every moment, continually) involves us in decision-making that includes an evaluating and evaluations which are unavoidably limited and thus unjust (even if they are the best we are capable of at the time), it also urges us toward a development of greater capacity for taking part in affairs and (as part of this capacity) for judging *well* in such assessing of what bears for better or worse on the life in us. In this reference, to judge well means to weigh and assess in such fashion as enables the life in us effectively to reach the 'more' which it wants to reach: it means to serve well the unfolding of the life within ourselves. Now because individually the capacity being developed eventually (beginning in youth) is to be exercised amidst youth's aspirational reaching for the 'more' as the higher-and-better, we are to exercise our developing judgment at that time in a reaching for culture as that perfected and transformed nature in ourselves through which we are capable of taking part in affairs at the highest level open to us in virtue of that nature and in the situation of our life. In order to follow well the pointer of aspiration and to discern well its concrete relevance, we need to become capable of allowing the different voices of the drives within us, and of each of life's different situations, to make themselves heard and of assessing and heeding better than ever before the harmony and dissonance of those voices as regards the achieving of this goal of culture.[41]

So far as the philosopher goes, however, there is a broader concern than his/her own individual future and growth. For since the truth he seeks concerns human life, what is at stake in it, and what would give it meaning, the philosophic grasp of this implicates the philosopher in a task, that of becoming the law-giver who, interpreting the at-stake, sets forth the law-- the way we ought to live and act-- that is grounded in the truth of life's nature. Just as the aim of the truth-seeking side of philosophy is at a universally-valid understanding of reality and of human life as human, on the legislative side the judging that would draw upon such understanding would attempt to reach beyond individual human life simply as individual and concern itself with human life as in virtue of its humanity an interconnected whole. Thus its guidance would concern the movement of humankind as a whole toward its true goal, toward what the drive in human life (as human) ultimately drives. This means that the philosopher, according to his/her own full nature, is not simply an interpreter of the problematic of existence but one who also stands in a commanding relation to others (even the host of scientific and learned human beings) and points out to them the culture-goals for humankind as a whole and the means for achieving such goals.[42] For the individual philosopher, this means looking at current human beings who bear humankind forward in a continuation of its movement into the future, and looking for a goal-- thus for a future condition that is to be worked for-- that has meaning not simply for those current humans but for humanity as such and as a whole. Looking backward and seeing how humanity has made its way in the past will teach the early stage of human becoming, but it will also disclose the path which humankind can and may not go on again. For the movement is forward, and in particular, forward beyond the errors of the past and to an assumption of responsibility for the unfolding of future human life on earth. Thus

> in that you want with all your strength [*Kraft*] to descry in advance how the knot of the future is going to be tied, your own life will acquire the value of an instrument and means of knowledge. You have it in your hands to achieve the absorption of all your experience-- your experiments, errors, delusions, faults, passions, your love and your hope-- into your goal without remainder. This goal is yourself to become a necessary chain of rings of culture and from this necessity to conclude to the necessity in the course of culture in general. When your gaze has become strong enough to see the bottom in the dark well of your nature and your knowledge, perhaps the distant constellations of future cultures will also be visible to you in its mirror.[43]

To function well as a law-giver, then, the philosopher must know inwardly *a life being lived in fullest and highest fashion* and, as part of this, must know a capacity-- developed in the reflective activity which is part of his/her living his/her own life, thus developed in the discipline of honest attention to and reflection upon the matters being disclosed in the depths of that living-- to *discern reflectively* what of the universally human and the collective human future is open to him to see.

4. The philosophizing embodied in HAH

In the preceding discussion, we have sketched out the main lines of Nietzsche's account of philosophy as it is given in HAH. Let us now consider more fully the form that it takes, and discern what we can of what Nietzsche is doing-- and what is happening to him-- in making this shift in the way he conceives his philosophizing and, more profoundly, in making a shift in the way he actually conducts inquiry. To help us here, let us begin by recalling what Nietzsche himself says later to indicate how in mid-life what he was doing earlier and what was happening to him then seems to him now.

In his retrospects, Nietzsche speaks of the altered way of undertaking philosophical inquiry which is manifest in the second phase of his writing and reflecting, and relates it back to his disillusionment at Bayreuth.[44] In that Bayreuth-experience certain influences which had dominantly inflected his initial philosophizing had appeared to him as of deeply questionable character, and that, together with his embarrassing and hard-to-be-borne sense of his own lack of courage and his resultant complicity in what seemed to him now overwhelmingly repugnant, had generated the strong need to alter his way of reflecting. But these factors also constrained the way he engaged now in reflection, and burdened it with needs and functions that did not allow him complete freedom in his re-thinking. What seemed to him at the time a way forward free of the objectionable features his reflection had taken on in his response to Wagner and Schopenhauer was a thinking that saw in (natural) science its model in spirit and method; and even more, it was a thinking which would pursue the problematic of existence and of life's meaning with a focus on life in a biological (and more pointedly) physiological vein, for that would enable him to deal with life without the temptation to get lost in idealities and to engage once more in idealistic self-deception. What accompanied, even dominated, his pursuit of reflection in this 'scientific' vein, however, was the need to purify himself of what now seemed to him contaminating in the idealistic reaching he had centered on before. The result was an impetus to reflection which was marked by a deeply-felt and forcefully-working animus: not an impartial concern to follow inquiry wherever it might take him, but a determination to pursue truth in those directions and to find it in those forms which would hurt, as if in self-punishment for his having wandered astray, as if his now acknowledged self-delusion had been a deliberate affair for which he felt guilty. He needed now both to prove himself no longer deluded and to remove all that he had previously allowed into his thinking that might be suspect and carry this earlier corruption. For this effort to succeed, a considerable strength was needed, a concentrated and focused attention to matters that was on the lookout above all for truth that might afford the sort of better understanding he now sought.

This freer but still (if differently) constrained effort which he was now launched upon included a self-conscious attempt to bring to clarity what he was now doing, the way he was now engaging in reflective inquiry. But the constraining burden of anger, impatience with himself, and the like, affected not only the shape he gave to inquiry but the way he made intelligible to himself the shape of this new manner of inquiring he was undertaking, and in particular whether and how what was involved in it might in its own way be corrupting, biasing, and prejudicing, his very advance. As he acknowledges in his later retrospects, his initial work of purification and its attendant self-understanding were not fully successful. Not only did his own animus lead him initially into extremes in his inquiry that, while countering what seemed now the extremes of his first-phase of thinking, were in fact still of a kind with the earlier ones: youth reacting against youth is still youth. But in particular, his animus did not permit him at the time to see in full transparency what he was now doing, nor did it allow him to see how, in his companion interpretation of what he had been doing in his first phase of thought, he was being disposed to a reading which above all would enable him to see it as worthy of rejection. Even later, when he does recognize more fully what was going on in this start on his new way of thinking, he still does not seem to see fully what was happening.

Two things in particular stand out as reference points for discerning his inadequate recognition, both at the time and even later in retrospect. One of these we will treat here, and the other we will treat in the course of the next subsection below. The latter is the nature and standing of obligation. What we will consider here is the unreflective nature of science and its impact as it serves the role which Wagner and Schopenhauer did before, as that into which Nietzsche could now project himself and, under that guise, could feel supported in his working with matters he felt the need to inquire into and understand.

What is reflection, the reflective mode of thought?

In his philosophizing Nietzsche has from the start been developing a thinking which finds its appropriate standpoint to be that of the agent who is involved in the affairs of existence and who, concerned by the problematic of existence, is responsive to it in such fashion as brings it to be matter for thought. The thinking which is to accomplish this is first called forth in the maturation period of youth, where its emergence is part of the assumption of responsibility for one's life. In that matrix, thinking becomes re-flective, 'bent back' to explore the problematic of existence that already is being responded to in one's living and acting but now comes forward for express attention in thought as it regards life-whole. When this reflection became philosophical in Nietzsche and initially explored the disclosure accessible in the time which brought the problematic home, it did this guided by the aspiration-element of the time and sensitive to dimensions of elevation and depth relating both to the experiencing of reality and to reality itself. But as we noted in considering BT and UHH, while the way in which he proceeded in his earliest thought made positive sense of the disclosiveness, it did so without adequately retrieving in his express reflection the time that enabled that temporality of his living, acting, and thinking, which he was addressing in his thought. His reflection then was re-flective, but carried out in a being-bent-back which was unable to bring the enabling conditions of life and activity (including itself) into full self-cognizance, or at least, full self-understanding.

When in HAH he brings his own previous way of engaging in reflection into question, his self-criticism not only fails to break this reflective obliviousness to the full nature of time as fundamental enabling condition, but it deepens the oblivion by the way its concentration becomes narrowed and focused in virtue of the revulsion he feels at fundamental features of his previous way of thinking that have now become clearly apparent to him. What is (in some regards) an increased self-awareness did in fact become both occasion and impetus for a rethinking of the disclosive character of the experience; it also offered an opportunity for overcoming what incompleteness obtained in the way he had been pursuing reflection. But the rethinking that ensued did not pursue the matter of the disclosive character of experience by effectively exploring and deepening his understanding of the enabling conditions which made the disclosure seem initially to be what he took it to be in the first phase of his thought; in other words, it did not take shape in a *more adequately reflective* form of reflection. Apparently he was unable to separate what was to be thought-- the disclosiveness of experience, its bearing on the problematic of existence, and the nature of thought that would be apt to such disclosiveness and able to discern that bearing-- from those interpretative guides (and their steering) who had led him to make what he did of it at first; due to the emotional reaction which seemed to overwhelm him at the time, he was unable to consider freely what it was in experience to which that experience itself and those guides seemed to him in that earlier time to be pointing, and both to enter upon reflection in a more deeply reflective way and to come to a better understanding and a re-affirmation of the original disclosiveness. Instead, the discovery of himself as implicated by his acceptance of those guides in much that he could no longer square with his own evolving sensitivity led initially to a drawing back away from such an exploration: apparently no way of crediting the disclosiveness of such experience, and of entering more fully into the reflective thrust of thinking, seemed evident and viable to him that did not seem to him to mean his being drawn back into what he was bent on escaping. As a result, his reflection became even more fully incomplete as reflection than it was before.

Out of this incomplete reflectiveness, Nietzsche was disposed to see in science (mainly natural science) an undertaking not only useful for his purification-purpose but also marked by certain features he valued now all the more as part of reflection. Science was determined by a commitment to inquiry seeking the truth. If the focus of its attention was upon the various fields of fact being explored, and when needed and appropriate, upon the interconnection of those fields so that the many-sidedness of the actual world can be brought comprehensively into intelligible focus, its heart lay in two things: one, a skeptical 'prove it by evidence' approach, a spirit of inquiring which involved doubt and self-criticism as essential elements; and two, a concern for the methods whereby fact could best be ascertained, an attention to the methodology of establishing fact. But what he did not pay sufficient attention to was that such spirit and concern are *not reflective in nature*. In scientific inquiry, the nature of science itself is not a scientific question, nor is express inquiry into the enabling conditions for inquiry, the ultimate factors which make such inquiry possible (let alone meaningful): these are simply taken for granted and moved within. Given its unreflective nature, there was no reflective element in science that would, *from out of itself*, remind him of the problematic nature of his own mode of inquiry (the philosophically reflective, in which the nature of philosophy is a philosophic question) and would prod or assist him in raising in his own inquiring the question of the *reflective* nature of the undertaking in which he was involved. Quite to the contrary, by its own focus-- primordially on subject-matter, secondarily on method-- it confirmed the animus which limited the scope of his critical address to his own previous mode of inquiry and its enabling conditions. All the more was this so because, in the fields of fact that attracted his attention most (namely, physics and evolutionary biology), it was finding an intelligibility to things which seemed useful to him within his own reflective inquiry.

Reinforced by his reaction against his previous ways and his resistance to a more deeply reflective exploration, what the strong appeal of science worked in particular now to support in him was a critical address which, claiming to be scientific, would understand our capacity for knowing by way of a strong opposition between feeling and reason. This opposition was understood as that between the irrational and the rational, or (more fundamentally, perhaps) between the non-cognitive and the cognitive. This horizon becomes embodied in his conception of the "free spirit", which he celebrates in HAH but later acknowledges was a fictional type not unlike his transformed-Schopenhauer and transformed-Wagner.

What was prominent in the conception of the free spirit was a freedom from tradition, or perhaps more broadly, from all that his environment and his incorporation of that environment held that represented a horizon for thought and which, having become conviction in himself, formed an obstacle to reflection. Included in tradition here were Schopenhauer and, in the more distant background, Kant. But important to the conception of the free spirit was also another side to freedom, that of freedom from emotional biasing factors.[45] In order for the freedom from tradition to be well used, it needs to be exercised out of an inner condition in which the involvement in the alternation of love and hate, as these introduce an emotional bondage which disturbs present vision and prevents letting the loved-or-hated past go, is eventually lessened to the point at which one "will not hate and despise existence, but neither will he love it: placed above it, he will look on it now with the eye of joy, now with that of sorrow, and like nature itself, be now in a summery, now in an autumnal mood."[46] Such liberation from emotional bondage, along with the resulting capacity to hover-freely-over and to see things from the different sides which different emotional registers make possible, marks the eventually-achieved standpoint of the reflective agent who would be free in his judging: such is his understanding now.[47]

The enduring condition of such a freedom to attend to and to see has, nonetheless, its own self-affirmed limiting horizon, that of time, and its own field, the sensible-and-sensuous that appears within time's horizon. Natural science, with its spirit and methods, addresses this field in pre-eminent fashion. Such science, as a discipline he can honor for its commitment to truth, offers as well a gradually-being-established content which can be drawn on and can serve as invitation for his reflections. It enables him to broaden the reach of 'history' that was important in UHH and SE, but also to reconceive it, making it free of the eternal (both the metaphysical and the time-less that is internal to the temporal). The content of two disciplines becomes important in his philosophizing: one is evolutionary biology, the other is psychology; together they are important for understanding life, and this, both as visible outwardly and from within, with psychology being all the more crucial now because elements of self-deception and motivation have gained prominence as themes for him in virtue of the self-disclosure made at Bayreuth.

The fruitfulness of the resources he can avail himself of from scientific disciplines works to strengthen his refusal to allow our disclosive power legitimately to reach to anything but the temporal. Yet in this restriction which he is now affirming, there lurks the still unrecognized inadequacy in his explicit view of time; accompanying it, now with greater consequence than before, is a companion inadequacy that is also unrecognized, namely, the undifferentiation in his notions of space and spatiality. Although responsible address to matters to be understood in reflection looks to reality as wholly temporal and spatial, *what time and space are and what it means for something to be temporal and spatial are nonetheless not explored but simply taken for granted.* The appeal to evolution, by providing an outward focus for psychology on the primitive (the earlier stages of evolution being the simpler and more primitive, according to this vision), makes for a reading of the earlier human condition as more primitive psychologically; the element of heredity, understood as the vehicle of the transmission of traits (including responsive dispositions), means that we retain the more primitive in ourselves and have access thus to the earlier human condition as a less developed one; and the treatment of our bodily being which makes certain assumptions concerning the non-differentiation of (say) mind and brain makes for an easy integration of the biological and psychological. All three of these ways of proceeding depend for their meaning on those inadequately differentiated notions of time and space, temporality and spatiality.

What then becomes featured in this indirect approach to life-- indirect both as making the external prominent, and as reading ourselves by the roundabout way of an inheritance and 'chemical' sublimation of what we have conjectured to have formed the more primitive inwardness of primitive life-forms-- is two things. One is a different temporal focus than that of his first-phase thought. Individual growth as maturation becomes displaced as central for reflection, in favor of what can be conjectured about development of the human race in the evolutionary movement of life on earth. In this way, the sun-measures view of time and temporality becomes even more important and definitive for how his thought develops now than in the first phase. The other is a constraint on what are increasingly subtle and sensitive psychological explorations; these not only must operate under presumptions about the temporal horizon of reality and the wholly-temporal status of all things psychological but also under presumptions about the physiological and evolutionary as providing significant vehicles for the reading of the meaning of psychological discoveries.

In short: In his account of 'historical philosophizing' as if that were now his way of addressing matters reflectively, Nietzsche proclaims a temporal (and spatial) horizon for thought about reality, without the disillusioning discovery that has called for his self-criticism and brought on a different reflective address to things having brought his awareness of time and space, temporality and spatiality, to attention in such way as invited, or required, reflective examination of the nature of time and space and the resultant nature of temporality and spatiality. Because science is an affair of thought *but not of reflective thought*, it also does not invite (or reinforce any invitation to) a reflection which wants to take it as paradigm to bring forth an express retrieval and understanding of space and time as conditions of being and action. Thus in virtue of the animus emerging responsively to the disillusion and the nature of the discipline (science) that he seems to be finding fruitful, Nietzsche's initial pursuit of reflection in this second phase, including his critical address to his own earlier embodiment of philosophical reflection and his constructive account of his current effort, embodies an inquiring that ventures within a particular horizon that does not allow important conditions of reflective inquiry, and thus essential features taking shape within those conditions, to come into view and receive adequate notice. Due to this limiting horizon, and the development of insights in terms that are skewed to make things intelligible within it, the advance which Nietzsche is making in this first work of the second phase of his reflection-- the increasingly subtle discernment of the inward, and the explorations that are bringing him closer to a satisfactory insight into the limits of the Kantian framework for understanding both reality and our understanding of reality, to mention only two facets of his advance-- is considerably ambivalent. Indeed, the more successfully he advances, and the more his grasp of the matters that concern him most seems to him purified and acceptable, the more it distorts and hides of the ultimate conditions of life and of essential elements in its proximate affairs. Matters are being forced, however much the ideal being aspired to is that of the "free spirit".

Once again, the hermit's question is relevant. To that question Nietzsche himself provides some answer-pointers in his later retrospects. But even there, it remains important to ask about those retrospective accounts as well: are they undertaken from a standpoint which could let the earlier and its limitations come *adequately* into view?

B. Agency

Speaking of the temperament which allows the free spirit to find that the after-effect of the knowledge that human life is deeply involved in fiction and error is a life "much simpler and emotionally cleaner than our present life is", Nietzsche says:

> Though at first the old motives of vehement desire would still have strength [*Kraft*] due to long inherited habit, they would gradually grow weaker under the influence of purifying knowledge. In the end one would live among humans and with oneself as in *nature*, without praising, blaming, flying into a passion, and as regards many things for which one formerly felt only fear, now feeding on them as though on a spectacle.[48]

For this to happen, such a free spirit would have to possess a certain good temperament, namely,

> a firm, mild, and at bottom cheerful soul, a frame of mind [*Stimmung*] which does not need to be on its guard against malice or sudden outbursts and in whose outward expressions there is nothing of snarling and sullenness ... . A man from whom the ordinary fetters of life have fallen to such an extent that he continues to live only in order to know ever better must ... be able, without envy or vexation, to forgo much, indeed almost everything upon which other men place value; that free, fearless hovering over human beings, customs, laws, and the traditional evaluations of things must *suffice* him as the most desirable condition. He gladly communicates his joy in this condition, and he *has*, perhaps, nothing else to communicate-- which involves, to be sure, one more privation and renunciation. If nonetheless one wants more from him, he will, with a benevolent shake of the head, point to his brother, the free man of action, and perhaps not conceal a certain mockery in doing so: for that man's 'freedom' is a peculiar matter.[49]

In his contrast of free spirit with free man of action, Nietzsche avails himself of a common distinction, between some human beings as "doers" and others as "thinkers". Taken as a way of speaking of human agency, the distinction can be misleading, since in both cases we are active. But a contrast within our agency does obtain, in that the activity of the doer, while entered upon inwardly by a decision-making, essentially involves overt behavior and results, whereas the activity of the thinker, also entered upon inwardly by a decision-making, does not. Now because our agency always involves both initiated activity of some sort and a decision-making whereby we enter upon it, his thinking on the different sorts of freedom realized in our agency can bring them forward in ways that reflect these differentiations. Thus the contrasts of the "man of action" with the "free man of action", and of the "fettered spirit" with the "free spirit", can center around the decision-making in each, whether it is fettered or free. In the contrast of the free spirit with the free man of action, however, while there is the common freedom of decision-making that makes them brothers, they are different not only because the one is a doer, the other a thinker, but because (as we will see) the freedom of the free spirit is somewhat more expansive than that of the free man of action.

The notions which make intelligible what Nietzsche is pointing to in his brother-metaphor arise when, inquiring within the horizon of intelligibility in which life is an evolutionary phenomenon, he treats of human agency and initiative with a particular attention to morality, and ventures on an exploration of "the origin and history of so-called moral sensations" and of "the posing and solving of sociological problems that are intertwined with (such sensations)".[50] Leaving aside this matter of the sociological (we will take it up in section C. below), let us begin our consideration of Nietzsche's treatment of agency with his account of it as a moral affair. That account has two stages. First is his attack upon the conception of agency according to which, if it would be a moral affair, it requires of us free will; the second is his analysis of morality itself, and in particular, morality freed from any notions of 'ought' and 'responsibility'. After exploring these, we will consider the basic elements of agency as he is now bringing it into view, and eventually seek to make intelligible the contrast he draws between the two brothers-in-freedom.

1. Freedom and responsibility

In the first phase of his thought, Nietzsche made morality, and in particular, a morality of responsibility, a primary element in his conception of the human being. In its basic character it was something natural, something for which our nature and the nature of things (that something is at stake in existence) fitted us and into which we would grow provided that our nature evolved as it was meant to from the start. We would by nature come into it as an actual first-hand affair in youth, and know it then in connection primordially with the matter of taking our own lives upon ourselves and venturing into the future as beings who are from then on responsible for our own lives. Thus his reflection tended to concentrate on our initiative as the enabling medium for this, and upon circumstance as functioning to support and favor it but as also introducing factors that obstruct and thwart our growth into it.

Within the limited horizon that marks this first work of his thought's second phase, Nietzsche expands his attentiveness to the inward, and conceives motivation and its variety of factors, our drives and their varied outworking, as wholly temporal factors which enter into the constitution of our active being. This attentiveness of his, in its extent and kind, forms a venture which he claims is novel: philosophy traditionally (that is, metaphysical philosophy) has avoided any psychological inquiry which (based on close observation) attempted to get below the surface. The result has been that even the greatest of philosophers has often taken as his point of departure a false understanding of human actions and sensations: for example, a false ethics has been built upon the misinterpretation of certain actions as "unegoistic".[51] In virtue of his own psychological probing, Nietzsche would re-conceive our agency: that is, he would purify the notion of agency and of the decision-making that forms the initiative of an agent, and in the course of this, would undermine those notions of agency and initiative which he conceives to be founded on fictions.

The most fundamental error he would lay before us concerns our initiating of activity (whether overt or the inward activity, say, of thinking). Activity is the vehicle of our participating in a larger course of events, and as such is interwoven with the larger context. According to his account, we have developed a conception of such activity as stemming from an initiative determined by our decision-making powers; and central to such decision-making is a "conscious will" which is "free" in the sense of having *no determining ground* beyond itself or internal and prior to its own act (that act whereby we determine and commit ourselves to some particular action). Freedom in this reference is absence of effective constraint exerted upon and limiting the act of the will and its determination of ourselves to doing-this or doing-that. Now when human activity is seen as part of that larger course, we must conceive it (so he asserts) as we would conceive, say, a waterfall. Regardless of how much a waterfall may seem by its curvings, twistings, and breakings, to express choice [*Belieben*] and freedom-of-will, everything there is necessary, and every motion is calculable mathematically. If one were all-knowing, one would be able to calculate every individual action, likewise every advance in knowledge, every error, every piece of wickedness. The actor himself is, to be sure, fixed in the illusion of free will. But if in any moment [*Augenblick*] the wheel of the world were to stand still, and there were an all-knowing, calculating intelligence there to make use of this pause, it could narrate the future of every being [*Wesens*] to the remotest ages and describe every track along which this wheel had yet to roll. The agent's [*Handelnden*] deception regarding himself, his erroneous assumption of free will, is itself part of the mechanism it would have to compute.[52]

In urging this manner of considering initiative,[53] Nietzsche proceeds somewhat as he did in UHH when speaking of the temporal consciousness of the animal. That is, he approaches the inward indirectly, by way of the outward, and speaks as if the involvement of our activity in the sphere of the outward meant that the terms of outward events are sufficient to account for the initiative involved in the activity. And to the extent that Nietzsche sees initiative as belonging to our (human) nature and constituting the 'out of itself' functioning of a nature which develops 'out of itself' over time, then he extends the 'necessity' which marks the course of events seen outwardly to cover not only the 'out of itself' of the development of our nature (our growth and maturation) but also the 'out of ourselves' character of our initiative. Such extension to embrace what is inward under the terms of what is outward is facilitated in Nietzsche's mind by his express conception of time, which becomes refined in this phase of his thought from the the conception of a series of discontinuous or discrete moments to a conception of a continuous, homogeneous, undivided, indivisible flowing[54] in which the present actualizes itself but does so without stretches (isolated stretches are fictional abstractions, not realities). With the inclusion of the ongoing of time as enabling condition for activity under this form of the sun-measures representation of time, we have the basis for the use of the waterfall as an apt image for ourselves in our functioning out of ourselves. That basis becomes built on to the extent that Nietzsche moves, without acknowledgement that this is a move across a genuine gap, to identify the moment of decision-making and initiative with an instantaneous state of the continuous flow of reality in time-- the "pause" starting from which the whole future could be calculated, to use the language of HAH-I/106. That pause is not a stretch but, at best, an imaginary instant; at it, a momentum is present (for reality is a flux, is motion), and a directional movement as well, whose 'necessity' (as regards measure, momentum, and direction) enables the calculation in question.

In HAH-II/WS (aphorisms 9-10), Nietzsche returns to this matter of free will and develops thoughts on it from a somewhat different perspective. This time he approaches it by way of the activity in which we find our nature, in its strongest elements, at work.

> Over one person, *necessity* stands in the shape of passions, over another as the habit of hearing and obeying, over a third as a logical conscience, over a fourth as whim and capricious pleasure in side-leaps. The freedom of their will, however, is sought by these four precisely there where each of them is most firmly fettered: it is as if the silkworm sought the freedom of its will precisely in spinning. Why do they do that? Evidently because each considers himself most free there where his *feeling of being alive* [*Lebensgefühl*] is greatest; thus, as we have said, in passion, in duty, in knowledge, in capriciousness respectively. That by means of which the individual human being is strong [*stark*], wherein he feels himself enlivened [*belebt*], he involuntarily thinks must also always be the element of his freedom: he counts dependence and dullness [*Stumpfsinn*], independence and the feeling of being alive [*Lebensgefühl*], as necessarily coupled.[55]

It would seem from this perspective that free will is an interpretation of a facet of the experience of ourselves in which we find ourselves active in a way that brings our strength into play and makes us feel most alive; in being so active, we feel ourselves to be most free, and free in the sense of independent, of not being determined from beyond ourselves but being self-determined by something in ourselves in the operation of which we feel ourselves most ourselves, most acting 'out of ourselves'. The reality of freedom which is being misinterpreted as a matter of free will in the sense of conscious and unconstrained deliberate choice among options is our *willing* involvement in effort, a responsive involvement in which our *wanting*-- what we above all want as living active beings-- is effectively being realized in the initiative and execution and we are acting in such way that the operation of the most forceful element in our own nature is leading the way into the future. The necessity here may in some sense be a firm fettering, but it is not that of some power constraining us from beyond; it is rather that of an operation of our very own nature in the responsive enacting of itself, an operation felt by us as a release and flow and a functioning as we, given our distinctive nature, really want to be functioning.[56] In this, freedom and necessity are one.

In a companion account, which focuses as well on the inward sense of our functioning but this time on our ordinary functioning, Nietzsche speaks of how, in our ordinary involvement in things, we do not *feel* our dependence on anything, and therefore (but falsely-- and in testimony of how "proud and lusting for dominance" we human beings are) regard ourselves as independent. But this sense that independence (and with it, a being in control, in charge) is our ordinary condition is mistaken, as is the companion assumption that if we were to become dependent on anything we would recognize this (the altered condition would be perceived by us, and felt to be antithetical to what we are accustomed to). In reality, we are always living in manifold dependence; it is just that we have become so accustomed to this that we no longer perceive "the pressure of the chains" and thence assume that we are free. "It is only from *new* chains that he now suffers: 'freedom of will' really means nothing more than feeling no new chains."[57] Presumably the chains here compare in one respect with the fetters of the previous aphorism, but they represent all the factors internally at work in us in our ordinary condition, as contrasted with those strongest factors in whose functioning in extraordinary times we feel ourselves alive. Our ordinary involvement is not marked by such a sense of 'being alive'; and yet we still regard ourselves in our ordinary condition as free, at least in the sense of not being determined or constrained to something from beyond ourselves. When we introduce a new factor, however (learn a new pattern of response, say), until this becomes habitual and we no longer notice what is really taking place, we feel we have become dependent. Again, the matter on Nietzsche's mind is the felt character of our functioning from out of ourselves as we are actively involved in things, which is being mis-taken as involving a conscious and unconstrained deliberate choice among options. There is a genuine difference in our varied (extraordinary and ordinary) conditions registered in our feelings, but neither condition justifies a concept of free will; the difference only involves a distinction within-- and in our awareness of-- the necessity at work in our involvement. There is necessitation in both cases, but somewhat different according as it is a strength, what makes us strong, that is at work or as it is something else within us.[58]

In the line of thought whose direction has just been sketched out, two complementary things are happening. In one case, (a modified version of) the inadequate express idea of time and temporal reality which marked Nietzsche's first-phase thought-- the idea now of time and the temporal as a continuous flow-- is being used to facilitate the extension of a notion of deterministic necessity from the outward realm to the inward and, by its denial of indeterminacy to the will, to refute the notion of free will. To that extent, the ideas being used operate in the self-purification vein whereby Nietzsche is ridding himself of what has become an embarrassment to him, and they do this work in keeping with the intellectual conscience that is central to being 'scientific'. In the other case, what is inward is being attended to in experientially discoverable features relating to our participation in activity, and being interpreted (to the extent that there is realized in it a flow of life and energy felt as coming from the heart of our nature) by way of a notion of "freedom" which is one with a "necessity" in the operation of our nature *out of itself* and which is mistakenly read if taken to signify the freedom of indeterminacy to the will. These two approaches would cohere *if* the inward functioning and flow could be taken as of a kind with, and intelligible by way of, the outwardly-visible flow.

For whatever reasons (perhaps among them, impatience engendered by his animus), the ideas here are not yet worked out very satisfactorily.[59] They involve a recasting of "necessity" as he treated it in WB, dropping the term "destiny" when speaking of nature, while at the same time stressing a necessity in the functioning of circumstance made intelligible by way of the refined sun-measures idea of time. But difficulty arises when these ideas of time and visible-reality-as-flux are applied inwardly; for this means denying the reality of stretches, thus of what make possible activity as a time-taking affair. The waterfall-image he uses also has further limitations important enough to make it of questionable (and at any rate, limited) value for making the inward and its temporality intelligible.

For one: the flow of a stream that forms a waterfall is not defined by the water alone but by things which are other than the water and which are not flowing but fixed-- the stream-bed, for example, and the land-forms generally, the changes in elevation, the force of gravity, and so on. Is there something comparable in the case of time and temporal reality? Not if time is the *ultimate* horizon of being, so that there is nothing beyond and outside it. In any case, there is this as well, that time (and with it temporal reality) has a *stable internal* reference-point (the present) in virtue of which the ongoing can be what it is-- the moving side of the present. But since the streams (of time and reality) are flux throughout, they have no such stable internal reference-point.[60]

For another: if the stream-flow images the continuous onward movement of time and temporal reality, there is no way in which such an image can account for (say) a remembering of the past; remembering calls back and holds the past expressly into the ongoing present, whereas the flow can at best image the continuous novel ongoing, whether it be of 'this water' ever moving onward downstream or of 'the continually new water here at this point of the stream-bed'.

Finally, in its application to human activity, other limits emerge. For example, when the image is extended to the inward and applied to our involvement in activity, it relates to our effort and its exertion of energy. Now these involve stretch-inflections of the continuously-ongoing-now whose continuing holds only *from our beginning onward* so long as we are. We did *begin*, and this, in a twofold sense. The one sense concerns the initiative in which we *start* activity as *our own*; such initiative has its own *beginning* or initial actuality in ourselves as agents, and with this, we ourselves have our beginning as *active* beings. This beginning is genuinely a first, discontinuous with any antecedent. The other sense concerns the nature which functions as *our own* in our initiating. We are active from the start as having (for one thing) a native endowment (a nature) which in our effort we draw on as 'already-there' and enabling for the effort being made and whose determinateness reflects an inheritance-relation of this endowment to our progenitors and ancestors. Even so, not only is our nature novel, but our activity itself drawing on that nature is nothing inherited, nothing that is continuous with what came before us, and in particular, nothing which was going on before our beginning. In short, there is radical discontinuity as part of the condition under which the effort and the flow of energy in it are such as they are, namely, *ours*, those of *another* active being than our progenitors or any other beings.[61] Such discontinuity is not acknowledged in and can not be accounted for by the image of a continual stream, however much any continuity of effort and flow of energy in our activity once started can give some limited purchase for the extension inward which the image makes.

However adequate or inadequate may be these first formulations of an attempt to reconceive the freedom involved in our agency, there are many consequences which follow from the rejection of an interpretation of our initiative as being (or involving) the work of a free will. Two are particularly noted by Nietzsche: one, that we can not be held accountable for our actions; and two, that any morality which makes a 'shall'/'should'/'ought' central and thereby presupposes free will is undermined. The second of these, the most important for our purposes, we will take up in the next section.

As for the first: Unlike in the first phase of his thought, Nietzsche's thoughts about responsibility in HAH focus not on the matter of responsibility for our lives and ourselves, but on our various actions, and the question whether or not these can be attributed to us as our responsibility in the sense of their being an outcome which we generate of our own free will. Here responsibility is a matter of an accountability that can be isolated to ourselves as decision-making agents. Can we rightly be held accountable for our actions? Not if those actions were not freely willed by us-- so Nietzsche would answer, in agreement with the proponents of free will. But for Nietzsche, since free will is a fiction, this means that we are not responsible for the consequences of our actions, nor for their motives, nor for the nature in us from which follow motives, actions, and consequences.[62] Merit and guilt are creatures of a fiction, and have reality only as such, not as themselves founded truly in reality.[63] And without merit and guilt, there is no passing judgment on human beings or their actions, no punishing or rewarding as a matter of justice; punishment and reward can only have the meaning of encouraging or deterring others, not of giving to the 'doer' what is his own.[64] "We do not accuse nature of immorality when it sends us a thunderstorm and makes us wet: why do we call the harmful human being immoral? Because in the second case we assume a free will holding sway in voluntary fashion [*willkürlich waltenden*], in the first necessity. But this distinction is an error."[65]

In HAH-II/WS, Nietzsche expands this attack on reward and punishment. If the will were free, then no deed could have a past, and therefore the practice of mitigating or increasing punishment according to the past of the doer (this is his first transgression, up to now he has been a good man; or this is his seventeenth, he is a habitual criminal) is illogical.[66] Or again, if the will were free, then reward and punishment are not pertinent. For we hold someone accountable for ill-doing only under certain conditions: he was able to employ his intelligence, and he acted for this-or-that reason and not unconsciously or under compulsion. But if he did what he did out of free will, he acted without reason or motive and his deed arose out of nothing. For that is the nature of free will, that it is not determined by anything beyond itself. According to our assumption concerning punishable deeds, however, such a deed should not be punished, since the perpetrator was not acting intentionally and for 'this'-reason, with 'this'-motive and 'this'-purpose, being determined so to act by his intelligence.[67]

2. Morality

The second major consequence which follows from rejection of an interpretation of our initiative as involving free will is that there is in that case no 'shall', 'should', 'ought'.[68] At first sight, this seems to mean: 'Shall', 'should', 'ought', are addressed to us only under the presupposition that we are free to act in this-way rather than in that-way, and that this freedom, making it equally possible for us to do or not do what we ought, is due to our having free will. Without free will, any 'thou shalt' in a morality has no meaning. But if this is so, what does that mean for the morality the idea of which Nietzsche had been developing in his first phase, the morality which is latent in our nature and grown into in time as part of our maturation? Does that morality involve a 'thou shalt'? Is it undermined? Or is the 'thou shalt' Nietzsche has in mind found only in (a) social morality?

So far as the psychological inquiry which Nietzsche now conducts reveals, what alone can be allowed by knowledge to stand as motives in ourselves as living beings are pleasure [*Lust*] and unpleasantness [*Unlust*], use [*Nutzen*] and injury [*Schaden*].[69] Pleasure is a feeling that is basically to be understood out of life's own nature and drive, as "the feeling [*Gefühl*] of one's own power [*Macht*], of one's own strong excitation [*Erregung*]".[70] Pleasure occurs both as register of the well-being the living being wants and also as motivating to the preserving and enhancing of that well-being [*Wohlbefinden*]. "Without pleasure, no life; the struggle over pleasure is the struggle over life."[70] Such motivational equipment includes nothing which is intrinsically moral, if that means dependent on free will. And yet, "morality" as Nietzsche would now focus his and our attention on it is able to be built up on this basis. How?

HAH provides a provisional sketch of several ways in which the development of morality can be seen to happen.

One direction for such development is set forth in an aphorism entitled "The three phases of morality hitherto".

It is the first sign that the animal has become human when his actions are no longer referred to momentary well-being [*Wohlbefinden*] but to enduring well-being, so that the person is oriented to the *useful*, the *purposive*: it is here that the free lordship [*freie Herrschaft*] of reason first breaks out. A still higher stage is reached when he acts according to the principle of *honor*; in virtue of this, he enters into orderly arrangements, and submits to common feelings [*gemeinsamen Empfindungen*], and this raises him high above the phase in which only personal usefulness guides him: he respects, and wants to be respected, and that means: he conceives use as dependent on what he thinks about others and what others think about him. Finally, on the highest stage of morality *hitherto*, he acts according to *his own* standard concerning human beings and things: he himself determines for himself and others what is honorable, what is useful; he has become the law-giver of opinion, in accordance with an ever more highly developed concept of the useful and the honorable. Knowledge makes him capable of [*befähigt*] preferring [*voranzustellen*] the most useful, that is, preferring the general and enduring use to the personal, preferring the honoring recognition of the general and enduringly valuable [*Geltung*] to the momentarily valuable: he lives and acts as collective-individual.[71]

The first phase involves morality as a work of a practical reason which, accepting the good our nature points us to-- our well-being-- and grasping it as an enduring affair, orients the individual to the useful. But morality does not end with the personal; it takes higher forms when, in our orderly association with others, we develop ideas of the honorable, and eventually grasp (with reason's help) not simply the enduring but the general as preferable to the momentary and personal.

Nietzsche tries out several sketches of a second direction for such development, one which maintains the sense of the ultimate motivational grounds in the individual as being pleasure and unpleasantness, use and injury, but expands on this sense of the moral as a social affair. Here, morality is an element in the creation of a social group.[72]

One sketch sees "the ground for all morality [*Moralität*]" as being

> first prepared when a greater individual or a collective-individuality (for example, society, the state) subjugates other individuals, that is, draws them out of their isolation and orders them within a collective [*Verband*]. Morality is preceded by *compulsion*, indeed it is for a time itself still compulsion, to which one accommodates oneself for the avoidance of unpleasantness [*Unlust*]. Later it becomes custom, later still voluntary [*freier*] obedience, finally almost instinct: then, like all that has for a long time been habitual and natural, it is associated with pleasure-- and is now called *virtue*.[73]

A second sketch speaks of the double pre-history of the concepts of good and evil. The soul of ruling tribes and castes is one source of such concepts; the soul of the subjected and powerless is another. The resulting concepts have rather different character and meaning. In the former case, it is the power [*Macht*] to repay [*vergelten*] (good with good, evil with evil) and the actual practice of such repaying (in gratitude and revenge) which makes one be counted good, while those who are powerless to repay in this manner are counted bad. The good, alike in this power and practice, feel bound together by this and form a caste; but the bad, the horde of the powerless, have no sense of belonging together. In the caste of the good, good and bad are for a long time the same thing as noble and base, master and slave; such goodness is inherited. In the case of the powerless, every *other* human being (be he noble or base) is "inimical, ruthless, exploitative, cruel, cunning". In fact,

> evil is the characterizing expression for humans, indeed for every living being one supposes to exist (e.g. for a god) ... . Signs of goodness, readiness to help, sympathy, are received fearfully as a trick, a prelude with a dreadful termination, a means of confusing and outwitting, in short, as refined wickedness. When this disposition exists in the individual, a community can hardly arise, at best the most rudimentary form of community: so that wherever this conception of good and evil reigns the downfall of such individuals, of their tribes and races, is near.[74]

In works to come, Nietzsche refines this sketch until, in *On the Genealogy of Morals*, it becomes an account of two basically different visions, marked terminologically by the two expressions, "good and evil" and "good and bad".

A third direction for such development, one presupposing morality as social morality, is concerned with the way this functions in the individuals that are members of the social group. If morality is a social affair which is eventually incorporated into individuals in a process of socialization, it becomes (as HAH-I/99 suggests) a matter of custom. Once it is that, to be moral or ethical [*moralisch, sittlich, ethisch*] is to act in accordance with custom, "in obedience to a long-established law or tradition". The content of the law or tradition does not matter, and neither does the degree of willingness or resistance which one feels to such submission: all that matters is that one submits, obeys.[75] Now of course, *what* the moral person does when acting morally does depend on the content of the accepted traditions; and if tradition is modified in any significant way, then what the moral person does will also change. But the 'what' does not define the morality of the doing.

Yet this is only one side of moral action within a traditional system. For the content of any morality as a social affair includes an order of rank of the things considered good; this hierarchical order opens up another dimension of what it means to be moral and act morally, in that the decision to act in accord with a lesser good in preference to a higher good will be seen as acting immorally, even if one is acting for a good which the system affirms and encourages and in that sense is acting morally.[76]

Now further, there is this that marks all the laws of custom of all times, that doing injury to one's neighbor is seen as injurious above all else, so that at the word 'evil' we now think especially of voluntarily doing injury to one's neighbor.[77] Nonetheless, this-- formulated in the contrast of 'egoistic' vs. 'unegoistic'-- is not a more fundamental antithesis for understanding morality than that of acting in accord with custom vs. acting in defiance of it. However, because of its persistent recurrence, this distinction has been often presented within our tradition as itself what makes the difference between moral and immoral in action. But in fact, the notion of 'unegoistic action' is a fiction. For "no human being has ever done anything that was done wholly [*allein*] for others and with no personal motivation [*Beweggrund*] whatever; how, indeed, should a person be *able* to do something that had no reference to himself, that is to say, lacked all inner compulsion [*Nötigung*] (which must have its ground in a personal need [*Bedürfnis*])? How could the *ego* act without the *ego*?"[78]

Within the framework of these three pointers into the origin and facets of morality, Nietzsche poses two questions which bring us back toward matters as he was understanding them in the first phase of his thought. Assuming that the fundamental motivational forces in the human being are the four he has enumerated, and that these figure in action the decision-making in which involves some more or less intelligent assessment of the way to satisfy the desire for well-being rational focus on which is the first step in the development of morality, why did impersonal actions come to be commended everywhere and the impersonal be regarded as the real distinguishing mark [*eigentliche Kennzeichen*] of moral action? The reason: on account of the general utility of such actions. But what in reality best answers to this standard of general utility? Is it really actions motivated by pity and compassion? We realize now that "it is in precisely the most *personal* possible consideration that the utility for the generality is at its greatest". For "to make a complete *person* [*ganze Person*] out of oneself, and in all that one does to have in view the *highest good* [*Wohl*] of this person"-- this does more to make us able to be useful to others than "those excitations and actions of pity" which are otherwise being promoted as most useful.[79] It is "strictly personal action" of this sort, then, that best measures up to the standard of general utility.

The aphorism in which the preceding questions and thoughts occur is entitled "The morality of the mature individual". It ends as follows.

> In truth, we are all suffering from paying too little attention [*Beachtung*] to the personal in us, it is badly cultivated-- let us confess it: we have forcibly diverted our minds [*Sinn*] away from it and offered it as a sacrifice to the state, to science, to those in need of help, as if what had to be sacrificed was something bad. Now we also want to work for our fellow human beings, but only to the extent that we discover our own [*eigenen*] highest advantage [*Vorteil*] in this work: no more, no less. All depends on this, namely, what one understands by *one's advantage*; precisely the immature, undeveloped, crude individual will understand it most crudely.[80]

In this aphorism, the being toward whose "enduring well-being" morality was oriented in its first phase (see page 212, above) is ultimately ourselves in our maturity, ourselves as complete persons whose concern in our activity is always our own highest good. We can only gain such maturity eventually, since it includes developed and refined capacities which take time and a cultivation-effort to gain and which the "immature, undeveloped, crude individual" therefore lacks; included in such capacities is a rational grasp of the useful as it relates to such a refined person. In claiming this, and seeing a being who is moral in this way as what is most useful also from the perspective of social morality, Nietzsche is making what is decisive morally in both references a matter of (individual or social) advantage or good. That is a revision of his earlier thinking. For in SE, he had grasped morality as naturally entered into as we respond in youth to the imperative call of conscience and seek to carry out concretely the responsibility we are assuming for our own being. Such a morality of responsibility is not founded in advantage and its calculation; its basis is rather an *imperative call*-- not, of course, the 'thou shalt' correlative with 'free will', but a call *internal* to life. The "realized higher self" of the morality of responsibility (SE) and the "complete person" of personal morality (HAH) are rather similar, but the morality involved in their becoming and being has a rather different basis.

There are other echoes of his earlier sense of morality, with a similar kinship-yet-difference. For one, in HAH-II/WS-45, Nietzsche can say:

> All those who do not have themselves sufficiently under their own control [*in der Gewalt*] and do not know [*kennen*] morality [*Moralität*] as a continual self-command [*Selbstbeherrschung*] and self-overcoming [*Selbstüberwindung*] practised both in great things and in the smallest, involuntarily become glorifiers of the good, pitying, benevolent impulses [*Regungen*], of that instinctive morality [*Moralität*] which has no head but seems to consist solely of heart and helping hands. It is, indeed, in their interest to cast suspicion on a morality [*Moralität*] of reason and to make of that other morality the only one.[81]

Here a self-command and self-overcoming, required as part of reason's refined morality of advantage,[82] may indeed serve the advantage both of the individual and the collective better than a morality of feeling. But that they are moral in virtue of reason's determination of advantage is different from their being moral as called for by the summons of life.

Seen overall, the various initial steps Nietzsche is tentatively taking now in his thinking on morality all start with the individual. In some, he sees morality forming and evolving in function of reason's referring an individual's activity to his/her own good or advantage at higher and more refined levels; in others, he sees morality as branching off to become a social affair so far as the individual is engaged with others in a collectivity and finds his/her activity as a member of that collectivity subjected to social arrangements which embody customary valuations whose ultimate rationale is their general utility (that is, their power to effect the highest good of the collectivity, namely, its preservation). On both paths of his thought, he is sorting out morality as a phenomenon much broader than the one which had come to monopolize the term in his times (i.e. Christian morality), and is claiming a root for this complex broader phenomenon which nowhere involves a 'thou shalt' that presupposes a 'free will' but which lies in the individual as engaged in activity in necessary fashion. That means, morality arises as the individual, seeking his/her own well-being and moved to act by the pleasant/ unpleasant and harmful/useful, is guided by a more-or-less intelligent grasp of the good.[83]

Such an analysis makes all of the phenomena in question-- higher and lower goods and moral systems, authoritative traditions and customs, utility and harm, motivations to action-- gain their intelligibility by reference to this facet of human being, that in our activity and existence there is something at stake which concerns us as active beings. In his first-phase thought, Nietzsche interpreted the *claiming* relation of the at-stake to our activity by speaking of the call of conscience, that is, life's summons to the living agent to take responsibility for his/her life and unique being. Revising his interpretation, he now replaces a "call" correlating in its imperativeness with our responsive will (readily misinterpreted as a free will) by a good toward which our wanting is necessarily drawn. In this notion of a *good* that we are *natured* to be *necessarily drawn toward*, he continues to acknowledge and integrate the claiming of the at-stake, but now hiddenly in the guise of the good's drawing power, not of life's imperative.[84] Correlative with this drawing power, which is effective in us by way of our responsive wanting, is the nature-expressing functioning whereby through our decision-making we concretely enact a seeking for the good as our current capacities can presently discern it.

The path on which Nietzsche's thought is now moving leads him, at the end of the chapter on the history of moral sensations, to a vision of the ideal human being not as a 'moral' human but as a 'wise or knowing' one in whom the working of intelligence (in both practical and reflective veins) is opening up a rather different human possibility than what Nietzsche takes to be present in the traditions of the past or in current humanity otherwise.[85] Thus after he has urged the complete unaccountability of human beings for their actions and their nature, he can claim:

> To gain insight into all this can be deeply painful, but there is a consolation: such pains are birth-pangs. The butterfly wants [*will*] to break out of its cocoon, it tears at it and tears it open, and it is then blinded and confused by the unfamiliar light, the realm of freedom. It is in such humans as are *capable* [*fähig*] of that sadness-- and how few of them there are!-- that the first attempt will be made to see whether humankind *could transform* itself from a *moral* to a *wise humanity*. The sun of a new gospel [*Evangeliums*] is casting its first beam on the highest peak in the soul of those individuals: there the mist is gathering more thickly than ever before, and the brightest shining [*Schein*] and the gloomiest twilight lie side by side. Everything is necessity, thus says the new knowledge, and this knowledge itself is necessity. Everything is innocence, and knowledge is the path to insight into this innocence. If pleasure, egoism, vanity are *necessary* for the production of the moral phenomena and their finest flower, the sense for truth and justice belonging to knowledge; if error and aberration of the imagination was the only means by which humankind was able gradually to raise itself to this degree of self-enlightenment and self-redemption-- who has the right to despise those means? Who could be sad when he becomes aware of the goal to which those paths lead? It is true that everything in the domain of morality has become and is changeable, unsteady, everything is in flux; but *everything is also flooding forward* [*in Strome*], and towards *one* goal. Even if the inherited habit of erroneous evaluation, loving, hating, does continue to rule in us, under the influence of increasing knowledge it nonetheless will grow weaker. A new habit, that of comprehending, not-loving, not-hating, surveying, is gradually implanting itself in us on the same soil, and in thousands of years will perhaps be strong [*mächtig*] enough to bestow on humankind the power [*Kraft*] of bringing forth the wise, innocent (conscious of innocence) human being as regularly as it now brings forth-- *not the antithesis but the necessary preliminary of such a being*-- the unwise, unjust, guilt-conscious human being.[86]

The "realm of freedom" to which Nietzsche alludes here is the realm spirit entered when, struggling to free itself from error and to discern truth, it was able finally to free itself from the basic errors of 'thou shalt' and 'free will' and, as continuation of a (knowledge-discerning) functioning in which it had been realizing in some fulness the freedom (free-functioning) of itself in its truth-seeking, was set to exploring the implications for humanity and the human future of this truthful insight into all functioning (including its own). In its struggling, and in the exploring ahead, spirit has been (and will continue to be) animated by the "sense for truth and justice" and thus has been seeking (and will continue to seek) understanding under the pressure of a "logical conscience" as the form of necessity which the inquirer feels is the element of his/her freedom.[87] Now spirit thinks its seeking has been brought to a self-enlightenment that opens out the whole world in a new light. If that seeking has indeed involved a search for evidence, a drawing of conclusions which are claimed as true because correctly drawn from and supported by that evidence, and so on, and if it has culminated in an insight into a necessity marking the functioning of all, we may properly ask here: What is the evidence that supports this conclusion, and what the inferences that lead to it? Even more fundamentally, we may ask: What does that insight mean? In particular, what does "necessity" here mean? For until we understand that, we can not aptly assess the validity of the claim being made in it.

We have seen something of what the claim means from the waterfall analogy, and have seen-- and are seeing-- the application of that analogy both to doing and knowing. But the application in the latter case is odd, and revealing. In HAH-II/WS-43 Nietzsche comes as close as he ever does in HAH to confronting an ambiguity, apparently unnoticed by him, in the term "necessity" as he is now using it. Entitled "Problem of duty toward truth", the aphorism reads as follows.

> Duty is a compelling [*zwingendes*] pressing-to-deed [*zur Tat drängendes*] feeling [*Gefühl*], which we call good and hold to be undiscussable (as to the origin, limits, and justification of this feeling, we do not want to talk about them or have them talked about). The thinker, however, holds all to be something which has become and holds all that has become to be something discussable; therefore he is a man without duty-- so long, that is, as he is merely thinker. As such, he would therefore also not acknowledge the duty to see and say the truth and would not feel this feeling; he asks: Whence does it come? Whither does it lead? This questioning, however, is regarded by him as itself worthy of question. But would this not have as its consequence, that the machine of the thinker no longer works correctly [*recht*], if in the act of knowing he could actually feel himself to be without duty [*unverpflichtet*]? Inasmuch as here the same element that is supposed to be being investigated by means of the machine seems needed for *heating* it.-- The formula would perhaps be: *assuming* that there was a duty to know the truth, how does truth sound in relation to any other type of duty?-- But is not a hypothetical feeling of duty a contradiction [*Widersinn*]?

The discussion here moves within the new horizon that Nietzsche has come to affirm-- the horizon of the temporal-as-all-- and takes up with the activity of thinking, and more specifically, with what is involved in that activity when it addresses the phenomenon of duty as a matter to be inquired about and its true nature discerned. The phenomenon which the thinker would understand-- duty-- is (subjectively) a feeling that functions in compelling fashion to press the person to some deed (the deed being duty in an objective form).[88] Duty in this sense is regarded as "good" but also as something whose origin, limits, and justification, need no discussion-- indeed, as something which is not properly subject to discussion. Presumably[89] this is because "duty" (as it is in question here) involves a "to be done" which is commanded unconditionally, categorically-- that is the nature of the compelling and pressing; and this dutiful-action is to be done without further ado and with no questions asked, in particular, without questioning the command. For in the case of a duty, there is only the unconditional pressure to do-this; there are no 'conditions' or 'reasons' (that is, no prudential reasons, extrinsic reasons) upon which one is to act in doing the deed or which would explain why 'this' (deed) is indeed a duty. The horizon of gain, profit, being excluded from matters of duty, there is nothing to discuss in that regard, 'this is simply one's duty, the right thing, and to be done as such'. Now in *this* sense of "duty", does the thinker (in his/her inquiring) have a duty (for example, to see and say the truth)? More pointedly, can the thinker, as thinker, act on a not-to-be-questioned feeling pressing him/her to such a dutiful deed? As Nietzsche understands the thinker (that is, the free spirit in its own proper activity), the latter can not treat anything as rightfully undiscussable, nor can the thinker enact duty in his/her own activity of thinking. For it is the thinker's task precisely to raise questions, and because any phenomenon he/she would consider is something which becomes and which in his/her thinking is to be explored, questioned, and discussed, as to the reasons that make it be and be intelligible as what it is, the thinker must bring duty into question when he/she seeks to understand it and must not be prohibited from inquiry by the authoritative and undiscussable nature of its pressure. Moreover, the thinker's thinking can not be an enacting of duty, because any such enacting must be unquestioning whereas the thinker's thinking can not be unquestioning about anything, itself and its own motivation included. In sum: in his/her thinking any thinker must address duty in a way that violates its not-to-be-discussed character (for understanding requires discussing), and in his/her approach the thinker can not be enacting any duty but rather must be un-dutiful.

There seems a paradox here, but does that seeming represent reality? If we reflect on the activity of thinking, we can not help but see it as one internally fraught with obligation.[90] Central to the determination of truth which is to take place in the course of inquiry is the operation of judgment in the making and considering of *claims* to truth, *claims* for relevance as evidence, *claims* for validity of inference, and the like. In that operation, the thinker forms his/her assessment under the *obligation*, in considering a truth-claim, to weigh and assess it by reference to evidence, and to judge it to be justified only if it has evidence and reasons sufficient to support it; or the thinker, when making a claim to truth, is under the *obligation* to offer evidence as a basis for the claim, or to attend to 'this' (but not 'that') as evidence for the truth being such-and-such, and so on. In other words, if there is any reason we *ought* to take any specific claims to be true (the claims, say, that 'there is no ought', or that 'the thinker should not heed any duty'), then the thinker making the claim is *obligated* to (that is, *must*) present the reason(s), and all parties (so far as they are thinkers) are *obligated* to (that is, *must*) consider the claim being made in that light, to weigh and assess the evidence offered and to accept or reject the claim according as *in their judgment* the evidence does or does not support it. In considering and offering reasoned accounts, then, the thinker is actively realizing a *morality essential to thinking itself*, a morality including demands for the honesty of the thinker in his/her thinking, for intellectual conscientiousness, etc.-- all as part of responsible inquiry that heeds the "logical conscience" and embodies the "sense for truth and justice" which is the "finest flower" of morality. Now the thinker can not carry out this process *except as free to form his/her judgment on the basis of the evidence alone and of his/her assessment of such evidence*. There can be no reasonable and rationally-compelling basis for claiming this-or-that is true, if there is no freedom in the act of thinking and thus no capacity on our part (say) to reject a claim because *in our judgment* it is insufficiently based or (say) to affirm that *in our judgment* there are sufficient reasons for concluding that 'this' is the case, and so on.

In short, in its *nature* thinking *is* an affair of duty in *this sense* of an activity acknowledging a multi-sided *obligation* to seek out, take up with, and sort out, matters to be understood and to make claims to understanding them according to the 'must', responsiveness to which marks the capacity and functioning which make thinking be what it is by nature. Thinking realizes the capacity ('can') for the responsive and willing submission to such multi-sided necessity ('must'); and given the finitude of our capacity as we enact the freedom complicit with this 'must', the risk of misjudging, of misconstruing what is relevant evidence and mistaking the validity of a claim, inescapably accompanies our attempts to see and say the truth. Nietzsche is not unmindful of this: indeed, his stress on the scientific spirit and the kinship in spirit between science and philosophy places inquiry, and thus the obligations of conscientious thought, at the heart of his thinking. However, *in the sense of "duty" which he has in mind* when claiming that dutiful action is unquestioning and unthinking (namely, as a 'thou shalt' imposed from beyond), thinking is *not* an affair of duty and, when it encounters duty as subject of inquiry, it must not be deterred by the thought that inquiry violates its undiscussable character. As for the element of *obligation* involved in thinking, rather than prohibiting inquiry into its own nature it makes such inquiry essential to *reflective* thinking and its intellectual conscience. There would be, however, this limit to what conclusion such reflective inquiry might conscientiously arrive at, that since in this inquiring (as in any other) the thinker is being responsive to obligation and is claiming whatever concluding-truth he/she does on the basis of an enacting of thinking as such an obligation-fraught affair, he/she can not then have as that concluding-truth a "denial" of obligation, a claim that there is nothing in reality which the term "obligation" stands for. For such an affirmation (such a denial of obligation) would be possible only because it was enabled by that very condition which is being denied and which thus makes the affirmation in question false. Such reflective exploration could therefore only be a *clarification* of an immanent enabling element in thinking (a clarification of its nature and status in reality, say), not a denial of the reality of that condition.

That thinking involves obligation (but not 'duty' as an affair of unquestioning obedience) is an implicit part of the thread of thought Nietzsche is developing in HAH, concerning the spirit of science and the kinship at their heart between philosophy (historical philosophizing) and science. At the same time, that the course of affairs is necessary is a second thread of thought in HAH, being developed by focusing on the intelligible process visible in the outward phenomena of the world as it is subject to scientific inquiry and by extending the necessity discerned there to what is taking place inwardly. We saw one manifestation of these two threads earlier, in his denial of free will based, on the one hand, on the waterfall-image, and on the other hand, on the grasp of activity as an out-of-ourselves engaging that manifests a freedom instinct with the necessity of our nature ("logical conscience" is one form of this) and misconstrued when taken as giving purchase to a notion of free will. In HAH, Nietzsche thinks these two threads fit together coherently in virtue of a complex notion of necessity, one expressed in the claim that "all is necessity, including this insight itself". If we would exhibit that coherence, we could do it as follows.

In the phrase "all is necessity", the term necessity initially has two different fields of application, and in one field, it has two different meanings which Nietzsche does not expressly differentiate. One field is outwardly-discernible affairs, and there necessity signifies a determination to functioning whose reasons necessitate that determination and its issue without the possibility of an alternative. The other field is the functioning of any natured-being as a matter of an out-of-itself affair; in the human case, our activity is necessary as determined out of our own nature, thus as a self-determined functioning which while taking place under the conditioning of what is alien issues freely and unhindered out of ourselves and so far forth takes its shape in accordance with our nature. Now our nature is such as harbors (among other things) the capacity for thinking; and in HAH the most important actualization of the necessity of self-determination is found in spirit and its functioning in thinking as an activity natural to itself. In virtue of its nature and as internal to its own self-determined functioning, the thinking of spirit involves necessity *in a further sense*, that of the 'must' of obligation in the various forms which are inherent in the conscientious and rigorous conduct of thoughtful inquiry. In HAH, Nietzsche does not expressly differentiate *this* necessity *internal to* thinking from the necessity of self-determination in virtue of which thinking is a natural activity for spirit; but in fact this (internal) necessity has its distinctive feature, that it is addressed to a responsive freedom of judgment without which there is no necessity of *that (obligating) sort*. Such freedom, necessitated to be ours by our nature, is not the indeterminacy of free will; instead, it belongs to thinking as a truth-seeking use of mind that is responsive to the disclosures of experience as evidential for some truth-claiming conclusion. In the exercise of our capacity for judging (evidence and conclusions) in inquiry, then, we have a functioning which is natural and thus 'necessary' as following from that nature, but one whose necessity in that sense involves internally to itself the *further and different necessity* of the 'must' of obligation. Now in the aphorism we have just been considering, Nietzsche takes this self-determined functioning in its general form, and singling out a specific form of it, likens spirit to a thinking-machine and its functioning to that of such a machine. This machine-image is a particularized adaptation of the waterfall-image, and under its likeness conveys the functioning of spirit as embodying necessity as it is meant in the first application. In the machine-image, then, the necessity of obligation is implicitly included under the broader necessity of self-determination, and this in turn is included under the necessity-without-alternative. Thereby spirit's distinctive functioning is presumably integrated with the larger necessity which the waterfall images.

But is such an ordered integration, which fits together the two applications and the three meanings of necessity and presents them as coherent with each other, in fact coherent? Is the coherence more than verbal?

The machine-image which Nietzsche uses represents our nature (or one facet of it in particular) as being a structured or ordered affair which is fitted to function in certain ways determined and limited by its own 'nature'. But for one thing, the necessity of (human) self-determination involves a spontaneity, a functioning arising out of-- and as part of-- our nature itself, whereas a machine has no spontaneity at all. For a second thing, our spontaneity is natured to be responsive in character and in particular to be responsive to an at-stake; in contrast, a machine's functioning takes place without register of an at-stake and simply in function of (not in response to) external impelling factors whose impetus is channeled by the design of the machine. Then for a third thing, thinking is a particular form of our spontaneity, a mental venturing whose creative effort to discern truth involves a heedfulness to multiple obligations and to the operative presence of multiple claims. Taking shape within such heedfulness by posing questions, assessing evidence, inferring conclusions, etc., thinking makes use of the leeway obligation presupposes in a responsive being, so that judging can heed in some manner *that* "must" and operate well or badly in its taking into account and assessing claims and in its drawing conclusions that claim to be warranted by the evidence. The leeway involved in this activity, being complicit with the distinctive necessity of obligation, is not free will; but without such leeway, in a machine-like world that knew only alternativeless determination, there could be no truth-seeking, and no judgments formed, conclusions drawn, by a responsible inquirer. Paradoxically, Nietzsche's image, if true, would undermine the very thinking in which he produced and used the image.

There is a more fundamental question even than that concerning the coherence or incoherence of the integration we have just been considering. That is this: If the free thinker, and the free man of action, are brothers, and if the former's insight is into 'all is necessity', then action must also be necessary. How is one to understand *this* necessity? Is it a fourth type, different from the other three: from alternativeless determination, from natural self-determination, and from obligation? Or does Nietzsche have in mind that the brothers-in-freedom are brothers not as having each a freedom internal to his activity (thinking or doing), but as having the same mother, a shared freedom of initiative that leads into thinking or into doing and makes them both free? If so, how is this freedom constituted? If decision-making is responsive to an at-stake and is necessitated to a seeking to secure its realization as the good, does the claim of the good at stake open decision-making to a distinctive freedom-- not that of free will, but ... ? But if the two brothers are both free as initiated out of the same freedom, how are they then different from each other? Simply because the forms of activity they involve (thinking and doing) are different? Or is there a further difference, in regard (say) to the matter of each having a further (and presumably different) freedom internal to themselves?

3. Activity

So far, it seems that our engaging in activity follows necessarily from our nature (we are natured to be active beings), and given the (human and complex) character of that nature, that engaging knows an internal self-forming through a decision-making by which we engage ourselves as whole beings in a particular activity, whether a form of thinking or a form of doing. This initiating and acting do not involve free will, or 'morality' so far as it involves free will. Yet their shape-taking, while it also reflects conditioning factors at work in it, necessarily also realizes the character and manner of the spontaneity of our nature, whatever they may be. So far we have been content to note *that* our decision-making is necessary without exploring the necessity in its operation; we have rather been attending to the necessity distinctive and internal to one form of activity natural to us (i.e. thinking). Let us concern ourselves now with the necessity in the operation of decision-making, and in particular, with how decision-making enables not just thinking but the thinking of the "free spirit".

In HAH-I/107, Nietzsche sketches out in brief fashion his understanding of our initiative and activity, once the notions of free will and of our accountability for our actions have been undermined. Let us take it as our starting-point for seeing how Nietzsche now treats these matters.

> The complete unaccountability [*Unverantwortlichkeit*] of man for his actions and his nature [*Wesen*] is the bitterest draught which the knower must swallow, provided that he was accustomed to seeing in accountability [*Verantwortlichkeit*] and duty his humanity's patent of nobility. All of his evaluations, his recognitions of this-or-that as distinguished, his antipathies, have thereby become false and devalued; his deepest feeling, which he accords to the sufferer, the hero, has rested on an error; he can no longer praise or censure, for it is absurd to praise or censure nature and necessity. Just as he loves a good art work but does not praise it because its goodness is not its own doing, just as he stands before the plants, so must he stand before the actions of human beings and before his own. He can admire their strength, beauty, fulness, but he may not find any merit in them: the chemical process and the strife of the elements, the torment of the sick man who thirsts for recovery, are as little merits as are those soul-struggles and states of distress which arise when we are torn back and forth by conflicting motives until (as we put it) we finally decide [*entscheidet*] for the most powerful of them (in truth, however, until the most powerful motive decides about us). But all these motives, however elevated the

names we give them, have grown up out of the same roots in which we believe evil poison to be dwelling; between good and evil actions there is no difference in kind, but at most one of degree. Good actions are sublimated [*sublimierte*] evil ones; evil actions are coarsened [*vergröberte*], stupidified [*verdummte*] good ones. It is the individual's longing [*Verlangen*] for self-enjoyment (that alone [*einzige*], together with the fear of losing it) which gratifies itself [*befriedigt sich*] under all circumstances, however, the person can (that is, must) act-- be it in deeds of vanity, revenge, pleasure, utility, malice, cunning, or those of sacrifice, sympathy, knowledge. The degrees of competence in judging [*Urteilsfähigkeit*] decide [*entscheiden*] whither each person will let this longing [*Verlangen*] draw him [*sich ... hinziehen lätzt*]; an order of rank of goods is continually present to every society, every individual, according to which he determines his own actions and judges those of others. But this standard [*Matzstab*] is continually changing, many actions are called evil but are only stupid, because the degree of intelligence which decided [*sich ... entschied*] for them was very low. Indeed, in a certain sense *all* present actions are stupid [*dumm*], for the highest degree of human intelligence which can now be attained will certainly be exceeded in the future; and then all *our* actions and judgments will seem in retrospect as circumscribed and precipitate as the actions and judgments of still existing primitive peoples now appear to us.

a. Self-enjoyment and power

In UHH, Nietzsche spoke of life as "that dark, driving power insatiably thirsting after itself". In the reconceiving HAH effects, this basic sense is retained, but recast within a somewhat different framework of interpretation. Nietzsche now thinks of the decision-making whereby we initiate activity as involving the responsive register of a drive in us which by nature we always heed with the strength and energy available to us at the time; that drive, he points us to by speaking of the individual's longing [*Verlangen*] for self-enjoyment [*Selbstgenutz*].[91] He makes intelligible the enjoyment in question with the help of a specific understanding of our basic motivational powers, namely, pleasure and unpleasantness; these relate to-- and motivate toward-- the achieving of the individual's well-being [*Wohlbefinden*]. Thus what UHH spoke of as life's thirsting after itself is understood now as life's struggle to maintain and enhance itself, which (as we saw earlier: 211 above) is a struggle over pleasure understood as "the feeling [*Gefühl*] of one's own power [*Macht*], of one's own strong excitation [*Erregung*]"[92]. It is such self-enjoyment, such a feeling of power, that represents the good we reach for, the at-stake as it by nature necessarily claims us and draws us to seek its realization.

The view of pleasure as the immediate register in feeling of our own power as individual agents, and in particular, of that power as aroused, excited, stimulated, recurs in a variety of contexts, but with various specifications of aspects of this exercise which make power a somewhat complex-- and perhaps ambiguous-- notion.

Thus in HAH-I/134, where Nietzsche is seeking to explain the feeling of redemption which the Christian interprets in one way, he speaks of "the pleasure in himself, the taking enjoyment [*Wohlbehagen*] in his very own power [*eigenen Kraft*]". Central in our sense of ourselves is the sense of a certain strength, energy, power-- it is all three, really, and closely connected with a sense of competence, capability: we *can* ... , we *are capable*. It is not a matter however of being capable of this or that, of some determinate capability; it is rather a matter of being *capable as human beings*, of being capable as human participants in affairs. We feel at the heart of ourselves as the individuals we are that, in this 'are capable humanly', we *are* someone.

Nonetheless, this sense of ourselves is always felt under different conditions and in connection with our exercise of particular capacities in various particular ways in various particular circumstances. For it is the capability of ourselves as responsive active beings that is in question, and that capability is realized only in that participation in the interacting with circumstance in which we are able to be ourselves. Such participation involves determinate particular capacities brought into play in the exercise of our decision-making and -executing capacity as human beings. In virtue of this, the sense of the individual's self-enjoyment as individual human being is inflected by-- and distinct cognizance of it may even on occasions be lost to our awareness and attention in-- the enjoyment of the particular capability, capacity, strength, exhibited on that occasion. For there is pleasure as well in this exercise, since the particular capabilities are a part of us and their exercise is the medium for the actualization of ourselves in our very own selfhood.

Various examples of this 'identification' are scattered through HAH. For instance, in HAH-I/103, while speaking of maliciousness not really having the suffering of others as its aim but rather its very own enjoyment [*eigenen Genutz*], Nietzsche interprets the enjoyment to be of "the feeling of revenge, or the stronger excitation of the nerves [*stärkere Nervenaufregung*]". "Even teasing shows how it gives satisfaction [*Vergnügen macht*] to vent [*auszulassen*] our power [*Macht*] on others and bring the pleasurable feeling of ascendancy [*Übergewicht*]". Then again, in regard to nature we take plea-sure in (for example) breaking tree-branches "in order thereby to become conscious of our power [*Kraft*]"; even pity contains elements of personal pleasure in itself and is in that way "self-enjoyment: first as pleasure in the emotion (the pity in tragedy), and then when this leads to action (the pleasure of gratification [*Befriedigung*] in the exercise of power [*Macht*])".

Or again, in noting how children and invalids try to arouse our pity, he urges that while the pity they evoke is a consolation, it is this because

> they know from it that, all their weakness notwithstanding, they *possess* at any rate one *power* [*Macht*]: the *power to hurt*. In this feeling of superiority of which the manifestation of pity makes the person conscious, the unfortunate one gains a sort of pleasure; the fancy rises up, of being still of sufficient importance to cause the world pain. The thirst for pity is thus a thirst for self-enjoyment [*Selbstgenutz*], and that, at the expense of one's fellow men; it shows human be-ings in the whole ruthlessness [*Rücksichtslosigkeit*] of their ownmost dear self.[93]

Or again, "in the conversation of society, three-quarters of all questions posed and answers given are meant to cause just a little pain to the other party; thus many men thirst after society: it gives them the feeling of their own power [*Kraft*]. In such numberless but tiny doses in which malice makes it-self felt, it is a powerful [*mächtiges*] stimulant [*Reizmittel*] of life ... ."[93]

Or again, in speaking of the ascetic, Nietzsche suggests that "certain men feel so great a need [*Be-dürfnis*] to exercise their strength [*Gewalt*] and lust to dominate [*Herrschsucht*] that, lacking another object or because their efforts in other directions have always failed, they finally hit upon the idea of tyrannizing over a certain part of their own nature, as it were sections or stages of themselves".[94] Thus the ascetic practices a defiance of himself which is "a close relative of the lust to dominate and yet gives even the most solitary the feeling of power [*Macht*]"[95].

These examples have in common the exercise of force in particular fashion against something (outside oneself, but also inside) in order, in the exercise itself, to feel and enjoy some particular strength in ourselves and, through the impact achieved in its exercise, to know ourselves to have a superiority in some regard. In this, we 'identify' ourselves-as-individuals with that particular strength and take the latter as signifying something about *ourselves*-- our worth, our being something-- in vir-tue of our power.

Now in contrasting love with honor, Nietzsche links love with desire and links honor with fear, and while explaining the latter, he claims: "he who honors recognizes power [*Macht*], that is, he fears it: his state is respect [*Ehr-furcht*: the German combines 'honor' and 'fear']. Love, however, recog-nizes no power, nothing which separates, contrasts [*abhebt*], involves hierarchical ordering above and below [*über- und underordnet*]."[96] The notion of such a distinguishing, contrasting, and ordering as belonging to the meaning of power is visible in one form in the preceding examples, but the higher-and-lower may also be realized differently than in those examples.

For instance, in HAH-I/262 Nietzsche speaks of Homer, and claims that all the spiritual and hu-man freedom which the Greeks attained can be traced back to Homer and to the fact that he was pan-Hellenic at such an early time in Greek history. Yet this early impact of Homer throughout the Greek world was also a fatality for Greek culture, in that by effectively centralizing that culture Homer leveled the cultural development of the Greeks and dissolved the instincts for independence. "From time to time, there arose out of the deepest grounds of the Hellenic the contradiction to Homer; but the latter always remained victorious. All great spiritual powers, beside their liberating effect, also exercise a suppressing effect; but of course, there is a difference if it is Homer or the Bible or science which tyrannizes human beings." If power involves hierarchy and some sort of constraint upon the lower by the higher, that constraint, while it may restrain what seeks to rise to the height of the higher and to challenge it as independent of it, also gives a place to the lower which liberates its function-ing-- so long, at least, as it operates at its own level and under the constraint imposed. From the point of view of the lower, the constraint is felt not only as providing the needed stable matrix within which the lower can function well out of itself and can be itself, but also as supporting, encouraging, as-sisting, the lower in achieving that level of functioning open to it. Thus in the terms of UHH, it pro-vides the fixed horizon within which the lower may live and realize its own vitality.[97]

When the hierarchy-creating power is a spiritual one, and thus not a matter of quantitatively great-er strength exerting constraint on lesser strength but of qualitatively more elevated strength exerting constraint on qualitatively lower and cruder strength, then Wagner, as Nietzsche spoke of him in WB, may exemplify it. For quite apart from his deliberately intending this, Wagner's music had such an impact on the musically-inclined of his day as, by its superior richness, novelty, and the like, to domi-nate the music world, other composers and the audiences of the day. But how was this possible? In HAH-I/170 ("Artist's ambition"), Nietzsche speaks of a cognate state of affairs: speaking of the am-bition of the Greek artists (he focuses on the tragedians in particular), he claims that it was to conquer, and that art among the Greeks can not be conceived apart from the notion of the contest. But referring to Hesiod's idea of the contrast of the good *Eris* (striving-and-strife) with the bad, he claims:

> this ambition demands above all that their work should preserve the highest excellence [*Vortreff-lichkeit*] in *their own eyes*, as *they* understand excellence, thus without reference to a dominant taste or the general opinion as to what constitutes excellence in a work of art; and thus Aeschylus and Euripides were for a long time unsuccessful until they had finally *educated* judges of art who assessed their work according to the standards they themselves laid down. It is thus they aspire to victory over their competitors according to their own assessment (of superior excellence), a victory before their own seat of judgment, they want actually to *be* more excellent; then they de-mand agreement from others as to their own assessment, and confirmation of their own judgment. To aspire to honor here means 'to make oneself superior and to wish that one appear superior in the public eye.' If the former is lacking and the latter is still demanded, one speaks of *vanity*. If the latter is lacking and its absence is not regretted, one speaks of *pride*.

In the case of spiritual powers, there is a qualitative hierarchy, and thus a superiority within an order, but one according to which power-over and superiority (such as relates to victory of the superior in the eyes of others) is only one (a conditioned) element in the aim, not *by itself* the aim.

There is another regard in which the thought here reminds of what is said in WB. There Nietzsche sought to portray the nature of Wagner as two-sided, involving on the one hand a love-full spirit, abounding in goodness and sweetness and gentle in voice, and on the other hand a vehement will which streamed precipitously on any and all paths in its reaching for the light and its longing for power. Acted upon, this personal will to power-- at first a boundless craving to tyrannize which moved restlessly along the paths of its reaching and longing-- found that love-full spirit drawing closer and found itself gradually transforming as the two achieved an integrated working; and the artistic creativity which eventually arose out of this integrated functioning was reached only upon re-nunciation of influence-and-power-over as the meaning of the power being sought. That renunciation led in time to an understanding, a thinking the nature of the world in events, and with this, the creat-ing of musical works in which the composer's own ultimate insights were effectively embodied. Only in the transformation of his will to tyrannize into a will of this sort did Wagner come into the power [*Kraft*] which his drive had been reaching for all along (but under a misreading of its nature); and only when, out of the nature of itself as power, this power was bodied forth and transmitted in his music to others, did that drive reach its appropriate fulfillment. That fulfillment lay in a connecting of creator with others in which, enabled by the overwhelming but stimulating influx they were receiving to find that feeling and perceiving which is *their very own,* those others were empowered to *stand as themselves over against* Wagner and everyone else. Here there was that same recourse by Wagner to higher standards and a higher sense of excellence that Nietzsche found among the Greek tragedians; but there was as well the sense of power-- superior power-- as assisting the others whom it liberated and challenging them to respond and complete the connection out of their own creativity. If in WB the will to power meant ultimately a vital and *power-fraught connection* which is established among beings creatively active out of themselves, in the reconception underway in HAH the *mutual* connection initially almost drops out of sight,[98] and the meaning of power for the creative self and creativity is stressed.

In thinking of power in the way these passages indicate, Nietzsche is continuing to make the articulation of heights and depths be central to his thought, and to grasp the heights as a qualitative and spiritual affair; the power which is achieved and discharged in higher activity at such heights or in function of having reached such heights is also regarded not simply as the highest but as the most powerful, in some meaning of "power" which is not to be understood if we look to-- let alone look simply to-- the effects of its discharge (namely, influence, control over). If life is a longing for self-enjoyment, and such self-enjoyment is found in its highest and *most powerful* form in such higher activity, then Nietzsche is still rehearsing the feel for life found in the first phase of his thought, even if he is on his way to a somewhat different conceptual framework for understanding it. At the very least, the shift in perspective in the second phase of thought involves an exploration of the notion of power that complicates its connection with the maturational development of the human being and the increase in capacity as human agent which was initially adumbrated in UHH and was subsequently amplified in SE and WB (especially in the latter, as regards the life and nature of Wagner). If in these previous works life's striving for 'more life' is part of youth's vision of the maturational process ahead, according to which we are eventually to achieve that realization of our primordial meant-to-be and stuff as a potency to be creative in the fullest way open to us in our individual nature, then power is something that relates to our individual being as a unified whole and to a functioning in which that whole is achieving its perfected realization. In HAH-I, Nietzsche is beginning to explore our empowerment without regard to some primordial (or any) 'meant-to-be' and to conceive it in close connection with the particularities of capacity and circumstance and the impact of the exercise of particular capacity. In this way he is entering on a path of thought which in time, after an increasingly expanded suggestion of various directions in which such "power" and "empowerment" are part of experience, will bring the variety of particularities and directions back into reference to some unity again. This time it will be under a general insight into the being of things-- all things, for humans are no exception here-- as constituted by a will-to-power. More on this later.

b. Motivation and responsive decision-making

The medium for the active involvement of ourselves in the affairs of existence is a responsive decision-making capacity which, in virtue of the structuring of our being, lies at the center of that being. As part of the present turn in his thinking, Nietzsche's reflections upon our involvement become more complex and subtle psychologically, yet operate within a fairly simple framework. As he would now understand the matter, what enters into-- and is responsively registered within-- the forming of initiative is not simply the longing for self-enjoyment which embodies (in the longing itself) the felt appeal of self-enjoyment as what is at stake; two further responsively registered facets of our nature also enter into such forming. One is the variety of feelings which operate as motivating powers to the extent that acting on them is anticipated to bring pleasure or to ward off unpleasantness. The other is intelligence. For example, the variety of motivating forces, circumstances, and alternatives, that are part of any decision-making situation requires an anticipatory weighing and assessing of the pleasant and unpleasant (thus a determination of the useful and harmful) in order that the to-be-decided-upon activity may move intelligently toward the self-enjoyment we long for. The direction of the venture in each case then depends on the degree of intelligence, the grade and constitution of the intellect, which is involved in the assessment of the various factors in life's practical situations and the determination in each case of what will bring the self-enjoyment we are drawn toward by nature.

The analysis of our being which makes it center on a decision-making capacity into which feeling and intelligence enter continues Nietzsche's thinking in the first phase in this regard, that our relation as active beings to ourselves and to circumstance is first and foremost a matter of feeling. But gone now is the sense which he expressed earlier, of feeling in a form that signifies an openness of some sort to reality deeper in the nature of things than ordinarily accessible: presentiment, say, as super-rational rather than (as now) sub-rational. Any more subtle sorting out of the non-rational that might discriminate, say, super- and sub-, is not attempted: the non-rational is simply the ir-rational, and our basic relation to things is to that extent an irrational one.

If our basic relation as active beings is irrational as based in feeling, it is also irrational in a second way. For since our acting involves interpretation and the operation of intelligence in our decision-making, and since (as we noted above in discussing philosophy as law-giving) even inclination and aversion (the immediate action-responses evoked by pleasure and pain) involve illogical and unjust evaluative judgments as part of what is included in their nature,[99] our active participation in things is deeply sunk in untruth and fiction.[100] We cannot live without evaluating, but all of our evaluative judgments have been formed illogically and are therefore unjust. Evaluative judgments are illogical because (a) they are based on very incomplete material, (b) that material is also the outcome necessarily of impure knowledge (our experience of another person, say, can never be complete, so that any total evaluation of him is premature), (c) the summative conclusions arrived at in such judgments are reached in invalid ways, and (d) the standard [*Matz*] by which we measure when making our evaluations (namely, our own being [*Wesen*]) is not itself an unalterable magnitude (we are subject to moods and fluctuations, but need to know ourselves as a fixed standard to be able justly to assess the relation between ourselves and anything else whatever).[101] Beginning with our feelings and passions, the illogical also permeates our language, our art, our religion, and in general all that endows life with value.

> It is only the all too naive human being who could believe that a person's nature could be transformed into something purely logical; but if there should be a degree of approximation to this goal, what all would have to be lost on this path! Even the most rational human being needs [*bedarf*] nature again from time to time i.e. needs again his own *illogical basic stance* [*Grundstellung*] *toward all things.*[102]

Our ultimate irrationality, then, is a mixed affair, involving feeling and intelligence in the above cited ways; and yet while there is a contrast and even a tension between the two factors, there is also a working together, an integrating, of these in our decision-making. This co-operating can take different forms but central to its structure is the working of intelligence (in the sorting out and assessing belonging to its practical operation) to enable the longing for self-enjoyment to be responsively acted on under different motivations and with a practically sufficient measure of consonance with reality (and first and foremost, that means current circumstance). It is the development, the amplification and refinement, of this capacity of intelligence, that it may better carry out this function, which Nietzsche stresses in HAH as central to our human agency.

In general, this practical functioning of intelligence, and with it, any improvement in that functioning, always takes place in a dynamic context some of whose various factors are inward, others outward.

Inwardly, intelligence operates in a motivational matrix which is complex and inherently dynamic. Nothing in it stands still; the forces involved exert pressure to be the moving forces in the agent's activity, to achieve the discharge of themselves which relieves the state of tension which marks themselves as emotional powers.[103] Intelligence functions, for one thing, to provide the interpretative ideas which guide the drives; and yet the various drives are just that, driving forces, and in the measure in which a drive is discharged, whatever the idea that guides its discharge may be (this-idea rather than that-idea), that drive not only maintains itself but is strengthened.[104] Even more, in the measure in which there is kinship among different forces, they can also align themselves with each other and the pressure they exert would further not only their own claims but the claims of what is kindred to them.[105] And then, for a second thing, intelligence functions to aid in the sublimation of feeling which is occasioned by the arousal of emotional tension to greater and greater heights and which makes for novel motivational forces which otherwise would not have been possible.[106] Finally, because the various drives bring into play the diverse capacities, talents, aptitudes, present in ourselves, and because these latter are themselves forces and powers in their own right, intelligence operates under the pressure of these forces as well: "every talent is a vampire, which sucks the blood and energy [*Kraft*] out of the remaining forces [*Kräften*]".[107]

Outwardly, intelligence operates in this matter of decision-making not simply under the pressures of motivational forces within but in the face of a complex context of circumstance and what is present in it. By its register in us, circumstance and its components arouse and stimulate us, occasioning the coming to the fore in us of certain drives in this circumstance and others in that. But it also forms the immediate condition under which whatever we are motivated to do is ventured. In this latter regard, intelligence operates to assess circumstance as to what its character means as condition for realizing the longing for self-enjoyment, and more specifically, for acting in the present circumstance on this or that motive and its pressure for its discharge. In the former regard, what circumstance occasions in us is not easily predictable, given the measure of our lack of understanding of ourselves and the possibility that it may touch on forces we were unaware were to be found in us.[108]

The function of intelligence in our decision-making in the concrete is to be an effective mediator between the inward (motivational) factors and outward (circumstantially occasioning and conditioning) factors. Its mediating has a particular character. In the citation of HAH-I/107 with which we began this consideration of activity,[109] we saw Nietzsche claiming that, in the determining to do-this or do-that, it is "the degrees of competence in judging" which "decide whither each person will let this longing (for self-enjoyment) draw" him/her. That is, within our responsiveness to this longing and under some interpretative grasp both of the self-enjoyment that is the natural end or purpose which activity is to serve and of the (inward and outward) factors involved in the situation of the agent, we "let" ourselves be drawn to act in this-direction rather than that-direction as (in our judgment) the one leading to the self-enjoyment our nature wants. This means different things, depending on the degree and quality of our intelligence. Now in that same aphorism, Nietzsche also spoke in 'correction' of our ordinary way of speaking of our decision-making: we find ourselves "torn back and forth by conflicting motives until we finally choose the most powerful of them-- so we say (in truth, however, until the most powerful motive chooses us)". This 'correction' seems intended to make a polemical point against the notion of decision-making as a wholly deliberate and intentional affair in which a conscious free will is central. When the reversed language-- a motive 'chooses' us-- is detached from polemics and its meaning understood in conjunction with the "let", it represents a metaphorical rendering with a two-fold significance. In part, it points us to our deciding as responsive to a pre-decisional pressure of various motivating forces: deciding is not 'free' as unaffected by any motivating forces, but in it many motives are calling for us to act upon them, so that our deciding is our allowing some already-urging motive to prevail over the others, namely, the one which is the 'most powerful' as having the strongest appeal within the horizon of judgment that is involved. In part, it points us to the decision as necessitated by way of a "letting" (-prevail) in which judgment has a role, and in that role functions according to its nature, with the necessity of its nature. Such judging is not a wholly conscious affair, so that we are never wholly conscious of what is being taken into account and of the account-taking itself. From the perspective of our 'ego' or the wholly-conscious side of ourselves, not all of the factors involved, even of the genuinely decisive one(s), are discernible.[110] Thus we are entered by our responsive powers of initiative into a decision which we do indeed make-- but not 'we' as conscious ego (let alone ego with free will), and not 'make' as an affair in which the conscious side of ourselves is necessarily much involved, let alone in complete control.

Because of the complexity of this affair of decision-making, we are continually being placed in a dilemma in it. For while the longing for self-enjoyment is one and our decision-making brings us into action whole, two sorts of problem arise.

For one thing, we ourselves and our circumstance are both complicated wholes, not simply in the sense that we are rational beings with a basic irrational relation to things, but also in the sense that we know an inward diversity and conflict on the irrational level of motivation and an outward range of possibility in circumstance. At the very least, we can not respond on all that lays claims on us at any time; and any action requires not only attendance to certain things rather than others in the circumstances of our situation at the time, but also attendance in this way with this emphasis rather than in that way with that emphasis. Decision-making thus involves selection, prioritization, and concentration, and correlatively, exclusion and disregard, all guided by a sense of how we would best spend our time and energy in the situation.

For a second thing, we are also evolving beings whose capacity for self-enjoyment changes in its nature as we ourselves become different, and whose capacity for practical judgment also changes with experience and practice. Earlier, we have seen Nietzsche speaking of the "highest good" of the individual, and that way of speaking points us not simply to a complexity of higher and lower at any time but to ourselves as continuing beings who at the time are marked by possibility and potential and have a future in which we ourselves can be different from ourselves as we are in our present actuality. In decision-making which has this possible futural difference in mind, the dilemma in which complexity places us is compounded. We must not simply decide and act in and for a particular situation we are presently in, with some anticipation of differences in the future; but must decide as knowing the task of integrating and organizing (so far as we can) the changing inner complexity and chaos of ourselves as living beings with potential, and knowing thus the possibility of facilitating through our decision-making a *higher* self-enjoyment (one of ourselves differently integrated and organized) than otherwise might come about. According to Nietzsche's current thought and in contrast with his first phase thought, life does not provide us an original meant-to-be as destining-pressure and pointer for our development as continuing beings. But it does provide us a nature-based standard, a guiding aim, under which this developmental work naturally takes place, namely, the self-enjoyment life longs for and fears to lose. As the enjoyment of ourselves in our capability as *ongoing and developing* individuals and whole human beings, the standard and aim in question are the highest and most intense self-enjoyment open eventually to us as such beings, or as it might be more proper to put it in this second phase of his thought, the ever increasingly higher and more intense self-enjoyment open to us as changing and evolving individuals. In the integrating whereby we make a "whole *person*" out of ourselves and the deciding in which we keep in mind "the *highest good* of this person", we are changing in capacity for self-enjoyment and in capacity to interpret what self-enjoyment is, and in the measure in which we become more refined in both regards what we hold before ourselves as the ultimate aim and purpose in our deciding and acting can and will vary.

The type of self-cultivation by which we might become the whole persons we can be and secure entry into the highest self-enjoyment that life makes us long for requires of us something like an artistic approach to the achievement of our own becoming. In this phase of his thought, Nietzsche shifts emphasis in his consideration of art away from art-works and toward the notion of artistic creativity as addressed first and foremost to a "becoming better [*besser*] and more beautiful as a person", that is, to a "creating *oneself*". One has only a fixed quantity [*bestimmtes Matz*] of such energy-and-strength [*Kraft*], and it should be expended on oneself first of all, then on art-works.[111] In HAH-II/MMO-174 ("Against the art of art-works"), he indicates what he means by this when he speaks of art generally as

> above all and especially *beautifying* life, thus making *ourselves* be bearable, and where possible pleasant, to others: with this task before its eyes, it restrains [*mätzigt*] and keeps a tight rein on us, creates forms of intercourse, binds the ill-bred with laws of proper behavior, of cleanliness, of politeness, of speaking and being silent at the right time. Then art is supposed to *conceal* or

reinterpret everything ugly, those painful, dreadful, disgusting things which, all efforts not-withstanding, in accord with the origin of human nature again and again will break forth: it is supposed to do so especially in regard to the passions and psychical fears and pains, and in the case of what is ineluctably or invincibly ugly it is supposed to let the *meaningful* shine through. After this great, indeed exceedingly great task of art, what is usually termed real art, *that of the work of art*, is merely an *appendage*. Someone who, within, feels a surplus [*Überschutz*] of such beautifying, concealing and reinterpreting powers [*Kräfte*] will in the end seek to discharge this surplus in works of art also; so, under the right circumstances, will an entire people.

Since we are as interacting with what is other than ourselves, our employment of the artist's capacity for harnessing our creative powers and mastering circumstance in this reference means creatively bringing ourselves and circumstance into a connection in which life's reaching in us for self-enjoyment is gradually expanded and intensified. For some of us, it may be useful to throw all our energy-and-strength [*Kraft*] into one domain, and to make out of ourselves (as it were) one monstrous organ. But "assuredly a *uniform* [*gleichmätzige*] development [*Ausbildung*] of his powers [*Kräfte*] is more useful and more happiness-bringing for the human being himself"; for one-sided development can bring even the most gifted human being almost to madness.[112] Likewise, "we must guard ourselves against grounding [*gründen*] our life on a too small basis [*Grund*] of desire [*Begehrlichkeit*]; for if one renounces the joys that position, honors, companionship, sensual pleasures, comforts, the arts, bring with themselves, the day can come when we notice that by doing without these things we have acquired for a neighbor not *wisdom* but *boredom with life*."[113] In any case, what is to our own highest advantage, when this is understood as the mature, developed, and refined individual would understand it, is such self-cultivation as achieves that wholeness in which (put in artistic terms) we have become a "good poem", a "fair statue".[114]

What this means for each individual, however, depends both on what that individual encounters as circumstance and upon what his/her own starting-points are, what components belong to us as our original stuff.[115] For even if there is no primordial meant-to-be, there is a primordial stuff, an original endowment. Since the horizon of intelligibility within which Nietzsche's inquiry is now oriented is that of life as an evolutionary affair and heredity as the transmission of facets of previous life to new life, his account of what we are at the beginning and are to realize in this artistic fashion-- what drives and aptitudes, but also what habits of sensibility and ways of interpreting things according to primeval errors that have come to maintain themselves in the total evolution of organic life and to be inherited by us[116]-- suggests that the starting-point depends in each case on the line of life which leads up to the individual in question. And depending on the way the elements of our endowment have been formed in the past and have been carried forward in the line of transmission until they have entered into our being as its endowment, we have different capacity to operate creatively with them, to trans-figure them as they function and/or develop in us. There are facets of our being-- constituents of our character-- which represent "an imprinted script of many millennia"[117]; because of his undifferen-tiation of inward and outward, Nietzsche can speak in physiological terms of our inheritance-- as in HAH-I/43 ("Cruel humans as left behind"), when he speaks of cruel humans as

> relict human beings whose brain has, through chance in the course of hereditary-transmission, failed to develop in as delicate and many-sided a way. They show us what we all *were* ... . Just as the form of certain human organs recalls the (evolutionary) state of fish, so in our brain there must also be grooves and convolutions that correspond to that cast of mind: but these grooves and convolutions are no longer the riverbed along which the stream of our sensibility runs.

There are other facets which reflect very recent (say, parental) imprints: for example, Nietzsche speaks[118] of the son as inheriting not only talent from his ancestors but also the energy [*Energie*] pos-sessed by the father at that stage of life when he produced the son. As individuals, we do not repre-sent an absolute or unconditioned beginning to life or to the endowment drawn into play in our initia-tive; our genetic derivativeness makes us (temporally speaking) continuators carrying gifts from previous living beings at the same time as we are novel living beings.

Because the realization of this endowment is always circumstantial, art should be applied to what Nietzsche calls the "closest things" above all-- things such as eating, housing, clothing, social intercourse: the needs, great and small, which the individual has in the course of the twenty-four hours of the day. Ordinarily we do not seriously attend to these and give them any consideration, intellectual or artistic, because the education we receive beginning in childhood as to 'what matters' deflects our seriousness to the salvation of the soul, the furthering of science, the service to the state, the accumulation of reputation and possessions-- all as means of serving the whole of humankind; but thereby we are led into committing offences against the most elementary laws of the body and spirit.[119] For example, through the lack of self-observation and observation of those who are to be brought up, and through the neglect of small facts, we allow our passions to develop into monsters, into devastating torrents, of which we become fearful-- this, instead of transforming them into joys.[120] For such transformation, it is needful to do more than overcome our passions; we must treat them as fertile ground in which we are to sow the seeds of good spiritual works.[121] Contrary to what present-day education teaches, we should give shape to our lives in future on the basis of two principles:

> First principle: life should be ordered on the basis of what is most certain and most demonstrable, not as hitherto on that of what is most remote, indefinite, and no more than a cloud on the horizon. Second principle: the order of succession of what is closest and less close, certain and less certain, should be firmly established before one orders one's life and brings it into a definitive direction.[122]

In the responsive decision-making of our individual initiative, then, we function according to the necessity of our nature, and so far as we have considered it, that means: in response to the native longing in ourselves as living beings for self-enjoyment, we find our powers to interpret, assess, and form judgments, called into play and operating amidst dynamic forces within and without, and we carry on our decision-making (well or ill) with a view to what is useful (as our judgment discerns it) for achieving individual self-enjoyment (now and into the future) under the circumstances. What is crucial in the decision-making is, on the one hand, the quality of our judging as it guides in a (more or less) competent way our allowing the longing for self-enjoyment to draw us in some particular direction, and on the other hand, the creative taking ourselves in hand whereby, according as how we decide, we further (or fail to) the integration and organization of the multiple facets and potentials of our own being and are able thereby gradually to increase the self-enjoyment which the conjunction of circumstance and our nature open to us. However well or ill the decision-making takes place in these regards, so far as the determination of initiative is nature-accordant, it is the necessary working of nature, its functioning extending the necessity of self-determination into the engaging in activity; but such necessitated out-of-itself functioning is not yet fully before us, since our decision-making and -executing capacity is an evolving affair. So far as our development in this regard is natural, the natural functioning of ourselves as agents initiating activity through the working of these powers and this capacity transforms over time and comes into its own native fulness only when this evolution reaches a certain point. Only then are we able to enter into activity in such fashion as embodies the full freedom of our functioning as initiators; and only as we enter upon thinking through such initiative can our taking part in the distinctive freedom-and-necessity that belongs to the nature of thinking be in the manner of the free spirit.

c. Opinion, and practical and philosophical reflection

The shift of emphasis in Nietzsche's second-phase pursuit of philosophical inquiry downgrades attention to the maturational movement in individual life and (say) to the rise of reflection in youth, and upgrades the perspective of the larger historical and evolutionary movement of life, one in which (say) among the ancient Greeks and in particular, in their philosophers, the human race develops for the first time the notions of reason and of knowledge as science. But downgrading is not rejection, and Nietzsche brings these two perspectives together in two places that can help us further our understanding of freedom and the necessity of our own nature, particularly as these concern initiative.

In an aphorism devoted to spiritual productivity (HAH-I/272), Nietzsche takes note of two complementary matters. One concerns the way in which a culture that is alive and growing maintains itself and advances over time. Successive generations are required for this because in the individual lives of most persons who become cultured there is, at the age of thirty, a kind of solstice, after which they are disinclined to make new spiritual changes. Instead, settling in they continue culture as a living affair at that point they have reached. The next generation, after resuming in itself the cultural development of the previous one, has sufficient inherited energy left over to advance a bit beyond the previous generation: the resuming is somewhat less time consuming in their case than the learning required of the previous generation, so that something of the inherited energy remains for expanding the cultural heritage. This second generation likewise has its limits, and there is need of another generation if there is to be further cultural advance. In a few individuals, however, there is, in addition to inherited talent, a significant degree of what Nietzsche calls the power of expansion [*Spannkraft*]-- stretchability-- which he sees as being given along with that talent. This is the power to take the given talent and with it to stretch and augment its productivity to the point where one reaches farther forward, in cultural terms, than the promise of one's talent by itself would seem to indicate as possible. Citing a man such as Goethe, he speaks of how, in a culture which is alive and advancing, creative persons like him, whose power of expansion is great, can advance culture far beyond where his contemporaries can reach, so that it takes several generations to catch up to where he is culturally. But that is unusual: the advance of a living culture is basically a generational accomplishment.

The second matter he takes note of extends this sort of observation to something which involves a much larger scale. Here he suggests that, when we look at the ordinary phases of culture attained to in the course of history, we see a movement which, in human beings of the present, is recapitulated in its phases in a very short order of time.

> Human beings at present begin their entry into the realm of culture as children affected religiously and in perhaps their tenth year these sensations are brought to their liveliest, then pass over into feebler forms (pantheism) while at the same time drawing closer to science; they come wholly beyond God, immortality and the like but fall prey to the charms of a metaphysical philosophy. At last they find this, too, unbelievable; art, on the other hand, seems to promise them more and more, so that for a time metaphysics continues and lives on transformed into art or as an artistically transfigured mood. But the scientific mind [*Sinn*] grows more and more imperious and leads the person away to natural science and history and especially to the most rigorous methods of knowing, while art is accorded an ever gentler and more modest significance. All this nowadays usually takes place within a human being's first thirty years. It is the recapitulation of a curriculum at which humankind has been laboring for perhaps thirty thousand years.

Because Nietzsche has this sense of a kinship of the path of individual development and the phases of human cultural evolution, he can urge that from close attention to the former we can gain insight into the latter.[123]

More to the immediate point here, however, is the sense of our individual maturation that this sketch points us to. What he addresses here is the time of life, and the conditions of that time, when our initiative-capacity naturally expands and transforms, to make engaging in activity a life-bearing affair. In his first phase thought he understood this to involve the call of conscience and the beginnings of moral responsibility. Now he calls our attention to this time using different notions. Thus in HAH-I/273 ("Retrogressed, not left behind"), his recall stresses the moving forces which are at work in it, and amidst which reflection is called forth.

> He who at present commences his own development from religious sensations and perhaps lives on after that for a longer time in metaphysics and art, has surrendered a good bit [*Stück*] and be-

gins his race with other modern men under unfavorable conditions [*Voraussetzungen*]: apparently he loses a bit of time. But because he has sojourned in those domains where heat [*Glut*] and energy [*Energie*] are unchained and power [*Macht*] continually streams out of inexhaustible wells [*unversiegbarer Quelle*] as a volcanic flow [*Strom*], he advances all the more quickly--provided only that he has separated himself at the right time from those domains: his feet are winged, his breast has learned to breathe more calmly, longer and more enduringly. He has moved back only in order to have sufficient room for his leap: thus something fearful and threatening can lie in this retrogression.

In this observation, the time of youth which is the time when reflection first arises amidst the reaching of aspiration and the passion of love is one in which feelings flow, and that flow can be nourished by religion, art, and metaphysics, so that what is felt in youth is felt deeply and strongly. If one can find oneself at home in these realms and their strengthening of feeling and of spirit's capacity to fly, and can then separate oneself from these vehicles when the time comes in our own development to move beyond them, then one knows a range of deeper and refined experience on the strength of which, in virtue of its inspirational power and its enhancing of one's 'breathing power', one is prepared for and initiated into an adulthood that will move ahead spiritually in quite forceful stride.

One can, however, seek to hold on to these vehicles (religion, art, metaphysics) and not move beyond them. For the intensity and depth of feeling that they nourish readily engenders in one conviction, a sense of 'knowing', such as (in EH) he saw in retrospect being characteristic of himself and being starkly expressed in BT. In HAH-I, he spends time on this matter of convictions; and if he does not often explicitly focus on the growth side we have just recalled, nonetheless he does ask:

> The demand that what a person says, promises, resolves, in passion, he advocate afterward when he has become cold and sober, belongs to the heaviest burdens which oppress human beings. ... Because we have sworn to be loyal, perhaps even to a purely fictional being like a god, because we have surrendered our heart to a prince, a party, a woman, a priestly order, an artist, a thinker, in a state of deluded madness [*verblendeten Wahnes*] that laid its bewitchment [*Entzückung*] over us and let that being seem to be worthy of every reverence, every sacrifice-- are we now ineluctably bound fast? Indeed, were we not ourselves deceived at that time? Was it not a hypothetical promise, made admittedly under a silent condition that the beings to whom we consecrated ourselves were really what they appeared to us to be in our idea? Are we obliged [*verpflichten*] to be loyal to our errors, even when we see that by this loyalty we do harm to our higher self? No, there is no law, no obligation [*Verpflichtung*] of that kind; we must be traitors, practise disloyalty, again and again surrender our ideals. We do not advance from one period of life into another without creating these pains of betrayal and continuing to suffer from this.[124]

Convictions become formed in youth when (as in his own personal case) the passion of love animates the youth, and at least part of the defense of our holding on to them is that we erroneously think that it is only vulgar advantage or personal fear that would lead anyone to a change in convictions. But that is to misunderstand the nature of conviction.

> Conviction is the belief that on some particular point of knowledge one is in possession of the unconditioned [*unbedingten*] truth. This belief presupposes that unconditioned truths exist, likewise that perfect methods of attaining to them have been discovered, and finally that anyone possessing a conviction has availed himself of these perfect methods. All three assertions demonstrate at once that the man of convictions is not the man of scientific thought; he stands before us as a child still innocent concerning theoretical matters, however grown up he may otherwise be. Yet whole millennia have lived under these childish presuppositions, and it is from them that humankind's mightiest sources of energy have flowed [*herausgeströmt*].[125]

Now countless numbers of persons have sacrificed themselves thinking they were doing so for unconditioned truth when in reality they not only were mistaken in *what* they believed (their 'truth') but were mistaken in their sense that they *had* to be in the right (eternal salvation, say, depended on believing, even if the belief's truth could not be proved). In such matters, intellect was all too heedful to the prompting of 'will'.

While convictions become formed in youth as a time of passion, the truth is that it is only opinion, not conviction, that grows directly out of passion, as how things *seem* to the impassioned youth, as what *seems* plausible in that passionate state. It is only because of a certain inertia [*Trägheit*] of the spirit that we let opinions stiffen into convictions, that is, into unexamined or ungrounded opinions, passionately held. And it is our convictions which in turn lead us to hold on to religion, art, and metaphysics, because in them we see our convictions-- the 'truths' we are convinced of-- expressed. This reference to spiritual inertia echoes a similar thought in SE when, using the ideas of a call of conscience and a youthful decision-making in which we are for the first time *also* assuming responsibility for our lives in one way or another as we enact our decision, he had claimed that most of us, due to a fearfulness and lack of courage, and to a certain inertia, indolence, laziness, they engender, turn away from the task of individual self-development and, taking refuge in a variety of roles assimilated from the 'times' and made second-nature in ourselves, give birth to ourselves as 'men of action'.[126] Here in HAH, he also sees role-playing as integral to this birth, claiming that men of action "are active as officials, businessmen, scholars, that is to say, generic creatures, but not as wholly determinate individual and unique human beings [*ganz bestimmte einzelne und einzige Menschen*]"[127]. But in keeping with the rationalistic stress of his thinking now, his present account of our becoming 'men of action' puts convictions at the heart of that birth-giving.

To understand this matter of convictions, we need to consider two things. First, where do these opinions come from that become turned into convictions. And second, what prevents this 'turning' from occurring in all of us so that we all end up men of action?

As for the source of the opinions which a person arrives at: "All the opinions of one's fellow human beings, of whatever kind they are and with whatever intensity they are held, are like their actions, necessary and something for which they can not be held to account"; for there is an "inner necessity of opinions" arising from "the inextricable interweaving of character, occupation, talent, surroundings". But in this interweaving, in virtue of which we may regard our own nature [*Wesen*] as a "changing sphere [*Sphäre*] of moods [*Stimmungen*] and opinions [*Meinungen*]"[128], how are we to understand the interplay of factors (character and talent, occupation and surroundings) that accounts for the opinions we form? Nietzsche see this interplay as a matter, generally, of the interweaving of the social and the personal, achieved in a living being who is developing.

Socialization is taking place from birth on into youth, and as a result of the assimilation into our developing selves of values, ideas, patterns of action and reaction, from persons around us, we are giving shape to a second nature in ourselves which reflects the social context. In this process, our nature is not simply operating out of itself under conditions but is entering those conditions responsively into its own development and doing this with capacities that are themselves in process of developing. Thus the power of thought, say, both as at work in practical intelligence and as a part of specific activities, is itself evolving and through this time up to youth is so constituted as to be still relatively limited in its capacity to apprehend and interpret. The assimilation being effected, then, not only brings our being on all of its levels to be affected, but does so with the help of a relatively impotent capacity for thought. Thus when we arrive at youth, "most of what young people think has not come forth [*ist nicht ... herausgeströmt*] from the abundance [*Fülle*] of their own [*eigenen*] nature but is a resonance [*Anklang*] and echo [*Nachklang*] of what has been thought, said, praised and blamed, in their vicinity [*in ihrer Nähe*] ... ."[129] Indeed, even for us adults, "the first opinion that occurs to us when we are suddenly asked about something is usually not our own but only the customary one pertaining to our caste, station, origin; our own opinions rarely swim to the top."[130] In our growing up and into our adulthood, then, socialization plays such a role-- and at the conscious level of our ordinary life and activity the socially-incorporated has such dominance-- that we ordinarily do not find even 'our' thought, let alone 'our' activity, coming from any deeper source within ourselves. Not only that, but socialization reaches deeply enough in us that the unconscious side of our activity is dominated by it as well.

By youth, then, surroundings have provided a particular matrix for the assimilation which we effect in socialization, and our character and talent have worked in that assimilation to contribute to the selectivity according to which certain things we assimilate sink in more deeply and forcefully than others, some things are ignored altogether, and many enter us and help shape us but without touching us deeply. In youth the affinity behind our selectivity continues to operate, now in the passion of love, in what draws out our love and what does not, thus in what promises a future for us. At this time we also find our passion-filled selves faced with taking our lives on ourselves, and discover opinions-- those which are to guide our entry into and living of our adult life-- coming to the fore as important, indeed crucial, for our future. Among them, we find ourselves initially drawn toward certain (usually familiar) ones as principles holding to which as guides we are comfortable committing ourselves to the future. And finally, as we prepare to enter into the adult world, to assume one occupation or another there, we are also readying ourselves to fit into the roles that appeal to us and to think in ways reflective of those roles. This is how the opinions which can become convictions arise in us and come to our attention in youth; it is not yet how, and why, they become turned into convictions, and we, into men of action.

As to why we do not all end up men of conviction and action: As in the first phase of his thought, so in HAH, Nietzsche conceives the youthful matrix full of feeling as also the natural birthplace of reflection, of a form of thought called forth as part of the process of assuming responsibility for one's life. Reflection is thinking arising in oneself as cast back upon oneself as having to assume responsibility; part of its dynamic is formed by a critiquing power harbored in it, one which by nature raises questions and seeks reasons on its way toward understanding. For that reason, with the birth of reflection comes by nature that questioning, that regarding as questionable, which makes of youth a time of rebellion, rejection, and as part of this, a time when philosophical reflection can also be born out of a practical thinking which has become reflective and critical of what one has accepted heretofore as a belief-worthy framework for living one's life. Youth then holds in principle the rise, within our decision-making capacity, of the power of reflective thinking with whose help we can and need to take up with and consider opinion critically, and in particular, those opinions which are to guide us in the life of our own which we are entering upon and taking responsibility for. So far as this power is able to operate in us, opinions-- even those which at first seem quite convincing to us-- are not allowed to become convictions. Quite the contrary: The free and restlessly-alive [*freien, rastlos lebendigen*] spirit inward to this power, aiming at an impossible certainty in its critiquing, turns opinions at best into precisely measured probabilities.[131] This turning knows no end. For by their very nature, reasoned opinions are held only as strongly as evidence warrants, and since new evidence can accumulate or new inquiry discover previously undetected evidence, the commitment to reason is commitment to a life of change.[132]

If in youth our practical intelligence, become reflective, can *effectively* enter the critiquing power of reason into the decision-making in which we are assuming responsibility for our lives, then in virtue of this freeing ourselves from the fetters of conviction we can initiate action as free men of action.[133] But as a consequence of this integration, we are also committing ourselves to living in unending change and to being wanderers in the sense sketched out by the aphorism (HAH-I/638) with which Nietzsche ends HAH-I. Entitled "The wanderer", it reads as follows.

> He who has come in any measure into the freedom of reason cannot feel other than a wanderer on the earth-- though not as a traveler *to* a final goal: for such a goal does not exist. But he will be on the lookout and keep his eyes open for all that is really going on in the world; for this reason, he may not let his heart attach too firmly to any individual thing; within him too there must be something wandering that has its joy in change and transience. To such a person there will, to be sure, come bad nights when he is tired and finds the gate of the town that should offer him rest closed against him; perhaps in addition the desert will, as in the Orient, reach right up to the gate, beasts of prey howl now farther off, now closer by, a strong wind arises, robbers lead off his beasts of burden. Then dreadful night may sink down upon the desert like a second desert, and his heart will be weary of wandering. When the morning sun then rises, burning like a

god of wrath, and the town opens up, perhaps he will behold in the faces of those who dwell there even more desert, dirt, deception, insecurity than lie outside the gate-- and the day will be almost worse than the night. Thus it may be that the wanderer shall fare; but then, as recompense, there will come the joyful mornings of other days and regions, when already in the first gray light of daybreak he shall see the Muses come dancing close by him in the mist of the mountains, when afterwards, if he relaxes quietly beneath the trees in the equanimity of his forenoon soul [*Vormittagsseele*], good and bright things will be thrown down to him from their tops and leafy hiding-places, the gifts of all those free spirits who are at home in mountain, wood and solitude and who, like him, are, in their now joyful, now thoughtful way, wanderers and philosophers. Born out of the mysteries of early-morning [*Frühe*], they ponder on how, between the tenth and the twelfth stroke of the clock, the day could present a face so pure, so light-filled, so cheerful and transfigured: they seek the *philosophy of the forenoon* [*Vormittags*].

Despite the fact that youth is a time when a reflective practical intelligence is born in all of us, that birth does not mean an equally effective presence of reason in everyone. Quite the contrary: For most of us, youth is the time when we are born men of action and conviction instead. Right at this very time we find our 'truth' and hold to it firmly. Such a person, who "has not passed through different convictions but remains attached to the belief in whose net he was first captured"[134], does not evolve culturally: he is unteachable, and incapable of grasping that there are other opinions; instead, he grasps at every means of carrying his own opinion onward. 'Convinced' spirits, not being free to learn beyond the confines of their convictions, are superficial. And yet because of their convictions, they are also stable, and a force for stability in a social group.

Now as we saw above Nietzsche appeals to a certain spiritual inertia in the persons in question to explain this. He says in another place:

> We unconsciously seek for the principles and dogmas [*Lehrmeinungen*] appropriate [*angemessen*] to our temperament, so that in the end it appears as though these principles and dogmas had created our character and given it firmness and assurance: whereas what has happened is precisely the reverse. Our thinking and judging (so it seems) subsequently are made into the cause [*Ursache*] of our nature; but in fact it is our nature [*Wesen*] that is the cause [*Ursache*] of our thinking and judging thus and thus. And what is it that determines [*bestimmt*] us to this almost unconscious comedy? Indolence [*Trägheit*] and love of ease [*Bequemlichkeit*] and not least the desire of our vanity to be found consistent through and through, homogeneous [*einartig*] in thought and being: for this procures respect and bestows confidence and power [*Macht*].[135]

But why this "indolence" and "love of ease", this inertia of the spirit, in most of us but not in all? Why do most of us let a concern for the way others think of us dominate us, so that it is from others that we derive our confidence and a sense of our own power? Why is the reason that is born in all of us at this time weak, constrained in its functioning, in most of us? Or seeing the question from the fullest maturational perspective: If our activity exhibits necessity and that necessity is one of nature, and if nature means for us a course of growth as human beings that, taking us beyond the passion of youth, carries us through this time for assuming responsibility having resisted the transformation of opinion into conviction and having developed it as reasoned opinion instead, why is this not what happens to every human being? Most of us do not emerge from this time of passage and transformation free in our initiating in virtue (basically) of reason's effective operation in it, but rather in bondage, constrained by our spiritual inertia and confined by our commitment to acting out various roles determined for us by our surroundings. Is this inertia natural? But if so, natural as expressive of the human nature in us, or of the individual nature of ourselves? Is it natural as ours in actuality from the beginning, or as ours as a natural development in nature's unfolding in us in the course of time? Do some of us have higher, some lower, natures, or more precisely, natural powers of initiative, as our native endowment?[136] Or is such inertia not a matter of nature but rather an outcome of circumstance, a de-naturing (so to speak) of our nature that emerges in almost all of us in the course of our interplay with circumstance? Or ... ?

d. Genius

In the free man of action, the practical intelligence operating in our decision-making has gained a reflective dimension and effectively integrated as well a power whose own nature demands that opinion become scrutinized and turned into reasoned truth. Given the decision-making context of this integration, when the questioning that arises naturally is allowed to have a place and be pursued without constraint it reaches back to the good that is at stake concretely in and for ourselves as active living beings as well as to the particular facets of the situation relevant for the decision-making. Here, the reaching of this reflective power for reasoned insight serves decision-making with its requirement for a guiding insight into the good (the highest good), as element in its effective achievement. That makes the freedom inward to the doing of the free man of action and definitive for his being consist in that necessary functioning of his nature (here, in its decision-making and -executing side) when his initiation of action brings a reflectively reasoned grasp of the (highest) good and of the practically-relevant facets of his situation as guide to and in the doing.

What this means is not what it seems at first sight to mean. For, to begin with, the reasoned grasp of the free man of action is not that of someone who *has* the *truth*; it is a grasp infused with the spirit of someone refusing to be hostage to conviction and determined to make the best workable (practically efficacious) reasoned insight be the guide. Secondly, the situation of practice is always concrete, and the agent unique; thus that reasoned grasp, such as it is, can not be the individual's holding and applying some borrowed general insight but his/her first-hand personal apprehension of the facets of his/her concrete situation: a refined nature's own grasp, say, of the highest good of *his/her* nature and of the factors appropriate to *its* achievement. Thus Nietzsche can say:

> I believe that everyone must have an opinion of his own [*eigene*] concerning everything about which an opinion is possible, because he himself is an individual, unique thing [*ein eigenes, nur einmaliges Ding*] which adopts a new stance towards all other things such as has never been adopted before. ... Freedom of opinion is like health: both are individual, one can not set up a universally valid concept of either. That which one individual needs [*nötig hat*] for his health is to another a cause of sickness, and many ways and means to freedom of spirit may to more highly developed natures count as ways and means to unfreedom.[137]

Such a demand-- a moral demand, as Nietzsche is now understanding morality-- calls for a practical thoughtfulness which he thinks of as meditative or contemplative in character. Such a demand then would (as he sees it) place an individual of his own times in tension with his world.

> From lack of repose, our civilization is turning into a new barbarism. At no time have the active, that is the restless who know no repose, counted for more. That is why one of the most necessary corrections to the character of humankind that have to be taken in hand is a considerable strengthening of the meditative-and-contemplative [*beschauliche*] element in it. Yet even now every individual who is calm and steady in head and heart has the right to believe not only that he has a good temperament but also that he is in possession of a universally useful virtue and even that, by preserving this virtue, he is fulfilling a higher task.[138]

The entry of reflection into the forming of the initiative that leads to action, then, makes for a participation in action inwardly steadied by the meditative/contemplative element within, and signifies an initiating which (by nature) is spiritually alive inwardly and unfettered by traditional roles and role-playing. This says nothing of how the carrying out of the particular deeds being initiated is constituted, that is, of any further freedom realized in doing itself as there is further freedom realized in thinking; it speaks only to initiating, and this, equally when it leads to thinking as to doing. Now when it leads to *thinking as a reflective affair*-- and not all thinking is--, then the initiating which enters the agent into (say) philosophical reflection brings the functioning of this reflective power, expanded beyond its practical role, to operate at the center of a particular truth-seeking activity. In that activity, philosophical reflection universalizes and broadens the individual practical reference of the thinking that is part of the decision-making that enters the agent into philosophizing; and in philosophical inquiry, the kind of freedom realized with reflection's help in our initiative as agents becomes extended into thinking as a particular activity. Then the reflection in question, while addressing its own distinctive problematic, can not only realize the obligating-necessity internal to any thinking but also a further freedom distinctive to itself.

This extension of the freedom brought naturally by practical reflection marks the emergence in principle of the free spirit, or more broadly, of the genius or "great superior fruitful spirit"[139]; it does not occur in most of us. Rather, the inertia of spirit that successfully obstructs the rise of initiative-freedom in most of us affects not only our doing but (when we make it our activity) our thinking, making it be that of a fettered spirit. Now if inertia is the obstacle, overcoming it would seem to call for energy. But what sort is needed, and coming from where?

In the first phase of his thought, Nietzsche celebrated such free-spirited or contemplative human beings under the terms "artist", "philosopher", "moral genius", or in general, "genius", and contrasted them with the scholar. But now, he would examine genius more closely regarding its nature and its origin. In his rethinking he dismisses as superstitious both the current vision of genius (as, say, someone who possesses certain miraculous faculties for acquiring knowledge in the form of a direct insight into the essence of reality, and for acquiring it thus by means quite different from those open to the rest of humankind), and the current vision of the origin of genius (a supra-human origin). Such views are not only mistaken but, if and when the genius thinks of himself in this way, such thinking leads him to cease practicing criticism of himself, and eventually

> that superstition digs at the roots of his strength-and-energy [*Kraft*] and perhaps even makes him into a hypocrite after his strength-and-energy has fled from him. For the great spirits themselves, it is therefore probably more beneficial if they acquire an insight into their strength-and-energy and its origin, if therefore they comprehend what purely human qualities have come together in them and what fortunate circumstances attended them: as for qualities, sustained [*anhaltende*] energy [*Energie*], resolute application to individual goals, great personal courage, and as for circumstances, the good fortune to receive an upbringing which offered in the early years the finest teachers, models, and methods.[140]

What then is the appropriate view of the genius and of his origin? Referring explicitly to SE, Nietzsche suggests now (HAH-I/252) that

> if it is true that, if the scholar is to come into existence, 'a host of very human drives, great and small, [*Triebe und Triebchen*] have to be moulded together', that the scholar, though a very noble metal, is not a pure one and 'consists of a tangled network of very various motives and stimuli' [*Antriebe und Reize*], the same likewise applies to the origin and nature of the artist, the philosopher, the moral genius-- and whatever the great names glorified in that essay are called.

He had spoken in SE with some irony concerning the scholar, but now, in his reaction against romanticism and turn to science, he claims: "*Everything* human deserves to be viewed ironically so far as its *origin* is concerned ... ." Now there is no question that, given the highly developed state of the human race at present, every human being acquires from nature access to many talents [*Talenten*]: such is the inheritance of each of us. But while we all possess inborn talent, our endowment is nonetheless different in its particularities. Is that difference the reason of genius, namely, superior inborn talent? Whatever the native talent, possession of it as potential is no guarantee of its actual development; and in regard to what is needed for that development, "only for a few is the degree of (inborn and acquired [*anerzogen*]) tenacity [*Zähigkeit*], perseverance [*Ausdauer*], and energy [*Energie*], such that he actually becomes a talent, that is to say, *becomes* what he *is*: which means, discharges it in works and actions."[141] Put more broadly:

> ... [T]he activity of the genius seems in no way fundamentally different from the activity of the inventor of machines, the scholar of astronomy or history, the master of tactics. All these activities are explicable if one pictures to oneself people whose thinking is active in *one* direction, who employ everything as material, and who always zealously observe their own inner life and that of others, who perceive everywhere models and incentives, who never tire of combining their means. Genius too does nothing except learn first how to put stones in place then how to build, except continually seek for material and continually try to fashion it. Every activity of human beings is amazingly complicated, not only that of the genius ... .[142]

What is involved in genius, then, is not some special faculty and special capacity for insight, some special talent given at the start, but (on the one hand) a developed capacity whose evolved state is fruit of certain inward qualities by which perhaps very ordinary talents have been developed in an extraordinary way, and (on the other hand) a conjunction of the working of those inward qualities with fortuitous supportive circumstance.

As for those inward qualities,

> one can name great men of all kinds who were very little gifted. They *acquired* greatness, became 'geniuses' (as we put it), by means of qualities the lack of which no one who knew what they were would boast of: they all possessed that seriousness of the efficient workman which first learns to construct the parts perfectly before it ventures to fashion a great whole; they allowed themselves time for it, because they took more pleasure in making the little, secondary things well than in the effect of a dazzling whole. The recipe for becoming a good novelist, for example, is easy to give, but to carry it out presupposes qualities one is accustomed to overlook when one says 'I do not have enough talent'.[143]

Outlining the steps that would lead someone to become a good novelist, and contrasting the effort involved in taking those steps with what most people do, he concludes: "Sometimes, when the needed character and reason [*Vernunft*] are lacking to form such a life-plan for being an artist, destiny [*Schicksal*] and need [*Not*] take their place and lead the future master step by step through all the conditions [*Bedingungen*] of his craft."[143]

If it is not gifts and talents (the inborn in this form) that make the 'genius', what does? Nietzsche has suggested that on the inward side it is the energy, application, and courage of the person in question. Where do these come from? Nietzsche himself asks this question when he is speaking of the free spirit as being weak in comparison with someone who has tradition on his side and requires no reasons for his actions, and weak especially in regard to action: he is aware of too many motives and points of view, and thus has at best an uncertain and unpractised hand.

> What means are there of nonetheless making him *relatively strong*, so that he at least makes his way successfully and does not perish without effect? How does the strong spirit (*espirt fort*) arise? This is, in any individual case, the question of the production of genius. Whence comes the energy [*Energie*], the unyielding strength [*Kraft*], the perseverance [*Ausdauer*], with which the individual, in opposition to tradition, endeavors [*trachtet*] to win [*erwerben*] a wholly individual knowledge of the world?[144]

Part of the answer has been given when speaking of the energy as something inborn. But the inborn is amplified by the acquired: how is this amplifying acquisition to be understood? What are its conditions?

Education immediately comes to mind as the instrument for such amplification: after all, Nietzsche has mentioned teachers, models, and methods, when speaking of the contribution of circumstance. In this second phase of his thought, Nietzsche maintains the notion of education he urged in the first, that it is not a process of introducing something (knowledge, say) from the outside but rather a matter of developing what is inside, on the occasion of and with the assistance of what is provided from the outside. But he develops this idea slightly differently now.

In HAH-I/242 ("Miracle-education"), Nietzsche speaks of the importance and interest that attach to education for those who have abandoned belief in a God and his loving care; but the current educational system is not formed within any such acknowledgement, express or implicit. Rather, it is in a state comparable to the state of medicine before miracle cures were abandoned; at present we believe only in a 'miraculous' education, and thus provide a system wherein "the most fruitful and mightiest human beings" are supposed to arise out of "the greatest disorder, confusion of objectives, unfavorable circumstances". And indeed, some do 'arise' in that matrix, but if one looks at those cases, one will find that

> under the same circumstances, countless men continually perish; the single individual who has been saved usually has become stronger [*stärker*] because, by virtue of an inborn, indestructible [*unverwüstlicher*] strength-and-energy [*Kraft*], he has endured these ill circumstances and has exercised and even augmented [*geübt und vermehrt hat*] this strength-and-energy [*Kraft*]. An education that no longer believes in miracles will have to pay attention to three things: firstly, how much energy [*Energie*] is inherited? Secondly, how can new energy be ignited [*entzündet*]? Thirdly, how can the individual be adapted [*angepatzt*] to the so-diversified demands [*Ansprüchen*] of culture without being troubled-and-disturbed [*beunruhigen*] by them and his individuality [*Eigenartigkeit*] dispersed [*zersplittern*]-- in short, how can the individual be set in place [*eingereiht*] within the counterpoint of private and public culture, how is it possible for the melody to lead and as melody to accompany?

True education-- one which recognizes that education is basically self-cultivation, that is, self-strengthening in the course of (and with the help of) learning-- presupposes nature (both talents and, here, inborn energy), and its furthering of self-cultivation takes the form of seeking to kindle new energy, to facilitate an acquiring of the new by an amplification of the inborn. As an indication of his meaning Nietzsche can speak (in HAH-I/256) of the value of practising a science for a while as lying not in the knowledge one gains (a small drop in the sea of knowledge) but rather in such practise yielding [*ergibt*] "an increase in energy [*Energie*], in the faculty of drawing conclusions, in the tenacity [*Zähigkeit*] of perseverance [*Ausdauer*]; one has learned to attain an *end* [*Zweck*] *in a purposeful way* [*zweckmätzig*]. So far forth, it is very valuable for all that one later does [*treibt*] once to have been a scientific human being."[145]

But how, more generally, can assistance to self-cultivation be provided by an educational system? In the midst of a series of aphorisms devoted to genius and its origin (HAH-I/231-235), Nietzsche looks to hints that nature herself provides and suggests a conclusion that might be drawn from them. Thus, in an aphorism entitled "The arising of genius" (HAH-I/231), he starts by saying:

> The wit with which a prisoner seeks after means for his liberation-- the most cold-blooded and tedious employment of every little advantage-- can teach what hand-hold [*Handhabe*] nature sometimes makes use of in order to bring into existence genius-- a word I ask to be understood without any flavor of the mythological or religious. She imprisons it in a prison and excites to an extreme its desire to free itself. Or, using a different image: anyone who has totally lost his way in the woods, but who strives with uncommon energy [*Energie*] after some direction out into the open discovers occasionally a new path which no-one knows: so arise the geniuses famed for their originality.-- It has already been remarked that a mutilation, a crippling, a significant lack of an organ, often offers the occasion [*Veranlassung*] for the uncommonly good development of another organ which is due to its having to perform its own function and that of the other as well. It is out of this that one may divine the origin [*Ursprung*] of many a glittering talent.-- From these general indications about the arising of genius, one may make an application to the special case of the arising of the perfected [*vollkommenen*] free spirit.

In the matter of the arising of such a free spirit, Nietzsche then points to something essential in the next aphorism (HAH-I/232: "Conjecture concerning the origin of free-spiritedness"). "Just as glaciers increase [*zunehmen*] when in the equatorial regions the sun bears down upon the sea with greater heat than before, so it may be that a very strong and aggressive [*sehr starke, um sich greifende*] free-spiritedness may also be evidence that somewhere the heat [*Glut*] of sensibility has grown [*ist gewachsen*] extraordinarily." Does the arising of a strong free spirit involve or depend, then, upon an increasing passionateness on the side of feeling? The next aphorism (HAH-I/233, "The voice of history") poses a form of that suggestion.

> In general history *seems* to offer the following instruction concerning the production of genius: mistreat and torment human beings-- thus it cries to the passions of envy, hatred, and competitive rivalry [*Wetteifer*]-- drive them to the extreme, one against the other, people against people, and do it for centuries on end; then perhaps the light of genius will flame up, like a spark of the fearful energy [*Energie*] kindled thereby which has fled aside from the rest; the will [*Wille*], like a horse made wild under the rider's spur, then breaks out and leaps over into another domain.-- He who came to be conscious of the production of genius and also wanted to proceed practically in the manner in which Nature ordinarily does in this matter, would have to be as evil and ruthless as Nature is.-- But perhaps we have misheard.

If "great energy [*starke Energie*]" is "the soil out of which great intellect and the powerful [*mächtige*] individual" (that is, in general, genius) grows, then if what socialists desire-- "a comfortable life for as many as possible"-- was ever achieved, humankind would have become too feeble [*matt*] to be able to produce the genius any longer.

> Must one therefore not desire that life should retain its violent [*gewaltsamen*] character and that savage forces and energies [*wilde Kräfte und Energien*] continue to be called up [*hervorgerufen*] again and again? At present the warm, sympathizing heart wants precisely the *abolition* of that savage and violent character of life, and the warmest heart one can imagine would long for it the most passionately; and yet precisely this passion has derived its fire, its warmth, indeed its very existence, from that savage and violent character of life. The warmest heart thus desires the abolition of its own foundation, the destruction of itself, which is to say it desires something illogical, it is not intelligent. The highest intelligence and the warmest heart cannot coexist in the same person, and the sage who pronounces judgment on life places himself above goodness as well and regards it only as something to be taken into account together with everything else in the total assessment [*Gesamtrechnung*] of life. The sage has to resist these extravagant desires of unintelligent goodness, because his concern is the continuance [*Fortleben*] of his type and the final arising [*endlichen Entstehen*] of the supreme intellect; at the least he will refrain from promoting the founding of the 'perfect state', inasmuch as only enfeebled [*ermattete*] individuals can have any place in it. Christ, whom we want to think of as the warmest heart, promoted the stupidifying of man, placing himself on the side of the poor in spirit and retarding the production of the supreme intellect. And this had consequences! And we may predict: his counter-image, the perfect sage, will just as necessarily obstruct the production of a Christ. The state is a prudent institution for the protection of individuals against one another; if one exaggerates its nobility, the individual will in the end be enfeebled by it, and indeed, dissolved by it-- that is to say, the original purpose of the state will be thwarted in the most thorough way possible.[146]

Looking at the matter in an evolutionary perspective, Nietzsche asks a final question about the production of genius.

> Perhaps the production of genius is reserved to only a limited time-period of humankind. For one cannot expect of the future of humanity that it will produce all at the same time things which required for their production quite definite conditions belonging to some period or other of the past: for example, the astonishing effects of religious feelings. Such feeling has had its time, and many very good things can never thrive again because it was only out of it that they could grow. So there will never again be a religiously-bounded horizon of life and culture. Perhaps also the saint, as type, is possible only with a certain narrowness [*Befangenheit*] of intellect, which (so it seems) is now done with for all future time. And so perhaps the high point of intelligence has been reserved for a single age of humankind: it appeared-- and continues to appear, for we are

still living in this age-- when an extraordinary, long-accumulated energy [*Energie*] of will in an exceptional fashion [*ausnahmsweise*] transferred itself [*sich ... übertrug*] through inheritance to *spiritual* goals. This high point will be past when that wildness and energy have ceased to be cultivated [*nicht mehr grotzgezüchtet werden*]. Perhaps humanity will approach closer to its real [*eigentlichen*] goals at the middle of its way, in the mid-period of its existence, than at its end. Forces [*Kräfte*] such as condition the production of art, for example, could simply die out; delight in lying, in the vague, in the symbolic, in intoxication, in ecstasy, could fall into disrepute. Indeed, if life were ever to be ordered within the perfect state, there would no longer exist in the present any motive whatever for poetry-and-fiction [*Dichtung*], and it would be only relict human beings who still had a desire for poetical unreality. These would in any case look back with longing to the times of the imperfect state, the time of half-barbarian society, to *our* times.[147]

Before we take up this suggestion about the future (see Section C. below), let us recall that we entered upon this consideration of genius as the final part of our effort to understand how Nietzsche is now thinking of our agency, and in particular, of the freedom appropriate to it. What have we found? By the necessity of our nature, we are agents initiating activity in a working together of powers native to us; such initiating is the nature-based functioning out-of-ourselves whereby we participate actively in existence. Because the initiative-capacity in us naturally evolves, our spontaneity changes character as we mature, and by the time of youth, we are natured for an initiating that takes shape through a transformed capacity that includes a practical reflection. In virtue of the questioning nature of a practical intelligence that has become reflective, our entry upon doing in a decision-making involving it can now be that of the free man of action, and will be *if* the element of reason involved is made sufficiently effective. Without that, we engage ourselves in action out of a spiritual inertia, thus as men of action and conviction, and when we engage in thinking, it is as fettered spirits who at best know the limited freedom of spirit operating responsively to the pressure of obligation on a truth-seeking mind. If, however, we are able to enter thinking as a reflective affair, in an entry that is like to the free man of action's entry into doing, then we can know (philosophical, say) reflection as the thinking of a free spirit. But again, with a proviso, namely, that we have energy enough-- tenacity, determination, commitment-- effectively to enact the freedom opened up by reflection. The energy needed by both the free man of action and the free spirit belongs in some measure to our nature as an inheritance, and what is native can in some measure also be amplified. Thus the fact that such energy, in a sufficing measure to make freedom actual, is present in only a few of us and not in all is due in part to the happenstance of heredity, in part to the chance of supportive and challenging circumstance, and in part to its own working in the concrete engagement with circumstance.

This understanding of freedom as involving reflection, reason, and energy, modifies what we saw in SE, but in an initial way that seems unfinished, the tentative outcome of an inquiring that is reaching for something but has not yet found it. In its unfinished state, however, such understanding seems of a piece in the direction in which it is moving with other but not-yet-connected thoughts on other matters: in particular, the understanding of reality as interactive in nature, and the various insights into power and its inherent relations of superiority and inferiority. The idea in which the thinking at work in these three threads is brought to an end-point satisfying to Nietzsche is the idea of reality as will-to-power. But that will enter into his published works only well after HAH.

C. Present, past, and future: the crisis

1. The present: a crisis concerning progress

In the first phase of his thought, Nietzsche's concern with his contemporary world was focused to a great extent on the German people, and on the ancient Greeks as providing a counterpart which not only embodied the human in a significant fulness of realization (the 'classical' as standard) but represented a historical source from which important facets of the contemporary were derived. Greek tragedy and German music, Socratic rationalism and modern science, represented variations on a theme-- an eternal theme; and the Alexandrian development of rationalism also provided the early historical source of the Renaissance and Enlightenment movements of modern Europe. Christianity was mainly an implicit factor and theme.

In this second phase, the framework for analysis of the contemporary alters significantly, and the interpretative stress in the treatment of the relevant historical background also shifts.

The alteration in the framework involves a rejection of the trans-temporal (the eternal and the perpetual or everlasting both) and the projecting of a vision of the indefinite past time before the coming-to-be of the earth, so as to set the extended evolutionary development of life on earth and the lengthy evolution of the human itself on an immense background, and to bring to mind the recent time (four thousand years) of recorded human history as a small segment of human evolution lost in this sea of temporality. Indeed, Nietzsche speaks of the modern age being distinguished for its having "for the first time demolished the ancient walls between nature and spirit, man and animal, morality and physics", and for its making possible thus a kind of "connected and lively recollection" which, if it were to become perfect and complete, would constitute a "cosmic self-consciousness".[148]

Concomitantly, the interpretative stress has now shifted away from the German people, to Europe, and while Greece remains an important source in the background of modern Europe, Christianity is becoming openly analyzed and discussed by Nietzsche as a part of recent human development. As he sees it now, the major force in modern Europe that is bringing both change and the promise of progress and the elevation of human life is the disciplined search for truth that is manifest in science; instead of the possibility of an artistic Socrates, the free spirit emerges as the ideal of the fulfilled greatness of the human being. The considerable difference between the two ideals attests the very positive and even primary place which knowledge and the spirit of science now have in making for-- even constituting the heart of-- a worthwhile existence, compared with their more questionable working in the first phase of his thought. The advocate of art and morality has become a promoter of the Enlightenment and knowledge.

Nietzsche still sees a crisis obtaining in his contemporary world, and in important respects its character remains (verbally, at least) what it was in the first phase. That common character can be noted by speaking of the present as a time in which the depth of the human involvement in untruth is being discovered, and in which the question is being raised of the bearing of this involvement on meaning: is it possible for us to live a meaningful life while residing consciously in untruth?[149]

In the first phase, this discovery was a component of the Silenic side to the Dionysian experiencing in BT; and it was found again in the modern world in connection with Kant's achievement of reason's discovery of its own limits and of our involvement in an 'appearance' which we ordinarily mis-take as ultimate reality. The answer to the question of meaning had involved (in BT) the recognition of Wagner as representing the renewal of tragedy in the modern world and the hope for the human being's regaining a tragic attitude toward existence and life. For it was with that, and the renewed touch with the eternal that it involved, that the meaningfulness which is possible in the life of a human being-- a meaningfulness dependent on squarely facing the fullest reach of negativity present in temporal human existence-- was to be found.

Now, however, this whole way of interpreting the crisis is regarded by Nietzsche as a mistaken reading of what is nonetheless a genuine crisis. Because there is nothing eternal, human existence is unable to find meaning by a renewed touch with the eternal, as in BT. Is a meaningful existence still possible then, if life bears at its heart this insight into the temporality of all, and into the unavoidable involvement of ourselves in the negativities of finite existence and the fictive apprehension of reality? If there is a positive answer to this question, it will involve a move into a new and different future, something fuller and deeper and more alive than the present; but what sort of move, and into what sort of future?

There are signs that seem to offer promise of a future that would (at the very least) signify genuine progress, but progress in the sense of the genuine elevation of human existence on earth, not in that of further travel on the paths of the old culture of 'progress'.[150]

One sign: In the historical self-consciousness dawning in us in virtue of the scientific spirit and the love of truth, we have become cognizant of ourselves as the inheritors of a build-up of an abundance-- indeed, an overabundance--- of deeply-stirring feelings. For this we have above all to thank Christianity and its spiritualizing refinement of our capacity for feeling, together with the various poets, musicians, and philosophers, of modern times. Seen in relation to our crisis, this abundance holds promise for the future, as the potential reservoir of energy and of refined capacity out of which a higher culture could be formed. But in the immediate present, "the sum of feelings, cognitions, experiences, thus the whole burden of culture, has become so great that an over-excitation of the nervous and thinking powers is now a universal danger-- indeed, the cultured classes of Europe have in fact become altogether neurotic ... ." What is needed in order to overcome the unhealthy side of this condition is, first and foremost, a

> lessening of that tension of feeling, of that crushing cultural burden which, even if it had to be purchased at a heavy cost, nonetheless gives us a basis for the great hope of a *new Renaissance*. ... In order that we not become overgrown by this overabundance, we must conjure up the spirit of science which on the whole makes one somewhat colder and more skeptical and especially cools down the fiery stream of belief in final conclusive truths.[151]

And in fact, led by science (both its spirit, and its increasing discovery of tentative truths), this coolant is not only present, but is also already in process of moving us out of a tropical zone of culture into a temperate zone.[152] If the Italian Renaissance represented a beginning of this moving out-- it contained within it all the positive forces to which we owe modern culture (liberation of thought, disrespect for authorities, victory of education over the arrogance of ancestry, enthusiasm for science and the scientific past of humankind, unfettering of the individual, a passion for truthfulness and an aversion to appearance and mere effect)--, the continuation and fulfillment of that start has nonetheless been held up for several centuries, primarily due to the German Reformation, then the counter-Reformation. The progressive impulses and tendencies that are leading into a new and different future-- impulses to freedom of spirit-- have not been strong enough to prevent the conjuring up in their midst of these regressive movements, which are revivals of earlier phases of humankind.[153] In virtue of them, the complete awakening and hegemony [*Herrschen*] of the sciences has been delayed for two or three hundred years; and the great task of the Renaissance-- that of the complete growing-together [*In-Eins-Verwachsen*] of the spirit of antiquity and the modern spirit-- was unable to be brought straightaway to completion. Yet that after an extended delay the Renaissance re-emerged, in the guise of the Enlightenment (although this dawning-again had a lesser lustre than an unchallenged continuation of the Renaissance might have had[154]) attests that those liberating forces were still powerful.

Thus the abundance of built-up energy and feeling-resources remain present, and the spiritual coolant which can quiet the unhealthy excesses involved in the build-up is present and gaining strength. Even so, the present remains locus of an ongoing struggle between progressive and retrogressive forces. The old ways of thinking, the old cultures, are still partly with us, and the new is not yet secure and habitual and therefore still lacks decisiveness and consistency. From in the middle of this transitional time, it looks at present as though everything is becoming chaotic; the old may be increasingly losing hold, but the new is not taking a shape that is proving useful and still seems vulnerable: witness the romanticism of which Schopenhauer and Wagner are leading voices in the world of culture. The time, then, is still a precarious one of struggle between the forward-looking and the backward-looking, and indeed is potentially calamitous. For if we are uncertain, even faltering, in our movement into a new future, we simply cannot return to the old, but *must* move forward. Even if genuine progress-- and that means, genuine elevation-- does not follow, we have no real choice but to make the venture.[155]

Another sign: This time of transition, uncertain as it is in its outcome, harbors another positive sign, additional to the presence both of the requisite reservoir of spiritual energy for a future higher culture and of the cooling power of disciplined reason currently needed that the energy not overexcite and thence debilitate us.

The less men are bound by tradition, the greater is the inner stirring of motives and in turn the greater the corresponding outward unrest, the mingling of human beings with one another, the polyphony of their strivings. For whom is there any longer a strong compulsion to bind oneself and one's posterity to a place? For whom is there still anything rigorously binding at all? Just as in the arts all the styles are imitated side by side, so are all the stages and types of morality, custom, culture.-- Such a time acquires its significance by the fact that in it the different world-views, customs, cultures, can be compared and lived through side by side: something not possible earlier, amidst the ever localized dominance of each culture, and the corresponding confinement of artistic styles to a place and time. Now an enlargement of aesthetic feeling will finally decide among so many forms offering themselves for comparison: it will allow most to die out-- namely, all which are rejected by such feeling. Likewise there is now taking place a choice in the forms and habits of higher morality [*Sittlichkeit*], the aim of which can be nothing other than the demise of lower moralities. It is an age of comparison! This is its pride ... .[156]

We have an unprecedented opportunity now for testing and assessing the various ways in which human beings have defined life for themselves, and for sorting them out on the basis of our own enlarged aesthetic sensitivity and our own elevated morality. But for what end, to what purpose? To what future are that enlargement and elevation, and the testing under their auspices, to contribute?

That future in question comes into perspective when we avail ourselves of the unprecedented retrospect on the past and its variety which the present offers.

There is a sad side to such a retrospect. For at the same time as we are discovering ourselves to be the inheritors of an abundance, we can not help but suffer from a feeling similar to that of someone who has inherited a riches won by unjust means, or to a prince who rules in virtue of the violent deeds of his forefathers. "He thinks with sadness on his origin and is often ashamed, often sensitive about it. The whole sum of energy [*Kraft*], life-will, joy, which he expends on his property, is often balanced by a profound weariness: he can not forget his origin. He looks to the future pained at heart, he knows in advance that his posterity will suffer from the past as he does."[157]

Even more profoundly, however: our unprecedented retrospect brings not only the ambivalent recognition of a treasure inherited and an inheritance felt as unjustly acquired, but it opens us to the possibility of bringing into an encompassing conscious cognizance the whole of humankind and the course of human existence up to the present. To the extent that we can do this, we can not help but have come home to us, forcefully enough even to make us feel despair, the problematic of our existence, and on that background, a lack which seems to threaten meaninglessness not simply to our individual human existence but to the existence of human beings on earth. For

humanity as a whole has *no* goal, and the individual human being, when he regards its total course, can find no support or comfort in it ... . If in all he does he has before him the ultimate goallessness of man, his actions acquire in his own eyes the character of useless-squandering. But to feel *squandered* as humanity as a whole (and not merely as an individual) in the way we see the individual fruits of nature squandered, is a feeling beyond all other feelings.[158]

The sense of despair, felt in our discovery of the apparent meaninglessness of human existence, is all the more intense because in the past-- and for many, still into the present--, we have believed that "a God broadly directs the destinies of the world and, despite all the apparent twists and turns in its path, is leading humanity gloriously upward".[159] But such a belief has ceased, such an idea is part of the fiction of which we have become cognizant: there is no God who looks out for us with loving care.[160] As for this 'we' who have become aware of ourselves as alone in this way: we are not simply isolated individuals or even members of a people, but are human in a humanity that connects us with *all* other human beings. What is felt strongly by us now, and felt as missing, is a meaningfulness to that connectedness of ourselves as all human, one that could be provided only by a goal for humankind as a whole. Without that, we lack what we, as *human* beings, need to find life worthwhile.

The crisis of the present, then, is understood by Nietzsche now as that of the seeming meaninglessness of earthly human existence discovered as we are now discovering such existence in truth to be. Our response to this can not call on some God or saving force beyond ourselves, but must amount to our assuming the responsibility which is ours as human beings, not simply for ourselves individually but for ourselves as together sharers of this earthly existence and needing to connect with each other as such.

2. The present: the momentum of disintegration, revolution and war

The crucial driving force of modern Europe, its vehicle for change, has been-- and still is-- the disciplined love of truth which is embodied in science and which Nietzsche sees as marking genuine (historical) philosophy. The work of this drive has been, above all, to expose our involvement in error, and thereby to challenge and overturn the foundations on which modern life has established itself and to which many would still like to cling.[161] At the same time that such a love opens the way potentially to genuine progress, its undermining of previous and still-held-to foundations has had-- and is increasingly having-- a disintegrative impact in modern life. Although we may at present have abundant treasure that was built up in-- and is being inherited by us from-- the past, the undermining of the foundations of belief within which that treasure was accumulated has loosed forces that threaten not only to dissipate the treasure but to create a future which is the reverse of progress. Counterposed to the gleam of light and hope which the love of truth introduces is not simply the darkness which clinging to what is being undermined represents (the darkness of regression), but another darkness, that introduced by the growing momentum of disintegration which the undermining of foundations is introducing as is spreads through all of the various areas of life. It is possible-- and above all, there is a question of whether it is indeed avoidable-- that the outcome of the disintegration set in motion by our truth-seeking will be a condition of darkness out of which human life can not find its way again, a manner of human existence which is meaningless in the extreme, given that we will have dissipated our inherited treasure and established ourselves world-wide in a life which lacks the impetus-- the creative impetus-- which alone could make life meaningful.

Disintegration is taking place in the various areas of life, and taking shape in different guises, but with something like the same spiritual sense and force. Nietzsche sketches out brief pointers that adumbrate his ideas on various facets of this development.

There is, for instance, the increasing triumph of a new conception of government.[162] The old conception, involving the regime and the people being separated into two spheres of power (one that is stronger and higher, the other that is weaker and inferior), still holds sway in most states; the new conception sees the regime as an organ of the people, instead of as a provident and venerable 'above' in relation to a 'below' which is accustomed to diffidence. Since the governmental relation is the (unconscious) model for many other social relations-- teacher and student, lord and servants, father and family, general and soldier, master and apprentice--, change to a democratic form of state will have much broader consequences than the merely political. Indeed, the shift is the first step in what could well be the death and disappearance of the state itself as an organizing force-- a not altogether unhappy prospect, indeed, but since one does not know what might emerge afterward, it is best for a while to work to preserve the state.[163]

Or again, there is the matter of social relations, and in particular, increasing tension concerning property and property-division. Here it is socialism that is the disintegrating and potentially revolutionary force. On the surface, it is a question of justice that is at issue here. But

when socialists show that the division of property among present-day humankind is the outcome of countless acts of injustice and violence, and repudiate wholly any obligation towards something having so unjust a foundation, they are looking at only one individual matter. The entire past of the old culture was erected upon force, slavery, deception, error; but we, the heirs and inheritors of all these past things, cannot decree away the concretizations of all that past and may not extract an individual part of them. The disposition to injustice inhabits the souls of the nonpossessors too, they are no better than the possessors and have no moral prerogative over them, for their own ancestors were at some time or other possessors. What is needed is not a forcible redistribution but a gradual transformation of mind [*Umschaffungen des Sinnes*]: the sense of justice must grow greater in everyone, the instinct for violence weaker.[164]

In reality, the socialist advocacy of 'justice' is a false front. Socialism is

> the fanciful younger brother of the almost expired despotism whose heir it wants to be; its endeavors are thus in the profoundest sense reactionary. For it desires an abundance of state power such as only despotism has ever had; indeed it outbids all the despotisms of the past inasmuch as it expressly aspires to the formal annihilation of the individual, who appears to it like an unauthorized luxury of nature which should be be improved by it into a useful *organ of the community*. ... But even this inheritance would be inadequate to its purposes ... . (Working) for the abolition of all existing *states*, socialism can hope to exist only for brief periods here and there, and then only by the exercise of the extremest terrorism. For this reason it is secretly preparing itself for rule through fear and is driving the word 'justice' into the heads of the half-educated masses like a nail so as to rob them wholly of their reason ... and to create in them a good conscience for the evil game they are to play. Socialism can serve to teach, in a truly brutal and impressive fashion, what danger there lies in all accumulations of state power, and to that extent to implant mistrust of the state itself. When its harsh voice takes up the cry 'as much state as possible' it thereby at first sounds noisier than ever: but soon the opposite cry comes through with all the greater force: 'as little state as possible'.[165]

Implicit in the socialistic fight for justice in property ownership is the ideal of "a comfortable life for as many as possible" As we noted earlier (in the discussion citing HAH-I/235), this means a life in which the soil out of which the great intellect and the powerful individual grows (namely, great energy) is destroyed, and humankind has become too feeble to be able to produce the genius.

Both the democratization of contemporary Europe, and the socialist upsurge, represent movements which tend toward a revolutionary overturning of the social order. But revolution in the outward sense-- the use of force to overthrow the established order of things-- does not automatically bring with it a fairer humanity; it rather brings the resurrection of the most savage energies stemming from excesses of distant ages: cf. the French Revolution, for example. And thus, while its dislocations may release sources of energy in a humankind that has grown feeble, it never works directly in constructive fashion, as a "regulator, architect, artist, perfecter, of human nature".[166]

More broadly, war in general may function in a dual way: destructively on the one hand, both as regards a culture that has grown feeble and also as regards those "men of the highest civilization" who "guarantee a good and abundant posterity" but who are sacrificed and squandered disproportionately in war;[167] on the other hand, by its brutalization of those involved,[168] war not only makes its participants more natural (at a primitive level of nature) but its excitation of energy enables, under favorable circumstances after the war ends, the "wheels in the workshops of the spirit" to turn "with new energy [*Kraft*]".[169] If however, we look at the current context of war, the prosecution of "grand politics", we find that subsequent circumstances are not likely to be favorable. For

> just as the greatest cost which war and the preparation for war bring to a people is not the expense of the war or the interruption to trade and commerce, nor the maintenance of standing armies ... but the cost involved in the removal year in, year out, of an extraordinary number of its energetic and industrious men from their proper professions and occupations so that they may become soldiers: so a people which sets about practising grand politics and ensuring to itself a decisive voice among the most powerful states does not incur the highest costs where these are usually thought to lie. It is true that from this moment on a host of the most prominent talents are continually sacrificed on the 'altar of the fatherland' or of the national thirst for honor, whereas previously other spheres of activity were open to these talents now devoured by politics. But aside from these public hecatombs, and at bottom more horrible, there occurs a spectacle played out continually in a hundred thousand simultaneous acts: every efficient, industrious, in-

telligent, aspiring human being belonging to such a people lusting after political laurels is dominated by this lust and no longer belongs wholly to his own domain, as he formerly did: questions and cares of the public weal, renewed every day, devour a daily tribute from the capital in every citizen's head and heart: the sum total of all these sacrifices and costs in individual energy and work is so tremendous that the political emergence of a people almost necessarily draws after it a spiritual impoverishment and enfeeblement and a diminution of the capacity for undertakings demanding great concentration [*Konzentration*] and one-sided-application [*Einseitigkeit*].[170]

As regards the uncovering or generating new energies, there is an alternative: surrogates for war can be developed. For example:

At present the English, who seem on the whole to have renounced war, are seizing on a different means of engendering [*erzeugen*] anew their fading energies [*Kräfte*]: those perilous journeys of discovery, navigations, mountain-climbings, undertaken for scientific ends (so they claim) but in truth so as to bring home with them surplus energy [*überschüssige Kraft*] from adventures and perils of all kinds. One will be able to discover many other such surrogates for war, but they will perhaps increasingly reveal that so highly cultivated and for that reason necessarily feeble [*matte*] humanity as that of the present-day European requires [*bedarf*] not merely war but the greatest and most terrible wars-- thus a temporary relapse into barbarism-- in order that their culture and their existence itself not suffer loss from the means of culture.[171]

But on the whole, there is a conflict between the political and the cultural: the seeking for and assertion of power [*Macht*] in a political venue by a people means spiritual loss, whereas being on the political sick-bed, or more broadly, being in politically-weak times, often allows rejuvenation, a rediscovery of itself spiritually.[172]

Viewed in larger perspective, then, the undermining of previous foundations which is part of the present-day crisis does not simply open up the potential for a different and progressive future; it generates a disintegrative movement that could possibly undermine the future in question, supposing even that we have the courage to venture upon it and the intelligence and discipline to formulate and work for the goal(s) that distinguish that future. Even if, in certain cases (war, for one) it discovers new energies, it does not by itself harness these to constructive ends but can diminish the possibility of a humanly-constructive outcome and future.

3. The present: hope and possibility for the future

According to Nietzsche's present understanding, the crisis of the contemporary world concerns the future of the human race as a whole in its existence on earth. The catalyst for this crisis-- the disciplined effort of inquiry animated by the love of truth-- has exposed the belief-foundations of modern European culture as fictional and consisting of error. In particular, it has brought into the open the discovery of ourselves-- we human beings-- as alone on earth without a God, without a guiding and supporting force from beyond ourselves. At the same time, we have discovered ourselves in a connectedness with each other as a race, together in this aloneness and facing a future in which we-- we as a race-- must find a meaningful manner of dwelling on earth which is commensurate with this knowledge. In virtue of its undermining of belief-foundations, however, and its opening up the prospect of a dwelling which is commensurate with truth, the very force which would free humanity from unwitting captivity to untruth has also initiated a disintegrating movement which is gaining momentum and has a potential outworking which might permanently undermine the possibility of meaningful existence.

This time of crisis is the time for a decision-making of ourselves as a race. If the catalyst and the leading forces bringing these things to pass are found concentrated in Europe, the need is nonetheless for a decision-making commensurate with human existence as a whole. In this situation, two things seem forcefully clear to Nietzsche.

The first: We human beings can-- and need to-- take responsibility for our (collective and individual) existence on earth, and as part of this, have confidence that we *can* consciously resolve to develop onward into a new and higher culture (not as previously, only develop unconsciously and fortuitously), and that we *can* now not only create better conditions for the arising of human beings and for their nutrition, education and instruction, but also *can* manage [*verwalten*] the earth as a whole economically and *can* weigh and set off against one another and institute and set in place [*einsetzen*] the various energies-and-forces [*Kräfte*] of human beings in general.[173] Nietzsche envisions in this regard a "still distant state of things in which the good Europeans will come into possession of their great task-- the direction [*Leitung*] and supervision [*Überwachung*] of the total culture of the earth"[174].

The second: As the basic side of such a new conscious culture arising from our taking responsibility for ourselves as a race, we can-- and need to-- set "ecumenical goals embracing the whole earth" so that all this 'can-do' gains a direction.[175] More specifically, we need to understand "the requirements [*Bedürfnisse*] of humankind"-- the variety of needs that require satisfying if a meaningful existence is to be created--, and setting a goal that expresses the morality of 'benefit the whole of humankind' as our standard, we need to recognize that, in the interest of achieving the various ecumenical goals various special tasks-- and under certain circumstances, even evil tasks-- may have to be set for whole expanses [*Strecken*] of humankind. Because the accomplishing of these tasks is needed for reaching those goals, and because these different tasks may mean that different things are required of different people, we need to recognize that different special moralities will be called for: the Kantian view of morality, in which the same thing being required of each and all is of the essence of morality, will need to be overcome.[176]

In short: we find ourselves in a time of decision-making when three paths into the future seem open to us and compete for affirmation in our collective decision-making.

One is that on which we hold to the old 'truths' despite what our love of truth seems to be disclosing to us; if the regressive or reactionary forces that call us to this path prevail, we have no truly human future, and would find the commitment of ourselves to truth-- our science and scientific philosophy-- suppressed.

A second is that on which modern European man is currently embarked, the path of 'progress' that involves, indeed, the disintegration of institutions which held the European together in the Middle Ages and their replacement by 'better', 'more progressive', institutions. However, the constructive forces here-- those embodied in 'modern ideas', in the democratic and socialist movements as they are taking shape in the present-- are too weak, their guiding ideas too shallow, to prevent the disintegration from ending in an existence which undermines in its own way the human future which the reactionary forces also oppose. It is possible, indeed, that the 'more progressive' institutions, while they are being built within too narrow a horizon of vision, could be eventually adapted to function in the future which provides the only resolution to the crisis compatible with our humanity.[177] But the current horizon is completely inadequate.

That path into the future which seems to Nietzsche alone adequate humanly-- the third path-- is something which can come to pass only if human beings effectively assume responsibility for the existence of human life on earth and are willing and able to venture in such way as makes of it something meaningful by the way they enlarge and enhance it. As Nietzsche puts it at the end of the aphorism about the present as an age of comparison: "We want to understand as grandly as we can the task which the age sets for us: so will posterity bless us for that-- a posterity that will know itself to be as much beyond the original closed-off people-cultures as it is beyond the culture of comparison, but will look back with gratitude on both kinds of culture as on venerable antiquities."[178]

A sketch of the vision of the future which could arise if we took responsibility in an effective way is found in HAH-II/WS-189, entitled "Reason and the tree of humanity". It reads as follows.

> That which in senile short-sightedness you fear as the overpopulation of the earth is precisely what offers to the more hopeful their great task: humankind shall one day become a tree that overshadows the whole earth, bearing many milliards of blossoms that shall all become fruit one

beside the other, and the earth itself shall be prepared for the nourishment of this tree. That the *still small* beginnings of this shall increase in sap and strength [*Kraft*], that the sap shall flow around for the nourishment of the whole and the individual parts through numberless canals-- it is from this and similar tasks that the *standard* is to be derived as to whether a man of the present is useful or useless. The task is unspeakably great and bold: let us all want to act for this, that the tree does not rot away before its time! Human being and action in the whole of time no doubt present themselves to the historical mind in the way in which the ant, with its cunningly raised up hills, presents itself. Judged superficially, one could allow all human existence, like that of the ant, to be grasped under the term 'instinct'. A more rigorous examination lets us perceive how whole peoples, whole centuries, toil to discover and *thoroughly to test* new means for promoting a great human collective [*Ganzen*] and finally the great collective [*Gesamt-*] fruit-tree of humanity; and whatever individuals, peoples and ages may suffer harm in the course of this testing, individuals have always become wise-and-prudent [*klug*] through this harm-suffering, and wisdom-and-prudence [*Klugheit*] slowly flows out from them over upon [*strömt ... über*] the regulative-measures [*Matzregeln*] of whole peoples and whole ages. Even the ants go astray and make mistakes; humanity may well be ruined and wither before its time through the folly of its means; neither for the one nor for the other is there an infallible instinct. What we must do, rather, is to look in the face our great task of *preparing* the earth for a growth of the greatest and most joyful fruitfulness-- a task for reason on behalf of reason!

Now if in our decision-making we respond to the crisis by deciding on a venture to achieve the conscious total-rule [*Gesamtregierung*] of humankind by itself and through it the realization of such a vision, we risk ourselves and the future on a venture which has no assurance in advance of success. Indeed, such a venture could turn out to be self-destructive. Above all this could be so because, if we are successfully to set the good of humanity as a whole as our unifying goal and as part of this to set particular goals serving this universal goal and (along with those particular goals) various tasks for various segments of humanity which must be carried out in order to reach those goals, then human beings must first of all have discovered a hitherto quite unprecedented knowledge [*Kenntnis*] of the conditions [*Bedingungen*] of culture, as a scientific standard [*Matzstab*] for such ecumenical goals. Herein lies the tremendous preparatory task that immediately faces the great spirits of the coming (that is, the twentieth) century.[179] But is such knowledge open to us-- to an 'us' who are inextricably entered into untruth and error?

What the preceding paragraphs summarize is the initial elements in Nietzsche's purified re-statement of the vision he set forth in SE. As in that earlier form, so here: the heart of the matter is culture, and culture as a two-sided affair, both a matter of individual growth and self-cultivation, and a matter of the connected realization of such culture in a social setting so that there is a shared public culture. If the movement into the future is effectively to engender a culture which, both on its higher side and in the community at large, is higher than what belonged to the past and continues on in the present, it needs to keep its eye on, and maintain, a basic contrast within society-- a contrast of types of human being, of a higher and a lower. Culture (both higher and lower) involves a natural and functional differentiation, thus a hierarchical ordering, as regards the creating and enjoying of culture. Nietzsche characterizes the presupposed differentiation in HAH-I/439 ("Culture and caste") as follows.

A higher culture can arise only where there are two different castes in society: that of the workers and that of the leisured [*Mützigen*] who are capable of [*Befähigten*] true leisure [*Mutze*]; or using a stronger expression: the caste of forced labor [*Zwangs-Arbeit*] and the caste of voluntary work [*Frei-Arbeit*]. The view-point of apportioning happiness is not essential when it is a question of the production of a higher culture; in every case, however, the caste of the leisured is the more capable of suffering and suffers more, its enjoyment of existence is less, its task greater. If an exchange between these two castes should take place, so that more obtuse [*stumpferen*], less spiritual families and individuals are demoted from the higher to the lower caste and the freer human beings in the latter obtain entry into the higher, then a state [*Zustand*] is attained beyond which there can be seen only the open sea of indeterminate desires [*Wünsch*]. Thus speaks to us the fading voice of ages past; but where are there still ears to hear it?

The future to be worked for, then, must be visualized in two references: one, in reference to the creating and embodying of an overall culture (the higher expression in the higher few, the lower in the communal whole); and two, in reference to the larger matrix-- of persons, classes, functions, works-- which is not itself cultural (higher or lower) but without which the realization of the cultural, in individuals and in the community, is not possible. In HAH, Nietzsche offers pointers in both regards, more suggestive than worked out, more sketches of aspects than elaborations expressing or seeking to express a connected and comprehensive formulation. The following seven points of focus show us the directions in which Nietzsche's thought on this matter is now moving.

One point of focus: The leading power in the assumption of responsibility called for is to be Europe, the European community. Such a community is arising.

> Trade and industry, intercourse by letters and books, the community [*Gemeinsamkeit*] of all higher culture, rapid changing of home and landscape, the nomadic life now lived by all who do not own land-- these circumstances are necessarily bringing with them a weakening and finally an abolition of nations, at least the European: so that as a consequence of continual crossing a mixed race, that of European man, must come into being out of them.[180]

The emergence of such a European community is being worked against, consciously or unconsciously, by an artificial nationalism that serves the interests of certain princely dynasties and certain classes of business and society. But "one should not be afraid to proclaim oneself simply a *good European* and actively to work for the amalgamation of nations: wherein the Germans are, through their ancient and tested quality of being the *interpreter and mediator between peoples*, able to be of assistance."[181] The mission and history of such a Europe is to be a continuation of that of the Greeks and to pursue a path first opened up by the Greeks of old. Implicated in this continuing of the light-bringing of the Greeks is to be a lead-taking with an eye to the human race as a whole, not simply to Europeans; and such lead-taking will involve a transforming of something from its Christian heritage.

> The Middle Ages exhibit in the church an institution with a wholly universal goal embracing all humankind, and one that is supposedly concerned with humanity's highest interests; in contrast, the goals of the states and nations exhibited by modern history produce an oppressive impression-- they appear petty, mean, materialistic and spatially limited. But this divergent impression on fantasy should not determine our judgment; for that universal institution responded to artificial needs reposing on fictions which, where they did not yet exist, it was obliged to invent (the need of redemption); whereas the modern institutions help do away with real states of distress. The time is coming when institutions will come into being to serve the true needs common to all men and to cast their fantastic archetype, the Catholic Church, into shadow and oblivion.[182]

Thus Europe would take the lead in understanding and responding to the crisis that concerns human existence on earth, and that would involve the setting of goals that would embrace all humankind and relate to genuine needs of all.

A second point of focus: The venture upon which the European is self-consciously to launch humanity is a real venture, one without any assurance of success in the near future, let alone in the long term. Indeed, in contemporary Europe there is present that spiritual abundance we have spoken of above.

> Culture has arisen like a bell, inside a casing of coarser, commoner stuff (untruth, violence, unlimited expansion of every individual ego, of every individual people: these have been this casing); has the time now come to remove it? Has what was molten [*Flüssige*] become solid [*erstarrt*], have the good, advantageous [*nützlichen*] drives, the habits of the nobler disposition [*Gemütes*], grown so secure and general that there is no longer any need to lean on metaphysics and the errors of the religions, and no need of acts of severity and violence as the strongest cement binding human being to human being, people to people? For the answer to this question, the nod of a god is no longer a help to us: our own insight [*eigne Einsicht*] must here decide.

> Man himself has to take in hand the rule on a grand scale of humanity over the earth [*die Erd-regierung des Menschen*]; it is his 'omniscience' that has to watch over the further destiny [*Schicksal*] of culture with a sharp eye.[183]

Even if we suppose that our reading of the need and the possibility are correct and our venture is to that extent realistic and well-founded, still any success we achieve may be only temporary.

> Perhaps the whole of humanity is no more than a stage in the evolution of a certain species of animal of limited duration: so that man has emerged from the ape and will return to the ape, with no one there to take any interest in this marvelous comic ending. Just as, with the decline of Roman culture and its principal cause, the spread of Christianity, a general uglification of man prevailed within the Roman Empire, so an eventual decline of the general culture of the earth could also introduce a much greater uglification and in the end animalization of man to the point of apelikeness. Precisely because we are able to maintain this perspective in view, we are perhaps in a position to prevent such an end of the future.[184]

We are to venture, then, self-aware to the possibility that even our best efforts may bring no lasting achievement but may lead to a condition in which what we have gained for a while is lost.

A third point of focus: The basic thrust of the venture is to achieve an elevated culture world-wide. Culture as we know it up to now is something developed within a people, only a limited segment of the human race. Still, what do we see there that we can anticipate will hold also for this elevated culture of the future, and will be thus of importance for the projection of the venture on the way to such a universal culture?

The branch of a people [*Volkes*] that preserves itself best is the one in which most persons, by virtue of sharing habitual and undiscussable principles (that is, by virtue of their common belief), have a living sense of community [*lebendigen Gemeinsinn*]; in that branch, sound custom grows strong, the individual learns subordination, and character (a gift at birth) is augmented in its firmness. The danger in such a community is a gradually increasing inherited stupidity, such as haunts all stability like its shadow. In such communities, it is the more unfettered, uncertain, and morally weaker individuals upon whom spiritual progress depends: tenderer and more refined natures who attempt new things, and in general, many things. While countless numbers of this kind perish unnoticed due to their weakness, they nonetheless loosen up the stable element of the community, and from time to time inflict an injury on it; and at this injured and weakened spot, the whole body is as it were inoculated with something new. Its strength must be as a whole sufficient to receive this new thing into its blood and to assimilate and incorporate it. And if that is so, then progress is possible.

Thus we can say: A community capable of continuity and progress contains a tension between many stronger natures (those which can preserve the type), and several weaker natures (those which can help it to evolve). Both types are needed, and need to interact in a certain constructive way. For the community gains stability through the union of the minds of most in belief and communal feeling, but it gains the possibility of progress, of a strengthening of itself by the attainment of higher goals, by virtue of degenerate natures who represent the partial weakening and injuring of the stabilizing force. A people that becomes somewhere weak and fragile but is as a whole still strong and healthy is capable of absorbing the infection of the new and incorporating it to its own advantage.

Now to assure its own survival and progress, the individual human beings within a community need to be educated in a certain way. The basic task of education is to imbue the individual with such firmness and certainty that he can no longer as a whole be in any way deflected from his path; then the educator has to inflict injuries upon him, or employ the injuries inflicted on him by fate, and when he has thus come to experience pain and distress something new and noble can be inoculated into the injured places. It will be taken up into the totality of his nature, and later the traces of its nobility will be perceptible in the fruits of his nature.[185]

What could this teaching of the past mean for a future in which peoples are no longer the vehicle of culture, for a future in which the human race as a whole is that vehicle? Do different peoples still have some role, but a different one than before? Or ... ?

A fourth point of focus: If this differentiation-yet-interplay between the few higher and the many inferior is something to be kept in mind in projecting the venture we are to undertake, it is the weaker few, as the culturally creative, that we must pay closest attention to and understand.[186] We have seen already that the free spirit-- the form of the culturally creative spirit that most occupies Nietzsche's attention at present-- is spirit liberated from tradition and thinking differently from what (on the basis of its origin, environment, its class and profession, or on the basis of the dominant views of the age) would be expected of it.[187] This liberation-from and thinking-differently is effected on the basis of an inner activity, a person's taking responsibility for forming his own opinion about things; in contrast, the fettered spirit-- the rule, in relation to which the free spirit is the exception-- is the one who takes over spiritual principles via socialization (a form of accustoming: *Gewöhnung, Angewöhnung*), and holds to them without appeal to reasons: whose relation to such principles, therefore, is one of 'faith'.[188] It is such faith, such unreasoned holding to 'truths', that gives their force [*Kraft*] and endurance to the various institutional arrangements within a society, including the state-- to "classes, marriage, education, law". And it is the fetteredness [*Gebundenheit*] of views which, through habit become instinct, leads to what is called 'strength of character'. This arises when someone acts from a few but always the same motives, so that his actions attain to a great degree of energy [*Energie*]; if those actions are in accord with the principles held by the fettered spirits, they receive recognition and produce in him who does them the sensation of the good conscience. Few motives, energetic action, and good conscience, constitute what is called strength of character. Now the human being of strong character lacks knowledge of how many possibilities of action there are and how many directions it can take; his intellect is unfree, fettered, because in any given case it presents to him perhaps only two possibilities. Such a limited view arises with the help of one's educational environment, in the measure in which, so far as it is an instrument of socialization, it seeks to present him with only a small range of possibilities, and thus to make him unfree. In such educating, the individual is treated by his educators as though, granted he is something new, what he ought to become is a *repetition*. If he appears at first as something unfamiliar, never before existent, he is to be made into something familiar, often before existent. A child is said to have a good character when it is visibly narrowly determined by what is already existent; by placing itself on the side of the fettered spirits the child first proclaims its awakening sense of community; it is on the basis of this sense of community, however, that it will later be useful to its state or its class.[189] In contrast, the free spirit is one who, during the time of his higher education [*Bildung*], has come to find everything interesting, and who knows how to quickly find the instructive side of a thing and to declare the point where a gap in his thinking can be filled with that instruction or a thought can be confirmed by it. With this quickening and the concentration of energy on the intellectually interesting, boredom vanishes more and more, as does excessive excitability of feeling. In the end the human being with such a spirit goes among human beings as a naturalist among plants, and perceives even himself as a phenomenon which stimulates strongly [*stark anregt*] only his drive to know [*erkennenden Trieb*].[190]

A fifth point of focus: The higher culture that is to be reached is two-sided in its nature, and marked by two sides in tension with each other. At the heart of the highly cultivated person-- now understood as the free spirit-- is the scientific pursuit of truth. For the inquirer, there is much satisfaction gained in that pursuit; but for others who receive the truths gained without themselves being inquirers, eventually these truths become as little sources of satisfaction as the multiplication-table. For most persons, then, science itself and its discoveries provide little pleasure, and indeed, the latter deprive such persons of pleasure by casting suspicion on the consolations of metaphysics, religion, and art. If that suspicion-casting is not countered in them, then

> that greatest source of pleasure to which humankind owes almost all its humanity will become impoverished. For this reason a higher culture must give to human beings a double-brain, as it were two brain-ventricles, one to feel [*empfinden*] science, one to feel non-science: lying side by side, without confusion, separable, able to be closed off. This is a demand of health. In one

realm lies the energy-source [*Kraftquelle*], in the other the regulator: the first must be heated with illusions, one-sidednesses, passions, but the evil and perilous consequences of overheating must be obviated with the aid of scientific knowing. If this demand of higher culture is not satisfied, then the future course of human evolution can be foretold almost with certainty: interest in truth will cease the less pleasure it gives; because they are associated with pleasure, illusion, error and fantasy will step by step gain by struggle the ground they formerly asserted; the ruination of science, a sinking back into barbarism, will be the immediate consequence; humankind will have to begin again at the weaving of its tapestry, after having (like Penelope) unwoven it at night. But who can guarantee to us that it will always find the strength [*Kraft*] for it?[191]

Whether this higher culture is being thought as it is found within the individual or within the community, what is involved is not simply any integration of different powers but such an integration of conflicting powers as sustains both sides in some modified fashion. In the case at hand, such integration is quite difficult. In an aphorism entitled "Parable of the dance" (HAH-I/278), Nietzsche speaks to this matter as follows.

Nowadays, it is to be considered the decisive sign of greater culture when one possesses sufficient strength [*Kraft*] and flexibility [*Biegsamkeit*] to be as pure and rigorous in knowing as at other times one is capable of (as it were) giving poetry, religion and metaphysics, a hundred paces advantage and entering into their power and beauty. Such a position between two so different claims [*Ansprüchen*] is a very difficult one, for science presses for the absolute dominance of its methods, and if this pressure is not relaxed there arises the other danger of a feeble vacillation back and forth between different drives. To open up a glimpse at the resolution of this difficulty, however, if only by way of a likeness, one might recall that the *dance* is not a feeble reeling back and forth between different drives. High culture will resemble an audacious dance: whence, as was said, a great deal of strength and suppleness [*Geschmeidigkeit*] are needed.

With the qualification that this aphorism speaks of higher culture in a time in which poetry, religion, and metaphysics are still important forces, there will be in future, in the contrast and tension of reason and passionate feeling, the same question involved. In culture as Nietzsche is anticipating it, the pull of different sides of our nature will bear on us in our decision-making and -executing as laying claim upon us for a place in the concrete shaping of our being. We need some sort of integration which acknowledges the strength and the strengths of the claim of both sides while effecting a realization of both which balances, harmonizes, them so far as possible. The inward strength which this takes, and the flexibility and adaptability on our part in our decision-making, is what makes high culture possible as a unified affair, both at present and in future.

A sixth point of focus: The spirits in whom the capacity for responsible decision-making about the human future on earth is to be found know an anticipatory envisioning of the higher cultural future which human beings can now project and work for as integral to the effort to give meaning to life. As we have seen earlier, in our discussion of philosophy, the ultimate work of the philosopher is that of a law-giving based on insight, that is, of setting the parameters and guiding the accomplishment of something, not simply of seeing truth. Of such a person, Nietzsche has several images, all in some fashion holding the sense of a force which shapes or moulds or builds, as in the case of a sculptor or an architect.

Thus he speaks of the "genius of culture": If someone wanted to imagine such a genius whose work is culture, he would imagine someone who "manipulates lies, force [*Gewalt*], the most ruthless personal usefulness, as his instruments, and does so with such assurance that he would only be called an evil, demonic being; but his aims [*Ziele*], which here and there shine through, would be great and good. He is a centaur, half animal, half human being, and in addition has angel's wings on his head."[192] Given the aims and goals of a higher culture in which the human reaches its fulfillment, he must make use of the materials he has, and do with current humanity as Cellini did when he was casting his statue of Perseus:

> the liquefied mass threatened to be insufficient, but the statue *shall be* [*sollte*]--thus he threw into it keys and plates and whatever else came to hand. Just so does that genius throw in errors, vices, hopes, delusions, and other things of baser as well as nobler metal, for the statue of humanity must [*mutz*] emerge and be completed; what does it matter if here and there inferior material is employed?[193]

The culture-former in the image of the sculptor might prefer to work only with the best material, but culture is a communal affair so that in the image of the statue of humanity Nietzsche addresses the integration of the culturally creative and the lesser but culturally receptive in one image-- that of the statue of humanity, or the human in its communal realization of the cultivated existence of the future.

Other ways of speaking of this genius stress other sides to the matter. As one example (HAH-I/109), Nietzsche is expressing the wish that one could exchange the falsities of the priest (concerning God and salvation) for truths that would be "as salutary, pacifying, and beneficial" as those errors are. But such truths do not exist; and yet if one has an intellectual conscience, one cannot believe the dogmas of religion and metaphysics, even if one recognizes that the development of humanity has left us "so delicate, sensitive and afflicted [*leidend*]" that one needs a potent means of cure and comfort. A romantic return, say, to Christianity in any form, is not permissible:

> given the current state of knowledge, one can no longer have any association with it without incurably dirtying one's intellectual conscience and abandoning that conscience in front of oneself and others. Those pains may be distressing enough: but without pains one cannot become a leader [*Führer*] and educator [*Erzieher*] of humankind; and woe to him who wants to attempt it but no longer possesses this clean conscience.

This means that any use of lies as tools can not involve one's own belief (or pretended belief?) in them. As another example (HAH-I/243), Nietzsche speaks of future physicians in contrast with present-day physicians.

> There is no profession which admits ascent to such height as that of the physician ... . The highest spiritual development of a physician is not reached when he knows the best and most recent procedures [*Methoden*] and has gained practice in them, and can draw those quick conclusions from effects to causes that make the celebrated diagnostician: he also has to possess an eloquence that adapts itself to every individual and draws out his heart, a manliness at the sight of which all timorousness [*Kleinmut*] (the wormrot of all invalids) takes flight, a diplomat's flexibility [*Geschmeidigkeit*] in mediating between those who require joy if they are to become well and those who for reasons of health must (and can) make others joyful, the astuteness [*Feinheit*] of an agent of police or a lawyer-advocate in comprehending the secrets of a soul without betraying them-- in short, a good physician now needs the art-skills and art-privileges of all the other professions; thus equipped he is then in a position to become a benefactor to the whole of society through the augmentation of good works, spiritual joy and fruitfulness, through the prevention of evil thoughts, intentions, acts of roguery (whose revolting source is so often the belly), through the production of a spiritual-physical aristocracy (as promoter and preventer of marriages), through the benevolent amputation of all so-called torments of soul and pangs of conscience: only thus will he come to be savior from being 'medicine-man', and need to perform no miracles, and have no need of having himself crucified.

The final point of focus: The future being anticipated is no utopia,[194] nor will it contain all of the excellences of earlier stages in the evolution of humankind.[195] But one can anticipate that the path there will involve the loosing of forces destructive of the culture of the past and present; at the same time, it will involve the developing of science and the effort to integrate into any construction of the culture to come its "unimpeachable truths" and to build "eternal works" using them.[196] Most fundamentally, however, when it emerges the highest sphere of that higher culture to come will be defined by a plurality of competing and conflicting creative spirits. Culture concerns a cultivation and refinement which involves taste, and within the sphere of taste, a sovereign authority [*Herrschaft*]. But in the future Nietzsche anticipates, this authority will lie in the hands of 'oligarchs', not a 'monarch'. Speaking of these "oligarchs of the spirit" (HAH-I/261), Nietzsche claims that

> despite their spatial and political separation, they constitute a society whose members not only belong together but *also know* and *recognize* one another .... The spiritual superiority which formerly divided and created hostility now tends to *unite*: how could the individual affirm himself and, against every current, swim on his own course through life if he did not see here and there others of his own kind living under the same conditions and take them by the hand, in struggle against both the ochlocratic character of the half-spirited and the half-educated and the attempts that occasionally occur to erect a tyranny with the aid of the masses? The oligarchs have need of one another, in one another they have their best joy, they understand the signs of one another-- but each of them is nonetheless free, he fights and conquers in *his own* place, and would rather perish than submit.

Any such oligarch will aspire to and embody power [*Macht*] in his own being and work, and have lordship [*Herrschaft*] in virtue of the impact of that power on others, as we saw earlier in our discussion of "power". That impact of the higher on the lower is liberating to the lower, but at the same time, by its dominance, confining as well, in a confinement which is felt (on the part of the lower) as the needed stable matrix within which it can function well. But so far as the higher culture of the future is to be achieved by way of a variety of creative figures in competition with each other for reaching the heights, it will have been anticipated by the Greeks, in (say) the figure of the Greek tragedians and their competition to be the best, the most excellent, and to define the standard itself of excellence.[197]

Epilogue

In HAH the free-spirited thinker has taken center stage in Nietzsche's delineation of humanity in its perfection, while the poet and poetry have taken a secondary place. Nonetheless, in HAH-II/ MMO-99 ("The poet as path-pointer for the future"), Nietzsche suggests a role which the poet could take in fostering the future which the thinker is envisioning. For of the poetic power [*Kraft*] available to human beings today, there is a surplus [*überschüssige*] that is not used up in giving form [*Gestaltung*] to life. That surplus "ought [*sollte*] without remainder to be dedicated not to representing the present or reanimating-and-condensing the past but to one purpose, namely, pointing the way to [*Wegweisen für*] the future." What he has in mind here is not that the poet should (say) portray in images a fantasy national economy of conditions favorable for a people and society and image as well the enabling of these. Rather, as earlier the artist created images of gods, so now he should imaginatively develop a fair image of the human being and scent out those cases in which, *in the midst of* our modern world and reality and without any artificial withdrawal from or warding off of this world, the great and beautiful soul is still possible, still able to embody itself in harmonious and well-proportioned states [*Zustände*] and thus acquire visibility, duration and the status of a model [*Vorbildlichkeit*]. In doing this, the poet would help to create the future through exciting envy and emulation.

> Strength [*Kraft*], goodness, mildness, purity and an involuntary inborn moderation [*Mass*] in persons and actions; a level ground which gives repose and joy to the feet; a luminous sky mirrored in countenances and events; knowledge and art blended to a new unity; the spirit dwelling together with its sister, the soul, without presumptuousness and envy and evoking from what sets them in opposition and contrast [*Gegensätzlichen*] not the impatience of contention but rather a graceful seriousness [*die Grazie des Ernstes*]--: all this would make up the embracing, universal, golden background upon which now first the delicate [*zarten*] distinctions between the different embodied ideals would then constitute the actual painting-- that of the ever increasing elevation of the human being.

It is clear, then, that his vision of the future centers in a certain conception of humanity, and in particular, of a higher-and-better humanity which, while exhibiting certain shared features, is bodied forth in different types. The image of such humanity is definite enough to allow of a poetic rendering, one that makes use of reality-- and thus nothing superstitious or fantastic, as with past poets-- but a "selected reality" only.[198] The point is to call forth in appeal, to create longing, and through this, to help bring the full reality to pass. In this idea, we have an anticipation of the poet-creator of TSZ.

CHAPTER 10
Dawn

In the second phase of Nietzsche's thought the work which follows HAH, entitled *Dawn*, breaks some important new ground but mostly explores and refines matters opened up on the paths which were taken in the preceding work. The composition is still aphoristic, with the 575 titled aphorisms being segregated into five untitled Books. In his retrospects, Nietzsche emphasizes its attention to morality, something pointed to by its sub-title ("Thoughts on moral prejudices"). But for our purposes, the work is significant more broadly, and in particular for refinements which confirm and expand upon the second main theme we considered in HAH, namely, human agency. But it addresses the first theme as well, namely, philosophy, and offers scattered points that are significant for our purposes on the third theme, concerning the crisis marking the present and relating to the future of human life on earth. As before, the concern here is to take note of those developments of themes which manifest his ideas of time and temporality; there are, however, no refinements or modifications of these ideas themselves, only important preparations for a significant modification that comes in GS.

A. Philosophy

At times Nietzsche has a way of speaking of philosophy oversimply, as a reflective transcription of an individual's life.[1] But it is no narration of that life as a temporal affair, nor simple characterization of it in its private and public features (the person's drives and habits, the events and happenings in it), that he has in mind. It is the person's thoughtful effort, drawing on what is becoming disclosed in his/her life as it unfolds, to gain an understanding which catches in truthful fashion the nature of the problematic of *human* existence, not simply of his/her own existence. Since the philosopher's seeking is open to others to attempt, others can discover in exploring their own lives the meaning of his ideas and confirm or dispute his interpretation of the matters of common concern.

In the self-critical turn which his thought took in HAH, we have seen Nietzsche raising questions about this matter of our access to truth, especially as it now seems to him that access is more problematic than he had noted in the works of his first-phase thought. "For whom is truth there?" That is the title of D/424, an aphorism which gives us a pointer into what enters into inquiry and its consummation as he now conceives these. Given that our primordial practical concern is with something other than truth, namely, meaning, to seek truth regardless of its bearing (favorable or otherwise) on our life's sharing in meaning requires of us the sort of disciplined effort which we have seen being pointed to in HAH. In this aphorism in D, Nietzsche claims two things: one is that truth ("*as a whole and interconnected thing*") is there *only for* souls which are "at once powerful [*mächtigen*] and harmless, full of joyfulness and peace"-- he names Aristotle as an example; the second is that not only are such souls alone able to find themselves in the presence of truth, but they alone are really seeking it. For, to begin with, no matter how proud others may be of their intellect and their freedom of thought, they are seeking cures for what is unhealthy in themselves, not truth. Moreover, truth is such that one needs strength to allow it to emerge whole and to face it. For given our need for meaning, we are prone to link truth and contribution to our sharing in meaning, and to discount that there are depressing, ugly, hostile truths. If we can not overcome the presumption that all truth is meaning-confirming, we can not allow ourselves to see what is truly there. In that case, our thinking must be (in greater or lesser measure) a form of wishful thinking. Successfully to overcome this presumption requires the strength of the powerful in soul, of a human being healthy in mind, body, and soul.

What else enters into and determines the character of inquiry, and likewise, the coming face to face with truth and the apprehension of it? Various further aphorisms in *Dawn* offer us pointers into the directions in which Nietzsche's thought is advancing now to make intelligible this matter in its various sides, moral and otherwise. Let us survey these aphorisms, and take up with them in an order that will bring us back to the question of D/424 and will suggest that-- and how-- Nietzsche's analysis, when sorted out, is taking place at different levels at different times.

D/539 ("Do you know what you want?") gives us our starting point.

> Has the anxiety never plagued you, that you might not be at all fit [*nicht ... taugen*] for knowing the truth? The anxiety that your mind [*Sinn*] may be too dull and even the subtle sensitivity [*Feingefühl*] of your seeing still much too coarse? If you noticed it at some time, what kind of will ruled [*waltete*] behind your seeing? For example, did you notice yesterday how you wanted to see *more* than someone else, today *differently* from someone else, or how from the very first you longed to find agreement with, or the opposite of, what others fancied they had found previously! Oh shameful craving [*Gelüste*]! Have you noticed how you sometimes were on the lookout [*ausspäht*] for something which affected you strongly [*Starkwirkenden*], sometimes for something that soothed [*Beruhigenden*] you-- because you happened to be tired! Always full of secret predeterminations of *how* truth must be constituted in order for you-- precisely you-- to be able to accept it! Or do you believe that today, since you are frozen and dry like a bright morning in winter and have nothing weighing on your heart, you had better eyes? Are warmth and enthusiasm not needed to provide *justice* to a thing of thought?-- *and that precisely is what is meant by seeing*! As though you *were able* to traffic with things of thought any differently from the way you do with human beings! In this traffic too there is the same morality, the same honorableness, the same reservations [*Hintergedanke*], the same slackness, the same timidity-- your whole lovable and hateful ego! Your physical tiredness [*Ermattungen*] will give to things a pale-and-tired [*matte*] coloration, your fever will make monsters out of them! Does your morning not shine upon things differently from your evening? Do you not fear finding again in the cave of every kind of knowledge your own ghost [*Gespenst*], as the fine-spun-veil [*Gespinst*] in which truth has hidden itself [*verkleidet*] from you? Is it not a horrible comedy in which you so thoughtlessly [*unbedachtsam*] want to play a role [*mitspielen*]?

While Nietzsche is here calling attention mainly to our encounter with thoughts, in the same way he would have us notice what we bring to bear when, attending to things in their presence, we seek to think them and do them justice. What is at issue is not the matter of simply noticing things sufficiently well to be able to make our way in the world: half-truths can readily serve us in that. The question is truth, and our effort is to grasp it, to see it accurately, to find and know things in their truth. Now there is considerable variation in the way we actually-- or even can, on any occasion-- register and notice, let alone understand, things; and this is so on a variety of grounds. We need a certain degree of sensitivity and certain sharpness of mind to register and discern some things. And even with these, honest and close attention is called for, but requires energies we may not have and cannot simply command at the time needed. In any case, different feelings and moods disclose even the same things differently, and incline us to pay attention in certain ways rather than others and to interpret the disclosure of things in this way rather than in another. Thus we always need to consider whether or not, when we say at any time that we "see" something truly, we are actually in the presence of things in their full and undistorted self-disclosure and are looking at them in a way that enables us to do justice to them.

Looked at closely, the apprehension of truth involves two complementary things: one, the register of and attention to presence and its disclosive force, and the other, the interpretation and understanding of what we are seeing. On the matter of interpretation and understanding, Nietzsche makes a differentiation, as in D/500 ("Against the grain").

> A thinker can for years on end force himself to think against the grain: I mean, to pursue not the thoughts which offer themselves to him from within him but those to which an office, a prescribed schedule, an arbitrary kind of industriousness, seem to oblige [*verpflichten*] him. In the end, however, he will fall sick; for this apparently moral overcoming of himself will ruin his nervous energy just as thoroughly [*gründlich*] as any regularly indulged in excess could do.[2]

The thoughts which offer themselves from within are those which come from out of one's very own self, and that means eventually, out of a self strong in itself, *strong in its capacity for responsibility*. Such thoughts are formed and enter into consciousness only of their own accord. Even when they emerge in the midst of disciplined inquiry, they do not do so in function of any method; there are no methods (and in particular, none in the 'scientific' form of inquiry which is now Nietzsche's model for responsible thought) which can guarantee the production of the needed insights and whose use alone can bring us knowledge. In any case, even while it is alone the self-generated thoughts of a person strong in this way that could reach into the heart of things, to discern and comprehend the truth visible there, not all such thoughts do this. In inquiry we need not only to test what appears to us, attending to it now in this way and now in that, trying out how it looks when we approach it with this-feeling and then again with that-feeling and address it in this-manner and then again in that-manner: only in this way can we bring it before ourselves with the clarity and fullness of disclosure that opens up the possibility of apprehending it in its truth.[3] We need as well to test even the thoughts which come from within us, and to recognize the need for marshalling evidence even for ideas that on first sight seem very illuminating and convincing. In this matter of weighing the disclosive power of various experiences and the aptness of our own interpretative efforts, we need an "audacious morality"[4], the morality of an adventurer and discoverer of new lands who is guided by the reaching for justice and is aware how readily our feelings may color and hide truth at the same time as they disclose something, and how limited the insight may be in even the thoughts which come from out of ourselves. In its fundamental nature, inquiry is an audacious essay and experiment.

On this matter of the thought-side of the effort, in D/426 ("Color-blindness of thinkers") Nietzsche speaks from a further perspective of this need for testing thoughts.

> *Every thinker paints his world and each thing in fewer colors than are actually there*, and is blind to certain individual colors. This is a deficiency, but not merely one. For by virtue of this approximation and simplification, he sees *in the things* harmonies of colors which possess great charm and can constitute an enrichment of nature. Perhaps it was only in this way that humankind first learned to take *pleasure* in the sight [*Anblick*] of existence: existence, that is, was in the first instance presented to them in one or two colors, and thus presented harmoniously. Humankind then as it were practised on these few shades before being able to go over to a greater range. And even today many an individual works himself out of a partial color-blindness into a richer seeing and distinguishing: in which process, however, he not only discovers new enjoyments but is also obliged to *give up and relinquish* some of his earlier ones.

Even at its best, our thinking renders things in simplified fashion, grasping them in limited ways and (on the strength of that) seeing connections, making sense of matters. But as we attend to presence more closely and more diversely, our thinking is capable of gaining complexity, grasping things which we did not see or were ignored before; and often enough this brings insight into the previously unnoticed limits of our prior thought, and not simply a more complex grasping of what is there to be seen. Richer distinguishing and seeing means loss as well as gain.

Yet even if thought becomes more complex, it operates for the most part with language, and at least seeks to bring things into speech to formulate and communicate itself. At the same time, what thinking is attentive to-- at least so far as inward affairs are the subject of reflection-- for the most part eludes the capacity of language to render it. For example, in regard to inner processes and drives we have words only for the superlative degrees of these; yet there are milder and middle degrees, and lower degrees, which are continually in play and which indeed do much to weave the web of our character and our destiny. In regard to these, exact observation and exact thinking are very difficult and painful. Because the more extreme is more obtrusive to our attention, and can be brought into words and be thought through with their help, it is easy for us-- even when we are the person in whom the processes and drives in question are operative-- to be misled. In fact,

> *we are none of us that* which we appear to be in accordance with the states for which alone we have consciousness and words, and consequently praise and blame; we misunderstand ourselves following those cruder outbursts with which alone we are familiar, we draw a conclusion from material in which the exceptions outweigh the rule, we misread ourselves in this apparently most intelligible [*deutlichsten*] of handwriting of our self.[5]

The way we attend to experience (indeed, for the most part are *able* to attend to it) is such that we naturally form a false opinion even of ourselves: for example, we take the conscious 'ego' as our self.[6]

On this matter of what we can register in the immediacy of our powers of receptivity, Nietzsche claims that however far we go in self-knowledge our image of the collective drives [*gesamten Triebe*] which constitute our being is incomplete. We can scarcely name even the cruder ones, and

> their number and strength, their ebb and flood, their play and counterplay among one another, and above all the laws of their *nourishing* remain wholly unknown to us. This nourishing is therefore a work of chance: our daily experiences throw some prey in the way of now this, now that drive, and the drive seizes it eagerly; but the whole coming and going of these events stands outside any rational connection with the nutritional requirements [*Nahrungsbedürfnissen*] of the collective drives. ... Every moment of our life lets some polyps-arms of our being grow, and others wither, in each case according to the nourishment which the moment bears or does not bear in itself. Our experiences ... are all means of nourishment in this sense, but the nourishment is scattered with blind hand, without knowing about that which is hungry and that which already has superfluity. As a result of this chance nourishment of the parts, the whole fully-grown polyp will be something just as accidental as its becoming has been.[7]

There is, then, a whole side to ourselves, unconscious, unknown to ourselves directly, which nonetheless enters constitutively into the nature of our own being and the character of our experiencing.

Finally, taking the preceding cautions about self-knowledge further, Nietzsche exclaims (in D/116, "The unknown world of the 'subject'"):

> What is so difficult for human beings to grasp is our ignorance [*Unwissenheit*] of ourselves, from the most ancient times till now! Not only in respect of good and evil, but in respect of what is much more essential! The primeval delusion is ever still alive, that one knows and knows quite precisely in every case *how human action is brought about*. ... Actions are *never* what they appear to us to be! We have taken so much pains to learn that external things are not such as they seem to us-- very well! it stands likewise with the inner world! Moral actions are in truth 'something else'-- more, we cannot say: and all actions are essentially unknown.

Of the matter at the very heart of our being, namely, our being active and our living life in active participation in things, we are deeply unknowing, even as we think we know.

So far we have seen Nietzsche thinking on how we can-- and do-- take up with what is given in experience and come in our inquiry to find the truth; certain problematic limitations have appeared as recognizable factors within our experience of inquiry. But so far the very originative base for our knowing, namely, our sensibility, has been taken for granted, and the question has not been raised of whether experience is in fact disclosive in a way that would allow us ever to be directly confronted with truth, leaving aside whether we could apprehend and comprehend it then. Reflection on the powers which open us to things and ourselves in the immediacy of experience-- our sense-powers-- leads us, however, to recognize limitations to this openness. In D/117 ("In prison") Nietzsche remarks on the confining (the imprisoning) character of this openness. "My eyes (however strong or weak) can see only a certain distance, and it is within the space encompassed by this distance that I live and move; the line of this horizon is my immediate fate (in great and small things) [*nächstes grosses und kleines Verhängnis*] from which I cannot escape. Around every being, there is a concentric circle of this sort, which has a mid-point and which is peculiar [*eigentümlich*] to it." Similarly with ears, and sense of touch.

> In accordance with these horizons in which (as in prison-walls) our senses enclose each of us, we *measure* the world, we speak of 'this is near' 'that far', 'this big', 'that small', 'this hard', 'that soft': this measuring, we call sensing [*Empfinden*]-- it is all error, intrinsically [*an sich*] error. According to the number [*Menge*] of experiences and excitations ordinarily [*durchschnittlich*] possible to us at any particular point of time, one measures one's life as being short or long, poor or rich, full or empty; and according to the average [*durchschnittlichen*] human life one measures that of all other creatures-- all of it an error, intrinsically error! If we had eyes a hundredfold sharper for nearness, the human being would appear to us monstrously long; indeed, organs are thinkable in virtue of which he would be sensed [*empfunden*] as immeasurable. On the other hand, organs could be so constituted that whole solar systems were sensed as contracted and packed together like a single cell; and to beings of an opposite order, a cell of the human body could exhibit itself as a solar system in motion, structure, and harmony. The habits of our senses have woven lie and deception into our sensibility [*Empfindung*]: these again are the bases of all our judgments and 'knowledge'-- there is absolutely no escape, no back-way or by-way into the *real world*. We exist within our net, we spiders, and whatever we may catch in it, we can catch nothing at all except that which allows itself to be caught in precisely *our* net.

The sense-medium through which we register things and ourselves in our encounter involves a judging (a measuring, in the examples in question here) in which we take the *appearance* of things to *our* sensibility to *be* things as *they are*. But this perceptual judgment is a function of two things: of what *our* senses can register of other things and ourselves as we interact with our surroundings, and of how this immediate register is taken up into judgment and judged to present things: the "habits of our senses" are actually "habits of the judgment that is part of our sensing". About many of the resultant mis-takings, we can-- and do-- make the attempt at undoing them, and do so concertedly when we try (in and as science) to sort out the 'merely subjective' from what is 'objectively there' and seek to discern correctly how the latter is constituted. But this attempt at rectification and ascertainment of what is 'really there' still takes sense-disclosure as providing the evidence and basis for such objective determination of what is; thereby it still does not address the deeper question, which is not that of whether human senses suffice for the exhaustive disclosure of phenomenal reality but that of whether-- and if so, how-- *any* sense-disclosure *ever* reveals *reality*.

This deeper question is approached in D/118, in which Nietzsche addresses briefly the question, "What is our neighbor?"

> What then do we comprehend [*begreifen*] of our neighbor [*Nächste*] but his bounds [*Grenzen*]: I mean, that with which he impresses and (as it were) engraves himself on and into us? We comprehend nothing of him except *the changes in us* of which he is the cause [*Ursache*]-- our knowing of him is like an empty space *that has been formed*. We attribute to him the sensations his actions evoke [*hervorrufen*] in us, and thus give him a false, inverted [*umgekehrte*] positivity. In accordance with our knowledge of ourselves, we form [*bilden*] him into a satellite of our own

system; and when he shines for us, or grows dark, and we are the ultimate cause of both-- we believe, nonetheless, the opposite! We live in a world of phantoms, an inverted, upside down, empty world which is dreamed of as *full* and *upright*.

There is the mistaking by which we judge a thing of experience (a dog, say) to *be small* by taking up its immediate appearance to us into a judging that attributes smallness to the dog itself. But there is a profounder mis-taking involved in our perception of the dog itself. For as Nietzsche sorts the matter out, what we call the registering in sensibility of a sensible reality (a dog with all its perceptible features) is something other than what it appears to us initially to be. What is really happening in our perceiving is that some other (but unknown and otherwise undisclosed) presence is making a *causal* impact upon ourselves which results in a sensation *in us;* because of the spatial intuition which enables us to register the sense-content in question, we 'see' that sense-content as 'out there' and judge it to belong to and manifest its cause. But what is that cause? Not the dog as a thing of our experience, for all of the component appearances which together make up the dog as a phenomenal thing (as itself *an* appearing thing with a shape, size, color, etc.) are likewise such projections, and projections which are attributed to a cause *which does not itself appear at all*. Thus Nietzsche speaks of the "inverted positivity" that we are projecting back upon the "empty world" (the world of the otherwise undisclosed and unapparent cause of our sensation). Of what character that cause actually is, we have *no direct evidence at all*. As regards it, we only know something bounding, limiting, us in the act of its impacting us causally. All we 'know' directly in our 'experience' of 'it' is *what it has caused* to arise in *our sensibility*-- its appearance as a dog, including the color, shape, and size, we see as belonging to it in those cases in which the sensation has arisen in our eyes; and while in our sensing this color, shape, and size *seem* to us not to be 'in us' but to belong to 'a thing out there', in fact they do not. Indeed, all that we perceive 'out there'-- all that composes the dog as a thing of our experience-- is on a par in this regard. What we directly know in such a case is only our sense-organs, or more precisely, the sensations and sense-contents that have been produced 'in' us. What is really 'there'-- or more precisely, what is the source of that 'appearance' 'out there'-- is a void to us so far as the immediacy of sense is concerned, and (so far as our experience goes) is simply that unrevealed, unknown and unknowable, 'something' which is not itself a content of our sense-experience but is 'causing' the impression that we have and that we project from ourselves back to that something and see as constituting or belonging to a 'thing of appearance'. Thus even in what seems to us our immediate register of things themselves in experience (dogs, trees, etc.), we find ourselves entered in truth into a "world of phantoms", a dream world, created unconsciously in function of the working of something upon us and the reaction which is our sensing.[8]

This view of sense-experience, which sees the experienced world as a kind of intermediate realm arising in the interaction of ourselves with other (unknown and unknowable) beings, depends on some notion of causality as part of the interaction of ourselves and other (otherwise unknown) realities which are impacting our receptivity. Our response to what is being generated in this causality (namely, image representations of the sources of causal impact) is looked at more fully in the latter part of D/119, whose beginning we discussed above. Nietzsche is speaking at the start of this aphorism of the drives at work in our experiencing, seeking nourishment from the states we find ourselves in as we encounter things. He continues the account of what takes place by suggesting that some drives-- for example, hunger-- gain no satisfaction with (in its case) dream food, only with real food; but many drives gain such satisfaction as they do only in a substitute way that compensates for the lack of real nourishment. For dreams (so he claims) are compensatory in nature, wish-fulfillments in the world of fantasy; they thereby give some scope and discharge to our drives, even if it is only in this fantasy way. He goes on to explain how he conceives dreams. The inventions which people our dreams are

interpretations of stimulations of our nervous system [*Nervenreize*] while we are asleep, *very free* and arbitrary interpretations of the motions of the blood and intestines, of the pressure of the arm and the bedclothes, of the sounds made by church bells, weathercocks, night-revellers and other things of the kind. That this text, which is in general much the same on one night as on another, is commented on [*kommentiert*] in such varying ways [*so verschieden*], that the inventive reasoning-faculty [*dichtende Vernunft*] imagines [*sich vorstellt*] today a cause for these same [*dieselben*] nerve-stimulations [*Nervenreize*] so very different from the cause it imagined yesterday: the reason [*Grund*] of this is that today's prompter [*Souffleur*] of the reasoning-faculty was different from yesterday's-- a different *drive* wanted to gratify itself, to be active, to exercise itself, to refresh itself, to discharge itself-- it was precisely in its high flood, and yesterday another was. Waking life does not have this *freedom* of interpretation possessed by the life of dreams (it is less inventive and unbridled)-- must I, however, add the detail that when we are awake our drives likewise do nothing but interpret nerve-stimulations [*die Nervenreize interpretieren*] and, according to their requirements [*Bedürfnisse*], posit [*ansetzen*] their 'causes'? that there is no *essential* difference between waking and dreaming? that even when we compare very different stages of culture the freedom of waking interpretation in the one is in no way inferior to the freedom exhibited in the other in dreaming? that our moral judgments and evaluations too are only images and fantasies concerned with [*über*] a physiological process [*Vorgang*] unknown to us, a kind of attendant [*angewöhnter*] language for designating [*bezeichnen*] certain nerve-stimulations [*Nervenreize*]? that all our so-called consciousness is a more or less fanciful commentary on [*über*] an unknown, perhaps unknowable, but felt [*gefühlten*] text? ... What then are our experiences? Much *more* that which we put into them [*hineinlegen*] than that which lies therein! Or must it even be said: in themselves, nothing lies in them? Experiencing [*Erleben*] is an inventive-poetizing [*Erdichten*]?

What waking life adds to life while asleep and dreaming is simply a fulness to the conscious side of our functioning. But all experiencing, conscious and unconscious, is internal to an interacting, and all involves in some way this inventive poetizing whereby the immediate register of nerve-stimuli occasioned by unknown sources is transcribed in fantasy and the resultant image is projected and given meaning of one sort or another.[9] The function of the poetized elements is first and foremost to clothe the 'void' with content that purports to be the appearance of the source of the stimulation that is occasioning the poetizing.

One final facet of this matter of experience. Beyond the drives which lead to further interpretation of the 'cause' of a sensation (that is, of the appearance we take to be that of the 'cause') so that we see the 'cause' differently in virtue of different drives animating the interpreting, feeling in general works in similar fashion, and even more broadly, the total inward condition of the human being as a whole. Thus for example, in D/210 ("The 'in itself'"), Nietzsche speaks of how we used to ask about the "laughable" as if there were things external to us which had this as their property, but now we ask about laughing and its origin. Similarly, "we have reflected and finally established that there is nothing good, nothing beautiful, nothing sublime, nothing evil in itself, but indeed there are soul-states in which we impose such words upon things outside and within us. We have again *taken back* the predicates of things, or at least remembered that it was we who *lent* them to things ... ." Or again, in an aphorism (D/114, "Of the knowledge of the sufferer") which speaks anonymously to his own condition and experience, Nietzsche speaks of the condition of a person suffering dreadful and protracted torment, but at the same time being undisturbed in mind.[10] He looks out upon things from this condition with a "terrible coldness", and

> all those small lying charms [*Zaubereinen*] in which things ordinarily swim when the eye of the healthy regards them have disappeared for him; indeed, he himself lies there before himself without color and plumage. If until then he has been living in some perilous world of fantasy [*Phantasterei*], this supreme sobering-up through pain is the means of extricating him from it-- and perhaps the only means.

The undisturbed mind that would seek to be just in its judgment would "think with contempt of the warm, comfortable misty world in which the healthy person thoughtlessly wanders; he thinks with contempt of the noblest and most beloved of the illusions in which he himself formerly indulged." And yet, such a mind would also resist the pressure and insinuation of pain to form a judgment about life on the basis of this insight into the naked colorless world, and that would mean: to conclude about it in pessimistic vein. With the first glimmering of relief, of convalescence, comes the desire not only to get beyond the pain but also to get beyond the struggle against pain: all has become too personal, what is needed now is a depersonalization.

> We gaze again at man and nature-- now with a more desiring [*verlangenderen*] eye: we recall with a sorrowful smile that we now know something new and different about them, that a veil has fallen-- but we find it so *refreshing* again to see *the subdued light of life* and to emerge out of the terrible sobering brightness in which as sufferers we formerly saw things and saw through things. We are not annoyed when the charms of health resume their game-- we look on as if transformed, gentle and still wearied. In this condition one cannot hear music without weeping.

If the world devoid of the "small lying charms" in which the things of the ordinary healthy human being swim is not itself reality but reality as it appears to a painfully suffering sick person, and if that same world gains an aura of enticement and allurement which is counterpart to the feelings and desires of the healthy person in everyday life and is not part of reality itself, then ... what is reality? In what condition do we see *truth*, see *reality itself* in its truth? Is there any? Or ... ?

Since the time when we posed the questions of what (according to Nietzsche) enters into and determines both the character of inquiry and the coming face to face with truth in such way that we may apprehend it, we have sketched out lines of thought suggested in a variety of aphorisms. These have pointed to various factors and limitations involved in our access to, our attention to, our interpretation of, and our apprehending of, the things of ordinary experience and even within scientific inquiry. And we have arrived at the suggestion of a basic limitation, whose import is briefly summarized in two aphorisms. In D/483 ("Satiety with the human") Nietzsche records the following brief anonymous exchange:

> A. Know! Indeed, but always as a human being! What? Always sit before the same comedy, play in the same comedy? Never able to see into things out of any eyes other than *these*? And what innumerable types of being may there be whose organs are better fit for knowledge! What at the end of all its knowledge has humankind known?-- its organs! And that means, perhaps: the impossibility of knowledge! Misery and disgust!-- B. This is an evil attack-- *reason* attacks you! But tomorrow you will again be in the midst of knowing and with that also in the midst of unreason, which means: in the midst of the *joy* of the human. Let us go down to the sea!

Now if knowledge were indeed impossible for us and we could know this, then the ultimate reason for that impossibility would seem summed up in abbreviated form in another aphorism, namely, D/438, entitled "Man and things": "Why does man not see things? He himself stands in the way: he conceals things."

In sum, in the series of aphorisms we have been considering, we have seen Nietzsche pointing to experience as involving us in a concealing as well as a revealing, due to the complex way in which our disclosive powers are constituted and function. Experience begins in the receptivity of pure sensing, becomes ramified by the judging inherent in sensing, and becomes even more elaborate due to the drives and feelings that affect and steer such judging. But not only are there experientially discernible reasons for questioning whether our efforts can genuinely lead to knowledge of the world of experience; there is also reason for thinking reality ultimately eludes us, being unknowable because knowing depends on sensing for the givenness of the to-be-known. And yet, we started our discussion from an aphorism (D/424) entitled "For whom is truth there?" How square this beginning and this end? As a step in this direction, we can recognize: Nietzsche's discussion here, as in his discussion of science in HAH, is taking place on different levels in different places.

Corresponding with the first level of the science discussion are discussions which take for granted the givenness of appearance in sensing and acknowledge the function of interpretation, the play of drives and feelings, the differentiation of conscious and unconscious, the limits of conscious cognizance of unobtrusive components, and the like. Reflection here accepts our senses as realistically disclosing the sensible world that we ordinarily encounter and engage with and that science concerns itself with when it seeks to sort out what is objectively the case and what is merely subjective.

Corresponding with the second level of the discussion of science is an interpretation of the distinctive and limiting character of human sense-organs and their immediate disclosure, according to which the sensibly-apparent world does not, in any of its apparent features, directly manifest reality as it seems to us ordinarily to do; what sense discloses is only a specious representation of an unknown (and in principle unknowable) source whose working on our receptivity occasions a perception which emerges by virtue of our transcription into sense-images of the nerve-stimuli resulting from this working and our projection (in what we call sense-perception) of such images back upon the presumed source. In the analysis which claims this conclusion, reflection relies at the start on the veracity of the disclosive immediacy of our perception of sensible-presence, but builds an objective account whose conclusion ends up undermining that veracity.[11]

Now in the discussions in HAH and D both, there is a third level, that on which Nietzsche himself is operating in his account of the matters on the other two levels. Here the same question about access to truth recurs, but as yet only the barest hint emerges of how Nietzsche will see the matter when his thought advances the recognition (begun in HAH) of reality as something lying *beyond the distinction of 'in itself' from 'in relation to us'*. That hint, provided in the aphorism with which we started this discussion in *Dawn*, points us to the strength, the power, of mature human capacity as enabling us to see-- and eventually to say-- reality in its truth. But how is this possible? We will return to this matter later; for the moment, let us simply raise the following questions.

If reality is an interactive affair and human experience is the disclosure-realm in and for the humans who are party to the interacting, then the strength and power of human capacity which enables truth to come to be there for the participant is something exercised in the interacting and must be such as enables this interacting itself to come into apt experiential disclosure in its interactive character. That is the meaning of the 'truth' being 'there'. But that would not be possible if understanding is always 'knowing objects', for the interacting can not be objectified, distanced as object. If, however, interactive reality can be understood 'from within' and if understanding can be other than objective knowing, then what about the understanding of this understanding itself, and with it, of the sense-perceiving which has a role in it? Since such understanding and its attendant sense-perceiving are elements in the human participation in such reality, we would presumably understand them in the way we understand reality, not in a knowing which objectifies. If that is so, the second-level analysis offered by Nietzsche can not be to the point, at least not fully. For failing to differentiate between cause in two different references and meanings ('cause *of* experience' vs. 'cause *within* experience'), it proceeds by giving an *objective* account of sense-perception as if it were *wholly phenomenal*, one *phenomenon* among others. That is, it regards sense-perception as having a being which after all is *not interactive*! If we can not do justice to sense-perception as a first-personally operative facet of a human being's being and activity by taking this path, what manner of address and what terms would be relevant for understanding it and its disclosive working within the interacting? How would it become intelligible to the participant to whose capacity and working it belongs as facet of his/her being and activity? And how would all this relate to the power (of soul) that Nietzsche alludes to in D/424?

B. Agency

Thinking is a kind of venturing, and in that way attests the nature of activity in general: in all that we undertake, our decision-making enters us upon a venturing in which something is at stake and we are risking in various ways-- wagering that doing-this is what is called for, and in doing-this, risking ourselves and our becoming in such a venturing, and so on. In HAH, Nietzsche has developed a critique of the way he understood this matter in the first phase of his thought, and in rejecting free will and obligation (so far as it presupposes free will), has sought to understand this venture character as an affair in which necessity reigns. In *Dawn*, he would bring this altered vision to expression by way

of a certain image found in D/130 (entitled "Purposes? Volitions?"). According to the account offered there, we have accustomed ourselves to believing in two realms: one is that of purpose and will,
the other that of accident. In the latter realm, things happen in a meaning-less way: there is no 'Why?
For what?' that is relevant, only stupid accident. The Greeks spoke of this realm as Moira, and the
Christians saw in this realm the face of the workings of a God whose ways and purposes were dark
and hidden but who would in the end 'bring all to glory'. In recent times, this Christian idea has
come to be doubted, but rather than go back to Moira, human beings have recast the old fable. Now
in what had been taken as the realm of purposes and reason, we have learned: not all that is called
'purpose' and 'will' is purpose or will. But

> if you wanted to conclude: 'Is there therefore only one realm, that of accident and stupidity'--
> you must then add: indeed, perhaps there is only one realm, perhaps there are neither purposes
> nor volitions, and we have only imagined these. Those iron hands of necessity which shake the
> dice-box of chance play their game for an infinite length of time, so that there *have* to occur casts
> which look perfectly similar to purposiveness and rationality of every degree. *Perhaps* our acts
> of will, our purposes, are nothing other than precisely such casts-- and we are merely too limited
> and too vain to comprehend our most extreme limitation, namely, that we ourselves shake the
> dice-box with iron hands, that we ourselves in our most intentional actions do nothing more than
> play the game of necessity. Perhaps!-- In order to get beyond this *perhaps*, one has already to
> have been a guest in the underworld and beyond all surfaces, and at the table of Persephone to
> have wagered and cast with the goddess herself.

The image involved here is meant to reinforce two things: that 'necessity' reigns, but that such
necessity is of a sort that works to produce casts of dice in a game in which something is at stake and
some wager is being made. If we are prone to thinking of this casting in our own case as an act of
conscious choice in which reason and purpose are decisively at work, this is a mistaking of the matter,
a misconstruing of what we are doing and involved in in such acts. But the matter being mis-taken
is in reality a casting, and one whose necessity involves risk, wagering, and chance; these take place
beneath the surface which is our consciousness, at the very heart of ourselves as active beings, and
take place in that very underground place-- and in company with that dominant underground power--
where all the life-and-death issues of existence are decided. However much or little the conscious
side of our venturing registers the matter, however much we may misinterpret it on that basis, our
casting has *this necessity* as its character, that it is *with our very own hands* that we make the casts
we do and take part in that deciding. In the image of this account, those hands are our nature as active
beings, and in particular, the decision-making power which is ours by nature.

1. Decision-making, development, and maturation

As in HAH, the focus of Nietzsche's concern in the matter of our initiative is with the activity that
arises out of it: presumably the casts of chance are of that character.[12] But in *Dawn*, the matter also
becomes taken up in some reference to the life for which we assume responsibility, and thereby a
theme of the first phase of his thought returns, its re-conception within the new horizon of his second
phase being further developed beyond what we saw in HAH.[13]

In D/560 ("What stands open to us"), Nietzsche speaks as follows.

> One can dispose of one's drives like a gardener and, although few know it, nurture the germs,
> buds, and shoots of anger, pity, pondering, vanity, as fruitfully and profitably as any beautiful
> fruit on a trellis; one can do it with the good or bad taste of a gardener, and as it were in French
> or English or Dutch or Chinese manner; one can also let nature rule [*Walten*] and be concerned
> [*sorgen*] only with a little embellishment and tidying-up here and there; one can, finally, without
> paying any attention to them at all, let the plants grow up in their natural favoring-conditions and
> hindering-conditions [*Begünstigungen und Hindernissen*] and fight their fight out among them-

selves-- indeed, one can take delight in such a wilderness, and desire precisely this delight even if one has his distress [*Not*] with it. All this stands open to us [*steht uns frei*], but how many know that it stands open? Do the majority not *believe* in *themselves* as in completed *fully-developed facts* [*vollendete ausgewachsene Tatsachen*]? Have the great philosophers not put their seal on this prejudice with the doctrine of the unchangeability of character?

It is not clear how this image relates to the account in D/119, except that at the very least it modifies somewhat the dependence on chance for the nourishment of the drives and feelings within. I say "somewhat", for the givenness of what will nourish is that, an ultimate complicity of the circumstantially other and of our own being amidst it. But within what is given overall, we may move to find the sunshine and rain that will nourish this or that bud, and may do so with some intentionality if we are able to recognize the connection, to identify the readiness of what is within, and to find the appropriate nourishing conditions from within circumstance.

In discussing HAH, we noted how in HAH-I/107 Nietzsche spoke of our decision-making as involving our "letting" the longing for self-enjoyment draw us in this direction or in that one, so that our drives came into effective play as motivating powers under the condition of this working of the decision-making capacity in us. Here the image is of the same 'inner act', but with a different side of it to the fore, namely, the inward issue of such letting. For acting on drives strengthens them, and according as we strengthen different drives in ourselves (or find different ones growing stronger, if we are not attentive in the manner of the gardener or are attentive only in minimal fashion), so we ourselves become different. Given the complexity of our being as agents, and given that it is not simply drives but (say) talents that clamor for attention and for our allowing them to come into play, the image here is another way of speaking of the basic task of the artist in ourselves working to shape our own becoming.[14]

Such attentiveness to what is within and (say) to its strengthening or weakening is particularly important at the crucial turning point which is youth, but it is significant far earlier than that. For even in childhood, what is present and happening within can receive reinforcement and become developed inwardly in virtue of the way the child's relatives and familiars act and the child's imitation of what he/she finds bodied forth in his/her surroundings. And his/her later condition can have developed with such strength as to be difficult to resist or modify in time, even if it is only the issue of "discipline and habit".[15]

The most striking refinement of Nietzsche's thought in this area of decision-making and our growth lies in the way he now also seeks to bring forward within the new framework of inquiry and thought an idea of that development which is central to our agency, namely, our maturation and the discovery and actualization of the creativity which is at the center of our life as mature agents. Much as Plato does in the *Symposium*, Nietzsche uses the image of pregnancy to convey a point quite kindred to that of the Platonic Socrates, that what lies at the heart of our being is a creative nucleus which evolves and flowers in a way that this image can readily convey. Thus in D/552 ("Ideal selfishness [*Selbstsucht*]"), he urges: in the holy condition of pregnancy, we do all that we do in the unspoken belief that it must somehow benefit what is coming to be within us, that because how we live and act will somehow affect the life that is developing within us we must live and act in such way as will be beneficial to it. Given our condition at this time, "everything is veiled, full of presentiment [*ahnungs-voll*], we know nothing of what is taking place [*wie es zugeht*], we wait and try to be *ready*." At the same time

a pure and purifying feeling of profound irresponsibility [*Unverantwortlichkeit*] reigns [*waltet*] in us, almost that which the spectator has before the curtain is raised. *It is growing, it* is coming to light: *we* have in hand nothing for determining either its value or the hour of its coming. The sole influence assigned to us is the indirect [*mittelbaren*] one of blessing and protecting. 'What is growing here is something greater than we are' is our most secret hope: we prepare everything for it so that it may come happily [*gedeihlich*] into the world: not only everything that may prove useful to it, but also the joyfulness and laurel-wreaths of our soul. It is in *this state of conse-*

cration that one should live! It is a state one can live in! And if what is expected is an idea, a deed-- towards every essential accomplishing [*wesentlichen Vollbringen*] we have no other relationship than that of pregnancy and ought [*sollten*] to blow to the winds all presumptuous talk of 'willing' and 'creating'. This is the right *ideal selfishness*: continually to watch over [*wachen*] and care for [*sorgen*] and to keep our soul still, so that our fruitfulness shall come to a fair [*schön*] fulfillment [*Ende*]! Thus in this indirect [*mittelbaren*] manner, we watch over and care for to the benefit of all; and the mood in which we live, this mood of pride and gentleness, is a balm which spreads far around us, even on to restless souls.

The image of pregnancy (whether it issue in a thought or a deed, thus whatever type of activity is involved in its birth) signifies our harboring somewhere deep within the makings and the embryonic life-form of some reflective or practical accomplishment. We know only that something is taking shape within us, gathering nourishment and growing, and we can only guess and hope about what will eventually come forth. In the meantime, we are drawn to live and act in a way that will facilitate its evolving until the time comes for its birth and entry into the world for all-- ourselves included-- to see. In EH, we see what eventually is to become of the idea sketched out here: the embryonic life is the agent's destiny, and more precisely, the organizing idea and task that is hiddenly at work long before it surfaces and is making itself felt in ventures that are (unknown to the agent) preparing him/her for eventually undertaking that task.[16]

Nietzsche speaks here of a selfishness, and means that, because of the primordial standing in us of life's drive toward self-enjoyment, our efforts involve an at-stake which requires of us above all the strengthening of our capacities for taking part in life. According to the image of D/522, that strengthening has brought us to the place of a capacity to order and organize life with a view to the development, then birth, of what it is that we are pregnant with. This matter of self-mastery, self-governance, in a way that includes the working of the 'gardener', is addressed in a further aspect in D/548. Entitled "The victory over strength [*Kraft*]", its focus is upon the person who in previous times has been honored as "genius", as "superhuman [*übermenschlicher*] spirit". Nietzsche's claim is that the vision of such a being has fallen far short of what is possible for a human being. In the traditional vision, we are

> still on our knees before energy-and-strength [*Kraft*] (after the ancient custom of slaves); yet when the *degree of worthiness to be revered* is fixed, only the *degree of rationality* [*Vernunft*] *in strength* is decisive. We must assess [*messen*] to what extent precisely energy-and-strength [*Kraft*] has been overcome by something higher, in the service of which it now stands as means and instrument. But for such an assessment [*Messen*] there are still far too few eyes, indeed the assessment [*Messen*] of the genius is still usually regarded as a sacrilege. So perhaps the most beautiful facet of the matter still appears, as it ever has, only in the dark, and sinks, scarcely born, into eternal night-- I mean, the spectacle of that energy-and-strength [*Kraft*] which a genius applies [*verwendet*] *not to works* but *to itself as a work*, that is, to its very own constraint [*Bändigung*], to the purification of its imagination, to order and selection in the influx [*Zuströmen*] of tasks and invading-notions [*Einfällen*]. The great human being is still, in precisely the greatest thing that demands reverence, invisible like a too distant star: his *victory over strength-and-energy* [*Kraft*] remains without eyes to see it and consequently without song and singer. As always still, the order of rank of greatness for all past humankind has not yet been established.

There is here, in the claim about the way of working of the creative person, a further element in the working of reason, concerned not simply with the overall living of life as it relates to what one is pregnant with, but with the particularities in him-/herself-- the discipline, the powers, the priorities-- that will facilitate the forming and the eventual birth of what is developing within. It is part of the creative person's work to organize his/her life and to prepare his/her energies so that the creative work-- the embryonic thought or deed, in the pregnancy-image account-- may best take shape and best be brought to eventual birth within the creative act itself. This is reason at work overcoming not simply what from beyond ourselves impacts the embryonic life within but also what in more inward (but still indirect) fashion bears on the giving-birth.

2. Decision-making and motivation

Because decision-making has both conscious and unconscious sides, it is not an affair which can be discussed as if everything involved was visible in the conscious side of the affair. In earlier discussion we saw Nietzsche urging that we are much more unknown to ourselves than we think, as regards how an action comes to be undertaken, what drives are at work in our interpretation of things, and so on. In several places, Nietzsche expands on this sense of things.

One realm of such expansion is in his account of decision-making itself. In D/129 ("The alleged conflict of motives"), he takes up with this in reference to our motivation for doing what we decide to do, and indicates how we commonly misunderstand the affair by ignoring or misinterpreting the role of various factors that are involved. Ordinarily, we think of the process leading up to the undertaking of a particular action as eventuating in a decision which involves one motive, that provided by the conscious deliberation upon anticipated consequences of different actions. When alternatives are considered for their consequences, the balance-scale upon which these are to be weighed is settled upon, and the factor of chance is taken into account, then the image of the consequences of the determinate action which on balance appear best provides *one* motive for undertaking that action. But

in the moment when we finally do act, the action is often enough determined by a different species of motives than ... that of the 'image of the consequences'. The way we habitually expend our energy [*die Gewohnheit unseres Kräftespiels*] has its effect then [*da wirkt*], or some slight instigation [*Anstotz*] from a person whom we fear or honor or love, or our love of comfort [*Bequemlichkeit*] which prefers to do what lies at hand, or the excitation of imagination brought on in the decision-making moment by some immediate trivial event; something bodily which emerges wholly unanticipated effects it [*es wirkt*], capricious waywardness effects it, the leap of some affect which by chance is precisely ready to leap effects it: in short, motives effect it [*es wirken*] which in part are unknown to us and in part very badly known and which we can *never* take into account beforehand. *Probably* a struggle [*Kampf*] takes place between these as well-- a propelling to and fro, a rising and falling of scale-weights-- and this would be the actual 'conflict of motives': something for us quite invisible and of which we are quite unconscious. I have calculated the consequences and results and with that set in place *one* very essential motive in the battle-line-- but this battle-line itself I have as little set up as I can see it: the struggle [*Kampf*] is hidden from me, and likewise the victory as victory. For although I certainly experience the deed I finally *do*, I do not experience which motive has therewith actually proved victorious. *But we are accustomed not* to bring all these unconscious processes into account but to think to ourselves the preparation for a deed only so far as it is conscious: and so we confuse conflict of motives with comparison of the possible consequences of different actions-- a confusion very rich in consequences and one highly fateful for the evolution of morality.[17]

A second but connected realm of such expansion relates to another kind of conflict of motivating powers. Nietzsche has spoken of the decision-making process as the locus for the establishing and exercise of self-mastery [*Selbst-Beherrschung*], and we have seen how various sides of this may be understood: the image of the gardener provides one perspective, that of the artist another. In D/109 ("Self-mastery and moderation and their final motive"), he is concerned with still another, and in particular, with a moderation which can be established in our drives, for the benefit of ourselves as a whole. Six essentially different methods of combating the vehemence of a drive and thereby exercising a restraint upon it are enumerated: (1) one can avoid opportunities for the gratification of the drive; (2) one can introduce a rigorously regular order into its gratification, enclosing its ebb and flow in a fixed time-period and freeing the intervals in between from its pressure; (3) one can engender satiety and disgust with it, by intentionally yielding to its wild and unrestrained gratification; (4) one can associate its gratification with a painful idea; (5) one can dislocate the collective mass of drives one has by directing one's thoughts and the play of one's physical forces on other paths (imposing on oneself some especially difficult and strenuous labor, say, or subjecting oneself intentionally to a new stimulus and pleasure) or by favoring for a time another drive (giving it ample opportunity for gratification and in that way expending the energy that would otherwise be at the bidding of the vehement drive); (6) one can aim at a general weakening and exhaustion of one's entire bodily and physical organization (as in asceticism). When he concludes this line of thought, he speaks as follows.

> *That* one *wants* to combat the vehemence of a drive at all does not stand within our power [*Macht*], any more than on what particular method it is that one happens to fall or whether one has success with this method. Rather, in this whole matter [*Vorgange*] our intellect is obviously [*ersichtlich*] only the blind instrument of *another drive* which is the *rival* of the one which torments us by its vehemence: be it the drive for repose, or the fear of disgrace and other bad consequences, or love. Thus while we think 'we' are complaining about the vehemence of a drive, at bottom it is one drive *which is complaining about another*; that is, the perception of suffering from any such vehemence presupposes that there is another drive equally vehement or still more vehement, and that a *struggle* impends in which our intellect must take part.

Because the choice and carrying out of combating-methods involves the operation of conscious intelligence, there is the temptation to think of this whole effort as the work of a conscious 'I' operating deliberately and with a motivation of its own. But in fact, what we consciously interpret as 'my' wish to combat the vehemence of a drive is a reflection in consciousness of an antecedent underground side to a decision-making in the living being in question. In that hidden side, the being's longing for self-enjoyment has already been interpreted in a listening to the clamor of a variety of drives with sufficient vehemence to motivate, in an interpreting and assessing of their claims and conflicts with each other, and in a favoring of one as the most-acceptable-in-our-best-judgment motivating power in the circumstances. It is this decision to let that one prevail following our best judgment which gives rise to our consciously-felt wanting. Our penchant, however, is to consciously (and mistakenly) interpret what appears in consciousness as something belonging to a conscious 'I', and as thus in 'our' power, an expression of something deliberate in 'ourselves', a testimony to 'our' free will. In truth this consciously-felt wanting is not in 'our' power in that sense, and the intellect, enlisted under the longing for self-enjoyment in the combating being discussed, in its operation is serving a drive which is not consciously known to itself (thus intellect is a "'blind' instrument").

A third realm of expansion, again connected with this matter of how motives become acted upon, emerges as Nietzsche speaks of how drives and feelings become interpreted and through the interpretation changed. This is part of the process which he thinks of in speaking of sublimation, and it takes a number of forms. His notice of two forms is in turn worth mention here. Thus in D/76 ("To think something bad is to make it bad"), he observes that by thinking the passions bad, we can make them so: witness Christianity and its transformation of Eros and Aphrodite-- great powers, capable of idealization-- into diabolical phantoms.[18] In D/110 ("That which sets itself in opposition"), he observes how a new desire [*Verlangen*], arising from the scent of a kind of new pleasure, can evoke opposition; if that opposition stems from persons we do not respect and considerations of a common sort, the goal of this new desire can become clothed with the feeling 'noble, good, praiseworthy, worthy of sacrifice': in this way "the whole inherited moral disposition [*Anlage*] takes it up into itself and adds it to the goals felt as moral", so that now we think of ourselves as striving not after a pleasure but after something moral. Our striving is now more confident than before.

In a fourth and final realm of expansion, Nietzsche speaks (in D/104: "Our evaluations") of how actions go back to evaluations, and of how evaluations themselves are of two types. They are either our very own [*eigene*], or are something we have adopted [*angenommene*]. As for the latter, which are by far the most, why do we adopt them?

> From fear: that is, we consider it more advisable to pretend they are our own, and we accustom ourselves to this pretence so that at length it becomes our nature. Our very own evaluation: this means, to assess a thing according to the extent to which it pleases or displeases us alone and no

one else: something extremely rare.-- But must not our evaluation of another, in which there lies the motive for our availing ourselves in most cases of *his* evaluation, at least proceed from *us*, be *our very own* determination? Yes, but we make it as *children*, and rarely re-learn; most of us thus are life-long fools of judgments acquired in childhood so far as concerns how we judge our neighbors (their spirit, rank, morality, whether they are exemplary or reprehensible) and find it necessary [*nötig*] to pay homage to their evaluations.

It is in this adopting of the evaluations of others (of those who are authority figures for us) that morality as a social affair enters into us.

3. Decision-making and morality

In HAH, Nietzsche addressed morality critically, rejecting 'free will' and the 'ought' and 'responsibility' based on it and central to morality, and seeking to reconstrue morality without these. Here in *Dawn*, he rephrases his account of what he is doing: he is "denying morality". According to D/103 ("There are two kinds of deniers of morality"), this phrase can mean two quite different things. One is to deny that the moral motives which human beings claim have inspired their actions have really done so; this means that morality is no more than words, there *is* no such thing as morality and we only deceive ourselves in thinking that there is. The other is to deny that moral judgments are based on truths. Accepting that there *are* in reality moral motives of action, this kind of denial simply regards as false the moral judgments which become motivating in action; they embody misunderstanding. Nietzsche claims that he is the second sort of denier of morality: he denies morality in the same way as he denies alchemy, accepting that there have been alchemists and moral agents who have believed in certain premises and acted on those beliefs, while denying that the premises are true.

But if moral judgments in the form in which he is treating them are real but mistaken judgments, are there real judgments which are based on truth and which serve the function of 'moral' judgments, that is, are genuine moral judgments? What is that function?

So far we have seen Nietzsche approaching the re-conception of morality from a perspective that acknowledges two things about human beings: one, that we are animated by life's reaching for self-enjoyment, so that to that extent there is a directionality which, in our decision-making, we register and discern and which we must judge how, in the concrete circumstances, best to achieve; and the other, that while this involves us in evaluative judgments that we must form with whatever capacities we have at the time, we also find ourselves amidst other human beings and entered into a socialization process as we grow up and develop our capacities. We have just seen how, because that process involves us in accepting valuations from authority-figures in our early life, our judging takes place in a developing matrix in which, according to the strength of the fearful impress on us of authority, we can come to heed such incorporated guides instead of forming our own judgments directly out of our register of things as these are referred to our register of life's reaching. The valuations we have accepted from without, and come to act upon as if they were our own (indeed, they eventually become our own even if not in the sense of being formed out of our very own self) are prescriptions of social morality, prescriptions relating to roles (to speak in compressed fashion). The basic rationale of such prescriptions relates to society, the social whole, and its maintenance-- its continued existence, and the accepted mode of living in which it has its distinctive character and identity. Socialization and its assimilation of these is meant to incorporate us into that society in such way as maintains it. Thus whatever their content may be-- and it varies from society to society--, such prescriptions are directed toward us as members of a particular collectivity, not as individuals. Or more strongly: they are directed *against* us as individual, and in no way want the individual's happiness.[19] If then we form our own evaluations out of ourselves, if we relate the impress of things on life's reaching in us and assess those things and our situation accordingly, if as a result we concretely enact the striving for more intense enjoyment of power (the good by nature) according to our own judging, we enter into conflict with the prescriptions of social morality-- if not in content, in the way in which they bear on us.

This matter of the bearing of 'morality' upon us is taken up in D/107 ("Our right [*Anrecht*] to our folly"). The aphorism opens with the posing of two questions: "How [*wie*] should [*soll*] one act? For what (end) [*wozu*] should [*soll*] one act?" These are the questions which, as formulated in the 'ought' language, are central to morality both in the form Nietzsche is rejecting it and in his re-conception of it. But they mean something different in the two cases. In each case, there is the end which is sought, and the deed in which the striving to achieve that end is embodied. Taking up the matter from the perspective of the individual, Nietzsche notes that in the case of the individual's most immediate and crudest needs [*Bedürfnissen*], these questions are easy enough to answer. The more refined [*feinere*], comprehensive, and weighty, the realms of action are into which one rises, however, the more uncertain, consequently the more arbitrary, will any answer be. But 'morality' bears on us with the force of a 'thou shalt' which is undiscussable, unquestionable. In these weightier realms, the "arbitrariness of decision should [*soll*] be excluded: so commands [*heischt*] the authority of morality". Rather than summoning us to individual decision and thought, morality bears on us in the immediacy of "an obscure fear and awe" and holds forth its prescriptions as what should guide [*leiten*] us in the decision-making for "those actions whose ends and means are least of all immediately [*sofort*] clear to one". In this way "the authority of morality paralyses thinking in the case of things about which it might be dangerous to think falsely: so it is accustomed to justify itself before its accusers." But to Nietzsche's mind, this is a specious apology, for what is really on the mind of the apologist as dangerous is that if the right to act arbitrarily [*willkürlich*] and foolishly [*töricht*], according to one's own [*eigener*] reason (be it greater or smaller), is granted to everybody, then the power and influence of the advocates of 'morality' may be diminished. And indeed, the defense is not merely specious and self-serving, but hypocritical. For the authorities

> make unhesitating use of the right of arbitrariness and folly for themselves-- they *command* even where the questions 'how should I act? for what (end) should I act?' are scarcely answerable-- or with difficulty. And if humanity's *reason* is so slow in its growth that it has often been denied that it has grown at all during the whole course of human existence, what is more to blame than the solemn presence-- indeed, omnipresence-- of moral commands which do not permit *individual* inquiring after How? and For what (end)? to be uttered. Have we not been raised *to feel passively* and to flee into the dark precisely when reason ought [*sollte*] to be taking as clear and cold a view as possible! that is, in the case of all our higher and weightier affairs?

Morality-- social morality-- speaks in an authoritative voice that tells us what to do (lays down commands which settle the matter without requiring the individual to think, let alone think on his/her own); and its manner of impressing itself on us is to command against such reflection.

It is the thrust of Nietzsche's thought in its second phase to reject this and, in his clarification of what is involved in decision-making, to offer another view of morality, a rational morality. Unlike Kant, who urges that reason can not be itself except as a spontaneous self-legislating power which freely determines itself in its judgments on grounds which it itself has laid down, Nietzsche sees reason in its practical function as a vital power that serves life, itself being by nature oriented toward life's good; as such, it not only acknowledges no 'ought' deriving from beyond life, but also knows no formal universal legislation and no categorical imperative. Rather, its prescriptions-- its interpretative translations of the good's claim into directives for decision-making-- would serve the individual life of the being to which it belongs. More precisely, its 'for what' is its interpretation of life's ever-more-intense individual self-enjoyment (the good by nature), and its practical determinations provide concrete interpretative orientation (via goals) for the individual on the singular path-making by which he/she is to realize this 'ever-more-intense'. In its goal-setting and means-determining, then, reason functions in nature-necessitated fashion not as obligated to think truth but as committed to an interpreting and guiding that is effectively to aid in achieving the good.

Now so far as we are individual *human* beings, there is an *essential* involvement of ourselves with *other human* beings: not simply a limited collective (social) involvement, but one concerning ourselves and others simply as human beings, as together constituting humankind. We have seen Nietzsche addressing the implications of this for the future which is rising into view in his own time, in the need for and possibility of ecumenical goals, say, for the governance of earth by human beings. In *Dawn* his pointing into this future is amplified in two aphorisms.

In D/106 ("Against the definition of the moral goal"), he speaks critically of that goal for humanity which defines the secular version of the morality which he is denying. His complaint: when the goal of morality is defined as the "preservation and advancement [*Förderung*] of humanity", that phrase is given no determinate content. What does it mean? Preservation *in what regard* [*worin*]? Advancement *to what* [*wohin*]? Because the 'in what regard' and 'to what' are left indeterminate, one cannot establish anything for a teaching of duty. If one implicitly has in view the longest possible existence of humanity, that is quite different from the greatest possible deanimalization [*Enttierung*] of humanity. And the resultant means-- the practical morality [*praktische Moral*]-- that would be involved in these two cases would have to be quite different. If one wanted to bestow on humankind the highest degree of rationality possible to it, this would not guarantee the longest period of duration possible to it. Or if the attainment of humankind's 'highest happiness' is the 'in what regard' and 'to what' of morality, would that mean: the highest degree of happiness that individual humans could gradually attain to, or the (in any case, not at all calculable) average-happiness which could finally be attained by all? And in either case, why would what we call "morality" [*Moralität*] be precisely the path to such ends? "Has not 'morality', seen overall, produced such an abundance of sources of displeasure that one could rather judge that with every refinement of morality [*Sittlichkeit*] human beings have hitherto become more dissatisfied [*unzufriedener*] with themselves, their neighbors and their own lot? Did not the hitherto most moral human being not believe that the only justified condition of a human being in face of morality is the profoundest misery [*Unseligkeit*]?"

If the current way of thinking of the goal of humanity which morality is to be oriented toward is unsatisfactory, is there a goal implied in Nietzsche's own re-conceived rational morality? That is, does life reach for something in us as human beings (not simply as individuals), so that discerning that, we may define a practical morality that would form the central element in the path whereby such an end is reached? We saw above, in considering one aspect of D/108 ("Some theses") that 'morality' as social morality does not-- and can not-- have individual happiness as its goal. Neither is its goal "the happiness and welfare of humankind (rigorous conceptions can not be united with those words, to say nothing of those words being guiding stars on the dark ocean of moral strivings)". Neither is 'morality' [*Moralität*]-- that which Nietzsche is denying-- something more favorable to the evolution of reason than is immorality. If there is to be a 'thou shalt' for humankind-- if human beings are to accept a morality which relates to ourselves as *human* beings--, it could only be under the condition that humankind possessed "a universally recognized-and-acknowledged [*anerkanntes*] goal"; then it would be possible to "propose 'such-and-such should [*soll*] be done'. But at present there exists no such goal. So one should [*soll*] not posit [*setzen*] the demands [*Forderungen*] of 'morality' in relation to humankind, this is irrational tomfoolery [*Unvernunft und Spielerei*]." Now about any such recognized-and-acknowledged goal, it can only be offered as a *recommendation* [*anempfehlen*], for only then is it thought of appropriately, namely,

> as something which lies in our own will-and-discretion [*in unserem Belieben ist*]. And supposing humankind found appealing [*beliebte*] what was proposed, it could also *give* [*geben*] itself a moral law in that reference, doing this out of its own will-and-discretion [*Belieben*]. But up to now the moral law has been supposed [*sollte*] to stand *above* our own will-and-discretion [*Belieben*]: one did not want actually to *give* [*geben*] oneself this law, but to *take* it from somewhere or *discover* it somewhere or *let it be commanded* from somewhere.

The sketch here is abbreviated, with no indication (for example) of the basis on which the proposed goal could be found appealing. But if it made itself felt as having the appropriate appeal, then a practical morality could arise as central to the path that would bring achievement of such a goal.

C. Present, past, and future: the crisis

In *Dawn* Nietzsche continues the development of the expanded version of the crisis of his time which came forward in HAH, filling it out in some respects and refining it in others.

When the present is seen on the background of the past, what is most visible in human history is how humankind has again and again 'surpassed itself', raised itself aloft, by errors as to its origin, its uniqueness, its destiny, and by the demands that have been advanced on the basis of these errors. If in consequence of the moralities involved and the errors that support them an unspeakable amount of suffering, mutual persecution, suspicion, misunderstanding, and even greater misery, have come into the world for the individuals involved, this has made the 'proud sufferer' into the highest type of human being so far.[20]

But now, in the course of modern and European times, something has happened which, while it is issue of one of these efforts at self-surpassing, has brought the human race as a whole into a condition where for the very first time it can (and must) see itself and assume its existence as a whole, and can (and must) venture in a radically different vein (that of ultimate human responsibility) than ever before. This is issue of a modern movement which has brought to light this past involvement in error: the Enlightenment, begun initially in the Renaissance and regaining impetus more recently. Speaking out of the German strand in this recent development, Nietzsche recalls the first half of the nineteenth century as being marked by the German hostility toward the Enlightenment. German philosophers went back to the first and oldest stage of speculation, in which thinkers were satisfied with concepts instead of explanations; in this way they brought to life again a pre-scientific form of philosophy. German historians and romantics sought to bring into honor older, primitive sensibilities-- the folk-soul, folk-lore, folk-speech, Christianity, the world of medieval times, oriental asceticism, the world of India. And German natural scientists fought against the spirit of Newton and Voltaire and sought to see nature as suffused with ethical and symbolic significance. The tendency in each case was to erect a cult of feeling in place of one of reason. But by his own day, Nietzsche sees a change: the very forces conjured up initially in resistance to the Enlightenment-- "the study of history, understanding of origins and evolutions, empathy for the past, newly aroused passion for feeling and knowledge"-- have ceased being ancillaries of the spirit of obscurantism and reaction. Instead they have

> assumed a new nature and now fly on the broadest wings above and beyond their former conjurers, as new and stronger genii of *that very Enlightenment* against which they were first conjured up. This Enlightenment we must now carry further forward, unconcerned that there has been a 'great revolution' and in turn a 'great reaction' against it and that indeed both still exist-- they are no more than the sporting of waves in comparison with the truly great flood in which *we* are-- and want to be-- moving![21]

One sign of the flood in which Nietzsche feels himself caught up, he alludes to in D/164 ("Perhaps premature").

> At the present time it seems that, under all kinds of false, misleading names and mostly amid great unclarity, those who do not regard themselves as being bound by existing laws and customs are making the first attempts to organize themselves and therewith to create for themselves a *right*: while hitherto, corrupted and corrupting, they had lived under the ban of outlawry and bad conscience, denounced as criminals, free-thinkers, immoral persons, and villains. One ought to find this on the whole *fair and good*, even though it makes the coming century a dangerous one and hangs a gun on everyone's shoulder: by this fact alone it constitutes a counter-force which is a constant reminder that there is no such thing as a morality with an exclusive monopoly on making-moral [*allein-moralisch-machende Moral*], and that every morality that affirms itself alone destroys too much good energy-and-strength [*Kraft*] and comes to be too dear a price to pay for humankind Human beings who deviate from the usual path and are so often the inventive and fruitful ones should [*sollen*] no longer be sacrificed; it should [*soll*] no longer be considered disgraceful to deviate from morality [*Moral*], either in deed or thought; numerous

new experiments should [*soll*] be made in life and society; a tremendous burden of bad conscience should [*soll*] be expelled from the world-- these most universal goals [*Ziele*] ought
[*sollten*] to be recognized and furthered by all who are honest and truth-seeking.

This wide-spread stirring of energies refusing to be confined by conventional morality makes of the
present a transition time which, in reference to morality, is a time of 'moral interregnum'. In D/453,
whose title is that phrase, Nietzsche speaks of how, since the foundations of 'moral' feelings and
judgments are defective and their superstructure is beyond repair, this morality will one day be done
away with-- supposing, of course, that its obligatory force [*Verbindlichkeit*] diminishes from day to
day, as it must if the binding force [*Verbindlichkeit*] of reason does not diminish.

> To construct anew [*neu aufbauen*] the laws of life and action-- for this task our sciences of
> physiology, medicine, society-and-solitude, are not yet sufficiently sure of themselves, and it is
> from them that the foundation-stones of new ideals (even if not the new ideals themselves) must
> come. So it is that, according to our taste and talent, we live an existence which is either a *pre-
> lude* or a *postlude*, and the best we can do in this interregnum is to be as far as possible our own
> kings and found little *experimental states*. We are experiments: let us also want to be them!

There is one precedent of sorts which our historical study can bring forward to reassure us that
what is happening in Europe can indeed succeed. For on a somewhat different level and scale, there
is the achievement of ancient India, namely, the displacement of the gods, then their discard, led by
the work of the Brahmins. And this was followed by the Buddha, and the displacement of the priests
by the religion of self-redemption which he taught.

> And finally, when all the observances and customs upon which the power of the gods and of the
> priests and redeemers depends will have been abolished, when (that is to say) morality in the old
> sense will have died, then there will come ... well, what will come then? But let us not speculate
> idly, rather let us first of all see to it that Europe overtakes [*nachholt*] what-- as commandment
> of thinking-- was done several thousand years ago in India, among the nation of thinkers! There
> are today among the various peoples of Europe perhaps ten to twenty million people who no
> longer 'believe in God'-- is it too much to ask that they should *give a sign* to one another? Once
> they have thus come to *know* one another, they will also have made themselves known to oth-
> ers-- they will at once constitute a power [*Macht*] in Europe and, happily, a power *between* the
> nations! Between the classes! Between rich and poor! Between rulers and subjects! Between
> the most unpeaceable and the most peaceable, peace-bringing human beings![22]

1. A limited future

If in the present our recollection reaches beyond the recent past, beyond the Greeks, beyond human existence, and into an indefinite past without human beings, so our anticipation has a kindred
reach. For as the truth of our situation dawns on us, a new sense of its temporality emerges here, one
fraught with the new basic feeling of our "conclusive transitoriness". In D/49 ("The new basic feeling: our conclusive transitoriness") Nietzsche calls attention to how we used to seek the feeling of the
grandeur [*Herrlichkeit*] of the human being by appeal to humanity's divine *origin*; but our knowledge
of evolution no longer allows that, for the ape lies in that direction. Now we try in the opposite direction: the way humankind is *going* shall serve as proof of human grandeur and kinship with God. But
this is also in vain: in this direction lies "the funeral urn of the *final human being*". For

> however high humankind may have evolved-- and perhaps at the end it will stand even lower
> than at the beginning--, it cannot pass over into a higher order, as little as the ant and the earwig
> can at the end of its 'earthly course' rise up to kinship with God and eternity. Becoming
> [*Werden*] drags the has-been [*Gewesensein*] along behind it: why should an exception to this
> eternal spectacle be made on behalf of some little star and in turn for any little species upon it!

Away with such sentimentalities!

In what perspective does the cognizance of the eventual end of the human race on earth place life and its meaning? The rejection of the eternal, the insistence on the temporal as the ultimate horizon, makes such a question pressing because we have in past linked meaning with the eternal. Is there something *within* the temporal which could serve to give meaning, something of such character that its own quality can enable us to stand equal not simply to our own individual death but to the death of the human race on earth?

In D/429 ("The new passion"), Nietzsche is speaking of where we human beings find ourselves at present, and in particular, of that new passion (for knowing) which makes ours a continuation of the age of the Enlightenment. We fear and hate a possible reversion to barbarism, but not because it would make men unhappier (a strong, firmly rooted delusion can provide happiness), rather because our drive to know has become too strong for us to be able to want happiness without knowledge. The unrest of conjecturing [*Erratens*] and discovering has such an attraction for us as to have become indispensable to us. Indeed, in us

> knowledge has been transformed into a passion which shrinks at no sacrifice and at bottom fears nothing but its own extinction; we sincerely believe that all humankind [*gesamte Menschheit*] must believe itself more comforted and exalted under the compulsion and suffering of *this* passion than it did formerly ... . Perhaps humankind will even perish of this passion for knowledge! Even this thought has no power over us. ... Are love and death not brothers? Indeed, we hate barbarism, and would all prefer the destruction of humankind to a regression of knowledge. Finally: if humankind does not perish of a *passion*, it will perish of a *weakness*: which is preferable? This is the main question: do we want for humankind an end in fire and light, or one in the sand?

Nietzsche develops this last suggestion in D/45 ("A tragic issue of knowledge"). He is speaking of the means whereby human beings elevate, exalt, their being, and calls to mind human sacrifice as something which at all times human beings have found exalting, elevating. And thus he suggests that the idea of a self-sacrificing humankind is one that could become victorious over all others.

> But to whom should humankind sacrifice itself? One could already take one's oath that, if ever the constellation of this idea appears on the horizon, the knowledge of truth would remain as the one tremendous goal commensurate with such a sacrifice, because for this goal no sacrifice is too great. In the meantime, the problem of the extent to which humankind can as a whole take steps to advance knowledge has never yet been posed; not to speak of what drive to knowledge could drive humankind far enough to die with the light of an anticipatory wisdom in its eyes. Perhaps if one day an alliance has been established with the inhabitants of other stars for the purpose of knowledge, and knowledge has been communicated from star to star for a few millennia: perhaps enthusiasm for knowledge may then rise to such a high-water mark!

In the first phase of his thought, tragedy and the tragic attitude were keys to meaningful life in a Dionysian world. The theme endures in this second phase, stripped of all reference to eternity and even (for the moment) to divinity. But in this bare form, what can the passion for knowledge, what can knowledge, introduce that could make the living being a match for death and make his/her living be meaningful even in the face of death? Is there something which life wants, and wants with such ultimacy and finality, that is found in such passion, in knowledge? In all knowledge? In just any knowledge? Or more precisely, in the passion for knowledge?

2. The immediate need: physicians and health

Nietzsche has a number of ways of characterizing the present in which he finds himself and of eliciting the nature of the crisis marking it. In HAH, we found him speaking of the present as a time in which an abundance, indeed overabundance, of the energy and resources for culture had been built up. This overabundance meant a kind of unhealthy condition, a sickness-- but such a sickness as pregnancy is: something attendant upon a new birth in the process of taking place. There was also present in his times another sickness which marked what was being left behind: the unhealthiness of a way of taking part in life that was caught up in unrecognized illusions, that was referred to non-existent conditions and beings for meaning, and that struggled with quack-cures for the suffering it knows, much of which has been-- and is being-- brought upon itself by the way it has sought to deal with genuine suffering.

In *Dawn*, the theme of health, and the figure of the physician who would diagnose the genuine causes and offer genuine cures of disease and illness, recurs in several connections. In each case, the theme relates primarily to mental and spiritual health.

Thinking of a physician in a relatively narrow focus, but thinking "physician" in a sense that means someone who addresses soul and body both, Nietzsche can speak (D/202: "For the promotion of health") of the promotion of mental and spiritual health as part of the transformation he sees the future to be bringing. The specific aspect of this he focuses on in this aphorism concerns the criminal, and a new way of thinking of the criminal, namely, as a mental patient, to be approached and treated with the prudence and good-will of the physician. This would mean getting beyond guilt, punishment, revenge, and those ways of thinking which express the morality of 'responsibility' and 'free will'. It would mean instead seeking to cure (say) the tyrannical drive which led to criminal behavior: to extinguish it, transform it [*Umbildung*], sublimate it [*Sublimierung*]; one should neglect nothing in the effort to restore the criminal to his courage [*guten Mut*] and freedom of heart [*Freiheit des Gemütes*]. At present, we have not arrived at such an enlightened approach, and above all, we can not carry through on it now for the lack of proper physicians, "physicians for whom that which has hitherto been called practical morality must have been transformed into a piece of their science and art of healing [*Heilkunst und Heilwissenschaft*]".

Again, thinking of a physician in a broader focus, Nietzsche asks (in D/52), "Where are the new physicians of the soul?" Much of the suffering present in current life is due to the way the genuine and unavoidable elements of suffering in life have been mis-diagnosed and mis-treated by alleviations and consolations which do not deal with the genuine suffering except in a fantasy fashion. By use of such fantasy means, something worse than what they were to overcome has been produced.

> Out of ignorance, one held the momentarily effective, anesthetizing and intoxicating, means-- the so-called consolations-- for actual cures; indeed, it was not noticed that these instantaneous alleviations often had to be paid for with a general and profound worsening of the suffering, that the invalid had to suffer from the after-effect of intoxication, later from the withdrawal of intoxication, and later still from an oppressive general feeling of restlessness, nervous agitation and ill-health. Past a certain degree of sickness, one never recovered-- the physicians of the soul, those universally believed in and worshiped, took care of that. It is said of Schopenhauer, and with justice, that he finally took seriously once again the sufferings of humankind; where is he who will take seriously the long-neglected antidotes to these sufferings, and put in the pillory the unheard-of quack-doctoring with which, under the most glorious names, humankind has hitherto been accustomed to treat the sicknesses of its soul?

Finally, in D/54 ("Thinking about illness!"), Nietzsche thinks (implicitly) of his own role in the times, and the effort to be such a physician. In that regard, he can say: "To calm the imagination of the invalid, so that at least he should not (as hitherto) have to suffer *more* from thinking about his illness than from the illness itself-- that, I think, would be something! It would be no small thing! Do you now understand our task?"

In all this, there is implicit an idea of health, but what idea? Derived and grounded how? In particular, what would it mean to speak of health, and specifically, mental and spiritual health, if (as Nietzsche urged in HAH-I/286) "health" is always *individual*, such as pertains to "an individual, only one-time thing which adopts a new stance towards all other things such as has never been adopted before"? In the HAH-aphorism just cited, he urges that no universally valid concept can be set up of health; and similarly, there can be no such concept of the means toward health. For "that which one individual needs [*nötig hat*] for his health is to another a cause of sickness, and many ways and means to freedom of spirit may to more highly developed natures count as ways and means to unfreedom." Is Nietzsche here confusing different things, or at least, speaking elliptically or loosely? For are these not two quite different things, what it means to be healthy, on the one hand, and on the other, the specific elements, conditions, functions, and the like, that are involved in being healthy? These latter may well differ from individual to individual, while the identical notion of what it means to be healthy may nonetheless apply and indeed serve as reference point for understanding that, and eventually why, one thing belongs to the health of this person but is unhealthy in another.

Supposing that there is some idea of health which in different individuals would be realized differently, an equally significant question can be raised about this idea of the spiritual physician. For in D/322 ("If possible live without a physician"), Nietzsche urges that when under the care of a physician, sick persons are more frivolous than if they had to take care of their health themselves. For in the former case, it is sufficient to adhere strictly to what has been prescribed; but in the latter case, they view their own health more conscientiously, noticing much more, ordering and forbidding themselves much more, than when a physician is in charge. The moral he advances is this: "All rules have the effect of drawing us away from the purpose behind them and making us more frivolous." He concludes the aphorism: "What heights of unrestraint and destructiveness would the frivolity of humankind have risen to if they had ever in perfect honesty surrendered everything to the divinity as their physician, following the words 'as God wills'!" But how would the spiritual physician he is envisioning function, if not by a diagnosis which issues in rules (of treatment, of conduct)? How could these function if not as distractions of the patient from the conscientious attention-paying needed if he/she is to share responsibly in care for his/her own health?

3. Ambivalent social conditions of the present

Dawn does little to advance Nietzsche's vision of the future, but it does something to fill out his understanding of the present and what in it bears on the character of the future.

The most significant element in the present whose part in the future he anticipates is that of the Jewish segment of the current Europe. In his view,[23] the twentieth century will see the decision as to the destiny of the Jews of Europe: are they to use their extraordinary psychological and spiritual resources to bring forth great men and works and to become masters of Europe, or will they lose Europe as they once lost Egypt?

In contrast with this element of promise, there are features, especially of the economic system, which work against the future he would affirm.

For example, in D/206 ("The impossible class"), Nietzsche speaks of the working class in his contemporary world. "Factory slaves" he calls them, capable of a kind of happiness, so long as they do not feel it to be in general a disgrace to be thus used, and used up, as a part of a machine and as it were to be a stopgap filling a hole in human inventiveness. The essence of their condition-- their impersonal enslavement-- is nothing which can be changed by higher wages; nor can the enhancement of this impersonality, achieved in a new society, transform the disgrace of slavery into a virtue. The very setting a price on oneself, in exchange for which one ceases to be a person and becomes a part of a machine, is disgraceful.

> Would you be accomplice in the current folly of the nations-- of wanting above all to produce as much as possible and to become as rich as possible? It should rather be your affair, to hold up before them a counter-reckoning: how great a sum of *inner* value is thrown away in pursuit of this external goal! But where is your inner value if you no longer know what it is to breathe freely? if you have not even scanty control over yourselves? if you all too often grow weary of yourselves like a drink that has been left too long standing? if ... ?

Or again, in D/173 ("Those who commend work") he sees fear of the individual present behind all the talk of the 'blessing of work'. In that talk, "work" means a "hard industriousness from early till late". But that is something which "powerfully [*kräftig*] hinders the evolution of reason, covetousness, desire for independence [*Unabhängigkeitsgelüstes*]"; it "uses up an extraordinary amount of nervous energy [*Nervenkraft*] and removes it from reflection, brooding, dreaming, worrying [*Sorgen*], loving, hating; it sets a small goal always in sight and guarantees easy and regular satisfactions". Thus a society in which there is continual hard work will have more security: indeed, in it security is worshiped as the supreme deity. But, in the current unrest in the working world, with its socialist agitation giving it a particular meaning, ironically "the 'worker' has become *dangerous*, and the place is swarming with 'dangerous individuals'! And behind them, the danger of dangers-- *the* individual!"

In D/175 ("Basic idea of a commercial culture"), Nietzsche speaks more generally of the culture that is coming into existence due to the presence and effect of the economic system in place currently. It is the culture of a society of which commerce is as much the soul as personal contest was with the ancient Greeks and war-victory-justice were for the Romans.

> The man engaged in commerce understands how to appraise everything without having made it, and to appraise it *according to the needs of the consumer*, not according to his own most personal needs [*eigenen persönlichsten Bedürfnisse*]: 'who consumes this, and how much' is his question of questions. This type of appraisal he then applies instinctively and all the time, to all things, and thus even to the production of the arts and sciences, of the thinker and scholar, the artist and statesman, of peoples and parties, of the whole age: in relation to all which is created, he asks after supply and demand, *in order to establish for himself the value of a thing*. This, made into the character of an entire culture, thought through without bound and in the subtlest detail and imprinted in every will and every faculty: it is this of which you men of the coming century will be proud ... .

Finally, in D/174 ("Moral fashion of a commercial society"), Nietzsche sees, behind the basic principle of current moral fashion, namely, that 'moral actions are actions performed out of sympathy for others', a companion attitude to the calculativeness of such consumerism. The morality expressed in social form is one of a timidity which hides behind an intellectual mask. It is a morality which desires, as what is highest, most important, and most immediate, that all the dangerousness which life once held should be removed from it, and that everyone should assist in this with all his might [*Kräften*]. Thus only those actions which tend towards the common security and society's sense of security are to be called 'good'. With such a moral attitude-- "such a tyranny of timidity", such a "tremendous intentionality of obliterating all the sharp corners and edges of life"--, we are "well on the way to turning humankind into sand". The human beings who uphold this attitude have very little joy in themselves.

CHAPTER 11
Gay Science

The first expression of the way of thinking which took shape in Nietzsche in response to the crisis at Bayreuth was HAH. Given the nature of that crisis, the tone of that work was strongly marked by an animus against certain things and by an assertion-- a defiant one indeed-- of certain other things. What followed, in D, continued exploration of matters along the lines set forth in HAH, but its mood was mellower, its thought less obviously agitated and burdened by the reactive animus of HAH. It is as if the venting of hostility in the three collections that constitute HAH had enabled him to calm down and to incorporate the expression of negative energy into a more incisive, more patient, more probing, effort. *Gay Science* represents a continuation of the advance being made in HAH and D, but again, one with a somewhat different character. A kind of joyfulness, exuberance, liveliness, surface here, but no longer those of his early youth but those of a Nietzsche matured to a noticeable degree. This altered mood, the sign of a revival of energy, a restoration of confidence, and a regaining of touch with the self that had been alive (but self-deceived and constrained) in his first phase, is conveyed in an expression of thought which in its own right seems surer, more coherent and subtle. The thought advances in part by reconceiving issues which had long concerned him and by re-covering and reworking themes and ideas from the first phase, purifying and further developing them within a new framework. But the change in horizon effected in HAH had been decisive and endured, indeed was stabilized by continued work on the horizon itself. Nietzsche himself has grown, and his thinking has also definitely moved onward. In GS he is progressively establishing himself within the altered framework, drawing on a richer and much more subtle receptivity and employing a more incisive and nuanced reflective capacity.

The overall structure of GS reflects its character both as continuing this second phase and as calling back in reworked form the first phase; but it also reflects its character as preparing for-- indeed, issuing in the opening passage of-- the first work of his third phase, namely, TSZ.

GS is composed of four Books[1] of 342 successively-numbered aphorisms. The beginning (GS/1: "The teachers of the purpose of existence") takes up with human life in the larger evolutionary and historical perspective which has become prominent in HAH and D, but the terms echo the focus on tragedy which began with BT. Singling out that aspect of what is at stake in life ('more life') which is the maintaining of the living in existence, he sketches out the task which life sets for human beings as members of the human race, namely, that their activity contribute to the maintenance of the exist-ence of the species; and he recalls how, as the at-stake becomes interpreted within the varied human groups and as various moralities and religions embody such interpretations, the history of the human race shows a repeated pattern. Each of these systems, as a reading of life which gives this-or-that rea-son for life and for living in this-way rather than that-way, gives itself off as 'the truth'; in fact, however, each is false, expressing and depending on fictions which have a certain utility, indeed, but miss truth. However, since the system defines what must be taken seriously by members of the group collected together to live under its guidance, it is vigorously defended by the group. But eventually, since each system is a limited one that is not able to answer to all of life's needs and demands, each breaks down or is undermined, its capacity to support life and to maintain the interest of group members in vital affairs having become exhausted. In this breakdown, it is the passion of the strongest and most evil spirits ('evil' in terms of the system in question) that is most instrumental in this destruction; but what takes shape in the establishment of a subsequent system suffers from the same basic limitations and vulnerability.[2] Thus the history of the human race so far has been a series of tragedies, in which limited systems taken as absolute have repeatedly collapsed. Seen from a slightly different vantage-point, this same phenomenon is a comedy, that of human pretense: 'serious' human beings taking 'seriously' rationalizations of life's meaning which unknown to themselves are fictive, and eventually going aground, only to be followed by others acting similarly and suffering the same fate.

The end (GS/342: "*Incipit tragoedia*") is an entryway into the fifth act[3] of this extended drama. In the fourth act, in virtue of the way 'morality' has been entered into one of these systems and 'knowledge' has come to be valued and pursued, the element of falsity in *all* of the previous systems-- and indeed, also in this very system within which 'morality' and 'knowledge' are to be found-- has come to light. Something radically new is emerging in human existence. The need for such systems has indeed become part of humanity, but we can no longer respond to it within that obliviousness which has allowed past humanity to claim absolute truth as the foundation for the way of life of a group of human beings. Indeed, we can no longer respond to it as simply members of a limited group: it is *as human* beings that we are finding ourselves now, and the human race is the 'group' for which meaning is somehow to be secured with the help of a guiding system which brings to self-consciousness what gives meaning to the existence of humankind on earth. What is the fifth act to be like? This is pointed to in the title of the final aphorism, "The tragedy begins"; it is the very narrative which opens TSZ, the first work in the third phase of Nietzsche's thought. In the Preface he added when GS was republished, Nietzsche comments on the handful of songs being added as an appendix, and remarking on them as expressive of the "foolishness, exuberance and 'gay science'" which mark the book, he continues:

> Alas, it is not only the poets and their beautiful 'lyrical sentiments' on whom the resurrected author has to vent his sarcasm: who knows what victim he is looking for, what monster of material for parody will soon attract him? '*Incipit tragoedia*' we read at the end of this seriously unserious book. Beware! Something downright wicked and malicious is announced here: *incipit parodia*, no doubt.[4]

It seems that the vision of TSZ and the figure Zarathustra who voices it form a parody of the previous moralities and religions and their founders, serious and yet not serious in the same way because self-conscious to their own lack of absoluteness. But that what is being presented in GS is preparatory for this next work is further underlined by the presence, in the aphorism immediately preceding this last one (GS/341: "The greatest weight"), of the idea which in EH Nietzsche claims is the central idea of TSZ, that of the eternal recurrence of the same. It is not developed here, only presented in an allusive and enigmatic fashion. But these two concluding aphorisms, by echoing the first aphorism in GS, and by the way they are built up to, particularly in Books III and IV, make clear that in GS we are verging on what is to come in TSZ.

Along the way between beginning and end, GS shows a thematic development and coherence which is often quite musical in character. The thought is less strident in its expression than in HAH, more orderly in a musical sense in its build-up than HAH or D, and as it proceeds, it seems to flow from ever deeper sources. While it becomes quite personal at times, at the same time it gains in sensitivity to and insight into the human generally. Two aphorisms point us in warning fashion to how we are to take what we are reading.

GS/298 ("Sigh") reads: "I caught this insight on the way and quickly seized the rather poor words that were closest to hand to pin it down lest it fly away from me again. And now it has died for me in these arid words and hangs attached and dangling in them-- and I hardly know any more when I look at it, how I could have had such happiness as I did when I caught this bird."

GS/286 ("Interruption") reads: "Here are hopes; but what will you hear and see of them if you have not experienced [*erlebt*] splendor, ardor, and dawns in your own souls? I can only remind you; more I cannot do. To move stones, to turn animals into human beings-- is that what you want from me? Alas, if you are still stones and animals, then better seek your Orpheus."

A. Philosophy

1. Experience and disclosure

Philosophy begins in experience, explores experience in its inquiries, and finds in experience the confirmation or disconfirmation of the ideas it develops which claim to embody understanding of what is being inquired after.

a. Beginning in experience

Of this beginning, Nietzsche speaks as follows.

> To stand in the middle of this *rerum concordia discors* [discordant harmony of things] and the whole marvelous uncertainty and ambiguity of existence *and not to ask questions*, not to tremble with eagerness and joy in questioning, not once to hate the questioner and perhaps also even faintly amuse oneself over him-- this is what I feel to be *contemptible*, and this feeling is what I look for first of all in anyone-- some folly persuades me ever again that every human being, as human, has this feeling.[5]

And yet, the expectation that Nietzsche expresses here is sadly disappointed: "*the great majority of people lack an intellectual conscience*". Such a lack means for Nietzsche this above all, that when someone asks of others that they exhibit such a conscience,

> everybody looks at you with strange eyes and goes right on handling his weighing-scales, calling this good and that evil. Nobody even blushes when you make it known that their weights are not full-weight-- people do not even feel outraged, perhaps they laugh at your doubts. I mean: *the great majority of people* do not consider it contemptible to believe this or that and to live ac-cordingly, *without* having in advance become conscious of the final and most certain reasons pro and con, and without even troubling themselves about such reasons afterward: the most gifted men and the noblest women still belong to this 'great majority'. But what is goodheartedness, refinement, or genius to me, when the person who has these virtues tolerates slack feelings in his believing and judging and when he does not account *the desire for certainty* as his inmost craving and deepest distress-- as that which separates the higher human beings from the lower.

In the first phase of his thinking, Nietzsche had pointed to youth and the emergence there of the call of conscience to become yourself,[6] and had given this call meaning by speaking of aspiration and of the self reached for in it as something high above-and-beyond yourself as you are at the time of hearing this call. This call and reaching formed the matrix for the beginning of reflection, including philosophical reflection and the intellectual conscience that forms part of it. Here in this aphorism of GS, Nietzsche focuses on the intellectual conscience which is part of the search for truth and the desire for certainty in a matter. Because we all enter into and live through youth, and because the call of conscience belongs to that time, his expectation is that everyone has heard and responded somehow to that call (that would be the natural thing to happen), and he looks thus for an intellectual conscience in everyone, only to find it missing in most.[7]

Two things are pointed to as matters for such conscience: the scales on which one weighs good and evil (whether or not they are full-weight), and the reasons for and against the practically-effective beliefs in accordance with which one lives (that the ultimate reasons relating to such beliefs are as secure as possible). The weighing (the judging concerning what-matters) and the reflective interpretation (the reading of why it matters) are affairs at the heart of practice. But amidst the uncertainty of action as a venturing, and the many ways of interpreting the meaning of things, there is need for a reflection which, while entered into the judging and the interpreting of the matter at hand in practical personal reference, readily moves beyond this into the philosophically reflective.

b. Exploration in inquiry

In the (practical and philosophical) reflection in question, it is one's own involvement with things, and what is coming to disclosure in it, that are the field for exploration in the development of questioning and the seeking for understanding. A number of aphorisms speak of that involvement, and to our reflective probing of it as part of our search for answers to our questions, and give us some idea of the complexity of the matter of experience and disclosure as Nietzsche is now conceiving it.

Occasionally (if rarely) we find ourselves involved in the sort of experiencing which was central in the first phase of his thought but whose disclosive import has become re-interpreted by Nietzsche in this second phase. Thus in GS/319 ("As interpreters of our experiences"), he speaks of a kind of honesty which he claims has been alien to creators of religions and their kind.

> They have never made their experiences a matter of conscience for knowledge. 'What have I really experienced? What happened then in me and around me? Was my reason bright enough? Was my will turned against all deceptions of the senses and brave in its warding off the fantastic?' None of them has asked these things, even today all the dear religious people still do not ask them. Rather they have a thirst for things which are *counter to reason*, and do not want to make it too difficult for themselves to satisfy it-- so they experience 'miracles' and 'rebirths' and hear the voices of angels! But we, we others, thirsty for reason, want to look our experiences in the eye as rigorously as a scientific experiment-- hour after hour, day after day. We ourselves want to be our experiments and experimental-animals.[8]

As we saw in HAH, when Nietzsche explored more closely the matter of (say) the Dionysian experiencing which he had made so much of in BT, he could not sustain his initial reading of it as disclosing a metaphysical reality. Apparently he judged in retrospect that his reason had not been bright enough in youth, and his will resistant and brave enough, so that he had misread the nature of the experience reflectively, and even in the experiencing itself had been making of presence something which, from that later perspective, was not warranted.

Ordinarily our experience is not of such seemingly great import, but even in this case-- perhaps especially in this case-- we need to look closely and honestly at our experience and ask the same questions: What am I really experiencing in my everyday life? How am I involved and operating in the experiencing? What sort of disclosure is really taking place? In GS/308 ("The history of every day"), Nietzsche observes:

> What is the history of every day in your case? Look at your habits of which it consists: are they the result of innumerable little cowardices and lazinesses, or of your courage and inventive reason? However different these two cases are, people might very well praise you equally and you might actually profit them equally this way and that. But while praise, profit, respectability, may be enough for those who merely want to have a good conscience, they are not enough for you, a reins-tester who knows [*Wissen*] about conscience [*Gewissen*]!

The sense of our being active in giving shape to our experience, and of how often we deceive ourselves in that activity, how easily and readily we fail to be conscientious and excuse our cowardice and laziness, and how much such self-deception and failures in attentiveness contribute to the character of our experience, runs deep in Nietzsche. Indeed, it leads him to speak of an essential moral component in *all* our experience. In GS/114 ("The sphere [*Umfang*] of the moral"), he asserts: "Any new image which we see we immediately construe with the help of all the old experience which we have had, and we do this *each time according to the degree* of our honesty and justness [*Gerechtigkeit*]. There are no experiences other than moral experiences, not even in the realm of sense-perception."

What then is involved in our experience, whether it be extraordinary or ordinary? There is something given and with it a disclosure of some sort, but there is also an interpreting in which we more or less honestly read the meaning of such disclosure and determine it to be such-and-such. To the extent that we are not honest and courageous, and do not genuinely seek to do justice to what is registering in us, we do not really know what is given and being disclosed: we make something of presence, indeed, but proceeding under a reading which is formed in more or less careless and inattentive fashion, we presume this-or-that represents the disclosure and live and act accordingly. And if, reflectively, we make use of such experience without exploring more closely what was happening in it, we can give it a value and import it does not deserve.

Nonetheless, if honesty and courage are needed in the making of experience itself as well as in the reflective use of the disclosures of experience, we can also recognize that in certain circumstances, and perhaps in some measure in all circumstances, all the honesty and courage which we can muster may not be enough to see what is genuinely present and happening at the time, and this, for good reasons grounded in the nature of life and our capacities as living beings. For as growing beings, not only do initial limitations mark our capacities of all sorts, including those for registering and interpreting, but there are more pressing needs than truth. For what is at stake in life is something other than truth. Thus in GS/ 307 ("In favor of criticism"), Nietzsche observes:

> Now something that you formerly loved as a truth or likelihood [*Wahrscheinlichkeit*] seems to you an error; you shed it and fancy that this represents a victory for your reason. But perhaps this error was as necessary for you then, when you were still a different person (you are always a different person) as are all your present 'truths', being a skin, as it were, that concealed and covered a great deal that you were not yet permitted to see. What killed that opinion for you was your new life and not your reason: *you no longer need it*, and now it collapses and unreason crawls out of it into the light like a worm. When we exercise criticism, this is no arbitrary and impersonal event; it is, at least very often, evidence of vital driving energies [*lebendige treibende Kräfte*] in us that are shedding a skin. We negate and must [*mützen*] negate because something in us *wants* to live and to affirm itself-- something that we perhaps do not know or see as yet.

The heart of the matter here is that ours is the experience of a living being, and that inherent in the life in us and its drive is the matter of our growth and development. We experience things as growing beings for whom something is at stake. Now so far as our growth in our decision-making capacity goes (including our capacities for registering, for interpreting, for weighing the bearing of presence on life's reaching), there is not only much which lies beyond our capacity at any time to see, but there are elements present but hidden from us in virtue of our own current state as participants in life's affairs. For in such participation, the 'truths' we hold to are useful representations which interpret things in ways that enable us (as we currently are) to live with the world; by our interpretation we support ourselves in our current involvement not only by seeing various things but by protecting ourselves from seeing (or seeing in particular ways) various other things which as yet we are not strong and capable enough to cope with. But as we gain strength as participants, find different drives evolving in ourselves, and discover our needs and capacities to be changing, so it is possible for what was given before but which at the time our 'truths' hid from us (altogether, or by distortion) to come out into the open and to be registered and be understood now, or to be registered now without the distortion of previous 'truth'. We no longer need to see the world through the lens of such readings, and freed from that need and the pressure to 'see the truth of things in this way' which it had been placing on us we can see how mistaken we were before. The 'could not see before' was in this case not a sign of lack of relevant presence at the time or of a deficient rational power in us then, but the expression of a vital need which is no longer ours.

Thus in our growth and development, the disclosure of our experience and our reading of that disclosure is at any time mixed, and in time to come can change for a number of different reasons. Looked at with the case in mind of this criticism in which we become critical of 'truths' of whose truth we were formerly convinced, we can see: one factor that makes for variation and change is our own capacity for discerning and interpreting. It can amplify, and indeed does so as we develop and use it and ourselves grow; and accordingly it is possible that we can discern and understand more or less at any time, in the very making of experience and in its reflective use, depending on how far and well developed our rational capacity is. But there are others factors as well that make for variation and change. The standpoint from which (that is, the place of judgment at which) we find things present and make our discernments and judgments at any time can alter in character, and (say) the strengths and resources for living which are available to us at this altered standpoint can allow to enter into express presence more than we could (or could allow ourselves to) find and see there before. This could be so, for one thing, because we are *stronger* now and not at the mercy of the same weaknesses and needs as confined us before. The strength in question here includes courage and honesty, drive and confidence, thus various aspects of a moral capacity which allow us to make the best use (so far as truth is concerned) of our developing capacity for discernment. If at the time we do not have the strength to be equal to the threat and the danger, if we can not resist its pressure toward indolence and inertia, if we can not counter the distraction and clamor of what is calling for attention and for our looking at things from 'its' standpoint, not *our own*, we can make only limited use of what capacity we have. The stronger we are, the better use we can make of that capacity. Or this could be so also for other reasons, because (say) with the growth of some particular facet of ourselves we have increased resources which enable presence to open up for us in fuller, more complex, more many-sided ways, than before, simply due to and in correlation to this particular development. Both this fuller particular entryway into presence, and any outgrowing of a need which we had as ourselves less developed and which previously required us to hold to a certain truth, can enable us now to see in critical fashion what we could not see before.

On this matter of experience and its disclosure, honesty and intellectual conscience are companion factors which Nietzsche emphasizes forcefully in GS. But there is another factor equally important for his thought in this work because just as decisive as that pair for the nature of our experience and for its employment in reflection. Our growth as human beings brings an expanded and refined capacity for receiving and registering which (as we have already seen him noting in UHH) opens us to-- and enters us into-- a (so to speak) vertical dimension of experience, an elevation and depth that belong both to experience and what is being experienced. In the difference Nietzsche sees between superior and inferior human beings, higher and lower humanity, participation in such heights and depths forms a complementary element to the presence of an intellectual conscience. What is meant by "expanded capacity" here is not merely (or mainly) a quantitative expansion, one achieved by the addition of more of the same. Rather, it is primarily a qualitative augmentation, a refinement, a becoming more subtle and sensitive, in virtue of which we open up in immediacy to this vertical dimension and to qualitative differences which relate to it. Thus we have elevated moods, for example, and so long as we are in them, we know our own having been raised above our self as we find ourselves in our ordinary experiencing, and know the distinctive disclosure which opens up in such states.[9]

As we noted in discussing HAH, Nietzsche tends to articulate the distinction of higher and lower (both within experience and also among human beings) by speaking of the contemplative vs. the active human beings. Put oversimply, the former (the contemplative and higher) "see and hear unspeakably more, and see and hear thoughtfully".[10] As a result, "for anyone who grows up into the heights of humanity, the world becomes ever fuller; ever more fishhooks of interest are cast after him; the number of things that stimulate him grows constantly, as does the number of different kinds of pleasure and displeasure. Indeed, the higher human being always becomes at the same time happier and unhappier." Growth in such persons enables them to attain, and eventually to maintain themselves in, the heights and to know in themselves an unequalled complexity in register as well as a refined awareness. It is such persons that Nietzsche also singles out not simply as embodying higher humanity; where their being has come to center itself in the passion for knowledge, they also represent nobility as we know it in the present day. The noble person is one who is focused in a kind of special passion, of whose specialness (its not being shared by others) the noble person is oblivious. That special passion involves

> the use of a rare and singular standard-- something close to madness [*Verrücktheit*]; the feeling of heat in things which for all others feel cold; a divining of values for which the scale has not yet been invented; a bringing sacrifice to altars which are consecrated to an unknown god; a courageousness that does not want honor; a self-sufficiency which has an overflow and communicates [that overflow] to human beings and things.[11]

Where the contemplative, with the elevated character of his experience, has come to be centered in the passion for knowledge, he is an exceptional human being as well, and the latest embodiment of the noble human being. His is a form of nobility which is more inward than ever before, but noble nonetheless, in virtue of the rarity of his passion (that for knowing), the singularity of his value-standard (making truth the highest value), and the unselfconsciousness involved.[12]

In the noble contemplative human being, then, experiencing becomes enriched by disclosure of a dimension and facets of things to which lesser human beings are oblivious. And yet the exploration of experience which reflection involves only gains greater complication thereby. For even in the noble human being with a potentially richer experience than others, there is no exemption from dishonesty in the formation of experience itself, given the person's sensitivity to dangers and threats, and to possibilities of suffering, which others do not-- perhaps can not, but at least do not allow themselves to-- register. Nietzsche's repeated calls to boldness and courage, and to hardness and severity in face of various facets of oneself and others, remind that, even-- or especially-- for the noble reflective human being, the exploration of experience out of a passion for knowledge is a task which requires above all a kind of moral strength if genuine knowledge is to result.

c. Knowing and experiential confirmation

If reflective inquiry begins in the immediacy which calls for questioning and summons us to an intellectually conscientious exploration of experience, and if that exploration discovers experience to be an affair which not only itself evolves in its disclosive reach as we become more capable of taking part in things but also has a moral dimension and holds different (higher and less high) levels to what is experienced and to experiencing itself, what is the character of the understanding in which such inquiry comes to its consummation, so far as consummation is possible at all? In GS/333 ("What is it to know?"), Nietzsche takes up with this matter of knowing and coming to know. He does so starting from a line from Spinoza, who is urging that we are "not to laugh, nor to lament, nor to detest, but to understand [*intelligere*]". But-- Nietzsche asks-- in the last analysis

> what else is *intelligere* than the form in which the other three are able to be felt by us at once? One-- a single-- result out of the different and mutually opposed drives of wanting-to-laugh, wanting-to-lament, wanting-to-detest? Before any knowing [*Erkennen*] is possible, each of these drives must first have brought its one-sided view of the thing or event forward; after this, the fight of these one-sidednesses arose and occasionally out of it a mean [*Mitte*], a quieting, an acknowledging of claims [*Rechtgeben*] on all three sides, a kind of justice and accord: for in virtue of this justice and accord, all these drives can be affirmed in their existence and carry their point against each other. We, in whom only the final reconciliation-scenes and conclusion-reckoning of this long process comes to consciousness, think accordingly that 'to understand' is something conciliatory, just, good, something essentially opposed to the drives; while it is only a *certain relating* [*Verhalten*] *of the drives to one another*.

A matter to be understood registers in us varyingly, according as different drives and feelings are involved in that register and disclose it as it bears on them and as it is felt from their standpoint. Thinking is a matter of gathering together the disclosive force of these diverse registers, and in adjudicating among their claims to reveal the matter at issue, attempting to do justice to the disclosure of each and to conclude to some interpretation in which those claims are heeded, done justice to and integrated.

> For the longest time, conscious thought was considered thought itself. Only now does the truth dawn on us that by far the greatest part of our spirit's activity runs along unconscious and unfelt. But I suppose that these drives which here fight with one another understand right well how to make themselves felt and hurt *one another* in this fight: that sudden and violent exhaustion by which all thinkers are visited may have its origin there (it is exhaustion on the battle-field). Indeed, perhaps there is in our fighting innards much concealed heroism, but certainly nothing divine, resting eternally in itself, as Spinoza thought. *Conscious* thinking, and especially that of philosophers, is the least forceful [*unkräftigste*] and therefore also the relatively mildest and most peaceful kind of thinking: and so precisely the philosopher can most easily be led astray about the nature of knowing.

Much of our thinking goes on unconsciously, some of it involves both conscious and unconscious functioning, and perhaps some of it is wholly conscious. But its eventual issue is an interpretative perspective on the matter under consideration which somehow integrates and reconciles the views of the various parties. The resultant reading constitutes our knowing, an apprehending which claims truth, but clearly, truth as *we* whose drives and feelings have provided the basic disclosure elements *can find and apprehend* it. But in this process of heeding the various claims, weighing and assessing them, and coming to some conclusion, what is the basis appealed to in drawing the conclusion, in weighing the evidence and deciding on its relevance and significance, and so on? Indeed, what is the standpoint at which the feeling-and-drive-disclosures are gathered together and 'felt together'? And what does the 'conclusion' have as basis for its claim to be just? Finally, since the varied disclosive vehicles are also motivational forces, how is their weight as motivational discounted so that the evidence is weighed 'impartially'?

Nietzsche provides no answer to any of these questions in the aphorism cited, nor does he place this matter of knowing in the growth-context we have just been noticing come forward in his treatment of much of our critical reflection. In his discussion of this latter case, something that wants to live, something which is growing stronger, is thereby changing the matrix of drives, feelings, and in general the factors and forces whose disclosive power is clamoring to be heard; what does that mean for the knowing-- or what claims to be knowing-- that consummates reflective inquiry? Does it matter what it is that wants to live and affirm itself and in so doing changes the disclosure matrix? Does it matter if it is the growth of one drive, say, or one skill or capacity, that is involved? Or is it more crucial that what is involved is a strengthening of our overall capacity for taking part in life's affairs, and that this strengthening brings all the clamoring into a new place, transforming the place of 'hearing' of the different claims and thus of the way those claims sound and resound for the judge who would hear them? Is it this overall strengthening of ourselves as participants in life's affairs that is decisive, and what most of all enables a different and better judgment of truth to be reached? And yet, is this possible without a certain measure of development on the side of particularity as well, and thus a new voice or voices to be taken into account, not simply a new place for the hearing and seeking to do justice to? Finally, does this overall strengthening of ourselves as participants, together with any development on the side of particularity, ever bring us to the place where we are (say) fully equal to any threat and distraction, where we might employ our capacity for discernment such as it is in full freedom? Even more, do our capacities (for disclosure, and for discernment) ever reach a peak, and if so, even if their exercise involves a fulness of freedom does it necessarily suffice for the task of discerning truth? Such questions bring us back to the problem of that eventuation which is being discussed in D/424,[13] where Nietzsche is speaking of the one for whom truth is there.

From what we see in such aphorisms as these, Nietzsche is continuing to reconstrue the sense of what it is to know that he developed in his first phase of thought in the context of maturation, using the altered framework of his second phase to reformulate the matter. Thus there endures the sense of ourselves as living growing beings, with life and growth being understood in reference both to a drive that is of the essence of life itself-- in the present phase, a drive toward self-enjoyment, toward enjoyment of one's own power-- and to a variety of particular drives and feelings which enter into the living of life and color the disclosure open to us through our powers of receptivity. In this matrix, the human being may develop a passion for knowledge which is, on the one hand, itself a drive which, as a vital affair, is one among other particular drives, and which, from the practical perspective, must be integrated with other drives somehow and allowed to develop in ways that answer to the drive toward self-enjoyment. But on the other hand, in terms of its own internal structure this passion for knowledge aims at truth, and since truth is not inherently life-enhancing or life-preserving, the conscientious and methodical pursuit of truth must avoid weighing things on the balance-scale of life itself.[14] Its own proper scale, however, must be internal to life, since its beginning, middle, and intended end, are affairs of life-experience, the instrument of its attainment is also a vital-power (reason), and its questioning concerns the very nature of life and reality. But because the power of reason can only function and operate with what experience provides, the foundation of the scales is the disclosure which the current-- and evolving, at least potentially-- engagement of the living being with things in the living of life provides. But the scale itself is that in which one weighs evidence, not life itself, and weighs the capacity of apparent disclosure to reveal truth, not the power of motivating factors to move one or the power of those factors to enable our achievement of self-enjoyment. If reason is the power which places the evidence on the scales, it does not itself provide the evidence: that is a function of life in other facets and sides of itself. Thus two questions confront any inquiry into-- and self-understanding of-- knowing: When (if ever) has life enabled the evidence to be assembled that is relevant and needed for knowledge of truth? And what determines the weight to be assigned the pieces of that evidence in each case, and more basically, what is the balance mechanism that would correctly register the outcome of placing the weight of evidence on the scale?

2. Life and reality

We have seen Nietzsche seeking to move beyond the distinction which Kant instituted between the thing in itself and the thing in relation to us, and groping for a way of understanding reality that does not depend on it. But the path on which he has been moving to do that has not yet reached a conclusion satisfactory to him. We find in a set of aphorisms at the end of Book I and the beginning of Book II the end-point of this movement in this second phase of his thought.

The initial aphorism in this set is GS/54 ("The consciousness of seeming [*Scheine*]"). It is an explication of an experiential discovery[15] crucial to his coming to the knowledge he has now finally gained of the-all of existence (of existence as an interconnected affair): he found himself as if waking up in the midst of a dream and, while continuing to dream on, at the same time being aware of his continuing dream and aware of himself aware of it. In the poetizing, loving and hating, and drawing inferences, that constitutes the core of his 'dream-making' participation in existence, he sees himself now participating in a way of functioning which has been going on throughout the human, the animal, indeed the sentient, past. And this continuing on of the constitutive activity for 'the dream' not only maintains the same sort of activity as went on in the past but carries in itself an inheritance from the past that inflects current activity, so that the way in which it works now is in part a reflection of this carry-over. In this 'dream-making' he exists as the active being he is, so that his continuing to exist depends on his continuing participation in this 'dream-making'. But now in his self-conscious participation in it, he finds an altered sense of reality, and with it, a strange sense of what he calls '*Schein*' or 'seeming'. More precisely:

> What is '*Schein*' to me now? Truly, not the opposite of some being [*Wesens*]-- what do I know

to say of any being but the predicates of its seeming. Truly, not a dead mask, which one puts on some unknown X and could just as well take away! *Schein* is for me the-living-and-working itself [*das Wirkende und Lebende selber*], which goes so far in its self-mocking to allow me to feel that here is mere-seeming [*Schein*] and mirage-light [*Irrlicht*: literally, light that leads astray] and ghost-dance [*Geistertanz*] and nothing more-- that among all these dreamers I too, the 'knower', am dancing my dance, that the knower is a means to prolong the earthly dance, and so far forth belongs to the festival-organizers of existence, and that the sublime consistency and connectedness of all knowledge is perhaps-- and will be-- the highest means of *maintaining the universality* of the dreaming and the universal intelligibility of all these dreamers to one another and thereby precisely *the enduring of the dream.*

Reality *is* a *living interacting* which harbors, internal to itself and as generated in the interacting, the 'world of appearance' which *seems* reality itself but which *in truth* is only deceptive in that regard; such seeming is indeed an *actual* facet of the interactive reality in question, but it is not itself reality nor real in the way it ordinarily seems. To an *awakened* participant this realm of appearance is reality mocking itself by seeming something without being it; yet this seeming not only genuinely belongs to reality, as its own dissembling appearance, but it is *this appearance* with which the *unawakened* dreamers are occupied as their everyday reality. Included among those unawakened dreamers are the knowers (in science) whose focus in their knowing is appearance, and more precisely, what within appearance is 'truly (i.e. objectively) there'; indeed, appearance is that the knowing of whose look (due to the consistency and connectedness of the apprehension involved[16]) is a means whereby the dreamers can make themselves understood to each other and all the better continue the dream-making.

According to the image, then, our active existence-- and that means, our interactive involvement with others beyond ourselves-- is (internally to that involvement) a 'dream'-making. Now ordinarily we think of the phenomenon of dreaming as an activity of our sleep; in that activity, we are oblivious to reality within and beyond us, and immersed instead in a 'world' which, as long as we are dreaming, seems real, seems reality itself, even though in truth it is our own creation-- although in a way of which we are oblivious so long as we are dreaming.[17] Already in HAH, Nietzsche has treated dreams in such a vein: thus in HAH-I/13 ("Logic of the dream")[18] he gives a waking-life account of dreaming as a creative activity of our sleep which is occasioned by a stimulus (a nerve-excitation aroused, say, by the sounding of bells). That means that even in sleep there is some register, unconscious indeed but genuine, of an occasioning-working of something upon us, and the dreamer's activity amounts to the creation of images which are meant as interpretative representation of the source of the im-mediate occasioning factor, as a (causal) reading of the meaning of the nerve-excitation which is be-ing registered. Supposing this is at least part of what Nietzsche has in mind when he uses the dream as an *image*, then the image here would seem to imply this, that as part of what takes place in the continual interacting which is our active existence, other parties to the interacting effectively (caus-ally) impinge on (among other things) our capacity to receive and register presence, and thereby occa-sion, in virtue of our own sensing and interpreting, the generation by us of the sensuous and sensible appearance which *seems to us ordinarily* to be *not* something we are responsible for but to be a part of the occasioning reality that is making its presence felt in and to us. As we form our activity and integrate this something-appearing into that forming, we become immersed in this appearance and are responsive to its various features *in obliviousness to* how all of this that we are attending to, while occasioned by the working of reality beyond us, is nonetheless mostly our own work, our way of representing and construing that occasioning reality. We mistakenly take *the content we are attentive to* as *itself belonging to the reality* other than ourselves with which we are interacting. But if it is not itself (part of) that reality, such appearance is nonetheless part of the way that reality which *is* other to us and with which we *are interacting* makes *its presence* known *in and to us*. Since this 'making known' is *by way of our* powers and their way of operating, that appearance is *at the same time* most-ly our own work in its content, an image-world which is occasioned by an effectively working inter-active reality of ourselves and others but which is itself at best an indirect manifestation of reality.

As Nietzsche uses the image in this aphorism, it is possible (unlike the case with actual dreaming) for us to 'wake up' without waking out of the dream. That is, in our active involvement we are continually 'dreaming' but on occasion, internal to that involvement and *additionally* to that 'dreaming', we can also become self-conscious to this creative working of ourselves (this poetizing, loving and hating, drawing conclusions) which we are otherwise wholly obliviously involved in; and thus we can become aware of how this 'reality' that forms the content of our experience is in truth our own creation like the dream world.[19] At this point, however, the dream-image becomes less adequate for what Nietzsche seems to wish to convey, and not simply because of the non-parallel with waking up.[20] For any dream is a wholly private affair: neither the dreaming itself, nor the content of the dream, is accessible to and shared with others. While they are dreaming, different dreamers can not talk with each other: in my dream, I can of course dream a figure that represents myself and dream a conversing of that figure with another figure in my dream, but in doing this I never get beyond *my* dream. If waking up is no more than becoming aware of my continued dreaming, it does not by itself open me out to *others*, let alone to them as also *themselves dreaming*. 'Themselves dreaming their own dreams out of themselves' is not the same as 'them dreaming in *my dream*'. Nietzsche's *intent*, however, is to speak of ourselves as *actually* interacting with and encountering each other as acting out of ourselves, and to point to how, in the interacting, we make each other and ourselves present to ourselves in significant dependence on activity (here, creative construing) of our own; he does not intend to construe us in solipsistic vein, as absolutely cut off from each other, even though that is part of the apparent force of the dream-image because it is the apparent meaning of the actual dream experience.

Whatever 'wakes us up' without discontinuing the 'dream' brings appearance to shimmer and not seem what it did before-- not seem 'reality', solid and stable, simply there and confronting us, other and independent--; appearance now shines peculiarly in its contrast with the interactive reality *within which* it is being generated, shining as 'semblance', 'mirage-light', 'ghost-dance', which both hides and discloses its generative matrix. We find ourselves then, one dreamer among others, but a dreamer dancing self-aware the dance of our involvement with things; and in our seeking knowledge, we are both participating in the dance and aware of that participating as a dreaming going on in our seeking. In this complex awareness, we contrast with those whose conscientious effort of discernment, embodied in the sciences, is as yet unawakened. In GS/57 ("To the realists"), Nietzsche addresses those not-yet-awake dancers who nonetheless claim superior knowledge over that of most people because their objective approach to things enables them to separate out the objective from the subjective and to determine what is 'really there'. That is, ironically they claim to lay hold of the 'real' content of the 'dream', in contradistinction from the merely subjective coloring we introduce. "You sober human beings, who feel well-armed against passion and fantasizing and would like to make of your emptiness a matter of pride and an ornament: you call yourselves realists and hint that such as the world appears to you, so it is really constituted: before you alone, all reality stands unveiled, and you yourselves would be perhaps the best part of it ... !" These "sober human beings" know what in UHH Nietzsche called the objectivity of indifference. But looked at more carefully, the sobriety of such persons is ironic, only the empty forefront of a being who, compared with the fish, is in the highest degree "passionate and dark". Not only does he harbor, as heritage from the past, "valuations of things that have their origin in the passions and loves of former centuries", but

> your sobriety still has a secret and inextinguishable drunkenness incorporated into itself. Your love of 'reality', for example-- oh, that is an old primeval 'love'. In every feeling [*Empfindung*], in every sense-impression, there is a piece of this old love; and some fantasy, some prejudice, some unreason, some ignorance, some fear, and ever so much else has contributed to it and worked on it. That mountain there! That cloud there! What is 'real' in that? Subtract from it the phantasm and every human *contribution*, my sober friends! If you could! If you could forget your descent, your past, your training-- all of your humanity and animality. There is no 'reality' for us-- not for you either, my sober friends. We are not nearly as different as you think, and perhaps our good will to transcend intoxication is as respectable as your faith that you are altogether *incapable* of intoxication.

Here as in the GS/54, Nietzsche conceives the very presence of a mountain, say, as the issue of a formative process in which we 'poetize, love and hate, draw conclusions'; and in the use of our capacity for sensing and feeling that this process involves, we carry onward and make effective in the creative process valuations and feelings that are a heritage from much earlier times, an endowment received from antecedent beings in the line of life from which we stem.[21] Since there can be no mountain there for us without feeling having been at work in making this possible, the 'emptiness' of the 'sober' human being for whom the 'face' *is* 'reality' is only the foreground absence of consciously obvious emotionality in a person whose very register of presence depends on feeling and sensing as an unconscious but enabling background in the encounter in question.

In this process whereby this 'intermediary world' which is appearance arises and operates within the interacting of ourselves with what is other than ourselves, it is not simply feeling that plays a significant role in making things present to us in the way they come to be. Language is also an important power, for it is not simply what things are in our experience (their immediate character as presences, say) but how we speak of them, the names we use and the meanings those names carry, that makes things 'actual' in the social dimension of our interaction with them.[22] Now in all this creative work, we 'dream-makers' are artists and as such are focused on certain things rather than others in our work, highlighting this and downplaying that. Like the lover of a woman who hates and refuses to pay attention to a woman's repulsive natural functions, or the lover of God of former years who ignored nature and mechanics in favor of God's will and action, we too bring certain things forward and dismiss others in our attending to things. Thus speaking of the God-lovers of former days, Nietzsche says (in GS/59: "We artists"):

> Oh, these men of former times knew how to *dream* and did not find it necessary to go to sleep first. And we men of today still know this art much too well, despite all of our good will toward the day and being awake. It is quite enough to love, to hate, to desire, simply to feel [*empfinden*]-- and *immediately* the spirit and power of the dream overcome us, and with our eyes open, cold toward any danger, we climb up on the most dangerous paths, up onto the roofs and spires of fantasy-- without any sense of dizziness, as if we had been born to climb, we somnambulists of the day! We artists! We ignorers of what is natural, we moonstruck and Godstruck ones! We wander, still as death, unwearied, on heights that we do not see as heights but as our plains, as places safe and secure for us.

In this creative work of ours, something is at stake such that we idealize as we do-- poetize, fictionalize-- and make ourselves a world in which we are at home and know security so far as possible. At issue first and foremost is not truth, but such interpretation as forms a grasp of things and ourselves which enables us to live and act in response to life's drive for 'more life'. If today we have developed a 'waking' condition which is that of ourselves as philosophically 'scientific and conscientious', this has emerged in an 'us' who are 'dreaming on' all the while we are seeking to 'transcend intoxication' and to honor the 'day' and our 'waking' condition. At the level of our 'dreaming', however, we are not fussy about the precise accuracy of our interpretations; it is enough that they work and enable us to dwell in a meaningful world.

In these aphorisms of GS, Nietzsche is advancing further a way of speaking of reality which began in HAH and D. There, after confining reality to the temporal, he challenged the notion of any reality "in itself" by venturing on a reading of the "in relation to" whereby reality is to be construed as an interactive affair. Now in GS, he suggests that what our experience discloses to us (if and when we are truly awake and aware of what is happening) is that our participating in that interacting involves our constructing a whole 'world' or 'realm' (that of appearance, seeming) which ordinarily we lose ourselves in *as if it itself were reality*. In other aphorisms in GS, he explicates aspects of this thought by extending two related threads present already in some form in HAH and D: he restates various of the 'truths' which we have developed and used in constructing our 'world-home', despite the fact that these 'truths' were fictions and not the truths we believed them to be;[23] and in GS/110 ("Origin of knowledge") he gives a version of the "physiology and history of the evolution of organisms and concepts" first voiced in HAH-I/10 and developed piecemeal here and there in HAH and D.[24]

According to the account of the latter offered in GS, for a tremendous period of time the intellect produced nothing but errors, but some of these proved useful, species-preserving, and those who hit upon them or inherited them succeeded better in the struggle for existence. Included in those fruitful errors whose continual inheritance has made them almost part of the human endowment are errors about what is other than ourselves and errors about ourselves. Among the former are erroneous beliefs that there are identical things, enduring things, substantial or bodily things, and that a thing is what it appears to be; among the latter are erroneous beliefs that our will is free, and that what is good for me is also good in itself [*an und für sich*]. Skepticism about such propositions has emerged only recently, and with it, a notion of truth (not utility for life) as a standard for judging such beliefs. But by this time in the evolution of the race, our organism had incorporated and become adapted to these basic errors, so that all its higher functions, sense perception and every kind of sensation, operated by way of them. Because of this, they had become a powerful force in us, even conditions of our life. And indeed, when the ideas of 'true' and 'untrue' arose, even the norms by which one measured these harbored these fictions: logic, say, involves them. Nonetheless, while skepticism about them, doubt and denial of them, at first seemed madness, exceptional thinkers like the Eleatics in classical Greece did just that, and urged a way of life in which such denial and knowledge of 'the truth' was made a guiding force. But to affirm what they did-- the idea of the sage and of an intuition which disclosed 'the truth'--, they had to *deceive* themselves about their own state: they had to attribute to themselves impersonality and changeless-duration they did not have, to mistake the essence of the knower, to deny the force of the drives in knowing, and in general, to grasp reason as completely free self-originating activity; they shut their eyes to the fact that even they had come into their propositions by contradicting what was commonly counted as valid, or by longing for repose or sole-possession of lordly-dominance. Eventually, the refined development of honesty and skepticism made clear that in their living and judging they were not what they claimed, but were dependent on primeval drives and basic errors belonging to all sensitive [*empfindenden*] existence. Nonetheless, their claims, and the refined development of honesty and skepticism that undermined them, began a process which had further fruits; for now that the basic errors had been brought to light (though still unrecognized as errors), the fascination with 'truth' and the process of judging it could expand: other propositions that agreed with them but stood in conflict with each other could be judged in regard to which was more useful for life, and others that were neither useful nor harmful could be considered in the intellectual play which had been started. Gradually as the variety of judgments and convictions became entered into the struggle to determine 'the true', other drives than usefulness-to-life and intellectual-pleasure became entered into the play, and the intellectual consideration of 'truth' became an occupation, a profession, even a duty, and in any case something dignified. Eventually, knowing and striving for the truth became a need [*Bedürfnis*] among other needs, and the testing of truth-claims, and the employment of denial, mistrust, and contradiction in service of such testing, became a power, and in the end, a good, one in which drives which before had been taken as evil (because challenging belief and conviction) were harnessed to the achieving of something good and were themselves seen as good.

The story does not end here, however.

One further stage is pointed to at the end of GS/11 ("Consciousness"): because the drive to know the truth has become not simply a part of life but one with increasing power, it has not only brought various basic errors to light *as errors*, but has raised a question for us. For those errors, as a power of long-standing and basic usefulness, and this recently developed drive, as a new but vital and increasingly powerful drive, are now colliding with each other; and the thinker is that human being in whom the drive to truth, on the one hand, and the life-preserving errors, on the other, are now engaging in struggle. The question at issue is this: how far can truth, now that it has become *a* life-preserving power, displace those basic errors and itself become incorporated into our being and eventually function as a condition of life-- indeed, *the* basic condition-- as error has done for such a long time? Can we ever do without those errors?

A second further stage is manifest in GS/54: we have reached a place in the seeking for truth in which it is not simply this or that error that has been called into question, but the whole 'world of appearance' in its dream-like status. Even if we could see this 'apparent world' truly, unconfined by the errors that have served us in past as 'truths', we have discovered that 'appearance' is not reality, even if it is not nothing, and two questions emerge: first, do we have the capacity not simply to see but to say the truth concerning reality as an interactive affair and seeming as an aspect of this? Second, can incorporation of that truth be life-supporting?

On reality as it is coming into focus in GS, two final considerations are worth noting.

One concerns the place of values in reality and its formation. We have seen Nietzsche speaking of our 'dreaming with our eyes open' as a creative involvement on our part in the interaction of ourselves with what is other than ourselves. In that involvement, there is something at stake, so that part of the creativity involves evaluations and part of what issues in the culmination of the creative process is a world permeated by values. If on the individual level this signifies a creativity which for each of us is our own, as involved with each other it remains that there are different levels on which we live and act and there is a creativity at the higher levels whose creations have broader meaning and function than simply for the life of the individual in question. When in GS/301 ("The fanciful delusion of the contemplative") Nietzsche is distinguishing higher from lower human beings, and claiming that the higher "see and hear unspeakably more, and see and hear thoughtfully", he is characterizing the contemplative person whose creativity, issuing in various works, contributes to the broader culture which colors the world in which all live. Now the contemplative person is prone to think of contemplation as the activity of a "*spectator* and *listener* placed before the great visual and acoustic spectacle that is life", and thereby to misread his own condition. For as with the conscientious person who awakens while still dreaming on, the contemplative person (of whatever form, philosopher or artist or whatever) is himself also "the authentic poet who keeps on poetizing life" [*der eigentliche Dichter und Fortdichter des Lebens*]. Now as poet of life, he is different from those who function as actors in the drama of life, the so-called active type of human being who plays one role or another and is busy as such a role-player. But while contemplative, he is no mere spectator to life either. For his contemplative power enables him to look upon that work of life which is emerging with the help of his functioning as creative participant (that is, as someone at work with a power of creativity that is missing in the active type of human being).

> We, the thinking-feeling-ones [*die Denkend-Empfindenden*], are those who are really [*wirklich*] and continually *making* something that had not been there before: the whole eternally growing world of valuations, colors, accents, perspectives, scales for measuring higher and lower [*Stufen-leitern*], affirmations, and negations. This poem invented by us is continually learned and practised and translated into flesh and actuality-- indeed, into the everyday-- by the so-called practical human beings (those we just called actors). Whatever has *value* in the present-day world has it not in itself, according to its nature-- value does not belong to nature as such-- but it has value at some time given to it, bestowed on it, and *we* are these givers and bestowers. We have first created the world *which is of any concern to human beings*!

In the contemplative human being, that 'seeing' out of which he produces his works-- that sensitivity to higher things, that thoughtful cognizance of such things-- is his cognizance of that re-creation of life which is taking place in his dream-involvement with things; and what he produces in the way of a vision of life, a perspective and an insight into life's possibilities, contributes to the horizon of intelligibility within which life in the group whose cultural horizon is involved is encouraged to take shape. In this way the roles that are honored, the ways of living and acting that are encouraged, the sense of life's meaning that is being instilled, derive from the vision of such creative contemplatives (artists and philosophers, for example). Thereby 'reality' as a shared public affair comes to be re-shaped, new meaning given to things, and life fostered in those who make that reality their own.

The other consideration worth noting concerns the interacting in which the world of experience is 'created'. In GS/310 ("Will and wave"), Nietzsche offers an initial hint of the ultimate nature of the interacting which the awake-dreamer sees and which we have been considering previously in various facets internal to it, those through which appearance is constituted. In the image which he advances here, he anticipates an important thought in TSZ, which conceives of temporal reality in its inclusive nature as will-to-power. The beginning is with a portrayal of waves advancing against the cliffs, then receding.

> How eagerly this wave comes on, as if it were concerned to obtain something! How it crawls with terrifying haste into the inmost nooks of this fissured rock-cliff! It seems that it wants to steal a march on someone; it seems that something is hidden there, which has value, high value.-- And now it comes back, somewhat slower, still quite white with excitement-- is it disappointed? Has it found what it sought? Does it feign disappointment?-- But already another wave draws near, still more eagerly and savagely than the first, and its soul also seems full of secrets and of the hankering [*Gelüste*] of treasure-digging. Thus live the waves-- so live we, those who will! More, I do not say.

There follows a monological dialogue with the waves:

> Really? You mistrust me? You are angry with me, you beautiful monsters? Are you afraid lest I wholly give away your secret? Well, be angry with me, arch your dangerous green bodies as high as you can, raise a wall between me and the sun-- as you are doing now! Truly, even now nothing remains of the world but green twilight and green lightning. Carry on as you want [*wollt*], you high-spirited-ones, roaring with joy and malice-- or dive downward again, throw your emeralds down into the deepest depths, and cast your infinite white mane of foam and spray over them. Everything suits me, for everything suits you so well, and I am so well-disposed toward you for everything; how could I betray *you*? For-- mark my word!-- I know you and your secret, I know your kind! You and I, we are of *one* kind!-- You and I, we have *one* secret!

In HAH, we found Nietzsche imaging the flux of temporal reality as a waterfall. Here we find the continuous flow imaged as a body of water whose leading edge is articulated on its surface into a series of waves; and the title of the aphorism suggests that this pulsating water body is an image for will. In the living of we who will, there is something at stake, something to be gained, obtained, attained; and the drive of life presses our wanting (to secure the at-stake) into all the nooks and crannies of what is other to us, that we may reach and gain the treasure in question, something of great value, and do so ahead of others. Life is a competitive affair, seeking for a hidden treasure. Whether or not our venture in any instance finds what is being sought, whether it succeeds or is disappointed (in reality or merely in pretense), it remains excited and ventures again, even more eager and wild with the hankering after what is to be obtained. Such is life, an unending onflow of wave after wave, ever and ever a seeking of something still to be gained. Yet what is revealed by Nietzsche here is revealed only hiddenly: the image betrays, but also conceals. What has been intimated so far is not the whole story. For the unfolding of that, and its connection with temporality as it is pointed to in GS/341 ("The greatest weight"), we will have to wait for TSZ.

3. A life of inquiry and knowing

It is the centering of life in the reflective modality of the contemplative that Nietzsche celebrates most forcefully in GS. He speaks with irony of the great majority who know thinking as a laborious affair, and know the intellect as "a clumsy, gloomy, and creaking, machine which is difficult to get going" (GS/327: "Taking seriously"). In contrast to such 'taking things seriously' and laboring to think well, he himself knows the thinking of 'gay science', a thinking instinct with laughter and dancing, with quick and co-ordinated movement. But above all, he knows an atmosphere and a spirit in which inquiry, thinking, knowing, all find themselves at home, and he characterizes it as a "bright, transparent, vigorous, electrified air", within which reflection demands of itself (and is capable of) a rigor, a speed of weighing and judging matters and passing judgment, and an inexorability in matters large and small, that may be intimidating to someone not at home in this element but that are quite natural and easy for anyone who is at home there.[25] Thinking is there play, not as amusement but as in "playing the piano".

This play takes place within the larger matrix of life as something lived in the interactive coming together of ourselves with what is beyond us. If in the 'dreaming' which is the primordial creative or artistic element in our participation in that interacting a world is being generated and is taking shape in such way as reflects our reading of the at-stake in life, it is the task and meaning of the re-flective thinking that operates playfully within this creative working to direct itself simply to deter-mining truth. Animated by the passion for knowledge-- an "unconditioned propensity and impetus [*Hang und Drang*]"--, it strives for reflective insight as its "ultimate, unconditioned" object: that is what it has a passion for.[26] In regard to the effort which this passion animates, Nietzsche remarks up-on that as his own life attests it at its mid-point.

> No! Life has not disappointed me! From year to year I have found it more true, more desirable and more mysterious-- from that day on when the great liberator came over me, the thought that life may be an experiment of the knower-- and not a duty, not a calamity, not a deceitful fraud! And knowledge itself: let it be for others something else, for example a bed to rest on or the way to such a bed or a diverting conversation or a form of leisure-- for me it is a world of dangers and victories, in which heroic feelings also have their places to dance and play. '*Life as a means to knowledge*': with this principle in one's heart one can not only live courageously but even gaily and laugh gaily! And who would really know well about living and laughing if he did not first of all understand war and victory well?[27]

It is possible, however, for such a life to be one-sided in detrimental fashion, despite the rooting of reflective inquiry in life whole. For inquiry leads to insight into cognitive and sensitive existence as conditioned by delusion and error, as involved universally in untruth and mendaciousness; and the honesty which leads to this, if that were the whole or the sole focal-point of life, would make life unbearable for us and would have nausea and suicide as its consequences. But there is a potentially effective counterforce against this issue of honest inquiry, namely, art as the good will toward appearance and seeming, as a type of cult of the untrue in a positive life-supportive sense. In our engagement with things, we are artists, we poetize, and to that extent can (or at least seek to) provide ourselves a circumstantial context in which life is bearable as an aesthetic phenomenon.[28] But we need more, and art can help us achieve more. In particular, we need the good conscience, and the hand and eye, to be able to make *ourselves* into such a phenomenon, into a work of art. For

> at times, we need to rest from ourselves, by looking away and down upon ourselves and, from an artistic distance, laughing *over* ourselves or weeping *over* ourselves. We must discover the *hero* but likewise the *fool* that lies hidden in our passion for knowledge; we must from time to time be joyful [*froh*] in our folly in order to be able to remain joyful in our wisdom. And precisely because in our ultimate ground we are grave and serious human beings-- really, more weights than human beings-- nothing does us as much good as a *fool's cap*: we need it in relation to ourselves-- we need all exuberant, floating, dancing, mocking, childish, and blissful art, lest we lose the *freedom above-and-beyond things* that our ideal demands of us. It would mean a *re-lapse* for us, with our irritating honesty, to get involved entirely in morality and, for the sake of the exceedingly severe demands that we place on ourselves in these matters, to become virtuous monsters and scarecrows. We should [*sollen*] be *able* also to stand *above-and-beyond* morality-- and not only to stand with the anxious stiffness of a person who is afraid of slipping and falling any moment, but also to float and play above it. How then could we possibly dispense with art-- and with the fool?-- And as long as you are in any way *ashamed* before yourselves, you do not yet belong with us.[29]

If, then, the reflective inquirer is to answer adequately to life's drive toward 'more life', his life must be more than a matter of inquiry; it must be an affair in which he is able to 'create' his own be-ing, artistically to give it beautiful form, and thereby to place the central drive and his passionate pursuit in perspective. Although Nietzsche does not use the word here-- and his language becomes increasingly wary on this point--, this is a delineation of how the morality of responsibility which we saw emerging in the first phase of his thought returns, to be articulated with almost no use of the word "morality" but mainly by artistic or aesthetic language. There is an accompanying re-emergence worthy of note, the echo of the ideal of the artistic or musical Socrates which we saw also in the first phase. Thus speaking (in GS/113: "On the doctrine of poisons") of the separate development but eventual coming together of the varied drives which have been harnessed together and disciplined within 'scientific' thinking, and recalling the difficulty for the drives to "conceive their beside-one-another and to feel themselves with each other as functions of an organizing force in one human being", he observes: "how far even now are we from this, that the artistic powers and the practical wisdom of life are found added to scientific thinking, and that a higher organic system is formed in respect to which the scholar, the physician, the artist, and the law-giver, such as we know these now, must appear as paltry antiquities."

B. Agency

1. Consciousness, will, and action

In the preceding discussion we have already begun the articulation of our agency as it is found in GS, speaking of it in those aspects which are most critical to the constituting of experience and the world of experience. There are, however, more extensive characterizations in GS of facets of our active being which further advance Nietzsche's developing delineation of it. Our activity is an affair central to which is the decision-making and -executing capacity in and by whose operation we enter into and carry out our part of the interacting in which existence takes concrete shape. Internal differentiations of various sorts mark the operation in question, one of the most important for Nietzsche being that of the conscious and the unconscious. For reasons he has noticed in earlier works, we have come to mis-take consciousness and to give it a standing and role which reflect that mistaken reading. We think of it as constituting "the *kernel* [*Kern*] of the human being", "what is abiding, eternal, ultimate, and most original in him"; and this enduring core, the factor which gives unity to the organism, is regarded as "a determinate given magnitude" not subject to growth or variation (intermittence, for example). But all of this represents a misunderstanding and an overestimation. In reality, seen in an evolutionary perspective, consciousness is "the last and latest development of the organic, and hence also what is most unfinished and lacking in strength [*Unkräftigste*] in it". Deeper and more important in the constitution of our being is the "conserving association [*erhaltende Verband*] of the instincts", whose power, exceeding by far that of consciousness, enables this unconscious side of our being to function on the whole as a regulator that prevents the human being from going aground due to consciousness and its "perverse judgments and fantasies with open eyes, its lack of thoroughness and its credulity". Co-operating with this regulative functioning of the unconscious is another (and in this case, conscious) constraint upon consciousness, namely, our very pride in our conscious being. For our mistaken high regard has this beneficial consequence, that it prevents an all too fast development of this still not yet fully developed function in ourselves, since because we believe we possess it as basically a fully developed power, we have not exerted ourselves much to acquire it.[30]

So far in our evolution as living beings, the consciousness which has developed in us has functioned basically to enable us to incorporate into our instinctive life the life-preserving errors which Nietzsche has detailed in HAH, D, and again in GS. But we have arrived at the place in the development of the conscious side of our life where, in virtue of the concern for truth that has arisen and become a power in us, we are now beginning consciously to realize what has been happening and to enter upon the task of incorporating the knowledge which we are developing in our disciplined scientific pursuit of truth and of making it instinctive along with (or in displacement of) the life-preserving errors.

As part of the truth-seeking self-consciousness which has emerged, we find ourselves seeing our agency differently in a variety of respects closely connected with this matter of the standing of the conscious and the unconscious. Not only do we (mistakenly) think of consciousness as the core of ourselves, we also misconceive our decision-making power. What is central to this, namely, will, we take to be the conscious and deliberate power of initiating action and bringing ourselves to take part, from out of ourselves, in the interaction with circumstance. We have seen Nietzsche being critical of will as free-will; now we find him focusing his critical eye on will as the cause of effects. It is not that we do not bring about effects and do this by initiating actions. It is simply that this initiation is rather more complex an affair than a wholly conscious act.

> Every thoughtless person thinks, 'the will achieves effects by itself alone [*das allein Wirkende*]; willing is something simple, plainly given, underivable, intelligible in itself'. He is convinced if he does something (strikes something, say), it is he who strikes, and he has struck because he *willed* to strike. He notices nothing at all of a problem in this, but the feeling of *willing* suffices for him, not simply for the assumption of cause and effect but also for the belief he *understands* the relation. Of the mechanism of the happening and the hundred-fold subtle work which must be done in order that the blow come about or equally of the incapacity of the will in itself even to do only the least part of this work, he knows nothing. Will is for him a magically working force: the belief in the will, as in the cause of effects, is belief in magically working forces.[31]

Leaving aside the question of the mechanism involved in that unconscious side of our functioning whereby our conscious willing is made effective, Nietzsche construes conscious will as itself a complex responsive affair. For he urges: (a) will comes into play in dependence on antecedent feelings of pleasure and displeasure; (b) those feelings themselves depend on the way the *interpreting* intellect, which for the most part works without our being conscious of it, interprets some strong [*heftiger*] stimulus-- one and the same stimulus *can* be interpreted as pleasure or displeasure. In its simplest form, then, what we think of as our conscious will is a power of (apparently) determining ourselves to action which is evoked and motivated by pleasure and displeasure and which initiates only as the impetus formed in it is carried into effect in a complex and basically unconscious fashion involving forces and a mechanism of which we know little and which are not themselves the work of will.

Clearly, when Nietzsche is rejecting the notion that conscious will is by itself sufficient for the initiation of action, he is seeking to separate such a mistaken notion from a more adequate one, in which the conscious is indeed one side of a functioning to initiate, other sides to which are unconscious. Even his more adequate idea is not will as he conceives it in speaking of life's drive toward self-enjoyment and our willing engagement in action responsive to that drive. Our initiative is more complex and inclusive than any conscious element; it is *ours*-- is *our own*-- even though we are unaware of all the forces at work in it and even though the conscious side of our functioning within it is not in control of the whole and does not, by itself alone and unaided, accomplish the initiative. The "our own" refers to a self which is deeper and more inclusive than any 'conscious ego'.

The degree to which we are superficial in our insight into our own agency is made further manifest, and manifest on other grounds, in another and lengthy treatment of the matter of action (GS/335: "Long live physics!"), this time in reference to what people call moral action. "How many people know how to observe something? Of the few who do, how many observe themselves? 'Everybody is farthest away from himself': all who try the reins know this to their chagrin, and the maxim 'know thyself!', addressed to human beings by a god, is almost malicious." Here it is not that there are things present but unobserved because they are part of our unconscious side; it is rather that we do not pay attention to what is there to be seen. Thus Nietzsche claims: Almost everybody talks about the essence of moral action in a way that attests the failure of self-observation; for they speak as if to say: when a human being judges 'this is right [*recht*]', then infers 'therefore it must [*mutz*] be done', and then proceeds to do what he has thus recognized as right and designated as necessary [*notwendig*]-- then the essence of his action is moral. The discussion which follows elicits a variety of deficiencies in self-observation which enable this statement to have a surface plausibility.

The first point of focus-- the judgment 'this is right'-- is initially addressed in terms of whether the judging to this effect, being itself an act, might not be carried through in an immoral as well as a moral manner. But regardless of how it is carried out, what is the basis of the judgment, what justifies its claim: why is precisely this what is right? A response in terms of conscience (conscience tells me, and it is never immoral but is what alone determines what is supposed to be moral) is in turn occasion for further questions, and here we see what Nietzsche calls intellectual conscience at work, seeking out the *reasons why* one should listen to conscience and regard its judgment as true and infallible, seeking out the origin of the judgment 'this is right' (the drives, inclinations, aversions, experiences and lack of experience, which are its origin in one), and seeking out what drives a person to give ear to his/her conscience in this way rather than in that way (for one may do so in many different ways). The point of the question-raising is to lay bare what is involved in taking this-or-that-judgment as the voice of conscience, and to raise the possibility that a person's feeling that something is right may have its ground in the fact that the person has never thought much about him-/herself and has simply accepted blindly what has been designated as *right* ever since childhood; and then too there is the possibility that the acceptance of this voice is grounded in what past acceptance of it has brought the person in rewards and honors, and that selfish stubbornness has joined with the incapacity to envision new ideals to make the holding to this voice so much a part of one's life that it has become a condition of one's existence. The conclusion Nietzsche draws here is that if one "had thought more subtly, observed better, and learned more", one would no longer think of 'duty' and 'conscience' in the way one has been doing.

The second point of focus-- the conclusion 'therefore it must be done'-- concerns the categorical or unconditional nature of the imperative involved. Simply because it is right, therefore it must be done, and that 'must be done' is valid not simply for the person in question but for everyone. But the universality here-- in such a case, everyone must judge as I do and therefore do as I do-- is suspect. Nietzsche treats it as an expression of selfishness [*Selbstsucht*] to experience *one's own* judgment as forming and imposing a *universal* law. But more fundamentally: it betrays that the person has not yet discovered his-/her self nor created for him-/herself an ideal of his/her very own [*eigenes, eigenstes*]-- for that could never be somebody else's and much less that of all!

> Anyone who still judges 'in this case everybody would have to act like this' has not yet taken five steps toward self-knowledge. Otherwise he would know that there neither are nor can be actions that are the same; that every action that has ever been done was done in an altogether unique and irretrievable way, and that this will be equally true of every future action; that all prescriptions for actions relate only to their coarse exterior (even the most inward and subtle prescriptions of all moralities so far); that these prescriptions may lead to some semblance of sameness, *but really only to a semblance*; that as one contemplates or looks back upon any action at all, it is and remains impenetrable; that our opinions about 'good' and 'noble' and 'great' can never be *proved true* by our actions because every action is unknowable; that our opinions, valuations, and tables of what is good certainly belong among the most powerful levers in the involved mechanism of our actions, but that in any particular case the law of their mechanism is undemonstrable.

The conclusion which Nietzsche draws from this critique of the way we ordinarily think of moral action is this: that we need to leave behind the contemporary chatter about the 'moral value of our actions' (it is not well founded in the realities of action), and to "*limit* ourselves to the purification of our opinions and valuations and to the *creation of our own* [*eigener*] *new tables of what is good*". What we want is this alone,

> *to become who we are*-- human beings who are new, unique, incomparable, who give themselves laws, who create themselves. To that end we must become the best learners and discoverers of everything that is lawful and necessary in the world: we must become *physicists* in order to be able to be *creators* in this sense-- while hitherto all valuations and ideals have been based on *ignorance of* physics or were constructed so as to *contradict* it. Therefore: Long live physics! And even more so that which *compels* us to turn to physics-- our honesty.

Our will-- not our deliberate conscious will, but our wanting as distinctive individual human be-ings-- is to become ourselves: that familiar idea from SE recurs here, along with the idea that the self in question is new, unique, and incomparable. What differs is that this becoming involves a self-crea-tion and a self-legislation: laws there were in SE, and a higher self, both grounded in and expressing our nature; but the stress now is on *our own interpreting* that higher self (providing ourselves thereby with a determinate ideal) and *our own establishing* the prescriptions under which we determine how we live and achieve that ideal. As the emphasis on necessity and the reference to physics indicate (physics is the study of natural necessity), to 'interpret' and 'establish' properly (honestly and truth-fully? morally?) we must study the necessary, the lawful, in circumstance and in ourselves, and form our prescriptions in such fashion as enables our ideal to be realized under the conditions of genuine reality. The purification of our opinions (our ideas of that reality) and of our valuations (the transfor-mation of these as part of our vision of our ideal self), together with the development of a sense of the goods appropriate within such an ideal and to the reality of circumstance: these are the areas of concern which Nietzsche would call us to take seriously.

Yet in speaking as he does, is Nietzsche being altogether consistent? Is not 'purify your opinions' a prescription, and one addressed to us, to others than Nietzsche himself? Does this point to a mor-ality (an 'ought', indeed), and a universal morality at that, but one commensurate with our being in-dividual human beings, one which does not violate the uniqueness of each of us or of our actions? Has the morality of SE reasserted itself in this altered context?

2. Morality

In GS the terminological shift which began in HAH has become consolidated: what is now being conceived under the name "morality" is no longer the phenomenon which in SE was centrally, indeed almost exclusively, the matter in mind when that term was used, but is primarily what we would call "social morality". GS/116 ("Herd instinct") attests the state of the matter now.

> Wherever we encounter a morality, we also encounter a valuation and an order of rank of human drives and actions. These valuations and rank-orderings are always the expression of the needs of a community and herd: whatever benefits *it* first-- and second and third--, that is also the su-preme value-standard for all individuals. With morality, individuals are led to be a function of the herd and only as such a function to ascribe to themselves value. Since the conditions for the preservation of one community are very different from those of another, there are very different moralities; and in respect to the impending essential transformations of herds and communities, states and societies, we can prophesy that there will yet be very divergent moralities. Morality is the herd instinct in the individual.

This focus on the social and its norms is accompanied by a way of speaking of virtues which makes of them separate and identifiable states, dispositions or habits, which can be generated in non-moral fashion and which have a meaning and function at odds with individual well-being. The degree to which this is so can be seen in GS/21 ("To the teachers of selflessness"). Enumerating as virtues "industriousness, obedience, chastity, filial piety, justice", Nietzsche urges that the praise of these and other such states is far from selfless, for virtues are usually harmful to their possessor, being drives that dominate them too violently and covetously and resist the efforts of reason to keep them in balance with other drives. "When you have a virtue, a real, whole virtue (and not merely a mini-drive for some virtue), you are its *victim*." Praise of such things is due to the fact that virtues are useful for others and for society. What is really being valued when virtue is praised, then, is both its instru-mental nature and the unreason in it in virtue of which the individual lets himself be transformed into a function of the whole-- the blind drive holding sway in it and not allowing it to be held in bounds by the overall-advantage [*Gesamt-Vorteil*] of the individual. The praise of virtue is the praise of something privately harmful-- the praise of drives which take from a human being his noblest self-ishness and weaken the capacity in him for his own highest self-protection.

What emerges as contrasting with morality and virtue in the sense just noted is the kind of self-ishness in which the individual applies his whole strength-and-energy [*Kraft*] and reason to *his own* preservation, evolution, elevation, furtherance, that is, to the enlargement (expansion and broadening) of his own power [*Macht-Erweiterung*]. In this application, reason functions to maintain attention to the overall advantage of the individual, and what is generated thereby is what Nietzsche occasionally calls a morality of reason but what he usually avoids using the term "morality" to designate. The key element in this application of energy and reason is the individual's setting up of his own ideal, establishing thereby that determinate vision from which he derives the law of his own life, the joys and the rights that are distinctively his own.[32] Because of the creative nature of this setting up, Nietzsche uses artistic language to speak of the phenomenon in question. We are to become the "poets of our life",[33] or even more inwardly, are "to give style to our character". This last phrase, Nietzsche explicates in GS/290 ("One thing is needful").

> He practises [this great and rare art] who surveys all which his nature offers in the way of strengths and weaknesses and who fits it into an artistic plan until each one appears as art and reason and even the weaknesses still enrapture the eye. Here a great mass of second nature has been added, there a piece of first nature removed-- in both cases, with long practice and daily work on it. Here something ugly which does not allow of being removed is hidden, there it is re-interpreted into the sublime. Much that is vague, and resists the forming, is saved and used for distant views-- it should beckon into the distant and immeasurable. In the end, when the work is finished, it becomes evident how the constraint of a single taste governed and formed everything large and small. Whether this taste was good or bad is less important than one might suppose, enough that it was a *single* taste!

The morality of responsibility has here become an agent's self-shaping to form an integrated and co-herent whole that expresses the lawfulness of the well-formed. The beauty that is manifest here is the appearance of life's power, such as it can be realized and show itself in the integration whereby the person in question has secured his expanded power.

Because there is discipline involved in such creativity, because the ideal envisioned stands in some contrast and tension with what happens to be the case at the time of its installation, there are elements of self-restraint, self-control, self-mastery, renunciation, and sacrifice, involved in this morality which is not being called "morality". But as the various aphorisms which speak to this indicate, these elements are subordinate and supportive elements in a reaching which would envision that ideal and create its embodying reality.[34]

3. Motivation

GS does little to advance the account of motivation that we have seen emerging in HAH and D. It remains that, as Nietzsche sees it, the basic motivational forces in ourselves as living beings with a variety of needs, drives, and feelings, are pleasure and displeasure. The close attunement of his thought from the first to the matters of suffering (especially as this raises the question of meaning) and of the joy of creativity (again, especially as this answers to that question) continues. And the theme of the inseparable interconnection of the two becomes rehearsed again within this second phase of his thought, this time in close connection with its emphasis on the centrality of disciplined ('scientific') thought to life. The refinement in sensibility which Nietzsche urges as important in life and important to the pursuit of truth means an increase both of displeasure and pleasure, and a functioning of both in the embracing drive of life toward 'more life'.[35] As his observation and self-observation have grown more subtle and refined, so his critique of pity, of the morality of selflessness, has become both stronger and more nuanced. One aphorism in particular crystallizes the sort of psychological sensitivity which he can draw upon in treating the religion of pity and the morality of selflessness. GS/338 ("The will to suffer and those who feel pity") also seems to speak closely to his own experience. It is placed toward the end of GS, where in the concluding series (333-342) he is bringing his thought in this work to the climax which opens out into TSZ: a sign of the importance of the theme.

The aphorism begins with questions about the value of pity, both for the sufferer being addressed in it and for the person feeling pity. His initial focus is on the impact of pity upon the sufferer. That from which we suffer in the profoundest and most personal way is incomprehensible and inaccessible to almost everyone else. But when our suffering is noticed, it is interpreted superficially and the attempt to benefit us in our distress-- something which is of the essence in pity-- involves a stripping away of what is personal in it.

> One simply knows nothing of the whole inner sequence and intricacies that distress [*Unglück*] means for *me* or for *you*. The whole economy of my soul and the balance effected by 'distress', the breaking open of new springs and needs, the healing of old wounds, the shedding of whole periods of the past-- all these things that can be involved in distress are of no concern to our dear pitying friends; they want to *help* and do not consider that there is a personal necessity to distress, that terrors, deprivations, impoverishments, midnights, adventures, risks, and blunders are as necessary for me and for you as are their opposites, indeed that (to express it mystically) the path to our own heaven always goes through the voluptuousness of our own hell.

If these 'benefactors' treated themselves as they do others, and sought to prevent and forestall all possible distress ahead of time, then their religion of pity would harbor in itself a religion of comfortableness. The comfortable know little of the happiness of human beings. Happiness and distress are sisters, even twins, that either grow bigger together or (as in such people) remain small together.

Turning now to the impact of pity on the persons who feel it, Nietzsche asks:

> How is it possible, despite all, to keep to *one's own* way? Constantly, some cry or other calls us aside; rarely does our eye behold anything that does not require us to drop our own affairs and instantly to help. I know, there are a hundred praiseworthy and decent ways of losing *my own* way, and they are truly highly 'moral'! ... [Indeed, all that arouses pity and calls for help] is secretly seductive, for our 'own way' is an affair too hard and demanding and too remote from the love and gratitude of others: we are not unhappy to run away from it-- and from our very ownmost conscience-- and to flee into the conscience of the others and into the lovely temple of the 'religion of pity'.

Like war, pitying allows one "to turn aside from one's own goal", and to do so with good conscience. But in contrast, Nietzsche claims that his morality [*Moral*] says to him:

> live in seclusion so that you *can* live for yourself. Live in ignorance about what seems most important to your age. Between yourself and today, lay a skin of at least three centuries; let the cry of today, the noise of war and revolution, be only a murmur to you. You will, indeed, want to help: but only those whose distress you *understand* entirely because they have with you *one* suffering and *one* hope-- your *friends*; and only in the manner in which you help yourself. I want to make them more stout-hearted, more persevering, simpler, gayer; I want to teach them what is understood by so few today, and least of all by the preachers of pity [*Mitleidens*]-- to share in joy [*Mitfreude*].

If the displeasure which is pain invites others who notice it to respond in pity, it also normally invites those who feel it to respond differently to it than to pleasure. Both pleasure and pain are motivational forces which work crudely to support life. In the case of pain, as it makes itself felt in most of us most of the time, it speaks with one voice.

> In pain I hear the ship-captain's command: 'Take in the sails!' The bold seafarer 'man' must have schooled himself in a thousand ways of setting his sails; otherwise he would be done for in no time, and the ocean would soon swallow him up. We too must learn to live with diminished energies: as soon as pain gives its safety signal the time has come to diminish them; some great danger or other, a storm is approaching, and we would do well to 'fill our sails with

air' [*aufzubauschen*] as little as possible.[36]

There are times, and people, however, in which pain works in a different way. There are

> human beings who hear precisely the opposite command when great pain approaches and never
> look-down-upon more proudly, in more warlike fashion, in happier fashion, than when a storm
> comes up; indeed, pain itself gives them their greatest moments. These are the heroic human
> beings, the great *pain-bringers* of humanity, those few or rare human beings who have need of
> the very same apology that pain needs-- and truly one should not deny it to them. They are spe-
> cies-preserving species-furthering forces of the first rank, were it only by the fact that they op-
> pose comfortableness and do not conceal their disgust when faced with this kind of happiness.[37]

Clearly, then, while pleasure and displeasure are the fundamental elements in the motivational set-up of our nature, Nietzsche does not focus on them as if that were all there were to understanding motivation. Indeed, two other factors have emerged in D as significant, one is the higher feeling called "love", the other is power. In GS, Nietzsche does not say much on either one, but what he does say is significant for TSZ.

In D/145 ('*Unegoistic*'), two rather different things have already been pointed out as going under the name of "love", one involving an emptiness which sought to fill itself by appropriating what is beyond itself, the other involving a fulness which would discharge and empty itself. D/449 ("Where are the needy in spirit?") hearkened back to the second case, focusing on the giving away and com-municating which stems from the passionate love of knowledge and truth and which aids others in need from out of the achievements of that love. And according to D/309, both forms of 'love' may involve an effort to elevate the person who becomes the object of love, to see as much beauty as one can in that person. Beyond echoing (in GS/14: "What is called 'love'") the first case of love, GS adds something new (GS/334: "One must learn to love"): in seeking for the person who would fill the inner void or would focus the outward overflow, one must learn to love. What that means, Nietzsche suggests by a musical example.

> First one must *learn to hear* a figure and melody at all, to detect and distinguish it, to isolate it
> and delimit it as a separate life. Thus one needs to make the effort and exercise the good will
> required to *tolerate* it in spite of its alienness, and to practice patience in face of its appearance
> and expression as well as kind-heartedness in face of its oddity; finally a moment arrives when
> we have become *accustomed* to it, when we anticipate it and sense that we should miss it if it
> were missing; and from then on it works its compulsion and magic and does not stop before we
> have become its humble and enraptured lovers who want nothing better from the world than it
> and it once again. This happens to us not simply in music; that is how we have *learned to love*
> all the things which we now love. In the end we are always rewarded for our good will, pa-
> tience, fairmindedness, gentleness, in face of what is strange by its slowly shedding its veil and
> displaying itself as a new and indescribable beauty. That is its *thanks* for our hospitality. Even
> he who loves himself will have learned it in this way; for there is no other way. Love, too, has
> to be learned.

In GS/13 ("On the teaching of the feeling of power [*Macht*]"), Nietzsche continues that expanded attention to power which we saw emerging in HAH. Here too it is still considered in limited fashion and in a determinate context, and the scope of presentation is not that which is implicit in the image of the waves (GS/310) which we considered earlier. The beginning point is with our benefiting and hurting others: in both, we are exercising our power [*Macht*] on them, and in each of the cases as he considers them, one wants nothing further than this. This is so when the hurting is an inflicting of pain in order to make others feel one's own power; it is also so where the benefiting is addressed to others who are already dependent on us in some way and whom (say) we would like to help to in-crease their own power so that our own power increases. Whether the benefiting or hurting involves a sacrifice on our part does not basically change the matter: martyrs even offer their lives as part of *their* desire for power, or for the purpose of preserving *their* feeling of power. What is decisive is the enjoyment of our own power, and as for the manner-- whether one prefers the slow or the sudden, the assured or the dangerous and audacious growth of power [*Machtzuwachs*]--, that is a matter of taste, of how (given one's temperament) one would spice one's life.

C. Present, past and future: the crisis

In the larger historical sweep with which GS opens, a pattern of 'tragedy' following on 'tragedy' marks the movement of history: the formation of a social group with stable moral and religious systems, its endurance for a while, and then, after a period of turmoil, the undermining of the social order and the emergence of a new order or orders. In any such society, the period of turmoil is normally considered a time of corruption; but if one looks at it from a different angle it is possible to see that, in the breakdown taking place and the loss of effective molding power on the part of the traditional way, there are also changes going on which eventually bring to birth individuals who represent the fruit of the culture at its highest stage. These fruits, fallen from the tree of a people, carry the seeds of another future; the individuals represent spiritual forces which colonize and give rise to new states and communities. "Corruption is merely a nasty word for the autumn of a people."[38]

The Europe of Nietzsche's own day seems to him to be experiencing such a time of turmoil. It knows a kind of unrest, dissatisfaction, of both a 'masculine' and a 'feminine' type, great enough to signify that it is sick but unable as yet to cure itself. The sickness means unceasing change, thus affliction taking different forms: constantly new conditions, constantly new dangers and pains. But it is a sickness which is generating an "intellectual excitability that almost amounts to genius, and is in any case the mother of all genius": that is, it is a sickness of the sort which pregnancy is.[39] In particular, the youth of Europe is restless, bored and craving to do something which would enable them to endure that boredom. In GS/56 ("The craving for suffering"), Nietzsche diagnoses their condition as one centered in a craving to suffer and to draw from their suffering a probable reason for acting, for deeds. But the young people of Europe, in this way demanding unhappiness rather than happiness, long for it to come from the outside, that they may engage it and involve themselves in a fight which would give their lives a meaning. But in this, they are mistaken.

> If these distress-cravers felt in themselves the strength-and-energy [*Kraft*] to benefit themselves from within themselves, to do something for themselves, they would then also understand how, from within themselves, to create for themselves a distress [*Not*] which is their very own. Their inventions could then be more subtle-and-refined, and their satisfactions could sound like good music, whereas at present they fill the world with their distress-cries and consequently all too often only with the *feeling of distress*. They do not understand how to begin anything with themselves, and so they paint the unhappiness of others on the wall: they ever need others! And ever again, other others!

Certainly there is enough in the world around them to support their feeling of distress. Nietzsche does little in GS to expand the portrayals of the current world we have seen in the preceding works. He does briefly speak to the economic system, and its dehumanization, but he adds to his previous characterization of these only in minor fashion. What comes out more forcefully instead is the sense of what concerns him in his own inner distress amidst the present world, namely, what is needed given the crisis which obtains now despite the failure of his contemporaries to focus in on it and to begin taking the steps called for to deal with it.

To his mind, what he needs and what the situation needs is others-- a few others at least-- who, emerging in the warlike age that is about to begin, can help him prepare the way and gather the strength-and-energy for an even higher age, one in which heroism is carried widely into the sphere of knowledge and a spiritual 'war' is waged on behalf of ideas and their consequences. His lengthy characterization of these "preparatory human beings" (GS/283) ends with this thought and description: they are "more endangered human beings, more fruitful human beings, happier human beings!

For believe me: the secret for harvesting from existence the greatest fruitfulness and the greatest enjoyment is to *live dangerously!*"

As he sees it-- and sees himself as alone seeing this for the moment-- we have, already in the present, "left land and embarked on ship. We have destroyed the bridges behind us-- even more, the land behind us." And thus he urges:

> Now, little ship! Be careful! Beside you lies the ocean: it is true, it does not always roar, and occasionally it lies there like silk and gold and reverie of goodness. But there are hours when you will know that it is infinite and that there is nothing more fearful than infinity. Oh, the poor bird who has felt free and now strikes on the walls of its cage! Woe, when you feel homesick for the land, as though there were more *freedom* there-- and there is no 'land' any longer![40]

The sense he has, both of the crisis and of himself as alone seeing it at present, is presented dramatically in GS/125 ("The madman"). In this aphorism, the 'God is dead' refrain, which first is sounded in GS/108 ("New struggles"), sounds again, this time with the further thought that 'we have killed him-- you and I!', and with an articulation as well of the feeling that must grow as more people become aware of what we have done and (provided they do not reject that feeling) seek to keep open to things within the question-filled emptiness that is engulfing them.

GS/125 focuses on the event itself and the feelings which recognition of complicity in the event evokes: 'we have killed him', we have undermined belief in him in virtue of our pursuit of truth. In doing that, we have rejected the point of reference for life as it has been going on, that which enabled us to have a sense of meaning to life, a sense of meaningful direction. But how can we bear life without that reference-point and its support, ourselves alone now and really alone for the first time ever? How can we atone for our murderous act? "Is not the greatness of this deed too great for us? Must we ourselves not become gods simply to appear worthy of it? There has never been a greater deed; and whoever is born after us-- for the sake of this deed, he will belong to a higher history than all history hitherto." The voice that sounds in EH is already sounding here. Within the aphorism, the madman finds no one who understands what he means.

> 'I come too early,' he said then, 'I am still not at my time. This tremendous event is still underway and wandering-- it has still not penetrated to the ears of human beings. Thunder and lightning need time, the light of the stars needs time, deeds need time, even after they are done, in order to be seen and heard. This deed is for them still more distant than the most distant stars-- *and yet they have themselves done it!*'

It is not simply the deed, but the lack of realization-- of widespread realization-- of what has been done, that marks the present as Nietzsche would here convey it. But that lack means: we also do not realize how much we must change, if we are to be faithful to the deed. GS/108 ("New struggles") speaks indirectly of what we have gotten ourselves into: not simply life on earth alone without a god, but life needing a radical reconstruing, that we might bring it forth in its truth and begin the process of incorporating truth into our living of life. "After Buddha died, his shadow was still shown for centuries in a cave-- a tremendous, gruesome shadow. God is dead; but given the way human beings are, there may still be caves for thousands of years in which his shadow will be shown.-- And we-- we must also still vanquish his shadow." This "shadow" is the set of ways of thinking whose conceptualization of reality (mistakenly) retains, in 'secularized' form, the ways of thinking reflected in the fictitious concept "God". GS/109 ("Let us beware!") enumerates some of these shadows and ends with questions: "But when will we be at an end with our caution and guardedness? When will all these shadows of God no longer darken us? When will we have wholly de-deified nature? When will we be allowed to begin to naturalize us human beings with a pure, newly discovered, newly redeemed nature?"

From the series of "let us beware" phrases which structure the aphorism, we can discern the directions in which Nietzsche's attempt to free himself from the fetters of traditional thinking is moving.

The first caution is against thinking of the world [*die Welt*] as a living being, an organism: the-living depends on what is beyond itself (thus can not be the character of the whole), and life (on earth: life as alone we know it) is a late, derivative, rare and accidental, phenomenon which ought not to be made into something essential, universal, and eternal.

The second caution is against thinking of the universe [*das All*] as a machine: it is not constructed for any purpose, calling it a machine honors it too much.

The third caution is against universalizing the celestial order in our neighboring stars: the astral order in which we live is an exception (look at the Milky Way); it and the suitable duration conditioned by it have enabled the exception of exceptions, the formation of the organic. But in all eternity the overall character of the world [*der Welt*] is chaos, not as lacking necessity but as lacking order, arrangement, beauty, wisdom-- all our aesthetic anthropomorphisms. Its temporality harbors (what to our reason are) unsuccessful casts as far and away the rule (even to speak of 'unsuccessful', how-ever, is to humanize in a way that violates the universe [*das All*]); and those few exceptions are not the secret goal. Indeed, there is no goal: the whole musical-box repeats eternally its tune, and that tune is no melody.

The fourth caution is against other forms of humanization, anthropomorphization: speaking of it as heartless and irrational, or their opposites; calling it perfect, or beautiful, or noble, and thinking it wishes to become any of these things. None of our aesthetic and moral judgments apply to it; nor does it have any drive for self-preservation, or any other drive.

The fifth caution is against an anthropomorphism common when we think of scientific know-ledge, namely, thinking there are laws in nature. Law involves commanding and obeying, and trans-gressing: none pertain to the universe. There are only necessities. A companion anthropomorphism which does not apply to nature is purpose: there are no purposes, and for that reason also no accidents-- there is no meaning to the word "accident" except in a world of purposes.

The sixth caution is against the differentiation we make within the world, between the living and the dead (that is, the inanimate): the living is only a type of the dead, and a very rare type.

Finally, the seventh caution is against a kind of infinity to the temporal world, involving the world eternally creating the new, or involving the world holding eternally enduring substances. Indeed, matter is just as much an error as the god of the Eleatics.

The cumulative impact of this set of cautions is to leave us with a sense of this encompassing matrix of our finite existence as a temporal whole in an infinite time, circling in some limited time so as to repeat itself endlessly in its movement; it is a whole which has none of the elements of order we are accustomed to project into it so as to grasp it as a whole or in regard to its basic properties (those of its structure, of its dynamic). It is rather an order-less or chaotic affair which (in its parts and as a whole) moves through time and operates as it does with necessity; and its components are all of a kind ('dead'), continually changing-- a monster of energy, as Nietzsche will later phrase it.

What is this "universe" of which Nietzsche speaks in this cautionary way? Is it the world-- the world of appearance-- as the scientific discernment of its truth discloses it? But if, as earlier dis-cussion has claimed, the framework within which we construe reality is fictional, if appearance is a fiction-constituted seeming, such a universe would only be the fiction-mediated rendering of what is basic in the nature of the world of appearance, and truths about it would only be 'truths'. Or is it reality somehow discerned beyond the framework of fiction, the living-and-working which includes as participant the awakened dreamer who, having wakened to the face of things as 'seeming' and not *itself reality*, has in that awakened awareness become cognizant of the interactive reality that is con-stituted by all these participants in the dance of existence-- participants whose face, which before seemed reality itself but now is visible as only seeming, has even so a place *within* the interacting and itself shares thereby in the living-and-working which is the reality in question? How is it possible for Nietzsche to have come to know truth in this matter? What is the knowing in which he knows these things and discerns that 'this' is the truth of reality? On what evidence is such a claim based? Is his the knowing of those 'powerful and harmless souls, full of joy and peace' of which he spoke in D/424 and claimed that it is alone for them that truth is there?

If we are participants in ongoing existence, and if our participation is driving itself now toward an incorporation of such knowledge into our living, how is it possible to find meaning in life lived within-- and in truthful cognizance of-- such a 'whole'? Three aphorisms point to the direction in which Nietzsche is thinking and indicate some important components of his answer.

In GS/285 ("Excelsior"), Nietzsche speaks of the character of the act in which, having pursued inquiry far enough to see that God is dead, he responded in keeping with that truth. He sees it as an act of renunciation which requires great strength.

> 'You will never pray again, never adore again, never again rest in boundless trust; you refuse to remain standing before an ultimate wisdom, a final goodness, an ultimate power, and to unharness your thinking there; you have no perpetual guardian and friend for your seven solitudes; you live without a view of mountains with snow on their peaks and fire in their hearts; there is no longer for you the ultimate hand of an avenger or improver; there is no reason any longer in what happens, nor love in what happens to you; there is no resting-place any longer that stands open to your heart, where it only has to find and no longer to seek; you resist any final peace, you will the eternal recurrence of war and peace.'

Renunciation on such a scale and in such matters requires considerable strength. Where can that be found, he asks. His answer:

> There is a lake that one day refused to flow off, and threw up a dam there where previously it flowed off. Since then this lake has been rising ever higher. Perhaps this very renunciation will also lend the strength with which the renunciation itself can be borne; perhaps man will rise ever higher from the time when he no longer *flows out* into a god.

To have the strength to push ahead in this vein is not enough. To give meaning to life in the universe that is emerging into view, something further is needed . In GS/341, the next to last aphorism of GS ("The greatest weight") Nietzsche speaks to this matter of meaning in such a world.

> What if some day or night a demon were to steal after you into your loneliest loneliness and to say to you: 'This life as you now are living it and have lived it, you will have [*müssen*] to live once more and innumerable times more; and there will be nothing new in it, but every pain and every joy and every thought and sigh and everything unutterably small or great in your life will have to return to you, all in the same succession and sequence-- even this spider and this moonlight between the trees, and even this moment and I myself. The eternal hourglass of existence is turned upside down again and again, and you with it, speck of dust!' Would you not throw yourself down and gnash your teeth and curse the demon who spoke thus? Or have you once experienced a tremendous moment when you would have answered him: 'You are a god and never have I heard anything more divine.' If this thought gained power over you, it would transform you as you are or perhaps crush you. The question in each and every thing, 'Do you want this once more and innumerable times more?' would lie upon your actions as the greatest weight. Or how well-disposed would you have to become toward yourself and toward life to *long for nothing more* than for this ultimate eternal confirmation and seal?

Time forcefully brings home to a mortal the question of meaning, yet it also can bring a tremendous transforming moment when, even in a person anticipating endlessly being brought back into this very same temporal existence, that question may find its answer, one which can continually invest and transform decision-making to the end. What moment is that?

A few aphorisms earlier (GS/337: "The 'humaneness' of the future"), Nietzsche points to a future possible feeling of happiness which might represent such a tremendous moment and might enable earthly human life to find meaning in keeping with such a reality. Speaking of what he sees when he looks back on the present age with the eyes of a distant future age, he says: there is nothing more remarkable in present-day human beings than their own characteristic virtue and sickness, namely, their 'historical sense'. This feeling is the beginning of something altogether new and strange, a seed [*Keime*] which given a few centuries or more might become a marvelous growth. We of the present day, without really knowing what we are doing, are beginning to form the chain of a very powerful future feeling. One element in that feeling is this:

> Anyone who knows how to feel, as *his own history*, the history of humanity as a whole will sense in an enormously generalized way [*Verallgemeinerung*] all the grief of an invalid who thinks of health, of an old man who thinks of the dreams of his youth, of a lover deprived of his beloved, of the martyr whose ideal is perishing, of the hero on the evening after a battle that has decided nothing but brought him wounds and the loss of his friend.

But

> if one endured-- if one *could* endure-- this immense sum of grief of all kinds while yet being the hero who, as the second day of battle breaks, welcomes the dawn and his fortune [*Glück*], being a person whose horizon encompasses thousands of years past and future, being the heir of all the nobility of all past spirit-- an heir with a sense of obligation, the most aristocratic of old nobles and at the same time the first of a new nobility, the like of which no age has yet seen or dreamed of; if one could take upon one's soul all of this-- the oldest, the newest, losses, hopes, conquests, and the victories of humanity [*Menschheit*]; if finally one could hold all this in *one* soul and crowd it into a *single* feeling--, this would surely have to yield a happiness [*Glück*] that the human being has not known so far: the happiness of a god full of power [*Macht*] and love, full of tears and laughter, a happiness that, like the evening sun, continually bestows out of its own inexhaustible riches, pouring its gifts into the sea, feeling richest, as the sun does, only when even the poorest fisherman is also rowing with golden oars! This godlike feeling would then be called humaneness [*Menschlichkeit*].

Such a feeling, temporal through and through, ingathering a few thousand years of future and past into a limited life and into an even more limited moment in that life-- one marked by a fulness of power and love--, would open up a giving, a creativity, which bodies forth one's meaningful connection with all humanity. But is the tremendous moment of such a feeling of connectedness enough to give *life* meaning? Does that suffice to enable one (even for a moment, let alone to the end of life) to bear-- indeed, to welcome and want-- the return of everything just as it is?

INTERLUDE

A SECOND PAUSE

CHAPTER 12
The Return

In Chapter 2 and again in brief form in Chapter 8, we considered the spiritual dynamic within which the published writings to which we attended in Part II came to birth. The dominant formative factors shaping that dynamic were three. First was Nietzsche's disillusion at Bayreuth, his revulsion in the face of what no longer seemed to be genuinely his own, and his desire to purify himself of that. Second was his initial fixation on science as the model and guide now if reflection is to make not only its rejection of the impure but its advance into a more adequate grasp of matters. Third was what eventually released him from the dominance of the science/sciences in which he was initially submerging himself, namely, the revival of his deeper self, his coming back to life again, and his discovery (as he puts it in EH[1]) of his task compelling him, imperiously, to return to authentic historical studies. As the three writings we have just considered one-by-one arose within this spiritual movement, HAH set forth the new horizon and the themes that were generated in the initial self-purification and 'scientific' effort which Nietzsche was making in response to the disillusion at Bayreuth. Then D and GS, as they elaborated and consolidated the initial fruit of his self-purification, began increasingly to enter into the altered idea-framework he was developing a treatment of themes which attested the maturer realization of himself which was taking place at the time. In D, but especially in GS, that realization was generating a feel for life which, while kindred to that of the youthful self voicing itself in the first phase of his thinking, was more complex and subtle in virtue of the fuller and the more refined realization of life that was emerging; in turn the thought that operated out of this expanded-and-expanding realization and more complex and nuanced feel and operated with what was being disclosed in virtue of these was bringing to pass two things at once: one was an increasing complexity, depth, and fulness, to the new framework, and the other was a fuller and more apt penetration into the matters that had been thematic in his first phase of thinking but which were now coming to fuller and richer disclosure in his more mature realization of life.

In Chapters 9-11 we have considered in a work-by-work fashion Nietzsche's treatment of those matters most relevant to our concern for understanding his ideas of time and temporality. The thematic developments we have noted, while formed within the spiritual dynamic and (in Nietzsche's phrasing) being its translation into reason, are nonetheless different from the dynamic itself. As the fruit of truth-seeking effort the resources for which were becoming available in the spiritual evolution, the ideas involved define certain pathways of reflection on the problematic of existence which Nietzsche was opening up seeking insight. Just as the underlying spiritual dynamic in which the reflective paths were taking shape and the ideas gaining birth eventually culminated in an initial maturity in which Nietzsche had decisively returned to himself, so the thinking being essayed in this matrix came to blossom in its own right in an integrated and coherent work (namely, TSZ), which was at once a manifestation of that maturity and the first work of the third phase of his thought. As final preparation for our study of TSZ, let us elicit from the ideas set forth in Part II the main markers on the thought-paths which his reflection is now forming and on which it is making its way (if only gropingly and unwittingly) toward the two basic ideas of time and temporal reality which will be presented in TSZ, namely, the eternal recurrence of the same, and reality as will-to-power.

A. One path

The decisive initial step on one path is taken in HAH, in a thinking animated by the first two factors in the spiritual dynamic; this step is to make time the enabling condition and horizon for the intelligibility of *all* reality, not just of a created part. But what does that mean? If all reality is temporal, is it all temporal in the same sense? What sort of affair is this time-enabled-and-conditioned whole which is reality? Can it be understood in its intrinsic character without grasping the nature and function of space and spatiality? and likewise, of causality as an interactive affair?

Involved in the way Nietzsche takes this first step of temporalizing all reality are two things that reflect the animus at work in this step and decisively affecting its character.

One is that his thinking is initially shunted away from any attention to, and rethinking of, the *nature* of time (and space too, for that matter), despite the fact that this condition is gaining a more fundamental status than before. Instead, the way time was conceived in his first-phase thinking (in particular, in UHH) is carried over unquestioned. One refinement is made: the earlier idea of its being composed of a succession of moments (brief stretches of time) is replaced by the notion of its movement-ahead as being a perfectly continuous flow. But throughout this second phase, time's nature is still being conceived in refraction of the outward, and Nietzsche's thought remains oblivious to the inadequacy of his idea as a rendering of time in its full structure as activity-enabling condition.

The other is that his thinking, responding to a problematic that concerns a living being and reacting against his previous romanticism, 'idealism', and metaphysical reading of certain higher experience, which made the inward the key to grasping life and reality, is disposed to model itself now on the (unreflective) venture of natural science. Where life is concerned, this means accepting the invitation of the science of biology, to think life with a focus on its outward (biological) aspects and to think of the broadest temporal horizon for understanding life and its problematic as that of evolutionary biology. In his first-phase thought evolution had been acknowledged and was important in SE; but it is now re-conceived, to dismiss the 'meant-to-be' both in individual life and in life's overall movement and to deny any metaphysical meaning to the achievements of life's reaching for 'more life'. Given this dismissal and denial, when he would now interpret life as he knows it from within (as his own and being realized in his own activity) he construes its nature and meaning wholly within the biological and evolutionary horizon as he now understands it. For example, he now sees life's reaching for 'more life' not as leading to some determinate meant-to-be 'higher' but as involving simply the production of increasingly sublimated forms of the lower. The problematic of existence is one for beings whose life is intelligible in this perspective.

In regard to this thoroughly-temporal reality which his reflection is focused on now, the second step on the developing path we are here tracing is taken when, focusing his reaction against Schopenhauer and Kant on the Kantian address to reality, he challenges Kant's distinction of thing in itself vs. thing in relation to us. The thrust of his thinking on this point in HAH is, initially, to reject the 'in itself' as pertaining to reality but at the same time to maintain the (Kantian) sense of ourselves as active and as functioning in a constructing mode in that activity. Thus we co-author what in our interacting we encounter as the things of experience; but given that the horizon for making intelligible even this ongoing and current interaction of the human being with its environing world is an evolutionary one, the intimately and directly accessible facets of a living being's interacting are interpreted by way of the filter of distant events indirectly accessible by inference from the outwardly visible. Thus our current constructing activity is seen, above all, as a kind of life-enabling fictionalizing which, at the same time as it carries with it a heritage from such constructing activity by earlier life-forms, extends the long-standing interpretative effort by the living that has this same character.

While the first two steps on this path of reflection attest the first two factors in the underlying spiritual dynamic, the third step, taken in D, is taken in function of the third ingredient in that dynamic. For as an early expression of the expanding and revivifying disclosive matrix for his thinking which was coming with the revival of his self, we find Nietzsche (in D/539, say) engaged in an increasingly subtle and sensitive notice of what enters into our thinking, and more broadly into our experiencing. Not only are there moods which color that experiencing, and various pre-determinations to interpret in this-or-that way and thereby either not to notice at all, or to notice only under pre-judgment, what is there for our attention; but (continuing this line of thought in GS/114, 319) all experience, even the apparently purest sense experience, has a moral dimension, its character depending on the measure of honesty or dishonesty involved in our attention, notice, interpretation, and the various other activities in which our constructing is taking the shape it does.

As part of this noticing of what enters into our thinking, we find Nietzsche (still in D) taking a fourth and decisive step, by beginning to bring back to our attention our own maturing as providing the enabling ground for a power counter to this fictionalizing. For as he understands it, the evolution of ourselves is a strengthening of our capacity to take part in life, and that strengthening, including particularly an increasingly demanding intellectual conscience, eventually brings by nature a power or powerfulness to the soul (D/424) whereby it is empowered to find the truth coming into the light and coming forward there for our potential discernment. But this evolution brings the light forth in a peculiar way. For in GS, as the effort to move beyond Kant toward an interactive vision of reality is taken up again and brought to its fruition in this phase of his thinking (in GS/54), this discovery in D is integrated into his thinking on the fictionalizing of our experience-constructing activity and gives it a significant twist. Thus he speaks now (GS/57) of the possibility of not simply constructing experience in this fictionalizing fashion but of awakening to this activity of ourselves while it is still going on and of finding ourselves thus at once both engaged in and beyond it. As part of this transcending of the intoxication of our poetizing-activity and awakening to its continued going-on, we are wakened to the interactive reality within which this is taking place. Such reality does not disclose itself any longer as if it were something 'lying behind' the appearance which we encounter and experience in our living and acting; rather it shows itself as holding such appearance as the face of the interacting beings which form it but which never wholly manifest themselves in their own face. In its own character, in its interactivity, reality as we can awaken to it is centered in a kind of energy and power being exerted, discharged, enacted, and thereby in a concrete powers-in-tension connection being formed, in the interpreting-and-constructing interplay of causally-effective centers.

What is the fundamental character of such reality when seen from the perspective of our participation in it out of a matured power in ourselves? In his second-phase writings we get at most a glimpse of the "truth that is there" for the "powerful soul": for example, GS/108-109 offers intimations of a vision of the universe as it manifests itself when our conceiving has become freed of the 'shadows of God'. Likewise GS/310. But the fully-blossomed idea of an interactive thoroughly-temporal reality whose very nature and essence is will-to-power gains its connected and explicit presentation only in TSZ.

B. A second path

The decisive initial step on a second path, also taken in HAH in a thinking animated by the first two factors in the spiritual dynamic, is the denial of human freedom as it was being understood in the first phase of his thinking. For that phase had involved not only a creational reality, the created side of which was marked by space, time, and individuation, but an interacting of the beings composing creation which was causal in nature. Yet it had involved as well that we humans, whose participation in this interacting entered us crucially into our own growth and maturation in capacity, would naturally find in youth's transforming capacity an imperative call of conscience and a freedom on our part responsively to heed this and eventually to participate creatively in affairs as responsible beings. So long as his reflection was focused on clarifying youth's aspirational reaching and on reading the ultimate (cultural) meaning of our answering to this imperative, Nietzsche had not closely scrutinized the freedom he was taking for granted. But disillusion at Bayreuth had meant a turning against the 'romanticism' of the first phase, and with it, the engendering of an animus against and suspicion of the 'idealism' of youth; at the same time, with the accompanying turn away from the inward as basic and toward the outward sphere in which causality is readily grasped as necessitation in the form of alternativeless-determination-from-beyond, there emerged an approach to our own activity which brought a rejection of the notion of our will as free (wholly undetermined) and an effort to see our human nature in a way more in keeping with nature at large.

The accomplishing of this initial step, operating with an idea of time which (unbeknownst to him) misses its full activity-enabling nature, looks at our time-enabled activity through a further filter that makes the outward (the biological and evolutionary) be primary point of reference. Thereby we active beings are seen as living beings who arise reproductively in the extended course of life's evolution on earth and who inherit genetically an extensive past in our initially given endowment and nature (HAH-I/2, 10, 12, 16, 18). It is due to this genesis and this endowment and nature that we have such capacities as we have for being active out of ourselves and that we are entered by a responsive decision-making capacity into an interacting with our environment in which we incorporate it somehow into the realization of the life in ourselves. In this circumstantially-conditioned functioning of ourselves as the living active beings which our nature makes us be, our ongoing interacting is grasped as oppositional in basic nature: what surrounds us circumstantially is '-posed' over against us ('op-') and comes to meet us as functioning out of itself independently of us. Yet because we interlock as we interact, we form a whole which, judging from the way what we encounter seems to us to function and from how we are now looking at ourselves as parts of this whole, seems to operate internally to itself (i.e. in the interacting) with the necessity of alternativeless-compulsion-from-beyond.

The initial effort in HAH to see our own participation in this interacting in this fashion, under the waterfall-image (HAH-I/106), is complemented by an approach which affirms in corrected form the grounds that are being mis-taken in our notion of free will, namely, a sense of the 'out of itself' functioning of ourselves as active, as forming and carrying out initiatives (HAH-II/WS-9). If we readily misconstrue our nature and natural functioning as attesting free will, this is because it does indeed embody a kind of freedom, one with two moments. For using an Aristotle-like notion of nature as an internal principle-and-beginning-point of motion, Nietzsche grasps the initial moment of such freedom (that of the unimpeded emergence from our nature of an activity-forming functioning which naturally brings forth over time the potential harbored in the initial endowment) as being modified in our responsive encounter with circumstance; in particular, it is expanded in a second moment of fluent and self-pro-ductive activity if and when circumstance allows (or even favors and enhances) an accumulative learning-to-function which brings that spontaneous functioning to appropriate our natural potential more fully than otherwise. We thus develop naturally and grow more capable humanly with the help of circumstance. The completion in HAH of the first step on the thought-path we are recalling (that of the rejection of free will) is accomplished when Nietzsche ventures (HAH-I/107) an understanding of the interacting involved in this functioning that includes the necessity of our nature's self-evolving via its own functioning under the necessity of alternativeless-determination-from-beyond that seems visible in the outward side of the world. Exclusion of free will by assimilating the decision-making expressive of our nature to the necessitation in outwardly-discernible 'nature' both 'naturalizes' our decision-making and -executing capacity and retains the (genuine) basis for the illusion of freewill.

Accompanying this first step is a second, taken also in HAH, which explores the decision-making and -executing functioning of ourselves to make apparent the necessity involved in the nature-based responsive freedom which is involved. Crucial here are two things: first, that the at-stake which we are responsively attuned to is a good (pleasure or self-enjoyment in the form of an enjoyment of our own power in the act of making an impact on something), and that by our nature we are necessarily drawn to seek to realize this good; and second, that the native powers involved in the decision-making are (on one side) various drives and talents and (on the other) a practical intelligence or mind, all operating according to the necessity of their own distinctive natures (HAH-I/102, 104, 107). If the functioning of our inclusive (human) nature is not distorted by the op-positional working of outward circumstance or by inept resolution of the inward conflicts of drives and talents competing to be the actual motivations of our deeds, we grow by nature to the place where the functioning of practical intelligence in the decision-making can become informed by the powers of reflection and reason that emerge in youth. With the natural emergence of reflective reason, we have the opportunity to grasp in a practically intelligent way our being as continuing beings and the at-stake in our activity (as it relates to our lives) as the self-enjoyment of ourselves as such beings. That means: we can envision and seek to realize the self-enjoyment of the fullest power open to us as evolving and changing beings. This focus on power as what the life in us reaches for and moves us toward (HAH-I/104) is accompanied in HAH by an exploration of the idea of power in various contexts (HAH-I/50, 103, 134, 137, 142, 170, 603, 609); linked with this is a suggestion that instrumental to the achieving of the highest power in ourselves is an energy, connected closely with passion, whereby we apply ourselves, endure frustrations and suffering, and can stretch our potential for creativity and make the most (the highest and best) of our talents (HAH-I/164, 230, 232, 233, 235, 242, 263, 272, 273, 589, 603).

Beginning with D in places, and then in GS in a dominant way, we find this path of thought being developed next in ways that reflect the third factor in the spiritual dynamic of this phase in Nietzsche's thinking, namely, the revival of his deeper self and the maturing of himself humanly. In particular, in D/130 Nietzsche links his conception of our agency-- our venturing amidst circumstance as agents, and our responsiveness in that venturing to an at-stake, both as intelligible through the notions of natural necessity, power and energy-- with the thought that most of what is operative in our decision-making and -executing is unconscious to ourselves, unnoticed in and to what is functioning consciously in us. And yet, the idea that we are ignorant of much of what makes our decision-making and our activity what they are is not offered as making the decision not our own, but rather as making it that of selves who are not reducible to their conscious egos. It is also not presented as incompatible with our capacity to assume responsibility for our lives and our evolving selves, whether as gardeners (D/560) or as pregnant mothers (D/552) or as artists (D/548).

Finally, in GS Nietzsche not only continues to stress that life calls us to the integrated realization of our higher self and thus to assume the responsibility of being gardener and artist of our own becoming, poets of our own life (GS/299); but he stresses that such realization of our own lives-- such becoming what we are-- requires of us an exploring of the necessities that form the ineluctable outward matrix for this realization and mark the efficacious realities of circumstance whose opposition challenges us, in favorable and unfavorable ways, to rise to our own heights and realize our own fullest power (GS/335). With the notion of the necessity in functioning of our own nature as issuing in the intensity of a realized capacity, energy, and power, amidst but also in tension and in complicity with the necessary functioning of circumstance, we are seeing the integrated culmination of the path on which Nietzsche is discovering how, because the interactive thoroughly-temporal reality he is gaining sight of includes us as participants, to fill out the idea of such reality as in its nature and essence will-to-power.[2]

C. Two questions implicit in the two paths

Immanent in Nietzsche's breaking of the two paths recalled here are two questions which place time and temporality into their most critical perspective.

1. First question

The thinking which is developing on the two paths and which issues in novel insights that become the heart of Nietzsche's next writing is that of a philosophic endeavor which is responsive to the problematic of existence that bears on us human beings as raising the question of meaning, of life's meaningfulness. When at the start of the first path we have just traced out Nietzsche denies to reality any transcendence of time, then the answer to the question of meaning which seemed plausible to him in his first-phase thought is undermined. For it involved the eternal, the timeless, and in particular, a creational reality in which time not only enabled the existence and functioning of the human creature who was caught up in the question of meaning but also enabled its answering, namely, the artistic-aesthetic participation of the human being in the consummation of creation. As he understands it now, there is no transcendent creation or eternity; instead we find ourselves involved in a reality whose pervasive temporality precludes such an answer-- indeed, precludes his previous understanding of the question itself, denying its roots in reality.

In HAH, the question of meaning arises again, this time to confront the 'man of knowledge', that is, the human being who is discovering not only the thoroughly-temporal character of reality and life but also how deeply immersed human life is in illusions, falsities, injustice. In reflection of the impact of the emergence of this question in this person, Nietzsche asks (for example) whether one can consciously reside in untruth (HAH-I/34), and speaks also of the bitter draught that we must now swallow when those things in which we have previously placed the patent of our humanity (namely, responsibility and duty) seem to be illusions (HAH-I/ 107). Given that included in what we are now grasping as illusion are all those visions of purpose which up to now have been offered as giving meaning to the existence of the race and to the efforts of individuals (HAH-I/33), is there something about reality and life as we are now discovering and acknowledging these to be which enables another answer to be found, one appropriate to them and their distinctive character? Indeed, what are the roots of the question itself now, since they no longer reside as before in the trans-temporal act of creation and the resultant constitution of the creature? Is there something at stake in this thoroughly temporal whole, something that is to be secured with our help, and something the securing of which makes our life meaningful? But what, and why that?

In HAH, Nietzsche grasps the question of meaning as rooted in the nature of life rather than in the nature of creation. What is at stake in life, that height of self-enjoyment (power) which life seeks, is what gives individual life direction to its striving and meaning with its achievement; and if we look at ourselves whole, see the way in which we human beings are essentially connected and are not simply disconnected individuals, and look to a collective achievement that would bring meaning, we would find it (so Nietzsche claims) in the future realization of what he calls the "great collective fruit-tree of humanity" (HAH-II/WS-189).

And yet, this reference to the future as the locus for the realization of meaning must be such that, if meaning is to be genuine and sufficient, we need to be equal to an implication of temporality which, while recognized ever since BT, looms all the larger now that nothing eternal can counterbalance it. Thus in D/49 he acknowledges: whatever we achieve in the future of our individual life, that life ends in death; but problematic as that is, it is not nearly as problematic as the collective end of human life on earth. Simply looking to the future for meaning, then, whether in the form of individual creativity or that of contributing to a collective realization of life, would not seem to be enough. For that makes the Silenic sense of time's implication prevail, or rather, it does so unless (as D/45 suggests) humankind could, collectively, face this lot by sacrificing itself for something higher: he alludes to the eventual communication of knowledge from star to star, to other beings on other planets, by us earthlings before we become extinguished. But this form of tragic end does not seem fully to satisfy him.

GS brings the intimation of a revised sense of what would provide meaning in the thoroughly temporal reality he is now thinking of. In an aphorism (GS/341) which already hints of the circular side of the conception of time that is to appear in TSZ, Nietzsche speaks of a "tremendous moment" which is sufficiently momentous that, if someone suggested to us that time implicates life in a round of existence which brings that moment and this life back again infinite times, we would feel such joy that, despite what else would also be brought back, we would wish for that endless return without reserve. But what sort of moment would that be? And what is life such that some momentary fulness and power which was through-and-through transient could suffice?

In GS/337 he alludes to the character of such a moment when, referring to a development of that 'historical sense' which he had addressed in UHH, he speaks of the powerful [*mächtigen*] future feeling he calls humaneness. In it one feels both futurally and historically, and in particular, feels the history of humanity as one's own, crowding all that past venturing of humankind into a single feeling. That feeling would include all the sadness one would have to feel over the suffering, failure, and loss, humanity has known but would integrate it into the "happiness of a god full of power and love, full of tears and laughter". But within a world that far outreaches temporally our determinate knowledge of its course, reaching beyond all that is the earth and its coming-to-be and all that is life and its coming-to-be, such a feeling, even if it encompassed human life and its whole coming-to-be and history, would pass; even such a person feeling that feeling in an enduring way to the end of life and being creative out of it would pass. How would such a moment, then, be enough? How would it suffice life's reaching for meaning? Indeed, would it if it did not include the knowledge, as part of it, that it would return over and over again? But how, beyond intensifying the moment, would such knowledge make something sufficing out of what otherwise would not be? Again, would such a feeling be enough if no one else felt it as well? Underlying these questions is the further one, of what provides the standard, the measure, for this "enough", this "sufficing". Is it really life that does this? Individual life? Collective life? Or is it existence at large? Or ... ?

There is a glimpse here in GS of how, as thought is culminating on the two paths in a vision of reality as will-to-power, time might not simply make the question of meaning pressing for a temporal being but might also enable a seemingly sufficient resolution to it in virtue of a fulness of power and love. But could one make sense of such a reolution under Nietzsche's second-phase idea of time's nature? Indeed, is that idea even apt for making intelligible the question which such a resolution is to answer?

2. Second question

The thinking which has been developing on the two paths we earlier sketched out and which is entered into the question of whether meaning is genuinely possible in a wholly temporal universe forms a phase in a reflective endeavor which we have been following from its start in BT. Our consideration of Nietzsche's thinking from that start, taking shape in consonance with the urging of EH which we noted in Chapter 1, has been twofold. On the one hand, we have been concerned with the thematic exposition and development in his writings of ideas of time and temporality which are fruit of reflective inquiry responsively attuned to the problematic of existence and which make a claim to truth; on the other hand, we have been concerned with that exposition and development as also being grounded in and manifesting his maturation as a human being and his acquiring thereby of the resources for inquiry needed for understanding time and temporality. The issue underlying this twofold concern can be formulated by asking: what is the nature of the standpoint, powers, and resources, needed for discerning the truth of the problematic of existence? But we may also phrase this issue in more general terms, namely, in temporal ones. Since Nietzsche's inquiry and his resources depend and draw upon his own realization of that temporality of human life which is growth and maturation, we may therefore ask: in what sense and way does time enable temporal beings to discern the truth of the problematic of existence, including the truth of its own (time's) nature? And implicit in that question: What is the nature of time itself, such that we temporal beings, made temporal under the enabling and conditioning of time, can reach such discernment (supposing that we can)?

Keeping in mind Nietzsche's own retrospective assessment of his writings as works of a maturity-manifesting truth-claiming sort, we have ourselves considered the works one by one, noting thematic elements in them and pointing to how-- and occasionally, how well or badly-- their content has been grounded in experience, and in particular, in the experiencing and resources available to him at the time, so far as this could be ascertained from the writings themselves. In particular regard to the writings of this second phase, we have seen a significant shift taking place from what we saw in the first phase: a shift in the form of the writing, in the perspective in which the themes have been developed, and in the maturational-condition and reflective standpoint of the thinker-author and the resources he was thus able to employ in inquiry. The form of writing is now aphoristic; the perspective of thematic development is that of time as the enabling condition for *all* beings and existence, and evolution as the temporal character of the larger life-context for understanding living beings and in particular human beings; and in virtue of a traumatic and explosive initial liberational surge, followed by a calming down and, in the course of this, the reviving and strengthening of a self that had earlier been submerged in others but is now emerging in its own right, the reflective standpoint has taken a changing shape which attests the developing of an increasingly refined sensitivity and a more determined reflective notice and attention to nuances and depths both. Are these three things connected, not just chance companions but intimately related?

In considering the transition between Nietzsche's first and second phases, we were faced with a radical shift in perspective and in form of writing, and a traumatic personal shift as well, but one which remained within the maturational condition of youth. The second phase begins, thus, as one of youth in disillusion and determined on rejection of what in itself seems alien to itself. In considering the two paths sketched out above, we have been pointing to the development of thought taking place as Nietzsche was on the way toward another transition. This transition would be one of a rather different character from the previous one, and the basic difference is to be found in the maturational element: the transition is culmination of a revival and maturing of the self that had been submerged in the first phase and which the purification effort was freeing. As that revival and augmenting in capacity was taking place, two things were happening: a tension was emerging in and for reflection, and a transformation was being prepared maturationally that would effect his initial entry into the maturity of his being beyond youth and would complete his return to himself.

The tension in question arises after Nietzsche, while unburdening himself of the submerging force of Schopenhauer and Wagner that had constrained his first-phase thought, initially burdens himself in cognate fashion with science (in HAH) and with its help strengthens the hold of his (now slightly modified) idea of time and makes it the horizon of all. As the previously submerged higher self in himself revives and begins to voice itself (in D, but especially in GS), this 'scientific' dress becomes shed without the 'scientific' being rejected: it is simply put in its secondary place. It is as if his thinking is finally breaking out of all alien confinements and is coming to form itself with some assurance, clarity, and purity, from out of himself. This coming into his own reflectively beyond even the 'scientific', because its matrix is the maturational transformation taking place in his own person, means that along with other themes from his first-phase thinking the temporality of human beings as growing and maturing beings comes back as reflectively-thematic counterpart to the changes in himself and his capacities. But more is happening than this reviving of a centering of himself-as-thinker back in himself as growing human being and his rehearsal in reflection of important facets of the earlier thinking by him that had a kindred centering. Or rather, there is an aspect of what is happening that is not as readily caught as these matters, and that is this: the growing tension between (on one hand) this reviving self, what is coming to be revealed in immediacy through it, and what his thinking is beginning to discern in that, and (on the other hand) the horizon of intelligibility in which his second-phase thought is working, one confined by time as he is now thinking it and by evolution. This tension is to a great extent resolved in the course of the dynamic which enters him into maturity and into a third phase of thinking and writing.

We can catch a glimpse of that tension-resolving dynamic by noting what the next work which he composes (namely, TSZ) attests, in its form and content. For in both regards, it is quite different from the works of this second phase.[3]

In TSZ, the idea of time which had carried over from the first phase with only a slight modification becomes significantly modified; a part of this new modification is hinted in GS, but it comes fully into sight only in TSZ. There the fully developed idea is the central idea of the whole work. While this represents one element in the resolution to the tension, achieved by bringing the concept of time more in line with what is being revealed in immediacy in virtue of his reviving self, it is not all. For out of what was happening and becoming disclosed to him, Nietzsche formed the determination to communicate his dawning insights into time in very different fashion from previously. To convey and share them, he shifts out of the aphoristic form into a dramatic form, and more specifically, a dramatic form into which a biographical element is entered. Thus the matter of growth and maturation, something decisive in which was happening in his own person, becomes embedded in the very form of TSZ so that this aspect of temporality inflects the medium for the presentation and communication of his ideas.

What do these two features of the next work-- one relating to its content, one to its form-- indicate about the impetus building while the second-phase works were being composed, the tension that this was introducing, and the disclosive matrix belonging to the completing of his return to himself? They suggest that the end of his youth and his entry upon maturity were marked by the strengthening revival of his sense of the *temporality* of human being as an affair of *maturation* (*power*), and that this revival *included an altered register of time itself*, not simply of temporality-- one sufficiently pressing to call attention to itself and to catch his attention reflectively. Bringing both temporality and time forcefully back to mind for reflection, this disclosive matrix of his entry into maturity was opening for him the opportunity for a fundamental re-conceiving of both time and temporality and thence for deepening his idea of both while also resolving the tension that had developed between time as he had been accepting it to be and how it was coming to light now in an ampler and subtler disclosive matrix. If the time of his life was bringing this enabling condition of being and determinant of temporality (namely, time) to presence as being at some odds with his previous idea of it and thus was drawing him to more deeply and thoroughly probe presence so as to better understand the nature of that condition, it remains to be seen how fully and aptly he was able to respond to the opportunity offered for the reconceiving that was needed. For that, we turn now to TSZ.

PART III

MATURITY

CHAPTER 13
Thus Spoke Zarathustra: a drama

The second phase of Nietzsche's thought began with a turn against the first, and developed by a purification of himself and a gradual advance toward thought that would recover and adequately voice the higher self in himself that had become obscured in his earlier efforts. As in the first phase, the set of works involved in the second was uniform in form, being a set of aphoristic writings in contrast with the initial set of essays. In the third phase of his thought Nietzsche operates out of a regained sense of self and presents the thoughts which form a horizon which he now feels is his own; having achieved his own words for his own things, he is discovering and working out his individual destiny in a self-aware fashion. His entry into this third phase is doubly dramatic. For *Thus Spoke Zarathustra* not only bursts on the scene with a lyric voice unknown in his previous works, but its form is also that of a drama. It is thus unlike in form to what precedes it, but also distinct in form from the works which follow and which elaborate on the horizon itself and the visible look of things within it. For this elaboration brings back the aphoristic form of the second phase, and even (in *On the Genealogy of Morals*) returns to something like the essay form of the first phase.

TSZ is a four Part work, the first three Parts of which were composed in short intense bursts of inspiration between February 1883 and January 1884.[1] The basic thoughts in those Parts were already formed in the years before the composition took place. That includes the idea of the eternal recurrence of the same, which in EH Nietzsche claims is the central idea in TSZ. The idea had first come to him in August 1881, eighteen months before the first burst of inspiration which issued in Part I of the work.[2] There are also numerous passages which closely echo aphorisms in the works of his second phase thought. What is new in the work is the dramatic form, the organizing and formulating of his thought and its presentation to make break-through ideas of temporality and reality (eternal recurrence, and will-to-power) the decisive ones, and the extent of the personal element in the presentation (something we saw increasing in Books III-IV of GS); also new is the work's dominant tonality, the intense pitch of its emotionality, which is sustained through a variety of shifts of mood, attempts at humor and sarcasm, and ventures into poetry, and which is persistently exhortatory as the state of things is characterized and the reader is urged to recognize it and to respond accordingly.

The drama is especially noticeable for two features, both of which depart from the way Nietzsche has been presenting his thought in writing.

To begin with, it is intentionally indirect. The central figure in the drama is someone called Zarathustra, and more specifically, is the historical religious figure with that name. But that figure appears as transfigured under Nietzsche's hand. In EH (Part IV, Section 3) Nietzsche points to part of the meaning of this figure being the main one in TSZ. "What constitutes the tremendous historical uniqueness of that Persian" was that he was the "first to consider the fight of good and evil the very wheel in the machinery of things: the transposition of morality into the metaphysical realm, as a force, cause, and end in itself, is *his* work". Given this, Nietzsche's use of Zarathustra has the following rationale, that

> Zarathustra *created* this most calamitous error, morality; consequently, he must also be the first to *recognize* it . ... Zarathustra is more truthful than any other thinker, his teaching, and only it, has truthfulness as the highest virtue ... . To speak the truth and to *shoot well with arrows*, that is Persian virtue. ... The self-overcoming of morality, out of truthfulness; the self-overcoming of the moralist, into his opposite-- into me-- that is what the name of Zarathustra means in my mouth.[3]

The kind of indirectness which the use of a transformed Zarathustra makes possible for Nietzsche's presentation of his thought needs careful understanding. Zarathustra is *not* Nietzsche, however much of himself Nietzsche enters into the delineation of the life, character, and experience of Zarathustra. The Zarathustra of TSZ is rather one-- the main-- figure in a work created by Nietzsche. So far as Nietzsche himself appears in the work, it is as narrator recounting a dramatic story and often disappearing into the speech of the figures in the story. But when he disappears into Zarathustra (which is much of the time), the latter is not presented as speaking *to the reader* but to other figures in the drama as well as to himself. In his speaking to others Zarathustra proceeds in some adaptation to the figure(s) whom he is addressing. We are meant, of course, to *overhear* Zarathustra's words: they are being narrated-- and that narration is being conveyed to us in writing-- in order for us to encounter them. But we are intended to hear them as addressed not directly to us but to one or another audience in the drama which the written work we are reading is conveying to us. What is addressed to us-- what functions to communicate to us *Nietzsche's* thought-- is the *whole* work: not simply Zarathustra, but the other figures and the dramatic action, all as integral facets of the *written* work which records the narrative and which we are *reading*.

Secondly, the primary dramatic element in what is narrated is the interplay between a Zarathustra who has come to feel he has something to say to others as teacher, and persons who are caught up in the affairs of their lives but are approachable at times and on occasions by this teacher-figure. This "has come to feel" is important. The actions and interplay of figures which form the main drama are narrated in such way as expressly introduces the larger matrix of the unfolding of Zarathustra's life as an essential element in the drama, and this, not simply as something which the narrator introduces but as something which Zarathustra himself recalls and avails himself of. Thus the narrator begins his narration with Zarathustra at the age of thirty withdrawing into the mountains, and here and there, either the narrator or Zarathustra himself directly or indirectly fill out a bit the youthful times before that and what has happened since, so that the overall movement of his life becomes made known to us as that larger matrix for Zarathustra's participation in the main dramatic events. This is more than a merely literary device. For not only is an important thematic of the first phase of Nietzsche's thought, namely, growth and maturation, thereby made part of the presenting of the teaching in the case of Zarathustra; but after the events of the Prologue, in which Zarathustra descends to the marketplace of the nearest town and finds his first effort to teach a failure, his resumption of this effort in another town (Motley Cow is its name) is with a speech which concerns three metamorphoses of the spirit. The subject of his first speech in Part I is thereby this very matter of growth and maturation. The function of this focus of Zarathustra's re-adjusted teaching and of this presentation of Zarathustra himself does not end with these matters internal to the work itself. For by its being a written work which is to communicate the thought of the author Nietzsche to his readers, the inclusion by TSZ of this dimension in the drama and this focus of the opening speech of Part I in it is meant to evoke a reader's response which, if it is commensurate with the presentation, registers the drama as drama and registers this emphasis in it. Such register in turn invites the reader to recognize that his/her own understanding of what Nietzsche wishes to communicate may well depend on his/her own growth and maturation and on the metamorphoses these have involved him/her in. That it is these that alone make available the experience and capacities that are needed for such understanding is in fact driven home in various further ways in the course of the work, and even comes to express notice in one place. For in "Reading and Writing", a speech (I/7) in Part I, Zarathustra begins: "Of all that is written, I love only what one has written with his own blood. Write with blood, and you will experience that blood is spirit. It is not easily possible to understand the blood of another: I hate reading idlers." In short: the dramatic interplay being narrated to us involves a Zarathustra and a narrator who are both cognizant of, and intent on emphasizing, speech as being charged with the life of the speaker, and this presentation to a reader is so formed as to invite the reader's register and attention to the drama as self-aware to how his/her listening is likewise charged with his/her life and only thereby granted such resources as he/she has and needs for listening to and adequately understanding Nietzsche's speech.[4]

What is the life-course of this Nietzschean-Zarathustra? According to the narrator's account (directly, and indirectly via Zarathustra's recollections, say), Zarathustra knew in youth various significant visionary experiences which inspired him: "glimpses of love", Zarathustra calls them, "divine moments", which in the later life of his teaching effort he recalls with peculiar force such that, although they died to him long ago, he can nonetheless say that they possess him still.

> How quickly you died to me! Today I recall you as my dead ones. From you, my dearest dead ones, comes to me a sweet aroma, loosening heart and tears. Verily, that aroma sends shudders through and loosens the heart of the solitary sea-farer. ... I am still the heir and the soil of your love, flowering in remembrance of you with motley virtues that have grown up wild, O you most loved ones.[5]

The 'death' of such moments was a 'murder'. In their own character as in his response to them, both parties-- those moments, and himself-- seemed fashioned for loyalty, "for tender eternities"; indeed, those "visions and dearest wonders", those "blessed spirits", inspired an idealistic sense of the future which Zarathustra recalls in phrases which voice his youthful purity and wisdom, namely, "All beings shall be divine to me" and "All days shall be holy to me". Neither party betrayed the other, but nonetheless something soon disillusioned the youthful Zarathustra: the youthful moments were strangled. Zarathustra does not identify or localize the responsible party or parties: he simply alludes to the impersonal "they", and to "enemies". If we may interpret Zarathustra's experience from Nietzsche's, part of the meaning here may reside in the educational system, part in the Silenic side of the nature of things. Or to put it in the image of TSZ, we may see here one side of the working of the spirit of gravity. In any case, what was alive in him then died an unnatural death, but not without having transmitted its life to the very inmost part of himself, his will, his will-to-life. That same will lives on in him, and within it what was left unfulfilled and unredeemed in his youth lives on as well.

The time through which Zarathustra was passing when this happened was a time of accumulating suffering and nausea. The other side to the idealism of youth was a question-raising, a thoughtfulness, which brought an awakening to and intensification of the negativity of things; and to the extent that this was confirmed by pessimistic philosophies-- as in Nietzsche's case, by Schopenhauer's--, so the positive side was called into question. At the same time there was a growing sense of separation from other human beings, and more specifically, of how the "well of joy" which is life is polluted by the way most people live and take part in social intercourse with each other. Growing nausea in this regard "created wings for me and powers to divine water-sources". The winged flight of spirit and the divination of higher spheres of experience where the well of joy was less subject to pollution by others enables him to escape from what otherwise was growing oppression.[6]

Thus we find that at the age of thirty, he withdrew to the mountains. This withdrawal is characterized by the saint whom Zarathustra first met on his way into the mountains and whom he encounters
again on his first venture down from them: he was then carrying his ashes to the mountains.[7] He himself uses the same expression about himself in I/3 ("The Afterworldly"). Speaking of a time in late
youth when, like Nietzsche himself, he had cast his fancy beyond humanity and had created a god,
he recounts: "out of my own ashes and fire this ghost came to me, and truly, it did not come to me
from beyond. What happened, my brothers? I overcame myself, the sufferer; I carried my own ashes
to the mountains. I invented a brighter flame for myself. And behold, then this ghost *fled* from me."[8]

In the heights of the mountains, Zarathustra "enjoyed his spirit and his solitude, and for ten years
did not tire of it" (Prologue/1).[9] In that enjoyment, he 'invented a brighter flame', that is, he developed the ability to see more and more, particularly concerning the capacity and promise in the lives
of human beings. Down below, the actuality of such lives-- the sense of dwelling amidst depressing
failures and mediocrity-- had been too strong; but here he gradually found the pull of potential-to-be-
actualized growing stronger, so much so that in time he felt the need to help the future come about,
to make a positive contribution and one that would run against the grain of the present.

Thus one day, at the age of forty now, he awoke and felt the need to give of his accumulating wisdom; for that, he needed to descend and go among human beings again. And this is where we meet
him at the beginning of TSZ, after his long withdrawal being about to come out of the mountains and
rejoin other human beings; bearing his wisdom as a gift, he would function as a herald whose communication of insight to others is meant to bring them to see an imminent crisis and to join in the
effort he has come to see called for on the part of present-day human beings.

The dramatic structure of TSZ is articulated by events that unfold over considerable time and
bring further changes in Zarathustra himself and in his life. The major articulation is provided by
Zarathustra's two descents from the mountains to the places where he finds others, in each case followed by his returns to the mountains and his solitude. The work ends with the arrival of signs that
mean that a third descent is on the verge of taking place.

A. The first descent

Zarathustra's first descent is articulated into two phases, which represent what happened in two
different places before he returns to the mountain heights.

1. First phase: speaking to all

In the Prologue, Zarathustra enacts his first educative reaching out to other human beings. On the
way down, he encounters a saint, and the brief encounter establishes not only a religious contrast: the
love that moves them (love of God vs. love of man) is quite different; it establishes as well that the
gift-giving which is at the heart of Zarathustra's love of man is self-aware to the insight that 'God is
dead'. When he reaches the market-place of the nearest town, he addresses a crowd which has gathered there for the performance of a rope-dancer. In this first teaching effort of his, he focuses on what
it is to be a human being and on the future at present for humankind on earth. A two-fold alternative
future is pointed to, marked by the contrast of the kind of humanity that will distinguish these futures:
on the one hand, the "last man", and on the other, the "overman". The human being whose venturing
will issue in the future that does arise, whichever of these it is, he characterizes as a venturer who, in
his venturing, gives up his current being for a being that is above-and-beyond what he is at the time.
It is this above-and-beyond which is at stake in human activity; it is this which activity is meant to
secure. His thought about the future then is this: the human being who would remain faithful to this
nature of the human as venturer -- who has the courage to do so: it is dangerous, and a risk-- must
now will self-consciously what has in fact always constituted the meaning of human life on earth,
namely, the realization in future of truly superior human beings (the "overman") in a supportive
community. It is time for human beings expressly to set this as the goal of humankind as such. The

only alternative for humanity at present is the abandonment of this striving above-and-beyond; but since it is this venturesome striving which makes the human being human, such abandonment means the retreat into an 'animal' existence, to become the "last man": clever but without aspiration, love, and creativity, that is, without what makes human life truly human and truly meaningful.

This first effort at teaching, with its practical thrust, is received by unresponsive ears. The crowd is uncomprehending, and eventually impatient: this is not the rope-dancer they were gathered in the market-place to see. Once Zarathustra grasps their response in its significance, he is convinced that in his teaching effort he should not be addressing himself to anyone-and-everyone: at most he might gain followers that way, but followers are of no value. Rather, he should be addressing himself to those who are potential companions, those 'alive' enough as human beings in the human reaching for 'higher life' that there is something in them that might resonate with his teaching and that he might assist, abetting its development by his words.

2. Second phase: speaking to some

Accordingly, in Part I this refocusing of his initial venture has shifted location: we find him teaching in the town 'Motley Cow',[10] that is, in the community of the educated-and-cultured, to those human beings who have some higher aspirations, capacities, and feelings.[11] Presumably this is a place where what he has to say might be heard by potential companions, and be heard in suitable company. And indeed, he does find some responsive listeners there as he sets forth in exhortatory fashion some of the more obvious and readily intelligible features of his vision of humanity, the human future, and reality as humans find themselves in it.

a. The first speech

The beginning (I/1: "The Three Metamorphoses") is with a central factor in the condition of human beings: they are venturers who know life as an affair of growth, and in particular, know the decisive phases of their maturation as human beings to involve them in fundamental metamorphoses of the spirit in themselves.

As Zarathustra treats them, the first metamorphosis (becoming a camel) arises in youth, when we want to take our own life on ourselves and assume responsibility for it. In this we involve ourselves in a decision-making for a life, not simply for this or that deed; and we assume the numerous burdens inherent in being responsible for our lives and test out our strength under them. These burdens are connected with what inspires love in us at the time, with what matches aspiration and imposes duties on us that we might follow out aspiration, and with the relationships we have formed with others and which are undergoing significant change. The heaviest burden of this time of life is connected with our desire to found our own lives on truth and to live it with a purity in keeping with what aspiration points to as the higher-and-better that we are to become. If we follow out our desire for truth and purity (our idealism), the accumulation of burdens that crystallize around this desire has the effect of something like a hastening of ourselves into a desert. Our sense of ourselves as solitary grows stronger, and we know the more forcefully the aloneness of ourselves in our assumption of responsibility.

In this desert, the second metamorphosis of the spirit takes place, into the lion. For if the problematic of the time of youth, namely, of what we are to do with our own life, requires of us reflection, and in particular requires of us thought which serves aspiration and our reverence for what-and-who inspires us, that reflection eventually needs to move beyond seeking to elicit what the summons to the higher-and-better means as revered others can help us interpret it. As part of the aloneness in which we eventually find ourselves, it must finally bring into question the very things-- the interpretative framework we have developed, the loves we have found inspiring, the reverence we feel for what nourishes and supports us-- that have been animating and guiding us at the same time as they have been burdening us with responsibilities and supporting our development under that burden. This is required of us because, in order to reach what we are wanting to reach, we must free ourselves eventually even from those who have inspired and helped us to pursue this dutiful life that has given our solitude substance. Every 'Thou shalt'-- the imperative that comes from the outside-- must be rejected, in order to create the freedom for *our own creation* of new values, of our own goal. This lion-spirit works critically then, beyond the criticism implied in the camel-spirit and its selectivity concerning what burdens are to be assumed, and its working deepens the solitude even further.

This lion-spirit, however, only creates the conditions-- the freedom-- for *our own* distinctive creativity to emerge, for our belief in *our own* self as creative center and for our expression of 'I will' in a creating that brings forth what is latent in ourselves as unique selves. In this creating of new values-- this re-shaping of the world to make it manifest the life and self in us which are taking their very own shape out of themselves now-- we have entered upon the third metamorphosis, our spirit's transformation into a child whose 'play' is the image of our own most fluent and effective functioning of ourselves as initiators and originators. In that functioning we are involved both in a forgetting (of precedents, say)[12] and in a new beginning: in a manifestation of our own originating power, our own originality, our own initiative as 'self-propelled wheels' and 'first movements' engaged in the child-like seriousness of 'play'.

b. The last speech

The end of the teaching at Motley Cow (I/22: "The Gift-giving Virtue") speaks to the character of the third of these metamorphoses, to the effect that it is a condition of power, and in particular, of power that overflows and constitutes the gift-giving virtue. Zarathustra is bidding farewell, leaving the town, and his disciples follow him. When they come to a crossroads, and he expresses his desire to walk alone, his disciples present him with a farewell gift-- a staff with a golden handle on which a serpent is coiled round the sun. Zarathustra uses it as an image by which he can address the matter of that power of creativity in which growth is to culminate, that power of one's fullest self-- supposing that that self (the 'child' which is the third metamorphosis) is indeed rich-and-great. The gifts of this virtue (the highest virtue) are the eventual issue of an assimilation of things from without, a transforming of them within oneself, and an outflow from out of the depths of our own being which carries to others ourselves and what has come of this assimilation and transformation. The self-seeking involved in this seeking out all things to take them into oneself is quite different from the self-seeking which ordinarily goes under the name of 'selfishness', the self-seeking of the sick and frustrated; the latter want all for themselves, simply to feed upon what is taken in and that is the end of it, simply to make it serve as nourishment for their own ego. In the person with the healthy self-seeking, however, there is at work a strength, capacity, and energy, which make for a characteristic sort of happening in the taking-in and transforming: a rising up and elevation in the working of the energies of the body which catches up the spirit in its joy and animates it to become lover and creator. There are numerous factors involved contributing to the emergence of such an overflow and numerous aspects of the creative outflow itself: it may amount to finding a way out of a distress whose depth concentrates one and gives rise to an overflowing heart; it may involve the strength and determination to endure the hard and disagreeable, with this enduring eventuating in a flow from the depths which raises one above good-evil praise-blame and into the wanting to re-shape as a lover the way things appear. But these are facets of one thing, the discovery and tapping of an energy deep within which, drawn into play and integrated with a guiding awareness and cognizance, engages one with the world in a giving fashion. This power unites a dominating thought with a wise soul around her: that is, it unites a guiding aim with our passions transformed and integrated to serve that aim. Or (in the staff-image) it unites a golden sun with the serpent of knowledge around it: that is, it unites the gift-giving love with that earthly wisdom which is insight into the meaning of life on earth.

Speaking further, but after a silence and in a changed tone, Zarathustra urges: let this virtue be employed faithfully to the earth. Much misinterpretation has entered into the creativity of the great men of the past; as a result, much virtue (and spirit) has flown away from earthly things. And this is not something simply past: much delusion and mistake still dwell in our body as an inheritance from the past trial and error of spirit and virtue. Thus over the whole of humanity there has ruled so far only non-sense: no meaning, or better, interpretations which seek to give meaning but miss the true meaning of life on earth. It is possible now, and high time, for human beings to guide the creative spirit and its virtue by an honest understanding of the human condition. That means: let spirit and virtue serve the sense (meaning) of the earth. For that, we need ourselves to become pure and elevated through knowing;[13] we need to heal ourselves and to find the many paths still open to humans and taking us over the earth as a place of human health and life. What Zarathustra envisages is that as a few awake here and there and are drawn into this healing solitude, they may eventually find each other and form a people, and from out of this community of self-chosen individuals who have drawn together to form a people may in turn arise the overman.[14] Thereby the earth can become a site of recovery from the sickness of the past and present.

c. The intervening speeches

In between beginning and end, the focus which Zarathustra established in I/1-- upon the movement of life as an affair of growth that is to culminate in mature creativity-- is taken up in orderly fashion; but the order is that in a musical progression, not in an argumentative sequence that draws logical consequences and then consequences of those consequences. First (I/2-10) he directs attention to the character of life and its movement as individual, and in particular, to the inwardness that marks it as such; and then (I/11-16) he shifts attention to its character as involving the relation of one human being with another and, within the interconnective side of our growth, as marked by a variety of relationships. Then in I/17 ("The Way of the Creator") he returns to the central theme-- namely, growth and maturation in the individual-- and considers more fully the character (and in particular, the difficulties) of the movement of life as it defines a path, the pathway to oneself. To find and become oneself and the creator in oneself, to pursue the path which brings one to oneself in that creative fulness, means to realize the uniqueness in one's being. This is something we mostly turn away from because of the hardships it promises us, especially from the unconditional honesty which is called for-- and this, even though the presentiment of what happiness is in store for us when we anticipate such realization is a powerful incentive to start off on this quest.[15] In the course of this speech, Zarathustra is intent on bringing out some of the negative sides to such a question, on correcting some misimpressions about what is involved, and on entering a caution.[16]

The path which brings us to ourselves requires us, first of all, to face a sense of guilt in separating ourselves off from others. For the herd instinct is strong in us, and has been strengthened by our socialization. Thereby such belongingness has been entered deeply into our being, and from its perspective, for us to be solitary is for us to have denied that belongingness, to have become guilty of betrayal of the group. If we are to be able to survive this constructively, we will have to face-- and answer in affirmative fashion-- the question of whether we have "the right and the strength" for such a becoming-ourselves. For if we do not, if we are only ambitious and lust for the heights (for glory and fame, for example), then such an effort is inappropriate. Most human beings in fact have their place, one appropriate to their own natures, in a functioning which is grounded in some belief or faith, some fixed foundation, which is set by others and accepted by them.[17] Their value depends on their maintaining themselves and functioning in an appropriate place on such a basis. But the sort of freedom and creativity Zarathustra has in mind here is for a few only, and is something for which their particular nature suits them. It involves throwing off the yoke of our present 'Thou shalt' and, rather than being free of any or substituting some other ready-made yoke (with some modifications or adaptations, perhaps), creating for ourselves our own good and evil, and functioning as judge and avenger of this law which we have established. That is to take responsibility for our lives in an absolute fashion; for that, most human beings have neither the strength nor the desire. But supposing we can answer the question affirmatively, the strength which enables and justifies our moving further on this path must enable us also to endure the isolation of solitude. We will not notice that isolation at first, when we are still suffering from the impositions of others and have our courage and hopes intact; but eventually it becomes wearing, and we will feel so isolated, abandoned, and at sea, as to feel that there is nothing genuine, all is false. Unless we can bear this and 'kill' this feeling, we will be slain ourselves; but can we be such a murderer-- take on such a responsibility? Supposing that we can, there is still this, that while living among human beings and having to do with them even as inwardly we are becoming more isolated from them, we will find being just to them difficult; for they will come to despise us, since we have forced them to relearn about us. Their envy, their injustice toward us, must be met with justice, not returned in kind; and particularly difficult will be doing justice to 'the good and just', whose intolerance toward the creative can have disastrous consequences for us. In the midst of this increasing difficulty marking relationships, any company or apparent company will tempt us to settle for that, and to draw back from pursuing the path which is bringing deepening isolation. But the hardest things to bear will come from within, from the surfacing of factors and aspects of ourselves from the depths. For this is something which must happen: the way to ourselves requires our retrieval of energies that are locked up in what we have become. The path then involves a purifying of ourselves, as part of what enables us to become new; but such purifying is possible only by means of the cleansing fire of unconditional honesty, and leads us (as we come to recognize our limits and inadequacies) into a contempt for what we presently are, in contrast with what we are reaching to become. This contempt is part of the impetus needed to sustain the movement and eventually to realize that self over-and-above-ourselves out of which we can be creative as our unique being fits us to be. The difficulties and demands of the way to our creative being, then, are considerable, even supposing that our being has anything in it of greatness humanly that could eventually come to realization. It is not the way for most human beings, but only for a few who could reach and sustain genuine spiritual independence and greatness in creativity.

In sum: In this first descent of Zarathustra's, we have a cautious venturing on his part of relatively surface elements in a fuller teaching, elements which could be formulated and assimilated without the deeper elements in that teaching having to be broached.[18] The focus of the teaching is on creativity and the creative self, and on the need (in one's creativity) to affirm the bodily-and-earthly. God is dead, humanity is alone, and the meaning of human life on earth is found in the overman, superior human beings who are able to be creative out of passion that has been transformed and ennobled and whose creative capacity harbors an honest and true self-consciousness to reality and to humanity and in particular to themselves as being the true and proper goal of humanity and thus what gives meaning to human existence. There is only one intimation of a deeper side: in the speech entitled "The Thousand and One Goals" (I/15), there is the phrase "will-to-power", which points us in advance to one of the deeper elements in the teaching, one that becomes central in the teaching that he initially offers in his second descent. For the moment, however, it is only mentioned once by name and not explained, and there is no reference at all to the central teaching of the work, the eternal recurrence.

The closing thoughts of the final speech of Part I express Zarathustra's wish for the immediate future and utter an anticipation of his return at some future time and then again at a second time. He is not withdrawing because he has exhausted his teaching. Instead, expressing his desire for solitude again for himself, he calls upon his disciples to leave him and to find themselves. For he sees them as sufficiently established in themselves for the moment, but as having come to revere him and believe in him. That is neither what he wants nor what is good for them. Urging them to find and establish themselves in their independence from himself, he anticipates a return to them when this has happened, and his loving them then with a different love from his present love: they will be his friends and creative companions then, and all will be children of a single hope, claimed by the vision of the human and the human future he has been sketching out for them. But eventually, he will withdraw again, to return when he can celebrate with them "the great noon". That is

> the great noon when humanity stands in the middle of its way between beast and overman, and celebrates its way to the evening as its highest hope: for it is the way to a new morning. Then will he who goes-under bless himself for being one who goes-over-and-beyond; and the sun of his knowledge will stand at high noon for him. '*Dead are all gods: now we want the overman*

to live'-- on that great noon, let this be our ultimate will.[19]

Such, at least, are Zarathustra's anticipations as he departs.

B. The second descent

The withdrawal of Zarathustra to the mountains lasted for "months and years", and then he found arising in himself an impatience to descend again, which desire was strengthened by a dream in which the need for him to return is underlined. Not only does he have more to give, but the dream-sign indicates that his initial teaching is being misunderstood and needs clarification so that misunderstanding may be removed. Once again, the teaching made between the time of his descent and his return to the mountains is articulated into phases, this time into three.

1. First phase: the descent proper

When Zarathustra descends this time, it is to the place where he can find his 'disciples', namely, the Blessed Isles.[20] They have indeed lost their way in his absence. But taking for granted the initial teaching, he sets about the task of clarification both by expanding his thoughts on the level and in the terms he had first employed, and by deepening the teaching itself, so that what was said previously can gain fuller intelligibility as some of the deeper thoughts which give context and expanded meaning to the first teaching are made explicit.

The teaching's first phase begins with "Upon the Blessed Isles" (II/2) and lasts through "Great Events" (II/18). Internally it is divided into two by a group of three songs ("Night Song", "Dancing Song", and "Tomb Song": II/9-11) which function as musical prelude to the introduction (in II/12: "Self-overcoming") of will-to-power; the speeches II/3-8 clarify by a contrast with manifestations of declining life, while the speeches II/13-18 do so by a contrast with defective manifestations of higher humanity. This two-part phase ends with "Great Events" (II/18), and in particular, with the mention there of a story of an apparition of Zarathustra flying through the air and being seen by some sailors. Passing overhead, it had cried out: "It is time, it is highest time!" The speech ends with Zarathustra pondering this reported incident: "What am I supposed to think of that? Why did the ghost cry: 'It is time! It is highest time!' *For what* is it highest time?" It turns out that it is high time for Zarathustra to reach even more deeply into himself and to bring forth his deepest teaching.

In its main lines, the amplification and clarification he undertakes in this phase proceeds by underlining the ultimacy of time as the horizon for understanding human life and its ordainment toward creativity. Because human life and its encompassing reality are thoroughly temporal, no meaning is to be found by reference to something eternal or timeless. But more: within that temporal reality, life (both human and non-human) is a structured and dynamic affair, with a directionality to the dynamic which, in the human case, makes mature creativity its *telos* but which, more deeply and more broadly, belongs to life as-- in essence and everywhere-- a will-to-power. For living beings individually, that means it is marked by a drive toward a power or potency to be gained by growth and development within their own type of being; for life collectively, it means that life is an evolutionary affair involving diversification of species. Given life as will-to-power, the characteristic act of the living is that of developing amplified inward resources for living and functioning out of its own nature, and doing this by integrating and appropriating what is initially outside and beyond itself; thus living beings are inherently involved in op-position to whatever appears in their circumstance, and in particular, they are entered into the dynamic of an interacting within which each is seeking to establish itself and function out of itself within the tension of struggle with others likewise engaged in such seeking. By its nature, the centering of life on power means the pervasive presence of hierarchy, of integration and subordination, of striving and conflict, of tension and opposition. Put even more abstractly, it means the conjunction of a dialectical unfolding of the living out of itself, with the interactive establishment of the diverse in tension with each other.

a. Experiential matrix: beauty

The start of the teaching here is thematically as decisive as it was in Part I. This time it is the experience of beauty, and its interpretation, which embody the dynamic and open the way for reaching more deeply into the nature of temporal reality. "It is autumn around us, and pure heavens and afternoon. Behold what fulness is around us! And from out of the overflow, it is beautiful to look out upon distant seas. Once one said 'God' when one looked upon distant seas; but now I have taught you to say 'overman'."[21] The immediacy which forms the occasioning matrix for creative response is a pregnant fulness to things; touching on our responsiveness and evoking our own inward overflow, it seems to us disclosive in some fundamental fashion. How understand what is being disclosed? Zarathustra poses and reiterates a contrast. In traditional thought its meaning has been interpreted by conjecture to an actuality deeper in the nature of things than what appears, one which, while it cannot be grasped directly by evidence accessible in experience in its immediacy, is taken nonetheless to explain its meaning. That is God. What is called for in that case is simply acknowledgement of an already existent reality, a creator God who is responsible for all this. In contrast, Zarathustra urges an interpretation of the meaning of the disclosure which sees such presence as calling for one's own becoming creative in fuller and deeper fashion than before and sees a creativity out of the fullest human capacity as providing the meaning of human existence on earth. That is the overman.

More fully: From the teaching in the first descent, we know that the drive of human life, at least in those with the noblest human capacity, is toward an overflowing of spiritual creativity out of mature power. We know as well that, being a drive toward a witting and willing sharing in such power, this drive develops internally to itself an interpretation of the meaning of itself and its creativity. Now in their immediacy times of the experience of beauty are times of a fulness and pregnancy (without and within) which are excitatory to a self finding itself elevated and brought alive amidst things and placed on-the-verge, so to speak, in their presence. At that place of height, a future opens out, imaged by the seas, and a sensing of that future (a 'looking out over') which it is beautiful to experience. At the heart of this experiencing the beauty involved exerts an appeal which calls one into a future that could be. The experience is in this way activating and inciting; and yet, in what direction is life being called to unfold itself in response to this appeal of beauty? If this call is a summons to be spiritually creative, and if that creativity is to have some intimate relation to reality, then how are we to understand such creativity, such reality, and the relation of the two to each other?

In the past,[22] the strength for a profoundly truthful reading of the meaning of such experience of beauty has been lacking. Instead, the creativity responsive in such times has been guided by a mistaken reading, to the effect that: (a) beauty is a mark of things placed in them by their source; (b) that source is not evident itself but (so the conjecture claims) stands beyond the realm of finite existence and experience and stands there as itself already perfect and timeless in reality. What appears as beautiful is thus itself unreal, but its beauty reminds us of its source and calls basically for an acquiescence on our part to a timeless non-sensible reality and (so far as our creativity goes) to a creating which provides images of beauty. But such images, and the creativity that generates them, are themselves excluded from the constitution of reality just as are the original beautiful presences which were understood as creations of the source. None of these things is a part of reality nor makes reality any different by the change they involve. For all of these are temporal, whereas all reality is eternal and unchanging. Under this interpretation, beauty-- to the extent that it pulls us toward reality-- calls in the direction which the saint whom Zarathustra met on his first descent epitomizes, toward withdrawal from the earthly and human as too imperfect and toward concentration on the divine and eternal in celebration of this divine reality.

Zarathustra understands the import of such experience differently, and sees in the traditional reading a failure to allow the full and genuine import of the experience to emerge into view and to be grasped honestly and truly. The traditional reading fails on two fundamental counts.

One: Experience of the sense-mediated interaction of ourselves with things is our only beginning-point and only genuine avenue for understanding. But the traditional interpretation does not exhaust or remain faithful to *all* that is being disclosed-- and to *how* it is being disclosed-- in and through the feeling and senses at work disclosively in our experience. Rather, it jumps too quickly beyond experience. Or put differently: it imports from outside the experience-- indeed, from outside experience altogether-- a concept, that of a source which already is, and would derive the meaning of the experience from that. But the will to truth represents above all an effort of "thinking through (our own) senses to the end", and thus demands above all the creation of ideas of reality that are grounded in the immediacy of experience. "Senses" here are the powers that open to us humans the visible and feelable; to think what is disclosed in this fashion through to the end, is to bring reality to light in its truth as this is accessible in the sense-mediated interconnectedness of ourselves with things. The conjecture to a God involves reference to something which is not part of the experience and is in principle beyond what is thinkable in such fashion.[23]

Two: By this conjecture to a timeless reality, the interpretation makes time-- the condition which enables us to participate in the only reality we know, that disclosed *in* experience-- something unreal, and with it, all passage, transience, becoming-- all that belongs to the temporal reality of our experience. But this is to miss time in its full meaning, and to fail to do justice to the sense which marks creativity, that it is taking place at the very heart of reality and real life and that what issues from it is above all real, indeed more intense in its reality than things otherwise. Thereby it devalues and threatens to undermine the creative effort itself.

Zarathustra's own interpretation seeks to remain faithful to the full meaning of the experience and to what is immediately disclosed in it, without introducing a conjecture that refers us beyond temporal reality. In his reading he would limit his conjecturing to what is thinkable by human beings when they think through the given and, in particular, limit it to what the creative will could bring to be. In that reading three things come to the fore.

One: Attending to all that is disclosed in the experience, there is nothing that points beyond experience altogether, nothing that requires or grounds any conjecture to some reality beyond experience in order to make intelligible the nature of this experienced reality or the called-for issue of the creative will. Rather, the experience discloses a reality which is properly acknowledged as altogether temporal. But while that means that it is an affair of passage, that is not the most fundamental aspect of its temporality. It means, more importantly, that in the passing of time real things are continually forming and re-forming themselves in their interacting with each other, and thus are continually shaping the future and re-shaping the present and past: this is part of the meaning of time as introducing perpetual change. In this light, the creativity-evoking appeal of beauty to ourselves-- a central element in the experience-- means that human creativity has (in principle) an integral place and participant-role in the working-together that constitutes such reality and makes of it a concrete affair.

Two: In its most fundamental dimension, the working of beauty in and on us opens out for us-- and calls us toward the realization of-- a possibility of human life on earth that could be a real issue of human creativity, namely, the overman. This possibility is one manifestation (the one in *human* life) of life's immanent directionality and purposiveness, its reaching *toward itself in higher and fuller forms*. In its own appropriate temporality, human life is not-- in any particular case or overall--an affair simply of passage, nor one simply of formative shaping and reshaping of future, past, and present. It is rather one of self-realization, of a realization that is a giving-birth to itself in a higher-and-fuller form. *Within* the human species, life harbors as the implicit goal or inherent end-point for its reaching in every human being a *high or elevated way of being human* which has always been there in human beings as potential but which needs to be *expressly discerned and affirmed* as such and made into the consciously-recognized *goal* for human effort. Only in virtue of the strengths available in the present is that way able honestly and truthfully to be discerned and affirmed in its true character and meaning. That goal and reference point-- that higher self-- is (for the individual) a certain maturity in capacity for being creative, and (for the race) certain superior creative human beings. As the latter, it is the communal goal around which the future human community can be ordered; further, it is a communal goal in which the past would also be brought to fulfillment, being the adequate realization of what was inadequately realized by human beings of the past. For past humans did not accurately and self-consciously understand life's pointing but mistook it and diverted their creativity in other (mainly other-worldly) directions.

Three: In being more than passage and more than formative shaping, in being self-transformation which is to eventuate in self-realization, the temporality of human life is directional toward an end-condition which is of a peculiar sort. Because it is a fulness in creative capacity, it is not an end which is itself fixed and unchanging. Quite the contrary, the self-realized self is such as by its own nature is creative beyond itself, and more fully, is such that the transforming of what is circumstantial and what is within and, on that basis, the production of what is beyond in a creative overflow is inherent to its very being. What has been reached in becoming a 'child' is the end of a growth, indeed, but an end which is the beginning of a fully-grown participation in life as a human being. The full-grown human being *is* and is *itself in* its creative transforming and overflowing and in *continuing* to be creative in this fashion out of the fulness and maturity of its capacity.

Put differently: The experience of beauty gives an intimation of meaning to human life which is made good on only when, aptly read and its practical implication brought to pass, the individual achieves the end-condition bodied forth by the overman and the human community achieves the ordering of itself which integrates such creative individuals into itself as its supreme achievement. But (focusing here on the individual) meaning is found by the individual only in achieving an end-condition which in its own nature is the realization of a creativity which discharges itself and places the creator in need of further creative reaching-beyond. That is, meaning is found *in* the participat*ing* which realizes the *maturity* of the individual, but that participating, being one in a creativity which engenders the need for further creativity, is inherently an indefinitely continuing or ongoing affair.

Put differently once more: Given that change is ongoing and given the centrality of feeling in our responsiveness, there is inherent an unavoidable suffering at the heart of our existence, connected with simple passage and the loss it brings, with the destruction of what was once built up but in time is torn down to make way for something else, and even with the dying of the old and the pangs of giving birth to the new self and what comes to birth with it. In that sense, time means suffering, unavoidably; but that is not all which it means. If time is condition of a reality at the heart of which is creativity, and if creativity arises out of self-transformation which eventually brings self-realization as a creative person, then the intimation of meaning which is found in the experience of beauty seems able to be made good on when, both despite and with the help of suffering, the self-realization is eventually attained and brings a joy and release from burdens which outweighs pain and suffering. But such a gift, received and accepted *in* the creating out of maturity, seems itself passing, although able to return as the participation in creativity revives. Further transformation seems in principle possible, and thus the ongoing generation of creative works and the experience in immediacy over and over again of the redemption of feeling-- the joy of creative participation, and the release from burdens that bear heavily on life. But equally, and again in principle, such achieving is each time transient. Thus questions arise, implicit here but addressed later: Does meaning deepen with successive recurrence? Is there an amplitude that would suffice, given that in a finite being this continuing can not extend endlessly? Is there an 'end' within this indefinitely extending *telos* where meaning suffices, without this signifying the cessation of ongoing creative involvement?[24]

In sum: "Upon the Blessed Isles" concerns the full and faithful reading of the disclosure and the pointing of the experience of beauty which evokes the creative will in ourselves as living beings. It affirms that the meaning of such disclosure and pointing is caught in the alternative intimated under the term "overman" rather than that intimated under the term "God". God is a deeper, time-less reality, over against which all else is unreal; and the alternative reading intended under the term signifies that the creative will being evoked contributes nothing that is ultimately real to reality. Overman is a fuller and temporal possibility for human beings, which could be brought into reality as issue in a willing commitment of effort and energy. Given that reality as disclosed in experience is not timeless but altogether temporal, and given that the creative will belongs to a power (life) whose temporality defines itself eventually in a fulness of the capacity for creative participation in the realization of reality at large, the realization of such an issue to the human creative effort being evoked would make a difference in reality itself. The reading intended under the alternative "overman", then, is to this extent adequately expressive both of the ultimate nature of reality and of the capacity of temporal beings to share in the realization of reality in keeping with their own natures. But is the eventual participation in the ongoing cycle-- that of a creative overflow followed by a time of recovery and regaining strength-- of itself sufficient for meaning in the life/lives of temporal beings? Or must the recurrent participation lead somewhere? But to a place *beyond* all cycles, or rather ... ?

b. Expanded experiential matrix: the dance of life

In the three songs (II/9-11) which introduce the second part of this phase, Zarathustra recalls the experiential matrix which opens out when the lion's will, animating reflective exploration,[25] enables other facets to come into view and to be taken into account. There is the deepening solitude and sense of being alone (II/9), but beyond that, there is the recognition and celebration of life as a love affair of a peculiar sort (II/10). In follow-up to the sadness and the questions concerning life that arise when the dance of Cupid and the girls is over and evening has come, Zarathustra recalls (II/11) times of youth long gone, times of loving vision which soon died of strangulation but not before their life and energy were bequeathed to and sustained in his will. They have come back in memory to him now, and bringing tears at their remembrance and at the recall of the premature death of their inspiration of him toward dancing, they bring Zarathustra to turn back to this matter of the will to truth.

Past wise men, insufficiently capable of the truth-seeking of the free spirit in whom life would cruelly cut into itself so as to increase knowing, have lacked the courage, strength, and honesty, to recognize that each time what they settle for as 'truth' is simply an imposition on their part of intelligibility on things which, in truth, are beyond such intelligible character. In their valuations and claims concerning good and evil as well as in their claims to truth, they have been creating an intelligible world which, rather than actually eliciting truth, achieves instead the spirit's will to dominate so that life may flourish. Not only are such thinkers unaware that this is the nature of their will to truth, but so too are the people, those in whom the valuations and truth-claims of such wise men have become effective, having been assimilated from the wise and then employed by the unwise in the making of their way through life. But life can never be confined by any particular set of such fictions for long; its drive, its will, resists permanent confinement by fiction. In II/12 ("Self-overcoming") Zarathustra proclaims the issue of his own exploration of the disclosures of experience as regards life's nature. That exploration, ranging over many paths and involving seeing matters from many different perspectives, has been able to allow reality to emerge without needing to conceal aspects of it and has discovered the following about life and its inherent drive.

Life is a power which structures itself hierarchically, in an ordering that involves a commanding and an obeying. Where the living being cannot obey its own commands, it is commanded from beyond itself; where it can obey its own commands, it knows in commanding a venturing, an experimenting, a hazarding, in which itself and any beings beyond itself who also obey its commands are basically at risk. Now in this commanding and obeying, what is it that is at stake? For what does the living continually place itself at risk? Claiming to have "crawled into the very heart of life and into the very roots of its heart", Zarathustra pronounces: the will of the living is a will to power; it is for power that the living risks itself. What is this matter which Zarathustra here calls "power"?

At the end of Part I, we have already seen him speaking of the gift-giving virtue, and saying: "Power is she, this new virtue: a dominant thought is she, and around her a wise soul; a golden sun, and around it the serpent of knowledge." This characterization is preceded by an extended pointer into the striving with which those (potentially superior) human beings who are 'alive' with any 'life' strive for such virtue, for such a consummating condition of their being. That striving is marked by a gathering of "treasures and gems", of "riches", an ingathering of what provides resources for the creativity in question, so that eventually, transformed, such things can "flow back out of your well as the gifts of your love". The striving in question is also marked along the way by the gradual building of the capacity for such gift-giving love. Crucial to such building are the times of immediate experience when we know in and through our senses an elevation, or more precisely and more fundamentally, a parable of the elevation of our 'body' as a whole. As 'body' (active beings), we are engaged with things as ourselves coming-to-be beings who are involved in a struggle, and know times of success in which our capacity for taking part is strengthened, our body 'elevated'; and as this registers in sense, so it also is taken up into spirit, the power within the 'body' which functions as herald for the whole and brings its conditions, its fights and victories, to speech. Naming good and evil, spirit brings to speech those times, and those more lasting conditions, in which the 'body' knows its own elevation, its augmentation in capacity. Such speech, parable-speech, points us back into those times and conditions which are building in one that capacity which, in its fullest form, is "virtue", is "power" as the gift-giving virtue. Thus the originative sources of our virtue are the times and conditions in which "your body is elevated and raised up", when the body's "rapture delights the spirit so that it turns creator and esteemer and lover and benefactor of all things".

> When your heart flows broad and full like a large river, a blessing and a danger to those living near: there is the origin of your virtue. When you are raised above praise and blame, and your will wants to command all things as a lover's will: there is the origin of your virtue. When you despise the agreeable and the soft bed and cannot bed yourself far enough from the soft: there is the origin of your virtue. When you are the willer of a *single* will and you call this turn-and-turning [*Wende*] of all your distress [*Not*] 'necessity' [*Notwendigkeit*]: there is the origin of your virtue. Truly, a new good and evil is she. Truly, a new deep roaring, and the voice of a new well [*Quelles*]![26]

Now at the mid-way point of Part II, Zarathustra broadens the reference and generalizes the meaning of power, seeing not simply in human beings but in all living beings such a striving for such a condition of creative participation, in each case with a creativity expressing *its own* distinctive nature and being. Much of his characterization in II/12 ("Self-overcoming") is addressed to the human, but the point is more general.

> Life confided this secret to me: 'Behold,' it said, 'I am *that which must always overcome itself.* Indeed, you call it a will to procreate or a drive toward a purposed-end, toward the higher, farther, more manifold; but all this is one, and *one* secret. Rather would I go under than renounce this one thing; and truly, where there is going-under and a falling of leaves, behold, there life sacrifices itself for power. That I must be struggle, and becoming, and purposive-end and contradiction of purposive-ends-- alas, whoever divines what is my will divines also on what *crooked* paths it must proceed'.[27]

What is the character of these paths by which the will seeks power, and what does it mean to call them "crooked"?

"That I must be struggle": The crooked character of the paths is rooted in the enabling structure of life itself, whereby it may realize itself in living beings. That structure is one of hierarchization and oppositioning of commanding and obeying centers of life and activity, so that they exist as living beings whose internal ordering fits them for involvement in an interacting which is a struggle [*Kampf*] with each other. Because of this structure, that power which the life in any one living being seeks and which that living being gains as *inward issue* in the growth and development *out of itself* of its own nature is achieved only *indirectly*, in a way that depends on the concrete interweaving of the living beings in their struggle with each other. Seen more fully, that interweaving takes shape in dependence first of all on the hazarding and risking in the midst of danger, the staking and casting of dice, which is our venturesome engagement with ... and in which we exert force and energy in order that a more vital-- more powerful-- mode of living arise. This exertion of force and energy is the first dialectical moment in the achievement of power, but the force and energy exerted are *not themselves* the power that is ultimately at issue nor is the exertion of these itself properly speaking a discharge of power in that sense.[28] In any case, the actual achievement of power is issue of an inward development of the living being out of itself and requires more than the living being's own initiative in that engagement; it needs that initiative to be complicit with the working of circumstance in such fashion that circumstance conditions and contributes to that development. Seen in terms of the structuring feature of commanding and obeying, circumstance so functioning may take the form of the other as able to be mastered and put to use, or may take the form of a place and function in a context of others where the living being's own obeying and serving what is other-and-commanding in that context can enable such increase, in part by the way serving enables the exercise of capacity which enacts such development and in part by providing the niche from which the servant may in turn command what is weaker and can put it to use to serve its own development. But in none of these alternatives, or of any other, is the living being's achievement of power direct, dependent only on the living being itself and its effort alone. Rather, it depends on how the *interaction* and the interlinking of living beings that is taking place in virtue of it works out, on whether the elements of control and dominance that are involved-- the exertion of force-- are sufficient and appropriate to *enable or foster* the increased vitality and capacity to take part creatively in life which life seeks. The indirectness which obtains in such achievement due to the primordial structure of active being (above all, the being dependent and conditioned by what is beyond for growth out of oneself) is the initial aspect of the "crooked" character of the paths in question.

"That I must be becoming": Power is an inward issue of the activity of a being as it is engaged in the struggle of existence. But it is an indirect issue, and this, not only in the way we have just noticed, namely, by way of the conditioning and contributing of what is beyond; it is indirect as attained in virtue of a growth and development of the active being out of itself (in the human case, of the maturation). Such growth and development involves activity as its enabling medium, but they form an evolution of ourselves which is *not a direct result* of any action or set of actions. Activity facilitates or makes difficult or even precludes our 'becoming', but does *not produce* this evolution as a *result* (direct or indirect) of itself. Moreover, when that coming-to-be does occur, its path-- the path of the becoming by which we arrive at power and thus are what we are-- is itself not a straight-ahead one, and the movement of this becoming is not a straightforward one. This is so in three important ways.

For one: Early in the teaching at Motley Cow in his first descent, Zarathustra sketched out the nature of ourselves in our agency, speaking (in I/3: "The Afterworldly") of ourselves as 'bodily' beings whose self is a creating, willing, valuing self. In I/4 ("Despisers of the Body"), he speaks of this in more detail: as such beings, we are complex in nature. For we are composed of a plurality of powers and drives (a "herd") which are to be developed and integrated according to a single sense by a unifying power (a "shepherd") operating at the center of ourselves as living beings. The developing and unifying work of this integrating power-- the true self in and of ourselves-- takes place over time, accomplishing in a structured and ongoing and evolving way its unification of the variety and in this accomplishing aiming at that eventual fulness to our being which is power. Since each of the plural elements has its own force and aim, the plurality and the unifying of this plurality involve much strife and accommodation (a "war" and a "peace"). Now the unifying in question goes on for the most part unconsciously (the work of the self or "great reason" in ourselves), yet not without involving the working of the powers that operate in our conscious experience ("little reason", "pleasure and pain"). These consciously-operating powers are "instruments and toys" of the creative self.

> Behind them lies the self. With the eyes of the senses and the ears of spirit, the self is seeking as well, ever seeking and listening: it compares, constrains and subdues, destroys. It governs [*herrscht*] and is governor [*Beherrscher*] even of the conscious-ego. Behind your thoughts and feelings, my brother, there stands a mighty ruler [*Gebieter*], an unknown sage-- who is called "self". In your body he dwells; he is your body. ... Your self laughs at your conscious-ego and at its bold leaps. "What are these leaps and flights of thought to me?" it says to itself. "A detour to my end [*Zwecke*], I am the leading strings of the conscious-ego and the prompter of its concepts." The self says to the conscious-ego, "Feel pain here!" Then the conscious-ego suffers and thinks how it might suffer no more-- and that is what it *is supposed* to think. The self says to the conscious-ego: "Feel pleasure here!" Then the conscious-ego is pleased and thinks how

it might often be pleased again-- and that is what it *is supposed* to think.[29]

Despite this "detour"-standing of the conscious-ego, spirit and sense tend to claim for themselves a more fundamental place in the whole of our being than they actually have, and we tend to form our sense of self around them-- this is our 'I' as conscious-ego, as center of deliberate will and thought. In so doing, we mistake ourselves. Even so, the self which operates at the center of ourselves and operates mainly in the unconscious side of ourselves, is governor within us as a whole, and so far as it is able to achieve its will in our interaction with things and we are able to grow and mature, it does this in a way that involves the *indirection* introduced by the differentiation-yet-unified-functioning of the conscious and the unconscious in the enabling activity of ourselves.

For a second: In the developing and integrating whereby the evolution of our creative capacity out of ourselves and the eventual realization of power take place, there is an essential place for a sub-limation in virtue of which the moving forces in ourselves develop by way of a transformation which elevates and refines. In I/5 ("Joys and Passions") Zarathustra speaks of it in one particular reference. Speaking of virtues or strengths-- the limited perfections which eventually contribute to the reali-zation of that highest virtue which is power or creative capacity--, he points to them as outgrowths of our nature, and thus as in each of us unique powers that body forth the individual being, the indi-vidual self, and express that self in vital moral strengths. In contrast with virtues as they are a function of socialization, these are strengths which have developed out of the elements of passion in ourselves, and developed in a transformation of passion.

> Once you had passions and called them evil. But now you have only your virtues left: they grew out of your passions. You placed your highest aim at the heart of these passions; then they became your virtues and your joys. And whether you came from the race of the choleric or the voluptuous or the fanatic or the vengeful: in the end all your passions became virtues and all your devils, angels. Once you had wild dogs in your cellar, but in the end they metamorphosed themselves into birds and lovely singers. Out of your poisons, you brewed your balsam; you milked your cow, melancholy, and now you drink the sweet milk of her udder.[30]

Now each of such virtues or strengths wants the energy of the whole human being to be devoted to itself: "each wants your whole spirit that it might become *her* herald; each wants you whole energy-and-strength [*Kraft*] in wrath, hatred, and love". The work of the creative self, then, does not end with the evolution of such powers, but involves integrating all these various forms of the good in turn, so that eventually something beyond any one or any set of them can emerge: virtue in that culminat-ing form which is power, the highest virtue.

For a third: The evolution of ourselves in maturation does not take place simply as an additive increase, nor simply by an integration of an additively-increasing multiplicity. Instead, it involves phases and an augmentation of our creative capacity which make it a metamorphic affair. We have already noticed the stress which Zarathustra places on this in his first-descent teaching, when he speaks of the crucial entryway into power as involving the metamorphic transformation of the spirit in ourselves in the way imaged by the camel, the lion, and the child.

In short: Life is structured to be an affair of activity in which something is at stake, but the secur-ing of what is at stake (power) is issue of a becoming of the active being which its active engagement enables but does not directly produce. At the heart of the enabling active effort is a venturing, a risk-ing, in which we give up what we presently are so that we may become more. That becoming-- that coming-to-be of ourselves out of ourselves enabled by this venturing in which we come-beyond-what-we-are-now-- has a complex character of its own which makes it *crooked* in a further way to that introduced by its dependence on conditions and support from without. Integral to the augmenta-tion of our creative capacity as whole human beings which is enabled as, in our activity, the con-flicting powers internal to ourselves are developed and integrated and harnessed to operate in our active engagement with circumstance are the indirection introduced by the differentiation of con-scious-unconscious in our activity and the winding path and twisting movement introduced into our evolution by sublimation and metamorphosis. Power is issue of an augmentation that does not take place as a merely additive affair but as a qualitatively expansive one which refines, elevates, and deepens, toward fulness our capacity to take part creatively in the affairs of life. In this maturation, activity is the foreground vehicle, while the qualitative expansion in question is the background event. If the former is continually onward moving and thus 'straight', the latter introduces a complex 'crookedness' into the movement and the path.

"That I must be purposive-end and contradiction of purposive-ends": If life is will-to-power, it is inherently purposive, being a drive and striving oriented toward an end; and this is so quite apart from the matter of consciousness, let alone of deliberate will. Now life is not localized in any one living being in isolation, but is an affair of the interactive connection of diverse living beings. The drive toward power which is present in all such beings seeks power as what can be gained only as life overcomes itself in this struggle. In the perspective of any individual, this means a self-overcoming achieved in the context of an engagement with others that establishes for itself a place at which it can grow; in such engagement and establishing, the individual who commands himself defines his own values and imposes them on all whom it can get to obey, and the individual who obeys others accepts the values defined for it by others. But the point of such dominance of values is the establishing of a place at which one is enabled effectively to reach toward power and a discharging of that creative capacity. And if that power and its discharge involve more elevated capacity than in the case of other individuals, if the power discharged is *greater in that way*, and if others can recognize and acknowledge it as such, then the higher life in the one individual *also* has an appeal and appellative force whereby its surpassing of its competition in quality *also* enables its dominance within the group. In this way life overcomes itself not simply within the inward evolution of the superior individual but in the interconnection of individuals where the creativity of any individual is in competition with that of others for defining the common life of the group.

Now if within any group the ends-- and the creativity-- of different individuals are at odds with each other and in competition for establishing the shared framework of the group as group, it is also the case that any common framework of purposes and values itself is located in a larger context in which it is at odds with other such frameworks of other groups. At this community level, Zarathustra speaks of a people as a group of human beings who have come together and given shape to themselves as a community through the working of creative love, or more precisely, through the working of "love which would rule [*herrschen*] and love that would obey"[31]. That love has created its own distinctive vision of good and evil, and created customs and law that embody that vision. And there is thus a common belief which holds them together and lies at the heart of the distinctive way of life which functions to facilitate life's reaching (in all involved) for the higher-and-better.[32] In I/15 ("The Thousand and One Goals"), Zarathustra has already spoken of this matter in a historical perspective like that with which we have become familiar in Nietzsche's previous works. There have been a thousand different peoples, each with their own horizon of good and evil-- their own "tablet of the good"; that tablet distinguished the people and set it apart from the others. In each case it represented the people's own overcomings, its "will-to-power".

> Praiseworthy is what is regarded by it as difficult; what is difficult and indispenable, it calls good; and what frees it in its highest distress-and-need [*Not*], the rare and most difficult, it praises as holy. What makes it that it rules and triumphs and shines, to the horror and envy of its neighbors: that is to it the high, the first, the measure, the meaning of all things. Truly, my brother, once you have recognized the need [*Not*], the land and heavens, and the neighbor, of a people, you may divine the law of its overcomings, and why it climbs on this ladder to its hope.[33]

Now this power of creating values that unite a people has manifest itself not only in such diversity but over time, in the history of humankind: where life affirms itself in such creation, it must soon oppose that creation.[34] The question of the present, however, is not properly posed by asking after which people and which tablet must arise now as the appropriate opponent that upholds life as unable to be exhausted in any particular framework. Now that human beings have recognized that values are a human creation, and it is esteeming that gives things a meaning (a human one), the question is:

> Tell me, who will constrain this [power], O brothers? Who will throw a yoke over the thousand
> necks of this beast? A thousand goals have there been so far, for there have been a thousand
> peoples. Only the yoke for the thousand necks is still lacking: the *one* goal is lacking. Humanity
> still has no goal. But tell me then, my brothers, if humanity still lacks a goal-- is humanity itself
> not still lacking too?[35]

Whether at the level of the individual or of the community, then, life seeks power with the help
of a goal-setting, a creation of values, a forming and carrying out of purposes, and all this, in such
way that whatever the particular framework, it is limited and is opposed and contradicted by that of
others. And whether seen in contemporaneous or in historical reference, there is no framework which
can suffice life for long. Once again, but this time in a third way, the paths on which life seeks power
in and through a people are "crooked", involving a self-defining and self-delimitation at work in the
creativity of any group, and thus the need for opposition, the unavoidable character of exhaustion
with the limits in time, and the demand thus for release of the energy in the old and its enlistment in
something new. Would the recognition of the human condition-- that God is dead, that we human
beings create values, that we need a value-creating now which is commensurate with humankind as
such and not simply with limited peoples-- make a difference in this regard? Looking toward the
future in which this recognition obtains, Zarathustra says:

> On a thousand bridges and spans they shall throng to the future, and ever more war and in-
> equality shall be placed between them: thus does my great love make me speak. In their hos-
> tilities they shall become inventors of images and ghosts, and with these they shall conduct the
> highest fight [*Kampf*] against each other! Good and evil, rich and poor, high and low, and all
> the names of values: they shall be weapons and clattering signs that life must overcome itself
> ever again. Life wants to build itself into the heights by way of pillars and steps; it wants to look
> into vast distances and out on bliss-engendering beauties-- *for that* it needs height. And because
> it needs height, it needs steps and contradiction among the steps and the climbers. Life wants
> to ascend and, ascending, to overcome itself.[36]

This passage in II/7 ("The Tarantulas") suggests that even within the recognition of the unity of humankind as a whole and the setting of a goal for it, the diversity of peoples will remain. Thus the
crooked path that is involved in history will presumably endure for humankind, just as it does for the
individual who comes to maturity and takes part creatively in the fulness of human existence.

2. Second phase: the summons

II/18 ("Great Events") ended with Zarathustra pondering the cry of the ghost, that it is time for
something: but "For what?" Zarathustra asks himself. In the speech, he had urged that "the greatest
events" are "our stillest hours".[37] In the four speeches which end Part II (II/19-22), the last of which
is entitled "The Stillest Hour", we learn what it is time for, namely, for Zarathustra to utter his deepest
thought to his fellow humans. When he resists, indeed refuses despite wanting to, he is commanded
to withdraw into solitude again and there to gather the strength which will enable him to bring his role
as teacher to culmination. In the pause and turning point in the drama which these four speeches represent, we get an intimation both of that thought and of the looming crisis whose resolution that
thought will provide the ultimate horizon for.

II/19 ("The Soothsayer") counterposes a soothsayer's depressing view of the human future--
namely, a 'lifeless' life is descending on humankind--, with a dream vision which Zarathustra had
when, made melancholy by the soothsayer's words, he eventually fell into a deep sleep and dreamed.
That dream concerned himself as night watchman and tomb-guardian, who was wakened one night
by a wind, a coffin carried by it, and laughter spilling out when the coffin burst open. While one of

his disciples interpreted the dream as symbolizing Zarathustra overcoming the weariness that had come to dominate life, the speech ends with Zarathustra, vowing to have a good meal and atone for bad dreams, looking for a long time in the face of the disciple who had interpreted the dream and shaking his head. Evidently, this speech does symbolize Zarathustra, although not in the way the disciple claims. It bodies forth in prophetic vein the first teaching which, at the market-place, he had offered in exhortatory vein, with its contrast of the last man and the overman. Zarathustra concedes that there is little standing in the way of the arrival of the long twilight which the soothsayer describes; but he hints that his task is to see that his light shall survive that coming and endure, to become eventually the light "for distant worlds and even more distant nights".[38] He would work against the total domination of that twilight, and would seek to make it not the last (enduring to the end of human existence) but a prelude to another kind of future.

The narrator turns our attention back, then, to Zarathustra and his present-day circumstances, and poses another side of the question raised by the soothsayer's anticipation. Even supposing that Zarathustra is right in suggesting that an averting of endless twilight is possible, can the futural achievement which through the working of the creative will realizes the overman-alternative beyond the coming twilight really suffice to bring meaning to the earthly existence of the human race as a whole? For much of humankind's existence-- many human beings-- lie in the past, and neither that past, nor this present that is currently drawing upon it, lie within the scope of the creative will as something it could bring to pass. The will is potent only in regard to the future, not the past or the present.[39] Does the inadequate realization of the human in that past not count, can we find meaning in an achievement in which *not all* human beings participate? II/20 ("Redemption") begins with Zarathustra's encounter with a hunchback; in the course of it Zarathustra speaks to the hunchback of how the human beings of his time appear to him: they are cripples lacking this or that organ, or inverse cripples who have too much of one thing and too little of everything else. Then speaking to his disciples as "a seer, a willer, a creator, a future himself and a bridge to the future-- and alas, also as it were a cripple at this bridge", he reframes the vision: it is as fragments and limbs of human beings that he sees the humans of the past and present; they are fragments of the future he envisions. His aspiring and poetizing aims to divine a unity that will unite all humans in temporal fashion, thus to poetize what is fragment and to redeem what is otherwise dreadful accident.

> To redeem those who lived in the past and to re-create all 'it was' into a 'so I willed it': that is what I call redemption. Will-- that is what the liberator and joy-bringer is called: thus I taught you, my friends! But now learn this too: the will itself is still a prisoner. Willing liberates; but what is that called which puts even the liberator himself in fetters? 'It was'-- that is the name of the will's teeth-gnashing and loneliest melancholy. Powerless against what has been done, it is an angry spectator to all that is past. The will cannot will backwards; and that it cannot break time and time's covetousness, that is the will's loneliest melancholy.[40]

In angry reaction to its powerlessness to will backwards, the imprisoned will seeks to get rid of its melancholy by wreaking revenge on all that can suffer and that does not share its wrath and displeasure. And this is what revenge is, the will's counter-will against time and its 'it was'. In virtue of this powerlessness and frustration, life and willing have been (mistakenly) interpreted as punishment, and existence has been (mistakenly) interpreted as a moral affair. But these are mistakings, fallacious readings which Zarathustra claims to have led his disciples away from by teaching them a different view of will.

> 'The will is a creator'. All 'it was' is a fragment, a riddle, a dreadful accident-- until the creative will says to it, 'But thus I willed it.' Until the creative will says to it, 'But thus I will it; thus shall I will it.' But has the will yet spoken thus? And when does that happen? Has the will been unharnessed yet from its own folly? Has the will yet become its own redeemer and joy-bringer? Has it unlearned the spirit of revenge and all gnashing of teeth? And who taught it reconciliation with time and something higher than any reconciliation? For that will which is the will-to-power

must will something higher than any reconciliation; but how does this happen to it? Who ever taught it to will backwards?[41]

Zarathustra stops suddenly at this point, and makes it clear that he is remaining silent about something. The speech ends with the hunchback asking, first, why did Zarathustra speak differently to him than to his disciples, and then, when Zarathustra acknowledges having indeed adapted his speech to the hunchback, the latter replies: "All right, and with pupils one may well tell tales out of school. But why does Zarathustra speak otherwise to his pupils than to himself?"

A third speech (II/21: "Human Prudence") follows the pointers and hints of the two preceding speeches, and provides an implicit answer to this question. It lays out an important facet of Zarathustra's inward condition, that he reaches out in his will in two different directions, one toward human beings as they are now, the other toward the overman; he is dangerously split, then, and has to dwell with present-day human beings prudently, in order that he not lose faith in the human, that he may not be overwhelmed by the disparity and the contrast of actuality with possibility. Prudently: that means, not letting guardedness against being deceived dominate his life, not letting the ugliness or the timidity of present-day man get him down. But that means: he must live with present-day human beings, even the best of them, by attending to misleading-- but hopeful-- surfaces, guises, and disguises, and by himself going about in disguise, that both parties may mistake one another.

In the final speech (II/22: "The Stillest Hour") Zarathustra tells his disciples why it is that he must now leave them and return into his solitude, his teaching as yet unfinished. In voiceless speech his stillest hour has functioned as a conscience, reminding him of something he knows but is not saying, and indeed, claims he does not yet have the strength to say even though he would like to. He is hesitant in the face of the summons to do what is most needed by all, namely, to command what is great-- and that means, in his case, to voice to others the words that will address them as a command and make of him, the herald of what must come, the enunciator of thoughts that will guide the world. In the face of his resistance to assume this commanding role and to lead the way into what must come to be, his stillest hour spoke saying: "O Zarathustra, your fruits are ripe, but you are not ripe for your fruits. Thus you must return to your solitude again; for you must [*sollst*] yet become mellow."

Zarathustra's descents have had a practical meaning, but while they have brought him to human beings, what he has said to them has not yet reached them in a way that makes a practical difference, at least the practical difference he wants. Now, knowing he has more-- and what is most decisive-- still to say, he is hesitant, and needs to regain his confidence and find the strength to venture once again and to bring to others his deepest insight. From the first two speeches in this little set, it would seem that that insight concerns time not simply as the condition which enters beings into an active existence in which something is at stake but also as a condition which enables them, in the nature of things, to find their way to a place at which this may be secured in some ultimate fashion, in keeping with the temporal nature of all beings and securings. It seems that time, in virtue of its directional movement, enables active existence (that is, will), and enables willing to liberate, both in the sense of release latent energies and in the sense of do so in a functioning which has been freed from what otherwise constrains and imprisons. But that very movement forward, which orients will in the futural direction and makes the future that which will brings into being in its creative working, perpetually leaves behind the past and perpetually adds thereby to what lies outside the will's capacity to impact since that capacity extends only forward into the future.[42] There may be ways in which will can relate to that past, and even do so by drawing upon it; but if will can only function in the way it wants in forward reference and if only in this reference (in achieving what we want through its creative action) is meaning possible, then time's continual devouring of the future in which the will might be potent and increasing the past over against which it is impotent imprison the will within what it can not create.[43] Is there any way to overcome the frustration at this impotence? Given the terms in which the question is posed, it seems that this could happen only if the will could also will backward. But that would be possible only if time were different from what it seems to be, or more fully, if time and temporal existence were different from what they seem to be.

In short, in this second phase in the teaching taking place on this second descent, a turning point is reached in his teaching effort and an impetus is given for Zarathustra's withdrawal from the Blessed Isles and gradual return to the mountains. As the speeches effect this turn, they also hint at the basic underlying problematic for humankind. That is time itself as it bears on human life and activity as temporal affairs; and more fully, it is time as bearing on the wanting-and-willing which is central to meaningful human participation in time, and as doing this in this present which is so problematic for humankind as to its existence as a race and its future on earth.

3. Third phase: return to the heights[44]

Unlike the case of Zarathustra's first descent, the withdrawal that belongs to this second descent is portrayed at length. It begins (III/1) with Zarathustra, alone, climbing a ridge around midnight on his way to the other coast of the island he is on. To reach his mountains, he has first to cross the sea and reach land again, and only then can he regain his mountain heights and his cave. Thus crossing the sea by ship (III/2-4), he comes to land, and on the way toward his mountains, he eventually returns to the town where he first taught (III/5-8), and finally reaches 'home' on the heights and settles down there once again (III/9-16). The way back is thereby an articulated one, with each articulation having its own disclosive function.

Along the way, we are made privy to some indications of his ultimate teaching concerning time, but not even in Part IV do we find him offering that teaching to humanity generally. Rather, it comes out in a speech entitled "Vision and Riddle" (III/2), enigmatically revealed to the 'sailors' he is sailing with, and then once again, in a speech entitled "The Convalescent" (III/13), where it is voiced (back to him, and for us to overhear) by his animals. Then it is incorporated into the song-speeches which end Part III (III/15-16: "The Other Dancing Song", "The Seven Seals"). Oddly, then, while the experience which fathoms the depths and cor-responds with the insight appears in two places in Part IV (IV/10: "At Noon"; IV/19: "The Drunken Song"), the fundamental idea of the whole work is never disclosed by Zarathustra to others in any straightforward way, and even less is it conveyed to us straightforwardly by the author Nietzsche. Let us note, then, not simply what is said to convey that idea but also how the disclosure is made, and seek to understand what is being claimed, and why the claim is being made in the way it is.

a. First sub-phase: the wanderer and mountain-climber

On his way across the ridge of the island to the coastal harbor where he will board ship, Zarathustra thought and talked to himself. Speaking with an interweaving of the literal and the metaphorical,[45] he recalls to himself how often since youth he has wandered alone and how many mountains, ridges, and peaks, he has already climbed. "I am a wanderer and a mountain climber, he said to his heart; I do not like the plains, and it seems I cannot sit still for long." In their literal force, these words point to a recurrent sense of himself, of the typical way in which he has found himself coming to-- and becoming disclosed to-- himself in his engagement with things.[46]

> In the end, one experiences [*erlebt*] only oneself. The time is gone when accidents [*Zufälle*] could still happen to me; and what *could* still happen to me [*zu mir fallen*] now that was not already my own [*mein Eigen*]? It merely returns, it comes home at last to me-- my own self [*mein eigen Selbst*], and what of my self has long been in the alien-and-strange and scattered among all things and accidents.[47]

Experience, lived experience, is disclosive, disclosive to and of a being that is becoming and disclosive of that which it is encountering at any time in its becoming. "The time is gone when ... " indicates that Zarathustra has reached that time in his becoming and experiencing when two things hold. One: the encountered circumstance which is characteristic matrix for his recurrent discovery of his very own self (the mountains) and the characteristic manner of engagement with that circumstance which facilitates that discovery (wandering and climbing), have worked their disclosure often enough to have become identified for their power in that regard; and two, that self discovered has gained such fulness and stability that he knows, over and again, the characteristic feel to such times: what is other, what is strange and alien, discovers itself in an affinity to himself, something of himself is being bodied forth in it, so that the discovery of himself in the encounter discloses himself to himself both within and without.[48] In their metaphorical sense, the words point to a more important characteristic, this time of the inwardness in this discovery-encounter, namely, that this self which is being disclosed to itself in his wanderings and climbings in the (physical) mountains, is at home-- is most itself-- when engaged in reflective inquiry which seeks understanding by way of heightened (elevated, refined) experience and with the aid of the disclosure which such heights (such peak experiences) make available to one whose climbing has enabled him to attain them.

In discussing BT, we have already pointed to Nietzsche's use of the metaphors of depth and elevation to address differences in our experiencing. There we also saw him addressing a differentiation within being itself by reference to the notion of depth, taking the latter to signify a vertical dimension within reality constituted by the polarity of a timeless source in contrast with the spatio-temporal creatures which are its offspring. Since the second phase of his thought, this latter usage has vanished. But another is emerging, relating this time to temporal things and their being and introducing into the notion of such being a differentiation on a vertical scale. The particular imagery in question, that of a well or spring as the source of flowing water, is complementary to the image of the mountain and its polar opposite, the sea, when these are used (as they sometimes are) to signify aspects of reality and not simply of experience. The well or spring image was introduced in I/22 ("The Gift-giving Virtue") in connection with the flow of life and creative love[49] and was considerably expanded in the speeches of Part II.[50] It is occasionally combined with the mountain-image, as in II/6 and the suggestion that while life is a "well of joy", that well may originate on the plains or in the mountain heights, signifying thereby a difference in the source of the flow of joy. The well-image will become appealed to particularly when the matter of time becomes explored, because as we shall see time itself, being an onflowing now that continually realizes the bounded present in a flow that comes from the depths, has a structure to it which that image can readily convey. That is, there is a horizontal dimension, that of the ongoing now of time, its onward movement enabling life's own concomitant movement and unfolding, its passage; and there is a vertical dimension, that of a greater or lesser depth to the present being realized in that now, such that the temporal living being draws on sources available to that ongoing life which are deeper or shallower and can do this because time itself in its own verticality harbors such levels for the sources.

On the way up the ridge, Zarathustra anticipates his own future: before he can return to teach men in greater openness, he must experience again that unity of peak and abyss which in their immediacy latently harbor time as he has already grasped it in the thought which he must now find the strength to convey to others face-to-face. Thus he must ascend again to that highest height at which he can see his 'stars' *beneath* him (that is, see his own virtues, including his honesty, as something he has, indeed, but does not identify with and make his life), and at which, when he looks away from himself, he can see "the ground and background of all things".[51] That peak-- that height of immediate experience, his ultimate peak-- must be regained, but he cannot do that without experiencing again the abyss of suffering, nausea, and despair, which is included in the experience of time but outweighed if and when he can reach the height in question.

Reaching the height of the ridge, he could see the sea lying spread out before him, and he recognizes what he sees as an image of his own lot.

> Alas, this black sorrowful sea below me! Alas, this pregnant nocturnal troubledness! Alas, destiny and sea! To you must I now climb *down*! Before my highest mountain I stand and before my longest wandering; to that end I must first climb down deeper than ever I climbed before-- deeper into pain than ever I climbed before, down into its blackest flood! So my destiny wants

it. Well, I am ready. Whence come the highest mountains? I once asked. Then I learned that they come out of the sea. The evidence is written in their rock and in the walls of their peak. Out of the deepest depth the highest must come to its height.[52]

It is only by passing through the fullest *experience* of the temporal, in its negative as well as its positive side, that he will be readied not to think time and the ultimate temporal character of things (he has already done that) but to communicate to others his thought and to stand exposed before all as the teacher of that thought.

Descending the ridge and drawing near to the sea, he speaks to it as wanting to deliver it from its evil dreams, and then catches the folly of his singing comfort to the sea. Laughing a second time, at the trust and love that had for the moment drawn him even to the sea-- so typical of his approach to things, trustful and ready to love and to lure anything that seemed alive--, he suddenly feels angry with himself, as if in his laughing he had been wronging the friends he loved and had left. With this the speech comes to its end. From the account, it seems clear that the standpoint required for forming and understanding the insight into time and temporality which Zarathustra bears with him as the profoundest issue of his reflective inquiry is a demanding one, not easy of access to nor easy to maintain in such way that one can form the judgments needed if it is to be understood and to be assessed in its claim to truth.[53] That insight has been something made in virtue of the disclosures of an ongoing life which has first brought a deepening of experience in its immediacy as his own self has matured, and then has brought such exploration of the deepening disclosure as has not only felt and acknowledged the intense negativity involved in being temporal but surmounted it and moved beyond it, to find an elevation, a peak, from which life seems visible in self-disclosure as a temporal phenomenon. It is time as enabling ground and background in this disclosure of the temporal phenomenon of life that he has come to see and is now on his way to gain the strength to be able to communicate.

b. Second sub-phase: pointers into the nature of time

The sub-phase which follows the first speech consists of speeches that are given on board ship while it is sailing from the island to the mainland. The first of these (III/2: "Vision and Riddle") is the most important for our purposes, for in it we get our first extended intimation of the nature of time and temporal existence overall, as Zarathustra has come to see these.

Zarathustra has embarked on board a ship and as they sail curiosity about him builds; but he remains silent, indeed deaf and closed off to the others, for the first two days. But then he opens his ears, and hears much that is unusual and dangerous; and finally he loosens his tongue, drawn to speak by a friendly feeling toward those who travel far and do not like to live without danger. What he says, then, is addressed to a specific audience, and at its end, Zarathustra returns to the character of the audience. In between, the speech itself develops in three stages.

The audience, and the speech as addressed to that audience: When Zarathustra begins to talk, he addresses his audience in specific terms.

> To you, bold seekers [*Suchern*], experimenters [*Versuchern*], and whoever embarks with cunning sails on fearful seas-- to you, drunk with riddles, rejoicing in twilight, whose soul flutes lure astray to every whirlpool because you do not want to grope along a thread with cowardly hand, and who hate to *deduce* where you are able to *divine* [*erraten*]-- to you alone, I tell the riddle that I *saw*, the vision of the loneliest.[54]

Clearly the speech is not meant for the ears of just anyone. It is offered as embodying in a riddling form a vision which represents an insight into something disclosed in experience; and it is *offered to those alone* with souls such that in general they find experiential riddles 'intoxicating', are readily lured to follow out the intimations they contain, and are eager to gain understanding of what so challenges them. As such souls know and love it, that gaining is characteristically not a matter of attending-to and puzzling-out by bringing presence deductively into the framework of insight already established; it rather emerges in a fathoming which boldly ventures beyond the horizon of what is already clear and proceeds by a divining and guessing that would elicit in the twilight of intelligibility the meaning of what is disclosing itself in this riddling fashion. That the conditions for understanding are this particular condition of soul is underlined by the reiteration, at the end of the speech, of the characterization of who it is addressed to. "You bold ones who surround me! You seekers, experimenters, and whoever embarks with cunning sails on fearful seas-- you who rejoice in riddles: divine for me this riddle which I then saw, interpret for me the vision of the loneliest. For it was a vision, and a foreseeing: *what* did I see then in a likeness? And *who* is he who one day must still come?"[55] Zarathustra goes on to point his hearers to answers to these questions. But before noting that, let us first take up with the three stages of the speech itself, keeping in mind the need to receive what is said into ourselves as ourselves knowing inwardly that condition of soul which Zarathustra indicates is that of those to whom alone he is uttering what he does and for whom he is putting it as he does.

First stage: The vision is conveyed by Zarathustra as having arisen in the course of a bit of mountain-climbing on his part. Not long ago, he was walking at dusk along a desolate mountain path and forcing his way upward against the weight of the spirit of gravity that, hunched on his shoulders, drew him downward toward the abyss. The spirit of gravity is all that weighs down and oppresses life, in the form of a spirit which Zarathustra characterizes as "half dwarf, half mole, lame himself and making others lame, dripping lead into my ear, leaden thoughts into my brain". Carrying this spirit on his back as he moved upward in a cheerless landscape, his climbing was defiant, determined to move onward and upward despite the heavy burden which pressed him downward toward the abyss of suffering and meaninglessness: what the sea symbolized in the previous speech. That burdensome spirit spoke to him mockingly: 'you stone of wisdom, you may be casting yourself into the heights, but every stone that is thrown upward must fall back down, and in this case, you must fall back down on yourself, being condemned to your own stoning.' Finally, after a period of continued climbing in silence, Zarathustra found that 'something' in himself which he calls "courage [*Mut*]"-- what has so far slain his every discouragement [*Unmut*]-- bid him to stand still and to say: "Dwarf! It is you or I!" In characterizing this courage-- his attacking courage, which advances with drums beating in triumphant fanfare and which is the best of slayers--, Zarathustra gives us an indication of what that abyss is toward which the dwarf is drawing him: the human being is the most courageous of animals, overcoming everything animal through its courage, and so far overcoming all pain ("human pain is the deepest pain"), as well as the response of pity in the face of suffering ("pity is the deepest abyss: as deeply as one sees into life, one also sees into suffering"), and finally even death ("for it says, 'Was *that* life? Well then! Once more!'"). In all these cases, it overcomes as well the dizziness engendered when the human being looks into abysses ("and where does man not stand at the edge of abysses?"). In pointing to these various facets of the abyss, Zarathustra is echoing the Nietzsche of BT and his account of the Silenic element in the Dionysian: in virtue of its temporal character, its involvement in some stake that must be gained that life may make sense, and its centering in feeling, life unfolds in a venturing which is risky, which seeks meaning as it moves forward toward death and finds itself entered into suffering and responding to suffering in the immediate feeling of pity that would alleviate and remove suffering. But the joint force of these factors in life is depressing, weighing against life's aspirational reach. How could courage surmount them all? In particular, how now, when the temporal has come to be seen as the ultimate horizon of existence, and strength to bear the oppressive weight can not be acquired by appeal to the non-temporal?

Second stage: Zarathustra continues speaking: "Stop, dwarf! It is I or you! But I am the stronger of the two of us. You do not know my abysmal thought. *That*, you could not bear!" That thought is absymal in a particular sense: it is formed out of an abysmal depth, an abyss deeper than the negative abyss which the dwarf's weight drags him toward; but this deeper depth is reached only by the courageous going-deeper that gathers up the depths of the negative and retains them within itself even when it has reached a light beyond. The dwarf, being curious, jumped down off his back, and crouched on a stone in front of him, close to an arched gateway. Zarathustra uses the gateway as focal point in an image of time and the temporality of existence.

The first part of the image consists of the gateway itself, with its two faces and with its overhead arch on which is inscribed its name, namely, "Moment" [*Augenblick*]. The arch gives the moment depth, while the two faces mark it as the unmoving passageway for what passes through it on the pathway which stretches out in the two directions which define the horizontal reach of time, future and past. While these two faces (future and past) are *its own*, the gateway structure with those two faces belongs to neither future nor past; rather it is that fixed point *relative to which* future and past are defined as what they are (future and past relative to the present), and defined as fundamentally different from each other, indeed opposite to each other. The Moment, then, is a structured affair, whose opening out to future and past integrate these different dimensions of time into itself, and in virtue of this internally differentiated but unified structure the Moment defines the unmoving locus for movement, for the ongoing of time and all that is temporal.

Now the image is richer than the gateway itself, including as a second element the pathway which runs under and through the gateway. But its greater richness does not initially include any element representing the moving character of time itself, nor any which represents the temporal things which are moving on the pathway. Instead, when Zarathustra speaks of these paths, it is as if he makes the Moment that *in and under which* the temporal being finds itself now walking, and as if he regards it as the point *from which* that being can look forward to the path ahead and look backward at the path behind. The characterization of the paths in this looking-forward and looking-backward perspective reflects not the perspective of time's movement, however, which is always forward, but the perspective of the looking from what is for the moment an unmoving place. Given that standpoint, he characterizes them as *two* paths, defined not simply as different from this central point but as extending in opposed directions-- on backward indefinitely (that path lasts an eternity), and on forward indefinitely (it too lasts an eternity). Looking at them from that same standpoint, he then speaks of these two as coming together under the arch; or more strongly, as if to stress the oppositeness of the two paths, he speaks of their coming together at (thus, under) the gateway as their contradicting each other, their striking head to head against each other. This way of speaking suggests a coming-together of things moving toward each other (here, the courses of the future and the past), whereas the first way of speaking suggests a growing farther and farther apart as each moves off indefinitely far in opposite directions. Now if the paths are in fact the course of time's future and past realization of its own movement, and thus that on which things continually move in the accompanying active engagement whereby they take ongoing part in existence, the image does not differentiate two quite different things: one is the movement of time itself, which is *always forward* and forward along *one* path, and the other is the *visualizing* of that movement *from* the middle-point which every being occupies as that of its being and which is the Moment itself that (continually and constantly) divides time into future and past. The undifferentiation reflects (at the very least) the difficulty of imaging time through spatial features, and more importantly, the continuation of an obliviousness which we found in UHH in the explicit idea of time developed in that early work. More on that later.

Zarathustra's description of the image to this point ends with a question to the dwarf: would someone who followed out either of these paths on and on find that the two paths contradict each other eternally? The spirit responds contemptuously: "All that is straight lies, all truth is curved, time itself is a circle." The response, while imaging the futility of the movement of time ('you get no-where, only back to where you started'), uses an image which in fact anticipates the structure of the horizontal movement of time which Zarathustra is about to set forth. Zarathustra greets the dwarf's comment with anger; reminding the dwarf of the height to which Zarathustra has carried him, thus of the vertical dimension of time which harbors-- but as only one possibility-- the depressing downward pull which is figured forth in the circle of the dwarf's response, he proceeds to a further development of the image which is needed before he can point to another and contrasting possibility.

> Behold this Moment! From this gateway, Moment, a long, eternal lane runs *backward*: behind us lies an eternity. Must not whatever of all things *can* run have already once run on this lane? Must not whatever of all things *can* happen have already once happened, been done, run by?

> And if all already has been, what do you think about this moment, dwarf? Must not this gateway also have already been? And are not all things so firmly knotted together that this moment draws *all* coming things after itself? *Therefore*-- also itself? For whatever of all things *can* run: *must* it not also run once more in this long lane *ahead*! This slow spider which crawls in the moonlight, and this moonlight itself, and I and you in the gateway, whispering together, whispering of eternal things-- must not all of us have already been? and return and run in that other lane, ahead, before us, in this long dreadful lane-- must we not eternally return?[56]

This development introduces the 'things' and the 'happenings' that run their course in the past and the future, and suggests: what is possible in the way of things and happenings is finite, whereas the courses of time past and future, being boundless, reach beyond the time it takes for *all* that *can* be-and-happen *actually* to be-and-happen. Thus this present moment, with all the beings and happenings present in it, must have occurred before, indeed must have occurred an infinite number of times before; and similarly, because of the connectedness with each other of the things and happenings which are running at this moment, this moment leads necessarily into a future which will bring all this back again, over and over without end.

The introduction of beings-and-happenings into the image seems again to involve significant un-differentiations, even if we adjust Zarathustra's image to allow the arched gateway to continue to arch over us as we move forward into the future. Such an adjustment is needed since, while the Moment is indeed always the time of our interacting and interconnecting as active beings to form current actual existence, it is as such the time of an ongoing which takes us not beyond the Moment but beyond the current moment and into the next moment. Accepting for the moment this modification to the imagery Zarathustra is using, we see that he has set forth a conception of temporal existence in-and-under the gateway as an affair of active beings jointly forming current existence by their interacting and interconnecting; in virtue of the Moment, this interactive existence continually opens out in a forward direction (future) and in a backward direction (past) and defines itself in the middle-ground which is the (current) Moment. In that defining-- the 'walking' or 'running' of beings-and-happenings-- existence moves forward into the future (the next moment) and does so in such way as involves continuing the interacting-and-interconnecting even as the concrete issue of this is changing. And for reasons Zarathustra does not state, this interacting-and-interconnecting eventually exhausts the possibility of new component beings-and-happenings. For this, time itself is not directly responsible: it depends on a disparity between the infinity (eternity in the durational sense) of time and the finitude of the 'can be'. But whatever the reason for the disparity, it means that in time the interconnectedness of what at any moment concretely is eventually issues in a return of the *same* concrete achievement of connectedness, and this, endlessly.

Third stage: As in ever softer voice he is recounting his story to the sailors, Zarathustra comes to the place where ... suddenly he had heard a dog howl nearby. That howl recalled him to a time in his childhood when he had heard a dog crying out like that. In that childhood time it had been in the stillest midnight, when the full moon was passing over the house, and the dog had been terrified. As a child he had taken pity on the dog, and likewise now. This time, the dog's howl had brought his attention to shift, and when he came back from childhood into the present he found himself in different circumstances from before. The dwarf, the gateway, the spider, the whispering: all were gone, as if he had dreamed them and was now awake. What he found himself in the midst of now was wild cliffs, a bleak moonlight, and there within sight, a man and a dog. The latter, seeing Zarathustra, howled again, a cry for help; and what Zarathustra now saw was something the likes of which he had never seen before.

> A young shepherd I saw, writhing, gagging, in spasms, his face distorted, and a heavy black snake hung out of his mouth. Had I ever seen so much nausea and pale dread on *one* face? Had he been asleep when the snake crawled into his throat, and there bit itself fast? My hand tore at the snake and tore in vain; it did not tear the snake out of his throat. Then it cried out of me: 'Bite! Bite its head off! Bite!' Thus it cried out of me-- my dread, my hatred, my nausea, my

pity, all that is good and wicked in me cried out of me with a *single* cry.[57]

Calling out to the sailors to interpret this vision-- this foreseeing vision-- and pointing in questions to the direction of interpretation called for ("*What* did I see then in a likeness? And *who* is it who still must come one day? *Who* is the shepherd into whose throat the snake thus crawled? *Who* is the human being into whose throat all the heaviest-and-most-grave, the blackest, will thus crawl?"), he completes his account of the vision. The shepherd bit as his cry had counseled him, and biting off the snake's head and spitting it out, he jumped up, "no longer shepherd, no longer human-- one transformed, radiant, *laughing*. Never yet on earth has a human being laughed as *he* laughed. My brothers, I heard a laughter that was no human laughter; and now a thirst gnaws at me, a longing that never grows still. My longing for this laughter gnaws at me; oh, how do I bear to go on living! And how could I bear to die now!"[58]

This conclusion to the speech is the vision of the future coming of the overman, that is, of the human being perfected in his capacity for taking creative part in temporal existence. Already we have seen such a vision-- that of the overman-- as issue in the reading of the meaning of the experience of beauty (II/2). But how is the vision here connected with the preceding stages of his speaking to the sailors? At the beginning of the second stage, Zarathustra alludes to an abysmal thought which, if he expressed it to the dwarf, would overcome the depressing effect of the spirit of gravity. In what immediately follows in the second stage Zarathustra prepares the way for such a thought by offering a conception of time and temporal existence, one side of which would strengthen gravity's pull. For by denying to the future any lasting or fundamental relief from the downward pull-- for time and temporal existence go in circles--, it would seem to signify no escape kindred (say) to the liberation from rebirth envisioned in the ancient Indian *Upaniṣads*. But is there another side to this conception, one which makes it possible to overcome the spirit of gravity? Is such an overcoming to be achieved by a thought which comes from a deeper depth than that of the negative, one enabled by time's own nature? And yet, if there is nothing about the achievement of such depth which surmounts the spirit of gravity *permanently*, if it is transient and does not preclude the return of the depressing, how does that *overcome* the spirit of gravity? Overcome in what sense? Overcome for whom?

The speech leaves many questions unanswered: it is an intimation which is not simply riddling but incomplete, pointing to certain facets of a fuller vision in the light of which such questions may be answered. For the moment, there are no answers, but the next two speeches give us some further intimations that can help.

The last speech (III/2) occurred on the evening of the second day at sea; on the fourth day, Zarathustra feels he has now surmounted the pain of leaving his friends behind and finds himself standing triumphantly and firmly on his destiny again. In a speech to a conscience that was rejoicing in his triumph (III/3: "Involuntary Bliss"), he thinks in a reflective mood on this venture he embarked on in his first descent from the mountains. The speech recalls it now from the present perspective, and amplifies in particular the moods and feelings that had been at work in both descents up to now.

Then early in the next day (III/4: "Before Sunrise"), in the last of his sea-journey speeches, Zarathustra addresses the heavens as they appear before sunrise and before dawn's color shows itself, when they are white from the light that is beginning to flood them. The purity and depth to the heavens at such a time, its being an "abyss of light", is an outward counterpart-- the "sister soul"-- to that insight that constitutes Zarathustra's own profundity but whose full disclosure still awaits us. Of that insight, we are provided a few hints in this speech.

Addressing the heavens, he speaks of an insight that has come as he has been able to ascend to himself above-and-beyond himself, and from there to carry the "blessings of my Yes" to all things. In a previous speech (III/1: "The Wanderer"), he had spoken of such ascent as animated by the desire to see the ground and background of things; here, he speaks of the insight he achieves as one into things-- into every single thing-- as having "been baptized in the well of eternity". As such they have a being which can not be made intelligible by means of terms such as "good" and "evil", or "purpose" (as in God's purposes); there is no 'eternal will' that effects its will through them, no 'eternal spider or spider web of reason' which makes existence a coherent rational system. Rather they show them-selves in their "most ancient nobility", chance [*Ohngefähr*], themselves ultimate in their happening and happening to be such-as-they-are. But how *are* they in this such-as-they-are? And what is this "well of eternity", what this submergence of things in its upwelling-and-flow? Nothing is yet said to answer these questions, but this much is said: in the happening of things, there is a "little reason, a seed of wisdom", that forms a part of things, a measure of coherence such as the one Zarathustra means when he speaks of the "(creative) self", the "unknown sage", the "great reason" of the "body", the coherence of life as a will-to-power. But it is the coherence in active beings which (in their hap-pening) are active out of themselves, in whose activity there is something at stake, and whose activity is a venturing, a risking, in which the at-stake is to be secured; it is the coherence in an interacting in which each participant is a "divine dice player" playing with "divine dice" on a "divine table". Thus Zarathustra (like Nietzsche in his second-phase thought) rejects the ways of making things intelligible associated with metaphysical philosophy and the unself-critical insistence on the truth of those useful and life-sustaining 'truths' which reflection exposes as truly fictions. But if "eternity" does not intro-duce the metaphysical, how is it to be understood?

The speech ends this address to the before-sunrise heavens when the first sign of dawn's color shows itself. "But you blush? Did I speak the unspeakable? Did I blaspheme, wishing to bless you? Or is it bashfulness in face of a second that makes you blush? Do you bid me go and be silent be-cause the *day* is coming now? The world is deep-- and deeper than day has ever been aware. Not everything may be put into words in the presence of the day. But the day is coming, so let us now part."[59] The day knows an intelligibility, that of the everyday, but it is superficial; the world has depths which are not disclosed in everyday experience, and can not be brought to speech and com-municated in everyday speech, not even as this speech is made more precise in the world of science. What is at issue here is a depth of experiencing which discloses depths in the temporal being of things, and if the experience reaches to the deepest depths, discloses above all the baptism of things out of the well of eternity, their being dipped in the flow of up-rising spring-water out of the deepest well in time as they function out of themselves. That is nothing which does (or could) make sense in everyday experience and its language. It is something coming to pass in a way more inward to life, and deeper in the living being, than what is a visible part of everyday conscious experience.

We will return to the image and thought here, for the present passage is only a first sounding that is re-sounded later, especially in III/15 and then again at IV/10 and 19. But the mention of things that can not be said in the presence of day recalls the question concerning Zarathustra's effort to teach, and points to one reason why he might not speak straightforwardly of the matters that are coming to focus in this sea-voyage-- indeed, one reason why he is not portrayed as straightforwardly offering his teaching concerning time to humanity at large. There are only certain conditions under which it is appropriate to utter it and possible for the few qualified ears to receive and genuinely hear it.[60]

c. Third sub-phase: landfall and the plains

Once Zarathustra's ship reaches land and he disembarks, he wanders for a while among humanity at large, desiring to experience what has become of it. The four speeches which occur here (III/5-8: "The Virtue that Makes Small", "Upon the Mount of Olives", "Passing-by", "The Apostates") con-tribute little to our understanding of his ultimate thoughts on time and temporality.

d. Fourth sub-phase: home and solitude again

In a colloquy with his solitude, Zarathustra celebrates his return to the mountain heights in the first of the eight speeches with which Part III ends (III/9: "Return Home"). Then in the next four (III/10-13) he sets forth in compressed fashion major features of his overall vision of reality and builds to a lyric climax (III/14-16). In two speeches, III/10 and III/13, he provides a significantly expanded disclosure to us of his conceptions of time and particularly of temporal existence.

In its major structure, III/10 ("Three Evils") recalls and echoes III/2 ("Vision and Riddle"). This speech has two main parts: one is a dream that concerns the nature of reality, the other is a waking imitation of that dream which concerns humanity and the future of humankind. In the dream, Zarathustra weighs the world and finds it a humanly good thing; the world as he treats it here includes all beings, living and non-living. This 'all' forms a single whole which, in virtue of the temporality of all its components, knows a becoming internal to itself of (at any moment) limited contemporaneous centers who by nature are entangled concretely with each other and with all others that have gone before and will come after in the circling of temporal existence. In his waking imitation, he weighs certain so-called evil features of human being (sex, the burning desire to be lord and master, self-ishness) and, throwing three questions onto the scales ("On what bridge does the present pass to the future? By what compulsion does the higher compel itself to the lower? And what bids even the highest grow still higher?"[61]) he addresses the energies at work in the human drive toward creative potency and sees these three 'evil' features as indispensable factors through which a human being passes into his own future in the movement of aspiration, elevating himself and eventually realizing that future which is the overman.

As for the dream disclosure: Zarathustra recalls to himself a dream[62] in which, urged on by his "laughing wide-awake day-wisdom which mocks all 'infinite worlds'", he stood on a promontory beyond the world, held a pair of scales, and weighed the world. "World" here is the inclusive existence within which human beings are co-participants, the interconnected multiplicity of interacting non-living and living beings which includes each of us as one. Giving no indication of the (non-metaphorical) location of this 'beyond' or what would be placed on the other balance pan and enable the weighing,[63] he nonetheless finds the world "measurable for him who has time, weighable for a good weigher, overflyable for strong wings, guessable for divine nutcrackers". For as his day-wisdom says: "wherever there is force-and-energy [*Kraft*], number will become mistress: she has more force-and-energy".[64] We have already seen that the essence of the living is will-to-power, which involves (as the case of man indicates) not simply a center of will but an environment with which that center is inherently bound up and which that center takes up with and develops itself in connection with. Zarathustra here expands that sense of reality, making the being of anything-which-is be constituted by energy-and-force [*Kraft*]: whatever-is is a center of active energy-and-force, exerting itself in struggle with other such centers. In saying that number is mistress in such a world, Zarathustra means that that world must be finite. For if reality is will-to-power as force-and-energy, then it is constituted in a polarity of opposed forces; a single force can not exist. If such a reality can not be 'one' but must be plural, it nonetheless is such only as the interconnected self-definition of a polar multiplicity, as a field of centers of energy-and-force defining themselves over against each other. In that defining of any one center in polar opposition to others, each enters into the being and self-definition of the other: the many can not be apart from each other, only in interaction with each other. But if that is so, then an infinite reality is impossible. It would lack the balance required for the poles within a polarity. Reality must be a finite plurality.

Thus the reason for the finitude of possibility which was assumed in III/2 ("Vision and Riddle") is now clear. Zarathustra was conceiving of the whole as a finite collection of things-- of centers of power, of energy-and-force-- that can walk down the path of time, that is, that are active and define their temporal existence in the ongoing engagement with each other. There is also a finitude of happenings that can occur in the interactive self-definition of things. "Number is mistress" then means that being is a temporally ongoing finite whole of opposing participants, existing in an infinite time.

Now not only is the world finite: it is such as includes man within itself as entered into op-positional relation to his environing circumstance and as able, in his engagement with environing things, also to discover the whole itself in which he exists and to reflect upon it *from within*. When he does this, then to one who looks upon this finite whole with assurance-and-security [*sicher*], unintimidated and free from the predisposition to look either for the new or for the old, it offers itself as if it were ... a ripe golden apple offering itself to his hand, or a tree waving to him and bending as support and footstool for the weary-traveller, or as a shrine carried toward him by delicate hands and open for the delight of bashful,[65] adoring eyes. The metaphors point us to a presence which, when aptly received and attended to, is supportive to the living being and alluring in this moment of its perfection, and in any case is "not riddle enough to frighten away human love, not solution enough to put to sleep human wisdom: a humanly good thing ... ." As Zarathustra earlier said (III/4: "Before Sunrise"), there is "a little reason", "a seed of wisdom" scattered here and there, thus sufficient coherence in things and sufficient intelligibility for the human being to be able to grasp it and effectively guide his/her participation in the affairs of life. Such a com-mensurateness of human capacity with the world as a temporal affair, such a limited aptness of human venturing and op-posing circumstance, suffices for an interlinking and being together which in principle can make life a meaningful affair.

As for the waking imitation of the dream-weighing: how could that participation take shape so as to take part in such eventuation? If such participation is essentially will-to-power, a venturing and striving to secure creative potency, what energies are needed and at work to enable such venturing to reach such a point? The second part of this speech concerns itself with this matter. It is not enough that, in this finite whole, human involvement with the environing world is supported out of its very nature sufficiently that it is *possible* for man to maintain himself and to thrive. Human beings must be *able* to take advantage of the opportunity offered by their existence in such a world and *actually* to come to thrive. To make clear his sense of the vital inward factors needed, Zarathustra undertook a waking-weighing which weighed certain factors "humanly well" so that he might know the answer to each of the three questions we mentioned earlier.[66] Those factors are the "three most evil things" according to the standards of the present.

First question: "On what bridge does the present [*Jetzt*] pass to the future [*Dereinst*]?" Sex is the bridge on which the present engenders the future. In the experience, it is (for free hearts) "the garden happiness of the earth, superabundant gratitude to the future in the present", and (for the lion-willed) "the great invigoration of the heart and the reverently reserved wine of wines". In itself, it is "the happiness that is the great likeness of a higher happiness and the highest hope".

Second question: "By what compulsion does the high compel itself to the lower?" The burning desire to be lord and master [*Herrschsucht*] is this compulsion. For while at the same time it is many other things, such ardent desire

> ascends alluringly to the pure and lonely and up to self-sufficient heights, glowing like a love that alluringly paints purple fulfillments on earthly skies. ... Who would call it lust [*Sucht*] when what is high longs [*gelüstet*] downward for power? ... That the lonely heights should not remain lonely and self-sufficient eternally; that the mountain should come to the valley and the winds of the heights to the low-plains-- oh, who could find the right baptism-and-virtue-name for such longing? "Gift-giving virtue"-- thus Zarathustra once named the unnameable.[67]

Third question: "What bids even the highest grow still higher?" Selfishness [*Selbstsucht*] in the form of "the wholesome healthy selfishness that wells up out a powerful soul [*aus mächtiger Seele quillt*]-- out of a powerful soul to which belongs the elevated body, beautiful, triumphant, refreshing, around which everything becomes a mirror-- the supple, persuasive body, the dancer whose likeness and epitome is the self-enjoying soul": this is what bids even the highest to grow higher. Selfishness here is the 'self-seeking' which pertains to the creative self, not to the 'ego'; it involves the strengthening of that self by ingathering riches into a being who *can* create and who eventually knows in his/her own person the highest form of virtue, the gift-giving virtue which is *power*, creative potency.

In the next speech, Zarathustra addresses the countering force at work in human life, one which works against the successful achievement of the movement of aspiration, against the elevating of oneself, and against the eventual realization of the gift-giving virtue and of that highest humanity which is the overman. III/11 ("The Spirit of Gravity") brings back that power which, in III/2 ("Vision and Riddle"), was the dwarf whom Zarathustra carried on his back up the mountain path and to whom the gateway-and-paths were pointed out as an image of time. In the fuller account given here, this spirit embodies those factors which work against life's becoming as (in its eventuality) a becoming light-- a dancing, a flying.

One aspect of this spirit: that one is-- in oneself and in one's own treasures-- hidden to oneself so as only to be able to come into one's own (one's being as a 'bird') through the most demanding of arts, namely, that of loving oneself. This art of self-love, the art of healthy selfishness, one must *learn* and employ, but for a long time (through childhood and youth) we work in the dark, blindly. It takes time, effort, skill, to achieve such learning: "it is of all arts the subtlest, the most cunning, the ultimate, and the most patient. For whatever is his own [*Eigenes*] is well concealed from its owner [*Eigener*], and of all treasures it is our own that we dig up last: thus the spirit of gravity makes it".[68]

A second aspect of this spirit: that in the process of growing up, one is laden "almost in the cradle" with values ("grave words": "'good' and 'evil' this gift is called") and is accepted by others so far as one heeds these and neglects to love oneself. Then in youth, "like a camel, he kneels down and lets himself be well loaded. Especially the strong, reverent spirit that would bear much: he loads too many *alien* grave words and values on himself, and then life seems a desert to him".[69] Still forbidden to love oneself, one faithfully carries this burden, and when the going becomes difficult, one is told that 'life is a burden', when it is only this alien burden that one is feeling weighed down by.

A third aspect of this spirit: that there is much in ourselves that is nauseating and slippery and hard to grasp (disgusting feelings and dispositions, for example), much that is a grave burden (incapacities, for example, and inner conflicts), and much (in ourselves and in others) that is difficult to discover because "often the spirit lies about the soul". That is, there is much in ourselves which, because of its character and because of our immediate response to it, is difficult for us to acknowledge and to accept, even to discover and to grasp as it is. We then are drawn to resist honest self-knowledge.

In short, the spirit of gravity represents factors which make life as an affair of growth a difficult affair. Some of them are able to be overcome by discarding, others by developing strength, others by learning to beautify, others by honesty. But the essential difficulty-- that of becoming oneself-- is surmounted in principle only when one has grown to the place where one can say 'this is *my* good and evil'. Such a person has discovered himself in that uniqueness whose values are also unique, and whose morality must be unique-- not a morality of 'good for all, evil for all' which makes one simply one of the herd. According to Zarathustra the way to such self-discovery is by learning to love oneself and to fly, by learning to say "I" and both "yes" and "no" (as opposed to tasting and being satisfied with everything), by learning to "love blood". But such learning involves much waiting-- waiting for oneself-- and much learning to wait, and above all learning to stand and walk and run and jump and climb and dance, all this before learning to fly. In his own case, Zarathustra speaks of it as having especially involved learning to climb and eventually flicker like a small flame visible to others on the high masts of knowledge.

> By many paths, in many fashions, I came to my truth: it was not on *one* ladder that I climbed to the height where my eye roams in the distance opening out to me. Only reluctantly did I ever inquire about the way-- this always went against my taste! I preferred to question and try out the ways themselves. All my going was a trying-out [*Versuchen*] and questioning-- and truly, one must also *learn* to answer such questioning. That, however, is my taste: not good, not bad, but *my* taste which I am no longer ashamed of and conceal. 'This is now *my* way, where is yours?'-- Thus I answered those who asked me 'the way'. For *the* way-- that does not exist.[70]

In the two preceding speeches, Zarathustra has spoken first to the upward-reaching heart of life in the finite world of opposed powers, and then to the downward-pulling factors which make the upward-reaching a struggle against what weighs it down. Now in III/12 ("Old and New Tablets"), Zarathustra brings forward a miscellany of new and old observations concerning this affair of life. Dramatically, it is a final rehearsing of thought and gathering of strength, in preparation for his effort to summon up his deepest thought. This summoning, the suffering he goes through in carrying it through, the seven days of his convalescence, and the pointer by his animals to further sides to his vision of life, of its existential context, and of time as it enables and bounds life and existence, are the dramatic substance of III/13 ("The Convalescent"). For our purposes, only one of the thirty sub-sections of III/12 (the second) provides something new and of interest. In it, he is speaking of himself as having undermined the conceit of human beings, that they know-- and have long known-- what is good and evil for man. He has done this-- and pointed to the creator as the one who gives to human existence on earth its meaning and future by creating humankind's goal and defining good and evil in that reference-- on the strength of this, namely, the "great strong-winged longing [*Sehnsucht*]" which sweeps him up and away into the heights and into distant futures which no dream had yet seen. Flying into the future like a "quivering arrow" due to his "sun-intoxicated rapture", he has found himself (to speak limpingly, he says, using further likenesses) there

> where all becoming seemed to me the dance of gods and the wanton-mischievousness [*Mut-willen*] of gods, and the world seemed released-and-freed and fleeing back to itself:-- as an eternal fleeing each other and seeking each other again of many gods, as a blessed contradicting each other, hearkening to each other again, belonging to each other again of many gods: where all time seemed a blissful mockery of moments [*seliger Hohn auf Augenblicke*], where necessity [*Notwendigkeit*] was freedom itself which blissfully played with the goad of freedom; where I also found again my old devil and arch-enemy, the spirit of gravity, and all that he created: constraint, statute, necessity [*Not*] and consequence and purpose and will and good and evil: for must there not be that *over which* one dances and dances away? Must there not be-- for the sake of the light and the lightest-- moles and grave dwarfs?[71]

The three preceding speeches prepare, dramatically speaking, for the III/13 ("The Convalescent"). In III/7, then III/10, 11, and 12, we have seen intimations of the notion of time and temporality that forms the central thought of TSZ. In the present speech, we have another such intimation. For now Zarathustra summons that "most abysmal thought" of his, and its emergence brings nausea. Indeed, it took seven days for him to recover sufficiently to "raise himself on his resting place, take a rose apple into his hand, smell it, and find its fragrance lovely". Presumably this echo of the Biblical creation story means that this summoning concerns the thought of the ultimate ground and background of all things, that thought which forms the basis for the creation of a new world, for the re-creation of the old one. In any case, when Zarathustra had recovered that far, his animals call him to step out of his cave and, responding to his welcome of their speech, they give a complementary elaboration of the first parts of III/2 (the gateway-image) and III/10 (the world-weighing dream), saying how things are for "those who think as we do".[72] To such

> all things themselves are dancing: they come and offer their hand and laugh and flee-- and come back. Everything goes, everything comes back; eternally rolls the wheel of being. Everything dies, everything blossoms again, eternally runs the year of being. Everything breaks, everything is fitted anew; eternally is built the same house of being. All things part, all greet each other again; eternally the ring of being remains faithful to itself. In every now [*Nu*] being begins; around every here rolls the sphere there. The center is everywhere. Curved [*krumm*] is the path of eternity.[73]

In this passage, one thing new appears. We have seen that the world as it is baptized out of the well of eternity is a finite affair in several senses. To begin with, each active being within it is finite as interactive with opposed circumstance, and that means, as it is put here, it is active out of a here which contrasts and stands in tension or opposition to the there which spatially locates, correlatively to this here, all else that exists and constitutes opposed circumstance for that active being. But secondly, the world-whole which includes *all* such active beings (not just those contemporaneous with any one being) is itself finite: not, however, as contrasted with anything beyond itself, but because a whole of energy-and-force must be finite. However, in virtue of the temporality that marks each of its component beings, it is *also* finite as *at any time* holding a limited segment of beings contemporaneous with each other and involved, in the ongoing of time, in carrying the interconnected concrete world-at-any-time onward through all of the possibilities of beings-and-happenings so as eventually to arrive back at this same contemporaneous segment. Thus being (the world-whole) *is* only in that becoming which is effected by its constituent beings, but *is in this becoming* only as it is inclusive spatially and temporally, thus as it runs through all those constituents over time and does so repeatedly and eternally, in ever the same course in each round. Thirdly, in *every* now each such active being (as a center of energy-and-force reaching for power) is initiating activity in its interaction with others. That means, seen collectively, that given the circular temporal movement of existents the conjoint initiative of the beings contemporaneous in any now is a *beginning* of being as a whole. For consistent with circularity, there can be no *first moment* (beginning) in contrast with other moments which *only* come afterward; in the circling of temporal things, every moment is the first moment, and in every moment being is being initiated. At the same time, seen individually or distributively, each component being in that being, as active out of its own here-and-now (its very own present), is not only at the *beginning* of being all the while it is active but *at the center of being*. For that whole, that interactive *field* of beings, *is* as composed of every here-and-now: *its own* 'center' is a distributively collective one, thus *is* all centers together; it is not located apart and in distinction from such centers. Each such center, itself finite in its spatiality and temporality, is center of being because in its here-and-now it is active participant in the interaction which *is* what is. The center of being is everywhere because being is *interactive* in its nature.

Zarathustra's response to the speech of his animals echoes the last part of III/2 (the riddling image of the shepherd): he voices (as something his animals know well) what had happened to him during these last seven days. He speaks of how, as the idea (of time and the temporal) re-emerged, a monster crawled down his throat and suffocated him; but he was able to bite off and spew out its head, and thus redeem himself from this "great disgust with man", the "long twilight" of the soothsayer's prophecy, and the near-despair at the eternal recurrence of man-in-his-smallness. He differs in one important respect from the shepherd: the latter jumped up immediately and laughed, while Zarathustra took seven days to recover, and even then he was still weary of his "biting and spewing".

As in the earlier cases, so here: this turn to the human and the human future in the second half of each speech (III/2, 10, 13) is expressive of the nature of time, that it *is* as a *condition* of *active engagement* in which something is at stake, and as a condition which enables movement not simply forward but also up and down. As regards what is at stake-- namely, power-- this movement in the up-and-down dimension of time is just as crucial as that in the on-and-on. For the achievement of power is issue of a deepening and elevating within the up-and-down dimension, an augmenting and intensifying which take place as we participate in the onward-moving interconnectedness with others and encounter and deal with life-enhancing or life-depressing elements of presence. Time means for us not simply passage, a being lived and enacted in an onward movement defining itself in interaction with others who are on the move, but also growth and maturation, a being lived and enacted as an affair of augmenting and intensifying capacity achieved as we are able to effect this movement within the up-and-down dimension of time. If, then, time implicates one in a becoming which can bring such depressing factors as the snake with it, that becoming also harbors through its temporality-- in particular, through the amplification of the center's actual potency which is the outworking of the drive toward power over time-- the possibility of gaining the strength to bite the head off this disgusting snake. And if in its accompanying up-and-down movement time makes possible such come-to-be strength as enables someone like Zarathustra to envision himself as implicated in an eternal recurrence of the same, it seems also to enable him to have attained-- in his own on-going and growing-up-- such power that he can find in himself (and even more, envisage in a future form) a human capacity sufficient to *affirm* life even as it includes the *infinite* recurrence of such a snake. But what enabled Zarathustra to find the strength for this, and the strength to recover as well as eventually to sing, we are not here told, although we may infer the kind of thing from III/10 ("Three Evils"), namely, the strength of his burning desire to be lord and master and of his selfishness-- and ultimately this means, the self-so of his being-such-as-he-is with such destiny as he has.

The speech ends with Zarathustra's animals urging him to fashion for himself a new lyre for his new songs, so that curing his soul with new songs, he may bear his destiny, to be (as he *must become*) the teacher of the eternal recurrence to human beings. And-- so his animals say-- if he wanted now to die, Zarathustra would speak of himself as mortal wholly, but as entangled in a knot of causes[74] which will create him again, *himself belonging to the causes of that recurrence.* With this, we have a pointer to what it would mean to *will* the *past* as an *actual future.*

The concluding three speeches of Part III-- really, songs-- provide the lyric ending to the Part being prepared for in II/13, and one in which the ultimate character of the positive side to the teaching concerning time and time's implication for human beings begins to emerge more fully (III/15: "The Other Dancing Song"). It is filled out fully, however, only in Part IV (IV/19: "Drunken Song") where the song in III/15 is repeated and is then called "Once More".

III/14 ("The Great Longing"), consisting of an extended series of brief lines all beginning with the invocation "O my soul", is a meditative song sung by Zarathustra to his own soul, basically to celebrate that longing which earlier he said had opened up for him the sense of reality as a dance of gods and gave him also the term "overman". As he addresses it here, soul is the feeling-ful inward-ness of his being, the sensitive receptivity and moving power within which thinking and willing operate, the feeling-heart of life and activity. In virtue of an initiative which is formed with the soul as primordial factor at work in it, Zarathustra has made many strides in learning and becoming, and he reviews some of these, beginning with "O my soul, I taught you to say 'today' and 'one day' and 'formerly', and to dance away your round-dance over all Here and There and Yonder." That is, the articulated facets of time and space as the dancing-ground of life have come to register. In the course of such learning and becoming, his soul has evolved in such way as provides purchase for various names, the most relevant ones for our purpose here being these: (1) "I myself gave you the name 'turn-and-turning [*Wende*] of all distress [*Not*]' and 'destiny' [*Schicksal*]", referring to the way the manifold of feeling eventually converges and presses to the forming of initiative in a way that realizes what was harbored inwardly as meant-to-be from the start; (2) "I gave you new names and colorful playthings: I called you 'destiny' [*Schicksal*] and 'circumference [*Umfang*] of circumferences' and 'umbilical cord of time' and 'azure bell'", referring to how over time feeling expands to encompass things more broadly and delicately in outward and upward reach, the way it functions as inward medium in which the deeper energies harbored in time and native to life feed and energize initiative, and the way it provides the atmosphere within which things are received. And overall, the focus is on the maturation of soul:

> O my soul, I gave your soil all wisdom to drink, all the new wines and also all the immemorially old strong wines of wisdom.
> O my soul, I poured every sun out on you, and every night and every silence and every longing: then you grew up for me like a vine.
> O my soul, overrich and heavy you now stand there, like a vine with swelling udders and crowded brown gold-grapes-- crowded and pressed by your happiness, waiting for the overflow and yet embarrassed about your waiting.
> O my soul, now there is not a soul anywhere that would be more loving and encompassing and comprehensive. Where would future and past dwell closer together than in you?[75]

Feeling has evolved, having been provided nourishment in various ways by his efforts, and develop-ing out of itself in actualization of its potential but developing amidst and with the aid of the receipt and register of immediacy and the assimilation of the reflective efforts of others; and in Zarathustra's case, that evolution meant a growing pregnancy and fruitfulness that is fruit of love and fruit that at this time in his life has for a while been-- and continues to be-- in need of being carried to others on the strength of "the longing of overfulness". What has been accumulated, built up, needs release, needs giving away, needs to be sung:

> And truly, even now your breath is fragrant with future songs; even now you are glowing and dreaming and drinking thirstily from all deep and resounding wells of comfort; even now your melancholy is resting in the blissfulness of future songs. O my soul, now I have given you all, and even the last I had, and I have emptied all my hands to you: *that I bade you sing,* behold, that was the last I had.[76]

What follows, dramatically speaking, is two songs which respond to this bidding and step by step reach more deeply into the nature of things.

The first (III/15: "The Other Dancing Song") is addressed to life, that power which harbors the soul and whose inwardness is soul. As "other" dancing song, it recalls the first dancing song (II/10): indeed its beginning echoes the first song, repeating the introductory "into your eyes I looked recently, O life". The earlier song was something Zarathustra sang as Cupid and some dancing girls danced together; having been walking through a forest seeking a spring, he had found an open meadow and some girls dancing there with each other, with Cupid asleep by a spring-- asleep in broad daylight! Chastising the god, and anticipating that he will ask the girls to dance, he volunteers to sing a song for the dance-- "a dancing and mocking song on the spirit of gravity, my supreme and most powerful devil". That song addressed life as a woman who is not deep and unfathomable (she has no other-worldly depth), only wild and changeable, and by no means virtuous. Among the three of them-- Zarathustra, life, and Zarathustra's wild wisdom--, Zarathustra claims: 'it is only life that I love from the ground up, but I am well-disposed toward wisdom because she reminds me so much of life'. In this second song this contrast of life and wisdom recurs, although the ambivalence of life (her shifting kaleidoscopic manifestation: on the one hand her allure, her invitation to him to dance, but on the other, her elusiveness, her flight, her malice, her treachery) is celebrated at length. Zarathustra claims he would follow and dance after her wherever traces of life are to be found; but that has meant encountering much that is ugly and hurtful, much that leads him to want to make her dance keeping time to his whip. In response to this extended expression of his ambivalence toward her, life responds:

> We are both two real good-for-nothings and evil-for-nothings. Beyond good and evil we found our island and our green meadow-- we two alone. Therefore we had better be well-disposed to one other. Indeed, we do not love each other from the ground up, but need we bear a grudge against each other for that? That I am well-disposed to you, often too well, that you know; and the reason is that I am jealous of your wisdom. O this mad old fool of a wisdom! If your wisdom ever ran away from you, then alas, my love would quickly run away from you too.[77]

At this point where this matter of their continued companionship is being raised, life changes her tone and admonishes: 'Zarathustra, you are not faithful enough to me, you do not love me nearly as much as you say; I know you are thinking of leaving me soon. There is a bell which sounds at night, all the way up to your cave; and as you hear this bell strike the hour at midnight, you think how you want [*willst*] to leave me soon.' And the acknowledgement of this by Zarathustra is intimated: yes, but ... I want to come back. When life expresses her amazement that Zarathustra knows of this matter of the return of the same, "we looked at each other and gazed on the green meadow over which the cool evening was running just then, and we wept together. But then life was dearer to me than all my wisdom ever was."[78] After the speech ends in this vein, the narrator records the sounding of the bell, its twelve strokes each being occasion for a line that, as line follows line, amounts to a poem-- the very poem taken up once again toward the end of Part IV (IV/19) and developed lyrically at some length as the "Drunken Song".

The second song which Zarathustra sings to end Part III (III/16: "The Seven Seals", sub-titled "The Yes and Amen Song") celebrates time, that ultimate condition which enables all life and all being. More precisely, it celebrates time as structured dimensionally to involve vertical and horizontal sides that are so ordered and integrated that the ongoing of the passing moment is the continual realization of the eternal Moment of the beginning of being. Even more precisely, it celebrates something harbored in the deepest depth of the structure of time, the ground of all becoming which he speaks of as the well-source from which wells up the spatially-polarized energy which takes shape as beings and is continually being realized in the active engagement whereby beings are and are as continually ongoing in the circular horizontal passage-side of time. This wellspring of the energy of being, he calls eternity and celebrates as a woman. The seven 'seals'-- each a separate sub-section of the song-- all end with the one refrain: "Oh, how should I not ardently desire eternity and the nuptial ring of rings, the ring of recurrence? Never yet have I found the woman from whom I wanted

children, unless it be this woman whom I love: for I love you, O eternity. *For I love you, O eternity!*"
But each celebrates a different facet of that condition of the temporal being of the human being in
whom this on-flowing energy has been deepened in its disclosive reach so as eventually to enable his
fathoming this source-of-all which is present in the depths of time.

In the first seal, he addresses the present as pregnant with the future: "if I am a soothsayer and full
of that soothsaying spirit which wanders on a high ridge between two seas, wandering like a heavy
cloud between past and future ... pregnant with lightning bolts that say Yes and laugh Yes, soothsaying lightning bolts-- blessed is he who is thus pregnant!"

In the second seal, he addresses the present as redeeming the past: "if ever my wrath burst tombs,
moved boundary stones, and rolled old tablets, broken, into steep depths; ... if ever I sat rejoicing
where old gods lie buried, world-blessing, world-loving, beside the monuments of old world-slan-
derers."

In the third seal, he addresses the present as locus of creative activity: "if ever one breath came
to me of the creative breath and of that heavenly need [*Not*] that constrains even accidents to dance
star-dances; if I ever laughed the laughter of creative lightning which is followed grumblingly but
obediently by the long thunder of the deed; if I ever played dice with gods at the gods' table, the
earth, till the earth quaked and burst and snorted up floods of fire-- for the earth is a table for gods
and trembles from creative new words and gods' throws".

In the fourth seal, he addresses the present as the locus of the intertwining of all things, of the
uniting of opposites: "if ever I drank full drafts from that foaming spice-and-blend-mug in which all
things are well blended; if my hand ever poured the farthest to the nearest, fire to spirit, joy to pain,
and the most wicked to the most gracious; if I myself am a grain of that redeeming salt which makes
all things blend well in the blend-mug-- for there is a salt that unites good with evil ... ".

In the fifth seal, he addresses the present as the locus of a venturing into the open: "if I am fond
of the sea and of all that is of the sea's kind, and fondest when it angrily contradicts me; if that delight
in searching which drives the sails toward the undiscovered is in me, if a seafarer's delight is in my
delight; if ever my rejoicing cried, 'The coast has vanished, now the last chain has fallen from me;
the boundless roars around me, far away gleam space and time; be of good cheer, old heart!'".

In the sixth seal, he addresses the present as the locus of a dancing and becoming light: "if my
virtue is a dancer's virtue and I have often jumped with both feet into golden-emerald delight; if my
sarcasm is a laughing sarcasm, at home under rose slopes and hedges of lilies-- for in laughter all that
is evil comes together, but is pronounced holy and absolved by its own bliss; and if this is my alpha
and omega, that all that is heavy and grave should become light; all that is body, dancer; all that is
spirit, bird-- and verily, that is my alpha and omega".

In the final (seventh) seal, he addresses the present as the locus of freedom's overflow into singing: "if ever I spread tranquil skies over myself and soared on my own wings into my own skies; if
I swam playfully in the deep light-distances, and the bird-wisdom of my freedom came-- but bird-wisdom speaks thus: 'Behold, there is no above, no below! Throw yourself around, out, back, you who
are light [*Leichter*]! Sing! Speak no more! For are not all words made for the heavy-and-grave?
Are not all words lies to those who are light? Sing! Speak no more!'"

Thus Zarathustra celebrates himself in that culminating temporal being out of which he is creative
in the most profound and far-reaching way and out of which, knowing life's limit in death, he is ardent for the unending return of this creative intimacy with this 'source' in the depths of time.

C. On the heights, alone but not alone

Part IV, the final one of the work, portrays Zarathustra on his mountain heights awaiting the signs
that are to signify that it is time for him to descend for the third and final time. Those signs arrive in
the last speech of the work (IV/20: "The Sign"). When at the end of Part II Zarathustra was shown
to be unready to teach his highest thoughts, his withdrawal opened the way to the dramatic renderings
of what he calls his hardest self-overcomings. The one is nausea; and Part III represents him as over-

coming this. The other is pity. Part IV is prefixed with a quotation from Part II (II/3: "The Pitying"), and that is indeed an accurate pointer to the main action of this Part. For in it Zarathustra is presented as facing his final trial, that of pity for higher men, those who are failures indeed but who represent the best in humanity so far.

In its overall structure, this Part begins with Zarathustra after months and years had passed by since his return, enough time that his hair had turned white. One day, sitting on a stone before his cave looking out on the sea over winding abysses, he ascended to the peak for solitude; the first speech of this Part (IV/1: "The Honey-sacrifice") is his talking to himself about his teaching mission, speaking of himself as a fisherman seeking to lure human fish with his happiness. He puts the matter in a way that implicitly prepares for what indeed happens, that certain figures come up into his mountains where he is waiting for the time for his descent to arrive.[79] The first (in IV/2: "The Cry of Distress") is the soothsayer, the prophet of the great weariness who had introduced the one danger (nausea) and who has come now to introduce the other. As they were conversing, they hear a cry of distress, and after the soothsayer has interpreted it for him ('it is higher man, come to seduce Zarathustra to his final sin'), Zarathustra leaves the soothsayer to stay at his cave while he goes in search of the source of the cry. In his search, he meets a series of figures (IV/3-9): two old kings, a leech-seeker, a magician, a retired pope, the ugliest man, a voluntary beggar, and finally his own shadow.[80] Although Zarathustra apparently does not recognize this, it is from them that that cry emanated. Nonetheless, he sends them on up to his cave, and after finding himself once again alone, he lies down to sleep at noon (IV/10: "At Noon"). Returning in late afternoon to his cave, he finds the cry of distress coming from it. Welcoming his guests while declaring they are not the higher men he is seeking (IV/11: "The Welcome"), he sees to the preparation of supper (IV/12: "The Last Supper"), during which nothing was discussed but the higher man (IV/13: "The Higher Man").

When Zarathustra retreats outside his cave, the old magician, claiming to be overcome by the spirit of melancholy, sings a song expressing it (IV/14: "The Song of Melancholy"). But the leech-seeker (the conscientious in spirit) responds by seeking to counter the seduction of the melancholy view of truth-seeking by instead celebrating science and its drive for certainty, conceived as fostered on the strength of fear (IV/15: "Science"). Zarathustra returns while the leech-seeker is talking and disputes the view of man underlying his account of science. Then as Zarathustra is about to leave the cave again, his shadow-and-wanderer calls out to him to stay, and he sings a strange song hearkening to the desert and southern spirit, in contrast with Europe and northern melancholy (IV/16: "Among Daughters of the Wilderness"). After Zarathustra does slip outside again, there follow two speeches about the Ass-Festival that these higher men celebrate, and noting Zarathustra's response to it when he discovers what they are doing (IV/17-18). Then, as one after the other of them stepped out into the "cool reflective night", Zarathustra initiates them into the ultimate mysteries of midnight and the midnight bell, disclosing in final form in this work his deeper thoughts (IV/19: "The Drunken Song").

The next morning brings the sign for his final descent to human beings: he has overcome his final temptation (pity for higher men) and, having thereby completed his maturation, is ready now to utter his deepest thoughts to humanity. And the time has come to do so: "this is *my* morning, *my* day is breaking: *rise now, rise, thou great noon!*" (IV/20: "The sign"). It is with this-- the suspense and anticipation of a future that is in process of arriving-- that the work as a whole comes to its conclusion. Of the speeches in Part IV, only two are important for our purpose.

1. At Noon (IV/10)

There are two speeches in Part IV which speak to the matter of time and temporality, and they do so through opposed images (here, that of noon, in the second, IV/19, that of midnight [but "midnight is also noon"[81]]). Both of them image times of highest sensitivity and insight.

In the present speech, the setting is of prime significance: Zarathustra has found himself alone again after this series of odd encounters, and in that solitude he discovers himself over and over again until finally he finds himself at high noon near a certain tree embraced by a grape-vine which held its abundant ripe grapes into the face of the wanderer. Feeling a slight thirst, but then the still greater desire to lie down beside the tree and sleep, he does the latter, lying down in the stillness and secrecy of the many-hued grass and falling asleep, though his eyes remain open seeing and praising the tree and the love of the grapevine.

All of this has its meaning beyond the sensuous face and the way it is taken up into the deepening inwardization that occurs. Thus the tree and the grape-vine represent as well the perfection of the human community;[82] the many-hued grass, the manifold living things; the ground, that in which all of these are rooted and upon which he too rests; and the hour of perfect noon when the sun is at its highest peak and giving the fullest light makes thereby the least shadow represents the time of clearest and amplest awareness and insight, when eternity comes fully to itself self-consciously, when the depths become transparent to the greatest extent possible.

So too the sleep into which he sinks is strange: a wakeful sleep[83] (his eyes open, "for they did not tire of seeing and praising ... "), it seems that inward stillness of the deepest and most delicate bliss, most alert and alive, contemplative counterpart to the stillness in the world around him.

In such a condition, Zarathustra speaks to his heart, urging it to be still and remarking on how the world has just now become perfect, and indeed he finds his soul becoming relaxed and settling inwardly back into itself.[84] It is as if this time of noon has brought the rest that belongs to the eve of a seventh day, a resting for the soul in closeness to the earth. The happiness of such a time urges the soul to sing, but Zarathustra urges it to be still: the world is perfect, and "old noon" himself sleeps, yet in that sleep, his mouth is moving, drinking a drop of golden happiness and laughing-- thus laughs a god! Feeling the happiness of his soul, Zarathustra thinks of how little is needed for the best happiness: "precisely the least, the softest, lightest, a lizard's rustling, a breath, a breeze, the glance of an eye" [*Augen-Blick*: an allusion to the Moment, *Augenblick* unhyphenated].

In response to the question, 'What happened to me?', he says:

> Listen! Did time perhaps fly away? Am I not falling? Did I not fall-- listen!-- into the well of eternity?
> What is happening to me? Still! I have been stung, alas-- in the heart? In the heart! Oh break, break, heart, after such happiness, after such a sting.
> How? Did not the world become perfect just now? Round and ripe? Oh, the golden round ring-- whither indeed does it fly? Shall I run after it? Quick! Still![85]

The experience he conveys has a peculiar intensity; in it the alive-and-moving seems drawn back into-- yet still in tension with-- the stillness of the depths of time. This is the becoming self-aware of the Moment in its fullest downward and onward reaches. That is: this is the self-aware discovery of the Moment as in its depth harboring the well-spring of all that is, the source of the continuous on-flow of temporal ongoing whose own fulness-as-ongoing is marked by the continuous joining of the-beginning and the-ending of the ring of passage, the continuous joining of future and past in their opposedness. In virtue of that fulness of depth and the horizontal together, this Moment is the 'time' of the beginning of creation and of the eve of the seventh day of creation. Thus the "golden round ball" of the perfected world and the "golden round ring" of time in its fulness and perfection are bound together in the Moment and discovered there together by Zarathustra as his soul, stretching out, falls into the well of eternity: that is, as his attention becomes absorbed and focused in this particular and intense way, to the dis-regard of the moving *simply as* passage.

Zarathustra seeks to wake himself: "'Up!' he said to himself; 'you sleeper! You noon-sleeper! Well, get up, old legs! It is time and more than time [*Überzeit*], many a good stretch of road still remains for you. Now you have slept away-- how long? Half an eternity! Well! Up with you now, my old heart! After such a sleep, how long will it take you to-- wake it off?'"[86] Time's passage has slowed, the moment is lasting on and on for 'half an eternity'; having become 'intoxicated' without even having partaken of the grape, he anticipates it will take time to recover from this drunken state of repose when he comes out of it. His soul resists his effort to summon it out of its absorption, but he tries again; finally he says to his soul: "Get up, you little thief, you little day-thief! What? Still stretching, yawning, sighing, falling into deep wells? Who are you? O my soul!" The inwardness he knows and the feeling-heart of his being wants to remain in touch with-- absorbed into-- these depths, at the same time as he knows in himself this urge to regain fuller self-awareness to time in its moving side.

At this point Zarathustra is startled, for a sunbeam falls from the heavens onto his face. And sitting up, sighing, he says: "O heaven above me! You are looking on? You are listening to my strange soul? When will you drink this drop of dew which has fallen upon all earthly things? When will you drink this strange soul? When, well of eternity? Cheerful, dreadful abyss of noon! When will you drink my soul back into yourself?"[87] So speaking, "he got up from his resting place at the tree as from a strange drunkenness; and behold, the sun still stood straight over his head. But from this one might justly conclude that Zarathustra had not slept long."

In this speech it is the depth of the Moment discovered in the peculiar light and stillness of noon that comes to the fore as claiming attention and as, in its holding attention much more fully than attention is normally held by anything, modifying the experience of time's ongoing side. In this speech, there are remarkable echoes of BT and the Dionysian element there. Thus for one thing, that "old noon" which was "just now drinking a drop of happiness, an old brown drop of golden happiness, golden wine", that noon "asleep" yet-- as he drinks "his happiness"-- laughing ("thus laughs a god"), points us to what has become of the Dionysus of BT. For a second thing, the sense of Zarathustra's soul as having come forth from the well of eternity and at some time going to be drunk back, points us to what has become of the manifesting of that true Dionysian reality in the individuality of appearance. Finally, Zarathustra's "strange drunkenness" in the moment points us back to the intoxication of possession by Dionysus when the bonds of such individuality are being burst ("Who are you? O my soul!"). The echoes are there, but they point us to how far we are from BT also. For in that initial work, for example, there was the split of the timeless and the temporal; we have now the perpetual upwelling of the flow of life and being out of the depths of time itself and into the circular ongoing of time, and we have also the joy of discovering oneself alive in those temporal depths.

Yet as there was tragedy in BT, so there is still tragedy here: Zarathustra's is a transient discovery, enabled in the inward becoming of a transient being as he becomes strong enough in that power which life seeks that he can become inadvertently plunged self-aware down into those depths. But it is transient discovery of a life 'eternal' in a dual sense: as sharing in the upwelling of energy in which all temporal things in the interconnected world of temporal existence exist, and as sharing in the ongoing movement that will eventually bring this being, Zarathustra, back as active participant once again in this very life and do so endlessly. If this participation in the ongoing can gain the strength to be such a self-aware participation in the creational flow, life has a fulness which allows the living being to affirm and love all that is as that in which it is implicated 'forever'. And if included in that 'all', there is mortality and finitude, suffering and pain, and if these are not simply negative factors but in their negativity inherent elements in the dynamic which makes such fulness possible, then would this preclude wanting that life in that whole back endlessly-- and not simply wanting it, but also rejoicing in its anticipated recurrence?[88]

2. The Drunken Song (IV/19)

This speech, the heart of which is certain events at midnight that celebrate the disclosive experience of time and temporality, is the counterpart in many respects to the speech on noon. Noon and midnight, solitude and company: the two sound against each other in these and numerous other complementary ways. It seems that after the celebration of the ass-festival, all those present had one by one stepped out into the "cool reflective night", and in the silence there, with the secrecy of the night coming closer to their hearts, even these defective 'higher men' come to recognize a change in themselves. Attributing it to Zarathustra, they provide their own rendering of eternal recurrence much as the spirit of gravity did of the circular nature of time. In keeping with his character, that spirit voiced the negative side of time's circularity-- its leading nowhere, its meaninglessness as mere onward-and-onward-- as if that were the whole; similarly these 'transformed' higher men voice the affirmation of life in the face of death ("Was that life? Well, then, once more!") only in a deficient way, reflecting their ultimate dependence on Zarathustra.

As this celebration was going on, Zarathustra stood there like a drunkard, having lost his senses and his spirit flying off into remote distances: the language used ("as it were 'on a high ridge', as it is written 'between two seas, wandering like a heavy cloud between past and future'") comes from III/1 ("The Wanderer"), the account of another midnight experience, and is echoed in the opening of III/16 ("The Seven Seals"). As Zarathustra is gradually coming back to himself, all at once he turns his head quickly as if he had heard something, and putting one finger to his mouth, he says, "Come!" Then with the stillness and secretness growing greater, the sound of a bell came up slowly from the depth, and as all were hearkening to it, Zarathustra says again: "Come! Come! Midnight approaches"; this time, he speaks in changed voice, but does not stir from the place. Finally, as everything becomes concentrated into a listening, he speaks again: "*Come! Come! Come! Let us wander now! The hour has come: let us wander into the night!*"

At this point, Zarathustra became desirous of saying into their ears what that midnight-bell is saying to him. In what follows we have the sounding of the remainder of the twelve strokes of midnight (the first three have occasioned the three "Come!" utterances), and with each, Zarathustra weaves it into a wild and lyric account which ends with one of the lines from the midnight-bellstroke song that we have encountered before (III/15: "The Other Dancing Song"). After the stroke of twelve, Zarathustra repeats the bare lines and gives the whole song a new title, "Once More". Throughout, his words, phrasing, and imagery, draw on earlier speeches and songs, and this gives added meaning and a kind of integrating function to this culminating speech-song in the whole work.

It all begins with a stress on two things. First: To hear what the bell, and Zarathustra, are saying requires an intense listening-for which brings what is being voiced to sound in an inner stillness and silence. The listener must listen, then, with a "nocturnal, exceedingly-awake [*überwache*]" soul, in a vigilant and expectant readiness for what is coming to be sounded that is 'above-and-beyond' normal wakefulness. Only in that extremely quiet and concentrated inner condition can the voicing be heard in an appropriate fashion. Second: That utterance being addressed to such an attentive listener is itself bringing to speech much that is not able to be voiced and aptly heard in the day, that is, in the receptivity and sensitivity which define the conscious experiencing of the everyday mind.[89]

Once Zarathustra has summoned his listeners and warned concerning what is being brought to speech, he accompanies the next bell-stroke by a pointer of the listener into an approaching time when the question implicit in his very first attempt to teach, in the Prologue of this work, must be raised: now that 'God is dead', who has the strength and the will to become lord of the earth, to form those thoughts and invent those values that will guide the world?[90] Again, the passage is filled with echoes of earlier passages, which call back into mind other speeches and their meanings.[91] But above all, it contains a warning, to the higher men to whom he is speaking but presumably indirectly to us as well: "This speech is for refined-and-delicate [*feine*] ears, for your ears." It must be listened to and understood with caution and care.

What is the bell saying?

As of now, human beings live a life that, in a way hidden to its everydayness, is entombed, in need of redemption; but there is in reality a love which, with the help of pain, has been able to come to a kind of fulness of happiness, one "with a fragrance and smell of eternity"-- a creative happiness that has as well a profounder basis than everyday life is cognizant of. To answer the question about the future of humankind, daylight clarity and brightness are not enough; one must see more deeply, with fuller clarity. "*The world is deep, deeper than day had been aware.*"

What answer to the question does one see then? "The purest shall be lords of the earth-- the most unknown, the strongest, the midnight souls who are brighter and deeper than any day." In such souls, the world knows a woe, a suffering-- "*deep is its woe.*" But it knows as well a joy, a "*joy*" which is "*deeper yet than agony*"-- the joy of the creative, of those superior human beings who take creative part in the ongoing of life. All that is as yet unripe, and that knows suffering in that condition, wants something different from itself-- "wants to live that it may become ripe and joyous and full of long-ing-- longing for what is farther, higher, brighter"; it wants children and heirs: in it, *"Woe implores, 'Go!'."* In contrast, the soul that has matured knows the joy of giving out of itself, and thus "wants itself, wants eternity, wants recurrence, wants everything eternally the same". There is a finality here, a completeness and arrival, that would not have things-- itself, or anything it is involved with-- differ-ent, even the suffering that is part of giving birth.

> Have you ever said Yes to a single joy? O my friends, then you said Yes to *all* woe. All things are entangled, ensnared, enamored; if ever you wanted one thing twice, if ever you said, 'You please me, happiness! Abide, moment!' then you wanted *all* back. All anew, all eternally, all entangled, ensnared, enamored-- oh, then you *loved* the world. Eternal ones, love it eternally and evermore; and to woe too, you say: go, but return! *For all joy wants eternity.*

Two things are central here: one, the affirmation which is implied in any joy (whether recognized and acknowledged in all it involves, or not), and the other, the concrete interconnectedness of things such that nothing can be what it is except as interconnected with all else. But is there a joy to which one can say, without qualification, 'Yes!'? If there is, what joy would that be? And what would give one the strength to say that?

> All joy wants the eternity of all things ... . *What* does joy not want? It is thirstier, more cordial, hungrier, more terrible, more secret, than all woe; it wants *itself*, it bites into *itself*, the ring's will strives in it; it wants love, it wants hatred, it is overrich, gives, throws away, begs that one might take it, thanks the taker, it would like to be hated; so rich is joy that it thirsts for woe, for hell, for hatred, for disgrace, for the cripple, for *world*-- this world, oh, you know it!
> You higher men, for you it longs, joy, the intractable blessed one-- for your woe, you failures. All eternal joy longs for failures. For all joy wants itself, hence it also wants agony. O happiness, O pain! Oh, break, heart! You higher men, do learn this, joy wants eternity. Joy wants the eternity of *all* things, *wants deep, wants deep eternity.*

It is not eternity as endless recurrence on the horizontal level alone that is wanted, but an eternity with depth: that is, it is the temporal in its fulness that is wanted, that wants itself. And in wanting itself-- itself as the joy of power, of the gift-giving virtue, of the productive act out of the matured strength of a human being--, it wants all temporal things, whatever their character may be.

The implication of this lyric culmination to TSZ seems to be that temporal reality, constituted by will-to-power (that is, by the dialectic of centers of force-and-energy interacting as they reach for a power that is to consummate their development out of themselves), comes fully into the meaning of its own temporal being in those centers-- and at those times-- when the center is ingathered in a cer-tain way. That ingathering, that concentration, is of the fully mature center in its own creative power and in the discharge of that power in a creative working which connects it with what is other than itself and does this in a way that supports and affirms in all the *dynamic* of time in virtue of which each takes part in being. In such creative power and its expression, the temporal has achieved a reali-zation of itself which is marked by finality and ultimacy and which, effectively beyond the frustration that generates revenge, affirms itself in its own dynamic without reserve. It is in the hands of human beings powerful in this way that the future of humanity lies.

CHAPTER 14
Thoughts on time and temporality

With TSZ, we have reached the final work to be considered in our study of Nietzsche's thoughts on time and temporality. In Chapter 13, we simply followed through the work, attending to and noting what we were being offered. What we found was a drama whose central activity is one of teaching and whose main figure-- the philosopher-teacher-- makes certain notions of time and temporality the ultimate horizon for the vision of life and reality that animated his educational effort. This dramatic medium which Nietzsche in turn uses for educatively communicating with us is constructed not simply to present the educative interplay of that main dramatic figure with others but also to do this in such way as points to the inclusive temporality of that figure's life-- in particular, his maturation-- as crucial to his forming and offering of the ideas. It is as if Nietzsche had not simply found his own entry into maturity the matrix for his gaining his insights into time and temporality, but that he had also come to recognize that this connection of matrix with insight was internal and enabling, not external and accidental. That being so, then effective communication of those insights to others in writing would initially depend on readers having and making use of a matching realization of the enabling condition in themselves. Thus to engage the reader in the most propitious way for achieving communication, he made use of a presentational form (drama) which made the enabling condition-- the self-aware culmination of the maturation of a human being over time-- a discernible feature of the form of the work in which he presented those insights; given that feature, a reader's response to the work would presumably bring that enabling condition (so far as it was present in him/her) into play in his/her reading and seeking to understand the work.

It is time now to complete our study with a thematic and critical consideration of what we have found. In preparation for this, let us observe the following two things.

First, although when seen on the background of preceding writings TSZ is a culmination to a development of thought which has been taking place over time, it is at the same time only a first realization of a mature thinking which, while it has finally landed on the new continent toward which it has been moving, needs time to explore that place and, as it makes itself at home there, to correct misleading initial impressions and to secure a well-grounded vision. In the case of the theme of time and temporality, the conceptual rendering in TSZ both goes beyond and culminates his previous thought; but it also represents a horizon which Nietzsche never advances beyond. The re-thinking needed if he was fully to overcome the limits that have been hedging in his previous thought on these matters has not been carried through in TSZ, nor is it ever carried through in his future published writings. In addressing in this chapter the end-point at which he has arrived, we will consider the ideas both as culminations and as incomplete rethinkings which can to some extent be seen in their deficiencies by taking note of time and temporality as these are implicitly conveyed in the treatment of temporal matters in the work.

Second, since TSZ only indirectly voices Nietzsche's thought, we need to elicit what *Nietzsche* is saying *to us*. If we may take Zarathustra as the main voice of the work, we must nonetheless recognize that that voice speaks directly only to others in the drama, never to us. In the thoughts voiced by Zarathustra to others, we are indeed to find something which we are to consider and take seriously as we respond to this work. But if we are to discern what *Nietzsche* has it in mind to say *to us* in presenting what he does, we must go beyond Zarathustra's words, even when those words are understood in their meaning as addressed-to-so-and-so-on-such-and-such-an-occasion; we must also go beyond Zarathustra's ideas. For what we are offered by Nietzsche is a drama in which Zarathustra is drawn back into solitude and then out of it and into an interacting with figures and a responding to events in the course of which the ideas of time and temporality that had been evolving in him and that had eventually come to form the heart of his thinking were being brought forward only in gradual, piecemeal and elliptical, fashion. This presentation manifests Nietzsche's thoughts on time and temporality in a complex way, and one that makes the thoughts of Zarathustra only a part of the manifestation. We find Nietzsche's speech to us about time and temporality by attending to the drama as drama (a temporal affair), to Zarathustra as a figure in that drama (his interacting with others being a temporal affair), to the structure of deepening involved in Zarathustra's offering of his teaching (this interplay being a deepening temporal affair), and to the life-matrix the narrator makes be part of his recounting of Zarathustra's venturings (the unfolding of his life being an embracing temporal affair). These all manifest in their own different ways Nietzsche's thoughts on time and temporality as he is communicating them to us for our thinking through and understanding and for our assessment as to their claim to truth. To ascertain and to assess his thoughts we need to consider all these and see the way they complement and condition each other.

But notice as well: Nietzsche is speaking in this dramatic fashion to us not simply to communicate to us something *he* thinks but also to stir us and to enable us, as we respond sensitively to the drama, to find ourselves there where we may not only engage with him-offering-the-fruit-of-his-reflection *but* may come to understand *more* than *his* ideas. For our response to the drama is to place us back into the problematic of existence itself as we know it in ourselves and our life-experience; the recollective discovery of this problematic means our recall to the immediacy of a presence which summons us to reflective thought ourselves. Not only that, but the drama recalls us to the way the drama of our own life and its events provides us the relevant first-hand presence and evidence on the basis of which we could, aptly attending to and interpreting such presence and evidence, appropriately understand the problematic in its nature and meaning. What Nietzsche is pointing us to as ultimately to be understood is *this problematic*: it is both the 'where' of the recall he would have us undergo as we read, and the ultimate 'what' of the understanding he would have us achieve. But only the *ultimate* 'what', and a 'what' of which the vehicle that recalls us to the place where we might understand it is itself an attempted thoughtful interpretation which we are to attend to, understand, grasp in its own claim to render that problematic in adequate fashion, and engage with reflectively. The more we can respond to TSZ as speaking to us in this complex way, the more it can help us in our ultimate task as philosophers.

A. Time

We have been looking at Nietzsche's thinking on time and temporality as part of an evolving reflection concerned with the problematic of existence and seeking to grasp the contemporary world as entered into that problematic in a historically crucial way. Over time his reflection showed significant advances, but not in the form of straightforward intellectual progress, rather in that of a spiritual deepening, fundamental transformations in its manner, and a re-casting of its overall horizons. Key to his thought was a youthful discovery of life which, deepening and growing more complex with time, he was all the while at work clarifying; but due to that very deepening and to the way his initial clarification had been conducted, he soon found the need to significantly re-cast his initial efforts if he would maintain the honesty and integrity of his inquiry.

In the course of considering the first phase of his thought and writing, we observed a tension between the temporal experiencing his thought was addressing and the express conception of time which he had taken over from others and had appealed to as if it sufficed to account for the possibility of such experiencing. Thus in BT, time was interpreted as a creational factor which was nonetheless able to be transcended in the participative aesthetic-artistic encounter with our eternal living source; but the Kantian-Schopenhauerian interpretational framework which Nietzsche was availing himself of was at odds with his account of such experience, given the framework's limitation of time to being the transcendental horizon of 'experience' in a limited sense of that word. And in UHH, when time was looked at more closely, the express account of time by way of the moment and an image of it (as a scroll and its detachable pages) was unable to do justice to the richness of the experience which he was drawing on and seeking to employ in his account of our historical being. In both cases, there was implicit in his recounting of our temporal being and experience a contrasting idea of time which would have done greater justice to matters if he had made it explicit and employed it instead of the idea he appealed to explicitly.

When we turned to the second phase works, we saw that his self-critical address to his prior way of thinking was initially dominated by an animus that did not allow it to reach deeply and reflexively enough to recognize the questionable character of his express idea of time and thus of its power to grasp the temporal matters he was treating; rather than retrieve time in its fulness as condition of our active being and undo the limited idea of it that he had been employing in his first phase, he instead expanded the horizon of his use of the inadequate sun-measures version, as if that would help him overcome what he had come to feel deficient in his first-phase thinking. In outward reference, that expansion focused on life as an evolutionary affair, and in complementary inward reference, his psychological probing took shape in a seeking for origins which was oriented, on the one hand, toward conjecturing the inwardness involved in the historical development from primitive to sophisticated, and on the other hand, toward seeing all that is higher in the human being as a sublimated development of the lower. In both references his explorations advanced his thought without challenging its horizon-defining notion of time. However, with the last work of this second phase (GS), we found numerous signs of the increasing revival in more mature form of the sense of his self that marked his first phase, and with this, the re-emergence of some significant consideration of the matter of growth and maturation. We found as well the first hint of a concern again for the nature of time itself, and the presence of what was to be the initial sub-section of the Prologue of TSZ.

With TSZ we have found a blossoming of these signs, hints, and considerations, in a lyric outburst which brought front and center his renewed sense of self and a re-engagement with the themes of his first phase. Along with this came the express revival of his early explicit conception of time. In the second phase of his thought, while he had rejected the creational function of time as he had conceived it in his first phase, and had made time the enabling ground of *all* reality, he had left untouched his early idea of the nature of time itself, except to refine his understanding of its movement to grasp it as a continuous affair instead of one of discrete moments; and when his inquiry expanded the field of that refined conception's application, it was guided by a kind of 'scientific' concern which did not invite, let alone require, an express consideration of time's nature. Neither did it invite, nor initially issue in, a comprehensive grasp of the nature of this wholly temporal reality beyond its being 'becoming'. Even so, in the course of the psychological detour which 'scientific' consideration of the temporal involved him in, he had developed various initially unconnected thoughts on 'power' in a variety of different senses and references. Eventually this not particularly obvious or stressed thread in the development of his thinking became transformed when, as this second phase concluded, it was brought together with two significant themes which were part of the revival of the first phase of his thought: one, the notion of life as driving toward more life (UHH), and the other, the notion (applied to Wagner, but admitted later to have had its roots in his own being) of a drive to dominate as central in a human being but as so constituted as to involve a reaching for and responsiveness to the light and thus having the potential for sublimation in virtue of its infusion by a higher side of the person's nature

(WB). Out of this confluence of revived early themes and a later reflective thread eventually emerged (in TSZ, as the teaching of Zarathustra) a universal conception of temporal reality at the heart of which is the notion of will-to-power as the nature and meaning of the energy whereby all beings (and not simply living-beings) *are* and are *as they are.*

When time emerges as the most fundamental theme in the Dionysian dithyramb which is TSZ, its close linkage with this novel reading of the nature of wholly-temporal reality as will-to-power means its own nature must be constituted so that it can be enabling condition for an interactive existence the participants in which, being internally constituted hierarchically and entered into a tension-marked venturing in which something is at stake, can transform qualitatively, grow and mature. To be enabling ground for such a reality, time must have (for one thing) a vertical as well as a horizontal dimension to its own nature. In TSZ we find Nietzsche's thinking amplifying his prior conception to accommodate this; but it does this by adding on to, not re-thinking, that previous idea, and thus, while it achieves significant modifications (ones that also bring his explicit idea closer to the implicit conception of time and temporality that continues to be harbored in his treatment of temporal matters), it does not basically transform the idea. If Nietzsche's evolving grasp of time and temporality arrives in TSZ at the final destination of the journey of inquiry he embarked on in BT, it still falls short of where the trail needs to reach in order to arrive at its most satisfactory end. His efforts to think through time and temporality as they are disclosed in the experiencing whose disclosive meaning his thought is attuned to and seeking to clarify are incomplete in even more fundamental fashion than we have noted so far. Let us now look to how this is so, and consider it first with regard to the vertical, then in regard to the horizontal, dimensions envisioned in his new idea.

1. Time's depth: eternity

The express conception of time in TSZ is first brought forward in the image of the gateway and path in II/2 ("Vision and Riddle"). It is an image which, while other than the image which Nietzsche used in UHH, retains the structural elements of the earlier image (together with the second-phase modification concerning continuity) but introduces two major features which amplify the conception of time being presented.

First, is the introduction into the conception of time (as the Moment) of an element of depth, a vertical dimension, to complement the horizontal dimension of the ongoing of time. In the gateway-image, this facet of the Moment is signified by the vertical arch. But that facet is further developed in another image which Zarathustra also employs to convey the dual-dimensionality of time, namely, the dynamic image of a well or spring. Here the ongoing of time is imaged as a flow carrying on a horizontal plane a welling up from the deepest depths of time, from that unchanging side whereby the Moment is *ever* the time of being. That deepest depth (namely, eternity) harbors being in each case in the form of a Self whose organized energy is ordered to center in the activity whereby as an existing temporal thing it moves with the ongoing of time. As the ongoing side of time is the continual spring-flow of its ever-unchanging side, so the ongoing activity of existing temporal beings continually enacts that Self which is the self of each being.

If we look at this explicit conception with Nietzsche's earliest writing in mind, we see this idea of a depth to time as recapturing, in a transforming reconstrual, the creational account which was Nietzsche's first attempt to interpret certain experience of his and was of cardinal importance in that work. But in BT, depth was interpreted as signifying a deeper side of being, a trans-temporal reality, the source of the temporal and surface side of being. In TSZ, it has become understood as a dimension (first) of time itself and (thence) of that reality which is enabled by time.

More fully, in BT reality is constituted by an eternal source engendering an existence composed of the many spatio-temporal individual creatures. Keeping in mind that in TSZ Nietzsche does not differentiate the moment of activity and the now that holds all contemporaneous beings (and eventually holds all beings since it has no inherent bounds), this creational structure has become internalized to time, as something grounded in the complex nature of time itself. According to that nature as it is now being construed, the Moment is structured so that there is not simply a differentiation-yet-unity of the unchanging and the ongoing sides of time (as in UHH) but, as the image of the well of eternity suggests, a depth or vertical expanse and a directional dynamic internal to the differentiation, the 'upwelling' dynamic of the realization of the same Moment in different ongoing moments. This upwelling internal to the Moment structures the continuing existence which it enables, so that individual Selves at the base (the unchanging side) of time become manifest in time's ongoing side as particular active beings, each entered in ongoing fashion into activity and involved in continual interaction with other such beings. These Selves, taken collectively as joined together in their interacting, have replaced the one trans-temporal 'creator' of BT; these particularized active beings have replaced the spatio-temporal 'creatures' of BT; and this manifestation of a Self in an active being has replaced the 'creating' of 'creatures' by the 'creator'. Put a bit oversimply, the Kantian account of time as an *a priori* intuitional form in the enabling of "experience" and the accompanying distinction of the in-itself from the in-relation-to have finally been overcome and replaced by an account of an interactive reality and of experience as the emergent element within such reality whereby it has become self-conscious, cognizant of itself from within. There is depth to such reality, but no longer as signifying something trans-temporal, rather as relating to an altogether-temporal being whose temporality accords with the complex internal structure of time itself. Thus such beings are Self-expressing centers of active energy, themselves hierarchically ordered internally, oppositionally and tensionally engaged with each other, and able to develop, grow, and mature: all as enabled to be such due to this structure of time (along with the conjoint enabling and structuring condition which is space, of course).

Much more is included in this conception of time as having a depth itself and as enabling a depth to the reality it conditions, and we will keep returning to this matter in later discussion. For the moment, however, we need to note that this idea of time as having a depth belongs to both the explicit and the implicit conceptions of time which are bodied forth in TSZ. In both cases time provides the ultimate horizon for understanding reality and giving meaning to the notion of "depth". But is time really such a bound of reality and horizon for its understanding? Originally, Nietzsche did not think so; something in his experience invited a creational account which grasped time as enabling condition for the created only. Later he came to think this reading was a mistake, but was it? If so, what was mistaken in it? Was it the reading of a fully-actual trans-temporal source? Or was it his attempt to formulate the creational reading using Kantian-Schopenhauerian terms? Or ... ? Whatever (if anything) may in fact have been faulty, Nietzsche focused his rejection on the notion of a trans-temporal source of creation. But if we are to assess the claim he is now putting forth, that time is an ultimate bound and horizon of all being, we must ask how he grounds this claim in supporting evidence. Or rather, since he offers us none, we might seek it out, and ask: Was there something in Nietzsche's own early experience which discloses the place, and the nature of the place, of time in reality but which his thinking, even in TSZ, did not retrieve and think through adequately?

Let us reflect on experience which Nietzsche himself appeals to in his early work. In SE he speaks of times when we discover "our wondrous [*wunderliches*] existence precisely in this Now [*Jetzt*]"[1] and find an inexplicableness [*Unerklärlichkeit*] in this, "that we live precisely today and yet had infinite time to arise, that we possess nothing but a short-spanned [*spannenlanges*] today and are supposed to show in it why and for-what we arose precisely now [*jetzt*]"[2]. Due to his focus at this place in SE, Nietzsche attended to the experience he was drawing upon here with an eye to the question of purpose, to the sense that such experience seems to disclose our being as meant to be where-and-when it is *for a reason*: it is as if something is at stake in our being *here-and-now* in *these* circumstances *rather than there-and-then* in *other* circumstances, and that to find meaning we need to discover that which we are suited for here-and-now, that the achieving of which was the purpose for our being precisely here-and-now. But if we recall our own experience of wonder's disclosive force, Nietzsche's seems to be a foreground focus and incomplete interpretation. For as a more fundamental facet of what is puzzling, as something 'deeper' and 'prior', there seems disclosed not the here-and-now *in contrast with* some *other* time and place, but the here-and-now *at all*: 'that we exist at all, that we are being held forth out of nothing and into being, that there is not nothing'. Such a puzzlement, dawning in us who *in some sense* are, both registers the fragility of that being and brings forward its questionable character for us in that being. Now such puzzling character to our being may well not register with sufficient strength for distinct notice in an attention which is caught by the question of meaning, but may be left unrecognized and undifferentiated from the question of purpose. Even so, the wonder that we are (more precisely, that anything at all is) seems to register something different and more fundamental than the wonder concerned with the here-and-now rather than there-and-then.

But what, more precisely, is this 'prior and deeper' that wonder is registering? What are this fragility and this questionableness that mark our being? Are they such as can make sense as well of the alternative-question relating to purpose and meaning? Wonder has this complex character to its immediacy, that it registers the being of things ('that we are, that we share in the miracle of being'), yet registers it not as finished fact, but rather as fragile and in the midst of a making/being-made whose dynamic is as yet unfinished. Not simply that, but internal to this dynamic is the reference of the in-the-making to an at-stake, the securing of which finishes the dynamic but requires that active effort of beings which at the same time completes their own making. If wonder discloses our being as *in-the-making* in this way and reveals the questionableness of an at-stake as belonging to that in-the-making, and if its register belongs to us as beings who *are* in the *midst of* our own making and who, in that 'midst', are participant in an interactivity that concretely involves others who as participants *are* also in the *midst of* their own making, how are we to understand this? How, in particular, if this 'in-the-making' is not itself temporal, yet requires time as enabling for the needed active effort?

Two phrases from "At noon" (IV/10) can help us pursue these questions: "Did the eve of a seventh day come to [my wondrous soul] precisely at noon?"; "When will you drink this drop of dew which has fallen upon all earthly things? When will you drink this wondrous soul? When, well of eternity? Cheerful, dreadful abyss of noon! When will you drink my soul back into yourself?"[3]

The seventh day that emerges at noon (at the time of the greatest light) is not the morning of the first day (the 'beginning' of on-going being which is the initial moment of the impetus of creation), but the time of that self-aware rejoicing in the completed creation wherein the impetus of creation is coming to consummation (its third moment). In this seventh-day completion of the impetus that brought the dawn of the first day, the soul (in the second moment) sinks down deeply into the depths of time, at once relaxing back self-aware toward the beginning-point of the nisus while stretching out "long, long-- longer" in the reach of ongoing time. At this consummation, she regains touch with a basis there at the beginning of the impetus of creation, a basis deeper in things than that wondrous on-going being which is her own. In his explicit thought, Zarathustra understands this basis as the eternity internal to time (to its unchanging side), which harbors the Self as the basic element in reality.

Yet there is a failure here to differentiate. For how could *this* well and abyss "drink back" this "drop of dew", this "wondrous soul"? In truth, such a 'drinking back' could not be *internal* to the moment of our active being, for the end of the on-going side of the moment (the end internal to the moment) is *ever* 'not yet' to the ongoing of that being. But because he has not differentiated the moment of our active existence and the now which is the embracing contemporaneous time of sun-measured time, Zarathustra can treat the end immanent in the moment as if it were the termination that can be located within the framework of external existence; and grasping the Now of such existence as if it were what harbors all ongoing in itself, he can see that ongoing as going on beyond the existence of the being. The 'drinking back' is then the 'becoming nothing' (the language of III/14) of this Self-manifesting-itself-as-particular-being and the relinquishing of its energy to other beings that are going on in the movement of the embracing Now.

If, however, we make the differentiation and focus on the more fundamental side in the experience of time, do we not find wonder (in its revelation of our being's fragility) pointing us to a nisus whereby (in Zarathustra's terms) there *is* conditioned being (Self *and* active-center) *and* its condition (that is, time)? But if what wonder discloses is the 'is' of 'unfinished (incomplete, uncompleted) fact', does that not mean that time itself *is* in its own 'unfinished' fashion, being an enabling factor 'arising' in the nisus whereby active beings 'arise' *from* a prior-to-time 'starting-point'? But then, how *are* this nisus and this starting-point? Could we say, using Nietzsche's language: They *are* as 'unfinished' factors in that 'out of itself' coming-to-be of being as a uni-verse of beings, a coming-to-be in which time also arises and has its being? The thought is difficult here, but while something like this seems implied in Nietzsche's account of temporal matters and of time itself in its depth, this thought-path leads us toward being as creational in a way beyond what was captured in BT *and* beyond TSZ's reconstrual of BT. More on this in subsection 3 below.

2. Time's directionality: recurrence?

The second amplifying feature to the conception of time in TSZ is the express introduction of the horizontal directional differentiation as *belonging to* the moment itself, making explicit thereby that the moment is a complex affair even on this horizontal level. In particular, on that level the moment is the fixed reference point for the forward and backward dimensions which found and enable the directional ongoing of time into the future that is continually taking place.

Because of the difficulty of representing time in spatial fashion, and because the point of using the representation in the context is to focus attention on the course of time rather than on time in its whole nature, the image which makes this point has certain peculiarities which we noticed in our initial consideration of the drama. Thus the gateway arches above the path which is the image-representation of the ongoing side of time, and thereby the arched gateway is not the present-moment on its passing side but rather is the unchanging and unmoving side of the present. The 'future' and 'past' which are grounded in and defined from this gateway-point of the Moment likewise are not the 'coming' and 'gone' moments themselves but the directional dimensions unmovingly determining the directionality that belongs to time in its ongoing side, a directionality which is anchored in the present as that in reference to which the future is future and the past is past. The moving and passing side of time, in contrast, is represented by a path that runs through the gateway; but because the spatially formed path itself does not move, this image of that side is defective: a circling treadmill stationed in the gateway would be a more apt spatial image, for it would enable the beings walking on the path continually to function in-and-under the gateway, *always in* the Moment even as the passing-moments which the walking-beings know are continually passing.

The focus of Zarathustra's use of the image is on this path which, as the enabling pathway for the movement ('walking') of the beings of reality, is the course of time's continuous ongoing. More specifically, the focus is on a viewing of this path from the perspective not of the actual moving side *as moving* (which is always forward) but from that of the moment as *unchangingly separating* future and past and allowing (in virtue of the spatial imagery) the *one* path to be considered as *two separate* paths which come together, butt heads and contradict each other, here at this point (this dividing instant) under the gateway. The claim is that if in thought[4] one followed the one path backward and followed the other path forward, one would not continually and endlessly move in opposite directions, ever into the novel and never in such way as to find the paths coming together again. Rather, temporal reality is what time (and space) enable it to be, namely, active beings (centers of the will-to-power) who are necessarily *finite* (first) in the time of their own existence (thus they come and go),[5] (second) in the diversity of relations which each establishes in its interactive involvement with other such beings (in that interaction, each is bounded by various others), and (finally) in their number. Time thus enables an existence of interconnected beings which is an inherently limited and circularly unfolding whole endlessly repeating itself in the unending movement of time.[6] But if that is the character of temporal reality, what of its enabling ground, namely, time itself? Is that passing moment in which the 'same' concrete confluence returns *itself* the 'same' moment? If so, is time itself then finite in a form imaged by a ring: ever moving into the future without stop, yet finite in its course because continually circling back upon itself?

The crux of the matter to be grasped here is a disparity between the nature of time's ongoing, and the reality for which it is time's function to be an enabling condition. But before approaching this matter, we need to consider in its own right Zarathustra's idea of the nature of time's ongoing.

In Chapter 5 above, when considering the image offered in UHH to represent time and convey

Nietzsche's conception of it at that time, we noted how the discussion of our historical being, and then again of life, carried an implicit sense and idea of time important features of which the express image and concept failed to enable us to understand. The failures in question related to the inherently bounded character of the present as enabling condition for an active being, to the function of the bounds (beginning and end) to define the directionality of the ongoing side of time (future and past), and to the convergent bearing of future and past within the bounds upon the ongoing-now so that the whole-- future and past together with what is already actual in the ongoing-now-- is held into the realization of time in the ongoing of the present. The failures we found could be traced back to the fact that Nietzsche offered a representation of the sun-measure version of time as if time in that form were primary and sufficed as enabling ground for active beings and their activity.

In the amplified image of time brought forward in TSZ, the concept Zarathustra offers is basically (but not wholly) the same as Nietzsche's earlier concept; and the deficiencies we noted in the first concept and its image are not overcome but persist and become compounded as the new image becomes used. I say the deficiencies persist, and mean this.

In TSZ, the new image (the gateway and path) conveys a concept which advances beyond that of the image in UHH in two main respects. One, it expressly includes the directionality of future and past as part of the unchanging structure of the Moment. Two, it makes the ongoing movement of time under the Moment-structure a continuous affair instead of a succession of discrete leaf-moments.

Despite these advances, the concept carried in the gateway element of the total image still ignores the bounds which make possible such directionality. Thus it treats the unchanging side of the present as if it were the instant or limit which *separates* future and past as matters *outside* (but implied by) that instant, whereas the diversification of the present by way of its bounds gives *inward* amplitude to the present so that the continuously-ongoing side of time is continuously integrating both the bounds and the contrasting inward expansiveness (future and past) into its ongoing realization of the present. The gateway side of time's image, then, embodies a concept of the 'now' which does not give it the amplitude needed if the present is to be an enabling basis for activity and agency.

Furthermore, while the pathway element of this complex image represents the ongoing movement of time as being continuous and to that extent would seem to provide for the ongoing movement of temporal realities (the beings who walk on the path) a basis for their own continuity in being active, the continuity as imaged by the pathway lacks the continual convergence of bounds and dimensions of future and past in the continuous and current ongoing of time that must enter into the nature of time's ongoing side if it is to enable activity. In addition, like other versions of the line-image that is popular for representing the movement of time, this image does not provide for the moment-inflection of the current ongoing of time which we called attention to in discussing UHH (pages 99-103, above) and which enables a 'walking' being to move 'step-wise' (activity by activity) over the path.

Granting, then, that Zarathustra's account of the nature of time in its ongoing side is deficient in these ways, why these defects? What is their root? We approach its discernment by observing that the TSZ concept has the same formative ground we noted as present when discussing the concept expressed in the UHH image. Time is not an outwardly visible phenomenon, but is an enabling condition to active existence; as such, it is directly accessible to an active being only inwardly. In UHH and TSZ both, the formative ground for the concepts of time being conveyed in their different images is an act of abstraction which avails itself of our inward access to isolate and retrieve some aspect of time as time is being disclosed inwardly. In UHH the focus of the abstracting is on the 'now' (the moment), and entering into the concept being conveyed in the scroll-and-leaves image is the 'now' in two forms that are left undifferentiated from each other-- the 'now' of brief moments of lived experience, and the 'now' which is involved in providing a public measure of time. In TSZ, the abstraction from time's inward register expands beyond the 'now' to retrieve as well the bounds-grounded directionality which is also accessible only inwardly to the agent and belongs to time as agent-enabling condition. In virtue of this more inclusive act of abstracting, the 'now' which is the time of time's continual ongoing is recognized more fully as temporal: it inherently involves future and past, in a way attested by the inscription of directional sign-posts on the outer faces of the gateway-arch. And the continuous ongoing which accords with this more complex stationary side to the 'now' is acknowledged in the image of a path which runs under the gateway arch. These advances in TSZ, while they make the concept of the Moment a somewhat fuller rendering of the inward reality of time, do nothing to remove the fundamental deficiency of the idea of time being conveyed.[7] That deficiency lies in the inadequacy of the retrieval of time as it is disclosed inwardly in our active participation in things. TSZ differs from UHH only in that the concept being formed reflects a less incomplete retrieval being effected in what is basically the same act of abstraction. But the abstracting involved ignores and detaches in such way as makes for a concept of time which does not grasp it in its full nature as directly enabling condition but which reduces it to the bound-lessly ongoing-into-the-future current moment in which things appear, operate, and disappear. What is offered in TSZ is only a somewhat fuller version of time as the latter is visible in refraction of the external, what we have called the sun-measures version. Without the abstraction and the reduction effected in this sun-measures approach, Zarathustra could not speak of the pathways into the future and past as end-less, and thus as implicated in an eternity in this sense. For time in its enabling function is itself always bounded.[8]

Given this understanding of the deeper deficiency of Zarathustra's conception of the nature of time's ongoing (that the idea stems from an incomplete abstracting address to time and involves an inattentiveness to the difference between the ongoing present of active engagement and the now of the sun-measures determination of that present), we can return to the issue that led us into the preceding discussion, namely, the disparity between the nature of time's ongoing and the reality for which time is an enabling condition. Given his way of conceiving time's nature and ongoing, Zarathustra claims: "this moment draws after it *all* that is to come" and therefore "itself too".[9] What is it that moves in circular fashion here? Is it time itself, or temporal reality, or both?

When Zarathustra speaks of time as involving an ongoing which is end-less, he is thinking of time in its movement forward as continually bringing new and different moments.[10] By itself, in virtue of its own character, it does *not* move *circularly*. But the time which ever moves onward has its own being as a *condition* for the being of something beyond itself, namely, a temporal reality. Such reality (so Zarathustra claims) is an energy field whose centers exist in a drive toward and struggle over power; it is and must be finite in nature, that is, limited in the variety and extent of difference in its 'can be'. Zarathustra does not seem to think that such a nature of the enabled reality requires that its enabling condition (time) itself be finite in its generation of novel moments, realizing only a number sufficient to enable the concrete run-through of all the different possibilities in temporal reality and then ending such generation.[11] Rather, he thinks of the continuous extending of the moment in the futural direction as endlessly bringing a next moment which is different from all moments preceding it, making therefore for a disparity between the movement of time and the movement of temporal reality. What are we to make of this disparity between the unending and continually novel nature of the conditioning power of time and the finite nature of the reality that is what it is (namely, a whole whose realization as such takes a circular course) under time's conditioning?

When (in III/13) his animals speak to the convalescing Zarathustra, they say: if you wanted to die now, you would say

> 'Now I die and vanish, and all at once [*im Nu*] I am nothing. The soul is as mortal as the body. But the knot of causes in which I am entangled recurs and will create me again. I myself belong to the causes of the eternal recurrence. I come again, with this sun, with this earth, with this eagle, with this serpent-- *not* to a new life or a better life or a similar life: I come back eternally to this same, selfsame life, in what is greatest as in what is smallest, to teach again the eternal recurrence of all things, to speak again the word of the great noon of earth and man, to proclaim the overman again to human beings. ... '[12]

"All things are entangled, ensnared, enamored",[13] and this, so that that very past which is said to be recurring now is among the causes which have brought on this recurrence.[14] Thus Zarathustra, speaking to the spirit of gravity, says:

'Behold, this moment! From this gateway, Moment, a long, eternal lane runs *backward*: behind us lies an eternity. Must not whatever of all things *can* run, have already once run on this lane? Must not whatever of all things *can* happen have already once happened, been done, run by? And if all already has been, what do you think, dwarf, of this moment? Must not this gateway also have already been? And are not all things so firmly knotted together that this moment draws after it [*nach sich zieht*] all coming things? *Therefore*-- also itself? For whatever of all things *can* run-- *must* [*mutz*] it not also run once more in this long lane *ahead*!'[15]

In such passages as these, Zarathustra is taking temporal reality to be not only an interactive one, such that *all* participants in it are *knotted together*, but also to be a finite whole and so entangled internally that the outworking of any being's present activity is causally co-responsible for bringing the eventual existence-again of the very same participants and concrete interweaving that obtains in the moment of the activity in question. This entanglement-connection of all means that harbored in that returning-but-at-present-futural being and its activity will be its connections with the prior (and at present, also futural) beings and events by which it will be conditioned and to which it will be bound all the way back to the present which is our initial point of reference. (One could speak similarly of the relation of a past condition with its repetition in the current present.) But what of that present (our reference point)? Zarathustra claims: The finitude of possibility and the knotting-together of actuality mean that any present is connected to *itself-as-past* as among *its own* causes. Is such a state of affairs truly possible, and if so, can the movement involved be spoken of as a recurrence of the (absolutely) same?

If the movement of time is continuously onward and if temporal reality is an interactive one involving an entangling of *all* things such that each is continually making a difference in the movement of *all* participants in that reality, then it would not seem possible for present actuality to be absolutely the same with any past actuality. For if, due to the entanglement-nature of reality, past actuality enters into and makes a difference in present actuality, then past actuality would, *at the same time*, be *ingredient in* the current present as (part of) its past *and be absolutely identical* with it: an impossibility. It could be absolutely identical only if there were no continuity and entangling in the ongoing of time, and thence no difference-making that carries any moment forward into all that is coming, including 'itself' when that eventually comes. Or even then, could it be *absolutely identical*?

Zarathustra's assertion of an absolute sameness of some reality with itself in another occurrence-- an impossibility, if the preceding thought holds-- is usually expressed in the language of return, recurrence. Thus his animals speak of his teaching "the great year of becoming" which "must, like an hourglass, turn over again and again" and "be identical [*gleich*] in what is greatest and also in what is smallest".[16] Now this way of speaking not only attests his assuming, when speaking of time and temporal reality, the perspective of the sun-measures rendering of time and his use thus of an abstract idea of time which misses time as the enabling condition for a concrete interactive reality; but it involves his rejecting the normal meaning of the language of such a perspective, since the return of autumn (say) is not the return of the identical, only of a concretely *diverse and subsequent* realization of the same season, thus of what may be same in type but is at best similar concretely and occurring at another time. Next autumn, the present autumn, and last autumn, all are different and successively occurring times even though they are 'recurrences' of the 'same' season. The plurality implied in any recurrence (even if the plural are total iconic likenesses) seems being confused with absolute identity.

Nonetheless, it is within a framework of ideas and language that reflect this perspective and this abstract rendering of time that he would do justice to the fact of time as enabling power for a concrete reality which he recognizes as absolutely singular in its ultimacy. The result is that his use of the idea of time as unending and boundlessly bringing the new divorces the enabling condition (time) from the enabled (temporal reality) in such way that another and novel time can be-- indeed, must be-- the basis for the same (absolutely same: supposing this could be) singular reality.[17] How this could be is not at all clear, since the indeterminateness of the enabling (time) does not seem consistent with the singularity of the enabled (singular beings interacting). The alternative would seem to be a conception of time as itself finite, and yet as endless because 'circling' through its finite course without cease. But how could it be finite, and at the same time be defined by future-and-past and by a movement-forward-futurally? For "futural" seems intrinsically to mean "novel" and (if novelty is inherent in such movement) to make impossible thereby a circularity to time itself. Time could be finite only if future and past did not mean what they mean in the conception of time to which Zarathustra is otherwise appealing.

3. Time's enabling, and the at-stake

In his explicit conception of time, Zarathustra grasps it as the horizontally and vertically structured Moment. The Moment in its depth holds eternity or the dynamic temporal stillness harbored in the prior unchanging side to the present-- that side in tension with which the moving side is a continual ongoing realization of this unchanging side in its priority.[18] This stillness lies at a depth from which the flow of time continually arises as the bubbling of a spring arising from within the earth. The image of the well of eternity is a way of signifying the inherent dynamic connection of the two sides to time and the priority of the vertical.

The time which has such a structure is an ultimate bound with an enabling and conditioning function. It makes possible an active existence in which there is something at stake which is to be secured in the interacting whereby such existence is as it is.[19] Activity thus is a venturing, a casting of the dice, in and through which something is to be achieved, gained, won. But what? And why that? Indeed, why *is* there any *activity* at all, any active beings and anything *at stake* in their interacting?

In BT, the at-stake is part of the creational structure of reality. Creation knew an originative impetus coming from the need for a continuing redemption of an original suffering on the part of a reality that was the beyond-time source of all else. Creation effectuated such redemption by its being the joyful engendering of individuated being that exists under the conditions of space and time and is implicated in causal interaction. Yet in virtue of the finitude that marked each and every being of this space-time-enabled causally-interacting reality, a comparable problematic was introduced for each individual being, namely, its own inherent involvement in suffering and thus in the need itself to participate creatively in the world of appearance in order to find meaning for itself in such an existence. What was at stake, then, in existence as BT envisioned it was, first of all, the redemptive consummation to the original being of the (trans-temporal) creator, and thence, that of the being of its various (temporal) creatures, this latter consummation being achieved (in the case of human beings, at least) in the creature's self-aware participation in the aesthetic-artistic immediacy of its own creative act. However, because such participation is to be self-aware, this creaturely consummation is complete, is fulfilled, only as it is a participation in which the creature is self-aware to itself *as creature* because aware in its own creativity of the creative activity of the creator. That is, creaturely consummation involves the creature's creative participation in the divine self-consummation.

In TSZ, however, reality is no longer conceived as creationally structured to have an ultimate beginning-point in a trans-temporal reality. Rather, the creational has been internalized to time and the temporally existent. This means: the timelessly-unitary source of BT has become reconstrued as a (collective) 'source' internal to time, namely, the diversity of Selves within the interactive whole of existence. Creatures are still the temporal active beings of ongoing existence, but the need responsible for the 'creational' emergence of these from the diversity of Selves is no longer seen in parallel with the need of the timeless source of BT for redemption from its original suffering-condition. Rather, each of these diverse Selves *wants* to create beyond itself and *needs* a vehicle for its will towards this.[20] The dynamic of the differentiation within the present, between the unchanging and the ongoing sides of time, conditions existence in every case to be structured in the 'creational' differentiation of (eternal) Self and (ongoing) active being; and that active being is so constituted by the Self of which it is the manifesting offspring and creaturely expression that it functions, in its activity, as the temporally ongoing means for the empowerment of that Self to the creativity it wants.[21] Because the 'trans-temporal source' (BT) is now a set of 'temporal sources' (diverse Selves) which are distinct but interactively-connected (under space and time) in their manifestation as finite activity-centers, what is at stake no longer includes a universal consummation of 'creation' as a whole (in BT, that of the one 'creator-source'), nor is there a creaturely consummation which, while distributive, includes the participation by the individual creature in that universal consummation. Rather, the only creational consummation is distributive and limited spatially-temporally: in each case it is the consummation in ongoing creative power of the Self being realized in some active being who comes and goes, whose existence is a continuing but passing engagement with circumstance, and whose engagement is the medium for achieving and expressing the creative power in question.

Two different lines of questioning arise here.

One concerns the nature of what is at stake. How could Self-realization be what is at stake in existence, if the active existence which time enables-- keeping in mind that the Moment of Zarathustra's explicit conception of time is undifferentiated from the now of the sun-measures version of time-- is a *continually interconnecting whole* (that limited set of beings which are contemporaneous) and not separate beings? The notion of Self-empowerment as what is at stake in existence seems to fall short of indicating what would be at stake if time, as the enabling condition of beings, is enabling for an *interactive existence*, thus for a *diversity* of beings becoming interwoven in their being as they interact. (More on this later.)

The other concerns the status of the at-stake in being. If time is the ultimate horizon for reality, and there is nothing beyond time to make it intelligible in its character or function, then the reality which is the interconnected active existence of diverse Selves with something at stake in their interacting is simply such as it is, and all reasons for any aspect of this lie internal to time. The eternal well-bottom present in the Moment in its depth and the ongoing movement within the Moment in its horizontal dimension simply hold 'this' rather than 'that'-- this Self, manifesting itself in this active manifestation, with this at-stake for its existence and activity because this Self wants its own realization in creativity. Everything is simply such as it is. As the ultimate horizon, then, time would thus seem to be a fate, the Nietzschean residue of the Moira of Homer. And fate can only be explored and discerned, not 'explained'.

But is time such an ultimate fact? Indeed, is time a fact at all? Or to approach the matter from another perspective: what is the *status* of the reflecting agent, and in particular, of the *standpoint* of the reflection in whose inquiry and exploration this matter of the *ultimate*-- of what ultimately is, of what is ultimate in being-- is being interpreted and decided upon? *Are* we, in our reflecting, *beings*? If so, in what sense of "be"? And how can we understand the being of anything, ourselves 'being' in *that* sense (whatever it is) in our effort to understand? In BT, Nietzsche had sought clarification of a certain matter of experience by way of a creational conception of a particular sort, one which appeals to an extant trans-temporal ground that is already fully existent. But in that Dionysian experiencing whose character we sketched out when considering BT, the agent called to reflection (here, Nietzsche called to clarify certain experience) does so as called into question in his/her being: not as called to account for being-in-this-way rather than in-that-way, but as made cognizant of his/her being as a *contingent* being that happens *for a while* to be held forth out of non-being, that is aware now of this peculiar contingency, and that (because in that being the agent is cognizant of being claimed by something at stake) is also reflecting as made cognizant of non-being as a *threat*, an inescapable threatening power. When, in his second and third phases, Nietzsche rejects the particular interpretative conception that had seemed to him at the earlier time apt to such a being in the light of the experience of finding meaning in the joy of his own creating, and in TSZ presents us with a Zarathustra who addresses the same experiencing but who would clarify it by an interpretation which sees its meaning in wholly intra-temporal terms, does he carry this through keeping in mind the contingency of his being and speaking in consonance with that status, making it the standpoint of his reflection? Indeed, did he keep it in mind in his original (BT) interpretation, or has Nietzsche-Zarathustra *in both cases*-- the earlier and the later-- failed to recognize the full import of the mode of his own being, and the implication of this for his reflection and for the understanding of what bears on his being in its peculiar mode?

In BT Nietzsche had spoken of this sense of contingency in connection with the Apollonian and dream-experience. In our dream-world, we delight in the immediate understanding of figures; all forms speak to us; there is nothing indifferent and unneeded. But even in the highest liveliness [*Leben*] of this dream reality, we still have, glimmering through it, the sensation that it is *mere-appearance* [*Schein*]: at least this is my experience, and for its frequency--indeed, normality-- I could adduce many proofs, including the sayings of the poets. Philosophical men even have a presentiment [*Vorgefühl*] that another, quite different reality lies beneath this reality in which we live and have our being, and that the latter is thus mere-appearance [*Schein*].[22]

The Dionysian is such an intensification of this sense of 'mere appearance' as swallows up the sense of intelligibility and order which the Apollonian also conveys, and brings home the sides of finitude otherwise kept concealed by the clear and intelligible. Both Apollonian and Dionysian take us beyond the "incompletely intelligible daily reality"[23] of our ordinary experience, and philosophical men find what in daily life seems solid reality showing itself in a dream-like fashion: no longer does it register as absorbing into itself our sense of reality, but it seems now itself unreal and as pointing us beyond itself for what is truly real. What so seems unreal includes ourselves: we are of a piece with this reality in which we live and have our being, ourselves phenomenal, appearances. In the terms he then was using, Nietzsche understood this pointing-beyond to be a pointing back to a trans-temporal reality underlying this phenomenal reality which is now being discovered in its true status, that of 'mere appearance', of pretending to a reality which it does not in fact have.[24]

On the way to TSZ, and in keeping with his second-phase rejection of such a creational interpretation of reality as he ventured in BT, Nietzsche invokes the notion of the dream in GS, using it to indicate how he would now get beyond the Kantian in-itself and get to a different (interactive) sense of reality. In GS/55, he uses the dream-image again, but in a different way from that in BT: our ordinary encounter with the things of everyday reality is in reality a dreaming with our eyes open (so to speak), in that, in this encounter, we are creating that reality as we do a dream in our dreaming: the inventing-loving-hating-inferring involved in our active reception of what we are encountering is what makes what appears appear as it does. And yet there are times when we awaken in the middle of this 'dream' and know the dreaming as still going on but now as something we are aware of. This awakening, however, is not to be taken as pointing us to some underlying trans-temporal reality; it is rather the way what-is-working-and-living (this appearing reality) is making us aware of its face as illusory in the sense of not the solid objective reality we take it to be ordinarily. In truth, it has the status of a construct being effected in our encounter with what is other than ourselves, but in a constructing taking place more deeply within our being than we normally are aware of. In the interpretation which is ventured in GS, then, the glimmering of contingency has been reinterpreted: not lost in its immediacy, but in the reinterpretation, lost in its challenge to *our own* being. We are no longer understood as having our being "in" contingent reality, as ourselves contingent; we have it "with" such reality, as in our own functioning 'constructive' of this 'dream-reality' but ourselves being in a functioning which itself is real in some non-constructed sense. But then, how *are* we who are so decisive in the shaping of what we meet and of our own meeting with it?

In TSZ, we find this challenge-loss maintained. Earlier we raised the question whether in fact Nietzsche-Zarathustra had fathomed depth to the bottom, and suggested that perhaps he had left undifferentiated something which needs differentiation. We can re-frame that question in the present context: When we discover ourselves in wonder held forth into a being which is a being-active-with what we are encountering, and when we find the dream-like presence of ourselves and others to ourselves glimmering in our wakened awareness with contingency in contrast with the solid unquestioning/unquestioned/provoking-no-question reality of ourselves and others ordinarily, what is the status of this being in which we and others are held suspended out of non-being? Is it simply *fact*, ultimate and unquestionable as such, simply such as it is? That interpretation gives to it a particular sense of being, that pertaining to a finished fact: is that the being we are finding as ours? Or does the glimmering shatter any mere-facticity to the being of what is, ourselves included? Are we discovering rather a being which, as a being-active-with, is *in-the-making*, nothing itself ultimate, final, complete in itself, even if ordained for an ultimacy, finality, completeness, which may come if ... ? Indeed, in the sense of an at-stake which concerns us in *this* being, are we discovering a being of ourselves whose in-the-making is such as it is as referred to a joint-- indeed, all-inclusive-- in-the-making, namely, that of the uni-verse?

In BT, Nietzsche seems to acknowledge a pointing-beyond in the experience of the contingency of being, but he interprets it in a particular way: it is a pointing to an *already fully existent* trans-temporal ground or beginning-point. But if that is questionable, is there no other and more appropriate meaning to the pointing-beyond? If there is a nisus whereby (spatio-) temporal reality *is* as held forth under the conditioning and enabling work of time (and space), must this start in or arise from an already fully existent beginning-point? What if any beginning, any nisus, and this spatio-temporal interactive existence, are not beings which *are in the mode of fact or facticity*, but are factors in a 'making' which itself (including its factors) 'is' in some other manner than as finished fact?[25] What if reality is (in regard to these factors) ever *yet to be*? and if the meaning of these factors lies in their enabling reality to be? Would that not signify that our being (as active beings engaged with each other and becoming ourselves out of ourselves) is what it is (temporal and spatial), and (in the activity whereby we are) has at stake what it does (namely, reality itself), because reality must 'become' *in order to be* itself? Is that why time (and space), as conditions of our being, are what they are, namely, such as enable and condition the being of beings to be an *active*-being such as *makes possible* the realization of reality? Is that why our being (the active being of participants in an interactive existence) is temporal, and temporal in the manner that it is, because it is part of reality in the midst of its happening, of its coming-to-be itself *from out of itself*-- from out of its own initiative? Is this the apt resolution to the problems of the Kantian dichotomy of in-itself and in-relation-to?

Nietzsche-Zarathustra does not expressly understand the matter of being in such a way, of course. Nonetheless, when Zarathustra speaks of the evening of the seventh day of creation, is the self-aware repose he alludes to one attuned (unawares to himself) to the dynamic of *this* 'making', not simply to that of the upwelling of the ongoing from the stillness of eternity within time? Could that be why Zarathustra (in IV/10) addresses his soul repeatedly with the exhortation, "Still!" [*Still*], and again "Listen!" [*Horch*]? Is attention a key to the register of the tension marking this dynamic?[26] If so, then temporal reality has an intelligibility and meaning which involve a deeper tensional basis than time itself and its tensions-- indeed, the latter become intelligible as what they are in virtue of this tensional basis--, and has an at-stake whose character and bearing become intelligible in the further tension they introduce by reference back to this not-as-yet-real basis. Is it this dynamic, whose tensions have not become differentiated from those implicated in time, which is unwittingly meant in his notion-- his mis-reading-- of being as through-and-through becoming? More on this later.

B. Temporality

Nietzsche's concern to understand time is one element in his concern to understand temporal exist-ence and what is at stake in such existence. We have traced the development of this inclusive concern, and observed how it grows out of his involvement as an individual human being in his contemporary world and how this outgrowth, beginning with a reading of current existence as problematic and of that problematic as related to the Germans as a people, evolved to the place where in TSZ the over-riding question that is at issue in his contemporary world is seen to concern humankind and its exist-ence on earth, and to be formulated, in a brief formula, as this: Who shall be lord of the earth? Let us recall and think critically on the sketch in TSZ of the temporality of existence by reference to three themes: first, the temporality of individual life as an affair of maturation (our temporality as intending our becoming lords inwardly); second, the temporality of communal human existence as an affair which in Nietzsche's own times is taking a turn with far-reaching consequences for the future (our temporality as intending the human race as lord of the earth, internally governed by lords among humans); and third, temporal reality and the at-stake as uni-versal and concerning us human beings in that uni-versality (something more fundamental than lordship).

1. The human individual: maturation, morality, and mortality

In TSZ Nietzsche's return to themes of the first phase of his thought, and in particular, to that of growth and maturation, moves well beyond GS and permeates the whole work. But the return brings those themes to a development now in a context marked by the conception of the whole of reality as enabled and bounded by time and as determined in its character to be will-to-power. As it has from the start where that side of reality which was temporal was concerned, the determination of reality by time still means the determination of beings[27] to be active centers involved in an interacting with each other in which something is at stake.[28] According to the specifics of the conception of reality that is formulated in TSZ, however, these beings are more or less complexly structured centers of energy, and in their interacting they know both the internal tension of a hierarchically-integrated energy-and-power-structure to their own being and the interrelational tension of conflict with other beings and a striving for dominance. In each case, that functioning by which such a complex center *is* in its interacting with others is also charged with a drive that orients effort toward something at stake in existence. Because that orienting drive is the will-to-power of the Self manifesting itself in that being, and because what is at stake is thus the realization of the creative power of that Self, the individual's initiative is a venturing, a risking, in the effort to secure such power. It is in such venturing, such risking, that the individual knows the ultimate tension that enters into its being, one which is resolved (to the extent that it ever is) only in partaking of power.

To make intelligible in its maturational meaning Nietzsche's conception of our functioning as such beings in such a reality, we need to begin by recalling two particular facets of our being.

One: As living active beings manifesting the Selves present in the depth of our own presents, we are actualities whose being harbors potentiality and who are capable, in our interacting with things, of drawing on an inward reservoir of resource and potential in our decision-making and -executing. Thereby we are active *out of ourselves*, both as initiating and (in that initiation) as drawing on what is within ourselves and is enabling for the forming and carrying out of our venturings.

Two: In virtue of the complexity of our actual being and the potential implicit in it, there are many facets of ourselves which, at the start of our existence, are susceptible of one type of development or another. There are, for example, the various organs of our being which, in their physical side, alter in their size and shape, and in general grow in some co-ordination toward an adult form. There are also various emotional energies and motivational forces, and a variety of talents and aptitudes, more inward facets of our being which know development in their own ways, toward further forms and without obvious predetermined ending-point for that development. Central to ourselves there is also the decision-making and -executing capacity whereby we operate as single and more-or-less-effectively-integrated beings in the forming and undertaking of activity; this capacity, and the facets thereof as functional elements in it, develops in its own way (via exercise and learning) and that development constitutes our maturation as human agents. Finally, there is the distinctive creative capacity which is also native to ourselves and which, as maturation brings us into the time of youth, is central to what we are to assume responsibility for and to discharge in activity that creates and that enters what is being created into the world beyond ourselves as agents. In all of these cases, it is by our *acting* out of ourselves that we also, in one way or another, *develop out of ourselves*.

Now this dual 'out of ourselves' (being active, developing) marks an engaging in which we are interacting with circumstance. To begin with, because in that interacting we humans are responsive in capacity, our encountering circumstance involves our registering and entering it responsively into the forming of our effort. What is more, circumstance not only holds conditions in dependence on which we exist but holds resources which bear on our development out of ourselves. Thus what develops in its own fashion and pace out of ourselves does so under the conditioning of circumstance and in an interacting which connects us with a circumstantial matrix which is more or less favorable to our development. As a concrete affair, such development is different according to what circumstantial resources are present, what our developmental needs are, and how our activity assimilates from circumstance what is originally alien and integrates and transforms it to use in our becoming. Finally, because circumstance is composed of beings which are independent of us, active out of themselves towards their own ends, and thus not only placed op-posite us but readily functioning in resistance and opposition to ourselves and our efforts, the primordial level of our dialectically-structured being is a being active in a selectively aggressive fashion toward others, not because that is the ultimate nature of our being active but because we need so to act if we are to maintain, appropriate, and develop, our being in such circumstance and to secure what is at stake in interaction with such beings.

In the different sides of ourselves we develop in different modes and manners and under different connections with circumstance. Yet our being is structured internally so that all other forms of development are ordered to two, namely, to the development of our decision-making and -executing capacity, and to the development of the distinctive creativity which is ours as singular human beings. In virtue of this-- an internally dialectical-- ordering of our being, the aggressive primordial mode of our being active and engaging with circumstance has its *ultimate* function and meaning in this, namely, that in our reaching for power (that is, in our wanting to grow and grow capable humanly and creatively) it *indirectly facilitates* our doing this, that is: it indirectly serves our maturing in our decision-making and -executing capacity and our eventually becoming creative participants who empower and enliven others out of our own power and life and who, in giving back creatively, make our ongoing interactive connection with circumstance a fruitful one.[29] Likewise, in keeping with this native internal ordering the functioning and development of the various further factors inward to ourselves as active beings is meant to achieve, with the help of a subordinating and integrating, the effective development of the primary factors, namely, the decision-making and -executing capacity, and our distinctive creative capacity.

The temporality which marks our human being is as complex as our being, and just as those parts of the active realization of that being which are maturation and the development and discharge of our creative capacity are central in our being as agents, so the temporality marking the realization of these is central to the temporality which is ours as structured and integrated active beings. That temporality exhibits a timing that involves what is taking place both in the ongoing and in the depth-elevation sides of time.

As to the ongoing side, there is, on the one hand, the timing which relates to the phases of maturation manifest in the actualization of our essential capacity out of ourselves; this has been a theme for Nietzsche since UHH, and it is important in TSZ, especially as concerns the movement through youth and the lengthy stretch of adulthood which Zarathustra is portrayed as living through by the time of the end of the work and which his speeches address here and there in its various features. On the other hand, there is the timing which relates to the way present circumstance-- including 'the times' (the 'contemporary world')-- enters into the development in question. Maturation not only takes time (likewise for the development of the creativity of the mature human beings), but at different times in the course of that time it involves different needs that are met by different circumstances or elements of circumstance. Maturation succeeds best when the timing of inward evolution is matched by the seasonable presence in circumstance of the different things that enable the growing being to meet the maturational needs of the time; in any case, maturation does not proceed automatically and regardless of circumstance, but knows propitious circumstances and favorable conditions which change as the development within brings inward changes and different needs as well as the need for a different fit with circumstance.

As to the concomitant depth-elevation side of time, Zarathustra conceives certain developmental features enabled by it to be integral to the character of our maturation and its phases. For the gradual actualization whereby the decision-making and -executing capacity develops over time toward its fulness involves (for one thing) an augmenting which elevates and deepens the responsiveness involved in this capacity as well as increases and extends the complexity of factors that are at work in it.[30] Such augmenting, with its metamorphic transition-times, brings us to "grow up", initially and then fully, with the initial "up" (of youth) opening us to a further "above-and-beyond" (the higher-and-better of aspiration) and to a potential fulness whose actualizing brings us to be fully grown up. Correlative to the augmenting capacity, its elevating and deepening responsiveness, and the new levels on which we can function, is our register of hitherto elusive distances, complexities, and subtleties, as well as heights and depths within reality, given our fuller capacity to take part in affairs. Of particular importance in this augmenting is the development of the various moral strengths which are sublimations and elevating refinements of our responsiveness that must be part of the exercise of our agential capacity if its responsiveness to what is at stake is to be effective and one which is eventually adequate to our full responsibility as creative beings.[31]

a. Noble morality

It was in SE that Nietzsche first expressly set forth a sense of our becoming which, when nature's meanings were aptly realized, saw it blossoming naturally in youth in a morality of responsibility, and saw it culminating naturally in what would be central for that responsibility, namely, our adult actualization of a distinctive creative capacity. In SE our growth into such a morality involved at its first crucial transition point-- that into the adult condition when we are 'grown up' in initial fashion-- the incursion of the call of conscience, the awakening of aspiration and love, and the heeding of the call despite solicitations that work against that. In TSZ, the heart of Zarathustra's speech "The Way of the Creator" (I/17) consists of a sketch of moral development that begins in youth and that relates to our bearing and exercising the distinctive creative capacity which is central to the life in us. There he characterizes landmarks on the path into solitude and toward our (creative) Self (the Self with the right and strength to command) and points to effective movement on that path during youth as requiring certain strengths. Above all, courage is needed, but also justice, restraint, the strength and determination for purification of elements of 'ego' and for the honesty and self-critique which reaches for truth, and all these, as powers for self-overcoming that are supportive of the aspiration and commitment to the pursuit of the higher self and in keeping with contempt for the lower self.[32] In effect, this is the reformulation in TSZ of the morality of responsibility of SE, highlighting (on the basis of Nietzsche's own more mature experiencing) the moral strengths ('virtues') which are needed if we are to shoulder the burden of self-responsibility in the way needed for us eventually to blossom in the unique creativity of our very own Self. It is the gaining of such capacity for self-responsibility which is the initial *telos* of our growth and maturation.

In the TSZ reformulation of the SE morality of responsibility, two things come to the fore and are stressed, in keeping with the sense of reality as will-to-power. One is becoming lord-and-master of ourselves; the other is becoming noble.

As we saw in considering III/11 ("The Spirit of Gravity") in Chapter 13, Zarathustra thinks we begin life hidden to ourselves and entered upon a development in which we gather into ourselves the burden of alien values accepted from others; and even when we enter upon youth, we can find as a counterpart to our aspiration an inspiration by others to whom we look up. Like the 'camel' of I/1 ("The Three Metamorphoses"), we then initially enter the alien into ourselves in this form as well, thinking it is lifting us upward-- as, in a way, it is-- and not at first recognizing how confining such yielding to others is and how much it is helping to conceal our Self from ourselves. Eventually, if we are to find our Self, we need freedom from even such inspiring figures: the 'camel' in us needs to become a 'lion'. However, the freedom-from which we thereby seek is not the end we want to reach (our Self), only a step on the way toward it. For in-dependence is not yet self-determination, and only in this latter have we taken responsibility for ourselves. The Self which we would reach, however, is not some 'ego' that 'consciously and deliberately' determines us to be this-or-that; it is that life-center whose *wanting* is the deepest heart of ourselves, which heart 'speaks' in quiet but 'commanding' fashion within us and *would have us heed* its voice and its determination of what is at stake, of what is valuable and what is to be striven for.

In II/12 ("Self-overcoming"), where Zarathustra claims to be speaking of what is of the essence in life, not just in human life, he claims it is an organization and functioning which makes command-and-obedience central to each being. In us human beings, this means that in the decision-making and

-executing capacity which is at the center of our being, there is cognizance of the wanting or willing of the life within us and a responsiveness to its summoning us to venturing and risking which would attain power. For all of us, there is this as well, that in such venturing and risking we come to be heedful of some commanding force imperative upon us; but that force may come to us from without, it need not stem from the Self within. For those of us who have not the courage and the strength to seek for, find, and heed that force within, there is the "will" nonetheless to be heedful to some commanding force from beyond which can enable us to reach what we want so far as we are capable of this. This will persuades us, say, to live inspired by some great human being, and to seek our own growth toward the heights and our sharing in '(creative) power' supported by such a commanding force-- but also constrained by it, as Nietzsche himself was constrained by Schopenhauer and Wagner, for example. In that service, there is for many of us such support as enables the mobilization of capacities and capacity to grow toward our own heights, and in this to function thereby in turn as commanding force for what is even weaker than ourselves.[33] But for the few, this is not what they want or are suited for. For them, there is indeed a yielding to what is higher, a heeding of some commanding power; but that power is their very own Self, and that commanding (to which they would obey, so that in their identifying with it they are Self-determined in their initiative) means their becoming both lord and servant in themselves, and at the same time a ruling force in and for those others who feel, and acquiesce in, the commanding force of the will of the Self-determined.[34] It is this Self-determination that consummates the morality of responsibility-- this power "to give yourself your own evil and your own good and hang your own will over yourself as a law", to "be your own judge and avenger of your law".[35] Youth enters us self-aware into the middle of this evolution of morality within, and opens the way to its fulfillment in the self-aware seeking, trying out, and testing, of early adult life whereby, as the moral powers involved become sufficiently strengthened (at least in a few), we eventually reach the condition of mature capability for responsibility, in which our Self has become lord-and-master in its own 'home'.[36]

In TSZ this morality of responsibility achieved via self-overcoming is also a noble morality,[37] where "noble" signifies a distinctive developed and elevated condition enabled by time in its two-sidedness. From its beginning in the experience of heights and depths which the aspiration of youth enters us into, and throughout its perfecting in the course of adult life, the moral element in our decision-making and -executing functions to enable apt concrete actualization of the "up" (as in "grown up") to our being and experiencing. From out of that "up", we discern not simply the "above-and-beyond" which aspiration opens to us, but also what is not-- or not yet-- at our height (let alone at that of the above-and-beyond us). This, we see as "beneath" us, as something "inferior" or "lesser": not so much ourselves in the childhood and childish condition we have outgrown, but other youth and adults who, at the heart of their becoming, have not grown up in important respects; their failure in one way or another-- they are grown-ups, yet have not grown up-- can be spoken of in many ways, but commonly we say they have remained children and are 'childish adults'. Zarathustra, however, sees the "not" in this moral reference (but not the "not yet"[38]) primarily as a smallness, pettiness, reflective of a congealed complacency that has its roots in (but hides) a lack of courage in virtue of which maturation has become arrested. For maturation takes place in dependence on a venturing, one in which we risk ourselves and are ever in danger. In the Prologue, Zarathustra, in his acknowledgement to the fallen and dying tight-rope walker that the latter has made danger his vocation, had shown a kind of compassion that reaches to the human being as such: "There is nothing contemptible in that. Now you perish of your vocation: for that I will bury you with my own hands."[39] Toward the end of TSZ, in IV/13 ("The Higher Man"), Zarathustra echoes this. Talking to certain (defective) higher men who have been drawn to his heights, he speaks of his love of man as drawn out by man as a going-above-and-beyond [*Übergang*] and a going-under [*Untergang*]-- as a venturer who will not rest in what he currently is but, surrendering himself-as-he-is by reaching for what is above-and-beyond, thereby risks himself, since there is no assurance of success. 'Higher man' is simply the human being who is resolute and stalwart as such a venturer, who will not give up his reverence for what lies above-and-beyond and thus his despising what does not measure up, and who while driven to despair by the pettiness around him even so will not surrender to its pressure and settle for the "petty prudences"-- the "resignation and diffidence and prudence and industry and consideration and the long etcetera of the small virtues"-- which the "small people" [*kleinen Leute*] preach.[40]

Now beyond these higher men around him who, while they have ventured and held out, have nonetheless not found their way but have gone astray, there are even "better ones of your kind" who will perish, lacking the courage sufficient to face suffering greater than these present men know: "to my mind you still do not suffer enough. For you suffer in regard to yourselves, you have not yet suffered *in regard to man*."[41] For higher man ('higher' in this moral sense) to persist and eventually, at the peak of his moral development, to become that lord-and-master of himself and commanding figure to others that is Zarathustra's version of the (morally) great human being in whom this (moral) evolution culminates, it will take that extraordinary courage which can be equal not only to the individual's own individual lot, but to the lot of the human race.

> Do you have courage, O my brothers? Are you brave [*herzhaft*]? *Not* courage before witnesses, but the courage of hermits and eagles, which is no longer watched even by a god. Cold souls, mules, the blind, and the drunken, I do not call brave. He has heart [*Herz*] who knows [*kennt*] fear but *conquers* [*zwingt*] it, who sees the abyss but with *pride*. He who sees the abyss but with the eyes of an eagle, who *grasps* the abyss with the talons of an eagle-- that man has courage.[42]

It is when such resolute and self-aware courage enables us not simply to be responsible for our own individual existence but also to assume the human condition self-aware and to be equal to the threat to *human* existence *as such* that we consummate our maturing.

The polar opposite to higher man in this moral vein is what Zarathustra calls the "small person" [*kleine Mensch*](III/13), or what he also calls (depending on context and emphasis) "the all-too-many, the superfluous" (I/11), "the most-of-all, the every-day, the superfluous, the many-too-many" (III/8), "the rabble [*Gesindel*]" (II/6), "the mob [*Pöbel*]" (IV/13). Integral to the underlying lack of courage which makes for the arrest of maturation, for the frustration and sense of impotence that arises from this, and for the resignation and the concealing complacency which also belong to this condition, is also a desire for revenge, and a teaching which Zarathustra sees as counter to justice. In II/20 ("Redemption") Zarathustra has spoken of revenge as the will's ill will against time and its 'it was': frustration at the inability to will the past, powerlessness to break the hold of time-- that it moves forward, that it opens up only the future as the realm where will can be effective-- and to will backward. Imprisoned in its frustration and powerlessness, the will strikes out: "'That which was' is the name of the stone he cannot move. And so he moves stones out of wrath and displeasure, and he wreaks revenge on whatever does not feel wrath and displeasure as he does. Thus the will, the liberator, became woe-maker; and on all who can suffer he wreaks revenge for his inability to go backwards."[43] Here, in regard to the small person, there is a kindred failure of will: in this case, the inability in youth to be equal to the challenge of self-responsibility and to will that future which aspiration holds out in prospect, and the failure thus to evolve effectively, to develop in accord with the upward reach of aspiration in the course of the movement of time forward. Out of the ensuing impotence there arises the frustrated effort to hurt others, to seek revenge against those who seem able to make the movement.[44] Thus in IV/13 ("The Higher Man"), recalling his failed first attempt to teach (his speech in the market-place of the town to which he had first gone on his initial descent), Zarathustra exclaims:

> You higher men, learn this from me: in the market place nobody believes in higher men. And if you want to speak there, very well! But the mob blinks: 'We are all equal.' 'You higher men'-- thus blinks the mob-- 'there are no higher men, we are all equal, man is man; before God we are all equal.' Before God! But now this god has died. And before the mob we do not want to be equal. You higher men, go away from the market place![45]

The "small person", in his cowardice and inward impotence, seeks to tyrannize over those who are on their way to or have achieved 'power' or mature creative capacity. Such an effort to tyrannize, masking itself in this way, expresses a forefront aggressiveness which, rather than serving the evolution of the agent within, makes effective instead the impotence of those whose lack of courage has arrested their evolution toward potency. If this leads to a particular use of the notion of human equality as a vengeance-weapon, and if Zarathustra emphasizes in contradiction to it the inequality of human beings, this does not signify that in Zarathustra's teaching and the morality he affirms there is no meaning to the notion of our equality as human beings. But such equality as he acknowledges is quite different in character from what is meant under the teaching of equality. In III/5 ("The Virtue that Makes Small"), he says: "I am Zarathustra the godless: where shall I find my equal? And all those are my equals who give themselves their own will and reject all resignation."[46] Anyone who has the courage and honesty and who not only *can* make his own way to his own Self but actually *wills* this is on an equal footing with Zarathustra in this moral reference.

As set forth in TSZ, this transformation of SE's morality of responsibility in which morality comes to express the reality of temporal existence as a matter of will-to-power not only gives considerable emphasis to the element of distance, especially that between higher and lower, superior and inferior. But into the speaking which makes this greater stress enters something else, something that was absent in SE but often present here when distance relates to something moral (courage and cowardice, in the case at hand), namely, a stridency which echoes of the kind of animus which came through so strongly in HAH and which marked Nietzsche's turn against his first-phase thought. This seems to betray that, in his sketch of the morally higher and superior (ourselves as lord-and-master of ourselves) and the morally inferior and base (ourselves as impotent, unable to be lord-and-master of our own selves), Zarathustra is involved in a kind of typing of human beings which seems at odds with the claim that we *are* in the temporal fashion which he has been describing. In what sense of "are" are there such things as "petty human beings" or "great human beings" or "higher human beings"? Granted that since we all are ever in process, obstacles and obstructions can arise so that the concrete path of development becomes blocked, at least for a while, and even becomes unwittingly blocked at times by ourselves; and granted also that the creative love with which Zarathustra approaches the human as such can harbor a despising that is part of the constructive urge and that that despising will be different from the "foaming fool's" contempt for his contemporaries which is rejected by Zarathustra (in "Passing-by": III/7) as itself nauseating because it stems from the swamp: still, the tone of his contempt for "the rabble" with their unclean and lustful thirst (II/6) and for "the most-of-all, the every-day, the superfluous, the many-too-many" (III/8) with their cowardice and complacency, and of his nausea at the "small man" and his eternal recurrence (III/13), does not seem consonant with the register of others in the in-process character of their being; and the extreme character of the condemnation, the intensity of the dissociation of himself from what is seen as impure and repulsive, do not seem the forefront of a creative love which, while it rejects the facets in question, affirms *the beings in their being* and acknowledges the potential implicit in the being whose becoming has become arrested.[47]

What seems to happen is that, in typing the 'moral failures' and the 'moral successes' as he does, Zarathustra does not simply bring different human beings under concepts which, by his own account of reality, can at best represent moments in a process. He goes further, to treat persons the condition of whose decision-making and -executing capacity, at some time and in passing, is intelligible by reference to a type, as if they were *reducible to-- were no more than--* what is contained under the fixation of the type. But reality is ever individual, in process, fraught with potential, and not reducible to what it is at the moment, let alone to a type or type-instance. And when such a reductionist type-subsuming of the individual (himself as superior, others as inferior) concerns what is essential in human being, the sense of higher and lower moral conditions is turned into an unbridgeable chasm humanly. But even where the obstruction which marks the lower never in fact becomes removed, the love of man that would help release the person can not justly judge the person only on that basis. Zarathustra's pronunciation of judgment by way of types turns developmental differences into fixed conditions which type-cast beings, to the detriment of reality. To that extent, his assessment bespeaks a stance other than that of the morality he is actually advocating.[48]

b. Noble creativity

The noble morality of responsibility opens the way to the actualization of the potential for creativity or the gift-giving virtue. As in the case of morality, so here: such actualization involves time both in its ongoing and in its depth-elevation sides. Unlike in the case of morality, which concerns us all in regard to our responsibility for our own lives and whose perfecting relates to the decision-making and -executing capacity which we share as human beings, the actualization of potential here (so Zarathustra claims) involves development of particular capacities which are not shared equally and whose development in the unfolding of the individual's life may not be very distinct and obvious, let alone noticeably seem central, when the capacities in question are relatively limited. Yet because the work of these capacities amplifies and extends the self-awareness that comes into being at the beginning of the moral, such actualization is intimately connected with the maturational development of the person in question.

What Zarathustra has in mind here is creativity only in those cases where the particular capacities are such that their development and actualization can manifest and amplify human greatness, not because of the amount of talent or degree of its development alone but because the supporting inward matrix for development and actualization is the perfecting of the moral. In SE, Nietzsche had recognized such greatness-manifesting creativity in the artist, philosopher, and saint, and had distinguished the creativity involved (as genius) from a lesser creativity of the same sort that would best be devoted to enabling this creative greatness of a few; he had also distinguished it from the modicum of unique creativity of various sorts which persons with lesser talents have by nature. Finally, he had distinguished all these from the receptivity to the greatest creativity on the part of the broad range of persons sufficient to compose a people. When he criticized his first-phase notion of genius in the second phase of his thought, he had sought to understand what was involved as more a fruit of energy, discipline, and circumstance, than of some innate and unusual (perhaps supernaturally granted) talent and capacity, and he had stressed the likeness of 'genius' with the creative as this may be found even beyond art and philosophy (the saint is no longer a 'higher human being' in the sense now being urged). But when he voices in TSZ his conception of humanity with superior creativity (the overman and those higher human beings who would be forerunners of such a person), Nietzsche seems to have in mind only those few human beings who are not simply capable of the moral self-governance just characterized but are also creative in a fundamental way that involves our higher spiritual capacities (the philosophic and artistic). What distinguishes the creativity operating with these capacities is three things. For one, it involves the flow of creative energy out of the depths of the individual being (its Self); for a second, it involves a continued elevating and deepening of experience and a disclosure of things that is achievable only by increasingly refined responsive capacities but that expands and builds on the morality (the honesty, the courage, and the like) that is maintaining open the way to the Self; and for a third, it involves the development and functioning of a skill in appropriating and giving shape to what is being discovered, so that the creative giving has its meaning as an expression of power that also empowers the recipient, the person capable of receiving it.

The creative greatness which is actualized in the gift-giving virtue is conceived by Zarathustra as that in which the will-to-power which marks the nature of reality in every being achieves its fullest consummation in the individual human being. Power in this sense completes human life. Such a consummating completion is a temporal condition and accordingly exhibits certain elements of limit in its nature and realization, directly and indirectly reflecting time itself.

In Zarathustra's explicit account of it, time has no intrinsic bounds (beginning or end), although it (the moment) has future and past as dimensional horizons for its moving (ongoing) side. For that reason any limitations there may be in the life-span of a temporal being (a beginning and end, a birth and death, say) are nothing intelligible as grounded directly in time as the moment. They can only be accounted for indirectly, by reference to the other beings that have generated us, are involved in interacting with us, and eventually contribute to our demise. Yet in his description of temporal matters, Zarathustra attests an implicit conception of time according to which bounds (birth and death) are intrinsic; and in both his implicit and explicit ideas of our temporality, he sees bounds inherent in our maturation humanly. For in life as an affair of growth, maturation is a transformational affair with limited phases proportioned to a mortal life. By nature, our growth in humanity culminates its first phase in our entry in youth into a capacity for bearing a bounded life upon ourselves, and involves us in the perfecting over the phase(s) of adult life of this capacity for bearing responsibility for ourselves. It is in this youthful beginning of adult life that creativity first finds its place in us. As part of the assumption of our lives upon ourselves at that time, we assume our capacities for the higher creative participation in life and we assume them as ours to realize responsively to aspiration and to realize in some (life-) work in the course of life ahead. Thus while in adult life we are perfecting our capacity for bearing our lives responsibly, we are concurrently seeking and entering into that (life-)work as the locus for our realization of the creativity native to our being. To the extent that we are successful in achieving such realization, to that extent we know a consummation of our responsibility beyond the moral, in our participation in that power in which our philosophic and artistic capacities are empowered to be creative. This empowering depends upon the moral capacity with which we are bearing our lives responsibly, for it is our moral strengths which allow us to become centered back in our very own Self as the source of creative energy in us and to maintain such a centering. In turn, in our higher creativity we are building upon and expanding the responsiveness which such responsible bearing involves. However intimate the connection of the moral and the creative and however closely their different developments occur in adulthood, the life-time in which our perfecting of our responsibility and our participation in creativity is to occur has an ultimate limit, death. Speaking of death (I/21: "Free Death"), Zarathustra urges a (moral) orientation toward it which sees in dying a life-fulfilling act in which death "comes to me because *I* want it. And when shall I want it? He who has a goal and an heir wants death at the right time for his goal and heir. And from reverence for his goal and heir he will hang no more dry wreaths in the sanctuary of life."[49] We can cling to life (existence) too long, beyond the time when we can effectively work in creative fashion;[50] or in contrast, we can become "open-and-willing toward death [*frei zum Tode*] and open-and-willing in death, a holy No-sayer when the time for Yes has passed [*wenn es nicht Zeit mehr is zum Ja*]: thus he has a superior understanding [*besser versteht er sich auf*] of life and death."[51]

The capacity for creativity is ours, then, as intrinsically limited (mortal and growing) beings, and knows a limited time for its realization (in the stretch between youth and death, Zarathustra's "time for Yes" to life). And finally, the energies and capacities with which we can carry out any creative work, accomplish any creative task, are themselves limited by nature, in a way apt to these conditions and limitations for their exercise. They are, indeed, capable of development over this time, of expansion and of deepening and elevating. However, even under the favorable condition that they are fully accessible and freely employable for the whole time between the beginning of adulthood and the arrival of death, they still represent only a limited 'can'. Even at our very best, we can only do 'so much'. (All this leaves aside limits which circumstance imposes.)

Now the doing which develops and employs these capacities in creative fashion under these limit-marked conditions does this in the accomplishing of some (life-) task or work. As for this work and this accomplishing, let us sketch it out in brief outline first, then expand the account.

In outline: That task or work which such doing works on is one thing, whereas the goal for which we are working in that exercise of our creativity is another. For example, Zarathustra sees the goal he is working for as a certain human future; but he sees his own work as that of a discerner, herald, and promoter, of that human future he would have arise.[52] Thus his work, in its preliminary phase, primarily centers in philosophic reflection, and thus in the creative employment of the capacities required for reflection, beginning with our responsive powers (of sensuous receptivity, attention, interpretation, conceptualization, etc.). In his case, that has meant (among other things) eventually thinking time and reality in their height, depth, and breadth, under the ideas of eternal recurrence and will-to-power. But this is only the generating of a gift; TSZ shows us Zarathustra carrying through the next phase of his work, that primarily of teaching, which requires further capacities than those involved in reflection, including the sensitivity to the human soul which is integral to speaking with others in an educative vein. Here we see Zarathustra's creativity in his addressing human beings in different ways as the drama of TSZ unfolds, searching for those with ears to hear, for his 'children' and potential companions. This phase of his work is preliminary as well, in that the gift-giving involved is preparatory for the final phase as he anticipates it, namely, the "great noon" of the awakening of the human race, the decisive event for its future on earth, indeed for the whole earthly existence of human beings. It is the final step in inducing this awakening that he is ready for at the end of TSZ, in his becoming for all men the teacher of eternal recurrence and in his subsequent assumption of a commanding role in the "great noon" that is soon to arise. This extended working at his work (in reflection, in teaching, in joining with others in the dialogue in which the human race comes to itself in a way that will be decisive for the human future) is all oriented toward a goal which is quite beyond him and what he is doing and can do personally. For the realization and completion of his vision of future human existence (all that is implied in the "overman" as symbol of the human future in a temporal reality which is will-to-power) is not his work, nor is it anything that could come to pass in his life-time. It is rather the work of his heirs and the heirs of his heirs. Thus he ends I/21 with the words: "Truly, Zarathustra had a goal; he threw his ball: now you, my friends, are the heirs of my goal; to you I throw my golden ball. More than anything, I like to see you, my friends, throwing the golden ball."[53] There must be others who are able to find their own (life-) work in working for the same goal, if that future he envisioned and worked for is to come to pass.[54]

More in detail: The temporal conditions which enter into the enabling of the higher creativity of which Zarathustra speaks bound and mark that creativity, but they do not of themselves define its nature. When Zarathustra speaks of its nature, he speaks of a creative love and a gift-giving. What do these terms "lover" and "gift-giver" mean?

Implicit in the aspiration, in response to which in youth the initial realization of the morality of responsibility takes place, is the implication of ourselves in a task in which we discharge our responsibility regarding the capacity for higher creativity which is ours. While that responsibility for ourselves and our own life's future is singular, the capacity with which we exercise it is a human one which implicates us in a connection with other human beings-- implicitly, with any and all, but concretely, with some. Thus our venturing is two-sided. One side, marked by our response to one side of the higher self in ourselves (ourselves perfected in our capacity for self-responsibility), knows the need for our own becoming stronger and more capable morally in this matter of bearing our own lives. The other side, marked by our response to the other side of our higher self (ourselves as creative), knows the need to enable the development of our own higher capacities and to find the work to which their development and exercise is to be put. Our response here knows a dynamic which is two-fold in a further and rhythmic way. Initially it involves the need for the healthy and holy selfishness which Zarathustra speaks of in I/22 ("The Gift-giving Virtue"). For the longing to become capable creatively involves a thirst, and

> this is your thirst, to become sacrifices and gifts yourself: and accordingly, you have the thirst to pile up all riches in your soul. Insatiably your soul strives for treasures and gems, because your virtue is insatiable in wanting to give. You compel all things to and into yourself that they shall flow back out of your well as the gifts of your love. Truly, such a gift-giving love must become a thief in regard to all values.[55]

Such thirst is healthy because of what it ultimately serves. For from the start in aspiration, there is another and deeper sense that enfolds this selfishness and gives it its nature and meaning: a sense that implicated in our own future is a fulfilling of this side of ourselves in which we give ourselves, sacrifice ourselves, out of the impetus of a certain love-- a love of humanity, and more precisely, a love of the human being as courageous venturer whose venturing brings him/her to become and be him-/herself at the risk of losing him-/herself along the way. The building of ourselves toward this condition in which we have something to give to others involves an ingathering of what of value we meet in our experience, in the course of which meeting we are also developing those capacities whereby we may eventually give back something out of ourselves. In Zarathustra's case-- that of someone whose capacities were strongly reflective--, what he would distribute and give back to others is a wisdom born of (reflective) attention that transforms the values encountered. Becoming-capable in this way and transforming what is encountered does not occur without transformation in himself: thus Zarathustra's withdrawal to the mountains, carrying his ashes with him, and the transformation which the saint notices when Zarathustra meets him again on his way back to human beings, this time carrying his wisdom as a gift: "Zarathustra has been transformed, he has become a child, Zarathustra is an awakened one".[56]

The issue meant in-- and giving meaning to-- such healthy self-love is a giving and gift which is carried to others on the overflow of a love of man that is responsively attuned to the human as an affair of venturing, risking, and becoming, and that would accordingly assist that becoming where possible. What is to be achieved in this giving is an empowered and empowering concrete connectedness with other human beings. To find the basis for this in himself, Zarathustra has had to withdraw into the mountains and solitude at the age of thirty. There, after enjoying his solitude for ten years without tiring of it, he finally found his heart transformed. He had spent enough time in reflection gathering his wisdom, he needed now to give it to others. Thus speaking to the sun one morning, he asks it to "bless this cup that wants to overflow, that the water may flow from it golden and carry everywhere the reflection of your delight. Behold! This cup wants to become empty again, and Zarathustra wants to become again a human being among humans".[57] This is the start of the gift-giving that is to bring to fulfillment in its meaning the first phase of his work, that of reflection.[58] It is animated by a love born in its initial seed in the maturational phase of youth and is enabled, on the one hand, by the moral self-perfecting which has been taking place and, on the other hand, by the employment of his spiritual capacities in creative fashion.

What he carries-- the wisdom of a sort capsulized in the phrase "God is dead"-- is a vision commensurate with the human condition; whatever is its content, his work now on the behalf of the arising of the future envisioned in it is concrete, here-and-now, with his contemporaries. Its gift-giving involves initially a reaching out that is a searching for any and all who have the ears to hear what he has to say and who could join him in working for the goal he envisions; the creativity involved here is exhibited in a way of teaching which would facilitate the release (in those who have the capacities) of their own capacity for reflective understanding, for centering reflection back in their own Self, and for functioning in thought then out of themselves.[59] There is a passage from BGE which expresses the sort of teaching that Zarathustra engages in. It concerns the "genius of the heart"

> whose voice knows how to descend into the netherworld of every soul, who does not say a word or cast a glance in which there is no consideration and element of enticement, whose mastery includes the knowledge of how to seem-- not what he is but what is to those who follow him one *more* constraint to press ever closer to him in order to follow him even more inwardly [*innerlicher*] and profoundly [*gründlicher*]--; the genius of the heart who silences all that is loud and self-satisfied, teaching it to listen, who smooths rough souls and lets them taste a new longing-- to lie still as a mirror, that the deep sky may mirror itself in them--; the genius of the heart who teaches the doltish and rash hand to hesitate and reach out more delicately, who guesses the concealed and forgotten treasure, the drop of goodness and sweet spirituality under dim and thick ice, and is a divining rod for every grain of gold that has long lain buried in the dungeon of much mud and sand; the genius of the heart from whose touch everyone walks away richer, not having received grace and surprised, not as blessed and oppressed by alien goods, but richer in himself, newer to himself than before, broken open, blown at and sounded out by a thawing wind, perhaps more unsure, tenderer, more fragile, more broken, but full of hopes that as yet have no name, full of new will and currents, full of new dissatisfaction and undertows.[60]

In the Prologue and Part I of TSZ we see Zarathustra adapting his teaching effort (in regard to both whom he will speak to, and how he will do so), and at the end of Part I he withdraws even from those who have been receptive, urging them to resist him, for one repays a teacher badly if one always remains nothing but a pupil. ... You had not yet sought yourselves: and you found me. ... Now I bid you lose me and find yourselves; and only when you have all denied me will I return to you. Truly, my brothers, with different eyes will I then seek my lost ones; with a different love will I then love you. And once again you shall become my friends and the children of a *single* hope-- and then I want to be with you the third time, that I may celebrate the great noon with you.[61]

When he returns, urged in part by a dream which saw those who had been responsive to him failing to find their own independence and becoming caught up in a distortion of his teaching, he would clarify and deepen his initial teaching and strengthen those who had been receptive so that when he withdrew again and had himself eventually found the strength to say fully what was on his mind, he could return to persons who had in the interim gained sufficient strength to be able to stand on their own feet and to become his companions.

In his teaching (and presumably when this celebration arrives), Zarathustra is enacting a love and engaging with others in a way that helps empower them to come to be out of themselves, to take up in creative reflection the question of life's meaning and to assess what he is saying out of that, and to become co-participants in the discussion and envisioning which is meant under the phrase "great noon". More precisely, he is engaging with those who *can* respond to his embodiment of a reflective humanity and to the ideas he has developed, and eventually he would be engaging with those who have been able to succeed in their own creative reflective venturing. But in this, he is leaving aside and behind those who cannot, and that means (to his mind) most human beings. For it is only a few who could reach such heights in their reflective endeavor, and not simply become lord-and-master of themselves morally but share in the spiritual leadership which, in developing the ideas that hold out hope for the human future, is needed if the life of humankind on earth is to be assumed in an act of collective responsibility and lived in meaningful fashion. It is this self-selected nobility-- this self-chosen few who eventually join together animated by a shared hope for the future and common commitment to being advance explorers who are catalysts and guides for others-- that Zarathustra wants soon to arise and wants himself to join with.[62]

Despite its form as a pronouncing and exhorting without the give and take of question and answer, the teaching which Zarathustra undertakes is a successful gift-giving only in the measure in which his listeners appropriate the gift as they receive it into themselves.[63] But what is it to appropriate in this case? It is not to accept pronouncements and regard them as truth; that might make one a believer with convictions, but that is no proper way to follow a creative person. Rather, the appropriate way is to draw closer to the person in responsiveness to the strength manifest in his being, to find oneself becoming able to follow that person ever more inwardly and profoundly because one is maturing and is developing in capacity, and eventually to make one's own what is being said. But that eventual making is possible and commensurate with the gift and the giving only as one becomes centered back in one's own Self, and this-- what Zarathustra as teacher wants-- makes the appropriation which gets in appropriate fashion to the heart of the teaching a creative one and turns the 'follower' into a 'companion'.[64]

In short: noble creativity is a concrete mortal-to-mortal affair of giving-and-receiving whose dynamic is that of a being empowered and an empowering in noble and creative vein. The gift Zarathustra would give (his own unique reflective re-valuation of the world, say) is the fruit of inward transformations that have brought a refined and elevated unfolding of his humanity and an enrichment of his spiritual life. Developed by way of a reflection enabled by and grounded in his life, the gift is a transmutation of his vitality into a conceptual rendering of reality, human life, and meaning as human beings may discover it investing their lives. The giving of this gift is animated by the love in which the mature capacity and vital energy of the creator overflow and carry what has been created forth to other human beings. But the meaning of the giving does not lie simply in the discharging of creative energy and the conveying of the created work of the creator. For that work is sent forth to exert a transformative force upon and in others who can respond to it. The meaning of the giving of such a work lies in the concrete connection which is to emerge, and ultimately, the connection of creative companions. Because the focal element in this connecting is a vision of the human future that is to be worked for, the connecting is eventually to bring further kindred connections as it itself becomes worked out in its practical ramifications. The consummation as Zarathustra is participant in it is in this way contributory to an ongoing history-making affair which culminates the human without terminating it in a fixed condition.

Numerous questions arise about this sort of finite creative connecting which Zarathustra claims to be that interacting in which a reality of will-to-power gains its highest human form. Let us consider two sets.

A first set of questions concerns the gift Zarathustra would give. Zarathustra speaks as a philosopher whose teaching effort arises because, in his personal will and determination to heed the summons of aspiration, his reflection has developed responsively to the matter at stake in life as needing (in human beings) to be brought to some understanding which in turn would make a difference in how the (thoughtful) human being lived life. Zarathustra understands the insights that have emerged through this will of his as truths which are commanding not simply for his own life but, since they illuminate the human condition, for other human beings as well.[65] Out of the love of humanity which emerges with the morality of responsibility of the maturing human being, and given his understanding of the common condition and needs of human beings, he would aid others in their own becoming and becoming reflective, and do this in a way that involves offering his insights to them in appropriate form and fashion, thereby sharing them (to the extent possible) as commanding insights that would be instrumental in and for their becoming. Now in this creative giving what is most important is that becoming, and within that, those truths not so much as truths but rather as facilitating to that becoming. Thus in III/3 ("Involuntary bliss"), Zarathustra says:

> Companions the creator once sought, and children of *his* hope; and behold, he discovered that he could not find them unless he first created them himself. Thus I am in the middle of my work [*Werke*], going to my children and returning from them: for his children's sake, Zarathustra must perfect himself. ... My children are still growing green in their first spring, standing close together and shaken by the same winds-- the trees of my garden and my best soil. And verily, where such trees stand together there *are* blessed isles. But I want one day to lift them out and place each by itself, so each may learn solitude and defiance and caution. Gnarled and bent and with supple hardness it shall then stand by the sea, a living lighthouse of invincible life. Where the storms plunge down into the sea and the trunk of the mountain range drinks water, there each one shall one day have his day and night watches, for *his* testing and knowledge. He shall be known and tested, whether he is of my kind and origin, whether he is the master [*Herr*] of a long will ... , so that he may one day become my companion and a fellow creator and fellow celebrant of Zarathustra-- one who writes my will on my tablets, to the greater perfection of all things.[66]

Now in what sense is Zarathustra's will, as he means it in the phrase "writes my will on my tablets", his own will? And why should others, whom in his gift-giving he is aiding to come to be themselves and who, as they succeed, are then creative out of *themselves* and not out of *his* self and who know thus 'their own' will, write *his* will on *his* tablets?

In his teaching, Zarathustra is looking for persons who are of his own "kind and origin", those who have been able to become "master of a long will". This latter will is not identical with the "my will" of "writes my will on my tablets". Rather, it is the will of the Self in oneself, a will to become realized in the activity and person of the person in question. To this will and this Self in his own case, Zarathustra alludes in II/11 ("Tomb song") when, speaking of the youthful visions of his that had died and become entombed in himself, he says:

> Indeed, in me there is something invulnerable, unburiable, something that explodes rock: that is *my will*. Silent and unchanged it strides through the years. It would walk its way on my feet, my old will, and its mind [*Sinn*] is hard of heart and invulnerable. Invulnerable am I only in the heel. You are still alive there and the same to yourself, most patient one. You have still broken out of every tomb. What in my youth was unredeemed lives on in you; and as life and youth you

sit here, full of hope, on yellow ruins of tombs.[67]

In virtue of this will and the way it has been able to walk on his feet (be effective and become realized in and through his active and willing participation in things), he has eventually become open to his own Self and creative in the way that has generated the reflectively-formed gift he is giving. That gift (those commanding ideas) carries what he whose personal will has succeeded in realizing that "long will" has eventually come to see as what he-- this unified and fulfilled being-- would have (what he 'wills', wants, commands, legislates) as horizon and guide for human life and in particular for the life of human beings on earth into the future.

Now in III/16 ("The Seven Seals"), in a refrain that ends each section Zarathustra speaks of never having found any woman from whom he wanted children "except" this woman "eternity". And in IV/1 ("Honey- sacrifice"), he speaks of "that great distant human kingdom, the Zarathustra kingdom of a thousand years" that one day "must come" and not be passed by; how much time it will take to come, he does not know, but he has this certainty: "with both feet I stand securely on this ground, on an eternal ground, on hard primeval-rock, on this highest, hardest, primeval mountain range, to which all winds come as to the 'weathershed' and ask: where? and from where? and to where?"[68] If his living and his reflecting have come to be stabilized in a way that allows a clear and fathoming register of eternity (the deepest depth of the Moment) and the directionality of the movement of temporal things as determined out of that depth (the eternal direction-determining rock), then how and in what sense is it 'his' will that is to be commanding for others?

In one sense of "will", that which relates to an active being as a whole, there is no will but 'his' or 'hers' or 'mine' or 'yours'-- in each case, the personal will of some singular being; and such will, as effective self-integrating and -realizing focal point in an active being who is the existent and temporal expression of a Self, can be enabled by its eventual transformation to become privy to its own eternal singular foundation (Self) and to the directionality at the basis of the movement of all temporal things.[69] But any expression of a Self-- any active being-- is singular and *not itself* the eternal, and its ongoing self-forming in activity takes its own concrete shape only as it is *interpretative*. If there is anything genuinely commanding in such a singular expression-- in its personal will--, it is not the singularity of its will but what, in its transformation, that singular will has become cognizant of and has formed itself in heedfulness to, namely, (at the very least) the will of its Self. But even if in the emerging cognizance in question the will becomes self-aware and reaches back in its reflections into the eternity and the eternal directional ground that is registering in the self-forming of itself as personal will, its self-awareness holds these (eternity and the eternal directional ground) only with the help of an interpretative rendering of them. The shape these reflections take in turn is a responsively-formed one which seeks to grasp these in their universal nature and meaning. In that effort, the will which operates in such reflection, the transfigured and empowered will, continues to be distinctive and singular, and the reflective attempt to bring clarity to the universal sense of elements of the problematic that concerns such a will practically can do this only as discerning in a universal reference what is commanding for itself as singular (namely, the will of the Self of the person in question). Even if it knows a courage and honesty that enables otherwise distorting factors to be transcended not only in its register (in practice) of what is found in the depths but also in its interpretation of such commanding presence in its universality, such reflection forms a limited and interpretative witness to the will of the Self as what is authoritatively commanding, not to itself-as-personal.

What is bodied forth, then, in reflection as commanding is an interpretation of the general nature of the Self's will, that in each and every Self its will is a will-to-power. What this means concretely is different in every case, but the universal meaning is one: a drive toward power is the ultimate directional factor throughout beings. Yet how well such an interpretation grasps the genuinely commanding and conveys it as it makes it intelligible depends on the way the reflective effort itself operates. In every case however, when reflecting out of our very own Selves and sharing in the power of creativity which rises from the depths within, we function as ourselves singular and as unable to claim our rendering even of the problematic we are involved in, let alone of what would resolve it, to be identical with, or different from but fully adequate to, what is being registered and interpreted by us. Nonetheless, our rendering makes a claim to truth, and so far as it was formed as founding itself in the relevant evidence, it commands the *attention* of any and all, but not-- apart from a testing it out and finding it to prove itself out-- the *assent* of anyone. In turn, any assent granted must be grounded in a cognate way, with the tester taking what is claimed back to what he/she has direct access to but only inwardly, and testing the claim in the face of what is commanding as so present. Given its nature, reflective thought concerning the problematic of existence can take as authoritative only immediate evidence, not 'commands' from the outside. It may be, of course, that Zarathustra's teaching effort can help such testing to take place, by its aiding others to gain touch with their own Selves and to function *out of themselves* in cognate creative vein.[70] But in this testing, his rendering of what is authoritative for human effort-- his commanding thoughts-- are not being accepted (supposing that they are) because they are his and express 'his will'. If they are worthy of acceptance, it can only be so far as they adequately formulate the directionality which the tester responsively knows inwardly to his/her own testing.

It is not *his* (singular) will, then, that others could or should write, nor their own will simply; what is written would rather be his and their responsibly willing interpretations of matters commonly accessible to the various parties (of the directionality immanent in reality, say). Those interpretations, reflectively articulating the wills of their Selves as these are responsively incorporated in the making of the reflective effort and being made manifest in their universal meaning in the ideas in question, are addressed to a matter to which all are privy inwardly, and they claim to render it in appropriate fashion and in a way that would command assent if others would look closely at the grounds of this rendering and see how well they ground it. This is what it is appropriate for Zarathustra to say if he would speak in keeping with his use of the phrase "fellow creators". For if creators are self-determining in the way he has claimed, then different creators may be responsive to the same problematic and in reflection of that responsiveness and what it discloses may even sound the same themes. But they will do so in their own way, and there is no appropriate way for any framing of the sameness of the problematic and of the various themes to identify it/these with one or another of the particular competing realizations or renderings. Nor is there any need for such identification; indeed, it is the very conflict of these 'different-renderings-of-the-same' that throws the clearest light on the sameness as different from any and all renderings, provided of course that that sameness, in its prior-to-rendering being and presence, is kept in mind in its immediacy and the variety is listened to on that background.

There is a whole complicated nest of questions on this matter of the creative teaching of creative thought and truth that are implicit here. But at this place, having pointed in their direction let us turn now to a second set of questions concerning the finite concrete connecting Zarathustra sees as issue of noble creativity, one which revolves around the matter of human nature as Zarathustra is delineating it. In a reality defined by energy, force, power, and concomitant elements of hierarchization so that its essence is will-to-power, the human is one type of living being whose variety of capacities are ordered to the decision-making and -executing capacity, and whose growth and maturation as human is constituted by the development of this essential capacity. Thus the human is complex, and if one focuses on the essential, then all human beings are capable of the same maturation regardless of their particular capacities. As regards both this maturation and the development of the particular capacities that are brought into play through the decision-making and -executing of the evolving essential-power, all human beings are by nature capable, even if circumstances and their own decision-making usually combine to bring failure rather than success. Such success as does take place involves, among other things, a movement marked by sublimation and transformation, in which our essential growth-- up, then into the perfection of our moral capacity-- is to arise on an initial (and within a persistent) basis of aggressive dominance-seeking; and this can happen if such seeking can indirectly enable that growth. But such a moral issue of activity is not assured: the inward development can well be (and usually is) unsuccessful in this upward reach, so that inward (maturational, moral) impotence rather than power marks the activity being initiated out of that inwardness.

Now youth represents a crucial time not simply for this evolution in our essential capacity but for the development of the various particular capacities that are to be employed in the activity which carries forward the life being assumed by ourselves. Certain of those particular capacities that enter as well into our decision-making and -executing capacity can be developed in their own right (beyond their role in our essential capacity), and can evolve as 'higher' powers within the transformed awareness (the aspirational cognizance) which the time of youth brings. Like all other particular capacities they are then exercised and developed only by the functioning of our decision-making and -executing capacity. But when such particular powers are developed in their own right, they are 'higher' because they can expand the cognizance of reality and life inherent both to the 'up' of the initially grown up and the 'above-and-beyond' of the still-being-perfected moral capacity. The exercise and development of these capacities, however, *will not actually expand that cognizance unless* their functioning is kept responsively grounded in the requisite inwardness. For if their exercise and development becomes severed from this aspirational base, it may refine and complicate capacity and experience in other regards but it will not *expand* the initiating cognizance.

Now Zarathustra speaks of these capacities as enabling a kind of higher spirituality, and sees their functioning as expanding adult human self-awareness in such way as justifies him saying that the human beings who are marked natively by such an endowment are by nature more fully human in their nature than others who lack the endowment. And where such endowment can be actually developed in an exercise out of a mature responsibility, such human beings are more fully human in their actuality, constituting humanity in its fullest and finest flowering.[71] A variety of questions arise at this point, which we can enter upon by asking: Is such a claim sustainable? More precisely, does such an assessment follow necessarily from the conception of temporal reality as will-to-power?

In discussion in Chapter 13 on the 'crooked' path on which the will seeks power, we saw that the being of a human being is defined within the elevation-depth side of time in a variety of different ways, the foundational one for which is the differentiation of the essential decision-making and -executing center from the rest. For the essential decision-making and -executing capacity is 'above' or 'superior' in relation to the variety of particular powers and capacities which it brings into play. But there is also the sense that this capacity itself is 'subordinate' to the Self of the being, operating on its behalf even when, in that operating, itself-as-center is not consciously aware of the Self that 'governs' its decision-making and -executing. In both cases, it is a functional distinction that is in question, and an above-below that relates directly to the distinguished factors as functional. But we also saw that growth and maturation, relating to the (so to speak) central decision-making and -executing capacity, is an affair in which the development here achieves an 'up' (that of growing up) in a transformation in which an 'above-and-beyond' is opened out for its future development. In neither case is the 'higher' a functional one. Rather they are qualitative in meaning, the 'up' referring to an initial completeness of the developmental expansion of the capacity which is functionally higher than the capacities it brings into play, and the 'above-and-beyond' to further completeness relating both to the decision-making and -executing capacity and to the employment of particular capacities.

Now in developing his thought from this point on, Zarathustra (Nietzsche) fails to differentiate matters that are significantly different, and his failure has important consequences. There is, on the one hand, the essential decision-making and -executing capacity that defines the human as a distinctive type of active being whose being is made concrete and brought to completion in a becoming which develops to (initial) fulness and (final) fulfillment this capacity for active engagement with things. Our growth here is in that potential of our being whereby we are, as whole active beings, the (distinctive human) beings we are. The culmination of this growth is the empowerment of ourselves to be, as distinctive active beings, responsible participants in the interaction which is reality. Whatever superiority and inferiority is involved here pertains to this development, not to the capacity and potentiality itself. On the other hand, and contrasting with this essential capacity, there are the particular capacities brought into play and developed by way of this evolving decision-making and -executing capacity, and with these, differences of a rather different order. For we are different, here, in particularities, not only in strong points and diversity, but in the levels at which such capacities can and do operate. These do not make us human, let alone more or less so; yet they are integral to the concrete realization of our being as human, so that we are not the *individual* human beings we are ex-cept as we are such as we are in the employment of them. This introduces many differences, but the question raised by Zarathustra's address to the matter is this: Are there any such differences that make a difference to our being human? This is not the question: are there any such differences which make us different (individual) human beings? The question is whether the differences made are differences in our humanity, in what makes us human.

What is it to be a human being? Zarathustra would answer this in a way that, while conceding that the crux is the decision-making and -executing capacity (and this, as a developing power in virtue of which we mature into a moral responsibility), sees the development of our humanity as continuing in the assuming responsibility for particular capacities, some of which are not simply different but are higher than others in nature. To his mind, the human is realized more fully in the responsible and creative disposition of such higher capacities, in virtue of which such persons not only have an inner life that is more elevated and complex than that of others, but have more-- a higher quality gift-- to give others. They actualize a higher humanity, then, than others do or even can.

In virtue of his reading of this matter, Zarathustra is preoccupied with what he calls the "order of rank". But the scale he would recognize here in fact involves not an expansion of the human, but rath-er an increase in the degree of express self-consciousness, which he treats as if *that* were the ap-propriate standard and measure of the human. But if the human is a matter of *agency*, and if respon-sibility is the capacity to assume our lives upon ourselves and to bring our particular capacities into play in a way that is effectively responsive to the at-stake in existence, then expansion of the human is found instead in the *effective-- and eventually, skillful and masterful-- exercise* of our decision-making and -executing capacity, such that whatever the life, the nature, and the available particular capacities involved, that concrete exercise is creative and is effective in the measure possible in con-tributing to the securing of the at-stake. Such effectiveness depends on our heedfulness to the at-stake successfully permeating our particular efforts (our employment of particular capacities) within the responsible assumption of life on ourselves; the discharge of the responsibility for whatever our capac-ities and potential are may thus be greater or lesser, more or less aptly effective in bringing our full being to participate in the attempt to help secure what is at stake. But the measure here is not a function of the capacities that are involved, neither the native endowment nor the developed form of such endowment, but of the effectiveness in concretely engaging oneself in the work of mature hu-manity in the course of life's unfolding.

Instead of proceeding to understand our humanity in this way, Zarathustra/Nietzsche extends the intellectualist horizon that marks much of Western philosophy, which sees in the philosopher's par-ticular strengths (discriminative thought and speech, understanding of broad conceptual frameworks, and so on) an indication of what constitutes humanity at its finest. For all of Zarathustra's insistence on ourselves as bodily beings ("body am I entirely, and nothing else; and soul is only a word for some-thing about the body": I/4), there is little feeling evidenced for such a thing (say) as farm work and farm life, and no recognition of how such work can engage one and occasion the commitment and the development of skillful creative effort-- in short, can expand the human core of a person and make the life and the work fully human, even if it is not as refined and elevated as (say) scholarly work. Creativity is a functioning of ourselves in which, within the responsible assumption of our lives and of the determinate side of our nature, particular capacities are brought into originative play in an original fashion from out of our very own Self. Such play is indeed animated by an aspirational love-- but not a love of human beings to the exclusion of other beings; and it is given over to a work-- but not a work whose goal excludes other beings than human beings. In such functioning we know (as Zarathustra claims) the discharge of that power which is the fulness of the being of ourselves as human beings and which enables the connectedness with what is beyond ourselves in which reality is being realized in its ultimacy and finality. But again, the connectedness of ourselves as fully human is not limited to a connectedness with other human beings.

In short: In his reading of the noble creativity of a human being, Zarathustra mistakes one ex-pression of it for the matter itself. For the higher-and-better to which we are pointed in youthful aspiration does have (as he indicates) its two-sidedness: the moral and the creative. In the realization of this higher-and-better, we fulfill the humanity in ourselves in this sense, that we come into that capacity for taking part in fully human fashion in the interaction which is reality. The evolving of the moral toward its own fulness is the ongoing matrix in which the (adult) development of our particular capacities in creative fashion is to occur; and the latter development, whatever the particular capacities that are involved, depends for the creativity in question primordially on the inward (moral) holding oneself open to one's Self which enables creative energy to flow from the deepest side of ourselves. In this holding-open and in the development of the skill in responding to that energy flow as we develop our particular capacities, we enact our responsibility for what we are as whole human beings, and that responsibility is effectively realized in increasing fashion as we gain in capacity and skill for such moral-creative working. The measure of the fulness of our humanity is how well we are able to be responsible in our participation in the ongoing interaction which is reality, responsible for ourselves in moral and thence creative veins, and able thus eventually to engage (and continue engaging) in such way as gives of ourselves as fully matured and whole beings.

There will be differences from person to person in the particular capacities that come into play in our creative work, and with these differences, an outworking of lives on a creative plane that is more elevated and refined in some cases than is the outworking when its creativity is centered in other capacities. But there is nothing *superior humanly* in our spiritual (philosophic, artistic) capacities and in an outworking centered in them, however superior in (say) sensitivity or intellectuality may be the being, the life, and the work, in question. What is definitive humanly is rather a becoming, a growth, whose eventuation is to be the achievement, in maturational and creative veins, of power as the overflow in and of a capacity for responsible participation in the affairs of life. Power in this sense, power as the gift-giving virtue, is the inward-but-overflowing issue born of care and effective concern. Where power comes to realization there is connection, and where it is human beings connecting, an empowering one. So far as it is beings conceived as Zarathustra does, that connecting will indeed involve a hierarchizing internal to the power-manifestation-and-being-empowered. (More on that later.) But important in such connecting is not power conceived abstractly and as if it were greater or lesser in that abstraction, but power as the ongoing concrete issue in the living of a mortal life, in a living that is eventually adequate to death.

2. Humankind: the future and the overman

In that preliminary phase of his work (the reflective phase) in which he began the realization of his own creativity, Zarathustra explored the problematic of existence and, seeking out the truth of the human condition, found-- beyond his deepest thoughts (on time and reality, the ideas of eternal recurrence and will-to-power)-- that his own times were those of a historical turning point for the collective existence of humankind on earth. Zarathustra speaks of this discovery in elliptical symbols, saying that in his times the "little people" [*kleinen Leute*] are lord-and-master [*Herr*], but in the times there is also the first dawning (in himself) of the fact that "God is dead", and with that the recognition of the need first for "the great noon" of a broader and future-decisive awakening and then for the assumption by "higher man" of the place of being lord-and-master.[72] The meaning of these insights is indicated but is not developed in detail; for the most part, it is set forth by broad contrasts such as that of the Prologue, between the "last man" and the "overman".

In the market-place where this contrast is drawn, Zarathustra is speaking to current human beings who, complacent with the lack of creativity in their being, still have in themselves the potential for creativity. But they have turned away from it, and given the sense Zarathustra has, that in addition to historical tradition evolutionary inheritance makes a difference in the endowment of human beings over time, he can say:

> The time has come for man to set himself his goal. The time has come for man to plant the seed
> of his highest hope. His soil is still rich enough for that. But one day this soil will be poor and

exhausted, and no tall tree will be able any longer to grow in it. Alas, the time is coming when man will no longer shoot the arrow of his longing beyond man, and the string of his bow will have unlearned how to whir. I say to you: one must still have chaos in oneself to be able to give birth to a dancing star. I say to you: you still have chaos in yourselves. Alas, the time is coming when man will no longer give birth to a star. Alas, the time of the most despicable human being is coming, he that is no longer able to despise himself. Behold, I show you the *last man*.[73]

The future foreseen here is one which the soothsayer also anticipates (II/19: "The Soothsayer"), one in which all the life has gone out of life: human beings have withered inwardly, their creative potential has vanished, they have grown weary, and it seems to them now that 'All is empty, all is the same, all has been'. Thus

'What is love? What is creation? What is longing? What is a star?' Thus asks the last man, and he blinks. The earth has become small, and on it hops the last man, who makes everything small. His race is as ineradicable as the earth-flea; the last man lives longest. 'We have invented happiness,' say the last men, and they blink. They have abandoned the regions where it was hard to live, for one needs warmth. One still loves one's neighbor and rubs against him, for one needs warmth. Becoming sick and harboring mistrust are sinful to them: one proceeds carefully. A fool, whoever still stumbles over stones or human beings! A little poison now and then: that makes for agreeable dreams. And much poison in the end, for an agreeable death. One still works, for work is an entertaining form of making a livelihood. But one is careful lest the entertainment be exhausting. One no longer becomes poor or rich: both are too troublesome. Who still wants to rule? who obey? Both are too troublesome. No shepherd, *one* herd! Everybody wants the same, everybody is the same: whoever feels different goes voluntarily into a madhouse. 'Formerly, all the world was mad,' say the most refined, and they blink. One is clever and knows everything that has ever happened: so there is no end of derision. One still quarrels, but one is soon reconciled-- else it might spoil the digestion. One has one's little pleasure for the day and one's little pleasure for the night: but one has a regard for health. 'We have invented happiness', say the last men, and they blink.[74]

The contrasting future is posed in terms of the overman, and the way to avert that future and hold open, through the "long twilight" of the increasing smallness to the potential of human beings, a rather different future is by the "great noon" of those who currently can command and can obey such commanding and can provide that nucleus of competitively creative current life which in time can strengthen and broaden itself and eventually make possible the overman.[75] The term "overman" is used by Zarathustra in a special sense which intends certain human beings of superior higher creativity who belong to the future. Such creativity has certainly existed in the past, but one thing was missing: it did not arise in a being who had seen the truth of man's aloneness ('God is dead') and did not involve creating out of a sense of ultimate human responsibility for the human future and in a faithfulness to human life as an affair of the earth. But as well, the creative potential (as Zarathustra is understanding it) has in past been one that has accumulated blindly in an unassisted evolutionary inheritance. It is part of the 'great noon' not simply to acknowledge that man is alone but also to recognize the responsibilities this entails, including that of seeking to understand and foster the conditions (external and internal) that make for the presence in future of human beings with extraordinary potential in favorable circumstances. It is the future of a humanity which has become self-consciously responsible for its existence under the leadership of a nobility of higher human beings that Zarathustra sees as the goal that would give meaning to human existence on earth. This is the thought of SE, as it is being reformulated in TSZ.

The future being urged by Zarathustra is that collective one in which the existence of the human race on earth is consummated in the fullest realization of the human. That means, first of all, it involves a race united in a way never before seen, for up to now human beings have seen themselves in connection with more restricted communities: thus the "thousand goals" (I/15) of the diverse peoples of past and present, each people united by its own table of goods, the product and manifestation of the creativity which in that table formulates the value-horizon which serves as the accepted orienting-horizon of the life of the community. The creativity which provides the uniting framework-- that of the wise among a people (II/12: "Self-overcoming")-- would distinguish the people in question from other people, set it apart competitively as well as orient the members of the collective body in question to what is worthy and worthwhile as seen within the 'world' of that people. But now a more far-reaching creativity is needed, a creative love and an esteeming of good-and-evil which is commensurate with humanity as such and which thereby rejects the ultimacy of the collectivity of distinctive peoples and their more restricted horizons. The humankind-responsible cognizance which, now that God is dead, acknowledges the need for a uniting goal for humanity as a whole has made its appearance in Zarathustra, and his teaching effort is an attempt to broaden such cognizance and to engage the creative segment of the human beings currently alive in an undertaking that would define that goal and what it implies for collective human effort now and into the future. Except in the broadest terms, Zarathustra does not indicate, let alone spell out, what this would (or could) mean (say) for current collective institutions or for future institutions that are in keeping with the focus. He points rather to a time of experimentation, a time of testing out various ways of life. And he speaks of a "Zarathustra kingdom of a thousand years"[76], to symbolize both the self-conscious unity and the limitedness of future human existence on earth at its culturally creative peak.

In his sketchy account of the immediate and long-run future, Zarathustra stresses one thing above all else. The 'great noon' he envisions is that of diverse and diversely creative individuals: it is a nobility that is to be at work in the initial shaping of the vision of the future of humankind-alone-on-earth; and that sense of a competing diversity of noble beings, and with this, diverse perspectives, endures even as the beings that are to carry the burden of self-aware leadership in future by embodying humanity at its creative finest are the overmen who at present exist only as his dream.[77] Thus the answer to the question which we recalled at the start ("Who will be lord of the earth?") is this: that "lord" is to be the spiritually creative within the human community, who have become lord-and-master of themselves morally and who have developed and exercise their spiritual capacities in masterful and creative fashion under the governance of their Selves. Specifically, that lord is to be the philosophically creative, who can and must venture on this task of commanding, of thinking and offering to others the thoughts which are to guide the world.[78] But what thoughts are those?

Ultimately they are the thoughts which interpret what bears directively, as claiming and giving direction, on the forming of our activity: both interpret it in its character and standing, and interpret it in its concrete meaning for activity that would be responsive to it.[79] Zarathustra himself has already accomplished the first, in his interpretation of what claims our decision-making and -executing capacity as the Self wanting power; and in his filling out of this interpretation in his vision of reality as a temporal affair of diverse beings (including the human) whose being takes shape in a will-to-power, he has also begun on the second. Thus he has given us his vision of human being and existence as implicating a future of the race which is now unavoidably in our own hands and requires of us our setting a goal for humankind as a whole. Now this (complex) thought commands as interpretatively mediating the directive or claiming factor itself; but for it successfully to function as command, it must be understood. Without an understanding of the thought, we have words, on the one hand, and the uninterpreted (or diversely interpreted) claiming power, on the other hand. But if we have words while the thought meant to be conveyed by them is not understood, then if we are to respond to them as a command we must give them a meaning intelligible to us and (supposing we accept them with that meaning and respond to the imperative form they take) we will act guiding ourselves by those meanings-- and not, therefore, by the original thought. Now under what conditions is it possible for reflective thought to be understood?

In our earlier discussion of Zarathustra's creative teaching, we saw how his communication of his thoughts required of him an address to others that would facilitate their rising to the heights; for only on those heights could his thoughts be understood in their meaning and assessed in their truth-claim. Something like that would be required of the participants in the "great noon", of any fellow-creators. But Zarathustra does not conceive these participants as anything but a few human beings: most persons are not capable of such understanding since they cannot rise to those heights. How then can such thoughts guide the world?

A possible way seems opened up when Zarathustra claims that there are others who, if they are not (or not yet) creators in the manner of great philosophers, can enter upon the struggle for knowledge as "warriors". In I/10 ("War and warriors"), while distinguishing himself from them (he was of their kind, and still is, though he is more and is also hostile to such warriors), he concedes a certain sublimity and grandeur to those who wage war on behalf of knowledge, who would war on behalf of their thoughts and (if those thoughts are vanquished) would have the honesty to feel triumphant in that outcome-- for it is truth that is at stake in that war. But speaking to such warriors, he urges:

> let your nobility be an obedience, let your very commanding be an obeying. To a good warrior
> 'thou shalt' sounds more agreeable than 'I will'. And everything that is dear to you, you should
> first let be commanded to you. Let your love for life be a love for your highest hope, and your
> highest hope be the highest thought of life. But let your highest thought be commanded to you--
> and let it sound: man is something which should be overcome.[80]

Presumably Zarathustra's reference to warriors of knowledge and their waging war is to the mobilization of disciplined ('scientific') inquiry in the search for the truths that would bear on the overcoming in question and whose apprehension would contribute to its accomplishment. In such inquiry, the orienting conceptual framework would be provided by the unquestioning acceptance of the 'should'-idea as its own directive, and inquiry into other things could proceed on such a basis. But how is this different from the 'thou shalt' character of morality Nietzsche rejected in his second phase thought? Then, too, quite apart from whether there are such truths-- whether 'overcoming' is the sort of thing that could be produced--, can the commanding thought in question be commanding and a guide if it is not understood? indeed, if the person in question is not even capable of understanding it? Is it clear what (say) "overcome" means in this 'should'-statement? Could it be clear to these warriors?

The question of understanding becomes even more pressing when we recall that it is "the world" that is to be guided by the philosopher's ideas, and that that world is not exhausted by the few creative philosophers together with those seekers-after-knowledge whose creativity is manifest in scientific inquiry obedient to a philosophic rendering of the larger life-perspective. If even these seekers are not thoughtful philosophically and not able to understand in its reflective meaning the guide for their own creative life-commitment, what of the mass of human beings for whom truth-seeking is not a focus of their life's work? If it were the Nietzsche of BT that was answering this question, the answer would be: myth would provide the orienting basis for life, the interpretative guide called for, and myth means religion. But it is Zarathustra, not early Nietzsche, we are concerned with now, and the places where one might expect pointers-- as in I/15 ("Thousand and one goals")-- are silent.[81]

3. The at-stake and temporal reality

Zarathustra, and Nietzsche, and we ourselves who are studying the thoughts of Zarathustra and Nietzsche: we are all human beings, whose reflecting and reflective studying is an activity of ourselves as beings who exist and whose existence is marked by (among other things) a concern for truth. In our case, what matters most directly is that we understand Zarathustra and Nietzsche, discern truly what they thought. But if we begin questioning that-- why does that matter?-- and child-like repeat that 'why?' to every answer offered, we find ourselves eventually driven to ask: have we found here an endemic feature of our existence? For this matter of 'something matters'-- not 'this matters' or 'that matters', but 'something matters'-- marks our very involvement in things, in life's affairs, so that even when 'nothing matters', the 'lifeless' condition signified in that phrase itself still matters to us: it is nothing we want to live with, indeed nothing we could live with if living on really did not matter.

Crucial in Zarathustra's understanding of this phenomenon is time as the enabling condition for existence. In virtue of the nature of time, a reality is enabled, one which is an interactive field of beings whose complex temporality has in every case a primordial reference to itself as active being, as center of activity who carries its whole being into its active engagement with other beings who are circumstantial to it. In each case, the being of such beings is, in its essence, will-to-power, and that means: it is constituted in such way that in its activity, there is something at stake which concerns it and is to be secured in and through its participation in activity. And that 'something' is 'power'. This being what time enables, the activity of each being is a venturing and risking, whose meaning is to be vehicle for the securing of power.

Although Zarathustra begins his approach to understanding the at-stake in existence with individual beings-- and in particular, the individual human being--, his thought develops a sense of the power that, when secured, culminates the being of a human being as a creativity, a gift-giving virtue. When we explore what this means, we find that the very meaning of power as the perfection of the individual is a creative participation in affairs which is marked by *something at stake beyond* this fulfillment of the creative agent, namely, a strengthening of the others to whom the creative agent is giving his/her gift-- a strengthening of *their* capacity to take part in affairs in such way as secures what is at stake as it concerns them. This understanding of the meaning of creativity as involving a broader at-stake is recurrently underlined by Zarathustra and phrased in diverse ways as if to make sure the point was understood and not confined by any particular phrasing. Thus in one phrasing:

> My ardent will to create impels me ever again toward man; thus is the hammer impelled toward
> the stone. O men, in the stone there sleeps an image for me, the image of my images. Alas, that
> it must sleep in the hardest, the ugliest stone! Now my hammer rages cruelly against its prison.
> Pieces of rock fly from the stone: what is that to me? I want to perfect it; for a shadow came to
> me-- the stillest and lightest of all things once came to me. The beauty of the overman came to
> me as a shadow. O my brothers, what are the gods to me now?[82]

According to this mode of speech, then, the creating in question involves a destroying which enables something harbored latently in the human being to emerge, something whose emergence would represent the perfection of the human being in question. That 'something' is the overman (the superior human being) latent in the actual being of the human being.

In a kindred mode of speech, Zarathustra speaks of himself as wandering among human beings

> as among fragments and limbs of human beings. This is what is terrible for my eyes, that I find
> man in ruins and scattered as over a battlefield or a butcher-field. And when my eyes flee from
> the present to the past, they always find the same: fragments and limbs and dreadful accidents--
> but no human beings. ... I wander among human beings as among the fragments of the future--
> that future which I envision. And this is all my poetizing and striving, that I poetize and carry
> together into unity what is fragment and riddle and dreadful accident.[83]

Here Zarathustra suggests that the claim of others upon him in his connecting with them reaches beyond the particular others in question, to include all human beings as members of the human community. Thus in his concrete connecting he is animated by a vision of how the whole human race might come into unity, and his creative involvement, so far as it concerns particular others, strives to foster that becoming in them whereby this inclusive future might come to be.

Whatever the phrasing, Zarathustra's point is that the power which marks creative activity as the expression of the fulness of the hierarchically-and-dialectically-structured being's Self is-- in the case of human beings-- manifestation of a love (of man) which would 'create' human beings: man is something which should be overcome, and other humans claim us in that vein. Accordingly, the encompassing issue of the creative address of one human being to another-- what seems at stake when this is grasped in its overall reach-- is the emergent connecting of human beings when interacting in a mutually creative fashion.[84]

And yet, why is what is at stake in Zarathustra's activity such a concrete connecting of himself with other human beings? Indeed, is it this which really is at stake there, that is, is Zarathustra's reading of the matter correct? If we trace this gift-giving connecting back to the aspirational register of the at-stake and see in the latter (as it registers in us) the two-sided call to a responsible participation in the realization of humanity-- to the agent's own fulness in being, and (in virtue of his/her human nature, and a special connection of human being with human being) to his/her working for the fulness of others--, have we thereby understood what is at stake, or grasped the full nature of the love harbored in our aspirational reaching? Although our human capacities make possible-- and indeed in some measure necessary-- a special connection with human beings, our aspiration-born love does not seem restricted to love of humanity. In all beings, there is a temporality that means for any being its being is centered in its activity out of itself; and in its so functioning, it is involved in interacting with other things as well as in its own becoming, such as it is. And there are times when other living beings (animals, say, or trees), or even places as complex gatherings of such beings under land-form and climate conditions, come home to us strongly in their being out-of-themselves, touching us at the heart of our own being and evoking a love, as if we were encountering our kin-- not (pretend, but actually sub-human) 'human' beings, but rather (say) other and strange beings who share in earthly existence. At such times and in such situations, we know a love of such beings and places, and with it, a distinctive claim upon our care, a summons to a connecting and connection in which we are supportive and affirmative of the being of such other beings, of their being as centered in a being active out of themselves by way of their own capacity. It may well be, as Zarathustra's conception of the matter stresses, that we have a primordial responsibility for ourselves individually, but this self-responsibility implicates us not simply in a responsibility to other human beings and humanity, but in a responsibility to beings, to all beings.

The encounter and touch which awakens this sense need not be oblivious to the complexity in what Zarathustra brings to attention when conceiving reality as temporal, and temporal reality as will-to-power: to the op-positional nature of active beings and the aggressive side of venturing, for one thing, and further, to the primordial place of self-responsibility for each human being within the fuller sense of responsibility that marks our maturity as human beings, and so on.[85] But it also need not accede to Zarathustra's restriction of the at-stake (as it concerns us human beings) to the human itself-- to the human being's own being, and to the being of the other human beings with whom he/she is engaged. There is, indeed, opposition in our relation to any beings, and aggression, as part of life in other beings as in ourselves. There is also contrast in the inwardness of beings, in the aggressive-outwardly side of the activity of different beings, and thus in the way other beings may enter out of themselves into the connection in which human beings are creative participants. The connecting then is not that of human with human, and not understood by treating other beings as diminutive or deficient human beings. Yet there is nonetheless a genuine connecting and sharing, however diverse in capacity the parties are and whatever the nature of the reciprocity involved.

Even within Zarathustra's way of thinking, there seems a basis for extending in this way the sense of the aspiration-founded love and of the connection which is at stake in our active involvement with things. For when Zarathustra takes time as the enabling bound of existence, it is of an interactive existence, and if in such a temporal existence there is something at stake it presumably relates to the being of that interactive whole and itself is of an interactive character. Now that whole *is* an interactive one, composed of participants and not itself something apart from these; and if the at-stake (in existence-whole) relates to these participants, it relates to them as including (but not being identical with) them as participants, as co-participants, as co-operating in the securing of itself in their concrete connecting.[86] Now such an at-stake does not simply relate to interactive existence and its constituent participants, but it also *concerns* the various beings, and does so in such way that into their being in each case is entered a reference, in their activity, to the at-stake as *to be secured* in and through their participation in the interacting whereby they are. That the at-stake concerns any participant does not mean that the whole burden of the at-stake falls on that participant alone, as what is to be secured in and through its active participation in existence. That burden is shared by *all* participants, and their activity can secure it only as a co-operative affair (thinking "co-operative" etymologically). In virtue of this sharing of the task and the co-operative character of the working of all, the at-stake concerns us each, but concerns us as something we are to share in the securing of, in its realization. Co-opera-tive (thought etymologically) does not necessarily-- or even often-- mean co-operative: that is, the working together is the working of op-posed beings each of which operates out of itself in the inter-acting and functions thus in a co-operating which, on the primordial level, aggressively seeks to secure a place in the interacting in which the being can continue its becoming. Such co-operating is rarely without conflict, competition, a contesting of wills.

Now if the at-stake that concerns each of us concretely is itself a connection of a certain sort which is to arise in our interacting with things and each other and whose nature includes the varied parties, then we may understand how, although what is at stake is neither simply our own being as distinct beings nor something which is a function of some part of our being, human beings, in their register of the at-stake in its concerning themselves, might construe it as Zarathustra does, in such way as em-phasizes the connecting of human with human and ignores other things. But even when, within the perspective Zarathustra is advocating, we notice this foreshortened reading and seek to correct it by extending the sense of the at-stake as it concerns us humans beyond human beings, to all beings, in the way attested by our own experience of nature, say, and on the basis just set forth, we still have not done enough to make the idea Zarathustra is advancing fully apt, but have unawares perpetuated the original failure of Zarathustra to make a differentiation which is crucial.

What is unfortunate in Zarathustra's approach to the matter of the at-stake is that, in beginning as he does with individual (human) beings and emphasizing as he does the call to self-responsibility, he fails to distinguish clearly and consistently the at-stake in existence from what is at stake for the individual in his/her activity. In BT, Nietzsche's creational reading of reality had opened the way to something like such a distinction, except that by grasping the trans-temporal source as already fully existent, the universal consummation of creation was found in the self-enjoyment of that source, and only so far as the creature, according to his distributive account of creaturely consummation, knew a self-awareness that included cognizance of this (the creator's) self-enjoyment was there any sense in which the creature knew a sharing in universality.[87] Once Nietzsche had rejected the trans-tem-poral, he went to the other extreme of acknowledging only the distributive consummation and seeing it as ultimate. In TSZ this ultimacy of the distributive remains, even as it is recognized that such con-summation is nonetheless interactive in the sense of involving a concrete connecting of human agents. But in keeping with the incomplete or one-sided ('perspectival') way Nietzsche had come to see the interactive nature of reality in the second phase of his thought and which even in TSZ he did not fully overcome, the full nature and implication of time as enabling condition of an *interactive existence* in which what is at stake is related to the *whole* and only thereby to the diverse participants did not come to be clearly seen and acknowledged. Thus in speaking of the human situation Zarathustra tends to treat what 'matters to us' as if it related simply to a need in us as human beings and at most concerned what is good for us. But if it is the nature of the whole that in *its* realization something matters and that this mattering represents an at-stake which concerns all participant beings in that whole as something to be secured in their participation, and if what 'matters to participants' signifies their share of this 'mattering' in the nature of things, then 'what matters to us' can not be an affair relating only to human beings and one simply of human good. Even for human beings, humanism, anthropocen-trism, is not-- and can not be-- a responsible perspective in such a world.

One final unfortunate side of Zarathustra's approach to the at-stake is found in the incompleteness of his consideration of the passing experience he makes so central. Granting that time involves ongo-ing, because his conception of time does not explicitly recognize the inherent bounds involved in that ongoing Zarathustra's account of our participation in the securing of what is at stake proceeds by pointing to a transient experience and to a depth and breadth he claims could suffice to outweigh all that threatens meaning for us as transient beings. But that immediacy, while a significant part of what is important, is only foreground and not by itself what gives the experience meaning. More decisive is the culmination in our becoming that is involved-- the coming-to-be in which we become, for a while, capable of taking part in existence in such way as shows this foreground and concentrates our life-whole for that while in such participation. It is this concentration which enables the experience to have *finality* and to give *life* meaning and which enables this finality and meaning-giving to endure beyond the passing moment-- so long, that is, as we endure in our con-centered *being*. Our being and that finality are not themselves a passing immediacy or some simply passing participation in the concrete realization of a connected reality in the event. We have touched on how and why that is so-- or begun to-- here and there in earlier discussion, but further inquiry into that matter is for another book, which takes us farther beyond Nietzsche than it is appropriate for us to go in this one.

Epilogue

We began this study of Nietzsche with EH, and in the main body have pursued it with his guidance in mind concerning that reading of his writings which would enable them to be understood properly. In general terms, he pointed us to his works as having his own coming-to-be as their generative matrix, and as being intelligible as works of an evolving capacity for living and thence for reflection, which are bringing to eventual self-consciousness his own life-task, that of himself as a mature human being. In that regard, the work with which we have completed this study, TSZ, is the culminating expression of his growing self-awareness, and at the same time the beginning of his self-conscious carrying out of that task. Like Zarathustra and his gift-giving descent from the mountains, in this particular written work Nietzsche has given us a gift shaped to provoke a response in us which completes the act on his part of giving his insights to us with an understanding on our part gained by searching out in our own lives the issues and the evidence that would facilitate understanding.

In his retrospects, Nietzsche acknowledges flaws that strongly color his earlier works, some simply reflecting youth, some reflecting his own way of realizing youth. But he treats TSZ as a work in which, having righted his ship and gradually recovered from his romantic aberration, he has finally overcome those flaws and has achieved something of the highest quality and perfection. As we have pursued our study, we have found deeper flaws in his writings than those which he himself retrospectively acknowledges, and in particular, have found that the treatment of time and temporality in TSZ exhibits significant deficiencies which he does not seem to see. Yet we have also found something quite remarkable, a reflection which from BT to TSZ has taken its stand at the heart of this matter of the problematic of existence and has been able, as he grew toward maturity and developed skill in reflection, to maintain itself there as disclosure altered, as initially exciting ideas lost their aura of sufficing the standard of truth, indeed as his whole way of going about philosophy initially proved unsatisfactory and required replacement with a different ('scientific') approach. The evolution in his reflective capacity did not stop there, but as he himself changed further he also grew capable of-- and responded to the need for-- a more subtle and incisive reflection which could sensitively grasp the richer disclosure of experience, especially as it concerned time and temporality. Even so, the maturity that lies behind TSZ was only an initial one which was by no means perfected but provided a disclosive matrix for reflection that was still obscured in important regards; and while it supported a demanding and capable reflection it did not allow (or at least, that reflection did not succeed in) a sufficiently self-critical address such as could make of what was open in disclosure something sufficient for discerning in explicit and clear fashion the truth of these matters of time and temporality.

All the same, it is underway toward an original and suggestive understanding that we have found Nietzsche from BT onward. In TSZ he is not yet open enough to see all that needs to be seen, nor free enough to make it out fully and faithfully. Yet he is 'there' somewhere in the middle of what he needs to be in the middle of, and his thinking is determined to explore and understand what he is finding disclosed. That makes the struggle to understand his thought-- to locate his themes, to recognize the experiential disclosure that went into the making of his sense of things, and to find the standpoint at which to apprehend the meaning and test the claim of his words-- eminently worthwhile.

Notes for PRELUDE

Chapter 1

1. Misunderstanding had characterized much of the reception of Nietzsche's writings from the beginning, and this was not the first notice he took of it in his published work. His disappointment, and his impatience with readers who do not seem to know how to read his writings, appear in a number of places in them. Three are important here. In a Preface that was added in late 1886 to one of his earlier works (*Dawn*), he indicates that the proper reading of any such book as *Dawn* is like that which a well-trained philologist would undertake. Philology, he claims, "teaches to read *well*, that means, to read slowly, deeply, looking forward and backward cautiously, with second-thoughts at open doors, with delicate fingers and eyes ... . My patient friends, this book wishes for itself only perfect readers and philologists: *learn* to read me well!" (S-I/1016 [H-D/5]). [Something further of what this means appears from *Antichrist*, aphorism 52 (S-II/1218 [K-A/635]), where Nietzsche characterizes philology or the art of reading well as one of "being able to read facts *without* falsifying them by interpretation, *without* losing caution, patience, delicacy, in the desire for understanding. Philology as *ephexis* in interpretation: whether it is a question of books, of the news in the newspaper, of destinies, or of weather-conditions-- not to speak of the 'salvation of the soul'."] Again, in 1887, at the end of the Preface to *On the Genealogy of Morals*, we find him addressing his readers: "If this book is incomprehensible to anyone and jars on his ears, the fault, it seems to me, is not necessarily mine. It is clear enough, supposing, as I do suppose, that one has first read my earlier books and has not spared some trouble in doing so: they are indeed not easily accessible." (S-II/769-70 [K-GM/22]). Finally, also in 1887, in Aphorism 381 of the later-added Part V of *Gay Science*, Nietzsche speaks on "The Question of being Intelligible" and says: "When one writes one does not wish only to be understood: one wishes just as surely *not* to be understood. It is by no means an objection to a book if someone finds it impossible to understand: perhaps that belonged precisely to the intention of the author-- he did not *want* to be understood by just 'anybody'. All the nobler spirits and tastes choose their audience when they want to communicate; and when they choose that, they at the same time erect barriers against 'the others'. All the more subtle laws of any style have their origin at this point: they at the same time keep away, create a distance, forbid 'entrance', understanding, as said above-- while they open the ears of those whose ears are related to ours." (S-II/256 [K-GS/343]).

[NOTE: In references to the various works of Nietzsche, I will normally cite them as follows: first, with a reference to the relevant pages in the Schlechta edition of his works (S-I/1016, for example, refers to Volume I of that edition, page 1016); then, with a reference to a readily accessible English translation (in the above cases, H-D/5 signifies the translation of *Dawn* by R. J. Hollingdale, page 5; K-A/635 and K-GM/22 and K-GS/343 refer to pages in the translations of *Antichrist*, *Toward the Genealogy of Morals*, and *Gay Science*, by Walter Kaufmann). Given that several of Nietzsche's works are translated by Hollingdale and several by Kaufmann and that all the translations I cite will be by one or the other of these two translators, such specific reference as (say) H-D or (say) K-EH will be needed for clarity and unambiguity. The abbreviations for all the Nietzsche-works to be cited-- represented here by D and EH-- are indicated in Note 2, Chapter 2. There is, however, this peculiarity to this way of citing the English translations, that the page numbers refer to volumes in English which in some cases do not bear the title in question (because they hold translations of two different works, say); they do, however, hold the translation being cited. For the volumes involved, their English titles, and which translations are contained in them, please consult the bibliography. Finally, please note that the English translation of passages cited in the text and in these notes is my own, not that found in the translations being cited.]

2. We shall take up with most of the import of the title, and in particular its religious significance, later in

the present chapter.

3. S-II/1069 (K-EH/221).

4. S-II/1067 (K-EH/219). The quote refers to hearing Zarathustra, but it would have the same meaning here. The full passage reads: "Above all one must *hear* aright the tone-- this halcyon tone-- which comes out of this mouth, in order not to do wretched injustice to the meaning of its wisdom."

5. Indeed, the books express his self, even preserve what was vital in his life: so he says in regard to the writings of his forty-fourth year, in the note we cited and discussed earlier (pages 3-4, above).

6. The quoted phrases are found at S-II/1074 (K-EH/226).

7. S-II/1072 (K-EH/224).

8. S-II/1071 (K-EH/223). The phrase occurs in a passage that reads: "Even that filigree art of grasping [*Greifung*] and comprehending [*Begreifung*], that finger for nuances, that psychology of 'seeing around the corner' and whatever else belongs [*eignet*] to me, was first learned at that time, is the authentic gift of that time, in which ... ". Nietzsche then continues: "From out of the perspective of the sick to look toward *healthier* concepts and values, and again conversely, from out of the fulness and self-certainty of a *rich* life to look down into the secret work of the instinct of decadence-- this was my longest training, my authentic experience, if I was master anywhere it was in this. I now have it in hand, I have the hand for this, *to reverse* [*umzustellen*] *perspectives*: the first reason why a 'revaluation of values' is perhaps possible for me alone."

9. The quoted phrases are found at S-II/1072 (K-EH/224). The "healthy" here refers mainly to psychical and spiritual health, and only secondarily to physical health. He brought himself 'back to life again', and yet remained life-long afflicted by various ailments and manifestations of physical problems.

10. S-II/1077, 1078 (K-EH/230, 231).

11. S-II/1093 (K-EH/252).

12. S-II/1094 (K-EH/253).

13. S-II/1072 (K-EH/224).

14. S-II/1085 (K-EH/240).

15. S-II/1095 (K-EH/254).

16. S-II/1098 (K-EH/258).

17. S-II/1090 (K-EH/247).

18. In the first section of the Preface he added (in 1886) to Volume I of *Human all-too-human*, Nietzsche speaks of these encounters and their initial impact in connection with a profound suspiciousness which, strengthening the sense of distance from others he had long ago recognized, had already entered into his attitude toward the world well before these encounters took place. See the discussion in Chapter 2 below, pages 19-20, 23.

19. For the passage containing this likeness to the birth of Athena, see Chapter 2, pages 22-23 below, and S-II/1095-1096 (K-EH/254-255).

20. S-II/1152 (K-EH/326).

21. S-II/1157, 1158 (K-EH/332, 333-334).

22. S-II/1152-1153 (K-EH/326-327). That the first book of the *Revaluation of all values* is entitled *The Antichrist* and that EH stresses the antagonism of Nietzsche to Christianity connects these two works closely.

23. We shall consider in Chapter 2 the retrospective assessments of the works treated in the rest of this study.

24. The immediately preceding quotes are to be found at S-II/1104 (K-EH/265).

25. S-II/1099 (K-EH/259).

26. S-II/1104 (K-EH/265).

27. S-II/1100 (K-EH/261).

28. S-II/1099 (K-EH/259).

29. A "good reader", "a reader as I deserve him", is one "who reads me the way good old philologists read their Horace." (S-II/1104-1105 [K-EH/266]). "When I imagine a perfect reader, he always becomes a monster of courage and curiosity; in addition, supple, cunning, cautious, a born adventurer and discoverer. In the end, I could not say better to whom alone I am speaking at bottom than Zarathustra said it: *to whom* alone will he relate his riddle? 'To you, bold seekers, experimenters, and whoever embarks with cunning sails on fearful seas-- to you, drunk with riddles, rejoicing in the twilight, whose soul flutes lure aside to every whirlpool, because you do not want to grope along a thread with cowardly hand; and who hate to *deduce* where you are able to *divine*.'" (S-II/1103 [K-EH/264]).

30. The first speech of Part II of *Thus Spoke Zarathustra* shows Zarathustra, alarmed that his teaching has been distorted by his enemies, returning to his friends to reawaken in them the true sense of his meaning. He does not return in order to set straight those whose distortions in his absence were working to confuse and undermine the beginnings of understanding in his friends. If this betrays Nietzsche's own attitude at the time, it would seem also to provide indirect confirmation for his not being concerned, in *Ecce Homo*, with clearing up

in the minds of most persons their ideas of him and his thoughts, but at most with rejecting such misunderstandings because they affected and distorted what the few who were receptive to his thought and might eventually come to genuine understanding of it were able to see.

31. S-II/1065 (K-EH/217). In aphorism 295 of *Beyond Good and Evil*, Nietzsche continues this characterization.

32. Nietzsche uses Dionysus basically as a symbol, and wavers between a characterization of him as a god and one of him as the human being realizing the powers that that god (to Nietzsche's mind) symbolizes. Such a wavering has its ground, of course, in the nature of the god himself and his relation to his followers. "The Crucified" has a similar duality (Jesus as man and as God). For a hint concerning the meaning of the religious form of Nietzsche's self-presentation, cf. *Gay Science*, aphorism 300.

33. S-II/1066 (K-EH/218).

34. S-II/1065 (K-EH/217).

35. In the Prologue in *Thus Spoke Zarathustra*, Zarathustra speaks of his descent to share his wisdom with others as animated by a love of humanity. The character of the love meant there is the same as here.

36. S-II/1066 (K-EH/218).

37. "I never speak to the masses" (S-II/1152 [K-EH/326]).

38. S-II/1152 (K-EH/326).

39. His work, *Schopenhauer as Educator*, dwells at length on the liberating effect on himself of Schopenhauer; yet that working was ambivalent, as he came to see, since it led him to project himself into Schopenhauer in a way that had to be undone if he was fully to come to himself.

Chapter 2

1. A further work, *Nietzsche contra Wagner*, is an edited compilation of passages from earlier works of his, which Nietzsche also completed in 1888 but which was published only posthumously.

2. Future references to these works will normally take an abbreviated form. In the case of *Ecce Homo*, the abbreviation will be EH. The other abbreviations are as follows: BT (for *The Birth of Tragedy*); UHH (for *The Utility and Harmfulness of History for Life*); SE (for *Schopenhauer as Educator*); WB (for *Richard Wagner in Bayreuth*); HAH-I (for Volume I of *Human all-too-human*); HAH-II/MMO and HAH-II/WS (for the two original appendices to HAH-I); D (for *Dawn*); GS (for *Gay Science*); TSZ (for *Thus Spoke Zarathustra*); BGE (for *Beyond Good and Evil*); GM (for *Toward a Genealogy of Morals*); TI (for *Twilight of the Idols*); A (for *The Antichrist*). With one exception, these will also be the abbreviations used in the references to pages in the translations; the exception is in references to pages of the translation of *Human all-too-human*, which translation contains both volumes in one.

3. Moreover, at this time he also added Part V to the original *Gay Science* and appended a set of poems to the whole, as counterpart to the "Prelude in German Rhymes" that had been the introductory part of the original work. Interestingly, the very first of the Prelude-poems speaks to the matter of reading his works; it runs as follows: "Take a chance with my fare, you who eat! Tomorrow it will taste better to you, and by day after tomorrow it will taste good! If at that time you want still more-- in that case for me my seven old things make for seven new moods." (S-II/17 [K-GS/41]). Entitled "Invitation", it invites the reader not simply to take the time needed to digest and savor GS but to follow up by reading his seven previously published works and taste them from that place to which GS has drawn one. One will find them tasting differently now.

4. It is worth noting here that the autobiographical turn expressed by these Prefaces (1886) and culminated in EH (1888) was initiated (if indirectly) in TSZ (1883-1885), with the account of Zarathustra's life forming a significant element in the dramatic framework of that work. We shall return to this matter when we come to TSZ; see Chapter 13 below.

5. There may be a question of how accurately Nietzsche is recalling his life in EH, but the answer is of as little importance to the philosophical intent and significance of the work as the question of the accuracy with which Plato presented Socrates in his dialogues. Our focus in this chapter will be wholly on what Nietzsche offers, in its individual, common human, and historical, dimensions, and not on questions of factual accuracy or inaccuracy in his memory of circumstance or event or, more precisely, in his representation of these.

6. Chapter 1, page 7 above; see S-II/1070, 1072 (K-EH/222, 224) for the relevant passages in EH.

7. S-II/1083, 1085, 1086, 1093, 1096 (K-EH/237, 240, 242, 252, 256).

8. S-II/1085 (K-EH/240).

9. S-II/1086 (K-EH/241). Keep in mind the positive meaning of this 'calamity'; see the discussion in Chapter 1, page 8 above.

10. In Nietzsche's usage, this term often includes what we call adolescence and early adulthood.

11. S-II/1091 (K-EH/249).

12. S-II/1090 (K-EH/247). Nietzsche means "relaxation-and-recreation" [*Erholung*] in the sense of the following comment about reading: "In my case, every kind of reading belongs among my relaxations-and-recreations: hence among the things that liberate me from myself, that allow me to walk about in strange sciences and souls-- that I no longer take seriously. Reading is precisely my relaxation-and-recreation from *my own* seriousness." (S-II/1087 [K-EH/242]).

13. S-II/1090 (K-EH/247).

14. S-II/1092 (K-EH/250-251).

15. S-I/437 (H-HAH/5). (HAH-I, Preface).

16. S-I/439 (H-HAH/6-7). (HAH-I, Preface).

17. S-I/437-438 (H-HAH/5-6). (HAH-I, Preface). Thus Nietzsche can say (in the opening section of the Preface to HAH-II): "When, in the third *Untimely Meditation*, I then brought to expression my reverence for my first and only educator, the *great* Arthur Schopenhauer-- I would now express it much more strongly, also more personally-- I was, so far as my own person was concerned, already in the midst of moral skepticism and destructive analysis, *that is to say, in the critique and likewise the deepening of pessimism as understood hitherto*, and already 'believed in nothing any more', as the people put it, not even in Schopenhauer: just at that time arose an essay I have refrained from publishing, 'On Truth and Lying in an Extra-moral Sense'." (S-I/737-738 [H-HAH/209]).

18. S-I/738 (H-HAH/210). (HAH-II, Preface).

19. S-I/438 (H-HAH/6). (HAH-I, Preface).

20. S-I/739 (H-HAH/210). (HAH-II, Preface).

21. S-II/1119 (K-EH/284).

22. S-II/1120 (K-EH/286).

23. "Ten years behind me, when the *nourishment* of the spirit in me had really come to a stand-still, when I had been learning nothing that was useful, when I had forgotten an absurd amount for the sake of a trash-pile of dusty erudition. Crawling scrupulously with bad eyes through ancient metrists-- that's what I had come to!-- It was with pity that I saw myself utterly emaciated, utterly starved: my knowledge simply failed to include *realities*, and my 'idealities' were worth nothing." (S-II/1120 [K-EH/286]). Nietzsche also notes: "it was then, too, that I first guessed how an activity chosen in defiance of one's instincts, a so-called 'vocation' which is the last thing to which one is called, is related to the need for *deadening* the feeling of desolation and hunger by means of a narcotic art-- for example, Wagnerian art." (S-II/1120 [K-EH/286-287]).

24. S-II/1121 (K-EH/287).

25. S-I/440 (H-HAH/7). (HAH-I, Preface).

26. S-I/443 (H-HAH/10). (HAH-I, Preface).

27. S-II/1094-1095 (K-EH/253-254).

28. S-I/444 (H-HAH/10). (HAH-I, Preface).

29. S-II/1095-1096 (K-EH/254-255). The "my capacities, ripened, leaped forth in their ultimate perfection" alludes to Athena's birth from Zeus.

30. For a very interesting and suggestive counterpart to all this, consider the Platonic Socrates as he is portrayed in the *Phaedo*, but also in the *Phaedrus* and *Symposium*. See my brief discussion in *Loving and Dying*, especially 107-115, but consider it not only in the context of the whole dialogue but in connection with the involvement with love and the confusing turn in life which Socrates adumbrates in his speech on love in the *Phaedrus*. (See *Loving and Dying*, 205-223, especially 220-222.)

31. S-I/439 (H-HAH/7). (HAH-I, Preface).

32. S-I/740-741 (H-HAH/211-212). (HAH-II, Preface).

33. S-I/740 (H-HAH/211). (HAH-II, Preface).

34. S-I/439-440 (H-HAH/7). (HAH-I, Preface).

35. S-I/439 (H-HAH/7). (HAH-I, Preface).

36. S-II/1120 (K-EH/286).

37. S-I/739-740 (H-HAH/211). (HAH-II, Preface). "One of the bravest" is an allusion to Wagner.

38. S-I/440 (H-HAH/7) (HAH-I, Preface) for all the quotations in this paragraph.

39. S-I/438-439 (H-HAH/6). (HAH-I, Preface).

40. S-II/1121 (K-EH/287-288).

41. S-I/741 (H-HAH/212). (HAH-II, Preface).

42. S-II/13 (K-GS/36-37). (GS, Preface). Nietzsche is here playing with a German expression for deceiving someone, namely, to pass off a *u* as an *x*; it relates to the use of V and X as Roman numerals, and means passing off a 'five' for a 'ten'. The "great suspicion" precludes the trust which allows such deception.

43. S-II/1072 (K-EH/224).
44. S-I/742 (H-HAH/212). (HAH-II, Preface).
45. S-I/742 (H-HAH/212). (HAH-II, Preface).
46. S-I/739 (H-HAH/210). (HAH-II, Preface).
47. S-I/741 (H-HAH/212). (HAH-II, Preface).
48. S-I/741 (H-HAH/212). (HAH-II, Preface). From his first work (BT) to the end, science is, for Nietzsche, the epitome of optimism, of knowledge claiming to be fit and able to improve life and life's conditions.
49. S-II/1071 (K-EH/223).
50. S-II/9-10 (K-GS/32-33). (GS, Preface).
51. S-I/742 (H-HAH/213). (HAH-II, Preface).
52. S-I/441 (H-HAH/8). (HAH-I, Preface).
53. S-I/441 (H-HAH/8-9). (HAH-I, Preface).
54. S-I/440-441 (H-HAH/8). (HAH-I, Preface).
55. S-I/442-443 (H-HAH/9). (HAH-I, Preface).
56. S-I/743 (H-HAH/213-214). (HAH-II, Preface).
57. S-II/13-14 (K-GS/37). (GS, Preface).
58. S-II/14-15 (K-GS/37-38). (GS, Preface). Concerning "Baubo", Kaufmann notes (38n8): "A primitive and obscene female demon; according to the *Oxford Classical Dictionary*, originally a personification of the female genitals."
59. In the preface Nietzsche composed (October, 1886) and added to the second edition of GS, he speaks of the philosopher who has passed through various kinds of health as having passed through an equal number of philosophies. For a philosopher "is simply un*able* to do anything but transpose his condition every time into the most spiritual form and distance: this art of transfiguration *is* philosophy. We philosophers are not free to separate body and soul as the people do; we are even less free to separate soul and spirit. We are not thinking frogs, nor registering and objectifying mechanisms with frozen innards: it is constantly the case that we must give birth to our thoughts out of our pain and, in motherly fashion, endow them with all we have in us of blood, heart, fire, pleasure, passion, agony, conscience, destiny, and fate. Life-- that means, for us, constantly transforming all that we are into light and flame-- also everything that befalls [*trifft*] us; we simply *can* not do otherwise." (S-II/12-13 [K-GS/35-36]).
60. S-I/10-11 (K-BT/18-19). (BT, Preface).
61. S-I/11 (K-BT/19). (BT, Preface).
62. "I would perhaps now speak more cautiously and less eloquently about such a difficult psychological question as that concerning the origin of tragedy among the Greeks." (S-I/12 [K-BT/20-21]). (BT, Preface). As EH makes clear, "now" he is *still* a disciple of Dionysus, even if no longer a novice initiate but a much more experienced and knowing one. See also TI (S-II/1032 [K-TI/562-563]), where he ends that work with a consideration of the tragic, and concludes: "And herewith I again touch that place from which I once went forth: *The Birth of Tragedy* was my first revaluation of all values. Herewith I place myself back again on the soil out of which my will, my *ability*, grows-- I, the last disciple of the philosopher Dionysus-- I, the teacher of the eternal recurrence." The uncongeniality to youth of the task-- the address to the problem of science-- seems to stem importantly from the penchant of youth, in the face of the need for reflection, to be impatient with the thorough thinking-through of matters such a philosophical task really requires; a youthful beginner on adult life wants reflection to do its work quickly, so that he/she can get on with life. Thus thought is not itself uncongenial to youth; indeed, youth is the beginning-time for reflection and reflective thought is needful to the maturational work of the time of life. But in all but those who are natured for the extended thinking-through that is part of philosophy, such thorough pondering is uncongenial; and even the youthful philosopher can become impatient with the dialectical, if the impetus and impetuousness of youthfulness itself gains an upper hand in the undertaking of his reflective effort.
63. S-I/9 (K-BT/17). (BT, Preface).
64. S-II/1109 (K-EH/271-272). In retrospect, Nietzsche sees in the insights into the Dionysian and into Socrates a further and connecting insight which, developed considerably in his later thought and put here in the language of that thought, he also claims to be a first: "I was the first to see the real opposition: the *degenerating* instinct that turns against life with subterranean vengefulness ... versus a formula for the *highest affirmation*, born of fulness, of overfullness, a Yes-saying without reservation, even to suffering, even to guilt, even to everything that is questionable and strange in existence. This ultimate, most joyous, most wantonly extravagant Yes to life represents not only the highest insight but also the *deepest*, that which is most strictly confirmed and upheld by truth and science. Nothing in existence may be subtracted, nothing is dispensable ... . To comprehend this requires *courage* and, as a condition of that, a surplus of *strength* [*Kraft*]: for precisely as far as courage *may*

venture forward, precisely according to that measure of strength one approaches the truth. Knowledge, saying Yes to reality, is just as necessary for the strong as cowardice and *flight* from reality-- the 'ideal'-- are for the weak who are inspired by weakness. They are not free to know: the decadents *need* the lie-- it is one of the conditions of their preservation." (S-II/1109-1110 [K-EH/272]).

65. Thus what expressed itself in the book was "a *strange* voice, the disciple of a still 'unknown god', one who concealed himself for the time being under the scholar's hood, under the gravity and dialectical ill humor of the German, even under the bad manners of the Wagnerian. Here was a spirit with strange, still nameless needs, a memory bursting with questions, experiences, concealed things after which the name of Dionysus was added as one more question mark. What spoke here-- as was admitted, not without suspicion-- was something like a mystical, almost maenadic soul that stammered laboriously and by force of will, as in a strange tongue, almost undecided whether it should communicate or conceal itself. It should have *sung*, this 'new soul'-- and not spoken! What I had to say then-- too bad that I did not dare say it as a poet: perhaps I would have been capable of it." (S-I/12 [K-BT/20]). (BT, Preface).

66. S-I/11-12 (K-BT/19-20). (BT, Preface).

67. S-I/11 (K-BT/19). (BT, Preface).

68. S-I/16 (K-BT/24). (BT, Preface).

69. S-I/16 (K-BT/24-25). (BT, Preface).

70. S-II/1113 (K-EH/276).

71. In the second later-added Preface to HAH, Nietzsche indicates that in chronological terms, the experiencing that lay behind the first three UM goes back to a time before the experiencing being brought to expression in BT. See S-I/737-738 (H-HAH/209). Since BT seems to have arisen from experiencing during his teaching days (starting in early 1869), the beginning of the experiencing brought to expression in UHH (published in 1873) would seem to go back at least to his university student days (1864-69), if not to his teenage days at Pforta (1858-1864).

72. S-II/1113 (K-EH/277).

73. S-II/1116 (K-EH/280-281).

74. Referring to WB, Nietzsche says: "Even psychologically all decisive traits of my own nature are projected [*sind ... eingetragen*] into Wagner's-- the close proximity of the brightest and the most calamitous forces, the will to power as no man ever possessed it, the ruthless courage in matters of the spirit, the unlimited power to learn without any stifling of the will to act." (S-II/1112 [K-EH/275]).

75. S-II/1112 (K-EH/275). The tragic-disposition passage in WB being alluded to is as follows: "The individual should be consecrated to something superpersonal-- that is what tragedy means; he should unlearn the terrible anxiety which death and time make [*macht*] the individual feel: for already in the smallest moment, in the briefest atom of his life-course, he can encounter something holy which abundantly outweighs all his struggle and all his distress-- this is what it means to be *of tragic mind and disposition* [*tragisch gesinnt sein*]. And if the whole of humankind must one day die-- and who may doubt that!-- so the goal is set for it, as the highest task for all coming times, to grow together into unity and community [*ins Eine und Gemeinsame*] in such way that humanity *as one whole* stands over against its impending going-under with a *tragic mind and disposition* [*tragischen Gesinnung*]. All ennobling of human beings lies included in this highest task; the final rejection of it would result in the saddest image which any friend of humanity could place before his soul: such is the way I feel. There is only *one* hope and *one* guarantee for the future of the human: it lies in this, *that the tragic mind and disposition not die out.* An unequalled cry of distress would necessarily resound over the earth if human beings should ever lose it completely; and conversely, there is no more blessed joy than to know what we know-- how the tragic idea has been born again into the world. For this joy is a wholly super-personal and universal one, a jubilation of humanity over the assured connection and progress of the human as such." (S-I/386 [H-WB/213]).

76. S-II/1111-1112 (K-EH/274).

77. S-II/1116-1117 (K-EH/281).

78. See page 20 above. Nietzsche's likening of his use of Schopenhauer and Wagner to Plato's use of Socrates is quite suggestive, and raises a (perhaps unanswerable) question of the same sort: how far was Plato making use of-- and mis-representing when that was useful for his purpose-- the actual Socrates, in those dialogues in which the central character is a man named Socrates? For a discussion of the dialogue form as Plato uses it, and the role which such a figure as Socrates might have in it, see my *The Temporality of Human Excellence: A Reading of Five Dialogues of Plato* (ix-xv, 197-207). For Nietzsche's point about himself, one might also notice how he speaks in SE of Schopenhauer when, asking about the experience (the "terrible vision") which is the key to his picture of life, he says: "One can prove that the youth had already seen this terrible vision, and one would like to believe that the child had also seen it. Everything that he later appropriated from life, books, and all fields of science-and-scholarship, was for him little more than color and means of expression. He even used a Kantian

philosophy above all as an extraordinary rhetorical instrument with which he believed he could express that picture more clearly, as Buddhist and Christian mythology also occasionally served this same purpose for him. He had only one task and a hundred-thousand means of accomplishing it: one meaning and countless hieroglyphs to express it." (S-I/350-351 [H-SE/182]).

79. See Chapter 1, pages 12-13 above, and S-II/1066 (K-EH/218). Note the kinship of Nietzsche's re-trospective judgment here, on his youthful idealizing self, and the broader judgment expressed when, after characterizing philosophy as he has come to live and understand it (a seeking out of the strange and questionable in existence, of what is placed under the ban of morality), he describes previous philosophers and philosophy, saying: "From long experience gained in the course of such wanderings *in what is forbidden*, I learned to look on the causes that so far have prompted moralizing and idealizing very differently from what may seem desir-able: the *hidden* history of the philosophers, the psychology of the great names, came to light for me."

80. And yet, note: Nietzsche's use of science was, almost wholly, an availing himself of second-hand thought, and thus a repeat of his use of Schopenhauer and Wagner in the first phase of his thought. I say "almost wholly" because, in the broad sense of "science" Nietzsche is using, his involvement in philology was a first-hand engagement in a scientific discipline. But that was not science as it was central to the thought of this second phase.

81. S-II/1118 (K-EH/283). That such liberation is not to be thought as a simply personal matter, Nietzsche himself indicates in the second of the later-added Prefaces of HAH. Speaking there of the three works being gathered together and republished as one work, he asks: "Shall my experience-- the history of an illness and recovery, for a recovery was what eventuated-- have been my personal experience alone? Only *my* 'human, all-too-human'? Today I would like to believe the reverse; again and again I feel confident that my travel-books [*Wanderbücher*] were not designed solely for myself, as has sometimes seemed to be the case.-- May I now, after six years of growing confidence, as an experiment send them on their way again? May I commend them espe-cially to the hearts and ears of those who are burdened with any kind of 'past' and who have sufficient spirit left still to suffer from the *spirit* of their past too? Above all, however, *to you* who have the hardest lot, you rare, most endangered, most spiritual, most courageous ones, who must be the *conscience* [*Gewissen*] of the modern soul and as such must have its *knowledge* [*Wissen*], and in whom what there can be today of sickness, poison, and danger, comes together-- whose lot means that you must be sicker than any other individual because you are not '*merely* individual', and whose consolation it is to know and alas! to go on the path to a *new* health! a health of tomorrow and the day after, you predestined, victorious ones, overcomers of your times, you healthiest and strongest, you *good Europeans*!" (S-I/742-743 [H-HAH/213])

82. S-II/596 (K-BGE/43).

83. S-II/1118-1119 (K-EH/283-284).

84. S-I/440 (H-HAH/7). (HAH-I, Preface). See also the remark in the Preface to HAH-II: "Optimism, for the purpose of restoration, so that at some future time I could again have the *right* to be a pessimist-- do you understand that?" (S-I/741-742 [H-HAH/212]). Speaking in EH of an uninterrupted three-day migraine head-ache, he says that in its midst "... I possessed a dialectician's clarity *par excellence* and thought through with very cold blood matters for which under healthier circumstances I am no mountain-climber, not subtle, not *cold* enough. My readers know perhaps in what way I consider dialectic as a symptom of decadence; for example in the most famous case, the case of Socrates." (S-II/1070-1071 [K-EH/222-223]). Finally, in the later-added Preface to GS, Nietzsche speaks of the "sickness of severe suspicion" (S-II/13-14 [K-GS/37]).

85. S-II/1122 (K-EH/288).

86. S-I/741 (H-HAH/212). (HAH-II, Preface).

87. S-I/444 (H-HAH/10). (HAH-I, Preface).

88. Because that wanderer was who and what he was, Nietzsche can speak of HAH as a book 'for free spirits', over which lies "something of that almost cheerful and inquisitive coldness of the psychologist who has *behind* and *under* himself a mass of painful things and who subsequently fixes them for himself and as it were *impales* them with the point of a needle". (S-I/738 [H-HAH/210]) (HAH-II, Preface).

89. S-II/1121 (K-EH/288).

90. Whether by accident or intention, the title-word of the work (in the German, *Morgenröte*, literally, morning-red, morning-blush, morning-flush) is suggestive metaphorically. Dawn breaks the darkness but does not yet bring full light. In comparison to the pale grey of morning's first light, however, the red color announces more fully the glow of the coming sun and signifies in colorful fashion the mid-way status of the dawning of which it is a part. Following this metaphorical suggestion, this book expresses the insights of someone who, as he digs underground and in darkness, is experiencing the first flush of vitality and life reviving again and giving things some color but who has by no means yet arrived at the fulness of vigor. The insight into things which is expressive of such a condition and such presence of things is intimative of more to be seen and seen into, more

so than it is indicative of matters already fully caught. In EH (S-II/1070 [K-EH/222]), Nietzsche puts the matter differently, alluding in passing to D as having been "produced" by "that sweetening and spiritualizing which is closely conditioned with an extreme poverty of blood and muscle", and speaking of "the perfect brightness and cheerfulness, even exuberance of spirit, which is reflected in this work" as compatible in his case not only with the most profound physiological weakness but with an excess of pain. (See Note 84 above, this Chapter, for the migraine-example he recalls here.)

91. See the sketch earlier in this chapter (pages 26-27) of the path of convalescence and of the sorts of distinctive condition he remembers along the way. This hints at some possible elements in the disclosive matrix he was operating within.

92. S-I/1011-1012 (H-D/2). (D, Preface).

93. S-I/1015 (H-D/4-5). (D, Preface).

94. S-I/1014 (H-D/4). (D, Preface).

95. Later in this same recollective assessment, Nietzsche observes that "the morality of decadence, the will to the end, has become accepted as morality-*in-itself*" (S-II/1125 [K-EH/291]). It is against morality in this sense, as morality in the sense of social morality, that the campaign is conducted; it is not against morality in all senses: the life-affirming noble (social) morality, say, or the life-affirming individual morality of the creative person.

96. S-II/1124 (K-EH/290).

97. S-II/1124-1125 (K-EH/290-291).

98. S-II/1124 (K-EH/290). The imagery in this EH passage echoes two other passages. One is in GS (aphorism 298): "*Sigh.*-- I caught this insight on the way and quickly seized the rather poor words that were closest to hand to make it fast in order that it not fly away from me again. And now it has died to me in those arid words and hangs and dangles in them-- and I hardly know any more when I look at it how I could ever have felt so happy when I caught this bird." (S-II/175 [K-GS/239]). The other is in BGE (aphorism 296): "Alas, what are you after all, my written and painted thoughts! It was not long ago that you were still so colorful, young, and malicious, full of thorns and secret spices, that you made me sneeze and laugh-- and now? You have already taken off your novelty, and some of you are ready, I fear, to become truths: they already look so immortal, so heart-breakingly decent, so boring! And has it ever been different? What things do we write down and paint, we mandarins with Chinese brushes, we immortalizers of things that *allow* themselves to be written-- what are the only things we are able to paint? Alas, always only what is on the verge of withering and is beginning to lose its fragrance! Alas, always only passing and exhausted storms and feelings that are late-in-the-season and yellow! Alas, always only birds that grew weary of flying and flew astray and now can be caught by hand-- by *our* hand! We immortalize what cannot live and fly much longer-- only weary and mellow things! And it is only your *afternoon*, you, my written and painted thoughts, for which I have colors, many colors perhaps, many motley caresses and fifty yellows and browns and greens and reds: but nobody will guess from that how you looked in your morning, you sudden sparks and wonders of my solitude, you my old beloved-- *wicked* thoughts!" (S-II/756 [K-BGE/ 236-237]).

99. The verses (at S-II/161 [K-GS/221]) read:

> With a flaming spear you
> parted the ice of my soul,
> so that, roaring, it rushes now
> to the sea of its highest hope:
> ever healthier and brighter,
> free in the most love-filled necessity--
> therefore my soul praises
> your wonders, fairest January.

100. S-II/9 (K-GS/32). (GS, Preface). Nietzsche gives meaning to this reference to winter in this same passage, speaking of what lies behind him now as an "icing up in the midst of youth"-- the condition out of which HAH was composed and one error after another was placed on the ice (see the end of the quote in the main text on page 36 above).

101. S-II/9 (K-GS/32). (GS, Preface).

102. See Chapter 2, pages 25-26 above, for Nietzsche's own language and for the citation of the connected passage. For the quotes just made, see S-II/13, 14 (K-GS/36, 37). (GS, Preface).

103. Thus in EH, Nietzsche can draw attention to "the hundred signs" in GS "of the proximity of something incomparable; in the end it even offers the beginning of *Zarathustra*, and in the penultimate section of the fourth

book the basic idea of *Zarathustra*." (S-II/1128 [K-EH/296])
104. S-I/12 (K-BT/20). (BT, Preface).
105. S-II/1130-1131 (K-EH/298-299).
106. S-II/1132 (K-EH/300-301).
107. S-II/1135 (K-EH/304-305).
108. These two energies are said by Nietzsche (in WB) to lie at the heart of Wagner's nature, but in EH he acknowledges that they were projected there by him from himself. See Note 74 above, this Chapter.
109. S-II/1135-1136 (K-EH/305-306). The passage comes from TSZ, III/12 (Section 19).
110. S-II/1134 (K-EH/303-304).
111. S-II/1133-1134 (K-EH/303).
112. S-II/1134 (K-EH/304).
113. S-II/10 (K-GS/33). (GS/Preface).
114. Thus Nietzsche can claim that in the philosophizing of the sick the philosophy that is engendered functions as "a supporting-prop, a pacifier, medicine, deliverance, exaltation, or self-alienation" and its aim at truth is not free to reach and serve truth. Rather, under the pressure of sickness, it is led-- and misled-- on "involuntary detours" and "side lanes", and led to "resting places, and sunny places of thought" on account of the distress and suffering that is at work impelling the reflection. "...(T)he sick body and its needs unconsciously urge, push, and lure the spirit"" toward the sun, stillness, mildness, patience, medicine, balm in some sense." "The unconscious disguise of physiological needs under the cloaks of the objective, ideal, purely spiritual, goes to frightening lengths-- and often enough I have asked myself whether, taking a large view, philosophy has not been merely an interpretation of the body and a *misunderstanding of the body*. Behind the highest value judgments that have hitherto guided the history of thought, there are concealed misunderstandings of the physical constitution-- of individuals or classes or even whole races. All those bold insanities of metaphysics, especially answers to the question about the *value* of existence, may always be considered first of all as the symptoms of certain bodies. And if in short such world affirmations or world negations lack any grain of significance when measured scientifically, they still give to the historian and psychologist valuable hints as symptoms of the body, of its success or failure, its plenitude [*Fülle*], power [*Machtigkeit*], and self-mastery [*Selbstherrlickeit*] in history, or of its frustration, weariness, impoverishment, its premonitions of the end, its will to the end." So widespread is this sickness-philosophizing that Nietzsche can ask about "all philosophizing hitherto", whether what was at stake in it was not at all truth but rather "health, future, growth, power [*Macht*], life". The quotes all come from the later-added Preface to GS (S-II/10-12 [K-GS/33-35]).
115. S-II/10 (K-GS/34). (GS, Preface).

Chapter 3

1. This involves a complementary enabling condition to time, namely, space. Of that, we will speak in later discussion.
2. Life and activity do not end here, but in our characterization of life we have reached that point at which Nietzsche's life ends and up to which *Ecce Homo* takes us. What needs to be said if we would sketch out, in the roughest of terms, the remainder of the movement of life as it seems meant to unfold, supposing sufficiently favorable circumstance, will emerge in the appropriate later places in this study of Nietzsche.
3. That the "up" is ended does not mean, of course, that all growth is over. But while growth continues in the future, it does so within the concludedness of the "up", and this is sustained even as a final transition time and transformation are to take place when old age and its debilities begin to make themselves felt and impending death draws closer and makes our mortality palpable. At worst, the affairs of the final phase can bring the threat-- and even the reality-- of a disintegration of the accomplishment which is represented by the "up", and thus the deterioration of this element of stability for reflection. But regression at the center, and a reflection which manifests and suffers from this, is not inevitable.

Notes for PART I

Chapter 4

1. S-I/11 (K-BT/18). (BT, Preface).
2. The phrases quoted in this paragraph all come from Section 4 of BT (see S-I/32 [K-BT/45]).
3. S-I/32 (K-BT/44).

4. S-I/32-33 (K-BT/44-45). In his retrospective characterization of the metaphysics asserted in the book, Nietzsche sees its focus being in "a 'god', if you please, but certainly only an entirely reckless and amoral artist-god who wants to experience, whether he is building or destroying, in the good and in the bad, his own same joy and self-mastery-- one who, creating worlds, frees himself from the *distress* of fulness and *overfulness* and from the *affliction* of the contradictions which are crowded together within himself. The world-- at every moment the *attained* salvation of God, as the eternally changing, eternally new vision of the most deeply afflicted, discordant, and contradictory being who can find salvation only in *appearance* ... ." (Preface to BT, S-I/14 [K-BT/22]). Note the difference, then, of the distress and affliction of the source from that of the finite creature; the former's creativity comes simply out of itself, while the latter's, even as it stems ultimately out of a kindred fulness-and-tensioned-richness within itself, must operate in a context and matrix of a space-time-and-circumstance-introduced negativity unknown to the former.

5. S-I/21 (K-BT/33).

6. S-I/22 (K-BT/34, 35).

7. S-I/23 (K-BT/35).

8. S-I/22-24 (K-BT/35-36).

9. S-I/25 (K-BT/37).

10. S-I/24-25 (K-BT/36-37).

11. S-I/93 (K-BT/104).

12. S-I/40 (K-BT/52).

13. S-I/33 (K-BT/45); 25 (K-BT/37); 43-44 (K-BT/55); 32 (K-BT/45); *et al.*

14. S-I/43-44 (K-BT/55); 59 (K-BT/71); 32 (K-BT/45); 33 (K-BT/45); *et al.*

15. S-I/38-39 (K-BT/51); also 92 (K-BT/104), 33 (K-BT/45), 50 (K-BT/62), and 99 (K-BT/109-110), which refer to the life, suffering, and contradiction, involved in the one as eternal.

16. Life: S-I/92 (K-BT/104); 47 (K-BT/59); 50 (K-BT/62); 99 (K-BT/109-110). Abiding indestructibly beyond all phenomena: 50 (K-BT/62); 92 (K-BT/104). Raging desire for existence and joy in existence: 93 (K-BT/104). Eternally being creative, eternally finding satisfaction in the change of phenomena: 93 (K-BT/104).

17. S-I/93 (K-BT/104). Nietzsche also speaks of the genius, in the act of artistic creation, as "fusing" [*verschmilzt*] with the "primordial artist of the world". (S-40 [K-BT/52]).

18. S-I/10 (K-BT/18). (BT, Preface).

19. In EH, Nietzsche says of BT, that "it smells offensively Hegelian": "an 'idea'-- the antithesis of the Dionysian and Apollonian-- translated into the realm of metaphysics; history itself as the development of this 'idea'; in tragedy this antithesis is sublimated into a unity; and in this perspective things that had never before faced each other are suddenly juxtaposed, are illuminated by each other, and are *comprehended*-- opera, for example, and the revolution." (S-II/1108-1109 [K-EH/270-271]).

20. S-I/35, 21 (K-BT/47, 33).

21. S-I/47 (K-BT/59).

22. S-I/48 (K-BT/60).

23. S-I/47, 48 (K-BT/59).

24. S-I/71 (K-BT/82).

25. S-I/440 (H-HAH/7). (HAH-I, Preface).

26. S-I/77 (K-BT/88).

27. S-I/76 (K-BT/87).

28. S-I/78-79 (K-BT/89).

29. S-I/82 (K-BT/92).

30. S-I/82 (K-BT/93). For other references to the music-practising Socrates, see S-I/87, 95 (K-BT/98, 106).

31. For another interpretation of this incident and its relation to the meaning of the whole dialogue, see my discussion in *Loving and Dying*, Chapter 2, 13-22.

32. In EH, Nietzsche observes: "Profound, hostile silence about Christianity throughout the book. That is neither Apollonian nor Dionysian; it *negates* all *aesthetic* values-- the only values recognized in *The Birth of Tragedy*: it is nihilistic in the most profound sense, while in the Dionysian symbol the ultimate limit of *affirmation* is attained. There is one allusion to Christian priests as a 'vicious kind of dwarfs', of 'subterraneans'." (S-II/1109 [K-EH/ 271]). In fact there are several allusions to Christianity: see the discussion at the end of the present section.

33. S-I/85 (K-BT/96).

34. S-I/98-99 (K-BT/109). See also S-I/99 (K-BT/110). Theoretical man is man finding an infinite delight in whatever exists because of its intelligibility and of his own joy in the process of uncovering its truth. (S-I/84 [K-BT/94]). "Socrates is the prototype of the theoretical optimist who, with his faith that the nature of things

can be fathomed, ascribes to knowledge and insight the power of a panacea and conceives error to be the intrinsically evil. To press into the depths and to separate true knowledge from appearance and error, seemed to Socratic man the noblest human calling, even the only truly human one. And since Socrates, this mechanism of concepts, judgments, and inferences has been esteemed as the highest occupation [*Betätigung*] and the most admirable gift of nature, above all other capacities [*Fähigkeiten*]." (S-I/86 [K-BT/97]).

35. S-I/128 (K-BT/138).

36. S-I/125-126 (K-BT/135-136).

37. S-I/126 (K-BT/136).

38. S-I/127 (K-BT/138).

39. "Our whole modern world is entangled in the net of Alexandrian culture. It proposes as its ideal the theoretical man equipped with the greatest forces of knowledge, and laboring in the service of science, whose archetype and progenitor is Socrates. ... We must not hide from ourselves what is concealed in the womb of this Socratic culture: unlimited self-deluding optimism." (S-I/99, 100 [K-BT/110, 111]).

40. S-I/100-103, 111-113 (K-BT/111-114, 122-123).

41. S-I/109 (K-BT/119-120).

42. S-I/101-102 (K-BT/112).

43. S-I/110 (K-BT/121).

44. S-I/87 (K-BT/98). For other references to the 'artistic' or 'music-practising' Socrates, see Note 30 above, this Chapter.

45. S-I/102 (K-BT/113). The future tragic culture which Nietzsche sees replacing Socratic/Alexandrian culture is one symbolized still by Socrates, but now the artistic or music-practising Socrates instead of the rationalist Socrates.

46. S-I/102 (K-BT/113).

47. S-I/108 (K-BT/119).

48. S-I/110 (K-BT/121).

49. S-I/112 (K-BT/123).

50. S-I/127 (K-BT/137).

51. S-I/114 (K-BT/124-125).

52. S-I/132-133 (K-BT/142-143).

53. S-I/128 (K-BT/138-139).

54. S-II/1109 (K-BT/271-272).

55. "Heart [*Herz*]" (S-I/119 [K-BT/129]) or "inner essence [*Wesen*]" (S-I/91 [K-BT/103]; S-I/95 [K-BT/106]) of the world, the "innermost heart [*Kern*] of things" (S-I/88 [K-BT/99-100]), the "innermost abyss [*Abgrund*] of things" (S-I/115 [K-BT/126]).

56. S-I/95 (K-BT/106), and S-I/99 (K-BT/109-110).

57. S-I/133 (K-BT/143).

58. S-I/48, 47 (K-BT/59): "the rapture of the Dionysian state with its annihilation of the ordinary bounds and limits of existence", and "that the state and society and, quite generally, the gulfs between man and man give way to an overwhelming feeling of unity leading back to the very heart of nature".

59. S-I/93 (K-BT/104-105); also "altogether one with": S-I/37 (K-BT/49); "unity with the innermost ground of the world": S-I/26 (K-BT/38).

60. S-I/47 (K-BT/59).

61. S-I/93 (K-BT/104).

62. S-I/91 (K-BT/103).

63. S-I/114 (K-BT/124).

64. Even more precisely: "For the rapture of the Dionysian state with its annihilation of the ordinary bounds and limits of existence contains, while it lasts, a *lethargic* element in which all personal experiences of the past become immersed. The worlds of everyday reality and of Dionysian reality are cut off from one another by this chasm of oblivion." (S-I/48 [K-BT/59]). In the rapture of the Dionysian experiencing, the 'ego' experience of the creature-oblivious-of-itself-as-such becomes itself submerged in an obliviousness belonging to the Dionysian, one which is the other side of our awakening to ourselves-as-creatures. As we put it commonly (and from the ego-perspective), we no longer recognize ourselves in such times.

65. S-I/93 (K-BT/105).

66. S-II/751-752 (K-BGE/229).

67. S-I/24 (K-BT/36).

68. In the Kantian/Schopenhauerian framework which forms the background Nietzsche is drawing on here, there is the immediacy of sensation, but there is the conceptualized integration of sensations to constitute the

objects in experience. Strictly, the empirical apprehension of actual objects is thus a (conceptually) mediated affair, but in the measure in which such apprehension does not involve inference and reference to principles or laws, thus the work of reason as reasoning or inference based on premises as providing grounds or bases, it can be spoken of by Nietzsche as instinctive and as immediate in a secondary sense. In any case, the empirical objects so constituted in and for our apprehension can come to be registered contemplatively as well, and registered as manifesting a meaning, a type. Thereby they have another sort of immediacy, that of aesthetic experience.

69. S-I/92 (K-BT/104). Note that "unconscious" here means "not the fruit of conscious reasoning", and "instinctive" means "at the level before conscious reasoning takes up with it".

70. The author of tragedy brings such wisdom to symbolic representation in the tragic drama, so that dramatist-poet and philosopher are centered in the same experientially-achieved wisdom and simply work with it differently. Nietzsche speaks of such symbolic representation as myth, or perhaps more accurately: Nietzsche thinks of myth as including such dramatic representations as vehicles for the conveying of Dionysian insight and the Dionysian myth. In general, myth (for Nietzsche) is a symbolic story in which events, persons, and things, have gained a universal (typal) and symbolic meaning within what claims to be a total symbolic image of reality. This overall image, when it is apt to the successful disclosure of reality, bodies forth the true insight of Dionysian wisdom. In contrast, the philosopher seeks to bring the vision of Dionysian reality-- the immediate intuition which is Dionysian insight-- into a conceptual rendering, aiming thus at "Dionysian wisdom grasped in concepts" (S-I/110 [K-BT/121]).

71. S-I/11, 12 (K-BT/19, 20). (BT, Preface).

72. S-I/11 (K-BT/19). (BT, Preface).

73. "I understand by the spirit of science the faith that first came to light in the person of Socrates-- the faith in the explicability [*Ergründlichkeit*] of nature and in the universal healing-power of knowledge [*Wissens*])." (S-I/95 [K-BT/106])

74. S-I/85 (K-BT/96).

75. S-I/84 (K-BT/95). Thus Socrates, known for exposing the ignorance (or pretence to know) of others, had no "correct and assured insight" [*richtige und sichere Einsicht*] into his own activity but practiced it only "out of instinct" and under an undiscovered and unrecognized illusion. (S-I/76 [K-BT/87])

76. S-I/76 (K-BT/87).

77. S-I/77 (K-BT/88).

78. See page 79 above, and the BT-quotation there (cited in Note 42 above).

Chapter 5

1. See Note 71, Chapter 2, for the time of the experiencing behind UHH. Regardless of whether (or not) that experiencing antedated his encounter with the writings of Schopenhauer (1865), his writing up and publication (in 1873) of the feeling he says UHH attempts to articulate eschews the language which we find in BT (published in 1872).

2. So he says in the opening passage (S-I/211 [H-UHH/61]): "Thus the animal lives *unhistorically*: for it is contained in the present like a number without any curious fraction left over; ... at every moment it appears wholly as what it is." But shortly after (S-I/213 [H-UHH/62]), he claims "it is possible to live almost [*fast*] without memory, and to live happily moreover, as the animal demonstrates". See also S-I/214 (H-UHH/63): "we have observed the animal, which is quite unhistorical and dwells within a horizon well-nigh point-like [*beinahe ... punktartigen Horizontes*], and which yet lives in a certain happiness ...". If the variation in language carries only stylistic meaning, that is one thing; but if it carries substantive meaning, it poses a problem for Nietzsche's whole account. Is animal consciousness one limited wholly to the present moment, or can it include (say) the immediate ('personal') past at least? I understand him to mean the former, and see passages like the following as confirming that interpretation. The opening paragraph of Section 1, in which animal consciousness is first characterized, ends with an imaginary 'conversation' between human and animal: "The human being might well ask the animal some time: why do you not speak to me of your happiness but merely gaze at me? The animal would indeed like to say in answer: that is because I immediately forgot what I wanted to say-- but it forgot this answer as well and was silent." This suggests that as soon as the current moment passes it becomes lost to animal consciousness and that the animal has no power of recall and no cognizance of its past as part of its current awareness at any time.

3. S-I/211 (H-UHH/61). Again, there is variation in Nietzsche's language, here relating to the meaning of "historical" and "unhistorical". The latter being the negation of the former, the question concerns what is being negated; does the historical include the past in all regards (even the personal past, say, as in one's "personal history"), or more narrowly, include only the trans-personal past, one that is shared, and in particular, is social,

collective? In the case of the animal, the use of "unhistorical" is inexact to the extent that the animal lacks any memory of even the personal past, let alone of some trans-personal past; properly, its mode of being would be ahistorical. In the case of human beings, Nietzsche seems to have in mind sometimes the broader, sometimes the narrower, meaning; but linguistically he makes no express distinction, and at least at times this creates problems for our understanding of particular passages, if it does not also reflect his not yet having thought the matter through far enough. The same indeterminateness holds regarding other temporal words and phrases-- for example, "it was", the "past", and even the "yesterday" and "today" which is disclaimed for animal consciousness. Sometimes the meaning is narrower, sometimes broader and inclusive; but throughout Nietzsche proceeds as if any such differences can be left without explicit marking for a reader, assuming as he does that so proceeding reflects no confusion of thought on his part but at most a looseness and imprecision of writing which the reader can see through on his/her own.

4. Thus Nietzsche says: "having as yet nothing of the past [*Vergangenes*] to disavow [*verleugnen*]", the child "plays in blissful blindness between the hedges of past [*Vergangenheit*] and future [*Zukunft*]". (S-I/212 [H-UHH/61]). The passage continues: "yet its play must be disturbed; all too soon it will be called [*wird ... heraufgerufen*] out of its state of obliviousness [*Vergessenheit*]. Then it will learn to understand the phrase 'it was', that password with which struggle, suffering, and boredom approach man to remind him what his existence is at bottom-- a never to be completed imperfect." The "as yet" and the "all too soon" point us to our growth as the context for Nietzsche's thought here; in its terms, we are, from beginning until youth, oblivious to ourselves as distinctive human beings who are other than all others and who are able to recognize the otherness of those others. As we grow during this time, we acquire language, we assimilate norms and patterns of response, we learn rudiments of historical knowledge, all from others; but all this enters into an 'us' whose self-awareness is still oblivious to ourselves as distinctive human beings. That obliviousness, pre-historical in nature (in the sense of being ours prior to our acquiring the capacity for the historical), is broken, and we are called out of the state of forgetfulness, as one side to what (in SE) he will speak of as the "call of conscience"; this call, at the heart of the transformation which enters us into youth beyond childhood, opens us to ourselves in our mortality, to our own mortal life as our own, to our own being as that of a distinctive human being, and also to our involvement in 'history' and its 'it was' (a 'sense of history'). Antecedent to that, we have a child's memory of the personal past we bear with ourselves, but our assimilation in childhood of what has 'historical' standing (language and other conventions, say) is oblivious to it *as historical*. As I understand Nietzsche's thought in this matter, then, while our blindness as children includes (secondarily) both our immersion in the immediate present and the limited reach of our anticipation and personal memory, it signifies primarily our obliviousness to the hedges of (historical) "past" and (historical) "future" which, while we are all the while as children playing between them (so to speak), become visible to us only as we become adults and the transformation in capacity involved in this becoming-adult opens our eyes to them. It does not imply that, as in the animal, the (human) child has no memory even of its own personal past (let alone no anticipation of its own future); what the child has no sense of is the 'it will be' and the 'it was' of history. And it is because the child has no cognizance of *this* 'past' that it has as yet no (historical) 'past' from which it could (desire to) dissociate itself. [Incidentally, this childhood state of forgetfulness as Nietzsche is understanding it can profitably be thought through in connection with (and in some contrast to) the notion of the Platonic Socrates, that knowledge is recollection and that from birth on for a while we live in a state of forgetfulness which is first broken when something we encounter recalls us to what we knew in the pre-existence of our soul. For one understanding of this, see my *Loving and Dying*, 52-61 (recollection and pre-existence in the *Phaedo*) and 214-223 (love and recollection in the *Phaedrus*).]

5. S-I/215 (H-UHH/63-64).

6. The human being "continually hangs on to the past: however far and fast he may run, this chain runs with him." (S-I/211 [H-UHH/61]). In him the past does not disappear from consciousness beyond retrieval, as it does in the animal, but is retained and can eventually come back into the conscious mind, in remembering. [Actually, because of the variation in language noted in Note 2 above, the disappearance of the moment for animal consciousness seems to mean it 'disappears into the sea of forgetfulness never to return to consciousness, or at best, almost never'. If the animal has memory of any sort, however, it would be cognate to the 'personal' memory in human beings, not one introducing or involving 'history'.]

7. *Toward a Genealogy of Morals* speaks at some length of this power, especially in the Second Essay.

8. S-I/212 (H-UHH/61). Note how Nietzsche speaks here: in contrast with the animal, man "braces himself against the great and ever greater burdening-load [*Last*] of what is past: it pushes him down or bends him sideways, it encumbers his steps as a dark, invisible burden [*unsichtbare und dunkle Bürde*] which he can make a show of disowning and which in traffic with his fellow men he gladly does disown so as to excite their envy." This is not simply a vivid way of saying that as we grow older we have more memories that can return into the present to complicate our life and movement there; it carries the more profound idea that we *feel* the increasing

burdening-weight of a proliferating memory, even though the memories stored in our minds are unconscious to ourselves ("dark, invisible").

9. Nietzsche's use of the idea of recall does not include an express treatment of its nature, and in fact is quite elliptical and as a result in places is confusing. But according to the discussion in UHH, we know two forms of recall, and two meanings of 'it was', which are different but become intimately connected in our historical mode of being. There is, to begin with, the recall of the memory of some moment in the earlier part of our own life, the remembering of our own earlier experience. This can reach back no farther than our own life and gives us how we experienced something *first-hand*. The capacity for it is part of us from the beginning, and it functions as a significant power in our childhood experience and learning. But there is, in contrast, the 'recall' of some *trans-personal* or 'historical' past *as historical*, as 'the past'. This is not a matter of personal remembering, but a form of recall which becomes possible for us only when the changes of youth open it up to us, namely, when in knowing our mortality we also know our own life-whole in contrast with what is beyond it in the direction of our past and what reaches us in transmission from that earlier time. Such recall in turn takes two shapes. One (the initial) is that of a knowing in the present (the apprehension of records, say, or of elements in a historical site) which enables us to become *indirectly* cognizant of things that happened before our personal existence began. Recall of this sort is not of one's personal experience or of anything so far as it was simply part of such experience; we would not verbalize such recall by saying 'I remember' such-and-such an event, say. But there is also a second shape of historical recall, which involves an interweaving of personal remembering with such historical recall. In it, once the ideas with which we first indirectly grasp and thus recall things of the trans-personal past have been formed by us in some present moment of our own lives, they pass out of our current present and become forgotten just as every current impression does. But because we bear them with us as elements in our experience of learning, we may find them becoming recalled at some time. At such times, the personal recall of our earlier learning-this-or-that includes the historical recall effected because the this-or-that is some historical trans-personal affair which is being brought to mind as something we once learned about and now know even though we have never had any first-hand or immediate acquaintance with it. In this more complex historical recalling, our personal recall is a vehicle by which, in an ignoring of its personal side and a focusing on what was once learned by us, we are entered into a recalling of something which has never been part of our personal experience. Nietzsche implicitly recognizes the personal and historical forms of recall; but he does not differentiate them linguistically, or discuss them in their difference, let alone go on to expressly distinguish the two forms of historical recall. Whether he can treat accurately the matters he wishes to treat and not enter into such discussion and adapt the language of his presentation accordingly, is an open question for the moment.

10. S-I/212 (H-UHH/61).

11. S-I/212-213 (H-UHH/62).

12. In a later part of the meditation (S-I/281-282 [H-UHH/120]), Nietzsche expands the meaning of "super-historical", to include art and religion as superhistorical powers. It is at that place that the discussion of BT concerning these powers would fit into the development of thought in UHH.

13. S-I/218 (H-UHH/67).

14. S-I/216-217, 218 (H-UHH/65, 67).

15. S-I/217-218 (H-UHH/66).

16. Especially in the opening section of UHH, Nietzsche phrases his exposition in a way that usually leaves (the experiencing of) time itself undifferentiated from (the experiencing of) things in time: "the moment" may mean either, or both together. Usually this creates no problems, and when it is important to do so the reader can make the distinction needed given the context and thrust of the thought being expressed. But sometimes Nietzsche's style seems to reflect not so much an omission of linguistic markers so that sentences can flow unimpeded, as a carelessness and/or confusion of thought on his part, a youthful failure to have thought a matter through sufficiently to see required distinctions. This is particularly the case in his presentation and use of the idea of "the moment".

17. Thus he can say: "It is a wondrous thing: the moment [*Augenblick*], suddenly there [*im Husch da*], suddenly gone-by [*im Husch vorüber*], previously a nothing, subsequently a nothing, nonetheless comes again as a ghost and disturbs the peace of a later moment." (S-I/211 [H-UHH/61]). See also his way of speaking of the horizon of the animal as almost "point-like" (S-I/214 [H-UHH/63]), and of the capacity of the human being (at the threshold of the moment) to forget the past and "without anxiety and dizziness to stand on a point [*Punkte*] like a victory-goddess" (S-I/212 [H-UHH/62]).

18. But see Note 2, above (this Chapter), for other language.

19. S-I/211 (H-UHH/60).

20. S-I/211-212 (H-UHH/61).

21. S-I/212 (H-UHH/61). Nietzsche plays on the German here in a way that is impossible to carry straight

over into English; he means a being which has a past as part of its being.

22. S-I/211 (H-UHH/61). Note how the image suggests that the moments are not *themselves* moving, but that the movement of time is a matter of the detaching of separate unmoving moments, one after the other, from the scroll. See our discussion below (pages 102-103) for the place of such an abstract idea in the measuring of time via the sun. And keep in mind here what we suggested in Chapter 3, that the *ongoing* of time is made possible by the finitude of the present and by the directionality thereby enabled for the moving that realizes time's ongoing within beginning and end.

23. To convey human memory by way of his image, Nietzsche speaks of a leaf which has dropped away being able to float back again and fall into the human being's lap, enabling the human being then to say 'I remember'. Presumably here the image has been modified in meaning to this extent, that the returning-leaf is not the original moment itself (that moment was as *current*) but that moment *as it now is, namely, as past* and as coming back into our conscious mind (falling into our lap) in what is the now-current moment.

24. Nietzsche's exposition of our 'historical' involvement with things often ignores differences which he recognizes at other places but which, at the point he is at in his presentation, seem unimportant for the point he is making. Unfortunately, in places his judgment is mistaken and his argument is flawed by his failure to accommodate differences which really are significant. On the matter of time, whether the latter is conceived in a personal or in a public reference is crucial, and his exposition does not sufficiently acknowledge that.

25. Note, then, that in virtue of such latency, any current moment, as the current forefront of the ongoing realization of one and the same present, would be differentiated from all others within that present by (at the very least) the past which is at work within it.

26. For example, if the past continues on in us in memory, consciously remembering would be finding-- or allowing-- that past-being-retained-in-memory to gain a place in the (conscious) functioning of ourselves in the current ongoing of the present. At the very least, this would amount to an extension of the way that that continuing-on past is making itself felt in our current functioning in that ongoing, and would modify the way what else is part of our functioning in that ongoing would-- or can-- operate. But while remembering could involve no more than minimally registering this returned-past as past, most remembering involves attending more or less consciously to what has come back into mind, noticing it in some fashion, and doing so selectively and interpretatively. Thus our 'remembering' can, say, be a mis-remembering, in virtue of our current feelings or habits or a variety of factors that affect our attending and noticing and that can give us a distorted register of what has come back for our conscious notice. This is only one of the things that makes remembering a much more complex phenomenon (and complex temporally) than the imagery can accommodate.

27. The moment as measuring factor may be (as for Aristotle) simply a limit and not itself a part of time, or may be (as presented in Zeno's paradoxes) an ultimate discrete and indivisible component (an atom) of time itself. In any case, Nietzsche does not linguistically distinguish between the moment in either of those meanings (abstractions which do not themselves exist) and a moment which is part of lived experience-- for example, a brief lived stretch which, even when very limited, is not (contrary to the way Nietzsche speaks at times) ever 'simply and wholly current'.

28. While Nietzsche's account of life is centered on individual living beings, it also treats powers that unite human beings and impact their living-- a culture, for example-- as themselves living beings with their own becoming. In what sense a culture is living, let alone itself a living being, is not something which he explores or expands upon.

29. That this is what Nietzsche has in mind seems evident both from the context and from the (at first sight) obvious questionableness of a claim that before youth we have no personal memory. It is the lack of express differentiation by him of personal and trans-personal remembering that makes such a specification of his meaning necessary here. Nonetheless, Nietzsche seems aware of a similar impact of personal remembering: it also involves a monitored allowing of the personal past to come back into our conscious minds and has (in life's plastic power) a regulative standard (thus a 'too much' and 'too little') for the life-and-health-supportive functioning of remembering.

30. S-I/213 (H-UHH/62). Note that "fatal" here does not mean that we perish as ongoing beings, but that the maturing life in ourselves is prevented from continuing its maturation and thus we 'die' humanly.

31. S-I/213 (H-UHH/62).

32. S-I/213-214 (H-UHH/62-63).

33. This alternative is extremely important to notice: the formation of a people, for example, involves a hierarchy, and the capacity to co-operate within such an ordering (thus, say, to form and maintain a common life and culture) depends on both sorts of horizon-forming. Nietzsche's phrasing here is: "a living thing can be healthy, strong, and fruitful, only within a horizon; if it is incapable [*unvermögend*] of drawing a horizon around itself and is at the same time too self-centered to enclose its own view within an alien one, then it feebly

languishes away or hastens to an early end." (S-I/214 [H-UHH/63]).

34. S-I/214 (H-UHH/63).

35. "As it currently is" means in a current actuality which is pregnant with a future and has a determinateness which is issue of its past development. Keep in mind that, as itself a temporal affair, life takes time to be lived; that time is the life-time span between the beginning and the end of our life. In the living along the way of the actualizing and extending of the actuality of this span, the life being lived does not ever exist as a fully actualized whole but rather as a *temporal whole in the process of being actualized* over time. That temporal whole, a bounded one, is ever concentrated whole in the ongoing actuality of our current living, but concentrated in keeping with its own temporal nature. Thus life's own future is there under the not-yet of the future, as element in the potential-and-possibility that is part of our present being; and its own past is there under the already-actual of the past, as element in the retained-as-gone-by-actuality of our being, and more precisely, as the unfolded-so-far which is internal to life's continuing unfolding in the moving present. Likewise, life's futural end (death) and its past beginning (conception or birth) are there, continually ingredient in temporal fashion in the actuality of ongoing life, ingredient there thus as the already-happened-beginning and the not-yet-arrived-end which belong inherently to the continuing-current-actualizing. At no other time *is* life but *in the ongoing-now of the present*, and yet in that ongoing-now it is never fully actual but *is* both as future-and-past-end-and-beginning-harboring (thus as whole) and as currently extending its actually-being in such way that our lives endure. Such extending is dual, meaning both continuing to actualize itself in an ongoing course and maintaining (inward to that actualizing and as belonging to life in its wholeness) an increasing span of the past-and-already-actual and a decreasing reservoir of the not-yet. Thus life is like activity as time-taking, and in its continuing realization in ongoing current activity, it exists in the continuous unfolding of itself as actual but not-yet-fully-actual, as having already begun and going to have an end but wholly ingathered now into this currently-continuing realization which is extending its actuality over a span of time between its beginning and end.

36. See, for example, "the innermost nature of a human being" (S-I/213 [H-UHH/ 62]), a phrase used when he is discussing the plastic power. Or again, "the inherited, hereditary nature" as an "inborn" "first nature" in contrast with a "second nature" which we develop in our interaction with circumstance (S-I/230 [H-UHH/76]).

37. For Nietzsche's more precise and refined statement of this matter, see the discussion of SE in our next chapter (pages 130-131 below, for instance).

38. The notions of time and temporality which would make sense of this idea of an 'initial' or 'original' 'inborn' nature are not expressly brought forward by Nietzsche, but this latter idea would scarcely seem possible without a somewhat different notion of time than his explicit idea, and one which introduces the element of finitude which we have been suggesting is part of a more fundamental idea than he ever expresses explicitly in UHH. Yet such a more fundamental idea can be pointed to by starting from the way Nietzsche speaks when giving his account of the historical mode of our engagement with things. As we have just seen, this account grasps time as continually retaining and integrating (whether subterraneously, or as 'ghostly' memories) into the ongoing-now the past moments which are made past by the going-onward of time. Thus the past is continually entering into the forming of our current activity, so that the activity in and by which life is realized takes shape under this pressure. There is, however, an exception to this. If there is a *start* of *our* activity, of that forming which continues life-long, this start involves no past of the sort in question (one that was once current). If for that start there is needed (say) resources 'already there' on the strength of which the start is made, what would be involved in that case would be a 'before' which never issued from the activity of a current moment and then became past and accumulated in the present; it would be something *already there* in some other sense *in and for* the *initial* forming. As for what might be 'already there', in the case of a living active being it would be the capacities for initiating activity, as harbored in the organization, constitution, and capacities, whose actuality and potentiality make up the original or inborn nature of the living being at the start of life, in a meaning of "nature" not so different from the Greek sense as it is attested in Aristotle. In short, it would be (or be very like) what Nietzsche is calling the original or inborn nature of the living active being. As to the 'already' of this 'already there', it signifies not some prior moment *within* the temporal existence of the being but one side of the *finitude of* the activity-enabling present, namely, the beginning *of* that present. Thus the factors that initially compose the nature of the living active being and enable its initial (and continuing) activity are 'already there' to the initial effort not *as part of* that being's own past but as part of its own beginning-to-be. The activity which takes shape in the current ongoing of the present which has *this* beginning is thus enabled to be what it is by the elements of that beginning-to-be which are there already for activity-- elements not simply actual but also potential. In the measure in which they include potential, in that measure the activity takes shape under the pressure of a future (grander or less grand, etc.) which weighs in the forming of activity now as a might-be-which-is-harbored-in-the-potential-that-is-ingredient-in-our-initial-nature. Nietzsche's failure expressly to recognize the *essentially* bounded/finite character of time's nature leads him to speak of this nature as "inherited" without sufficiently

exploring the gap (and the consequences following from that gap) that is required for such inheritance to be and be what it is, involving as it does the beginning of *another* being, not the continuing of a previous being.

39. S-I/275-276, 283 (H-UHH/115, 121).

40. More on all three of these points when we reach SE.

41. For example, he characterizes as follows the man who, seized by a vehement passion for a woman or for a great idea, finds his whole world becoming altered: "Looking behind him he feels he is blind, listening around him he perceives what is alien only as a dull, meaningless noise; whatever he does perceive, however, he perceives as he has never perceived before-- all is so palpably close, colorful, resounding, illuminated, as though he apprehended it with all his senses at once. All his valuations are altered and disvalued; there are so many things he is no longer capable of evaluating at all because he can hardly feel [*fühlen*] them any more: he asks himself why he was for so long the fool of the words and opinions of others; he is amazed that his memory revolves unwearingly in a circle and yet is too weak and weary to make even a single leap out of this circle. It is the most unjust condition in the world, narrow, ungrateful to the past, blind to dangers, deaf to warnings, one is a little vortex of life in a dead sea of night and oblivion: and yet this condition-- unhistorical, anti-historical through and through-- is the womb not only of an unjust deed but of every just deed too; and no painter will paint his picture, no general achieve his victory, no people attain its freedom, without having first desired and striven for it in an unhistorical condition of this kind." (S-I/215-216 [H-UHH/64]). See also his contrast of the narrow (but healthy and vigorous) human being, with the far more just and learned (but sicker and weaker) human being (S-I/214 [H-UHH/63]).

42. Or analogously, later in life: Nietzsche's analysis, while centered in youth, is conceived to extend beyond that, to adult life at any time.

43. In BT, Nietzsche speaks of illusion as intrinsic to our condition in two ways in particular. First, is in relation to creation: appearance seems all, seems to be being. Second, art is illusion-creating; even that art in which truth comes to its fullest voicing (the Dionysian art of tragedy) operates in the medium of illusion (enlisting the Apollonian, for instance). Neither of these matters is a focus in this meditation, although the matter of art does achieve some mention.

44. In BT, we saw Nietzsche conceiving art as a capacity to use illusion in a constructive and life-supporting fashion. In UHH, he focuses on other ways in which illusion can function in this fashion.

45. "... (B)ut it is only in love, only when shaded by the illusion of love, that is to say, only in the unconditional belief in the perfect and the just, that a human being is creative." (S-I/252 [H-UHH/95]). Note the Platonic coloring involved here, and the kinship (if also difference) to what Socrates points us to in the *Symposium*, concerning the good and beautiful, love and creation.

46. "All living things require an atmosphere around them, a mysterious misty vapor; if one takes this enveloping mist from them, if one condemns a religion or art or genius to revolve as a star without atmosphere, one should no longer be surprised if they quickly wither and grow hard and unfruitful. It is the same with all great things, 'which never succeed without some illusion', as Hans Sachs says in the *Meistersinger*. But every people too, indeed every human being, that wants to become *mature* needs a similar enveloping illusion, a similar protective and veiling cloud; ... ." (S-I/254 [H-UHH/97]).

47. See aphorism 307 in GS for an excellent statement of Nietzsche's on this point. Of course there is no guarantee that the critical work of reflection may not lead to the replacement in the supportive horizon of an old illusion with a new one rather than with a genuine truth. Even so, what is essential is not truth in and of itself, but the function of knowledge and of self-criticism.

48. S-I/252 (H-UHH/95).

49. S-I/229 (H-UHH/76). See also S-I/216 (H-UHH/64): "As he who acts is, in the words of Goethe, always without a conscience, so is he also always without knowledge; he is oblivious to most things in order to do one, he is unjust toward what lies behind him and knows only one claim, the claim of that which should [*soll*] now come to be. Thus everyone who acts loves his deed infinitely more than it deserves to be loved; and the best deeds take place in such a superabundance of love that however incalculably great their value may otherwise be they must in every case be unworthy of this love."

50. Thus, in speaking of "historical justice" and its judgments (always annihilating in character) on elements of the past, Nietzsche can say: "If there is no drive to construct at work behind the historical drive, if the destroying and space-clearing is not taking place in order that a future already alive in hope build its house on the ground thus liberated, if justice alone holds sway [*waltet*], then the creative instinct is weakened [*entkräftet*] and discouraged." (S-I/252 [H-UHH/95]).

51. S-I/252 (H-UHH/95).

52. For Nietzsche, education in the most proper sense of that word is a fundamental element in the process of cultivation

53. S-I/266-267 (H-UHH/107-108). See also the portrayal of the learned and just human being at S-I/214 (H-UHH/63) for part of what Nietzsche has in mind.

54. S-I/231-232 (H-UHH/78).

55. S-I/233 (H-UHH/79); also S-I/255 (H-UHH/98).

56. S-I/237-238 (H-UHH/83-84). Included in what Nietzsche says here: "He who wants to conceptualize, calculate, understand, there in the moment during which he should in extended shuddering be holding fast to the unintelligible [*Unverständliche*] as sublime, may be called intelligent [*verständig*], but only in the sense of Schiller's epigram ...: there are things he does not see which even a child sees, things he does not hear which even a child hears; and these things are precisely the most important. Because he does not understand these, his intelligence [*Verstehen*] is more childish than the child's and more simple than simplicity-- and this in spite of the many cunning folds of his parchment scroll and the virtuosity of his fingers in unravelling the entangled."

57. In disputing the claim of modern education to produce "free personalities", Nietzsche comments on the meaning of free in that phrase: it signifies "truthful toward itself, truthful towards others, in both word and deed". He continues: "It is only through such truthfulness that the distress, the inner misery, of modern man will come to light, and that, in place of that anxious concealment through convention and masquerade, art and religion, true ancillaries, advance together to implant a culture which corresponds to true needs [*Bedürfnissen*] and does not, like present-day universal education teaches, merely teach us to deceive ourselves [*sich ... belügen*] as to those needs and thereby become a walking lie [*Lüge*]." (S-I/239-240 [H-UHH/84-85]).

58. Nietzsche notes (S-I/243 [H-UHH/87]) that lack of self-control is what the Romans called *impotentia* [impotence].

59. S-I/238-240 (H-UHH/83-85). Included here: "... [H]e has lost and destroyed his instincts, and having lost his trust in the 'divine animal', he can no longer let go the reins when his reason falters and his path leads him through deserts. Thus the individual grows fainthearted and unsure and dares no longer believe in himself: he sinks into himself in his interiority, which here means into the accumulated lumber of what he has learned but which does not make itself effective outwardly, of instruction which does not become life. If one watches him from outside, one sees how the expulsion of the instincts by history has transformed man almost into mere *abstractis* and shadows: no one dares to be his own person, but masks himself as a cultivated man, as a scholar, as a poet, as a politician." Nietzsche also speaks of "our contemporary men of letters, popular figures, officials, politicians" and claims: "they are not human beings but only flesh-and-blood compendia and as it were abstractions made concrete. If they possess a character and type [*Art*] of their own it is buried so deep it cannot get out into the light of day: if they are human beings they are so only to him 'who tries the reins'. To anyone else they are something different, not human beings, not gods, not animals, but creatures [*-gebilde*] of historical culture [*Bildungs-*], altogether culture [*Bildung*], image [*Bild*], form without demonstrable content and, unhappily, merely bad form, and in addition, uniform. And so let my proposition be understood and pondered: *history can be borne only by strong personalities, weak ones are utterly extinguished by it.* The reason is that history confuses the feelings and sensibility when these are not strong enough to measure the past by themselves. He who no longer dares to trust himself but involuntarily asks of history 'How ought I to feel about this?' finds that his timidity gradually turns him into an actor and that he is playing a role, usually indeed many roles and therefore playing them each badly and superficially." (S-I/240-241 [H-UHH/85-86]).

60. S-I/232 (H-UHH/78).

61. "... [H]ow despairing the proposition sounds: we Germans feel in abstractions; we have all been ruined through history-- a proposition which would destroy at its roots all hope of a future national culture. For any such hope grows out of the belief in the genuineness and immediacy of German feeling [*Empfindung*], out of the belief in a sound and whole interiority. What is there left to hope for or believe in if the source [*Quell*] of belief and hope is muddied, if our interiority has learned to leap, to dance, to paint itself, to express itself in abstractions and calculatively and gradually to lose itself! And how should the great productive spirit continue to endure among a people which is no longer secure in its unified interiority and which has fallen asunder into the cultivated with a miseducated and misled interiority and the uncultivated with an inaccessible interiority! How should that spirit endure if unity of feeling among the people has been lost, and if, moreover, it knows that this feeling is falsified and colored precisely among that part of the people which calls itself the cultured part and lays claim to possession of the national artistic spirit?" (S-I/236 [H-UHH/81-82]).

62. S-I/232 (H-UHH/78).

63. Thus Nietzsche claims: the foreigner is to some extent at least justified in maintaining that German interiority "is too feeble and disorganized to work effectively outward and give itself a form. The interiority of the Germans can well show itself to be delicately receptive to an exceptional degree, serious, powerful, inward, and perhaps even richer than that of other peoples; but as a whole it remains weak because all these beautiful threads are not wound together into a powerful knot: so that the visible act is not the total-act and self-revelation

of this interiority but only a feeble or crude attempt on the part of one or other of these threads to pass itself off as being the whole." (S-I/235 [H-UHH/81]).

64. S-I/232 (H-UHH/78).

65. S-I/243-244 (H-UHH/88-89). Included in this passage: "If he were a cold demon of knowledge, he would spread about him the icy atmosphere of a dreadful superhuman majesty which we would have to fear, not revere: but that he is a human being and yet nonetheless tries to ascend from indulgent doubt to strict certainty, from tolerant mildness to the imperative 'you must', from the rare virtue of magnanimity to the rarest of all virtues, justice; that he resembles that demon without from the start being anything other than a poor human being; and above all, that he has every moment to atone for his humanity and is tragically consumed by an impossible virtue-- all this sets him on a solitary height as the most *venerable* exemplar of the species man; for he wants truth, and yet not simply as cold knowledge which has no consequences, but as a regulating and punishing judge; truth, not as the egoistic possession of the individual, but as the sacred authorization to overturn all the boundary-stones of egoistic possessions; in a word, truth as the judgment of the world, and certainly not, for instance, as the captured prey and joy of the individual huntsman."

66. Continuing the quotation from the previous Note: "Only insofar as the truthful person possesses the unconditional will to be just is there anything great in that striving for truth which is everywhere so thoughtlessly glorified; while to the duller eye, a whole host of the most various drives such as curiosity, flight from boredom, envy, vanity, the desire for amusement, for example-- drives which in reality have nothing whatever to do with truth-- flow together with that striving for truth which has its root in justice. Thus the world seems to be full of those who 'serve truth', and yet the virtue of justice is rarely present, even more rarely recognized and almost always mortally hated; while on the other hand the horde of those who only seem virtuous is at all times received with pomp and honor. In truth few serve truth because only a few have the pure will to be just, and again even of these, very few have the strength [*Kraft*] to be able to be just." (S-I/244 [H-UHH/89]).

67. Yet Nietzsche is loathe to credit them here, where he puts a reference to them in quotation marks: men welcome "those 'servants of truth' who possess neither the will nor the strength [*Kraft*] to judge and set themselves the task of seeking 'pure' knowledge 'without any consequences', or more clearly, truth that eventuates in nothing." (S-I/245 [H-UHH/89]).

68. S-I/246-247 (H-UHH/91).

69. S-I/244-245 (H-UHH/89).

70. S-I/245-246 (H-UHH/89-90).

71. Nietzsche does not seem to consider that the correlation might be to a restraint in the employment of resources, not to a lack of them, or might even be to a restraint in drawing upon what one's resources disclose, in subservience to a method which is fitted to draw into knowledge only a limited facet of actuality.

72. "If ... you live yourself into the history of great men, you will learn from it a supreme commandment: to become mature and to flee the jurisdiction of that paralyzing education [*Erziehungs-*] of the present age which sees utility for itself in not allowing you to mature, so as to rule and exploit you, the immature." (S-I/251 [H-UHH/94-95]). Cf. also S-I/275-276 (H-UHH/115-116), where Nietzsche claims that "*the excesses of the historical sense from which the present day suffers are deliberately furthered, encouraged, and employed.* They are employed ... against youth, so as to train them up to that mature manhood of egoism which is striven for everywhere; they are employed so as to break the natural resistance of youth by a transfiguring (in this case, scientific-magical) illumination of that manly-unmanly egoism. We know, indeed, what history can do when it gains a certain ascendancy, we know it only too well: it can uproot the strongest instincts of youth, its fire, defiance, self-forgetting, and love, damp down the heat of its feeling for justice, suppress or repress its desire to mature slowly with the counter-desire to be ready, useful, fruitful as quickly as possible, cast sickly doubt on its honesty and directness of feeling: indeed, it can even deceive youth about its fairest privilege, its power to implant in itself in an over-full confidence a great idea and to allow it to grow out of itself into an even greater idea. A certain excess of history can do all this, we have seen it do it: and it does it by no longer allowing a person to feel and act *unhistorically*, due to continually shifting the horizon-perspectives, due to removing the protective atmosphere. From an infinite horizon he then returns to himself, to the smallest egoistic enclosure, and there he must become withered and dry: it is likely he attains to cleverness, but never to wisdom. He listens to reason, calculates and accommodates himself to the facts, does not get emotional, blinks and knows how to seek his own or his party's advantage in the advantage and disadvantage of others ... ."

73. Thus speaking of historiography become a scientific study of the past, and as such not being pursued in subservience to some inner drive to construct, he claims such study of the past "does nothing but destroy" and "in the long run makes its instruments enervated [*blasiert*] and denatured [*unnatürlich*]" (S-I/252 [H-UHH/96]). Then returning to his theme after two examples, he speaks of the present age, one not of "ripened [*fertig*] and mature, of harmonious personalities but of labor of the greatest possible common utility", and says: it requires

"that men ... be adjusted to the purposes of the age so as to be ready for employment as soon as possible; they must labor in the factories of the general good before they are mature, indeed, so that they shall not become mature-- for this would be a luxury which would deprive the 'labor market' of a great deal of its workforce." (S-I/254-255 [H-UHH/97-98]). Then finally, he speaks of the student of the past as "the heir of an all-too-early enfeeblement [*Blasiertheit*] already visible almost before he has ceased to be a boy. He has acquired the 'methods' for doing work of his own, the right technique and the noble bearing of the master; a wholly isolated little chapter of the past has fallen victim to his astuteness and the methods he has learned; he has already produced, indeed to use a prouder word, he has 'created' something, through the deed he has now become a servant of truth and a lord in the realm of the world of history. If already as a boy he was 'ripe' [*fertig*], now he is 'over-ripe' [*überfertig*]: one needs only to shake him and wisdom falls with a clatter into one's lap; but the wisdom is rotten and there is a worm in every apple. Believe me: if men are to labor and be useful in the factory of science before they are mature, science will soon be ruined just as effectively as the slaves thus employed too early." (S-I/256 [H-UHH/98-99]). ·

74. For Nietzsche the noblest form is philosophy, the "honest naked goddess" who is "the most truthful of all the sciences" (S-I/240 [H-UHH/85]). [Presumably, she is the most truthful because honest and disclosive about the most fundamental and fearful problem, that of meaning.] Eventually he will speak of philosophy as having to be judge of the past and present but more profoundly, having to be legislator and creator of the future.

75. In BT, this conceiving of thought as 'reason' was epitomized by Socrates, and the sense of the distinctively human as appropriately accounted for by speaking of 'reason' was conceived to be a departure from the earlier Greek notion of the nature of human beings, namely, that notion crystallized in tragedy. According to the sense of things bodied forth in tragedy (its 'wisdom'), the human being is centered in the capacity to see directly and to acknowledge the Dionysian constitution of reality and to found life in the joy of a creativity that can accept-- and does accept-- the negativity of existence but takes it into activity that has deeper and positive sources, which give activity meaning even in the face of such (accepted) negativity. Given the focus of UHH, the development of thought in which this contrast is made central is ignored and another contrast introduced and characterized without the Greek terms and tonality. One might also note: it is not often recognized-- or recognized appropriately and sufficiently-- how much the various conceptions of our power of thought as 'reason' differ, not only among the Greeks but (say) between the Greeks and the Christians who have assimilated Greek thought to make it a vehicle of their own, and among the variety of moderns from (say) Descartes and Spinoza through Kant and Hegel to 21st century thinkers. There is not one thing called reason, but a power which is interpreted to be such-as-this by so-and-so but such-as-that by someone-else, and which is nonetheless called by a term which (in English) we would render by "reason". Too often we moderns unwittingly introduce into the interpretation of the Greeks, say, a modern conception of the nature of reason, and miss what in fact those Greeks were thinking of.

76. See the discussion in the next section for such a sense and its focus.

77. S-I/258-259 (H-UHH/100-101). The reference to Hesiod's prophesy is to *Works and Days*, lines 180ff.

78. S-I/259-260 (H-UHH/101-102).

79. S-I/262 (H-UHH/104).

80. S-I/262-263 (H-UHH/104).

81. S-I/263 (H-UHH/104).

82. S-I/263 (H-UHH/104-105).

83. The phrase is from the Preface to Hegel's *Foundations of the Philosophy of Right*.

84. S-I/274 (H-UHH/114).

85. S-I/273 (H-UHH/113).

86. UHH does not reject what is central in BT-- a creational sense of the whole, the metaphysical meaning of artistic creativity, a created world indelibly stamped with suffering, art as consolation to creatures in such a world--, but simply ignores it and addresses another side to life in what is nonetheless the same basic world.

87. Thus it is (as in BT) the Socratic focus upon knowledge, continued in the Alexandrian culture, which modernity has developed "so grandly and fruitfully" through (among other means) "our universal history [*Historie*]". (S-I/261 [H-UHH/103]).

88. S-I/254 (H-UHH/97).

89. S-I/239 (H-UHH/85).

90. S-I/221-222 (H-UHH/69).

91. S-I/236 (H-UHH/81-82).

92. S-I/236 (H-UHH/82). See also S-I/257 (H-UHH/100).

93. S-I/270 (H-UHH/111).

94. Note thus that while for Nietzsche there is a sense of directionality implicit in the involvement of

individuals in active existence, and a sense which concerns our being together as human beings (our individual being as human and as implicated by that humanity in a distinctive connectedness with other human beings), this does not form the basis of a single movement of "history". It is rather the basis for a recurrent but non-progressive realization of such directionality at different times and places. Here and in his first-phase works generally, Nietzsche not only differs from Hegel but also from his later thinking. In the latter, there emerges something more in the way of a connective thread to human life on earth. Involved in it is a venturing which, in many ways blind during its actuality up to now, achieves a decisive turning-point in the self-aware discovery of the unity of all human life on earth and the facing of the question of 'Who is to be lord of the earth?' This movement, however, has no "rational necessity" which guides and compels it toward any final and fulfilling stage.

95. S-I/270 (H-UHH/111). "End" here means "temporally last"; the highest examples occur here and there in time, not as the last, yet nonetheless form the end or culmination, and this, as something which nature "aims at" in some fashion. For a fuller sense of this, see SE and the discussion in the next Chapter.

96. S-I/272 (H-UHH/112).

97. "Ask yourself for what you are here as an individual, and if no one can tell you, attempt just once to justify the meaning of your existence as it were *a posteriori*, by the fact that you set before yourself a goal, an aim, a for-this, a high and noble for-this. If you go aground on it-- I know no better life-purpose than to go a-ground on the great and impossible, *animae magnae prodigus*." (S-I/272 [H-UHH/112]).

98. S-I/272 (H-UHH/112-113).

99. S-I/277 (H-UHH/116).

100. "One must be young to understand this protest; indeed, in view of the premature greyhairedness of our present-day youth one can hardly be young enough if one is to feel [*spüren*] what is here really being protested against." (S-I/277 [H-UHH/116]). Note the distinctions implied here: of young-age chronologically from youth as a time of life with a certain natural character, and of both from the maturation according to which one may become formed (at a young age and under contrary-to-nature conditions) in such way as amounts to 'premature greyhairedness'! One may, of course, become formed otherwise in such maturation at the time.

101. See page 109 above, this Chapter.

102. S-I/275 (H-UHH/115).

103. S-I/276 (H-UHH/115).

104. S-I/278 (H-UHH/117-118).

105. S-I/278 (H-UHH/117-118). Something of the motivation for this in the case of Nietzsche himself seems alluded to in S-I/236-237 (H-UHH/82), where he speaks of the great productive spirit, frustrated by the lack of solidarity with a people, finding nothing left but to "turn his inspired hatred against that hindering interdiction, against the barriers erected in the so-called culture of his people, so as at least to condemn as judge what to him, as a living and life-producing [*Lebenzeugenden*] being, is destructive and degrading: thus instead of the divine joys of creating and helping he receives in exchange a profound insight into his destiny and ends as a solitary knower and satiated sage. It is the most painful of spectacles: he who beholds it will know a sacred compulsion: here, he says to himself, I must render aid, that higher unity in the nature and soul of a people must again be produced, that breach between inner and outer must again vanish under the hammer-blows of necessity [*Not*]. But what weapons should he now reach for? What does he have but, again, his profound knowledge; expressing and spreading this, sowing it with full hands, he hopes to implant a need [*Bedürfnis*], and out of a strong need there will one day arise a strong deed. And so as to leave no doubt of the source of our example of that necessity [*Not*], that need [*Bedürfnisses*] , that knowledge, let me expressly attest that it is for *German unity* in the highest sense that we strive, and strive more ardently than we do for political reunification, *the unity of German spirit and life after the abolition of the antithesis of form and content, interiority and convention.*"

106. S-I/278-280 (H-UHH/118-119). The reference to "babblers and bunglers" is presumably to the two sides to human activity, namely, speech and overt action.

107. S-I/280 (H-UHH/119).

108. S-I/281 (H-UHH/119-120).

109. S-I/281 (H-UHH/120).

110. In SE, Nietzsche takes up this theme at some length. See Section 1 of that work in particular.

111. S-I/281 (H-UHH/120).

112. Note that this is not the superhistorical in the sense adumbrated in Section 1 of UHH (see also A.1. of the present Chapter, pages 96-97 above), but the superhistorical in a broader meaning.

113. S-I/282 (H-UHH/120).

114. S-I/282 (H-UHH/120-21).

115. S-I/282-3 (H-UHH/121).

116. S-I/264 (H-UHH/105).

117. S-I/265 (H-UHH/106-107).
118. S-I/284 (H-UHH/122-123).
119. S-I/285 (H-UHH/123).
120. S-I/283-284 (H-UHH/122).

Chapter 6

1. S-I/290 (H-SE/129).
2. S-I/290 (H-SE/129).
3. S-I/292 (H-SE/131).
4. S-I/298 (H-SE/136).
5. Even more broadly, Nietzsche speaks of what is happening at large in modernity as a kind of consuming and squandering of the moral capital we have inherited from our forefathers. In historical terms, we live amidst a declining Christianity, unable to go back to Greek naturalness but no longer believing in Christian ideals. Thus we live in vacillation, and in dire need of moral educators who embodied and could educate us in an appropriate morality for our condition. But none have as yet arisen among us, although in this work Nietzsche is prone to speak as if Schopenhauer were such a man, even if he is as yet unrecognized as such among the Germans of Nietzsche's day.

6. Recall Nietzsche's characterization of life in UHH: it is a "dark, driving [*treibende*] power that insatiably craves itself [*unersättlich sich selbst begehrende Macht*]" (S-I/229 [H-UHH/76]).

7. One has to go back to Plato to find a Western philosopher whose sensitivity to matters of childhood experience-- say, to the way need makes itself felt in us as children and to the way we feel and respond to claims upon our capacity then-- plays an important part in his thinking. I think, for example, of the Platonic Socrates in the *Phaedrus* and his account of the soul's pre-existence. See my discussion in *Loving and Dying* (214-223).

8. Thus as we saw in UHH Nietzsche can speak of the crux of the maturational work to be accomplished in youth as involving the discovery and recovery in ourselves of the 'right and honest feeling' that forms the heart of the life in our own selves and which reason and the historical, as we become capable of these, are to illuminate and serve. Likewise, in the early phase of our lives, the requisite sensitivity is not present and available in us for recognition of obligation and morality: as children we are as innocent of these as we are of reason and 'the historical'. This matter, and even Nietzsche's way of expressing it, can profitably be thought out in connection with the *Republic* of Plato, and the Socratic account of the evolving human being and of education in that dialogue. See my discussion of the dialogue in *The Beginnings of Philosophy in Greece*, Chapter 7.

9. The analysis and language used in UHH and SE to address the ambivalent state of our condition at this beginning-point are different, but when thought together the ideas in the two works are complementary, indeed mutually reinforcing. Particularly suggestive is UHH's pointer to youth as a time when we find in ourselves the desire to feel growing within us a coherent living system of experiences of our very own, when this thought is brought together with SE's notion of the call of conscience recalling us to the life in ourselves and placing us back amidst aspiration. Neither work, however, speaks as fully as it might to the developmental reasons for the common experience in youth, of an inward not-being-equal to the demands and hardships of taking responsibility for ourselves. Why the doubts and timidity, the lack of confidence and courage, that make it difficult for us to follow out adequately the directive and direction that claims us in youth and that make it easy for us instead to turn away and lose ourselves in the masses, in social roles and the sociability of association in such terms?

10. S-I/298 (H-SE/136).
11. S-I/307 (H-SE/144).
12. S-I/313-314 (H-SE/150).
13. S-I/313 (H-SE/149-150).
14. S-I/316-318 (H-SE/152-154).
15. S-I/318-320 (H-SE/154-155).
16. The account implicitly expands upon the creational sense of reality in BT, concentrating on the meaning of genesis which the artist-author (Nature) has introduced within the created world.

17. S-I/323-324 (H-SE/158-159).
18. S-I/324 (H-SE/159).
19. S-I/326 (H-SE/160-161). Note how, in this characterization of the saint, we have an echo in a minor key of the full positivity of the Dionysian experience which was central to BT. Both seem renderings of something which Nietzsche himself felt strongly, even if as his thought develops both early formulations are rejected and a more refined rendering emerges and becomes central in TSZ.

20. S-I/326 (H-SE/161).

21. S-I/350 (H-SE/181). In connection with this, Nietzsche sees Kant as having had the inborn nature and drive to be a philosopher, but as having remained "in a (so to speak) state of pupation". (S-I/349-350 [H-SE/181]). That is, because he never became a "real" human being, his thinking never became great as that of a philosopher, but remained that of a scholar-and-scientist. In a kindred contrast, the real (strong and whole) human being whose thinking concerning the meaning of life incarnates greatness is contrasted with the human being with the talent for thinking but who, because of his failure humanly, has become at best merely "a clattering thinking-and-calculating machine" (S-I/302 [H-SE/140]).

22. S-I/350 (H-SE/181). He continues: such a person "will never see things for the first time and never himself be such a first-time seen thing; both belong together, however, in a philosopher, because he must take most of his learning from himself and because he himself serves as illustration and abbreviation of the whole world." Nietzsche speaks of the experiential matrix of philosophical reflection in connection with the philosophical 'genius', "who looks on things purely and lovingly, like a poet, and cannot immerse himself too deeply in them". (S-I/355-356 [H-SE/186]). This is in contrast with the scholar's filtering of presence (inward and outward) through various opinions he has picked up here and there and which color his receptivity to things-and-himself so that he never really receives and registers them apart from reference to that filtering framework. In his later thought, Nietzsche insists still on this distinction of philosopher from scientist-and-scholar, but formulates it a bit differently. Thus in aphorism 381 ("The Question of being Intelligible") of the later-added Part V of *Gay Science*, he speaks as a philosopher and says: "our task is and remains above all not to mistake ourselves for others. We *are* something different from scholars, although it is unavoidable for us to be also, among other things, scholarly. We have different needs, a different growth, a different digestion: we need more, we also need less. There is no formula for how much a spirit needs for its nourishment; but if its taste is directed toward independence, toward swift coming and going, toward wandering, perhaps toward adventures for which only the swiftest are a match, it prefers living free with little to eat to living unfree and stuffed. It is not fat but the greatest possible suppleness and strength that a good dancer wants from his nourishment-- and I would not know what the spirit of a philosopher might wish more to be than a good dancer. For the dance is his ideal, also his art, and finally also his only piety, his 'service of God'." (S-II/257 [K-GS/345-346]).

23. S-I/350 (H-SE/181).

24. S-I/304 (H-SE/141-142). At the practical level, Nietzsche speaks of such reading of the hieroglyphics of the outward world in connection with the second consecration to culture: "For now the transition is to be made from the inner event to the judgment of the outer event, our view is to be directed outward in order to find again in the great animated world that desire for culture as we know it from those first experiences. The individual is to use his own struggles and longings as the alphabet with which he can now interpret the strivings of humanity. But he must not stand still even here, he must climb to a higher level: culture demands not only inner experience, not only the judgment of the exterior world streaming around him, but finally, and chiefly, it demands action ... ." (S-I/329 [H-SE/163])

25. "Every great philosophy ... as a whole, always says only: this is the picture of all life, and learn from it the meaning of your own life." (S-I/304 [H/141]) See also the quotation in the preceding Note.

26. The whole as Nietzsche is thinking it is not the sum of its parts, although it has numerous sides and knowledge is possible of those various sides. Still, without a "regulative overall picture" of the whole, indeed a "steady view of the overall picture of life and existence", one can not see how the parts fit and have a role within the whole, and drawing upon the truths developed by the various sciences-and-scholarly-endeavors can be harmful. For by themselves such disciplines can not provide guidance to life, but are merely "threads which nowhere lead to an end [*Ende*] and only make our life's course all the more confused and labyrinthine". (S-I/304 [H-SE/141])

27. The heart of Schopenhauer's philosophy for Nietzsche is his embodiment of life as a heroic truth-seeking affair. In speaking of the Schopenhauerian ideal as becoming visible in the "happiness-engendering, even intoxicating, intuitive-perception" [*Anschauung*] of single moments, Nietzsche says: "our commerce with this ideal *begins* with these sudden intervals of light and shade, intoxication and nausea", but it does not end there. (S-I/320-321 [H-SE/156]). The "intoxication and nausea" recall the Dionysian experiencing of BT, and indeed it seems one and the same experience which the youthful Nietzsche reads in BT as making intelligible the phenomenon of Dionysus among the Greeks and in SE as making Schopenhauer intelligible. This means a slightly different emphasis and meaning is allowed to be given to the experience in the two cases, epitomized by the contrast of satyr with saint as the figures in whom the disclosure in each case is said to be realized in its full meaning. These are not, of course, the "satyr" and "saint" that appear in contrast in EH.

28. In the measure in which we can respond to this pointing and dedicate ourselves accordingly, we can live with a "presentiment [*Vorgefühl*] for all those who are in the process of becoming and for all fighters, and the most inward conviction that we meet nature almost everywhere in her need-and-distress, as she presses toward

man, as she painfully feels that her work has again failed, as she nevertheless succeeds in the most wonderful beginnings, outlines, and forms, so that the people with whom we live resemble a field covered with fragments of the most precious sculptural projects which all call out to us: 'Come, help, complete, bring together what belongs together! We long immeasurably ourselves to become whole!'" (S-I/329 [H-SE/163])

29. S-I/324 (H-SE/159).

30. S-I/326 (H-SE/161).

31. S-I/304, 305 (H-SE/142, 143).

32. S-I/328 (H-SE/162-163).

33. S-I/350 (H-SE/182).

34. S-I/307 (H-SE/144). For the philosopher as "the judge of life", see S-I/308 (H-SE/145).

35. S-I/304 (H-SE/142).

36. "The only criticism of a philosophy which is possible, and which also proves something-- that of seeing if one can live by it-- has never been taught at the universities: but always criticism of words by words." (S-I/356 [H-SE/187]).

37. S-I/302 (H-SE/140).

38. S-I/303 (H-SE/141). Nietzsche is alluding here to Heinrich von Kleist's response to the Kantian claim that truth may not reach to reality but only to appearance: he felt wounded to the core, his aim of basing life on truth being undermined by this possibility.

39. S-II/1116 (K-EH/281).

40. S-I/365 (H-SE/194).

41. S-I/354 (H-SE/185).

42. S-I/364 (H-SE/193).

43. The three images of humanity-- those of Goethe, Rousseau, and Schopenhauer-- represent alternative developments of the future immanent in youthful individuals, alternative types of the fuller humanity which is to be realized in the future of youth. Thus after a brief characterization of Schopenhauerian man, Nietzsche can say: "I should think that the heart of anyone who places such a life-direction before his own soul would necessarily open out [*weit werden*] and an ardent longing arise in him to be such a Schopenhauerian man." (S-I/317 [H-SE/153]). The type gives a determinate rendering (and in the case being envisaged, a relevant one) of the higher-and-better which aspiration reaches for, and in that determinateness elicits (with the force of 'must') a responsive welcoming and an accordant longing, in following out which various moral powers already present as part of youth are strengthened and the concerted effort in which they are employed is oriented in a certain direction (by Schopenhauer, e.g., toward being truthful whatever the cost, in belief that only a truthful existence is worth living).

44. That is, if the everyday spirit dominates, since it is basically conformist in nature and since what is being conformed to is basically extant and determinative already, what would arise as future would be of a piece with the present. But even supposing one had accurate and thorough knowledge of the current state of things, a future dictated by the 'times' and by the conformist thrust of its predisposing could still only be relatively predictable. An obvious example would be a present dominated by 'progress': continued conformity to this guiding idea and value is quite compatible with (say) 'revolutionary' technological advances that would make the future unpredictably different in many regards.

45. Nietzsche's exposition focuses on the great human being, and upon a greatness that is exemplified in SE by Schopenhauer. Thus he characterizes the decision-making by saying, for example: "If every great man is wont to be considered as a genuine child of his times, and in any event suffers more strongly and grievously [*empfindlicher*] from all its maladies than do lesser people, then the struggle of such a great man *against* his times is apparently a mere senseless and destructive struggle against himself. But only apparently, for he is fighting that in his times which prevents him from being great, which for him means being free and wholly himself. Consequently, his enmity is basically directed against only that which to be sure is in him but which is not authentically himself, namely, against the impure confusing-and-juxtaposing [*Durch- und Nebeneinander*] of the uncombinable and eternally irreconcilable [*Unvereinbarem*], against the false soldering of the timely to his untimeliness; and in the end the alleged child of his times shows himself to be a stepchild of the same. Thus Schopenhauer, from early youth onward, struggled against that false, vain and unworthy mother-- his times-- and by so-to-speak banishing her from inside himself, he purified and healed his being and found himself again in the health and purity which belong to him." (S-I/308-309 [H-SE/145-146]). It should be kept in mind, however, that the decision-making that makes the future could involve the piety and faithfulness in spirit whereby the present becomes locus for a continuation of the past which is not 'everyday' but which maintains with new life the tradition in which one finds oneself. See the discussion in UHH of antiquarian historiography.

46. Note the questions arising for this way of thinking. Anticipation would be difficult enough if it were

only a matter of the individual as a singular human being, in contrast with the individual as part of the collective humanity and the future as a collective one. In that case, there would be aspiration's pointer into the 'higher-and-better', and the 'law' of individual evolution and functioning under the meant-to-be of the higher-and-better self; but creativity, while operating under the obligating pressure of these, would be giving birth to what 'must be' in the concrete, in the medium of particularity (within and circumstantial), and the future here, given creativity and particularity, would scarcely be anticipatible in any concreteness and with any definiteness. If the future in question were communal, however, and not simply individual, the matter would be considerably more complex. There would be, for example, the diversity within the collective: not simply the contrast of the creative few and the masses, but the conflict in the interplay of the creative; and there would further be the question of the dynamic within the whole that integrates the creative and the masses. If we looked to the few as defining the future, the problems of anticipation would be multiplied by recalling the discussion in UHH of what is central in history-making and history-writing: Is the new life one taking shape aided by monumental recall of an earlier variation on the same thematic meaning, or rather by a critical or an antiquarian recall? The kind of intelligibility to the future provided by the past functioning supportively in these different ways would be different, and in any case not very concrete. But further: if it is a collective future in question, what of the masses and their needs, and the 'laws' of the demands which arise in such neediness? Would these not provide the preponderant momentum into the future? If the future can not help but involve the enduring presence of a mass of human beings, then perhaps its nature would be anticipatible in some regards on these rather different and non-creative grounds-- supposing that one could also anticipate how the changes in spiritual life which the few introduce could be anticipated in the effect they would have on the masses. If such problems of anticipation are not enough, keep in mind that the philosopher, as law-giver, is not concerned with simply anticipating the future but with giving it shape, with legislating as a new future is opening out through the creative appropriation of the potential of the situation by the great. What could it mean to "legislate" here? A final point: notice that in UHH, Nietzsche had focused on the individual and the moment of the decision-making which is the recall to the native chaos within, to what is genuine in oneself (as regards stuff and meant-to-be), and had said little of what might come of this as the future implicated there (whether collective or personal or both) gains determination in the creative appropriation in question. SE, however, is attempting an advance beyond that, and thus the new issues and problems.

47. Nietzsche expresses at some length this idea that Nature aims at an effect but only in a clumsy way, such that we can-- and need to-- aid her and enable her to achieve her end skillfully. Thus, for example, at S-I/345-346 (H-SE/177-178), he speaks of Nature as always wanting to be "useful to all [*gemeinnützig*]" but not understanding "how to find the ways and means [*Mittel und Handhaben*] that are best and most suited for this purpose". Given her own "pressing need for redemption [*erlösungsbedürftigen Drange*]", "Nature wishes to make existence explicable [*deutsam*] and meaningful [*bedeutsam*] for human beings by the production of the philosopher and the artist"; but her efforts are uncertain, weak and dull, indeed often without effect at all, especially in regard to the philosopher. In the realm of culture, she is as wasteful as she is in planting and sowing; "she fulfills her ends [*Zwecke*] in a general and clumsy manner, whereby she sacrifices much too much energy [*Kräfte*]". "The artist and the philosopher are proofs against the suitableness of nature's means, although they give the best proof for the wisdom of her ends [*Zwecke*]." "The artist makes his work according to nature's will for the good of others, there is no doubt of this. Nevertheless, he knows that none of these other human beings will understand and love his work as he himself understands and loves it. Because of the unskilled disposition [*Verfügung*] of nature, a high and unique degree of love and understanding is necessary in order that a lower degree might arise: the greater and nobler are used as a means to bring about the lesser and ignoble. Nature is not a prudent manager; her outlay is far greater than the profit [*Ertrag*] she aims at [*erzielt*]: for all her wealth she must eventually destroy herself. She would arrange things more rationally if her household rule were to minimize the costs and maximize the profits. If, for example, there were only a few artists, and these were of weaker powers, and if there were numerous appropriators [*Aufnehmende*] and receivers [*Empfangende*] who were of a stronger [*stärkerer*] and more powerful [*gewaltigerer*] type than the type of artists themselves, then the effect [*Wirkung*] of the work of art would be a hundredfold stronger response." "It often looks as though the artist, and especially the philosopher, existed in his times *by chance*, as a recluse or wanderer who has lost his way and been left behind. Let one only feel deeply how great Schopenhauer is in every way-- and how absurdly small his effect!" After commenting on the "powers and impotencies" that account for the minimal influence Schopenhauer has had, Nietzsche continues (S-I/347-348 [H-SE/179-180]): "Whoever, then, has recognized the unreason in the nature of this time, will have to think of means for helping a little here; his task will be to acquaint the free spirits, and those who suffer deeply from their times, with Schopenhauer, to gather them together, and through them to produce a current strong enough to overcome the clumsiness which nature ordinarily shows in using the philosopher as she does even today. Such men will realize that the same obstacles which hinder the effect of a great philosophy also stand in the way of the production of a great philosopher. Therefore they can

define their goal [*Ziel*] as the preparing for a re-creation of a Schopenhauer, that is, of a philosophical genius. But from the first what opposed the effect and dissemination of his teachings and in the end what wants with all its means to make vain [*vereiteln*] the rebirth of the philosopher is the perversity [*Verschobenheit*] of current human nature: for which reason all great men in their coming-to-be [*werdenden*] must waste an incredible amount of energy [*Kraft*] in order to free [*retten*] themselves from this perversity. The world into which they now enter is full of false pretenses. These in truth are not necessarily only religious dogmas, but are also such pretentious concepts as 'progress', 'universal education', 'national', 'modern state', 'cultural struggle'; indeed, one can say that all general terms now carry artificial and unnatural finery, for which reason a more enlightened posterity will reproach our time as being twisted and stunted to the highest degree, however loudly we may boast of our 'health'. ... The genius in process of becoming is most hindered by the fact that such wondrous concepts and whimsical needs are in vogue in his times. This is the leaden weight which so often, unseen and inexplicable, forces his hand down when he wants to drive the plow-- in such a way that even his highest works, because they freed themselves violently, must carry, to a certain extent, the mark [*Ausdruck*] of this violence."

48. S-I/328-329 (H-SE/163).

49. See S-I/329-330 (H-SE/163-164), which says that anyone who is capable of feeling this call to action "is immediately surprised at *how extraordinarily rare and scanty our knowledge is of this goal* [*Ziel*], how universal on the other hand is the preoccupation [*Bemühen*] with culture, and how unspeakably great in amount are the forces-and-energies [*Kräfte*] used in its service. One asks oneself in astonishment: 'Is such knowledge perhaps not necessary? Does nature reach her goal even though most people falsely determine the purpose of their own efforts?' He who has become accustomed to having a high regard for the unconscious purposefulness of nature will perhaps have no trouble in answering: 'Yes, so it is! Let people think and say what they will about their final goal [*Ziel*]. They still, in their blind instinct [*Drange*], are conscious to themselves of the right way.' One must have some experience to be able to contradict this. He who is convinced, however, that the goal [*Ziele*] of culture is to further the arising of the true *human beings* and nothing else, and then compares how now, with all the display and splendor of culture, the genesis [*Entstehung*] of these men is not much different from continued cruelty to animals-- he will find it necessary that a conscious will be put in place of that 'blind instinct' [*dunklen Drangs*]. And particularly for a second reason: so that it is no longer possible to use that impulse [*Trieb*] which is unclear about its goal [*Ziel*], the famous blind instinct [*dunklen Drang*], for quite different purposes, and to lead it on ways where the highest goal [*Ziel*], the production of the genius, can never be reached. For there is a kind of *misused and enlisted culture*-- one has only to look around! And just those forces that are at present most actively promoting culture have ulterior motives and do not have a pure and disinterested attitude in their commerce with culture."

50. S-I/311-312 (H-SE/148). "Therefore, I concern myself here with a species of human being whose teleology goes somewhat beyond the weal of the state, with philosophers, and with these only in respect to a world which is fairly independent of the weal of the state, the world of culture. Of the many interlocking rings which compose the human community, some are of gold, and some of brass." The 'gold' and 'brass' presumably allude to the account by the Platonic Socrates in the *Republic*, of the diverse natures of the functionally-differentiated classes in the ideal *polis* which he is constructing in his conversation with Glaucon and Adeimantus.

51. In his discussion of the immediate future, however, concerned as it is with the conflict of the philosopher and philosophy with the current institutional system for education (in particular, with university professorships in philosophy), he seems to suggest there is an essential tension between cultural institutions and other institutions in the society (political, economic, and the like). It would seem that, to be themselves, future cultural institutions mediating the cultural ring within the whole would stand apart from and in tension with the other institutional structures which mediate the other rings which, together with the cultural, compose a society.

52. S-I/342-343 (H-SE/175).

53. S-I/343-344 (H-SE/176).

54. S-I/344 (H-SE/176).

55. This whole matter can be thought out in a way that is helpful to addressing Nietzsche's thoughts, by study of the *Bhagavad-gītā*. See my translation and commentary, especially 71-76, 100-107, and more generally, the treatment of *dharma* in that work.

Chapter 7

1. Keep in mind, of course, that in his later retrospects, Nietzsche acknowledges that the Wagner of this meditation is a figure into which he has projected himself as he was in youth.

2. This *Blick*, Nietzsche speaks of in EH as "the authentic Zarathustra-gaze" (S-II/1112 [K-EH/275]). It is an immediate viewing which brings the whole of life into view, and from a point in the middle of the ongoing

of that life, envisions the becoming involved in it-- and not simply the becoming up to that point, but the futural part of that becoming as it is immanent in that point as well. Is it with such a vision of his own life that Zarathustra enters into and carries out his teaching in TSZ? In any case, Nietzsche links WB with TSZ in a further way, claiming that "that great noon at which the most elect consecrate themselves for the greatest of all tasks" is his later transformation of "the idea of Bayreuth" (S-II/1112 [K-EH/274]). As for a parallel in the structure of WB with that of EH, in which (so the note between the Preface and the main body of that work suggests) Nietzsche lays out his own life out of a kindred concentration of the whole, see the discussion in Chapter 1 above (especially pages 2-4).

    3. S-I/380-381 (H-WB/209).
    4. S-I/382-383 (H-WB/210-211).
    5. S-I/381 (H-WB/210).
    6. S-I/384 (H-WB/212).
    7. S-I/387 (H-WB/214).
    8. S-I/387 (H-WB/214).
    9. S-I/387-388 (H-WB/214-215).
   10. S-I/393 (H-WB/219).
   11. S-I/388 (H-WB/215).
   12. S-I/390 (H-WB/217).
   13. S-I/391 (H-WB/218).
   14. S-I/395 (H-WB/221).
   15. S-I/395-396 (H-WB/221).
   16. S-I/396-397 (H-WB/222).
   17. Nietzsche does liken these two: see S-I/380 (H-WB/208).
   18. S-I/397-398 (H-WB/223).
   19. S-I/400-401 (H-WB/225-226).
   20. S-I/401-402 (H-WB/226).
   21. S-I/399 (H-WB/224).
   22. S-I/400 (H-WB/225).
   23. S-I/396 (H-WB/221-222).
   24. S-I/404 (H-WB/228-229).
   25. S-I/374 (H-WB/203).
   26. S-I/374 (H-WB/203).
   27. S-I/373 (H-WB/202-203).
   28. S-I/376 (H-WB/205).
   29. S-I/376-377 (H-WB/205).
   30. S-I/379 (H-WB/208).
   31. The preceding four quotes all come from S-I/402-403 (H-WB/227).
   32. S-I/403-404 (H-WB/228).
   33. S-I/407 (H-WB/231).
   34. S-I/409 (H-WB/233).

    35. For light thrown on this matter by the ancient Hindu, see the discussion of freedom in my *Bhagavad-Gītā: Translation and Commentary*, 108-115.

    36. S-I/422 (H-WB/244). The "necessary" here concerns the doing which makes the elements of the work fit together to form a meaningful whole. The idea here uncannily prefigures the gift-giving virtue of TSZ (Part I, last speech).

    37. In its fuller form, the quotation introduced at the end of Section A of this chapter reads: "Even if the way [*Art*] it came-to-be should betray a purposiveness, who could clearly name the purpose for its being there at all? Out of a blessed presentiment-and-suspicion [*Ahnung*] one may ask: should the greater really exist for the lesser, the greatest giftedness for the good of the smallest, the highest virtue and holiness for the sake of the frail? Must true music resound because humankind *deserved it least but needed* [*bedurften*] *it most?*" (S-I/396-397 [H-WB/222]). In speaking earlier in WB of the appearance of German music in modern times, which times are otherwise "an existence striving mightily upwards and struggling for *conscious freedom* and *independence of thought*", Nietzsche says of this appearance that it is no chance event: "it is not chance but necessity that rules here." (S-I/387 [H-WB/214]) Similarly recall the opening of WB, in which Nietzsche anticipates a joint achievement of greatness on the part of composer and audience as what is about to happen at the performances at Bayreuth; the cor-respondence of composer and audience represents a necessary fit being realized, not a mere affair of chance but a coming together of the diverse in a way such that what happens must happen and happen

as it does. Finally, the suggestion that Wagner's appearance has its intelligibility and meaning in one side of the neediness of the times (the sickness of language and the need for correct feeling to find outward expression in culture) faintly echoes Kṛṣṇa's explanation of his descent and incarnation when times get bad, in the *Bhagavad-Gītā*, Chapter IV, vss. 7-8 (see my translation, on page 17).

38. S-I/346 (H-SE/178).

39. S-I/380 (H-WB/208-209).

40. S-I/409 (H-WB/233). That the perfected community would be no utopia, Nietzsche intimates in saying: "May good reason preserve us from the belief that humanity will at any future time find a final ideal order of things, and that happiness will then necessarily shine down upon such an order with unwavering ray like the sun of the tropics: with such a belief Wagner has nothing to do, he is no utopian." (S-I/430-431 [H-WB/251]).

41. S-I/384 (H-WB/212). See the quotation of this passage on page 155 above, this Chapter.

42. S-I/384-385 (H-WB/212).

43. S-I/386 (H-WB/213).

44. S-I/426 (H-WB/247).

45. S-I/428-429 (H-WB/249).

46. S-I/429-430 (H-WB/250).

47. S-I/431 (H-WB/251-252).

Notes for INTERLUDE

Chapter 8

1. D/424 ("For whom truth is there"). The aphorism, to be returned to in Chapter 10 (pages 417, 429-430 below), contains a suggestion to the effect that "truth (*as a whole* and interconnected affair) exists only for souls which are at once powerful [*mächtigen*] and harmless, and full of joyfulness and peace (as was the soul of Aristotle), and equally, only such souls will be in a position *to seek truth*. For no matter how proudly they think of their intellect and its freedom, the others are seeking *cures* for themselves, they are *not* seeking truth. This is why those others take so little genuine joy in science, and make of the coldness, dryness and inhumanity of science a reproach to it: this is the judgment of the sick on the games of the healthy." (S-I/1220 [H-D/182]).

2. S-I/741 (H-HAH/212). The quotation comes from section 5 of the Preface to HAH-II.

3. For imagery concerning this period as one of winter and harboring an icing up relative to which GS is a thawing, see Chapter 2 above, pages 26 and 38.

4. S-II/1128 (K-EH/296). The last aphorism of the original GS (342) is the first section of the Prologue of TSZ, and the penultimate aphorism is GS/341.

Notes for PART II

Chapter 9

1. HAH-I/436. Except in the case of the two later-added Prefaces, reference to passages in HAH will normally be by aphorism number and (where helpful) title.

2. HAH-I/164 ("Danger and gain in the cult of genius").

3. HAH-I/4 ("Astrology and what is related").

4. For Nietzsche's account of this in BT, see Chapter 4 above.

5. HAH-I/1 ("Chemistry of concepts and feelings [*Empfindungen*]"). Note that this phrasing sketches out the structure of HAH-I, which after this beginning on first and last things proceeds: II. On the History of the Moral Sensations; III. The Religious Life; IV. From the Souls of Artists and Writers; V. Signs of Higher and Lower Culture; VI. Man in Society; VII. Woman and Child; VIII. A Glance at the State; IX. Man alone with himself. Presumably, then, the rest of the work contributes to such a chemistry.

6. For signs of Nietzsche's own recognition of this, see the passing acknowledgement in the first later-added Preface to HAH (S-I/437 [H-HAH/5]: he took shelter in scientificalness, among other things), and the additional suggestion in the second later-added Preface (S-I/741-742 [H-HAH/212]: he had recourse to optimism-- that is, that native to science-- for the sake of self-restoration).

7. HAH-I/6 ("The spirit of science powerful in its parts, not in the whole").

8. HAH-I/27 ("Substitute for religion").

9. HAH-I/131. For an element in the contrast of philosophy with the special sciences, see HAH-II/WS-171 ("The employees of science and the others"), where Nietzsche contrasts the philosopher with the employees and employers in science, and speaks of philosophers as those "rarer, rarely successful and wholly mature natures 'for the sake of whom science exists'". Themselves possessed of the qualities of the workers in science and utilizing what those workers have ascertained, philosophers are nonetheless different, being marked by a particular limitation: "they can live only *in their own* [*eigenen*] *atmosphere*, on their own soil". Theirs is a task which is peculiarly personal, an inquiry guided not by the needs of the science(s) but by their own needs. Thus they require a peculiar freedom to move in directions which answer to those needs. If they cultivate individual areas in a science, they do so only in those areas in which "the fruit and seeds they themselves need [*nötigen*] will prosper [*gedeihen*]"; and more generally, from the sciences (whether they are participants in them or not) they bear home with them to their own atmosphere and dwelling all that 'belongs to them', their own 'property' [*Eigentum*]. "If they are prevented from constructing their own [*eigenen*] nest, they perish like houseless birds; unfreedom is wasting-away [*Schwindsucht*] to them." Lacking all impersonal participation in a problem of knowledge, they are themselves personalities through and through, and all their insights and acquirements in the field of knowledge [*Kenntnisse*] grow together into a personality (a living manifold whose individual parts depend on one another, cleave to one another, are nourished by the same food, and as a whole possess their own atmosphere and aroma). Thus philosophic natures, by producing structures of knowledge which have this person-like character to them, give the illusion of having produced something finished, something that has reached its goal; in fact, it is rather the *life* in that structure which gives this impression.

10. HAH-I/109 ("the rigorous method of truth" and a "clean" "intellectual conscience"); HAH-I/3 ("spirit ... claimed by rigorous thinking"). In HAH-I, Nietzsche is prone to stress certainty (HAH-I/19, 635), and the capacity of the "little homely truths", because they are "certain" and "enduring", to be "rich in consequences for any further development of knowledge" (HAH-I/3). Occasionally he will state the matter with greater precision: in HAH-I/22 he speaks of "unimpeachable [*unantastbaren*] truths in the sense of truths which have survived all the assaults of skepticism and disintegration". Eventually, in HAH-II/MMO-7, what he has in mind becomes set forth simply and straightforwardly: "Strictly understood" we are "never able to speak of truth but only of probability and degrees of probability".

11. HAH-I/8 ("Spiritualistic explanation of nature"); see also HAH-I/270 ("The art of reading"), pointing to the eventual discovery by philologists of correct methods for elucidating texts, and claiming that only when such an art of correct reading was perfected did science of any kind acquire continuity and constancy.

12. HAH-I/113, 271 ("The art of drawing conclusions"), 631, 13 (this last aphorism contrasts the correct use of the faculty of drawing conclusions with the way conclusions are drawn in dreams). See also HAH-I/265, on schools having no task more important than to teach "rigorous thinking, cautious judgment, and consistent reasoning".

13. HAH-I/3 ("Valuing unpretentious truths"), on the laborious struggle involved, contrasted with the miraculous and easy means of inspiration and direct seeing. HAH-I/633-637 contrast the tentative holding-for-true with conviction, and insist that the scientific spirit rests upon an insight into methods and expresses "an instinctive mistrust of the straying-ways [*Abwege*] of thinking", a mistrust "which, as a consequence of long practice, has struck root in the soul of every scientific man" (HAH-I/635).

14. HAH-I/261, 634.

15. HAH-I/3.

16. HAH-I/630.

17. HAH-I/10 ("Harmlessness of metaphysics in the future").

18. HAH-I/19 ("Number").

19. HAH-I/11 ("Language as alleged science"), 18, 19.

20. It is not simply arithmetic but geometry as well that involves us in fictions: "in nature there is no exactly straight line, no real circle, no absolute magnitude". (HAH-I/11).

21. HAH-I/19.

22. HAH-I/19.

23. HAH-I/11.

24. HAH-I/11. See also HAH-II/WS-11 ("Freedom of will and isolation of facts"), where, in connection with a discussion of the freedom of the will, Nietzsche speaks of the false assumption that there are "*identical* facts", indeed a "graduated order of *classes* of facts which corresponds to a graduated world-order: we thus *isolate* not only the individual fact, but also again groups of supposedly identical facts (good, evil, sympathetic, envious actions, etc.)-- in both cases erroneously." He continues: "The word and the concept are the most visible reason why we believe in this isolation of groups of actions: we do not merely *designate* things with them, we think originally that through them we grasp the *true* in things. Through words and concepts we are still continu-

ally misled into thinking things to be simpler than they are, separate from one another, indivisible, each existing in and for itself. A philosophical mythology lies concealed in *language* which breaks out again at every moment, however careful one may be otherwise."

25. Behind Nietzsche's discussion of science in HAH lies Kant, who distinguished natural science (as epitomized by Newtonian mechanics, and as secured in its relevance to experience by his transcendental analysis) from the life-sciences, whose basic conceptualization (that of life, the organic) involves purpose and purposes and thus notions which go beyond those integral to the determination of an object as such. If (in some analogy to Kant) the evolutionary account which Nietzsche is drawing on is 'scientific' but in a sense other than that of the (natural) 'science' which Kant focused on, then in order for Nietzsche's account of "the physiology and history of the evolution of organisms and concepts" to make a valid claim to truth it would have to involve two things: one, an accurate conceptualizing of living beings without using the fiction-concepts of 'nature', 'substance', 'cause', 'number', etc.; two, a different conception of the status of space and time. For if the conceptual frame for understanding life has meaning only granting the intuitional-falsities of space and time, it would still be only a 'truth' relating (in this case, accurately and not simply approximatingly) to the falsity-stabilized appearance amidst which living beings appear and thus be unable to give (or be basis for) any *true* (corresponding-with-what-is-real) account.

26. How does he know that such a disparity exists? He would have to claim (and justify that claim) that reality itself is (say) a flux and thus such that all truth-claims that impose fixity on it are false. But would that claim not undermine itself, being itself a fixed and unchanging (linguistic and mental) reality (so long as it is being made)? Yet how else could it be tested and confirmed or disconfirmed if it did not stand still in this way? In reality, in HAH Nietzsche is beginning on a skeptical inquiry into the foundations of scientific knowledge which, addressing and criticizing a certain modern view of nature (as a system of substances interacting in mechanical fashion that is made intelligible by mathematical laws of motion, etc.: a view which Kant enshrines), will lead to a revised view of nature, intelligible under different notions (involving energy and process, say), and not to an ultimate skepticism or denial of the possibility of any genuine knowledge. But his unqualified way of phrasing matters here at the start really precludes any insight into reality as an intelligible energy-and-process system, and will have to be modified if such insight is to be possible.

27. For example, HAH-I/9 ("Metaphysical world") suggests that there could be a metaphysical world (the absolute possibility is hardly to be disputed), but "one could assert nothing at all of the metaphysical world except that it was a being-other, an inaccessible, incomprehensible being-other; it would be a thing with negative qualities. Even if the existence of such a world were never so well demonstrated, it would stand fast that knowledge of it would be the most indifferent of all knowledge". For "we behold all things through the human head and cannot cut off this head; while the question nonetheless remains what of the world would still be there if one had cut it off. This is a purely scientific problem and one not very much suited to bother people; but all that has hitherto made metaphysical assumptions *valuable, terrible, delightful* to them, all that has begotten these assumptions, is passion, error and self-deception; the worst of all methods of acquiring knowledge, not the best of all, have taught belief in them. When one has disclosed these methods as the foundation of all extant religions and metaphysical systems, one has refuted them!" In this aphorism, Nietzsche verges on confusing two different senses of the "in itself" when he claims that the question of "what of the world would still be there" is a *scientific* one. For if one cut off the human head, the 'objective world'-- what science and scientific knowledge determine as the "in itself" of *things of experience*-- would also disappear; it is rather the "in itself" *beyond* experience that would remain, and this is nothing which science and its knowledge have anything to say about. See also HAH-I/29 ("Drunk from the odor of blossoms"). More precisely stated, the thought of the two aphorisms seems to be that, while in philosophical vein one may think of a 'metaphysical world' (the 'in itself' of reality) beyond experience, that thinking is quite empty; all color and character attributed to such a world, and any pretense to knowing it as having such color and character, are spurious, and amount to the projection onto that empty 'in itself' *beyond* experience of experiential coloration which, in fact, arises and has its being only subjectively, in our encounter with the scientifically-determinable 'in itself' of the world *of experience*.

28. S-I/457-458.

29. The 'thing' to which sensible content is being attributed as part of *its* appearance to us (the thing of experience) is thus *not* the reality (thing-in-itself, or even that thing as affecting our sensibility) involved in the impacting that originally generated the sensible content; this 'thing' is at best the experiential surrogate for that originative reality, which in no way directly discloses how this reality might be constituted in its nature and existence as something independent and apart from anything else (as the 'thing in itself').

30. In Kant the phrase "in relation to us" may signify things as affecting us so that there is something given to us in our sensibility (the interacting whereby there is such affecting is not part of experience but presupposed by experience), but it may signify the appearing thing of experience which is a construct of ours reflecting what

we have made of the given when we conceptualize it. While rejecting the "in itself", Nietzsche does not specify the "in relation to" as he means it but allows the phrase to mean either or both: the relative-to-us character of other beings so far as they are party to the pre-experiential interactive matrix within which experience is generated, or the dependent relation of the thing of experience on the capacities of ours that constitute the experienced thing and make it different from the thing in itself.

31. How the reality of others *appears to us* is different from how that reality is being realized out of itself in the interacting, and is different as well from the *appearing* of that reality *to us*. In this initial moving beyond Kant, Nietzsche seems unwittingly to take up with the interacting in disregard for the multi-party participation in any disclosure, and for how the disclosure (even that in only one party: ourselves, say) is the manifestation of the *multi-* in the interacting. There is no *interacting* if there is only one 'party' self-enclosed to itself, and there would be no disclosure of *any party* in the interacting (no disclosure of ourselves to ourselves, say) if disclosure were reducible simply to a 'semblance' which 'appeared' within the self-enclosure of one 'party'. For that 'party' would be no participant in an interacting. We are disclosed to ourselves *only as participants*, and find ourselves as such *only as we find others also* as such-- the others with whom we are interacting. Here at the beginning, Nietzsche not only disregards the interacting as *interacting*, but abstracts the 'disclosive' experiencing from ourselves-*participating* (as if the disclosing were not disclosive in and to a participating party which, as such, is involved with what is beyond itself and is finding disclosure as disclosure of this interacting). In this first work of the second phase of his thought, Nietzsche is still Kantian in ways he does not yet recognize, however much he may be attempting to deny the Kantian; and the way he initially proceeds indicates that he is still stuck with 'in relation to', and with the focus on disclosive conscious experience, as the proper remainder once the 'in itself' is rejected. By the time of *Beyond Good and Evil*, however, he can remark (aphorism 15): "To carry on physiology with a good conscience, one must insist that the sense organs are *not* phenomena in the sense of idealistic philosophy; as such they could not be causes! Sensualism, therefore, at least as a regulative hypothesis, if not as a heuristic principle.-- What? And others even say that the external world is the work of our organs? But then our body, as a part of this external world, would be the work of our organs! But then our organs themselves would be-- the work of our organs! It seems to me that this is a fundamental *reductio ad absurdum*, assuming that the conception of a *causa sui* is something fundamentally absurd. Consequently, the external world is *not* the work of our organs--?" (S-II/579 [K-BGE/22-23]).

32. What is happening in the shift taking place in Nietzsche's philosophizing can be framed by way of the duality in the meaning of "becoming" which we found in Nietzsche's usage in UHH. There is that becoming which is internal to the being of a temporal thing, and which amounts to the becoming more fully itself of the being in question-- the actualization of its potential, say; and there is the becoming which involves novelty and change, a becoming in which a being becomes other and different as time moves on. Both involve the continual ongoing of time, but mean a different aspect of what is happening in the course of that ongoing. Now in any realization of the 'historical' mode of philosophizing, reflection could attend to things as becoming-beings, seek temporal origins and beginnings, and utilize the reflective agent's own becoming-being as entryway and resource for inquiry, in all this giving emphasis to what is temporal in either of these senses. Seen in this reference, we can characterize the shift in Nietzsche's way of philosophizing by saying: in the first phase of his thinking, the inward 'becoming what one is' received primary emphasis and focus, and the temporal (including the evolution of life) became explored with attention mainly to the matter of individual (human) growth-and-maturation; but in the second phase of his thought, Nietzsche's emphasis and focus shift to becoming as change. Not simply that, but it is change that is visible in the outward side of life that dominates attention and calls for primacy in our understanding of life. The biological and evolutionary being the most plausible frame of reference for understanding living beings (including ourselves) in their outward face, the first-phase reading of evolution, now deprived of the creational-and-cultural-end-and-meaning that (in SE, say) illuminated evolutionary life by way of our grasp of individual growth-and-maturation, becomes replaced by a second-phase psychological probing which seeks to reverse the perspective and to make intelligible the moving forces in the outwardly visible evolutionary development of life (pre-human and human) by recourse to the *primitive* (*not the culminating*) elements of a living being's inwardness and to subsequent complications of those elements. Our current being and experience then become grasped as derivative (subsequent and higher) outcomes of the ages-long process of life's most primitive reaching. This means, for one thing, that we cannot take ourselves-as-we-currently-are as, in and by our full current determinateness, manifesting the constitution of our own (= human) being as it has always been and will always be. And given that our own (= human) being is changing over the course of evolution, it means, for a second thing, that we can not take our inquiring-and-truth-ascertaining powers to represent something unchanging and always available to us; the powers found in human beings of later ages and generations are different and, so far as the ascertaining of truth is concerned, greater. As we shall see, various complications (indeed, conflicts) arise as a result of this new approach, particularly when it comes to understanding

the moral but also in regard to the matters at issue here, namely, responsible thought and understanding of reality. For the terms in which one readily approaches these in the indirect outward-emphasizing address of this second phase make difficult (indeed, impossible) adequate understanding of the normative both in morality and in asserting and assessing truth claims. More on this later.

33. HAH-I/2 ("Hereditary failure of philosophers").

34. HAH-I/16 ("Appearance and thing-in-itself").

35. HAH-I/16.

36. As we will see in discussion later in this chapter, this register, which in the first phase thought of SE (see Chapter 6, pages 134-137 above) is of a claiming in the mode of the normative (obligation), becomes understood in the explicit thought of HAH with a stress on *Not* in meanings (need, distress) that are not necessarily and expressly normative as commonly intended. In his discussion, however, Nietzsche seems *implicitly* to keep the normative alive in his sense of the bearing (in this modality, that of need) of the at-stake on the decision-making in ourselves as active beings.

37. HAH-I/31 ("The illogical as necessary").

38. HAH-I/32 ("Being unjust as necessary"); see also /103 ("The innocent element in wickedness") and /104 ("Self-defense").

39. Thus Nietzsche can affirm (in HAH-I/518: "The human lot"): "he who considers more deeply knows that, whatever his acts and judgments may be, he is always wrong [*unrecht hat*]."

40. HAH-I/32.

41. HAH-I/618.

42. Thus in HAH-I/282, Nietzsche can speak of the philosopher as having, in contrast with the scholar, "the quite different and higher task of commanding [*befehligen*] from a lonely position the whole militia of scientific and learned men and showing them the paths to and goals of culture". Even if others acknowledged the philosopher's concern was for an at-stake underlying all human life (including their own), what would give the philosopher authority as a commander? Would it be his possession of a 'compelling truth', due to his having responsibly sought out in reflection and adequately discerned the at-stake for human life and having determined on that basis the goals of culture and the paths toward those goals? Or would it be something about his/her own person and being as a conscientious thinker that would be (quite apart from any deliberate intention) compelling for the will of others (as in the case of the impact of Schopenhauer's courage and honesty on Nietzsche, say)? Or ... ?

43. HAH-I/292.

44. See Chapter 2, pages 20-29, and Chapter 8, pages 186-189, for discussion of his retrospective accounts of this turn and of the way he initially made his way forward after the disenchantment marking the turn.

45. See HAH-I/34, for example.

46. HAH-I/287. See also HAH-I/291 ("Prudence of free spirits").

47. The longing for, and achieving of, such freedom has larger life-consequences. See HAH-I/288 ("Accessory success"): "He who earnestly [*ernstlich*] wants to be free will thereby (as accompaniment, and without any compulsion) lose the inclination toward faults and vices; he will likewise be assailed by annoyance and ill-humor less and less often. For his will [*Wille*] wants nothing more ardently [*angelegentlicher*] than knowing [*Erkennen*] and the means to this, that is: the enduring condition [*andaurenden Zustand*] in which he is most capable [*tüchtigsten*] of knowing [*Erkennen*]." Also HAH-I/464 ("Moderation"): "The full resoluteness of thinking and inquiring, thus free-spiritedness that has become a property of character, makes for moderation in action; for such resoluteness weakens covetousness, draws much of the available energy to itself for the promotion of spiritual purposes, and shows the merely half-usefulness or the total uselessness and perilousness of all sudden changes."

48. HAH-I/34 ("On tranquilizing").

49. HAH-I/34.

50. HAH-I/37.

51. HAH-I/37.

52. HAH-I/106 ("At the waterfall"). As Nietzsche uses the term "necessity", it means numerous things. In denying the freedom of the will, one of his reference points is Kant and Schopenhauer, and the thought of causal necessity. Thus he agrees with Schopenhauer that "the insight into the strict necessity of human actions is the boundary line which divides *philosophical* heads from others", and he affirms: "we *are* in prison, we can only *dream* ourselves free, not make ourselves free". (HAH-II/MMO-33). But the hidden tension of different meanings used as if they were one, comes out in HAH-II/MMO-363 ("The fatalist"), when he says: "You *have to* [*du mutzt*] believe in fate-- science can compel [*zwingen*] you to." In the "have to" and the "compel", there is no causal necessity at work, but necessity of a quite different order, one of obligation and one that depends for its working on the freedom to think otherwise.

53. Nietzsche also approaches this matter in a different vein, when he is detailing (in HAH-I/18: "Basic

questions of metaphysics") the various fictionalizations which are at the root of scientific knowledge. There he speaks of our false belief "that all sensations and actions are acts of free will. When the sentient [*fühlende*] individual observes itself, it regards every sensation, every change, as something *isolated* (that is, unconditioned, disconnected): it emerges out of us independently of anything earlier or later. (We are hungry, say, but originally [*ursprünglich*] we do not think that the organism wants to sustain itself; this feeling seems rather to be asserting itself [*sich ... geltend zu machen*] without reason [*Grund*] or purpose, it is isolated and taken as will-full [*willkürlich*].)" Nietzsche reiterates this approach in HAH-II/WS-11 ("Freedom of the will and isolation of facts"). There he urges that in virtue of our usual imprecise mode of observation, we isolate a group of phenomena as a unit and call it a fact, separating it off by an empty space from other facts; but "in truth, all our acting and knowing is no succession [*Folge*] of facts and empty spaces, but a continuous flux." Belief in the freedom of the will is incompatible with the idea of a "continuous, homogeneous, undivided, indivisible flowing: it presupposes that *every individual action is isolated and indivisible*; it is an *atomism* in the domain of willing and knowing." [One might note this paradox about such an approach: if it is in a fictionalizing (a grasping of continuity as discontinuous) that we in effect generate what we call facts, then not only are individual actions and acts of will fictive, so are the words and the language which speak of matters in this way and make the claims we do.]

54. See HAH-II/WS-11 for the characterizing phrase, which relates directly to our activity and indirectly to the time which enables it.

55. HAH-II/WS-9 ("Where the doctrine of free-will has arisen"). Nietzsche ends this aphorism by claiming that in this linkage of pairs, we are transferring to the metaphysical domain a coupling that is part of experience in the socio-political domain. For in the latter domain, the strong man is also the free man, "lively feeling [*lebendiges Gefühl*] of joy and sorrow, elevation of hope, boldness in desire, powerfulness in hatred" being properties of "the rulers and the independent, while the subjected man, the slave, lives dull [*stumpf*] and oppressed. The teaching of the freedom of the will is an invention of *ruling* classes."

56. Thus Nietzsche can speak (in HAH-II/WS-61: "Turkish fatalism") of how each human being (including his follies and his acts of intelligence) is himself a "piece of fate". In this meaning of "fate", it is not something external to the human being and compelling it against its will (what is envisioned in Turkish fatalism), but is the person him-/herself: "you yourself ... are the invincible *moira*, enthroned even above the gods, in regard to whatever comes; you are the blessing or the curse and in any event the fetters in which the strongest lies captive; in you the whole future of the world of man is predetermined [*vorherbestimmt*] ... ." Yet if one is only one "piece of fate", how is the world of man as a whole predetermined in oneself? In HAH-I/208 ("The book almost becoming a human being"), Nietzsche phrases the matter in another way:"If one now considers that every action of a human being ... becomes in some manner [*auf irgendeine Art*] occasion [*Anlatz*] for other actions, decisions, thoughts, that all that happens is indissolubly knotted fast with all that will happen, so one knows the actual *immortality* which there is, that of motion: what has once moved, is included and eternalized in the total-union of all that is [*dem Gesamtverbande alles Seienden*] like an insect in amber." Things are knotted fast together in a peculiar way so that, in occasioning other things, any action is effective as tied in with everything else. This is what later becomes conceived as the "fate" of Nietzsche's "love of fate" [*amor fati*].

57. HAH-II/WS-10 ("Feeling no new chains").

58. Nietzsche's account has its predecessor in Spinoza, who develops it in his *Ethics* by contrasting freedom with bondage. Thinking Nietzsche through with Spinoza in mind is very fruitful, here and elsewhere.

59. In HAH, Nietzsche is venturing in various directions at once, and beginning on paths of thought which within that work not only are unfinished but are also not being constrained by their current apparent inconsistency with each other. At the same time as he is criticizing a certain notion of nature, he is appealing to an aspect of it and employing it, and connecting it with another notion of nature that has its roots in the Greeks (Aristotle, in particular) but is becoming shaped by himself somewhat differently. It is as if he trusts that when he has pursued the various paths thoroughly what will emerge on them will fit together well enough, and that a too early concern about consistency and system will only stifle the needed development of thought. That makes for difficulty in understanding him at times. In GS, Nietzsche provides an appropriate characterization of what is taking place in HAH, and indeed, in larger perspective, in his own evolution over time, and of its baffling character to his readers. An aphorism from Part 5 (371: "We incomprehensible ones [*Unverständlichen*]") reads (in part): "Have we ever complained of being misunderstood, misjudged, misidentified, slandered, misheard, and not heard? Precisely this is our lot-- oh, for a long time yet! let us say (to be modest) until 1901-- it is also our distinction; we would not hold ourselves sufficiently in honor if we wished that it be otherwise. We are misidentified because we ourselves are growing, we keep changing, we shed our old tree-bark, we shed our skins every spring, we keep becoming ever younger, fuller of future, taller, stronger, we drive our roots ever more powerfully into the depths-- into evil-- while at the same time we embrace the heavens ever more lovingly, more broadly, and drink into ourselves their light every more thirstily with all our twigs and leaves. Like trees,

we grow-- this is difficult to understand, like all life!-- not in *one* place only, but everywhere, not in *one* direction only but equally upward and outward and inward and downward; our energy pushes simultaneously into trunk, branches, and roots, we are no longer free to do only one particular thing, to *be* only one particular thing ... ."

60. HAH-I/39 ("The fable of intelligible freedom").

61. Nietzsche seems to be thinking (in HAH-I/39) that since our *nature* (including the transmitting endowment which is presupposed and involved in our activity 'out of ourselves') is "a completely necessary consequence" which "is concretized from elements and influences of past and present things", it follows that our activity, so far as it is the operating of that nature, is thereby itself necessitated to be what it is. But that would be so only under certain meanings of "completely necessary consequence", "concretized", and "necessitated". If among the given elements of our nature or natural endowment is to be found (say) a *responsive* power of initiative, then because of the nature of such a power the initiative and activity formed in its functioning would not be *causally* determined at all; but neither would they be "free" in the sense of "formed by a free will". They would, however, be expressions-- direct natural expressions-- of the responsive power of our nature, of the responsive spontaneity of that nature.

62. In HAH-I/39, Nietzsche is critical of Schopenhauer's claim that our 'consciousness of guilt' signifies that we are genuinely responsible for our actions. To make this intelligible while nonetheless conceding that our actions run their course with necessity, Schopenhauer urges that the 'consciousness of guilt' points to a freedom related only indirectly to our actions but directly to our nature: we are free to be such-and-such, not to do such-and-such, and what we *are* is determined by our will. Since our actions follow from our nature (being such-and-such, we act in such-and-such ways), the guilt relates back to the will as the basic cause of the character of the being of the individual, and as indirectly responsible thereby for actions which take place with necessity out of the nature which the will has freely determined upon. Nietzsche simply dismisses the consciousness of guilt as founded on an error. But in this matter, there is implicitly raised two important issues. One concerns the nature of nature: in what sense (if any) is it determinative of action? The second concerns the difference between being responsible for our lives and natures, and being responsible for our actions. If the latter is a responsibility for generating some result in function of our initiative, the former is not of that character at all; responsibility in that case is a matter of taking our nature into our care as that for which we are now the party whose activity is the vehicle for realizing that nature in accord with its meant-to-be. How Nietzsche now treats this matter of responsibility for our lives and natures, we shall see later.

63. HAH-I/39.

64. HAH-I/105 ("Justice that rewards").

65. HAH-I/102 ("A human being's actions are always good").

66. HAH-II/WS-28 ("Capriciousness in the apportionment of punishment").

67. HAH-II/WS-23 ("Whether the adherents of the doctrine of free-will have the right to punish?").

68. "There is no longer an 'ought'; morality, insofar as it was an 'ought', is negated by our manner of considering matters just as religion is" [*ein Sollen gibt es nicht mehr; die Moral, insofern sie ein Sollen war, ist ja durch unsere Betrachtungsart ebenso vernichtet wie die Religion.*]. HAH-I/34.

69. HAH-I/34.

70. HAH-I/104. According to HAH-I/107 ("Non-accountability and innocence"), life's drive is toward self-enjoyment, and accordingly, toward the enjoyment of power or the excitation of the feeling of power: this is what the life in us wants; if it is power that is at-stake for us as living beings, then, and this registers in us as what we want, what is the mode of its appeal? In his first-phase thought, it would be normative, in the vein of obligation, as in the call of conscience-- a call construed as the summons of the life in us. Now when in this second-phase Nietzsche rejects the 'shall', 'should', 'ought', what he mainly has in mind is the 'thou shalt' that comes from without; but in keeping with the altered sense of nature, he also no longer speaks of the call of conscience (which seems unavoidably to introduce the normative rather explicitly) and speaks instead of the mode of appeal of the life in us as that of a *Not* in the sense of "need, distressing-need". While explicitly this does not carry the normative in the obvious way the idea of the call of conscience did, it nonetheless seems *implicitly* to carry the normative claim of the at-stake, and more precisely, to maintain the normative hiddenly because *in undifferentiation from* something further which gives it a non-normative face and allows him to proceed as if the normative has been eliminated altogether. Nietzsche's express rejection of the 'shall', then, and his elimination of the language of the call of conscience (which seems overtly normative in its appeal) in favor of the language of *Not,* is not quite what it seems, but is a forefront modification which continues to reflect his failure to differentiate the at-stake and its claiming-bearing on our initiative from life's urgency-- a failure which indeed may attest how things seem in youth but which nonetheless is still a failure. See the discussion on pages 214-215 below for another way of putting this thought.

71. HAH-I/94 ("The three phases of morality up to now").

72. The close verbal link of morality [*Sittlichkeit*] and custom [*Sitte*] in German is reflected in Nietzsche's association of the two, and indeed, his reading of one meaning of morality (the morality of piety) as simply the feeling for custom as normative. Thus in HAH-II/MMO-89 ("Custom and its sacrifices") he can argue that customs express two valuative principles: 'the community is worth more than the individual', and 'an enduring advantage is to be preferred to a transient one'; thus customs are socially expressed and enforced patterns which have greater weight than anything individual (individual well-being, lasting advantage, or even survival). Morality [*Sittlichkeit*] then is nothing more than "the feeling for the whole sum-total [*ganzen Inbegriff*] of customs [*Sitte*] under which we live and have been raised-- and raised, not as individual but as member of the whole, as a cipher in a majority. So it continually comes about that the individual, by means of his morality, makes himself part of the majority." For some refinements on the earliest parts of the thought-path which would derive morality from the social, the incorporation of the social, and the transformation of this within us, see HAH-II/WS-40, -44. WS-44 ("Stages of morality") is of particular interest. According to it, morality is first of all a means of preserving the community and warding off its destruction, then a means of preserving the community at a certain height and in a certain quality [*Güte*] of existence. Its motive forces are fear and hope, which are applied the more severely, powerfully, and coarsely, the stronger the inclination to perversity, one-sidedness, and the purely personal, remains. Morality, and further means of attaining its objectives, develops in broad stages, roughly indicated by speaking of the commands of a god, and "further and higher", the commands of the concept of unconditional duty with its 'thou shalt'; then comes the morality of inclination, of taste, and finally, of insight-- the last being above and beyond all illusionary motive forces of morality and holding a clear real-ization of why for long ages humankind could possess no other motive forces. As with all his attempts to a-moralize morality via the social, the scheme presupposes in the social group's members an inward sense of an at-stake and a correlative wanting-and-willing, both of which are left unexplored by Nietzsche and simply presumed to be intelligible without acknowledgement of the claim-and-obligation mode of receptivity to the at-stake that is part of the human condition.

73. HAH-I/99 ("The innocent element in so-called evil actions").

74. HAH-I/45 ("The dual pre-history of good and evil").

75. HAH-I/96 ("Custom [*Sitte*] and customary [*sittlich*]").

76. HAH-I/42 ("The order of goods and morality").

77. HAH-I/96.

78. HAH-I/133.

79. HAH-I/95 ("The morality of the mature individual").

80. HAH-I/95.

81. S-I/900 (H-HAH/322). The aphorism is entitled "The morality of pity in the mouth of the intemperate". In HAH-II/WS-305 ("The most needful gymnastic"), Nietzsche speaks of such self-mastery as involving e.g. self-denial. "A lack of self-mastery [*Selbstbeherrschung*] in small things brings about a crumbling of the ca-pacity [*Fähigkeit*] for it in great ones. Every day is ill employed and a danger for the next day, in which one has not denied oneself some small thing at least once; this gymnastic is indispensable if one wants to preserve in one-self the joy of being one's own master."

82. The self-mastery which is important in the morality of reason is something which requires persistent practise. See HAH-II/WS-305, cited in the preceding Note. Self-denial may be a deliberate practise with no governing concern beyond showing that one can deny oneself this or that, but it may also serve (indeed be simply the by-product of) a concentration of interest and attention in certain directions rather than others and reflect the need to keep attention focused on what is most important and to disregard, resist the solicitations of, anything else. Nietzsche speaks as if there was no real difference between the two.

83. In HAH-II/WS-20 ("Not to be confused"), Nietzsche speaks of "moralists" in contrast with other types of person. Genuine moralists treat the dispositions and soul-states of truly good men and women as problems and seek to discover their origin by exhibiting the complexity in the apparent simplicity and directing the eye to the interlocking of motives, to the delicate conceptual illusions woven into it, and to the individual groups of sensations inherited from of old and slowly intensified. But there are those persons with whom such moralists are readily confused but who have no belief at all in these dispositions and states of soul, and suppose that greatness and purity are only an outward show concealing behind them a paltriness similar to their own. The moralists say: 'here there are problems', while persons of the second type say: 'here there are deceivers and de-ceptions'; thus the latter deny the existence of that which the former are intent upon explaining. Although Nie-tzsche sees himself as a moralist, in his treatment of 'ought' and 'morality' he often seems more like a person of the second type due to the way he exposes the subtle conceptual illusions he sees being involved.

84. Nietzsche's account, then, by recognizing the claiming of the at-stake in the form of the appeal of the good, returns to what is historically prior to the 'free will' of the Christian, namely, to the teleology of the Greek,

particularly in an Aristotelean vein.

85. Nonetheless, note how close Nietzsche is to a Socratic view. Indeed, HAH-I/102 ("The human being's actions are always good") ends as follows: "Socrates and Plato are right: whatever a human being does, he always does what is good, that is: that which seems to him good (useful), each time in accordance with the grade of his intellect, with the measure of his rationality at the time."

86. HAH-I/107 ("Non-accountability and innocence"). The butterfly-image, one of metamorphosis, will recur later (TSZ, for example) in another form, as apt to the growth and maturation of the human being, its coming into its own being in metamorphic movement.

87. See pages 208-209 above, and the passage from HAH-II/WS-9 cited there.

88. In what sense of the term "feeling" is duty a feeling? Is it an emotion and, as such, a motivational force-- "feeling" in that sense? Or is it a responsive register of something impressing itself on us and making itself felt in us through our register of it-- "feeling" in that sense? Or put from a slightly different perspective: What is necessitating in duty, what feeling registers or feeling itself as emotional motivating power? When Nietzsche speaks of duty as if it were the "heat" that makes the thinking-machine operate, it would seem to be the duty-feeling-as-emotion that he has in mind. But if implicit here, and undifferentiated from 'emotion', there is also the *register* of something, it would seem *ultimately* to be a register of the at-stake as claiming human effort, so that feeling (in *this* sense) is thereby a mediating factor for the presence of a power which is normatively at work (by way of our receptivity) in the forming of our initiative. In the aphorism, Nietzsche's focus is on the "duty to see and say the truth", that is, on that feeling (= emotion) which motivates us *to* thinking (it is our duty to think); but if his discussion leaves unacknowledged but hidden in this a feeling in the other sense (= register of the at-stake as claiming), it ignores altogether the extension of this latter *within* thinking so that our application of our mind is *thinking because* internal to the effort (to see-and-say the truth) is a responsiveness to a necessitating which, as it bears on effort, necessitates it to (say) the basing of its conclusions on evidence. That necessitating in which truth is at stake and claims our effort as to-be-sought-and-secured is a limited inflection of the necessitating of the at-stake on our effort generally, including that involved in any duty and determination to think (thus to see-and-say the truth).

89. When Nietzsche makes duty not discussable, he seems to be thinking of it as it is presented by a parent to a child: it is a 'thou shalt' which is presented from an external source, and that source simply says 'this is your duty, do it, no questions asked'. That 'duty' (in the form of an external 'thou shalt' which is 'unconditional' in the sense that no questions are allowed) is a hang-over from childhood, seems suggested by the discussion in HAH-II/WS-52 ("Content of conscience"), where Nietzsche is speaking of conscience quite differently from earlier. In SE, for example, he knows a call of conscience which is the call of our nature which summons us away from heedfulness to the voice of other human beings in ourselves ('public opinion') and toward a heedfulness to our own higher self. In this aphorism in WS, conscience is simply the repository of "all that was regularly demanded [*gefordert*] of us in childhood without reason by persons whom we feared or honored. Thus that feeling of 'must' ("I must do this, omit this")-- the feeling which does not ask, '*why* must I?'-- is aroused by conscience. In all cases where a thing is done with a 'because' and 'why', the human being acts *without* conscience, but not for that reason counter to conscience. The belief in authorities is the source of conscience: it is therefore not the voice of God in the breast of man, but the voice of some human beings in the human being." Nietzsche does not probe into what is involved in 'demand' and 'authority' here, but proceeds as if these could be grasped without any reference to an 'ought'. But what is authoritative about an authority figure the force of whose authority is simply the threat of harm? What is a demand which does not voice the right and the just as what claims it?

90. In its full nature, thinking is an essentially creative effort of inquiry, involving address to a problematic in an exploring, an interpreting, a connecting, a testing of implications and of coherence, and the eventual bringing of these various component activities together in the culminating exercise of thought in which an integration of the offering and assessing of truth claims and a judgment concerning the strength of such claims is central. In the preliminary or subordinate facets of thinking as well as in the culminating facet, there is obligation and thus, say, the demand to proceed in such ways as enable the eventual seeing-and-saying of truth. But we-- Nietzsche included, at times-- tend to focus on the culminating facet in which the obligation-informed activity is particularly concerned with assessing conclusions drawn from premises connected in formally satisfactory ways. But to focus on such formal connections themselves, important as they are in and for our judging, is to miss the nature of the *activity* of thinking and to reduce thinking to a manipulation of content in formal terms. Development and use of computers in the 20th-21st centuries provides a more recent version of the machine-image, and an added impetus to such reduction. In any case, such terms are in no way definitive of obligation itself, not even of the obligation to test claims according to formal standards. (Nietzsche eventually moves beyond the machine-image of thinking; see e.g. Chapter 2, Note 59, for a citation of Nietzsche's eventual claim, made in the later-added Preface to GS, that "we are not thinking frogs, nor registering and objectifying mechanisms with

frozen innards.")

91. Given such a drive, Nietzsche can speak of morality (in its most inward and highest form: rational morality) as that way of self-ordering in which one is able to achieve such self-enjoyment in the highest fashion possible for oneself as individual human being. In virtue of this line of thought, Nietzsche can re-assess Socrates as he understood him in the first phase of his thought, and can speak now (HAH-II/WS-86) of how the time will come when, "to further ourselves morally-rationally" we will take up the memorabilia of Socrates rather than the Bible. "The pathways of the most various philosophical modes of life [*Lebensweisen*] lead back to Socrates; at bottom they are the mode of life of the various temperaments established and confirmed [*festgestellt*] by reason and habit and all of them pointedly directed towards joy [*Freude*] in living and in one's own [*eignen*] self; from which one might conclude that Socrates' most characteristic feature was a participation in every temperament. Socrates excels the founder of Christianity in being able to be serious cheerfully [*die fröhliche Art des Ernstes*] and in possessing that *wisdom full of roguishness* that constitutes the finest state of the human soul. And he also possessed the greater intellect."

92. HAH-I/104.

93. HAH-I/50 ("Wanting to arouse pity").

94. HAH-I/137.

95. HAH-I/142.

96. HAH-I/603 ("Love and honor").

97. The complexity of this matter is visible when we find Nietzsche also saying (HAH-II/MMO-407: "The glory of the great"): "Of what account is genius if it does not communicate to him who contemplates and reveres it such freedom and elevation [*Höhe*] of feeling that he no longer has need of [*bedarf*] genius! *Making themselves superfluous*-- that is the glory of all great men." This thought echoes the remark in WB on Wagner's communicating his own overflowing higher self in such way as empowers listeners to a feeling and perceiving that are their very own. See Chapter 7 above, discussing Wagner the dithyrambic artist.

98. There is a trace of it in the idea of an oligarchy of the creative set forth in HAH-I/261 ("The tyrants of the spirit").

99. Even prior to this, Nietzsche claims that the experiencing of any sort of psychical pleasure or displeasure involves illusion, and one of the illusions involved takes the shape of belief in the identity of certain facts and sensations. For one experiences psychical pleasure or displeasure by comparing one's present state with past ones and declaring them identical or not, as happens in all recollection. (HAH-II/WS-12: "Fundamental errors").

100. HAH-I/34.

101. HAH-I/32.

102. HAH-I/31. Thus Nietzsche can urge that while science calls for a de-personalization of the inquirer and the attempt to function as a purely cognitive being, the scientist as a human being is led to inquiry and to have an interest in science by the joy of knowing and the utility of what is known. "If we had not remained to some extent *unscientific* human beings, what meaning could science possibly have for us?" The commitment to 'objective inquiry' is itself subjective, personal and ego-related. (HAH-II/MMO-98).

103. HAH-I/138.

104. HAH-I/212 ("Old doubts about the effect of art"); see also HAH-I/121 ("Dangerous game").

105. HAH-I/121.

106. HAH-I/138. In HAH-I/130 ("The religious cult lives on in the heart"), Nietzsche indicates that while feelings involve an interpretative element, they are detachable from the original interpretative element and are able to gain other interpretative sides, or even to be free altogether. Thus although the presuppositions behind certain feelings of earlier human beings are no longer believed, the consequences of such a belief-- in the capacity to feel such feelings-- are still present, in the form of the 'inner world of the sublime, affected, full of foreboding, deeply contrite, hope-blessed moods'.

107. HAH-I/260.

108. In HAH-I/72, he urges that "the degree of moral inflammability [*moralischen Erhitzbarkeit*]" of ourselves is unknown to us in advance. "Whether or not our passions glow red hot and direct [*lenken*] the whole of our life depends on whether or not we have had certain emotionally-shocking sights and impressions-- a father unjustly condemned, killed or tortured, for example, an unfaithful wife, a cruel and hostile unexpected attack. No one knows whither circumstances ... may drive him, no one knows the degree of his inflammability." On this matter of how circumstances impact one, Nietzsche further observes (HAH-II/MMO-228: "Travelers and their grades") that we travel through the whole journey [*Wanderschaft*] of life as travelers who are very different in the way we relate to the things we encounter-- different not only from person to person, but even from time of life to time of life in one person's own journeying. Thus he would distinguish five grades of traveler: "The travelers of the first and lowest grade are such as travel and become seen-- they become indeed traveled but are

as it were blind; the next actually themselves see into the world; the third experience [*erleben*] something in consequence of this seeing; the fourth absorb [*leben ... hinein*] what they experienced [*Erlebte*] into themselves and bear it onward with them; finally, there are a few human beings of the highest energy [*Kraft*] who, after all that they have seen has been experienced [*erlebt*] and become absorbed [*eingelebt worden*], in the end must also necessarily live it out of themselves again [*wieder aus sich herausleben mützen*] in works and actions [*Handlungen und Werken*] as soon as they have returned home."

109. See pages 219-220 above.

110. Nietzsche develops this line of thought further in *Dawn*: see the discussion in Chapter 10, pages 267-269 below.

111. HAH-II/MMO-102 ("On the excuse for many a fault").

112. HAH-I/260.

113. HAH-II/MMO-337 ("Danger in renunciation").

114. HAH-II/MMO-172 ("Poets no longer teachers").

115. In the case of the (potential) thinker, Nietzsche suggests (HAH-II/WS-267: "There are no educators") that this involves an emphasis on self-education. "The education of youth by others is either an experiment carried out on an as yet unknown and unknowable subject, or a leveling on principle in order to *make* the new being (whatever it may be) conform to the customs and habits then prevailing: in both cases, therefore, something unworthy of the thinker, the work of elders and teachers whom a man of rash honesty once called *nos ennemis naturales*.-- One day, when one has long since been educated as the world understands it, one *discovers oneself*; here begins the task of the thinker. Now the time has come to call on him for assistance-- not as an educator but as someone who has educated himself and who thus has experience." This would seem to suggest that perhaps in late youth, when one has been 'educated', one can come to discover the beginning point for true education, and thus the task of being the artist of the becoming of oneself (in this case, the becoming of someone with the potential for being a thinker). Thus one can understand how Nietzsche can speak of the degrading character of dependence on teachers, and can say (in HAH-II/WS-282: "The teacher a necessary evil"): "As few people as possible between the productive spirits and the spirits who hunger and receive! For *mediators* almost involuntarily falsify the nourishment they mediate: in addition, they want too much *for themselves* as payment for their mediation, and this must be taken from the originating, productive spirits: namely interest, admiration, time, money and other things. Thus we must always regard the *teacher* as a necessary evil, just like the tradesman: as an evil we must make as small as possible."

116. HAH-I/16,18.

117. HAH-I/41 claims: "That character is unalterable is not in the strict sense true; instead, this beloved principle only means that during the short life-span of a human being, the effective motivation can not scratch deeply enough to destroy the imprinted script of many centuries. If one thought of a human being of eighty-thousand years, then one would have in him an absolutely altered character: an abundance of different individuals would have developed out of him, one after the other."

118. HAH-I/272 ("Annual rings of individual culture").

119. HAH-II/WS-5 ("Linguistic usage and reality"), -6 ("Earthly frailty and its chief cause").

120. HAH-II/WS-37 ("A kind of cult of the passions").

121. HAH-II/WS-53 ("Overcoming of the passions").

122. HAH-II/WS-310 ("Two principles of the new life").

123. HAH-I/274.

124. HAH-I/629 ("Of conviction and justice").

125. HAH-I/630.

126. See the discussion in Chapter 5 on UHH (pages 96, 108, 116, 118) and in Chapter 6 on SE (pages 148, 149).

127. HAH-I/283 ("Chief deficiency of men of action"). See HAH-I/200 for brief examples (in writing and teaching) which give some concrete indication of the meaning of the distinction Nietzsche is making, between the person as individual self and the person in his/her role-activity (as writer, teacher, etc.), and also between activity as bodying forth one's very own self and activity as role-enacting. Cf. also HAH-I/51 ("How seeming becomes being") for one way in which one incorporates roles into oneself.

128. HAH-I/376 ("Of friends").

129. HAH-I/613 ("Age and tone of voice").

130. HAH-I/571 ("Our very own opinions").

131. HAH-I/637.

132. In HAH-I/636, Nietzsche speaks of a certain kind of genius, that of "justness" [*Gerechtigkeit*], as particularly hostile to conviction (or as he puts it: "to what men call 'conviction': among women, it is called

'faith'"). This is spirit seeking to do justice to things, and thus "with hearty indignation avoiding all that confuses and blinds judgment about things. Consequently it is an *enemy of conviction*, for it wants to give to everything (be it alive or dead, a thought or a reality) its own-- and for that, it must know it purely. It thus places every thing in the best light and circles it with careful eye. In the end, it gives even to its enemy, blind or short-sighted conviction ... , what belongs to it as conviction-- and this, for the sake of truth." Reasoned opinion, formed in a judging that is as clear-sighted and pure as humanly can be, is the closest approximation to knowledge we have.

133. It is not clear how much an initiative-power transformed to include the functioning of such practical reflection is being conceived to accomplish beyond the prevention of the conversion of opinion into conviction. If the decision-making that makes for the 'man of action' enters the agent into activity-- into doing, in this case-- in such way as effects a turning away from individual self-development and amounts to a conviction-guided functioning according to one role or another, does a decision-making which holds to the discernment of individual self beyond any roles mean not only a reasoned-opinion guided participation in doing but one in which the agent as 'free man of action' is freed from any role-playing at all? Clearly in the 'free man of action', role-playing is not definitive, but is that because the 'free man of action' is entered into a doing that involves no role-playing at all, or does it mean that he is able to do what the 'man of action' can not do, namely, maintain touch with his own individual being and subordinate any role-playing to it, making any role be a vehicle for self-realization (in tension, presumably, with the pressure of the role upon the role-player to conform to social expectations related to the role). Nietzsche seems to lean toward the former alternative (no role-playing at all), but he does not seem to have thought the matter through very far.

134. HAH-I/632.

135. HAH-I/608 ("Cause and effect confused").

136. Nietzsche is prone to speak of a differentiation within human nature, but to characterize it somewhat differently at different times, depending on the point he would like to make. For example, in HAH-I/627 ("Living [*Leben*] and experiencing [*Erleben*]") he speaks as follows: "When one observes how some individuals know how to be concerned with [*umzugehen*] their experiences-- their insignificant everyday experiences-- in such way that they become arable soil that bears fruit three times a year, while others-- and how many there are!-- are driven through the wave-beat of the most exciting [*aufregendsten*] destiny, the multifarious currents of the times and the peoples, and yet always remain on top like a cork; one is then tempted in the end to divide humankind into a minority (a minimality) of those who know how to make much of little, and a majority of those who know how to make little of much." Does this difference in human beings reflect an original difference in nature, or only a different outworking of an originally identical nature, or ... ?

137. HAH-I/286 ("The extent to which the man of action is lazy").

138. HAH-I/285 ("The modern unrest").

139. HAH-I/164 ("Danger and gain in the cult of genius").

140. HAH-I/164.

141. HAH-I/263 ("Endowment").

142. HAH-I/162 ("Cult of the genius out of vanity").

143. HAH-I/163 ("The seriousness of a craft").

144. HAH-I/230 ("*Esprit fort*").

145. The title of this aphorism ("The ability [*Können*], not the knowing [*Wissen*], exercised by science") points us to the skill itself and its amplification in the endeavor and learning-how of the practice of a science as something to be distinguished from results in the form of knowledge gained and as something to be valued as issue of such practice. Nietzsche is not always as clear verbally about the difference as he is here.

146. HAH-I/235 ("Genius and the ideal state in contradiction"). It is important to understand the mutual exclusion posed here, between strong feeling and supreme intellect, in its context. In HAH-II/MMO-196 ("Two-horse carriage"), Nietzsche speaks differently, but means something quite compatible with what is being said here. He speaks of the link of "a warm benevolence and desire to help [*herzhaftes Helfen, Gönnen und Wohlwollen*] with the drive to purity [*Reinlichkeit*] and clarity of thinking, to moderation [*Mätzigung*] and restraint [*Ansichhalten*] of feeling". Passion as meant in HAH-I/235 is passion acquiesced in unconditionally and without restraint, in contrast with the warmth referred to in MMO-196. There is an echo in MMO-196 of WB, and of the way in which the higher and lower spheres, at first opposites that would stand in conflict, accede to each other and become modified without the tension and difference being altogether eliminated. Keep in mind that moderation and restraint are not absence of feeling, and not less intense feeling; the refinement brings greater intensity, but less of the excitability which would subordinate everything else to itself.

147. HAH-I/234 ("Value of the mid-point of the way").

148. HAH-II/MMO-185 ("Genius of humanity"). Together with this larger temporal context, and with that, the suggestion of a kind of intelligibility in which previous barriers have been broken down, there is also a note

of mockery concerning the human penchant for looking on ourselves as the purpose [*Zweck*] of the existence of the whole world, and for (in all seriousness) being content with ourselves only when we can see ourselves as having a "world mission". But as for our uniqueness in the world: "it is an all too improbable affair. Astronomers ... give us to understand that the drop of *life* in the universe is without significance for the total character of the tremendous ocean of becoming and passing away: that uncounted stars possess similar conditions for the production of life as the earth does-- very many thus do, though of course they are only a handful compared with the limitless number which have never experienced the eruption of life or have long since recovered from it; that measured against the duration of their existence life on each of these stars has been a moment, a sudden flickering up, with long, long spaces of time afterwards-- and thus in no sense the goal [*Ziel*] and ultimate objective [*Absicht*] of their existence." (HAH-II/WS-14: "Man, the world's comedian"). In his focus on the outward and its magnitude, Nietzsche seems here to forget a number of things he otherwise recognizes, including e.g. the sense that a goal is not to be identified with a final state (HAH-II/WS-204), thus that the outward context, extensive as it is and dwarfing (spatially and temporally) so long as one looks in that direction as the sole or primary one, may not provide the whole story. There may be something to Kant's awe in face not simply of the starry heavens but of the moral law, even if Kant's rendering of the matter's nature and grounds is questionable.

149. HAH-I/34 ("On tranquilizing").
150. HAH-I/24 ("Possibility of progress").
151. HAH-I/244 ("In the vicinity of madness").
152. HAH-I/236 ("The zones of culture").
153. HAH-I/26 ("Reaction as progress").
154. HAH-I/237 ("Renaissance and Reformation").
155. HAH-I/248 ("Consoling words of a progress grown desperate").
156. HAH-I/23 ("Age of comparison"). In HAH-II/MMO-179 ("Good fortune of the times"), Nietzsche points to his own present-day time as fortunate in two regards, one concerning its future and the other its past. As for the past, the present contrasts with the earlier cultures in this, that they were capable of enjoying only themselves and not what lay outside themselves, whereas we know a past which holds all the cultures that have ever been and their productions. We can thus nourish ourselves with the noblest blood of every age.
157. HAH-I/249 ("To suffer from the cultural past"). Yet there is also a heroic side in all that past, so that in HAH-II/MMO-184 ("How the history of nature is to be told"), Nietzsche urges to the telling of "the history of the war of spiritual-moral force against anxiety, fantasy, inertia, superstition, folly, and its victory over them", and doing this in a vein such that "everyone who hears it is irresistibly swept up into a striving after spiritual and bodily health and vigor, into the glad feeling of being the heir and continuator of humankind, and into the need of ever-nobler undertakings."
158. HAH-I/33 ("Error regarding life as necessary for life").
159. HAH-I/25 ("Private and world morality").
160. HAH-I/242 ("Miracle-education").
161. Ultimately, it is not simply modern life that is involved, but also human life up to modern times. In HAH-II/WS-350 ("Golden rallying-cry") Nietzsche speaks of the many chains that human beings have laid upon themselves "so that he should unlearn behaving like an animal". As a result of such chains, the human being "has in truth become gentler, more spiritual, more joyful, more reflective, than any animal is. Now, however, he suffers from having worn his chains for so long, from being deprived for so long of pure air and free movement:-- these chains, however, I shall never cease from repeating, are those weighty and meaning-filled errors contained in the ideas of morality, religion, and metaphysics. Only when this sickness from one's chains has also been overcome will the first great goal have wholly been attained: the separation of the human being from the animals. We stand now in the midst of our work of removing these chains, and we need to proceed with the greatest caution." See HAH-I/40 also, for a similar view of morality and its rigorous laws.
162. HAH-I/450 ("New and old conception of government").
163. HAH-I/472 ("Religion and government").
164. HAH/I-452 ("Property and justice").
165. HAH-I/473 ("Socialism in regard to its means").
166. HAH-I/463 ("A delusion in the doctrine of revolution").
167. HAH-I/442; also HAH-I/481.
168. HAH-I/444.
169. HAH-I/477 ("War indispensable").
170. HAH-I/481 ("Grand politics and its cost").
171. HAH-I/477.
172. HAH-I/465 ("Resurrection of the spirit"). In HAH-I/474 ("Evolution of the spirit as feared by the

state"), Nietzsche speaks of the Greeks and the Greek *polis* in this vein, to the effect that the Greek *polis*, like every organizing political power, was mistrustful of the growth of culture and sought almost exclusively to paralyse and inhibit it. This culture evolved in spite of the *polis*.

173. HAH-I/24 ("The possibility of progress"). In HAH-II/WS-183, Nietzsche speaks of "the idea of a progress of all progresses" and means here a future which transcends "wrath and punishment". He concludes the aphorism as follows: "Let us go forward with one another, my friends, a few thousand years. There is a *great deal* of joy still reserved for humankind, of which men of the present day have not had so much as a scent! And we may hope for ourselves this joy, indeed promise and take an oath to it as something necessary, only provided that the evolution of human reason *does not stand still!* One day we shall *no longer bring upon our heart* the *logical* sin that lies concealed in wrath and punishment, whether an individual's or society's; one day, when heart and head have learned to dwell as close to one another as now they still stand far apart. That they *no longer* stand *as far apart* as they originally did is fairly apparent if we look at the total course of humankind; and the individual who has a life of inner labor to survey will with proud joy be conscious of distance overcome and closer proximity achieved, so that he may venture even greater hopes on that basis."

174. HAH-II/WS-87 ("Learning to write well").

175. HAH-I/25 ("Private and world morality"). In HAH-II/MMO-179 ("The good fortune of the times"), Nietzsche claims: "there opens out before us, for the first time in history, the tremendous far-flung prospect [*ungeheure Weitblick*] of human-ecumenical goals embracing the entire inhabited earth. At the same time we feel conscious of forces [*Kräfte*] in ourselves that allow [*dürfen*] us without presumption to take this new task [*Aufgabe*] in hand without requiring [*bedürfen*] supernatural assistance; indeed, let our undertaking eventuate as it may, even if we have overestimated our strength [*Kräfte*], there is in any case no one to whom we owe a reckoning except ourselves: henceforth humanity can do with itself [*mit sich anfangen*] whatever it wishes."

176. HAH-I/25.

177. Thus in HAH-II/WS-275 ("The age of cyclopean building") Nietzsche suggests that the democratization of Europe is the building of institutions which, as currently conceived, are indeed quite inadequate but which might be adapted to suit the future he is envisioning. This democratization has a current momentum which makes it irresistible, and yet posterity may one day "regard the democratic work of a succession of generations somewhat as we regard the building of stone dams and protective walls-- as an activity that necessarily gets a lot of dust on clothes and faces ... but who would wish such work undone on that account. The democratization of Europe is, it seems, a link in the chain of those tremendous *prophylactic measures* [*Matzregeln*] which are the conception [*Gedanke*] of modern times and through which we separate ourselves from the Middle Ages. Only now is it the age of cyclopean building! We are finally securing the foundations, so that the whole future can safely build upon them. We are making it henceforth impossible for the fruitful fields of culture again to be destroyed overnight by wild and senseless torrents. We are erecting stone dams and protective walls against barbarians, against pestilences, against *physical and spiritual enslavement!* And all this coarsely and literally at first, but gradually in a higher and more spiritual sense, so that all the measures [*Matzregeln*] here indicated seem to be an inspired collective preparation for the supreme artist of horticulture, who will be able to apply himself to his real task only when these preparations have been fully carried out. To be sure, given the great length of time which lies between means and end, and given the great, very great energy and spirit of centuries-spanning labor needed even to create or procure each one of these means, we must not hold it too much against those who are working on the present-day if they loudly decree that the wall and trellis *are* the end and final goal; since no one, indeed, can yet see the gardener or the fruit-plants *for whose sake* the trellis exists." The transformed sense of democracy which would eventuate, Nietzsche alludes to in HAH-II/WS-293 ("Aim and means of democracy"): "Democracy wants to create and guarantee as much independence as possible: independence of opinion, of mode of life and of employment. To that end it needs to deprive of the right to vote both those who possess no property and the genuinely rich; for these are the two impermissible classes of human beings at whose abolition it must work continually, since they continually call its task into question. It must likewise prevent everything that seems to have for its objective the organization of parties. For the three greatest enemies of independence in the above-named three-fold sense are the indigent, the rich, and the parties. I am speaking of democracy as of something yet to come. What now calls itself democracy differs from the older forms of government solely in that it drives with *new horses*: the streets are still the same old streets, and the wheels are likewise the same old wheels."

178. HAH-I/23 ("Age of comparison").

179. HAH-I/25.

180. HAH-I/475 ("European man and the abolition of nations").

181. HAH-I/475. What Nietzsche here refers to as an amalgamation of nations [*Verschmelzung der Nationen*], he speaks of (in HAH-II/WS-292: "Victory of democracy") as "a European league of nations [*Völker-*

bund] " which he anticipates will be the practical outcome of the democratization of Europe. In that league, "each individual nation [*Volk*], delimited according to geographical fitness, will possess the status and rights of a canton."

182. HAH-I/476 ("Apparent superiority of the Middle Ages").

183. HAH-I/245 ("Bell-casting of culture").

184. HAH-I/247 ("Circular course of humanity").

185. HAH-I/224 ("Ennoblement through degeneration").

186. Between higher and inferior, there is not only difference and interplay but also tension. See, for example, HAH-II/MMO-191 ("Pro and contra needed"), where Nietzsche says: "Whoever has not grasped that every great human being has not only to be furthered but, for the good of the general well-being [*der allgemeinen Wohlfahrt wegen*], also *opposed* [*bekämpft*], is certainly still a great child-- or himself a great human being." More broadly, in HAH-II/MMO-186 ("Cult of culture") Nietzsche can speak of the need for both higher and lower, even as there is tension between them: "To great spirits there has been joined the repellent all-too-human aspects of their nature [*Wesens*], their blindnesses, deformities, extravagances, so that their mighty influence, that can easily grow all too mighty, shall be continually kept within bounds by the mistrust these qualities inspire. For the system of all that which humanity has need of [*hast nötig*] for its continued existence is so comprehensive, and lays claim [*nimmt.. in Anspruch*] to so many and such varied [*verschiedenartige*] forces [*Kräfte*], that humanity as a whole would have to pay heavily for any *onesided* preference, whether it be science or the state or art or trade, to which these individuals would drive [*treiben*] it. It has always been the greatest fatality for culture when men have been worshipped ... . Next to the cult of the genius and his force [*Gewalt*] there must always be placed, as its complement and palliative [*Heilmittel*], the cult of culture [*Kultur*], which knows how to accord to the material, humble, base, misunderstood, weak, imperfect, onesided, incomplete [*Halben*], untrue, merely apparent, indeed to the evil and fearful, an intelligent appreciation [*eine verständnisvolle Würdigung*] and the admission *that all this is necessary* [*nötig*]. For the harmonious endurance of all that is human [*Zusammen- und Fortklang alles Menschlichen*], attained through astonishing labors and lucky accidents and as much the work of ants and cyclops as of genius, must [*soll*] not be lost to us again. How, then, could [*dürften*] we dispense with the common, deep and often uncanny groundbass without which melody cannot be melody?"

187. HAH-I/225 ("Free-spirit a relative concept").

188. HAH-I/226 ("Origin of faith [*Glaubens*]").

189. HAH-I/228 ("The strong, good character").

190. HAH-I/254 ("Increase of what is interesting").

191. HAH-I/251 ("Future of science").

192. HAH-I/241 ("Genius of culture").

193. HAH-I/258 ("The statue of humanity").

194. So far as Nietzsche does think in utopian fashion, he sketches out the perfection of the hierarchical order he has been pointing to. Thus in HAH-I/462, entitled "My utopia", he says: "In a better ordering of society, the heavy work and exigencies [*Not*] of life will be apportioned to him who suffers least as a consequence of them, that is, the most insensible [*Stumpfsten*], and thus step by step up to him who is most sensitive [*empfindlichsten*] to the most highly sublimated [*sublimiertesten*] species of suffering and who therefore suffers even when life is alleviated to the greatest degree possible."

195. HAH-I/239 ("Fruit out of season").

196. HAH-I/22.

197. HAH-I/170 ("Artist's ambition").

198. HAH-II/MMO-114 ("Selected reality").

Chapter 10

1. D-553 is a good example of this. Entitled "On by-ways", he speaks in it of his philosophy as "translating" the "constant and strong drive" of his life into "reason". [Note: Except in the case of the Preface, reference to passages in D will normally be by aphorism number and (where helpful) title.]

2. Putting one's mind to things and thinking them out according to the dictates of one's role is one form of what Nietzsche has in mind; others involve (say) accepting the Christian interpretation of things and thinking things out along such externally-assimilated lines (see D/86 for one case of this). Nietzsche's own relation to Schopenhauer and Wagner offers another case where internalization of an originally alien framework provided a diversion of his attention from the thoughts that offered themselves to him from within and that he did not follow out-- had not the courage to follow out, so he claims.

3. D/432 ("Inquirer and experimenter").

4. D/432.

5. D/115 ("The so-called 'I'").

6. There is another side to this, pointed to by Nietzsche in D/105 ("Pseudo-egoism"). In the course of discussing egoism, he contrasts our ego (meaning here, self) with a kind of pseudo-ego, the idea of ourselves which is formed in the heads of others and communicated to us and with which we identify ourselves; in virtue of seeing ourselves in this way, as refracted through others, people "live together in a fog of impersonal, half-personal opinions and arbitrary, so to speak poetic valuations, each alive in the heads of others, and those others in the heads of further others: a marvelous world of phantasms .... . This fog of habits and opinions lives and grows almost independently of the people it envelops."

7. D/119 ("Experience [*Erleben*] and invention [*Erdichten*]"). Later in the same aphorism Nietzsche offers what he calls a clearer exposition of one side of the matter: "Suppose a drive finds itself at the point at which it desires gratification (or exercise of its strength [*Kraft*], or discharge of its strength, or satiation of an emptiness: all are metaphors), it then looks on every event [*Vorkommnis*] of the day to see how it can employ it for its purposes; whether a person is running or resting or is angry or is reading or speaking or fighting or rejoicing, the drive will (in its thirst) as it were taste every condition [*Zustand*] into which the person may enter, and as a rule will discover nothing for itself there and will have to wait and go on thirsting. In a little while it will grow faint, and after a couple of days or months of non-gratification it will wither away like a plant without rain."

8. Nietzsche is still entangled here in the Kantian distinctions which he is nonetheless moving away from. Thus he does not clearly and consistently distinguish the thing of experience (the dog, say) from the thing in itself (the unknown reality whose causal activity is the originating ground for the sense-perceiving in which the thing of experience appears as, say, the dog-over-there). In particular, he never makes clear how the causal activity of the originating ground relates to the phenomenal causal chain whereby he seeks to make the phenomenon of dreams intelligible (see the immediately forthcoming discussion).

9. At this time in his thought, Nietzsche has not yet fully grasped the implications of the fact that "nerve-stimulations" are themselves only part of the phantom world of appearance, like the "motions of the blood and intestines", "the pressure of the arm and bedclothes" and "the sounds made by church bells, weathercocks, night-revellers and other things of the kind". It may be that when we are attending only to what is taking place *within* that world, we may speak of ourselves asleep as not being aware of these 'objective causes' and only feeling the stimulation deriving from somewhere and interpreting its source in our dream. But all of the factors appealed to here belong to the world of phantoms, and what is unknown within that world (whether unknown in the sense of our 'not being aware of', or unknown in the sense of our 'not knowing the physiology involved') is unknown in a quite different sense than is the 'cause' and 'causal impact' involved in the generation of the whole phantom world of appearance. If knowing is a matter of the grasp of things of experience, the 'cause' of 'experience' is unknowable in principle whereas what is subject of the not-knowing of the physiology is not. Nietzsche is as yet also unable to make (or consistently to adhere to) the distinction of the register of the unknown 'impacting cause' working on the unknown 'ourselves-receptive-to-such-causal-impact', from the register of nerve-stimulations whose source is unknown to us in sleep but in principle discernible scientifically by us when awake.

10. If we take up the indication of this aphorism and relate it to Nietzsche himself in this second phase of his thought, we would need to see Nietzsche as burdened in his reflection not only by his reaction against his previous self-deception but by the suffering that marked and colored his condition at the time. In his reflective effort to do justice to things under these twin burdens, he is operating under pressures which impact that effort by coloring the way things and life did-- and could-- appear to him in their immediacy at the time. And yet while that poses a problem for the attempt to 'do justice to' things-and-life within and beyond that time, he will none-theless insist (as in D/82: "Spiritual assault") "we are free to refrain from forming an opinion about this thing or that, and thus to spare our soul distress. For things themselves are by their nature incapable of *forcing* [*ab-nötigen*] us to make judgments." Things, in complicity with our own condition, do however invite, press, solicit, our judgment along certain lines rather than others, and it takes courage and strength to resist this and to form our judgments on sound bases (if we form any judgment at all).

11. When Nietzsche speaks of sense-perception as a *causal* affair, he does not inquire into what causality means in this case (cause *of* experience), as contrasted with the application of causality to matters within experience where both cause and effect are part of experience (cause *within* experience). Nor does he discuss why an objective account (of sensation as the transcription of the resultant nerve-stimulation and of our projection of this sensation back on the presumed source) based on a trust in the immediate disclosive force of sense-perception and concluding to the non-disclosive character of sensation does not undermine itself. For the whole nerve-stimulus account is itself founded in evidence presented in sense, which evidence (according to the account) can not be trusted to disclose reality.

12. In D/128 ("Dream and responsibility [*Verantwortlichkeit*]"), Nietzsche gives us another pointer into the

perspective within which he is working when he attempts to see our initiative in the perspective of necessity. The aphorism is a challenge, followed by a pointer. The challenge: "You want to be responsible [*verantwortlich*] in everything! only not for your dreams! What miserable weakness, what a lack of the courage to be consistent! Nothing is *more* your own [*eigen*] than your dreams! Nothing more *your* work! Stuff, form, duration, play-actor, spectator-- in these comedies, you are all of this yourself! And it is precisely here that you shrink back and become embarrassed in face of yourselves, and even Oedipus, the wise Oedipus, knew how to draw consolation from the thought that we can do nothing about what we dream! I conclude from this that the great majority of human beings must be conscious of horrible dreams. If it were otherwise, how greatly would one have exploited his nightly poetizing on the behalf of human arrogance!" The pointer: "Must I add that the wise Oedipus was right, that we actually are not responsible for our dreams-- but just as little, for our waking life, and that the teaching of the freedom of the will has its mother and father in pride and the feeling of power [*Machtgefühl*] of human beings? Perhaps I say this too often, but at least it does not thereby become an error."

13. In discussing HAH-II/MMO-174 (Chapter 9, 226-227 above), we saw Nietzsche speaking of ourselves becoming artists of our own becoming. The thoughts here continue at greater length and with further refinement that sort of consideration of our decision-making.

14. D/507 gives one pointer to what gardening might involve in one person. Entitled "Against the tyranny of the true", it reads: "Even if we were crazy enough to hold that all our opinions are true, we still would not want them alone to exist--: I would not know why it would be desirable for truth alone to dominate and be all-powerful; to me it would suffice that it has a *great power* [*Macht*]. But it must be able to *struggle* and have opponents, and one must be able to have relief from it now and then in untruth-- otherwise it becomes boring, powerless and tasteless, and makes us be that also." It is a sense of overall life that is the ultimate reference point for any 'gardener's' attending to the development of this or that in ourselves-- supposing that such gardening is to serve life.

15. See D/111 ("On the admirers of objectivity"), for example, which treats of such a development. Nietzsche is not careful consistently to differentiate, either linguistically or conceptually, between that development of feeling which amounts to its being strengthened and evolving out of itself into more refined form as it is drawn into play, from the development of a habit which involves (among other things) the importing and incorporating of what is alien, bringing a modification to feeling which does not arise because (or involve that) feeling which is already there is *evolving out of itself*. He is also not careful consistently to distinguish between imitating overt behavior and imitating feelings. The former does not involve the latter; indeed, in a strict sense, feelings can not be imitated at all, but can only develop within the person as that person's imitating behavior becomes matrix for the person's own feeling. In any case, the thought of the aphorism is that we evolve emotionally according to what we put our energy toward (and that would include discipline as self-discipline in the sense of learning the feel of our feelings and distinguishing things in their immediacy) and according to our response to what is apparent to us in what is around us. In this latter case, our learning includes not simply assimilating in an accepting fashion what is exemplified for us (intentionally or not) but also rejecting what we see as something to be followed (where, say, behavior angers or annoys or irritates us: we see hypocrisy, for example, or unfairness). What was said in D/104 about valuation and the value-judgments we take over from others holds broadly: it is our own feelings that have prior standing, not anything that approaches us from without.

16. For the mature form of this thought, see the discussion in Chapter 1, subsection 2a (pages 6-8).

17. As often, when Nietzsche speaks of these motives as "unconscious", the stress is upon their being "not a part of the deliberate consideration" which forms the heart of our conscious functioning. He does not always mean that we are wholly unaware of what is 'unconscious' in that sense.

18. In D/502 ("One word for three different conditions"), Nietzsche remarks that the word "passion" [*Leidenschaft*] signifies three different conditions. One is an outbreak of the savage, dreadful, and unendurable, beast. A second is an elevation of oneself into a height and grandeur [*Grötze*] and splendor compared with which one's normal state of being [*sonstiges Sein*] appears needy, impoverished and paltry [*dürftig*]. A third is the noblest storm and stress-- noble through and through-- in which one becomes nature in its wild beauty, more profound than what is represented ordinarily in a noble person, namely, nature in its quiet beauty. In D/471 ("Another kind of neighbor-love"), he speaks of "great passion", presumably representing the second condition, and comments on its dwelling within "like a quiet dark glow [*Glut*]" and "assembling there all that is hot and ardent"; such passion leaves a person looking outwardly cold and indifferent, and impresses upon that person's features a certain impassivity. It also makes the person's neighbor-love different from that of persons who are sociable and anxious to please: it is a "gentle, reflective, relaxed friendliness".

19. The aphorism making this claim (D/108, "Some theses"), speaking of that self-enjoyment which the life in the individual wants as "happiness", also claims: because individual happiness springs from "one's own [*eigenen*] laws unknown to anyone", prescriptions as to the path to the individual's happiness that come from

without can only hinder and obstruct the individual's evolution and movement toward that end.

20. D/425 ("We gods in exile!").

21. D/197 ("German hostility to the Enlightenment").

22. D/96 ("*In hoc signo vinces*"). This Latin phrase ("in this sign you will conquer") was the motto of Constantine.

23. D/205 ("Of the people of Israel").

Chapter 11

1. When the second edition was printed, Nietzsche not only added a Preface and an Appendix of some songs, but a fifth Book of aphorisms (343-383), entitled "We Fearless Ones". Since this was composed after TSZ was completed, we shall not be considering these aphorisms here.

2. See GS/4 ("What preserves the species") for an account of this work of such spirits. [NOTE: Except in the case of the later-added Preface, reference to passages in GS will normally be by aphorism number and (where helpful) title.]

3. In GS/153 ("*Homo poeta*"), Nietzsche writes (speaking in the voice of man): "I myself, who absolutely on my own [*höchsteigenhändig*] have made this tragedy of tragedies so far as it is finished; I, who first tied the knot of morality into existence and drew it fast so that only a god can loosen it (which is what Horace demands!), I myself have now in the fourth act brought down all gods, out of morality! What should now become of the fifth? From where am I to take the tragic solution? Must I begin to think about a comic solution?"

4. As *incipit tragoedia* means "the tragedy begins", so *incipit parodia* means "the parody begins".

5. GS/2 ("Intellectual conscience").

6. This thought is repeated in GS/270 ("What does your conscience say?"); it reads simply: "You shall [*sollst*] become the (person) you are." It is no chance matter that the preceding aphorism, GS/269 ("In what do you believe?") reads: "In this, that the weights of all things must be determined anew."

7. In GS/25 ("Not predestined for knowledge"), Nietzsche speaks of an affliction which makes a person unfit to become a devotee of knowledge; he calls it "an imbecilic but not uncommon humility" and says: "The moment a person of this type perceives something out of the ordinary, he turns on his heel, as it were, and says to himself: 'You have made a mistake. Where has your mind been? This cannot [*darf nicht*] be the truth.' Then instead of looking and listening again but more carefully, he runs away from the unusual thing, as if he had been intimidated, and seeks to strike it from his head as fast as he can. For his inner canon says: 'I do not want to see anything that contradicts the prevalent opinion on things. Am *I* made for the discovery of new truths? There are already too many old ones.'" There are echoes here of the Nietzsche's early understanding (in SE) of the reason why in youth most people do not respond to the call of conscience, namely, because of an inertia and laziness, and beneath that, the paralyzing fear which the honesty needed for assuming responsibility for one's life engenders in most of us.

8. In GS/41 ("Against remorse"), Nietzsche claims that the thinker looks on his own actions as experiments [*Versuche*] providing answers to questions. In GS/51 ("Sense of truth"), he adds: "I favor any skepticism to which it is allowed me to answer: 'Let us try [*versuchen*] it!' But I do not want to hear anything more of things and questions which do not allow an experiment. This is the limit of my 'sense of truth': for there, courage has lost its rights."

9. See GS/288 ("Elevated moods").

10. GS/301 ("The fanciful delusion of the contemplative"). According to the claim in this aphorism, it is differences in this receptive, interpretative, and attentional, capacity that differentiates not merely higher from lower human beings, but human beings from animals, and higher animals from lower animals.

11. GS/55 ("The ultimate noblemindedness").

12. In GS/3 ("Noble and common"), Nietzsche contrasts the common or vulgar person (as one who cannot rise above the perspective of selfish advantage, of calculativeness in this regard) with the noble (as a person able to give in to a passion such as that for knowledge). In this case, nobility is defined by a passion for something singular which is also higher, namely, knowledge. In both aphorisms, the singular character of the noble standard of value means that the noble judges the ordinary, the common, the mass, unfairly, seeing it only as not measuring up to its standard (and puzzlingly so, since the noble assumes its standard is a shared one) and missing how the "usual, nearest, and indispensable" is not only what above all preserves the species but also makes a valuable contribution without which the higher could not be.

13. See Chapter 10 above (pages 255-256, 262-263).

14. GS/121 ("Life no argument"): reads: "We have arranged for ourselves a world in which we are able to live-- with the assumption of bodies, lines, surfaces, causes and effects, movement and rest, form and content:

without these articles-of-faith no one perseveres in living. But with this, there is still nothing proven. Life is no argument; among the conditions of life could be error."

15. The imagery which Nietzsche uses here reflects how the original Apollo-Dionysus dichotomy of BT is becoming transformed; the Apollonian dream-world is now a facet of the inclusive Dionysian reality.

16. That Nietzsche does not speak of "truth" here but of "consistency and connectedness" reflects that the scientific grasp of things is one founded in fictions. The self-awareness which is the subject of this aphorism-- the awakened self-awareness of the intellectually conscientious philosopher beyond the scientist-- is being thought as not confined by those fictions but as able not only to see such fiction as fiction but truly to see the true (that is, the-living-and-working). How that seeing can be said, however, is another and difficult matter.

17. Depending on whether one is asleep or awake, what appears in the dream as the dream world seems real, or seems merely fictional. For if we limit ourselves to dream-consciousness, *in it* we are unaware of the world which enters into our waking consciousness and is taken as the real world; we are aware only of that dream world as what is real. We need to bring both modes of experience (waking and dreaming) together in order to recognize the dream world *as dream world* and not see it as reality.

18. The aphorism reads: "In sleep, our nervous system is continually under stimulation by a manifold of inner occasioning-factors [*Anlässe*]: almost all the organs are active, the blood is making its vigorous circulation, the position of the sleeper presses on individual limbs, his bedcovers influence [*beeinflussen*] his sensibility in various ways, his stomach is digesting and disturbing other organs with its motions, his intestines twist and turn, the position of his head brings unaccustomed muscle-states, his feet-- unshod, and not pressing with their soles on the ground-- produce an unaccustomed feeling as does the difference in the way the whole body is clad-- all this, according to its daily alteration and degree, stimulates the whole system by its out-of-the-ordinary character, right up to the functioning of the brain; and thus there are a hundred occasions [*Anlässe*] for the spirit to be puzzled and to seek after the *grounds* [*Gründen*] of this stimulation. The dream, however, is the *seeking and representing of the causes* for that stimulated sensibility, and that means, of the presumed [*vermeintlichen*] causes. For example, someone whose feet are girded round by two straps may well dream that two snakes are coiled around his feet: this is at first a hypothesis, then a belief, with an accompanying representation and poetization in images: 'these snakes must be the cause of that feeling which I, the sleeper, have'-- so judges the spirit [*Geist*] of the sleeper. The immediate past to which he has thus concluded becomes a present [*Gegenwart*] to him through the stimulated fantasy. Each of us knows from experience how quickly the dreamer weaves into his dream any strong sound pressing in on him (for instance, the sound of bells, the firing of cannon), that is, how quickly he clarifies *afterwards* from the dream so that he *thinks* [*meint*] he experiences first the occasioning circumstances and then that sound. How does it come about that the spirit of the dreamer always blunders in this way, while the same spirit is accustomed in wakefulness to be so sober, cautious, and skeptical in relation to hypotheses?-- so that for the dreaming spirit, the first best hypothesis suffices as explanation of a feeling, so as immediately to believe in its truth? (For in our dreams we believe in the dream as if it were reality, that is, we hold our hypothesis to be fully proven.) I believe [*meine*]: how at present the human being still concludes in dreams, so humanity concluded *also in waking experience* through many centuries: the first cause which comes to the spirit to explain something which needs explanation suffices it and is taken as truth. (So according to the tales of travelers savages even today still proceed.) In dream, this primeval piece of humanity practices on in us, for it is the foundation [*Grundlage*] on which the higher reason developed itself and in every human being still develops itself: dream brings us back into the distant condition of human culture and gives us a means for better understanding it. Dream-thinking is at present so easy for us because, in the tremendous stretches of the evolution of humanity, we have become so well drilled in precisely this form of fantastic and cheap explanation out of the first arbitrary idea [*Einfalle*]. To that extent the dream is a relaxation for the brain which during the day has satisfied the more rigorous demands which are placed on thinking by higher culture." Note how Nietzsche here addresses life in a perspective which not only leaves undifferentiated the spatially inward and the spatially outward, but also (given that undifferentiation) proceeds as if memory (an inward capacity) could be *identified with* (or understood as a *function of*) a brain process (an outwardly located affair), and more broadly, as if the immediate register of the sound of bells could be *identified with* the register (in the brain, presumably, even though this is an outwardly located organ) of a stimulation of our physical organ for hearing which is transmitted to the brain by way of the nervous system. Given such assumptions, and given as well the interpretation of the living being as an organism (that is, as a being identified with a facet of its outward organization as a center of life and activity) whose present form reflects and carries on the evolutionary process which has brought it forth, he can not only understand the interpretative process carried on by ourselves asleep as a matter which is *identical with* or a *function of* a brain-process, but he can likewise grasp the activity in question as being the continuing on in ourselves (as evolutionary descendants) of a long-practised form of thinking found in the waking activity of earlier human beings but found in ourselves, who are later in evolutionary terms and conse-

quently more fully developed, mainly in sleep. It is as if the spatially outward and spatially inward are not poles of a whole which is spatially unified in a way that maintains their contrast and whose maintenance alone enables activity and interaction as a concrete affair, but lie as different but causally interacting factors on a continuous plane (some plane that spans them and enables an 'interaction' of the differently placed).

19. "Waking" may eliminate the obliviousness-to-reality-and-to-self that is central to dreaming, but the awakened-awareness that is now integral to our dreaming-on itself can-- and indeed, always does-- in its own way focus, concentrate, and interpret, so as to dis-regard as well as regard, be oblivious to as well as be attentive to. If this were not so, then Nietzsche would be reviving the 'romantic' view of knowing that he otherwise sees as marking his first phase of thinking and as having been rejected by him at the start of this second phase. Even if the free spirit is awake to reality and to itself as participant in reality, it is still finite, determinate, and not absolute, unconditional, in its illuminating.

20. In actual dreaming, the dreamer is not *as such* part of the dream. He may indeed dream a figure which is himself as a part of the dream, but this is not himself *as dreamer*. That self, *as such*, is wholly outside the dream world. When we wake up, we become aware of ourselves as *having been dreaming*, but that still is not awareness of our ongoing dream*ing*. What, and who, is the self who is both continuing to dream *and* awake, and whose awakened-awareness is both of his/her dreaming as his/her dreaming and of his/her being awake as well?

21. Thus D/35 ("Feelings and their derivation from judgments") says: "'Trust your feelings!'-- But feelings are nothing ultimate, original, behind feelings stand judgments and evaluations which are inherited by us in the form of feelings (inclinations, aversions). The inspiration which stems from feelings is the grandchild of a judgment-- and often of a false one!-- and in any case not your very own! Trust your feelings-- that means, heed one's grandfather and grandmother and their grandparents more than the gods present in *us*: our reason and our experience." D/30 ("Refined cruelty as virtue") also comments: "thoughts are not hereditary, only feelings".

22. GS/58 ("Only as creators") claims that "what things are called is incomparably more important than what they are"; "the reputation, name, and appearance, what a thing counts as, the usual measure and weight of a thing-- in origin almost always an error and arbitrariness cast over the thing like a dress and wholly alien to its nature and even its skin-- has (so to speak) grown onto and into the thing due to belief in it and growth of that belief from generation to generation. What was at first mere appearance [*Schein*] at last almost always becomes essence and *works* as essence!" Thus this 'thing', which is in good measure our own creation already (in its sensible appearance, and in the interpretative reading of that), is further modified in the way it works in our lives and actions by how we bring it into the language which enables us to communicate with each other; by naming it, we define it for ourselves as speakers of that language, and bring it to stand has having a certain 'reality' for us and in our intercourse with it and each other. But of course, because such giving things the validity which their name signifies is our work-- the work of our language creators--, by re-interpreting and creating new evaluations and giving new names, we can to that extent change that 'reality'. If 'reality' is 'effective working', then not only the occasioning working of things which makes for the sensuous presence we regard as theirs is reality, but also this, namely, that presence as something which works upon us as focus of our attention and draws out our care, and finally this, namely, the naming that so attaches a name to a presence that for the most part we see that presence only as the name singles it out and categorizes it for us: these amplify that 'reality' or 'effective working' which things have in our living and acting. Thus reality [*Wirklichkeit*] is gaining a complex articulation as Nietzsche moves away from his Kantian and Schopenhauerian beginning-point. In GS/152 ("The greatest change"), Nietzsche presents the outcome of such a re-creation, claiming that "the illumination and color of all things have changed" so that (for one thing) "we no longer wholly understand how ancient man felt the closest and most frequent things (e.g. the day, and waking): by the fact that the ancients believed in dreams, waking life had a different light. And likewise a whole life, with the back-lighting of death and its significance: our 'death' is a wholly different death. All experiences shone differently because a god shone out of them. All decisions and perspectives on the remote future, too; for they had oracles and secret portents and believed in prophecy. 'Truth' was experienced differently, for the insane could be accepted formerly as its mouthpiece-- which makes *us* shudder or laugh." He concludes: "We have colored things anew; we go on painting them continually."

23. Several aphorisms accomplish this in one respect or another. Thus GS/111 ("Origin of the logical") treats of the rise of logic out of the illogical, and the development of the concept of substance, refining and expanding the account of HAH-I/11, 19. GS/112 ("Cause and effect") adds this erroneous belief to the list, urging that while we treat it as explaining something, it is in reality only a description of temporally successive events. Explanation would involve genuine understanding of reality; but "we operate only with things that do not exist: lines, planes, bodies, atoms, divisible time-spans, divisible spaces. How should explanations be possible when we first make everything into an *image*, into our image! It is enough to consider science as the most faithful [*getreue*] possible humanizing [*Anmenschlichung*] of things; when we describe things and their one-after-another, we are learning how to describe ourselves more and more precisely." Properly speaking, the

category of cause-effect means one thing as applicable to phenomena in the 'world of appearance'; but as explanatory, it could relate only to the reality of will, of initiative and activity. But if we do this in relation to the *appearance* of will-- that is, our initiative as we regard it phenomenally--, we miss the reality in question, namely, the exertion of energy, effort, the 'waves' which break against the cliffs (see the discussion of GS/310 below). Nietzsche proceeds somewhat carelessly here when he discusses cause-effect as a duality which we apply not simply to outward affairs but to inward ones as well. In this application, we treat cause as bringing about effect, thus as the condition of the existence of the latter. But "in truth, we are confronted by a continuum out of which we isolate a couple of pieces, just as we perceive motion only as isolated points and then infer it without every actually seeing it. The suddenness with which many effects stand out misleads us; actually, it is sudden only for us. In this moment [*Sekunde*] of suddenness, there is an infinite number of processes that elude us. An intellect that would see cause and effect as a continuum, not according to our type of arbitrary division into parts and pieces-- who would see the flux of what is happening [*Geschehens*]-- would repudiate the concept of cause and effect and deny all conditionedness [*Bedingtheit*]." This way of treating cause-effect, as a fiction that introduces a conditionality into what is only a continuous flux, removes the sense that in the initiative by which we engage in activity we might be 'determined' by 'the past', 'caused' to act and thus 'lacking in free-will' because of this causation. But such an approach, which makes reality temporal as bodying forth the sun-time measure of temporality, creates more problems than it resolves for understanding agency, including thinking and the activity which (among other things) claims that this is the true conception of temporal reality. For even if it enables the present to be the continuously ongoing exertion of effort in keeping with the nature of the exerting center's constitution at the time, how the past enters into that effort, and in what way possibility and potentiality and thus the future enter into it, are left a puzzle, to say nothing of how such continuity comports with the sort of differentiation involved in initiating different activities. On this matter of our agency, and of errors involved in conceiving it, see also GS/115 ("The four errors"), which claims that certain errors about ourselves are the basis on which we have evolved and come to distinguish ourselves as human from the animals.

24. For example, HAH-I/11, 18, 19, 37, 39, 634 (see also 2, 16). For refinements on the notion of errors involved in our sensing and judgment, see also D/117, 210, 424, 426, 539.

25. GS/293 ("Our air").

26. GS/123 ("Knowledge as more than a means"). Note how Nietzsche treats "science" as quite capable of being pursued without this passion: indeed, the latter has very rarely manifest itself in science. Yet it is the heart of philosophy or reflective thought as Nietzsche (or any genuine philosopher) pursues it.

27. GS/324 ("*In media vita*" [that is, in mid-life]).

28. The echo here of the phrasing of BT is presumably intentional.

29. GS/107 ("Our ultimate gratitude to art"). The thought here is echoed at the end of the series of aphorisms which end Book III and which, in EH, Nietzsche stresses as "granite words in which a destiny finds for the first time a formula for itself, for *all* time". (S-II/1127 [K-EH/293]. The quote is part of the EH discussion of GS.). Taking that series as beginning with GS/265 ("Ultimate doubt"), it reads: "What are man's truths ultimately? His irrefutable errors." GS/266 ("Where cruelty is needed"): "Those who have greatness are cruel to their virtues and to secondary considerations". GS/267 ("With a great goal"): "With a great goal, one is superior even to justice, not only to one's deeds and one's judges." GS/268 ("What makes one heroic?"): "Going out to meet at the same time one's highest suffering and one's highest hope." GS/269 ("In what do you believe?"): "In this, that the weights of all things must be determined anew." GS/270 ("What does your conscience say?"): "You shall become that which you are." GS/271 ("Where are your greatest dangers?"): "In pity." GS/272 ("What do you love in others?"): "My hopes." GS/273 ("Whom do you call bad?"): "Those who always want to put to shame." GS/274 ("What do you consider most humane?"): "To spare someone shame." GS/275 ("What is the seal of achieved-liberation [*erreichten Freiheit*]?"): "No longer being ashamed in front of oneself."

30. GS/11 ("Consciousness").

31. GS/127 ("The after-effects of the most ancient religiosity"). Nietzsche goes on to urge that our notions of cause-effect and of their applicability everywhere stemmed from this sense of ourselves as personal willing beings, generalized so that we believed that wherever we saw something happening a will had to be at work. This belief in a personal will at work everywhere, although it has become superseded by notions of mechanical causality (with the accompanying ideas of substances, impersonal forces, and the like), remains our instinctive belief even today, an atavism of very ancient origin.

32. In GS/143 ("The greatest advantage of polytheism"), Nietzsche points out how the art of creating a multiplicity of gods (polytheism) gave scope and cover to this drive toward an individual ideal, enabling it to "discharge, purify, perfect, and ennoble itself'. Morality, even in polytheistic societies, was hostile to such a drive: there was only one norm, namely, man, and every society thought it possessed this one ultimate norm. But in the world of the gods, one could see a plurality of norms: one god was not considered a denial of another

god. Monotheism, in contrast, by its faith in the one normal god, reinforced the moral doctrine of one normal human being. In virtue of that it endangered humanity, threatening it with premature stagnation. "In polytheism, the free-spiritedness and many-spiritedness of man lay pre-formed: the strength-and-energy to create eyes for ourselves, new and our own, ever again new and ever more our own-- so that for man alone among all animals, there are no eternal horizons and perspectives."

33. The phrase comes from GS/299 ("What we should learn from artists"), in which Nietzsche asks how we can make things beautiful, attractive, desirable for us when they are not. His answer is to learn from physicians, but even more from artists. If the subtle power by which they achieve this usually comes to an end in their case where art ends and life begins, we should be wiser than they are and apply it to life, and first of all in the smallest and most everyday matters.

34. See GS/27, 285, 294, 304, 305, for various aspects of this matter.

35. See, for example, GS/12 ("On the goal of science") and GS/302 ("The danger of the happiest"). The first attacks a common aim whose achievement is set for science in modern times, the providing to human beings as much pleasure as possible and as little displeasure. Pleasure and displeasure are linked so as to be diminished together, or increased together. The second recalls the happiness of Homer, and the fact that someone with a Homeric happiness in his soul is also more capable of suffering that any other creature under the sun.

36. GS/318 ("Wisdom in pain").

37. In a comparable vein, GS/19 ("Evil") speaks of life-favoring conditions. "Examine the lives of the best and most fruitful human beings and peoples, and ask yourselves whether a tree that is supposed to grow proudly into the heights can dispense with bad weather and storms; whether misfortune and external resistance, some kinds of hatred, jealousy, stubbornness, mistrust, hardness, avarice, and violence, do not belong among the *favorable* conditions without which any great growth even of virtue is scarcely possible. The poison of which weaker natures perish strengthens the strong-- nor do they call it poison."

38. GS/23 ("The signs of corruption").

39. GS/24 ("Diverse dissatisfaction").

40. GS/124 ("In the horizon of the infinite").

Notes for INTERLUDE

Chapter 12

1. S-II/1120 (K-EH/286).

2. In BGE (36) Nietzsche points us in condensed fashion into what has been happening hiddenly in his second-phase thought, when he writes as follows: "Suppose that nothing else were 'given' as real except our world of desires and passions, that we could not get down or up to any other 'reality' than precisely to the reality of our drives-- for thinking is only a relation of these drives to one another: is it not permitted to make the experiment and pose the question whether this given *is* not *sufficient* for also understanding, out of this kind of thing, the so-called mechanistic (or 'material') world? I mean, not as a deception, a 'mere appearance', an 'idea' (in the sense of Berkeley and Schopenhauer), but as having the same reality-rank as our affects-- as a more primitive form of the world of the affects, in which everything that later (in the organic process) is ramified and developed (and as is fair, becomes tenderer and weaker) still lies contained in a mighty unity-- as a type of drive-life in which all the organic functions, including self-regulation, assimilation, nourishment, excretion, metabolism, are synthetically integrated into one another-- as a *pre-form* of life?-- In the end, not only is it permitted to make this experiment; it is demanded by the conscience of *method*. Not to assume several kinds of causality until the experiment of making do with a single one has been driven to its outermost limit (to the point of nonsense, if I may say so)-- that is a morality of method which one may not shirk today-- it follows 'from its definition', as a mathematician would say. In the end the question is whether we really [*wirklich*] recognize the will as *effective* [*wirkend*], whether we believe in the causality of will: if we do-- and at bottom our belief in causality itself is the belief *in that*-- then we *must* make the experiment of positing will-causality hypothetically as the only causality. 'Will' can by nature operate [*wirken*] only on 'will', and not on 'stuff' (not on 'nerves', for example): enough, one must venture the hypothesis whether everywhere where 'effects' [*Wirkungen*] are recognized will is not working [*wirkt*] on will, and whether all mechanical happening (insofar as a force [*Kraft*] is active in it) is not just will-force, will-working [*Willenskraft, Willens-Wirkung*]. Suppose, finally, that we were successful in explaining our whole drive-life as the development and ramification of *one* basic form of will, namely, the will-to-power (as *my* proposition has it); suppose that one could trace all organic functions back to this will-to-power and that one could find in it also the solution to the problem of procreation and nourishment

(it is *one* problem); then one would have gained the right to define [*bestimmen*] *all* efficacious force [*wirkende Kraft*] univocally as *will-to-power*. The world seen from within, the world determined and designated in its 'intelligible character': this would be precisely 'will-to-power' and nothing else.--"

3. One might think on this in connection with Nietzsche's characterization in EH of the work that comes after TSZ, namely, BGE. After calling it the beginning of the No-saying after the Yes-saying part of his task has been solved in TSZ, and speaking of it as a critique of modernity, Nietzsche speaks as follows: "When you consider that this book follows *after* Zarathustra, you may perhaps also guess the dietetic *régime* to which it owes its origin. The eye that had been spoiled by a tremendous need [*Nötigung*] to look *afar* ... is here compelled to grasp in acute and penetrating fashion what is nearest, the times, the *around-us*. In all parts, above all also in its form, you will find the same *deliberate* turning away from the instincts [*Instinkten*] out of which a Zarathustra was possible. The refinement in form, in intention, in the art of *silence*, is in the foreground, psychology be-comes practised with an admitted hardness and cruelty-- the book is devoid of any good-hearted word. All this is recuperation: in the end who would guess *what* kind of recuperation such a profuse lavishing of goodness as Zarathustra is makes necessary?" (S-II/1141-1142 [K-EH/310-311]). There was a condition-- certain instincts, a tremendous need, an abounding good-heartedness-- out of which TSZ was composed, making it a work shaped by these and expressive of a good-hearted reaching out to share. And as we see from his characterization of TSZ as "music" (S-II/1128 [K-EH/295]) and his characterization of GS as containing "a hundred signs of the prox-imity of something incomparable" (S-II/1130 [K-EH/296]), there was something already gathering force in the writing of GS that makes it a spring-board for TSZ. The signs are not simply the aphorism that contains the beginning of TSZ, and the aphorism that holds its basic idea, but e.g. the increasing coherence, the greater per-sonal presence, the musical development of themes, which we noted in our earlier discussion of GS.

Notes for PART III

Chapter 13

1. Each of the first three parts was initially printed for the public separately and quite soon after being com-pleted. The fourth was completed in 1885, and was printed and circulated privately among a few friends until 1892, when it too was published for the public. When Nietzsche speaks of TSZ in EH, he seems to have in mind the work of three parts which was by then known to his public, not the work of four parts which he had actually composed and was known to very few persons.

2. S-II/1128 (K-EH/295). [References to passages in TSZ will normally be either to a section of the Prologue (for example, Prologue/3 refers to the third section of the Prologue), or to a speech in one of the Parts (for example, I/7 refers to the seventh speech in Part I, entitled "Reading and Writing").]

3. S-II/1153-1154 (K-EH/327-328).

4. That it is also the listening, and not simply the understanding, that requires life-resources can be con-firmed by recalling what Nietzsche writes in speaking of his books in EH. See the quotation from EH in Chapter 1, page 10 above, about the ears which enable one to hear something.

5. II/11 ("Tomb Song"). (S-II/367 [K-TSZ/222]).

6. II/6 ("The Rabble") conveys this sense of the direction he moved in; outwardly, it is imaged by a retreat into the mountains and to the mountain heights.

7. See Prologue/2 (S-II/278 [K-TSZ/122]). The saint is commenting on how changed Zarathustra is as he makes his way down from the mountains, compared with how he was when he first withdrew. He has become a child, an awakened one, his eye pure and the nausea and disgust has disappeared from his mouth.

8. S-II/297-298 (K-TSZ/143). Zarathustra continues: "Suffering and incapacity-- this created all after-worlds, this and that brief madness of happiness which is experienced only by those who suffer most deeply. Weariness that wants the ultimate with *one* leap, with one fatal leap, a poor ignorant weariness that does not want to want any more: this created all gods and afterworlds. Believe me, my brothers: it was the body that despaired of the body-- that touched the ultimate walls with the fingers of a deluded spirit. Believe me, my brothers: it was the body that despaired of the earth-- that heard the belly of being speak to it. With its head (and not only with its head), it wanted through those ultimate walls-- over there to 'that world'. But 'that world' is well hidden from the human being, that dehumanized inhuman world which is a heavenly nothing; and the belly of being does not speak to the human being except as human being." This is the way the criticism of metaphysical philo-sophy, first formulated in HAH, comes eventually to be framed.

9. In II/6 ("The Rabble"), Zarathustra speaks of having had to fly to the heights to find the well of joy that would replace the one which was polluted by the rabble: "Oh, I found it, my brothers! Here, in the highest

heights, the well of joy wells up for me! And there is a life of which the rabble does not also drink. ... Gone is the hesitant gloom of my spring! Gone the malice of my snowflakes in June! Summer have I become entirely, and summer noon! A summer in the highest heights with cold wells and blissful silence: oh come, my friends, that the silence may become still more blissful. For this is *our* height and our home: we live here too high and steep for all the unclean and their thirst. Cast your pure eyes into the well of my joy, friends! How should it become muddy on that account? It shall laugh back at you in *its own* purity." (S-II/355-356 [K-TSZ/ 210]). In EH, and speaking of Zarathustra, Nietzsche claims that it was precisely Zarathustra's "knowledge of the good, the 'best', that made him shudder at man in general; it was from *this* aversion that he grew wings 'to soar off into distant futures' ... ." (S-II/1156 [K-EH/331]).

10. In I/8 ("The Tree on the Mountainside"), he is to be found in the mountains surrounding the town.

11. For "motley" as signifying (present-day) culture, see II/14 ("The Land of Culture"). For the "cow" as symbol of the ruminant and of rumination, see I/2 ("The Teachers of Virtue"), and recall the connection of this sort made in UHH.

12. This is an echo of the 'unhistorical' as UHH speaks of it.

13. Nietzsche's urging to this effect pervades the second phase of his thought.

14. That the chosen people is to arise through dedicated and knowing effort is a thought echoing what was urged in SE, where the matter at stake was an affair of higher culture.

15. The theme being sounded here is much like what we found in SE.

16. Because of its focus on the elements of negativity involved in the reaching for the heights which the assumption of responsibility enters us into, this speech helps us understand something of what was involved in that burning of himself which created the ashes which Zarathustra carried to the mountains.

17. The theme being sounded here echoes UHH and its notion of a horizon as being requisite; for those unable to draw one for themselves, it is needful for them to fit themselves into one drawn by others.

18. In a letter to Peter Gast (Nr. 183, dated at the end of August, 1883), Nietzsche speaks of having received from the printer the proofs of the first two parts of TSZ. In the course of expressing his impression of the two he speaks of the first part as "comprising a circle of feelings which is a *presupposition* for the circle of feelings which constitute the second part". And a bit later he says: "Probably I would, from artistic motives, have chosen darker and more somber and garish colors for the first two parts-- if I had kept my soul cheerful [*heiter*] and bright [*hell*] this year -- for the sake of what happens at the end. But this year the solace of more cheerful [*heiterer*] and airy colors was *vitally necessary* to me, and so in the Second Part I have cavorted about almost like a jester-clown [*Possenreitzer*]. In its particulars, there is incredibly much personal experience and suffering which is only intelligible to me-- some pages seemed to be almost bloody." (S-III/1212-1213). [NOTE: Is "the end", that of Part III, with its lyrical ending? Or is it that of Part IV?]

19. I/22 (Section 3) ("The Gift-giving Virtue"). In EH, we saw Nietzsche speaking of this "great noon" as follows: "My task of preparing a moment of the highest self-examination for humanity, a *great noon* when it looks back and looks forward, when it emerges from the dominion of accidents and priests and for the first time poses, *as a whole*, the question of Why? and For what?-- this task follows of necessity from the insight that humanity is *not* all by itself on the right way, that it is by *no* means governed divinely, that, on the contrary, it has been precisely among its holiest value concepts that the instinct of denial, corruption, and decadence, has ruled seductively." (S-II/1125 [K-EH/291]).

20. In EH, Nietzsche characterizes the time he spent with Wagner at Tribschen as "days of trust, of cheerfulness, of sublime accidents-- of *profound* moments" (S-II/1090 [K-EH/247]), and thus speaks of Tribschen as "a distant isle of the blessed" (S-II/1119 [K-EH/284]). This intimate and fruitful time seems to have been the model for, and reason of, his use of the term as he does here in TSZ.

21. II/2 ("Upon the Blessed Isles") (S-II/343-344 [K-TSZ/197]). The beginning of Part II echoes the beginning of Part I, in that the time of life of the metamorphoses is that when beauty is also of utmost significance. Throughout TSZ, Nietzsche is working to clarify what Plato was seeking likewise to understand; in this case, the beginning with beauty as Zarathustra treats it is implicitly sounded to contrast with the account of the Platonic Socrates in the *Phaedrus* and the *Symposium*, in particular, the ideas of *erōs* and beauty and creativity presented in those dialogues. On this Platonic presentation, see my *Loving and Dying*, 162-174 and 205-223, for a discussion of the two dialogues in regard to such ideas.

22. But also in Nietzsche's own first-phase thought; for this is part of the way he develops his thought in BT and of what he rejects in his second-phase thought.

23. Keep in mind that, as GS/54 suggested and as Nietzsche will be reaffirming here in TSZ in his notion of the will-to-power, reality is what is vital and operative in such interconnecting, so that the thinking which discerns such truth is an element in the responsiveness involved actively in the establishing of such real-interconnection. That is, it is an element in the responsiveness by which we are creating (and re-creating) the 'world'

of experience. The question is whether the spiritual creativity involved is sufficiently powerful (well-founded in courage and honesty, thence also capable and skillful on its interpretative side) to discern reality truthfully as we are finite participants in its making.

24. For thematic parallels with Plato's *Phaedo*, see my *Loving and Dying*, 48-52 and 61-63.

25. This will is the positive focus in the preceding speech (II/8: "The Famous Wise Men"), which in this side of itself leads into the three songs, and in particular, into the rehearsal of the solitude of the lover who gives but knows no gift-giving from others.

26. I/22 (Section 1) ("The Gift-giving Virtue") (S-II/337-338 [K-TSZ/187-188]). This transformatory integration of capacity and resources which turns distressful need into a responsive answering that does the need-ful: such is "necessity" for Zarathustra here. Recall, for example, the account Nietzsche gives in EH, of inspir-ation (Section 3 in the discussion of TSZ in Part III of the work as a whole), and recall as well his account of the distress of the creator in BT. This is not "willing" in the deliberate conscious sense that involves 'choice', but also not something involving reference to a cause compelling something from beyond it; it rather speaks to such participation as comes from deeper sources within (indeed, from one's own deepest self within) and as answers to need not simply in the sense of the at-stake as we are responsive to it but to the need for release, discharge, of built-up tension and energies in a creative act. To understand Nietzsche here, it is important to maintain quite stubbornly-- and faithfully-- the standpoint of the agent participant in creative activity: something very difficult to do without inadvertently slipping into the spectator's perspective and at the very least raising questions that are external and irrelevant to the matter that is being intended to be understood here.

27. S-II/371 (K-TSZ/227).

28. Nietzsche does not use language with technical consistency, and particularly when he generalizes beyond the human situation and speaks of everything that is alive at any level as a center of the will-to-power or when he analyzes the human condition and separates out different components and treats them as alive in their own way and thus as centers of the drive toward power, he will use the term "power" [*Macht*] and the phrase "discharge [*Auslassung*] of power" in ways that belie what has just been said. Not every occurrence of the term, or even of the phrase "will to power", signifies power in the sense presently under discussion. Further linguistic complication enters because *Kraft* (force, energy, strength) and *Energie* (energy) and their deployment are integral to the living being and have a variety of relevant functions related to power and the achievement of power in the sense presently being considered, without this meaning that their presence and functioning is itself the presence and functioning of power or even a sign of such presence and functioning. Indeed, exertion of force can well be an expression of impotence or the lack of power in the sense being discussed here.

29. S-II/300-301 (K-TSZ/146-147).

30. S-II/302 (K-TSZ/148-149).

31. S-II/323 (K-TSZ/171). The phrase comes from I/15 ("The Thousand and One Goals").

32. See I/11 ("New Idols"), especially S-II/313-314 (K-TSZ/160-161).

33. S-II/322 (K-TSZ/170).

34. II/12 ("Self-overcoming") (S-II/371 [K-TSZ/227]).

35. S-II/323-324 (K-TSZ/172). The passage comes from I/15 ("The Thousand and One Goals").

36. S-II/358-359 (K-TSZ/213).

37. S-II/386 (K-TSZ/243). The speech is mostly a dialogue between Zarathustra and a figure called the "fire hound", a spokesman for the revolutionary movements which promise a transformation of humanity and are the liberal, utopian, forefront of the progress in modern and contemporary times to which Nietzsche has been point-ing in mostly negative terms in the second phase of his thought. It is not revolution and freedom in political-eco-nomic terms that is most important, however much noise is made about them. It is rather the revolution which 'God is dead' is bringing, and the inward freedom out of which the new values that can sustain the new world that is emerging are invented, that are central.

38. S-II/389 (K-TSZ/246).

39. We have seen, in UHH, one way in which the will is potent in regard to the past, namely, in the creative appropriation of it which brings it to serve the achieving of new life in the future. But the matter goes deeper here. Not only does such appropriation reshape and distort, but it operates with something which (in relation to the current will) is already there and was not willed by the will in question. Such a will might reconcile itself with what was, but that is not the same as creating what was.

40. S-II/394 (K-TSZ/251).

41. S-II/395-396 (K-TSZ/253).

42. Note that while this disables the will in regard to all that becomes past, such disabling is exacerbated when what is left behind and can not be willed any longer is missed possibility and opportunity, failure that is unchangeable, and in general, those occasions on which the will was not able effectively to reach toward power

and was becoming frustrated in its aspiration. Such parts of the 'It was' become an added burden which cumulatively works to intensify in the will the feeling of being hemmed in.

43. Note that while the matter at issue is not itself death, passage means the dying of each moment in the ongoing movement of life toward its end in death, and the dying out of the future as possibility, hence the increasing loss of time for achieving potency as the past increases and the future diminishes.

44. Parts II, III, and IV, are each prefaced by brief quotations from earlier in the work, and the quotations underline something about the Part they introduce. In the case of Part II, the quote concerns the return of Zarathustra to his lost ones, this time with different eyes and a different love from before. (The quote is from I/22, the end of Part I.) In the case of the present (third) Part, the quote concerns elevation, and conveys a contrast of his audience (who look up when they feel the need for elevation) and himself (who, already elevated, looks down). It concludes: "Who among you can laugh and be elevated at the same time? Whoever climbs the highest mountains laughs at all tragic plays and tragic seriousness." (The quote is from I/7, also in Part I.)

45. Speaking of TSZ in EH, and setting forth the experience of inspiration which was the matrix of the composition of TSZ, Nietzsche says: "The involuntariness of image, of likeness, is most remarkable of all; one no longer has any notion of what is image or likeness: everything offers itself as the nearest, most appropriate, simplest expression. It actually seems (to recall something Zarathustra says) as if the things themselves approached and offered themselves as likenesses." (S-II/1132 [K-EH/301]).

46. In BGE/70, Nietzsche writes: "If one has character, one also has one's typical experience, which recurs repeatedly." (S-II/626 [K-BGE/80]).

47. S-II/403 (K-TSZ/264). The passage is from III/1 ("The Wanderer").

48. The recurrence and the stability are such that he can anticipate that "whatever still comes now as destiny and experience [*Erlebnis*]-- there will be a wandering in it, and a mountain-climbing ... ." (S-II/403 [K-TSZ/264]).

49. D/491 has a very suggestive use prior to TSZ. Entitled "Another reason for solitude", it reads: "A. So you want to return to your desert?-- B. I am not quick-moving, I must wait for myself-- it is always late before the water comes to light out of the well of my self, and I often have to endure thirst for longer than I have patience. That is why I am going into solitude-- in order not to drink out of the cistern meant for everybody. Among the many I live as the many do and do not think as I do; after a time it always is for me as if they want to banish me from myself and rob me of my soul-- and I become angry at everyone and fearful of everyone. I need the desert then in order to become good again." (S-I/1244-1245 [H/201]).

50. In II/6 ("The Rabble"), we find it used extensively, centering around the opening phrase "Life is a well [*Born*] of joy [*Lust*]". In the speech Zarathustra speaks of having to retreat to the highest heights to find again the well of joy which had been polluted at the lower level where the rabble drink the well-water. See also II/8 ("The Famous Wise Men") for "the inmost wells [*Brunnen*] of the spirit"; II/9 ("Night Song") for the soul as a "gushing fountain" [*Brunnen*]; and II/10 ("Dancing Song") for the spring [*Brunnen*] beside which Cupid lies and the dancing girls dance.

51. S-II/404 (K-TSZ/265). This is the experience which, in BT, is the experience of Dionysian reality and (as he interpreted it there) of a 'timeless' reality beyond 'experience'. What was involved there is no longer understood as 'timeless' in that sense.

52. S-II/405 (K-TSZ/266).

53. Recall here Nietzsche's earlier adumbrations of this standpoint and of who can find and stand on it in the way needed: it is that of the "powerful soul" of D/424, and of the "awakened dreamer" of GS/54.

54. S-II/406 (K-TSZ/267-268). In EH, Nietzsche refers to this passage to explain whom he is writing for: "when I imagine an image of the perfect reader, he always becomes a monster of courage and curiosity; moreover, supple, cunning, cautious; a born adventurer and discoverer. In the end, I could not say better to whom alone I am speaking at bottom than Zarathustra said it: *to whom* alone will he relate his riddle?" (S-II/1103 [K-EH/264]). The passage quoted in our text follows.

55. S-II/410 (K-TSZ/271-272).

56. S-II/408-409 (K-TSZ/270).

57. S-II/410 (K-TSZ/271).

58. S-II/410 (K-TSZ/272).

59. S-II/416 (K-TSZ/278).

60. Is something like this involved in what Nietzsche means when, in the 1886 Preface to GS (Section 4), he speaks of no longer believing that truth remains truth when the veils are withdrawn, and of having respect for the bashfulness with which nature has hidden behind riddles and iridescent uncertainties? The peculiar way in which this insight is being voiced in TSZ-- elliptically and enigmatically, with careful concern for how (and when, and to whom) it is or could be voiced-- is not a merely literary device but something intrinsic to the sense

of the appropriate mode of communication of this highest and deepest of insights. But is it only communication that is in question, and not disclosure? Does it also reflect the natures of that whose truth is being disclosed, of the being to whom it is being disclosed, and of the disclosure-relation of the disclosed-affair and the being-to-whom-disclosure-is-being-effected?

61. S-II/436 (K-TSZ/300).

62. Zarathustra characterizes the dream in language that recalls III/2 ("Vision and Riddle") and its characterization of his seafaring companions: it is "a bold sailor, half-ship, half-hurricane, taciturn as butterflies, impatient as falcons". The whole dream image symbolizes a time of disclosure which reaches sufficiently to the heart of the interconnecting in which the whole is taking shape that the bearing of larger circumstance on the human capacity for engaging and finding a meaningful place in existence can be assessed.

63. Presumably the promontory beyond the world is a place within the depths of the present but beyond the active beings (the 'world') which time enables, and the judgment which takes shape at that standpoint concerns the character (infinite or finite) of the interactive existence of beings in the ongoing of time. What forms the counterweight which decides the issue between the alternatives is the nature of reality as will-to-power, that is, the energy-field character of reality.

64. S-II/435 (K-TSZ/299).

65. In the later added Preface to GS, Nietzsche speaks of having unlearned the youthful madness in the love of truth that would "by all means" "unveil, uncover, and put into a bright light whatever is kept concealed for good reasons". "We no longer believe that truth remains truth when the veils are withdrawn." The "bashful" or "modest" here signifies a gaze respectful of and apt to life's concealing ways, aware of these as a participant; the truth of life is not discoverable except in the living, and its self-conscious and reflective recognition is one that is matched to the nature of the truth itself.

66. This weighing is characterized as taking place on the promontory also, but that location is more fully described: here the scales are held "over the rolling sea", and the weighing has a witness ("you, solitary tree, fragrant and broad-vaulted, that I love"). That witness would seem to symbolize the end to be reached by human beings, what in HAH-II/WS-189 ("Reason and the tree of humanity") was called the tree of humanity. A similar tree-image, this time with a slight twist, recurs later in TSZ (IV/10), and again in BGE/258 (the fundamental faith of a good and healthy aristocracy has to be "that society must *not* exist for society's sake but only as the foundation and scaffolding on which a choice type of being is able to raise itself to its higher task and to a higher state of *being*-- comparable to those sun-seeking vines of Java ... that so long and so often enclasp an oak tree with their tendrils until eventually, high above it but supported by it, they can unfold their crowns in the open light and display their happiness" [S-II/728 {K-BGE/202}]).

67. S-II/437-438 (K-TSZ/301-302). The language here closely echoes the characterization Nietzsche made of Wagner's nature and development in WB, with its two forces and their loyalty to each other, which is further interpreted in EH as having belonged to himself ("the close proximity of the brightest and the most calamitous forces, the will to power as no human being ever possessed it": S-II/1112 [K-EH/275]).

68. S-II/440 (K-TSZ/305).

69. S-II/441 (K-TSZ/305).

70. S-II/442-443 (K-TSZ/307).

71. S-II/444-445 (K-TSZ/309). In the next sub-section, Zarathustra says that it is there (in those distant futures where becoming, time, and necessity, seemed such as he has just characterized them) that he picked up the word 'overman', and the thought that man is something to be 'overcome', not an end but a bridge to something over-and-above.

72. In his response to his animals, Zarathustra claims that the world that belongs to any soul is different from that which belongs to another soul. This language, hearkening back to GS and his second-phase thought, means, beyond the fact that all experiencing is first-personal, that the immediacy of the world as we are experiencing it is something we have been creatively involved in constituting, each of us a bit differently. When we talk and 'communicate', we tend to forget this, and are prone to think of language and words as forming a bridge between these two separate beings. But that does not make the difference specious, it only encourages us to ignore it. Souls are eternally other, and they are not dissolved in their distinctness by speech-- words and sounds; but by bringing things to name and sound, we can dance over things in forgetfulness of this being-eternally-other.

73. S-II/463 (K-TSZ/329-330).

74. In the second phase of his thought, Nietzsche was critical of the notion of cause, calling it a fiction, while at the same time he gave some sense to the notion in explicating sense-perception. What is meant here is not a one-sided external or from-beyond necessitation, but the *joint* responsibility for what happens which is characteristic of interactive reality where *all* contribute *out of themselves* (*according to their own natures*) to the character and direction of the happening between them. Cf. III/12 (Section 2) on becoming as the dance and

wanton-mischievousness of gods.

75. S-II/468 (K-TSZ/334-335).

76. S-II/469 (K-TSZ/336).

77. S-II/471-472 (K-TSZ/338).

78. S-II/472 (K-TSZ/339).

79. He speaks of himself as also awaiting "what must come", formulated as "our great distant human kingdom, the Zarathustra kingdom of a thousand years". The contrast in EH of 'Dionysus vs. the Crucified' is anticipated in numerous ways in TSZ, where on occasion Christianity and Christian ideas (here, the kingdom of God and the millennium) are also transformed and secularized by Zarathustra.

80. The two kings seem to represent the old hierarchical order that is a vestige of nobility being eliminated in the leveling movement of modernity. The leech-seeker represents the conscientious spirit of scientific inquiry, what is good in science and scholarship-- yet only as this is specialized and intent on some small certainties. The magician seems to represent Wagner, the human being who is actor through and through. The last pope represents hierarchy in religious guise, a man seeking someone of genuine 'piety' (even that of a non-believer such as Zarathustra), now that his own god has died. The ugliest man is the one who has killed that god, and who is now fleeing the pity of man. The voluntary beggar seems to be man seeking restoration of the spirit of Jesus, in face of nausea toward present-say human beings and in flight from mob-arrogance. Finally, his own shadow or earlier free-spirit self appears, representing the early HAH-part of his second-phase thought. All have something higher which they symbolize, something noble or superior; but all are badly flawed.

81. S-II/556 (K-TSZ/435). The phrase comes from IV/19, Section 10.

82. See the reference in Note 66 above, to BGE/258, where the tree represents society or the mass of dependent human beings on whom-- as on a foundation and scaffolding-- a choice type of being (the vines) is able to raise itself to its higher task and to a higher state of being.

83. This is TSZ's counterpart of the 'awakened dreamer' of GS/54 (see Chapter 11, pages 286-288 above).

84. See II/13 ("Those who are Sublime"), for another type of such experience, in that case the elevation beyond the straining of the sublime, that stilling of torrential passion in beauty. "But precisely for the hero the *beautiful* is the most difficult thing. No vehement will can attain the beautiful by exertion. A little more, a little less: precisely this counts for much here, this matters most here. To stand with relaxed muscles and unharnessed will: that is most difficult for all of you who are sublime. When power becomes gracious and descends into the visible-- such descent I call beauty." (S-II/374 [K-TSZ/230]).

85. S-II/514 (K-TSZ/389).

86. S-II/514 (K-TSZ/389).

87. S-II/515 (K-TSZ/390).

88. Another echo of BT, and the conception there of the deepest joy of the creator with whom we become one for a while at times. See sections 7, 8, 17, and 22, in particular, for the early characterizations of experience such as this.

89. In III/4 ("Before Sunrise"), we find (see page 342, above): "The world is deep-- and deeper than day has ever been aware. Not everything may be put into words in the presence of the day." (S-II/416 [K-TSZ/278]).

90. "Who has heart enough for it? Who shall be lord of the earth? Who will say: *thus* shall you run, you big and little streams!" (S-II/554 [K-TSZ/432]). The warning about refined-and-delicate ears is pertinent particularly for the hearing and understanding of the "lord of the earth" language. In II/22 ("The Stillest Hour"), his stillest hour had said to Zarathustra: "It is the stillest words that bring on the storm. Thoughts that come on doves' feet guide the world. O Zarathustra, you shall go as a shadow of that which must come: thus you will command and, commanding, lead the way." (S-II/401 [K-TSZ/258-259]).

91. In IV/10 ("At Noon"), Zarathustra has said: "What happened to me? Listen! Did time perhaps fly away? Am I not falling? Did I not fall-- listen!-- into the well of eternity?" (S-II/514 [K-TSZ/389]). And earlier, in III/2 ("Vision and Riddle"), Zarathustra refers to the presence of moonlight, both when the gateway Moment appears to him and the spirit of gravity, and in that scene recalled from his childhood (a dog barking at the moon) by a dog's howling. Then again, not only is there a spider crawling in the moonlight of the Moment-gateway scene, but in III/5 ("The Virtue that Makes Small") Zarathustra speaks of the virtuousness of the men of today as "a spider web and a spider, which lives on the blood of the future" (S-II/421 [K-TSZ/283]), and in III/4 ("Before Sunrise") he claims there is no "eternal spider or spider web of reason" (S-II/416 [K-TSZ/278]).

Chapter 14

1. S-I/288 (H-SE/128).

2. S-I/288-289 (H-SE/128).

3. S-II/513, 515 (K-TSZ/388, 390).

4. "In thought", because all actual walking is forward into the future.

5. If time had no inherent bounds, endings and beginnings would be sheer accidents. But that does not square with the sense that has been part of Nietzsche's thought from the beginning, that 'space, time, causality' define 'individuation' (as BT puts it), and with this, the bounds and limits which introduce (among other things) suffering as inherent in temporal being. Implicitly, that is, Nietzsche is understanding time to imply, as part of its *nature* and not as an accident, our finitude in the ongoing side of itself. But that remains only a part of the *implicit* conception of time he attests in his treatments of matters of experience, not something he introduces into his *express* conception of time.

6. Despite the close affinity which Nietzsche feels with Spinoza, on this point of the finitude of temporal reality the two philosophers exhibit a strong contrast. For Spinoza the modal expression of the nature of God is infinite, a boundless universe of spatio-temporally finite centers of striving, effort, energy.

7. It remains, however, that the conception of time expressed in the image, while inadequate to time itself, has a usefulness for certain purposes that involve the outward-and-external and events and happenings as they appear in that region.

8. Oddly and hiddenly, the further characterization of the forward and backward reaches as if they represented two paths whose directionality was convergent would seem implicitly reflective of the way future and past within the bounds of an agent's present do converge on the ongoing current realization in the middle between beginning and end. Yet *this* convergence does not relate to the pathways, whereas that in the image does.

9. S-II/409 (K-TSZ/271). The phrase comes from III/2 ("Vision and Riddle").

10. Note how the Moment is now becoming, in its realization, a series of moments much as in the first-phase conception and in some tension (at least) with the continuity of the flow of time in the second-phase refinement.

11. At first sight, it seems possible to think time as itself finite and yet unending because circular in its onward movement, generating next moments which, while in each case different from their preceding moments, are eventually not different from all preceding moments but the recurring of earlier moments. At second sight, however, such a conception seems problematic. For example, is the notion of a recurrent moment (the occurrence again of the same moment) a self-consistent idea? If "same" were understood in the sense of "absolutely identical", "absolutely the same", a moment could be the same only with itself, not with a moment which is in any sense another; for 'another' involves some difference and thus the lack of absolute identity or sameness, although not, of course, the lack of identity or sameness in every respect. Now a recurrence (here, of the 'same' moment) would seem to involve by its very nature at least a duality-- only then is there a "re-" of an occurrence. But if that is so, one could not properly speak of any moment as the recurrence of some prior moment *with which it is absolutely the same*. Since 'prior' introduces difference and undermines the 'absolutely', the 'prior' could only be the same in this or that respect with the 'subsequent'. Absolute identity allows only the moment itself in its only occurrence.

12. S-II/466-467 (K-TSZ/333).

13. S-II/557 (K-TSZ/435). The phrase comes from IV/19 (Sect. 10) ("The Drunken Song").

14. Note the implications of this from an explanatory point of view. It means that if we seek to explain the current present by way of the past, we are in reality trying to explain the current present by a past present which is identical with it. That is, we can only explain it by itself, and that means presumably, by what is *internal* to itself and its forming.

15. S-II/408-409 (K-TSZ/270). The passage comes from III/2 ("Vision and Riddle"). The language is not unambiguous, in that "moment" is being thought with considerable emphasis on what is present in the moment; but it seems to mean the moment itself as well. This could perhaps return if, because all things in it are so connected that time's movement forward brings their return, time brings itself back in the form of 'this moment' as their unique enabling time. But can that be?

16. S-II/466 (K-TSZ/332): the passage comes from III/13 ("The Convalescent"). Notice that the notion of "year" can readily mislead, since it refers to a pattern: time measured not in its own ongoing, but measured in regard to temporal things and patterns which they show (the seasons, for example). Next autumn is, as "next", different and not the same, though it may be the same as "autumn" (yet even here, not identical concretely).

17. As we have seen, Zarathustra's notion of time's depth involves reconstrual of Nietzsche's creational account in BT; in TSZ, time is enabling condition for a unique centered-and-active-being that is expression of a unique Self. Inward to the uniqueness of each such active being is much that is typical, universal and common, particular and different, etc.; but each being is singular, unique, as is the interactive whole or universe. Zarathustra gives no explanation for why the 'beginning-points' for such a creational reality (the various Selves) are finite in number: apparently it just happens to be that way, or as he puts it, number (that is, a finite field) happens to

be stronger ("Wherever there is force [*Kraft*], *number* will become mistress: she has more force." III/10: "Three Evils" [S-II/435 {K-TSZ/ 299}]). No further argument or evidence is offered to justify the idea.

18. In this reference, "eternal" here does not mean timeless or beyond time, nor everlasting; it means the still but dynamic source, within the Moment, of its own ongoing realization.

19. In the SE passage we considered above (pages 360-361), the wonder about our being here-and-now is linked by Nietzsche with the sense of being questioned about a why? and for-what? that concern us in our being: there is something to be discovered and shared in in the 'today' of our being. *That* we are *at all* is of such a nature as to implicate us-who-are in an at-stake for our activity and being, and in virtue of this there is a reason and a for-this to our being and activity, even if we do not (at least for the early while of our lives) comprehend *what* it is and *why*.

20. If this 'wanting' belongs to the Self as a tension in the creator-before-the-act-of-creating, and if this tension is grasped as (or as introducing) a kind of suffering (something which Nietzsche is prone to claim), then the difference between the BT conception and the TSZ conception is lessened. Because Nietzsche's appeal to a Self echoes Upaniṣadic language known to him, it is pertinent to note that in the Upaniṣads, as in the *Bhaga-vad-gītā*, the notion of the ultimate source of things as a holy power contains, in the term *brahman*, an etymological suggestion of a power that is expansive in nature and whose expanding beyond itself engenders a spatio-temporal creation. (See my *Bhagavad-gītā. Translation and Commentary*, especially 117; also my *The Beginnings of Philosophy in India*, especially 57-58.) Thinking Nietzsche on this background can be quite helpful.

21. I/4 ("Despisers of the Body") does much to adumbrate this vision, doing so in speaking of ourselves as bodily in our being and of the great reason of that bodily being as the ordering and organizing power of the Self and its will to create beyond itself.

22. S-I/22 (K-BT/34).

23. S-I/23 (K-BT/35). The incompleteness involves the concealment to ourselves of much, including the contingency of our being; it also involves the muting of the element of threat in the reference of ourselves to an at-stake and in the nature of activity as a venturing and risking.

24. Zarathustra seems to be echoing this in II/2 ("Upon the Blessed Isles"), in his contrast of the interpretations of the experience of beauty, God vs. overman.

25. Keep in mind how Aristotle, while making the question of being refer in ultimate fashion to *ousia*, does not thereby reduce all being to *ousia*. We have difficulty understanding these 'factors' for the reason that (1) out of our being as we are in our participating in the making, we are prone to envision them as 'fact' in a sense that is based on our apprehending the face of things in a certain abstract or oblivious fashion, and (2) we are prone to insist they must *be* in that way if they *are* at all. But this notion of 'fact' is itself an abstraction developed by us in-- and relevant to a facet of a factor in-- this in-the-making which itself *is* in another sense (one which we are dis-regarding in its own character, even though we ourselves are in this fashion and its being as it is is a precondition of our being and of our functioning in this abstracting fashion); our abstracting (and the facet which is being apprehended in that abstracting) are in truth intelligible *as they are* only when grasped in their place and standing within the in-the-making and its manner of being. By trying to apply a derivative and univocal conception of 'fact' to the preconditions which make possible its forming, we try the impossible and fail to think with the subtlety even of Aristotle, let alone of a sort that is needed.

26. Note how, if this were so, the emphasis in Upaniṣadic philosophy upon *yoga* and the discipline of our power of *buddhi* as central consequence for our participation in being would make sense. See also the *Bhaga-vad-gītā* for a broader notion of *yoga* than that of meditative discipline (see my commentary, 88-93, 101-103).

27. Often Zarathustra is speaking explicitly of all living beings. But the all-inclusive claim, which Nietzsche ventures explicitly in BGE/36, is implied in TSZ in such places as III/10 ("Three Evils"), where Zarathustra speaks of the world as "energy, force" [*Kraft*], and III/13 ("The Convalescent"), where his animals speak of the wheel or house or ring of being.

28. If time were differently constituted in its nature as condition of existence (such as, say, in the vision of it seen in refraction of the external), what it enables would be temporal in different fashion: not active beings, but (say) processes of one sort or another, which do not (in their being) occupy time (as activity does) but rather take place 'in' time and are present for a greater or lesser length of time. In such a temporal reality, there could be no human beings, no human activity, no human understanding, for the temporality of these requires that their enabling condition (time) be differently constituted.

29. In the German language as Nietzsche uses it, there are a number of words that become important in his expression of his thought, such as *Macht*, *Kraft*, and *Energie*. Each of these (and other) words has a multiplicity of meanings, some of which coincide or overlap in some measure with meanings of others. His use of these is fairly fluid, without the strict consistency of a technical vocabulary. This creates some initial confusion at times on what precisely he means, and while context can usually help select out the meaning occasionally even this

does not suffice. One recurrent question arises concerning *Macht*. In works such as D and GS, its use and meanings do not give it the sense of *Macht* in his later phrase *Wille zur Macht*, although his thought and the meanings involved in his use of the term in those works is anticipating or moving toward the use and meaning it will have in that phrase. In TSZ, *Macht* gains meanings which reflect that the sense of reality which the work would convey is that of an energy system, a system of forces and powers of rather different kinds and relation. He makes no effort to capture the multiplicity of differences involved in the system as he conceives it by use of a multiplicity of different words, one for each difference; rather, he avails himself of a multiplicity of inflections of the (more or less overlapping) meanings of a few key words. Thus even when the phrase *Wille zur Macht* becomes important, the use of the term *Macht* is still varied; and perhaps more importantly, the use of the phrase *Wille zur Macht* is itself variable in the sense (for example) that it may stand for the whole of a certain phenomenon or for some aspect of it that he is stressing in a certain context. A case in point: There is no question but that life, as inherently determined in its character by will-to-power, includes an aggressive element, and thus elements of the exertion of control over, manipulation of, domination and exploitation of, what is other than the living being and what is being subordinated to its needs; and sometimes the phrase "will-to-power" may be used with this limited reference in mind, instead of the more complex phenomenon which is the nature of life and which includes this element in subordination to others. Where the phrase in its full meaning is involved, the phenomenon is a drive in the living being to grow, that is, increase in capacity to be creative in the fashion relevant to its determinate nature; and "power" then stands for the fulness in such capacity and the exercise of it in which the living being 'has' that power. Such growth depends on a measure of aggressive exploitation, indeed, but it is not a matter of increasing capacity for such exploitation. Likewise, such power and its expressions have impacts on others, but their meaning as power or powerful does not lie in such impacts as controlling the beings who are being impacted.

30. See the discussion in Chapter 13 above, pages 326, 329-331.

31. See the discussion in Chapter 13 above, pages 317-318, 319-322, 324-325.

32. The characterization of moral forces here focuses on the lion-form of the three metamorphoses (I/1), but there are strengths needed also in the preceding camel-form, to say nothing of the continuing strengths called for in the child-form.

33. Zarathustra speaks very elliptically here, thus in broad-brush which oversimplifies and to that extent can readily mislead. The passage in II/12 which I have been rephrasing is a reformulation of the SE notion of the world of culture as involving the few great creative figures and many who are much lesser in their creative capacity but are creative at their own level and in their own way in responsiveness to the creativity of the few and within the world opened up by those few. Because there is a difference, however, between maturation morally and the development of creative capacity, the 'commanding' of the few would have a different nature and character for the lesser in the two different domains of reference, being a reinforcing of responsibility in the moral but providing a creative horizon as well as shelter and support for work within it in the creative. At the lowest end of the hierarchy, however, there is the question of the whole range of persons who (in the language of TSZ) are parasites, whose inward incapacity and impotence (a moral weakness) is what marks their being and what makes their efforts focus on outward control as a substitute for inward growth. In them, genuine (moral-based) creativity is lacking and the 'commanding' presence of the creative (great few, many lesser) is no reinforcement of moral responsibility; rather, because these lowest members of the hierarchy mis-take control-over and dominance-of in the aggressive mode for what is at-stake, they respond to the horizon provided by the higher for creative effort under a mis-reading of it, as if it were the horizon within which and under whose guidance they are to seek "power" in the form of "enjoyment of the exercise of control over".

34. This is Nietzsche's version of the Kantian idea of the autonomy of the moral will, its capacity of self-legislation. Nietzsche's notion is quite different from Kant's, of course.

35. S-II/326 (K-TSZ/175). The passage is from I/17 ("The Way of the Creator").

36. Already in HAH-II/WS-266 ("The impatient"), Nietzsche had spoken of the steps in this becoming. Characterizing youth as impatient, refusing to wait until its picture of men and things is completed, thus taking over from others such a picture, he says: "he casts himself from the heart on a philosopher or poet and then has for long to deny himself and serve as a vassal. He learns much in the process: but often a youth forgets while doing so what is most worth learning and knowing: himself; he remains a partisan all his life. Alas, much boredom has to be overcome, much sweat needed, before one has found one's own colors, one's own brush and canvas!-- And even then one is far from being a master [*Meister*] of one's own art of living-- but at least one is master [*Herr*] in one's own workshop." The double meaning of the English word "master" is worth noting: the becoming lord-and-master of ourselves as TSZ characterizes it involves, first, the becoming 'master in our own workshop', and then, in following out the pointer of aspiration and the Self that becomes disclosed to ourselves in the freedom of being master in that sense, we learn and eventually become a 'master of our own art of living'.

The former sense signifies being freed from domination by others, the second our having developed the skill to follow our Selves well, effectively, 'masterfully', and knowing how to do this amidst changing circumstance.

37. Speaking of TSZ in EH, Nietzsche explains his use of Zarathustra as the main figure in TSZ as expressing an effort on his part to let the Nietzschean-Zarathustra undo the accomplishment of the historical Zarathustra ("the transposition of morality into the metaphysical realm, as a force, cause, and end in itself"): "The self-overcoming of morality, out of truthfulness; the self-overcoming of the moralist, into his opposite-- into me-- that is what the name of Zarathustra means in my mouth." (S-II/1153-1154 [K-EH/328]). If one does not see his writings in their developmental place and interpret his use of terms in context, such phrasing can easily be misunderstood, and this, despite the fact that he immediately goes on to say: "my term *immoralist* involves two negations", one, of a type of human being ("the good, the benevolent, the beneficent") and the second, of a type of morality (a type "that has become prevalent and predominant as morality itself-- the morality of decadence, or, more concretely, *Christian* morality"). (S-II/1154 [K-EH/328]). In TSZ as earlier, Nietzsche's is a thinking which affirms morality, but in a more apt realization than the Christian, namely, that of the morality of responsibility, or as it is called here, of strength, of ascending Yes-saying life. TSZ is pervaded by this morality-- by the morality of this 'immoralist' (to pose the linguistic paradox), by a morality which enables the creative life to come into its own. The frequent polemical function of the term "immoralist" in the writings of Nietzsche from TSZ on has its antecedents in the second phase of his thought, with its development of a variety of critiques of "morality" in various forms, of accounts of the origin of "morality" in non-moral sources, and of a rejection of the notion of free-will and 'ought' as these were conceived as affairs of conscious choice and duty ('thou shalt'). But his vaunting his "immoralist" way of thinking in these later writings expresses more his allowing to prevail verbally the pretension of Christian morality to *be* morality itself and his accepting the negative opposite to it as a term for himself. Because in TSZ and later he so much uses the term "morality" in the limited sense that the EH passage indicates, the morality that was at work and acknowledged in the thinker in these earlier critiques and accounts-- and what in EH is called the morality of ascending life and in BGE the morality of good and bad (that beyond good and evil)-- is rarely spoken of as morality in TSZ.

38. See I/8 ("The Tree on the Mountainside"), where Zarathustra is talking with a youth who is "not yet free", and note the manner of his address to him.

39. S-II/286 (K-TSZ/132). The image suggests that the human condition-- that of human agency (decision-making and -executing, thus living life as human)--- places us beyond being simply an animal but short of being all that we can be. This is a place marked by danger, and a place where activity is a risky venturing: we are on-the-way toward-- and must cross above an abyss to reach-- that 'all-we-can-be'; and while we can look back in historical recollection and can allow ourselves to shudder in the face of danger and stop, we also can do as the tight-rope walker did, accept our condition as a dangerous one and summon the courage to make the crossing (to follow the above-and-beyond). We may fail, as he does, and even if there are those who, like the jester (whose motley clothes signify a cultured human being), surpass us in venturing, nonetheless the resolve to venture-forward is courageous and worthy of honor. Every human being who is able not only to feel the danger but to summon the courage to venture in spite of it is on that basis alone a higher human being, however defective otherwise.

40. S-II/523 (K-TSZ/399).

41. S-II/525 (K-TSZ/401).

42. S-II/524 (K-TSZ/400).

43. S-II/394 (K-TSZ/251-252).

44. In I/4 ("Despisers of the Body"), Zarathustra speaks in similar fashion, and in clear temporal terms: the Self wants to create above-and-beyond itself, but if it becomes no longer capable of such creating (of what is dearest to it and its whole fervor), if it has become too late for that, then it wants to go under. Thus is generated the despising of the body, as a reflection of this no longer being capable of such creating and of this turning of the living Self against itself.

45. S-II/522 (K-TSZ/398).

46. S-II/420 (K-TSZ/283). Presumably in this sense the tight-rope walker who (in the Prologue) fell and died was his equal.

47. In the second phase of his thought, Nietzsche seemed to recognize that the measure of a person's potential can not be fathomed by others and that the potential releasing agent for it can accordingly not be discerned by them. See, for example, HAH-I/72 on the unknowability even to ourselves of our "moral inflammability". But even more broadly, recall the discussions in his second-phase works of the unknowability of actions (see Chapter 10, page 258; Chapter 11, pages 294-297). In his response to the 'small person', Zarathustra seems to have surmounted this ignorance, and to be ready and able to pronounce final and condemnatory judgment; but this, along with the attempt to 'overcome' his nausea at the small and the unavoidable presence of the small in

the world, seems to attest an enduring element of resentment and distaste, such as marked the extreme animus with which the second phase of his thought opened. Nonetheless, it may also be seen as an embittered form of something already present in SE; consider the following passages from Section 6, for example. "And precisely this disposition should be planted and built into a young human being, that he understand himself so-to-speak as a failed work of nature but at the same time as a witness to the grandest and most marvelous intentions of the artist: in his case, nature has done badly, he should say to himself, but I will honor its great intention by serving it so that one day it may do better." (S-I/328 [H-SE/162]). "Almost everywhere we encounter nature in her distress pressing towards man and again and again feeling her work painfully failing, yet everywhere succeeding in the most marvelous beginnings, traits and forms: so that the human beings we live among resemble a field over which is scattered the most precious sculptural sketches, where everything calls to us: come, assist, complete, bring together what belongs together, we have an immeasurable longing to become whole." (S-I/329 [H-SE/163]).

48. It is interesting to consider how the Nietzsche of GS would see and interpret this attitude of Zara-thustra's. Speaking of intellectual conscience (GS/2), Nietzsche speaks of the folly that marks himself, one that persuades him that every human being has the feeling which generates intellectual conscience, namely, that it is contemptible to stand amidst "this whole marvelous uncertainty and ambiguity of existence *without questioning*". This folly, the expectation that "every human being has this feeling, simply because he is human", is of a piece with what (in GS/3: "Noble and common") he speaks of as another folly of the noble, namely, the passion for knowledge. Here, the noble person has a singular value standard, but posits its values and disvalues as generally valid. "Very rarely does a higher nature retain sufficient reason for understanding and treating everyday people as such; for the most part it believes that its own passion is present but kept concealed in all human beings, and precisely in this belief the higher nature is full of fire and eloquence. But when such exceptional human beings do not feel themselves to be exceptions, how should they ever be able to understand common natures and be able to evaluate the rule fairly? Thus they, too, speak of the folly, inexpedience, and fantasies of humanity, full of wonder how insanely the world runs and why it won't acknowledge what 'is needful'. This is the eternal injustice of those who are noble." From the perspective of the claim that the noble has faults, even characteristic faults, and thus does injustice to (say) the common, how does Zarathustra's attitude toward 'the small' seem? Even if it is not an expression of the folly of the noble and a misjudging of the persons in question, the question itself raises the larger question about what it is in Zarathustra which leads to his judgment of 'the small'. Is it what he seems to claim, genuine insight, or is this colored by other things that might distort his sight and lead to misjudgment? One might think here of the animus which marked the Nietzsche of HAH: how just was he being toward himself and others in that case?

49. S-II/334 (K-TSZ/184).

50. In the speech in question, Zarathustra proclaims: "Truly, I do not want to be like the ropemakers: they drag out their threads and always walk backwards." That is, I do not want to approach death blindly, dragging out life as long as I can. He continues: "Some become too old even for their truths and victories: a toothless mouth no longer has the right to every truth. And everybody who wants fame must take leave of honor betimes and practice the difficult art of leaving at the right time. ... There are sour apples, to be sure, whose lot wants that they wait till the last day of autumn; and they become ripe, yellow, and wrinkled all at once. In some, the heart grows old first; in others, the spirit. And some are old in their youth; but late youth keeps others young long. For some, life turns out badly: a poisonous worm eats its way to their heart. Let them see to it that their dying turns out that much better. Some never become sweet; they rot already in the summer. It is cowardice that keeps them on their branch. All-too-many live, and all-too-long they hang on their branches." (S-II/334-335 [K-TSZ/184-185]). In the face of death's impending, then, how one has lived and come to be, and in particular, how one has matured and is realizing-- has realized so far-- the creativity in oneself makes for different ways in which death registers for one and for different ways in which one responds in the face of approaching death.

51. S-II/335 (K-TSZ/185).

52. Thus in III/3 ("Involuntary Bliss"), Zarathustra speaks of himself as, in the afternoon of his life, "in the middle of my work" (S-II/411 [K-TSZ/273]), meaning the effort of teaching whereby, given the thinking that lies behind and animates it, he is seeking to create companions and set in motion the forces needed to bring about the future which is envisioned in his thoughts and is the goal of his efforts. See also IV/13 (Section 11) ("The Higher Man"), where "your work, your will" is what Zarathustra urges higher men (creators) to attend to. Finally, in IV/20 ("The Sign") just before the signs appear, he says: "I want to go to my work, to my day"; and after they have arrived, as he realizes their significance, he says: "I am concerned with my *work*! ... Zarathustra has ripened, my hour has come: this is *my* morning, *my* day is breaking: *rise now, rise, thou great noon!*"

53. S-II/336 (K-TSZ/186).

54. Given such thoughts, one can see why Nietzsche, when referring to WB, could speak in EH as follows:

"'the idea of Bayreuth' was transformed into something that should not puzzle those who know my *Zarathustra*: into that *great noon* at which the most elect consecrate themselves for the greatest of all tasks." (S-II/1112 [K-EH/274]). The concluding thought ("Who knows? The vision of a feast that I shall yet live to experience.") proved a bit optimistic.

55. S-II/336-337 (K-TSZ/187).

56. S-II/278 (K-TSZ/123). The quote is from Prologue/2.

57. S-II/277 (K-TSZ/122). The quote is from Prologue/1.

58. Note that the phases of his work are not wholly successive affairs: as the work is being entered into the second phase (teaching), the first phase (reflection) continues (especially in the time of withdrawal after the first descent and before the second). Thus, seen in large terms, in mid-life his work on the second phase (teaching) is suspended while he concentrates again on the first (reflection), and then eventually he returns to the second (teaching) in his second descent.

59. The whole sense of Zarathustra descending from the mountains and teaching as he does is a refined and transformed version of feelings adumbrated in WB. There, while characterizing Wagner as dithyrambic dramatist, Nietzsche speaks of the mixture of feelings and impulses involved: "in the midst of all the noisy summonses and importunities of the day", Wagner stands as if he were "the only one awake, the only one aware of the true and real"; at the same time, in addition to the uncanny sense of his being surrounded by people asleep, he knows the "longing to descend from the heights into the depths, the loving longing for the earth, for the joy of communion". The solitary creator feels "the longing at once to take all that is weak, human and lost, and like a god come to earth 'raise it to Heaven in fiery arms'". Wagner's approach to others through his music, Nietzsche also characterizes as at once communicating his "overflowing nature" and "its energy" [*Kraft*], and having this impact, that the recipient participates in that energy in such way as, through Wagner, to have been empowered against him, strengthened in himself to be himself. See WB, Section 7, for these thoughts and references (S-I/397-402 [H-WB/222-226]).

60. S-II/1106-1107 (K-BGE/268-269). The passage is from BGE/295.

61. S-II/339-340 (K-TSZ/190). The passage is from I/22 (Section 3) ("The Gift-giving Virtue").

62. Thus in I/22 (Section 2), Zarathustra can speak to those initial disciples he is leaving, saying: "Wake and listen, you that are lonely! From the future come winds with secret wing-beats; and good tidings go forth to delicate ears. You that are lonely today, you that are withdrawing, you shall one day be a people: out of you, who have chosen yourselves, there shall grow a chosen people-- and out of them, the overman." (S-II/339 [K-TSZ/189]). The idea of a self-chosen community giving rise to a transformed future refines and transforms a thought which occurs in UHH, where Nietzsche alludes to the example of the band of a hundred men on whose shoulders the culture of the Renaissance was raised. The passage reads: "Supposing that someone believed that it would require no more than a hundred men educated and actively working in a new spirit to finish off the culture which has just now become the fashion in Germany, how must it strengthen him to perceive that the culture of the Renaissance was raised on the shoulders of just such a band of a hundred men." (S-I/221-222 [H-UHH/69]).

63. Zarathustra uses a variety of images when he speaks of himself in relation to others as teacher. For example, in IV/1 ("The Honey-sacrifice") he speaks of himself as a fisherman, who casts his happiness out far and wide as bait, to see if "many human fish might not learn to wriggle and wiggle at my happiness until, biting at my sharp hidden hooks, they must come up to *my* height ... . For at bottom and from the start, *that* is what I am, reeling, reeling in, raising up, raising, a raiser [*Zieher*], cultivator [*Züchter*], and disciplinarian [*Zuchtmeister*], who once counseled himself, not for nothing: 'Become who you are!'" (S-II/479 [K-TSZ/ 351]). Note the idea of teaching as an effort to foster the *elevation* of those who are responding to the teaching.

64. Under an earlier understanding of its character and meaning, what is involved here is portrayed in SE, in Nietzsche's own response to Schopenhauer. It involves a gift-giving which fosters the *moral* and (beyond it) the *creative* evolution. One can see the same thing in Nietzsche's own personal growth, first with the help of Schopenhauer and Wagner, then in his movement beyond them.

65. We need to keep in mind the contrast between Zarathustra's thoughts as commanding as regards truth, and as commanding as regards himself and others in their living and the will-to-power in themselves. In the former case, the commanding is the appellative force of the insights offered as claiming truth, and the question of truth does not concern the bearing, say, of the insights in a practical reference. Rather, it relates to the evidence on which the claim to truth is based and correlatively to the functioning of the person open to the evidence in the judgmental interpretation and use of it; in regard to this the question of where the judgment is to take place is important, since in not every place is the evidence accessible, and there can be no justified claiming or adequate testing of reflective truth which is not, in the person claiming or testing, referred to immediacy accessible to the person in question. In the latter case, however, the commanding relates to the practical reference of what

is being communicated, and the meaning of command relates to a heeding of the command, through which the evolution and fulness of life is to be fostered in the one who is to heed it. Here the appellative force involved is the power to stir and move and engage, to evoke an active engagement that will affect for the better the being of the person in question.

66. S-II/411-412 (K-TSZ/273).

67. S-II/369 (K-TSZ/224-225). As often, Zarathustra speaks elliptically here, but in a way clarified by a brief passage in IV/11 ("The Welcome"), where he is speaking to the higher men who have gathered at his cave. "You may indeed all be higher men, but for me you are not high and strong enough. For me-- that means, for the inexorable in me that is silent but will not always remain silent." (S-II/518 [K-TSZ/394]). The inexorable (his will) is his Self but not his 'ego' or himself-as-conscious-being, which is at best a 'part' of the himself-as-active-being. The will of himself-as-active is also not the 'conscious deliberate volition' of the ego, yet neither is it his Self as will. It is rather the determination of himself-as-active-being which, at times, may be grounded self-aware in his Self as will and thus embody this-- and be "will" in two different but connected senses.

68. S-II/480 (K-TSZ/352).

69. Nietzsche's non-differentiation of the Now of sun-time (with its inclusion of all contemporaries) and the Now of activity (which is singular in its immediate bearing) allows him to proceed without noticing the leap he is making from the inward directional ground and that which pertains to contemporaneous beings and is worked out in their interacting.

70. In SE Nietzsche spoke of how Schopenhauer functioned as educator for him, but in that case he became (like the initial followers of Zarathustra in TSZ) caught up *also* in the ideas being offered and for a while became confined thereby in a way he eventually outgrew. The medium of the teaching was, directly, ideas, but the teaching-learning was a human-being to human-being affair in which the e-ducating depended on a responsiveness to the person (the courage and honesty of Schopenhauer, for example) to provide the enabling atmosphere in which such a focus and such teaching-learning could be fruitful. But providing an atmosphere is one thing, a student using it effectively is another: thus Zarathustra's first withdrawal, for example. But even that is no guarantee: again, witness the distortions that crept in and the need of Zarathustra to descend again, both to strengthen the followers in themselves and to counter such distortions (indirectly, as it turns out, by re-stating and deepening the initial teaching).

71. As is indicated by the quotations from SE in Note 47 above, this sense of not simply a hierarchization of human nature but of the meaning of that hierarchization as implying fuller and lesser humanity did not first arise in TSZ and under the conception of reality as will-to-power.

72. S-II/522-523 (K-TSZ/398-399). The thoughts are part of IV/13 ("The Higher Man"), Sections 2-3.

73. S-II/283-284 (K-TSZ/129).

74. S-II/284-285 (K-TSZ/129-130).

75. In the second section of I/22 ("The Gift-giving Virtue"), Zarathustra says: "You that are lonely today, you that are withdrawing, you shall one day be a people: out of you, who have chosen yourselves, there shall grow a chosen people-- and out of it, the overman. Truly, the earth shall yet become a site of recovery. And even now a new fragrance surrounds it, bringing a healing-and-salvation [*ein Heil*]-- and a new hope." (S-II/339 [K-TSZ/189]).

76. S-II/480 (K-TSZ/352). The phrase appears in IV/1 ("The Honey-sacrifice").

77. "A *new nobility* is needed ... . Many who are noble are needed, and noble men of many kinds [*vielerlei*], that there may be a nobility." (S-II/449 [K-TSZ/ 315]): the passage is in III/12 ["Old and New Tablets"], Section 11. Again, in Section 12: "O my brothers, I dedicate and direct you to a new nobility: you shall become procreators and cultivators and sowers of the future ... . Not whence you come shall henceforth constitute your honor, but whither you are going! Your will and your foot which has a will to go out over-and-beyond yourselves-- that shall constitute your new honor."

78. His 'stillest hour' speaks to Zarathustra (II/22) of his being someone who, though he has the power, is now hesitating to "rule" and "command great things". To Zarathustra's response that he lacks the lion's voice for commanding, it replies: "It is the stillest words that bring on the storm. Thoughts that come on doves' feet guide the world. O Zarathustra, you shall go as a shadow of that which must come: thus you will command and, commanding, lead the way." (S-II/401 [K-TSZ/258-259]). In IV/19 (Section 7) ("Drunken Song"), Zarathustra is interpreting the strokes of the bell at midnight, and says: "Leave me! Leave me! I am too pure for you. Do not touch me! Did not my world become perfect just now? My skin is too pure for your hands. Leave me, you stupid, doltish, dullish day! Is not the midnight brighter? The purest shall be lords of the earth-- the most unknown, the strongest, the midnight souls who are brighter and deeper than any day." (S-II/555 [K-TSZ/433]).

79. Given that activity takes its shape in an active being in a responsive fashion that gives to other powers than thought an antecedent and more fundamental role in the decision-making and -executing, it is clear that it

can not in any simple way guide the world, especially if it is reflective thought that could not be understood by many in its reflective meaning. Take, for example, the case of a warrior-inquirer. The relevant decision-making for his inquiry is first of all the decision to engage in inquiry at all, and then, to inquire in such fashion that this command-expressing thought orients inquiry. Thought's role in such decision-making is a subordinate and dependent one, that of a clarifying and reinforcing achieved by interpreting what is commanding and by proclaiming that this is its meaning (in this case namely, that 'I should engage in inquiry' and that 'in that inquiry, I should be guided by the command that "man should be overcome"'). But the actual decision-making involves the antecedent responsive register in immediacy of the at-stake and of all else as bearing on the forming of activity in this reference; and through this immediate responsive register, what is originally guiding for the forming of responsive effort is what-is-commanding itself. Thought comes into the forming as a mediating power which assists by clarifying and reinforcing this directive power and presence and which also furthers the forming by enabling it to take shape cognizant of a complex variety of interpretative ideas that relate to fact and possibility and other facets of the situation. In the inquiry itself, the inquirer can not accept any orienting idea for the undertaking except as he/she has already entered upon the act of inquiring in a decision-making which has by its own responsive formation already incorporated with the help of interpretation (implicitly, and occasionally also explicitly) what-is-commanding in the inquirer's own living; and even if there is a thought or idea which in the inquiry decided upon is accepted as its orienting conceptual basis, the inquiring is not-- and can never be-- carried forward without guidance deriving from immediacy and involving ongoing direct responsive adjustment to what is being disclosed. For even if the attention involved in inquiry is (as part of the intentionality of the activity) steered and inflected in its focusing by an idea, register of presence is fuller and wider, and response takes shape by reference to this whole register. Register is of a present richness fuller than what the steering idea may focus it on, and of a broader presence complementing peripherally what is being brought to focus but eluding the focus. The latter is formed as a care-inflected regarding that selectively limits notice while attention as a whole lets register what is much wider and richer than what may fall within the thought-frame-and-filter in question.

80. S-II/313 (K-TSZ/160).

81. Thoughts on such matters begin to show themselves in BGE. See e.g. BGE/203 for a sounding of the need, and /61-62 for how Nietzsche is assessing religion as a possible vehicle. See also /208-213 on the philosopher as Nietzsche is now thinking of him.

82. S-II/345-346 (K-TSZ/199-200). The passage is from II/2 ("Upon the Blessed Isles").

83. S-II/393-394 (K-TSZ/250-251). The passage is from II/20 ("Redemption").

84. Keep in mind here the narrow focus of Zarathustra's love of man, that his attention and concern are focused on certain differences in the forms or media of creativity, not on the responsibility being exercised by others in those forms, let alone on that responsibility being exercised in the creative involvement of the capacities of others whatever they are. That is, his notion of humanity involves superior and inferior in a form that makes human beings superior and inferior by nature, according as their native endowment is of one sort or another. But if that is his love-- of human beings in an order of rank of inferior and superior by nature and by development of that nature--, his is not simply a love of humanity as such but a love claimed by certain human particularities and most intense in regard to the (in his sense) higher and highest of human beings.

85. Nor need it be oblivious to what Nietzsche came to stress particularly in the second phase of his thought, namely, the evolutionary perspective on life. Nietzsche's treatment of other living beings and of nature generally seems, however, to be theoretical and aesthetic, and on the whole distant, without sign of the intimacy of interaction with such beings which might make vivid the thought that he nonetheless affirms at his distance, namely, that the primordial aggressive-in-outward-reference aspect of the activity of all living beings is to enable and support an inward growth whose culmination is in a way of taking part in relation to other beings which may be quite different in character, as the human testifies in the creative outworking in which others are affirmed as growing beings. Unfortunately, the phenomenon of evolution invites an attention to living beings from the outside, and fits readily with a conception of the human in which (for whatever reason) humans form a living species that is cleverer and more powerful than other species at modifying and controlling other living beings and the earth's resources. In TSZ, Zarathustra's attention is almost exclusively focused on human beings and their relations to one another; yet in the very nature of a will-to-power reality, and given that what is at stake for human beings is (in his account) their own humanity and that alone, the aggressive forefront of human activity involves the establishing of connections not only with other human beings but with all beings including the earth itself. And although among human beings one might (and Zarathustra attempts to) keep in mind that the meaning of this aggressiveness does not lie in itself but in enabling the growth and maturation and creative connecting of human beings with each other, the conception of this 'with each other' as that in which the at-stake for human beings lies would seem to imply the subordination (so far as human activity goes) of all other beings and the

earth itself essentially to the human, making all else a means to and setting for an ongoing human community. If the phrase "lord of the earth" speaks not to who is leader in the way the human race is eventually to live out its future on earth but to the human race as itself the dominant living power of those on earth, then the spirit of subordination is already attested in HAH-II/WS-189 (entitled "Reason and the tree of humanity"), which encourages preparation of the earth for the great collective fruit-tree of humanity that one day shall overshadow the whole earth. Zarathustra's conception of the at-stake for human beings as restricted to the human would seem to make the interaction of humans with the diverse living beings on earth, as it plays a role in the securing of the at-stake, to be essentially anthropocentric in nature, and consequently inadequate.

86. Keep in mind the etymology of "concrete", in *con-cresco* (to grow together). These co-operating agents grow together in the interacting whereby they participate in the securing of the at-stake, and harbored in this concreteness is the fulness of reality.

87. There is confusion, however, created by the way Nietzsche speaks of the Dionysian on occasion: the dissolution of barriers and the experience of unity among creatures is not the removal of space-time-causality, for the tragic maintains these and the elements of suffering which go with them while muting their force in the joyful participation in the joy of the creator-god's creating.

BIBLIOGRAPHY

Sections I and II list the works which have been used as reference in the main text.
Section III is concerned with studies of Nietzsche's life and thought which are alternative in their approach, assessment, and conclusions, to the present work.

I. Nietzsche's Works: German

Friedrich Nietzsche: Werke in drei Bänden. Karl Schlechta, Editor. Published by Carl Hanser, Munich: 1956.

A more extensive and critically superior, but less handy, version of the collected works (published and unpublished, including notes and other materials) is *Nietzsche Werke: Kritische Gesamtausgabe* (ed. Giorgio Colli and Mazzino Montinari; published by Walter de Gruyter, Berlin and New York: 1967-).

II. Nietzsche's Works: English translations

Hollingdale, R. J. *Untimely Meditations.* Cambridge University Press: 1983. [This book contains translations of four separately published works, whose titles are rendered as *David Strauss, the confessor & the writer*; *On the uses and disadvantages of history for life*; *Schopenhauer as educator*; *Richard Wagner in Bayreuth.* The second work here is the same work whose title I translate as *The Utility and Harmfulness of History for Life.*]

Human, all too human. Cambridge University Press: 1986. [This book contains translations of the work originally published under this name, and of the two continuations-appendices which were originally published separately but were subsequently gathered together as Volume II of the re-published original work. Included here, then, are *Mixed Maxims and Opinions*, and *The Wanderer and his Shadow.*]

Daybreak. Cambridge University Press: 1982. [This is the same work whose title I translate as *Dawn.*]

Kaufmann, Walter. *The Birth of Tragedy* and *The Case of Wagner.* Random House, Inc., New York: 1967.

The Gay Science. Random House, Inc., New York: 1974.

The Portable Nietzsche. The Viking Press, Inc.: 1954. [Among other things, this book contains complete translations of the following: *Thus Spoke Zarathustra*; *Twilight of the Idols*; *The Antichrist*; *Nietzsche contra Wagner.*]

On the Genealogy of Morals and *Ecce Homo.* Random House, Inc., New York: 1967. [R. J.

Hollingdale collaborated on the translation of *On the Genealogy of Morals*.]
Beyond Good and Evil. Random House, Inc., New York: 1966.

Many other English translations of separate works or sets of such works are available, of varying accuracy and value.

In addition, translations of selections of notes which Nietzsche left behind are also available. Two in particular are worthy of attention. One is *The Will to Power*, translated by Walter Kaufmann and R. J. Hollingdale (Alfred A. Knopf, Inc. and Random House, Inc., New York: 1968). The other is *Philosophy and Truth: Selections from Nietzsche's Notebooks of the early 1870s*, edited and translated by Daniel Breazeale (Humanities Press, Atlantic Highlands, NJ: 1979).

III. Nietzsche literature

We have been concerned with only those accounts of his life and works which were offered by Nietzsche himself in his published writings. As a result we have not made reference to biographical accounts by others, nor to studies of his writings. The following two works represent in English the genre of biographical accounts which include some measure of critical address to his ideas and some attention to the development of his thought.

Hayman, Ronald. *Nietzsche: a Critical Life*. Oxford University Press: 1980.
Hollingdale, R. J. *Nietzsche: The Man and His Philosophy*. Louisiana State University Press, Baton Rouge, Louisiana: 1965.

Studies of Nietzsche's thought, in some facet of it, or as found in some work or works, or as a whole, have ranged widely in approach, degree of responsible address to the subtlety and complexity of the thought, and measure of insight achieved and expressed in the presentation. Only in the case of Martin Heidegger have these been the work of first-rate philosophers; most are the work of students of philosophy who are concerned with one or another influential or controversial side of his thought, often in its relation to contemporary issues. In the present work we have taken no notice of any such writings, and that means, of thousands of books and articles composed mainly in English, German, and French, but also in other languages. For listings of titles which give an idea of the variety in question, one may look to the bibliographies or bibliographic elements in the following works.

Hilliard, B. Bryan. *Nietzsche Scholarship in English: A Bibliography, 1968-1992*. North American Nietzsche Society, Urbana, Illinois: 1992.
Kaufmann, Walter A. *Nietzsche: Philosopher, Pyschologist, Antichrist*. Princeton University Press, Princeton, New Jersey: 3rd rev. ed, 1968.
Reichert, Herbert W. and Karl Schlechta. *International Nietzsche Bibliography*. University of North Carolina Press, Chapel Hill, North Carolina: rev. and expanded, 1968.

One may also find bibliographical compilations of varying length at various sites on the internet (one by John Fredrick Humphrey, another by John Knoblock, a third by Kathleen Higgins, etc.).

INDEX

A.

activity (human: essential nature)
  effort to secure a thing, formed under sense of something-at-stake in and for it, 45-47
    threefold at-stake in and for activity, making activity a dramatic affair, 45-47, 65, 66, 161-166
    venturing nature of activity, 46, 133, 263-264, 330, 338, 370
  enabled to be by time and space. (*See* time *and* space.)
  engage in activity via initiative (decision-making-and-executing) capacity, 49-50
  engages agent with circumstance as op-positional presence for a situated being, 48, 147, 168, 170-171, 309, 310, 323, 328-329, 343-344, 346, 360, 370-371, 391
    primordial level: selectively aggressive engaging, 371
  medium for:
    actualizing and unfolding human being and life over time, 45-48, 49, 64, 104, 105-106, 132, 166-171
    in phases, 50-51
    in stretches, 49, 61
    integrating circumstance and incorporating 'times' into realization of own nature and life, 104, 118, 148
  takes time (a stretch of time) to be, 100
  always unique, 296

art
  art powers (divine: Apollo, Dionysus), 70-71
    and art-works, 71
    capacity to beautify life vs. to produce art-works, 226-227
    art-works are educative symbolically, 174
  as good-will toward appearance (the untrue), 243
  human being as living work of art, 70-71, 226-227, 293
  and life, 31, 84, 173-175
  metaphysical meaning of, 69, 70, 74, 75
  and religion, 74, 122, 125, 192
  unified with knowledge, 253, 294

artist, artistic
  artistic approach to self-development, 226-227,
    265, 267, 293-294, 298
  artistic involvement in formation of experience, 289, 291, 293
  creative out of higher spiritual capacities, 376, 386
  look at science from perspective of artist, 31
  Nature as artist, 145
  one form of true human being, 141-142, 145, 151, 376

aspiration
  animating directional factor (toward higher-and-better) in youth, 56-57, 58, 59, 95-96, 111-113, 122-123, 129, 135, 136-137, 139, 150, 201, 230, 343, 373, 385-386
    needing interpretation, 130
      interpretation aided by recall of loves, 130-131
  its pointing, 65-66, 378
  to own meant-to-be higher self, 55, 132, 137
  ways (three) of enacting aspiration-faithful movement into future, 111

at stake
  basis for question of meaning (to life), purpose (in existence), 70, 73, 83, 130, 141, 142, 278-279, 311-312, 318, 326, 360-361, 392-393
  claiming register of, in human beings, 50, 134-136, 184, 186, 214-215
    good which necessarily draws us to seek to realize it, 214-215, 220, 223, 310, 311, 390
    'need', 'must', obligation, 50, 135
    undifferentiated vs. differentiated register of, 135
  in and for activity, 45-47, 66, 134
    something matters, it makes a difference what we do, 106, 166, 389-391
  in and for activity vs. in existence, 392
  in existence, 47, 56, 57, 63, 66, 200, 366-367, 370, 389-391, 392
    introduces problematic of existence. (*See* existence.)
    the at-stake in existence concerns humans as responsive agents, 56, 63, 66, 391-392
    the at-stake in existence is interactive in its nature, 391-393
      a cultured human community?, 142-143
      an interactively-achieved concrete reality

philosopher
contemplative being (along with artist), 291
great human being as well as great thinker, 143
must take most learning from himself, not from
    others, and himself serve as illustration and
    abbreviation of the whole world, 144
contrasts with any-and-all (a scholar e.g.) who
    allow concepts/opinions/things-past/books
    to come between self and things, 144
'untimely' being, 143-147
    critic of his 'times', 32, 147
legislator, 145-146, 147, 200-202
    addressing youth about the future, 147-152
true human being (along with artist, saint), 141-
    142, 145-146

philosophy
begins in youthful moral questioning, 143-144
involves law-giving, 200-202
    Zarathustra's law-giving, 382-383
issues in insight into whole, and interpretation of
    its meaning for the living, 144-145
    Nietzschean-Schopenhauer's insight and in-
        terpretation, 145-146
Nietzsche's characterizations:
    contrasting ways of philosophizing: historical
        vs. metaphysical, 191-192, 193, 197,
        215
        his own historical philosophizing, 192,
            202-206
    reflective effort to bring intuitive Dionysian
        wisdom to concepts, 90-91
    reflective transcription of an individual's life,
        29, 255
practical impact of, 146-147
reflective concern with problematic of existence
    and meaning, 3, 12, 23, 41-42, 43, 45, 57,
    89, 143-144, 190, 202, 203, 204, 255, 280-
    281, 307, 311
    common agential standpoint for such concern,
        yet reflection there is concretely formed
        thus diverse, 56-57, 89-90
    Nietzsche's youthful (agent) standpoint,
        made definite by Dionysian experienc-
        ing, 89, 90-91
    time's enabling of a standpoint from which
        the truth of the problematic of existence
        can be discerned, 312
test for truth of philosophical insight, 144-146
vs. science (grasp of meaning of life vs. grasp of
    fact, vision of whole vs. grasp of parts), 144-
    145
Wagner as philosophizing in sound (thinking the
    essential nature of the world in events), 165,
    222-223

philosophical writing
aim is communication, 9
    Nietzsche's aim: a communication that

provokes a reflective and life-changing
    response, 3, 11, 316-317, 356-357, 393
conveys reflection and truth-claims rooted in
    life/being of author, 41-44
form and content both important for commun-
    ication (e.g. EH), 1-2, 5-6, 9-10
    different forms in Nietzsche's writings
        (essays, aphorism-collections, drama, auto-
        biography), 43, 187, 313, 315
    evolving content conveyed in Nietzsche's
        writings, 34-35, 39, 43
    form/content changes of Nietzsche's writings
        convey evolving reflective issue of his
        self-becoming, 29-41, 43
reading philosophical writing with understanding
    requires: courage, 13; shared experience, 9-10
reading and understanding writings by Nietzsche
    (the reader's task), 4-5, 9, 15-16, 43, 44,
    279-280
    assessment (Nietzsche's) of effectiveness of
        communication via his writing, 1, 6, 9-10,
        15
    EH: Nietzsche's use of autobiography (self-
        disclosure as living being centered in
        reflective activity) to communicate about
        his own writings, 1-2, 4-5, 15

physician
Nietzsche (re self), 7, 26
of the future, 252
    promoter of physical and psychical health,
        274-275

poetize. (*See* dream [dream-like], *also* reality [in-
teractive {forming itself ... dream-making}], *also*
fiction,... .)

power [*Kraft*]. (*See* energy.)

power [*Macht, Kraft*] (broadly)
divine power(s):
    Apollo and Dionysus as art-powers, 69-71
    eternal original art-force that calls phenom-
        enal world into existence, 86-87
in sphere of living beings:
    life wants, 220-223, 310, 311, 347, 353, 371,
        373
    the good by nature, 264
    paths (crooked) on which life seeks power,
        328-332
in sphere of reality: energetic-force which separ-
    ates, contrasts (introduces opposition/con-
    flict), hierarchically orders (subordinates
    and integrates), 221, 239, 323
will-to-power. (*See* will.)

power [*Macht, Kraft*] (human)
in connection with particularities of capacity and
    circumstance, 220-223
    decisive thing is to enjoy the feeling of power,
        300-301
in a political reference, 155, 244, 245, 273

reflection (nature, kinds) (cont.)

testing of purported insight: relates to phenomenon as immediately accessible, 43, 44, 52, 53-54, 383

but is it ever fully accessible, adequately registered, and aptly interpreted, while we are still alive?, 67-68

reflection (philosophical: nature), 41-42, 43, 57, 82, 144, 190-191, 232, 234, 280-286

concerned with the problematic of existence in its universality. (*See* existence.)

engaged in *in concreto*, and out of an ingatheredness and concentratedness, and an experiential disclosiveness, that can vary widely in many respects, 89-90

engaged in with evolving capacity for reflective insight, culminating in powerful awakened soul for whom truth is there, 308

developing life-matrix. (*See below*, life-matrix.)

learn how to reflect well (discipline the capacity for reflection), 42-43

skill in reflecting, 38, 39, 41-42, 44

experiential character of reflective inquiry, making life (life-experience) the means to knowledge, 293

takes place within the life-matrix of the thinker, 15, 39, 41-44, 82, 89, 188, 308

in general, includes:

inquirer's augmenting/developing responsiveness (sensibility/sensitivity), 82, 282-284, 308

inquirer's augmenting/developing skill in reflection, 42-43

thinker's maturation as human agent, 52, 308

moral strength of the inquirer, 143

in Nietzsche's case:

animation of reflection by: the 'cold' of 'winter', 36; mid-life's fuller being, 31; mid-life's overflowing health, 40, 41; 'thawing wind' of 'April', 39; youth, 29, 30-31, 32, 34; youth rejecting 'youth', 38

attentive to experience as ongoing variably disclosive affair, 42-43, 82

centrality of Dionysian experience for his reflection, 82-87

Dionysus elevates the capacity for immediate awareness that reflective insight presupposes, 12

philosophy made out of his will to health, to life, 26

method of reflective inquiry (Nietzsche's), 93

modes of philosophical reflection (Nietzsche's formulation of the nature of philosophical inquiry):

as protective rationalization, 53

'reason'-guided (Kant, Socrates), 92

reflective transcription of one's life, 255

Schopenhauerian Nietzsche's account: seeks insight into life/existence as a whole, and an interpretation that makes visible life's meaning for all humans, 145

in contrast with science:

seeks out dangerous and difficult truths of life and its meaning, vs. the indifferent truths of the sciences, 144

looks at painting as an interwoven whole, with a creator-introduced order manifesting its meaning for life, vs. the sciences as isolating and understanding the canvas/colors of the painting, 144-145

thinking which is 'beyond reason' and which brings intuitive Dionysian wisdom to conceptual rendering, 92

as 'scientific' (Nietzsche: historical vs. metaphysical), 190-192, 192-193, 202-203, 204, 307, 313

Nietzsche's actual conduct of historical philosophizing, 192, 202-206

more/less adequate realization of reflective nature of philosophical reflection, 190, 203-204

reflection (philosophical: nature, adequate realization)

assumes appropriate standpoint for such reflection: that of agents concerned to gain universal insight into the problematic which bears on them as agents, 89

three-fold foundation, best standpoint for reflection. (*See* reflection [nature, kinds], *under* shared features ... .)

carries on using best focus and best foundation for reflection, 59-68

conduct of inquiry allowed to change character according to agent's changing capacity for engaging, 44

conducted as venturing (exploring, testing), 179

embodies 'audacious morality' of adventurer/discoverer, 257

inquiry accords central place to logical conscience (intellectual conscience, sense for truth and justice), 19, 36, 37, 192-193, 208, 215-217, 280-281, 296

inquiry involves:

awareness of simplifications which thinking effects, 257-258

awareness of limitations to self-knowledge (in fact and in principle), 258, 295-296

awareness of sensibility as imprisoning, 259

honesty in cognizance of others-and-self in our interacting, 281-283

self-critical approach to all matters at issue, 14, 52-53, 54, 232

Z.